UNIVERSITY CASEBOOK SERIES®

CONTRACTS

CASES AND COMMENT

TENTH EDITION

by

JOHN P. DAWSON
Late Charles Stebbins Fairchild Professor of Law
Harvard University

WILLIAM BURNETT HARVEY
Late Professor of Law and Political Science
Boston University

STANLEY D. HENDERSON
F.D.G. Ribble Professor of Law Emeritus
University of Virginia

DOUGLAS G. BAIRD
Harry A. Bigelow Distinguished Service Professor
The University of Chicago

FOUNDATION PRESS

© 1959, 1969, 1977, 1982, 1987, 1993, 1998, 2003 FOUNDATION PRESS
© 2008 by THOMSON REUTERS/FOUNDATION PRESS
© 2013 by LEG, Inc. d/b/a West Academic Publishing
610 Opperman Drive
St. Paul, MN 55123
1-800-313-9378

Printed in the United States of America

ISBN: 978–1–60930–211–5

Mat #41328484

PREFACE TO THE TENTH EDITION

With the appearance of the Tenth Edition, the book is now well into its sixth decade. More than a thousand teachers and hundreds of thousands of law students across the country have subjected the book to the scrutiny of the classroom. This edition, the seventh for one of us and the second for the other, carries forward the main themes put in place by Jack Dawson and Burnett Harvey. We remain committed to preserving and building upon the book's distinctive character, especially its use of canonical cases, its sensitivity to the history and evolution of doctrine, and its close attention to the legal consequences of breach.

This is a teaching book, a vehicle for the formal study of contract law's rules and processes and the values they are supposed to serve. There is an informational base and a culture to be passed on, a critical and inquiring element to be shared. Every case tells a story, and every story presents a problem rooted in a particular context. Having entered the realm of legal rules, a territory containing an assortment of landmarks, many blurred or at odds with one or more others, students must consider the possible ways of handling a problem, and defend choices when alternative outcomes are possible by reason of competing facts or principles. It is a range of possibilities, not facile answers to hard questions, that one must master.

Since the beginning, the editors of this book have believed that contract law is best understood—the broad conceptions as well as the formal rules and technical formulations—by beginning with a focus on the nature of the legally enforceable promise. The underlying purposes of contract law (what it seeks to protect, and how it hopes to accomplish its aims) are revealed most clearly when problems are looked at from a perspective of taking care of harms or losses, or gains held unjustly. Students must see that the limitations of contract in our society are no small part of the story of its functions, and that the business of "enforcing" (perhaps dismantling) unkept bargains has much to contribute in the fixing of those limits and, accordingly, the forming of a working understanding of the law of contract as a whole. In a word, when a dispute over an obligation voluntarily assumed ends up in court, the great question of "when" to enforce cannot be detached from the also-great question of "how" to enforce.

There are a few additional introductory points. One is that the materials used to educate law students—particularly students in their first year—typically focus on the past, on disputes courts have already considered and decided, often long ago. But there is a larger sense in which history, long a particular emphasis of this book, is important, indeed indispensable. Legal rules and standards, if they are to attract a following in law offices and courts, must be explained, which is to say, understood. And if we are to truly understand where we are in contracts today, we need to have a feel for where we once were, and how and why it happened that there was movement from one rule or doctrine to another, from one dividing line to a different test altogether for division. So a book purporting to organize the field of contract in order to facilitate understanding of the subject must, in some fashion, track the evolution of modern law. Only then will the nature of common law reasoning be fully revealed, and the process of "thinking like a lawyer" begin for the uninitiated. It must be remembered that the ideas making up the core subject matter of contract, as with most of the common law's major subdivisions, are constructed ideas. The problem, as we shall see, is that they are also undergoing constant reconstruction.

Students should also understand that a number of the problems raised in this book are unlikely to come through the door of today's practicing commercial lawyer. In the year 1869 an uncle rises to speak at a joyous family occasion, promising a favored nephew (then fifteen) a very large sum of money if the nephew, in the six years left before his twenty-first birthday, gives up alcohol, tobacco, swearing, and gambling. The nephew agrees and remains true to his word, presumably at some cost, but the uncle dies many years later (eighteen in fact) without having kept his side of the bargain. Even earlier in the 1800s, a farmer, learning of his brother's death in the farm country some seventy miles distant, writes to his brother's widow saying that he has more land than he can tend and that he wants her and her children "to do well." The letter concludes: "If you will come down and see me, I will let you have a place to raise your family." The widow and children make the move, again presumably at some cost, emotional as well as financial. They are given land to work, plus a house, but it all ends abruptly a year or two later, when they are evicted (we are not told why).

In both cases, we want to know whether the promises are legally enforceable, whether the victim of the broken promise can call upon the state to hold the other to it, by force if necessary. Each is an artifact of its own time and place. No giant corporation, no sophisticated bargain, is involved. Nevertheless, such situations provide excellent vehicles for exploring basic principles—such as the extent to which the law should enforce any promise seriously made and reasonably relied upon. Mastery of these and other cases that have become part of the canon increase our confidence in distinguishing between the hard and easy cases. Even more telling, they guide our deliberations in classifying the vast expanse of cases that properly fall somewhere between hard and easy. It is no small matter that the term "artifact," as commonly defined, denotes a thing "showing human workmanship or modification, a product of civilization or artistic endeavor." Again, it is the collective yield of cases litigated by many courts over many decades that gives "commonness" to our common law.

Those familiar with the book will see that this edition's general order of march is largely unchanged. Nevertheless, times of economic dislocation create their share of important legal disputes, and the last several years have been no exception. This edition introduces a number of new principal cases. It is worth noting, however, that these cases, many of which involved large corporate transactions involving tens of millions, or in one case hundreds of millions of dollars, call on the same themes and indeed often cite cases that have long been part of this text. The new material puts in clearer perspective the developments of the twentieth century and their implications for the twenty-first. As always, we have attempted to keep the materials to manageable length, and notwithstanding the addition of the new cases, this edition is about the same length as the previous one.

Much of the newly-added material is designed to further consolidate topics within the book's customary structure and headings. The effort to reduce the number of main and ancillary cases has continued. It must be stressed, however, that these alterations in no sense signal a departure from the case or "problem" method. The cases remain the principal source of problems for classroom discussion; the accompanying text, whatever its form, is designed to illuminate those problems and expand the base for discussion. Moreover, by keeping the text on as objective level as possible, this edition again seeks to accommodate differing conceptions and modes of analysis of contract, as well as divergent views of legal method. Students should understand that a single book in the hands of different teachers can be a quite different thing. Through classroom approach and emphasis, aided by handouts and assigned readings, every teacher makes choices with a view to "personalizing" the course in Contracts. A particular challenge in organizing any casebook—especially one aimed at a national audience—is to steer a sufficiently "center-lane" path so as to allow the instructor room to provide the ultimate "take" on what it is that the book puts before the students.

We acknowledged in previous editions the contributions and support of many law teachers, now a list too long to repeat here. We are especially indebted to those in the academy who continue to offer suggestions (and criticisms). A special word of gratitude is again due Harvard's Clark Byse. His help and advice given over many years, first to his colleague and devoted friend Jack Dawson, and then to us, reaches far beyond contracts and the covers of this book.

Jack Dawson and Burnett Harvey are no longer here, but teachers who know about the study of contract in our nation's law schools will also know that Jack and Burnett created something worth preserving. We are privileged to be able to carry that tradition forward.

STANLEY D. HENDERSON

DOUGLAS G. BAIRD

Charlottesville, Virginia
Chicago, Illinois
January 2013

JOHN P. DAWSON
1902–1985

WILLIAM BURNETT HARVEY

1922–1999

ACKNOWLEDGMENTS

We are indebted to the following authors and publishers for permission to reprint excerpts from copyrighted material:

Charny, Hypothetical Bargains: The Normative Structure of Contract Interpretation, 89 Mich.L.Rev. 1815 (1991). Reprinted with permission of the Michigan Law Review.

Cohen, The Basis of Contract, 46 Harv.L.Rev. 553 (1933). Reprinted with permission of the Harvard Law Review Ass'n.

Corbin, Conditions in the Law of Contracts, 28 Yale L.J. 739 (1919). Reprinted with permission of the author, the Yale Law Journal Co., and Fred B. Rothman & Co.

A. Corbin, Corbin on Contracts, vols. 3, 3A (1960). Reprinted with permission of Yale University Law School.

Dawson, Economic Duress—An Essay in Perspective, 45 Mich.L.Rev. 253 (1947). Reprinted with permission of the Michigan Law Review.

Dawson, Judicial Revision of Frustrated Contracts: The United States, 64 B.U.L.Rev. 1 (1984). Reprinted with permission of the Boston University Law Review.

Dawson, Unconscionable Coercion: The German Version, 89 Harv.L.Rev. 1041 (1976). Reprinted with permission of the Harvard Law Review Ass'n.

J. Dawson, Gifts and Promises 216-218 (1980). Reprinted with permission of the Yale University Press.

Fuller, Consideration and Form, 41 Colum.L.Rev. 799 (1941). Reprinted with permission of the author and the Columbia Law Review.

Fuller & Perdue, The Reliance Interest in Contract Damages (pt. 1), 46 Yale L.J. 52 (1936). Reprinted with permission of the authors, the Yale Law Journal Co., and Fred B. Rothman & Co.

Gilmore, Law, Logic, and Experience, 3 How.L.J. 26 (1957). Reprinted with permission of the Howard Law Journal.

Goetz & Scott, Enforcing Promises: An Examination of the Basis of Contract, 89 Yale L.J. 1261 (1980). Reprinted with permission of the authors, the Yale Law Journal Co., and Fred B. Rothman & Co.

Henderson, Promises Grounded in the Past: The Idea of Unjust Enrichment and the Law of Contracts, 57 Va.L.Rev. 1115 (1971). Reprinted with permission of the Virginia Law Review Ass'n and Fred B. Rothman & Co.

Holmes, The Path of the Law, 10 Harv.L.Rev. 457 (1987). Reprinted with permission of the Harvard Law Review Ass'n.

Kessler, Contracts of Adhesion—Some Thoughts About Freedom of Contract, 43 Colum.L.Rev. 628 (1943). Reprinted with permission of the author and the Columbia Law Review.

Konefsky, How to Read, or at Least Not Misread, Cardozo in the *Allegheny College* Case, 36 Buffalo L.Rev. 645 (1988). Reprinted with permission of the author and the Buffalo Law Review.

Kull, Mistake, Frustration, and the Windfall Principle of Contract Remedies, 43 Hastings L.J. 1 (1991). Reprinted with permission of the author and the Hastings College of the Law.

Llewellyn, What Price Contract?—An Essay in Perspective, 40 Yale L.J. 704 (1931). Reprinted with permission of the author and the Yale Law Journal Co.

K. Llewellyn, The Bramble Bush (1951). Reprinted with permission of Oceana Publications, Inc.

Nyquist, "By My Watch—Which Was a Correct Time Piece": Gray v. Gardner and the Arrival of the Ship Lady Adams, The Log of Mystic Seaport, Spr. 1992. Reprinted with permission of the author and Mystic Seaport Museum, Inc.

Patterson, An Apology for Consideration, 58 Colum.L.Rev. 929 (1958). Reprinted with permission of the Columbia Law Review.

Patterson, Constructive Conditions in Contracts, 42 Colum.L.Rev. 903 (1942). Reprinted with permission of the author and the Columbia Law Review.

Posner, The Law and Economics of Contract Interpretation, 83 Tex. L. Rev. 1581 (2005). Reprinted with permission of the author and the Texas Law Review Association.

Rakoff, Good Faith in Contract Performance: Market Street Associates Ltd. Partnership v. Frey, 120 Harv. L. Rev. 1187 (2007). Reprinted with permission of the Harvard Law Review Association permission conveyed through Copyright Clearance Center, Inc.

Schultz, The Firm Offer Puzzle: A Study of Business Practice in the Construction Industry, 19 U.Chi.L.Rev. 237 (1952). Reprinted with permission of the author and the University of Chicago Law Review.

Shapiro, Courts, Legislatures, and Paternalism, 74 Va.L.Rev. 519 (1988). Reprinted with permission of the author, the Virginia Law Review Ass'n, and Fred B. Rothman & Co.

Sharp, Pacta Sunt Servanda, 41 Colum.L.Rev. 783 (1941). Reprinted with permission of the Columbia Law Review.

Sharp, Promissory Liability (pts. 1 & 2), 7 U.Chi.L.Rev. 1, 250 (1939-1940). Reprinted with permission of the University of Chicago Law Review.

A.W.B. Simpson, A History of the Common Law of Contract (1975). Reprinted with permission of the author and Oxford University Press.

Whittier, The Restatement of Contracts and Mutual Assent, 17 Calif.L.Rev. 441 (1929). Reprinted with permission of the California Law Review.

S. Williston, A Treatise on the Law of Contracts, vol. 6 (3d ed. 1962). Reprinted with permission of Baker, Voorhis & Co., Inc.

Wormser, The True Conception of Unilateral Contracts, 26 Yale L.J. 136 (1916). Reprinted with permission of the Yale Law Journal Co. and Fred B. Rothman & Co.

The photo of Chief Justice Roger J. Traynor is reproduced with the permission of the Traynor Family, as well as the copyright holder, Moulin Studios of San Francisco. The photos of John Dawson, Oliver Wendell Holmes, Learned Hand, and Benjamin Cardozo are courtesy of Historical and Special Collections, Harvard Law School Library. Burnett Harvey's photo is from the collection of Boston University, and the photo of Karl Llewellyn is from Special Collections, University of Chicago Library. The photo of Michael Jordan is with the permission of Warner Brothers/Getty Images.

We remain indebted to the American Law Institute for permission to quote from the Restatement (First) of Contracts, copyright © 1932 by The American Law Institute; the Restatement (Second) of Contracts, copyright © 1981 by The American Law Institute; the Restatement of Restitution, copyright © 1937 by The American Law Institute; the Restatement (Second) of Trots, copyright © 1965 by The American Law Institute; and ALI Proceedings, copyright © 1926, 1965, 1967, and 1971 by The American Law Institute; all excerpts from which are reprinted with the permission of The American Law Institute.

Once again, we acknowledge permission to reprint provisions of the Uniform Commercial Code, copyright © 1991 by The American Law Institute and the National Conference of Commissioners on Uniform State Laws. Reprinted with permission of the Permanent Editorial Board for the Uniform Commercial Code.

SUMMARY OF CONTENTS

TABLE OF CONTENTS

TABLE OF CASES

The principal cases are in bold type.

TABLE OF CITATIONS TO THE RESTATEMENT OF CONTRACTS

TABLE OF CITATIONS TO THE UNIFORM COMMERCIAL CODE (2002 OFFICIAL TEXT)

UNIVERSITY CASEBOOK SERIES ®

CONTRACTS

CASES AND COMMENT

TENTH EDITION

CHAPTER 1

THE LEGALLY ENFORCEABLE PROMISE: BASIC AND RECURRING THEMES

INTRODUCTORY NOTE

Not all promises are legally enforceable. Indeed, at common law, the background understanding was to the contrary. A promise without more was not legally enforceable. Chapter 2 of this book explores the question of what is required beyond a simple promise to make it enforceable in court. But before one can answer this question and assess whether it makes sense to hold a particular promise enforceable, it is useful to know the stakes. One should know the consequences that follow when a court finds a promise is enforceable. Determining when the law's intervention into voluntary exchanges is appropriate cannot be separated from the problem of setting sanctions when promises are broken. Moreover, what contract law is attempting to accomplish—that is to say, its underlying premises and objectives, and recurrent themes—is revealed most clearly in its approach to remedies and measures of recovery.

In one of the best known lectures on the common law, Holmes, The Path of the Law, 10 Harv.L.Rev. 457, 458–469 (1897), Oliver Wendell Holmes gave the following account of what it meant to say that a promise was legally enforceable:

> The duty to keep a contract at common law means a prediction that you must pay damages if you do not keep it—and nothing else. If you commit a tort, you are liable to pay a compensatory sum. If you commit a contract, you are liable to pay a compensatory sum unless the promised event comes to pass, and that is all the difference.

Holmes captures in this passage the idea that someone who breaks a legally enforceable promise is, in the usual case, obliged only to pay compensation. The person is neither punished nor forced to perform. Holmes, however, offers no justification for the rule, identifies no qualifications or exceptions, and does not explain what it means "to pay a compensatory sum." We explore all of these questions in this chapter, beginning with the question of how this "compensatory sum" is measured.

In thinking about the question of how to measure compensation, consider the possible measures. In a path-breaking article published in 1936, Professor Lon Fuller set out and discussed various possibilities. He suggested the term *restitution interest* to describe the interest of a party in recovering values conferred on the other party through efforts to perform a contract, the term *reliance interest* to describe a party's interest in recovering losses suffered by virtue of reliance on the contract, whether or not there was a corresponding gain to the opposite party, and the term *expectation interest* to describe the interest of a party in realizing the value of the expectancy that was created by the other's promise. These terms—*restitution*, *reliance*, and *expectancy*—are now an essential part of the law and the literature of contract. Professor Fuller used them to distinguish three principal purposes or policies an award of money damages might serve.

The goal in protecting the restitution interest is the prevention of gain by the defaulting promisor at the expense of the promisee—i.e., "the prevention of unjust enrichment." When damages are awarded not for the purpose of recapturing enrichment of the promisor but to reimburse the promisee for a change of position in reliance on the contract, the object is to put the promisee "in as good a position as he was in before the promise was made." And by seeking to give the promisee the value of the expectancy which the promise created, the aim is to put the promisee "in as good a position as he would have occupied had the defendant performed his promise." See Fuller & Perdue, The Reliance Interest in Contract Damages (pt. 1), 46 Yale L.J. 52, 56–57 (1936).

Understanding the interests protected by these ideas lies at the heart of understanding the consequences that follow from making a promise legally enforceable at common law. We need to understand why the compensation principle makes sense, how one goes about implementing it, and what limits need to be placed upon it.

SECTION 1. THE GOALS OF CONTRACT LAW

The cases in this sequence are directed mainly at the law of contract damages, yet they offer as well important insights about the distinctive features of contract liability. In order to enhance those insights, the materials in the book draw into question comparisons between contract and tort, fields that overlap and have common aims (even corresponding doctrines) but which are said to involve different requirements. For example, in the case that follows, the claim brought in contract is successful but the claim in tort, for negligence, is not. Liability for breach of contract is understood to be "strict"; the promisor who fails to keep a promise ordinarily cannot defend by showing good motives or the practice of due care.

––––––

Hawkins v. McGee

Supreme Court of New Hampshire, 1929.
84 N.H. 114, 146 A. 641.

Assumpsit against a surgeon for breach of an alleged warranty of the success of an operation. Trial by jury. Verdict [of $3,000] for the plaintiff. The writ also contained a count in negligence upon which a nonsuit was ordered, without exception.

Defendant's motions for a nonsuit and for a directed verdict on the count in assumpsit were denied, and the defendant excepted. During the argument of plaintiff's counsel to the jury, the defendant claimed certain exceptions, and also excepted to the denial of his requests for instructions and to the charge of the court upon the question of damages, as more fully appears in the opinion. The defendant seasonably moved to set aside the verdict upon the grounds that it was (1) contrary to the evidence; (2)

against the weight of the evidence; (3) against the weight of the law and evidence; and (4) because the damages awarded by the jury were excessive. The court denied the motion upon the first three grounds, but found that the damages were excessive, and made an order that the verdict be set aside, unless the plaintiff elected to remit all in excess of $500. The plaintiff having refused to remit, the verdict was set aside "as excessive and against the weight of the evidence," and the plaintiff excepted.

The foregoing exceptions were transferred by SCAMMON, J. The facts are stated in the opinion.

BRANCH, J. The operation in question consisted in the removal of a considerable quantity of scar tissue from the palm of the plaintiff's right hand and the grafting of skin taken from the plaintiff's chest in place thereof. The scar tissue was the result of a severe burn caused by contact with an electric wire, which the plaintiff received about nine years before the time of the transactions here involved. There was evidence to the effect that before the operation was performed the plaintiff and his father went to the defendant's office, and that the defendant, in answer to the question, "How long will the boy be in the hospital?" replied, "Three or four days, not over four; then the boy can go home and it will be just a few days when he will go back to work with a good hand." Clearly this and other testimony to the same effect would not justify a finding that the doctor contracted to complete the hospital treatment in three or four days or that the plaintiff would be able to go back to work within a few days thereafter. The above statements could only be construed as expressions of opinion or predictions as to the probable duration of the treatment and plaintiff's resulting disability, and the fact that these estimates were exceeded would impose no contractual liability upon the defendant. The only substantial basis for the plaintiff's claim is the testimony that the defendant also said before the operation was decided upon, "I will guarantee to make the hand a hundred per cent perfect hand or a hundred per cent good hand." The plaintiff was present when these words were alleged to have been spoken, and, if they are to be taken at their face value, it seems obvious that proof of their utterance would establish the giving of a warranty in accordance with his contention.

The defendant argues, however, that, even if these words were uttered by him, no reasonable man would understand that they were used with the intention of entering "into any contractual relation whatever," and that they could reasonably be understood only "as his expression in strong language that he believed and expected that as a result of the operation he would give the plaintiff a very good hand." It may be conceded, as the defendant contends, that, before the question of the making of a contract should be submitted to a jury, there is a preliminary question of law for the trial court to pass upon, i.e. "whether the words could possibly have the meaning imputed to them by the party who founds his case upon a certain interpretation," but it cannot be held that the trial court decided this question erroneously in the present case. It is unnecessary to determine at this time whether the argument of the defendant, based upon "common knowledge of the uncertainty which attends all surgical operations," and the improbability that a surgeon would ever contract to make a damaged part of the human body "one hundred per cent perfect" would, in the absence of countervailing considerations, be regarded as conclusive, for there were other factors in the present case which tended to support the contention of the plaintiff. There was evidence that the defendant repeatedly solicited from the plaintiff's father the opportunity to perform this operation, and the theory was advanced by plaintiff's counsel in cross-examination of defendant that he sought an opportunity to "experiment on skin grafting," in which he had little previous experience. If the jury accepted this part of plaintiff's contention, there would be a reasonable basis for the further conclusion that, if defendant spoke the words attributed to him, he did so with the intention that they should be accepted at their face value, as an inducement for the granting of consent to the operation by the plaintiff and his father, and there was ample evidence that they were so accepted by them. The question of the making of the alleged contract was properly submitted to the jury.

The substance of the charge to the jury on the question of damages appears in the following quotation: "If you find the plaintiff entitled to anything, he is entitled to recover for what pain and suffering he has been made to endure and for what injury he has sustained over and above what injury he had before." To this instruction the defendant seasonably excepted. By it, the jury was permitted to consider two elements of damage: (1) Pain and suffering due to the operation; and (2) positive ill effects of the operation upon the plaintiff's hand. Authority for any specific rule of damages in cases of this kind seems to be lacking, but, when tested by general principle and by analogy, it appears that the foregoing instruction was erroneous.

"By 'damages,' as that term is used in the law of contracts, is intended compensation for a breach, measured in the terms of the contract." Davis v. New England Cotton Yarn Co., 77 N.H. 403, 92 A. 732. The purpose of the law is "to put the plaintiff in as good a position as he would have been in had the defendant kept his contract." 3 Williston Cont. § 1338; Hardie–Tynes Mfg. Co. v. Eastern Cotton Oil Co., 150 N.C. 150, 63 S.E. 676. The measure of recovery "is based upon what the defendant should have given the plaintiff, not what the plaintiff has given the defendant or otherwise expended." 3 Williston Cont. § 1341. . . .

The present case is closely analogous to one in which a machine is built for a certain purpose and warranted to do certain work. In such cases, the usual rule of damages for breach of warranty in the sale of chattels is applied, and it is held that the measure of damages is the difference between the value of the machine, if it had corresponded with the warranty and its actual value, together with such incidental losses as the parties knew, or ought to have known, would probably result from a failure to comply with its terms. . . .

The rule thus applied is well settled in this state. "As a general rule, the measure of the vendee's damages is the difference between the value of the goods as they would have been if the warranty as to quality had been true, and the actual value at the time of the sale, including gains prevented and losses sustained, and such other damages as could be reasonably anticipated by the parties as likely to be caused by the vendor's failure to keep his agreement, and could not by reasonable care on the part of the vendee have been avoided." Union Bank v. Blanchard, 65 N.H. 21, 18 A. 90; . . . P.L. ch. 166, § 69, subd. 7. We therefore conclude that the true measure of the plaintiff's damage in the present case is the difference between the value to him of a perfect hand or a good hand, such as the jury found the defendant promised him, and the value of his hand in its present condition, including any incidental consequences fairly within the contemplation of the parties when they made their contract. 1 Sutherland, Damages (4th

Ed.) § 92. Damages not thus limited, although naturally resulting, are not to be given.

The extent of the plaintiff's suffering does not measure this difference in value. The pain necessarily incident to a serious surgical operation was a part of the contribution which the plaintiff was willing to make to his joint undertaking with the defendant to produce a good hand. It was a legal detriment suffered by him which constituted a part of the consideration given by him for the contract. It represented a part of the price which he was willing to pay for a good hand, but it furnished no test of the value of a good hand or the difference between the value of the hand which the defendant promised and the one which resulted from the operation.

It was also erroneous and misleading to submit to the jury as a separate element of damage any change for the worse in the condition of the plaintiff's hand resulting from the operation, although this error was probably more prejudicial to the plaintiff than to the defendant. Any such ill effect of the operation would be included under the true rule of damages set forth above, but damages might properly be assessed for the defendant's failure to improve the condition of the hand, even if there were no evidence that its condition was made worse as a result of the operation.

It must be assumed that the trial court, in setting aside the verdict, undertook to apply the same rule of damages which he had previously given to the jury, and, since this rule was erroneous, it is unnecessary for us to consider whether there was any evidence to justify his finding that all damages awarded by the jury above $500 were excessive.

Defendant's requests for instructions were loosely drawn, and were properly denied. A considerable number of issues of fact were raised by the evidence, and it would have been extremely misleading to instruct the jury in accordance with defendant's request No. 2, that "the only issue on which you have to pass is whether or not there was a special contract between the plaintiff and the defendant to produce a perfect hand." Equally inaccurate was defendant's request No. 5, which reads as follows: "You would have to find, in order to hold the defendant liable in this case, that Dr. McGee and the plaintiff both understood that the doctor was guaranteeing a perfect result from this operation." If the defendant said that he would guarantee a perfect result, and the plaintiff relied upon that promise, any mental reservations which he may have had are immaterial. The standard by which his conduct is to be judged is not internal, but external. . . . Defendant's request No. 7 was as follows: "If you should get so far as to find that there was a special contract guaranteeing a perfect result, you would still have to find for the defendant unless you also found that a further operation would not correct the disability claimed by the plaintiff." In view of the testimony that the defendant had refused to perform a further operation, it would clearly have been erroneous to give this instruction. The evidence would have justified a verdict for an amount sufficient to cover the cost of such an operation, even if the theory underlying this request were correct. . . .

New trial.

NOTE

On the eve of the new trial ordered in the principal case, Dr. McGee paid Hawkins $1,400 and settled the lawsuit. McGee then sued his liability insurance carrier, in the federal district court for New Hampshire, to recover that sum and an additional $2,850 in expenses, mostly attorneys' fees. (Counsel for the insurance company had participated in the trial of Hawkins v. McGee, assisting Dr. McGee's lawyer throughout, even though the insurance company had notified McGee at an early point in the proceedings that it disclaimed any liability, under its policy, because of McGee's alleged guaranty of the results of the operation.) The federal court denied McGee's claim, holding that the policy in question did not cover the "special contract" made with Hawkins but was limited by its terms to liabilities "in consequence of any malpractice, error, or mistake." Since the negligence count had been dismissed from the *Hawkins* litigation, McGee's insurer was therefore free to deny all liability under its policy. This ruling was affirmed in McGee v. United States Fidelity & Guaranty Co., 53 F.2d 953 (1st Cir.1931), where the court's opinion reveals that Hawkins' complaint in the suit against McGee (the principal case reported above) had alleged that Hawkins had been hospitalized for three months at the time of the operation, and that "the new tissue grafted upon said hand became matted, unsightly, and so healed and attached to said hand as to practically fill the hand with an unsightly growth, restricting the motion of the plaintiff's hand so that said hand has become useless to the plaintiff wherein, previous to said operation[,] [it] was a practical, useful hand." Additional information derived from later interviews with family members and Hawkins' lawyer can be found in Roberts, Hawkins Case: A Hair–Raising Experience, 66 Harv.L.Rec. 1 (1978). It seems the $1,400 settlement was used to take George to Montreal to determine whether another operation might reduce the hand's deformity. Doctors there concluded that nothing could be done for him. A comprehensive review of the trial itself and the competing accounts of Hawkins and McGee respectively can be found in O'Gorman, Expectation Damages, the Objective Theory of Contracts, and the "Hairy Hand" Case: A Proposed Modification to the Effect of Two Classical Contract Law Axioms in Cases Involving Contractual Misunderstandings, 99 Ky.L.J. 327 (2010).

Groves v. John Wunder Co.

Supreme Court of Minnesota, 1939.
205 Minn. 163, 286 N.W. 235.

STONE, J. Action for breach of contract. Plaintiff got judgment for a little over $15,000. Sorely disappointed by that sum, he appeals.

In August, 1927, S.J. Groves & Sons Co., a corporation (hereinafter . . . Groves), owned a tract of 24 acres of Minneapolis suburban real estate. It was served or easily could be reached by railroad trackage. It is zoned as heavy industrial property. But for lack of development of the neighborhood its principal value thus far may have been in the deposit of sand and gravel which it carried. The Groves company had a plant on the premises for excavating and screening the gravel. Nearby defendant owned and was operating a similar plant.

In August, 1927, Groves and defendant made the involved contract. For the most part it was a lease from Groves, as lessor, to defendant, as lessee; its term seven years. Defendant agreed to remove the sand and gravel and to leave the property "at a uniform grade, substantially the same as the grade now existing at the roadway . . . on said premises, and that in stripping the overburden . . . it will use said overburden for the purpose of maintaining and establishing said grade."

Under the contract defendant got the Groves screening plant. The transfer thereof and the right to remove the sand and gravel made the consideration moving from Groves to defendant, except that defendant incidentally got rid of Groves as a competitor. On defendant's part it paid Groves $105,000. So that from the outset, on Groves' part the contract was executed except for defendant's right to continue using the property for the stated term. (Defendant had a right to renewal which it did not exercise.)

Defendant breached the contract deliberately. It removed from the premises only "the richest and best of the gravel" and wholly failed, according to the findings, "to perform and comply with the terms, conditions, and provisions of said lease [respecting] the condition in which the surface of the demised premises was required to be left." Defendant surrendered the premises, not substantially at the grade required by the contract "nor at any uniform grade." Instead, the ground was "broken, rugged, and uneven." Plaintiff sues as assignee and successor in right of Groves.

As the contract was construed below, the finding is that to complete its performance 288,495 cubic yards of overburden would need to be excavated, taken from the premises, and deposited elsewhere. The reasonable cost of doing that was found to be upwards of $60,000. But, if defendant had left the premises at the uniform grade required by the lease, the reasonable value of the property on the determinative date would have been only $12,160. The judgment was for that sum, including interest, thereby nullifying plaintiff's claim that cost of completing the contract rather than difference in value of the land was the measure of damages. The gauge of damage adopted by the decision was the difference between the market value of plaintiff's land in the condition it was when the contract was made and what it would have been if defendant had performed.* The one question for us arises upon plaintiff's assertion that he was entitled, not to that difference in value, but to the reasonable cost to him of doing the work called for by the contract which defendant left undone.

1. Defendant's breach of contract was willful. There was nothing of good faith about it. Hence, that the decision below handsomely rewards bad faith and deliberate breach of contract is obvious. That is not allowable. Here the rule is well settled, and has been since Elliott v. Caldwell, 43 Minn. 357, 45 N.W. 845, that where the contractor willfully and fraudulently varies from the terms of a construction contract he cannot sue thereon and have the benefit of the equitable doctrine of substantial performance. That is the rule generally. . . .

Jacob & Youngs, Inc. v. Kent, 230 N.Y. 239, 129 N.E. 889, is typical. It was a case of substantial performance of a building contract. (This case is distinctly the opposite.) Mr. Justice Cardozo, in the course of his opinion, stressed the distinguishing features. "Nowhere," he said, "will change be

---

* [It appears this statement contains an error. The trial judge (jury trial having been waived by the parties) in fact described the damage formula as "the difference between the reasonable value of the property in the condition in which it was left by the defendant and what would be its reasonable market value had the defendant complied in all respects with the grading provisions of the contract." (Record, p. 258).

The trial judge had found (Record, p. 241) that the land was "without any value" on May 1, 1934, the date it was surrendered to Groves. This finding was based on the testimony of two witnesses who had testified at the trial in early December 1936. One of them, a real estate broker specializing in business and industrial properties, had stated (Record, p. 189): "You couldn't sell it now for any purpose; the value of real estate is the use to which it can be put, and I can't conceive of any use to which this property could be put in its condition, with the economical conditions as they were as of May 1st, 1934."—Eds.]

tolerated, however, if it is so dominant or pervasive as in any real or substantial measure to frustrate the purpose of the contract." Again, "the willful transgressor must accept the penalty of his transgression."

2. In reckoning damages for breach of a building or construction contract, the law aims to give the disappointed promisee, so far as money will do it, what he was promised. (9 Am.Jur., § 152.) It is so ruled by a long line of decisions in this state, beginning with Carli v. Seymour, Sabin & Co., 26 Minn. 276, 3 N.W. 348, where the contract was for building a road. There was a breach. Plaintiff was held entitled to recover what it would cost to complete the grading as contemplated by the contract. . . .

Never before, so far as our decisions show, has it even been suggested that lack of value in the land furnished to the contractor who had bound himself to improve it [provides] any escape from the ordinary consequences of a breach of the contract.

A case presently as interesting as any of our own is Sassen v. Haegle, 125 Minn. 441, 147 N.W. 445. The defendant, lessee of a farm, had agreed to haul and spread manure. He removed it, but spread it elsewhere than on the leased farm. Plaintiff had a verdict, but a new trial was ordered for error in the charge as to the measure of damages. The [court said], 125 Minn. 443, 147 N.W. [at] 446: "But it is also true that the landlord had a perfect right to stipulate as to the disposal of the manure or as to the way in which the farm should be worked, and the tenant cannot evade compliance by showing that the farm became more valuable or fertile by omitting the agreed work or doing other work. . . . The question is not whether plaintiff made a wise or foolish agreement. He had a right to have it performed as made, and the resulting damage, in case of failure, is the reasonable cost of performance. Whether such performance affects the value of the farm was no concern of defendant."

Even in case of substantial performance in good faith, the resulting defects being remediable, it is error to instruct that the measure of damage is "the difference in value between the house as it was and as it would have been if constructed according to contract." The "correct doctrine" is that the cost of remedying the defect is the "proper" measure of damages. Snider v. Peters Home Bldg. Co., 139 Minn. 413, 167 N.W. 108.

Value of the land (as distinguished from the value of the intended product of the contract, which ordinarily will be equivalent to its reasonable cost) is no proper part of any measure of damages for willful breach of a building contract. The reason is plain.

The summit from which to reckon damages from trespass to real estate is its actual value at the moment. The owner's only right is to be compensated for the deterioration in value caused by the tort. That is all he has lost. But not so if a contract to improve the same land has been breached by the contractor who refuses to do the work, especially where, as here, he has been paid in advance. The summit from which to reckon damages for that wrong is the hypothetical peak of accomplishment (not value) which would have been reached had the work been done as demanded by the contract.

The owner's right to improve his property is not trammeled by its small value. It is his right to erect thereon structures which will reduce its value. If that be the result, it can be of no aid to any contractor who declines performance. As said long ago in Chamberlain v. Parker, 45 N.Y. 569, 572: "A man may do what he will with his own, . . . and if he chooses to erect a monument to his caprice or folly on his premises, and employs and pays another to do it, it does not lie with a defendant who had been so employed and paid for building it, to say that his own performance would not be beneficial to the plaintiff." To the same effect is Restatement, Contracts, § 346, Illustrations of Subsection (1), par. 4.

Suppose a contractor were suing the owner for breach of a grading contract such as this. Would any element of value or lack of it, in the land, have any relevance in reckoning damages? Of course not. The contractor would be compensated for what he had lost, i.e., his profit. Conversely, in such a case as this, the owner is entitled to compensation for what he has lost, that is, the work or structure which he has been promised, for which he has paid, and of which he has been deprived by the contractor's breach.

To diminish damages recoverable against him in proportion as there is presently small value in the land would favor the faithless contractor. It would also ignore and so defeat plaintiff's right to contract and build for the future. . . . This factor is important when the subject matter is trackage property in the margin of such an area of population and industry as that of the Twin Cities. . . .

The genealogy of the error pervading the argument contra is easy to trace. It begins with Seely v. Alden, 61 Pa. 302, a tort case for pollution of a stream. Resulting depreciation in value of plaintiff's premises, of course, was the measure of damages. About 40 years later, in Bigham v. Wabash–Pittsburg T.R. Co., 223 Pa. 106, 72 A. 318, the measure of damages of the earlier tort case was used in one for breach of contract, without comment or explanation to show why. That case was followed [in cases decided in the states of Washington and Kentucky], with no thought given to the anomaly of using in a case in contract a standard ordinarily applicable only in cases of tort. . . .

The objective of this contract of present importance was the improvement of real estate. That makes irrelevant the rules peculiar to damages to chattels, arising from tort or breach of contract. . . . In tort, the thing lost is money value, nothing more. But under a construction contract, the thing lost by a breach such as we have here is a physical structure or accomplishment, a promised and paid for alteration in land. That is the "injury" for which the law gives him compensation. Its only appropriate measure is the cost of performance.

It is suggested that because of little or no value in his land the owner may be unconscionably enriched by such a reckoning. The answer is that there can be no unconscionable enrichment, no advantage upon which the law will frown, when the result is but to give one party to a contract only what the other has promised; particularly where, as here, the delinquent has had full payment for the promised performance.

3. It is said by the Restatement, Contracts, § 346, Comment b: "Sometimes defects in a completed structure cannot be physically remedied without tearing down and rebuilding, at a cost that would be imprudent and unreasonable. The law does not require damages to be measured by a method requiring such economic waste. If no such waste is involved, the cost of remedying the defect is the amount awarded as compensation for failure to render the promised performance."

The "economic waste" declaimed against by the decisions applying that rule has nothing to do with the value in money of the real estate, or even with the product of the contract. The waste avoided is only that which would come from wrecking a physical structure completed, or nearly so, under the contract. The cases applying that rule go no further. . . . Absent such waste, as it is in this case, the rule of the Restatement, Contracts, § 346, is that "the cost of remedying the defect is the amount awarded as compensation for failure to render the promised performance." That means that defendants here are liable to plaintiff for the reasonable cost of doing what defendants promised to do and have willfully declined to do. . . .

The judgment must be reversed with a new trial to follow.

OLSON, J. (dissenting). . . . [The] premises were to be used by defendant "for the purpose of removing the sand and gravel therefrom." The cash consideration was $105,000, plus defendant's covenant to level and grade the premises to a specified base. There was no segregation or allocation of the cash consideration made applicable to any of the various items going into the deal, and the instrument does not suggest any sum as being representative of the cost of performance by defendant of the leveling and grading process. Nor is there any finding that the contractor "willfully and fraudulently" violated the terms of its contract. All that can be said is that defendant did nothing except to mine the sand and gravel purchased by it and deemed best suited to its own interest and advantage. No question of partial or substantial performance of its covenant is involved since it did nothing in that behalf. The sole question here is whether the rule adopted by the court respecting recoverable damages is wrong. . . . [Plaintiff's] sole contention before the trial court and here is that upon [the] findings the court, as a matter of law, should have allowed him the cost of performance, $60,893.28, plus interest since date of the breach, May 1, 1934, amounting to more than $76,000.

Since there is no issue of fact, we should limit our inquiry to the single legal problem presented: What amount in money will adequately compensate plaintiff for his loss caused by defendant's failure to render performance? . . .

We have here then a situation where, concededly, if the contract had been performed, plaintiff would have had property worth, in round numbers, no more than $12,000. If he is to be awarded damages in an amount exceeding $60,000 he will be receiving at least 500 percent more than his property, properly leveled to grade by actual performance, was intrinsically worth when the breach occurred. To so conclude is to give him something far beyond what the parties had in mind or contracted for. There is no showing made, nor any finding suggested, that this property was unique, specially desirable for a particular or personal use, or of special value as to location or future use different from that of other property surrounding it. . . . [I]t seems clear that what the parties contracted for was to put the property in shape for general sale. . . .

 The theory upon which plaintiff relies for application of the cost of performance rule must have for its basis cases where the property or the improvement to be made is unique or personal instead of being of the kind ordinarily governed by market values. His action is one at law for damages, not for specific performance. As there was no affirmative showing of any peculiar fitness of this property to a unique or personal use, the rule to be applied is, I think, the one applied by the [trial] court. . . . Damages recoverable for breach of a contract to construct is the difference between the market value of the property in the condition it was when delivered to and received by plaintiff and what its market value would have been if defendant had fully complied with its terms. . . . Sandy Valley & Elkhorn Ry. Co. v. Hughes, 175 Ky. 320, 194 S.W. 344. It is interesting to note that in the

Kentucky case the court reversed its former opinion, [saying] (175 Ky. 320, 321, 194 S.W. 344):

"... From plaintiffs' avowal on the first trial it appears that it would cost at least $15,000 to do the work required by the contract, and from other testimony in the record it is by no means improbable that the cost would be far in excess of that sum. If this be true, the cost would far exceed the market value of the entire farm. If the contract had been performed, plaintiff would have had a farm with the place from which the earth and stone were taken reduced to the level of the railroad grade and in condition for building purposes. As the case stands, this provision of the contract has not been complied with. What, then, was plaintiff's damage? *Manifestly, not what it would cost to do the work, for, if the work had been done, plaintiff would not have received the cost of the work, but would have been benefited only to the extent that the work increased the market value of his land.* We, therefore, conclude that the measure of damages is the difference between the market value of the farm in its present condition and what its market value would have been if the land from which the earth and stone were removed had been reduced to the level of the railroad grade and left in condition for building purposes." (Italics supplied.)

The principle for which I contend is not novel in construction contract cases. It is well stated in McCormick, Damages, § 168, pp. 648, 649: "In whatever way the issue arises, the generally approved standards for measuring the owner's loss from defects in the work are two: First, in cases where the defect is one that can be repaired or cured without undue expense, so as to make the building conform to the agreed plan, then the owner recovers such amount as he has reasonably expended, or will reasonably have to spend, to remedy the defect. Second, if, on the other hand, the defect in material or construction is one that cannot be remedied without an expenditure for reconstruction disproportionate to the end to be attained, or without endangering unduly other parts of the building, then the damages will be measured not by the cost of remedying the defect, but by the difference between the value of the building as it is and what it would have been worth if it had been built in conformity with the contract." ...

In 1 Restatement, Contracts, § 346, Illustrations of Subsection (1), par. 3, reads: "A contracts with B to sink an oil well on A's own land adjacent to the land of B, for development and exploration purposes. Other exploration wells prove that there is no oil in that region; and A breaks his promise to sink the well. B can get judgment for only nominal damages, not the cost of sinking the well." And in Guardian Trust Co. v. Brothers (Tex.Civ.App.) 59 S.W.2d 343, a case in substance much like ours, the court said: "The loss or injury actually sustained by the obligee, rather than the cost of performance by the obligor, is the proper measure of damages for the breach of a contract...."

If this were a case to recover damages for tortious injury the applicable rule is the difference in the market value and not the cost of restoring the premises to the former condition if such exceeds the diminution in value.... If, then, the landowner received full compensation by this measure, why is he not also fully compensated by receiving the same amount in the case before us? Once it has been held that the market value wholly restores the landowner when his property is permanently damaged, it must be held that he is also entirely repaid by the same measure in our present situation. So it would seem that whether plaintiff's damages are to be measured by the rule applicable to the theory of breach of contract cases or that of tortious conduct the extent of his recovery can be no greater than his actual loss. In either case he may not be heard to complain that because the equivalent to defendant's performance will cost a larger amount than that, therefore he should receive such greater amount rather than his real loss. . . .

No one doubts that a party may contract for the doing of anything he may choose to have done (assuming what is to be done is not unlawful) "although the thing to be produced had no marketable value." (45 N.Y. 572.) In 1 Restatement, Contracts, § 346, Illustrations of Subsection (1), par. 4, the same thought is thus stated:

"A contracts to construct a monumental fountain in B's yard for $5,000, but abandons the work after the foundation has been laid and $2,800 has been paid by B. The contemplated fountain is so ugly that it would decrease the number of possible buyers of the place. The cost of completing the fountain would be $4,000. B can get judgment for $1,800, the cost of completion less the part of price unpaid."

But that is not what plaintiff's predecessor in interest contracted for. Such a provision might well have been made, but the parties did not. They could undoubtedly have provided for liquidated damages for nonperformance, . . . or they might have determined in money what the value of performance was considered to be and thereby have contractually provided a measure for failure of performance.

The opinion also suggests that this property lies in an area where the owner might rightly look for future development, being in a so-called industrial zone, and that as such he should be privileged to so hold it. This he may of course do. But let us assume that on May 1, 1934, condemnation to acquire this area had so far progressed as to leave only the question of price (market value) undetermined; that the area had been graded in strict conformity with the contract but that the actual market value of the premises was only $12,160, as found by the court and acquiesced in by plaintiff, what would the measure of his damages be? Obviously, the limit of his recovery could be no more than the then market value of his property. . . . In what manner has plaintiff been hurt beyond the damages awarded? As to him "economic waste" is not apparent. Assume that defendant abandoned the entire project without taking a single yard of gravel therefrom but left the premises as they were when the lease was made, could plaintiff recover damages upon the basis here established? The trouble with the prevailing opinion is that here plaintiff's loss is not made the basis for the amount of his recovery but rather what it would cost the defendant. No case had been decided upon that basis until now.

Plaintiff asserts that he knows of no rule "giving a different measure of damages for public contracts and for private contracts in case of nonperformance." It seems to me there is a clear distinction to be drawn with respect to the application of the rule for recoverable damages in case of breach of a public works contract from that applicable to contracts between private parties. The construction of a public building, a sewer, drainage ditch, highway, or other public work, permits of no application of the market value doctrine. There simply is and can be no "market value" as to such. And for this cogent reason there can be but one rule of damages to apply, that of cost of completion of the thing contracted to be done. I think the judgment should be affirmed.

[One judge joined in the dissent; two others did not participate. The vote was 3 to 2. Not quite 20 years later, the Supreme Court of Minnesota, in discussing Groves v. John Wunder Co., commented that "[t]he majority opinion is based, at least in part, on the fact that the breach of contract was willful and in bad faith"—a deliberate "failure to perform at all," distinguished from a situation where a defective performance is accompanied by a "substantial good-faith effort" to fulfill the contract. H.P. Droher & Sons v. Toushin, 250 Minn. 490, 85 N.W.2d 273 (1957).]

NOTE

Counsel in the principal case have provided some later history of the Groves tract. After the decision reported above, the case was compromised and defendant paid $55,000 in a cash settlement. The land remained in the same condition until 1951, when a corporation controlled by Frank Groves, to which he had meanwhile transferred it, leveled a portion of the surface without removing any of the overburden. In 1953, approximately three-fifths of the tract was sold for $45,000. The cost of leveling this portion had been about $6,000. The purchaser bought with the intention of using the land for the erection of factories that required railroad trackage. The leveling done rendered the land suitable for this purpose, though the grade and elevation remained higher than they would have been if the overburden had been removed in accordance with the lease to the Wunder Co.

––––––––

Peevyhouse v. Garland Coal & Mining Co.
382 P.2d 109 (Okl.1962), cert. denied, 375 U.S. 906 (1963)

Plaintiffs leased 60 acres of their 120–acre farm, which contained coal deposits, to defendant for a period of five years. It was understood that defendant would extract the coal from the leased premises by strip mining. The lease expressly provided that defendant, at the conclusion of its operations, would fill in all pits and smooth the surface. Defendant performed none of these remedial measures, which, the evidence at trial showed, would have required moving "many thousand cubic yards" of dirt at a cost estimated by the plaintiffs' expert witness to be $29,000. The defendant introduced evidence showing that these measures would increase the value of the farm by not more than $300. Plaintiffs sued for $25,000 damages and in the trial court recovered a judgment (based on a jury verdict) for $5,000. The Oklahoma Supreme Court (4 to 3) modified the judgment, reducing it to $300. The majority opinion pointed out that $5,000 was more than the value of the farm had the remedial work been done, that the primary object of the contract was "the economical recovery and marketing of coal from the premises, to the profit of all the parties," and that the remedial work promised was merely "incidental." The majority also relied on an Oklahoma statute providing that "no person can recover a greater amount in damages for breach of an obligation than he would have gained by the full performance thereof on both sides." In the court's view, this statute limited plaintiffs' damages to diminution in value "in spite of the agreement of the parties."

The majority dealt with the relevant case law in this manner: "Groves v. John Wunder Co. is the only case . . . in which the [cost] rule has been followed [where] the cost of performance greatly exceeded the diminution in value resulting from the breach. . . . [T]hree out of four appellate courts have followed the diminution in value rule [in such] circumstances. . . . We do not think either [the building and construction contract analogy used in *Groves* or the grading and excavation analogy used by the other courts] is strictly applicable [here]. The primary purpose of the lease contract [was neither construction nor grading but] merely to accomplish the economical recovery and marketing of coal from the premises. The . . . remedial work [was] incidental to the main object involved.

"Even in the case of . . . building and construction contracts, the authorities are not in agreement as to the factors to be considered in determining whether the [cost] or value rule should be applied. [The court here quotes Restatement of Contracts § 346(1)(a), which is reproduced infra p. 16.] [T]he Restatement makes it clear that the 'economic waste' referred to consists of the destruction of a substantially completed [structure]. . . . [N]o such destruction is involved [here]. On the other hand, in McCormick, Damages, § 168, it is said with regard to [building] contracts that '. . . where the defect is one that can be repaired or cured without *undue expense*' the cost of performance is the proper measure of damages, but where [the defect] 'is one that cannot be remedied without *an expenditure for reconstruction disproportionate to the end to be attained*' (emphasis supplied) the value rule should be followed. The same idea was expressed in Jacob & Youngs, Inc. v. Kent, 230 N.Y. 239, 129 N.E. 889, as follows: 'The owner is entitled to the money which will permit him to complete, unless the costs of completion is grossly out of proportion to the good to be attained. When that is true, the measure is the difference in value.' . . .

"In view of the unrealistic fact situation in the instant case [an outlay of $29,000 for improvements to property that would increase its value about $300], and [the Oklahoma statute which bars a plaintiff from receiving greater damages for a breach than would have been realized from a contract's full performance], we are of the opinion that the 'relative economic benefit' is a proper consideration here. . . . We therefore hold that where, in a coal mining lease, . . . the [agreed] remedial work is not done, the measure of damages . . . is ordinarily the reasonable cost of performance of the work; however, where the contract provision breached was merely incidental to the main purpose in view, and where the economic benefit . . . to the lessor by full performance of the work is grossly disproportionate to the cost of performance, the damages . . . are limited to the diminution in value [of the premises]."

The dissenting opinion argued that all the costs and difficulties in performing defendant's promise could have been foreseen when the contract was made and that, by defendant's own admission, the plaintiffs had insisted on inclusion of the remedial provision and had indicated that without it they would not sign the lease. The dissent urged that the cost of the promised performance should have been awarded, as in Groves v. John Wunder Co., and that the majority's solution "completely rescinds and holds for naught" the solemn contract of the parties, "taking from the plaintiffs the benefits of the contract and placing those benefits in defendant." [The factual background of the case is examined in great depth in Maute, The Unearthed Facts of *Peevyhouse v. Garland Coal & Mining Co.*, in Contracts Stories 265–303 (2007). Professor Maute points out that the Peevyhouses, in insisting on remediation, gave up a $3,000 payment the coal company typically gave to landowners. She also suggests that their lawyer, who was used to handling tort cases, exaggerated the costs of remediation and that these may in fact have been close to the jury verdict of $5,000. Do either of these facts change the way you look at the case? In the decades after the lawsuit, the Peevyhouses continued to live on the farm. Even now, the land has not been restored. It can be viewed at: http://www.google.com/maps?f=q&hl=e&q=stigler,+oklahoma&ie=UTF8&t=k&om=1&z=18&ll=35.17465,-5.142851&spn=0.001995,0.005322&iwloc=A.]

COMMENT: COST OR VALUE IN GENERAL CONTRACT LAW

The Restatement of Contracts, to which both *Groves and Peevyhouse* refer, was issued by the American Law Institute (ALI), a private organization whose elected membership includes prominent lawyers, judges, and law teachers interested in improving the law and its administration. The group was formed in 1923, as a result of a study reporting that the two chief defects in our law were its uncertainty and its complexity. Accordingly, over the years the ALI has prepared and published in condensed form "Restatements"—now in a third series—of the principal subject-matter areas of American private law (it has also undertaken numerous codification projects, model acts, and studies). The first of these projects was the Restatement of Contracts, which was completed in 1932. Its purpose was "to state clearly and precisely in the light of the decisions the principles and rules of the common law," including "the law which has grown from the application by the courts of generally and long adopted statutes." Work on a revised contracts Restatement was begun in the early 1960s and completed in 1979. One particular aim of the Restatement, Second, of the Law of Contracts, was to take account of the formulations of contract principles appearing in Article 2 (Sales) of the Uniform Commercial Code (UCC), a comprehensive statute on commercial law which was also sponsored (in part) by the Institute and which has been adopted in all of our states except Louisiana. There will be many occasions ahead for referring to both contracts Restatements and to the UCC. Both provide useful ways of accessing the common law of contracts. At the same time, both have significant limitations. The UCC, when adopted by a legislature, becomes a set of fully authoritative rules, binding on the courts. Article 2, however, only applies to contracts involving the sale of goods. Many, indeed perhaps most, of the contracts that the practicing lawyer encounters—from merger agreements to real estate transactions to employment contracts—do not involve goods. Article 2 applies in these cases only by analogy. Article 2 itself is now more than fifty years old. The ALI engaged in a large-scale effort to revise it in the 1990s, but the revised version did not win any adoptions.

The Restatement aspires to apply to contracts of every type, but it is not law and, technically speaking, not binding on anyone. Courts generally have accorded to the Restatements a status of "persuasive" authority, commensurate with the Institute's claim, made in the first Restatement of Contracts, that its formulations of rule and doctrine "may be regarded as . . . the product of expert opinion as well as the expression of the law by the legal profession." It is accurate to say that the influence of the ALI's work is widespread, and that many of its Restatements have been accorded an authority greater than that of any legal treatise.

Section 346 of the first Restatement, on which both opinions in *Groves* rely in drawing their opposing conclusions, stated the principles that were believed to be appropriate for calculating damages for breach of construction contracts. Section 346(1)(a) provides that for "defective and unfinished construction," the aggrieved party can get judgment for either:

> (i) the reasonable cost of construction and completion in accordance with the contract, if this is possible and does not involve unreasonable economic waste; or

> (ii) the difference between the value that the product contracted for would have had and the value of the performance that has been received by the plaintiff, if construction and completion in accordance with the contract would involve unreasonable economic waste. . . .

It then gives several illustrations, of which we repeat the two quoted by the dissenter in *Groves*:

> 3. A contracts with B to sink an oil well on A's land adjacent to the land of B, for development and exploration purposes. Other exploration wells prove that there is no oil in that region; and A breaks his promise to sink the well. B can get judgment for only nominal damages, not for the cost of sinking the well.

> 4. A contracts to construct a monumental fountain in B's yard for $5000, but abandons the work after the foundation has been laid and $2800 has been paid by B. The contemplated fountain is so ugly that it would decrease the number of possible buyers of the place. The cost of completing the fountain would be $4000. B can get judgment for $1800, the cost of completion less the part of the price unpaid.

The general principles stated in § 346 of the first Restatement are preserved in Restatement, Second §§ 347, 348, with some changes in terminology—most notably abandonment of talk of "economic waste." Thus, § 348(2), which replaces former § 346 on breaches resulting in defective or unfinished construction, recognizes the customary alternative bases for calculating the injured party's loss in value, but in these terms: "diminution in the market price of the property" or "the reasonable cost of completing performance or of remedying the defects if that cost is not clearly disproportionate to the probable loss in value to him."

———

Landis v. William Fannin Builders, Inc.

Court of Appeals of Ohio, 2011.
193 Ohio App. 3d 318, 951 N.E.2d 1078.

KLATT, J. . . . In 2004, Landis and his wife, Weidman, decided to build a custom home on land that Landis owned in Pleasantville, Ohio. After interviewing three builders, they chose Fannin Builders to construct their home. On May 4, 2004, appellees signed a contract with Fannin Builders, in which Fannin Builders agreed to construct appellees' home in accordance with the plans and specifications attached to the contract for $356,750.

The specifications for appellees' home called for T1–11 exterior siding covered with two coats of stain in a color of appellees' choice. T1–11 siding is a plywood siding with one-inch-deep vertical grooves spaced 11 inches apart. Appellees chose T1–11 siding for their home because it provided a more natural, rustic look than other types of siding. Before signing the construction contract, appellees sought, and received, assurances from Fannin Builders that it had experience with installing and staining T1–11 siding.

For the most part, the contract specifications indicated certain types of materials appellees wanted (i.e., ceramic tile floors or marble countertops), but did not list specific brands, designs, or colors of the materials. Throughout construction, Fannin Builders would request that appellees choose the brands, designs, or colors as the home progressed to the point where Fannin Builders needed to install the materials. When the time came to apply the stain to the exterior siding, Fannin Builders provided appellees with a brochure entitled "Semi–Transparent & Semi–Solid Color Palettes for all Cabot Colors." The brochure depicted stains in over 30 colors, each available in two different pigment levels: semitransparent (lightly pigmented) or semisolid (extra pigment). Appellees chose a semitransparent stain in a green color, which Cabot, the stain manufacturer, named "allagash." Landis communicated his and his wife's choice to Fannin Builders in a September 2, 2004 e-mail.

Fannin Builders subcontracted with 84 Lumber for the procurement and installation of the T1–11 siding. Unfortunately, 84 Lumber underestimated the amount of siding needed to completely clad appellees' home. Consequently, the company 84 Lumber hired to stain the T1–11 siding, Precision Applied Coating Enterprises ("PACE"), stained the 19 additional sheets separately from the majority of the siding. Although PACE stained both batches of siding with Cabot semitransparent allagash stain, one batch of siding turned out a noticeably darker hue than the other batch.

Weidman visited the construction site after 84 Lumber delivered the siding, and she saw that one stack of siding appeared darker in shade than the other stack. Weidman asked Jeff Klinger, Fannin Builder's field superintendent, if the different color would be a problem. According to Weidman, Klinger answered "no" and assured her that a second coat of stain, applied after the siding was in place, would blend the two shades so that they would match.

. When installing the siding, 84 Lumber did not attempt to group same-colored siding together. Instead, 84 Lumber placed darker and lighter siding at random intervals around the perimeter of the house and unattached garage. As a result, appellees' home acquired a striped or patchwork appearance.

The closing on appellees' home was scheduled for January 4, 2005. While Fannin Builders had substantially completed construction by that date, certain tasks remained undone. One of these tasks was the application of the second coat of stain on the siding. Fannin Builders told appellees that the stain should not be applied in temperatures below 50 degrees Fahrenheit, so appellees consented to delay application of the second coat of stain until spring 2005.

At the closing, appellees paid Fannin Builders almost the entire contract price, withholding only $2,000 in escrow to be paid out once Fannin Builders finished all work on the house. During the closing, appellees received from Fannin Builders a number of documents, including a homeowner's manual, a 20–year limited warranty on the home's structural components, and a one-year limited warranty on various aspects of the home's materials and construction.

Shortly after they moved into their new house, appellees observed workers applying a second coat of stain to the exterior siding outside their dining room. Appellees contend that eventually, the whole house and the garage received a second coat of stain. Although appellees did not see the entire staining process, they base their contention on the fact that green stain appears on all the grey trim that edges the siding. Because PACE stained the trim at its facility, the green stain on the trim could have come only from the sloppy application of a second coat of stain after both the siding and trim were installed.

Contrary to Klinger's earlier assurances, the second coat of stain did not improve the patchwork appearance of the siding. Appellees and Fannin Builders discussed various ways in which to fix the patchwork appearance. In spring 2005, appellees allowed Fannin Builders to remove siding from the back of the garage in order to try stain matching. The attempt was unsuccessful in producing a uniform color.

On June 14, 2005, representatives from Fannin Builders, 84 Lumber, and PACE met at appellees' home to confer about the siding problem. At that meeting, 84 Lumber agreed to provide and install new siding, and PACE agreed to stain the new siding. . . .

84 Lumber delivered the replacement siding to appellees' home in early September 2005. When appellees examined the siding, they discovered that it was yellow, not green. Appellees contacted Fannin Builders immediately, explained that the siding was the wrong color, and stated that they did not want the siding installed without discussion of the problem.

When subsequent communication with PACE revealed that PACE had, indeed, stained the replacement siding with the correct stain, appellees and Fannin Builders disagreed about the appropriate next course of action. Fannin Builders wanted to restain the siding on the house, while appellees advocated restaining the replacement siding. Landis told Fannin to delay any additional staining until they could arrive at a mutually agreeable solution. Despite Landis's instruction, a Fannin Builders' subcontractor attempted to blend the two stain colors on the siding on the front of the garage. Both appellees and Fannin Builders agree that the result looked horrible.

The same day that the subcontractor tried to fix the siding with additional stain, Fannin Builders had 84 Lumber remove the replacement siding from appellees' property. As Fannin later explained, he had 84 Lumber remove the replacement siding because appellees "rejected the color of the new siding [and] it makes no sense to put a siding on [the] home with a color [appellees] do not like and hope we can re-stain it to something acceptable." However, Fannin Builders did not inform appellees of its decision to recall the replacement siding or the reasoning behind that decision before implementing it.

After discovering the botched fix and the absence of the siding, Landis e-mailed Fannin Builders instructing it not to do any additional work relative to the siding problem without appellees' prior notice and approval. In a telephone call following that e-mail, Scott Gramke, owner and general manager of PACE, suggested that a solid stain in the allagash color would cover the patchwork appearance of the siding. Appellees were reluctant to use a solid stain because it could not render the natural, rustic look that appellees wanted. Unlike a semitransparent stain, a solid stain masked, rather than highlighted, the grain and natural imperfections of the T1–11 siding. Nevertheless, Landis agreed to test the solid stain by applying it to a sheet of siding that appellees had taken from the replacement batch of siding. Unfortunately, appellees were displeased with both the color and opacity of the solid stain.

Over the next year and a half, appellees and Fannin Builders periodically discussed potential solutions for fixing the patchwork appearance of the siding, but they could not come to any agreement. . . .

The trial court determined that appellees' damages amounted to $66,906.24, and after setting off the $3,908.98 that appellees owed Fannin Builders under the construction contract, the trial court awarded appellees $62,997.26. . . .

In the case at bar, the parties do not dispute that the evidence establishes that Fannin Builders fell below local industry standards in constructing a house with siding of such disparate color. Fannin admitted that the siding is unacceptable under industry standards. The BIA report states that the color variance in the siding "does not comply with professional standard's [sic] in the residential construction industry." Finally, appellees' expert witness testified that the patchwork appearance of the siding does not meet industry standards. Given this evidence, we conclude that the trial court did not err in finding that Fannin Builders' failure to provide siding in a uniform color amounted to a breach of contract. Because the siding does not conform to industry standards, Fannin Builders breached its implied duty to perform in a workmanlike manner. . . .

Fannin Builders argues that the trial court erred in awarding appellees damages based on the cost to replace the mismatched siding, instead of the difference in the market value of the house as contracted for and as received. We disagree.

Generally, the appropriate measure of damages in an action for a breach of a construction contract is the cost to repair the deficient work, that is, the cost of placing the building in the condition contemplated by the parties at the time they entered into the contract. Some Ohio courts subscribe to an exception to this general measure of damages. Although never adopted by this court, various other Ohio appellate courts have applied the economic-waste rule to determine damages for the breach of a construction contract. Under the economic-waste rule, if repair of a construction defect "will involve unreasonable economic waste, damages are measured by the difference between the market value that the structure contracted for would have had and that of the imperfect structure received by the plaintiff." Ohio Valley Bank v. Copley (1997), 121 Ohio App.3d 197, 210, 699 N.E.2d 540. Economic waste arises when the total cost to remedy a construction defect is grossly disproportionate to the good to be attained. . . .

The economic-waste rule emanates from courts' disinclination to award windfalls. Sometimes, the owner of a defective structure receives sufficient value from the builder's work that he or she will decide not to fix the defect, and instead, will pocket any damages awarded based on the cost of repairs. . . .

Similar concerns about unjust enrichment underlie the rule establishing the measure of damages for temporary injury to real property. In Ohio Collieries v. Cocke (1923), 107 Ohio St. 238, 248–249, 140 N.E. 356, the Supreme Court of Ohio held that if wrongful injury to real property can be repaired, then:

> [T]he measure of damages is the reasonable cost of restoration, plus reasonable compensation for the loss of the use of the property between the time of the injury and the restoration, unless such cost of restoration exceeds the difference in the market value of the property before and after the injury, in which case the difference in market value becomes the measure.

Like the economic-waste rule, this rule seeks to preclude the injured party from receiving a monetary windfall. In the case of temporary injury to real property, the injured party achieves this windfall by choosing to sell the property rather than restore it, resulting in a profit to the extent that the restoration costs exceed the diminution in market value.

Recently, in *Martin v. Design Constr. Servs., Inc.*, 121 Ohio St. 3d 66, 2009-Ohio-1, 902 N.E.2d 10, the Supreme Court of Ohio limited the rule enunciated in *Ohio Collieries*. The court recognized the relevance of evidence regarding the diminution in market value of injured property in setting a damage award. However, the court abjured *Ohio Collieries'* automatic limitation of damages to the loss of market value when the cost of restoration exceeded that loss. In the place of the *Ohio Collieries* rule, the court imposed a reasonableness test. While diminution in market value remains a consideration, "the essential inquiry is whether the damages sought are reasonable." Id. at ¶ 25.

The economic-waste rule and the rule expressed in *Ohio Collieries* developed in different contexts. The economic-waste rule restricts the damages recoverable for breach of contract. The rule governing imposition of damages for the temporary injury to real property originated from, and is generally applied to, tort cases. Nevertheless, we conclude that the reasonableness test announced in *Martin* precludes a strict application of the economic-waste rule.

"The fundamental rule of the law of damages is that the injured party shall have compensation for all of the injuries sustained." Fantozzi v. Sandusky Cement Prods. Co. (1992), 64 Ohio St.3d 601, 612, 597 N.E.2d 474. Thus, in both contract and tort actions, the appropriate measure of damages is that which will make the injured party whole. Consequently, both the economic-waste rule and the rule governing temporary injury to real property share the same objective. Moreover, as we explained above, both rules emerged from a desire to prevent the injured party from receiving a windfall. Given the rules' identical purpose and origin, we conclude that the economic-waste rule, like the *Ohio Collieries* rule, must cede in favor of the reasonableness test.

Therefore, in a case involving a breach of a construction contract where the breaching party seeks to limit damages to the diminution in value, a fact-finder must determine whether under the facts of that case, it is more reasonable to award damages based on the cost of the remedy or based on the diminution in value. Although a fact-finder may consider whether the cost of the remedy grossly exceeds the difference in the value of the structure with and without the defect, that consideration will not necessarily control the amount of the damage award. Since the goal of any damage award is to make a party whole, a fact-finder must determine which measure of damage best accomplishes that goal without exceeding the bounds of reasonableness.

Here, the trial court awarded appellees the cost to replace the siding because it determined that damages based on loss of market value could not fully compensate appellees. Because the purpose of the contract was the construction of a custom-built home with the aesthetics appellees desired, Fannin Builders' failure to achieve those aesthetics warranted an award of damages that would allow appellees to correct the defect. We find the trial court's decision to award appellees the cost of replacement, rather than the loss of market value, reasonable in this case.

As appellees testified, they contracted for the construction of a custom-built home. Appellees decided to build such a home because they wanted a particular house design and the ability to choose any material and finish they liked. Appellees explained to Fannin Builders that they wanted their house to have a natural, rustic look and that to achieve this look, they wanted T1–11 exterior siding stained with a semitransparent stain. Although the contract did not designate any particular stain opacity, Fannin conceded in his trial testimony that under the contract, Fannin Builders was obligated to apply stain with the opacity that appellees chose. Indisputably, appellees chose a semitransparent stain.

Because appellees placed such importance on the natural appearance of their home, they repeatedly rebuffed Fannin Builders' suggestion that they accept a solid stain. Appellees hired Fannin Builders to construct their "dream home," in which they planned to live many years. Consequently, appellees vigorously opposed Fannin Builders' attempts to get them to compromise on their desire to have T1–11 siding with a semitransparent stain.

According to 84 Lumber's expert witness, the market value of appellees' home is $8,500 less than it would be if it was stained a uniform color. The expert witness arrived at this valuation because the cost to apply two coats of solid stain to the siding is $8,500. Under the economic-waste rule, appellees' damages might have amounted to only $8,500, as opposed to the $66,906.24 necessary to replace the siding.[1] We, however, concur with the trial court that $8,500 could not fully compensate appellees. Given that appellees contracted for a custom home and that appellees place a high value on the rustic look, the cost to achieve the rustic look is the only reasonable measure of damages. Thus, the trial court did not err in awarding appellees damages based on the cost to replace the siding. . . .

––––––––––

[1] We question the likelihood of this outcome. Courts outside of Ohio exempt cases from the economic-waste rule and award damages based on the cost of remedy when aesthetic values make correction of the defect particularly important to a homeowner. As one court observed:

> If a proud householder, who plans to live out his days in the home of his dreams, orders a new roof of red barrel tile and the roofer instead installs a purple one, money damages for the reduced value of his house may not be enough to offset the strident offense to aesthetic sensibilities, continuing over the life of the roof.

Gory Assoc. Industries, Inc. v. Jupiter Roofing & Sheet Metal, Inc. 358 So.2d 93, 95 (Fla. App. 1978).

Acme Mills & Elevator Co. v. Johnson

Court of Appeals of Kentucky, 1911.
141 Ky. 718, 133 S.W. 784.

CLAY, COMMISSIONER. On April 26th, 1909, appellee J.C. Johnson executed and delivered to appellant Acme Mills & Elevator Co. the following contract:

"April 26th, 1909.

"I have this day sold to Ernest W. Steger, for Acme Mills & Elevator Co., 2,000 bushels No. 2 merchantable wheat, mill scale to apply, sacks to be furnished, to be paid for on delivery at Hopkinsville, Kentucky, at $1.03 per bushel, to be delivered from thresher 1909."

Appellee failed to deliver the wheat at the time agreed upon, and appellant brought this action to recover damages in the sum of $240 and for the further sum of $80, being the value of 1,000 sacks which appellant had furnished to appellee for his use in delivering the wheat. Appellee admitted the execution and breach of the contract, but denied that appellant was damaged. He further pleaded that he threshed his wheat after the 25th of July; that this was the time fixed for delivery, and wheat was then worth only about 97½ cents per bushel. He also pleaded that, at the time fixed for the delivery of the wheat, appellant had suspended business, was unable to comply with its contract, and had no money to pay for the wheat. In another paragraph he admitted his indebtedness for the item of $80 covering the sacks furnished him by appellant, and offered to confess judgment for that amount. The allegations of the answer were denied by reply. Subsequently appellant tendered and offered to file an amended reply, wherein it pleaded that on the 13th day of July, 1909, appellee, of his own wrong and without right or legal authority or the consent of appellant, sold his wheat to the Liberty Mills at Nashville, Tennessee, at the price of $1.16 per bushel, and that by reason of this fact he was estopped to plead in his answer that his wheat was not threshed until after the 25th of July, or that the market price for said wheat at the date of said threshing did not exceed $1 per bushel. The court declined to permit this amended reply to be filed, but entered an order making it a part of the record. The trial resulted in a verdict for appellant in the sum of $80 for the sacks, whereupon judgment was entered against appellee for $80 and costs. From that judgment this appeal is prosecuted.

The evidence for appellee is to the effect that he did not begin threshing his wheat until after the 25th of July; he completed his threshing about the 29th. . . . This fact is established by appellee and his brother and the testimony of two or three other witnesses who passed appellee's field while he was engaged in the work of threshing. There is no evidence to the contrary. At the time he finished threshing, wheat of the kind which he had contracted to sell appellant was not worth over $1 per bushel. This fact is established by the evidence of several witnesses, and there is practically no evidence to the contrary. Appellee attempted to justify his conduct in breaching the contract by certain rumors to the effect that appellant had suspended business and was unable to pay for the wheat. While there may have been rumors to this effect, the evidence fails to establish the fact that appellant had suspended business. About the 14th or 15th of July, appellee sold his wheat to the Liberty Mills at Nashville for $1.16 per bushel. On the 24th of July the price of wheat began to fall, until it reached about $1 per bushel on the 29th.

[Appellant's evidence] is devoted, chiefly, to establishing the fact that appellant did not suspend business and was fully able to pay for the wheat contracted for. While their evidence tends to show that the price of wheat, from the 14th or 15th of July to the 24th, was far in excess of the contract price, they practically admit that wheat was not worth more than a dollar per bushel at the time appellee claims he finished threshing.

One of the errors relied upon is the failure of the court to permit appellant's amended reply to be filed, wherein it attempted to plead that appellee was estopped by his conduct, in selling the wheat, from claiming that he threshed it at a later date or that appellant was not damaged by reason of the breach of the contract. In this connection it is insisted that appellee had no right to violate his contract by selling the wheat to another at a price far in excess of the contract price, using for that purpose the sacks appellant had furnished, and then claim that as a matter of fact he had not threshed the wheat until a later date, and at that time the market price of wheat was below the contract price.

In contracts for the delivery of personal property at a fixed time and at a designated place, the vendee is entitled to damages against the vendor for a failure to comply and the measure of damages is the difference between the contract price and the market price of the property at the place and time of delivery. (Miles v. Miller, 12 Bush 134). This principle of law is so well settled . . . that it is no longer open to discussion. There is no reason why this rule should not apply [here]. The evidence clearly established the fact that the threshing was not completed until about the 29th of July. There is nothing in the evidence tending to show that appellee fraudulently delayed the threshing of the wheat for the purpose of permitting the market price . . . to go down. Indeed, all the circumstances pointed to an advance rather than a decline in the price, and appellee had no reason to anticipate that the market would decline. As he finished threshing on the 29th of July, and the wheat was to be delivered from the thresher, and appellant was not to accept and pay for the wheat until the time fixed for the delivery, that is the time which determines whether or not appellant was damaged. If appellee had sold his wheat on July 14th or 15th, at $1.16 and the price on July 29th was $1.50 per bushel, appellant would not be contending that the measure of his damages was the difference between the contract price and the price appellee received for it on July 14th or 15th, but would insist that he was entitled to the difference between the contract price and $1.50 per bushel. Besides, appellee was not required by his contract, to deliver to appellant any particular wheat. Had he delivered other wheat of like quantity and quality, he would have complied with the contract. When he sold his wheat on July 14th or 15th, for a price in excess of the contract price, and, therefore, failed to deliver to appellant wheat of the quantity and quality contracted for, he took the chances of being mulcted in damages for the breach of the contract. Estoppel can only be invoked where a party by his conduct has led another to act to his prejudice. There is nothing in the facts of this case to justify the application of that doctrine.

. . . As stated before, the evidence overwhelmingly established the fact—indeed, it is practically admitted—that the market price of wheat of the kind and quality contracted to be delivered at the time and place designated in the contract did not exceed $1 per bushel. That being true, appellant, instead of being damaged by the breach of the contract, was actually benefited to the extent of about three cents per bushel. Had the jury upon this state of facts found anything for the appellant, it would have been the duty of this court to reverse the judgment because the verdict was flagrantly against the evidence. . . .

Judgment affirmed.

QUESTIONS

(1) Suppose in *Acme Mills* the market price of wheat had been $1.16 on July 29, and that Liberty Mills appeared for the first time as Johnson was finishing up the threshing that day. If Liberty Mills offered $1.16 for the wheat, should Johnson sell?

(2) Some breaches of contract are "opportunistic," meaning, as one court put it, "the promisor wants the benefit of the bargain without bearing the agreed-upon cost, and exploits the inadequacies of purely compensatory damages." Patton v. Mid–Continent Systems, 841 F.2d 742, 751 (7th Cir.1988). Such breaches presumably are to be deterred. How are we to determine whether a breach such as Johnson's sale to Liberty Mills is to be characterized as "opportunistic"?

––––––––

Laurin v. DeCarolis Constr. Co., Inc.
372 Mass. 688, 363 N.E.2d 675 (1977)

Plaintiffs purchased from defendant a wooded lot on which a dwelling was then under construction. During the finishing of construction and prior to the closing of the transaction, defendant removed gravel from the property without plaintiffs' approval. Plaintiffs sought and were awarded damages of $6,480 for the fair market value of the gravel removed—360 truckloads found to have an average fair market value of $18 per load. An intermediate appellate court reversed the judgment on the ground that the court below had improperly awarded the value of the gravel on a tort theory of "conversion." Since plaintiffs were not in (or entitled to) possession at the time the gravel was removed, this court reasoned that plaintiffs had no action in tort for conversion but were limited to contract damages measured by the diminution in the value of the premises. On further appeal, *held*, damages measured by the fair market value of the gravel removed are proper here.

Justice Braucher spoke for the court: The rights of a land purchaser are contract rights. The case must be decided not as a tort action for injury to or conversion of property, but "as a claim for a deliberate and willful breach of contract." Plaintiffs make no claim to recover the cost of restoring the premises to the bargained-for condition, nor do they seek the net proceeds of wrongful sales of gravel made by defendant. "In similar cases involving a tortious conversion of property, we have held that the diminution in the value of the premises is a proper measure of damages; alternatively, at the owner's election, we have upheld the award of the fair market value of the material removed. . . . Here the gravel was actually removed, and proof of its value is not confusing or speculative. Particularly where the defendant's breach is deliberate and willful, we think damages limited to diminution in value of the premises may sometimes be seriously inadequate. 'Cutting a few trees on a timber tract, or taking a few hundred tons of coal from a mine, might not diminish the market value of the tract, or of the mine, and yet the value of the wood or coal, severed from the soil, might be considerable. The wrongdoer would in such cases be held to pay the value of the wood and coal, and he could not shield himself by showing that the property from which it was taken was, as a whole, worth as much as it was before.' . . . This reasoning does not depend for its soundness on the holding of a property interest, as distinguished from a contractual interest, by the plaintiffs. Nor is it punitive; it merely deprives the defendant of a profit wrongfully made, a profit which the plaintiff was entitled to make." But a recovery in contract should not include the value added by defendant's labor in severing the gravel and loading it on trucks. Since the lower court determined the value of the gravel loaded on trucks rather than its value as it lay in the land, the case must be remanded for a redetermination of damages.

[Another court has said: "Since the purpose of [contract] damages is to compensate the injured party for the loss caused by the breach, those damages are generally measured by the plaintiff's actual loss. While on occasion the defendant's profits are used as the measure[,] . . . this generally occurs when those profits tend to define the plaintiff's loss, for an award of defendant's profits when they greatly exceed plaintiff's loss and there has been no tortious conduct [by defendant] would tend to be punitive, and punitive damages are not part of the law of contract damages." United States Naval Institute v. Charter Communications, Inc., 936 F.2d 692 (2d Cir.1991)].

―――――――

NOTE

The term "estoppel" mentioned in *Acme Mills* describes a general and most flexible doctrine of American law; it will be encountered in various contexts, in this course and others. Literally, to estop is to stop, to bar or prevent. What may seem to be a simple misspelling is the product of a period in history (reaching into the seventeenth century) when the language of the English common law was French of a peculiar hybrid type. The English verb "stop" was Gallicized and in the process became a word of art.

In the law of property one encounters "estoppel by deed," which rests on the principle that a party to a deed cannot contradict or disprove a statement contained in the deed, especially if that party is a grantor seeking to diminish or destroy the language of grant. Also much used in our law is "estoppel in pais," usually called "equitable estoppel," which operates similarly to prevent a litigant from repudiating a representation that has reasonably induced reliance by the person to whom it was made. It is commonly said that the party to be estopped must intend or reasonably expect that his representations will be acted upon by the party asserting the estoppel; if foreseeable reliance follows, the maker of the representation is forbidden to deny it in court, that is, "turn the tables" on the unsuspecting party. There is, on its face, a tort-like quality to such a doctrine. A classic example of "ordinary" estoppel resting on a false representation of fact can be found in the next chapter (American Nat'l Bank v. A.G. Sommerville, Inc., infra p. 285). Much attention also will be given in this course to so-called "promissory estoppel," which involves application of the estoppel principle not to a factual representation about the past or present, but to a promise of future action.

It appears that Acme Mills was invoking standard equitable estoppel against the defaulter Johnson. Note the reason the Kentucky court gave for refusing to apply estoppel.

————

COMMENT: DAMAGES AS PUNISHMENT FOR CONTRACT BREACH

A tort obligation is commonly described as a duty imposed by law to avoid causing injury to others. A person may therefore be liable in tort when there is no contract in the picture at all, as well as when there has been a breach of a duty of reasonable care distinct from contractual obligations. There are, in addition, some kinds of aggravated misconduct for which so-called "exemplary" or "punitive" damages may be awarded under the law of torts (only a few states fail to recognize a common law right to seek punitive damages, requiring instead a statute authorizing their award). Such awards are determined not by the extent of a victim's injury but by the desire to punish (and thus deter) misconduct deemed highly offensive. Standard examples would be deliberate fraud, assault and battery, defamation, or intentional destruction of property. Often the intention to cause harm is very clear and the misconduct so destructive that the legislature has been moved to make it a crime. In such situations, one objection to punitive damages in civil actions is that the defendant is denied the safeguards applicable in a criminal prosecution—proof beyond a reasonable doubt, the privilege against self-incrimination, and so on. Another more general objection to punitive damages is that jurors will be left free to award money in amounts that are measured only by the degree of their disapproval of the defendant's conduct. Likewise, judges, exercising the powers of review described earlier, will have no basis in the evidence and no standard derived from some external source to use in determining whether the penalty and its amount are justified. The arguments to the contrary, in favor of punitive damages, are that public prosecutors are usually too preoccupied to deal with relatively minor offenses and that public prosecutions, even when they are brought and are successful, aim only to vindicate the public interest and seldom include any indemnity to those injured. And so, the argument proceeds, an added incentive for those injured to sue will serve the double purpose of reimbursing private parties for their losses (including litigation costs) and deterring misconduct by others. These dual goals of compensation and deterrence provide much of the thinking behind our system of tort law.

Are punitive damages appropriate as a sanction for breach of contract? It is usually said in tort actions that punitive damages are available only in limited circumstances, that negligence, even "gross" negligence, or a barebones intentional act, is not enough, and that to justify such awards the misconduct must be "outrageous," "wanton," or at least "malicious"—i.e., particularly objectionable in nature (in the words of many courts, "morally reprehensible"). A special money sanction, one exceeding the actual injury suffered, is therefore thought necessary if aggravated forms of otherwise wrongful acts are to be deterred. It is, of course, quite possible for a breach of contract to be accomplished by conduct that is "outrageous" and independently wrongful—for example, an employee of a common carrier evicts a ticket-carrying passenger and in the process injures the passenger in an unprovoked and violent assault. In almost all of the contract cases in which an award of punitive damages has been sustained there has been this combination of contract breach and independent tort accompanied by some element of aggravation. Where the tort element is missing altogether, modern decisions overwhelmingly assert that neither punishment of the breacher nor "setting an example" for others can justify a damage award that is isolated and identified as having only this purpose. E.g., Morrow v. L.A. Goldschmidt Assoc., 112 Ill.2d 87, 492 N.E.2d 181 (1986) ("tort and contract law are founded on different policies which justify separate rules" respecting punitive damages); Paiz v. State Farm Fire & Cas. Co., 118 N.M. 203, 880 P.2d 300 (1994) ("the amount of recovery should not depend on the manner in which the contract was breached, and the nonbreaching party should not be able to extract an extra bonus from a breach characterized by a high degree of fault or resulting from a low degree of care"). Even the court that produced Groves v. John Wunder Co. has adhered to the view that a willful, malicious, or bad-faith breach of contract is itself neither tortious—that is to say, independently unlawful—nor a proper basis for imposing punitive damages. Barr/Nelson, Inc. v. Tonto's, Inc., 336 N.W.2d 46 (Minn.1983); Wild v. Rarig, 302 Minn. 419, 234 N.W.2d 775 (1975).

One question today is whether there has been a shift in direction—whether, as some have claimed, there exists a greater willingness by courts to award punitive damages in actions that appear to be primarily contractual. It is true that a fair number of our state legislatures, in passing "unfair and deceptive trade practices" acts applicable generally to consumer transactions, have provided for punitive awards in the private causes of action created. There are, in addition, modern statutes providing for the "doubling" and "tripling" of any compensatory damages awarded for certain types of conduct (e.g., trespass to land and unauthorized removal of timber). Also, beginning in earnest in the 1970s, courts have significantly expanded liability for punitive damages in insurance disputes, holding that a company's unjustified refusal to pay or settle a claim can constitute the tort of "bad faith breach of contract." See, e.g., Gruenberg v. Aetna Ins. Co., 9 Cal.3d 566, 108 Cal.Rptr. 480, 510 P.2d 1032 (1973). In the employment area, expanded tort theories have similarly been used by the courts to reexamine, and break down, the longstanding at-will doctrine, as we shall see later (Sheets v. Teddy's Frosted Foods, Inc., p. 649).

With the gradual expansion of tort liability, presumably more types of conduct, including conduct relating to bargains, will come to be viewed as independently wrongful. But the fighting issue is whether punitive damages will be awarded directly in noninsurance cases when the breach of a contract is found to be objectionable in a moral or ethical sense, but not tortious. It appears only a very small number of courts have taken that step. The reluctance of courts to depart from the "independent tort" requirement in contract actions is discussed in Sullivan, Punitive Damages in the Law of Contract: The Reality and the Illusion of Legal Change, 61 Minn.L.Rev. 207 (1977). For the story of the general refusal of courts to extend the tort doctrine of "bad faith" breach beyond the insurance cases, in California, the initiating state, and elsewhere, see Seaman's Direct Buying Service, Inc. v. Standard Oil Co., 36 Cal.3d 752, 206 Cal.Rptr. 354, 686 P.2d 1158 (1984), and Freeman & Mills, Inc. v. Belcher Oil Co., 11 Cal.4th 85, 44 Cal.Rptr.2d 420, 900 P.2d 669 (1995) (overruling Seaman's and approving rule precluding tort recovery for noninsurance contract breach, absent violation of independent tort duty other than "bad faith denial of the existence of, or liability under, the breached contract").

———————

Missouri Furnace Co. v. Cochran

United States Circuit Court, W.D. Pennsylvania, 1881.
8 F. 463.

ACHESON, DISTRICT JUDGE. This suit, brought February 26, 1880, was to recover damages for the breach by Cochran of a contract for the sale and delivery by him to the plaintiff of 36,621 tons of standard Connellsville coke, at the price of $1.20 per ton, . . . deliverable on cars at his works, at the rate of nine cars of 13 tons each per day on each working day during the year 1880. After 3,765 tons were delivered, Cochran, on February 13, 1880, notified the plaintiff that he had rescinded the contract, and thereafter delivered no coke. After Cochran's refusal further to deliver coke, the plaintiff made a substantially similar contract with one Hutchinson for the delivery during the balance of the year of 29,587 tons of Connellsville coke at four dollars per ton, which was the market rate for such a forward contract, and rather below the market price for present deliveries on February 27, the date of the Hutchinson contract. The plaintiff claimed to recover the difference between the price stipulated in the contract sued on, and the price which the plaintiff agreed to pay Hutchinson under the contract of February 27. But the court refused to adopt this standard of damages, and instructed the jury that the plaintiff was "entitled to recover, upon the coke which Cochran contracted to deliver and refused to deliver to the plaintiff the sum of the difference between the contract price—that is, the price Cochran was to receive—and the market price of standard Connellsville coke, at the price of delivery, at the several dates when the several deliveries should have been made under the contract." Under this instruction there was a verdict for the plaintiff for $22,171.49. . . .

The plaintiff moved the court for a new trial. . . . But we are not convinced that the instruction complained of was erroneous.

Undoubtedly it is well settled . . . that when contracts for the sale of chattels are broken by the vendor failing to deliver, the measure of damages is the difference between the contract price and the market value of the article at the time it should be delivered. Sedgwick on the Measure of Damages (7th Ed.) 552. In Shepherd v. Hampton, 3 Wheat. 200, this rule was distinctly sanctioned[:] . . . "[T]he price of the article at the time it was to be delivered is the measure of damages." Nor does the case of Hopkins v. Lee, 6 Wheat. 118, promulgate a different doctrine; for, clearly, "the time of the breach" there spoken of is the time when delivery should have been made under the contract.

It is said in Sedgwick [(7th Ed.) 558]: "Where delivery is required to be made by instalments, the measure of damages will be estimated by the value at the time each delivery should have been made." In accordance with this principle the damages were assessed in Brown v. Muller, Law Rep., 7 Ex. 319, and Roper v. Johnson, Law Rep., 8 C.P. 167, which were suits by vendee against vendor for damages for failure to deliver iron, in the one case, and coal, in the other, deliverable in monthly instalments. In one of these cases suit was brought after the contract period had expired; in the other case before its expiration; but in both cases the vendor had given notice to the plaintiff that he did not intend to fulfill his contract. To the argument, there urged on behalf of the vendor, that upon receiving such notice it is the duty of the vendee to go into the market and provide himself with a new forward contract, Kelly, C.B., in Brown v. Muller, said: "He is not bound to enter into such a contract, which might be to his advantage or detriment, according as the market might fall or rise. If it fell, the defendant might fairly say that the plaintiff had no right to enter into a speculative contract, and insist that he was not called upon to pay a greater difference than would have existed had the plaintiff held his hand.". . .

In this case I fail to perceive anything to call for a departure from that standard. There was no evidence of any special damage to the plaintiff by the stoppage of its furnaces or otherwise. Furthermore, the contract with Hutchinson . . . was made at a time when the coke market was excited and in an extraordinary condition. Unexpectedly and suddenly coke had risen to the unprecedented price of four dollars per ton; but this rate was of brief duration. The market declined about May 1, 1880, and by the middle of that month the price had fallen to one dollar and thirty cents per ton. The good faith of the plaintiff in entering into the new contract cannot be questioned, but it proved a most unfortunate venture. By the last of May the plaintiff had in its hands more coke than was required in its business, and it procured—at what precise loss does not clearly appear—the cancellation of contracts with Hutchinson to the extent of 20,000 tons. As the plaintiff was not bound to enter into the new forward contract, it seems to me it did so at its own risk, and cannot fairly claim that the damages chargeable against the defendant shall be assessed on the basis of that contract.

The motion for a new trial is denied.

NOTE

The sudden rise in the price of coke in the early months of 1880 may have been due to an agreement among Pennsylvania producers to cut coal production, by closing down three days a week, in order to raise prices (this was before the passage of antitrust legislation such as the Sherman Act). This agreement was reported in the New York Times for Saturday, February 14, 1880, but with no specific reference to coke, of which Connellsville, Pa., was a well-known source. It may also be that the rise in the price of coke was due to the prospect of strikes that might affect supply. On Sunday, February 15, 1880, the New York Times reported that the coal miners of the Cumberland region, numbering some 20,000, had given notice on February 13 that they would strike ten days later unless their wage demands were met; and most of them did strike accordingly on February 23 (Boston Herald, February 23, 1880). There was no nation-wide strike of the miners during the late winter and early spring of 1880, since a union capable of conducting such a strike had not yet been organized. In various places in Pennsylvania, however, there were local strikes that had begun in the last two weeks of February (New York Times, March 7, 1880).

COMMENT: THE BUYER'S DAMAGES ON BREACH BY ANTICIPATORY REPUDIATION

The day before Missouri Furnace breached, it had Cochrane's promise to take care of all its needs for coke for the whole year in exchange for its promise to pay $1.20 a ton. After Cochrane breached, Missouri Furnace had to promise to pay $4 a ton to get someone else to promise to do the same thing—to satisfy its need for coke for the entire year. To put Missouri Furnace in the same position it had been in before Cochrane broke its promise, it would seem Missouri Furnace needed damages based on the difference between $4 and $1.20.

Missouri Furnace entered into its contract with Cochrane in the first place because it had decided not to buy on the spot market. Missouri Furnace bargained for the benefit of a forward contract. Missouri Furnace did not want to buy on the spot market. It wanted to pay a fixed price for the coke. For that reason Missouri Furnace bargained for a forward contract with Cochrane, and it is this benefit that it lost when Cochrane broke his contract. To be made whole Missouri Furnace needs the amount it would cost to enter into another forward contract.

This reasoning suggests that, contrary to the conclusion that the court reached in Missouri Furnace, awarding the forward price would be consistent with the expectation damages principle. But is there anything the matter with the legal rule the court adopted? It would seem that providing the nonbreaching party with spot price might be easier to apply. The spot price is usually readily available, while in many cases there will not be a forward market that the buyer can reenter. Once a spot-market rule is in place, Missouri Furnace can just buy coke in the spot market and send Cochrane the bill. It is not any worse off. Even if the forward contract measure is conceptually correct, is there anything the matter with the spot price measure? The price could prove higher or lower after the fact, but is there anything systematically wrong with it? In an interesting article, Thomas Jackson argues that the spot market measure is indeed wrong. Although such a remedy is worse for the innocent party in Missouri Furnace itself, over the course of many cases this measure is overcompensatory. Using this measure tends to give the nonbreaching party more than it needs to be put back in the position it would have been in had there been performance. See Jackson, "Anticipatory Repudiation" and the Temporal Element of Contract Law: An Economic Inquiry into Contract Damages in Cases of Prospective Nonperformance, 31 Stan.L.Rev. 69 (1978).

Neri v. Retail Marine Corp.

Court of Appeals of New York, 1972.
30 N.Y.2d 393, 334 N.Y.S.2d 165, 285 N.E.2d 311.

GIBSON, J. The appeal concerns the right of a retail dealer to recover loss of profits and incidental damages upon the buyer's repudiation of a contract governed by the Uniform Commercial Code. This is, indeed, the correct measure of damage in an appropriate case and to this extent the code (§ 2–708(2)) effected a substantial change from prior law, whereby damages were ordinarily limited to "the difference between the contract price and the market or current price." . . . [T]he courts below erred in declining to give effect to the new statute and so the order appealed from must be reversed.

The plaintiffs contracted to purchase from defendant a new boat of a specified model for the price of $12,587.40, against which they made a deposit of $40. They shortly increased the deposit to $4,250 in consideration of the defendant dealer's agreement to arrange with the manufacturer for immediate delivery on the basis of "a firm sale," instead of the delivery within approximately four to six weeks originally specified. Some six days after the date of the contract plaintiffs' lawyer sent to defendant a letter rescinding the sales contract for the reason that plaintiff Neri was about to undergo hospitalization and surgery, in consequence of which, according to the letter, it would be "impossible for Mr. Neri to make any payments." The boat had already been ordered from the manufacturer and was delivered to defendant at or before the time the attorney's letter was received. Defendant declined to refund plaintiffs' deposit and this action to recover it was commenced. Defendant counterclaimed, alleging plaintiffs' breach of the contract and defendant's resultant damage in the amount of $4,250, for which sum defendant demanded judgment. Upon motion, defendant had summary judgment on the issue of liability tendered by its counterclaim; and Special Term directed an assessment of damages, upon which it would be determined whether plaintiffs were entitled to the return of any portion of their down payment.

[I]t was shown [at trial] that the boat ordered and received by defendant in accordance with plaintiffs' contract of purchase was sold some four months later to another buyer for the same price as that negotiated with plaintiffs. From this proof the plaintiffs argue that defendant's loss on its contract was recouped, while defendant argues that but for plaintiffs' default, it would have sold two boats and have earned two profits instead of one. Defendant proved, without contradiction, that its profit on the sale under the contract in suit would have been $2,579 and that during the period the boat remained unsold incidental expenses aggregating $674 for storage, upkeep, finance charges and insurance were incurred. Additionally, defendant proved and sought to recover attorneys' fees of $1,250.

The trial court found "untenable" defendant's claim for loss of profit, inasmuch as the boat was later sold for the same price that plaintiffs had contracted to pay; found, too, that defendant had failed to prove any incidental damages; further found "that the terms of [UCC 2–718(2)(b)] are applicable and same make adequate and fair provision to place the sellers in as good a position as performance would have done" and, in accordance with [2–718(2)(b)], awarded defendant $500 upon its counterclaim and directed that plaintiffs recover the balance of their deposit, amounting to $3,750. The ensuing judgment was affirmed, without opinion, at the Appellate Division, and defendant's appeal to this court was taken by our leave.

The issue is governed in the first instance by [UCC] 2–718 which provides, among other things, that the buyer, despite his breach, may have restitution of the amount by which his payment exceeds: (a) reasonable liquidated damages stipulated by the contract or (b) absent such stipulation, 20% of the value of the buyer's total performance or $500, whichever is smaller (§ 2–718(2), pars. a, b). As above noted, the trial court awarded defendant an offset in the amount of $500 under paragraph (b) and directed restitution to plaintiffs of the balance. Section 2–718, however, establishes, in paragraph [(3)(a)] an alternative right of offset in favor of the seller, as follows: "(3) The buyer's right to restitution under subsection (2) is subject to offset to the extent that the seller establishes (a) a right to recover damages under the provisions of this Article other than subsection (1)."

Among "the provisions of this Article other than subsection (1)" are those to be found in § 2–708, which the courts below did not apply. [Section 2–708(1)] provides that "the measure of damages for non-acceptance or repudiation by the buyer is the difference between the market price at the time and place for tender and the unpaid contract price together with any incidental damages provided in this Article (§ 2–710), but less expenses saved in consequence of the buyer's breach." However, this provision is made expressly subject to subsection (2), providing: "(2) If the measure of damages provided in subsection (1) is inadequate to put the seller in as good a position as performance would have done then the measure of damages is the profit (including reasonable overhead) which the seller would have made from full performance by the buyer, together with any incidental damages provided in this Article (§ 2–710), due allowance for costs reasonably incurred and due credit for payments or proceeds of resale."

The provision of the code upon which the decision at Trial Term rested [§ 2–718(2)(b)] does not differ greatly from the corresponding provisions of the prior statute (Personal Property Law, § 145–a(1)(b)), except as the new act includes the alternative remedy of a lump sum award of $500. Neither does the present reference [in § 2–718(3)(a)] to the recovery of damages pursuant to other provisions of the article differ from a like reference in the prior statute (§ 145–a(2)(a)) to an alternative measure of damages under § 145 of that act; but § 145 made no provision for recovery of lost profits as does [UCC 2–708(2)]. The new statute is thus innovative and significant and its analysis is necessary to the determination of the issues here presented.

Prior to the code, the New York cases "applied the 'profit' test, contract price less cost of manufacture, only in cases where the seller was a manufacturer or an agent for a manufacturer" (1955 Report of N.Y. Law Rev.Comm., vol. 1, p. 693). Its extension to retail sales was "designed to eliminate the unfair and economically wasteful results arising under the older law when fixed price articles were involved. This section permits the recovery of lost profits in all appropriate cases, which would include all standard priced goods." (Official Comment 2, [UCC] § 2–708.) Additionally, and "in all cases the seller may recover incidental damages" (id., Comment 3). The buyer's right to restitution was established at Special Term upon the motion for summary judgment, as was the seller's right to proper offsets, in each case pursuant to § 2–718; and, as the parties concede, the only question before us, following the assessment of damages at Special Term, is that as to the proper measure of damage to be applied. The conclusion is clear from the record—indeed with mathematical certainty—that "the measure of damages provided in subsection (1) is inadequate to put the seller in as good a position as performance would have done" ([UCC] § 2–708(2)) and hence—again under subsection (2)—that the seller is entitled to its "profit (including reasonable overhead) . . . together with any incidental damages[,] . . . due allowance for costs reasonably incurred and due credit for payments or proceeds of resale."

It is evident, first, that this retail seller is entitled to its profit and, second, that the last sentence of subsection (2), as hereinbefore quoted, referring to "due credit for payments or proceeds of resale" is inapplicable to this retail sales contract.[2] Closely parallel to the factual situation now before us is that hypothesized by Dean Hawkland as illustrative of the operation of the rules: "Thus, if a private party agrees to sell his automobile to a buyer for $2,000, a breach by the buyer would cause the seller no loss (except incidental damages, i.e., expense of a new sale) if the seller was able to sell the automobile to another buyer for $2000. But the situation is different

---

[2] The concluding clause, "due credit for payments or proceeds of resale," is intended to refer to "the privilege of the seller to realize junk value when it is manifestly useless to complete the operation of manufacture". . . . The commentators who have considered the language have uniformly concluded that "the reference is to a resale as scrap under . . . Section 2–704" (1956 Report of N.Y. Law Rev.Comm., p. 397 . . .). Another writer, reaching the same conclusion, after detailing the history of the clause, says that " 'proceeds of resale' previously meant the resale value of the goods in finished form; now it means the resale value of the components on hand at the time plaintiff learns of breach" (Harris, Seller's Damages, 18 Stan.L.Rev. 66, 104).

with dealers having an unlimited supply of standard-priced goods. Thus, if an automobile dealer agrees to sell a car to a buyer at the standard price of $2000, a breach by the buyer injures the dealer, even though he is able to sell the automobile to another for $2000. If the dealer has an inexhaustible supply of cars, the resale to replace the breaching buyer costs the dealer a sale, because, had the breaching buyer performed, the dealer would have made two sales instead of one. The buyer's breach, in such a case, depletes the dealer's sales to the extent of one, and the measure of damages should be the dealer's profit on one sale. Section 2–708 recognizes this, and it rejects the rule developed under the Uniform Sales Act by many courts that the profit cannot be recovered in this case." (Hawkland, Sales and Bulk Sales 1958 ed., pp. 153–154. . . .)

The record which in this case establishes defendant's entitlement to damages in the amount of its prospective profit, at the same time confirms defendant's cognate right to "any incidental damages provided in this Article (§ 2–710)"[3] ([UCC], § 2–708(2)). . . . [I]t is too clear to require discussion that the seller's right to recover loss of profits is not exclusive and that he may recoup his "incidental" expenses as well. . . . Although the trial court's denial of incidental damages in the uncontroverted amount of $674 was made in the context of its erroneous conclusion that [§ 2–718(2)(b)] was applicable and was "adequate . . . to place the sellers in as good a position as performance would have done," the denial seems not to have rested entirely on the court's mistaken application of the law, as there was an explicit finding "that defendant completely failed to show that it suffered any incidental damages." We find no basis for the court's conclusion . . . inasmuch as the proper items of the $674 expenses (being for storage, upkeep, finance charges and insurance for the period between the date performance was due and the time of the resale) were proven without objection and were in no way controverted, impeached or otherwise challenged, at the trial or on appeal. Thus the court's finding of a failure of proof cannot be supported upon the record and, therefore, and contrary to plaintiffs' contention, the affirmance at the Appellate Division was ineffective to save it.

The trial court correctly denied defendant's claim for recovery of attorney's fees incurred by it in this action. Attorney's fees incurred in an action such as this are not in the nature of the protective expenses contemplated by the statute ([UCC], § 1–106(1); § 2–710; § 2–708(2)). . . .

It follows that plaintiffs are entitled to restitution of the sum of $4,250 . . . less an offset to defendant in the amount of $3,253 on account of its lost profit of $2,579 and its incidental damages of $674.

The order of the Appellate Division should be modified, with costs in all courts, in accordance with this opinion, and, as so modified, affirmed.

NOTE

A detailed analysis of the UCC sections bearing on the question of damages for a lost-volume seller can be found in R.E. Davis Chemical Corp. v. Diasonics, Inc., 826 F.2d 678 (7th Cir.1987), including a discussion of whether 2–708 should be "relegated to a role inferior to that of 2–706 and 2–709 and [whether] one can turn to 2–708 only after [it is] concluded that neither 2–706

---

[3] "Incidental damages to an aggrieved seller include any commercially reasonable charges, expenses or commissions incurred in stopping delivery, in the transportation, care and custody of goods after the buyer's breach, in connection with return or resale of the goods or otherwise resulting from the breach" ([UCC], § 2–710).

nor 2–709 is applicable." The court rejected that latter view, at least as concerns 2–706, concluding, in line with most courts, that a reselling lost-volume seller is free to bypass 2–706's damage measure and to proceed under 2–708. The *R.E. Davis* court, however, questioned Neri's conclusion that market-based damages are inadequate in these cases "with mathematical certainty."

> [U]nder some circumstances, the measure of damages provided under 2–708(1) will not put a reselling seller in as good a position as it would have been in had the buyer performed because the breach resulted in the seller losing sales volume. However, we disagree with the definition of "lost volume seller" adopted by other courts. Courts awarding lost profits to a lost volume seller have focused on whether the seller had the capacity to supply the breached units in addition to what it actually sold. In reality, however, the relevant questions include, not only whether the seller could have produced the breached units in addition to its actual volume, but also whether it would have been profitable for the seller to produce both units. . . . As one commentator has noted, under "the economic law of diminishing returns or increasing marginal costs[,] . . . as a seller's volume increases, then a point will inevitably be reached where the cost of selling each additional item diminishes the incremental return to the seller and eventually makes it entirely unprofitable to conclude the next sale." (Shanker, [The Case for a Literal Reading of UCC Section 2–708(2) One Profit for the Reseller), 24 Case W.Res.L.Rev. 697 (1973)] at 705. Thus, under some conditions, awarding a lost volume seller its presumed lost profit will result in overcompensating the seller, and 2–708(2) would not take effect because the damage formula provided in 2–708(1) does place the seller in as good a position as if the buyer had performed. Therefore, on remand, [plaintiff] must establish, not only that it had the capacity to produce the breached unit in addition to the unit resold, but also that it would have been profitable for it to have produced and sold both.

On remand, plaintiff met this burden. See R.E. Davis Chemical Corp. v. Diasonics, Inc., 924 F.2d 709 (7th Cir.1991). There is an abundance of law-journal writing on lost-volume damage claims, including a most helpful discussion in Goldberg, An Economic Analysis of the Lost–Volume Retail Seller, 57 So.Cal.L.Rev. 283 (1984).

Illinois Central R.R. Co. v. Crail

Supreme Court of the United States, 1930.
281 U.S. 57, 50 S.Ct. 180.

STONE, J. . . . Respondent, plaintiff below, a coal dealer in Minneapolis, purchased, while in transit, a carload of coal weighing at shipment 88,700 pounds. On delivery at destination, the respondent's industrial siding, there was a shortage of 5,500 pounds. At the time of arrival, respondent had not resold any of the coal. It was intended to be, and was, added to his stock of coal for resale, but the shortage did not interfere with the maintenance of his usual stock. He lost no sales by reason of it, and purchased no coal to replace the shortage, except in carload lots. In the course of his business, respondent could and did, both before and after the present shipment, purchase coal of like quality in carload lots of 60,000 pounds or more, delivered at his siding, at $5.50 per ton, plus freight. The market price in Minneapolis for like coal sold at retail in less than carload lots was $13 per ton including $3.30 freight. . . .

It is not denied that a recovery measured by the wholesale market price of the coal would fully compensate the respondent, or that the retail price, taken as the measure of the recovery allowed below, includes costs of delivery to retail consumers which respondent did not incur, and a retail profit which he had not earned by any contract of resale. But respondent contends, as was held below, that the established measure of damage for nondelivery of a shipment of merchandise is the sum required to replace the exact amount of the shortage at the stipulated time and place of delivery, which, in this case, would be its retail value, and that convenience and the necessity for a uniform rule require its application here.

This contention ignores the basic principle underlying common-law remedies that they shall afford only compensation for the injury suffered, and [give] only a right of recovery for "actual loss." The rule urged by respondents was applied below in literal accordance with its conventional statement. As so stated, when applied to cases as they usually arise, it is a convenient and accurate method of arriving at an amount of recovery which is compensatory. As so stated, it would have been applicable here if there had been a failure to deliver the entire carload of coal, since the wholesale price, at which a full carload could have been procured at point of destination, would have afforded full compensation, or, in some circumstances, if respondent had been under any constraint to purchase less than a carload lot to repair his loss or carry on his business, for in that event the measure of his loss would have been the retail market cost of the necessary replacement. But in the actual circumstances the cost of replacing the exact shortage at retail price was not the measure of the loss, since it was capable of replacement, and was, in fact, replaced in the course of respondent's business from purchases made in carload lots at wholesale market price without added expense.

There is no greater inconvenience in the application of the one standard of value than the other, and we perceive no advantage to be gained from an adherence to a rigid uniformity, which would justify sacrificing the reason of the rule, to its letter. The test of market value is at best but a convenient means of getting at the loss suffered. It may be discarded and other more accurate means resorted to, if, for special reasons, it is not exact or otherwise not applicable. In the absence of special circumstances, the damage for shortage in delivery by the seller of fungible goods sold by quantity is measured by the bulk price rather than the price for smaller quantities. . . Likewise, we think that the wholesale market price is to be preferred as a test over the retail when, in circumstances like the present, it is clearly the more accurate measure. . . .

Reversed.

NOTE

Does the principle underlying *Crail* apply in contexts other than the sale of goods? Louise Caroline Nursing Home, Inc. v. Dix Constr. Corp., 362 Mass. 306, 285 N.E.2d 904 (1972), involved breach of a contract to build a nursing home. Part way through construction, defendant contractor halted its work without justification. An auditor found, however, that plaintiff nursing home suffered no compensable damages as a result, since the cost to complete the structure at the time of the breach was less than the contract price minus what had already been paid to defendant. Plaintiff appealed the denial of its motion to recommit the auditor's report, arguing that it was entitled to "the difference between the value of the building as left by Dix and the value it would have had if the contract had been fully performed." The reviewing court rejected this argument, upholding the auditor's findings. The court reasoned that compensation is the fundamental principle of damages. "Compensation," the court explained, "is the value of the performance of the contract, that is, what the plaintiff would have made had the contract been performed. . . . The plaintiff is entitled to be made whole and no more." Accordingly, in failure-to-complete cases such as this, "[t]he measure of the plaintiff's damages . . . can be only in the amount of the reasonably cost of completing the contract and repairing the defendant's defective performance less such part of the contract price as has not been paid."

———————

Watt v. Nevada Central R.R. Co.
23 Nev. 154, 44 P. 423 (1896)

Defendant's ~~locomotive~~, through what was found to be negligence in its operation, set fire in October 1893 to a hay stack and hay press on plaintiff's ranch. The hay had been produced on the ranch and was stored there as a reserve supply to feed plaintiff's cattle in the event of a recurrence of the severe winter that, in 1889–1890, had caused plaintiff to lose $100,000 worth of cattle through starvation. Plaintiff testified that half of these cattle could have been saved if, at the time, he had had on hand the quantity of hay (700 tons) that defendant's locomotive destroyed. He also testified that he had no other use whatever for the hay and had used none of it since he began storing hay in 1890, four years before. There was no market for hay nearer than Austin, Nevada, which was 37 miles distant by rail. Hay of the quality of that destroyed, when baled, sold in Austin for $10 to $12 a ton. The cost of baling was $2 a ton and the cost of transportation by rail between plaintiff's ranch and the Austin market was $6.50 a ton. The trial judge (jury trial being waived) gave plaintiff a judgment for the hay valued at $10 a ton. On defendant's appeal, this judgment was reversed and judgment was entered for the lost hay valued at $3.50 a ton, the top Austin price of $12 less $8.50 baling and transportation costs. On plaintiff's own testimony, said the court, the hay had no value for use as feed. Whether it would be used on the ranch in the future was so uncertain and so conjectural that no estimate of its value for this purpose could provide a basis for damage recovery. Plaintiff contended that the cost of baling and transportation between Austin and the ranch should be added to, not subtracted from, the Austin price, but the court rejected this claim, commenting that such a recovery would give plaintiff a sum far in excess of his loss and that the fire would then be a "source of great profit." Plaintiff did not buy any hay in Austin to replace the hay destroyed, "evidently for the reason that the cost would have greatly exceeded the value of the hay." Nor had plaintiff introduced at trial any evidence showing his costs of growing and storing the hay. But as to the hay press, plaintiff can recover the purchase price of another press, $80 in Lake Valley, plus the $30 cost of transporting it to the ranch, or $110.

QUESTIONS

(1) Although the damages in this case arise out of a tort, they could easily arise out of a breach of contract action. Under the expectation damages principle, we would look for a way to measure how much the hay was worth to Watt. What if Watt had replaced the hay promptly by purchasing an equal quantity in Austin? What if he regularly sold hay in Austin?

(2) The court noted that Watt had failed to offer any evidence of the cost of producing and storing the destroyed hay. What if he had shown these costs to be $5 per ton?

WHY NOT RELIANCE?

The law's preference, it seems, is relief based on the expectation interest. But there will be times when a court may choose to measure damages on the basis of a promisee's reliance losses. Indeed, we will soon discover that there has developed a considerable body of law authorizing reliance recoveries for breach of contract. Still, why isn't reliance the normal rule of damages? Consider the following passages drawn from the writings of Professors Sharp and Dawson.

Sharp, Promissory Liability (pt. 1)
7 U.Chi.L.Rev. 1, 20–21 (1939)

"[Fuller and Perdue] observe that a good, and doubtless in many cases, a sufficient justification for applying the measure of expectation damages, is that it is the surest and simplest device for protecting parties against the risks of reliance. Reliance is often difficult to prove . . . and when proved it may be difficult to measure. The propriety of protecting people to the extent of their reliance on contracts is fairly apparent. It may well follow that in a commercial community the expectation measure should be applied without too much opportunity for considering whether in every case it is entirely appropriate.

"Apart from these considerations, there may be other justifications for the general application of an expectation measure. If one promises a child to take him to a baseball game, he may be much disappointed by default. The distress and insecurity occasioned in mature life by failure to keep promises may be an adequate reason for our judgment that contracts should be performed or compensation awarded in such a way as to give as nearly as possible the equivalent of performance.

"Again it is sometimes said that a credit economy depends, to a peculiar extent, on the keeping of promises, or at least of contracts, and so the equivalent of performance should be given in case of breach. It is to be noted that if one understands credit in a limited sense, the force of this observation is likely to be lost. Credit in the sense of relations analogous to those of lender and borrower, could be taken care of by restitution. A more exact statement of the relations between our economy and expectation damages, seems to depend on the observation that this is not only an industrial and credit economy, but also a risk taking, profit making, more or less gambling economy. This may mean not only that harmful reliance, in fluctuating markets, is best remedied by expectation damages, but also that the profits dependent on good guesses about the future are generally to be assured to the person who is willing to gamble on his judgment.

"For whatever reason, the ordinary man apparently thinks naturally that promises should be performed or the equivalent of performance given."

———

Dawson, Restitution or Damages?
20 Ohio St.L.J. 175, 187–188 (1959)

"[T]he factor of potential gain through breach . . . has probably been a powerful factor in establishing the promisee's expectancy as the normal and accepted measure of damages for breach of contract. The point emerges more clearly if one considers the group of cases that most regularly adopt reliance loss as the measure and limit of recovery—i.e., the land contract with vendor defaulting in 'good faith.' If the vendor is unable to convey a clear title and had no reason to know at the inception of the contract that he would be thus disabled, a considerable number of states restrict the purchaser's damage recovery to purchase price paid plus cost of title search plus perhaps a few other types of wasted expenditure. A still larger number of states reject this limitation for various reasons. In the kaleidoscopic stream of reasons they give there constantly flicker into view two recurring reasons that really add up to one—this measure of recovery leaves the vendor free to 'speculate without risk' and exposes the vendor to temptation if the land has subsequently risen in value. . . . [T]he situation highlights one main objection to rules of contract damages that *limit* recovery to reliance losses." [The line of authority noted by Prof. Dawson stems from the famous English case of Flureau v. Thornhill, 2 WM.Bl. 1078 (1776), which was decided long before rules of contract damages were generalized into a theory of "compensation" with protection of expectancies the accepted goal. The *Flureau* or "English" rule, applicable only in a vendee's damage suit against a vendor of land, failed to achieve general acceptance in Anglo–American law (the courts in all but perhaps 15 or so of our states award the usual benefit-of-the-bargain damages to land-contract vendees irrespective of vendors' motives or reasons for defaulting). For more on the subject of adopting reliance loss as the measure and limit of recovery, see D. Dobbs, Law of Remedies 822–825 (2d ed. 1993).]

———

Chicago Coliseum Club v. Dempsey

Appellate Court of Illinois, First District, 1932.
265 Ill.App. 542.

WILSON, J. [The plaintiff] brought its action against William Harrison Dempsey, known as Jack Dempsey, to recover damages for breach of a written contract executed March 13, 1926, but bearing date of March 6 of that year.

Plaintiff was incorporated as an Illinois corporation for the promotion of general pleasure and athletic purposes and to conduct boxing, sparring and wrestling matches and exhibitions for prizes or purses. The defendant . . . was well known in the pugilistic world, and, at the time of [the] contract in question, held the title of world's Champion Heavy Weight Boxer.

Under [the] written agreement, the plaintiff was to promote a public boxing exhibition in Chicago, or some suitable place to be selected by the promoter, and had engaged the services of one Harry Wills, another well known boxer and pugilist, to engage in a boxing match with the defendant Dempsey for the championship of the world. By the terms of the agreement Dempsey was to receive $10, receipt of which was acknowledged, and the plaintiff further agreed to pay Dempsey the sum of $300,000 on the 5th day of August 1926,—$500,000 in cash at least 10 days before the date fixed for the contest, and a sum equal to 50 percent of the net profits over and above the sum of $2,000,000 in the event the gate receipts should exceed that amount. In addition the defendant was to receive 50 percent of the net revenue derived from moving picture concessions or royalties received by the plaintiff, and defendant agreed to have his life and health insured in favor of the plaintiff in a manner and at a place to be designated by the plaintiff. Defendant further agreed not to engage in any boxing match after the date of the agreement and prior to the date on which the contest was to be held. . . .

March 6, 1926, the plaintiff entered into an agreement with Harry Wills [to engage in] a boxing match with [Dempsey]. Under this agreement the plaintiff . . . was to deposit $50,000 in escrow in the National City Bank of New York City, . . . to be paid over to Wills on the 10th day prior to the date fixed for the holding of the boxing contest. . . . There is no evidence in the record showing that the $50,000 was deposited nor that it has ever been paid. . . . This contract between the plaintiff and Wills appears to have been entered into several days before the contract with Dempsey.

March 8, 1926, the plaintiff entered into a contract with one Andrew C. Weisberg, under which it appears that it was necessary for the plaintiff to have the services of an experienced person skilled in promoting boxing exhibitions. . . . It appears further from the agreement that it was necessary to incur expenditures in the way of traveling expenses, legal services and other costs in and about the promotion of the boxing match, and Weisberg agreed to investigate, canvass and organize the various hotel associations and other business organizations for the purpose of securing accommodations for spectators and to procure subscriptions and contributions from such hotels and associations and others for the erection of an arena and other necessary expense in order to carry out the enterprise and to promote the boxing match. . . . Weisberg was to furnish the funds for such purposes and was to be reimbursed out of the receipts from the sale of tickets for the expenses incurred by him, together with a certain amount for his services.

Both the Wills contract and the Weisberg contract are referred to at some length, inasmuch as claims for damages by plaintiff are predicated upon these two agreements. Under the terms of the contract between the plaintiff and Dempsey and the plaintiff and Wills, the contest was to be held during the month of September, 1926.

July 10, 1926, plaintiff wired Dempsey at Colorado Springs, Colorado, stating that representatives of life and accident insurance companies would call on him for the purpose of examining him for insurance in favor of the Chicago Coliseum Club, in accordance with the terms of his contract, and also requesting the defendant to begin training for the contest not later than August 1, 1926. In answer to this communication plaintiff received a telegram from Dempsey, as follows:

BM Colorado Springs Colo July 10th 1926

B.E. Clements

President Chicago Coliseum Club Chgo

Entirely too busy training for my coming Tunney match to waste time on insurance representatives stop as you have no contract suggest you stop kidding yourself and me also Jack Dempsey.

World Wide Photos

TUNNEY—DEMPSEY

We are unable to conceive upon what theory the defendant could contend that there was no contract, as it appears to be admitted in the proceeding here and bears his signature and the amounts involved are sufficiently large to have created a rather lasting impression on the mind of anyone signing such an agreement. It amounts, however, to a repudiation of the agreement and from that time on Dempsey refused to take any steps to carry out his undertaking. It appears that Dempsey at this time was engaged in preparing himself for a contest with Tunney to be held at Philadelphia sometime in September, and on August 3, 1926, plaintiff, as complainant, filed a bill in the superior court of Marion county, Indiana, asking to have Dempsey restrained and enjoined from engaging in the contest with Tunney, which complainant was informed and believed was to be held on the 16th day of September, and which contest would be in violation of [the] agreement entered into between the plaintiff and defendant [on March 13].

Personal service was had upon the defendant Dempsey in the proceeding in the Indiana court and on August 27, 1926, he entered his general appearance, by his attorneys, and filed his answer in said cause. September 13, a decree was entered in the [Indiana] superior court, finding that the contract was a valid and subsisting contract between the parties, and that the complainant had expended large sums of money in carrying out [the] agreement, and entering a decree that Dempsey be perpetually restrained and enjoined from in any way, wise, or manner, training or preparing for or participating in any contracts or engagements in furtherance of any boxing match, . . . and particularly from engaging or entering into any boxing match with one Gene Tunney, or with any person other than the one designated by plaintiff.

It is insisted . . . that the costs incurred by the plaintiff in procuring the [Indiana] injunctional order were properly chargeable against Dempsey for his breach of contract and recoverable in this proceeding. Under the evidence in the record . . . there appears to have been a valid subsisting agreement between the plaintiff and Dempsey [that Dempsey has refused to perform], and the plaintiff, as a matter of law, was entitled at least to nominal damages. For this reason, if for no other, judgment should have been for the plaintiff.

During [this proceeding] it was sought to introduce evidence for the purpose of showing damages, other than nominal damages, and in view of the fact that the case has to be retried, this court is asked to consider the various items of expense claimed to have been incurred and various offers of proof made to establish damages. . . . Under the proof offered, the question of damages naturally divides itself into the four following propositions:

1st. Loss of profits which would have been derived by the plaintiff in the event of the holding of the contest in question;

2nd. Expenses incurred by the plaintiff prior to the signing of the agreement between the plaintiff and Dempsey;

3rd. Expenses incurred in attempting to restrain the defendant from engaging in other contests and to force him into a compliance with the terms of his agreement with the plaintiff; and

4th. Expenses incurred after the signing of the agreement and before the breach of July 10, 1926.

Proposition 1: Plaintiff offered to prove by one Mullins that a boxing exhibition between Dempsey and Wills held in Chicago on September 22, 1926, would bring a gross receipt of $3,000,000, and that the expense incurred would be $1,400,000, leaving a net profit to the promoter of $1,600,000. The court properly sustained an objection to this testimony. The character of the undertaking was such that it would be impossible to produce evidence of a probative character sufficient to establish any amount which could be reasonably ascertainable by reason of the character of the undertaking. The profits from a boxing contest of this character, open to the public, is dependent upon so many different circumstances that they are not susceptible of definite legal determination. The success or failure of such an undertaking depends largely upon the ability of the promoters, the reputation of the contestants and the conditions of the weather at and prior to the holding of the contest, the accessibility of the place, the extent of the publicity, the possibility of other and counter attractions and many other questions which would enter into consideration. Such an entertainment lacks utterly the element of stability which exists in regular organized business. This fact was practically admitted by the plaintiff by the allegation of its bill filed in the [Indiana court] asking for an injunction against Dempsey [and charging]: "That by virtue of the premises aforesaid, the plaintiff will, unless it secures the injunctive relief herein prayed for, suffer great and irreparable injury and damages, not compensable by any action at law in damages, the damages being incapable of commensuration, and plaintiff, therefore, has no adequate remedy at law."

Compensation for damages for a breach of contract must be established by evidence from which a court or jury are able to ascertain the extent of such damages by the usual rules of evidence and to a reasonable degree of certainty. . . . [T]he performance in question is not susceptible of proof sufficient to satisfy [these] requirements[;] the damages, if any, are purely speculative. . . .

Proposition 2: Expenses incurred by the plaintiff prior to the signing of the agreement between the plaintiff and Dempsey.

The general rule is that in an action for a breach of contract a party can recover only on damages which naturally flow from and are the result of the act complained of. O'Conner v. Nolan, 64 Ill.App. 357. The Wills contract was entered into prior to the contract with the defendant and was not made contingent upon the plaintiff's obtaining a similar agreement with the defendant Dempsey. Under the circumstances the plaintiff speculated as to the result of his efforts to procure the Dempsey contract. It may be argued that there had been negotiations pending between plaintiff and Dempsey which clearly indicated an agreement between them, but the agreement in fact was never consummated until sometime later. The action is based upon the written agreement which was entered into in Los Angeles. Any obligations assumed by the plaintiff prior to that time are not chargeable to the defendant. Moreover, . . . the $50,000 named in the contract with Wills, which was to be payable upon a signing of the agreement, was not and never has been paid. There is no evidence in the record showing that the plaintiff is responsible financially, and even though there were, we consider that it is not an element of damage which can be recovered for breach of the contract in question.

Proposition 3: Expenses incurred in attempting to restrain the defendant from engaging in other contests and to force him into a compliance with [his] agreement with the plaintiff.

After the repudiation of the agreement by the defendant, plaintiff was advised of defendant's match with Tunney which . . . was to take place in Philadelphia in the month of September and was in direct conflict with [the] agreement entered into between plaintiff and defendant. Plaintiff's bill, filed in the superior court of [Indiana], was an effort on the part of the plaintiff to compel defendant to live up to the terms of his agreement. The chancellor in the Indiana court entered his decree, which apparently is in full force and effect, and the defendant in violating the terms of that decree, after personal service, is answerable to that court. . . . The expenses incurred, however, by the plaintiff in procuring that decree are not collectible in an action for damages in this proceeding; neither are such similar expenses as were incurred in the trips to Colorado and Philadelphia, nor the attorney's fees and other expenses thereby incurred. Cuyler Realty Co. v. Teneo Co., 188 N.Y.S. 340. The plaintiff having been informed that the defendant intended to proceed no further under his agreement, took such steps at its own financial risk. There was nothing in the agreement regarding attorney's fees and there was nothing in the contract in regard to the services of the defendant from which it would appear that the action for specific performance would lie. After the clear breach of contract by the defendant, the plaintiff proceeded with this character of litigation at its own risk. . . . [T]he trial court properly held that this was an element of damages which was not recoverable.

Proposition 4: Expenses incurred after the signing of the agreement and before the breach of July 10, 1926.

After the signing of the agreement plaintiff attempted to show expenses incurred by one Weisberg in and about the furtherance of the project. Weisberg testified that he . . . was in the employ of the Chicago Coliseum Club under [the March 8, 1926] contract during all of the time that his services were rendered in furtherance of this [contract]. Under its terms Weisberg was to be reimbursed out of the gate receipts and profits derived from the performance. His compensation depended entirely upon the success of the exhibition. Under his agreement with the plaintiff there was nothing to charge the plaintiff unconditionally with the costs and expenses of Weisberg's services. The court properly ruled against the admissibility of the evidence.

We find in the record, however, certain evidence which should have been submitted to the jury on the question of damages. . . . The contract on which the breach of the action is predicated shows a payment of $10 by the plaintiff to the defendant and the receipt acknowledged. It appears that the stadium . . . known as Soldier Field was considered as a site for the holding of the contest and plaintiff testified that it paid $300 to an architect for plans in the event the stadium was to be used for the performance. This item of damage . . . was sufficient to go to the jury. There were certain elements in regard to wages paid assistant secretaries which may be substantiated by evidence showing that they were necessary in furtherance of the undertaking. If these expenses were incurred they are recoverable if in furtherance of the general scheme. The defendant should not be required to answer in damages for salaries paid regular officials of the corporation who were presumed to be receiving such salaries by reason of their position, but special expenses incurred are recoverable. The expenses of Hoffman in going to Colorado for the purpose of having Dempsey take his physical examination for insurance, if before the breach and reasonable, are recoverable. The railroad fares for those who went to Los Angeles for the purpose of procuring the signing of the agreement are not recoverable as they were incurred in a furtherance of the procuring of the contract and not after the agreement was entered into. The services of Shank in looking after railroad facilities and making arrangements with the railroad for publicity and special trains and accommodations were items which should be considered and if it develops that they were incurred in a furtherance of the general plan and properly proven, are items for which the plaintiff should be reimbursed.

The items recoverable are such items of expense as were incurred between the date of the signing of the agreement and the breach of July 10, 1926, by the defendant and such as were incurred as a necessary expense in furtherance of the performance. . . .

For the reasons stated in this opinion the judgment of the circuit court is reversed and the cause remanded for a new trial.

HARRY WILLS

NOTE

Jack Dempsey fought Gene Tunney in Philadelphia on September 23, 1926, losing the heavyweight title. The injunction against Dempsey issued by the Indiana court operated only for the month of September 1926. Dempsey appealed from this decree, but the appeal was dismissed in 1928 (on mootness grounds), without a determination of the propriety of the injunction. 88 Ind.App. 251, 162 N.E. 237. Apparently no contempt proceedings were ever started against Dempsey in Indiana.

The gate receipts of the Dempsey–Tunney fight in Philadelphia on September 23, 1926, were reported to be $1,895,000. On September 22, 1927, Tunney again defeated Dempsey at Soldier Field in Chicago, in a fight whose gate receipts were reported to be $2,658,000. Would evidence of the gate receipts from these two fights dispose of the court's objection that the anticipated profits of the Dempsey–Wills fight were too uncertain?

————

Security Stove & Mfg. Co. v. American Ry. Express Co.

227 Mo.App. 175, 51 S.W.2d 572 (1932)

Security Stove brought an action for damages against the Express Co. for its failure to transport from Kansas City to Atlantic City, for exhibition at a gas association convention, a combination oil and gas burner that plaintiff had designed. The burner was not intended to be sold at the convention; plaintiff's object was to interest a particular company that distributed such equipment. Plaintiff wrote to the Express Co. on September 18, 1926, stating that it had engaged a booth at the convention for the week beginning October 11, and that "in order to get this exhibit in place on time it should be in Atlantic City not later than October the 8th." An agent of the Express Co. stated that, to meet that deadline, it would need to have the shipment in its hands by October 4; plaintiff actually delivered the burner to the Express Co. on October 2. Plaintiff's president went to Atlantic City to install the exhibit and found there, properly delivered, all but one of the twenty-one packages into which the shipment had been divided. The missing package was the part that controlled the flow of gas into the burner, the most important part and irreplaceable. A tracer was sent out for the missing package but it did not arrive in Atlantic City until the convention had closed. Plaintiff sued for and recovered: (1) $147 charges paid to the Express Co. for shipment of the exhibit; (2) $45.12 freight on the return shipment of the exhibit to Kansas City; (3) $101.39 railroad and pullman fares to and from Atlantic City, for plaintiff's president and an employee who had accompanied him; (4) $48 hotel costs for the two; (5) $150 for the president's time; (6) $40 for the wages of the accompanying employee; and (7) $270 for rental of the booth, which plaintiff had been unable to use.

Judgment for plaintiff for these sums was affirmed on appeal. Plaintiff had informed defendant of the necessity of prompt delivery of the shipment. "It is no doubt the general rule that where there is a breach of contract the party suffering the loss can recover only that which he would have had, had the contract not been broken. . . . But this is merely a general statement of the rule and is not inconsistent with the holdings that, in some instances, the injured party may recover expenses incurred in relying upon the contract, although such expenses would have been incurred had the contract not been breached." No profits were contemplated here, but "there is no contention that the exhibit would have been entirely valueless and whatever it might have accomplished, defendant knew of the circumstances and ought to respond for whatever damages the plaintiff suffered. In cases of this kind the method of estimating the damages should be adopted which is the most definite and certain and which best achieves the fundamental purpose of compensation." Even though the booth space had been rented before plaintiff contracted with defendant, plaintiff had arranged for the exhibit knowing that it could call on defendant to perform its common law duty to accept and transport the shipment with reasonable dispatch. The whole damage, therefore, was suffered in contemplation of defendant's performing its contract, which it failed to do, and all of plaintiff's losses were caused by defendant's breach.

COMMENT: *EQUITY RELIEF IN ADVANCE OF TRIAL*

The purpose of the Indiana proceeding initiated by the Coliseum Club was to obtain a court order restraining Dempsey from engaging in the match with Tunney. This type of remedy, aimed at compelling a party to do (or not do) something, rather than at compensating in money for an injury already inflicted, is called "equitable." We will consider such remedies later in this chapter. For now, it is necessary to note a striking feature of such relief—its availability in some circumstances in advance of a trial on the merits.

Such orders fall into two categories: temporary restraining orders and temporary injunctions (also sometimes called preliminary or interlocutory injunctions or injunctions pendente lite). A temporary restraining order may be issued without any notice to the defendant, or opportunity to be heard, if the plaintiff's need is sufficiently compelling to warrant restraint for a brief period (usually not more than ten days). Before a temporary restraining order terminates, or, if such ex parte relief could not be justified initially, the plaintiff may seek a preliminary injunction, after notice to the defendant and a hearing, typically abbreviated and perhaps simply on the basis of affidavits submitted. The standards for granting preliminary relief have been stated in various forms (e.g., plaintiff must show a reasonable likelihood of success on the merits), but the basic idea is to preserve the suit for an *effective decision* after a full trial. Therefore, where the harm to the plaintiff would be irreparable if preliminary relief were withheld, and such relief would not be irreversible so as to make a later decision against the plaintiff ineffective, the court may appropriately act before a full trial. Where the consequences of granting or withholding preliminary relief seem irreversible and not clearly compensable in money, the court must balance the hardships to the parties in reaching its decision. In the end, the benefits to the plaintiff from the injunction must be found to outweigh the injury that the defendant might suffer. Most temporary relief is cast in a negative form to prevent some prejudicial change in the existing situation, but mandatory injunctions ordering affirmative action can be issued.

Since preliminary relief necessarily involves some impingement on due process values, special procedural safeguards have been introduced. For example, it is customary to require from the plaintiff an injunction bond to indemnify the defendant if the injunction is later found to have been improvidently issued. Also, some procedural systems permit an appeal from the decision on a motion for a preliminary injunction, even though it is not a "final order," and the operative effect of the injunction may be stayed pending appeal, particularly if it is mandatory.

The power to issue preliminary injunctions in equity cases obviously adds to the remedial resources available to trial judges. Even with the safeguard of an injunction bond, the power may be exercised so as to bear down heavily on the party enjoined. It will usually be difficult to organize any effective review by appellate courts, if only because the time factor will be crucial, and it is recognized everywhere that the terms, scope, and conditions of the preliminary injunction are left largely to trial court discretion. Appellate courts often exhort trial judges to use their powers with restraint.

Again, the primary purpose of a temporary injunction is to preserve the *status quo*. The difficulty in defining this elusive phrase is illustrated by the injunction issued by the Indiana court against Dempsey's fighting Tunney in Philadelphia. If the injunction had been enforceable and compliance had been compelled, it would have given the Coliseum Club a much firmer grip on Dempsey, but it would also, no doubt, have caused severe losses and a considerable change in the situation for the promoters of the Philadelphia fight.

Yet the basic assumption is that the interlocutory injunction, "temporary" or "preliminary" though it be, must be obeyed and that a court, if it has means to do so, not only can but properly should punish any disobedience. If Dempsey had ventured back into Indiana before the case was formally held to be moot (so that the injunction was dissolved), the Indiana court clearly had power to punish him for contempt and might well have levied at least a money fine for his disobedience. The disabilities of the Indiana court were due to (1) the basic limitation that the process of a state court has no legal effect outside the boundaries of the state in which it sits, and (2) the conception of contempt as an offense against the court issuing the order, so that that court alone can punish. Such limitations might lead a court in its discretion not to enter on so difficult an enterprise, but they did not mean that the Indiana court, if proper service in Indiana of a summons on Dempsey had been secured, lacked power or acted improperly in giving this "interlocutory" relief.

———

RESTATEMENT OF CONTRACTS, SECOND

Section 349. Damages Based on Reliance Interest

As an alternative to the [expectation interest measure of damages], the injured party has a right to damages based on his reliance interest, including expenditures made in preparation for performance or in performance, less any loss that the party in breach can prove with reasonable certainty the injured party would have suffered had the contract been performed.

Comment:

a. . . . If the injured party's expenditures exceed the contract price, it is clear that at least to the extent of the excess, there would have been a loss. . . . Often the reliance consists of preparation for performance or actual performance of the contract, and this is sometimes called "essential" reliance. It may, however, also consist of preparation for collateral transactions that a party plans to carry out when the contract in question is performed, and this is sometimes called "incidental" reliance.

Illustrations: . . .

4. A contracts to sell his retail store to B. After B has spent $100,000 for inventory, A repudiates the contract and B sells the inventory for $60,000. If neither party proves with reasonable certainty what profit or loss B would have made if the contract had been performed, B

can recover as damages the $40,000 loss that he sustained on the sale of the inventory.

———————

L. Albert & Son v. Armstrong Rubber Co.

United States Court of Appeals, Second Circuit, 1949.
178 F.2d 182.

L. HAND, CIRCUIT JUDGE. Both sides appeal from the judgment in an action brought by the Albert Co., which we shall speak of as the Seller, against the Armstrong Co., which we shall call the Buyer. The action was to recover the agreed price of four "Refiners," machines designed to recondition old rubber; the contract of sale was by an exchange of letters in December, 1942, and the Seller delivered two of the four "Refiners" in August, 1943, and the other two on either August 31st or September 8th, 1945. Because of the delay in delivery of the second two, the Buyer refused to accept all four in October, 1945—the exact day not being fixed—and it counterclaimed for the Seller's breach. The judge dismissed both the complaint and the counterclaim; but he gave judgment to the Seller for the value without interest on a part of the equipment delivered—a 300 horse-power motor and accessories—which the Buyer put into use on February 20th, 1946. . . .

[In an omitted passage, the court held that the seller was entitled to recover from the buyer the fair market value of the equipment and accessories actually delivered (an amount set at $4,590) along with interest. The court went on to conclude that the buyer had justifiably rejected the four refiners, and thus affirmed dismissal of the seller's complaint for the price. Judge Hand then turned to the buyer's appeal.]

[Buyer] does not claim any loss of profit, but it does claim the expenses which it incurred in reliance upon the Seller's promise. These were of three kinds: its whole investment in its "reclaim department," $118,478; the cost of its "rubber scrap," $27,555.63; the cost of the foundation which it laid for the "Refiners," $3,000. The judge in his opinion held that the Buyer had not proved that "the lack of production" of the reclaim department "was caused by the delay in delivery of plaintiffs' refiners"; but that that was "only one of several possible causes." Such a possibility is not sufficient proof of causation to impose liability on the plaintiffs for the cost of all machinery and supplies for the reclaim department." The record certainly would not warrant our holding that this holding was "clearly erroneous"; indeed, the evidence preponderates in its favor. The Buyer disposed of all its "scrap rubber" in April and May, 1945; and, so far as appears, until it filed its counterclaim in May, 1947, it never suggested that the failure to deliver two of the four "Refiners" was the cause of the collapse of its "reclaim department." The counterclaim for these items has every appearance of being an afterthought, which can scarcely have been put forward with any hope of success.

The claim for the cost of the foundation which the Buyer built for the "Refiners," stands upon a different footing. Normally a promisee's damages for breach of contract are the value of the promised performance, less his outlay, which includes, not only what he must pay to the promisor, but any expenses necessary to prepare for the performance; and in the case at bar the cost of the foundation was such an expense. The sum which would restore the Buyer to the position it would have been in, had the Seller performed, would therefore be the prospective net earnings of the "Refiners" while they were used (together with any value they might have as scrap after they were discarded), less their price—$25,500—together with $3,000, the cost of installing them. The Buyer did not indeed prove the net earnings of the "Refiners" or their scrap value; but it asserts that it is nonetheless entitled to recover the cost of the foundation upon the theory that what it expended in reliance upon the Seller's performance was a recoverable loss. In cases where the venture would have proved profitable to the promisee, there is no reason why he should not recover his expenses. On the other hand, on those occasions in which the performance would not have covered the promisee's outlay, such a result imposes the risk of the promisee's contract upon the promisor. We cannot agree that the promisor's default in performance should under this guise make him an insurer of the promisee's venture; yet it does not follow that the breach should not throw upon him the duty of showing that the value of the performance would in fact have been less than the promisee's outlay. It is often very hard to learn what the value of the performance would have been; and it is a common expedient, and a just one, in such situations to put the peril of the answer upon that party who by his wrong has made the issue relevant to the rights of the other. On principle therefore the proper solution would seem to be that the promisee may recover his outlay in preparation for the performance, subject to the privilege of the promisor to reduce it by as much as he can show that the promisee would have lost, if the contract had been performed. . . .

[I]t appears to us . . . that the reported decisions leave it open to us to adopt the rule we have stated. Moreover, there is support for this result in the writings of scholars. The Restatement of Contracts [§ 333(d)] allows recovery of the promisee's outlay "in necessary preparation" for the performance, subject to several limitations, of which one is that the promisor may deduct whatever he can prove the promisee would have lost, if the contract had been fully performed. Professor McCormick thinks, [McCormick on Damages, § 142] that "the jury should be instructed not to go beyond the probable yield" of the performance to the promisee, but he does not consider the burden of proof. Much the fullest discussion of the whole subject is Professor Fuller's in the Yale Law Journal [46 Yale L.J. 52, 75–80]. The situation at bar was among those which he calls cases of "essential reliance," and for which he favors the rule we are adopting. It is one instance of his "very simple formula: We will not in a suit for reimbursement of losses incurred in reliance on a contract knowingly put the plaintiff in a better position than he would have occupied, had the contract been fully performed." . . .

. . . To the allowance for the motor and accessories will be added interest from February 20th, 1946. The Buyer will be allowed to set off $3,000 against the Seller's recovery with interest from October, 1945, subject to the Seller's privilege to deduct from that amount any sum which upon a further hearing it can prove would have been the Buyer's loss upon the contract, had the "Refiners" been delivered on [time]. Judgment [affirmed] as so modified.

Decision.

NOTE

This contractual dispute should be seen against the background of the Second World War. The war cut off many sources of rubber to the United States at the same time the demand for rubber grew dramatically. As a result, the market for reconditioned rubber grew. Once the war ended, rubber could once again be imported, and the business of reconditioning rubber suddenly became far less attractive.

————

Mt. Pleasant Stable Co. v. Steinberg
238 Mass. 567, 131 N.E. 295 (1921)

The court confronted the question of harmonizing reliance and expectation damages. "The parties entered into a written contract dated June 25, 1914, by which the plaintiff was to furnish at an agreed price, single and double teams to do the defendants' trucking. There was evidence that after the parties had operated under the contract for a few months the defendants broke the contract. The auditor found that at the time of the breach the contract had 450 days to run; that the defendants were using during the period on an average 'four and one-half teams a day,' and that the profit to the plaintiff would be $1 for each team, making the total profit $2,025. He also found that the plaintiff purchased for special use in the defendants' business, two 'Cliest' horses for which it paid $625 and sold them for $485, sustaining a loss thereby of $140. . . .

"The contract did not preclude the plaintiff from carrying on as many other contracts as it saw fit. Its time did not belong to the defendants and the contract did not call for personal services on the part of the plaintiff. The defendants having broken the contract became liable to the plaintiff for all damages which would compensate it for its loss and such as the parties were supposed to have contemplated would result from its breach. The plaintiff was entitled to recover damages measured by the difference between the contract price and what it would have cost it to have performed the contract, or, as found by the auditor, a profit of $1 on each team from the time the contract was broken until its expiration according to its terms."

The court went on to hold that the plaintiff was not entitled to recover for the loss on the sale of the two horses in addition to recovering the lost profits: "If the plaintiff had completed the contract, it could recover only the contract price. This expenditure for preliminary outlays could not be received in addition, and by recovering the profits on the contract, full compensation is given for its loss." The court specifically noted, however, that it was not reaching the question whether the plaintiff could recover expenses in preparing for its performance, where the profits cannot be determined. [Did it make sense for the court to exclude consideration of whether the breach allowed the plaintiff to take on additional contracts?]

————

COMMENT: THE ECONOMICS OF CONTRACT REMEDIES

The compensation principle does not punish those who break their promises. As Holmes characterized the law (recall the Introductory Note, supra p. 1), it gives those who make promises a choice to perform or pay a compensatory sum, but takes no position on whether keeping promises is either good or bad. He explained as follows (The Path of the Law, 10 Harv.L.Rev. 457, 458–469 (1897)):

The first thing for a business-like understanding of the matter is to understand its limits, and therefore I think it desirable at once to point out and dispel a confusion between morality and law, which sometimes rises to the height of conscious theory, and more often and indeed constantly is making trouble in detail without reaching the point of consciousness. You can see very plainly that a bad man has as much reason as a good one for wishing to avoid an encounter with the public force, and therefore you can see the practical importance of the distinction between morality and law. A man who cares nothing for an ethical rule which is believed and practised by his neighbors is likely nevertheless to care a good deal to avoid being made to pay money, and will want to keep out of jail if he can.

I take it for granted that no hearer of mine will misinterpret what I have to say as the language of cynicism. The law is the witness and external deposit of our moral life. Its history is the history of the moral development of the race. The practice of it, in spite of popular jests, tends to make good citizens. . . . When I emphasize the difference between law and morals I do so with reference to a single end, that of learning and understanding the law. For that purpose you must definitely master its specific marks, and it is for that I ask you for the moment to imagine yourselves indifferent to other and greater things.

I do not say that there is not a wider point of view from which the distinction between law and morals becomes of secondary or no importance, as all mathematical distinctions vanish in presence of the infinite. But I do say that that distinction is of the first importance for the object which we are here to consider,—a right study and mastery of the law as a business with well understood limits, a body of dogma enclosed within definite lines. I have just shown the practical reasoning for saying so.

If you want to know the law and nothing else, you must look at it as a bad man, who cares only for the material consequences which such knowledge enables him to predict, not as a good one, who finds his reason for conduct, whether inside the law or outside of it, in the vaguer sanctions of conscience. The theoretical importance of the distinction is no less, if you would reason on your subject aright. The law is full of phraseology drawn from morals, and by the mere force of language continually invites us to pass from one domain to the other without perceiving it, as we are sure to do unless we have the boundary constantly before our minds. . . .

The confusion with which I am dealing besets confessedly legal conceptions. Take the fundamental question, What constitutes the law? You will find some text writers telling you that it is something different from what is decided by the courts of Massachusetts or England, that it is a system of reason, that it is a deduction from principles of ethics or admitted axioms or what not, which may or may not coincide with the decisions. But if we take the view of our friend the bad man we shall find that he does not care two straws for the axioms or deductions, but that he does want to know what the Massachusetts or English courts are likely to do in fact. I am much of his mind. The prophecies of what the courts will do in fact, and nothing more pretentious, are what I mean by the law. . . .

Nowhere is the confusion between legal and moral ideas more manifest than in the law of contract. Among other things, here again the so called primary rights and duties are invested with a mystic significance beyond what can be assigned and explained.

OLIVER WENDELL HOLMES, JR.
1841–1935

Holmes was a legal pragmatist. His project was to describe the world. He ignored the moral underpinnings because they tended to obscure an understanding of the law; so he took no view on whether keeping promises was good or bad. In our own time, Richard Posner is the judge/scholar who has thought most explicitly—and controversially—about the compensation principle. In his view, expectation damages are to be preferred to reliance damages because protecting expectancies forces those who make promises to internalize the costs the breach imposes on the other party. Someone who makes a promise in an expectation damages regime has no incentive to break the promise unless he has better opportunities elsewhere. And—and this is the controversial point—if he has better opportunities elsewhere, it is desirable that he take advantage of them. Holmes made no judgment about whether keeping a promise was good or bad; Posner appears to take the view that what he calls "efficient" breach is normatively desirable.

The following example generally captures Posner's notion of efficient breach. I promise to mow your lawn on Saturday for $10. It will cost you $15 to have someone else do it, once the aggravation and inconvenience are taken into account. If I must pay you $5 damages in the event that I breach, I have no reason to breach unless I have an opportunity that brings me a benefit of more than $15. The expectation damages rule is thus uniquely sensible. If damages were less, I would have an incentive to breach even when my time was best spent mowing your lawn. If damages were greater, I would sometimes still mow your lawn, even though my time was better spent elsewhere. Only expectation damages ensure that the promise is kept if and only if keeping the promise remains mutually beneficial.

Law and economics scholars who built on Posner's insight looked at other ways in which contract remedies affected the incentives of both parties. Ensuring that the promisor internalize the costs of breach is not the only objective of contract law. The remedy imposed in the event of breach also affects the behavior of the beneficiary of the promise. As noted above, the virtue of enforcing promises derives in large measure from allowing the other party to rely on the promise. But there can be too much of a good thing. A world in which the innocent party recovers full expectation damages induces overreliance.

Let us assume that I am building a hotel and acting as my own general contractor. I expect to be finished by January 1, but I recognize that a delay of a week or more is possible. I start to book rooms and conventions in advance. I must decide whether to book two conventions in the month of January. I look at the numbers for the convention in the first week of January. Even if the hotel is finished on time, I shall end up losing a little money, so I decide not to book it. The numbers for the convention in the second week of January are more promising. If the hotel is built on time, I stand to make a significant profit. But if some unusual event comes my way, I shall either owe a large amount to the disappointed conventioneers or be forced to incur enormous expenses to finish the hotel on the original schedule. I decide the risk of a delay is too great, and I decide not to book this convention either even though it would be profitable if everything finished on time.

My incentives change in an expectation damages world when I hire you to build the hotel for me, and you promise to finish it by January 1. With your promise in hand, I treat the finishing of the hotel on schedule as a sure thing. Either you complete the hotel on time, or you put me in the same economic position I would be in if you had. Nevertheless, I still elect not book the hotel for the first week of January, as I lose money if you finish on time and expectation damages will leave me with the same loss even if you do not. But the second convention is a different matter. I receive the profit from the second convention if you finish on time or expectation damages in the same amount if you do not. My profit from the second convention is guaranteed. If the hotel does not open on time, I can shift onto you all the costs of dealing with disappointed conventioneers, such as paying them damages or finding them alternative accommodations. Expectation damages, as conventionally calculated, give me an incentive to "overrely," to treat performance as more certain than I would even if I were doing it myself.

To ensure that we both have the right incentive, expectation damages should be reduced to the amount necessary to put me in the same position I would be in if I had taken optimal precautions. Such a rule imposes enormous burdens on the courts. Instead of looking at my actual expenses, the court has to imagine my expenses in the counterfactual world in which I take account of the possibility that performance on your part is not certain. A court has no easy way of knowing what conventions I should or should not be booking.

The law does not explicitly require such an inquiry. Nevertheless, the common law developed a large number of doctrines that collectively have much the same effect. We turn to these limitations on the compensation principle in the next section. The innocent party has a duty to mitigate damages once a breach occurs. Moreover, a breaching party is not liable for all the damages that an innocent party suffers, but only those that are reasonably foreseeable. If the innocent party faces special circumstances that would make breach especially costly, it must take precautions itself or at least inform the other party at the time of the contracting. As we shall see, these doctrines significantly limit the overreliance problem as an issue in contract law.

The problem of overreliance is not, however, a reason to prefer reliance damages, the principal alternative measure of damages. Reliance damages, the amount necessary to return the parties to the same position in which they found themselves before the promise was made, induces overreliance as well. In the hotel example, I shall still book the second convention in January. (If the hotel opens on time, I enjoy the profits. If it does not, you pay for any losses.) But now I shall book the first one as well.

In a reliance-based regime, I enjoy the profits on the second convention only if you finish on time. In the event of breach, I recover only my reliance costs. The tidy profits that I receive in an expectation damages regime are gone. Hence, in a reliance-based regime, I am no longer indifferent to whether you perform or pay damages. I want you to perform so I can profit from the second convention. I shall search for ways of imposing costs on you to give you an added incentive to finish on time. Booking the first convention in early January does this. The prospect that you will have to compensate not one but two groups of disappointed conventioneers will lead to you to move heaven and earth to finish by January 1. The small loss from the first convention in the event the hotel opens on time may be worth incurring if it ensures you will finish on time and allow me to enjoy the profits on the second convention, profits I shall not receive if you breach. Steven Shavell, Damage Measures for Breach of Contract, 11 Bell J. Econ. 466 (1980). Hence, reliance damages increase my incentive to act even more inefficiently than I would have if I were building the hotel myself (booking both January conventions rather than just one). Because of the overreliance problem, an expectation damages scheme is unambiguously better than a reliance damages scheme. Expectation damages force you to internalize the costs of breaking your promise, and although I incur inefficient expenses as a result of having your promise, I do not incur as many as I do in a reliance-based regime.

Law and economics scholars must be cautious about overemphasizing the importance of a rule that induces efficient breach and optimal reliance. The value of such a rule is necessarily tempered by the costs of renegotiation at the time of performance. See Richard Craswell, Contract Remedies, Renegotiation, and the Theory of Efficient Breach, 61 S.Cal.L.Rev. 629 (1988). If I have an opportunity that is worth more than performing my promise to you, you and I should be able to renegotiate our contract and reach a deal that will leave us both better off.

Suppose you promise to sell me a unique machine for $1 million that will give me $200,000 in additional profit. Before you deliver it to me, you find someone for whom it will generate $500,000 in additional profit. It might seem that a damage rule allowing you to breach your contract with me and pay me $200,000 is socially desirable. After all, the third party values the machine more than I do. But things are not so simple. Instead of using the machine myself, I might have been able to sell it to a third party. More to the point, once you find the other buyer, you can always renegotiate with me and the machine will end up in that person's hands regardless of what the damage remedy is. The costs of renegotiation limit the benefits of an optimal damage remedy.

In short, the importance of a contract damages rule that promotes efficient breach turns largely on the costs of renegotiation. When these are low, the problem of inefficient breach is not that serious. Indeed, in a world in which it is costly to search for potential buyers, it may make sense to have a legal rule that requires specific performance so that at a given moment only one of us has the incentive to look for buyers. Negotiation is costly, but so too is the implementation of expectation damages.

In addition to uncertainties respecting transaction costs, the cases and examples we have seen—the "scarred land," the "ugly fountain," the "perfect hand"—suggest the hazards of analyzing breach of contract as if a market value were always readily accessible. One concern, evident in the trial court's findings in *Groves* (and underscored ahead in Vines v. Orchard Hills, Inc., p. 134) is the inherent limitation any judge or juror faces in estimating damages. A true expectation damages remedy requires identifying the amount of money that would have made the plaintiff indifferent to whether the promise had been kept. In many situations—such as the value of the "perfect hand" in *Hawkins*—this value is inherently subjective and cannot be measured precisely. Invocations of economic language and markets in such circumstances may imply a precision that is illusory. Moreover, for the defendant to internalize properly the costs of the breach to the plaintiff, expectation damages must reflect the value the plaintiff himself attaches to the promise, not the value others put upon it. For this reason, a focus on markets may lead to damage awards that are undercompensatory. The Peevyhouses may put a much higher value on having their land fully restored than would be reflected in the market price.

We shall return to Holmes's "bad man" conception of the common law and the contributions of Richard Posner and other law-and-economics scholars. Many question whether Holmes' figure of the "bad man" is the appropriate starting place for understanding contract law. In particular, such an account of contract may slight the moral dimension of the law. A modern exemplar is Charles Fried, Contract as Promise: A Theory of Contractual Obligation (1981). See also Shiffrin, The Divergence of Contract and Promise, 120 Harv.L.Rev. 708 (2007). As Lon Fuller observed, The Law in Quest of Itself 92–95 (1940), "it is a peculiar sort of bad man who is worried about judicial decrees and is indifferent to extra-legal penalties, who is concerned about a fine of two dollars but apparently not about the possible loss of friends and customers."

SECTION 2. LIMITATIONS ON THE COMPENSATION PRINCIPLE

Rockingham County v. Luten Bridge Co.
United States Court of Appeals, Fourth Circuit, 1929.
35 F.2d 301.

[The Luten Bridge Co. sued to recover the sum alleged to be due under a contract with Rockingham County for the construction of a bridge. On January 7, 1924, the board of commissioners of the county, by a vote of 3 to 2, awarded the contract to the plaintiff. As a result of continuing dissension over the issue, Pruitt, one of the commissioners who had voted in the affirmative, on February 11, 1924, sent a letter of resignation to the county's clerk of the superior court. The clerk immediately accepted the resignation and noted his acceptance on the letter. Later that same day, Pruitt telephoned the clerk and withdrew his resignation and subsequently confirmed this in writing, but the clerk ignored the withdrawal and appointed one Hampton as Pruitt's replacement. Hampton took an oath of office and thereafter attended the advertised meetings of the commissioners. Neither Pruitt nor the other two commissioners who had voted for the construction of the bridge attended any further advertised meetings of the commissioners.

On February 21, 1924, three commissioners (two holdovers and Hampton), at a regularly advertised meeting, unanimously adopted a resolution, of which a copy was sent to the plaintiff, to the effect that the contract for the construction of the bridge was not valid and that plaintiff should proceed no further under it. At the same meeting, the three commissioners rescinded action previously taken looking to the construction of a hard surface road for which the bridge was to be a connecting link. By February 21, plaintiff had expended in labor and materials a sum estimated at $1,900. After receiving the notice of the votes at the February 21 meeting, plaintiff proceeded to construct the bridge. On November 24, 1924, plaintiff brought the present action claiming $18,301.07 as the contract price for the bridge. Three days later, on November 27, Pruitt and the other two commissioners who had voted for the construction of the bridge but who, unlike Pruitt, had not attempted to resign, met with an attorney and prepared an answer to plaintiff's suit which admitted the county's liability. A newly-elected board of commissioners took office on December 1, 1924. It voted to repudiate this answer by Pruitt and his two colleagues and also to contest the county's liability under the contract with the plaintiff.

The trial judge ruled that the answer filed by Pruitt and his colleagues was a valid answer by a majority of the commissioners and was binding on the county. The judge therefore directed the jury to render a verdict for the plaintiff and the jury complied. In passages here omitted, the Court of Appeals held this instruction to be erroneous on two grounds. First, though North Carolina statutes made no provision for the resignation of county commissioners, a public officer under common law rules had a power to resign if the resignation was accepted by the proper authority, which in this case was the clerk of the superior court. Second, the November 27 meeting of Pruitt and his two colleagues had not been advertised so that the three, even if they had constituted a majority of the board, were not empowered to bind the county at this informal meeting.]

"Fishing Creek Bridge"—Built by Luten Bridge Co., 1924

PARKER, CIRCUIT JUDGE. . . . Coming, then, to the third question—i.e., as to the measure of plaintiff's recovery—we do not think that, after the county had given notice, while the contract was still executory, that it did not desire the bridge built and would not pay for it, plaintiff could proceed to build it and recover the contract price. It is true that the county had no right to rescind the contract, and the notice given plaintiff amounted to a breach on its part; but, after plaintiff had received notice of the breach, it was its duty to do nothing to increase the damages flowing therefrom. If A enters into a binding contract to build a house for B, B, of course, has no right to rescind the contract without A's consent. But if, before the house is built, he decides that he does not want it, and notifies A to that effect, A has no right to proceed with the building and thus pile up damages. His remedy is to treat the contract as broken when he receives the notice, and sue for the recovery of such damages as he may have sustained from the breach, including any profit which he would have realized upon performance, as well as any other losses which may have resulted to him. [Here,] the county decided not to build the road of which the bridge was to be a part, and did not build it. The bridge, built in the midst of the forest, is of no value to the county because of this change of circumstances. When, therefore, the county gave notice to the plaintiff that it would not proceed with the project, plaintiff should have desisted from further work. It had no right thus to pile up damages by proceeding with the erection of a useless bridge.

The contrary view was expressed by Lord Cockburn in Frost v. Knight, L.R. 7 Ex. 111, but, as pointed out by Prof. Williston (Williston on Contracts, vol. 3, p. 2347), it is not in harmony with the decisions in this country:

> There is a line of cases running back to 1845 which holds that, after an absolute repudiation or refusal to perform by one party to a contract, the other party cannot continue to perform and recover damages based on full performance. This rule is only a particular application of the general rule of damages that a plaintiff cannot hold a defendant liable for damages which need not have been incurred; or, as it is often stated, the plaintiff must, so far as he can without loss to himself, mitigate the damages caused by the defendant's wrongful act. . . . If a man engages to have work done, and afterwards repudiates his contract before the work has been begun or when it has been only partially done, it is inflicting damage on the defendant without benefit to the plaintiff to allow the latter to insist on proceeding with the contract. The work may be useless to the defendant, and yet he would be forced to pay the full contract price. On the other hand, the plaintiff is interested only in the profit he will make out of the contract. If he receives this it is equally advantageous for him to use his time otherwise.

The leading case on the subject [is] Clark v. Marsiglia, 1 Denio (N.Y.) 317. . . . [D]efendant had employed plaintiff to paint certain pictures for him, but countermanded the order before the work was finished. Plaintiff, however, went on and completed the work and sued for the contract price. In reversing a judgment for plaintiff, the court said: "The defendant, by requiring the plaintiff to stop work upon the paintings, violated his contract, and thereby incurred a liability to pay such damages as the plaintiff should sustain. Such damages would include a recompense for the labor done and materials used, and such further sum in damages as might, upon legal principles, be assessed for the breach of the contract; but the plaintiff had no right, by obstinately persisting in the work, to make the penalty upon the defendant greater than it would otherwise have been."[*]

We have carefully considered the cases . . . upon which plaintiff relies; but we do not think that they are at all in point. Roehm v. Horst [178 U.S. 1] merely follows the rule of Hochster v. De La Tour, 2 El. & Bl. 678, to the effect that where one party to any executory contract refuses to perform in advance of the time fixed for performance, the other party, without waiting for the time of performance, may sue at once for damages occasioned by the breach. . . . [I]n none of [these cases] was the point involved which is involved here, viz. whether, in application of the rule which requires that the party to a contract who is not in default do nothing to aggravate the damages arising from breach, he should not desist from performance of an executory contract for the erection of a structure when notified of the other party's repudiation, instead of piling up damages by proceeding with the work. As stated above, we think that reason and authority require that this

---

[*] [The court in Clark v. Marsiglia also stated: "To hold that one who employs another to do a piece of work is bound to suffer it to be done at all events, would sometimes lead to great injustice. A man may hire another to labor for a year, and within the year his situation may be such as to render the work entirely useless to him. . . . In all such cases the just claims of the party employed are satisfied when he is fully recompensed for his part performance and indemnified for his loss in respect to the part left unexecuted; and to persist in accumulating a larger demand is not consistent with good faith towards the employer."—Eds.]

question be answered in the affirmative. It follows that there was error in directing a verdict for plaintiff for the full amount of its claim. The measure of plaintiff's damage, upon its appearing that notice was duly given not to build the bridge, is an amount sufficient to compensate plaintiff for labor and materials expended and expense incurred in the part performance of the contract, prior to its repudiation, plus the profit which would have been realized if it had been carried out in accordance with its terms. . . .

Our conclusion, on the whole case, is that there was error in failing to strike out the answer of Pruitt, Pratt, and McCollum, [and] in directing a verdict for plaintiff. The judgment below will accordingly be reversed, and the case remanded for a new trial.

————

Leingang v. City of Mandan Weed Board

468 N.W.2d 397 (N.D. 1991)

The city's Weed Board awarded Leingang a contract to cut weeds on municipal lots of more than 10,000 square feet in size. Another contractor was given a contract to cut smaller lots. Leingang brought suit upon discovering that the Weed Board had improperly assigned large lots to the small-lot contractor. The city admitted its breach at trial, conceding that the contract price for the work that should have gone to Leingang was $1,933. Leingang urged that his damages should be $1,722, calculated by subtracting from $1,933 the further sum of $211, which, he testified, represented the total of gas, oil, repair, and blade-replacement expenses he had avoided by not performing the work wrongfully taken from him. The city argued that only "net profits" were recoverable, and that, in calculating such profits, some of Leingang's overhead expenses—items beyond those he testified he had avoided—should be attributed to the contract in question and deducted from the contract price of the lost work. The trial court adopted this approach. By subtracting four categories of expenses reported on the business schedule of Leingang's tax returns (insurance, repairs, supplies, and vehicle expenses) from the weed-cutting income reported on those returns, the court arrived at "a profit margin of 20 percent." Accordingly, the court awarded Leingang 20 percent of the price of the lost work, or $386. *Held*, this was error; there must be a new trial on damages. A plaintiff is to be compensated for all the detriment caused by the breach. "Where the contract is for service and the breach prevents performance of that service, the value of the contract consists of two items: (1) the party's reasonable expenditures toward performance, including costs paid, material wasted, and time and service spent on the contract, and (2) the anticipated profits." A plaintiff ordinarily proves profits "by reducing the contract price by the [total] amount it would have spent to perform." But "constant overhead expenses" are not included as a cost of performance because a plaintiff must pay them whether or not the contract was breached. In fact, a plaintiff is compensated for overhead by recovering "the contract price, reduced only by expenses saved because the contract did not have to be performed." It was therefore error to calculate a "net profit margin" by deducting Leingang's general costs of doing business "without determining whether these costs remained constant" regardless of the city's breach. "The reduction from the contract price of a portion of the 'fixed,' or constant expenses, effectively required Leingang to pay that portion twice."

————

Kearsarge Computer, Inc. v. Acme Staple Co.
116 N.H. 705, 366 A.2d 467 (1976)

Kearsarge performed data-processing services for Acme under a one-year contract. About halfway through the year Acme terminated the contract on the ground that Kearsarge's performance was unsatisfactory. Kearsarge sued for damages. The trial court adopted a master's report which found for Kearsarge on all issues and awarded damages for the full balance of the contract price, $12,313.22, with no reductions. On appeal, Acme contended that the recovery of the contract price should have been reduced in the amount of (1) "certain savings" realized by Kearsarge as a result of the breach, and (2) "income from new business" generated by Kearsarge after termination of the contract. *Held*, there was no error in the master's denial of Acme's claims for reduction of damages. The breach did not produce "substantial savings." Kearsarge "would not have spent significantly more on salaries, machine rental, or other overhead expenses if it continued to provide Acme with data processing services. With respect to labor costs, if a plaintiff cannot reduce his work force because of the breach, no savings result.... No layoffs were possible in this case because each of Kearsarge's three employees performed separate functions.... Kearsarge's operating costs—notably the rentals on computers and other equipment—were substantially fixed. The reduction of output due to the breach did not result in savings. R. Posner, Economic Analysis of the Law 59 n.7 (1972)." Moreover, Kearsarge's only remaining performance was the running of equipment and the delivery of the results to Acme. "The cost of performance was the cost of paper, electricity and transportation of data to and from the offices of the parties.... The costs of performance were trivial in relation to the contract price. Because the breach did not relieve Kearsarge of a costly burden, the master did not err in awarding Kearsarge the full contract price.... The fact that plaintiff did not introduce evidence of the cost of paper, electricity and delivery of data does not bar recovery because the defendant has the burden of proving savings."

Nor is there evidence that Kearsarge could not have serviced its "new" (i.e., post-breach) clients "but for" Acme's breach. "The general rule is that 'gains made by the injured party on other transactions after the breach are never to be deducted from the damages that are otherwise recoverable, unless such gains could not have been made, had there been no breach.' ... In contrast to an employee's suit for breach of a personal services contract, no deduction is allowed if the plaintiff sells to a third party a product that can be produced according to demand. The theory is that the second sale would have occurred even if the defendant did not breach this contract. See Locks v. Wade, 36 N.J.Super. 128, 114 A.2d 875 (App.Div.1955)." The contract here is neither purely for personal services nor the sale of goods. It involves "a combination of personal skills and labor, materials, equipment and time. In these respects, a contract for data processing services is similar to a construction contract... The builder's profits on contracts entered into after the breach do not mitigate the damages unless the first contract required the builder's personal services to such an extent that concurrent performance of another contract would be impossible.... The reason is that, like manufacturing, these businesses are deemed to be expandable. The law presumes that they can accept a virtually unlimited amount of business so that income generated from accounts acquired after the breach does not mitigate the plaintiff's damages.... We hold that in the absence of evidence to the contrary a data processing contract does not involve unique personal services to such an extent that when the provider of such services seeks new business after a breach of contract, the income from such new business mitigates the damages owed to him by the breaching party."

QUESTION

The *Leingang* and *Kearsarge* cases illustrate the problems that can arise in applying the *Luten Bridge* damage formula, including the problem of distinguishing overhead or "fixed" costs from "variable" costs, which are said to vary with the plaintiff's business activity. The nonbreaching parties stand in a position different from that of the builder in *Luten Bridge*. The issue is not whether they should be paid for expenses they incurred on the contract after the breach, but rather what damages they should be able to enjoy when they ceased performing and turned to work elsewhere. Judge Cudahy, writing in Hallmark Ins. Adm'rs v. Colonial Penn Life, 990 F.2d 984, 990 (7th Cir.1993), offered this analysis:

> . . . [A] party harmed by another's breach of contract is entitled to collect those lost net revenues that would have helped defray fixed costs and contributed to profit. [The amount by which revenue net of variable costs exceed fixed costs is "profit" in the sense that term is commonly understood.] A central element in making this calculation . . . is the ascertainment of which costs vary with output and which do not (i.e., are truly fixed). . . . If a business operates more than one activity [is a multiple-activity firm], fixed costs are not usually deducted from gross revenues since the business would be expected to continue operating [despite one broken contract] and "fixed" costs would continue to be incurred. The owner would be entitled, in this situation, to collect the contribution toward fixed expenses that it would have received but for the breach.

Had the bridge company stopped work upon receiving notice of the county's repudiation, diverting its workers and equipment to other bridge jobs, what deductions would have been proper in figuring the plaintiff's damages?

––––––––

Parker v. Twentieth Century–Fox Film Corp.

Supreme Court of California, 1970.
3 Cal.3d 176, 89 Cal.Rptr. 737, 474 P.2d 689.

BURKE, J. Defendant Twentieth Century–Fox Film Corp. appeals from a summary judgment granting to plaintiff the recovery of agreed compensation under a written contract for her services as an actress in a motion picture. . . . [W]e have concluded that the trial court correctly ruled in plaintiff's favor and that the judgment should be affirmed.

Plaintiff is well known as an actress,* and in the contract between plaintiff and defendant is sometimes referred to as the "Artist." Under the contract, dated August 6, 1965, plaintiff was to play the female lead in defendant's contemplated production of a motion picture entitled "Bloomer Girl." The contract provided that defendant would pay plaintiff a minimum "guaranteed compensation" of $53,571.42 per week for 14 weeks commencing May 23, 1966, for a total of $750,000. Prior to May 1966 defendant de-

––––––––

* [Better known under the name Shirley MacLaine.—Eds.]

cided not to produce the picture and by a letter dated April 4, 1966, it notified plaintiff of that decision and that it would not "comply with our obligations to you under" the written contract.

By the same letter and with the professed purpose "to avoid any damage to you," defendant instead offered to employ plaintiff as the leading actress in another film tentatively entitled "Big Country, Big Man" (hereinafter, "Big Country"). The compensation offered was identical, as were 31 of the 34 numbered provisions or articles of the original contract.[1] Unlike Bloomer Girl, however, which was to have been a musical production, Big Country was a dramatic western type movie. Bloomer Girl was to have been filmed in California; Big Country was to be produced in Australia. Also, certain terms in the proffered contract varied from those of the original.[2] Plaintiff was given one week within which to accept; she did not and the offer lapsed. Plaintiff then commenced this action seeking recovery of the agreed guaranteed compensation.

The complaint sets forth two causes of action. The first is for money due under the contract; the second, based upon the same allegations as the first, is for damages resulting from defendant's breach of contract. Defendant in its answer admits the existence and validity of the contract, that plaintiff complied with all the conditions, covenants, and promises and stood ready to complete the performance, and that defendant breached and "anticipatorily repudiated" the contract. It denies, however, that any money is due to plaintiff either under the contract or as a result of its breach, and pleads as an affirmative defense to both causes of action plaintiff's allegedly deliberate failure to mitigate damages, asserting that she unreasonably refused to accept its offer of the leading role in "Big Country."

---

[1] Among the identical provisions was the following found in the last paragraph of Article 2 of the original contract: "We [defendant] shall not be obligated to utilize your [plaintiff's] services in or in connection with the Photoplay hereunder, our sole obligation, subject to the terms and conditions of this Agreement, being to pay you the guaranteed compensation herein provided for."

[2] Article 29 of the original contract specified that plaintiff approved the director already chosen for "Bloomer Girl" and that in case he failed to act as director plaintiff was to have approval rights of any substitute director. Article 31 provided that plaintiff was to have the right of approval of the "Bloomer Girl" dance director, and Article 32 gave her the right of approval of the screenplay.

Defendant's letter of April 4 to plaintiff, which contained both defendant's notice of breach of the "Bloomer Girl" contract and offer of the lead in "Big Country," eliminated or impaired each of those rights. It read in part as follows: "The terms and conditions of our offer of employment are identical to those set forth in the 'Bloomer Girl' Agreement, Articles 1 through 34 and Exhibit A to the Agreement, except as follows:

"1. Article 31 of said Agreement will not be included in any contract of employment regarding 'Big Country, Big Man' as it is not a musical and it thus will not need a dance director.

"2. In the 'Bloomer Girl' Agreement, in Articles 29 and 32, you were given certain director and screenplay approvals and you had preapproved certain matters. Since there simply is insufficient time to negotiate with you regarding your choice of director and regarding the screenplay and since you already expressed an interest in performing the role in 'Big Country, Big Man,' we must exclude from our offer of employment in 'Big Country, Big Man' any approval rights as are contained in said Articles 29 and 32; however, we shall consult with you respecting the director to be selected to direct the Photoplay and will further consult with you with respect to the screenplay and any revisions or changes therein, provided, however, that if we fail to agree . . . the decision of . . . defendant with respect to the selection of a director and to revisions and changes in the said screenplay shall be binding upon the parties to said Agreement."

Plaintiff moved for [summary judgment], the motion was granted, and summary judgment for $750,000 plus interest was entered in plaintiff's favor. This appeal by defendant followed.

The familiar rules are that the matter to be determined by the trial court on a motion for summary judgment is whether facts have been presented which give rise to a triable factual issue. The court may not pass upon the issue itself. Summary judgment is proper only if the affidavits or declarations in support of the moving party would be sufficient to sustain a judgment in his favor and his opponent does not by affidavit show facts sufficient to present a triable issue of fact. The affidavits of the moving party are strictly construed and doubts as to the propriety of summary judgment should be resolved against granting the motion. Such summary procedure is drastic and should be used with caution so that it does not become a substitute for the open trial method of determining facts. . . .

The general rule is that the measure of recovery by a wrongfully discharged employee is the amount of salary agreed upon for the period of service, less the amount which the employer affirmatively proves the employee has earned or with reasonable effort might have earned from other employment. . . . However, before projected earnings from other employment opportunities not sought or accepted by the discharged employee can be applied in mitigation, the employer must show that the other employment was comparable, or substantially similar, to that of which the employee has been deprived; the employee's rejection of or failure to seek other available employment of a different or inferior kind may not be resorted to in order to mitigate damages. . . .

[D]efendant has raised no issue of *reasonableness of efforts* by plaintiff to obtain other employment; the sole issue is whether plaintiff's refusal of defendant's substitute offer of "Big Country" may be used in mitigation. Nor, if the "Big Country" offer was of employment different or inferior when compared with the original "Bloomer Girl" employment, is there an issue as to whether or not plaintiff acted reasonably in refusing the substitute offer. . . . [N]o case cited . . . holds or suggests that reasonableness is an element of a wrongfully discharged employee's option to reject, or fail to seek, different or inferior employment lest the possible earnings therefrom be charged against him in mitigation of damages.[3]

Applying the foregoing rules[,] . . . with all intendments in favor of the party opposing the summary judgment motion—here, defendant—it is clear that the trial court correctly ruled that plaintiff's failure to accept defendant's tendered substitute employment could not be applied in mitigation of damages because the offer of the "Big Country" lead was of employment both different and inferior, and that no factual dispute was presented on that issue. The mere circumstance that "Bloomer Girl" was to be a musical review calling upon plaintiff's talents as a dancer as well as an actress, and was to be produced in Los Angeles, whereas "Big Country" was a straight

---

[3] Instead, in each case the reasonableness referred to was that of the *efforts* of the employee to obtain other employment that was not different or inferior; his right to reject the latter was declared as an unqualified rule of law. Thus, Gonzales v. Internat. Assn. of Machinists, 213 Cal.App.2d 817, holds that the trial court correctly instructed the jury that plaintiff union member, a machinist, was required to make "such *efforts* as the average member of his union desiring employment would make at that particular time and place" (italics added); but, further, that the court *properly rejected* defendant's *offer of proof of the availability of other kinds of employment* at the same or higher pay than plaintiff usually received and all outside the jurisdiction of his union, as plaintiff could not be required to accept different employment or a nonunion job. . . .

dramatic role in a "Western Type" story taking place in an opal mine in Australia, demonstrates the difference in kind between the two employments; the female lead as a dramatic actress in a western style motion picture can by no stretch of imagination be considered the equivalent of or substantially similar to the lead in a song-and-dance production.

Additionally, the substitute "Big Country" offer proposed to eliminate or impair the director and screenplay approvals accorded to plaintiff under the original "Bloomer Girl" contract, and thus constituted an offer of inferior employment. No expertise or judicial notice is required in order to hold that [the] infringement of an employee's rights held under an original employment contract converts the available "other employment" relied upon by the employer to mitigate damages, into inferior employment which the employee need not seek or accept. (See Gonzales v. Internat. Assn. of Machinists, fn. 3, supra.) . . .

In view of the determination that defendant failed to present any facts showing the existence of a factual issue with respect to its sole defense—plaintiff's rejection of its substitute employment offer in mitigation of damages—we need not consider plaintiff's further contention that for various reasons, including the provisions of the original contract set forth in footnote 1, ante, plaintiff was excused from attempting to mitigate damages.

The judgment is affirmed.

SULLIVAN, ACTING C.J. (dissenting). The basic question [is] whether or not plaintiff acted reasonably in rejecting defendant's offer of alternate employment. The answer depends upon whether that offer (starring in "Big Country, Big Man") was an offer of work that was substantially similar to her former employment (starring in "Bloomer Girl") or of work that was of a different or inferior kind. . . . [T]his is a factual issue which the trial court should not have determined on a motion for summary judgment. . . .

The familiar rule requiring a plaintiff in a tort or contract action to mitigate damages embodies notions of fairness and socially responsible behavior which are fundamental to our jurisprudence. Most broadly stated, it precludes the recovery of damages which, through the exercise of due diligence, could have been avoided. Thus, in essence, it is a rule requiring reasonable conduct in commercial affairs. This general principle governs the obligations of an employee after his employer has wrongfully repudiated or terminated the employment contract. Rather than permitting the employee simply to remain idle during the balance of the contract period, the law requires him to make a reasonable effort to secure other employment.[1] He is not obliged, however, to seek or accept any and all types of work which may be available. Only work which is in the same field and which is the same quality need be accepted.

---

[1] The issue is generally discussed in terms of a duty on the part of the employee to minimize loss. The practice is long-established and there is little reason to change despite Judge Cardozo's observation of its subtle inaccuracy. "The servant is free to accept employment or reject it according to his uncensored pleasure. What is meant by the supposed duty is merely this, that if he unreasonably reject, he will not be heard to say that the loss of wages from then on shall be deemed the jural consequence of the earlier discharge. He has broken the chain of causation, and loss resulting to him thereafter is suffered through his own act." (McClelland v. Climax Hosiery Mills, 252 N.Y. 347, 169 N.E. 605 (1930), concurring opinion.)

SHIRLEY MacLAINE

Over the years the courts have employed various phrases to define the type of employment which the employee, upon his wrongful discharge, is under an obligation to accept. Thus in California alone it has been held that he must accept employment which is "substantially similar," . . . "comparable employment," . . . employment "in the same general line of the first employment," . . . "equivalent to his prior position," . . . "employment in a similar capacity," . . . employment which is "[not] of a different or inferior kind. . . ."

For reasons which are unexplained, the majority . . . select from among the various judicial formulations [one] particular phrase, "Not of a different or inferior kind," with which to analyze this case. I have discovered no historical or theoretical reason to adopt this phrase, which is simply a negative restatement of the affirmative standards set out in the [cases], as the exclusive standard. . . . However, the phrase is a serviceable one and my concern is not with its use as the standard but rather with what I consider its distortion.

The relevant language excuses acceptance only of employment which is of a *different kind*. . . . It has never been the law that the mere existence of *differences between two jobs in the same field* is sufficient, as a matter of law, to excuse an employee wrongfully discharged from one from accepting the other in order to mitigate damages. Such an approach would effectively eliminate any obligation of an employee to attempt to minimize damage arising from a wrongful discharge. The only alternative job offer an employee would be required to accept would be an offer of his former job by his former employer.

Although the majority appear to hold that there was a difference "in kind" between the employment offered plaintiff in "Bloomer Girl" and that offered in "Big Country," an examination of the opinion makes crystal clear that the majority merely point out differences between the two *films* (an obvious circumstance) and then apodictically assert that these constitute a difference in the *kind of employment.* The entire rationale of the majority boils down to this: that the *"mere circumstances"* that "Bloomer Girl" was to be a musical review while "Big Country" was a straight drama "demonstrates the difference in kind" since a female lead in a western is not "the equivalent of or substantially similar to" a lead in a musical. This is merely attempting to prove the proposition by repeating it. . . .

. . . The inquiry in cases such as this should not be whether differences between the two jobs exist (there will always be differences) but whether the differences which are present are substantial enough to constitute differences in the *kind* of employment or, alternatively, whether they render the substitute work employment of an *inferior kind.* . . .

It is not intuitively obvious, to me at least, that the leading female role in a dramatic motion picture is a radically different endeavor from the leading female role in a musical comedy film. Nor is it plain to me that the rather qualified rights of director and screenplay approval contained in the first contract are highly significant matters either in the entertainment industry in general or to this plaintiff in particular. . . . Nevertheless, the trial court granted the motion, declaring that these approval rights were "critical" and that their elimination altered "the essential nature of the employment." . . .

[T]he relevant question in such cases is whether or not a particular contract provision is so significant that its omission creates employment of an inferior kind. This question is, of course, intimately bound up in what I consider the ultimate issue: whether or not the employee acted reasonably. This will generally involve a factual inquiry to ascertain the importance of the particular contract term and a process of weighing the absence of that term against the countervailing advantages of the alternate employment. In the typical case, this will mean that summary judgment must be withheld. . . .

———

Billetter v. Posell

94 Cal.App.2d 858, 211 P.2d 621 (1949)

Defendants employed plaintiff to work in defendants' store from July 1, 1946, to June 30, 1947, as "floor lady and designer," at a salary of $75 a week plus a Christmas bonus of $500. This contract had been proposed by defendants to counter a similar offer made to plaintiff by another employer. During the Christmas holidays, defendants notified plaintiff that they had decided to employ another designer and to have plaintiff take the place of another floor lady at $55 a week, a sum they later offered to raise to $60 a week. Unwilling to accept these terms, plaintiff left defendants' employment on December 31, 1946. Plaintiff then sued for her salary of $75 a week from January 1 to June 30, 1947, and for $300 unpaid on the promised $500 Christmas bonus. Judgment for plaintiff for these amounts affirmed. (1) Defendants are not entitled to credit for the unemployment compensation that plaintiff received from the state unemployment compensation fund during the ensuing six months. "Such funds are not deductible as compensation received from other employment in mitigation of damages. Benefits of this character are intended to alleviate the distress of unemployment and not to diminish the amount which an employer must pay as damages for the wrongful discharge of an employee." (2) Nor are defendants entitled to credit for the $60 a week they offered to pay her for serving as floor lady. An employee is not required to perform the same work for less pay in mitigation of damages. Moreover, the offer of $60 was not qualified by any protective condition saving her rights to be paid $75 a week under the original contract, so that if she had accepted the offer she would have lost her right to a higher wage. "An employee, upon wrongful discharge [that prevents the employee from performing], should not be required to accept a new employment under circumstances which permit the claim that [she] consents to a modification of the original contract and an abandonment of her right of action under it."

QUESTIONS

(1) What if defendants on December 30 had offered plaintiff a position as sales clerk in the appliance department, at $75 a week?

(2) What if plaintiff on January 2 had been offered a position as waitress at the Star Restaurant, one block away, at $90 a week?

(3) What if plaintiff accepted the Star Restaurant position and held it until June 30?

(4) What if plaintiff on January 2 had learned that a store in a town 30 miles from her home was advertising a position of "floor lady and designer" at $75 a week?

(5) What if defendants on December 30 had offered plaintiff her old job on the exact same terms?

––––––––

Metoyer v. Auto Club Family Insurance Company

536 F. Supp. 2d 664 (E.D. La. 2008)

Metoyer sustained damage to his New Orleans home as a result of Hurricane Katrina and filed suit on March 1, 2007 to recover sums alleged due under his insurance contract with Auto Club. Additionally, he was awarded a $150,000 grant from the Louisiana Recovery Authority to rebuild his home and a $10,000 grant from the U.S. Small Business Association. Autocredit argued that it should be able to credit these recoveries against its obligation to pay damages. Metoyer argued that the grants were "collateral sources." In tort actions, courts have usually found that damages should not take into account recoveries from a "collateral source" such as an insurance policy. Courts, however, have only infrequently confronted the question whether such a "collateral source" rule applied in contracts cases, and they have not provided consistent answers. See John G. Fleming, The Collateral Source Rule and Contract Damages, 71 Cal. L. Rev. 56, 56 & n. 1 (1983); Richard C. Witzel, Jr., The Collateral Source Rule and State–Provided Special Education and Therapy, 75 Wash. U. L.Q. 697, 703 n.27 (1997). There is dictum in some cases to the effect that the collateral source rule does not apply in contract cases and that damages are therefore reduced by recoveries from third parties, but there are few holdings to that effect. See Joseph M. Perillo, The Collateral Source Rule in Contract Cases, 46 San Diego L. Rev. 705 (2009).

The most common reason put forward in tort cases for not taking the collateral source into account is that a defendant should not be allowed to profit from the outside benefits provided to the plaintiff. The classic formulation of the rule is that a tortfeasor's liability should be the same, regardless of whether the plaintiff had the foresight to buy insurance. But there is an element of punitive damages to a collateral source award and in general the law "prohibits punitive or exemplary damages in contract actions." In contract law there is a concern that allowing the nonbreaching party to recover from a collateral source and also collect damages is overcompensatory. The court in *Metoyer* concluded, however, "There cannot be a blanket prohibition of the application of the collateral source rule" in contract cases. First, even in contract cases, the innocent party with insurance should not have a lower recovery than one who did not. Allowing a party to recover damages as well as collect on the insurance policy recognizes that the insured party has paid insurance premiums. Moreover, in many cases, including the one before the court, "there is no danger of a double recovery or windfall." The Louisiana Recovery Authority required that, when it awards a grant, it will be subrogated to the rights of the homeowner with regard to insurance payments. The LRA will have the right to step into the shoes of any recipient and assert whatever rights it has. This "subrogation right negates the negative effects of the collateral source rule in a contract claim." Thus, "if the Defendant's position is adopted, it will amount to a windfall, not for plaintiffs, but for [the defendants]."

In re WorldCom, Inc.

United States Bankruptcy Court, Southern District of New York, 2007.
361 Bankr. 675.

GONZALEZ, BANKRUPTCY JUDGE. . . . On or about July 10, 1995, Jordan and the Debtors entered into an endorsement agreement (the "Agreement"). At that time, Jordan was considered to be one of the most popular athletes in the world. The Agreement granted MCI a ten-year license to use Jordan's name, likeness, "other attributes," and personal services to advertise and promote MCI's telecommunications products and services beginning in September 1995 and ending in August 2005. The Agreement did not prevent Jordan from endorsing most other products or services, although he could not endorse the same products or services that MCI produced. In addition to a $5 million signing bonus, the Agreement provided an annual base compensation of $2 million for Jordan. The Agreement provided that Jordan would be treated as an independent contractor and that MCI would not withhold any amount from Jordan's compensation for tax purposes. The Agreement provided that Jordan was to make himself available for four days, not to exceed four hours per day, during each contract year to produce television commercials and print advertising and for promotional appearances. The parties agreed that the advertising and promotional materials would be submitted to Jordan for his approval, which could not be unreasonably withheld, fourteen days prior to their release to the general public. From 1995 to 2000, Jordan appeared in several television commercials and a large number of print ads for MCI.

On July 1, 2002, MCI commenced a case under chapter 11 of title 11 of the United States Code (the "Bankruptcy Code") in the Bankruptcy Court for the Southern District of New York. [T]he Debtors rejected the Agreement . . . pursuant to § 365 of the Bankruptcy Code. Following that rejection of the Agreement, Jordan filed Claim No. 36077 (the "Claim") in the amount of $8 million . . . .

MCI argues that Jordan had an obligation to mitigate his damages and failed to do so. MCI argues that . . . the Claim should be reduced to $4 million. MCI argues that it is under no obligation to pay Jordan for contract years 2004 and 2005.

Jordan argues for summary judgment allowing the Claim in full and overruling and dismissing MCI's objections to the Claim. . . . Jordan argues that the objection should be overruled and dismissed for three independent reasons (1) Jordan was a "lost volume seller" and thus mitigation does not apply, (2) there is no evidence that Jordan could have entered into a "substantially similar" endorsement agreement, and (3) Jordan acted reasonably when he decided not to pursue other endorsements after MCI's rejection of the Agreement. . . .

The doctrine of avoidable consequences, which has also been referred to as the duty to mitigate damages, "bars recovery for losses suffered by a non-breaching party that could have been avoided by reasonable effort and without risk of substantial loss or injury." Edward M. Crough, Inc. v. Dep't of Gen. Servs., 572 A.2d 457, 466 (D.C. 1990). The burden of proving that the damages could have been avoided or mitigated rests with the party that committed the breach. The efforts to avoid or mitigate the damages do not have to be successful, as long as they are reasonable. . . .

Jordan argues that MCI's mitigation defense does not apply here because Jordan is akin to a "lost volume seller." Jordan points to testimony demonstrating that he could have entered into additional endorsement contracts even if MCI had not rejected the Agreement. Thus, he argues, any additional endorsement contracts would not have been substitutes for the Agreement and would not have mitigated the damages for which MCI is liable.

"A lost volume seller is one who has the capacity to perform the contract that was breached in addition to other potential contracts due to unlimited resources or production capacity." Precision Pine & Timber, Inc. v. United States, 72 Fed. Cl. 460, 490 (Fed. Cl. 2006). A lost volume seller does not minimize its damages by entering into another contract because it would have had the benefit of both contracts even if the first were not breached. The lost volume seller has two expectations, the profit from the breached contract and the profit from one or more other contracts that it could have performed at the same time as the breached contract. "The philosophical heart of the lost volume theory is that the seller would have generated a second sale irrespective of the buyer's breach" and that "[i]t follows that the lost volume seller cannot possibly mitigate damages." D. Matthews, Should the Doctrine of Lost Volume Seller Be Retained? A Response to Professor Breen, 51 U. Miami L. Rev. 1195, 1214 (July 1997).

The lost volume seller theory is recognized in the Restatement (2d) of Contracts, §§ 347, 350 (1981) (the "Restatement (2d)"). The lost volume seller theory applies to contracts for services as well as goods. See Restatement (2d), § 347, ill. 16.

This case offers a twist on the typical lost volume seller situation. In what the Court regards as the typical situation, the non-breaching seller has a near-inexhaustible supply of inventory. In the typical situation, when a buyer breaches an agreement to buy a good or service from the seller, the item is returned to inventory and the lost volume seller continues in its efforts to sell its goods or services. However, the transactions that occur following the breach are not necessarily the result of the breach but fundamentally the result of the seller continuing efforts to market its goods and services. It is this continuous effort coupled with a virtually limitless supply that warrants the lost volume exception to mitigation. As stated above, the transactions that may occur after the breach would in the context of the lost volume seller have occurred independent of the breach. Here, Jordan lacked a nearly limitless supply and had no intention of continuing to market his services as a product endorser . . . .

In his arguments, Jordan focuses primarily on his *capacity* to enter subsequent agreements, arguing that the loss of MCI's sixteen-hour annual time commitment hardly affected his ability to perform additional endorsement services. On this prong alone, Jordan likely would be considered a lost volume seller of endorsement services because he had sufficient time to do multiple endorsements. Although he does not have the "infinite capacity" that some cases discuss, a services provider does not need unlimited capacity but must have the requisite capacity and intent to perform under multiple contracts at the same time.

Contrary to Jordan's analysis, courts do not focus solely on the seller's capacity. The seller claiming lost volume status must also demonstrate that it *would* have entered into subsequent transactions. Jordan has not shown he could and *would have* entered into a subsequent agreement. Rather, the evidence shows that Jordan did not have the "subjective intent" to take on additional endorsements. The testimony from Jordan's representatives establishes that although Jordan's popularity enabled him to obtain additional product endorsements in 2003, Jordan desired to scale back his level of endorsements. Jordan's financial and business advisor, Curtis Polk ("Polk"), testified that at the time the Agreement was rejected, Jordan's desire was "not to expand his spokesperson or pitchman efforts with new relationships." Polk testified that had Jordan wanted to do additional endorsements after the 2003 rejection, he could have obtained additional deals. Jordan's agent, David Falk ("Falk"), testified that "there might have been twenty more companies that in theory might have wanted to sign him" but that Jordan and his representatives wanted to avoid diluting his image. Jordan's Memorandum for Summary Judgment stated that at the time the Agreement was rejected, Jordan had implemented a strategy of not accepting new endorsements because of a belief that new deals would jeopardize his ability to achieve his primary goal of National Basketball Association ("NBA") franchise ownership. . . .

Because the evidence establishes, among other things, that Jordan would not have entered into subsequent agreements, Jordan has not established that he is a lost volume seller. This theory thus does not relieve Jordan from the duty to mitigate damages. . . .

Jordan argues at length that MCI must show that Jordan could have entered a "substantially similar" endorsement contract in order to mitigate damages. However, this is not the law of the mitigation of damages or the avoidable consequences theory. This language stems from federal employment cases concerning back pay and mitigation, which this case, while similar in many respects, is not. . . .

Several of the justifications for the "substantially similar or equivalent" standard of employment law, aside from the general remedial policy of making the non-breaching party whole for losses caused by the breaching party, show why there is less concern here regarding a "substantially equivalent" opportunity as Jordan was not an employee of MCI. For one, the standard exists in part to ensure the employee's future advancement by mandating that the employee's promotional opportunities and status should be virtually identical to the prior position. Since Jordan was never an employee of MCI, this is not relevant. Second, to require acceptance of inferior employment can mean "that one who has been discriminated against would be obliged, in order to mitigate damages, to submit to the very discrimination of which he complains." This, obviously, has no application here. Finally, the employee's duty to make reasonable efforts in finding substantially equivalent employment is "based both on the doctrine of mitigation of damages and on the policy of promoting production and employment." See N.L.R.B. v. Miami Coca–Cola Bottling Co., 360 F.2d 569, 575 (5th Cir.1966).

The main case relied on by Jordan for this argument regarding a "substantially similar" opportunity is a case analyzed under employment law and one that presented a completely different factual and procedural background. See Parker v. Twentieth Century–Fox Film Corp., 3 Cal. 3d 176, 89 Cal.Rptr. 737, 474 P.2d 689 (1970). In *Parker*, the plaintiff, a leading movie actress, agreed to perform in a musical-type film in California. The employer studio later decided not to make the movie and offered to the plaintiff as a substitute the leading role in a dramatic "western type" movie set in an opal mine and to be filmed in Australia. The plaintiff turned down that offer, sued for damages on the original agreement, and the trial court ruled on a summary judgment motion that the earnings from this substitute employment that the plaintiff refused could not be applied in mitigation because the second offer was "different" and "inferior." The California Supreme Court affirmed.

More accurately, MCI must show the absence of reasonable efforts by Jordan to avoid consequences or minimize his damages. . . .

Since "reasonable efforts in the form of *affirmative steps* are required to mitigate damages," see Robinson v. United States, 305 F.3d 1330, 1334 (Fed. Cir. 2002) (emphasis added) (citing Restatement (2d) § 350), MCI carries its burden by showing that Jordan has not taken affirmative steps to mitigate damages. Jordan admits in his brief that at the time of the rejection of the Agreement, "Jordan had already implemented a business strategy of not accepting new endorsements." Falk testified that a replacement telecommunications company was not approached. Polk testified that Jordan did not return to the endorsement marketplace to try and replace the revenue he was to be paid under the Agreement. Polk explained that Jordan did not wish to expand his "pitchman efforts with new relationships" because of his primary goal of becoming the owner of an NBA team. Although Jordan points to his discussions with another company, Nextel, as showing that he was willing to listen to endorsement agreements after MCI's bankruptcy, MCI effectively responds that responding to an inquiry by giving them contact information and indicating a willingness to respond to another call "is not trying to find an alternative" agreement—it is, in effect, "doing nothing." Based on the foregoing, and drawing all permissible factual inferences in favor of Jordan, the Court determines that MCI has established that Jordan did not take affirmative steps to mitigate damages. . . .

Jordan cites the risk that entering another endorsement contract could dilute his impact as an endorser or damage his reputation or business interests. . . .

Jordan's dilution argument is not convincing. Jordan's agent Falk testified that although there were no "fixed numbers" for the amount of endorsements, Jordan and his representatives were wary about dilution and sensitive about "protecting the brand" of Jordan. Jordan does not set forth any facts showing that Jordan's image was at risk of dilution. MCI convincingly responds that adding an agreement to replace a lost one is merely maintaining the status quo, not a dilution of Jordan's impact by addition. MCI's expert stated that Jordan had previously had sixteen endorsement agreements in place, which further weakens Jordan's dilution argument and casts doubt on Falk's statement that Jordan and his advisors "always felt that less is more" in terms of endorsements. While the Court recognizes that Jordan's image is the true commodity here and its market value could be diluted from overexposure, MCI has shown that Jordan's image was not at risk of dilution by replacing the MCI endorsement agreement with another one. The only statements Jordan offers to support his argument that he behaved reasonably by not seeking another endorsement in 2003 because of a concern with diluting his image are conclusory in nature and contradicted by the available evidence. The contention that pursuing an endorsement opportunity would dilute the image Jordan wished to cultivate as one befitting an NBA team owner . . . may well raise factual issues regarding the impact an endorsement may have on a team owner's image but that impact is irrelevant to Jordan's duty to mitigate damages for his "rejected" endorsement contract. There is no genuine issue of material fact that dilution did not excuse Jordan's duty to mitigate damages. . . .

Under the risk to reputation theory Jordan cites, an injured party is not allowed to recover from a wrongdoer those damages that the injured party "could have avoided without undue risk, burden or humiliation." *See* Restatement (2d), § 350(1). Jordan's "harm to reputation" argument is flawed because the envisioned harm to Jordan's reputation does not rise to the level of harm found in the cited case law.

The cases cited by Jordan illustrate the harm to reputation that will excuse a party's duty to mitigate. In Eastman Kodak Co. v. Westway Motor Freight, Inc., 949 F.2d 317 (10th Cir. 1991), Kodak shipped a load of sensitized photographic material on a truck operated by the defendant. Most of the material was destroyed in transit because of the defendant's mishandling. The Tenth Circuit held that Kodak was not required to sell the damaged merchandise to mitigate damages, stating that the record revealed that Kodak's reputation, which it spent considerable resources in developing, "could be harmed if it was required to sell damaged merchandise in order to mitigate damages." *Id.* at 320.

Another case cited by Jordan is similar to *Eastman Kodak*. In Sony Magnetic Products, Inc. of America v. Merivienti O/Y, 668 F. Supp. 1505 (S.D. Ala. 1987), the plaintiff's merchandise, cassette tapes, had been damaged while it was being loaded onto a ship. The plaintiff refused to allow the cassettes to be marketed as "seconds" with only a non-warranty sticker on them and without removal of the marks identifying the cassettes as plaintiff's products. The court stated it was "convinced that as a matter of public policy a manufacturer which has spent years and millions of dollars developing a reputation in the marketplace should not be required to jeopardize that reputation under [those] circumstances." *Id.* at 1515.

Those cases show the uncontroversial maxim that a plaintiff faced with the choice of (1) selling a sub-standard product to the public to mitigate damages caused by the breach of another and (2) doing nothing—can choose to do nothing, but Jordan was not confronted with those circumstances. While Jordan's reputation is considerable and obviously the result of careful development, there are no factual assertions that support the proposition that Jordan's choosing another endorsement opportunity is akin to being forced to sell damaged goods, as was the case in *Eastman Kodak* and *Sony Magnetic Products*.

Jordan also cites District Concrete Co. v. Bernstein Concrete Corp., 418 A.2d 1030, 1037 (D.C. 1980), for the proposition that it is not unreasonable for a plaintiff "to take into consideration . . . consequences such as injury to reputation" as a factor in post-breach decisions. Bernstein had sued its concrete supplier, District Concrete, for breach of a requirements contract. Bernstein was the sub-contractor for a construction project building an apartment complex. After the complex's roof was poured with concrete, defects in the concrete were found. Bernstein considered two approaches to cure the problem (1) tearing out the slab and replacing it, or (2) building a "composite slab" over the defective area. Bernstein estimated the cost of each approach to be about $100,000 but considered that the highly visible "tear-out method" could damage Bernstein's and the general contractor's reputations. Although the chosen "composite slab" approach ended up costing more than anticipated, the court held that the choice of this method was reasonable when made, given that the "costs and time involved" for each were comparable *and also* considering the consequences of possible reputation damage.

That case is of little help to Jordan. For one, any harm to Jordan's reputation arising from MCI's bankruptcy is not comparable to the reputation damage a construction contractor faces from building a defective roof. As MCI's expert testified, consumers do not believe that celebrity endorsers are experts in the products they endorse, while a consumer would expect a builder to build a defective-free roof. If the roof fails, consumers would blame the builder. If a company fails, consumers do not blame the company's celebrity endorsers. Also, Jordan has not shown that he faced two reasonable approaches to mitigate his damages, with one of those approaches carrying a risk to his reputation. Jordan has stated that he was faced with two choices (1) mitigate damages, which he alleges could harm his reputation, or (2) concentrate on a venture that has no connection to the mitigation of damages. This situation is thus not comparable to *District Concrete*.

The above analysis also applies to Jordan's cited case of Citizens Fed. Bank v. United States, 66 Fed. Cl. 179 (Fed. Cl. 2005). There, the court held that the breaching party cannot engage in "Monday-morning quarterbacking" to criticize the wronged party's choice of mitigation. *Id.* at 185. "Where a choice has been required between two reasonable courses, the person whose wrong forced the choice can not complain that one rather than the other was chosen." *Id.* Here, MCI is not complaining about the choice between "two reasonable courses" of mitigation. MCI is arguing that choosing to take no steps to mitigate is not a reasonable course.

In arguing that Jordan acted reasonably by avoiding further endorsements based on a belief that those efforts would harm his business interests or reputation, Jordan argues essentially that he would be harmed by doing precisely what he originally contracted to do under the Agreement and what he has been doing for other clients for a number of years— endorsing products and services. The Court recognizes the possibility of Jordan's market saturation being a valid concern but Jordan's argument that he wanted to get out of endorsements to pursue other ventures does not relieve the duty to mitigate. Furthermore, MCI's expert stated that an additional endorsement agreement would not have harmed Jordan's reputation by either diminishing Jordan's image in the endorsement marketplace or harming Jordan's goal of becoming an NBA team owner. Jordan has not asserted any facts to refute those assertions nor did he undermine the credibility of the expert making such assertions. Based on the foregoing, there is a no genuine issue of material fact as to whether reasonable endorsement efforts done to mitigate damages would have harmed Jordan's reputation. The Court notes that even if there were a genuine issue of material fact as to whether another endorsement would negatively impact his becoming an NBA team owner, for the reasons set forth below, such would be irrelevant to the issue of mitigation regarding his endorsement contract. . . .

In this case, there has been no determination and no evidence presented of what Jordan could have reasonably earned had he fulfilled his obligation to mitigate damages by entering the endorsement marketplace following MCI's rejection of the Agreement. It is not clear that Jordan could have found an endorsement agreement in 2003 that paid him $2 million a year for the contract years 2004 and 2005. It is also unlikely that Jordan would have been obligated to accept a large number of endorsements of smaller value to make up the $2 million, due to the dilution effect such a number would have, because such efforts would likely be unreasonable. However, the facts may reveal that one or more endorsements could have been found without "diluting" his image and partially or completely mitigating the damages. Although MCI's expert stated that he believed that Jordan could have easily earned $2 million from an additional endorsement in 2003, that opinion was not presented with any objective evidence of the marketplace, such as what other celebrity endorsers of Jordan's stature earned that year and which companies were in the market for an endorser of Jordan's stature. Although the Court finds that as a matter of law Jordan has not mitigated damages, there must be an evidentiary hearing on how much his claim should be reduced to reflect what portion would have been mitigated had he used reasonable efforts to do so. . . .

Warner Brothers/Getty Images

Michael Jordan in *Space Jam*

NOTE

The advertising campaign at issue in *WorldCom* focused on MCI's consumer telephone services. The ads featured Michael Jordan and co-stars from the movie *Space Jam*. These advertisements can still be found on-line. See, e.g., http://www.youtube.com/watch?v=BV0yQcOXc_Y. By the time that its parent company found itself in bankruptcy, MCI had discontinued its consumer phone business. It had no further need for Jordan's services. It therefore wanted to terminate its contract with him. The breach in bankruptcy, as outside, gives the nonbreaching party a claim for damages. The bankruptcy lawyer must apply the common law of contract damages in the same fashion as every other lawyer. Because of the bankruptcy, Jordan might not be able to collect in full, but this is no different from having a claim against someone outside of bankruptcy who lacks the assets to satisfy a judgment.

In considering how these damages might be calculated, consider how Jordan's work with MCI had foreclosed and limited his other opportunities. While Jordan might have the ability to endorse many products, his work for MCI may have made him less attractive to other telecommunications companies. Similarly, his ability to run ads with his *Space Jam* co-stars might be compromised as well. The novelty of seeing him with Daffy Duck might wear thin.

––––––––––

Hadley v. Baxendale

Court of Exchequer, 1854.
9 Exch. 341.

At the trial before Crompton, J., at the last Gloucester Assizes, it appeared that the plaintiffs carried on an extensive business as millers at Gloucester; and that, on the 11th of May, their mill was stopped by a breakage of the crank shaft by which the mill was worked. The steam-engine was manufactured by Messrs. Joyce & Co., the engineers, at Greenwich, and it became necessary to send the shaft as a pattern for a new one to Greenwich. The fracture was discovered on the 12th, and on the 13th, the plaintiffs sent one of their servants to the office of the defendants, who are the well known carriers trading under the name of Pickford & Co., for the purpose of having the shaft carried to Greenwich. The plaintiffs' servant told the clerk that the mill was stopped, and that the shaft must be sent immediately; and in answer to the inquiry when the shaft would be taken, the answer was, that if it was sent up by twelve o'clock any day, it would be delivered at Greenwich on the following day. On the following day the shaft was taken by the defendants, before noon, for the purpose of being conveyed to Greenwich, and the sum of £2. 4s. was paid for its carriage for the whole distance; at the same time the defendants' clerk was told that a special entry, if required, should be made to hasten its delivery. The delivery of the shaft at Greenwich was delayed by some neglect; and the consequence was, that the plaintiffs did not receive the new shaft for several days after they would otherwise have done, and the working of their mill was thereby delayed and they thereby lost the profits they would otherwise have received.

[The defendants] objected that these damages were too remote, and that the defendants were not liable with respect to them. The learned Judge left the case generally to the jury, who found a verdict with £25 damages beyond the amount paid into Court.

Whateley, in last Michaelmas Term, obtained a rule nisi for a new trial, on the ground of misdirection.

Keating and Dowdeswell (Feb. 1) showed cause.—The plaintiffs are entitled to the amount awarded by the jury as damages. These damages are not too remote, for they are not only the natural and necessary consequence of the defendants' default, but they are the only loss which the plaintiffs have actually sustained. The principle upon which damages are assessed is founded upon that of rendering compensation to the injured party.... [PARKE, B.—The sensible rule appears to be that which has been laid down in France, and which is declared in their code [and] translated in Sedgwick: "The damages due to the creditor consist in general of the loss that he has sustained, and the profit which he has been prevented from acquiring.... The debtor is only liable for the damages foreseen, or which might have been foreseen, at the time of the execution of the contract, when it is not owing to his fraud that the agreement has been violated. Even in the case of non-performance of the contract, resulting from the fraud of the debtor, the damages only comprise so much of the loss sustained by the creditor, and so much of the profit which he has been prevented from acquiring, as directly and immediately results from the non-performance of the contract."] If that rule is to be adopted, there was ample evidence in the present case of the defendants' knowledge of such a state of things as would necessarily result in the damage the plaintiffs suffered through the defendants' default....

ALDERSON, B. We think that there ought to be a new trial in this case; but, in so doing, we deem it to be expedient and necessary to state explicitly the rule which the Judge, at the next trial, ought, in our opinion, to direct the jury to be governed by when they estimate the damages. It is, indeed, of the last importance that we should do this; for if the jury are left without any definite rule to guide them, it will, in such cases as these, manifestly lead to the greatest injustice. . . .

Now we think the proper rule in such a case as the present is this:— Where two parties have made a contract which one of them has broken, the damages which the other party ought to receive in respect of such breach of contract should be such as may fairly and reasonably be considered either arising naturally, i.e., according to the usual course of things, from such breach of contract itself, or such as may reasonably be supposed to have been in the contemplation of both parties, at the time they made the contract, as the probable result of the breach of it. Now, if the special circumstances under which the contract was actually made were communicated by the plaintiffs to the defendants, and thus known to both parties, the damages resulting from the breach of such a contract, which they would reasonably contemplate, would be the amount of injury which would ordinarily follow from a breach of contract under these special circumstances so known and communicated. But, on the other hand, if these special circumstances were wholly unknown to the party breaking the contract, he, at the most, could only be supposed to have had in his contemplation the amount of injury which would arise generally, and in the great multitude of cases not affected by any special circumstances, from such a breach of contract. For, had the special circumstances been known, the parties might have specially provided for the breach of contract by special terms as to the damages in that case; and of this advantage it would be very unjust to deprive them. Now the above principles are those by which we think the jury ought to be guided in estimating the damages arising out of any breach of contract. It is said, that other cases such as breaches of contract in the nonpayment of money, or in the not making a good title to land,* are to be treated as exceptions from this, and as governed by a conventional rule. But as, in such cases, both parties must be supposed to be cognisant of that well-known rule, these cases may, we think be more properly classed under the rule above enunciated as to cases under known special circumstances, because there both parties may reasonably be presumed to contemplate the estimation of the amount of damages according to the conventional rule.

Now, in the present case, if we are to apply the principles above laid down, we find that the only circumstances here communicated by the plaintiffs to the defendants at the time the contract was made, were, that the article to be carried was the broken shaft of a mill, and that the plaintiffs were the millers of that mill. But how do these circumstances show reasonably that the profits of the mill must be stopped by an unreasonable delay in the delivery of the broken shaft by the carrier to the third person? Suppose the plaintiffs had another shaft in their possession put up or putting up at the time, and that they only wished to send back the broken shaft to the engineer who made it; it is clear that this would be quite consistent with the above circumstances, and yet the unreasonable delay in the delivery would have no effect upon the intermediate profits of the mill. Or, again, suppose, that, at the time of the delivery to the carrier, the machinery of the mill had been in other respects defective, then, also, the same results would follow. Here it is true that the shaft was actually sent back to serve as a model for a new one, and that the want of a new one was the only cause of the stoppage of the mill, and that the loss of profits really arose from not sending down the new shaft in proper time, and that this arose from the delay in delivering the broken one to serve as a model. But it is

---

* [The court is referring to the doctrine of Flureau v. Thornhill, noted supra p. 38—Eds.]

obvious that, in the great multitude of cases of millers sending off broken shafts to third persons by a carrier under ordinary circumstances, such consequences would not, in all probability, have occurred; and these special circumstances were here never communicated by the plaintiffs to the defendants. It follows, therefore, that the loss of profits here cannot reasonably be considered such a consequence of the breach of contract as could have been fairly and reasonably contemplated by both the parties when they made this contract. For such loss would neither have flowed naturally from the breach of this contract in the great multitude of such cases occurring under ordinary circumstances, nor were the special circumstances, which, perhaps, would have made it a reasonable and natural consequence of such breach of contract, communicated to or known by the defendants. The Judge ought, therefore, to have told the jury that, upon the facts then before them, they ought not to take the loss of profits into consideration at all in estimating the damages. There must therefore be a new trial in this case.

Rule absolute.

NOTE

In Black v. Baxendale, 1 Exch. 410 (1847), an action brought seven years earlier against the same carrier, it appeared that defendant had undertaken to transport haycloths from London to Bedford and that through delay in shipment plaintiff had been unable to sell the cloths in Bedford and had had to reship them to another town for sale. In an action for the expense of reshipment and for the personal expenses of plaintiff's employee who had been sent to Bedford to receive and sell the cloths, all the judges agreed that whether these expenses were "reasonable" was entirely for the jury. One of the judges was Baron Alderson, who wrote the opinion in Hadley v. Baxendale; another *Hadley* judge, Baron Parke, was also on the panel. Chief Baron Pollock added that notice to defendant that delivery was required at a particular time might perhaps increase defendant's liability for expenses incurred by plaintiff, "but whether any particular class of expense is reasonable or not depends upon the usage of trade, and other circumstances. It is not a question for the Judge, but for the jury, to decide what are reasonable expenses."

Globe Refining Co. v. Landa Cotton Oil Co.

Supreme Court of the United States, 1903.
190 U.S. 540, 23 S.Ct. 754.

HOLMES, J. This is an action of contract brought by the plaintiff in error, a Kentucky corporation, against the defendant in error, a Texas corporation, for breach of a contract to sell and deliver crude oil. The defendant excepted to certain allegations of damage, and pleaded that the damages had been claimed and magnified fraudulently for the purpose of giving the United States circuit court jurisdiction, when in truth they were less than $2,000. The judge sustained the exceptions. He also tried the question of jurisdiction before hearing the merits, refused the plaintiff a jury, found that the plea was sustained, and dismissed the cause. The plaintiff excepted to all the rulings. . . . If the rulings and findings were right, there is no question that the judge was right in dismissing the suit but the grounds upon which he went are re-examinable here.

The contract was made through a broker . . . in the following letter:

Dallas, Texas, 7/30/97.

Landa Oil Company, New Braunfels, Texas.

Gentlemen: Referring to the exchange of our telegrams to-day, we have sold for your account to the Globe Refining Co., Louisville Kentucky, ten (10) tanks prime crude C/S oil at the price of 15¾ cents per gallon of 7½ pounds, f.o.b. buyers' tank at your mill. Weights and quality guaranteed.

Terms: Sight draft without exchange b/ldg. attached. Sellers paying commission.

Shipment: Part last half August and balance first half September. Shipping instructions to be furnished by the Globe Refining Co.

Yours truly,
Thomas & Green, as *Broker.*

Having this contract before us, we proceed to consider the allegations of special damage over and above the difference between the contract price of the oil and the price at the time of the breach, which was the measure adopted by the judge. These allegations must be read with care, for it is obvious that the pleader has gone as far as he dared to go, and to the verge of anything that could be justified under the contract, if not beyond.

It is alleged that it was agreed and understood that the plaintiff would send its tank cars to the defendant's mills, and that the defendant promptly would fill them with oil (so far, simply following the contract), and that the plaintiff sent tanks. "In order to do this, the plaintiff was under the necessity of obligating itself unconditionally to the railroad company (and of which the defendant had notice) to pay to it for the transportation of the cars from said Louisville to said New Braunfels in the sum of $900," which sum plaintiff had to pay, "and was incurred as an advancement on said oil contract." This is the first item. The last words quoted mean only that the sum paid would have been allowed by the railroad as part payment of the return charges had the tanks been filled and sent back over the same road.

Next it is alleged that the defendant, contemplating a breach of the contract, caused the plaintiff to send its cars a thousand miles, at a cost of $1,000; that defendant canceled its contract on the 2d of September, but did not notify the plaintiff until the 14th, when, if the plaintiff had known of the cancelation, it would have been supplying itself from other sources; that [defendant] did so wilfully and maliciously, causing an unnecessary loss of $2,000.

Next it is alleged that, by reason of the breach of contract and want of notice, plaintiff lost the use of its tanks for thirty days—a loss estimated at $700 more. Next it is alleged that the plaintiff had arranged with its own customers to furnish the oil in question within a certain time, which contemplated sharp compliance with the contract by the defendant; "all of which facts, as above stated, were well known to the defendant, and defendant had contracted to that end with the plaintiff." This item is put at $740, with $1,000 more for loss of customers, credit, and reputation. Finally, at the end of the petition, it is alleged generally that it was known to defendant, and in contemplation of the contract, that plaintiff would have to send tanks at great expense from distant points, and that plaintiff "was required to pay additional freight in order to rearrange the destination of the various tanks and other points." Then it is alleged that by reason of the defendant's breach, the plaintiff had to pay $350 additional freight.

Whatever may be the scope of the allegations which we have quoted, it will be seen that none of the items was contemplated expressly by the words of the bargain. Those words . . . go no further than to contemplate that when the deliveries were to take place the buyer's tanks should be at the defendant's mill. Under such circumstances the question is suggested how far the express terms of a writing, admitted to be complete, can be enlarged by averment and oral evidence; and, if they can be enlarged in that way, what averments are sufficient. When a man commits a tort, he incurs, by force of the law, a liability to damages, measured by certain rules. When a man makes a contract, he incurs, by force of the law, a liability to damages, unless a certain promised event comes to pass. But, unlike the case of torts, as the contract is by mutual consent, the parties themselves, expressly or by implication, fix the rule by which the damages are to be measured. The old law seems to have regarded it as technically in the election of the promisor to perform or to pay damages. It is true that, as people when contracting contemplate performance, not breach, they commonly say little or nothing as to what shall happen in the latter event, and the common rules have been worked out by common sense, which has established what the parties probably would have said if they had spoken about the matter. But a man never can be absolutely certain of performing any contract when the time of performance arrives, and, in many cases, he obviously is taking the risk of an event which is wholly, or to an appreciable extent, beyond his control. The extent of liability in such cases is likely to be within his contemplation, and, whether it is or not, should be worked out on terms which it fairly may be presumed he would have assented to if they had been presented to his mind. For instance, in the present case, the defendant's mill and all its oil might have been burned before the time came for delivery. Such a misfortune would not have been an excuse, although probably it would have prevented performance of the contract. If a contract is broken, the measure of damages generally is the same, whatever the cause of the breach. We have to consider, therefore, what the plaintiff would have been entitled to recover in that case, and that depends on what liability the defendant fairly may be supposed to have assumed consciously, or to have warranted the plaintiff reasonably to suppose that it assumed, when the contract was made.

This point of view is taken by implication in the rule that "a person can only be held to be responsible for such consequences as may be reasonably supposed to be in the contemplation of the parties at the time of making the contract." [Hadley v. Baxendale, 9 Exch. 341, 354.] The suggestion thrown out . . . in Gee v. Lancashire & Y. R. Co. 6 Hurlst. & N. 211, 218, that perhaps notice after the contract was made and before breach would be enough, is not accepted by the later decisions. The consequences must be contemplated at the time of the making of the contract.

The question arises, then, What is sufficient to show that the consequences were in contemplation of the parties, in the sense of the vendor taking the risk? It has been held that it may be proved by oral evidence when the contract is in writing. But, in the language quoted, with seeming approbation, by Blackburn, J., from Mayne on Damages, 2d ed. 10, in Elbinger Actien–Gesellschafft v. Armstrong, L. R. 9 Q. B. 473, 478, "it may be asked, with great deference, whether the mere fact of such consequences being communicated to the other party will be sufficient, without going on to show that he was told that he would be answerable for them, and consented to undertake such a liability." Mr. Justice Willes answered this question . . . in British Columbia & V. I. Spar, Lumber, & Saw–Mill Co. v. Nettleship, L. R. 3 C. P. 499, 500: "I am disposed to take the narrow view that one of two contracting parties ought not to be allowed to obtain an advantage which he has not paid for. . . . If that [a liability for the full profits that might be made by machinery which the defendant was transporting, if the plaintiff's trade should prove successful and without a rival] had been presented to the mind of the ship owner at the time of making the contract, as the basis upon which he was contracting, he would at once have rejected it. And though he knew, from the shippers, the use they intended to make of the articles, it could not be contended that the mere fact of knowledge, without more, would be a reason for imposing upon him a greater degree of liability than would otherwise have been cast upon him. To my mind, that leads to the inevitable conclusion that the mere fact of knowledge cannot increase the liability. The knowledge must be brought home to the party sought to be charged, under such circumstances that he must know that the person he contracts with reasonably believes that he accepts the contract with the special condition attached to it." . . . See also Benjamin, Sales, 6th Am. ed. § 872.

It may be said with safety that mere notice to a seller of some interest or probable action of the buyer is not enough necessarily and as matter of law to charge the seller with special damage on that account if he fails to deliver the goods. With that established, we recur to the allegations. With regard to the first, it is obvious that the plaintiff was free to bring its tanks from where it liked,—a thousand miles away or an adjoining yard,—so far as the contract was concerned. The allegation hardly amounts to saying that the defendant had notice that the plaintiff was likely to send its cars from a distance. It is not alleged that the defendant had notice that the plaintiff had to bind itself to pay $900, at the time when the contract was made, and it nowhere is alleged that the defendant assumed any liability in respect of this uncertain element of charge. The same observations may be made with regard to the claim for loss of use of the tanks and to the final allegations as to sending the tanks from distant points. It is true that this last was alleged to have been in contemplation of the contract, if we give the plaintiff the benefit of the doubt in construing a somewhat confused sentence. But, having the contract before us, we can see that this ambiguous expression cannot be taken to mean more than notice, and notice of a fact which would depend upon the accidents of the future.

It is to be said further, with regard to the foregoing items, that they were the expenses which the plaintiff was willing to incur for performance. If it had received the oil, these were deductions from any profit which the plaintiff would have made. But, if it gets the difference between the contract price and the market price, it gets what represents the value of the oil in its hands, and to allow these items in addition would be making the defendant pay twice for the same thing.

It must not be forgotten that we are dealing with pleadings, not evidence, and with pleadings which, as we have said, evidently put the plaintiff's case as high as it possibly can be put. There are no inferences to be drawn. . . . It is a simple question of allegations which, by declining to amend, the plaintiff has admitted that it cannot reinforce. This consideration applies with special force to the attempt to hold the defendant liable for the breach of the plaintiff's contract with third persons. The allegation is that the fact that the plaintiff had contracts over was well known to the defendant, and that "defendant had contracted to that end with the plaintiff." Whether, if we were sitting as a jury, this would warrant an inference that the defendant assumed an additional liability, we need not consider. It is enough to say that it does not allege the conclusion of fact so definitely that it must be assumed to be true. With the contract before us it is in a high degree improbable that any such conclusion could have been made good.

The only other allegation needing to be dealt with is that the defendant maliciously caused the plaintiff to send the tanks a thousand miles, contemplating a breach of its contract. So far as this item has not been answered by what has been said, it is necessary only to add a few words. The fact alleged has no relation to the time of the contract. Therefore it cannot affect the damages, the measure of which was fixed at that time. The motive for the breach commonly is immaterial in an action on the contract. It is in this case. Whether, under any circumstances, it might give rise to an action of tort, is not material here. . . .

Judgment affirmed.

————

Lamkins v. International Harvester Co.

207 Ark. 637, 182 S.W.2d 203 (1944)

The dispute grew out of a sale of a farm tractor. The buyer had told the seller at the time of the contract that he wanted lighting equipment so that he could use the tractor at night. The tractor was delivered on May 1, 1942, without lighting equipment, and the seller's agent promised that lighting equipment would be supplied within three weeks; it was not supplied until nearly a year later. The buyer alleged that without lights he could not work the tractor at night and therefore was unable to plant and harvest a 25–acre tract on his farm, on which he would have grown soy beans if the tractor had had lights. The court quoted from an earlier Arkansas case: "Where the damages arise from special circumstances, and are so large as to be out of proportion to the consideration agreed to be paid for the services to be rendered under the contract, it raises a doubt at once as to whether the party would have assented to such liability had it been called to his attention at the making of the contract unless the consideration to be paid was also raised so as to correspond in some respect to the liability assumed." In the present case, even if the buyer's testimony were believed, "there is nothing in the testimony showing circumstances surrounding and connected with the transaction which were calculated to bring home to the dealer knowledge that appellant expected him to assume liability for a crop loss which might amount to several hundreds of dollars, if he should fail to deliver a $20 lighting accessory. There was, of course, no such express contract on the dealer's part, and the facts and circumstances are not such as to make it reasonable for the trier of facts to believe that the dealer at the time tacitly consented to be bound for more than ordinary damages in case of default on his part." [The "tacit agreement" test embraced by the *Lamkins* court is usually attributed to Justice Holmes' rationalization of *Hadley* in *Globe Refining*.]

————

Victoria Laundry (Windsor) Ltd. v. Newman Indus., Ltd.

[1949] 2 K.B. 528

Plaintiffs carried on a business as launderers and dyers. In April 1946, they contracted with defendant, an engineering company, to purchase a large boiler, 19 feet high and capable of 8,000 pounds per hour of "heavy steaming." During negotiations plaintiffs had expressed their intention to put the boiler into use "in the shortest possible space of time." The parties arranged for its delivery on June 5, but on June 1 an accidental fall so damaged the boiler that plaintiffs refused to accept it, and defendant was unable to complete repairs and deliver it until November 8. Defendants knew at the time of the contract that plaintiffs were launderers and dyers and wanted the boiler for use in their business. *Held*, plaintiffs can recover for loss of "business profits" during the period June 5 to November 8, though not for the profits that plaintiffs could have made on certain "particularly lucrative" dyeing contracts of which defendant, at the time of the agreement, had not been specifically told. Lord Justice Asquith said:

"In cases of breach of contract the aggrieved party is only entitled to recover such part of the loss actually resulting as was at the time of the contract reasonably foreseeable as liable to result from the breach. What was at that time reasonably so foreseeable depends on the knowledge then possessed by the parties, or, at all events, by the party who later commits the breach.

"For this purpose, knowledge 'possessed' is one of two kinds; one imputed, the other actual. Everyone, as a reasonable person, is taken to know the 'ordinary course of things' and consequently what loss is liable to result from a breach of contract in that ordinary course. This is the subject matter of the 'first rule' in Hadley v. Baxendale. But to this knowledge, which a contract-breaker is assumed to possess whether he actually possesses it or not, there may have to be added in a particular case knowledge which he actually possesses, of special circumstances outside the 'ordinary course of things,' of such a kind that a breach in those special circumstances would be liable to cause more loss. Such a case attracts the operation of the 'second rule' so as to make additional loss also recoverable.

"In order to make the contract-breaker liable under either rule it is not necessary that he should actually have asked himself what loss is liable to result from a breach. . . . [P]arties at the time of contracting contemplate not the breach of the contract, but its performance. It suffices that, if he had considered the question, he would as a reasonable man have concluded that the loss in question was liable to result. . . .

"The defendants were an engineering company supplying a boiler to a laundry. We reject [defendant's claim] that an engineering company knows no more than the plain man about boilers or the purposes to which they are commonly put by different classes of purchasers, including laundries. . . . [T]hey knew they were supplying the boiler to a company carrying on the business of laundrymen and dyers, for use in that business. The obvious use of a boiler, in such a business, is surely to boil water for the purpose of washing or dyeing. . . . No commercial concern commonly purchases for the purposes of its business a very large and expensive structure like this—a boiler 19 feet high and costing over £2,000—with any other motive, and no supplier, let alone an engineering company, which has promised delivery of such an article by a particular date, with knowledge that it was to be put into use immediately on delivery, can reasonably contend that it could not foresee that loss of business (in the sense indicated above) would be liable to result to the purchaser from a long delay in the delivery thereof."

In another passage, Lord Justice Asquith pointed out that the statement of facts in Hadley v. Baxendale was misleading since Baron Alderson's opinion indicated that defendant's clerk knew only that the article to be carried "was the broken shaft of a mill and that the plaintiffs were the millers of that mill." The Lord Justice commented that if defendant's clerk had been informed also that the mill was stopped, "the court must, one would suppose, have decided the case the other way round; must, that is, have held the damage claimed was recoverable under the second rule."

———

NOTE: "LIABLE TO RESULT"

In The Heron II, 3 All E.R. 686 (House of Lords, 1967), defendant, owner of the vessel Heron II, contracted with plaintiff, owner of 3,000 tons of sugar, to load the sugar on the Heron II at the Black Sea port of Constanza, Rumania and carry it through the Suez Canal to Basra, Iraq. Plaintiff intended to sell the sugar upon its arrival at Basra; defendant did not know this, knowing only that there was a market for sugar there. The voyage to Basra would normally take about 20 days. In breach of contract, the vessel stopped at three other ports and as a result was nine days late arriving at Basra. During that interval an 8,000 ton cargo of sugar arrived at Basra from Formosa, the market price of sugar in Basra dropped, and plaintiff on sale of the sugar in Basra realized £4,183 less than he would have if the Heron II had not delayed its arrival. Judgment for plaintiff for this sum, awarded below, was unanimously affirmed in the House of Lords, despite little agreement among the judges on the proper phrasing of the *Hadley* principle.

Five law lords gave "speeches which restated each others' views at great length." One suggested that plaintiff, the shipper, might have wanted to stockpile sugar in Basra, or fill a previous contract for delivery there, so that the state of the Basra market could have been a matter of indifference to him. Some of the lords seemed to be concerned with whether defendant should have anticipated the fall in the sugar price that occurred through the arrival of Formosan sugar. Without distinguishing between the issues they were addressing, the lords spent much time discussing the phrases proposed by Asquith, L.J. in *Victoria Laundry*. In choosing the words to describe how probable the loss must appear to be at the time of the contract, the vote was in favor of "a real danger" (3 to 1) and "a serious possibility" (3 to 1), but against "odds on" (4 to 0). The vote was 5 to 0 against "on the cards." Indeed, some severe disapproval of this phrase was expressed, for, as Lord Reid said, in an unshuffled pack of cards the probability that the top card will be a diamond is 1 in 4 (apparently this 25 percent probability would be high enough for him), but the chance that it will be the 9 of diamonds is 1 in 52—not nearly high enough odds (a mere 2 percent chance) to make the damage compensable, though, Lord Reid observed, it would clearly be "on the cards." For most of the lords, "not unlikely" seemed to be acceptable. Some thought that Asquith's "liable to result," though somewhat indeterminate, could not after all be improved upon.

QUESTIONS

In applying *Hadley's* rule, should a distinction be drawn between a contract to sell machinery and a contract to transport machinery? Should a seller's knowledge that the purchaser is a dealer in goods of the kind sold be treated differently from knowledge that the purchaser has made a contract to resell the goods?

————

Hector Martinez & Co. v. Southern Pacific Transp. Co.
606 F.2d 106 (5th Cir.1979), cert. denied, 446 U.S. 982 (1980)

Defendant carrier was a month late in delivering a dragline which shipper intended to use in strip mining. The trial court, applying *Hadley*, dismissed the shipper's claim for the fair rental value of the dragline for the period of delay. *Held*, reversed. *Hadley* rests on the belief that, absent specific notice, the shaft was not an indispensable element of the mill. Here, it is obvious the dragline itself has use value. Cases suggesting that loss of use of a machine are not foreseeable results of delayed transport, "because [the injury] is not a usual consequence although it is a proximate consequence," are arbitrary extensions of the *Hadley* rule. "It might be quite foreseeable that deprivation of the machine's use because of carriage delay will cause a loss of rental value during the delay period." Moreover, defendant's contention that it was as foreseeable that the dragline was to be sold to another rather than used in plaintiff's operations "proves too much," for the test is what "should have been foreseen." A plaintiff need not show that the harm suffered was "the *most* foreseeable of possible harms." It is enough to show that a harm was "not so remote as to make it unforeseeable to a reasonable person at the time of contracting." Had this dragline been shipped for sale, not use, it cannot be said that delay in shipment would cause no recoverable loss.

————

NOTE: FORESEEABILITY TODAY

For an incisive critique of *Globe Refining*, see Larry T. Garvin, *Globe Refining Co. v. Landa Cotton Oil Co.* and the Dark Side of Reputation, 12 Nev. L.J. 659 (2012).

Outside of a few jurisdictions, courts have generally not followed *Globe Refining's* tacit agreement test. Judges nominally accept both parts of the rule of *Hadley v. Baxendale*. As a matter of blackletter law, a promisor is liable for all the consequential damages that flow from the breach as long as the other party communicates its special circumstances. On the face of it, consequential damages are available even if it seems extraordinarily unlikely that the promisor would have ever agreed to bear them, tacitly or otherwise.

One should not, however, accept the second half of *Hadley* uncritically. First, one of minority jurisdictions that appears to accept the *Globe Refining* test is New York. See Kenford Co., Inc. v. County of Erie, 73 N.Y.2d 312, 537 N.E.2d 176, 540 N.Y.S.2d 1 (1989); Bi–Economy Market, Inc. v. Harleysville Ins. Co. of New York, 10 N.Y.3d 187, 886 N.E.2d 127, 856 N.Y.S.2d 505 (2008). Many contracts, especially ones involving large corporate transactions, turn on

New York law. Moreover, a number of qualifications on the second part of *Hadley* have grown up over time in other jurisdictions. These qualifications lack theoretical coherence, but they leave us in much the same place as if the tacit-agreement test were the law. When the promisee gives notice of special circumstances, the promisor does become liable for the reasonably foreseeable damages that flow from the new circumstances, but only if they can be calculated with certainty and only if the promisee could not have avoided the damages. There is also the suggestion that promisee's damages cannot be grossly disproportionate to the amount paid to the promisor.

The Restatement, Second tracks the Code in formulating the *Hadley* requirement objectively, as a test of what the party in breach had reason to foresee. But observe that the restaters have added a further limitation (subsection (3)), one not found in the first Restatement:

§ 351. Unforeseeability and Related Limitations on Damages

(1) Damages are not recoverable for loss that the party in breach did not have reason to foresee as a probable result of the breach when the contract was made.

(2) Loss may be foreseeable as a probable result of a breach because it follows from the breach

(a) in the ordinary course of events, or

(b) as a result of special circumstance, beyond the ordinary course of events, that the party in breach had reason to know.

(3) A court may limit damages for foreseeable loss by excluding recovery for loss of profits, by allowing recovery only for loss incurred in reliance, or otherwise if it concludes that in the circumstances justice so requires in order to avoid disproportionate compensation.

The apparent justification for subsection (3) of § 351 is a belief that there will be times when it is not good policy to require the defendant to pay for all of the foreseeable loss that is caused by a breach of contract. On the assumption that it is wise "not to go too far," what are the factors that should guide the courts in defining the requirements of "justice"? The restaters, in comment on § 351(3), speak of such things as "informality of dealing," which presumably signals a failure of the parties themselves to allocate risks, and the familiar problem of "disproportionate losses." The *Lamkins* case, among others, is given as an illustration of the limitation. Perhaps this newly-stated discretionary power over damage recoveries is a natural outgrowth of developments observed by Grant Gilmore, The Death of Contract 50–53 (1974):

In the hundred odd years since the case was decided, the compendious [*Hadley*] formula has meant all things to all men. . . . "Foreseeability" and "communication" are, evidently, manipulable concepts. During the period of the [distinctly hostile nineteenth-century reaction to *Hadley*'s allowance of special damages, these concepts] were manipulated, with great sophistication, in favor of defendants and against plaintiffs seeking large damage awards.

More on the power of exclusion granted courts by § 351(3) can be found in Harvey, Discretionary Justice Under the Restatement (Second) of Contracts, 67

Cornell L.Rev. 666 (1982). Guidance on the general question of reducing the extent of a promisor's risk is provided in Garvin, Disproportionality and the Law of Consequential Damages: Default Theory and Cognitive Reality, 59 Ohio St. L.J. 339 (1998).

The distinction between "general" and "consequential" damages, though clear in principle, can be elusive at times. Similarly, the line between "incidental" and "consequential" damages is occasionally blurred (not so as concerns the $674 of expenses awarded the seller in *Neri*). Locating that line in goods cases can matter a lot, for under the UCC consequentials are a buyer's, not a seller's, remedy. See UCC §§ 2–710 and 2–715. This has led to disputes over whether a particular item claimed by a seller is properly classified as "incidental" rather than "consequential" damage—e.g., additional interest expense incurred in the interval between the breach and the seller's cover sale, deemed incidental in Afram Export Corp. v. Metallurgiki Halyps, S.A., 772 F.2d 1358 (7th Cir.1985), in disagreement with the district judge.

––––––––

Valentine v. General American Credit, Inc.

Supreme Court of Michigan, 1984.
420 Mich. 256, 362 N.W.2d 628.

LEVIN, J. Sharon Valentine seeks to recover mental distress damages arising out of the alleged breach of an employment contract. Valentine claims that, under the contract, she was entitled to job security and the peace of mind that is associated with job security. Because an employment contract providing for job security has a personal element, and breach of such a contract can be expected to result in mental distress, Valentine argues that she should be able to recover mental distress damages. She also asks for exemplary damages.

The Court of Appeals affirmed the decision of the trial court dismissing the claims for mental distress and exemplary damages. We affirm. . . .

Employers and employees [are] free to provide, or not to provide, for job security. Absent a contractual provision for job security, either the employer or the employee may ordinarily terminate an employment contract at any time for any, or no, reason. The obligation which gave rise to this action is based on the agreement of the parties; it is not an obligation imposed on the employer by law. This is an action for breach of contract and not a tort action.

Valentine may not recover mental distress damages for breach of the employment contract, although such damages may have been foreseeable and she might not be "made whole" absent an award of mental distress damages.

Valentine relies on the rule of Hadley v. Baxendale. . . . [T]hat rule has not been applied scrupulously. As stated by Professor Dobbs in his treatise on remedies, a "difficulty in the *Hadley* type case is that the test of foreseeability [i.e., whether damages 'arise naturally'] has little or no meaning.

The idea is so readily subject to expansion or contraction that it becomes in fact merely a technical way in which the judges can state their conclusion."[1]

Under the [*Hadley*] rule, literally applied, damages for mental distress would be recoverable for virtually every breach of contract. . . . In Stewart v. Rudner, 349 Mich. 459, 84 N.W.2d 816 (1957), this Court said that "all breaches of contract do more or less" cause "vexation and annoyance"; similarly, see Kewin v. Massachusetts Mut. Life Ins. Co., 409 Mich. 401, 295 N.W.2d 50 (1980).

Yet the general rule, with few exceptions, is to "uniformly den[y]" recovery for mental distress damages although they are "foreseeable within the rule of Hadley v. Baxendale." The rule barring recovery of mental distress damages—a gloss on the generality of the [*Hadley*] rule—is fully applicable to an action for breach of an employment contract.

The denial of mental distress damages, although the result is to leave the plaintiff with less than a full recovery, has analogy in the law. The law does not generally compensate for all losses suffered. Recovery is denied for attorney's fees, for mental anguish not accompanied by physical manifestation, and "make-whole" or full recovery has been denied where the cost of performance exceeds the value to the promisee. The courts have not, despite "make whole" generalizations regarding the damages recoverable, attempted to provide compensation for all losses. Instead, specific rules have been established that provide for the calculation of the damages recoverable in particular kinds of actions. In contract actions, the market price is the general standard.

. . . [T]he courts of this state have qualified the general rule, pursuant to which mental distress damages for breach of contract are not recoverable, with a narrow exception. Rather than look to the foreseeability of loss to determine the applicability of the exception, the courts have considered whether the contract "has elements of personality"[2] and whether the damage suffered upon the breach of the agreement is capable of adequate compensation by reference to the terms of the contract. [*Kewin*, 409 Mich. [at] 417, 295 N.W.2d 50.]

The narrow scope of those verbal formulas appears on consideration of the limited situations in which this Court has allowed the recovery of mental distress damages for breach of contract. In Vanderpool v. Richardson, 52 Mich. 336, 17 N.W. 936 (1883), recovery was allowed for breach of a promise to marry. In Stewart v. Rudner, a doctor who failed to fulfill his promise to deliver a child by caesarean section was required to pay mental distress damages. In Miholevich v. Mid–West Mut. Auto Ins. Co., 261 Mich. 495, 246 N.W. 202 (1933), the plaintiff, who was jailed for failure to pay a liabil-

---

[1] Dobbs, Remedies, § 12.3, p. 814. See also Dobbs, § 12.3, p. 804; 5 Corbin, Contracts, § 1007, pp. 70–71. [Most of the court's footnotes have been omitted; those retained are renumbered.—Eds.]

[2] *Stewart*, supra, 349 Mich. [at] 471, 84 N.W.2d 816. In *Stewart*, the Court also said that mental distress damages are recoverable in cases "where a contract is *made* to secure relief from a particular inconvenience or annoyance, or to confer a particular enjoyment." (Emphasis supplied.) See also *Kewin*, supra, in which the Court emphasized that, for mental distress damages to be recoverable, the parties must have formed "a contract *meant* to secure [the] protection" of personal interests. (Emphasis supplied.)

ity judgment, recovered mental distress damages from an insurer who had failed to pay the judgment.[3]

Loss of a job is not comparable to the loss of a marriage or a child and generally results in estimable monetary damages. In *Miholevich*, the breach resulted in a deprivation of personal liberty.

An employment contract will indeed often have a personal element. Employment is an important aspect of most persons' lives, and the breach of an employment contract may result in emotional distress. The primary purpose in forming such contracts, however, is economic and not to secure the protection of personal interests. The psychic satisfaction of the employment is secondary.

Mental distress damages for breach of contract have not been awarded where there is a market standard by which damages can be adequately determined. Valentine's monetary loss can be estimated with reasonable certainty according to the terms of the contract and the market for, or the market value of, her service. . . . [B]ecause an employment contract is not entered into primarily to secure the protection of personal interests and pecuniary damages can be estimated with reasonable certainty, . . . a person discharged in breach of an employment contract may not recover mental distress damages.

Valentine has not separately argued her exemplary damage claim. In *Kewin*, this Court said that "absent allegation and proof of tortious conduct existing independent of the breach [citation omitted], exemplary damages may not be awarded in common-law actions brought for breach of a commercial contract." Valentine failed to plead the requisite purposeful tortious conduct, and therefore she may not recover exemplary damages.

Affirmed.

————

Hancock v. Northcutt

808 P.2d 251 (Alaska 1991)

"The view that contracts pertaining to one's dwelling are not among those contracts which, if breached, are particularly likely to result in serious emotional disturbance is reflected in numerous cases. . . . [B]reach of a house construction contract is . . . not so highly personal and laden with emotion as contracts where emotional damages have typically been allowed to stand on their own. . . . Further, the typical damages for breach of house construction contracts can appropriately be calculated in terms of monetary loss. By contrast, the damages in contracts of a more personal nature in which emotional disturbance damages are allowed are usually intangible. Thus, there would ordinarily be only a nominal recovery unless emotional disturbance damages were allowed." [California's highest court, endorsing the *Hancock* position in Erlich v. Menezes, 21 Cal.4th 543, 87 Cal.Rptr.2d 886, 981 P.2d 978 (1999), added: "[T]o permit emotional distress damages [on a contract claim for] negligent construction of a personal residence [would] make the financial risks of construction agreements difficult to predict. Contract damages must be clearly ascer-

---

[3] Humphrey v. Michigan United R. Co., 166 Mich. 645, 132 N.W. 447 (1911), concerned the duty of a common carrier to a passenger. This duty is imposed by law without regard to contract.

tainable in both nature and origin. . . . Moreover, adding an emotional distress component to recovery for construction defects could increase the already prohibitively high cost of housing in California, affect the availability of insurance for builders, and greatly diminish the supply of affordable housing. . . . [And] [p]ermitting damages for emotional distress on the theory that certain contracts carry a lot of emotional freight provides no useful guidance. Courts have carved out a narrow range of exceptions . . . where emotional tranquility is the contract's essence. [This] reflects a fundamental policy choice. A rule which focuses not on the risks contracting parties voluntarily assume but on one party's reaction to inadequate performance, cannot provide any principled limit on liability."]

———————

NOTE: EMOTIONAL DISTRESS DAMAGES

Sharon Valentine had included in her complaint a claim for intentional infliction of mental or emotional distress, which is either an independent tort (indeed, a very young tort in some states, dating from the 1970s) or, if it will not support a recovery "on its own," a standard element of tort damages in limited types of negligence cases—e.g., the mental anguish that accompanies a physical injury caused by another's tortious act. In any case, Valentine apparently did not pursue a tort theory on appeal.

The practice of adding the separate tort of intentional (or, alternatively, negligent) infliction of emotional distress to what is essentially a contract action has increased considerably in recent times. An example is provided by Brown v. Fritz, 108 Idaho 357, 699 P.2d 1371 (1985), where a vendor contracted to sell land a portion of which he had previously sold to another—inadvertently, the vendor claimed, though the jury apparently thought otherwise. The purchaser's recovery below included damages of $2,100 for misrepresentation of the condition of the property (insulation, septic tanks, and boundary lines) and $15,000 for negligent infliction of emotional distress. The trial judge had permitted the latter issue to go to the jury, but refused to let the jury hear the purchaser's claim for punitive damages. Only the award for emotional distress was appealed. The court reversed, holding emotional distress damages unrecoverable in a suit for breach of a contractual relationship:

> [I]t is clear that any damage, pecuniary or emotional, which fell upon [the purchaser] resulted from the negotiations for and the consummation of a contract to convey real property. The damage did not result from an "independent" tort involving a physical or a constructive contact between two parties who were not in a contractual relationship. It did not involve the harassment of another or the libeling or slandering of another. . . . The distinction is far from clear [between] an action based upon breach of contract and an action for tortious breach of contract. . . . [O]ur allowance of an action . . . for negligent infliction of emotional distress resulting from a breach of contract can do little except muddy the already murky waters.

> We note the close parallel between allowable damages for breach of contract under the terminology of "emotional distress" and for punitive damages. . . . We hold that there is no significant, if in fact any, difference between conduct of a defendant which may be

seen to justify an award of punitive damages, and conduct which may justify an award of damages for emotional distress. Justification for [emotional distress damages, like punitive damages,] seems to lie in the quantum of outrageousness of the defendant's conduct. . . . We also suggest that the enormous differences that exist between individuals as to their ability to withstand mental stress, frustration, embarrassment or humiliation make next to impossible the application of a reasonableness standard as to plaintiffs whom defendants must expect to encounter in contractual dealings. While we have stated that in tort cases a defendant must take a plaintiff as he is found, including excessive fragility and the like, we know of no such standard applicable to the psychological state of a [contract] plaintiff which a defendant might encounter.

In reversing, the Idaho court concluded that the trial judge should have the benefit of its views on plaintiff's emotional distress claim (again, the only issue appealed). The case was therefore remanded for a new trial solely on the question of punitive damages.

The Restatement, Second § 353 provides: "Recovery for emotional disturbance will be excluded unless the breach also caused bodily harm or the contract or the breach is of a kind that serious emotional disturbance was a particularly likely result." As *Valentine* indicates, exceptions to the general rule against recovery for mental distress have been limited, usually involving contracts between carriers and innkeepers and their passengers and guests, contracts for the carriage and disposition of dead bodies, and contracts for the delivery of messages concerning death. McAfee v. Wright, 651 A.2d 371 (Me.1994). Under § 353, would George Hawkins have been entitled to emotional distress damages from Dr. McGee? What of a contract to care for one's child or elderly parent?

————

MindGames, Inc. v. Western Publishing Co.

United States Court of Appeals, Seventh Circuit, 2000.
218 F.3d 652.

POSNER, CHIEF JUDGE. This is a diversity suit for breach of contract, governed by Arkansas law because of a choice of law provision in the contract. The plaintiff, MindGames, was formed in March of 1988 by Larry Blackwell to manufacture and sell an adult board game, "Clever Endeavor," that he had invented. The first games were shipped in the fall of 1989 and by the end of the year, 75 days later, 30,000 had been sold. In March of 1990, MindGames licensed the game to the defendant, Western, a major marketer of games. Western had marketed the very successful adult board games "Trivial Pursuit" and "Pictionary" and thought "Clever Endeavor" might be as successful. The license contract, on which this suit is premised, required Western to pay MindGames a 15 percent royalty on all games sold. The contract was by its terms to remain in effect until the end of January of 1993, or for another year if before then Western paid MindGames at least $1.5 million in the form of royalties due under the contract or otherwise, and for subsequent years as well if Western paid an annual renewal fee of $300,000.

During the first year of the contract, Western sold 165,000 copies of "Clever Endeavor" and paid MindGames $600,000 in royalties. After that, sales fell precipitously (though we're not told by how much) but the parties continued under the contract through January 31, 1994, though Western did not pay the $900,000 ($1.5 million minus $600,000) that the contract would have required it to pay in order to be entitled to extend the contract for a year after its expiration. In February of 1994 the parties finally parted. Later that year MindGames brought this suit, which seeks $900,000, plus lost royalties of some $40 million that MindGames claims it would have earned had not Western failed to carry out the promotional obligations that the contract imposed on it, plus $300,000 on the theory that Western renewed the contract for a third year, beginning in February of 1994; Western sold off its remaining inventory of "Clever Endeavor" in that year.

The district court granted summary judgment for Western, holding that the contract did not entitle MindGames to a renewal fee and that Arkansas's "new business" rule barred any recovery of lost profits. 944 F.Supp. 754 (E.D.Wis.1996); 995 F.Supp. 949 (E.D.Wis.1998). Although the victim of a breach of contract is entitled to nominal damages, MindGames does not seek them; and so if it is not entitled to either type of substantial damages that it seeks, judgment was correctly entered for Western. By not seeking nominal damages, incidentally, MindGames may have lost a chance to obtain significant attorneys' fees, to which Arkansas law entitles a prevailing party in a breach of contract case.

The rejection of MindGames' claim to the renewal fee for the second year (and *a fortiori* the third) was clearly correct. . . .

The more difficult issue is MindGames' right to recover lost profits for Western's alleged breach of its duty to promote "Clever Endeavor." A minority of states have or purport to have a rule barring a new business, as distinct from an established one, from obtaining damages for lost profits as a result of a tort or a breach of contract. The rule of Hadley v. Baxendale often prevents the victim of a breach of contract from obtaining lost profits, but that rule is not invoked here. Neither the "new business" rule nor the rule of [*Hadley*] stands for the *general* proposition that lost profits are never a recoverable item of damages in a tort or breach of contract case.

Arkansas is said to be one of the "new business" rule states on the strength of a case decided by the state's supreme court many years ago. The appellants in Marvell Light & Ice Co. v. General Electric Co., 162 Ark. 467, 259 S.W. 741 (1924), sought to recover the profits that they claimed to have lost as a result of a five and a half month delay in the delivery of icemaking machinery; the delay, the appellants claimed, had forced them to delay putting their ice factory into operation. The court concluded, however, that because there was no indication "that the manufacture and sale of ice by appellants was an established business so that proof of the amount lost on account of the delay . . . might be made with reasonable certainty," "the anticipated profits of the new business are too remote, speculative, and uncertain to support a judgment for their loss." It quoted an earlier decision in which another court had said that "he who is prevented from embarking in [*sic*—must mean 'on'] a new business can recover no profits, because there are no provable data of past business from which the fact that anticipated profits would have been realized can be legally deduced." Central Coal & Coke Co. v. Hartman, 111 Fed. 96, 99 (8th Cir.1901). That quotation is taken to have made Arkansas a "new business" state, although the rest of the

Marvell opinion indicates that the court was concerned that the anticipated profits of the *particular* new business at issue, rather than of every new business, were too speculative to support an award of damages. On its facts, moreover, *Marvell* was a classic [*Hadley*] type of case—in fact virtually a rerun of *Hadley*, except that the appellants alleged that they had notified the seller of the icemaking machinery of the damages that they would suffer if delivery was delayed, and the seller had agreed to be liable for those damages. The decision is puzzling in light of that allegation; it is doubly puzzling because, assuming that by the time of the trial the ice factory was up and running, it should not have been difficult to compute the damages that the appellants had lost by virtue of the five and a half month delay in placing the factory in operation. Presumably it would have had five and a half months of additional profits.

Marvell has never been overruled; and federal courts ordinarily take a nonoverruled decision of the highest court of the state whose law governs a controversy by virtue of the applicable choice of law rule to be conclusive on the law of the state. But this is a matter of practice or presumption, not of rule. The rule is that in a case in federal court in which state law provides the rule of decision, the federal court must predict how the state's highest court would decide the case, and decide it the same way. Law, Holmes said, in a controversial definition that is, however, a pretty good summary of how courts apply the law of other jurisdictions, is just a prediction of what the courts of that jurisdiction would do with the case if they got their hands on it. Holmes, "The Path of the Law," 10 Harv.L.Rev. 457, 461 (1897). Since state courts like federal courts do occasionally overrule their decisions, there will be occasional, though rare, instances in which the best prediction of what the state's highest court will do is that it will *not* follow its previous decision.

That is the best prediction in this case. *Marvell* was decided more than three quarters of a century ago, and the "new business" rule which it has been thought to have announced has not been mentioned in a published Arkansas case since. The opinion doesn't make a lot of sense on its facts, as we have seen, and the Eighth Circuit case on which it relied has long been superseded in that circuit. The Arkansas cases decided since *Marvell* that deal with damages issues exhibit a liberal approach to the estimation of damages that is inconsistent with a flat rule denying damages for lost profits to all businesses that are not well established. Jim Halsey Co. v. Bonar, 284 Ark. 461, 683 S.W.2d 898, 902–03 (1985); Tremco, Inc. v. Valley Aluminum Products Corp., 38 Ark.App. 143, 831 S.W.2d 156, 158 (1992); Ozark Gas Transmission Systems v. Barclay, 10 Ark.App. 152, 662 S.W.2d 188, 192 (1983). The *Ozark* decision, for example, allowed an orchard farmer to recover for the damages to a *new* orchard. The "new business" rule has, moreover, been abandoned in most states that once followed it, and it seems to retain little vitality even in states like Virginia, which purport to employ the hard-core per se approach.

Western tries to distinguish *Ozark* by pointing to the fact that the plaintiff there was an established orchard farmer, albeit the particular orchard represented a new venture for him. This effort to distinguish that case brings into view the primary objection to the "new business" rule, an objection of such force as to explain its decline and make it unlikely that Arkansas would follow it if the occasion for its supreme court to choose arose. The objection has to do with the difference between *rule* and *standard* as methods of legal governance. A rule singles out one or a few facts and makes it or them conclusive of legal liability; a standard permits consideration of all or at least most facts that are relevant to the standard's rationale. A speed limit is a rule; negligence is a standard. Rules have the advantage of being definite and of limiting factual inquiry but the disadvantage of being inflexible, even arbitrary, and thus overinclusive, or of being underinclusive and thus opening up loopholes (or of being *both* over- and underinclusive!). Standards are flexible, but vague and open-ended; they make business planning difficult, invite the sometimes unpredictable exercise of judicial discretion, and are more costly to adjudicate—and yet when based on lay intuition they may actually be more intelligible, and thus in a sense clearer and more precise, to the persons whose behavior they seek to guide than rules would be. No sensible person supposes that rules are always superior to standards, or vice versa, though some judges are drawn to the definiteness of rules and others to the flexibility of standards. But that is psychology; the important point is that some activities are better governed by rules, others by standards. States that have rejected the "new business" rule are content to control the award of damages for lost profits by means of a standard—damages may not be awarded on the basis of wild conjecture, they must be proved to a reasonable certainty—that is applicable to proof of damages generally. The "new business" rule is an attempt now widely regarded as failed to control the award of such damages by means of a rule.

The rule doesn't work because it manages to be at once vague and arbitrary. One reason is that the facts that it makes determinative, "new," "business," and "profits," are not facts, but rather are the conclusions of a reasoning process that is based on the rationale for the rule and that as a result turns the rule into an implicit standard. What, for example, is a "new" business? What, for that matter, is a "business"? And are royalties what the rule means by "profits"? MindGames was formed more than a year before it signed the license agreement with Western, and it sold 30,000 games in the six months between the first sales and the signing of the contract. MindGames' only "business," moreover, was the licensing of intellectual property. An author who signs a contract with a publisher for the publication of his book would not ordinarily be regarded as being engaged in a "business," or his royalties or advance described as "profits." He would be surprised to learn that if he sued for unpaid royalties he could not get them because his was a "new business." Suppose a first-time author sued a publisher for an accounting, and the only issue was how many copies the publisher had sold. Under the "new business" rule as construed by Western, the author could not recover his lost royalties even though there was no uncertainty about what he had lost. So construed and applied, the rule would have no relation to its rationale, which is to prevent the award of speculative damages.

Western goes even further, arguing that even if it, Western, a well-established firm, were the plaintiff, it could not recover its lost profits because the sale of "Clever Endeavor" was a new business. On this construal of the rule, "business" does not mean the enterprise; it means any business activity. So Western's sale of a new game is a new business, yet we know from the *Ozark* decision that an orchard farmer's operation of a new orchard is an old business.

The rule could be made sensible by appropriate definition of its terms, but we find it hard to see what would be gained, given the existence of the serviceable and familiar standard of excessive speculativeness. The rule may have made sense at one time; the reduction in decision costs and uncertainty brought about by avoiding a speculative mire may have swamped the increased social costs resulting from the systematically inadequate damages that a "new business" rule decrees. But today the courts have become sufficiently sophisticated in analyzing lost-earnings claims, and have accumulated sufficient precedent on the standard of undue speculativeness in damages awards, to make the balance of costs and benefits tip against the rule. In any event we are far in this case, in logic as well as time, from the ice factory whose opening was delayed by the General Electric Co. We greatly doubt that there is a "new business" rule in the common law of Arkansas today, but if there is it surely does not extend so far beyond the facts of the only case in which the rule was ever invoked to justify its invocation here. There is no authority for, and no common sense appeal to, such an extension.

But that leaves us with the question of undue speculation in estimating damages. Abrogation of the "new business" rule does not produce a free-for-all. What makes MindGames' claim of lost royalties indeed dubious is not any "new business" rule but the fact that the success of a board game, like that of a book or movie, is so uncertain. Here newness enters into judicial consideration of the damages claim not as a rule but as a factor in applying the standard. Just as a start-up company should not be permitted to obtain pie-in-the-sky damages upon allegations that it was snuffed out before it could begin to operate (unlike the ice factory in *Marvell*, which did begin production, albeit a little later than planned), capitalizing fantasized earnings into a huge present value sought as damages, so a novice writer should not be permitted to obtain damages from his publisher on the premise that but for the latter's laxity he would have had a bestseller, when only a tiny fraction of new books achieve that success. . . .

This is not to suggest that damages for lost earnings on intellectual property can never be recovered; that "entertainment damages" are not recoverable in breach of contract cases. That would just be a variant of the discredited "new business" rule. What is important is that Blackwell had no track record when he created "Clever Endeavor." He could not point to other games that he had invented and that had sold well. He was not in the position of the bestselling author who can prove from his past success that his new book, which the defendant failed to promote, would have been likely—not certain, of course—to have enjoyed a success comparable to that of the average of his previous books if only it had been promoted as promised. That would be like a case of a new business launched by an entrepreneur with a proven track record.

In the precontract sales period and the first year of the contract a total of 195,000 copies of "Clever Endeavor" were sold; then sales fizzled. The public is fickle. It is possible that if Western had marketed the game more vigorously, more would have been sold, but an equally if not more plausible possibility is that the reason that Western didn't market the game more vigorously was that it correctly sensed that demand had dried up.

Even if that alternative is rejected, we do not see how the number of copies that would have been sold but for the alleged breach could be determined given the evidence presented in the summary judgment proceedings (a potentially important qualification, of course); and so MindGames' proof of damages is indeed excessively speculative. Those proceedings were completed with no evidence having been presented from which a rational trier of fact could conclude *on this record* that some specific quantity, or for that matter some broad but bounded range of alternative estimates, of copies of "Clever Endeavor" would have been sold had Western honored the contract. MindGames obtained $600,000 in royalties on sales of 165,000 copies of the game, implying that Western would have had to sell more than 10 million copies to generate the $40 million in lost royalties that MindGames seeks to recover.

When the breach occurred, MindGames should have terminated the contract and sought distribution by other means. The fact that it did not do so—that so far as appears it has made no effort to market "Clever Endeavor" since the market for the game collapsed in 1991—is telling evidence of a lack of commercial promise unrelated to Western's conduct.

Although Western in its brief in this court spent most of its time misguidedly defending the "new business" rule, clinging to *Marvell* for dear life (a case seemingly on point, however vulnerable, is a security blanket that no lawyer feels comfortable without), it did argue that in any event MindGames' claim for lost royalties was too speculative to ground an award of damages for that loss. The argument was brief but not so brief as to fail to put MindGames on notice of a possible alternative ground for upholding the district court's judgment; we may of course affirm an award of summary judgment on any ground that has not been forfeited or waived in the district court. MindGames did not respond to the argument in its reply brief. It pointed to no evidence from which lost royalties could be calculated to even a rough approximation. We find its silence eloquent and Western's argument compelling, and so the judgment in favor of Western is

Affirmed.

––––––

Freund v. Washington Square Press, Inc.
34 N.Y.2d 379, 357 N.Y.S.2d 857, 314 N.E.2d 419 (1974)

Plaintiff author and college teacher granted defendant exclusive rights to publish and sell in book form a manuscript on modern drama. The agreement called for Publisher to pay Author a $2,000 advance plus royalties. In addition, publisher agreed to publish a hardbound edition if it did not terminate the agreement within sixty days of receipt of the manuscript. Publisher paid the advance in full but merged thereafter with another company and ceased publishing hardbound books altogether. Though it never terminated the agreement as the contract allowed, Publisher refused to publish the book in any form. Author sued, seeking damages and specific performance. The trial court denied the request for specific performance but identified three categories of damages possibly arising from the breach: (1) delay in academic promotion; (2) loss of royalties that would have been earned; and (3) the cost of publication if plaintiff had made his own arrangements to publish. Ultimately, it found no delay in advancement and denied recovery of lost royalties without discussion. The court ruled, however, that plaintiff was entitled to that amount of money that would allow him to publish the manuscript, which it assessed at $10,000. The intermediate appellate court affirmed (3 to 2), and Publisher appealed. *Held*, plaintiff may recover nominal damages only. The law, so far as is possible, "attempts to secure to the injured party the benefit of his bargain. . . ." The lower court's analogy to a breach of construction contract was therefore inapposite. In that case, "[t]he value of the promised performance to the owner is the properly constructed building." But here, "unlike the typical construction contract, the value to the plaintiff of the promised performance—publication—was a percentage of sales of the books published and not the books themselves. Had the plaintiff contracted for the printing, binding and delivery of a number of hard-bound copies of his manuscript, to be sold or disposed of as he wished, then perhaps the construction analogy, and measurement of damages by the cost of replacement or completion, would have some application." Because the royalties plaintiff would have realized were not ascertained with adequate certainty, "the order of the Appellate Division should be modified to the extent of reducing the damage award of $10,000 for the cost of publication to six cents, but with costs and disbursements to the plaintiff."

––––––––

Fera v. Village Plaza, Inc.
396 Mich. 639, 242 N.W.2d 372 (1976)

Plaintiffs signed a 10–year lease for a "book and bottle" shop in defendants' proposed shopping center; the rent was a monthly minimum of $1,000, plus a percentage of annual receipts exceeding $240,000. The center eventually opened despite problems and delays, but plaintiffs' space was given to another tenant. Defendants' offer of alternative space was refused by plaintiffs as unsuitable for their planned venture. In the suit that followed, a jury awarded plaintiffs $200,000 for profits prevented by the breach. An intermediate appellate court, believing that a new business is barred from recovering lost profits and finding that plaintiffs' proofs of anticipated profits were "entirely speculative," ordered a new trial on damages. *Held*, the trial court's judgment based on the jury's verdict should be reinstated. Earlier decisions indicating reluctance to award an untried business lost profits "should not be read as stating a rule of law which prevents *every* new business from recovering" such damages. As Corbin has observed, the problem is not with profits as such but with the requirement that damages be proved with "certainty," that a plaintiff "lay a basis for a reasonable estimate of the extent of [harm], measured in money." Here, "there were days and days of testimony. . . The proofs ranged from no profits to [plaintiffs' own testimony of $270,000] over a ten-year period. . . . The weaknesses of plaintiffs' specially prepared budget were thoroughly explored on cross-examination. . . . The jury weighed the conflicting testimony and determined that plaintiffs were entitled to damages of $200,000. . . . 'Where injury to some degree is found, we do not preclude recovery for lack of precise proof. We do the best we can with what we have. . . . Particularly is this true where it is defendant's own act or neglect that has caused the imprecision.' While we might have found plaintiffs' proofs lacking had we been [the jury], that is not the standard of review we employ."

––––––––

Restatement of Contracts, Second § 352, Comment b (1981)

"*Proof of Profits*. The difficulty of proving lost profits varies greatly with the nature of the transaction. If, for example, it is the seller who claims lost profit on the ground that the buyer's breach has caused him to lose a sale, proof of lost profit will ordinarily not be difficult. If, however, it is the buyer who claims lost profit on the ground that the seller's breach has caused him loss in other transactions, the task of proof is harder. Furthermore, if the transaction is more complex and extends into the future, as where the seller agrees to furnish all of the buyer's requirements over a period of years, proof of the loss of profits caused by the seller's breach is more difficult. If the breach prevents the injured party from carrying on a well-established business, the resulting loss of profits can often be proved with sufficient certainty. Evidence of past performance will form the basis for a reasonable prediction as to the future. . . . However, if the business is a new one or if it is a speculative one that is subject to great fluctuations in volume, costs or prices, proof will be more difficult. Nevertheless, damages may be established with reasonable certainty with the aid of expert testimony, economic and financial data, market surveys and analyses, business records of similar enterprises, and the like."

SECTION 3. THE RESTITUTION ALTERNATIVE

INTRODUCTORY NOTE

The prevailing theory of contract damages aims to give the injured party the money equivalent of the promised performance. This means that damage rules, as they are usually phrased, protect both the expectation and the reliance interests; the defaulter, it is commonly said, must account for "gains prevented" as well as "losses caused," the latter because the nondefaulter normally will have acted in reliance on the contract. Thus, the court in Rockingham County v. Luten Bridge Co. embraced familiar doctrine in measuring damages by "labor and materials expended and expense incurred in the part performance of the contract, prior to its repudiation, plus the profit which would have been realized if it had been carried out in accordance with its terms."

The question raised by the present section is whether there are alternatives to the full enforcement of expectations through a money substitute for the promised performance.

———————

Boone v. Coe

Court of Appeals of Kentucky, 1913.
153 Ky. 233, 154 S.W. 900.

CLAY, C. Plaintiffs, W.H. Boone and J.T. Coe, brought this action against defendant, J.F. Coe, to recover certain damages, alleged to have resulted from defendant's breach of a parol contract of lease for one year to commence at a future date. . . [D]efendant was the owner of a large and valuable farm in Ford County, Tex. Plaintiffs were farmers, and were living with their families in Monroe County, Ky. In the fall of 1909 defendant made a verbal contract with plaintiffs, whereby he rented to them his farm in Texas for a period of 12 months, to commence from the date of plaintiffs' arrival at defendant's farm. Defendant agreed that if plaintiffs would leave their said homes and businesses in Kentucky, and with their families, horses, and wagons, move to defendant's farm in Texas, and take charge of, manage, and cultivate same in wheat, corn, and cotton for the 12 months next following plaintiffs' arrival at said farm, the defendant would have a dwelling completed on said farm and ready for occupancy upon their arrival, which dwelling plaintiffs would occupy as a residence during the period of said tenancy. Defendant also agreed that he would furnish necessary material at a convenient place on said farm out of which to erect a good and commodious stock and grain barn, to be used by plaintiffs. The petition further alleges that plaintiffs were to cultivate certain portions of the farm, and were to receive certain portions of the crops raised, and that plaintiffs, in conformity with their said agreement, did move from Kentucky to the farm in Texas, and carried with them their families, wagons, horses, and camping outfit, and in going to Texas they traveled for a period of 55 days. It is also charged that defendant broke his contract, in that he failed to have ready and completed on the farm a dwelling house in which plaintiffs and their families could move, and also failed to furnish the necessary material for the erection of a suitable barn; that on December 6th defendant refused to permit plaintiffs to occupy the house and premises, and failed and refused to permit them to cultivate the land or any part thereof, that on the ___ day of December, 1909, they started for their home in Kentucky, and arrived there after traveling for a period of 4 days. It is charged that plaintiffs spent in going to Texas, in cash, the sum of $150; that the loss of time to plaintiffs and their teams in making the trip to Texas was reasonably worth $8 a day for a period of 55 days, or the sum of $440; that the loss of time to them and their teams during the period they remained in Texas was $8 a day for 22 days, or $176; that they paid out in actual cash for transportation for themselves, families, and teams from Texas to Kentucky the sum of $211.80; that the loss of time to them and their teams in making the last-named trip was reasonably worth the sum of $100; that in abandoning and giving up their homes and business in Kentucky they had been damaged in the sum of $150, making a total damage of $1,387.80 for which judgment was asked. Defendant's demurrer to the petition was sustained and the petition dismissed. Plaintiffs appeal. . . .

The statute of frauds (§ 470, sub-secs. 6 & 7 (Ky. Statutes)) provides as follows: "No action shall be brought to charge any person: 6. Upon any contract for the sale of real estate, or any lease thereof, for longer term than one year; nor 7. Upon any agreement which is not to be performed within one year from the making thereof, unless the promise, contract, agreement, representation, assurance or ratification, or some memorandum or note thereof be in writing, and signed by the party to be charged therewith, or by his authorized agent; but the consideration need not be expressed in the writing; it may be proved when necessary, or disproved by parol or other evidence." A parol lease of land for one year, to commence at a future date, is within the statute. Greenwood v. Strother, 91 Ky. 482, 16 S.W. 138.

The question sharply presented is: May plaintiffs recover for expenses incurred and time lost on the faith of a contract that is unenforceable under the statute of frauds? . . . It is the general rule that damages cannot be recovered, for violation of a contract within the statute of frauds. . . .

To this general rule there are certain well-recognized exceptions. . . . [I]t has been held that, where services have been rendered during the life of another, on the promise that the person rendering the service should receive at the death of the person served a legacy, and the contract so made is within the statute of frauds, a reasonable compensation may be recovered for the services actually rendered. It has also been held that the vendee of land under a parol contract is entitled to recover any portion of the purchase money he may have paid, and is also entitled to compensation for improvements. . . .

And under a contract for personal services within the statute an action may be maintained on a quantum meruit. [Myers v. Korb, 50 S.W. 1108, 21 Ky.Law Rep. 163.] The doctrine of these cases proceeds upon the theory that the defendant has actually received some benefits from the acts of part performance; and the law therefore implies a promise to pay. In 29 Am. & Eng. Ency. 836, the rule is thus stated: "Although part performance by one of the parties to a contract within the statute of frauds will not, at law, entitle such party to recover upon the contract itself, he may nevertheless recover for money paid by him, or property delivered, or services rendered in accordance with and upon the faith of the contract. The law will raise an implied promise on the part of the other party to pay for what has been done in the way of part performance. But this right of recovery is not absolute. The plaintiff is entitled to compensation only under such circumstances as would warrant a recovery in case there was no express contract; and hence it must appear that the defendant has actually received, or will receive, some benefit from the acts of part performance. It is immaterial that the plaintiff may have suffered a loss because he is unable to enforce his contract." . . .

In the case under consideration the plaintiffs merely sustained a loss. Defendant received no benefit. Had he received a benefit, the law would imply an obligation to pay therefor. Having received no benefit, no obligation to pay is implied. The statute says that the contract defendant made with plaintiffs is unenforceable. Defendant therefore had the legal right to decline to carry it out. To require him to pay plaintiffs for losses and expenses incurred on the faith of the contract, without any benefit accruing to him, would, in effect, uphold a contract upon which the statute expressly declares no action shall be brought. The statute was enacted for the purpose of preventing frauds and perjuries. That it is a valuable statute is shown by the fact that similar statutes are in force in practically all, if not all, of the states of the Union. Being a valuable statute, the purposes of the lawmakers in its enactment should not be defeated by permitting recoveries in cases to which its provisions were intended to apply.

The contrary rule was announced by this court [in] McDaniel v. Hutcherson, 136 Ky. 412, 124 S.W. 384. There the plaintiff lived [in] Illinois. The defendant owned a farm in Mercer County, Ky. The defendant agreed with plaintiff that if plaintiff and his family would come to Kentucky and live with defendant the defendant would furnish the plaintiff a home during defendant's life, and upon his death would give plaintiff his farm. It was held that, although the contract was within the statute of frauds, plaintiff could recover his reasonable expenses in moving to Kentucky, and reasonable compensation for loss sustained in giving up his business elsewhere. Upon reconsideration of the question involved, we conclude that the doctrine announced in that case is not in accord with the weight of authority, and should be no longer adhered to. It is therefore overruled.

Judgment affirmed.

NOTE

In all of our states there are statutes modeled on the English Statute of Frauds of 1677. The key phrases in the original statute were that "no action shall be brought . . . whereby to charge the defendant . . . unless the agreement upon which such action shall be brought, or some memorandum or note thereof, shall be in writing, and signed by the party to be charged therewith, or some other person thereunto by him lawfully authorized." There are five classes of agreements for which this requirement is commonly imposed:

(1) contracts for the sale of an interest in land;

(2) contracts for the sale of goods for a price exceeding a specified amount ($500 or more in the Uniform Commercial Code, § 2–201);

(3) promises "to answer for the debt, default or miscarriage of another" (i.e., suretyship or guaranty);

(4) contracts "not to be performed within one year";

(5) contracts in consideration of marriage.

A discussion of the history and the general scope and operation of the statute of frauds can be found in the Appendix. The general aim of the statute, it seems, is to encourage parties to memorialize certain types of agreements by putting them in writing. The court in Boone v. Coe appears to have concluded that the lease agreement in question fell within the "not-to-be-performed-within-one-year" clause of the Kentucky statute, if not the land clause, which included long-term leases, as well. You should consult the Appendix on these two clauses generally.

Mobil Oil Exploration & Producing Southeast, Inc. v. U.S.

Supreme Court of the United States, 2000.
530 U.S. 604.

BREYER, J. Two oil companies, petitioners here, seek restitution of $156 million they paid the Government in return for lease contracts giving them rights to explore for and develop oil off the North Carolina coast. The rights were not absolute, but were conditioned on the companies' obtaining a set of further governmental permissions. The companies claim that the Government repudiated the contracts when it denied them certain elements of the permission-seeking opportunities that the contracts had promised. We agree that the Government broke its promise; it repudiated the contracts; and it must give the companies their money back. . . .

A description at the outset of the few basic contract law principles applicable to this action will help the reader understand the significance of the complex factual circumstances that follow. "When the United States enters into contract relations, its rights and duties therein are governed generally by the law applicable to contracts between private individuals." United States v. Winstar Corp., 518 U.S. 839, 895, 116 S.Ct. 2432, 135 L.Ed.2d 964 (1996) (plurality opinion) (internal quotation marks omitted). The Restatement of Contracts reflects many of the principles of contract law that are applicable to this action. As set forth in the Restatement of Contracts, the relevant principles specify that, when one party to a contract repudiates that contract, the other party "is entitled to restitution for any benefit that he has conferred on" the repudiating party "by way of part performance or reliance." Restatement (Second) of Contracts § 373 (1979) (hereinafter Restatement). The Restatement explains that "repudiation" is a "statement by the obligor to the obligee indicating that the obligor will commit a breach that would of itself give the obligee a claim for damages for total breach." Id., § 250. And "total breach" is a breach that "so substantially impairs the value of the contract to the injured party at the time of the breach that it is just in the circumstances to allow him to recover damages based on all his remaining rights to performance." Id., § 243.

As applied to this action, these principles amount to the following: If the Government said it would break, or did break, an important contractual promise, thereby "substantially impair[ing] the value of the contract[s]" to the companies, then (unless the companies waived their rights to restitution) the Government must give the companies their money back. And it must do so whether the contracts would, or would not, ultimately have proved financially beneficial to the companies. The Restatement illustrates this point as follows:

> A contracts to sell a tract of land to B for $100,000. After B has made a part payment of $20,000, A wrongfully refuses to transfer title. B can recover the $20,000 in restitution. The result is the same even if the market price of the land is only $70,000, so that performance would have been disadvantageous to B. *Id.,* § 373, Comment *a*, Illustration 1....

In 1981, in return for up-front "bonus" payments to the United States of about $156 million (plus annual rental payments), the companies received 10-year renewable lease contracts with the United States. In these contracts, the United States promised the companies, among other things, that they could explore for oil off the North Carolina coast and develop any oil that they found (subject to further royalty payments) provided that the companies received exploration and development permissions in accordance with various statutes and regulations to which the lease contracts were made "subject."...

In October 1992 ... petitioners joined a breach-of-contract lawsuit brought in the Court of Federal Claims. On motions for summary judgment, the court found that the United States had broken its contractual promise ..., in particular the provision requiring Interior to approve an Exploration Plan that satisfied [the Outer Continental Shelf Lands Act (OCSLA)'s requirements] within 30 days of its submission to Interior. The United States thereby repudiated the contracts. And that repudiation entitled the companies to restitution of the up-front cash "bonus" payments they had made....

The record makes clear (1) that OCSLA required Interior to approve "within thirty days" a submitted Exploration Plan that satisfies OCSLA's requirements, (2) that Interior told Mobil the companies' submitted Plan met those requirements, (3) that Interior told Mobil it would not approve the companies' submitted Plan for at least 13 months, and likely longer, and (4) that Interior did not approve (or disapprove) the Plan, ever. The Government does not deny that the contracts, made "pursuant to" and "subject to" OCSLA, incorporated OCSLA provisions as promises. The Government further concedes, as it must, that relevant contract law entitles a contracting party to restitution if the other party "substantially" breached a contract or communicated its intent to do so. Yet the Government denies that it must refund the companies' money....

[T]he Government argues that repudiation could not have hurt the companies. Since the companies could not have met the [Coastal Zone Management Act's] consistency requirements, they could not have explored (or ultimately drilled) for oil in any event. Hence, OBPA caused them no damage. As the Government puts it, the companies have already received "such damages as were actually caused by the [Exploration Plan approval] delay," namely, none. This argument, however, misses the basic legal point. The oil companies do not seek damages for breach of contract. They seek restitution of their initial payments. Because the Government repudiated the lease contracts, the law entitles the companies to that restitution whether the contracts would, or would not, ultimately have produced a financial gain or led them to obtain a definite right to explore. If a lottery operator fails to deliver a purchased ticket, the purchaser can get his money back—whether or not he eventually would have won the lottery. And if one party to a contract, whether oil company or ordinary citizen, advances the other party money, principles of restitution normally require the latter, upon repudiation, to refund that money. . . .

United States v. Algernon Blair, Inc.

United States Court of Appeals, Fourth Circuit, 1973.
479 F.2d 638.

CRAVEN, CIRCUIT JUDGE. May a subcontractor, who justifiably ceases work under a contract because of the prime contractor's breach, recover in quantum meruit the value of labor and equipment already furnished pursuant to the contract irrespective of whether he would have been entitled to recover in a suit on the contract? We think so, and, for reasons to be stated, the decision of the district court will be reversed.

The subcontractor, Coastal Steel Erectors, Inc., brought this action under the provisions of the Miller Act,* 40 U.S.C.A. § 270a et seq., in the name of the United States against Algernon Blair, Inc., and its surety. . . . Blair had entered a contract with the United States for the construction of a naval hospital in Charleston County, S.C. Blair had then contracted with Coastal to perform certain steel erection and supply certain equipment in conjunction with Blair's contract with the United States. Coastal commenced performance of its obligations, supplying its own cranes for handling and placing steel. Blair refused to pay for crane rental, maintaining that it was not obligated to do so under the subcontract. Because of Blair's failure to make payments for crane rental, and after completion of approximately 28 percent of the subcontract, Coastal terminated its performance. Blair then proceeded to complete the job with a new subcontractor. Coastal brought this action to recover for labor and equipment furnished.

The district court found that the subcontract required Blair to pay for crane use and that Blair's refusal to do so was such a material breach as to

---

* [Congress enacted the Miller Act in 1935; its purpose was to provide protections for subcontractors and suppliers on government projects. The legislation requires prime contractors to furnish payment bonds, for the benefit of subs and suppliers, as a condition of the finalization of contracts with the federal government. The Act gives a sub or supplier the right to bring suit on the bond if the prime contractor fails to pay the subcontract price in full within 90 days of completion of the sub's or supplier's performance. The suit, which is brought in the name of the United States, falls under the jurisdiction of federal district courts.—Eds.]

in quantum meruit = a reasonable amount

justify Coastal's terminating performance. This finding is not questioned on appeal. The court then found that under the contract the amount due Coastal, less what had already been paid, totaled approximately $37,000. Additionally, the court found Coastal would have lost more than $37,000 if it had completed performance. Holding that any amount due Coastal must be reduced by any loss it would have incurred by complete performance of the contract, the court denied recovery to Coastal. While the district court correctly stated the "'normal' rule of contract damages," we think Coastal is entitled to recover in quantum meruit.

In United States for Use of Susi Contracting Co. v. Zara Contracting Co., 146 F.2d 606 (2d Cir.1944), a Miller Act action, the court was faced with a situation similar to that involved here—the prime contractor had unjustifiably breached a subcontract after partial performance by the subcontractor. The court stated [at 610]:

> For it is an accepted principle of contract law, often applied in the case of construction contracts, that the promisee upon breach has the option to forego any suit on the contract and claim only the reasonable value of his performance.

. . . [T]he right to seek recovery under quantum meruit in a Miller Act case is clear. Quantum meruit recovery is not limited to an action against the prime contractor but may also be brought against the Miller Act surety, as in this case. Further, that the complaint is not clear in regard to the theory of a plaintiff's recovery does not preclude recovery under quantum meruit. Narragansett Improvement Co. v. United States, 290 F.2d 577 (1st Cir.1961). A plaintiff may join a claim for quantum meruit with a claim for damages from breach of contract.

In the present case, Coastal has, at its own expense, provided Blair with labor and the use of equipment. Blair, who breached the subcontract, has retained these benefits without having fully paid for them. On these facts, Coastal is entitled to restitution in quantum meruit.

> The 'restitution interest,' involving a combination of unjust impoverishment with unjust gain, presents the strongest case for relief. If, following Aristotle, we regard the purpose of justice as the maintenance of an equilibrium of goods among members of society, the restitution interest presents twice as strong a claim to judicial intervention as the reliance interest, since if A not only causes B to lose one unit but appropriates that unit to himself the resulting discrepancy between A and B is not one unit but two.

Fuller & Perdue, The Reliance Interest in Contract Damages, 46 Yale L.J. 52, 56 (1936).

The impact of quantum meruit is to allow a promisee to recover the value of services he gave to the defendant irrespective of whether he would have lost money on the contract and been unable to recover in a suit on the contract. Scaduto v. Orlando, 381 F.2d 587 (2d Cir.1967). The measure of recovery for quantum meruit is the reasonable value of the performance, Restatement of Contracts § 347 (1932); and recovery is undiminished by any loss which would have been incurred by complete performance. 12 Williston on Contracts § 1485 (3d ed. 1970). While the contract price may be evidence of reasonable value of the services, it does not measure the value of the performance or limit recovery. Rather, the standard for measuring the reasonable value of the services rendered is the amount for which such services could have been purchased from one in the plaintiff's position at the time and place the services were rendered.

Since the district court has not yet accurately determined the reasonable value of the labor and equipment use furnished by Coastal to Blair, the case must be remanded for those findings.[1] When the amount has been determined, judgment will be entered in favor of Coastal, less payments already made under the contract. . . . [T]he decision of the district court is [r]eversed and remanded with instructions.

NOTE

The sub, Coastal, was permitted to disregard terms of the contract by claiming "quantum meruit." What justifies this? Judge Learned Hand, faced with a similar claim in Schwasnick v. Blandin, 65 F.2d 354 (2d Cir.1933), considered just ahead, p. 132, remarked: "When [the promisee] has fulfilled the condition [of the promise], and the promisor has broken his promise, he [the promisee] sues upon that wrong. True, he does not seek the equivalent in money of what was promised; but it is the breach which gives him the power to call off the contract and raises the obligation to restore him to the status quo ante. The action is therefore a remedy for the breach, though it requires the equivalent of something which the promisor has never undertaken to perform." Judge Hand's last observation underscores the power of restitution in the setting of total breach. It is no objection that the remedy requires the defendant to do something that was never promised.

———

Kearns v. Andree

107 Conn. 181, 139 A. 695 (1928)

Plaintiff owned land on which stood a house then under construction but almost finished. Plaintiff contracted to sell the property to defendant for $8,500, of which $4,000 was to be paid in cash and the balance of $4,500 by the defendant's assumption of a first mortgage in that amount. There was no mortgage on the property at the time, but plaintiff undertook to find a lender and to execute a mortgage which defendant could then assume. Defendant thereafter became dissatisfied with the contract, but finally agreed to go through with it if plaintiff would make certain alterations and finish the house with paint and wallpaper chosen by defendant. Plaintiff did these things. Then defendant refused to complete the purchase. The way in which the house had been finished at defendant's urging made the property less saleable, but plaintiff finally succeeded in reselling the house and lot to another purchaser for $8,250, after repainting and repapering to meet that purchaser's objections. Plaintiff sued to recover (1) expenses incurred in finishing the house as defendant had requested, (2) repapering and repainting expenses to adapt it to the second purchaser's desires, and (3) the difference between the contract and resale prices. *Held*, the written contract was fatally indefinite as to the mortgage that defendant was to assume, since the identity of the mortgagee and the terms of payment were left

---

[1] Under the view of the case taken by the district court it was unnecessary to precisely appraise the value of services and materials rendered; an approximation was thought to suffice because the hypothetical loss had the contract been fully performed was greater in amount. [Most of the court's footnotes are omitted; this footnote is renumbered.—Eds.]

undetermined. The contract was therefore wholly unenforceable. But there are cases where a plaintiff who cannot bring an action on the contract for some reason other than his own default is permitted a recovery for the reasonable value of his services, without regard to whether those services have benefitted the other party. These are situations where "the law [will] imply an agreement" to make reasonable compensation. "The basis of that implication is that the services have been requested [by the defendant] and have been performed by the plaintiff in the known expectation that he would receive compensation, and neither the extent nor the presence of benefit to the defendant . . . is of controlling significance." The principle applies where, as here, the attempted contract, unenforceable though it was, showed the parties' expectation that compensation was to be made.

Accordingly, "the sums . . . for the repapering and repainting, which was done after the defendant refused to purchase [item (2)], do not fall within the [applicable] principles. . . . To allow them in this action would be, in effect, to permit a recovery upon an unenforceable contract, which may not be done. But, if the work done on the property to adapt it to the desires of the defendant [item (1)] was done under the terms of an oral agreement for the sale of the premises, in good faith, and in the honest belief that the agreement was sufficiently definite to be enforced, the plaintiff is entitled to recover reasonable compensation therefor. In fixing the amount of that compensation, however, a proper deduction must be made for any benefit that has accrued to the plaintiff himself by reason of the work he did upon the premises at the defendant's request."

NOTE

A situation similar to Kearns v. Andree was presented in Farash v. Sykes Datatronics, Inc., 59 N.Y.2d 500, 465 N.Y.S.2d 917, 452 N.E.2d 1245 (1983). Plaintiff claimed that the parties had entered into an agreement whereby defendant would lease for two years a building owned by plaintiff, who was to modify the building in certain respects and complete its renovation. Plaintiff made the modifications, but no agreement was ever signed and defendant refused to occupy the building. Plaintiff's suit survived defendant's motions in the trial court but was dismissed by the Appellate Division for failure to state a cause of action. The Court of Appeals (4–2), invoking *Kearns*, thought otherwise:

> Plaintiff pleaded three causes of action. . . . The first was to enforce an oral lease for a term longer than one year. This is clearly barred by the Statute of Frauds (Gen. Obligs. Law, § 5–703). The third cause of action is premised on the theory that the parties contracted by exchanging promises that plaintiff would perform certain work in his building and defendant would enter into a lease for a term longer than one year. This is nothing more than a contract to enter into a lease; it is also subject to the Statute of Frauds . . . [and] was properly dismissed.

> Plaintiff's second cause of action, however, is not barred by the Statute of Frauds. It merely seeks to recover for the value of the work performed by plaintiff in reliance on statements by and at the request of defendant. This is not an attempt to enforce an oral lease or an oral agreement to enter a lease, but is in disaffirmance of the

void contract and so may be maintained. . . . That defendant did not benefit from plaintiff's efforts does not require dismissal; plaintiff may recover for those efforts that were to his detriment and that thereby placed him in a worse position (see Kearns v. Andree, 107 Conn. 181, 139 A. 695 . . .).

In pleading the second cause of action, plaintiff's complaint had alleged that "[p]laintiff, in reliance on statements made [by] the defendant and at its request, performed work, provided labor and material to the defendant," and that "[d]efendant has failed to compensate the plaintiff for monies and other expenses incurred by the plaintiff in preparing the property . . . to the defendant's needs," resulting in damages of $400,000. It seems plaintiff's third cause of action also sought $400,000 damages, which sum, the dissenting judge pointed out, happened to be the annual rent allegedly agreed upon by the parties.

The dissent made two arguments to show that plaintiff's second cause of action was also barred by the statute of frauds. One was that quasi-contract was not available because the plaintiff had failed to demonstrate any "unjust enrichment." The other, premised on plaintiff's failure to allege a specific promise of compensation for the work to be performed, was that the second cause of action was nothing more than a rephrasing of the third—i.e., a claim for damages for defendant's alleged breach of an oral agreement to enter into a two-year lease. Accordingly, plaintiff should not be permitted to do indirectly what it cannot do directly.

Did the dissent have the better of the argument? It seems not, if the *Kearns* line of authority is to be believed.

A student commentator, writing long ago about recoveries for part performance of a contract (Note, 44 Harv.L.Rev. 623, 627 (1930)), concluded: "The true concept underlying the decisions seems to be not one of restitution based on quasi-contractual principles, but rather one of indemnification sounding in tort." Does that characterization fit cases such as *Algernon Blair*, *Kearns*, and *Farash*?

———————

Olsson v. Moore
590 N.E.2d 160 (Ind.Ct.App.1992)

Plaintiffs, the Moores, answered defendant Olsson's advertisement of a house and lot for sale. Plaintiffs indicated their willingness to buy the property, but because the Olsson house was unsuitable for winter habitation and the closing on the sale of their current home was imminent, plaintiffs asked permission to begin renovations on the house immediately. Olsson agreed, and by mid-December 1988, after placing the utility services in their name, plaintiffs had repaired the kitchen floor, renovated a total of four rooms, and reroofed the entire house. Throughout this period the parties were negotiating the purchase price of the property. Plaintiffs wanted more land than the one acre offered in the original advertisement. Forrest Moore testified he thought the deal was the house and 40 acres for $70,000; though Olsson had a survey drawn up for a sale of the house and five acres, he conceded there had been no definite agreement about acreage or price; Nancy Moore testified that the price changed so often she "couldn't keep track of it." On December 16, the day after plaintiffs closed on the sale of their home, the Olsson house was totally destroyed by a fire of accidental origin. Olsson was insured and collected $40,000 under his policy; no part of this payment was for the Moores' improvements. Plaintiffs then tendered a bill for $5,000 to Olsson, for labor and materials supplied, but Olsson refused to pay. Plaintiffs thereupon filed suit and, following a bench trial, were awarded a $4,800 judgment for their labor and materials. The judgment was affirmed on appeal.

Judge Baker, for the Court of Appeals, reasoned as follows: No contract of sale, written or oral, existed at the time of the fire; the parties' minds did not "meet" as required by standard contract doctrines. The fact neither party requested specific performance is further proof that, at most, negotiations produced only "an agreement to agree." Yet Olsson is wrong in contending "he received no benefit" from plaintiffs' improvements. Even if it be granted that plaintiffs' work was intended and understood to be for their own benefit, not Olsson's, "the fact remains that Olsson was the legal and equitable owner [on] the day of the fire" and, as Olsson concedes, "The Moores' work increased the value of the home." Thus, the conclusion that Olsson benefited from the improvements "is inescapable." Moreover, Olsson "consented to" and "sanction[ed]" the improvements, since he told plaintiffs they could do "whatever they needed to do" to make the house habitable when he might have stopped the work simply by giving notice. It is critical here that no contract of sale was made. Absent such a contract, the property remained exclusively Olsson's— because it cannot be said that "equitable ownership" passed to plaintiffs under the prevailing rule, followed in Indiana, that upon entry into a real estate contract the purchaser becomes the "equitable owner" who must assume the risk of loss from destruction of buildings or other improvements on the land. Olsson therefore "bear[s] the cost of the benefits he [received and] ratified," where there was "the opportunity to decline." The trial court's award of "the cost of [plaintiffs'] labor and expenses in bestowing the benefits" is proper.

———

COMMENT: THE "DOING AND GIVING" PROBLEM

An illustration accompanying Restatement, Second § 370 states: "A contracts to sell B a machine for $100,000. After A has spent $40,000 on the manufacture of the machine but before its completion, B repudiates the contract. A cannot get restitution of the $40,000 because no benefit was conferred on B." This illustration is intended to pose the so-called "doing and giving" problem, where, as concerns the restitution remedy, much depends on a determination of what it was that the party in breach "requested" and agreed to pay for. The grand case of Curtis v. Smith, 48 Vt. 116 (1874), is representative of the considerable authority that was the basis for the conclusion given by the restaters.

Plaintiff had contracted in writing to build stone "wing walls" around defendant's bakery, at a stipulated price for each completed yard of wall. Defendant repudiated before any installation had begun, though plaintiff had already quarried stone from his own quarry for use in building the walls. Plaintiff sued to recover the value of his work in quarrying the stone. The Vermont high court, reversing a judgment for plaintiff entered below on a jury verdict, held that the suit on the common counts for the value of plaintiff's work in quarrying the stone must fail. There simply was no ground for a recovery in restitution:

Q. Has benefit been conferred?

> If the completed work is not delivered so that the defendant re-
> ceives a benefit from it, the plaintiff, by his work and material, does
> not lay the foundation for a recovery under the common counts,
> however wrongfully the defendant may have prevented the comple-
> tion and delivery of such perfected work. . . . The defendants did not
> contract with the plaintiff for his labor, but for the wing walls com-
> pleted. The plaintiff, in quarrying stone from his own quarry, was
> not at work for the defendants, but was at work for himself, getting
> out material that he might or might not use in the erection of the
> wing walls. The stone when quarried belonged to the plaintiff, and
> he could put [it] to any use he saw fit. The plaintiff had performed
> no labor for the defendants, or that had enured to their benefit. . . .
> The *gravamen* of his complaint [is] that he has not been allowed to
> realize this expectation by reason of the act of the defendants in
> wrongfully terminating the contract. If he would recover for this, he
> should declare upon the contract specially, and for the breach there-
> of of which he now complains.

The wall builder's remedy, the court noted, was a suit for damages ("he
should declare upon the contract specially"). Note also that the result stated in
the Rest.2d § 370 illustration quoted above is that the seller "cannot get restitution." Nothing is said about damages. The emergence of the alternative
Dempsey theory of recovery—damages measured by loss through reliance on
the contract, not the expected profit—has no doubt meant that the need for the
restitution remedy is greatly lessened. Still, as *Boone*, *Kearns*, and *Farash* all
illustrate, a fair number of the "preparation" cases will involve agreements that
are unenforceable for some reason, often because a writing was not made. A
damage remedy is therefore unavailable, even one restricted to reliance loss.
The well-known case of Santoro v. Mack, 108 Conn. 683, 145 A. 273 (1929),
provides another example of the consequences when contractual efforts fall
short of the bargained exchange. The purchaser, relying on an oral contract for
the sale of land, employed an architect to draw plans for improvements and an
electrician to give cost estimates for wiring. Recovery for these expenditures
was denied, since the agreement was within the statute of frauds and the sums
expended were not "at the request" of the defaulting seller.

The most troubling cases remain those found in the Restatement's illustration reproduced above—substantial outlays to produce something that, by
virtue of the defendant's substantial breach, is never delivered or installed. The
product may have been planned with the special needs of the defendant in
mind. In Curtis v. Smith, for example, the activity required to produce the specified "wing walls"—the quarrying and the shaping of the stone—may have rendered the stone of little use for other building projects. What should be the
function of the restitution remedy in such cases? Can the bargain itself—the
terms of the exchange—provide a satisfactory basis for answering that question?

PROBLEM

B contracts with S to buy S's used car for $900, paying $100 down. S repudiates before the deal is carried through. The market value of the car at the

time of S's repudiation is proved to be $700. Is B entitled to restitution of the $100 payment?

————

Oliver v. Campbell

43 Cal.2d 298, 273 P.2d 15 (1954)

Plaintiff, a lawyer, agreed in writing to represent defendant in a pending action brought by defendant's wife for separate maintenance, later changed by amendment to an action for divorce. The contract provided for a total fee of $850. The divorce trial, at which plaintiff represented defendant, lasted 29 days. After the trial ended, the court indicated its intention to give defendant's wife a divorce, but before the court's findings were signed defendant dismissed plaintiff from the case and thereafter represented himself in the proceeding. The court then filed its findings in favor of the wife, and (by implication) it appears that a decree of divorce was entered. In this action based on the employment contract, the reasonable value of plaintiff's services was found to be $5,000. *Held*, plaintiff can recover only $300, the unpaid balance of the $850 contract fee. Where an employment contract is terminated by wrongful discharge before performance is completed, the contract does not operate as a limit on recovery. "Inasmuch as the contract has been repudiated by the employer before its term is up and after the employee has partly performed and the employee may treat the contract as 'rescinded,' there is no longer any contract upon which the employer can rely as fixing conclusively the limit of the compensation—the reasonable value of services recoverable by the employee for his part performance." But here the trial was at an end, the court had indicated its intention to give judgment for the wife, and all that remained was the signing of findings and judgment. Plaintiff had "in effect" performed and was therefore limited to the contract price, in accordance with the settled rule of Restatement, Contracts § 350: "The remedy of restitution in money is not available to one who has fully performed[,] . . . if the only part of the agreed exchange for such performance that has not been rendered by the defendant is a sum of money constituting a liquidated debt."

————

NOTE: DISCONTINUITY AT FULL PERFORMANCE

In *Algernon Blair*, had Coastal not stopped work when the general contractor refused to pay for crane rentals, but completed performance in full before bringing suit, would Coastal still recover in quantum meruit? Oliver v. Campbell provides a reliable guide as to the authorities.

One court has offered the following explanation for the rule applied in Oliver v. Campbell: "There is excellent reason to look to the terms of a contract . . . to govern the measure of compensation. The contract provisions will disclose, as they do in the instant case, what the contracting parties thought was appropriate, thus obviating an extended inquiry into external sources of information as to what may be fair compensation." Fay, Spofford & Thorndike, Inc. v. Massachusetts Port Authority, 7 Mass.App.Ct. 336, 387 N.E.2d 206 (1979). Another court has said that remedial rights in the event of a plaintiff's full performance are "rooted in the nature of the remedy that restitution affords," adding:

"[B]ecause the remedy in restitution is designed to prevent unjust enrichment of the party responsible for a material breach of an enforceable contract, the remedy is measured not by the loss suffered by the *injured* party but by the gain received by the party in breach." John T. Brady & Co. v. City of Stamford, 220 Conn. 432, 447, 599 A.2d 370, 377 (1991). Is there in fact "excellent reason" (perhaps "reasons") for limiting a party who has fully performed to a remedy "on the contract" when the other party's breach is a failure to pay the money price of that performance?

In Noyes v. Pugin, 2 Wash. 653, 27 P. 548 (1891), plaintiff had only partly performed when defendant breached the contract. The court said: "It is difficult to perceive why [plaintiff] should receive more compensation for the labor actually performed by him [than] he would have received for the same services had the contract not been broken by the [defendant]. The authorities which hold the contrary doctrine, and maintain that the plaintiff in such cases may recover what his labor was actually worth, without regard to the contract, proceed upon the theory that, if one party to an agreement sees fit to violate it, the law will then step in and imply a new and different one in favor of the other party to the contract. But we think it is rather the province of the law to provide remedies for enforcing contracts, and for indemnifying parties injured by their breach, than to make new and different ones."

There is one further point to keep in view. As the question which opened this Note suggests, a party facing the other's breach by nonperformance alone (e.g., *Algernon Blair*, where there was no explicit repudiation) may, by its manner of responding to the breach, affect the availability of the restitution remedy. Consider the situation in Clark–Fitzpatrick, Inc. v. Long Island R.R. Co., 70 N.Y.2d 382, 521 N.Y.S.2d 653, 516 N.E.2d 190 (1987). A construction contractor sued a railroad, alleging causes of action sounding in breach of contract, quasi-contract, fraud, and negligence. An appellate court agreed that the quasi-contract claim was properly dismissed below, saying: "The existence of a valid and enforceable written contract governing a particular subject matter ordinarily precludes recovery in quasi-contract for events arising out of the same subject matter. . . . [Of course,] where rescission of a contract is warranted, a party may timely rescind and seek recovery on the theory of quasi-contract. . . . It is impermissible, however, to seek damages in an action sounding in quasi-contract where the suing party has fully performed on a valid written agreement, the existence of which is undisputed, and the scope of which clearly covers the dispute between the parties. . . . Here [the] relationship between the parties was defined by a [full and complete] written contract. . . . Notwithstanding plaintiff's claim that defendant breached the contract, plaintiff chose not to rescind the agreement, but instead to complete performance . . . and sue to recover damages, which of course was plaintiff's right. Having chosen this course, however, plaintiff is now limited to recovery of damages on the contract, and may not seek recovery based on an alleged quasi-contract."

COMMENT: THE COMMON COUNTS AND RESTITUTION

Judge Craven's labeling of the recovery in *Algernon Blair* as "quantum meruit" (similar language was used in the *Boone* case) requires further explanation.

Quantum meruit describes a simplified and standardized form of pleading that is used to collect payment for services rendered. The pleading form typically reads as follows:

Work and Labor Done
(often called *quantum meruit*)
Title of Court and Cause

The plaintiff complains of the defendant and for cause of action alleges:

1. That on the ___ day of ___, 20__, in the county of ___, state of ___, the defendant was indebted to the plaintiff in the sum of $___, for the labor and services of the plaintiff, by him before that time done and bestowed in and about the business of the defendant, at his request, and being so indebted, the defendant, in consideration thereof, then and there promised the plaintiff to pay him the said sum of money on request.

2. That the defendant, though requested, has not paid the same, or any part thereof, to the plaintiff, but refused to do so.

Wherefore, plaintiff prays judgment against the defendant for the sum of $___, with interest thereon from the ___ day of ___, 20__, and costs of suit.

Virtually identical pleading forms are used for "goods sold and delivered" (often called *quantum valebat* or valebant) and for "money had and received." These two forms differ from quantum meruit only in that they mention different types of performances—goods or money rather than labor and services. This style of pleading alleges that after a performance was rendered, there was a subsequent promise to pay. For reasons explained below, the allegation of a subsequent promise is a mere formality; no such promise need be proved. These pleading forms, which disclose essentially nothing except the nature of the performance already rendered, are known as the "common counts." There are a few other less "common" counts (e.g., money lent, account stated, land sold and conveyed), but they have the same features and can be ignored for the present. The cryptic language and carefully designed ambiguity of the common counts present obviously great attractions to plaintiffs' lawyers. These features may help to explain the survival of the counts and their frequent use even today (recall, for example, the second cause of action in the *Farash* case). We need to know how and why they were invented, however, in order to throw some light into the dark corners where remedies aimed at unjust enrichment and those grounded on conventional theories of enforcement provide alternative routes to a money recovery.

The first point is that the early English lawyers (say, before 1500) were only vaguely aware of broad classifications such as the distinction between contract and tort. Their main concern was with the "forms of action," i.e., the writs with which common law actions were commenced. Before 1500, there were only three writs or forms of action that could be used to enforce duties that arose from contract, as that term would be understood today. One was the action of *covenant*, which was limited to the enforcement of promises under seal, a subject considered in Chapter 2. The writ of detinue could conceivably be used in some cases. It provided a remedy for an owner to recover possession of goods, and might possibly be used, for example, by a buyer in a sale of goods—after title had passed but before possession had been delivered. The writ that most nearly approached a generalized contract remedy was the writ of *debt*, which was not limited to liabilities arising from contract but could be used to collect a sum of money due for any reason, including contract, statute, or local custom. The most serious defect of the action of debt was that the defendant could escape liability altogether by "waging his law," that is, by securing twelve persons who were willing to swear that they believed the defendant told the truth in denying that the debt was owed. It is easy to understand the desire of litigants for an improved remedy by which they could escape from this archaism, whose main effect was to give incentives to perjury.

The escape route from the procedural inadequacies and hazards of the action of debt followed a tortuous course, becoming entangled along the way with the evolution of *trespass*—the form of action that always showed the greatest capacity for growth and change—and with the damage remedy that was to become the standard sanction of the common law for breach of contract. We make a giant leap over years of development during which the trespass action—originally designed to deal with violent breaches of the peace—had been extended to deal with miscellaneous wrongs that we would now call torts. This extended form of trespass acquired its own name—*trespass on the case*—and was gradually extended to provide a damage remedy for negligent acts that also involved breaches of promises, e.g., driving a nail too far into a horse's hoof while performing a promise to shoe the horse. In the early development, the action would lie only where a promisor performed negligently and caused injury ("misfeasance"); it was unavailable if the promisor failed to perform at all. In the sixteenth century, however, a major transition occurred when relief became available for "nonfeasance," failures to act as promised. With this transition accomplished, the breach of promise remedy through trespass on the case came to be recognized as sufficiently distinct to have a title of its own, *assumpsit* ("he undertook" or "he promised").

The action of trespass on the case and its offspring assumpsit could be brought in either the Court of King's Bench or the Court of Common Pleas; the older action of debt could be brought only in the Common Pleas. Since judges derived their income from litigants' fees, it is not surprising that competition for judicial business developed between these two central courts. The economic interest of the judges, combined with whatever attraction they found in law reform, led the King's Bench first to permit assumpsit to be used in any case where a new promise was made to pay a debt already due. An illustration would be a simple contract to sell goods—say, a horse for a £10 price. If the horse had been delivered to the buyer, the seller could sue in debt (Common Pleas) and recover £10. But if the buyer, having received the horse, had made a second promise to pay the overdue debt, the seller could sue in assumpsit (Common Pleas or King's Bench). A pleading form reflecting this extension developed, called *indebitatus assumpsit* ("being indebted, he promised"). You will see this phrase often, even today.

Indebitatus assumpsit (often called general assumpsit) was transformed into a complete substitute for debt, available whenever debt would lie, by the decision in Slade's Case, 4 Coke 926 (1602). This was a simple suit involving an express contract for the sale of a specific quantity of grain for £16. Plaintiff, the seller, alleged that the buyer, after the debt arose, had made a second promise to pay the £16 price. But plaintiff was unable to prove this. All the judges of England were assembled in solemn conclave; after extensive debate, they decided that the second promise did not have to be proved. The judges understood that by this pleading fiction they were making available to litigants a remedy to collect debts in which disputes over facts would be decided by juries, so that debtors could not escape payment by the wager of law, that is, simply by finding twelve friends willing to perjure themselves on the debtor's behalf. Thereafter, debt remained available, but it was a poor competitor with assumpsit and its more rational procedure. Eventually, debt faded out as a contract remedy and assumpsit occupied the field, with its "counts" or pleading forms becoming "common" indeed.

We must pursue the development of assumpsit a bit further. Consider the following situations:

> Case 1. Debtor borrows $3,000 from Creditor and promises repayment at the rate of $200 on the first of each month until the whole sum is paid. Debtor makes 10 payments (totaling $2,000) on time and at midpoint in the series also makes one extra prepayment of $500; the balance due is therefore $500. Forgetting about this extra $500 payment and calculating the balance to be $1,000, Debtor pays Creditor $1,000. Can Debtor recover the $500 over-payment made through mistake?

> Case 2. Owner of a car delivers it to Repairshop under an agreement calling for specified repairs for a price of $425. The repairs completed, Owner tenders $425 and demands the car. Repairshop refuses to return it unless paid $600. Owner pays this sum. Can Owner recover the $175 over-payment exacted by "duress"?

> Case 3. Jay Walker is run over in a street accident and lies unconscious on the curb. Dr. Smith, a physician, is called to the scene, renders services, and accompanies Walker in an ambulance to the hospital. There Dr. Smith administers further treatment but without success; Walker dies without ever regaining consciousness. Though no contract was ever made, should Dr. Smith be allowed to recover the reasonable value of the medical services from Walker's estate?

In the years after Slade's Case, while assumpsit was establishing itself as the principal remedy for breach of an express contract, the English courts began to hold that claims like these could be brought in general or indebitatus assumpsit. The appeal of claims of this type was that the defendant had been enriched by something the plaintiff had provided or done; allowing the defendant to retain the benefit without payment seemed unjust. It therefore mattered not in the least that the defendant had made no promise to repay the mistaken or coerced payment, or pay for unrequested services, for the English courts (and much later, the American courts) explained the result—recovery in assumpsit—by saying that a promise by the defendant to pay should be "implied." This fiction of a contract to ground assumpsit helped to popularize the term "quasi-contract" to describe a basis for restitution in law actions, ordinarily leading to money judgments, that has been greatly expanded in modern American law. The "quasi" is meant to indicate that liability does not rest on contract after all, and that, like other restitution remedies, the aim is to prevent the alleged unjust enrichment of one person at the expense of another. Such an objective indeed has broad dimensions, and a wide appeal. The suit by

Dr. Smith against Jay Walker's estate (Case 3 above) illustrates quasi-contract in its most obvious form—a recovery resting on an implication of law in circumstances wholly lacking any basis for finding an actual contract. To be sure, use of the term "quasi-contract" and talk of promises "implied in law" in such noncontractual settings produce confusion and, occasionally, unwarranted results. The failure of courts and commentators to settle on a common language to describe the restitutionary claim—especially when it arises in the absence of any semblance of promissory obligation—is no small part of the problem. But the historical terminology remains in use today, and you must be familiar with it.

We must emphasize again that the pleading forms of the "common counts" are entirely neutral and disclose nothing at all as to the source from which the debt arose, except the type of performance the plaintiff had supplied (rendering services, delivering goods, paying money). The counts also can be used to enforce a liability that arises through and is measured by the terms of an express contract, as in Slade's Case itself. How is this possible? As we have said, general assumpsit developed as a full substitute for the action of debt. It was only natural that courts and litigants, through use of the pleading forms of the common counts, should think the assumpsit action available to collect the "debt" arising through full performance of a contract to perform services or deliver goods in return for the payment of money. In Oliver v. Campbell, then, where the recovery was precisely the sum promised by express contract, a count for work and labor done (quantum meruit) would have been entirely suitable. This, of course, is not quasi-contract; plaintiff's recovery was limited to the contract price. The phrases quantum meruit and quantum valebat are probably most often used, however, to suggest a recovery that does not aim at all at enforcing a contract but, quite the contrary, at recovering the value of a performance rendered—enforcing restitution. This was the sense in which quantum meruit was used by Judge Craven in imposing on Algernon Blair, Inc. what was clearly viewed as quasi-contractual liability. It is the standard work of the restitution remedy where performance of a contract has been brought to a halt by one party's substantial breach.

We will not be concerned in general with the grounds for restitution, other than those that arise following a disruption (e.g., unforeseen events) or a substantial breach of an actual or supposed contract. The breach can be by the recipient of a requested performance (as in *Algernon Blair*) or by the performing party, who usually seeks restitution because a substantial default bars recovery on the contract. Because the common counts are used frequently in actions to enforce a contract, as well as to claim restitution in the absence of an enforceable contract, we stress again that you cannot reliably identify the basis of the action from the pleading form used. The problem is compounded by the great variety and irregularity of bargaining transactions that become derailed and require unwinding. It should be added that the law of restitution that emerged in the course of the nineteenth century has produced an assortment of remedies, many of which award not a money judgment but specific relief in one form or another (and thus are conceived of as "equitable"). We will see only a few of these remedies in this book. The point to be clear about at this stage is that restitution is not exclusively a "legal" or an "equitable" remedy; it is both, and it is routinely ordered in law and equity proceedings alike. Whether it is properly viewed as one or the other in a given case depends mainly on what is being sought by a claimant, money or something else.

It must also be said, however, that restitution's association with unjust enrichment—the origins of which, as the basis for an independent cause of action, lie largely in equity—invites talk of "equitable" factors and considerations, whatever the type of restitution claim. Since the restitution remedy is often focused on whether, in light of circumstances and the parties' conduct, a particular outcome is "fair" or "just," "equitable" or "inequitable," "conscionable" or "unconscionable," courts commonly speak of restitution as "equitable in nature." Kull, Rationalizing Restitution, 83 Cal. L.Rev. 1191 (1995), is helpful on these characterization questions. As the next case suggests, cases can arise in which, under a restitution measure, the conduct of the breaching party itself affects the calculation of damages.

Watson v. Cal-Three, LLC
Colorado Court of Appeals, 2011.
254 P.3d 1189.

CASEBOLT, J. . . . This case arises from a real estate project initiated by Brandon Park, LLC (Brandon Park). In 1999, Brandon Park borrowed money from First United Bank (FUB) to develop and construct townhomes in the project. In return, FUB obtained a first deed of trust. Watson agreed to guarantee repayment of the loan in exchange for a fee to be paid from the project's proceeds.

Calahan Construction Company (whose principal is Gordon Calahan) was the general contractor for the first phase of the project. When Brandon Park began having problems paying Calahan and others, Calahan initiated an action against it.

In June 2002, the parties mediated the dispute between Calahan and Brandon Park, resulting in the execution of a number of connected settlement agreements that resolved all issues. In one agreement, Brandon Park transferred all its rights in the project to Cal–Three, an entity formed by Gordon Calahan for the express purpose of becoming the owner and developer of the project.

Watson was not a party to that lawsuit but attended the mediation, was heavily involved in the negotiations and subsequent preparation of the modification and settlement agreements, and agreed to accept a reduced guarantor fee from the project. The agreements established a new fee due to Watson and a repayment plan for FUB and all other creditors, to be funded by the sale of completed townhomes.

In August 2002, Watson sent a notice to Cal–Three asserting that it was in default of the new agreements for failing to pay the outstanding balance on the FUB loan, failing to pay real estate taxes and homeowners association dues, failing to cure and resolve mechanics' liens, failing to obtain a construction loan, and failing to preserve and maintain the premises. Cal–Three did not respond to this notice.

On or about October 24, 2002, a sale of a completed townhome was scheduled to close. Watson sent a payoff letter to the title company in connection with the closing. Because the title company had asked Watson for the payoff amount for that one unit but Watson responded with a payoff amount for the entire project, the closing did not occur.

One day later, Watson commenced this action seeking a receiver, and one was appointed. In December 2002, having paid the remaining balance owed to FUB, Watson filed an action . . . to foreclose the deed of trust. Cal–Three did not appear . . . .

At the foreclosure sale in February 2003, Watson successfully bid on the property. The redemption period expired, and title to the property was transferred to Watson, who sold the remaining three completed townhome units in the project for $414,326.55 and the remaining raw land for $783,000.

Cal–Three eventually filed an answer and counterclaims in this, the receivership action, including claims for tortious interference with contract, breach of contract, and breach of the covenant of good faith and fair dealing. Watson responded to the counterclaims and included an affirmative defense of failure to mitigate damages.

Following a bench trial, the court ruled in favor of Cal–Three on its breach of contract and covenant of good faith claims. The court concluded that Cal–Three had not been in default on any obligation when Watson had sent the August 2002 letter. The court found that Cal–Three had been damaged in the amount of the profits realized by Watson—$414,326.55 resulting from the sales of the three existing townhomes, and $783,000 resulting from Watson's sale of the remaining raw land. The trial court also awarded Cal–Three $50,000 in punitive damages for what it found to be Watson's willful and wanton behavior.

After this appeal was filed and at issue, Watson and Local Service Corporation filed petitions in bankruptcy. Approximately three years later, the parties jointly petitioned for relief from the automatic stay, which the bankruptcy court granted. . . .

Watson asserts that the trial court's compensatory damages award must be vacated because it is premised upon an erroneous measure of damages and is not supported by the evidence. We agree that the damages award cannot stand.

In a breach of contract action, a plaintiff generally may recover the amount of damages that is required to place him in the same position he would have occupied had the breach not occurred. Pomeranz v. McDonald's Corp., 843 P.2d 1378, 1381 (Colo.1993). This amount is commonly called the "expectancy" interest.

The expectancy interest may include past lost profits. Colo. Nat'l Bank v. Friedman, 846 P.2d 159, 174 (Colo. 1993). As the court explained in Boyle v. Bay, 81 Colo. 125, 130-31, 254 P. 156, 158-59 (1927):

> [With respect to lost profits] it is . . . well settled that the profits which would have been realized had [a] contract been performed, and which have been prevented by its breach, are included in the damages to be recovered in every case where such profits are not open to the objection of uncertainty or of remoteness, or where from the express or implied terms of the contract itself, or the special circumstances under which it was made, it may be reasonably presumed that they were within the intent and mutual understanding of both parties at the time it was entered into.

Future lost profits, or those that a party would have made if it had been allowed to complete work under a contract, are also recoverable.

The expectancy interest is not the only interest that is protectable by an award of damages in a breach of contract case. While generally a mere breach of contract will not make a defendant liable for return of the profits it achieves as a consequence of breach, under some circumstances, a party to a contract may recover profits obtained by the breaching party under a remedy of disgorgement. EarthInfo, Inc. v. Hydrosphere Res. Consultants, Inc., 900 P.2d 113, 118–19 (Colo. 1995).

In *EarthInfo*, the parties had entered into contracts to develop a number of products to exploit information collected by governmental agencies. The contracts provided for payment of fixed fees as well as royalties. A dispute developed concerning whether certain new derivative products were subject to royalty payments. In the subsequent litigation, the trial court determined that EarthInfo had breached its contracts when it unilaterally suspended royalty payments. In a later damages hearing, both parties sought rescission of the contracts and restitution as a remedy. The trial court found that the breach was substantial, that damages would be inadequate, and that rescission was appropriate. It ordered EarthInfo to pay the net profits it had realized from the date it stopped making royalty payments until the rescission date.

On appeal, the Supreme Court phrased the issue as whether a party that breaches a contract can be required to disgorge to the nonbreaching party any benefits received as a result of the breach. The court explored the subtle conflict between the law of restitution and the law of contracts and, rather than announcing a general rule, held that whether the breaching party's profits can be awarded to a nonbreaching party must be determined on a case-by-case basis, a determination within the discretion of the trial court. If the breaching party's wrongdoing is intentional or substantial, or there are no other means of measuring the wrongdoer's enrichment, recovery of the breaching party's profits may be granted. The court stated:

> [T]he [trial] court must resort to general considerations of fairness, taking into account the nature of the defendant's wrong, the relative extent of his or her contribution, and the feasibility of separating this from the contribution traceable to the plaintiff's interest. Thus, the more culpable the defendant's behavior, and the more direct the connection between the profits and the wrongdoing, the more likely that the plaintiff can recover all defendant's profits. The trial court must ultimately decide whether the whole circumstances of a case point to the conclusion that the defendant's retention of any profit is unjust.

Id. at 119.

Accordingly, we reject Watson's contention that an award of Cal–Three's lost profits is the only measure of damages available here.

Further, contrary to Watson's argument, we do not perceive that disgorgement of profits is available only when rescission of a contract is sought and obtained. While those were the factual circumstances in *EarthInfo*, the court did not limit its holding only to cases in which rescission is sought. Indeed, Restatement (Third) of Restitution § 39(1) (Tentative Draft No. 4, 2005), which appears to formulate a general rule in synthesizing breach of contract cases allowing recovery of a defendant's profits, notes that liability in restitution with disgorgement of profits is an alternative to liability for contract damages measured by injury to the promisee.

Accordingly, the trial court did not err in employing the disgorgement of net profits remedy.

Here, the court concluded that Watson had entered into the settlement agreements in bad faith and that he had also exercised bad faith in responding to the townhome closing payoff request with a payoff for the entire project rather than the smaller amount agreed to in the settlement agreements. The court also concluded that Watson had acted deliberately in breaching the contracts and found that he had acted willfully and wantonly. The record supports the trial court's findings.

Watson testified that he provided the figure in the payoff letter, which ultimately led to Cal–Three's inability to sell the remaining units, because he believed the title company was requesting a payoff amount for the entire project as opposed to one unit. However, the letter indicated that the payoff was referring to the specific unit, not the entire project. The trial court found that Watson's testimony was not credible and that his payoff letter was sent in bad faith.

Watson asserted that Cal–Three breached its agreement by failing to pay the FUB loan, thus requiring that he pay it. The trial court held that no documentation supported this allegation and found Watson's testimony not credible and his position not defensible. Indeed, the settlement agreements provided for the payment of the FUB loan from the proceeds of the townhome sales.

Watson asserted that Cal–Three had failed to obtain a construction loan within the time allegedly required by the agreements. The trial court found that no deadline had been set in the agreements for obtaining the loan and that the failure to obtain a loan was due to the actions of Watson, not Cal–Three.

Watson testified that Cal–Three failed to pay real estate taxes on the project. The trial court found that there was no indication of delinquent taxes on the property and that the evidence available suggested Cal–Three had been paying taxes as required.

Watson testified that Cal–Three had failed to resolve numerous mechanics' liens. The trial court noted that no testimony or evidence was offered to support this position and the available evidence suggested the subcontractors were being paid pursuant to the escrow settlement agreement.

Watson testified that Cal–Three had failed to maintain the premises, make payments to the homeowners association, and pay utility bills. Again, the trial court found that Watson failed to provide any documentation in support of these allegations.

In our view, the trial court's findings are sufficient under *EarthInfo* to justify its exercise of discretion to order disgorgement of Watson's profits. The question remains, however, whether the trial court correctly determined Watson's profits. We conclude it did not do so.

Here, the trial court found that Watson's profit on the sale of the three units was $414,326.55 and that Watson sold the remaining raw land for $783,000. As a result, the court found Watson received profits of $1,197,326.55, and the court determined to award Cal–Three that sum as damages.

However, it was undisputed at trial that Watson had paid the FUB loan in full. It was likewise undisputed that the outstanding balance was $66,366.80 when he paid it, and that Cal–Three was liable for that sum.

But the trial court did not subtract or otherwise account for this amount in its award.

In addition, the court did not undertake to apportion the profits attributable to the benefits produced by Cal–Three and those earned by Watson's efforts and investment. While the burden of proving expenses to be deducted from gross profits generally will fall to the defendant, and the trial court found here that Watson had testified about expenses but had not provided documentation for them, we are loath to hold Watson fully accountable for failing to produce such evidence because Cal–Three requested damages in large part based upon a recovery of its lost profits, not a restitutionary recovery of Watson's profits. The vast majority of Gordon Calahan's damages testimony concerned Cal–Three's anticipated gross income and expenses, and he only fleetingly mentioned Watson's gross profits. Under these circumstances, we cannot conclude that Watson has failed to satisfy his burden to prove expenses.

Because the trial court made no findings with respect to the relative contributions of each party, or whether they are inseparable, we must remand the damages determination to the trial court. In light of the fact that the trial judge has recused herself, we conclude the proper remand is for a new trial on damages before a different judge. And because the decision to award disgorgement of profits as a remedy for breach of contract is a discretionary determination, we also conclude that Cal–Three should again be permitted to present evidence on its lost profits so that the court can determine whether to award its lost profits or order disgorgement of Watson's net profits. The court may also consider the factors set forth in *Restatement (Third) of Restitution* § 39 in reaching its conclusion. . . .

———

RESTATEMENT (THIRD) OF RESTITUTION AND UNJUST ENRICHMENT

§ 39. Profit From Opportunistic Breach

(1) If a deliberate breach of contract results in profit to the defaulting promisor and the available damage remedy affords inadequate protection to the promisee's contractual entitlement, the promisee has a claim to restitution of the profit realized by the promisor as a result of the breach. Restitution by the rule of this section is an alternative to a remedy in damages.

(2) A case in which damages afford inadequate protection to the promisee's contractual entitlement is ordinarily one in which damages will not permit the promisee to acquire a full equivalent to the promised performance in a substitute transaction.

(3) Breach of contract is profitable when it results in gains to the defendant (net of potential liability in damages) greater than the defendant would have realized from performance of the contract. Profits from breach include saved expenditure and consequential gains that the defendant would not have realized but for the breach, as measured by the rules that apply in other cases of disgorgement.

Comment:

a. General principles and scope; relation to other sections. In exceptional cases, a party's profitable breach of contract may be a source of unjust enrichment at the expense of the other contracting party. The law of restitution treats such cases in the same way that it treats other instances of intentional and profitable interference with another person's legally protected interests, authorizing a claim by the injured party to the measurable benefit realized as a result of the defendant's wrong. The claim described in this section is accordingly an instance of restitution for benefits wrongfully obtained. . . .

Judged by the usual presumptions of contract law, a recovery for breach that exceeds the plaintiff's provable damages is anomalous on its face. A breach of contract—whatever the actor's state of mind—is not usually treated in law as a wrong to the injured party of a sort comparable to a tort or breach of equitable duty. There is substantial truth, though not of course the whole story, in the Holmesian paradox according to which the legal obligation imposed by contract lies in a choice between performance and payment of damages. But the observation is most accurate where it matters least: in those transactional contexts where damages can be calculated with relative confidence as a full equivalent of performance.

By contrast, there are numerous legal relations—including some created by contract—in which a legal entitlement receives insufficient protection when the remedy for violation is limited to compensation in the form of damages. The traditional "inadequacy" test for the availability of equitable remedies may be largely a historical artifact, but it appropriately emphasizes this vital justification for supplemental relief. It is not generally the case, in short, that a person is free to choose whether to respect another's legal entitlement or pay damages for interference. It is precisely where a potential damage claim affords inadequate protection to a recognized entitlement that a court will enjoin a threatened interference. If a profitable interference has already occurred, the law of restitution allows a claim to disgorgement of profits, as an alternative to damages, in cases of intentional interference with legal entitlements of any kind.

Compared to other forms of legal entitlement, contract rights may often be easier to value in money; but they would be vulnerable to the same risks of underenforcement if the exclusive remedy for breach were an action for money damages. Where a party's contractual entitlement would be inadequately protected by the legal remedy of damages for breach, a court will often reinforce the protection given to the claimant by an order of injunction or specific performance. Restitution affords comparable protection after the fact, awarding the gains from a profitable breach of a contract that the defendant can no longer be required to perform.

The restitution claim described in this section is infrequently available, because a breach of contract that satisfies the cumulative tests of § 39 is rare. At the same time, the cases in which such a remedy is appropriate are generally uncontroversial and in some instances even well known. The innovation of the present section consists, not in proposing that defendants in such cases be liable to disgorge profits derived from a deliberate breach, but in stating a rule to generalize these commonly accepted outcomes. . . .

———

In the restitution cases considered up to this point, restitution served as an alternative path to recovery for the nonbreaching party. Cases also arise in which the breaching party asserts a restitution action. Notwithstanding the breach, this party attempts to recover the benefits that have been bestowed upon its contracting opposite. The two cases that follow present contrasting approaches. While the view put forward in the second case has largely prevailed, the view presented in the first remains an undercurrent in the law.

———

Stark v. Parker

Supreme Judicial Court of Massachusetts, 1824.
19 Mass. (2 Pick.) 267.

This was an action of *indebitatus assumpsit* brought to recover the sum of [$27.33], as a balance due for services rendered by the plaintiff on the defendant's farm. . . .

At the trial, . . . the defendant admitted that the plaintiff had performed the service set forth in the declaration, and for the price therein stated, and that he, the defendant, had paid him from time to time, before he left the defendant's service, money amounting in the whole to about [$36], and on account of his labor, but the defendant proved that the plaintiff agreed to work for him a year, for the sum of [$120], and that he, the defendant, agreed to pay him that sum for his labor. He also proved that the plaintiff voluntarily left his service before the expiration of the year, and without any fault on the part of the defendant, and against his consent.

The judge thereupon instructed the jury, that the plaintiff would be entitled to recover in this action a sum in proportion to the time he had served, deducting therefrom such sum, if any, as the jury might think the defendant had suffered by having his service deserted; and if such sum should exceed the sum claimed by the plaintiff, they might find a verdict for the defendant. The jury having returned a verdict for the plaintiff, the defendant filed his exceptions to this instruction. . . .

LINCOLN, J. This case comes before us upon exceptions filed. . . . The exceptions present a precise abstract question of law for consideration, namely, whether upon an entire contract for a term of service for a stipulated sum, and a part-performance, without any excuse for neglect of its completion, the party guilty of the neglect can maintain an action against the party contracted with, for an apportionment of the price, or a *quantum meruit*, for the services actually performed. . . . The direction to the jury was, "that although proved to them, that the plaintiff agreed to serve the defendant for an agreed price for a year, and had voluntarily left his service before the expiration of that time, and without the fault of the defendant, and against his consent, still the plaintiff would be entitled to recover of the defendant, in this action, a sum in proportion to the time he had served, deducting therefrom such sum, (if any,) as the jury might think the defendant had suffered by having his service deserted." If this direction was wrong, the judgment must be reversed, and the case sent to a new trial. . . .

It cannot but seem strange to those who are in any degree familiar with the fundamental principles of law, that doubts should ever have been entertained upon a question of this nature. . . . The true ground of legal demand in all cases of contracts between parties is, that the party claiming has done all which on his part was to be performed *by the terms of the contract*, to entitle him to enforce the obligation of the other party. It is not sufficient that he has given to the party contracted with, a right of action against him . . . .

Upon examining the numerous authorities, . . . it will be found, that a distinction has been uniformly recognised in the construction of contracts, between those in which the obligation of the parties is reciprocal and independent, and those where the duty of the one may be considered as a condition precedent to that of the other. In the latter cases, it is held, that the performance of the precedent obligation can alone entitle the party bound to it, to his action. It is assumed by [plaintiff's counsel], that the service of the plaintiff for a year was not a condition precedent to his right to a proportion of the stipulated compensation for that entire term of service, but that upon a just interpretation of the contract, it is so far divisible, as that consistently with the terms of it, the plaintiff, having labored for any portion of the time, may receive compensation *pro tanto*. That this was the intention of the parties is said to be manifest from the fact found in the case, that the defendant from time to time did in fact make payments expressly toward this service. [However] the parties may have intended between themselves, we are to look to the construction given to the contract by the court below. The jury were . . . instructed, that if the contract was entire, in reference alike to the service and the compensation, still by law it was so divisible in the remedy, that the party might recover an equitable consideration for his labor, although the engagement to perform it had not been fulfilled. The contract itself was not discharged; it was considered as still subsisting, because the loss sustained by the defendant in the breach of it was to be estimated in the assessment of damages to the plaintiff. A proposition apparently more objectionable in terms can hardly be stated. . . . The plaintiff sues in *indebitatus assumpsit* as though there was no special contract, and yet admits the existence of the contract to affect the amount he shall recover. The defendant objects to the recovery of the plaintiff [on] the express contract which has been broken, and is himself charged with damages for the breach of an implied one which he never entered into. The rule that *expressum facit cessare tacitum*, is as applicable to this, as to every other case. If the contract is entire and executory, it is to be declared upon. Where it is executed and a mere duty to pay the stipulated compensation remains, a general count for the money is sufficient. Numerous instances are indeed to be found in the books, of actions being maintained where the specific contract has not been executed by the party suing for compensation, but in every case it will be seen that the precise terms of the contract have been first held, either to have been expressly or impliedly waived, or the non-execution excused upon some known and settled principle of law. . . . Nothing can be more unreasonable than that a man, who deliberately and wantonly violates an engagement, should be permitted to seek in a court of justice an indemnity from the consequences of his voluntary act; and we are satisfied that the law will not allow it.

That such a contract as is supposed in the exceptions before us, expresses a condition to be performed by the plaintiff precedent to his right of action against the defendant, we cannot doubt. The plaintiff was to labor one year for an agreed price. The money was to be paid in compensation for the service, and not as a consideration for an engagement to serve. Otherwise, as no precise time was fixed for payment, it might as well be recovered before the commencement of the labor or during its progress, as at any subsequent period. While the contract was executory and in the course of execution and the plaintiff was in the employ of the defendant, it would never have been thought an action could be maintained for the precise sum of compensation agreed upon for the year. The agreement of the defendant was as entire on his part to pay, as that of the plaintiff to serve. The latter was to serve *one year*, the former to pay *one hundred and twenty dollars*. Upon the construction contended for by the plaintiff's counsel, . . . there is no rule by which the defendant's liability can be determined. The plaintiff might as well claim his wages by the month as by the year, by the week as by the month, and by the day or hour as by either. The responsibility of the defendant would thus be affected in a manner totally inconsistent with the terms of his agreement to pay for a year's service in one certain and entire amount. Besides, a construction to this effect is utterly repugnant to the general understanding of the nature of such engagements. The usages of the country and common opinion upon subjects of this description are especially to be regarded. . . . [I]n no case has a contract in the terms of the one under consideration, been construed by practical men to give a right to demand the agreed compensation, before the performance of the labor, and that the employer and employed alike universally so understand it. The rule of law is in entire accordance with this sentiment. . . .

The performance of a year's service was in this case a condition precedent to the obligation of payment. The plaintiff must perform the condition, before he is entitled to recover any thing under the contract, and he has no right to renounce his agreement and recover upon a *quantum meruit*. . . . The decisions in the English cases express the same doctrine, and the principle is fully supported by all the elementary writers.

But it has been urged, that whatever may be the principle of the common law, and the decisions in the courts of New York on this subject, a different rule of construction has been adopted in this commonwealth; and we are bound to believe that such has sometimes been the fact, from the opinion of the learned and respectable judge who tried this cause, and from instances of similar decisions cited at the bar, but not reported. The occasion of so great a departure from ancient and well established principles cannot well be understood. It has received no sanction at any time from the judgment of this Court within the period of our Reports. . . . The law indeed is most reasonable in itself. It denies only to a party an advantage from his own wrong. It requires him to act justly by a faithful performance of his own engagements, before he exacts the fulfilment of dependent obligations on the part of others. It will not admit of the monstrous absurdity, that a man may voluntarily and without cause violate his agreement, and make the very breach of that agreement the foundation of an action which he could not maintain under it. Any apprehension that this rule may be abused to the purposes of oppression, by holding out an inducement to the employer, by unkind treatment near the close of a term of service, to drive the laborer from his engagement, to the sacrifice of his wages, is wholly groundless. It is only in cases where the desertion is voluntary and without cause on the part of the laborer, or fault or consent on the part of the employer, that the principle applies. Wherever there is a reasonable excuse, the law allows a recovery. To say that this is not sufficient protection, that an excuse mtay in fact exist in countless secret and indescribable circumstances, which from their very nature are not susceptible of proof, or which, if proved, the law does not recognise as adequate, is to require no less than that the law should *presume* what can never legally be established, or should admit that as *competent*, which by positive rules is held to be wholly *immaterial*. We think well established principles are not thus to be shaken, and that in this commonwealth more especially, where the important business of husbandry leads to multiplied engagements of precisely this description, it should least of all be questioned, that the laborer is worthy of his hire, only upon the performance of his contract, and as the reward of fidelity.

The judgment of the Court of Common Pleas is reversed, and a new trial granted at the bar of this Court.

————

Britton v. Turner

Supreme Court of New Hampshire, 1834.
6 N.H. 481.

[Plaintiff agreed to work on defendant's farm for one year, from March 1831 to March 1832, at a wage of $120 for the year. After working until December 27, 1831, just over 9½ months, plaintiff abandoned performance. Plaintiff's suit in assumpsit included a count in quantum meruit alleging the worth of the work done to be $100. The defense was that the work had been done under a "special contract" which was unfulfilled, though defendant offered no evidence of damages resulting from plaintiff's departure.

The trial judge instructed the jury that plaintiff was entitled to recover under the quantum meruit count what his labor "was reasonably worth," even though he had left the job without defendant's consent and without good cause. The jury gave plaintiff a verdict for $95.]

PARKER, J. . . . It may be assumed, that the labor performed by the plaintiff, and for which he seeks to recover a compensation in this action, was commenced under a special contract to labor for the defendant the term of one year, for the sum of one hundred and twenty dollars, and that the plaintiff has labored but a portion of that time, and has voluntarily failed to complete the entire contract. It is clear, then, that he is not entitled to recover upon the contract itself. . . . But the question arises, can the plaintiff . . . recover a reasonable sum for the service he has actually performed, under the count in *quantum meruit*. Upon this, and questions of a similar nature, the decisions to be found in the books are not easily reconciled.

It has been held, upon contracts of this kind for labor to be performed at a specified price, that the party who voluntarily fails to fulfil the contract by performing the whole labor contracted for, is not entitled to recover any thing for the labor actually performed, however much he may have done towards the performance, and this has been considered the settled rule of law upon this subject. [Stark v. Parker, 2 Pick. 267] That such rule in its operation may be very unequal, not to say unjust, is apparent.

A party who contracts to perform certain specified labor, and who breaks his contract in the first instance, without any attempt to perform it, can only be made liable to pay the damages which the other party has sustained by reason of such non performance, which in many instances may be trifling—whereas a party who in good faith has entered upon the performance of his contract, and nearly completed it, and then abandoned the further performance—although the other party has had the full benefit of all that has been done, and has perhaps sustained no actual damage—is in fact subjected to a loss of all which has been performed, in the nature of damages for the non fulfilment, of the remainder, upon the technical rule, that the contract must be fully performed in order to a recovery of any part of the compensation. By the operation of this rule, then, the party who attempts performance may be placed in a much worse situation than he who wholly disregards his contract, and the other party may receive much more, by the breach of the contract, than the injury which he has sustained by such breach, and more than he could be entitled to were he seeking to recover damages by an action.

The case before us presents an illustration. Had the plaintiff in this case never entered upon the performance of his contract, the damage could not probably have been greater than some small expense and trouble incurred in procuring another to do the labor which he had contracted to perform. But having entered upon the performance, and labored nine and a half months, the value of which labor to the defendant as found by the jury is $95, if the defendant can succeed in this defence, he in fact receives nearly five sixths of the value of a whole year's labor, by reason of the breach of contract by the plaintiff, a sum not only utterly disproportionate to any probable, not to say possible damage which could have resulted from the neglect of the plaintiff to continue the remaining two and an half months, but altogether beyond any damage which could have been recovered by the defendant, had the plaintiff done nothing towards the fulfilment of his contract.

[In an omitted passage, the court noted the leading case of Lantry v. Parks, 8 Cow. 63 (N.Y.1827), which held that an employee who left a job after completing just over 10 months of a one-year contract could recover nothing for his labor.]

There are other cases, however, in which principles have been adopted leading to a different result. It is said, that where a party contracts to perform certain work, and to furnish materials, as, for instance, to build a house, and the work is done, but with some variations from the mode prescribed by the contract, yet if the other party has the benefit of the labor and materials he should be bound to pay so much as they are reasonably worth. . . . It is in truth virtually conceded in such cases that the work has not been done, for if it had been, the party performing it would be entitled to recover upon the contract itself. . . .

Those cases are not to be distinguished, in principle, from the present, unless it be in the circumstance, that where the party has contracted to furnish materials, and do certain labor, as to build a house in a specified manner, if it is not done according to the contract, the party for whom it is built may refuse to receive it—elect to take no benefit from what has been performed—and therefore if he does receive, he shall be bound to pay the value—whereas in a contract for labor, merely, from day to day, the party is continually receiving the benefit of the contract under an expectation that it will be fulfilled, and cannot, upon the breach of it, have an election to refuse to receive what has been done, and thus discharge himself from payment. But we think this difference in the nature of the contracts does not justify the application of a different rule in relation to them.

The party who contracts for labor merely, for a certain period, does so with full knowledge that he must, from the nature of the case, be accepting part performance from day to day, if the other party commences the performance, and with knowledge also that the other may eventually fail of completing the entire term. If under such circumstances he actually receives a benefit from the labor performed, over and above the damage occasioned by the failure to complete there is as much reason why he should pay the reasonable worth of what has thus been done for his benefit, as there is when he enters and occupies the house which has been built for him, but not according to the stipulations of the contract, and which he perhaps enters, not because he is satisfied with what has been done, but because circumstances compel him to accept it such as it is. . . .

If on [a] failure to perform the whole, the nature of the contract be such that the employer can reject what has been done, and refuse to receive any benefit from the part performance, he is entitled so to do, and in such case is not liable to be charged, unless he has before assented to and accepted of what has been done, however much the other party may have done towards the performance. He has in such case received nothing, and having contracted to receive nothing but the entire matter contracted for, he is not bound to pay, because his express promise was only to pay on receiving the whole, and having actually received nothing the law cannot and ought not to raise an implied promise to pay. But where the party receives value—takes and uses the materials, or has advantage from the labor, he is liable to pay the reasonable worth of what he has received. 1 Camp. 38, Farnsworth v. Garrard. And the rule is the same whether it was received and accepted by the assent of the party prior to the breach, under a contract by which, from its nature, he was to receive labor, from time to time until the completion of the whole contract; or whether it was received and accepted by an assent subsequent to the performance of all which was in fact done. If he received it under such circumstances as precluded him from rejecting it afterwards, that does not alter the case—it has still been received by his assent.

In fact we think the technical reasoning, that the performance of the whole labor is a condition precedent, and the right to recover any thing dependent upon it—that the contract being entire there can be no apportionment—and that there being an express contract no other can be implied, even upon the subsequent performance of service—is not properly applicable to this species of contract, where a beneficial service has been actually performed; for we have abundant reason to believe, that the general understanding of the community is, that the hired laborer shall be entitled to compensation for the service actually performed, though he do not continue the entire term contracted for, and such contracts must be presumed to be made with reference to that understanding, unless an express stipulation shows the contrary. . . .

It is easy, if parties so choose, to provide by an express agreement that nothing shall be earned, if the laborer leaves his employer without having performed the whole service contemplated, and then there can be no pretence for a recovery if he voluntarily deserts the service before the expiration of the time.

The amount, however, for which the employer ought to be charged, where the laborer abandons his contract, is only the reasonable worth, or the amount of advantage he receives upon the whole transaction, . . . and, in estimating the value of the labor, the contract price for the service cannot be exceeded. . . . If a person makes a contract fairly he is entitled to have it fully performed, and if this is not done he is entitled to damages. He may maintain a suit to recover the amount of damage sustained by the non performance.

The benefit and advantage which the party takes by the labor, therefore, is the amount of value which he receives, if any, after deducting the amount of damage; and if he elects to put this in defence he is entitled so to do, and the implied promise which the law will raise, in such case, is to pay such amount of the stipulated price for the whole labor, as remains after deducting what it would cost to procure a completion of the residue of the service, and also any damage which has been sustained by reason of the non fulfilment of the contract.

If in such case it be found that the damages are equal to, or greater than the amount of the labor performed, so that the employer, having a right to the full performance of the contract, has not upon the whole case received a beneficial service, the plaintiff cannot recover.

This rule, by binding the employer to pay the value of the service he actually receives, and the laborer to answer in damages where he does not complete the entire contract, will leave no temptation to the former to drive the laborer from his service, near the close of his term, by ill treatment, in order to escape from payment; nor to the latter to desert his service before the stipulated time, without a sufficient reason; and it will in most instances settle the whole controversy in one action, and prevent a multiplicity of suits and cross actions. . . .

Applying the principles thus laid down, . . . the plaintiff is entitled to judgment on the verdict. The defendant . . . does not appear to have offered evidence to show that he was damnified by [the] breach, or to have asked that a deduction should be made upon that account. The direction to the jury was therefore correct, that the plaintiff was entitled to recover as much as the labor performed was reasonably worth, and the jury appear to have allowed a *pro rata* compensation, for the time which the plaintiff labored in the defendant's service. . . . Judgment on the verdict.

NOTE

Should the restitution claim of the employee who quits without legal justification be affected by the moral quality of the employee's conduct? For a long, long time in this country, employees who abandoned employment contracts without compelling reason were refused relief in restitution, even though in other settings—e.g., a purchaser's default under a land contract—the character or quality of the breach might well be accorded less weight by the courts. Where the employee, discharged for "cause" (a good reason), had nevertheless made an effort to perform, courts adhering to the strict view occasionally softened their resistance to quasi-contractual relief. Today, though prediction is not easy (i.e., cases granting an employee restitution, without much attention given the reasons why performance was abandoned or proved defective, continue to appear regularly in the reports), the strictest tests probably are still applied to defaulters under service contracts not involving the construction or repair of buildings. See, e.g., Bright v. Ganas, 171 Md. 493, 189 A. 427 (1937) (misconduct amounting to "moral depravity"—here, revealing a fixation on the employer's spouse—bars all recovery, on an express contract and in quantum meruit for work already done); Stiff v. Associated Sewing Supply Co., 436 N.W.2d 777 (Minn.1989) ("gross misconduct" involving dishonesty and disloyalty triggers common law's longstanding "forfeiture doctrine," under which employer owes employee nothing).

———

Thach v. Durham

120 Colo. 253, 208 P.2d 1159 (1949)

This case involved a sale of sheep out of which a defaulting buyer sought restitution of a $3,100 down payment. The court rejected Professor Williston's suggestion that, to prevent serious forfeiture, equitable principles might require the seller to account for the excess of payment received over the damage suffered. "Such a requirement would place on the seller willing to perform his contract the burden of establishing the amount of his damage, which might frequently be uncertain and impossible of accurate determination; it would require him to hold payments received on the purchase price available for refund in case the purchaser tired of his bargain; in brief, it would deprive the seller of the protection which it was the very purpose of the down payment to furnish; it would encourage the violation of contracts and promote litigation. The rule as laid down by the decisions seems to exist independent of any provision in the contract for forfeiture or liquidated damages. It is generally just. . . . One who breaks his contract should not be favored over one who takes his loss and faithfully completes performance, nor should he be favored over the other party to the contract who is willing to perform. In situations where the rule effects injustice;—where equitable grounds of fraud or surprise or unavoidable accident or ignorance, not willful, appeal to the conscience of the court, equity will intervene. None such here appear, and the trial court erred in allowing plaintiff recovery of the down payment."

[The solutions adopted by the Uniform Commercial Code for restitution to a defaulting buyer of goods appear in § 2–718, which was applied in Neri v. Retail Marine Corp., supra p. 30. The defaulting seller of goods, under UCC 2–607, is allowed recovery for partial deliveries at an apportioned contract rate—minus the buyer's § 2–713 damages, of course. Observe that neither § 2–718 nor § 2–607 makes any distinctions based on the motive or moral excuse for the breach.]

———

NOTE: THE "GRAND TRADITION"

The opinion in Britton v. Turner warrants a brief word on judicial style. As Stark v. Parker suggests, the great weight of authority was contrary to the *Britton* result. Justice Parker's effort, under any test of balloting, surely qualifies for the Contracts Hall of Fame. It seems appropriate to recall the following passage from Professor Karl Llewellyn's memorable discussion of judges and judging (The Bramble Bush 157–158 (1951)):

> But I am concerned here with one special phase of the conditioning machinery of judges which goes not only unplanned but substantially unnoticed: that of the period-style of the law-crafts. It seems to me essential to health of our law and legal work that student, bar and bench should know that the Grand Tradition of the Common Law is our rightful heritage and needs complete and conscious recapture. They should read enough in the reports of the 1830's or 1840's (and a single volume read in sequence is commonly enough) to recognize as a prevailing style a handling of material as essentially made up of principle rather than of mere precedent, and of that finer type of principle which has perceptible reason and

makes perceptible sense in life. They should come to recognize the court's steady quest for rules which satisfy the needs of the Grand Tradition—each rule with a singing reason apparent on its face, each rule a rule whose reason guides and often even controls application according to the double maxim: *the rule follows where its reason leads; where the reason stops, there stops the rule.* They should come to recognize the steady and open checking of results against sense and decency as an of-courseness of our system of precedent when that system is working right; to recognize as of the essence a following because reason dictates following, a distinguishing or developing or shift in direction because reason dictates as the case may be distinction or development or shift.

Only then can student or bar or bench perceive that the conceptions of precedent as a static something, of movement as queer or improper or "departure," of figuring a court's prospective result without taking full account of the guidance the court rightly seeks *also* from its sense of decency and sense—that such conceptions are an aberration which crept upon and into lawyers' thinking in those least happy days of our legal system, the 80's and 90's of the Nineteenth Century. Not every court fell prey to the new formal style of work at the same time.... But the thinking of the whole bar about the proper way of judicial work had taken shape by 1910 as if the Grand Tradition had never been. It is against a rediscovery of the latter that student, bar and bench can then come, and come at once, to recognize that the picture of our appellate courts over the past thirty years, and increasingly with each of the decades, is one not of departing from the "good" old ways but rather of a groping, almost instinctive struggle to recapture the truly good and older ways which to the discredit of the work of law had slid into the bog.

Of course there is confusion when courts seek to work in the Grand Manner but still seek to write in the Formal Style. For esthetic comfort, work and opinion should match in style. For clarity of mind in judging, a man's verbal tools should fit comfortably into the jobs he is seeking to do with them. For consistency of results, a man needs conscious knowledge of the kind of result he has the job of gunning for—else again and again, and quite unpredictably, he fails to aim or aims in the wrong direction. Finally, for the sure pride of craft and craftsmanship which comforts and strengthens, which gives courage and infuses beauty and vision, for that a man needs not only personal knowledge of his finer craft traditions, but recognition by his fellows that he has such knowledge and that he works with it in the little as in the large.

———

Pinches v. Swedish Evangelical Lutheran Church

Supreme Court of Errors of Connecticut, 1887.
55 Conn. 183, 10 A. 264.

BEARDSLEY, J. The plaintiff claims to recover upon the counts for work and materials furnished in the erection of a church edifice for the defendants. A written contract was entered into by the parties, providing that the plaintiff should erect the edifice upon the land of the defendants, in accordance with certain plans and specifications. The plaintiff completed the building on the twenty-first day of January, 1885, when the defendants entered into the full possession and occupancy of the same. The building varies from the requirements of the contract in several material particulars. The ceiling is two feet lower, the windows are shorter and narrower, and the seats are narrower than the specifications require, and there are some other variations and omissions. The defect in the height of the ceiling is due to the combined error of the plaintiff and the defendants' architect. The other changes and omissions occurred through the inadvertence of the plaintiff and his workmen. The defendants knew of the change in the height of the ceiling when they took possession of the building, and of the changes in the windows and seats shortly afterwards, and objected to the changes as soon as they discovered them.

The plaintiff, in doing the work and furnishing the materials, acted in good faith, and the building, as completed, is reasonably adapted to the wants and requirements of the defendants, and its use is beneficial to them. It would be practically impossible to make the building conform to the contract without taking it partially down and rebuilding it. The defendants . . . offered evidence to prove the amount it would cost to make the building conform to the contract; claiming that they were entitled to such sum as damages. The court excluded the evidence, and the only error assigned is the exclusion of that evidence. The defendants' claim rests upon the assumption that the liability of the plaintiff to damages is not affected by the fact that his deviation from the contract was unintentional, nor by the advantageous use of the building, but that it is the same as it would have been if he had willfully departed from the contract, and they had rejected the building, and received no benefit from it.

The defendants' claim is undoubtedly supported by decisions of courts of eminent authority in England and this country, which hold that no recovery can be had for labor or materials furnished under a special contract, unless the contract has been performed, or its performance has been dispensed with by the other party.

The hardship of this rule upon the contractor who has undesignedly violated his contract, and the inequitable advantage it gives to the party who receives and retains the benefit of his labor and materials, has led to its qualification; and the weight of authority is now clearly in favor of allowing compensation for services rendered and materials furnished under a special contract, but not in entire conformity with it, provided that the deviation from the contract was not willful, and the other party has availed himself of and been benefited by such labor and materials, and, as a general rule, the amount of such compensation is to depend upon the extent of the benefit conferred, having reference to the contract price for the entire work. . . . In cases where only some additions to the work are required to finish it according to the contract, or where . . . the defects in it may be remedied at a reasonable expense, it seems proper to deduct from the contract price the sum which it would cost to complete it, as was done in that case.

In the present case the result of the plaintiff's labor and materials is a structure adapted to the purpose for which it was built, and of which the defendants are in the use and enjoyment, but which cannot be made to con-

form to the special contract, except by an expenditure which would probably deprive the plaintiff of any compensation for his labor.

We think that the court below properly deducted from the contract
price the amount of the diminution in the value of the building by reason of
the plaintiff's deviation from the contract. There is no error.

PARK, C.J., and CARPENTER, J., concurred. PARDEE and LOOMIS, JJ.,
dissented.

NOTE

Judge Learned Hand's analysis in Schwasnick v. Blandin, 65 F.2d 354 (2d
Cir.1933), may be helpful here. A lumberman who had contracted to cut timber
on defendant's land left the job when defendant, claiming the work was defective, refused to pay a salary installment. The lumberman then sued on the
common counts and recovered a judgment based on a jury's verdict.

Judge Hand reversed and remanded the case for a new trial. The trial
court's charge to the jury was found to be erroneous in that the jury was told
that (1) if plaintiff had failed to perform the work in a workmanlike manner,
even in "bad faith," he might nevertheless recover the reasonable value of his
services; and (2) defendant had the burden of proving that the plaintiff had
broken the contract. Observing also that the "whole action was misconceived"
below (the case apparently was tried as one in special assumpsit for damages,
when in fact it "could be nothing else" but on the counts for restitution), Judge
Hand declared:

> When the promisee has not performed, he obviously cannot re-
> cover on the [defendant's] promise.... Yet when the default is not
> willful and deliberate, it is generally agreed that he may recover so
> much as his efforts have actually benefited the promisor. [Citing
> cases, including Pinches.] The theory is that it is unjust for the
> promisor to profit, even though his promise has never become abso-
> lute. Furthermore, if the promisee has performed so far as he has
> gone, and the promisor breaks his promise, the promisee may aban-
> don the contract and sue for restitution, in which he can recover the
> reasonable value of his services, measured by what he could have
> got for them in the market, and not by their benefit to the
> promisor....

> This difference in the recovery is in accord with principle. When
> the promisee has not fulfilled the condition of the promise, and
> cannot charge the promisor with a breach, he may invoke only the
> equitable intervention of a court, though the remedy is legal in form.
> Justice demands no more than that the promisor shall not profit at
> the promisee's expense....

> The charge upon the burden of proof was [also wrong], because
> if the plaintiff wished ... to recover on the theory that though he
> had not performed, he was not in willful and deliberate default, he
> was ... bound to prove that he was not, since that too was a condi-
> tion upon the implied obligation to restore any benefits received....
> [T]he burden was on him to prove the amount of that benefit; that
> is, by how much the defendants were enriched, notwithstanding any
> injuries done to their [land, tools, or timber]. [T]he jury should have

been told to find the net benefit of the plaintiff's services to the defendant after deducting any injuries so done by defective work.

Observe Judge Hand's assertion that the law's different treatment of the restitution recovery when it is the plaintiff, not the defendant, who is in substantial default is "in accord with principle." Is it difficult to find the "principle" for defining the objective of restitution differently in cases like *Britton* or *Schwasnick*?

Putting the willfulness disqualification aside, it is fair to say that courts have not been in agreement on the principles for determining whether the plaintiff's own nonperformance precludes a restitution remedy. In some places (the state of New York, for one), it has long been true that a building contractor whose work fails to add up to "substantial performance" is denied relief in quasi-contract altogether. Steel Storage & Elevator Constr. Co. v. Stock, 225 N.Y. 173, 121 N.E. 786 (1919), remains the leading authority. The view with a much larger following holds that a contractor who fails to satisfy the test of substantial performance may recover in quasi-contract for the value of work done (less, of course, the other's damages). E.g., Levan v. Richter, 152 Ill.App.3d 1082, 504 N.E.2d 1373 (1987). We will see more of these doctrines in this book, especially "substantial performance."

———

Kelley v. Hance

108 Conn. 186, 142 A. 683 (1928)

Plaintiff agreed to excavate to the proper level and construct a concrete sidewalk and curb in the front of defendant's property, for a price of $420. Plaintiff removed a strip of earth, 12 feet wide and 8 feet deep, then left the premises and did not return. Defendant notified plaintiff that the contract was cancelled. Plaintiff sued to recover the reasonable value of the work done, which was found to be $158.60, and in the trial court recovered judgment for that amount minus $25, the value of earth removed by plaintiff. *Held*, reversed. In a construction contract like this a contractor who has deviated slightly from the contract, not willfully but in good faith, can recover if there has been a "substantial performance" (citing *Pinches*). Even where the performance is not substantial but the breach is merely negligent, recovery can be allowed, not on the contract but in quasi-contract. Also, a voluntary acceptance of benefits may raise an implied promise, but acceptance will not be implied from a mere retention of possession of land on which work has been done where the benefit cannot be returned. Here, however, plaintiff abandoned the work without justification before any part of the sidewalk and curb was built and no acceptance by defendant has been shown. Plaintiff can recover nothing.

———

NOTE: "WILLFUL" BREACH

As Learned Hand noted in *Schwasnick*, a "willful and deliberate" breach—this phrase was written into the first Restatement, § 357—is commonly said to preclude restitution (indeed, all relief). An "intentional" deviation from a contract, particularly a construction contract, may be given the effect of willfulness. E.g., Material Movers, Inc. v. Hill, 316 N.W.2d 13 (Minn.1982). See also

Smedley v. Walden, 246 Mass. 393, 141 N.E. 281 (1923) (disapproving jury instruction distinguishing good faith from intentional breach, because "an intentional departure [in performance] is in itself such bad faith as bars recovery, regardless of the presence or absence of an intent to gain or obtain some advantage thereby"). If the many stern denials found in the opinions are to be believed, one would expect to find that restitution is withheld regardless of the size of the forfeiture. Yet a search of the restitution cases—even a search limited to the construction cases, one of the most active groupings—fails to reveal many instances of judicial tolerance of clearly severe forfeiture.

The court that decided Britton v. Turner has invoked that decision to cast doubt on the customary view that "willful" conduct bars a restitution recovery. See, e.g., R.J. Berke & Co., Inc. v. J.P. Griffin, Inc., 116 N.H. 760, 367 A.2d 583 (1976) ("[t]he quality of the breach bears no logical relationship to the theory of quantum meruit recovery"). The court that in the 1920s decided Kelley v. Hance has, a half-century later, cited that decision as evidence of Connecticut's approval of the proposition that "a contractor who is guilty of a 'wilful' breach cannot maintain an action upon the contract." Vincenzi v. Cerro, 186 Conn. 612, 442 A.2d 1352 (1982). Still, that court was quick to add:

> The contemporary view, however, is that even a conscious and intentional departure from the contract specifications will not necessarily defeat recovery, but may be considered as one of the several factors involved in deciding whether there has been full performance. 3A Corbin, Contracts § 707; 2 Rest.2d, Contracts § 237, comment d. The pertinent inquiry is not simply whether the breach was "wilful" but whether the behavior of the party in default "comports with standards of good faith and fair dealing." 2 Rest.2d, Contracts § 241(e); see comment f. Even an adverse conclusion on this point is not decisive but is to be weighed with other factors, such as the extent to which the owner will be deprived of a reasonably expected benefit and the extent to which the builder may suffer forfeiture, in deciding whether there has been substantial performance.

In keeping with this approach, the Restatement, Second's provision on restitution for a party in breach, § 374, drops any mention of willfulness, explaining in a Reporter's Note that the section is intended to be "more liberal in allowing recovery in accord with the policy behind UCC § 2–718(2)."

We shall return to the factor of willfulness or bad faith in Chapter 6. That issue, as well as restitution for defaulters generally, is discussed fully in 1 G. Palmer, The Law of Restitution §§ 5.1–5.15 (1978).

––––––––

Vines v. Orchard Hills, Inc.

Supreme Court of Connecticut, 1980.
181 Conn. 501, 435 A.2d 1022.

PETERS, J.* This case concerns the right of purchasers of real property, after their own default, to 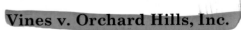 recover moneys paid at the time of execution of a

––––––––

* Ellen Ash Peters was a member of the Connecticut high court from 1978 to 2000; she served as Chief Justice from 1984 to 1996. Prior to her appointment to the bench, she was the Southmayd Professor of Law at the Yale Law School, teaching and writing in the field of com-

valid contract of sale. The plaintiffs, Euel D. Vines and his wife Etta Vines, contracted, on July 11, 1973, to buy Unit No. 10, Orchard Hills Condominium [in] New Canaan, from the defendant Orchard Hills, Inc. for $78,800. On or before that date, they had paid the defendant $7880 as a down payment toward the purchase. Alleging that the sale of the property was never consummated, the plaintiffs sought to recover their down payment. The trial court [overruled] the defendant's demurrer to the plaintiffs' amended complaint [and], after a hearing, . . . rendered judgment for the plaintiffs for $7880 plus interest. The defendant's appeal maintains that its demurrer should have been sustained, that its liquidated damages clause should have been enforced, and that evidence of the value of the property at the time of the trial should have been excluded.

. . . When the purchasers contracted to buy their condominium in July, 1973, they paid $7880, a sum which the contract of sale designated as liquidated damages.[1] The purchasers decided not to take title to the condominium because Euel D. Vines was transferred by his employer to New Jersey; the Vines so informed the seller by a letter dated January 4, 1974. There has never been any claim that the seller has failed, in any respect, to conform to his obligations under the contract, nor does the complaint allege that the purchasers are legally excused from their performance under the contract. In short, it is the purchasers and not the seller whose breach precipitated the present cause of action.

. . . [T]he purchasers established that the value of the condominium that they had agreed to buy for $78,800 in 1973 had, by the time of the trial in 1979, a fair market value of $160,000. The trial court relied on this figure to conclude that, because the seller had gained what it characterized as a windfall of approximately $80,000, the purchasers were entitled to recover their down payment of $7880. Neither the purchasers nor the seller proffered any evidence at the trial to show the market value of the condominium at the time of the purchasers' breach of their contract or the damages sustained by the seller as a result of that breach. . . .

The ultimate issue on this appeal is the enforceability of a liquidated damages clause as a defense to a claim of restitution by purchasers in default on a land sale contract. Although the parties, both in the trial court and here, have focused on the liquidated damages clause per se, we must first consider when, if ever, purchasers who are themselves in breach of a valid contract of sale may affirmatively invoke the assistance of judicial process to recover back moneys paid to, and withheld by, their seller.

The right of a contracting party, despite his default, to seek restitution for benefits conferred and allegedly unjustly retained has been much disputed in the legal literature and in the case law. See 5A Corbin, Contracts §§ 1122–1135 (1964); Dobbs, Remedies § 12.14 (1973); 1 Palmer, Restitution, c. 5 (1978). . . . Although earlier cases often refused to permit a party to bring an action that could be said to be based on his own breach, see

---

mercial law. Justice Peters' scholarly works include a highly influential article that remains a classic today, Remedies for Breach of Contracts Relating to the Sale of Goods Under the Uniform Commercial Code: A Roadmap for Article Two, 73 Yale L.J. 199 (1963). [Eds.]

[1] Paragraph 9 of the contract of sale provided: "DEFAULT: In the event Purchaser fails to perform any of the obligations herein imposed on the Purchaser, the Seller performing all obligations herein imposed on the Seller, the Seller shall retain all sums of money paid under this Contract, as liquidated damages, and all rights and liabilities of the parties hereto shall be at an end."

e.g., [Ketchum & Sweet v. Evertson, 13 Johns. 359, 365 (N.Y.1816)],* many of the more recent cases support restitution in order to prevent unjust enrichment and to avoid forfeiture. See, e.g., [Freedman v. Rector, Wardens & Vestrymen of St. Mathias Parish, 37 Cal.2d 16, 230 P.2d 629 (1951); De Leon v. Aldrete, 398 S.W.2d 160 (Tex.Civ.App.1965)].

A variety of considerations, some practical and some theoretical, underlie this shift in attitude toward the plaintiff in breach. As Professor Corbin pointed out in his seminal article, "The Right of a Defaulting Vendee to the Restitution of Installments Paid," 40 Yale L.J. 1013 (1931), the anomalous result of denying any remedy to the plaintiff in breach is to punish more severely the person who has partially performed, often in good faith, than the person who has entirely disregarded his contractual obligations from the outset. Only partial performance triggers a claim for restitution, and partial performance will not, in the ordinary course of events, have been more injurious to the innocent party than total nonperformance. Recognition of a claim in restitution is, furthermore, consistent with the economic functions that the law of contracts is designed to serve. . . . The principal purpose of remedies for the breach of contract is to provide compensation for loss, . . . and therefore a party injured by breach of contract is entitled to retain nothing in excess of that sum which compensates him for the loss of his bargain. Indeed, there are those who argue that repudiation of contractual obligations is socially desirable, and should be encouraged, whenever gain to the party in breach exceeds loss to the party injured by breach. Birmingham, "Breach of Contract, Damage Measures, and Economic Efficiency," 24 Rut.L.Rev. 273, 284 (1970); Posner, Economic Analysis of Law § 4.9, pp. 89–90 (2d Ed.1977). To assign such primacy to inferences drawn from economic models requires great confidence that the person injured by breach will encounter no substantial difficulties in establishing the losses for which he is entitled to be compensated. It is not necessary to push the principle of compensatory damages that far, or to disregard entirely the desirability of maintaining some incentives for the performance of promises. A claim in restitution, although legal in form, is equitable in nature, and permits a trial court to balance the equities, to take into account a variety of competing principles to determine whether the defendant has been unjustly enriched. . . .

In this state, at the turn of the century, in Pierce v. Staub, 78 Conn. 459, 62 A. 760 (1906), this court acknowledged the equitable claim of a purchaser in breach to recover moneys paid under a contract to purchase real property. Pierce v. Staub is distinguishable from the case before us, because the court there found that the parties had, after the buyer's breach, rescinded the contracts in question. In view of this rescission, the purchaser's widow was held to be entitled to a return of the $60,000 paid on the purchase price of $150,000. . . . Apart from Pierce v. Staub, we have never directly decided whether a purchaser of real estate may, despite his breach, recover payments made to his seller. But Pierce v. Staub is an impressive, and an impressively early, guidepost toward permitting such a cause of action. The court's narrow reliance on the possibly artificial conclusion of mutual rescission should not obscure the breadth of its language deploring for-

---

* [The *Ketchum* court denied defaulting vendees recovery of a $700 down payment on a farm, saying: "It would be an alarming doctrine to hold that the plaintiffs might violate the contract and, because they chose to do so, make their own infraction of the agreement the basis of an action for money had and received. Every man who makes a bad bargain, and has advanced money upon it, would have the right to recover it back that the plaintiffs have."— Eds.]

feiture. . . . We therefore conclude that a purchaser whose breach is not willful has a restitutionary claim to recover moneys paid that unjustly enrich his seller. In this case, no one has alleged that the purchasers' breach, arising out of a transfer to a more distant place of employment, should be deemed to have been willful. The trial court was therefore not in error in initially overruling the seller's demurrer and entertaining the purchasers' cause of action.

ELLEN ASH PETERS
Chief Justice Retired, Connecticut Supreme Court

The purchaser's right to recover in restitution requires the purchaser to establish that the seller has been unjustly enriched. The purchaser must show more than that the contract has come to an end and that the seller retains moneys paid pursuant to the contract. To prove unjust enrichment, in the ordinary case, the purchaser, because he is the party in breach, must prove that the damages suffered by his seller are less than the moneys received from the purchaser. Schwasnick v. Blandin, 65 F.2d 354 (2d Cir.1933). . . . It may not be easy for the purchaser to prove the extent of the seller's damages, it may even be strategically advantageous for the seller to come forward with relevant evidence of the losses he has incurred and may expect to incur on account of the buyer's breach. Nonetheless, only if the breaching party satisfies his burden of proof that the innocent party has sustained a net gain may a claim for unjust enrichment be sustained. Dobbs, Remedies § 12.14 (1973); 1 Palmer, Restitution § 5.4 (1978).

In the case before us, the parties themselves stipulated in the contract of sale that the purchasers' down payment of 10 percent of the purchase price represents the damages that would be likely to flow from the purchasers' breach. The question then becomes whether the purchasers have demonstrated the seller's unjust enrichment in the face of the liquidated damages clause to which they agreed.

This is not a suitable occasion for detailed review of the checkered history of liquidated damages clauses. Despite the judicial resistance that such clauses have encountered in the past[,] . . . this court has recognized the principle that there are circumstances that justify private agreements to supplant judicially determined remedies for breach of contract. Berger v. Shanahan, 142 Conn. 726, 118 A.2d 311 (1955). . . . This court has however refused to enforce an otherwise valid liquidated damages clause upon a finding that no damages whatsoever ensued from the particular breach of contract that actually occurred. Norwalk Door Closer Co. v. Eagle Lock & Screw Co., 153 Conn. 681, 220 A.2d 263 (1966).

Most of the litigation concerning liquidated damages clauses arises in the context of an affirmative action by the party injured by breach to enforce the clause in order to recover the amount therein stipulated. In such cases, the burden of persuasion about the enforceability of the clause naturally rests with its proponent. See, e.g., [*Norwalk Door*], supra, 688, 220 A.2d 263. In the case before us, by contrast, where the plaintiffs are themselves in default, the plaintiffs bear the burden of showing that the clause is invalid and unenforceable. . . . It is not unreasonable in these circumstances to presume that a liquidated damages clause that is appropriately limited in amount bears a reasonable relationship to the damages that the seller has actually suffered. See Rest.2d., Contracts [§ 374], esp. subsection (2).[2] The sellers damages . . . include not only his expectation damages suffered through loss of his bargain, and his incidental damages such as broker's commissions, but also less quantifiable costs arising out of retention of real property beyond the time of the originally contemplated sale. 1 Palmer, Restitution §§ 5.4, 5.8 (1978). . . . A liquidated damages clause allowing the seller to retain 10 percent of the contract price as earnest money is presumptively a reasonable allocation of the risks associated with default. . . .

The presumption of validity that attaches to a clause liquidating the seller's damages at 10 percent of the contract price in the event of the pur-

---

[2] Section [374] of the Restatement (Second) of Contracts (Tent. Draft No. 14, 1979) provides: "Restitution in Favor of Party in Breach. (1) Subject to the rule stated in Subsection (2), if a party justifiably refuses to perform on the ground that his remaining duties of performance have been discharged by the other party's breach, the party in breach is entitled to restitution for any benefit that he has conferred on the injured party by way of part performance or reliance.

(2) To the extent that, under the manifested assent of the parties, a party's performance is to be retained in the case of breach, that party is not entitled to restitution if the value of the performance as liquidated damages is reasonable in the light of the anticipated or actual loss caused by the breach and the difficulties of proof of loss."

chaser's unexcused nonperformance is, like most other presumptions, rebuttable. The purchaser, despite his default, is free to prove that the contract, or any part thereof, was the product of fraud or mistake or
unconscionability. . . . In the alternative, the purchaser is free to offer evidence that his breach in fact caused the seller no damages or damages substantially less than the amount stipulated as liquidated damages. See
[*Norwalk Door*], supra, 153 Conn. 689, 220 A.2d 263.

The trial court concluded that the plaintiff purchasers had successfully
invoked the principle of [*Norwalk Door*] by presenting evidence of increase
in the value of the real property between the date of the contract of sale
and the date of the trial. That conclusion was in error. The relevant time at
which to measure the seller's damages is the time of breach. Zirinsky v.
Sheehan, 413 F.2d 481 (8th Cir.1969). . . . Benefits to the seller that are
attributable to a rising market subsequent to breach rightfully accrue to
the seller. Beckley v. Munson, 22 Conn. 299, 313 (1853). . . . There was no
evidence before the court to demonstrate that the seller was not injured at
the time of the purchasers' breach by their failure then to consummate the
contract. Neither the seller's status as a developer of a condominium project nor the absence of willfulness on the part of the purchasers furnishes a
justification for disregarding the liquidated damages clause, although these
factors may play some role in the ultimate determination of whether the
seller was in fact unjustly enriched by the down payment he retained.

Because the availability of, and the limits on, restitutionary claims by
a plaintiff in default have not previously been clearly spelled out in our
cases, it is appropriate to afford to the purchasers herein another opportunity to proffer evidence to substantiate their claim. What showing the
purchasers must make cannot be spelled out with specificity in view of the
sparsity of the present record. The purchasers may be able to demonstrate
that the condominium could, at the time of their breach, have been resold
at a price sufficiently higher than their contract price to obviate any loss of
profits and to compensate the seller for any incidental and consequential
damages. Alternatively, the purchasers may be able to present evidence of
unconscionability or of excuse, to avoid the applicability of the liquidated
damages clause altogether. The plaintiffs' burden of proof is not an easy
one to sustain, but they are entitled to their day in court.

There is error, the judgment is set aside, and the case is remanded for
further proceedings in conformity with this opinion.

––––––––––

De Leon v. Aldrete

398 S.W.2d 160 (Tex.Civ.App.1965)

In May 1960, plaintiff contracted to purchase defendants' land for $1,500,
payable in installments the last of which was due April 1, 1961. All of plaintiff's
payments were late. By July 6, 1961, the date of his last payment, plaintiff had
paid a total of $1,070. He had also paid an architect $250 for plans for a residence on the land. In February 1962, defendants declared a default and sold
and conveyed the land to a third person for $1,300. *Held,* plaintiff can recover
$870 plus the $250 for the architect's fee. The majority rule in this country denies to a defaulting purchaser the right to recover monies paid under the contract. But dogmatic application of the forfeiture rule leads to "indefensibly absurd results." Because the amount of the forfeiture is determined by the stage

to which performance has progressed, "the purchaser's loss increases as the seriousness of his breach decreases." Moreover, the "can't-create-your-own-cause-of-action" rationalization is unpersuasive. The purchaser's default, standing alone, does not qualify the defaulter for restitution; nor does it terminate the contract or the vendor's contract rights. "It merely creates in the vendor a power to terminate the contract. Until he exercises such power, the vendor, apart from his right to damages, has the remedy of specific performance." Accordingly, the Texas cases have embraced the more salutary rule that restitution depends on the equities of each case. "[This] leaves room for the consideration of all relevant factors, especially the all-important considerations of the amount which the purchaser has paid and the extent to which the vendor has been injured by the breach. . . . At least in the absence of a forfeiture clause, the obvious intent of the parties [in such cases] is that all payments are to be treated simply and only as payments on the purchase price." Here, plaintiff has paid $1,070 and defendants' damages are $200. Defendants would be enriched unjustly were they permitted to retain more than the $200. "This result can be justified only if we are prepared to hold that plaintiff must be punished for his breach. Punitive damages are alien to the law of contract. The fundamental principle of [compensation] will afford sufficient protection to the innocent party, and this is the only interest . . . which the social welfare demands should be the subject of judicial solicitude."

QUESTION

Defendants did not appeal the portion of the trial court's judgment awarding plaintiff the $250 it had paid the architect. Could defendants have successfully challenged this item?

↳ looks like reliance, but breached.

NOTE: THE FORFEITURE RULE

New York's forfeiture rule for real estate purchases was judicially established in 1881. A century later, in Maxton Builders, Inc. v. Lo Galbo, 68 N.Y.2d 373, 509 N.Y.S.2d 507, 502 N.E.2d 184 (1986), the Court of Appeals reexamined its position, unanimously concluding that the policy of denying defaulting purchasers recovery of down payments on real estate contracts should be retained.

After observing that, "in most areas of the law," courts and legislatures have now adopted rules generally permitting a defaulter to recover the net benefit conferred by a part performance, and that the New York legislature had enacted UCC 2–718(2) respecting goods but failed to adopt similar proposals covering real estate transactions, the *Maxton* court declared:

> The rule permitting a party in default to seek restitution for part performance has much to commend it in its general applications. But as applied to real estate down payments approximating 10% it does not appear to offer a better or more workable rule than the long-established "usage" in this [s]tate with respect to the seller's right to retain a down payment upon default.
>
> In cases, as here, where the property is sold to another after the breach, the buyer's ability to recover the down payment would depend initially on whether the agreement expressly provides that the

seller could retain it upon default. If it did, the provision would probably be upheld as a valid liquidated damages clause in view of the recognized difficulty of estimating actual damages and the general acceptance of the traditional 10% down payment as a reasonable amount.

If the contract itself is deemed to pose no bar, then the buyer would bear the burden of proving that the amount retained exceeded the actual damages. As the authorities note, this is a difficult burden in any case involving real estate sales, and is not likely to be met in suits on down payments or first installments where the actual damages will generally be very close to the amount of the traditional 10% retained. Thus, in most cases, a change in the law will provide a forum for the disputants to further dispute their differences, but cannot be reasonably expected to save any party from true financial loss. Indeed in the case now before us the defendants made no effort to show that the actual damages were less than the plaintiff alleged or that there was, in fact, a net benefit conferred.

Finally, real estate contracts are probably the best examples of arm's length transactions. Except in cases where there is a real risk of overreaching, there should be no need for the courts to relieve the parties of the consequences of their contract. If the parties are dissatisfied with the [present rule], the time to say so is at the bargaining table.

The court explicitly reserved decision on "installment payments beyond a 10% down payment," emphasizing that the vendee's default in this case did not raise that issue.

SECTION 4. CONTRACTUAL CONTROLS ON THE DAMAGE REMEDY

INTRODUCTORY NOTE

The doctrines examined in this section say that a contract clause fixing damages in the event of breach is enforceable only if it constitutes a reasonable forecast of the injury resulting from breach, and then only if the injury is difficult to measure. A damages clause that is found to do something else will be classified as a "penalty" and held unenforceable.

The case of Pacheco v. Scoblionko, 532 A.2d 1036 (Me.1987), provides a starting place. Plaintiff had for several years sent his child to defendant's summer camp. Since early payment of fees entitled a camper to a tuition reduction, plaintiff registered his child before February 1, paying in full the reduced charge of $3,100. The contract plaintiff signed was on a preprinted form supplied by defendant; it included a paragraph on "refunds" and "liquidated damages," as follows:

> The $500 deposit will be refunded if a request is received by the camp prior to February 1st, less a $25 administrative processing fee. If a refund request is received on or after February 1st and prior to May 1st, then no refund of the $500 deposit will be made. If a refund request is received on or after May 1st, the entire sum then paid to date shall be retained by the camp. The parties agree that any de-

posit so retained would constitute liquidated damages for cancellation of the contract.

The camp season was to commence in July. On June 14, plaintiff was informed that his child, a high school student, had failed a final exam in Spanish and would be required to attend summer school. That same day plaintiff telephoned defendant, saying that his child would be unable to attend camp and asking for return of the fee paid. When defendant refused to refund any portion of the $3,100, plaintiff sued to recover it.

What was defendant's purpose in putting the "refund/liquidated damages" clause in the contract? Does a clause of this type serve any substantial and legitimate business interest?

The Maine Supreme Court, affirming a judgment for plaintiff for the full $3,100, agreed with the trial court that the clause in question was an "unenforceable penalty." The test of enforceability, said the court, is two-pronged: whether damages are "difficult to estimate accurately" and whether the amount fixed is a "reasonable forecast" of what is required to "justly compensate" the injured party. Here, defendant, who as the proponent of the clause bore the burden of proof of its validity, had failed to offer evidence as to what damages, if any, were anticipated or actually suffered as a result of plaintiff's cancellation. The amount declared forfeited was therefore "excessive" and "disproportionate to the contract price," suggesting that the clause was placed in the contract "for its in terrorem effect."

Is *Pacheco* an "easy" case to decide? Do you suppose that parents' last-minute withdrawals of their children is a recurring problem for summer-camp operators? Absent such a clause, how would a camp operator's damages be measured?

In approaching the materials that follow, it may be helpful to consider two differing perspectives:

The rationale for the rule against enforcing penalties in contract cases is not crystal clear. But it is not hard to imagine why a court might be loath to enforce a contract provision specifying a disproportionately large sum—which courts call a penalty—for breach of the contract. The parties may make such an agreement far in advance of the dispute and may not appreciate the full impact if the unlikely breach does occur. Contract damages, broadly speaking, aim at compensation, not at punishment. Finally, courts do not like results that appear unjust. Xerox Fin. Serv. Life Ins. v. High Plains, 44 F.3d 1033 (1st Cir.1995) (Boudin, J.).

Parties are more likely to make a reasonable estimate of the harm from a breach of contract than judges are—it is the parties' money that is on the line, after all—even though the parties are making it in advance whereas the judges would be assessing harm after it had occurred as a result of the breach. If the parties make a mistake they have only themselves to blame; why should the courts get involved? Of course it is settled doctrine . . . that a party can complain that a liquidated damages provision to which it freely and knowingly consented was actually a penalty and therefore void. . . . But the party making this paternalistic argument has the burden of proof. First Nat'l Bank v. Atlantic Tele–Network, 946 F.2d 516 (7th Cir.1991) (Posner, J.).

————

Muldoon v. Lynch
Supreme Court of California, 1885.
66 Cal. 536, 6 P. 417.

MYRICK, J. The question [is] whether a sum named in a contract as a forfeiture is to be regarded as liquidated damages or as a penalty.

The plaintiffs and defendant executed a written contract, by which the plaintiffs were to furnish and complete certain improvements on the cemetery lot of defendant in a cemetery in San Francisco, viz., grading, brickwork, stone-work, monument, sarcophagus, etc., in which lot the remains of defendant's deceased husband had been interred. The monument was to be of the best article of hard Ravaccioni Italian marble. The amount to be paid for the whole was $18,788, four installments of $1,725 each, to be paid as the work progressed to the point of being ready for the reception of the monument, and the balance, $11,887, on the completion of the whole. The contract contained the following clause:

> All the work, with the exception of monument, to be completed within four months from date of contract, and the balance in twelve months from the date of this contract, under forfeiture of ten dollars per day for each and every day beyond the stated time for completion.

The monument was procured in Italy, but was delayed nearly two years in reaching the point of destination for the following reason: The monument was of four large blocks of marble; one of them [weighed] twenty tons. The marble was transported from the quarry to a seaport in Italy for shipment, and was there delayed waiting for a vessel. As one of the plaintiffs testified: "We had to wait until we got a ship; we got the Ottilio; it was the first vessel that left there for two years for this port. Owing to the size of the blocks, the only way to bring them here was by ships directly from Italy; the largest block would not have been allowed on a railroad car."

As soon as the marble reached San Francisco it was set up, and everything was according to the contract, without question being made, except as to the matter of time; that was the only point of controversy.

The plaintiffs claim that the defendant is indebted to them in the sum of $11,887, with interest from the day of the completion of the monument, and that the sum of ten dollars per day, mentioned in the contract as a forfeiture, is a penalty, and not matter of defense or set-off, without proof of actual damage; while defendant claims that the said sum of ten dollars per day is to be taken as liquidated damages; and the same amounting to $7,820, is to be deducted from the sum of $11,887, leaving defendant indebted in the sum of $4,067 only.

There is no doubt that parties to a contract may agree upon the amount which shall constitute the damage for its breach. It is declared in § 3301, Civil Code, that "no damages can be recovered for a breach of contract which are not clearly ascertainable in both their nature and origin"; but § 1671 of the same code declares that "the parties to a contract may agree therein upon an amount which shall be presumed to be the amount of damages sustained by a breach thereof, when, from the nature of the case, it would be impracticable, or extremely difficult, to fix the actual damage." When parties have endeavored to contract with reference to damages— when they have explicitly declared that a sum named by them shall be taken as stipulated damages—it may be that such declaration would be taken as conclusive, and that courts would not attempt to relieve the losing party from his unfortunate or ill-advised engagement. But where it appears on the face of the contract that the sum named was intended by the parties to be considered as a penalty—a spur—courts will not enforce another construction, especially when the result would be the payment of a sum largely disproportionate to any reasonable idea of actual damage. The contract reads, "under forfeiture of ten dollars per day for each and every day beyond the stated time for completion." The general rule is, that damages are and ought to be purely compensatory; they should be commensurate with the injury, neither more nor less. There is nothing in this case to indicate that the defendant has suffered any actual damage which can be measured or compensated by money. It is true, she had the right to contract to have the monument erected in memory of her deceased husband, and to have it at a certain time; and possibly the agreement might have been so drawn that her disappointment should have received adequate compensation; but, referring to the words used by the parties, we are not prepared to say that either had thought of compensation, as such. The word "forfeiture" is the equivalent of the word "penalty"; it imports a penalty.

It has been held that in an agreement to convey land, and on default to pay a certain sum of money, or where the contractor agreed to do certain work, with a provision to pay a certain sum for each day's delay beyond the day fixed, or an agreement not to carry on a certain business at a named place, with a promise to pay a sum in case of violation of the agreement (Streeter v. Rush, 25 Cal. 71), if it appears that the parties intended the sum named to be considered liquidated damages, courts will not interfere with the contract, even if it might seem to have been an improvident agreement. But where it appears that the parties intended the sum named to be a forfeiture or penalty, it has been generally held that the party in whose favor the penalty or forfeiture exists must prove his damage.

In the case before us, there is no claim of special damage; it might have been quite difficult for the defendant to show any damage of a pecuniary nature, for the non-completion of the monument at the time specified, though its completion might have been of great comfort and consolation to her affectionate remembrance. . . .

[W]e are of opinion that the sum named is to be regarded as a penalty, and that the plaintiffs were entitled to recover the whole of the balance unpaid.

Judgment and order affirmed.

———

Yockey v. Horn

880 F.2d 945 (7th Cir.1989)

Two former business partners entered into a settlement agreement intended to resolve all disputes arising from their failed relationship. The settlement included a promise by Horn not to "voluntarily participate in any litigation against Frank Yockey" for events up to the date of the agreement (Yockey gave Margaret Horn a similar promise), as well as a clause fixing liquidated damages of $50,000 for either's breach by "voluntary participation in any lawsuit by anyone" against the other. A few months after signing the settlement, Horn, apparently disturbed by Yockey's business practices, contacted one Schrock, a business acquaintance who had invested money with Yockey. Although the substance of the Horn–Schrock conversations was not revealed, Schrock thereafter successfully sued Yockey for fraud and securities violations, recovering damages of $111,000. It was in that litigation that Horn, not under subpoena or other court process, gave a deposition which was received into evidence at the Schrock–Yockey trial. Yockey then sued Horn for breach of the settlement agreement, alleging that Horn, by giving the deposition, had violated her "covenant not to voluntarily participate" in litigation against Yockey. The trial court found a breach and awarded Yockey $50,000 in liquidated damages. *Held*, judgment affirmed "despite the rather harsh result." In the absence of clear Illinois precedent, we rely on general principles, notably Rest.2d § 356 [reproduced infra p. 147], which calls for enforcement of a liquidated damages clause if the amount estimated is reasonable either at the time of contracting or at the time of injury—provided the nonbreaching party has suffered some actual damage. On one view, it appears that Yockey suffered no injury by virtue of Horn's breach. Even if Horn had refused to testify without a subpoena, she could easily have been subpoenaed to give the same testimony. Moreover, Yockey concedes that Schrock's judgment against him was in no part based on Horn's deposition. But "[t]his analysis fails to account for other types of damage that Horn's breach might have caused. . . . Yockey's business reputation might have been significantly damaged in the eyes of investors or lenders when Horn, his former [partner], participated in litigation against him." Such damages are "difficult to evaluate" and, accordingly, the "proper subject" for a contract clause; they are also "what was anticipated." It follows that the $50,000 estimate was reasonable when made. "[A] great deal of damage might have been caused by Horn's breach."

QUESTION

What if the delay in completion of the work in *Muldoon* had been only 10 days?

COMMENT: THE PENAL BOND

In the early stages of the common law's development, the recovery of a penalty was a frequently used sanction for nonperformance of a contract. For planned transactions in which there was much at stake, it became customary to use the so-called "penal bond," which was a promise under seal to pay a specified sum of money if by a certain date a particular event did not occur—e.g., a sum of money was not paid, a house under construction was not completed, services promised were not rendered. The penalty—often a sum twice the amount of the actual obligation owed—was recoverable in the common law action of covenant. By the sixteenth century, however, the Chancery, concerned about oppression and extortion, had established the practice of intervening, regularly and predictably, to enjoin the collection of penal sums promised in bonds under seal. The underlying Chancery attitudes of disapproval were in time absorbed by the common law, aided by an English statute of 1687, and these have influenced our modern attitudes toward contractual penalties, as was noted in Muldoon v. Lynch. The interplay of ideas in this development has been summarized by Professor A.W.B. Simpson (A History of the Common Law of Contract 123–125 (1975)):

> [T]here existed for many centuries a divorce between contractual theory and contractual practice. This divorce can in its turn be understood if it is seen as reflecting a tension between two ideas. On the one hand we have the idea that the real function of contractual institutions is to make sure, so far as possible, that agreements are performed; the institution of the penal bond and the practice of the courts in upholding such bonds exemplified this idea. On the other hand we have the idea that it suffices for the law to provide compensation for loss suffered by failure to perform agreements. This second idea is not, of course, necessarily incompatible with the pursuit of the aim of encouraging contractual performance, but it is bound to impose a limitation upon the enthusiasm with which that aim is pursued, and there can well be contexts (for example, contracts for personal service) in which a positive value is attached to the right to break the contract so long as the defaulting party is made to pay compensation. Now if securing performance is the aim to be pursued, the use of penalties *in terrorem* of the party from whom performance is due is the natural and obvious technique. Thus today the decree of specific performance is given teeth by the threat of imprisonment for contempt, and in the criminal courts we are familiar with such institutions as the granting of bail and the entry into recognizances to keep the peace, which institutions, to those who are not over-impressed by labels, are nothing more than modern versions of the conditioned bond used to bind persons to the performance of contracts. What has happened is not that contracts *in terrorem* have been outlawed, or that the use of penal mechanisms no longer plays any part in contract law, but only that the courts have come to acquire a monopolistic control over the use of terror. It is today the courts which may do things which in former ages private citizens might do. Nobody who is familiar with the modern practice of hire-purchase, or other forms of usury could doubt that there is still a demand for private trafficking in penalties; the general trend is, however, to resist this demand.

> In early law this demand is not resisted; hence the prevalence in more or less primitive communities of the use of the pledge or hostage, at least in the case of important contracts, as a device for securing performance; where men cannot trust each other, and the machinery of the law is weak, the contracting party must place some important stake at the mercy of the other party. The penal bond for securing performance was a sophisticated form of self-pledge, and Shylock's bond with its forfeit of a pound of flesh neatly illustrates the fact that the best pledge of all is the body of the contractor, which in early law he could have used as security. The provision of security for performance is still a common practice today, but the general triumph of the compensatory principle has radically altered

its character; so far as the law is concerned, security has come to be non-penal where the device is used by private persons. The decline in the use of the penal bond, and the corresponding shift in the centre of gravity of contract law from the law of debt *sur obligation* to the law of the action on the case upon an assumpsit represents a major step in social evolution.

It would be a mistake, however, to suppose either that the decline in the popularity of the bond was rapid, or that the granting of relief against penalties deprived it of all usefulness. Commercial and legal habits do not change overnight, and even if the law only permits contracting parties to stipulate for liquidated damages of a compensatory character there can still be advantages in adopting this course rather than leaving the question open to later settlement in litigation or negotiation—for example, in contracts where the determination of compensatory damages is necessarily speculative. Furthermore there can be exceptions to the general principle, and ways of getting round it. Thus even today the use of the penal bond is not wholly obsolete in private transactions.

For some purposes, the practice of expressing formal obligations in the form of the ancient penal bond (a promise of a sum of money, followed by an express condition discharging the promisor in the event stated obligations are performed) is common even now. But the operative effect of such instruments— for example, a surety bond of the type sued on in *Algernon Blair*—is much different from that of its remote ancestor. As we shall see later, the conventional "interpretation" of the surety bond today converts what is stated as a condition of defeasance into a promise, with the sum promised functioning as an upper limit of liability and the principle of compensation measuring actual liability. Stated differently, a term fixing a flat sum as a penalty for the nonoccurrence of the condition of the bond is deemed unenforceable to the extent it exceeds the actual loss caused by such nonoccurrence.

RESTATEMENT OF CONTRACTS, SECOND

Section 356. Liquidated Damages and Penalties

(1) Damages for breach by either party may be liquidated in the agreement but only at an amount that is reasonable in the light of the anticipated or actual loss caused by the breach and the difficulties of proof of loss. A term fixing unreasonably large liquidated damages is unenforceable on grounds of public policy as a penalty.

Comment:

. . . [T]wo factors combine in determining whether an amount of money fixed as damages is so unreasonably large as to be a penalty. The first factor is the anticipated or actual loss caused by the breach. The amount fixed is reasonable to the extent that it approximates the actual loss that has resulted from the particular breach, even though it may not approximate the loss that might have been anticipated under other possible breaches. . . . [Alternatively,] the amount fixed is reasonable to the extent that it approximates the loss anticipated at the time of the making of the contract, even though it may not approximate the actual loss. . . . The second factor is the difficulty of proof of loss.

The greater the difficulty either of proving that loss has occurred or of establishing its amount with the requisite certainty . . ., the easier it is to show that the amount fixed is reasonable. . . . If the difficulty of proof of loss is great, considerable latitude is allowed in the approximation of anticipated or actual harm. [If] the difficulty of proof of loss is slight, less latitude is allowed in that approximation. If, to take an extreme case, it is clear that no loss at all has occurred, a provision fixing a substantial sum as damages is unenforceable.

NOTE: ONE LOOK OR TWO?

The first Restatement of Contracts § 339 embraced the historical "time of contracting" test of validity (the reasonableness of the forecast when made, taking account of the difficulty of accurate estimation); any "hindsight" inquiry in light of actual damages caused by the breach was rejected. The Reporter's Note to § 356(1) of the second Restatement, reproduced above, states that the section "has been redrafted to harmonize with Uniform Commercial Code § 2–718(1)," with only slight changes in terminology. The UCC's 2–718(1), calling for greater flexibility in the evaluation of damage clauses, was before the New York's high court in Equitable Lumber Corp. v. IPA Land Dev. Corp., 38 N.Y.2d 516, 381 N.Y.S.2d 459, 344 N.E.2d 391 (1976). That court said:

> The first sentence of § 2–718(1) focuses on the situation of the parties both at the time of contracting and at the time of breach. Thus, a liquidated damages provision will be valid if reasonable with respect to *either* (1) the harm which the parties anticipate will result from the breach at the time of contracting or (2) the actual damages suffered by the non-defaulting party at the time of breach (see *Hawkland*, A Transactional Guide to the [UCC], § 1.–280101). Interestingly, § 2–718(1) does, in some measure, signal a departure from prior law which considered only the anticipated harm at the time of contracting. . . . Thus, decisions which have restricted their analysis of the validity of liquidated damages clauses solely to the anticipated harm at the time of contracting have, to this extent, been abrogated by the [UCC] in cases involving transactions in goods. . . . Having satisfied the test set forth in the first part of § 2–718(1), a liquidated damages provision may nonetheless be invalidated under the last sentence of the section if it is so unreasonably large that it serves as a penalty rather than a good faith attempt to pre-estimate damages. . . .

It is clear that the law of liquidated damages has evolved over time. Assessing "reasonableness" at either the time of contract formation or at the time of the breach (a "second look") presumably means there is to be a larger role for damage clauses. Indeed, a leading decision asserts broadly that, in commercial transactions between parties with comparable bargaining power, the "modern trend" is toward enforcing stipulated damages clauses. Wasserman's Inc. v. Middletown, 137 N.J. 238, 645 A.2d 100 (1994) (reserving the issue of validity as concerns consumer contracts). Nevertheless, some courts (by one count, perhaps as many as 22), at least in the common law (non-UCC) cases, many involving real estate contracts, continue to adhere to the first Restatement's time-of-formation test. E.g., Watson v. Ingram, 124 Wash.2d 845, 881 P.2d 247 (1994) ("the prospective approach [of § 339] better fulfills the underlying purposes of liquidated damages clauses and gives greater weight to the parties' expectations"). One such case, Kelly v. Marx, 428 Mass. 877, 705 N.E.2d 1114

(1999), involved facts similar to Vines v. Orchard Hills, supra p. 134, in that the seller, within weeks of the breach, resold the property for $5,000 more than the contract price. The breached agreement had included this clause: "If the BUYER shall fail to fulfill the BUYER'S agreements herein, all deposits made hereunder by the BUYER shall be retained by the SELLER as liquidated damages." The court, limiting inquiry to a prospective or "single look," permitted the seller to keep the buyer's five percent deposit, explaining:

> [A] damages clause in a purchase and sale agreement will be enforced where, at the time the agreement was made, potential damages were difficult to determine and the clause was a reasonable forecast of damages expected to occur in the event of a breach. . . In addition to meeting the parties' expectations, the "single look" approach helps resolve disputes efficiently by making it unnecessary to wait until actual damages from a breach are proved. By reducing challenges to a liquidated damages clause, the "single look" approach eliminates uncertainty and tends to prevent costly future litigation. The "second look," by contrast, . . . increases the potential for litigation by inviting the aggrieved party to attempt to show evidence of damage when the contract is breached. . . . The plaintiffs argue that application of a "second look" approach would allow the court to guard against undue windfalls, such as the one the defendants would receive here if they were to keep the deposit, because the defendants suffered no loss from the breach of the sale. We disagree. In essence, the plaintiffs want to undo the agreement between the parties, who expect to receive stipulated damages, not damages resolved by a court examining postbreach circumstances. The parties agreed to the extent of their damages when they agreed on a liquidated damages clause. . . .

The Kelly v. Marx court, addressing Rest.2d § 356(1) specifically, made two points worth noting. One was a reiteration of agreement with the section's second sentence—a term fixing "unreasonably large" damages is an unenforceable penalty. The second was a flat rejection of any suggestion that § 356(1)'s comments and illustrations mean that a clause found "reasonable in light of anticipated loss" could, nevertheless, be unenforceable if the nonbreacher does not suffer a loss. Consider whether there is any inconsistency here.

———

Wilt v. Waterfield

273 S.W.2d 290 (Mo.1954)

Plaintiffs' complaint alleged that defendant, owner of an 825–acre farm, had contracted to sell it to them for $19,000; that they had paid defendant $1,900 on the purchase price; and that defendant, in breach of contract, then sold the farm to someone else. The lower court entered judgment for plaintiffs for $7,000 damages. Defendant appealed, urging that plaintiffs' recovery was limited by a printed clause in the contract, providing: "If either party hereto fails or neglects to perform his part of this agreement, he shall forthwith pay and forfeit as liquidated damages to the other party a sum equal to ten percent of the agreed price of sale." The evidence showed that after signing the contract with plaintiffs, defendant had conveyed the farm to one Windon for $26,000 and had paid $1,900 to the agent who arranged the second sale. Plaintiffs contended that the quoted clause was a penalty and did not limit their recovery of actual damages. *Held*, plaintiffs are correct. The parties' intention, drawn from their words, governs the construction of clauses fixing damages. To arrive at that intention, a court "may consider whether the agreement contains various stipulations of various degrees of importance, the breaches of which would be easy to calculate in damages as to some and difficult as to others, in which event the sum specified would be construed as a penalty and not as liquidated damages. . . . [U]nder [this] contract defendant was bound to convey the full 825 acres; to share the 1951 crops of corn, oil beans and hay; to hold plaintiffs' check until September 19; to cut none of the lespedeza crop; to furnish abstract of title, to deliver deed and possession by February 20. [Plaintiffs say] these are of varying degrees of importance and would each give cause to a different amount of damages in case of failure to perform, bearing no relation to the amount fixed by the contract. . . . It seems apparent that if the defendant . . . had failed or neglected to perform [any part of any one of these duties], the damages accruing thereby to the plaintiffs might in some of such instances be entirely disproportionate to the $1,900 stipulated in the contract. Being so, such arbitrary amount would constitute a penalty. . . ." Given the proofs of the farm's value, the verdict of $7,000 was well within the difference between the purchase and market prices.

COMMENT: APPLYING DAMAGE CLAUSES

The *Wilt* case raises the problem of the "undifferentiated" clause. The conventional view is that a damage formula that "is invariant to the gravity of the breach," that is, applies to a variety of breaches of varying degrees of importance, is not a reasonable effort to estimate damages. Lake River Corp. v. Carborundum Co., 769 F.2d 1284 (7th Cir.1985). This is especially true when the fixed sum greatly exceeds losses likely to flow from minor breaches. It should be obvious that the doctrines operating here require careful attention, else the loophole of escape from agreed terms will be too readily accessible. One might ask why it is not a good idea to limit the "reasonableness" test to the breach that actually occurred and is sued upon, or why a defaulter should escape a contract term by drawing attention to "what might have been" had a different breach occurred.

These problems serve as a reminder of the overriding importance of "interpretation," determining what the parties intended a given clause to do or to be. If a contract term on remedies does not reach a dispute at all, there is of course no occasion to confront the term's "reasonableness" in the circumstances.

Consider the following situations:

(1) Plaintiff, a city, contracted with a contractor (defendant) for the construction of a parking garage. Various disputes arose during construction, including the question of defendant's entitlement to progress payments. As a result, defendant left the job some five months before the designated completion date (a breach, said the trial court). Plaintiff was forced to retain another contractor to finish the project, which delayed the garage's opening. Plaintiff's suit against the contractor included a claim for liquidated damages, under the following clause: "As actual damages for any delay in completing the work . . . are

impossible to determine, the Contractors and their Sureties shall be liable for [the sum of $1,000] as fixed, agreed and liquidated damages for each calendar day of delay from the above stipulated completion date until such work is satisfactorily completed and accepted." At trial, plaintiff recovered only actual damages. On appeal, the denial of liquidated damages was affirmed. The damage clause, by its terms, dealt only with "delay"; the language used failed to clearly indicate that the parties also intended to cover "abandonment" of the work, "an entirely separate eventuality." It followed that liability under the clause did not attach "until the contractor had fulfilled its agreement." Plaintiff's contention that the court's reading of the clause would encourage contractors to abandon projects in order to avoid contractual delay damages was found unavailing, since owners were always free to negotiate for delay damages even in the event of abandonment. City of Elmira v. Larry Walter, Inc., 76 N.Y.2d 912, 563 N.Y.S.2d 45, 564 N.E.2d 655 (1990).

Would the result have been different had the clause provided for liquidated damages until "the entire completion of the work"? At least one court has given a "yes" answer. City of Boston v. New England Sales & Mfg. Corp., 386 Mass. 820, 438 N.E.2d 68 (1982) (liquidated damages recoverable beyond date of abandonment but time taken to complete work with another contractor must be "reasonable"; the injured party must act promptly to complete work).

(2) Plaintiff contractor sued to recover $21,300 withheld by the defendant city from the price it agreed to pay plaintiff for constructing four piers for a bridge across the Mississippi River. The contract fixed a time limit of 350 days for completion of the piers. A clause in the contract stated that the bridge was to be operated as a toll bridge, and that "delay in completion will cause interference with the traffic and losses, such as lost earnings, interest on investment, administration expenses and other tangible and intangible loss" and will inconvenience the public. To partially cover such losses and expenses, the city was given the right to deduct as liquidated damages $250 for each day that completion of the piers was delayed. Plaintiff was late by 96½ days. For access to the western end of the bridge, which was on the Arkansas shore, the state of Arkansas had agreed to construct a highway. Because of that state's delay in constructing the highway, the entire bridge was completed at least 30 days before the bridge could be used, since there was no access at the western end. Under these circumstances, a deduction of $250 a day for the 96½ day period would, said the court, be "inequitable and unreasonable and would amount to the infliction of a penalty." The parties intended to provide for losses "caused by a delay in completion," that is, their purpose was to guard against losses caused by delay in completing the bridge when this delay was due to plaintiff's delay in building the four piers. Here the bridge could not be used anyway. "[I]f the contingency upon which the presupposition [of the damages a breach would incur] is based never happens, the presupposition must vanish." Massman Constr. Co. v. City Council of Greenville, Miss., 147 F.2d 925 (5th Cir.1945).

Is this "interpretation"? The Rest.2d § 356(1), through comment and illustration, indicates that the *Massman* clause, in the circumstances of that case, is "unenforceable on grounds of public policy," a penalty.

(3) A farmer contracted to sell to a canning company all the tomatoes grown on the farmer's six-acre farm during the 1944 season, for a price of $28 a ton. The contract provided in Clause 12:

[I]f Grower shall fail to deliver to the Company any part or all of the Tomatoes herein contracted for, . . . the Company will sustain substantial damages, uncertain in amount, and not readily susceptible of proof under the rules of evidence, and great and irreparable damage to the Company will result from a breach of this agreement on the part of the Grower, and Grower hereby covenants and agrees with the Company that in case of such failure on Grower's part Grower shall and will pay to the Company the sum of $300 as liquidated damages and not as a penalty.

After delivering 10.99 tons of tomatoes to the company, the farmer sold the balance of the crop (about 44 tons) on the open market at prices varying between $33 and $36 a ton. A vice-president of the company testified that, from past experience, the company had learned that it would normally be advantageous to a grower to deliver one-third of the crop under contract during the "glut" period when tomato prices were low, and to sell two-thirds in the open market when prices had risen; and that the $300 figure in this contract was based on an estimate of $50 an acre as the company's loss in such a case, through calculation of the average yield per acre of this grower's six-acre farm and the range of tomato prices the previous year. On motion, the trial judge struck out this testimony. The appellate court held this was not error. The sum fixed was the same for both total and partial breach. Furthermore, "the specified damages are in no way proportionate to the possible extent of the prospective breach, nor do we find that the prospective damages for failure to deliver tomatoes having a ready market are incapable or difficult of ascertainment. . . . [C]lause 12 of the contract is a penalty and hence unenforceable." H.J. McGrath Co. v. Wisner, 189 Md. 260, 55 A.2d 793 (1947).

Can this be right? Observe that the court appears to treat the difficulty of estimating possible damages as a requirement or test with independent significance. Further, absent explicit language, should it be presumed that contracting parties intend a damages provision to apply only to "material" and not "partial" breaches? Cases illustrating one state's consistent position on nonmaterial breaches are collected in United Air Lines, Inc. v. Austin Travel Corp., 867 F.2d 737 (2d Cir.1989).

PROBLEM

Company breached a vice-president's two-year employment contract by discharging the officer without cause. The contract provided: "Should this Agreement be terminated by Company without cause and prior to its expiration date, Company will be responsible for fulfilling the entire unpaid salary obligation of this Agreement for the full period of two years." The vice-president is entitled to $75,000 under this provision. Shortly after the dismissal, the vice-president went to work for another firm, in a similar position, and was paid $50,000 for the balance of the term of the breached contract.

(1) Is evidence of the $50,000 earnings relevant on the issue of the validity of the clause in question?

(2) Will the vice-president recover $75,000 from Company?

(3) Would your answers change if the vice-president had been paid $150,000 by the second employer?

––––––––––

Samson Sales, Inc. v. Honeywell, Inc.

Supreme Court of Ohio, 1984.
12 Ohio St.3d 27, 465 N.E.2d 392.

[Plaintiff, operator of a pawn shop, contracted with Morse Signal for a burglar alarm system, agreeing to pay $1,500 at the installation and $150 a month thereafter for five years. Defendant Honeywell subsequently acquired Morse Signal, assuming the contract with plaintiff. A burglary occurred at plaintiff's shop, but defendant refused to pay more than $50 for the loss. Plaintiff sued, seeking $68,303 for merchandise lost in the burglary; it alleged that defendant's negligent failure to transmit the alarm signal to the police, as the agreement required, was a breach of contract. Defendant invoked the following provision of the agreement:

> It is agreed by and between the Parties that Company is not an insurer; and that this Agreement in no way binds Company as an insurer of the premises or of the property of the Subscriber, and that all charges are based solely on the value of the service, maintenance and installation of the system. In the event of loss or damage to Subscriber resulting by reason of failure of the performance of such service or the failure of the system to properly operate, Company's liability, if any, shall be limited to the sum of Fifty Dollars ($50.00) as liquidated damages and not as a penalty and this liability shall be exclusive.

The trial court awarded plaintiff summary judgment, but limited damages to $50. An intermediate appellate court reversed on the ground the contract clause was an unenforceable penalty.]

KERNS, J. The only issue of any consequence in this appeal is whether the exculpatory clause limiting Honeywell's liability to $50 is valid and enforceable.

While some jurisdictions have rejected such contract provisions on policy grounds, clauses in contracts providing for reasonable liquidated damages are recognized in Ohio as valid and enforceable. Jones v. Stevens, 112 Ohio St. 43, 146 N.E. 894 (1925). However, reasonable compensation for actual damages is the legitimate objective of such . . . provisions and where the amount specified is manifestly inequitable and unrealistic, courts will ordinarily regard it as a penalty. Hence, Honeywell's standard reference "to the sum of Fifty Dollars ($50.00) as liquidated damages and not as a penalty" is by no means conclusive or controlling in this case.

Whether a particular sum specified in a contract is intended as a penalty or as liquidated damages depends upon the operative facts and circumstances surrounding each particular case, but time has apparently had no undermining influence upon the guiding principles initially set forth in Jones v. Stevens, supra[:]

> Where the parties have agreed on the amount of damages, ascertained by estimation and adjustment, and have expressed this agreement in clear and unambiguous terms, the amount so fixed should be treated as liquidated damages and not as a pen-

alty, if the damages would be (1) uncertain as to amount and difficult of proof, and if (2) the contract as a whole is not so manifestly unconscionable, unreasonable, and disproportionate in amount as to justify the conclusion that it does not express the true intention of the parties, and if (3) the contract is consistent with the conclusion that it was the intention of the parties that damages in the amount stated should follow the breach thereof.

With reference to the initial test suggested in *Jones*, the court of appeals expressly noted that "the damages here are patently estimable," and this finding is attuned to the indisputable fact that the damages in this case would be as readily ascertainable as the damages in a multitude of other conceivable situations involving negligence and/or breach of contract. As to the second guideline recommended by this court, the stated sum of $50 in the contract involved in this case is manifestly disproportionate to either the consideration paid by Samson or the possible damage that reasonably could be foreseen from the failure of Honeywell to notify the police of the burglary. And with particular emphasis upon the third condition proposed in [*Jones*], it is beyond comprehension that the parties intended that damages in the amount of $50 should follow the negligent breach of the contract.

In other words, an examination of the minute type used in the standard contract issued by Morse, as well as a fair construction of the contract provision as a whole, fails to evince a conscious intention of the parties to consider, estimate, or adjust the damages that might reasonably flow from the negligent breach of the agreement. Surely, Samson, which apparently had some business experience, did not pay $10,500 for the mere possibility of recouping $50 if Honeywell provided no service at all under the terms of the contract. Characteristically, therefore, and by way of analysis, the nominal amount set forth in the contract between Samson and Honeywell has the nature and appearance of a penalty.

Accordingly, the judgment of the court of appeals is affirmed.

NOTE

Courts regularly assert that liquidated damage provisions are unenforceable if they lead to awards that are unreasonably small as well as too large, but cases such as *Samson* in which a court actually holds liquidated damages unreasonably low are rare. It would be odd if things were otherwise. Contracting parties often agree to waive consequential damages, and such waivers are routinely enforced. Limitations on damages seem the same. Moreover, instead of limiting damages, a contracting party can merely limit its obligations under the contract in the first instance. How is an artificially low liquidated damages clause any different from an exceedingly modest promissory undertaking? Even on its facts, *Samson* is an unusual case. The majority of suits against suppliers of alarm systems come out the other way. See, e.g., Fretwell v. Protection Alarm Co., 764 P.2d 149 (1988) (*Samson*-type clause which "makes no attempt to reasonably forecast just compensation for the harm caused, [but] is clearly an attempt to limit damages, is neither unconscionable nor against public policy"); Better Food Markets v. American Dist. Tel. Co., 40 Cal.2d 179, 253 P.2d 10 (1953) (clause akin to that in *Samson* is a provision for liquidated damages and valid in circumstances). Parties bringing these suits against alarm companies often employ a tort theory (perhaps joining a contract claim with the tort claim). The tort commonly asserted is negligence. Language often will be decisive here; a failure to include the terms "negligence" or "tort" has led to the conclusion that an intention to limit noncontractual liability has not been sufficiently demonstrated. Compare Schrier v. Beltway Alarm Co., 73 Md.App. 281, 533 A.2d 1316 (1987), with DCR Inc. v. Peak Alarm Co., 663 P.2d 433 (Utah 1983). Often the cases that sound in contract in which courts refuse to enforce clauses with low liquidated damages are cases in which the breach is willful and wanton. See, e.g., Core-Mark Midcontinent, Inc. v. Sonitrol Corp., __ P.3d __, 2012 WL 2994956 (Colo. App. 2012); ADT Security. Services., Inc. v. Swenson, 276 F.R.D. 278, 301 (D. Minn. 2011); Fed. Ins. Co. v. Honeywell, Inc., 641 F. Supp. 1560, 1562 (S.D.N.Y. 1986).

————

COMMENT: THE PENALTY RULE AND "EFFICIENCY"

Judicial scrutiny of agreed damages provisions has received criticism from some academics using economic analysis. An example is Goetz & Scott, Liquidated Damages, Penalties and the Just Compensation Principle: Some Notes on an Enforcement Model and a Theory of Efficient Breach, 77 Colum.L.Rev. 554 (1977).

The authors make these points, among others:

(1) One explanation for judicial limitations on the parties' contract-making power may be sought in the belief that an overly-compensatory damage clause signals some impairment of the process by which agreement was reached, such as fraud, duress, or mistake. But this explanation does not justify the general rule invalidating penalty clauses, for invalidation occurs even when the clause is shown to have resulted from a fairly-bargained exchange. Furthermore, modern contract law provides an arsenal of more particularized weapons for striking down agreements that do not result from fair bargaining. A blunderbuss rule invalidating all penalty clauses is not needed in order to deal effectively with defects in the agreement process.

(2) Those who argue in support of "efficient breaches" (efficient in the sense that at least the breacher is better off and the justly-compensated innocent party is no worse off) fear that an *in terrorem* penalty clause would, if valid and enforceable, discourage efficient breaches. But there are countervailing arguments. One is that the efficient breach would not necessarily be precluded by recognizing the validity of a penalty clause. It would remain open to the parties to renegotiate, after the breach, the allocation of efficiency gains between breacher and non-breacher.

(3) The postulated objective of the damage remedy, just compensation, is not necessarily achieved if the law's measurement rules do not recognize as provable, or compensable, all of the losses—perhaps idiosyncratic or subjective values—that the promisee may contemplate or suffer. What a court sees as a penalty clause may instead be an effort to bargain for an amount that is in fact what is needed to put the injured party in the same position he or she would be in had the other performed.

Are these arguments persuasive? If penalty-type clauses generally seem associated with a breakdown in the bargaining process, or perhaps inattention at the time of contracting, is there something to be said for a flat rule rather than a fact-specific inquiry into the reasons for imbalance? Moreover, is it likely that most—or even many—liquidated damages clauses are intended to protect idiosyncratic or subjective values?

Before leaving liquidated damages and the question of allowing parties to set damages themselves, it is worth noting the direction one is led when approaching the question of contract remedies from an economic perspective. Return to Holmes's basic insight that a damages-based contracts regime essentially gives the person who makes a legally enforceable promise a choice between performing and paying a sum of money. For some modern law-and-economics scholars, it is but a short step to the conclusion that every contract includes an option in the technical sense. In lieu of performance, the promisor has an option to pay a fixed amount of money. Damages, seen in this light, are merely the price promisors pay to release themselves from the obligation to perform. So, the problem of determining the appropriate damage award is simply a matter of option pricing. What amount would two sophisticated parties agree upon if they were negotiating explicitly for this option? Indeed, we should imagine that when two parties negotiate at arm's length, one of the issues they should settle is the price the promisor must pay if he chooses not to perform. And if they do, why should we think that expectation damages—or any of the other measures we have explored—is a good prediction of the price of this option? Given all the variables that must be taken into account—mitigation, overreliance, imperfect information, costly renegotiation, imperfect factfinding after the fact—there may be little reason to think that the parties should fix on an option price that is equal to expectation damages. This is the view some scholars have advanced. Robert E. Scott & George Triantis, Embedded Options and the Case Against Compensation in Contract Law, 104 Colum. L. Rev. 1428 (2004).

The remedy for breach is, from this perspective, no different from any other term in a contract. It may be in the parties' mutual interest that the goods be sold with a warranty. So, too, it may be in their mutual interest that the promisor have the option of paying expectation damages in the event of breach. But the parties may be better off without a warranty. So, too, the parties may be better off if the price of nonperformance were something other than expectation damages. From this perspective, the problem of contract damages is simply a problem of establishing a sensible default rule. Alternatively, it may suggest that the law should take a different path—instead of providing for damages, the law might require breaching parties actually to perform. This issue is explored in the next section.

SECTION 5. ENFORCEMENT IN EQUITY

INTRODUCTORY NOTE

The preceding section opened up the question of agreed remedies, attempts by the parties themselves to regulate damage awards. In a grand case that suggests what is to come in this section, Manchester Dairy System v. Hayward, 82 N.H. 193, 132 A. 12 (1926), the parties' agreement included two provisions addressed to remedies in the event of breach.

Plaintiff Dairy System (the Ass'n) entered into a contract with Hayward by which he agreed to sell to the Ass'n, for three years, all the dairy products produced on his farm. The Ass'n agreed to pay a monthly base price and to distribute the balance of each year's net earnings among its members, including Hayward, according to the quantity and quality of dairy products furnished. The contract recited that it was one of a series of identical contracts made between the Ass'n and its members, that it would be impracticable and extremely difficult to determine damages from any breach, and therefore each member agreed to pay the Ass'n $5 per cow as liquidated damages for any breach through selling milk or dairy products to other buyers. The contract also provided that, in the event of breach or threatened breach by a member, the Ass'n "shall be entitled to an injunction to prevent breach or threatened breach thereof, or to a decree for specific performance hereof." It was provided also that the Ass'n could not replace by purchase in the open market any dairy products that members failed to deliver.

In the Association's action for specific performance against Hayward, the trial court found that he had never delivered any milk from his 12 cows. The evidence showed that "there was plenty of milk to be had in the open market in the territory covered by the Manchester Dairy System." The trial court concluded that the contract was binding on Hayward, but refused an injunction against selling to others since the court knew him to be "a man of honor" who would perform his duties once he understood them. The court added that even if an injunction were issued and Hayward persisted in violating it, the result would have to be either fine or imprisonment—punishments that would be "neither merited by, nor a reasonable remedy for, a breach of his duty to deliver to this plaintiff the milk of his twelve cows." The trial court therefore denied all equitable relief. On appeal, the Supreme Court reversed, on this reasoning:

(1) The contract clause expressly providing for equitable relief was ineffective. "Jurisdiction over the subject matter of a controversy cannot be created or conferred by the agreement of the parties."

(2) But equity can enforce a contract, even one relating to personal property, where the legal remedy is not adequate. This contract was one of a series which together constituted a single agreement binding all member-subscribers to the Ass'n and to each other. It was a condition of the multi-party compact that the Ass'n could not replace in the open market milk that any member failed to deliver. Each withdrawal by a member would cast a larger share of the group's operating expenses on the remaining members. If one member could breach with impunity, so might others, and each withdrawal "would inevitably tend to promote further withdrawals and impair the ability of the Ass'n to secure new members."

(3) The provision for liquidated damages of $5 per cow did not make the legal remedy adequate, since, for the reasons noted, the harm done was more far-reaching and could not be measured. Nor did this clause show the parties' intent that defendant was to have an option either to perform or pay the $5. Strict performance by members was essential to the survival of the Ass'n and far more important to it than this small sum. Any doubt on this issue was removed by the clause calling for an injunction or specific performance in the event of breach.

(4) The trial court was right in denying affirmative specific performance. This would have been "a cumbersome and expensive process" and could have

been accomplished "only by placing the defendant's milk-producing operations in charge of the officers of the court." But there is no such objection to the negative form of order, an injunction against selling to others, which amounts to indirect enforcement by relying on defendant's own interest to induce him to perform.

(5) It may be that enforcement of the decree would impose on the defendant some burden that would be out of proportion to the benefit accruing to the plaintiff. The case must therefore be returned to the trial court so that it might examine this question. But the hardship involved in fine and imprisonment, punishments imposed if Hayward persisted in his defiance of the court's injunctive order, would not be the kind of hardship that could be taken into account at all, since it would be due only to his own disobedience.

Manchester Dairy, it might be noted, was handed down by the same court that three years later authored Hawkins v. McGee.

––––––––

Edge Group WAICCS LLC v. Sapir Group LLC

United States District Court, Southern District of New York, 2010.
705 F. Supp. 2d 304.

DOLINGER, UNITED STATES MAGISTRATE JUDGE. Plaintiff Edge Group WAICCS, LLC ("Edge Group") commenced this lawsuit to seek specific performance of a contract for the sale of an interest in a limited liability company. The anticipated transaction would have involved a payment of $20 million by defendant Sapir Group LLC ("Sapir") in exchange for a 50 percent interest in WAICCS Las Vegas 2 LLC, a limited liability company that was the sole member of another limited liability company, WAICCS Las Vegas 3 LLC. WAICCS 3 in turn holds a 20.4 percent undivided ownership interest in a parcel of undeveloped real estate in Las Vegas, Nevada. . . .

[On May 1, 2008, Sapir entered into a binding contract for the sale to Sapir of Edge Group's interest in WAICCS 2.] The closing was scheduled for May 30, 2008. Before the scheduled closing, plaintiff delivered to Sapir all required documents for the transaction to close. On May 29, 2008, however, Sapir notified Edge Group that it had decided not to go through with the closing and purchase. The decision by Sapir was not based on any failure of Edge Group to perform. Instead, defendant stated that it had decided to abandon the transaction because of the speculative nature of the project planned for development on the site.

Plaintiff commenced suit on June 4, 2008, seeking principally specific performance. It amended its complaint a few days later, and Sapir filed an answer, including several affirmative defenses, on September 16, 2008. The principal thrust of the answer is that, under the Amended Option Agreement, plaintiff's only remedy for the breach is payment of the escrow funds. . . .

Both sides seek summary judgment on the question of whether Edge Group should be awarded specific performance. That form of relief involves an exercise of the court's equitable powers. For Edge Group to justify its entitlement to such a remedy, it must first establish the existence of a contract with Sapir, Sapir's breach of that contract by non-performance, Edge Group's substantial performance of its obligations under the Option

Agreement and its ability and willingness to undertake any additional steps required of it under the contract. In addition, Edge Group must demonstrate that the invocation of the court's powers in equity is justified by the absence of an adequate remedy at law.

There is no dispute in this case that a valid and binding contract providing an option to Sapir was entered into by way of the assignment of the original option from Credit Suisse to Sapir in conjunction with amendments to the Option Agreement. There is also no real dispute that, pursuant to the terms of that amended Agreement, defendant gave notice of its exercise of the option on May 1, 2008, within the contractual period for doing so, and that this step created a binding contract for the sale to Sapir of Edge Group's interest in WAICCS 2. The record also reflects that Edge Group fulfilled all of its pre-closing obligations under the contract, that Sapir communicated on May 29—one day before the scheduled closing—its refusal to go ahead with the purchase, and that that decision was not a consequence of any failure by Edge Group to perform or of any other form of misconduct by plaintiff.

In sum, there is no question that the parties entered into a valid contract for the sale of plaintiff's interest in WAICCS 2 and that defendant breached its contractual obligation to purchase that interest. The remaining question is whether, in these circumstances, it is appropriate for the court to order specific performance of that contract by Sapir because of the inability of legal damages to compensate plaintiff fully.

In assessing this question, we note that the guiding consideration is " 'the difficulty of proving damages with reasonable certainty.' " Van Wagner Adver. Corp., 67 N.Y.2d at 193, 501 N.Y.S.2d at 632, 492 N.E.2d 756 (quoting Restatement (Second) of Contracts § 360[a] (1981)). Although case law refers, in appropriate circumstances, to the uniqueness of the product that was the subject of a breached contract in a sale context, that is ultimately not the test; rather, in all cases the court must address the practical question of whether the damages of the aggrieved party can be reliably determined:

> The point at which breach of a contract will be redressable by specific performance thus must lie not in any inherent physical uniqueness of the property but instead in the uncertainty of valuing it. "What matters, in measuring money damages, is the volume, refinement, and reliability of the available information about substitutes for the subject matter of the breached contract. When the relevant information is thin and unreliable, there is a substantial risk that an award of money damages will either exceed or fall short of the promisee's actual loss. Of course this risk can always be reduced—but only at great cost when reliable information is difficult to obtain. Conversely, when there is a great deal of consumer behavior generating abundant and highly dependable information about substitutes, the risk of error in measuring the promisee's loss may be reduced at much smaller cost. In asserting that the subject matter of a particular contract is unique and has no established market value, a court is really saying that it cannot obtain, at reasonable cost, enough information about substitutes to permit it to calculate an award of money damages without imposing an unacceptably high risk of undercompensation on the injured promisee."

Id. at 193, 501 N.Y.S. 2d at 632, 492 N.E. 2d 756 (quoting Anthony T. Kronman, "Specific Performance", 45 U. Chi. L.Rev. 351, 362 (1978)).

In applying this test, the trial court has broad discretion, although certain parameters have been recognized by the New York courts. Thus, real estate is deemed to be inherently unique, a notion that has led to a pattern of decisions granting purchasers specific performance of real-estate sale contracts. Similarly, the courts have typically held that the shares of closely held corporations are not readily appraised and hence that specific performance is properly granted on contracts for the sale of those shares. More generally, the courts look to the specific circumstances of the case to determine whether there is a sufficiently reliable means of measuring value for purposes of awarding contract damages. E.g., JMG Custom Homes, Inc. v. Ryan, 45 A.D.3d 1278, 1281, 844 N.Y.S.2d 817, 819–20 (4th Dep't 2007) (granting specific performance of an oral agreement to exchange two all-terrain vehicles and a snowmobile for a discount on the purchase price of a home because of the difficulty of calculating the value of the vehicles); Garber v. Siegel, 194 Misc. 966, 969, 87 N.Y.S.2d 597, 600 (Sup. Ct. Kings County 1948), modified on other grounds, 274 A.D. 1068, 1068, 86 N.Y.S.2d 456, 456 (2d Dep't 1949) (granting plaintiff specific performance of contract for sale of carbonated-beverage route and business where plaintiff helped develop business serving specific customers for many years and his loss of future profits could not readily be ascertained). See also Destiny USA Holdings, LLC, 69 A.D.3d at 221–22, 889 N.Y.S.2d at 801–02 (granting preliminary injunction requiring bank to fund draw requests on construction loan because of uncertainty in calculating damage to plaintiff's reputation and other harm stemming from inability to complete "groundbreaking" and "unprecedented" environmentally-friendly development project).

In this case, Sapir argues that measuring damages from its breach is not so inherently imprecise as to justify specific performance. It also argues that specific performance should be denied here based on two other equitable principles. It first cites plaintiff's obligation to mitigate its damages, and then asserts that specific performance should not be granted because it does not currently have the cash in hand to perform its end of the bargain, that is, to pay the $19 million owed for the purchase over and above the escrowed funds, an argument premised on the notion that specific performance will not be ordered if performance is impossible. *See Restatement (Second) of Contracts* § 357 cmt. C (1981). We address these arguments separately. . . .

In support of the contention that, as a matter of law, a legal remedy is adequate here, defendant notes that contract damages are normally measured by the difference between the value to the injured party of the performance that should have been provided by the breaching party and what the plaintiff was left with in the wake of the breach. Applying this principle, defendant contends that the difference between the $20 million purchase price and the value of Edge Group's interest in WAICCS 2 at the time of defendant's breach may be reliably determined. For this proposition, Sapir relies principally on the fact that an appraisal of the real estate parcel owned in common by WAICCS 3 and other parties was performed shortly after defendant's breach, and resulted in a valuation of $788 million. Defendant further asserts that this valuation should be binding on plaintiff because the appraisal was prepared on behalf of the property owners, including Edge Group, outside of the context of this litigation, and was later used to extend the payment schedule for a loan secured by the property. As further evidence of value, defendant also mentions, albeit without documentation, that Sapir itself paid approximately $21 million at about the same time for a share of a company that was a co-tenant of the Las Vegas property. Based on these facts, defendant asserts that the court can value the Edge Group's interest that Sapir failed to purchase for $20 million, and that in fact the value of that interest exceeded the purchase price, thus—unless the one million dollar deposit is considered liquidated damages—compelling the conclusion that plaintiff is entitled to no damages. We consider these arguments in turn.

The appraisal of the property owned in part by WAICCS 3—which Sapir cites to establish the value of Edge Group's interest in WAICCS 2—was undertaken in June 2008 at the request of Credit Suisse, not Edge Group, although that fact is not crucial for present purposes. More relevant, however, are certain details about both the context of the appraisal, the substance of the appraisal report, and the testimony of the person who prepared it.

The appraisal was of the Las Vegas parcel itself, not of the value of an interest in WAICCS 2, which was the asset to be sold under the Option Agreement. This distinction is important for several reasons.

Edge Group's ownership interest was in WAICCS 2, which in turn had an ownership interest in WAICCS 3, which in turn had an interest, in the form of an undivided tenancy-in-common with several other entities, in the undeveloped real property that was appraised. Moreover, the terms that governed the tenancy-in-common of the parcel sharply limited the ability of WAICCS 3—in which Edge Group held an interest through WAICCS 2—to sell its interest in the property. Thus, WAICCS 3 was precluded from selling a majority of its interest absent the unanimous consent of the other co-tenants in the Las Vegas parcel, and it could not sell even a minority of its interest to any broadly-defined competitor of those co-tenants. It is not surprising, then, that the sale of the Edge Group interest in WAICCS 2 was characterized by Credit Suisse as "very complicated to say the least."

The June 2008 appraisal of the parcel, cited by Sapir, did not consider the impact of these restrictions since it was looking only to the prospects for sale of the real estate rather than of the encumbered Edge Group interest in one of the two LLCs in the ownership chain. Necessarily, then, that appraisal would not reflect a valuation of the Edge Group's interest, much less an assessment of the viability of valuing that interest.

Apart from the general irrelevance of the June 2008 appraisal to the question of the adequacy of a legal remedy in this case, the substance of the appraisal report—viewed in light of the testimony of the appraiser—reflects that it has no probative weight even as an assessment of the value of the parcel at the time of defendant's breach, much less as an indicator that one could reliably value the LCC interest of plaintiff. The same appraiser had performed an appraisal of the property in January 2008 and offered the figure of $788 million. He then performed a comparable appraisal in June of that year and, in an identically-worded report, he arrived at the same figure. In his deposition testimony, however, he conceded that he had found no comparable sales during the relevant period and hence had simply utilized the prior number. Moreover, he conceded that he had had no pertinent data or information on which to base an appraisal, stating "we didn't have evidence to get to our conclusions."

The market conditions at that time only underscore the absence of a basis for the June 2008 appraisal. As all parties concede, the appraisal was made during the period of the recent financial and real-estate bubble collapse and accompanying major economic downturn, including a collapse in the market for commercial real estate on the Strip in Las Vegas. Indeed, as the appraiser testified, there was a major downturn in business during this period, including in the gaming industry, and there were no sales of comparable properties from late 2007 to April 2009. Indeed, it was apparently at least in part because of these conditions (1) that Edge was very anxious to sell its interest, (2) that Sapir was the only potential buyer that Credit Suisse could locate, (3) that Sapir decided at the last minute to repudiate its contractual obligation to purchase because the investment was too "speculative," and (4) that Alex Sapir testified that "[i]t wouldn't be a good deal to put any new money in this deal in the current environment."

Under all of these circumstances, . . . the appraiser could not be a competent expert on the valuation of the parcel itself as of June 2008, much less on the value of the Edge Group's interest in WAICCS 2. Necessarily, then, the appraiser's June 2008 appraisal of the parcel cannot be deemed at all probative as to the availability of a reasonably accurate valuation of the plaintiff's interest in WAICCS 2.

As for defendant's brief allusion to its asserted purchase of an interest in another entity, which purportedly had an interest in the parcel at issue, it offers no details or documentation, and relies solely on a passing reference by Alex Sapir. That brief and conclusory testimony is plainly not sufficient to establish that the value of plaintiff's interest in WAICCS 2 can be reliably determined.

Given that doubts about the adequacy of a damage remedy should be resolved in favor of awarding specific performance, Restatement (Second) Contracts § 359 cmt. a (1981), and in light of the fact that none of the methods that defendant has devised for calculating the value of Edge Group's interest in WAICCS 2 at the time of defendant's breach are reliable, we conclude that Edge Group is entitled to summary judgment on the inability to calculate, and therefore the inadequacy of, its legal damages. . . .

To the extent that defendant may be relying on two other arguments targeting the propriety of specific performance under traditional equitable principles, we review them briefly. First, Sapir has asserted in its answer that all relief should be denied because plaintiff failed adequately to mitigate its loss. Additionally, Sapir contends that it would be impossible for it to perform its obligations under the contract to purchase Edge Group's interest. We review these claims in turn.

Insofar as Sapir asserts that plaintiff failed to mitigate its damages, the argument fails first and foremost because mitigation is not required in order to justify specific performance. In addition, defendant cannot demonstrate, as a matter of law, that plaintiff failed to make reasonable attempts to mitigate. There is no dispute that Credit Suisse attempted to find a buyer on behalf of plaintiff, and could locate only Sapir, which in turn defaulted on its purchase contract, apparently as a result of market conditions. Moreover, as plaintiff points out, during the pendency of this lawsuit—filed only days after the default—it engaged in efforts to sell its interest to Sapir, albeit at a reduced price, and that effort apparently led to the scheduling of a closing, only to be frustrated when Sapir once again backed out at the last minute. In short, the evidentiary record is consistent with reasonable efforts by plaintiff to mitigate.

Additionally, Sapir argues that specific performance may not be awarded because it is incapable of performing. In support of that contention, it proffers a declaration by Alex Sapir, asserting in entirely conclusory terms and without the benefit of any documentation, that defendant currently—or at least when Alex Sapir executed his declaration—has only $4,000 in cash and cash equivalents on hand and is more than $250,000,000 in debt. This skeletal assertion is plainly inadequate to demonstrate as a matter of law that defendant cannot perform even if ordered by a court to do so.

Both sides concur that impossibility may bar specific performance, but they differ on the precise scope of this rule. Plaintiff asserts that the test is whether the defendant was capable of performing at the time of the breach, not later on, and in support of this contention it notes that otherwise a breaching party may manipulate the outcome by deliberately divesting itself of the capacity to perform after its breach. Applying this standard, Edge Group asserts that Sapir was plainly capable of performing at the time of the breach, for which proposition it cites the deposition testimony of Alex Sapir that Sapir had the $20 million dollar purchase price available on the closing date. It also cites testimony to the effect that Alex Sapir and his company had available to them essentially limitless financing from Alex's father, Tamir Sapir, who was to provide the funds to purchase Edge Group's interest on the original closing date. It further offers facts from which one could draw the inference that defendant's finances have been deliberately manipulated to permit it to claim financial incapacity to pay for the option that it contracted to purchase less than two years ago.

Defendant does not meaningfully dispute that it had the capacity at the time of the breach to pay for Edge Group's interest in WAICCS 2. Indeed, Alex Sapir admitted at his deposition that it could have done so, saying that "[a]t the time we decided we had better uses for our funds" and that it could have closed had it wanted to do so. As noted, it even represents that it purchased an interest in another entity for more than $21 million only days before the cancellation of the closing with the Edge Group. In its opposition papers it asserts, however, that it has since lost the ability to perform—although it does not even attempt to document this assertion—and it presses the notion that this incapacity precludes equitable relief for the plaintiff.

We conclude that specific performance may be precluded by impossibility of performance either at the time of breach or at the time that court relief is sought. The courts have long recognized that impossibility (or even impracticability) of performance at the time that performance was due may excuse enforcement of a contract if the impossibility was brought about by *force majeure,* or circumstances that were not caused by the party. In such a case, the court will read into the contract a clause excusing performance if an essential element to the contract ceases to be available prior to the time at which performance is due absent the fault of either party. In those circumstances, the aggrieved party cannot establish the existence of an enforceable contract at the time that performance was due, and therefore the remedy of specific performance will not be available to it.

It is equally the case, however, that if a party cannot perform at the time of the application for specific performance, that fact will preclude the grant of specific performance. See Restatement (Second) of Contracts § 357 cmt. c (1981) ("[A] court will not order a performance that is impossible.") As the New York Court of Appeals has made plain, a court should not order specific performance, or other equitable relief, unless the defendant is capable of complying: "The court will not make what may prove to be a futile order." S.E.S. Importers., Inc. v. Pappalardo, 464, 442 N.Y.S.2d 453, 458, 425 N.E.2d 841 (1981).

As we have observed, there is no question on the current record that defendant was able to perform as of May 30, 2008. As for whether it is now unable to do so, its bare proffer to that effect plainly does not justify a determination, as a matter of law, that specific performance is unwarranted. Indeed, defendant's financial status is likely to be a fairly complex matter to unearth, and it makes no effort whatsoever to justify its bare contention other than by allusion to cash or equivalents on hand and the amount of its debt, and the conclusory assertion by Mr. Sapir that the company cannot perform. Moreover, and most strikingly, Mr. Sapir's representation is seemingly in direct conflict with testimony that he gave at his deposition less than two months prior to his execution of his July 30, 2009 supplemental declaration; at that deposition, he testified that Sapir could still close the sale if it wanted to do so. In short, the record does not remotely justify . . . relief for defendant on this aspect of plaintiff's case based on impossibility or impracticability.

There remains for consideration whether plaintiff has itself adequately justified, as a matter of law, the appropriateness of equitable relief. For the reasons that we have noted, the record reflects that a remedy at law, in the form of damages, is not likely to be adequate because of the undisputed circumstances that render any attempt to value Edge Group's interest at the time of defendant's breach mere speculation. That interest was in an unlisted limited-liability company for which there was no apparent market at the time. Moreover, it appears that valuation of plaintiff's interest was in any event likely to be highly chancy since the company was restricted in its ability to sell its interest in the LLC, and the ability to value that interest was further clouded by the facts (1) that the LLC had an interest only in another LLC (also apparently not publicly or actively traded), (2) that that LLC's value was contingent on the valuation of the undeveloped Las Vegas parcel in which it had a tenancy-in-common with a number of other entities and for which there was no apparent market during the relevant time, and (3) that that LLC was significantly restricted in its ability to transfer its interest in the tenancy-in-common to another entity. In short, specific performance appears amply justified provided that Sapir is capable of complying with such an order or that any incapacity to do so is attributable to its own deliberate actions designed to frustrate relief in this case.

Defendant's showing on impossibility of performance is at best thin to evanescent. Moreover, insofar as it relies solely on the declaration of Alex Sapir, it runs into the well-established rule in this circuit that a party may not evade summary judgment by proffering an affidavit (or declaration) that directly contradicts the affiant's prior deposition testimony. On its face Mr. Sapir's declaration appears to do precisely that. The only possible way to avoid that conclusion would be if defendant could demonstrate that between the time of Mr. Sapir's deposition on June 4, 2009 and the date of the execution of his supplemental declaration on July 30, 2009 some new event occurred that so altered Sapir's financial position as to fundamentally undermine its conceded ability in June 2009 to pay $20 million to acquire Edge Group's interest in WAICCS 2.

Because that question is not answered on the current record, we are prepared to conduct a brief evidentiary hearing on that narrow issue in the event that Sapir can offer competent evidence in support of the notion that its financial status materially changed between June 4 and July 30, 2009 so as preclude its ability to perform its obligations under the Option Agreement as amended. Absent Sapir's ability to make such a showing— and subject to our ruling below regarding the purported preclusive effect of the escrow provision of the Option Agreement—we conclude that Edge Group has established the appropriateness of the equitable remedy of specific performance for Sapir's breach. . . .

———

Curtice Bros. Co. v. Catts

72 N.J.E.Q. 831, 66 A. 935 (Ch.1907)

Complainant, operator of a canning plant, sued for specific performance of a contract wherein defendant, a farmer, had agreed to sell his entire tomato crop from specified land. Vice–Chancellor Leaming rejected defendant's claim that the court was without power to grant equitable relief, saying: "The fundamental principles which guide a court of equity . . . are essentially the same whether the contracts relate to realty or to personalty. [Because] damages for the breach of contract for the sale of personalty are, in most cases, easily ascertainable and recoverable at law, courts of equity . . . withhold equitable relief. Touching contracts for the sale of land, the reverse is the case. But no inherent difference between real estate and personal property controls the exercise of the jurisdiction. Where no adequate remedy at law exists, specific performance of a contract touching the sale of personal property will be decreed with the same freedom as in the case of a contract for the sale of land. . . .

"Complainant's factory has a capacity of about one million cans of tomatoes. The season for packing lasts about six weeks. The preparations made for this six weeks of active work must be carried out in all features to enable the business to succeed. These preparations are primarily based upon the capacity of the plant. . . . With this known capacity and an estimated average yield of tomatoes per acre the acreage of land necessary to supply the plant is calculated. To that end, the contract now in question was made, with other like contracts, covering a sufficient acreage to insure the essential pack. . . . [A] refusal of the parties who contract to supply a given acreage to comply with their contracts leaves the factory helpless, except to whatever extent an uncertain market may perchance supply the deficiency. The condition which arises from the breach of the contracts is not merely a question of the factory being compelled to pay a higher price for the product. Losses sustained in that manner could, with some degree of accuracy, be estimated. The condition which occasions the irreparable injury by reason of the breaches of the contracts is the inability to procure at any price at the time needed and of the quality needed the necessary tomatoes to insure the successful operation of the plant. . . . [T]he very existence of contracts [of this nature] proclaims their necessity to the economic management of the factory. This aspect of the situation bears no resemblance to that of an ordinary contract for the sale of merchandise in the course of an ordinary business. [This] business and its needs are extraordinary. . . . The breach of the contract by one planter differs but in degree from a breach by all.

"The objection that to specifically perform the contract personal services are required will not divest the court of its powers to preserve the benefits of the contract. Defendant may be restrained from selling the crop to others, and, if necessary, a receiver can be appointed to harvest the crop. A decree may be devised pursuant to the prayer of the bill."

––––––––

COMMENT: THE HISTORY OF EQUITY

The division between "law" and "equity" is a peculiarity of the Anglo–American legal order. There has never existed in any other developed system of law the strange phenomenon of two separate sets of courts, administered by different judges and giving different types of remedies, on grounds that were radically different. Yet this was the state of affairs in Anglo–American law for about 500 years. Both in England and the United States attempts began more than a century ago, through legislation, to combine the two competing systems of law and equity. But the 500 years of history that came before still leave an enduring mark on our legal system.

The explanation for the basic division between law and equity can be stated briefly—English law was built and perfected much too soon. This would have been no misfortune at all if the early lawyers and judges had not then proceeded to enclose themselves in their system, refusing to admit new forms of writs, new grounds of action or defense, and new conceptions of morality and policy. The freezing of doctrine and, behind that, the freezing of minds, were never complete, for slow growth and change continued within the common law system. But the freeze was already quite deep by the year 1300. Thereafter, when gross injustices or inadequacies in the legal system were revealed, there was no place to turn but to the King. One might wonder why appeal was not made to the legislature. The Parliament, it is true, had emerged as a somewhat representative assembly, with a share of legislative power, but its members did not conceive it to be their task to grind out correctives to rules of private law. Furthermore, the Parliament came to be dominated by lawyers, who had a stake in the established order and who, it seems, believed that rules of law should not be casually tinkered with. The Parliament did legislate occasionally, but through most of this formative period it stood as a center of resistance to change, not as a source of innovation.

As protest developed and the grievances of suitors multiplied, it was natural that the Chancellor should be the main repository of complaints. The Chancellor was the chief officer of state, equivalent to a modern Prime Minister, as well as the head of the chief secretariat of the Crown and custodian of the King's Great Seal. In the Chancellor's name were issued the ordinary, standard writs through which common law actions were started. It was simply good administration to turn over to the Chancellor's staff the devising of ways for dealing with new problems. In this period the Chancellors were churchmen—bishops at least—and this fact must have influenced their innovations, whether they drew on canon law, reflected religious ideas, or merely acted as educated citizens unencumbered by the technical limitations of the common law. We must stress that the Chancellor was a very high magistrate, with a large responsibility for the administration of royal justice. At this stage in European history, and not only in England, kings had a personal and inescapable duty to render justice to their subjects. This duty could be assigned to courts but the delegation could not wholly discharge the King's responsibility. It was as hard then as it is now to determine precisely what is "justice," but the King's high officials had to seek an answer.

The reforms and innovations accomplished by the English Chancellors had far-reaching consequences throughout private law, including the law of contract. As we shall see in Chapter 2, until the end of the middle ages the common law remedies for enforcing promises were extremely limited. The action of *debt* carried most of the workload. It could be used whenever a promised exchange had been completed on one side so that an obligation on the other side to pay a "sum certain" in money had arisen. If a promise was made in an instrument under seal, the action of covenant was available. But for an array of informal promises, there simply was no common law action to provide a remedy. It seems clear, though the evidence is indirect, that by the year 1400 the Chancery had begun to enforce informal promises. Perhaps the Chancellors were influenced, as common lawyers quite surely were not, by theories of canon law that urged the sanctity of promises and condemned breaches as violations of faith reposed. Recurring and predictable interventions by the Chancellors must have put pressure on the common law judges to extend their remedies, as they eventually did through development of the action of assumpsit, a subject that we have discussed before, supra pp. 111–116, and to which we shall return at the start of the next chapter.

The methods of enforcement developed by the Chancellors differed markedly from the money judgment that became virtually the exclusive sanction of the common law. Specific remedies ordering the defendant to do or not do a particular act were not unusual in the earliest stages of development of the common law, but most of them rapidly became obsolete. There are some survivals of course—e.g., replevin to enable an owner to recover goods and ejectment to recover possession of land that another holds illegally. The so-called "extraordinary remedies" (mandamus, prohibition, quo warranto, habeas corpus, and certiorari) also continue to be used to control inferior courts, public officials, or state-created agencies like corporations. But in the main-stream development of the common law, it was the judgment for money damages that became the standard remedy. If the judgment debtor did not pay voluntarily, the debtor's assets were subject to seizure and sale by a court officer. If no assets could be found, a common law court would do nothing more. In earlier times, the judgment defendant could be imprisoned for nonpayment, but this severe compulsion was eliminated when nineteenth century reforms abolished imprisonment for debt.

The approach of the Chancellors was different from the beginning. The core idea inspiring the Chancellor's enforcement proceedings was contempt, which in its earlier forms meant disobedience or subversion of duly-constituted authority. The primitive idea of contempt was quite undifferentiated. Contempt could consist of armed entry into the King's palace, infringement of a protection given by the King to a particular person, or a refusal to appear before the King or his council. There could even be contempt of a feudal lord or of a manorial or borough court. From this same central source also stemmed contempt of a legislative assembly, which includes the refusal of a witness to testify in a legislative inquiry. There could also be contempt of a common law court. Both common law and equity judges can punish as contempt any conduct that seriously interferes with the orderly exercise of judicial functions—disturbances in the court room, refusal of witnesses to testify, bribery of jurors, misconduct or corruption on the part of officers of the court, insulting comment by lawyers, and even published statements that undermine public confidence in the courts.

The special feature of the Chancellors' remedies in enforcing contracts was that punishment for contempt was used for simple disobedience of a judicial order. The order could be affirmative (to execute and deliver a deed of land) or negative (for Catts to deliver his tomatoes to no one but Curtice Bros.), or both. In the framing of orders, the Chancellor claimed and exercised a wide discretion, a discretion suitable for an official who spoke in such a special sense on behalf of the King himself. The primary sanction for contempt of the Chancellor was, from the outset, personal arrest. The duration of the arrest, the terms for release from arrest, and any supplementary sanctions were all at the Chancellor's discretion. On the whole, modern legislation has done little to control or limit this discretion.

Within the last century, American courts have attempted to refine and differentiate further within the limits of their inherited powers. Primary for this purpose is the distinction between civil and criminal contempt, a distinction that existed vaguely for a long time but is now being drawn more sharply. *Civil contempt* usually is described as a proceeding whose sole (or primary) aim is to give a remedy to the party in whose interest the equity decree was originally issued. If the sanction used is imprisonment, the contemnor is to be jailed only to enforce compliance; if the contemnor obeys, release must follow (stated in extreme form: "the keys to prison are in the defendant's own pocket"). If a money fine is assessed against the contemnor, as it clearly may be, the fine is then to be measured by the injury caused through breach of the decree, and it is to be paid, as damages, to the opposite party, for whose protection the decree was issued. Similarly, if other coercive measures are used, such as seizure of the contemnor's assets through so-called "sequestration," the purpose of such measures in civil contempt is the enforcement of compliance, so that the pressure must end when compliance ensues. On the other hand, the purpose of *criminal contempt* is primarily to punish in order to vindicate the authority of the court and to "preserve the dignity of the law." Criminal contempt is a kind of crime, but a special crime since it is an offense against the particular court and only that court can punish the guilty party. For that matter, it is clear in civil contempt also that the court whose decree has been violated is the only court that can entertain contempt proceedings. If a money fine rather than imprisonment is used in criminal contempt, a wide discretion is reserved to the court, subject only to review for abuse of discretion. The fine assessed is payable, not to the injured litigant, but to county, state, or federal government.

The "adequacy-of-legal-remedies" test comes from this history. The work done by the Chancellors was always understood as interstitial. Their self-restraint came from inertia and tradition. The Chancellors never sought to develop a complete system that might displace the common law; they were to supplement the common law and ameliorate its harshness. The correctives of equity courts were intended for those cases for which the common law did not adequately provide. Then who was to judge what was "adequate"? From the beginning, and always, the Chancellor.

There was a brief episode in the early 1600s when lawyers, led by Sir Edward Coke, seem to have aimed to set up controls that would, in some degree, have transferred to common law judges the power to decide when equitable relief was justified. The writ of habeas corpus, which was later to become the

Great Writ for the defense of individual freedom against government repression, had at that time a highly indeterminate role. There were some strong indications that common law judges sought to use habeas corpus to cut back the Chancellors' power to imprison for contempt (and thereby to review indirectly the grounds for decision in equity cases). Another line of attack was suggested by the writ of prohibition that was issued in 1616 by the King's Bench, in Bromage v. Genning, 1 Rolle 368, with Sir Edward Coke presiding. It was addressed not to the Court of Chancery itself, but to a lesser court of equity sitting in Wales, and directed it *not* to decree specific performance of a promise by an owner of land to lease the land to another. The reason given by the King's Bench for this intervention seems at this distance somewhat contrived—that an order for specific performance would "subvert" the promisor's choice either to perform or pay damages. If this line had been pursued, it would have meant that in 1907 in New Jersey (whose law and equity were still separately administered), a judge sitting on the "law" (i.e., the jury) docket could have issued a prohibition to Vice Chancellor Leaming in Curtice Bros. v. Catts, forbidding him, under the threat of going to jail himself, from issuing or enforcing the injunction that he had decided to give to Curtice Bros. As a result of other acts of aggression against the Chancery, Coke was removed from judicial office shortly thereafter. This was a stunning event at the time and made a lasting impression. It seems most unlikely that Coke or the other common law judges intended to eliminate equitable remedies altogether, for they had become indispensable to the working of English society, as they clearly are in our own. But after the defeat of Coke, it was finally and forever established that the adequacy test and the other self-denying ordinances that restrict equitable relief would be administered by the judges who were sitting "in equity," as components of the decision whether the equitable relief requested of them should be given and, if so, in what form.

During the nineteenth century, in this country and in England, there were strong movements aiming at basic reforms and modernization of court organization and procedure. The program that became most widely known (and adopted in over 30 states) was the Field Code of Civil Procedure. Many ideas advanced by the Field Code were included in other reform programs, some of them equally comprehensive. Since the middle of the last century, the Federal Rules of Civil Procedure have provided a model for further reforms through state legislation or judicial rule-making. One common feature of these reform programs is the organization of a unified court system, with the same judges sitting on both law and equity cases. Separate dockets are maintained only because in actions that were historically brought "at law" jury trial must be made available, this being a requirement of the Seventh Amendment of the United States Constitution for the federal courts and a requirement of some state constitutions as well. There are now only a few states in which separate law and equity courts are maintained. In a couple of these states, the importance of the separation is considerably reduced by introducing jury trial as the standard means for finding disputed facts in equity cases. So almost everywhere the historical distinctions have become much blurred. It remains to be seen whether they have disappeared altogether.

Mainly for historical reasons, therefore, the remedial system of Anglo–American law starts with the money judgment as the standard remedy for breach of contract. Specific relief is reserved for situations in which the aggrieved party can show that a money-judgment remedy would be "inadequate" for some particular reason. Some very different solutions developed in Europe are described in Dawson, Specific Performance in France and Germany, 57 Mich.L.Rev. 495 (1959). On the question whether specific performance is granted in this country for reasons other than "inadequacy," a most useful discussion can be found in Laycock, The Death of the Irreparable Injury Rule, 103 Harv.L.Rev. 687 (1990).

Before leaving this sketch of history, we should recall an additional dimension of equity practice that was relevant to the problems facing the buyer in Curtice Bros. v. Catts. If court dockets were as crowded in 1907 as they are today, it may seem surprising that Curtice Bros. could have expected an equity suit to succeed in getting timely delivery of vine-ripened tomatoes suitable for canning. The decision to pursue that remedy may be made understandable by recalling a standard feature of equity practice, the power of trial judges to issue orders in advance of a full trial on the merits. We saw this power exercised in the Indiana phase of the litigation involving Dempsey (see Comment, supra p. 46).

———

RESTATEMENT OF CONTRACTS, SECOND

Section 360. Factors Affecting Adequacy of Damages

In determining whether the remedy in damages would be adequate [to protect the expectation interest of the injured party], the following circumstances are significant:

(a) the difficulty of proving damages with reasonable certainty,

(b) the difficulty of procuring a suitable substitute performance by means of money awarded as damages, and

(c) the likelihood that an award of damages could not be collected.

[The UCC's provision on a buyer's right to specific performance, § 2–716(1), states: "Specific performance may be decreed where the goods are unique or in other proper circumstances." It is generally understood that this section preserves the historical "adequacy" test of equity jurisdiction. Will the factors entering into a decision as to the adequacy of damages under UCC 2–716(1) be much different from those enumerated in Rest.2d § 360?]

———

Paloukos v. Intermountain Chevrolet Co.

99 Idaho 740, 588 P.2d 939 (1978)

Paloukos paid a $120 deposit and signed a form agreeing to purchase from intermountain a 1974 Chevrolet pickup truck for $3,650. It was understood that the pickup was to be ordered from the manufacturer. Intermountain returned the deposit five months later, informing Paloukos by letter that the dealership would be unable to deliver the vehicle "because of a product shortage." *Held*, dismissal below of a claim for specific performance was proper. Where goods "are unique or in other proper circumstances," UCC 2–716(1) makes specific performance available to a purchaser. "Although the UCC may have liberalized some of the old common law rules, see [§ 2–716, Comment 1], specific performance nevertheless remains an extraordinary remedy generally available only where other remedies are in some way inadequate." Paloukos alleged no facts suggesting anything unique about the pickup or indicating why damages would not be adequate relief. Market value was readily ascertainable. Moreover, Paloukos does not allege that Intermountain has in its possession a conforming pickup it could sell to him. "[T]he courts will not order the impossible, such as ordering the seller to sell to the buyer that which the seller does not have." [Another court found § 2–716's "other proper circumstances" for granting specific performance, reasoning that a particular auto's "mileage, condition, ownership and appearance"—in this case, a limited edition 1977 Corvette "Indy Pace car," of which only 6,000 were manufactured—can make it "difficult, if not impossible, to obtain its replication without considerable expense, delay and inconvenience." Sedmak v. Charlie's Chevrolet, Inc., 622 S.W.2d 694 (Mo.Ct.App.1981).]

NOTE

As concerns goods, the typical specific performance situation today probably involves a long-term output or requirements contract. While a buyer's inability to cover is evidence of UCC 2–716's "other proper circumstances," ability to cover does not itself foreclose equitable relief. Take, for example, Eastern Rolling Mill v. Michlovitz, 157 Md. 51, 145 A. 378 (1929). Plaintiffs, wholesalers at Harrisburg, Pa., bought and sold iron and steel scrap. In October 1927, they contracted to buy from Eastern, a manufacturer of sheet steel in Baltimore, all the scrap steel that would accumulate during the next five years as a by-product of Eastern's milling operations. The price to be paid was variable. For deliveries made during each quarter, the price was to be $3 a ton less than the price quoted at the beginning of that quarter by the Iron Age, a trade publication, as the market price in the Philadelphia market for scrap of the type Eastern produced. For nine months, deliveries were made and paid for, but in the summer of 1928 Eastern repudiated the contract, which by its terms was to run until September 30, 1932. Specific performance, sued for by the plaintiffs, was held properly granted, on this reasoning: There will be no difficulties in enforcing equity's decree, since the subject matter is the actual scrap made and accumulated at a specific plant. But the quantity of scrap defendant will produce in its operations is uncertain; if the plant suffers an interruption or closes down, there will be none. How could a jury determine the contract price, derived from a variable market price, during the years yet to come? Any estimate of damages would be "speculative," not compensatory. To remit plaintiffs to an action at law would be to force them "to sell their profits at a conjectural price." A court will do that, "substitute damages by guess" for a contractual performance, only when "there's no equity stirring."

––––––

COMMENT: THE VENDEE'S EQUITY ACTION

When a duty to transfer an interest in land is in question, the buyer (the vendee) enjoys the special treatment the law of specific performance accords contracts for the sale of land.

The case of **Gartrell v. Stafford,** 12 Neb. 545, 11 N.W. 732 (1882), is representative of the standard analysis and outcome. The vendor, a resident of California, agreed in writing to sell land in Nebraska to plaintiff, who lived in the Nebraska County in which the land was situated. When the vendor refused to convey, plaintiff, in Nebraska, sued for and was awarded specific performance of the contract. On appeal, the court summarily rejected the vendor's arguments for a reversal:

> The first objection made by the appellant is, that an action of this kind can only be brought where the defendant resides or may be summoned. But this objection is not well taken. An action to enforce specific performance of a contract for the conveyance of real estate is of two-fold character, viz: *in rem* and *in personam*. In the one case the decree of the court operates directly upon the land. In the other, where the court has jurisdiction of the parties, it may compel them to perform, although the land may be situated outside the state. . . . There is no doubt that an action may be brought against a non-resident in the county where the land in controversy is situated.

> The second objection . . . is that the plaintiff has an adequate remedy at law in an action for damages. The rule contended for by the appellant undoubtedly applies to contracts for the sale of personal property, the reason being that damages in such cases are readily calculated on the market price of property such as wheat, corn, wool, etc., . . . and thus afford as complete a remedy to the purchaser as the delivery of the property. Adderley v. Dixon, 1 Sim. & Stu., 607. But the rule is a qualified one and is limited to cases where compensation in damages furnishes a complete and satisfactory remedy. . . . The jurisdiction of courts of equity to decree specific performance of contracts for the sale of real estate is not limited, as in cases respecting chattels, to special circumstances, but is universally maintained, the reason being that a purchaser of a particular piece of land may reasonably be supposed to have considered the locality, soil, easements, or accommodations of the land, generally, which may give a peculiar or special value to the land to him, that could not be replaced by other land of the same value, but not having the same local conveniences or accommodations. [Story's Eq., § 746.] An action for damages would not, therefore, afford adequate relief.

1. Adequacy of Legal Remedy

Does the judge writing in Gartrell v. Stafford convince you that damages cannot be an adequate remedy for land-contract vendees? Suppose, for example, that the subject of the sale is Lot 101 in Broadmoor Subdivision and that the entire subdivision is flat and treeless and has not been built on at all, so that if some vandal ran off with the lot-number stakes no one but a surveyor could come within a hundred yards of locating Lot 101? Would it be harder to measure damages in such a case than, for instance, in the sale of a 2003 Ford SUV with the seller refusing to perform?

One can find many judicial opinions (e.g., Curtice Bros. v. Catts, p. 165) saying that there is "no inherent difference" between contracts for the sale of land and contracts for the sale of goods, and that they are simply governed by different presumptions—of inadequacy of damages in sales of land, of adequacy in the sale of anything else. In land contracts the presumption of inability to value land is, most of the time, conclusive. It is a working rule, about as firm as any working rule we have, that the vendee can have specific performance of such a contract if *adequacy of the legal remedy* is the only objection. There are perhaps 15 other objections that may prevent specific performance, but you will find that if an interest in land is to be transferred through the contract the inadequacy of the legal remedy is presupposed.

Anyone asserting legal propositions in such sweeping terms must be ready to retreat here and there, where the line is over-extended. We, too, have learned this. So what about the case where the vendee has contracted to sell the land in question to a third party and has no purpose other than to turn the land into money? If the vendee has made a resale contract at a higher price, is not a money judgment for the difference satisfaction in full? At least one court has reached this conclusion and therefore denied specific performance (Hazelton v. Miller, 25 App.D.C. 337 (1905)); another has held that equity should refuse its aid to "such bare-faced gambling," since one of the curses of the country is the "speculative craze" that drives people into the search for "easy money" (Schmid v. Whitten, 114 S.C. 245, 103 S.E. 553 (1920)). This issue was confronted more directly in Loveless v. Diehl, 235 Ark. 805, 364 S.W.2d 317 (1962). There the vendees had an option, granted as one of the terms of a lease, to buy land for $21,000. They exercised the option at a time when they had already contracted to sell the land to another for $22,000. The vendees admitted that they could not pay for the land themselves, and could buy it only if the resale contract went through as planned. The first reaction of the Supreme Court, "exercising the sound discretion" of a court of equity, was that the vendees should be awarded only the $1,000 difference, since this would put them precisely where they aimed to be. But on rehearing the court confessed, almost with embarrassment, that it had erred: in land contracts *"it is as much a matter of course for a court of equity to decree its specific performance as for a court of law"* to give damages (the court repeated that it was *a matter of course* three times, each time with italics). Whether the vendees "kept it, sold it, or gave it away was no concern of the sellers." It should be noted, however, that there was one other reason why the court became so aroused—the vendees had invested $5,000 in improvements while occupying as lessees, and these would accrue to the vendors if specific performance were denied, but if it were granted the vendees could get at least $1,000 back. You will run across this issue—the effect of vendee's resale—later in this book. In general, it can be said that the position taken in Hazelton v. Miller does not appear to have many adherents. See, e.g., Miller v. LeSea Broadcasting, Inc., 87 F.3d 224 (7th Cir.1996); Justus v. Clelland, 133 Ariz. 381, 651 P.2d 1206 (Ct.App.1982). Apart from the ordinary practice regarding land contracts, the fact that a vendee who has made a contract to resell the property would itself be in breach unless specific performance could be obtained, is, in most places, an added consideration favoring that remedy. Texaco, Inc. v. Creel, 310 N.C. 695, 314 S.E.2d 506 (1984).

As one other small qualification, we should note that decisions in Idaho have limited land vendees to the damage remedy unless they can show that the land is needed for some "particular, unique purpose." Watkins v. Paul, 95 Idaho 499, 511 P.2d 781 (1973); Wood v. Simonson, 108 Idaho 699, 701 P.2d 319 (Ct.App.1985). We are not aware that these decisions have made any impression anywhere else.

At a later point, we shall encounter the vendor's suit for specific performance. One question will be whether a vendor's equity action also depends on a finding of an inadequate legal remedy (as Idaho, with consistency, says it does, Suchan v. Rutherford, 90 Idaho 288, 410 P.2d 434 (1966); Perron v. Hale, 108 Idaho 578, 701 P.2d 198 (1985)), or whether other doctrines enter in. We shall see that the reason most commonly given for allowing the vendor specific performance of a land contract is "mutuality" and not inadequacy. But, as we shall also see, equity's special conception of mutuality may involve the vendor in other and related difficulties.

2. *In Rem* and *In Personam*

The phrases *in rem* and *in personam* carry a great load of procedural technicalities, exploration of which can wait till a much later stage. But the problem is evident. The land involved in *Gartrell* was in Nebraska; the owner-vendor was in California and apparently intended to stay there. The process of a state court is effective only within the boundaries of the state, and even if suit had been brought in a federal court the plaintiff could not have secured a writ that could be served or would generate sanctions against a nonresident defendant. It is not merely a question of the ineffectiveness of process. It is quite fundamental to our thinking about the powers of courts that personal service of process is necessary within the territorial limits in which the court operates, if a judgment or decree is to impose a personal liability of any kind on a litigant. There are important exceptions to this statement, but they will have to be examined in other courses.

In traditional practice, an equity decree giving specific performance of a promise to convey land was enforced primarily by imprisonment or threat of imprisonment of the promisor, to compel execution of a deed. The process in the older equity cases was *in personam* in the highest degree—against the body of the defendant. What then is the court to do about Stafford, basking in the sunshine of California?

The explanations are to be found in two types of statutes that have enlarged the traditional powers of equity courts. Both types were in force in Nebraska at the time of Gartrell v. Stafford. The first contributed the so-called "self-executing decree." If a litigant has been ordered by a court to execute a conveyance or release, such statutes provide that the decree itself will operate as a conveyance or release if the person to whom the order was directed has not complied within the time limit set. Some statutes provide as alternative machinery that the county sheriff (or a deputy) will execute a deed. In that case, the sheriff would obviously serve as a purely ministerial officer, whose authority would be derived from the court order, not from the disobedient litigant. It is usual for such statutes to add that the decree (or sheriff's deed), if it involves an interest in land, can be recorded as a conveyance in the local title registry, and to confer on the court power to issue a "writ of possession" and put the prevailing litigant in possession of the asset involved.

Statutes providing for self-executing decrees are very common. Many of these statutes, by explicit statement or by the inclusiveness of statutory language, also authorize decrees for the transfer of title to identified personal property. Rule 70 of the Federal Rules of Civil Procedure now has a similar provision applying to the decrees of federal courts.

The opinion in Gartrell v. Stafford suggested another sense in which a specific performance action could be *in rem*—that it could be brought in the county where the land in controversy was located, against a nonresident defendant. The implication was clear that a court sitting in that county could operate "directly on the land," even though there had not been and could not be any personal service of process within the state on the absent party. The power to act in this way was the product of another type of legislation that was already very common by the late 1800s and was in force at the time in Nebraska. The power is most often employed in litigation over interests in land, though some statutes include other kinds of property. Instead of personal service of process, the statutes authorize "service by publication" (sometimes called "substituted service"). This consists of publication of a specified number of notices for a specified number of weeks in a local newspaper, with a further requirement that a copy of the notice be sent by registered mail to the last known address of the absent owner. The thought behind such legislation is that the asset in question, situated within the governmental area over which the court's power extends, can be brought under the "control" of the court by a symbolic act such as posting a notice on the premises. If the provisions for mailed as well as locally-published notices are fully satisfied, it is clear that there can be no objections on due process or other constitutional grounds. Whether land contracts in which vendees seek a transfer of the vendor's legal title are included in such legislation will obviously depend on statutory language. They usually are included.

As Gartrell v. Stafford also indicated, the power of a court at the situs of the land to act *in rem* did not in any way diminish the historic power to act *in personam* against a land-contract vendor on whom personal service of process had in fact been made. The classic forms of coercion—imprisonment and money fine—could then be used to compel the vendor to execute a deed, even of land in another state. An example is Bell v. Wadley, 206 Ark. 569, 177 S.W.2d 403 (1944), where it was held that an Arkansas court had acted within its powers in ordering conveyance of land in Missouri. Then what if the defendant in the action skips off beyond the reach of the court that issued the decree? Should the decree be recognized as *res judicata*, decisive of the issues, by a court that sits at the situs of the land? Suppose in the case just mentioned that the plaintiff in the Arkansas action simply took a certified copy of the decree to Missouri, showed it to the court in the county where the land was situated, and asked for judicial confirmation of his or her right to the land. It has not yet been held that the Missouri court in such a case would be bound by the federal constitution to give "full faith and credit" to the Arkansas decree, but on essentially these facts it was held as early as Burnley v. Stevenson, 24 Ohio St. 474 (1873), that the court at the situs should and would do so. R. Weintraub, Commentary on The Conflict of Laws 421–427 (3d ed. 1986), discusses the subject.

3. Equitable Ownership and the Trust Analogy

There is another dimension of the vendee's equity action. In early times, it was quite easy for Chancellors working in a separate court to effect a transfer of ideas—to infer from the equitable remedy, granted so routinely, that equitable rights had been created and that the vendee was "equitable owner" of the land described in the contract. This could only occur, of course, where the contract was still "executory," where the vendor had merely promised to convey legal title by deed and the object of the equity suit was to compel performance of the promise. In any case, this manner of speaking ("equitable owner") appears often in our law and it has a number of important consequences. Suppose, to take one example, that after agreeing to convey to A, the vendor wrongfully conveys the same land to B. Instead of suing for damages, the vendee A would have an option to sue the vendor in equity, joining as defendant the grantee B. If B, now invested with the legal title, had given "value" without notice, either actual or imputed, of A's contract, the action against B would fail. As a bona fide purchaser of the legal title for value, B would be protected as against A's prior "equity." But if B had either knowledge or reason to know of A's contract, or if B gave or promised no "value," then A would probably succeed and B would be ordered by court decree to reconvey to A.

One way to explain this result is to say that the first vendee, A, became "equitable" owner from the inception of the contract with the vendor. Quite obviously, this is nothing more than a shorthand way of expressing the predisposition of an equity court to order specific performance. But this phrasing at once suggests another familiar situation in which legal and "equitable" ownership of the same asset are conceived to co-exist. The analogy invoked is of course the express *trust*, which is usually created by the owner of some asset (land, goods, stocks, etc.), who transfers legal title to the asset to a trustee with directions to hold, administer, or dispose of the asset for the benefit of another (a minor child, a relative or friend, a church or other "charitable" organization, or perhaps even the transferor). At least by the fifteenth century, the Chancellors had begun to enforce such directions that the transferor (usually called the "settlor") had imposed, and to prevent the transferee-trustee from appropriating the asset entrusted. The Chancellors continued in later centuries to enforce such restrictions and protect the interests of the beneficiary (usually called the *cestui que trust*, degenerate French for "he who trusts"). The ease with which the legal title of the trustee was thus subjected to the controls of equity courts led before long to a manner of speaking—that, though the trustee might be legal owner, the beneficiary was the "equitable owner," to the extent and in the ways that the original transfer from settlor to trustee had directed. You can see that the trust provides at least an analogy to contracts for the sale of land, which, as we have seen, equity courts also enforce with regularity.

It was this manner of thinking which led, in cases like the example given above (the vendor wrongfully conveys to B land previously contracted to A), to a further extension of land-contract remedies. Some courts came to allow the vendee to sue the defaulting vendor in equity and recover, not the land itself, but, if the vendee so elected, the money proceeds of the vendor's wrongful resale. E.g., Timko v. Useful Homes Corp., 114 N.J.Eq. 433, 168 A. 824 (1933). This was explained by labelling the vendor a "trustee" of the land, accountable like any other trustee for profits made through misappropriation of trust assets ("wrongful conduct," said the *Timko* court of the breach in selling the vendee's lots). Again, the word "trust" in this context was understood by all to express no more than the regularity with which specific performance is given the parties to land contracts. In fact, the remedy awarded here—a money judgment in equity, measured by the proceeds realized from the resale—might well be thought of as a sort of substituted specific performance. Of course, a similar claim brought at law, in an action framed as one for damages measured by the gains of the defaulter, would likely encounter the doctrine applied in *Acme Mills*.

It is a different question whether it is useful to describe the vendee, from the inception of the land contract, as a trustee of the purchase money. If one were to look at the executory land contract from this angle of vision and to equate it with a trust, what element would usually be missing?

———

Fitzpatrick v. Michael

Court of Appeals of Maryland, 1939.
177 Md. 248, 9 A.2d 639.

[Plaintiff, a nurse then 52, was employed by defendant Michael in the summer of 1936 to give nursing care to defendant's wife; plaintiff cared for the wife until the wife's death in February 1937. At that time, plaintiff informed defendant of her intention of leaving, but defendant, who was then 76, asked plaintiff to stay on for a few days. She did so, and defendant then told her that he wanted company, someone to manage his house, drive his car, and care for him when he was ill. Defendant stated that if plaintiff would remain with him for the rest of his life and provide such company and services, defendant would pay her $8 a week, would provide a home and board for her in his house in Aberdeen, and would at his death leave her by will a life estate in the house, the life use of its furnishings, and full title to his automobiles. Plaintiff "accepted the offer" and continued to serve until April 6, 1939, managing defendant's home and garden, driving him to and from his office and on long trips, and nursing him during periods of illness. Defendant expressed to neighbors during this period his complete satisfaction with plaintiff's services, and in three successive wills executed by him the promised life estate in home and furnishings and the gift of the cars were all included. Then suddenly all was changed, plaintiff's explanation being that distant relatives had "poisoned his mind" against her. On April 4, 1939, defendant left his house and did not return. On April 6, defendant tried to force plaintiff to leave the house by cutting off the electricity, water, heat and telephone, and food supplies, and, when that blockade proved ineffective, he had plaintiff arrested for trespass. While she was under arrest defendant locked up the house so that plaintiff could not enter it, though she had property of her own inside.]

OFFUTT, J. . . . Following her removal from Michael's home, Miss Fitzpatrick on May 9th of this year filed the bill of complaint in this case, [asking] that the respondent Michael be required to specifically perform his contract with her, and that a receiver be appointed to take charge of "all the estate, both real and personal, of the respondent, to collect all money, rents, etc., and to pay this complainant the weekly sum of eight dollars ($8.00) per week as long as the respondent lives, and to provide her in the respondent's Aberdeen residence a home with board and lodging so long as the respondent lives, upon the complainant looking after the respondent's home, flowers, driving his automobile, and nursing and caring for the respondent in compliance with her said agreement, with the said respondent."

The defendant demurred to the bill for a general want of equity, the demurrer was sustained and the bill dismissed, and from that decree the plaintiff appealed.

There can be no possible doubt that upon those facts the plaintiff should be entitled to some relief against the defendant, but the question . . . is whether the remedy is equity.

A contract to make a will is not invalid because of its subject matter (69 A.L.R. 18), for, since one may bargain, sell, give away, or otherwise surrender every right and property interest which he has, there can be no sound reason why he cannot also validly agree to dispose of it by will. . . . Nor, since Michael may not have lived for a year after it was made, can it be said that, apart from any question of part performance, that the contract is invalid because it was not embodied in a writing signed by the party to be charged, as required by clause 5 of the fourth section of the Statute of Frauds[,] . . . because there was a possibility that it might be performed within a year. . . . But, as it relates to an interest in land, it is within clause 4 of the section[,] . . . and unenforceable unless the bar of the statute is removed. Fry on Spec.Perf., § 561 et seq. That may be done by sufficient proof that the plaintiff has performed it in part, and is willing and able to continue to do those things which she undertook to do. . . . The doctrine of part performance,* however, is peculiar to equity, and may not be invoked in courts of law[,] . . . so that, unless the facts present a case of equitable jurisdiction, the appellant has no remedy on the contract either at law or in equity. 69 A.L.R. 20.

But no ground of equitable jurisdiction can be found in the facts stated, unless it be that she has no adequate remedy at law. But even though there is no adequate remedy at law, equity will not, ordinarily, specifically enforce a contract for personal service, for these reasons, one, that the mischief likely to result from the enforced continuance of the relationship incident to the service when it has become personally obnoxious to one of the parties is so great that the best interests of society require that the remedy be refused (Fry on Spec.Perf. 5th Ed., secs. 110, 112), for, as stated by Fry, "The relation established by the contract of hiring and service is of so personal and confidential a character that it is evident that such contracts cannot be specifically enforced by the court against an unwilling party with any hope of ultimate and real success. . . ." The other reason is, that courts have not the means nor the ability to enforce such decrees. Pomeroy, Spec.Perf., secs. 22, 310.

Nevertheless there is a class of cases in which, although the contract is not actionable under the Statute of Frauds, it has been performed by the rendition of services the value of which cannot be estimated in terms of money, and in such cases, when it appears that a monetary award will not place the parties in statu quo, or adequately compensate the complaining party, equity may grant relief in the nature of a specific performance of the contract. . . . Executory contracts, are not, however, within the scope of that principle, which can only be invoked where the employment has been terminated by the expiration of the term of employment, by the death of one of the parties, or in some other manner inconsistent with the possibility of future or continuing service under the contract. For, during the term of employment, where it is for an indefinite period, when both parties are living and specific performance would mean compelling one party to accept and the other to render services, the reasons for the refusal of courts of equity to decree specific performance of such contracts apply, and that relief will be refused even though there be no adequate remedy at law, for it would result in a species of peonage on the part of the servant, or an enforced association with an obnoxious employee on the part of the master, which would be intolerable. . . .

---

* [The "part performance" doctrine in equity is examined in Chapter 2, infra p. 234.—Eds.]

The limitation which the rule imposes upon equitable jurisdiction at times results in the denial of any adequate remedy to one who has been injured by the breach of such a contract, and courts have striven to discover some alternate remedy which, in cases of unusual and extreme hardship, would afford to the promisee some measure of relief. So in England, where such contracts contained [express] negative covenants, while the courts at first, in cases where specific performance of the affirmative covenants could not be enforced, also refused to enforce the negative covenants, later, beginning with Lumley v. Wagner, 1 DeG.M. & G. 604, their power to enforce negative covenants was recognized, although that might indirectly result in compelling the specific performance of the affirmative covenants. . . . There is a distinction between cases in which the contract provides merely for employment and compensation, in which a refusal to serve or to pay is the negation of a promise to pay or to serve, and cases where the services involve and imply some rare and unusual quality in the promisor which, if given to a competitor of the promisee might cause him a loss by the diversion of custom in addition to what he might suffer from the loss of custom which the services of the promisor might attract, and that consideration apparently underlies the decisions in many of the cases enforcing negative covenants. There are, however, cases in which the doctrine of the enforcement of implied negative covenants has been carried far beyond the present state of law in England, and beyond what seems to be the weight of the best considered authority here, but, taking the law as we find it, it may safely be said that equity will not enforce a negative covenant, express or implied, in a contract which it cannot specifically enforce, unless a breach of the negative covenant will cause a loss to the promisee distinct from that resulting from the mere failure of the promisor to carry out his affirmative promise. Applying that principle to contracts for personal services, the sounder rule is that equity will not enforce negatively a contract which it could not enforce affirmatively, nor will it enjoin the breach of a negative covenant, express or implied, unless the breach will cause a loss to the promisee independent of the loss caused by the mere failure of the promisor to keep and perform his affirmative covenants. . . .

Applying those principles to the facts of this case, the conclusion that the plaintiff is not entitled to any relief in equity seems inevitable. The contract was essentially one for the rendition of personal services. They were varied, it is true, but they required no extraordinary or unusual skill, experience, or capacity. Under the employment, the appellant acted as nurse, chauffeur, companion, gardener, and housekeeper, and, while it may be difficult to appraise in monetary terms the value of services so varied, nevertheless they involved no more than [things customarily done] as a part of the ordinary routine of life. The reasons for the general rule that equity will not specifically enforce contracts for personal service apply with plenary force to the facts conceded here. Assuming that appellee broke the contract, that the breach was whimsical, arbitrary, and unjust, and induced by the intrigue of greedy relatives, nevertheless its enforcement would compel him to accept the personal services of an employee against his wish and his will. The court can no more compel him to accept her services under such conditions, than it could compel her to render them if he demanded them and she were unwilling to give them. It follows that the decree must be affirmed.

NOTE

The agreement fell within the land clause of the statute of frauds because Fitzpatrick was promised a life estate in defendant's residence. The court's reasons for concluding that it did not come within the "not-to-be-performed-within-one-year" clause represent the standard interpretation of that clause, as is explained in the Appendix.

Recall also that Fitzpatrick asked the court to appoint a "receiver" to take charge of defendant's residence, collect and pay plaintiff her wages, and ensure her occupancy. The appointment of a receiver is one of the administrative devices available to a court exercising equity powers. This possibility was suggested in Curtice Bros. v. Catts (p. 165). Rule 70 of the Federal Rules of Civil Procedure provides for this as well as other enforcement measures:

> If a judgment directs a party to execute a conveyance of land or to deliver deeds or other documents or to perform any other specific act and the party fails to comply within the time specified, the court may direct the act to be done at the cost of the disobedient party by some other person appointed by the court and the act when so done has like effect as if done by the party. On application of the party entitled to performance, the clerk shall issue a writ of attachment or sequestration against the property of the disobedient party to compel obedience to the judgment. The court may also in proper cases adjudge the party in contempt. If real or personal property is within the district, the court in lieu of directing a conveyance thereof may enter a judgment divesting the title of any party and vesting it in others and such judgment has the effect of a conveyance executed in due form of law. When any order or judgment is for the delivery of possession, the party in whose favor it is entered is entitled to a writ of execution or assistance upon application to the clerk.

Receivers can be used for a variety of purposes. Since it is generally understood that the principal justification for a receiver is to secure property in dispute from waste or loss, the device is often seen where there are allegations of mismanagement or fraud. Courts usually do not appoint receivers in order to grant ultimate relief; rather, appointments are viewed as a measure ancillary to the enforcement of some recognized equitable right—e.g., the collection of rents during a lengthy proceeding to foreclose a mortgage on the rental property, as in Hartford Fed. Sav. & Loan Ass'n v. Tucker, 196 Conn. 172, 491 A.2d 1084 (1985). A common use of the equity receivership formerly was in the rehabilitation of business enterprises that had experienced financial difficulties. Today, reorganizations are handled under Chapter 11 of the Bankruptcy Code, which is itself a linear descendant of the equity receivership and which still bears many of its distinctive features. The aim of the receivership (as with the modern statutory proceeding) usually was not, as in traditional bankruptcy, a prompt liquidation with sale of assets and payment of the proceeds to creditors. The aim was rather to administer the assets, often over years, to scale down or extend fixed money obligations, and generally to restore an ailing enterprise to health.

An example of successful use of a receiver in the enforcement of a private contract is Madden v. Rosseter, 114 Misc. 416, 187 N.Y.S. 462 and 117 Misc. 244, 192 N.Y.S. 113 (1921), where plaintiff, a resident of New York, and defendant, a resident of California, owned a thoroughbred stallion jointly. Their agreement provided that defendant was to have possession of the stallion in California in 1919 and 1920 and plaintiff was to have the horse in Kentucky during 1921 and 1922. Plaintiff secured personal service of process on defendant in an action for specific performance in New York state, and persuaded the court to appoint a receiver with power to go to California, retrieve the horse, and deliver it to plaintiff in Kentucky. The receiver carried out the order "with tact and diplomacy," without litigation, and was allowed $5,000 for his services, to be paid by defendant.

————

Lumley v. Wagner

Lord Chancellor's Court, 1852.
1 DeG, M. & G. 604, 42 Eng. Rep. 687.

[Benjamin Lumley, who ran the opera company at Her Majesty's Theatre, engaged Johanna Wagner to sing for the season exclusively for him. Frederick Gye, who ran the rival opera company at Covent Garden, persuaded Wagner to break her contract with Lumley and to sing for him instead. Lumley then tried to prevent Wagner from singing with his competitor.]

LORD ST. LEONARDS, L.C. The question which I have to decide . . . arises out of a very simple contract, the effect of which is, that the defendant Johanna Wagner should sing at Her Majesty's Theatre for a certain number of nights, and that she should not sing elsewhere (for that is the true construction) during that period. . . . [T]he points taken by the defendants' counsel . . . in effect come to this, namely, that a court of equity ought not to grant an injunction except in cases connected with specific performance, or where the injunction being to compel a party to forbear from committing an act (and not to perform an act), that injunction will complete the whole of the agreement remaining unexecuted. . . .

The present is a mixed case, consisting not of two correlative acts to be done, one by the plaintiff and the other by the defendants, which state of facts may have and in some cases has introduced a very important difference, but of an act to be done by Johanna Wagner alone, to which is superadded a negative stipulation on her part to abstain from the commission of any act which will break in upon her affirmative covenant—the one being ancillary to, and concurrent and operating together with the other. The agreement to sing for the plaintiff during three months at his theatre, and during that time not to sing for anybody else, is not a correlative contract. It is, in effect, one contract, and though beyond all doubt this court could not interfere to enforce the specific performance of the whole of this contract, yet in all sound construction and according to the true spirit of the agreement, the engagement to perform for three months at one theatre must necessarily exclude the right to perform at the same time at another theatre. It was clearly intended that Johanna Wagner was to exert her vocal abilities to the utmost to aid the theatre to which she agreed to attach herself. I am of opinion that if she had attempted, even in the absence of any negative stipulation, to perform at another theatre, she would have broken the spirit and true meaning of the contract as much as she would now do with reference to the contract into which she has actually entered.

Wherever this court has not proper jurisdiction to enforce specific performance, it operates to bind men's consciences, as far as they can be bound, to a true and literal performance of their agreements, and it will not suffer them to depart from their contracts at their pleasure, leaving the party with whom they have contracted to the mere chance of any damages which a jury may give. The exercise of this jurisdiction has, I believe, had a wholesome tendency towards the maintenance of that good faith which exists in this country to a much greater degree perhaps than in any other, and, although the jurisdiction is not to be extended, yet a judge would desert his duty who did not act up to what his predecessors have handed down as the rule for his guidance in the administration of such an equity.

It was objected that the operation of the injunction in the present case was mischievous, excluding the defendant Johanna Wagner from performing at any other theatre while this court had no power to compel her to perform at Her Majesty's Theatre. It is true that I have not the means of compelling her to sing, but she has no cause of complaint if I compel her to abstain from the commission of an act which she has bound herself not to do, and thus possibly cause her to fulfil her engagement. The jurisdiction which I now exercise is wholly within the power of the court, and, being of opinion that it is a proper case for interfering, I shall leave nothing unsatisfied by the judgment I pronounce. The effect, too, of the injunction, in restraining Johanna Wagner from singing elsewhere may, in the event of an action being brought against her by the plaintiff, prevent any such amount of vindictive damages being given against her as a jury might probably be inclined to give if she had carried her talents and exercised them at the rival theatre. The injunction may also, as I have said, tend to the fulfilment of her engagement, though, in continuing the injunction, I disclaim doing indirectly what I cannot do directly. . . .

Pingley v. Brunson

272 S.C. 421, 252 S.E.2d 560 (1979)

Brunson, an auto mechanic by trade, was also a part-time organ player for various businesses in and around Mullins, S.C. In late 1977, he entered into a contract to play the organ for Pingley's restaurant, three nights a week for $50 per night, for a period of three years. The contract stated that Pingley was to purchase musical instruments costing $4,262.96 for Brunson's use at the restaurant, and that the monthly payments for the instruments were to be made by deductions from Brunson's paychecks. The instruments were to be Brunson's when paid for, but any breach by Brunson would result in a forfeiture of his claim to the instruments. Brunson began playing for Pingley the night of December 6, performed on nine evenings thereafter, and then refused to perform further. Pingley sued for and was awarded both specific performance and an order enjoining Brunson from playing musical instruments for any other establishment during times in conflict with the Pingley contract. *Held*, reversed. Equity courts will not ordinarily decree specific performance in this type of case, particularly where, as here, personal services are to be performed on a continuous basis over a period of time. There is an exception "where the performer possesses unique and exceptional skill or ability in his area of expertise." Even though Pingley's witnesses asserted Brunson's "exceptional talent as a major attraction to an area establishment," the evidence revealed that "five other organists of comparable ability were available for hire in the Mullins area." Thus the substantial equivalent of the subject matter of this contract is readily obtainable by means of a money payment. So "we cannot conclude . . . that appellant's musical talent is of such a unique quality as to warrant an award of specific performance." The lower court's injunctive relief was also erroneous. The contract did not contain an express covenant not to compete or perform elsewhere. Absent an express negative covenant, a court as a rule does not enjoin an employee's furnishing of services to another during the term of a breached contract.

QUESTION

Suppose that Pingley, upon receiving the news of his defeat in South Carolina's high court, then brought a suit joining as defendants each restaurant in Mullins that had, in the interim, employed Brunson as an organist. Pingley asked for an injunction preventing these restaurants from making use of Brunson's services. How should such a suit come out?

––––––––

ENFORCING NONCOMPETE PLEDGES

Assume Pingley's contract with Brunson had included this provision: "For a period of one year following Brunson's termination of employment under this agreement, whatever the basis or cause of the termination, voluntary or involuntary, Brunson agrees not to play any musical instrument in public, for compensation paid by any person, within a radius of 50 miles of Mullins, S.C." A leading decision, ABC v. Wolf, 52 N.Y.2d 394, 438 N.Y.S.2d 482, 420 N.E.2d 363 (1981), describes the law's general approach to an employee's promise to refrain from postemployment competition:

> After a personal service contract terminates, the availability of equitable relief against the former employee diminishes appreciably. Since the period of service has expired, it is impossible to decree affirmative or negative specific performance. Only if the employee has expressly agreed not to compete with the employer following the term of the contract, or is threatening to disclose trade secrets or commit another tortious act, is injunctive relief generally available at the behest of the employer. . . . Even where there is an express anticompetitive covenant, however, it will be rigorously examined and specifically enforced only if it satisfies certain established requirements. . . . Indeed, a court normally will not decree specific enforcement of an employee's anticompetitive covenant unless necessary to protect the trade secrets, customer lists or good will of the employer's business, or perhaps when the employer is exposed to specific harm because of the unique nature of the employee's services (see, e.g., . . . 6A Corbin, Contracts, § 1394). And, an otherwise valid covenant will not be enforced if it is unreasonable in time, space or scope or would operate in a harsh or oppressive manner. . . . There is, in short, general judicial disfavor of anticompetitive covenants contained in employment contracts. . . .

> Underlying the strict approach to enforcement of these covenants is the notion that, once the term of an employment agreement has expired, the general public policy favoring robust and uninhibited competition should not give way merely because a particular em-

ployer wishes to insulate himself from competition.... [Thus, the] rules governing enforcement of anticompetitive covenants and the availability of equitable relief after termination of employment are designed to foster [the legitimate] interests of the employer without impairing the employee's ability to earn a living or the general competitive mold of society.

The digested case that follows illustrates the difficulties—and the divergent views—in applying these principles, especially when the question is what to do by way of relief.

————

Fullerton Lumber Co. v. Torborg

270 Wis. 133, 70 N.W.2d 585 (1955)

Plaintiff, a Minnesota corporation, operated retail lumber yards in Wisconsin and other states. Plaintiff hired Torborg in 1938, in a "managerial capacity," and, on Torborg's return from military service in 1946, appointed him manager of its lumber yard in Clintonville, Wisconsin. Torborg signed an employment contract agreeing that if he ceased to be employed by plaintiff for any reason, he would not work for any other establishment or on his own account, handling lumber or building material at retail, for a period of 10 years thereafter, within a radius of 15 miles of any city or town in which he had been employed by plaintiff as a manager. The Clintonville yard was successful; in three years under Torborg's management, its business tripled. Torborg worked for plaintiff until November 1953, when he quit and set up his own yard in Clintonville. Plaintiff sued to enjoin him from working in Clintonville. The trial court dismissed the complaint, finding the contractual restraint unreasonable and not necessary to protect plaintiff's interests. On appeal, the court was clear that the time limit of 10 years imposed in Torborg's 1946 contract was excessive, so that the restrictive covenant was an unreasonable and illegal restraint of trade. Under earlier Wisconsin decisions, a clause producing an unreasonable restraint was wholly void, whether the clause was attached to a sale of a business or applicable to an employee whose employment had terminated. But the court, with one dissent, reconsidered these decisions and emphasized the employer's need for protection in an activity largely dependent on customer contacts, especially where the employer was a foreign corporation whose officers and supervisory employees resided outside the state. The case was remanded to the trial court to determine the length of time that would be reasonable and necessary for plaintiff's protection, and to enter an injunction accordingly. The Supreme Court suggested that the evidence would support a finding that the minimum period was three years; Torborg himself had built the Clintonville yard's business up to a fairly constant level in three years and "it must be assumed" that another manager could do the same. The period selected should run from the date of the decree, rather than from the date of termination of Torborg's employment in 1953, because he had in the interval engaged in competition with plaintiff, employing the advantage that he had gained in its service. [The case is discussed in 54 Mich.L.Rev. 416 (1956).]

NOTE

Two years after the *Torborg* decision, the Wisconsin legislature enacted the following statute (Wis.Stat. § 103.465):

> A covenant by an assistant, servant or agent not to compete with his employer or principal during the term of the employment or agency, or thereafter, within a specified territory and during a specified time is lawful and enforceable only if the restrictions imposed are reasonably necessary for the protection of the employer or principal. Any such restrictive covenant imposing an unreasonable restraint is illegal, void and unenforceable even as to so much of the covenant or performance as would be a reasonable restraint.

Wisconsin's Chief Justice, Shirley Abrahamson, dissenting in Tatge v. Chambers & Owen, 219 Wis.2d 99, 579 N.W.2d 217, 227–228 (1998), summarizes some additional information about the 1957 effort leading to § 103.465:

> The drafting record . . . includes a letter by Rep. Richard Peterson [to] the legislative reference library giving drafting instructions for § 103.465. [He] explained that he wanted a bill drafted to reverse *Fullerton Lumber v. Torborg*, in which the court enforced the reasonable aspects of an invalid covenant not to compete[,] [stating his] concerns about *Fullerton* as follows: "[A]t the time the contract was entered into, the bargaining position of the two contractors appears to me to be relatively unequal in that the party seeking employment must, if he desires employment with the contracting party, consent to almost any restrictive covenant imposed. The effect [of *Fullerton*] is to give to the employer complete latitude" in setting forth the terms of the agreement, including the geographical and time limits imposed. Rep. Peterson wanted the bill [written so] as to put the two contracting parties in more equal bargaining positions and to avoid giving "a green light" to employers in writing agreements not to compete.

Other courts have followed *Torborg's* lead and awarded partial enforcement of covenants not to compete. See, e.g., Johnson Controls, Inc. v. A.P.T. Critical Systems, Inc., 323 F. Supp. 2d 525, 539 (S.D.N.Y. 2004) ("Absent overreaching, coercive use of dominant bargaining power, or other anti-competitive misconduct, partial enforcement, as opposed to invalidating the entire covenant, is justified."); BDO Seidman v. Hirshberg, 93 N.Y.2d 382, 712 N.E.2d 1220 (1999).

————

Much of the material considered earlier in this chapter dealt with "enforcement difficulties" in a larger sense, that is, obstacles to recovery for losses actually incurred, through limitations imposed for reasons of fairness or practicability—e.g., mitigation, foreseeability, certainty. In this section, enforcement problems have centered mainly on when an "inadequate" damage remedy leads to relief in equity. An inevitable part of this landscape—recall, for example, *Manchester Dairy* and *Curtice Bros.*—is the practical problem of the ways and means of compelling compliance with an equity decree. When will difficulties anticipated in ordering specific enforcement result in the decision to withhold such a remedy?

The answer usually given is that specific performance will be refused when the decree will require extensive and unduly burdensome court supervision. So, for example, construction contracts, involving a large element of labor or services, traditionally have been viewed as instances where the burden of supervision calls for caution in the exercise of discretionary powers. E.g., Northern Delaware Indus. Dev. Corp. v. E.W. Bliss Co., 245 A.2d 431 (Del.Ch.1968) ("a court of equity should not order specific performance of any building contract in a situation where it would be impractical to carry out such an order"). The *Ammerman* and *Grayson–Robinson* cases, immediately below, should be read against this general landscape.

————

City Stores Co. v. Ammerman

266 F.Supp. 766 (D.D.C.1967)

Defendants owned land at Tyson's Corner, Fairfax County, Virginia, on which they hoped to construct a large shopping center. This would require rezoning by the Board of County Supervisors. Defendants earlier had applied to the Board for rezoning; a similar application was already pending from a rival group of developers, who planned a shopping center at a nearby site. The county planning commission, in a report to the Board, had recommended against the rezoning of defendants' site at Tyson's Corner. Plaintiff, owner of Lansburgh's Department Store in Washington, D.C., had been negotiating for a lease at the rival site. He was then asked by defendants to lend support for defendants' application, by expressing to the Board a preference for the Tyson's Corner site and a willingness to become a major tenant there, if the site were rezoned and developed. Defendants in writing assured plaintiff that if it supported their application plaintiff would be given an "opportunity" to become one of defendants' major tenants, "with rental and terms at least equal to that of any other major department store in the center." Plaintiff wrote the letter as requested, defendants' application for rezoning was granted, and defendants made leases to both the Woodward & Lothrop and the Hecht department stores, whose main stores also were located in Washington, D.C. When defendants then refused to lease to plaintiff a site in the center, plaintiff sued for specific performance. *Held*, defendants had given plaintiff an option with only two conditions—approval of the necessary rezoning and execution by defendants of leases to other major tenants which "could provide the essential terms of a lease to be offered to plaintiff." Both conditions have occurred and plaintiff has exercised the option so as to produce a valid contract. Plaintiff can have specific performance.

An order can be fashioned by examining the other leases. "Even though none of the stores in the center will be identical in design, it is apparent from defendants' own leases that complete equality of material terms governing occupancy, including amount of space and cost per square foot, and substantially equal terms on less material aspects of the lease, is within the customary contemplation of parties entering into shopping center agreements of the type at issue in this case." The lessors' own income was tied to the success of their lessees so that it will be to the lessors' advantage to ensure that one tenant be given "no distinct competitive advantage over another." All of the stores were to be subject to the overall design requirements of the center. Defendants were obligated, and will be ordered, to construct a building; there is no insuperable objection to this, especially since it is to be built on defendants' own land, so that plaintiff could not hire another contractor to build it at defendants' expense. If the parties should not be able in good faith to reach agreement on details, the court will appoint a special master to help them settle their differences, unless the parties prefer voluntarily to refer them to arbitration.

The essential criterion for a court of equity in deciding whether to enforce such contracts is the relative inadequacy of legal remedies. Here, even if it were possible, as it was not, to measure damages for breach of a contract to lease a store in a shopping center for a long period of years, money damages could not compensate plaintiff for the "almost incalculable future advantages that might accrue to it as a result of extending its operations into the suburbs."

[The decision was affirmed in a per curiam opinion, 394 F.2d 950 (D.C.Cir.1968). The reviewing court emphasized that "damages could hardly compensate for the loss of the sought for opportunity to raise Lansburgh's image and economic position in the Metropolitan Washington area by its anticipated expansion into the suburbs." It also asserted that relief ordering building construction should not be withheld "unless the difficulties of supervision by the court outweigh the importance of enforcement to the plaintiff."]

––––––––

Grayson–Robinson Stores v. Iris Constr. Corp.
8 N.Y.2d 133, 202 N.Y.S.2d 303, 168 N.E.2d 377 (1960)

Iris, owner of a tract of vacant land in Levittown, in 1955 agreed in writing with Grayson to erect on the tract a building, part of a shopping center, to be rented to Grayson as a retail department store for a term of 25 years. Possession was to be delivered to Grayson on or before September 1, 1957. The agreement called for arbitration of any disputes that might arise and incorporated the rules of the American Arbitration Association, which, among other things, empowered an arbitrator to award any just or equitable relief "including specific performance." After a public groundbreaking ceremony had been held and excavation for the shopping center had been commenced, Iris informed Grayson that it could not go further with the project because of difficulties in borrowing needed funds, unless Grayson agreed to an increase in rent. Grayson refused to pay more. Pursuant to the parties' contract, the dispute was submitted to a panel of arbitrators, who rejected the excuse offered by Iris that it could not borrow the money it needed. The arbitrators entered an award ordering Iris to "proceed forthwith with the improvements of the leased premises in accordance with the terms of said lease." The New York arbitration statute then in force provided that a written agreement to submit to arbitration any controversy thereafter arising "confers jurisdiction on the courts of the state to enforce it and to enter judgment on an award." The statute also directed that "the court shall not consider whether the claim with respect to which the arbitration is sought is tenable, or otherwise pass upon the merits of the dispute." By a 4–to–3 vote, the New York Court of Appeals affirmed a lower court order that defendant build the building, though as the dissent pointed out, the building would cost $5,000,000 and defendant had applied unsuccessfully to 27 lending institutions to secure the loan needed to undertake it. [In the end, the building was not completed, a court-appointed referee awarded plaintiff $3,287,483.10

for rental value lost as a result, and the case was settled by the parties for $550,000 to be paid by the defendant.]

———————

COMMENT ON ARBITRATION

The readiness of the New York court in *Grayson–Robinson* to carry out the mandate of the arbitrators, in an enterprise so extensive but also so unlikely to succeed, reflects a considerable reversal of early common law attitudes. Today, a preference for arbitration over ordinary judicial procedures has shown itself in a vast expansion in the use of arbitration clauses in many kinds of commercial transactions. Large segments of both the legal and the commercial worlds are now familiar with the uses and advantages of arbitration, and the reasons commonly given in support of the arbitral method of dispute settlement include much more than the claim that arbitration helps to relieve congestion in the courts. The emancipation of arbitrators from rules of judicial procedure can open a wider range of inquiry and at the same time speed decision. The parties can create their own forum and choose for it persons with specialized backgrounds and expertise. Experienced, professional arbitrators (organized into subject-matter panels by private organizations like the American Arbitration Association) frequently are familiar with the practices and expectations that have developed around transactions of the type involved in the dispute. Consequently, arbitrators may be able to find solutions that are more acceptable to the parties themselves. This reliance on "transaction-sense" reflects the fact that arbitrators are free to disregard established rules of law and to apply their own sense of fairness, informed by standards of acceptable conduct in the trade or business to which the parties belong. In fact, large-scale resort to such devices as arbitration or mediation can represent an appeal *against* the law, a reaction to its deficiencies. This was clearly true in the intermediate period in the growth of English equity (the sixteenth and seventeenth centuries), when the Chancellors enlisted the aid of informed and responsible lay people in restoring common sense to the legal system.

The status of arbitration at common law was a strange hybrid. The agreement to submit to arbitration was not specifically enforceable; indeed, it was revocable by either party at any time prior to rendition of the arbitration award. This view was first expressed by Sir Edward Coke, who declared in a dictum in 1609 that any agreement to submit a dispute to arbitration was "of its own nature revocable." Vynior's Case, 8 Coke Rep. 81b (1609). The doctrine of "inherent revocability" was later put on the broad ground that a delegation of judicial powers to lay persons "ousted the courts of jurisdiction" and was therefore against public policy and void.[1] Accordingly, either party could repudiate the agreement, revoke the authority conferred (by contract) on an arbitrator, and bring a court action on the disputed claim. But the agreement to submit to arbitration was not in a strict sense illegal, nor was it wholly without legal effects. A damage remedy for breach of the promise to arbitrate was theoretically available.[2] More important, if an arbitrator was actually appointed and pro-

———————

[1] The decisions are collected in 135 A.L.R. 79 (1941). 6A A. Corbin, Contracts § 1433, contains a critical evaluation of the notion of "ouster of jurisdiction."

[2] The damage remedy was usually inadequate because of the view at common law that only nominal damages are recoverable for breach or repudiation of the promise to arbitrate. See,

ceeded to render an award, the award was enforceable both at law and in equity. If it ordered payment of a sum of money, the successful claimant could sue on the award in an action of debt. If it established a duty to convey an interest in land, the one subject to the duty could be sued—again, on the award—for damages, or, since land was involved, specific performance.

Arbitration agreements are enforceable today principally because of legislation reversing common law attitudes. Most states have adopted arbitration statutes that provide for irrevocability of an arbitration agreement and for streamlined procedures for judicial enforcement.[3] The salient feature of the more advanced statutes is the prescription that written agreements to arbitrate any dispute, existing or prospective, are "valid, enforceable and irrevocable."[4] A party aggrieved by the other's refusal to honor a promise to arbitrate may simply move a court to compel arbitration. If suit is filed on a claim allegedly covered by an arbitration agreement, the defendant may similarly move the court to stay the action pending arbitration. For the enforcement of awards, the modern acts make available summary procedures to review and to ensure prompt implementation of the results of arbitration. The first major step was to eliminate the need to start an entirely new action. Now an arbitrator's award can be filed with the local trial court, and, under simplified procedures, it becomes a judgment enforceable directly by the court's own processes. Above all else, arbitration statutes attempt to limit judicial involvement by restricting the issues a court may fairly consider.

The role given courts to uphold arbitration reflects the considerable respect for freedom of contract that arbitration statutes embody. The system is created, administered, and controlled through the parties' agreement. Though arbitration acts establish limited requirements for an effective agreement, such as the formality of a writing, they do not initiate or create an obligation to arbitrate. Nor do they delineate substantive law or attempt in any way to regulate business transactions. The statutory scheme presumes the existence of an agreement created by mutual assent, and it does not purport to displace the

---

e.g., Rubewa Products Co. v. Watson's Quality Turkey Products, Inc., 242 A.2d 609 (D.C.App.1968).

[3] Modern arbitration legislation first appeared in the New York Arbitration Act of 1920 (now N.Y.Civ.Prac.Law §§ 7501–7514 (McKinney 1998)), which served as a model for other states and the federal government. The United States Arbitration Act (or Federal Arbitration Act, commonly referred to as the "FAA") followed in 1925, providing for arbitration solely in contracts involving maritime transactions and those evidencing transactions in interstate or foreign commerce. Act of Feb. 12, 1925, ch. 213, 43 Stat. 883–886, as amended, 9 U.S.C.A. §§ 1–14 (West 1999). As early as 1924, the Commissioners on Uniform State Laws drafted a model act; their efforts culminated in the Uniform Arbitration Act of 1955 (UAA). Uniform Arbitration Act (7 U.L.A. §§ 1–25). A large number of states have enacted the UAA in its entirety or with minor changes; others have departed from the model, although incorporating the essential elements of a modern arbitration statute. See M. Domke, Commercial Arbitration §§ 7:1–7:9 (3d ed. 2006). In 2000, the Uniform Law Commissioners adopted major revisions to the UAA, resulting in the revised Uniform Arbitration Act (RUAA). The preemptive effect of the FAA, the federal counterpart to the UAA, on state arbitration law is currently a most active question.

[4] A "modern" arbitration act is said to qualify for that designation by containing the following provisions: (1) irrevocability of agreements to arbitrate future disputes; (2) judicial power to compel a party to arbitrate at the request of the other; (3) judicial power to stay, pending arbitration, a court action instituted in violation of an arbitration agreement; (4) court authority to appoint arbitrators and fill vacancies when the parties fail to do so; (5) restrictions on judicial power to review awards of arbitrators; and (6) specification of the grounds for attack of awards, such as fraud or "evident mistake." Domke, § 7:1.

usual tests of contract formation and enforceability. A court order compelling arbitration is not a determination of substantive rights under the contract; it merely shifts the dispute to the agreed forum.

Yet when an arbitration award comes before a court for enforcement (and limited review), there is always present an important question of policy—to what extent should private parties be allowed by contract to transfer judicial functions to persons who may be wholly untrained in law and ready to disregard well-established rules? That legislatures have gone some distance in answering that question in favor of private autonomy is indicated by the following provision of the New York arbitration statute (McKinney's New York CPLR, § 7501):

> A written agreement to submit any controversy thereafter arising or any existing controversy to arbitration is enforceable without regard to the justiciable character of the controversy and confers jurisdiction on the courts of the state to enforce it and to enter judgment on an award. In determining any matter arising under this article, the court shall not consider whether the claim with respect to which arbitration is sought is tenable, or otherwise pass upon the merits of the dispute.

Does this mandated deference to arbitration extend also to remedies? In cases like *Grayson–Robinson*, for example, if the claim for specific enforcement had been presented initially to a court, it seems likely that problems of supervision would have led to a denial of relief. Yet the Commercial Arbitration Rules of the American Arbitration Association expressly provide that an arbitrator may grant any remedy or relief deemed "just and equitable and within the scope of the [parties'] agreement, including, but not limited to, specific performance of a contract." Should a court have to ignore its doubts because an arbitrator chosen by the parties has awarded specific relief? Does freedom of contract *require* the court to implement whatever remedy the arbitrator has ordered?

In a case decided the year before *Grayson–Robinson*, the New York Court of Appeals upheld an arbitration award that directed the "reinstatement" to his former position of a corporate manager of production and engineering. The arbitrators had found that the manager had been improperly discharged under an eleven-year contract that still had six years to run. Staklinski v. Pyramid Electric Co., 6 N.Y.2d 159, 188 N.Y.S.2d 541, 160 N.E.2d 78 (1959). Again, three judges dissented. They asked the question whether, if the employee had breached the agreement and an arbitrator had awarded specific performance, the employer could secure a court order forcing the employee to work for the corporation. Another question could be whether a court will enforce an arbitrator's award which specifically enforces a restrictive noncompetition covenant, even to the extent of enjoining an individual from engaging in like employment for a period of many years in the future. The New York Court of Appeals said "yes" in Matter of Sprinzen and Nomberg, 46 N.Y.2d 623, 415 N.Y.S.2d 974, 389 N.E.2d 456 (1979), deferring to the arbitrator's resolution of the issues of the restriction's reasonableness and necessity: "While there may be some doubt whether we would have enforced the restrictive covenant now before us had this dispute been adjudicated in the courts, such consideration is irrelevant to the disposition of this case, for courts will not second-guess the factual findings or the legal conclusions of the arbitrator."

Still a third question could be whether a court will enforce an arbitration award of punitive damages. As we shall see in many other cases involving arbitration, much turns on the preemptive effect of the Federal Arbitration Act. See Mastrobuono v. Shearson Lehman Hutton, Inc., 514 U.S. 52 (1995). A useful discussion can be found in Ware, Punitive Damages in Arbitration, 63 Ford.L.Rev. 529 (1994).

————

CHAPTER 2

THE DOMAIN OF LEGALLY ENFORCEABLE PROMISES

SECTION 1. INTRODUCTION

We are morally and ethically obliged to keep our promises, but it does not follow that promises should be legally enforceable on that account alone. Legal enforceability raises the stakes considerably. Holding a promise legally enforceable empowers one private citizen to call upon the state to use force (if necessary) against another. It is not something to be done lightly, especially when the judge must try to reconstruct the promise from evidence that is often conflicting and incomplete.

In this chapter, we focus upon the way in which common law courts have met the challenge of deciding when promises we are morally obliged to keep are also ones the state can force us to keep. We share intuitions about the cases at the extremes. The written promise of a giant corporation to sell goods to another giant corporation should be legally enforceable. A casual promise one friend makes to another in a social setting—perhaps about meeting for lunch or dinner—should not be. It would be surprising if any modern legal regime provided otherwise. But those trained in the law must learn exactly what mechanism a particular legal system uses to draw the line.

Under the Anglo–American law of contracts, whether a promise is legally enforceable turns in the first instance on whether there was a bargained-for exchange. For the cases at the extremes, this sorting mechanism works well. Social promises are not, by and large, bargained-for exchanges while virtually all transactions in the marketplace are. In the next section of this chapter, we explore exactly how this principle works in operation by focusing on unusual cases, such as promises made in a family setting that may or may not constitute a bargained-for exchange. We then go on in subsequent sections to see how an alternative ground for enforcing promises—that of promissory estoppel—took hold during the last century. To provide the necessary background, this introduction first explores alternative ways of distinguishing enforceable promises from those that are not and sets out the historical path that leads to where we are today, a place where courts refuse to enforce some promises, even when seriously made.

One way for a legal system to demarcate legally enforceable promises is to require a legal form, a particular ritual, that must be followed. German law, dating from the year 1900, provides a good example. It provides that promises of gift are void unless notarized. Another clause of the German Civil Code (BGB, art. 516(1)) defines a gift as a transfer by which "one person out of his property enriches another," if both parties "are agreed that the [transfer] is to occur without recompense." The latter feature of the definition—that both parties must have agreed on the absence of any recompense—was no doubt de-

193

signed to separate the gift from other transactions, notably those including an element of agreed exchange.

Notarization in European countries is very different from what it is in the United States. The European notary is not one who merely certifies, by signing and affixing a seal, that statements in a writing are made under oath. The notary in Europe is a licensed public official, trained in law, who is required to keep full records of the documents that are sworn to by private parties. It is the notary's duty to ensure that these documents are fully understood, to interrogate their makers if necessary, and to inform signers of the legal consequences of their acts.

The drafting commission that prepared the German Code first reviewed the long experience with strict requirements for making valid gifts, both gifts by present transfer and by promises performable in the future. The commission's own conclusion was that requirements of form would be needed only for promises of gift. They were needed, the commission said, "to prevent over-hasty promises of gift to exclude the doubt that often arises whether a serious promise had been made or only an expression of an intent to give in the future, and also to prevent, so far as possible, evasion of the requirements of form for testaments and gifts *causa mortis* [i.e., with death impending] and to eliminate disputes over gifts alleged to have been made by persons already dead. A mere requirement of a writing is not enough. Notarization must be required in view of the broad grounds for formalizing such transactions that transcend the interests of the parties involved. The evidence is preserved if the donor makes his promise before a court or notary. It is not necessary that acceptance by the donee be expressed in this form. It can be entirely informal, even his silence can be enough."

Formal rules indeed offer distinct advantages, as Professor Lon Fuller noted long ago in one of the most important law review articles ever written, an article that even today bears careful study, in particular the passage that follows.

―――――――

Fuller, Consideration and Form
41 Colum.L.Rev. 799, 800–801 (1941)

"[I]t is said that enforcement is denied gratuitous promises because such promises are often made impulsively and without proper deliberation. . . . [T]he objection relates, not to the content and effect of the promise, but to the manner in which it is made. Objections of this sort, which touch the form rather than the content of the agreement, will be removed if the making of the promise is attended by some formality or ceremony, as by being under seal. On the other hand, it has been said that the enforcement of gratuitous promises is not an object of sufficient importance to our social and economic order to justify the expenditure of the time and energy necessary to accomplish it. Here the objection is one of 'substance' since it touches the significance of the promise made and not merely the circumstances surrounding the making of it.

"The task . . . is that of disentangling the 'formal' and 'substantive' elements in the doctrine of consideration. [We examine first] in general terms the formal . . . bases of contract liability. . . .

"The Evidentiary Function—The most obvious function of a legal formality is, to use Austin's words, that of providing 'evidence of the existence and purport of the contract, in case of controversy.' The need for evidentiary security may be satisfied in a variety of ways: by requiring a writing, or attestation, or the certification of a notary. It may even be satisfied, to some extent, by such a device as the Roman *stipulatio*, which compelled an oral spelling out of the promise in a manner sufficiently ceremonious to impress its terms on participants and possible bystanders.

"The Cautionary Function—A formality may also perform a cautionary or deterrent function by acting as a check against inconsiderate action. The seal in its original form fulfilled this purpose remarkably well. The affixing and impressing of a wax wafer—symbol in the popular mind of legalism and weightiness—was an excellent device for inducing the circumspective frame of mind appropriate in one pledging his future. To a less extent any requirement of a writing, of course, serves the same purpose, as do requirements of attestation, notarization, etc. . . .

"The Channeling Function—Though most discussions of the purposes served by formalities go no further than the analysis just presented, this analysis stops short of recognizing one of the most important functions of form. That a legal formality may perform a function not yet described can be shown by the seal. The seal not only insures a satisfactory memorial of the promise and induces deliberation in the making of it. It serves also to mark or signalize the enforceable promise; it furnished a simple and external test of enforceability. . . .

"If we look at the matter purely from the standpoint of the convenience of the judge, there is nothing to distinguish the forms used in legal transactions from the 'formal' element which to some degree permeates all legal thinking. Even in the field of criminal law 'judicial diagnosis' is 'facilitated' by formal definitions, presumptions, and artificial constructions of fact. The thing which characterizes the law of contracts and conveyances is that in this field forms are deliberately used, and are intended to be so used, by the parties whose acts are to be judged by the law. To the business man who wishes to make his own or another's promise binding, the seal was at common law available as a device for the accomplishment of his objective. In this aspect form offers a legal framework into which the party may fit his actions, or, to change the figure, it offers channels for the legally effective expression of intention. It is with this aspect of form in mind that I have described the third function of legal formalities as 'the channeling function.' "

COMMENT: FORMALISM AND THE SEAL

Long before developments in the sixteenth and seventeenth centuries brought a search for the criteria of enforceable promises, formality had played an important role in identifying the relatively few promises that were enforced. We can only speculate as to how well modern justifications for the use of formalities may have been understood by the early lawyers. It suffices to say that when the making of the promise was attended by solemn, ceremonial acts, enforcement by official agencies seemed justified. Indeed, at these early times it was probably normal to think of enforceability and formality as two sides of the same coin.

By the late Middle Ages, English law had developed the seal, a highly serviceable, all-purpose formality. It was used to authenticate transfers of ownership, especially transfers of interests in land by way of "deed," and also to make promises enforceable. For breach of a promise under seal the action of covenant, leading to a judgment for damages, became a standard common law remedy. Indeed, until about 1500 it was almost the only remedy available for breach of promise. There was, it is true, the still more ancient action of debt, which we saw in Chapter 1 (pp. 111–116). But debt's utility was limited, since it could be used only to recover a sum of money already due and fixed in amount. It was not until later—the sixteenth century—that common law courts developed a generalized damage remedy for breach of contract, special assumpsit, which gave damages for breach of a variety of informal promises that did not fit debt's pattern of the half-completed exchange. Until then, and indeed for a long time thereafter, especially in transactions that had been carefully planned because the interests at stake were important, the contract under seal was the prototype for consensual transactions.

Viewed in light of Professor Fuller's description of the functions that legal formalities can perform, the seal in its heyday deserved a high rating. The requirements were strict. In the early seventeenth century, according to the testimony of a well-known judge-reporter, Sir Edward Coke, it was necessary for a valid seal that heated wax, impressed with a mark, be actually affixed to the document that was to be authenticated. As to the mark itself there was some leeway. Persons of importance would no doubt use their family seals embellished with mottos, but the impression could be made with a signet ring, a finger, or, according to one early report, the bite of a foretooth. Heating the seal and placing an imprint on the document would be quite likely to arrest the participants' attention. Signature or a mark by the person making the transfer or promise was also required. And there was one more step, delivery—a physical surrender of the document to the grantee or promisee or an authorized representative. A ceremony with all these elements was surely calculated—deliberately calculated, it seems, by those who conceived it—to produce persuasive evidence, to make a sharp impression on the participants, and to provide visible signs of authenticity.

If the prescribed formalities were followed, nothing more was needed to make a promise "under seal" enforceable. The requirement of consideration, which we will soon encounter, was invented as a control over informal (unsealed) promises long after promises under seal had come to be regularly enforced. Some modern decisions have mentioned a "presumption" of consideration that the seal produces, but in states where the seal still has its common law effects the presumption is conclusive (in other words, consideration is not needed). One question to keep in mind is whether persons who are fully competent should have power to bind themselves by promise merely because they seriously intend to do so. One way to confer this power is to provide a ceremonial—a stereotyped formality—such as the signing, sealing, and delivery of a written document. In more than half our states this is no longer possible.

In its classical development during the fifteenth and sixteenth centuries, common law doctrine made the sealed promise not only enforceable but almost invulnerable to attack. The person whose signature and seal appeared on a document could no doubt show that both were placed there through forgery. If a party did in fact sign and seal, it could also be shown that the very nature of the document itself had been misrepresented to the signer at the time of execution ("fraud in the factum"). But no other kind of fraud or mistake could be shown in a common law action (e.g., "fraud in the inducement," as where the buyer complained that a diseased horse had been fraudulently described as healthy by the seller). Nor could a promisor show that the other party's performance promised in return had not been received, or that the promisor had in fact fully performed but had neglected to secure a sealed cancellation or release of the obligation, or that the agreement evidenced by the sealed document had been superseded by a subsequent informal agreement of the parties.

These attitudes of common law courts were less than half the story, since the Chancellor adopted very different attitudes. Indeed, relief against misuse or abuse of sealed instruments had become, by the sixteenth century at least, a major activity of the Chancery. Fraud or mistake in the making of sealed contracts, payment without securing cancellation or release, and subsequent modification by informal agreement became standard grounds for intervention by the Chancellors. The correctives they introduced served to bring the sealed instrument back within the framework of a rational scheme of contract law. Some of these correctives were so obviously needed that they were gradually absorbed within the common law system. It has been true for a long time, for example, that payment can be pleaded by the obligor as a defense when sued at law on a sealed instrument. In many states, this is also true of fraud or mistake in the formation of the transaction. In other states, a legacy remains in the form of a distinction making the defenses of fraud, mistake, or breach by the opposite party "equitable" issues that must be decided by a judge rather than a jury. There were other problems that took longer to solve, such as the invulnerability of sealed promises to modification or revision by mutual agreement (the older law required an instrument of "equal dignity") and the limitation of the right to sue to the parties to the covenant (thus barring suit by beneficiaries and undisclosed principals). Difficulties of this kind were not inherent or inevitable features of formalized legal transactions. They reflected the technicality and rigidity that the common law showed in many other areas as well.

In order to preserve a legal formality a price must be paid. The history of the seal makes it plain that the opinion-makers in Anglo–American law did not consider the advantages gained to be worth the price. That history can be summarized briefly: gradual erosion of the requirements of form drained off the solemnity of the occasion and thereby destroyed the usefulness of the seal. The erosion occurred in several ways. Dilution of the requirement of delivery can illustrate the mental processes at work. It has been clear for a long time that the mere physical surrender of a document is meaningless by itself—the parties' purpose may be merely to permit another person to inspect it. The essential factor is the intent of the transferor to endow the document, by that act, with legal consequences. So a delivery to some third person or various kinds of "symbolic" delivery should do just as well, and restrictions or qualifications desired by the transferor (e.g., postponing all legal effect until some future event should occur) should be enforced. If, then, it was intent, not acts, that counted, why insist on the ancient formalities; was it really necessary to heat up wax and stick it on a piece of paper? Why not use another piece of paper on which a mark of some kind had already been made and stick it on with adhesive? Or why was it not enough for the signer merely to recite in the document that it was deemed to be under seal?

As printed forms came into wider circulation, it became common practice simply to print after the space provided for signature the word "seal" or the letters "L.S." Even signers who remembered some Latin would have no particular reason to know that L.S. is short-hand for the Latin phrase *locus sigilli*, meaning "place of the seal." These various dilutions of the ancient formality clearly were inspired by impatience with what seemed to be purely external trivia. Accepting these various substitutes could seem fully justified by the result—enlarging the power of promisors to bind themselves if they used the right words or did the right acts. The irony was that the words and acts used lost meaning, especially as they became standard features of widely-used printed forms. It is no wonder that the impulse grew stronger to cut off this path to promissory obligation and destroy the power altogether.

The attitudes that inspired modern legislation were expressed by the New York Law Revision Commission in 1941, in recommending a statute that deprived the seal of all legal effect (Report, pp. 359–360):

> The seal has degenerated into a L.S. or other scrawl which, in modern practice, is frequently a printed L.S. upon a printed form. To the average man it conveys no meaning, and frequently the parties to instruments upon which it appears have no idea of its legal effects. Moreover, under the present law, the character of an instrument which bears the magic letters, but which contains no recital of sealing, is left uncertain as to whether it is sealed, depending upon parol evidence of intent to be later adduced. . . . It would seem, therefore, that if a method of making promises binding without consideration is desirable, some method should be devised which more clearly than the seal brings to the attention of the promisor what he is doing, and which fixes the character of the instrument as of the time of its execution. . . .

> Concerning the broader question whether, and to what extent, a person should be able to bind himself by a promise without consideration, the Commission doubts the wisdom of any device that is applicable to all kinds of promises under all circumstances. Certainly the seal is not the best device, assuming that some such device is desirable.

Today, more than half of the American states have legislation, cast in general terms, depriving the seal of all legal effect (i.e., abolishing any distinction between sealed and unsealed contracts).[1] To these should be added another handful of states where the seal is not "abolished" but made merely "presumptive evidence" of consideration.[2] And for transactions in goods, the Uniform Commercial Code, adopted in all states except Louisiana, uses somewhat elliptical language (§ 2–203) but the effect seems clear enough—in a written contract for the sale of goods the "affixing" of a seal adds nothing. There are, however, still some states in which the use of a seal (perhaps only the word "seal" or the letters "L.S.") in a consensual transaction other than a sale of goods will have some legal consequences. The most important consequence, of course, is

---

[1] E.g., Cal.Civ. Code §§ 1614, 1629 (West); Iowa Code Ann. §§ 537A.1–537A.3 (West).

[2] E.g., N.J.Stat.Ann. § 2A:82–3 (West).

that consideration or some equivalent reason for enforcement does not need to be established. Quite often, also, a much longer period for the start of a court action after breach has occurred (a "statute of limitations") is provided for sealed instruments. There may be other procedural consequences, such as law-equity distinctions in fact-finding on certain issues, as we have suggested above. A state-by-state analysis of the seal's modern status is provided in 1 S. Williston, Contracts § 2:17.

A few additional pieces of history will bring the story of formality to the present day. For a brief interval in the 1700s, English law hesitated on the brink of making a mere writing a sufficient form, at least in commercial disputes between merchants. These efforts, led by Lord Mansfield, were emphatically rejected by the House of Lords in 1778, when it was made clear—if there had been any doubt—that the requirement of consideration was to apply to written as well as oral contracts.

Much later there appeared in this country a type of statute, usually one brief sentence in length, which provided that a "written instrument is presumptive evidence of consideration." Presently, in roughly 15 states, the incorporation of an agreement in a written instrument is declared by statute to "import" or give "presumptive evidence" of consideration.[3]

A different solution—indeed, in practical effect a substitute for the seal—was proposed in 1925 by the Commissioners on Uniform State Laws. That group's proposals for uniform legislation have been widely adopted by state legislatures over the years, including the Commissioner's joint effort with the American Law Institute in drafting and sponsoring the Uniform Commercial Code. The Uniform Written Obligations Act, which the Commissioners proposed in the 1920s, and whose adoption was urged by Professor Williston and other distinguished academics in the decades that followed, provides that a written release or promise, signed by the releasor or promisor, shall not be invalid for lack of consideration if the writing contains "an additional statement, in any form of language, that the signer intends to be legally bound." But this recommended statute did not receive as warm a reception as was the case with the Commissioners' other proposals. The Uniform Act was adopted in only two states; it is now in force only in Pennsylvania.

Congregation Kadimah Toras–Moshe v. DeLeo

Supreme Judicial Court of Massachusetts, 1989.
405 Mass. 365, 540 N.E.2d 691.

LIACOS, C.J. Congregation Kadimah Toras–Moshe (Congregation), an Orthodox Jewish synagogue, commenced this action [to] compel the administrator of an estate to fulfil the oral promise of the decedent to give the Congregation $25,000. The Superior Court . . . rendered summary judgment for the estate and dismissed the Congregation's complaint. [We now affirm.]

---

[3] This type of provision appears in, e.g., California (West's Civ.Code § 1614); Iowa (West's Code Ann. §§ 537A.2, 537A.3); Kansas (Stat. §§ 16–107, 16–108); New Mexico (Stat.Ann. § 38–7–2); Tennessee (Code Ann. § 47–50–103).

The facts are not contested. The decedent suffered a prolonged illness, throughout which he was visited by the Congregation's spiritual leader, Rabbi Abraham Halbfinger. During four or five of these visits, and in the presence of witnesses, the decedent made an oral promise to give the Congregation $25,000. The Congregation planned to use the $25,000 to transform a storage room in the synagogue into a library named after the decedent. The oral promise was never reduced to writing. The decedent died intestate in September, 1985. He had no children, but was survived by his wife.

The Congregation asserts that the decedent's oral promise is an enforceable contract under our case law, because the promise is allegedly supported either by consideration and bargain, or by reliance. . . . We disagree.

The [trial] judge determined that "[t]his was an oral gratuitous pledge, with no indication as to how the money should be used, or what [the Congregation] was required to do if anything in return for this promise." There was no legal benefit to the promisor nor detriment to the promisee, and thus no consideration. See Marine Contractors Co. v. Hurley, 365 Mass. 280, 310 N.E.2d 915 (1974); Gishen v. Dura Corp., 362 Mass. 177, 285 N.E.2d 117 (1972) (moral obligation is not legal obligation). Furthermore, there is no evidence in the record that the Congregation's plans to name a library after the decedent induced him to make or to renew his promise. Contrast Allegheny College v. National Chautauqua County Bank, 246 N.Y. 369, 159 N.E. 173 (1927) (subscriber's promise became binding when charity implicitly promised to commemorate subscriber).

As to the lack of reliance, the judge stated that the Congregation's "allocation of $25,000 in its budget[,] for the purpose of renovating a storage room, is insufficient to find reliance or an enforceable obligation." We agree. The inclusion of the promised $25,000 in the budget, by itself, merely reduced to writing the Congregation's expectation that it would have additional funds. A hope or expectation, even though well founded, is not equivalent to either legal detriment or reliance. . . .

The Congregation cites several of our cases in which charitable subscriptions were enforced. These cases are distinguishable because they involved written, as distinguished from oral, promises and also involved substantial consideration or reliance. See, e.g., Trustees of Amherst Academy v. Cowls, 6 Pick. 427, 434 (1828) (subscribers to written agreement could not withdraw "after the execution or during the progress of the work which they themselves set in motion"). . . . [We have] refused to enforce a promise in favor of a charity where there was no showing of any consideration or reliance. . . .

[W]e are of the opinion that in this case there is no injustice in declining to enforce the decedent's promise. . . . The promise to the Congregation is entirely unsupported by consideration or reliance.[1] Furthermore, it is an oral promise sought to be enforced against an estate. To enforce such a promise would be against public policy.[2]

---

[1] We need not decide whether we would enforce an oral promise where there was a showing of consideration or reliance. [Most of the court's footnotes are omitted; those retained are renumbered.—Eds.]

[2] The defendant argues that, if the decedent was aware of impending death, yet made no gift during life, then the promise is in the nature of a promise to make a will, which is unenforceable, by virtue of the Statute of Frauds. See G.L. c. 259, §§ 5, 5A (1986 ed.). Under the view we take, we need not consider this argument.

Judgment affirmed.

NOTE

It is useful to remember that our legal system requires formalities for certain purposes. To make a will in most places in this country, a testator must perform the ceremonial of signing in the presence of witnesses, who must then sign in the testator's presence and in the presence of each other (if witnessing is dispensed with, other forms are usually prescribed). To accomplish a transfer of chattels or choses in action by gift, "delivery" is needed. To pass title to real estate, by gift—e.g., the *Fischer* case, just ahead—or bargain, a deed must ordinarily be signed and delivered. And, as we have seen, for promises falling within the statute of frauds enforceability depends on a writing signed by the "party to be charged."

In *DeLeo*, it appears the decedent was serious about his promise, for he repeated it on four or five occasions, with witnesses present. Of course, the decedent might have demonstrated his seriousness of purpose by writing a check for $25,000 and handing it to the congregation's representative. Should a court in a case like *DeLeo* take into account the promisor's failure to make a completed gift?

The transaction in the principal case—a promise of a gift made to a charitable, religious, or other nonprofit organization—will surface again in the materials ahead. Our concern then will be the court's indication that a showing of reliance might alter the outcome in such cases. For the moment, the *DeLeo* decision is noteworthy because the court chose not to rule on the question whether an "oral promise" of this nature would be enforceable even though supported by consideration or reliance. Had the promise been in writing, and consideration or reliance shown, it seems liability would not have been in doubt. What is the basis for dividing the field of gratuitous promises in the manner the court suggests? Note also the court's statement that enforcement of this promise against this defendant would be "against public policy."

––––––

Pitts v. McGraw–Edison Co.

329 F.2d 412 (6th Cir.1964)

Plaintiff was a manufacturer's representative until his retirement from the business on July 1, 1955. For 25 years prior to that date, he sold defendant's products on a commission basis in an assigned territory working wholly independently of defendant and managing his own business, and employees, as he saw fit. Plaintiff had no contract of employment with defendant; their relationship was terminable at will by either at any time; defendant's sole obligation to plaintiff was to compensate him for sales made in the assigned territory; plaintiff was free to handle competitor's products, which he did for a time. Nevertheless, for five years after the parties' relationship ended by mutual agreement in 1955, defendant continued to pay plaintiff a 1% commission on all its sales in plaintiff's previous territory. When these payments were stopped in 1960, plaintiff sued alleging breach of a "retirement contract." Plaintiff sought to show that negotiations leading to his retirement were in substance "an offer [by defendant] that if he would retire as a manufacturer's representative on July 1, 1955, and turn over to his successor representative all of his customer account records[,] [defendant] would pay him monthly thereafter a 1% over-write commission on [its] sales within the territory." Defendant countered that there could be no "retirement" of one who was never its employee and free to do as he pleased about employment; that it had simply terminated a business re-lationship it was authorized to end; that it had made no offer nor undertaken any contractual obligation to plaintiff respecting payments; and that even if its dealings with plaintiff could be construed as a retirement contract, any such contract lacked consideration. The trial court dismissed the complaint. On ap-peal, *held*, affirmed. Even assuming a promise of retirement benefits can be found, there remains the question of what "passed from plaintiff" to make the promise enforceable. Plaintiff says that although he made no express promise, the turning over of his valuable customer records, at defendant's request, con-stitutes consideration. But the findings below do not support this claim, for nothing defendant said at the time, orally or in writing, required plaintiff "to do anything whatsoever" or "circumscribed his actions in any manner." Plaintiff himself testified that, at and after his retirement, he did things for defendant he was not required to do. Hence the five-year payments to plaintiff were with-out consideration, "the result of voluntary action [by] defendant, [and] mere gratuities terminable at will."

In re Bayshore Yacht & Tennis Club Condominium Ass'n, Inc.
336 Bankr. 866 (Bankr. S.D.Fla.2006)

In 1981, Coletta purchased three penthouse units in Bayshore Condomin-ium (the debtor), which units were located on the eleventh floor of the building. At the time of purchase, as Coletta knew, elevator service within the building ceased at the tenth floor. Upon purchasing the units, Coletta attempted to con-vince Bayshore to provide elevator access to the eleventh floor. According to Coletta, on numerous occasions Bayshore's representatives committed to providing elevator access to the eleventh floor at no expense to Coletta. Howev-er, no action was ever taken on this alleged commitment, purportedly because Bayshore lacked sufficient funds. Coletta eventually sued Bayshore, alleging a contract to extend the elevator at Bayshore's expense. Bayshore maintained that it never promised to pay for any elevator extension. A bankruptcy court rejected Coletta's claim, saying, "'A mere gratuitous promise of a future gift, lacking consideration, is unenforceable.' ... Even assuming arguendo that the Debtor and its representatives did orally promise to provide elevator access to the eleventh floor at the Debtor's expense and Coletta subsequently accepted such a promise, Coletta cannot point to any consideration that he provided to induce a promise obligating Bayshore to pay for an alteration Coletta would otherwise have to pay for himself, nor is there any evidence that he detrimen-tally relied on such a promise.... Simply, the record reflects that Coletta asked, the Debtor allegedly promised and nothing happened over a span of twenty years...."

SECTION 2. THE BARGAINED–FOR EXCHANGE

INTRODUCTORY COMMENT

In the nineteenth century, courts relied largely on the idea of "consideration" to distinguish the promises that were legally enforceable from those that were not. While theories of consideration were not spun out until that time, they all include a deposit from a much more distant past. We must speak again of the old forms of action, and in particular of special assumpsit. The history of consideration is tied in with special assumpsit in two quite different ways. First, and most obviously, there was no very great problem in defining the limits of promissory liability until the 1500s, when special assumpsit was made over into a generalized damage remedy for breach of informal promises. Second, the earliest origins of special assumpsit left an impression on lawyers' minds and may have helped to shape the ultimate doctrine of consideration.

With the action of covenant restricted to the enforcement of promises under seal, the early common law had only one form of action that could be used widely to enforce informal (unsealed) promises. This was the action of *debt*. Debt would lie to enforce any kind of a duty to pay a "sum certain" in money; the duty could arise from statute, custom, or promise. But if the promise was not under seal, there was a requirement that hardened into a rule—there must be a *quid pro quo* received by the promisor. In the standard cases where debt was used, the meaning of this term was plain enough. The plaintiff would have loaned money to the defendant and would be suing to enforce an express but unsealed promise of repayment; or goods would have been delivered or services rendered in reliance on an express promise of a money price. Situations of this type were appealing for a number of reasons, and the English common law, like early Roman law, responded by giving a remedy that was essentially contractual. But no general theory of contract was needed to justify enforcement of the unperformed promise in this type of case. There was the plain fact that the defendant had bargained for and actually received a gain, whose retention without payment would be unjust. The payment of money, the transfer of goods, or the rendition of services could not ordinarily be expected to occur without compensation. The performance actually rendered would, therefore, perform an evidentiary function; it would also confirm the plaintiff's contention that a promise of payment had in fact been made. Cases of this type have been aptly described as cases of "half-completed exchange" (Fuller, Consideration and Form, 41 Colum.L.Rev. 799, 815 (1941)). They were indeed exchanges, the product of agreement, but the dominant fact was that the exchange had been carried out only on one side.

The context from which the special assumpsit remedy gradually emerged was quite different. Trespass on the case was modeled on and derived from the writ of trespass, omitting the allegation of "force and arms." By the fifteenth century, trespass on the case was expanding steadily in various directions and was well on its way toward being, as it later became, the generalized tort remedy of the common law. To say that trespass on the case was a tort remedy in the fifteenth century is to read back modern classifications of which lawyers of that century were only vaguely aware. Yet they surely were aware of them, for they clung tenaciously to the idea that the defendant's "misfeasance" was the test for the availability of the special form of trespass on the case that came to be called special assumpsit. Typical of the thinking about the small cluster of cases that defined the line of growth is a comparatively early statement (the year was 1436) by Newton, a common lawyer who was soon to become Chief Justice:

> I fully agree that it is the law that if a carpenter promises me to make a house good and strong in a certain form and he makes me a house that is weak and bad and in another form, I will have an action of trespass on my case. So if a smith promises me to shoe my horse well and properly and he shoes him and drives in a nail, I shall have a good action. Also if a leech undertakes to cure me of my illnesses and he gives me medicines but does not cure me I shall have an action on my case. . . . And the cause is in all these cases that there is an undertaking and . . . the plaintiffs have suffered a wrong. (Year Book, 14 Henry VI, no. 58).

As a group, these illustrative cases were thought to share a common pattern: a loss was incurred by virtue of affirmative action taken in a manner not conforming to duty. Thus, a promisee who had relied on the representations implicit in a promisor's "undertaking," suffering harm as a result, was viewed as the victim of a "wrong"—in effect, a tort—for which an expanded assumpsit provided a remedy.

Where the informal promise was made but performance was not begun at all, the issue of enforceability was raised more sharply. During the fifteenth century, the transition period, the Year Book lawyers debated at length the distinction between "misfeasance" (cases of the type described above) and "nonfeasance" (a total failure to perform). Between these concepts lay a great white line, gray though it might be on the fringes. The common lawyers did not cross the line until the early 1500s, and even then, it seems, only with great reluctance and perhaps mainly to meet the competition of Chancery's expanding remedies. This development involved cases that today we would describe as an overlap between tort and contract, that is, instances in which wrongs were committed and losses caused in relations that had originated from agreement. The agreement or promise had the important function of defining the level of duty owed.

When it was agreed in the early part of the sixteenth century that trespass on the case (assumpsit) could provide a remedy where the promisor did not act at all, as well as where a promisor acted affirmatively but not in accordance with duty, some new and harder questions loomed up. The expanded remedy of assumpsit did not have a built-in limitation like the requirement of *quid pro quo* in debt. Should every informal promise now be enforceable? No limiting principle had yet been formulated in English law, and thus there was no good English term available to express the vague sensation that it was necessary to fix a cut-off point somewhere for obligation derived from promises.

The common lawyers had a very small vocabulary with which to describe the elements needed to make a promise enforceable. They had a few phrases that had been used for other purposes and that no doubt helped to precipitate thought in new directions. "Consideration" was at the outset the most pallid and least meaningful of these phrases. "Consideration" was only one of the words that began to appear to reflect this notion. Sometimes "consideration" was made synonymous with the *causa* that continental lawyers believed would clothe naked promises and make them respectable; at other times, the term was used interchangeably with the familiar *quid pro quo* of debt; at still other times the term was really pallid and in effect became part of a "whereas" clause, as in pleadings or other documents that recited "in consideration that A" had paid money or done some other act, "B promised," etc. In short, the term "consideration," on its first appearance, merely expressed (obscurely, to be sure) the feeling that there should be some sufficient reason, ground, or motive that would justify enforcement of a promise.

After the Statute of Uses in 1535, common law judges began to enforce contracts for the sale of land that before could be enforced only in Chancery. They continued to use "bargain and sale," the familiar phrase the Chancellor had used in such cases. But the common law judges were bent on expanding the range of promissory transactions they would enforce. The main directions that the extensions would follow were fixed not by any theory preordained at the outset, but by the reasons urged by lawyers and pleaders for court intervention. More and more it became standard to allege that the promise had been given "for" some asset or act that the pleader proceeded to specify, and if this kind of connection was not shown, the action was likely to fail. As time went on, the something "for" which the promise was made was described increasingly as "the consideration," though the word carried a load of vaguer meanings, suggesting other motives for promising that might or might not be good enough. Over time, most of these vaguer meanings were stripped away and "consideration" was made over, from an amorphous word drawn from common speech, into a technical requirement for contract formation.

During the decades that followed the courts struggled to define the "request" that would transform into a present exchange some action by another that had produced a result desired by the promisor. That their success in these efforts was far from complete matters not at all for the present purpose. It became abundantly clear as the sixteenth century progressed that common law courts had created the means for enforcing, and were prepared to enforce, a great variety of exchange transactions. In the transactions that were enforced there was one recurring element: each party had in fact desired some act or abstention of the other in return for which something would be given.

It must be stressed again that the thinking of lawyers around the year 1600 was centered on procedure and the forms of action. The practical question at the time was: "When will assumpsit lie?" A lawyer who would answer the question would surely have to take account of the assimilation of debt and assumpsit that was accomplished by Slade's Case in 1602 (recall the discussion of the Common Counts and Restitution, supra pp. 111–116).

Any generalization concerning the outer limits of contract liability, in the sixteenth century and later, had to include the two quite different core situations or cases: the "half-completed exchange" of debt (with its allegations that the promise in question had been given "for" some asset or performance) and the loss-through-fault situations of early assumpsit. Roughly corresponding to these two elements are *benefit to the promisor and detriment to the promisee*, either of which will suffice as consideration according to conventional statements of the modern doctrine. But the correspondence is only rough. In particular, the concept of detriment was rapidly generalized (and attenuated) so as to include much more than visible and measurable losses, caused by incompetent carpenters and blacksmiths. The common lawyers were practical people who thought in terms of particular cases. They were dimly aware that not every benefit or detriment would do, but it was not until much later—the nineteenth century—that another limiting principle, that of exchange through bargain, emerged as the core of consideration doctrine.

While courts would not necessarily inquire into the nature of the bargain or the fairness of the exchange, this conception of consideration required that there in fact be a bargain. A transaction that merely mimics the form of a bargained-for exchange is, under this view, suspect. In this sense, the doctrine of consideration is different from a legal formality such as a seal, where the ritual itself is all that matters.

Oliver Wendell Holmes (The Common Law 293-94 (1881)) offered his own formulation of this idea of consideration consisting of a bargained-for exchange:

> [I]t is the essence of a consideration that, by the terms of the agreement, it is given and accepted as the motive or inducement of the promise. Conversely, the promise must be made and accepted as the conventional motive or inducement for furnishing the consideration. The root of the whole matter is the relation of reciprocal conventional inducement, each for the other, between consideration and promise.

The question we pursue in this chapter concerns the extent to which it makes sense to enforce only those promises that are part of a bargained-for exchange. We look at how courts went about identifying the presence or absence of consideration and how, over the course of the twentieth century, they supplemented the idea of bargained-for consideration with an additional idea—that promises seriously made should be enforced if they were reasonably relied upon, at least to the extent of that reliance.

The next case focuses explicitly on the idea of the bargained-for exchange as the identifier of an enforceable promise, and thus on that unique feature of the common law of contracts, the doctrine of consideration.

Hamer v. Sidway

Court of Appeals of New York, 1891.
124 N.Y. 538, 27 N.E. 256.

Appeal from order of the General Term of the Supreme Court[,] made July 1, 1890, which reversed a judgment in favor of plaintiff entered upon a decision of the court on trial at Special Term and granted a new trial.

The plaintiff presented a claim [on an alleged contract] to the executor of William E. Story, Sr., for $5,000 and interest from the 6th day of February, 1875. She acquired it through several mesne assignments from William E. Story, 2d. The claim being rejected by the executor, this action was brought. It appears that William E. Story, Sr., was the uncle of William E. Story, 2d; that at the celebration of the golden wedding of Samuel Story and wife, father and mother of William E. Story, Sr., on the 20th day of March, 1869, in the presence of the family and invited guests, he promised his nephew that if he would refrain from drinking, using tobacco, swearing, and playing cards or billiards for money until he became twenty-one years of age he would pay him a sum of $5,000. The nephew assented thereto and fully performed the conditions inducing the promise. When the nephew arrived at the age of twenty-one years and on the 31st day of January, 1875, he wrote to his uncle informing him that he had performed his part of the agreement and had thereby become entitled to the sum of $5,000. The uncle received the letter and a few days later on the sixth of February, [1875,] he wrote and mailed to his nephew the following letter:

"W.E. Story, Jr.:

"Dear Nephew—Your letter of the 31st ult. came to hand all right, saying that you had lived up to the promise made to me several years ago. I have no doubt but you have, for which you shall have five thousand dollars as I promised you. I had the money in the bank the day you was 21 years old that I intend for you, and you shall have the money certain. Now, Willie, I do not intend to interfere with this money in any way till I think you are capable of taking care of it and the sooner that time comes the better it will please me. I would hate very much to have you start out in some adventure that you thought all right and lose this money in one year. The first five thousand dollars that I got together cost me a heap of hard work. You would hardly believe me when I tell you that to obtain this I shoved a jackplane many a day, butchered three or four years, then came to this city, and after three months' perseverence I obtained a situation in a grocery store. I opened this store early, closed late, slept in the fourth story of the building in a room 30 by 40 feet and not a human being in the building but myself. All this I done to live as cheap as I could to save something. I don't want you to take up with this kind of fare. I was here in the cholera season '49 and '52 and the deaths averaged 80 to 125 daily and plenty of smallpox. I wanted to go home, but Mr. Fisk, the gentleman I was working for, told me if I left then, after it got healthy he probably would not want me. I stayed. All the money I have saved I know just how I got it. It did not come to me in any mysterious way, and the reason I speak of this is that money got in this way stops longer with a fellow that gets it with hard knocks than it does when he finds it. Willie, you are 21 and you have many a thing to learn yet. This money you have earned much easier than I did besides acquiring good habits at the same time and you are quite welcome to the money; hope you will make good use of it. I was ten long years getting this together after I was your age. Now, hoping this will be satisfactory, I stop. . . .

Truly Yours,

"W.E. Story.

"P.S.—You can consider this money on interest."

The nephew received the letter and thereafter consented that the money should remain with his uncle in accordance with the terms and conditions of the letter. The uncle died on the 29th day of January, 1887, without having paid over to his nephew any portion of the said $5,000 and interest.

PARKER, J. The question . . . at the foundation of plaintiff's asserted right of recovery [is] whether by virtue of a contract defendant's testator William E. Story became indebted to his nephew William E. Story, 2d, on his twenty-first birthday in the sum of five thousand dollars. The trial court found as a fact that "on the 20th day of March, 1869, . . . William E. Story agreed to and with William E. Story, 2d, that if he would refrain from drinking liquor, using tobacco, swearing, and playing cards or billiards for money until he should become 21 years of age then he, the said William E. Story, would at that time pay him, the said William E. Story, 2d, the sum of

$5,000 for such refraining, to which the said William E. Story, 2d, agreed," and that he "in all things fully performed his part of said agreement."

The defendant contends that the contract was without consideration to support it, and, therefore, invalid. He asserts that the promisee by refraining from the use of liquor and tobacco was not harmed but benefited; that that which he did was best for him to do independently of his uncle's promise, and insists that it follows that unless the promisor was benefited, the contract was without consideration. A contention, which if well founded, would seem to leave open for controversy in many cases whether that which the promisee did or omitted to do was, in fact, of such benefit to him as to leave no consideration to support the enforcement of the promisor's agreement. Such a rule could not be tolerated, and is without foundation in the law. The Exchequer Chamber, in 1875, defined consideration as follows: "A valuable consideration in the sense of the law may consist either in some right, interest, profit or benefit accruing to the one party, or some forbearance, detriment, loss or responsibility given, suffered or undertaken by the other." Courts "will not ask whether the thing which forms the consideration does in fact benefit the promisee or a third party, or is of any substantial value to anyone. It is enough that something is promised, done, forborne or suffered by the party to whom the promise is made as consideration for the promise made to him." (Anson's Prin. of Con. 63.)

"In general a waiver of any legal right at the request of another party is a sufficient consideration for a promise." (Parsons on Contracts, 444.) "Any damage, or suspension, or forbearance of a right will be sufficient to sustain a promise." (Kent, vol. 2, 465, 12th ed.)

Pollock, in his work on contracts, page 166, after citing the definition given by the Exchequer Chamber already quoted, says: "The second branch of this judicial description is really the most important one. Consideration means not so much that one party is profiting as that the other abandons some legal right in the present or limits his legal freedom of action in the future as an inducement for the promise of the first."

Now, applying this rule to the facts before us, the promisee used tobacco, occasionally drank liquor, and he had a legal right to do so. That right he abandoned for a period of years upon the strength of the promise of the testator that for such forbearance he would give him $5,000. We need not speculate on the effort which may have been required to give up the use of those stimulants. It is sufficient that he restricted his lawful freedom of action within certain prescribed limits upon the faith of his uncle's agreement, and now having fully performed the conditions imposed, it is of no moment whether such performance actually proved a benefit to the promisor, and the court will not inquire into it, but were it a proper subject of inquiry, we see nothing in this record that would permit a determination that the uncle was not benefited in a legal sense. . . .

We must now consider the effect of the letter, and the nephew's assent thereto. Were the relations of the parties thereafter that of debtor and creditor simply, or that of trustee and [beneficiary]? If the former, then this action is not maintainable, because barred by lapse of time. If the latter, the result must be otherwise. No particular expressions are necessary to create a trust. Any language clearly showing the settler's intention is sufficient if the property and disposition of it are definitely stated.

A person in the legal possession of money or property acknowledging a trust with the assent of the [beneficiary], becomes from that time a trustee if the acknowledgment be founded on a valuable consideration. His antecedent relation to the subject, whatever it may have been, no longer controls. If before a declaration of trust a party be a mere debtor, a subsequent agreement recognizing the fund as already in his hands and stipulating for its investment on the creditor's account will have the effect to create a trust. . . .

The order appealed from should be reversed and the judgment of the Special Term affirmed, with costs payable out of the estate.

NOTE

Louise Hamer, the nominal plaintiff in the case, was Willie's mother-in-law. The assignment to her was gratuitous and was done at the same time that others on Willie's side of the family consolidated all the rights they had against the uncle's estate to her. At the time he died, the uncle had two nieces of a deceased brother living with him. They seem the most likely beneficiaries of the estate. For a review of the trial record and suggestions about the dynamics underlying the case, see Baird, Reconstructing Contracts: *Hamer v. Sidway*, in Contracts Stories 265–303 (2007).

––––––––

Earle v. Angell

157 Mass. 294, 32 N.E. 164 (1892)

Mary Dewitt said to her nephew, the plaintiff, that if he would agree to attend her funeral in the event that he outlived her, then Mary would give him $500 and pay his traveling expenses. Plaintiff testified that he made the promise as requested, and that after her death he attended Aunt Mary's funeral. Mary left a paper in a sealed envelope, reading as follows: "$500.00. Oxford, August 14th, 1883. If Benjamin A. Earle should come to my funeral, I order my executor to pay him the sum of five hundred dollars. Mary Dewitt." *Held*, plaintiff can recover from Mary's executor. The jury was warranted in finding a promise given for a promise. The case in its other aspects, said Holmes, J., is unexceptional. It is settled that "a contract to pay money after one's own death is valid." There is no legal difficulty with a contract "to pay a person $500, conditioned upon his attending the promisor's funeral, and in consideration of his promise to do so."

––––––––

Whitten v. Greeley–Shaw

520 A.2d 1307 (Me.1987)

The parties had engaged in an intermittent extra-marital relationship for a number of years. Defendant, complaining that plaintiff had not kept his promises in the past, then asked for "something in writing." Plaintiff allegedly replied, "[y]ou figure out what you want and I will sign it." Defendant thereupon drew up a one-page, typewritten document (entitled "agreement") which plaintiff signed without objection. The agreement required plaintiff to perform various "conditions made by [defendant]," including payment to her of $500 monthly, reimbursement of specified expenses, visits and phone calls at stated intervals, trips together, and gifts of jewelry (one trip and one piece of jewelry per year). No "condition" was explicitly imposed on defendant, though the agreement did provide that "[u]nder no circumstances will there be any calls made to my homes or offices without prior permission from me." Also, at some point in their relationship, plaintiff loaned defendant $64,000 to purchase a home, taking from her a mortgage on the property to secure a promissory note. When defendant defaulted on the note, plaintiff brought a foreclosure action in which defendant filed a counterclaim based on the parties' written agreement. The trial court denied defendant's counterclaim, ordering foreclosure of the mortgage. *Held*, judgment below affirmed; the agreement plaintiff signed is legally unenforceable. Defendant's promise not to call plaintiff without his permission could serve as consideration for plaintiff's return promises, since it is a promise "to forbear from engaging in an activity that she had the legal right to engage in." But such a promise must be "sought after" by plaintiff and "motivated by" his request that defendant not disturb him. There is no evidence whatsoever of this. The only clause in the agreement operating in plaintiff's favor was put there by defendant, not plaintiff, and only because, defendant testified, "she felt the plaintiff should get something in exchange for his promises." Clearly, the clause was neither "bargained for" by plaintiff nor "given in exchange for" his promises. It cannot constitute the consideration necessary to bind plaintiff to a contract.

NOTE

Suppose it had been shown in Earle v. Angell that Mary's nephew would have attended her funeral regardless of the promise of $500—e.g., that he had never missed a relative's funeral and that, on many occasions, he had said privately that he would be sure to get to Mary's funeral. Does the rationale of Hamer v. Sidway reach such a case?

It was noted earlier that donative promises made in social or family settings figure "prominently in the discussion of consideration." In fact, decisions on the doctrine of consideration have involved a wide assortment of conduct, ranging from the mere act of opening an envelope to "bringing about a miracle" (winning a lottery, allegedly by virtue of a bargained-for appeal, through prayer, to a specified saint). See, e.g., Harris v. Time, Inc., 191 Cal.App.3d 449, 237 Cal.Rptr. 584 (1987); Pando v. Fernandez, 127 Misc.2d 224, 485 N.Y.S.2d 162 (Sup.Ct.1984). If consideration is found in unusual circumstances (that is, social or noncommercial settings), courts typically explain that the concepts "benefit" and "detriment" have "technical meanings" in contract law, and that "legal detriment" is to be distinguished from "detriment in fact." For example, a modern court has said that "a promise to give up smoking may be a benefit to the promisee's health, but [it] is also a legal detriment and sufficient consideration to support a contract." Davies v. Martel Laboratory Services, Inc., 189 Ill.App.3d 694, 545 N.E.2d 475 (1989). You might think about why it is that consideration tests continue to be phrased in technical formulas (e.g., "real value in the eye of the law") which reveal little about the classes of transactions that are enforceable. Consider also whether it is appropriate to think of consideration, at least in one aspect, as little more than a formality which must be complied with as a condition of enforcing a promise in court. For example, if Aunt Mary's promise of $500 is enforceable even though the nephew would have agreed to attend her funeral without any pay at all, it seems not easy to say that the doctrine of consideration is a "substantive" rather than formal requirement of general contract law.

As you work through this chapter it may be useful to keep in mind the great variety of human activities that can be brought within the tests of consideration, tests which, as the pliability of the term "detriment" indicates, make possible the enforcement of a great many promises. Is every promise complying with the test deserving of enforcement? Look again at the court's analysis in Whitten v. Greeley–Shaw. Is there something in the case the court is not talking about?

Marmer v. Kaufman

Massachusetts Superior Court, 2009.
2009 WL 2002945, affirmed, 922 N.E.2d 862.

FEELEY, ASSOCIATE JUSTICE. . . . From approximately 1976 to 2000, Paul [Marmer] worked as a pharmacist at a family owned retail pharmacy. The pharmacy's stock was owned equally by Paul and his father Henry Marmer ("Henry"). As Henry aged, and the pharmacy became more reliant on technology, Paul assumed more responsibilities in operating the pharmacy. In recognition of Paul's additional responsibilities and duties in operating the pharmacy, Henry provided Paul certificates of deposit ("certificates") issued by a local bank. The certificates were issued in the name of Henry, as trustee for Paul. Upon the maturity of each certificate, rather than cashing out the certificate, the certificate automatically renewed.

In December 2002, Henry executed a Durable Power of Attorney in favor of June, his daughter and Paul's sister. Henry also provided June with the proceeds of numerous bank accounts and other assets in an attempt to become eligible for Medicaid assistance. Sometime after December 2002, June, acting under the durable power of attorney provided her by Henry, cashed in the certificates that had been issued for Paul's benefit. After learning of June's actions, Paul sued her in the Essex Probate and Family Court seeking to recover the amounts due him under the certificates. Paul's claim was dismissed, and the court's decision was affirmed by the Appeals Court.

On November 11, 2006, June died. June was survived by her three children, Richard, David, and April (collectively, the "children"). As a result of June's death, the family—the children and Paul—attempted to reconcile past family differences. This reconciliation included trying to deal with June's cashing of the certificates, as well as her actions to reduce Henry's wealth by placing his assets in her name in an attempt to make him Medicaid eligible for nursing home services. Richard, as the administrator of June's estate, repeatedly spoke with Paul regarding June's estate. At one point, Richard acknowledged that June may have improperly taken Paul's certificates, as well as other property that would have passed to Paul upon Henry's death, and even stated "we (the children) want to give you back what she (June) took from you (Paul)."

Shortly after June's death (November 2006) and until approximately August 2007, the children and Paul discussed entering into an agreement regarding the distribution of June's assets to settle their disputes. A proposed agreement which was never signed included terms requiring Richard, as the administrator of June's estate, to: (1) pay Paul $136,000 (plus what appears to be accrued interest) as reimbursement for the certificates; (2) give Paul one-half of June's assets; and (3) pay for Henry's nursing home care until Henry qualified for Medicaid. No agreement was ever signed reflecting the above mentioned terms, or any other terms. In his deposition testimony, Paul stated that he was not required to do anything in exchange for being repaid the amount owed on the certificates. Paul also stated that he owed neither Richard nor anyone else any obligation in return for one-half of June's assets. On November 9, 2007, Paul filed the present action seeking to enforce the oral agreements he claims he entered into with Richard. . . .

Richard seeks summary judgment arguing that even if his oral statements to Paul about making up for June's conduct—by repaying the $136,000 from the certificates and allowing Paul to receive one-half of June's assets—formed a contract, the contract is unenforceable and is invalid as it was not supported by consideration. Paul contends that the contract was supported by consideration, in the form of family unity and/or the substantial estate tax savings enjoyed by June's estate as a result of the agreement.

Even assuming Richard felt that Paul was entitled to the monetary value of the certificates' and half of June's assets because June wrongfully converted Paul's certificates and Henry's assets, that feeling, in and of itself, is not sufficient to establish contractual consideration. Additionally, any thawing of the family relations that Richard and the children hoped would result from the agreement constitutes neither a legal detriment to Paul, nor a legal benefit to Richard. Therefore, Paul's argument that improved family unity was sufficient to establish consideration in return for the value of the certificates and one-half of June's assets must fail. Essentially, Richard's statements are gratuitous promises that cannot be enforced for want of consideration.

Paul's argument that the substantial Massachusetts estate tax savings June's estate would enjoy constitutes consideration, and therefore makes the contract enforceable, is not persuasive. Richard's reason for his promises to Paul was simply to repay Paul what June had taken from him, it was not to improve the tax position of June's estate. The possible reduction in the estate's tax liabilities, if such was the case, was merely a side benefit that would attach to June's estate if money was given to Paul. Any tax benefit experienced by June's estate was not sought by Richard as his reason for entering into the agreement; Richard's desire for entering into the agreement was based on his desire to make amends for June's actions. Richard did not seek the tax benefit in exchange for his promise to Paul, and therefore any tax benefit experienced by June's estate does not constitute consideration.

Morever, any benefit to June's estate in the form of tax savings, was not a benefit conferred on Richard by Paul. Clearly, Paul did not give Richard any possible estate tax benefit in exchange for Richard's promise to pay him money from June's estate. The same argument made by Paul herein, could have been made in the *DeLeo* case, where the promissor would have earned a tax deduction if his oral promise to contribute money to the congregation had been complied with. The Supreme Judicial Court in *DeLeo* found the gratuitous promise to donate money unenforceable for lack of consideration, despite an obvious tax benefit to the promissor derived from donating money to a religious organization. Here, any gratuitous promise to give money to Paul, despite any possible estate tax benefit, similarly fails for lack of consideration.

Since Richard received no benefit (and certainly none from Paul) in exchange for his promise to reimburse Paul $136,000 for the certificates and give Paul one-half of June's assets, and because Paul suffered no legal detriment in exchange for Richard's promises, any oral promises by Richard are unenforceable for lack of consideration. . . .

RESTATEMENT OF CONTRACTS, SECOND

Section 71. Requirement of Exchange; Types of Exchange

(1) To constitute consideration, a performance or a return promise must be bargained for.

(2) A performance or return promise is bargained for if it is sought by the promisor in exchange for his promise and is given by the promisee in exchange for that promise.

(3) The performance may consist of

(a) an act other than a promise, or

(b) a forbearance, or

(c) the creation, modification, or destruction of a legal relation.

(4) The performance or return promise may be given to the promisor or to some other person. It may be given by the promisee or by some other person.

Section 81. Consideration as Motive or Inducing Cause

(1) The fact that what is bargained for does not of itself induce the making of a promise does not prevent it from being consideration for the promise.

(2) The fact that a promise does not of itself induce a performance or return promise does not prevent the performance or return promise from being consideration for the promise.

[Rest.2d § 81 is intended to make explicit a limitation on § 71's "bargained for" test of consideration. A comment to § 81 observes that a promisor—even the typical commercial bargainer—may have more than one motive in negotiating an exchange, adding: "Unless both parties know that the purported consideration is mere pretense, it is immaterial that the promisor's desire for the consideration is incidental to other objectives and even that the other party knows this to be the case."]

Fischer v. Union Trust Co.

Supreme Court of Michigan, 1904.
138 Mich. 612, 101 N.W. 852.

Bertha Fischer presented a claim against the estate of William Fischer, Sr., deceased, for damages for an alleged breach of a covenant in a deed. The claim was allowed by the commissioners, and the Union Trust Co., administrator, appealed to the circuit court. There was judgment for claimant on a verdict directed by the court, and defendant brings error. Reversed.

On December 21, 1895, William Fischer, Sr., conveyed by warranty deed certain property in the city of Detroit to the claimant, Bertha Fischer, his daughter, who had been incompetent for a number of years, and so remains, and is at present at the retreat for the insane at Dearborn. The deed was a warranty deed, in the usual form, with a covenant against all incumbrances, excepting two mortgages, which the grantor "agrees to pay when the same become due." The land described in the deed comprised the homestead where the father and daughter lived, and the adjoining lot, with the house thereon. Mr. Fischer, after signing and acknowledging it, handed it to claimant, saying, "Here is a deed of the Jefferson and Larned street property." He said it was a "nice Christmas present." She took it and read it. One of her brothers gave her a dollar, which she gave to her father, who took it. She then handed the deed to her brother Alexander, and asked him to take care of it. He put it in his safe, and did not record it until June 30, 1902, about a year after the grantor's death, and 6½ years after its date. The reason given by the son for not recording is that there were unpaid taxes, in consequence of which, under the statute, it could not be recorded.

After the delivery of the deed, both grantor and grantee continued to live together on part of the property so conveyed. Mr. Fischer continued until his death to manage and control it, and to receive the rents therefrom, just as he had done before the giving of the deed. During that time he took care of his daughter the same as before. At the time of the execution of the deed, the grantor was considered by his sons to be worth about $50,000. He had no debts except the two mortgages, one of $3,000 and the other of $5,000. If he was then worth that amount, the larger part of it was in some way disposed of in his lifetime. The $3,000 mortgage was foreclosed for nonpayment, and satisfied out of part of the property conveyed. The claim at bar is based upon this appropriation of her property to pay the mortgage.

GRANT, J. The facts and circumstances of the delivery of the deed are not in dispute. Counsel differ only in the conclusion to be drawn from them. We think that the conceded facts show a delivery. After the deed was signed and acknowledged, the grantor made manual delivery of it to the grantee. She took it and handed it to her brother, evidently to be kept by him for her. The grantor reserved no control over it, and retained no right to withdraw or cancel it. He never attempted to. Under those circumstances the delivery was complete.

The meritorious question in the case is: Was the claimant in position to enforce the executory contract in the deed against her father while living, and to enforce it against his estate now that he is dead, or to recover damages at law for nonperformance? To say that the one dollar was the real, or such valuable consideration as would of itself sustain a deed of land worth several thousand dollars, is not in accord with reason or common sense. The passing of the dollar by the brother to his sister, and by her to her father, was treated rather as a joke than as any actual consideration. The real and only consideration for the deed and the agreement, therein contained, to pay the mortgages, was the grantor's love and affection for his unfortunate daughter, and his parental desire to provide for her support after he was dead. The consideration was meritorious, but is not sufficient to compel the performance of a purely executory contract. The deed was a gift, and the gift was consummated by its execution and delivery. The title to the land, subject to the mortgages, passed as against all except the grantor's creditors. The gift was expressly made subject to the mortgages, and coupled with it was a promise to pay them. This promise has no additional force because it is contained in the deed. It has no other or greater force than would a promise by him to pay mortgages upon her own land, or to pay her $8,000 in money, or his promise to her evidenced by a promissory note for a like amount, and given for the same purpose and the same consideration. . . .

If Mr. Fischer had voluntarily paid the mortgages, he would then simply have carried out his nonenforceable contract and have completed his gift, as, perhaps, he then intended to do. For some reason, perhaps a good one, he chose not to pay them. A void promise is no more effective than no promise, and the void promise in the deed had no more effect than if it had been omitted therefrom. If it is void for one purpose, it is void for all, and cannot be made available, either directly or indirectly. Only performance of the promise can be of any avail to the claimant.

A gift of personalty can be consummated only by an unconditional delivery of the thing. A gift of realty can be consummated only by the execution and delivery of a deed. If either is incumbered, the donor gives only what he had to give. He cannot give the interest of a third party in the property. However clear may be the intention of the donor to pay the incumbrances and thus give the entire property, he can accomplish this only by actually paying them. Neither his promise without a valuable consideration, nor his intention as evidenced by such promise, is of any avail to the donee. . . .

Judgment is reversed, and new trial ordered.

COMMENT: "NOMINAL" AND "MERITORIOUS" CONSIDERATION

The one dollar handed from brother to Bertha to father is a recurring episode in the case law. It raises the problem of "nominal" consideration, a problem which for a long time was associated with a famous statement in English legal history—"when a thing is to be done by the plaintiff, be it never so small, this is a sufficient consideration to ground an action," Sturlyn v. Albany, 1 Cro.Eliz. 67, 78 Eng.Rep. 327 (1587). Talk of nominal consideration led naturally to a somewhat more general idea, the "peppercorn theory of consideration."

An illustration attached to Restatement, Second § 79 reads as follows: "In consideration of one cent received, A promises to pay $600 in three yearly installments of $200 each. The one cent is merely nominal, and is not consideration for A's promise." This illustration is intended to make the point that a "nominal" consideration, in the situation described, does not satisfy conventional tests. Why not?

Consider Schnell v. Nell, 17 Ind. 29 (1861), which provided the inspiration for the Restatement's illustration. In an elaborate document replete with "whereas" clauses (and signed, under "seal," by all parties), Zacharias Schnell promised to pay three persons $200 each in three annual installments. These three persons had been given legacies of $200 each by the will of Zacharias' deceased wife, Theresa, but her will was ineffective because all of the property she owned was held jointly with her husband and passed to him at her death. These facts were recited in the document, and the promise of Zacharias was

[handwritten margin notes: made promise in exchange for 1 cent. / void upon its face, nominal consideration / parties weren't really making a bargain / clearly disproportional]

stated to be given "in consideration of all this, and the love and respect he bears to his wife." The document also acknowledged that Zacharias had received one cent from the promisees, who, it was recited, had agreed to pay that sum "in consideration of" Zacharias' promise. In an action by the promisees to collect the money promised, Zacharias was held to have a complete defense. Though the Indiana court was clear that inadequacy of consideration ordinarily will not vitiate a contract, this was not true where the exchange is of unequal sums of money (things of "fixed," not "indeterminate," value). Moreover, a promise to pay $600 for one cent "is an unconscionable contract, void, at first blush, upon its face, if it be regarded as an earnest one." This is so because "the one cent is, plainly, in this case, merely nominal, and intended to be so." Nor would Zacharias' belief that he must carry out his wife's intentions—a "moral consideration" at best—support a promise; similarly, his wife's services in the past, and the love he bore her, were but "past considerations," insufficient to make him liable on a promise.

To be sure, at the time Zacharias Schnell signed the impressive document he had no doubt employed a lawyer to create, he was a person bent on giving a binding promise. He had gone to some considerable trouble in arranging his formal commitment. The court's words—"merely nominal, and intended to be so"—go far to explain his inability to accomplish what he most certainly had intended to accomplish.

We will see more of nominal consideration. It would be a mistake to conclude either that the problem has disappeared or that the law no longer makes provision for an effective nominal consideration. For the time being, however, you should ask whether courts are distinguishing between actual bargains, regardless of whether they seem lopsided, and interactions that merely mimic the form of a bargain.

Justice Grant's reference to "meritorious consideration" in Fischer v. Union Trust Co. refers to a doctrine that emerged in the courts of equity. As to promises without consideration, equity courts have often expressed their adherence to common law requirements by repeating the familiar slogan that "equity will not aid a volunteer," meaning by "volunteer" a promisee in a simple promise of gift. There were, however, exceptions to the refusal of relief to the volunteer. A court of equity may be induced to act if a donor has attempted to carry out the gift but the actions taken are in some way incomplete or defective, and the donor has died in ignorance of this. An example would be a gift of land executed by the delivery of a deed which describes the subject of the gift incorrectly, perhaps by including too little land or by describing the wrong tract. The donor, if still living, normally could secure judicial reformation of the incorrect deed; often, the mistake could be corrected merely by the donor's making of a new deed. Where the donee is a near relative, "a natural object of bounty," and there are no competing claims of greater moral force, the intended donee will usually be allowed reformation—despite the status of a "volunteer." The consideration is deemed "meritorious." A critical fact in these cases is that the donor has died believing the transfer to be fully effective. If the donor were still alive, and resisting correction of a defective or incomplete document of gift, it is extremely unlikely that a reformation action by the donee would succeed.

Sharon v. Sharon

68 Cal. 29, 8 P. 614 (1885)

The plaintiff brought an action to enforce the defendant's written promise reading as follows: "Palace Hotel, San Francisco, Nov. 7, 1880. I hereby agree to pay Miss S. A. Hill two hundred and fifty dollars for each and every month of the year A.D. 1883. Wm. Sharon." Defendant's answer admitted the execution and delivery of the document and his non-payment of three of the monthly installments and alleged "that to induce plaintiff to desist from making unwelcome visits and annoying and disturbing him in his rooms, and on the consideration that she would cease to disturb and annoy him, or make any demands upon him" he executed the document in question. Defendant's answer contained also the statement that defendant "denies that there was ever any consideration for the note" sued on. *Held*, in this condition of the pleadings, judgment must be ordered for plaintiff for the un-paid installments.

Military College Co. v. Brooks

107 N.J.L. 28, 147 A. 488 (1929)

A military school brought an action on a $927 promissory note executed by defendant to cover his son's tuition and equipment for the year 1926–1927. Defendant claimed that his son was wrongfully dismissed in the middle of the first semester, and that he gave his note to cover the year's tuition and equipment because "at the time I had financial difficulties and [the note was given] rather than have a lawsuit which I thought would greatly injure my credit." In holding that the trial court was correct in ordering summary judgment for plaintiff on the note, the Supreme Court said: "Defendant does not seem to deny that the contract was for the full school year. If his son was rightfully dismissed, it is at least arguable that the full year's fee would be nevertheless payable. Defendant claimed the dismissal was wrongful, and plaintiff that it was rightful; and this raised a legitimate dispute of fact and perhaps of law also as to defendant's liability. In this situation defendant being so situated financially that a lawsuit, whatever its result, would in his judgment be disastrous to him, elected to buy his peace for the time being by giving the first note, which postponed any such suit until the maturity of that note, not to mention that by a renewal or renewals it was further postponed until February 18th, 1928, or nearly a year. This, under our decisions, was adequate consideration to support the note."

RESTATEMENT OF CONTRACTS, SECOND

Section 74. Settlement of Claims

(1) Forbearance to assert or the surrender of a claim or defense which proves to be invalid is not consideration unless

    (a) the claim or defense is in fact doubtful because of uncertainty as to the facts or the law, or

    (b) the forbearing or surrendering party believes that the claim or defense may be fairly determined to be valid.

(2) The execution of a written instrument surrendering a claim or defense by one who is under no duty to execute it is consideration if the execution of the written instrument is bargained for even though he is not asserting the claim or defense and believes that no valid claim or defense exists.

Illustrations:

1. A, a shipowner, has a legal duty to provide maintenance and care for B, a seaman. B honestly but unreasonably claims that adequate care is not available in a free public hospital and that he is entitled to treatment by a private physician. B's forbearance to press this claim is consideration for A's promise to be responsible for the consequences of any improper treatment in the public hospital.

2. A, knowing that he has no legal basis for complaint, frequently complains to B, his father, that B has made more gifts to B's other children than to A. B promises that if A will cease complaining, B will forgive a debt owed by A to B. A's forbearance to assert his claim of discrimination is not consideration for B's promise.

QUESTIONS

(1) The first Restatement of Contracts § 76(b) required "an honest and reasonable belief" in the "possible validity" of an invalid claim or defense in order for forbearance or surrender of the claim or defense to operate as consideration. Why do you suppose Restatement, Second § 74(1) drops that test and substitutes the different formulation?

(2) In a case adopting Restatement, Second § 74(1) as "the better reasoned approach," Dyer v. National By–Products, Inc., 380 N.W.2d 732 (Iowa 1986), the court assumed the invalidity of the forborne claim in issue and stated: "The requirement that the forbearing party assert the claim in good faith sufficiently protects the policy of the law that favors the settlement of controversies. . . . [However,] the issue of the validity of [the] claim should not be entirely overlooked. . . . [Such evidence] is relevant to show a lack of honest belief in the validity of the claim asserted or forborne." Did the Iowa court read § 74(1) correctly?

(3) Is there any reason why standard consideration doctrine (e.g., Duncan v. Black) should stand in the way of the result called for by § 74(2)? Incidentally, the essential idea of § 74(2) is not a recent innovation; it was embraced by a number of our courts in the nineteenth century, including the United States Supreme Court, in Sykes v. Chadwick, 85 U.S. (18 Wall.) 141 (1873).

SECTION 3. PROMISES GROUNDED IN THE PAST

INTRODUCTORY COMMENT

The history of English law reveals two early groupings of cases in which a transaction was linked to a later, enforceable promise. One is indeed familiar at this point—the development whereby the action of assumpsit, through the offshoot writ of indebitatus assumpsit, was made available as a general alternative to the action of debt. See Chapter 1, pp. 111–116. Here, expansion of assumpsit was accomplished by giving effect to the new promise of a debtor to pay a debt earlier incurred, the later promise being enforceable solely because of the support extended by the old debt. After Slade's Case in 1602, which eliminated the necessity of proving the subsequent promise, the significance of the past transaction was diminished by the procedural ease with which a creditor could use assumpsit on a simple contract claim. Nevertheless, despite the lessened importance of the pleading fiction, the proposition that a precedent debt is "consideration" (that is to say, a reason for enforcement) for a subsequent promise to pay the debt was carried forward in Anglo–American law. Corbin is clear about the situation today: "A past debt, still existing and enforceable, is a sufficient basis for the enforcement of a new promise by the debtor to pay it. This is true, whether the past debt is contractual or quasi-contractual in character." 1A A. Corbin, Contracts § 211.

A second line of cases associated with the notion of an operative "past" consideration is traceable to assumpsit actions in the early seventeenth century. Even with the expansion of assumpsit accomplished by Slade's Case, that action was still grounded on an express promise—the promise giving rise to the antecedent debt. Until the period 1610–1620, there was great reluctance to "imply" promises from conduct, as we so readily do today, or from requests that did not include express promises of payment. It was then recognized that if services were performed at the recipient's request, but without express promise of payment, the past act rendered at request was sufficient reason to enforce a later promise of payment. E.g., Lampleigh v. Brathwaite, 80 Eng.Rep. 255, Hob. 105 (K.B.1616). Under this analysis, of course, the previous request and the subsequent promise may well assume the form of a single transaction; hence many of these problems eventually came to be handled by the theory of implied contract. Still, here was another situation in which promises could be enforced because of acts done in the past.

Another episode from history, dating from the late 1770s, should be mentioned. Lord Mansfield, a high Tory in politics, was in legal matters a notable reformer. You will learn later of his contributions to Commercial Law, particularly the assimilation of the "custom of merchants" into the common law. As to the doctrine of consideration, among Mansfield's efforts to dismantle the conventional requirement (one was an attempt to reduce it to a mere requirement of evidence) was a series of decisions identifying consideration with "moral obligation" or duty resting on "conscience." (A brief sketch of the story can be found in T. Plucknett, A Concise History of the Common Law 653–656 (5th ed. 1956).) Even though Mansfield's doctrines equating consideration with moral obligation were repudiated in England in the mid 1800s, the notions of "moral duty" and "conscientious obligation" continued to circulate in American decisions.

In fact, "moral obligation" is commonly invoked to explain three special situations in Anglo–American law: the promise to pay an obligation on which the statutory period of limitations has run; the bankrupt debtor's promise to pay a discharged debt; and the promise to pay a contract obligation incurred while a minor. Mills v. Wyman introduces these standard "exceptions" to the bargain test of consideration.

Mills v. Wyman

Supreme Judicial Court of Massachusetts, 1825.
20 Mass. (3 Pick.) 207.

. . . [A]ssumpsit brought to recover a compensation for the board, nursing, etc. of Levi Wyman, son of the defendant, from the 5th to the 20th of February, 1821. The plaintiff then lived at Hartford, in Connecticut; the defendant at Shrewsbury, in this state. Levi Wyman, at the time when the services were rendered, was about 25 years of age, and had long ceased to be a member of his father's family. He was on his return from a voyage at sea, and being suddenly taken sick at Hartford, and being poor and in distress, was relieved by the plaintiff in the manner and to the extent above stated. On the 24th of February, after all the expenses had been incurred, the defendant wrote a letter to the plaintiff, promising to pay him such expenses. There was no consideration for this promise, except what grew out of the relation which subsisted between Levi Wyman and the defendant, and Howe, J., before whom the case was tried [in] Common Pleas, thinking this not sufficient to support the action, directed a nonsuit. To this direction the plaintiff filed exceptions.

PARKER, C.J. General rules of law established for the protection and security of honest and fair-minded men, who may inconsiderately make promises without any equivalent, will sometimes screen men of a different character from engagements which they are bound *in foro conscientiae* to perform. This is a defect inherent in all human systems of legislation. The rule that a mere verbal promise, without any consideration, cannot be enforced by action, is universal in its application, and cannot be departed from to suit particular cases in which a refusal to perform such a promise may be disgraceful.

The promise declared on in this case appears to have been made without any legal consideration. The kindness and services towards the sick son of the defendant were not bestowed at his request. The son was in no respect under the care of the defendant. He was twenty-five years old, and had long left his father's family. On his return from a foreign country, he fell sick among strangers, and the plaintiff acted the part of the good Samaritan, giving him shelter and comfort until he died. The defendant, his father, on being informed of this event, influenced by a transient feeling of gratitude, promised in writing to pay the plaintiff for the expenses he had incurred. But he has determined to break this promise, and is willing to have his case appear on record as a strong example of particular injustice sometimes necessarily resulting from the operation of general rules.

It is said a moral obligation is a sufficient consideration to support an express promise; and some authorities lay down the rule thus broadly; but upon examination of the cases we are satisfied that the universality of the rule cannot be supported, and that there must have been some pre-existing obligation, which has become inoperative by positive law, to form a basis for an effective promise. The cases of debts barred by the Statute of Limitations, of debts incurred by infants, of debts of bankrupts, are generally put for illustration of the rule. Express promises founded on such pre-existing equitable obligations may be enforced; there is a good consideration for them; they merely remove an impediment created by law to the recovery of debts honestly due, but which public policy protects the debtors from being compelled to pay. In all these cases there was originally a *quid pro quo*, and according to the principles of natural justice the party receiving ought to pay; but the legislature has said he shall not be coerced; then comes the promise to pay the debt that is barred, the promise of the man to pay the debt of the infant, of the discharged bankrupt to restore to his creditor what by the law he had lost. In all these cases there is a moral obligation founded upon an antecedent valuable consideration. These promises, therefore, have a sound legal basis. They are not promises to pay something for nothing; not naked pacts, but the voluntary revival or creation of obligations which before existed in natural law, but which had been dispensed with, not for the benefit of the party obliged solely, but principally for the public convenience. If moral obligation, in its fullest sense, is a good substratum for an express promise, it is not easy to perceive why it is not equally good to support an implied promise. What a man ought to do, generally he ought to be made to do whether he promise or refuse. But the law of society has left most of such obligations to the interior forum, as the tribunal of conscience has been aptly called. Is there not a moral obligation upon every son who has become affluent by means of the education and advantages bestowed upon him by his father, to relieve that father from pecuniary embarrassment, to promote his comfort and happiness, and even to share with him his riches, if thereby he will be made happy? And yet such a son may, with impunity, leave such a father in any degree of penury above that which will expose the community in which he dwells, to the danger of being obliged to preserve him from absolute want. Is not a wealthy father under strong moral obligation to advance the interest of an obedient, well disposed son, to furnish him with the means of acquiring and maintaining a becoming rank in life, to rescue him from the horrors of debt incurred by misfortune? Yet the law will uphold him in any degree of parsimony, short of that which would reduce his son to the necessity of seeking public charity.

Without doubt there are great interests of society which justify withholding the coercive arm of the law from these duties of imperfect obligation, as they are called; imperfect, not because they are less binding upon the conscience than those which are called perfect, but because the wisdom of the social law does not impose sanctions upon them.

A deliberate promise in writing, made freely and without any mistake, one which may lead the party to whom it is made into contracts and expenses, cannot be broken without a violation of moral duty. But if there was nothing paid or promised for it, the law, perhaps wisely, leaves the execution of it to the conscience of him who makes it. It is only when the party making the promise gains something, or he to whom it is made loses something, that the law gives the promise validity. And in the case of the promise of the adult to pay the debt of the infant, of the debtor discharged by the statute of limitations or bankruptcy, the principle is preserved by looking back to the origin of that transaction, where an equivalent is to be found. . . .

For the foregoing reasons we are all of opinion that the nonsuit directed by the Court of Common Pleas was right, and that judgment be entered thereon for costs for the defendant.

QUESTION

Could Mills, showing that his services were reasonably worth $50, recover that sum from Levi Wyman's estate? The trial record tells us that Mills was an innkeeper. Watson, In the Tribunal of Conscience: *Mills v. Wyman* Reconsidered, 71 Tulane L. Rev. 1749, 1759 (1997). Does this change your view of the case?

COMMENT: PROMISES TO PAY BARRED OBLIGATIONS

New promises to perform obligations barred by the statute of limitations have long been subjected to special treatment. This was due in part to some accidents of history. A comprehensive statute of limitations was not adopted in England until 1623, when theories as to the grounds for, and limits on, contract liability were still relatively undeveloped. For more than one hundred years thereafter, the notion still circulated freely that "moral obligation" could suffice as a reason for enforcing promises (as we have said, that view lasted in England until the middle of the nineteenth century). Furthermore, it was not at all unnatural that the courts should minimize the effect of a not very ancient statute and regard it as precluding affirmative enforcement, but to not cut off the "honest debt" that survived. It followed that the protection given the obligor by the statute could be "waived" through a new promise, if the obligor chose.

When bankruptcy proceedings were more fully developed, so that they went beyond the liquidation of the bankrupt's assets to grant a discharge of existing obligations, the analogy was close enough to warrant transferring the same modes of thought to a new promise made after bankruptcy discharge. Indeed, it may have been still easier to think that an "honest debt" survived where the legal immunity was due merely to the fact that the debtor had become over-extended, was unable to perform, and needed a fresh start.

It also became well established that new promises can lift the protections from contract obligations that are accorded to minors. Until the twenty-first birthday arrives (or, pursuant to modern legislation in many states, the eighteenth), the young person is legally an "infant." All transfers or promises made during infancy can be disaffirmed (i.e., liability defeated), unless the securing of "necessaries" was involved. However, when the minor reaches the age of majority these "voidable" promises can be affirmed, in which event the promise acquires full legal effect. Making a new promise is one way to affirm. There is no particular harm in lumping minors' promises with obligations made unenforceable by a limitation statute or by bankruptcy discharge. But it is worth noting that infancy is only one of numerous grounds for making transactions voidable—fraud, duress, mental incompetency, even basic mistake can produce the same result. The explanation usually given in such cases is not that affirmance constitutes a "new promise." Rather, it is said that the disadvantaged party has exercised a choice to affirm rather than to rescind a voidable transaction, and this seems more descriptive of minors' promises also.

As to the prototype—the obligation barred by the statute of limitations—it should be stressed that our courts have not been as free in their treatment of statutes of limitation as they have been with statutes of frauds. Courts often assert that time limits on the bringing of actions serve desirable purposes, such as achieving finality for transactions long treated as closed and eliminating "stale" claims after evidence has been lost and memories have faded. Thus, a clause inserted at the inception of a contract, by which a party agreed not to plead the statute of limitations in the event of breach, would probably be held void everywhere. On the other hand, after default has occurred or is in prospect, a promise by the particular obligor not to plead the statute would quite surely be enforceable if there was bargain consideration meeting the usual tests. A firm assurance of this kind, even without a "bargain," would often justify a creditor in delaying suit and preclude a plea of the statute by the one who gave the assurance.

The vigilance of creditors may be relaxed as a result of conduct falling short of an express promise of the kind just described. Suppose a debt is in default on which the debtor, without comment, makes a part payment—e.g., by mailing a check. Suppose also that the applicable statute of limitations sets a time limit of six years for the start of suit. Should the six years be counted from the original date when the default occurred or from the date of the last payment? A literal reading might point to the date of default, for this is when a "cause of action" accrued. But this would mean that the creditor would be compelled to sue within the six-year limit even though the debtor had continued to make delayed payments, strung out perhaps over several years. This would be hard on the "honest" though delinquent debtor, but it would be even harder on the lenient creditor who may have been led to believe that the debt would be paid without the trouble of a lawsuit. Certainly the creditor should not be penalized for practicing leniency. Accordingly, it has long been agreed that not only delayed part payment of a contract debt but, in any kind of contract obligation, a new promise to perform (or an acknowledgment of liability) made after default and before the statutory period has expired will start the statute running all over again. (All of this can be found in Restatement, Second § 82.) A doctrine framed in these broad terms must be explained, at least in part, by the effect of part performance or a new promise in inducing creditors not to act and to trust that their indulgence would not leave them worse off. An unusually candid statement of this rationale appears in Graves v. Sawyer, 588 S.W.2d 542 (Tenn.1979).

It seems worth repeating that extension of periods of limitations in the circumstances just discussed—part payment, acknowledgment, or new promise before the statutory period has expired—need not take the form of a new agreement. Unilateral action by the debtor is enough. Nor is it necessary to demonstrate the requirements for some version of estoppel.

restarting SoL

The court in Mills v. Wyman had in mind a situation that was quite different, one in which the statutory bar had already fallen. Assume that a new promise was then made by the obligor to perform some or all of the barred obligation, though nothing new was received by the obligor in exchange for the promise. It has long been true that such promises are fully valid and take on what might be called a life of their own. Any conditions or limitations that they express ("I'll pay the whole debt when I sell my barn"; "I owed you $750 but I'll only pay $500") will be given full effect. E.g., Mun Seek Pai v. First Hawaiian Bank, 57 Haw. 429, 558 P.2d 479 (1977) (new promise to pay when "more or less financially able to" enforced upon finding condition of ability fulfilled). And the statutory period of limitation will start running on the new promise from the date it was made. This can hardly be explained as "waiver" of a waivable defense. As an explanation, waiver becomes still less convincing where the obligor makes no new promise at all but merely "acknowledges" the obligation or makes a part payment on the barred debt without saying or writing a word. If the statute of limitations created the bar, either acknowledgment or part payment will revive the debt. But with debts barred by discharge in bankruptcy, the courts were more demanding and only a new *express* promise would suffice;

a promise implied from part payment or acknowledgment would not do. This insistence on the formality of an express promise is usually attributed to a belief that today the statutory discharge in bankruptcy reflects a more compelling public policy than is the case with a statute of limitations. See Restatement, Second § 83, comment a.

As one would expect, there has been much litigation over the sufficiency of acknowledgments, especially as concerns limitation periods or bars. Snyder v. Baltimore Trust Co., 532 A.2d 624 (Del.Super.Ct.1986), is representative of the approach commonly taken. There must be a "clear, distinct and unequivocal" acknowledgment of the debt; a "vague or loose" admission will not do (e.g., "I'm going to look out for you"; "[t]he farm is big enough to pay you").

In explaining the revival of obligations rendered unenforceable by law, some courts speak of "past consideration." Of course, such phrasing hardly disguises the absence of present exchange which modern theories have made a crucial element in tests of consideration. More often courts invoke "moral obligation," as in Jones v. Jones, 242 F.Supp. 979, 982 (S.D.N.Y.1965) ("there must be a new contract, consideration for which is the moral obligation to pay the original debt"). Corbin, too, spoke of the "moral obligation" to pay the barred debt—something wholly unaffected by the law's bar of limitations—as amounting to an operative past consideration for any new promise. 1A A. Corbin, Contracts § 214. Other explanations typically given are that the statute of limitations merely raises a rebuttable presumption of payment, that it only bars the remedy and does not destroy the right, or, as already noted, that the new promise or acknowledgment creates no new legal duty but merely "waives" a defense. Whatever its choice of language, a court usually will take care to make clear that it is invoking a very special kind of moral duty, a ghostly survival from the parties' past relations, and that these past relations continue to set limits on the obligor's power to make a binding promise.

Suppose, for example, a money debt of $1,000 that had been barred by time-limitation. The sheltered debtor, perhaps filled with remorse, then makes a new promise to pay $1,500. The legal effect is clear: the promise would be valid up to the amount of the barred debt; as to the $500 excess it would be void, for lack of consideration. But no, we must quickly take some of that statement back—some of the $500 might be viewed as payment of accrued interest. It may seem somewhat incongruous to think of interest running on an uncollectible debt, but with practice one can become accustomed even to this. Or suppose that the creditor, after the bar had fallen, assigned the original claim to a third party and the debtor then made a new promise. To whom is the money due? The answer is, to the assignee, for "something of the original vitality of the debt continues to exist" and the claim, though all remedies to enforce it were barred at the time, was assignable. Stanek v. White, 172 Minn. 390, 215 N.W. 784 (1927). A good discussion of the various legal effects of unenforceable debts (plus a collection of the cases) can be found in Webster v. Kowal, 394 Mass. 443, 476 N.E.2d 205 (1985).

The effect of new promise, acknowledgment, or part payment on obligations barred by the statute of limitations is so well known and widely accepted that statutes in all but a half-dozen or so of our states regulate such conduct by requiring a writing signed by the debtor for the promise or acknowledgment (but not the part payment) to have any legal effect. Modern federal bankruptcy law sharply limits the enforceability of a bankrupt's promises to repay discharged debts. This extensive body of regulation, which includes requirements for bankruptcy-court approval of reaffirmation agreements and a grant of power to the debtor to rescind such agreements in specific circumstances, appears in 11 U.S.C. § 524(c), (d). See, e.g., Lumby v. Lumby, 116 Wis.2d 347, 341 N.W.2d 725 (App.1983) (letter reaffirming discharged debt invalid since not in compliance with § 524's specified standards).

Webb v. McGowin

Court of Appeals of Alabama, 1935.
27 Ala.App. 82, 168 So. 196.

Action by Joe Webb against N. Floyd McGowin and Joseph F. McGowin, as executors of the estate of J. Greeley McGowin, deceased. From a judgment of nonsuit, plaintiff appeals.

BRICKEN, P.J. . . . The complaint [in assumpsit] as originally filed was amended. The demurrers to the complaint as amended were sustained, and because of this adverse ruling by the court the plaintiff took a nonsuit, and the assignment of errors on this appeal are predicated upon said action or ruling of the court.

A fair statement of the case presenting the questions for decision is set out in appellant's brief, which we adopt.

"On the 3d day of August, 1925, appellant while in the employ of the W.T. Smith Lumber Co., a corporation, and acting within the scope of his employment, was engaged in clearing the upper floor of Mill No. 2 of the company. While so engaged he was in the act of dropping a [75–pound] pine block from the upper floor of the mill to the ground below; this being the usual and ordinary way of clearing the floor, and it being the duty of the plaintiff in the course of his employment to so drop it. . . .

"As appellant was in the act of dropping the block to the ground below, he was on the edge of the upper floor of the mill. As he started to turn the block loose so that it would drop to the ground, he saw J. Greeley McGowin, testator of the defendants, on the ground below and directly under where the block would have fallen. . . . Had he turned it loose it would have struck McGowin with such force as to have caused him serious bodily harm or death. . . . The only safe and reasonable way to prevent this was for appellant to hold to the block and divert its direction [by] falling with it to the ground below. Appellant did this, and by holding to the block and falling with it[,] he diverted the course of its fall in such way that McGowin was not injured. In thus preventing the injuries to McGowin, appellant himself received serious bodily injuries, resulting in his right leg being broken, the heel of his right foot torn off and his right arm broken. He was badly crippled for life and rendered unable to do physical or mental labor.

"On September 1, 1925, in consideration of appellant having prevented him from sustaining death or serious bodily harm and in consideration of the injuries appellant had received, McGowin agreed with him to care for and maintain him for the remainder of appellant's life at the rate of $15 every two weeks from the time he sustained his injuries to and during the remainder of appellant's life; it being agreed that McGowin would pay this sum to appellant for his maintenance. Under the agreement McGowin paid or caused to be paid to appellant the sum so agreed on up until McGowin's

M death →

Paid until death + it continued

death on January 1, 1934. After his death the payments were continued to and including January 27, 1934, at which time they were discontinued. Thereupon plaintiff brought suit to recover the unpaid installments accruing [after January 27, 1934,] up to the time of the bringing of the suit.

"The material averments of the different counts of the original complaint and the amended complaint are predicated upon the foregoing statement of facts." . . .

1. The [complaint shows] that appellant saved McGowin from death or grievous bodily harm. This was a material benefit to him of infinitely more value than any financial aid he could have received. Receiving this benefit, McGowin became morally bound to compensate appellant for the services rendered. Recognizing his moral obligation, he expressly agreed to pay appellant as alleged in the complaint and complied with this agreement up to the time of his death; a period of more than 8 years.

Had McGowin been accidentally poisoned and a physician, without his knowledge or request, had administered an antidote, thus saving his life, a subsequent promise by McGowin to pay the physician would have been valid. Likewise, McGowin's agreement . . . to compensate appellant for saving him from death or grievous bodily injury is valid and enforceable.

agreement is valid

Where the promisee cares for, improves, and preserves the property of the promisor, though done without his request, it is sufficient consideration for the promisor's subsequent agreement to pay for the service, because of the material benefit received. . . .

In Boothe v. Fitzpatrick, 36 Vt. 681, the court held that a promise by defendant to pay for the past keeping of a bull which had escaped from defendant's premises and been cared for by plaintiff was valid, although there was no previous request, because the subsequent promise obviated that objection; it being equivalent to a previous request. On the same principle, had the promisee saved the promisor's life or his body from grievous harm, his subsequent promise to pay for the services rendered would have been valid. Such service would have been far more material than caring for his bull. Any holding that saving a man from death or grievous bodily harm is not a material benefit sufficient to uphold a subsequent promise to pay for the service, necessarily rests on the assumption that saving life and preservation of the body from harm have only a sentimental value. The converse of this is true. Life and preservation of the body have material, pecuniary values, measurable in dollars and cents. Because of this, physicians practice their profession charging for services rendered in saving life and curing the body of its ills, and surgeons perform operations. The same is true as to the law of negligence, authorizing the assessment of damages in personal injury cases based upon the extent of the injuries, earnings, and life expectancies of those injured.

Body has pecuniary values - measurable in dollars + cents (physicians)

In the business of life insurance, the value of a man's life is measured in dollars and cents according to his expectancy, the soundness of his body, and his ability to pay premiums. The same is true as to health and accident insurance.

It follows that if . . . appellant saved J. Greeley McGowin from death or grievous bodily harm, and McGowin subsequently agreed to pay him for the service rendered, it became a valid and enforceable contract.

2. It is well settled that a moral obligation is a sufficient consideration to support a subsequent promise to pay where the promisor has received a

material benefit, although there was no original duty or liability resting on the promisor. . . .

The case at bar is clearly distinguishable from [cases] where the consideration is a mere moral obligation or conscientious duty unconnected with receipt by [the] promisor of benefits of a material or pecuniary nature. . . . Here the promisor received a material benefit constituting a valid consideration for his promise.

3. Some authorities hold that, for a moral obligation to support a subsequent promise to pay, there must have existed a prior legal or equitable obligation, which for some reason had become unenforceable, but for which the promisor was still morally bound. This rule, however, is subject to qualification in those cases where the promisor having received a material benefit from the promisee, is morally bound to compensate him for the services rendered and in consideration of this obligation promises to pay. In such cases the subsequent promise to pay is an affirmance or ratification of the services rendered carrying with it the presumption that a previous request for the service was made. . . .

4. . . . [I]n in saving McGowin from death or grievous bodily harm, appellant was crippled for life. This was part of the consideration of the contract declared on. McGowin was benefited. Appellant was injured. Benefit to the promisor or injury to the promisee is a sufficient legal consideration for the promisor's agreement to pay. . . .

5. Under [the complaint] the services rendered by appellant were not gratuitous. The agreement of McGowin to pay and the acceptance of payment by appellant conclusively shows the contrary.

6. The contract declared on was not void under the statute of frauds (Code 1923, § 8034). The demurrer on that ground was not well taken. . . .

From what has been said . . . the court below erred [in] sustaining the demurrer, and for this error the case is reversed and remanded.

SAMFORD, J. (concurring). The questions involved in this case are not free from doubt, and perhaps the strict letter of the rule, as stated by judges, though not always in accord, would bar a recovery by plaintiff, but following the principle announced by Chief Justice Marshall in Hoffman v. Porter, 2 Brock. 156, 159, where he says, "I do not think that law ought to be separated from justice, where it is at most doubtful," I concur in the conclusions reached by the court.

[On petition to the Supreme Court of Alabama, certiorari was denied, Justice Foster writing for the Supreme Court. 232 Ala. 374, 168 So. 199 (1936).]

FOSTER, J. We do not in all cases in which we deny a petition for certiorari to the Court of Appeals approve the reasoning and principles declared in the opinion, even though no opinion is rendered by us. It does not always seem to be important that they be discussed, and we exercise a discretion in that respect. But when the opinion of the Court of Appeals asserts important principles or their application to new situations, and it may be uncertain whether this court agrees with it in all respects, we think it advisable to be specific in that respect when the certiorari is denied. We think such a situation here exists. . . .

The opinion of the Court of Appeals . . . recognizes and applies the distinction between a supposed moral obligation of the promisor, based upon some refined sense of ethical duty, without material benefit to him, and one in which such a benefit did in fact occur. We agree with that court that if the benefit be material and substantial, and was to the person of the promisor rather than to his estate, it is within the class of material benefits which he has the privilege of recognizing and compensating either by an executed payment or an executory promise to pay. . . . The reason is emphasized when the compensation is not only for the benefits which the promisor received, but also for the injuries either to the property or person of the promisee by reason of the service rendered.

Writ denied.

————

Harrington v. Taylor
225 N.C. 690, 36 S.E.2d 227 (1945)

Defendant had assaulted his wife, who took refuge in plaintiff's house. The next day defendant gained access to the house and resumed the attack; his wife grabbed an ax, knocked defendant down, and was about to split his head open when plaintiff intervened, catching on her hand the blow intended for defendant. Defendant's life was thereby saved, but plaintiff's hand was badly mutilated. Subsequently, defendant promised "to pay the plaintiff her damages." After paying only a small sum, defendant failed to pay anything more. *Held*, on demurrer, these facts fail to allege a cause of action. "[H]owever much the defendant should be impelled by common gratitude to alleviate the plaintiff's misfortune, a humanitarian act of this kind, voluntarily performed, is not such consideration as would entitle her to recover at law."

[handwritten margin notes: "was a gift"; "not consideration, humanitarian act, voluntarily performed"; "Distinguished from Webb — expected payment"]

Restatement of Restitution § 112, Illustrations 2, 3 (1937)

"2. In the belief that with some assistance A will become a valuable citizen, B makes a gift to A of $1000. Upon receiving the money, A immediately begins to squander it, destroying all of B's expectations. B is not entitled to restitution, even of the unspent portion. 3. During A's absence and in the belief that A will be willing to pay for the work, B improves A's land, which is worth and is offered for sale at $5000, to such an extent that upon A's return he sells the land for $8000. B is not entitled to restitution from A. . . .

Comment:

"b. *Exceptional Situations.* Under some conditions, it is desirable to encourage persons to interfere with the affairs of others. . . . [A] person or his belongings may be in such jeopardy that a stranger is privileged to intervene and to recover for his salvage services. . . . [These are] the types of situations in which the unasked-for conferring of benefit has been regarded as unofficious. Other similar situations may arise in which the desirability of permitting restitution is equally great and, if so, restitution should be granted in accordance with the principle that compensation for benefits conferred is denied only to officious intermeddlers or to persons who do not desire or who manifest no desire to have compensation for their services."

[The second branch of the "principle" stated—the actor's intention to charge where intervention is justified—is elaborated in the Restitution Restatement's § 114, comment c: "[A] person who acts entirely from motives of humanity is not entitled to restitution. The fact that the person acting is in the business of supplying the things or is acting in the course of his profession, is evidence of an intent to charge. On the other hand, a non-professional person who gives a comparatively small amount of service normally would be considered as having no intent to charge for the services, in the absence of evidence of such intent."]

––––––––

NOTE: RESTITUTION ABSENT THE LATER PROMISE

Would Webb have recovered anything if McGowin had made no subsequent promise of compensation? Would the rescuer of the bull (Boothe v. Fitzpatrick, discussed in the principal case) have recovered anything if the owner had not promised to pay for the bull's care and keep?

The *Webb* court likened the case before it to one in which an "accidentally poisoned" McGowin is saved by an unrequested physician, and a grateful McGowin then promises payment for the services rendered. Can this be right, given that doctors are typically allowed to recover even without such a promise? See Cotnam v. Wisdom, 83 Ark. 601, 104 S.W. 164 (1907). But the physician's case does not depend on a later promise. What does this suggest about how we should think about *Webb*? Consider a modern discussion of benefits conferred in the absence of bargain, Goldstick v. ICM Realty, 788 F.2d 456 (7th Cir.1986), where Judge Posner wrote in part:

> A person who confers benefits gratuitously—officiously—obtains no legal claim for compensation. If [plaintiff, a lawyer seeking payment of a legal fee for tax work,] had appeared at a meeting of [defendant's] shareholders and serenaded them with his violin, and the shareholders had listened raptly, still [plaintiff] would have no claim of restitution against [the defendant company] for benefits conferred; he would have had to negotiate a contract with [defendant] in advance. . . . [Also, if plaintiff had a contract with another party,] plaintiff cannot bring [defendant] in through the back door by pointing out that [his] contractual performance conferred benefits on [defendant]. To illustrate, if you do work pursuant to a contract with X, you don't expect that Y, a nonparty, will pay you if X defaults, merely because Y was benefitted by your work; and expectation of payment is an essential element of a claim for restitution. For the doctrine of restitution does not make altruism a paying proposition. As its synonym "contract implied in law" brings out, it allows damages to be recovered in settings where (unlike our example of the unsolicited serenade) the parties would have agreed that there was a contractual obligation had the point occurred to them.

––––––––

Henderson, Promises Grounded in the Past: The Idea of Unjust Enrichment and the Law of Contracts

57 Va.L.Rev. 1115, 1157–1161 (1971)

"[T]he law of consideration developed and prospered for the very reason that it was thought to be well-suited to the task of marking off and excluding sterile transactions. Thus, it would be difficult to overstate the extent to which the informal gratuitous promise has been a subject of central concern [in discussions] of the various rules of consideration. . . . At times, the disposition not to inquire into the adequacy of consideration, which provides doctrinal legitimacy for enforcement of the mixed gift, encourages the notion that close distinctions between bargain and gift are not of great weight. Yet the factor of motive has always been recognized as critical to bargain theory, and it has generally received sensitive and evenhanded treatment in the decisions. . . .

"Why, then, has the common law been reluctant to explore motivations for the purpose of distinguishing the promise to pay for benefit earlier received from the simple promise of a gift? The [answer] surely cannot be that these promises are indistinguishable. Once undertakings based clearly on gratitude or sentiment are isolated—as the case law of bargain theory has long done and as [§ 86] of the second Restatement envisions—a promise to do something in return for benefit already in hand is most persuasively explained on the basis of motivations of reciprocity, not benevolence. . . . [P]romises prompted by enrichment already taken can fairly be associated with the idea of exchange that forms the essential support for the whole of bargain contract. So long as the promisee acted originally with an expectation of compensation, or even where it is not clearly established that a gift-making motivation controlled [the] conferring of benefit, the net effect of a promise of a return is to conclude a kind of exchange. There is no intelligible reason to require the trailing promise to stand apart from the chain of events which sponsored it. . . . [E]ven assuming that such transactions cannot be fitted within expanded notions of bargain, at the very least they ought to be legally operative for the limited purpose of negating the assumption of gift which stands as an obstacle on the general question of liability.

". . . [I]t is settled beyond recall that unjust enrichment, viewed independently or as reinforcement of bargain, itself constitutes a substantive ground for the enforcement of promises. [Moreover,] the impressiveness of the [benefit] ground is enhanced when the enrichment factor is coupled with a promissory confession that it has created in the recipient a sense of moral obligation. . . .

"Perhaps the most obvious conclusion to be drawn from a study of the [benefit cases] is that concern about ill-considered promise making is largely misplaced. Given the usual sequence in which events unfold—i.e., a performance on one side, resulting in an often identifiable gain in the hands of the other party, followed by the other's promissory response—the transaction itself involves natural safeguards equivalent to those of form or present exchange. The time lag between performance and promise affords an opportunity for deliberation and the exercise of caution, as well as an evaluation of 'price,' not present in most conventional bargains. Still, promises to return benefit are traditionally not enforced in spite of the strong likelihood that they were seriously intended when made. To the extent that the decisions accept the natural guaranties of the benefit cases, they do so implicitly and usually only in connection with recoveries placed on the material benefit rule of moral obligation."

———

RESTATEMENT OF CONTRACTS, SECOND §

Section 86. Promise for Benefit Received

(1) A promise made in recognition of a benefit previously received by the promisor from the promisee is binding to the extent necessary to prevent injustice.

(2) A promise is not binding under Subsection (1)

(a) if the promisee conferred the benefit as a gift or for other reasons the promisor has not been unjustly enriched; or

(b) to the extent that its value is disproportionate to the benefit.

Comment:

a. "Past consideration"; "moral obligation." Enforcement of promises to pay for benefit received has sometimes been said to rest on "past consideration" or on the "moral obligation" of the promisor, and there are statutes in such terms in a few states. Those terms are not used here: "past consideration" is inconsistent with the [conventional] meaning of consideration, and there seems to be no consensus as to what constitutes a "moral obligation." The mere fact of promise has been thought to create a moral obligation, but it is clear that not all promises are enforced. Nor are moral obligations based solely on gratitude or sentiment sufficient of themselves to support a subsequent promise. . . .

i. Partial enforcement. . . . [W]here a benefit received is a liquidated sum of money, a promise is not enforceable under this [s]ection beyond the amount of the benefit. Where the value of the benefit is uncertain, a promise to pay the value is binding and a promise to pay a liquidated sum may serve to fix the amount due if in all the circumstances it is not disproportionate to the benefit. See [Webb v. McGowin]. A promise which is excessive may sometimes be enforced to the extent of the value of the benefit, and the remedy may be thought of as quasi-contractual rather than contractual. In other cases a promise of disproportionate value may tend to show unfair pressure or other conduct by the promisee such that justice does not require any enforcement of the promise.

NOTE

When § 86 was before the annual meeting of the American Law Institute in 1965, Reporter Robert Braucher introduced this new category of binding promise with the comment that the accustomed ways of classifying and talking about the decisions giving effect to past consideration or moral obligation were a "rather unsatisfactory way to leave these cases." He proceeded to explain (42 A.L.I.Proc. 273–274):

> Actually, when you go through the cases in which this problem has been raised, it seemed to us that you discover that there is a principle, and so we have tried to capture the principle, although I think it is more of a principle than it is a rule.

If you look at [§ 86], it bristles with nonspecific concepts; in particular, the qualification that the promise is binding to the extent necessary to prevent injustice would be entirely at large if we did not add subsection (2) which refers to the concept of unjust enrichment.

[I think] the principle takes on meaning, and I think there is not a division here between a majority view and a minority view. . . . What you have, really, is a line of distinction between essentially gratuitous transactions and cases which are on the borderline of quasi-contracts, where promise removes difficulty. . . . If you look through the cases, the cases are a wide variety of miscellany, but we think there is a principle.

The cases digested below (*Edson*, *Muir*, and *Schoenkerman's Estate*) are part of the "miscellany" referred to by Reporter Braucher. Do they yield the "principle" of which he spoke? Despite the appearance of § 86, one continues to see promises for benefit received discussed in the consideration-based language of "material benefit" and "moral obligation." See, e.g., Worner Agency, Inc. v. Doyle, 133 Ill.App.3d 850, 479 N.E.2d 468 (1985) (receipt of " 'beneficial' or 'meritorious' consideration [imposes] a moral obligation yielding an implied consideration" for a subsequent promise by the person benefitted). The conventional explanation of the moral obligation cases in terms of restitution—the approach of § 86 and most commentators—is challenged in Thel & Yorio, The Promissory Basis of Past Consideration, 78 Va.L.Rev. 1045 (1992).

Edson v. Poppe

24 S.D. 466, 124 N.W. 441 (1910)

Plaintiff, at the request of a tenant in possession of land owned by defendant, drilled a 250–foot well on the property and installed casing. Plaintiff alleged that the value of the labor and material expended was $250, that the well added to the value of the land and later occupants have regularly used it, and that after the well had been completed defendant promised to pay plaintiff the reasonable value of the work and materials. Plaintiff recovered a jury verdict below. Defendant appealed, claiming only past consideration was alleged. *Held*, judgment for plaintiff affirmed. "The allegation . . . here is that the digging and casing of the well in question inured directly to the defendant's benefit and that, after he had seen and examined the same, he expressly promised and agreed to pay plaintiff the reasonable value thereof." The circumstances did not indicate that plaintiff's drilling was "gratuitous" or "an act of voluntary courtesy to the defendant." The subsequent promise was therefore supported by sufficient consideration.

Muir v. Kane

55 Wash. 131, 104 P. 153 (1909)

Defendants employed plaintiff, a real estate broker, to find a purchaser for their home. The arrangement was oral, and by a state statute of frauds any agreement authorizing a broker to secure a buyer or seller of real estate was "void" unless in writing. Plaintiff secured a buyer, and a written contract of sale was prepared and signed by both the buyer and defendants. One clause of the contract contained a promise by defendants to pay plaintiffs $200 "for services rendered." *Held*, plaintiff can recover this sum. The contract clause did not comply with the statute, since it was not the written authority to the broker that the statute required. Furthermore, plaintiff's service had already been rendered when the contract of sale was signed. Nevertheless, though declared by the statute to be "void," there was no moral turpitude in the prior oral agreement. Defendants had a moral obligation to pay for the service that was fully as strong as that continuing after a statute of limitations has barred a once-enforceable debt.

_____

In re Schoenkerman's Estate
236 Wis. 311, 294 N.W. 810 (1940)

Schoenkerman's wife died in 1928. There were two children of the marriage, a daughter then 17 and a son 13. Schoenkerman asked his wife's mother and sister, who lived in Chicago, to move to Milwaukee, live in his home to take care of the children, and to manage the household for them all. They did so, living in and managing his home until shortly before his death in 1939. A year earlier, in May 1938, Schoenkerman had executed two notes, promising $500 to his mother-in-law and $1,500 to his sister-in-law, on which they sued after his death. *Held*, the decedent was manifestly under a moral obligation to pay the claimants for their 10 years of service to him. Defendant, executor of Schoenkerman's estate, was right in contending that household services rendered and received by persons living together as a family are presumed to be gratuitous and that an express contract to pay would have had to be proved to overcome this presumption. But defendant was wrong in contending that there must have been at one time a legally enforceable obligation. In giving the notes, Schoenkerman plainly acknowledged a moral obligation that "afforded more than ample consideration." But the claim of the sister-in-law for the full value of her services, which she asserted to be $4,610, was correctly disallowed as to the excess over the $1,500 promised.

SECTION 4. RELIANCE ON A PROMISE

Seavey v. Drake
Supreme Court of New Hampshire, 1882.
62 N.H. 393.

Bill in Equity, for specific performance of a parol agreement of land. At the hearing the plaintiff offered to prove that he was the only child of Shadrach Seavey, the defendants' testate, who died in 1880. In January, 1860, the testator, owning a tract of land, and wishing to assist the plaintiff, went upon the land with him and gave him a portion of it, which the plaintiff then accepted and took possession of. The plaintiff had a [promissory] note against his father upon which there was due about $200, which he then or subsequently gave up to him. Subsequently his father gave him an additional strip of land adjoining the other tract. Ever since the gifts, the plaintiff has occupied and still occupies the land, and has paid all taxes upon it. He has expended $3,000 in the erection of a dwelling-house, barn, and stable, and in other improvements upon the premises. Some of the lumber for the house was given him by his father, who helped him do some of the labor upon the house.

The defendants moved to dismiss because no cause for equitable relief was stated, and because the parol contract, which is sought to be enforced, was without consideration, and is executory. The bill alleges a gift of the land to the plaintiff and a promise to give him a deed of it. The defendants also demurred, and answered denying the material allegations of the bill.

If the bill can be sustained on proof of these facts, or if not on these facts, but would be with the additional proof of a consideration for the promise, there is to be a further hearing, the plaintiff having leave to amend his bill. If on proof of these facts, either with or without proof of consideration, the bill cannot be sustained, it is to be dismissed.

SMITH, J. The bill alleges a promise by the defendants' testator to give the plaintiff a deed. The plaintiff offered to prove that the deceased gave him the land, and that he thereupon entered into possession and made valuable improvements. We assume that the plaintiff in his offer [of proofs] meant that he was induced by the gift of the land to enter into possession and make large expenditures in permanent improvements upon it. The evidence offered is admissible. Specific performance of a parol contract to convey land is decreed in favor of the vendee who has performed his part of the contract, when a failure or refusal to convey would operate as a fraud upon him. Johnson v. Bell, 58 N.H. 395. . . . The statute of frauds (G.L., c. 220, s. 14) provides that "No action shall be maintained upon a contract for the sale of land, unless the agreement upon which it is brought, or some memorandum thereof, is in writing, and signed by the party to be charged, or by some person by him thereto authorized in writing." Equity, however, lends its aid, when there has been part performance, to remove the bar of the statute, upon the ground that it is a fraud for the vendor to insist upon the absence of a written instrument, when he has permitted the contract to be partly executed.

It is not material . . . whether the promissory note given up by the plaintiff was or was not intended as payment or part payment for the land, for equity protects a parol gift of land equally with a parol agreement to sell it, if accompanied by possession, and the donee has made valuable improvements upon the property induced by the promise to give it. . . . There is no important distinction in this respect between a promise to give and a promise to sell. The expenditure in money or labor in the improvement of the land induced by the donor's promise to give the land to the party making the expenditure, constitutes, in equity, a consideration for the promise and the promise will be enforced. Crosbie v. M'Doual, 13 Ves. 148; Freeman v. Freeman, 43 N.Y. 34, 39. . . . Case discharged.

COMMENT: PART PERFORMANCE OF LAND CONTRACTS

There is much authority granting specific performance in equity after the kind of "part performance" that occurred in Seavey v. Drake. The land-contract clause in the statute of frauds quoted in *Seavey* is in substance the standard phrasing. There is of course no exception in the statutory language for the kind of "fraud" that involved no more than a refusal by the executor to perform the oral promise made by the father in his lifetime. It may be that this disregard of exact language began because of an original understanding that the statute of frauds did not apply to actions in equity. An early draft of the statute indicated this. But the language of the English statute of 1677, as finally adopted, drew no such distinction. Nor do most American versions, save for a small number that expressly authorize equitable relief after part performance of the kind discussed here (e.g., New York's Gen.Oblig.Law, § 5–703(4) states that "[n]othing contained in this section abridges the powers of courts of equity to compel the specific performance of agreements in cases of part performance").

The standard situation in which the part-performance doctrine displaces the statute of frauds does not involve a promise to convey land by way of gift, as in Seavey v. Drake, but an oral contract to sell land for money—an exchange in which the vendor has failed to sign a sufficient memorandum. In this context, the doctrine is certainly misdescribed. The most obvious and direct "part performance" of an ordinary land contract will be part payment of the purchase price, but it is agreed everywhere that mere payment of the price, in full or in part, will not make specific performance available. Jasmin v. Alberico, 135 Vt. 287, 376 A.2d 32 (1977), tells why: "[T]he reliance [must] be something beyond injury adequately compensable in money." If the vendee-promisee can be made whole by ordering restitution, there is no need for equity's intervention to protect the reliance of the performing party. Entry into possession by the promisee, with the promisor-owner's acquiescence, is the critical element. A substantial group of states has held that this is enough. In other states, entry into possession plus payment of some part of the price will suffice. Probably in most states possession plus permanent improvements will do. However, some states, like Massachusetts, have tied the whole doctrine explicitly into the reliance factor and require a showing that the oral purchaser has become committed in such a way that "irreparable" (meaning "unjust and unconscientious") injury will occur unless specific performance is given. Andrews v. Charon, 289 Mass. 1, 193 N.E. 737 (1935). Finally, at the other end of the spectrum are a few states which have firmly rejected "part performance" as a justification for specific performance of oral land contracts, though this has led to some peculiar results on the damage remedy side. 2 A. Corbin, Contracts § 443, tells the story in these states.

No elaborate effort is usually made to justify the part-performance route around the statute, but some clues to the reasons do appear. Occupancy by the vendee over an extended stretch of time, with no sign of protest from the vendor, does suggest that some fairly firm oral assurances have been given. When "improvements"—substantial repairs or new construction—are added, there emerges a course of conduct that gives direct and visual confirmation to the occupant's claim that entry was under a contract of sale. The vendor-owner can be called on to give some other explanation, if there is one—e.g., that there was an oral lease or other arrangement. Thus, conduct provides a kind of *evidence* that can be said to take the place of a signed memorandum, the evidence called for by the statute.

It is true that the "evidentiary" test tends to be strict. The plaintiff's actions, it is commonly said, must be "unequivocally referable"—even "exclusively referable"—to the alleged oral agreement; in some places, a higher standard of proof (e.g., "clear and convincing") is also added. Accordingly, if the conduct urged as "part performance" is readily explainable on other grounds (or not sufficiently substantial), or the underlying agreement alleged to have induced the conduct is not sufficiently demonstrated, the escape from the statute is lost. It must be remembered that part performance is both an equity doctrine and an "exception" to a formal requirement of general contract law. Hence the search for "what equity requires," especially at the pleading stage, is usually thorough, perhaps even grudging. E.g., Messner Vetere Berger v. Aegis Group, 93 N.Y.2d 229, 689 N.Y.S.2d 674, 711 N.E.2d 953 (1999).

The argument that appears in Seavey v. Drake and in many cases enforcing oral land contracts, that denial of specific performance because of the statute of frauds would itself produce "fraud," appears on first view to be little more than verbalism. Still, there are problems that this phrasing most inadequately defines, especially in the common case where the occupier has made "improvements" or incurred other expenses. Can these outlays be reimbursed if the occupier cannot have the land? If the occupier paid money or contributed work and labor that the vendor bargained for as part of the orally-agreed exchange, no difficulty would arise. It is agreed everywhere that the statute of frauds is no obstacle to quasi-contract restitution of performances rendered as part of the agreed exchange by a party not in default under an oral contract within the statute. But improvements, taxes, or other charges paid, and other expenditures that were not "requested" by the owner-vendor, are another story. Where such outlays are made by the vendee's own choice and fall outside the range of the oral agreement, there is real doubt whether any recovery can be allowed at all, even though the value of the real estate may have been permanently enhanced. See, e.g., Breen v. Phelps, 186 Conn. 86, 439 A.2d 1066 (1982) ("It is not evident from the complaint that restitution would be available [or] would provide an adequate remedy [for plaintiff's outlays of $6,300 for] labor and materials toward the repair and renovation of the premises"). You will see at once that the problem becomes one of reimbursing reliance losses. Can a *damage* remedy be given to reimburse for reliance losses where the breach, if any, is of an unenforceable contract? The case of Boone v. Coe (p. 98) has something to contribute on this.

In general, in the equity decisions on part performance as a ground for specific performance, there is a constant shuttling back and forth between the *evidence* that an oral contract was made, supplied by the conduct of the parties, and the *reliance* element that would make a refusal of specific performance a "fraud" on the vendee. Sometimes one of these elements seems to be uppermost in a court's mind, sometimes the other, and the facts of individual cases are exceedingly diverse. Also, as was true in *Seavey*, the equity cases giving specific performance after "part performance" tend not to devote much attention to the consideration defense (if one is raised). The primary issue—i.e., the most difficult—is thought to be the need to satisfy or circumvent the statutory writing requirement. Yet these equity cases can be added to the list of situations in which the reliance interest is protected (again, under a misdescribed doctrine), even though important requirements of contract formation and enforceability have not been met.

There has been some spillover of the *Seavey* doctrine to related situations. For example, there is respectable authority approving specific performance after "part performance" of oral contracts that are not performable within one year (2 A. Corbin, Contracts § 459). Then there is another category that might be described as "full performance," though that phrase is not always used. (It was used in Estate of Gorton, 167 Vt. 357, 706 A.2d 947 (1997): "[F]ull performance by one party in reliance on the agreement may support equitable enforcement where the parties cannot be returned to their former position.") Suppose, for example, an oral contract for the sale of land for money. If there were no more than this—no action taken by either party—neither vendor nor vendee could enforce the contract, in equity or at law, against the opposite party who pleaded the statute. But what if the vendor then proceeded to convey the legal title, thus rendering *in full* the performance promised? It plainly would be unjust for the vendee to keep the land without paying for it. One alternative would be to cancel the deed and order a reconveyance if the vendee refused to pay. But the deed itself would be persuasive evidence of a seriously-intended transaction, which had been so far performed that there was nothing left to do except pay money. The usual conclusion would be that by the vendor's conveyance the contract was "taken out" of the statute, and the vendee's promise to pay, though proved only by oral evidence, could be enforced, even at law. See also Nichols v. Nichols, 139 Vt. 273, 427 A.2d 374 (1981) (oral agreement to leave family farm to son if he farmed it, paid off bills, and cared for mother until her death specifically enforced where son fully performed agreement). Even with contracts that are "not to be performed within one year," decisions tend toward the same result and allow enforcement of the unperformed oral promise by the party who has fully performed. Mason v. Anderson, 146 Vt. 242, 499 A.2d 783 (1985), and Glass v. Minnesota Protective Life Ins. Co., 314 N.W.2d 393 (Iowa 1982), are representative examples. Cases on full performance by one party are collected in Willamette Quarries, Inc. v. Wodtli, 308 Or. 406, 781 P.2d 1196 (1989).

One of the haunting questions raised by the part-performance cases was whether there were compelling reasons, logical or historical, why judges sitting on law dockets should be impervious to proof of reliance on oral promises. They clearly were supposed to be under the traditional conception of "part performance." The avenue it opened was to equity only; a damage action would not lie on the same oral contract that the very same judge, if the case had been brought on the nonjury docket, would cheerfully enforce.

The first question, of course, was why the presence of a jury should make that much difference. Arguments began to be heard in 1677, when the statute of frauds was passed, that no effective means existed for controlling juries, and that the restrictive rules of evidence (such as the disqualification of the parties as witnesses) made perjury harder to detect. Furthermore, contract law itself was still relatively primitive, especially in its lack of restraints on damage recoveries (no requirements of foreseeability, mitigation, certainty, etc.). To some critics, the statute seemed more and more an anachronism. At the least, it seemed plausible to assert that the policies supporting the statute were not clear enough—or strong enough—to preclude redress for substantial reliance losses where the remedy of restitution was inadequate and damages alone could give indemnity.

The traditional view was not so easily dislodged, however, as a 1941 Washington case suggests.

Owners of an apartment building agreed orally to give Tenant a three-year written lease of an apartment then occupied by another tenant. Owners "understood" that Tenant would buy the occupant's furniture. Tenant did so, paying down $2,437.25 and obligating himself for an additional $2,600. Tenant entered into possession at once and paid rent for the next three months, but when he tendered the rent for the fourth month, he was informed by Owners that the building had been purchased by one Stone, who proceeded to evict him. Tenant defaulted on his contract to buy the furniture, forfeiting the payments already made. Tenant then sued for this loss (also for $58 spent in improving the apartment), and the jury rendered a verdict of $2,655.25 in his favor. Judgment on this verdict was reversed. It was improper to submit to the jury the question whether the conduct of the parties was "part performance," for that was an equitable issue for the judge and "in the very nature of things a judge cannot delegate his chancery powers to a jury under any imaginable circumstances." Equitable estoppel, as its name indicates, applied only in equity. Goodwin v. Gillingham, 10 Wash.2d 656, 117 P.2d 959 (1941).

There will be more ahead on the workings of the reliance principle as concerns a damage remedy for breach of an oral agreement deemed to fall within the statute of frauds.

————

Kirksey v. Kirksey
Supreme Court of Alabama, 1845.
8 Ala. 131.

Assumpsit by the defendant, against the plaintiff in error. The question is presented [upon] a case agreed, which shows the following facts:

The plaintiff was the wife of defendant's brother, but had for some time been a widow, and had several children. In 1840, the plaintiff resided on public land, under a contract of lease, she had held over, and was comfortably settled, and would have attempted to secure the land she lived on. The defendant resided in Talladega county, some sixty, or seventy miles off. On the 10th of October, 1840, he wrote to her the following letter:

"Dear sister Antillico—Much to my mortification, I heard, that brother Henry was dead, and one of his children. I know that your situation is one of grief, and difficulty. You had a bad chance before, but a great deal worse now. I should like to come and see you, but cannot with convenience at present. . . . I do not know whether you have a preference on the place you live on, or not. If you had, I would advise you to obtain your preference, and sell the land and quit the country, as I understand it is very unhealthy, and I know society is very bad. If you will come down and see me, I will let you have a place to raise your family, and I have more open land than I can tend; and on the account of your situation, and that of your family, I feel like I want you and the children to do well."

Within a month or two [of] receipt of this letter, the plaintiff abandoned her possession, without disposing of it, and removed with her family, to the residence of the defendant, who put her in comfortable houses, and gave her land to cultivate for two years, at the end of which time he notified her to remove, and put her in a house, not comfortable, in the woods, which he afterwards required her to leave.

A verdict being found for the plaintiff, for two hundred dollars, the above facts were agreed, and if they will sustain the action, the judgment is to be affirmed, otherwise it is to be reversed.

ORMOND, J. The inclination of my mind is, that the loss and inconvenience, which the plaintiff sustained in breaking up, and moving to the defendant's a distance of sixty miles, is a sufficient consideration to support the promise, to furnish her with a house, and land to cultivate, until she could raise her family. My brothers, however, think that the promise on the part of the defendant, was a mere gratuity, and that an action will not lie for its breach. The judgment of the Court below must therefore be reversed, pursuant to the agreement of the parties.

Ricketts v. Scothorn

Supreme Court of Nebraska, 1898.
57 Neb. 51, 77 N.W. 365.

SULLIVAN, J. . . . [T]he plaintiff, Katie Scothorn, recovered judgment against the defendant, Andrew D. Ricketts, as executor of the last will and testament of John C. Ricketts, deceased. The action was based upon [this] promissory note[:] "May the first, 1891. I promise to pay to Katie Scothorn on demand, $2,000, to be at 6 per cent. per annum. J. C. Ricketts." In the petition the plaintiff alleges that the consideration for the execution of the note was that she should surrender her employment as bookkeeper for Mayer Bros., and cease to work for a living. She also alleges that the note was given to induce her to abandon her occupation, and that, relying on it, and on the annual interest, as a means of support, she gave up the employment in which she was then engaged. These allegations of the petition are denied by the administrator. The material facts are undisputed. . . . John C. Ricketts, the maker of the note, was the grandfather of the plaintiff. Early in May—presumably on the day the note bears date—he called on her at the store where she was working. What transpired between them is thus described by Mr. Flodene, one of the plaintiff's witnesses: "A. Well, the old gentleman came in there one morning about nine o'clock, . . . and he unbuttoned his vest, and took out a piece of paper in the shape of a note; . . . and he says to Miss Scothorn, 'I have fixed out something that you have not got to work any more.' He says, none of my grandchildren work, and you don't have to. Q. Where was she? A. She took the piece of paper and kissed him, and kissed the old gentleman, and commenced to cry." It seems Miss Scothorn immediately notified her employer of her intention to quit work, and that she did soon after abandon her occupation. The mother of the plaintiff . . . testified that she had a conversation with her father, Mr. Ricketts, shortly after the note was executed, in which he informed her that he had given the note to the plaintiff to enable her to quit work; that none of his grandchildren worked, and he did not think she ought to. For something more than a year the plaintiff was without an occupation, but in September, 1892, with the consent of her grandfather, and by his assistance, she secured a position as bookkeeper. . . . On June 8, 1894, Mr. Ricketts died. He had paid one year's interest on the note, and a short time before his death expressed regret that he had not been able to pay the balance. In the summer or fall of 1892 he stated to his daughter, Mrs. Scothorn, that if he could sell his farm in Ohio he would pay the note out of the proceeds. He at no time repudiated the obligation.

We quite agree with counsel for the defendant that upon this evidence there was nothing to submit to the jury, and that a verdict should have been directed peremptorily for one of the parties. The testimony of Flodene and Mrs. Scothorn, taken together, conclusively establishes the fact that the note was not given in consideration of the plaintiff pursuing, or agreeing to pursue, any particular line of conduct. There was no promise on the part of the plaintiff to do, or refrain from doing, anything. Her right to the money promised in the note was not made to depend upon an abandonment of her employment with Mayer Bros., and future abstention from like service. Mr. Ricketts made no condition, requirement, or request. He exacted no quid pro quo. He gave the note as a gratuity, and looked for nothing in return. So far as the evidence discloses, it was his purpose to place the plaintiff in a position of independence, where she could work or remain idle, as she might choose. The abandonment of Miss Scothorn of her position as bookkeeper was altogether voluntary. It was not an act done in fulfillment of any contract obligation assumed when she accepted the note. The instrument in suit, being given without any valuable consideration, was nothing more than a promise to make a gift in the future of the sum of money therein named. Ordinarily, such promises are not enforceable, even when put in the form of a promissory note. But it has often been held that an action on a note given to a church, college, or other like institution, upon the faith of which money has been expended or obligations incurred, could not be successfully defended on the ground of a want of consideration. In this class of cases [involving promises to charities] the note in suit is nearly always spoken of as a gift or donation, but the decision is generally put on the ground that the expenditure of money or assumption of liability by the donee on the faith of the promise constitutes a valuable and sufficient consideration. It seems to us that the true reason is the preclusion of the defendant, under the doctrine of estoppel, to deny the consideration. . . .

. . . [I]s there an equitable estoppel which ought to preclude the defendant from alleging that the note in controversy is lacking in one of the essential elements of a valid contract? We think there is. An estoppel in pais is defined to be "a right arising from acts, admissions, or conduct which have induced a change of position in accordance with the real or apparent intention of the party against whom they are alleged." [A]s shown by the record before us, the plaintiff was a working girl, holding a position in which she earned a salary of $10 per week. Her grandfather, desiring to put her in a position of independence, gave her the note, accompanying it with the remark that his other grandchildren did not work, and that she would not be obliged to work any longer. In effect, he suggested that she might abandon her employment, and rely in the future upon the bounty which he promised. He doubtless desired that she should give up her occupation, but, whether he did or not, it is entirely certain that he contemplated such action on her part as a reasonable and probable consequence of his gift. Having intentionally influenced the plaintiff to alter her position for the worse on the faith of the note being paid when due, it would be grossly inequitable to permit the maker, or his executor, to resist payment on the ground that the promise was given without consideration. The petition charges the elements of an equitable estoppel, and the evidence conclusively establishes them. . . . The judgment is right, and is affirmed.

QUESTIONS

(1) It seems that Katie Scothorn's grandfather, like Willie Story's uncle, wanted something, perhaps some action. Are you satisfied that there was no bargain here?

(2) The court asserts that Katie Scothorn "alter[ed] her position for the worse." What do you understand the court to mean by its phrase "for the worse"? In a similar case, a grandfather's written promise of $17,000, given to

enable a granddaughter to purchase a house available for that sum, was followed by the granddaughter's payment of $2,000 from her own savings for an extended "option contract" on the property. A Colorado court also applied "the equitable doctrine of estoppel," citing Ricketts v. Scothorn for the proposition that "a gift of the donor's own note may be sustained if the donee, in reliance on the note, has expended money or incurred liabilities which will, by legal necessity, cause loss or injury to the donee if the note is not paid." In re Estate of Bucci, 488 P.2d 216, 219 (Colo.Ct.App.1971).

———

Prescott v. Jones

69 N.H. 305, 41 A. 352 (1898)

Defendant insurance agents had insured plaintiff's buildings for a year ending February 1. On January 23, they wrote plaintiff that they would renew the policy for another year on the same terms, "unless notified to the contrary." Plaintiff made no reply and defendants failed to renew the insurance. The buildings were destroyed by fire on March 1. Plaintiff brought suit alleging that he had understood the January 23 letter to be an agreement to insure, and that he relied on it, believing that a reply was unnecessary. A demurrer to plaintiff's complaint was entered below. *Held*, demurrer sustained. Defendants made an offer to insure, but there was no acceptance by plaintiff. An acceptance requires words or other overt action. As plaintiff neither paid the premium nor communicated a promise to do so, there was no acceptance and no contract. "Nor is there any estoppel against the defendants on the ground that the plaintiff relied upon their letter. . . . The letter was a representation only of a present intention or purpose on their part. 'It was not a statement of a fact or state of things actually existing, or past and executed, on which a party might reasonably rely as fixed and certain, and by which he might properly be guided in his conduct. . . . The intent of a party, however positive or fixed, concerning his future action, is necessarily uncertain as to its fulfillment, and must depend on contingencies, and be subject to be changed and modified by subsequent events and circumstances. . . . [The doctrine of estoppel] does not apply to such a representation. The reason on which the doctrine rests is that it would operate as a fraud if a party was allowed to aver and prove a fact to be contrary to that which he had previously stated to another for the purpose of inducing him to act and alter his condition. . . . But the reason wholly fails when the representation relates only to a present intention or purpose of a party, because, being in its nature uncertain, and liable to change, it could not properly form a basis or inducement upon which a party could reasonably adopt any fixed permanent course of action.' . . . To sum it up in a few words, the case presented is, in its legal aspects, one of a party seeking to reap where he had not sown, and to gather where he had not scattered." [This case, you will note, was decided the same year that the Nebraska court was delivering Ricketts v. Scothorn.]

NOTE

It was noted earlier that equitable estoppel or estoppel in pais normally operates on representations of fact (see Note accompanying the *Acme Mills* case, supra p. 25). When equitable estoppel is applied, how would you describe the mechanics or "theory" of the doctrine? Courts commonly say that it "ordinarily is used defensively," to "prevent the assertion of an otherwise unequivocal right." E.g., Chrysler Credit Corp. v. Bert Cote's L/A Auto Sales, 707 A.2d 1311 (Me.1998). The court in Prescott v. Jones was faithful to history in distinguishing promises of future action from factual representations about the past or present, and in limiting equitable estoppel to the latter. We shall see more of that distinction in the materials ahead. It is not too early to begin to think about how a "statement of fact" differs from a "statement of intention," and why such a distinction should matter.

Allegheny College v. National Chautauqua County Bank

Court of Appeals of New York, 1927.
246 N.Y. 369, 159 N.E. 173.

CARDOZO, C.J. The plaintiff, Allegheny College, is an institution of liberal learning at Meadville, Pennsylvania. In June 1921, a "drive" was in progress to secure for it an additional endowment of $1,250,000. An appeal to contribute to this fund was made to Mary Yates Johnston of Jamestown, New York. In response thereto, she signed and delivered . . . the following writing:

"Estate Pledge,

"Allegheny College Second Century Endowment

"Jamestown, N.Y., June 15, 1921.

"In consideration of my interest in Christian Education, and in consideration of others subscribing, I hereby subscribe and will pay to the order [of] Allegheny College . . . the sum of Five Thousand Dollars; $5,000.

"This obligation shall become due thirty days after my death, and I hereby instruct my Executor, or Administrator, to pay the same out of my estate. This pledge shall bear interest at the rate of . . . per cent per annum, payable annually, from . . . till paid. The proceeds of this obligation shall be added to the Endowment of said Institution, or expended in accordance with instructions on reverse side of this pledge.

(	"Name	Mary Yates Johnston,
(	"Address	306 East 6th Street.
(		"Jamestown, N.Y.
(	"Dayton E. McClain	Witness
(	"T.R. Courtis	Witness"

On the reverse side of the writing is the following indorsement: "In loving memory this gift shall be known as the Mary Yates Johnston Memorial Fund, the proceeds from which shall be used to educate students preparing for the Ministry. . . . This pledge shall be valid only on the condition that the provisions of my Will, now extant, shall be first met. Mary Yates Johnston."

The subscription was not payable by its terms until thirty days after the death of the promisor. The sum of $1,000 was paid, however, upon account in December, 1923, while the promisor was alive. The college set the money aside to be held as a scholarship fund for the benefit of students preparing for the ministry. Later, in July, 1924, the promisor gave notice to the college that she repudiated the promise. Upon the expiration of thirty days following her death, this action was brought against the executor of her will to recover the unpaid balance.

The law of charitable subscriptions has been a prolific source of controversy in this State and elsewhere. We have held that a promise of that order is unenforceable like any other if made without consideration. . . . On the other hand, though professing to apply to such subscriptions the general law of contract, we have found consideration present where the general law of contract, at least as then declared, would have said that it was absent. . . .

BENJAMIN N. CARDOZO
1870–1938

A classic form of statement identifies consideration with detriment to the promisee sustained by virtue of the promise. Hamer v. Sidway, 124

N.Y. 538, 27 N.E. 256. . . . So compendious a formula is little more than a half truth. There is need of many a supplementary gloss before the outline can be so filled in as to depict the classic doctrine. "The promise and the consideration must purport to be the motive each for the other, in whole or at least in part. It is not enough that the promise induces the detriment or that the detriment induces the promise if the other half is wanting," Wisconsin & Mich. Ry. Co. v. Powers, 191 U.S. 379, 386. . . . If A promises B to make him a gift, consideration may be lacking, though B has renounced other opportunities for betterment in the faith that the promise will be kept.

The half truths of one generation tend at times to perpetuate themselves in the law as the whole truths of another, when constant repetition brings it about that qualifications, taken once for granted, are disregarded or forgotten. The doctrine of consideration has not escaped the common lot. As far back as 1881, Judge Holmes in his lectures on the Common Law (p. 292), separated the detriment which is merely a consequence of the promise from the detriment, which is in truth the motive or inducement, and yet added that the courts "have gone far in obliterating this distinction." The tendency toward effacement has not lessened with the years. On the contrary, there has grown up of recent days a doctrine that a substitute for consideration or an exception to its ordinary requirements can be found in what is styled "a promissory estoppel" (Williston, Contracts, §§ 139, 116). Whether the exception has made its way in this State to such an extent as to permit us to say that the general law of consideration has been modified accordingly, we do not now attempt to say. Cases such as Siegel v. Spear & Co., 234 N.Y. 479, 138 N.E. 414, and DeCicco v. Schweizer, 221 N.Y. 431, 117 N.E. 807, may be signposts on the road. Certain, at least, it is that we have adopted the doctrine of promissory estoppel as the equivalent of consideration in connection with our law of charitable subscriptions. So long as those decisions stand, the question is not merely whether the enforcement of a charitable subscription can be squared with the doctrine of consideration in all its ancient rigor. The question may also be whether it can be squared with the doctrine of consideration as qualified by the doctrine of promissory estoppel.

We have said that the cases in this State have recognized this exception, if exception it is thought to be. Thus, in Barnes v. Perine, 12 N.Y. 18, the subscription was made without request, express or implied, that the church do anything on the faith of it. Later, the church did incur expense to the knowledge of the promisor, and in the reasonable belief that the promise would be kept. We held the promise binding, though consideration there was none except upon the theory of a promissory estoppel. . . . So in Roberts v. Cobb, 103 N.Y. 600, 9 N.E. 500, and Keuka College v. Ray, 167 N.Y. 96, 60 N.E. 325, the bounds of consideration as fixed by the old doctrine were subjected to a like expansion. Very likely, conceptions of public policy have shaped, more or less subconsciously, the rulings thus made. Judges have been affected by the thought that "defences of that character" are "breaches of faith toward the public, and especially toward those engaged in the same enterprise, and an unwarrantable disappointment of the reasonable expectations of those interested." W.F. Allen, J., in Barnes v. Perine, supra, [at] 24. . . . The result speaks for itself irrespective of the motive. Decisions which have stood so long, and which are supported by so many considerations of public policy and reason, will not be overruled to save the symmetry of a concept which itself came into our law, not so much from any reasoned conviction of its justice, as from historical accidents of practice and procedure (8 Holdsworth, History of English Law, 7 et seq.). The concept survives as one of the distinctive features of our legal system. We have no thought to suggest that it is obsolete or on the way to be abandoned. As in the case of other concepts, however, the pressure of exceptions has led to irregularities of form.

It is in this background of precedent that we are to view the problem now before us. The background helps to an understanding of the implications inherent in subscription and acceptance. This is so though we may find in the end that without recourse to the innovation of promissory estoppel the transaction can be fitted within the mould of consideration as established by tradition.

The promisor wished to have a memorial to perpetuate her name. She imposed a condition that the "gift" should "be known as the Mary Yates Johnston Memorial Fund." The moment that the college accepted $1,000 as a payment on account, there was an assumption of a duty to do whatever acts were customary or reasonably necessary to maintain the memorial fairly and justly in the spirit of its creation. The college could not accept the money, and hold itself free thereafter from personal responsibility to give effect to the condition. . . . More is involved in the receipt of such a fund than a mere acceptance of money to be held to a corporate use. . . . The purpose of the founder would be unfairly thwarted or at least inadequately served if the college failed to communicate to the world . . . the title of the memorial. By implication it undertook, when it accepted a portion of the "gift," that in its circulars of information and in other customary ways, when making announcement of this scholarship, it would couple with the announcement the name of the donor. The donor was not at liberty to gain the benefit of such an undertaking upon the payment of a part and disappoint the expectation that there would be payment of the residue. If the college had stated after receiving $1,000 upon account of the subscription that it would apply the money to the prescribed use, but that in its circulars of information and when responding to prospective applicants it would deal with the fund as an anonymous donation, there is little doubt that the subscriber would have been at liberty to treat this statement as the repudiation of a duty impliedly assumed, a repudiation justifying a refusal to make payments in the future. Obligation in such circumstances is correlative and mutual. A case much in point is New Jersey Hospital v. Wright, 95 N.J.L. 462, 113 A. 144, where a subscription for the maintenance of a bed in a hospital was held to be enforceable by virtue of an implied promise by the hospital that the bed should be maintained in the name of the subscriber. . . . A parallel situation might arise upon the endowment of a chair or a fellowship in a university by the aid of annual payments with the condition that it should commemorate the name of the founder or that of a member of his family. The university would fail to live up to the fair meaning of its promise if it were to publish in its circulars of information and elsewhere the existence of a chair or a fellowship in the prescribed subject, and omit the benefactor's name. A duty to act in ways beneficial to the promisor and beyond the application of the fund to the mere uses of the trust would be cast upon the promisee by the acceptance of the money. We do not need to measure the extent either of benefit to the promisor or of detriment to the promisee implicit in this duty. "If a person chooses to make an extravagant promise for an inadequate consideration it is his own affair" (8 Holdsworth, History of English Law, p. 17). It was long ago said that "when a thing is to be done by the plaintiff, be it never so small, this is a sufficient consideration to ground an action" [Sturlyn v. Albany, 1587, Cro.Eliz. 67]. The longing for posthumous remembrance is an emotion not so weak as to justify us in saying that its gratification is a negligible good.

We think the duty assumed by the plaintiff to perpetuate the name of the founder of the memorial is sufficient in itself to give validity to the subscription within the rules that define consideration for a promise of that order. When the promisee subjected itself to such a duty at the implied request of the promisor, the result was the creation of a bilateral agreement. Williston, Contracts, §§ 60–a, 68, 90, 370. . . . There was a promise on the one side and on the other a return promise, made, it is true, by implication, but expressing an obligation that had been exacted as a condition of the payment. A bilateral agreement may exist though one of the mutual promises be a promise "implied in fact," an inference from conduct as opposed to an inference from words. . . . We think the fair inference to be drawn from the acceptance of a payment on account of the subscription is a promise by the college to do what may be necessary on its part to make the scholarship effective. . . . Moreover, the time to affix her name to the memorial will not arrive until the entire fund has been collected. The college may thus thwart the purpose of the payment on account if at liberty to reject a tender of the residue. It is no answer to say that a duty would then arise to make restitution of the money. If such a duty may be imposed, the only reason for its existence must be that there is then a failure of "consideration." To say that there is a failure of consideration is to concede that a consideration has been promised since otherwise it could not fail. No doubt there are times and situations in which limitations laid upon a promisee in connection with the use of what is paid by a subscriber lack the quality of a consideration, and are to be classed merely as conditions (Williston, Contracts, § 112; Page, Contracts, § 523). "It is often difficult to determine whether words of condition in a promise indicate a request for consideration or state a mere condition in a gratuitous promise. An aid, though not a conclusive test in determining which construction of the promise is more reasonable is an inquiry whether the happening of the condition will be a benefit to the promisor. If so, it is a fair inference that the happening was requested as a consideration" (Williston, supra, § 112).* Such must be the meaning of this transaction unless we are prepared to hold that the college may keep the payment on account, and thereafter nullify the scholarship which is to preserve the memory of the subscriber. The fair implication to be gathered from the whole transaction is assent to the condition and the assumption of a duty to go forward with performance. . . . The subscriber does not say: I hand you $1,000, and you may make up your mind later, after my death, whether you will undertake to commemorate my name. What she says in effect is this: I hand you $1,000, and if you are unwilling to commemorate me, the time to speak is now.

The conclusion thus reached makes it needless to consider whether, aside from the feature of a memorial, a promissory estoppel may result from the assumption of a duty to apply the fund, so far as already paid, to

---

* [Professor Williston preceded the quoted passage with an illustration that became quite famous in legal education. The illustration, known as the "tramp case," is as follows: "If a benevolent man says to a tramp: 'If you go around the corner to the clothing shop there, you may purchase an overcoat on my credit,' no reasonable person would understand that the short walk was requested as the consideration for the promise, but that in the event of the tramp going to the shop the promisor would make him a gift. Yet the walk to the shop is in its nature capable of being consideration. It is a legal detriment to the tramp to make the walk, and the only reason why the walk is not consideration is because on a reasonable construction it must be held that the walk was not requested as the price of the promise, but was merely a condition of a gratuitous promise."—Eds.]

special purposes not mandatory under the provisions of the college charter (the support and education of students preparing for the ministry), an assumption induced by the belief that other payments sufficient in amount to make the scholarship effective would be added to the fund thereafter upon the death of the subscriber. . . .

The judgment of the Appellate Division and that of the Trial Term should be reversed, and judgment ordered for the plaintiff as prayed for in the complaint, with costs in all courts.

KELLOGG, J. (dissenting). The Chief Judge finds in the expression "In loving memory this gift shall be known as the Mary Yates Johnston Memorial Fund" an offer . . . to contract with Allegheny College. The expression makes no such appeal to me. Allegheny College was not requested to perform any act through which the sum offered might bear the title by which the offeror states that it shall be known. The sum offered was termed a "gift" by the offeror. . . . I can see no reason why we should strain ourselves to make it, not a gift, but a trade. . . . To me the words used merely expressed an expectation or wish on the part of the donor and failed to exact the return of an adequate consideration. But if an offer indeed was present, then clearly it was an offer to enter into a unilateral contract. The offeror was to be bound provided the offeree performed such acts as might be necessary to make the gift offered become known under the proposed name. This is evidently the thought of the Chief Judge, for he says: "She imposed a condition that the 'gift' should be known as the Mary Yates Johnston Memorial Fund." In other words, she proposed to exchange her offer of a donation in return for acts to be performed. Even so there was never any acceptance of the offer and, therefore, no contract, for the acts requested have never been performed. The gift has never been made known as demanded. Indeed, the requested acts, under the very terms of the assumed offer, could never have been performed at a time to convert the offer into a promise. This is so for the reason that the donation was not to take effect until after the death of the donor, and by her death her offer was withdrawn. (Williston on Contracts, § 62.) Clearly, although a promise of the college to make the gift known, as requested, may be implied, that promise was not the acceptance of an offer which gave rise to a contract. The donor stipulated for acts, not promises. "In order to make a bargain it is necessary that the acceptor shall give in return for the offer or the promise exactly the consideration which the offeror requests. If an act is requested, that very act and no other must be given. If a promise is requested, that promise must be made absolutely and unqualifiedly." (Williston on Contracts, § 73). "It does not follow that an offer becomes a promise because it is accepted; it may be, and frequently is, conditional, and then it does not become a promise until the conditions are satisfied; and in case of offers for a consideration, the performance of the consideration is always deemed a condition." (Langdell, Summary of the Law of Contracts, § 4.) It seems clear to me that there was here no offer, no acceptance of an offer, and no contract. Neither do I agree with the Chief Judge that this court "found consideration present where the general law of contract at least as then declared, would have said that it was absent" in the cases of Barnes v. Perine, 12 N.Y. 18 [and] Keuka College v. Ray, 167 N.Y. 96. In the Keuka College case an offer to contract, in consideration of the performance of certain acts by the offeree, was converted into a promise by the actual performance of those acts. This form of contract has been known to the law from time immemorial (Langdell, § 46) and for at least a century longer than the other type, a bilateral contract. (Williston, § 13.) It may be that the basis of the decision in Barnes v. Perine was the same as in the Keuka College case. . . . However, even if the basis of the decisions be a so-called "promissory estoppel," nevertheless they initiated no new doctrine. A so-called "promissory estoppel," although not so termed, was held sufficient by Lord Mansfield and his fellow judges as far back as the year 1765. Pillans v. Van Mierop, 3 Burr. 1663. Such a doctrine may be an anomaly; it is not a novelty. Therefore, I can see no ground for the suggestion that the ancient rule which makes consideration necessary to the formation of every contract is in danger of effacement through any decisions of this court. To me that is a cause for gratulation rather than regret. However, the discussion may be beside the mark, for I do not understand that the holding about to be made in this case is other than a holding that consideration was given to convert the offer into a promise. With that result I cannot agree and, accordingly, must dissent.

POUND, CRANE, LEHMAN and O'BRIEN, JJ., concur with CARDOZO, C.J.; KELLOGG, J., dissents in opinion, in which ANDREWS, J., concurs.

Konefsky, How to Read, or at Least Not Misread, Cardozo in the *Allegheny College* Case

36 Buffalo L.Rev. 645, 683–687 (1988)

"Exactly what was the problem Cardozo faced in this case? Litigation is easiest when strong facts mesh with firm law, but a good lawyer can make do with either strong facts or firm law. At first blush, Cardozo had neither. . . . [I]f anything was clear about classical contract law, it was that donative promises were unenforceable. . . .

"[Hamer v. Sidway] was hardly a secure precedent around which a great edifice had been erected. Indeed, it was more of a lighthouse than a castle. And promissory estoppel was hardly developed beyond the most classic of charitable subscription cases. With facts as weak as in *Allegheny College*, it would have been difficult for most judges to move the doctrine along in the direction that Cardozo wished. Normally, strong facts drag the doctrine with them. Yet, here again Cardozo's craft shows how much can be done with just a few raw materials, for he manages to push forward simultaneously on both doctrinal fronts. Simply by using *Hamer*, drawing a few inferences about the nature of reasonable conduct, and turning a piece of Holmes's objective theory on its head to create liability rather than limit it, Cardozo was able both to reinforce *Hamer* as a precedent and suggest a new and at the same time familiar way of thinking about what might be consideration. . . .

"By positioning, if only in dictum, promissory estoppel not as an exception to consideration doctrine, but squarely within it, Cardozo opened the possibility (though never realized by him or his court) that in the next case promissory estoppel could be found in a commercial circumstance. Bargain theory was used to make all doctrinal moves appear as mainstream as possible. To make such gains, in a two-front war with such poor troops on such unpromising terrain, bordered on the inspired.

"What are we left with at the end of this opinion? . . . [W]hatever consideration is, it is, at the least, an expansive, flexible and adaptable doctrine. . . . [A]s evidence of that insight, the concept of promissory estoppel is introduced, not as an exception to consideration doctrine, but as a continuation of the process of enlarging it. In other words, promissory estoppel is used informatively, as an historical lesson, and instrumentally, as a means to expand consideration."

––––––––

Siegel v. Spear & Co.
234 N.Y. 479, 138 N.E. 414 (1923)

Decided four years before *Allegheny College*, this case was one of the "signposts on the road" identified by Judge Cardozo. Siegel had purchased furniture from Spear & Co., giving a mortgage to secure payment of the price and a promise not to remove the furniture from his New York apartment until it was paid for. Desiring to leave the city for the summer months, Siegel visited Spear's credit officer, McGrath, to discuss storing the furniture. McGrath agreed to "keep it for him free of charge." Siegel alleged that these arrangements included a promise by McGrath to insure the furniture for Siegel's benefit, made in this way: "At that time he said, 'You had better transfer your insurance policy over to our warehouse.' I said 'I haven't any insurance. I never thought of taking it out. . . .' But I said: 'Before the furniture comes down I will have my insurance man, who insures my life, have the furniture insured and transferred over to your place.' He said, 'That won't be necessary to get that from him; I will do it for you; it will be a good deal cheaper; I handle lots of insurance; when you get the next bill—you can send a check for that with the next installment.'" Siegel delivered the furniture to Spear in May. A month later it was destroyed by fire. No insurance had been purchased. Siegel sued Spear for his loss, recovered judgment below, and preserved his victory in the Court of Appeals against the claim that McGrath's promise lacked consideration. That court (including Cardozo) proceeded in this way:

"[T]here was in the nature of the case a consideration. . . . It is, of course, a fact that the defendant undertook to store the plaintiff's property without any compensation. The fact that it had a chattel mortgage [on the property] did not affect its relationship as a bailee without pay. Under these circumstances it was not liable for the destruction of the goods by fire unless due to its gross neglect. . . . There is no such element in this case.

"But if in connection with taking the goods McGrath also voluntarily undertook to procure insurance for the plaintiff's benefit, the promise was part of the whole transaction and was linked up with the gratuitous bailment. The bailee . . . was then under as much of an obligation to procure insurance as he was to take care of the goods.

"When McGrath stated that he would insure the furniture it was still in the plaintiff's possession. It was after his statements and promises that the plaintiff sent the furniture to the storehouse. The defendant or McGrath entered upon the execution of the trust. It is in this particular that this case differs from Thorne v. Deas (4 Johns. 84, 99) so much relied upon by the defendant. In that case A and B were joint owners of a vessel. A voluntarily undertook to get the vessel insured but neglected to do so. The vessel having been lost at sea it was held that no action would lie against A for the nonperformance of his promise, although B had relied upon that promise to his loss. It was said that there was no consideration for the promise. In that case there was the mere naked promise of A that he would insure the vessel. B parted with nothing to A.

He gave up possession of none of his property to A, nor of any interest in his vessel. The case would have been decided differently, no doubt, if he had. As Chancellor Kent said in referring to the earlier cases: 'There was no dispute or doubt, but that an action upon the case lay for a misfeasance, in the breach of a trust undertaken voluntarily.' . . .

"Where one had gratuitously undertaken to carry the money of a bailor to a certain place and deliver it to another and after receiving the money the bailee gave it to a neighbor who undertook to make delivery and lost it, it was held that the bailee had violated his trust in handling the money, that he was guilty of gross negligence in not fulfilling the terms of the bailment. . . .

"From this aspect of the case we think there was a consideration for the agreement to insure. This renders it unnecessary to determine whether the plaintiff in refraining from insuring through his own agent at the suggestion of McGrath surrendered any right which would furnish a consideration for McGrath's promise.

"I find that Thorne v. Deas (supra) has been seldom cited upon this question of consideration and whether or not we would feel bound to follow it today must be left open until the question comes properly before us."

NOTE

A decade after *Siegel*, a lower New York court, faced with another gratuitous promise respecting insurance (a promise to file an insured's proofs of loss in a timely manner), sought to reconcile the relevant New York precedents. It concluded: "The Court of Appeals having, in [*Siegel*], declined to overrule Thorne v. Deas, and having, in [*Allegheny College*], extended the doctrine of promissory estoppel only to the law relating to charitable subscriptions, we think we should go no further." Thorne v. Deas was therefore held controlling where defendant was at most guilty of nonfeasance. Comfort v. McCorkle, 149 Misc. 826, 268 N.Y.S. 192 (N.Y.Sup.Ct.1933). It should be noted that, during this period, courts elsewhere were applying promissory estoppel (and § 90 of the first Restatement), not the misfeasance-nonfeasance test, when gratuitous promises to insure were found to have induced serious reliance. E.g., Lusk–Harbison–Jones, Inc. v. Universal Credit Co., 164 Miss. 693, 145 So. 623 (1933).

I. & I. Holding Corp. v. Gainsburg
276 N.Y. 427, 12 N.E.2d 532 (1938)

Defendant Gainsburg signed a pledge to pay $5,000 in four annual installments to the Beth Israel Hospital Ass'n, "to aid and assist the . . . Ass'n in its humanitarian work and in consideration of others contributing to the same purposes." Beth Israel assigned its rights to plaintiff, who sued on the pledge alleging that "the said Beth Israel Hospital Ass'n proceeded in its humanitarian work, obtained other like subscriptions, expended large sums of money and incurred large liabilities." *Held*, the complaint stated a cause of action. Under these allegations, evidence could be admitted to prove that the subscription agreement was an offer of a unilateral contract binding when acted on. An invitation or request to perform the services need not be expressed, it can be implied. It is true that court decisions sustaining subscriptions for charitable purposes are subject to criticism "from a legalistic standpoint," but they have been enforced for a long time. It is not necessary to base the decision on promissory estoppel. It is enough that a request or invitation to the promisee to go on with its work can be implied.

LEHMAN, J., dissented, urging that there must be allegation and proof that the promise constituted a request which induced the promisee to promise or perform some act that it would not have promised or performed except for the inducement. "[Plaintiff] must prove that [it] changed its position . . . because of the promise, or—if we accept the doctrine of promissory estoppel—as a consequence of the promise. . . . Mere continuance of its charitable work as it might have done even if no promise had been made does not constitute consideration for the promise or give rise to a promissory estoppel."

————

RESTATEMENT OF CONTRACTS, SECOND

PROMISSORY ESTOPPEL

Section 90. Promise Reasonably Inducing Action or Forbearance

(1) A promise which the promisor should reasonably expect to induce action or forbearance on the part of the promisee or a third person and which does induce such action or forbearance is binding if injustice can be avoided only by enforcement of the promise. The remedy granted for breach may be limited as justice requires.

(2) A charitable subscription or a marriage settlement is binding under Subsection (1) without proof that the promise induced action or forbearance.

————

Salsbury v. Northwestern Bell Tel. Co.
221 N.W.2d 609 (Iowa 1974)

Defendant by letter promised to contribute $15,000 to a newly-formed college. The college failed after a brief period of operation, and defendant did not pay its pledge. Iowa's highest court held the promise enforceable without proof of detrimental reliance, reasoning that a requirement of evidence of reliance might result in the enforcement of fewer charitable promises. After criticizing cases that enforce charitable subscriptions "only on a fictional finding of consideration," the court rested on this ground: "Restatement of Contracts, Second, includes a new subparagraph, § 90(2), [providing that] 'A charitable subscription or a marriage settlement is binding . . . without proof that the promise induced action or forbearance.' We believe public policy supports this view. . . . It is true some fund raising campaigns are not conducted on a plan which calls for subscriptions to be binding. In such cases we do not hesitate to hold them not binding. . . . However, where a subscription is unequivocal the pledgor should be made to keep his word."

NOTE

In Congregation Kadimah Toras–Moshe v. DeLeo, supra p. 199, the court required consideration or reliance for enforcement of gift promises to charities. Moreover, in portions of the opinion not reproduced earlier, the *DeLeo* court (1) rejected plaintiff's claim that the Massachusetts decisions on charitable subscriptions "require[ ] so little consideration or reliance that, in practice, none is required," and (2) bypassed plaintiff's invitation to adopt Rest.2d § 90(2), concluding that this provision, when read in the light of its official comment and the language of § 90(1), means that consideration or reliance are not "absolute requirements" but remain "relevant considerations." The court then proceeded to find "no injustice" in refusing to enforce the decedent's promise of $25,000, finding it "entirely unsupported" by either consideration or reliance. 405 Mass. at 368, 540 N.E.2d at 693–694. The promise in *DeLeo* was oral, not in writing. Look back at the opinion to see what, if anything, the court might have done differently had consideration or reliance been shown.

The few courts that have explicitly addressed the *Salsbury* decision seem to have rejected it. E.g., Arrowsmith v. Mercantile–Safe Deposit & Trust Co., 313 Md. 334, 545 A.2d 674 (1988) ("the legislative process is more finely and continuously attuned for the societal fact-finding and evaluating required for resolution of this exclusively public policy-based argument"). Nevertheless, it is commonly believed that charitable subscriptions are enforced in this country, and that courts that have enforced such promises on the basis of promissory estoppel have done so despite the absence of significant reliance.

Stewart v. Cendant Mobility Services Corp.

Supreme Court of Connecticut, 2003.
837 A.2d 736.

PALMER, J. This appeal arises out of an action brought by the plaintiff, Elizabeth M. Stewart, against the defendant, Cendant Mobility Services Corporation (Cendant), her former employer, for damages resulting from Cendant's allegedly wrongful termination of her employment. Following a trial, a jury returned a verdict in part for the plaintiff, finding in her favor on her claims of promissory estoppel and . . . and awarding her $850,000 on those claims. The trial court rendered judgment in accordance with the jury verdict from which Cendant appeals. . . .

The jury reasonably could have found the following facts. The plaintiff and her husband were employed by Cendant, which provides relocation services to domestic and international corporations and their employees. Among other things, Cendant assists its corporate clients in finding new homes for their relocating employees and in selling those employees' old homes. The plaintiff worked in the sales division and was considered one of the top producers in the relocation services industry. The plaintiff's husband was an executive in the operations division at Cendant.

In April 1998, Cendant underwent a major corporate reorganization. Soon thereafter, Cendant terminated the plaintiff's husband from employment. At the time of her husband's termination, the plaintiff held the position of vice president of sales.

Because the plaintiff believed that her husband was likely to seek employment with one of Cendant's competitors in the relocation services field, she spoke with James Simon, Cendant's executive vice president of sales and the plaintiff's immediate supervisor, about the matter shortly after her husband's termination. The plaintiff explained to Simon that she was concerned about how her employment with Cendant might be affected if her husband ultimately accepted a position with a competitor. Simon told the plaintiff that she should not be concerned and that her husband's reemployment in the relocation services business would have no bearing on her employment with Cendant. Simon further represented to the plaintiff that Kevin Kelleher, Cendant's president and chief executive officer, also wished to assure the plaintiff that she had no reason to be concerned about her continued status as a highly valued employee in the event that her husband were to become associated with a competitor. On the basis of Simon's assurances, the plaintiff continued in her position with Cendant and did not pursue other employment opportunities.

On or about March 5, 1999, Cendant learned that the plaintiff's husband was performing consulting services for a competing firm. Upon obtaining this information, Cendant reduced the plaintiff's duties and limited her interaction with clients. Cendant also requested that the plaintiff verbally agree to the provisions of a document drafted by Cendant that purported to delineate her obligations to Cendant in relation to her husband's work on behalf of any competitor of Cendant. On June 11, 1999, Cendant allegedly terminated the plaintiff's employment when she declined to agree to the provisions of that document.

Thereafter, the plaintiff commenced this action against Cendant. In count one of her complaint, the plaintiff alleged that her conversation with Simon gave rise to an oral contract of employment and that her discharge by Cendant constituted a breach of that contract. In count two, the plaintiff claimed that her discharge violated an implied covenant of good faith and fair dealing. In count three, which is predicated on a theory of promissory estoppel, the plaintiff alleged that she had relied to her detriment on Simon's promise that her employment with Cendant would not be affected adversely by her husband's probable future employment with a competitor. . . .

Following a trial, the jury returned a verdict in favor of Cendant with respect to the plaintiff's claims of breach of contract and breach of an implied covenant of good faith and fair dealing. The jury returned a verdict in favor of the plaintiff with respect to her claims of promissory estoppel and . . . awarded her $850,000. Cendant filed motions to set aside the verdict and for judgment notwithstanding the verdict on the promissory estoppel and negligent misrepresentation claims, contending that the evidence was insufficient to support the jury's verdict in favor of the plaintiff on those claims. The trial court denied Cendant's postverdict motions and rendered judgment in accordance with the jury's verdict, from which Cendant appealed.

On appeal, Cendant challenges the trial court's denial of its motions to set aside the verdict and for judgment notwithstanding the verdict. Cendant renews its contention that the evidence was insufficient to support the jury's verdict with respect to the plaintiff's promissory estoppel claim. Cendant's contention is essentially twofold. First, Cendant claims that its purported promise to the plaintiff lacked the requisite clarity and definiteness necessary to establish promissory estoppel. Second, Cendant claims that the plaintiff failed to present evidence sufficient to establish that she had relied to her detriment on any such promise. We reject both of these claims and, therefore, affirm the judgment of the trial court inasmuch as the jury award of $850,000 is sustainable on the basis of the plaintiff's promissory estoppel claim. . . .

Cendant first contends that the jury reasonably could not have found that Simon's representations to the plaintiff were sufficiently clear and definite to constitute a promise for purposes of a claim of promissory estoppel. We disagree.

The following additional evidence and procedural history are necessary to our resolution of this issue. On direct examination, the plaintiff testified that, after her husband was fired, she became concerned that his termination and likely reemployment in the relocation services industry adversely would affect her employment with Cendant. The plaintiff testified that she "specifically asked [Simon] what would happen [to her] if [her husband competed] in the industry." According to the plaintiff, Simon replied that "he had absolutely no concerns about [her husband] entering the marketplace." The plaintiff also testified that Simon told her that "he had tremendous respect for both [the plaintiff] and [the plaintiff's husband and] that [they] had a lot of integrity." The plaintiff testified further that Simon told her that "[h]e had trust and faith in [her] and in [the plaintiff's husband] and he knew that [they] would be able to keep [their] lives separate and [that] he had absolutely no concerns about [her husband] entering the marketplace." According to the plaintiff, Simon "said that he would talk to [Kelleher] on her behalf . . . [and] assured [her] that this was not going to be a problem and that [she] was a highly valued employee and there was nothing to worry about."

The plaintiff further explained that Simon thereafter reported to her that "he had spoken to [Kelleher] about [her] concerns and that [Kelleher] wanted [Simon] to assure [her] that [she] was very highly valued, that [she] was an integral part of the company, [that] he had tremendous respect for [her] integrity and [that] there were no problems whatsoever with [the plaintiff] continuing the job in the event [that her husband] competed." On cross-examination, the plaintiff acknowledged that when she and Simon spoke, they were discussing a hypothetical future occurrence because she was not certain whether her husband would join another relocation services company. The plaintiff further testified on cross-examination that she did not believe that she was negotiating an employment contract when she spoke with Simon.

At the conclusion of the court's instructions to the jury, the jury was provided with a special verdict form containing interrogatories relating to each of the plaintiff's claims. With respect to the plaintiff's breach of contract claim, the jury was asked, inter alia, whether it found that Cendant had "made a definite offer sufficient to form a contractual agreement with the plaintiff. . . ." The jury answered no. With respect to the plaintiff's promissory estoppel claim, the jury was asked, inter alia, whether it found that Cendant had "made a clear, definite promise to [the plaintiff] . . . upon which it should have expected she would rely. . . ." The jury responded in the affirmative.

The following legal principles govern our analysis of Cendant's claim. "Under the law of contract, a promise is generally not enforceable unless it is supported by consideration. . . . This court has recognized, however, the development of liability in contract for action induced by reliance upon a promise, despite the absence of common-law consideration normally required to bind a promisor. . . . Section 90 of the *Restatement [(Second) of Contracts]* states that under the doctrine of promissory estoppel [a] promise which the promisor should reasonably expect to induce action or forbearance on the part of the promisee or a third person and which does induce such action or forbearance is binding if injustice can be avoided only by enforcement of the promise. [1 Restatement (Second), Contracts § 90, p. 242 (1981).] A fundamental element of promissory estoppel, therefore, is the existence of a clear and definite promise which a promisor could reasonably have expected to induce reliance. Thus, a promisor is not liable to a promisee who has relied on a promise if, judged by an objective standard, he had no reason to expect any reliance at all." D'Ulisse-Cupo v. Board of Directors of Notre Dame High School, 202 Conn. 206, 213, 520 A.2d 217 (1987).

Although the promise must be clear and definite, it need not be the equivalent of an offer to enter into a contract because "[t]he prerequisite for . . . application [of the doctrine of promissory estoppel] is a *promise* and not a bargain and *not* an *offer*." (Emphasis added.) 3 A. Corbin, Contracts (Rev. Ed. 1996) § 8.9, p. 29; This, of course, is consistent with the principle that, although "[a]n offer is nearly always a promise"; 1 E. Farnsworth, Contracts (2d Ed.1998) § 3.3, p. 188; all promises are not offers. See 1 Restatement (Second), supra, at § 24, comment (b), p. 72 ("[w]hether or not a proposal is a promise, it is not an offer unless it specifies a promise or performance by the offeree as the price or consideration to be given by him").

Additionally, the promise must reflect a present intent to commit as distinguished from a mere statement of intent to contract in the future. "[A] mere expression of intention, hope, desire, or opinion, which shows no real commitment, cannot be expected to induce reliance"; 3 A. Corbin, Contracts, supra, at § 8.9, pp. 29-30; and, therefore, is not sufficiently promissory. The requirements of clarity and definiteness are the determinative factors in deciding whether the statements are indeed expressions of commitment as opposed to expressions of intention, hope, desire or opinion. Finally, whether a representation rises to the level of a promise is generally a question of fact, to be determined in light of the circumstances under which the representation was made.

Applying the foregoing principles, we conclude that there was sufficient evidence to support the jury's finding that Simon's representations to the plaintiff were sufficiently clear and definite to constitute a promise that her employment with Cendant would not be affected adversely if her husband subsequently secured employment with a competing relocation services firm. The plaintiff testified that: (1) she had approached Simon because she was concerned that her husband's employment with a competitor would have a negative effect on her employment with Cendant; (2) she expressed that concern in plain terms to Simon; and (3) Simon responded in equally unambiguous terms, in his own capacity and on behalf of Kelleher, that the plaintiff had no need to worry because her husband's future employment with a competitor would pose "no problems whatsoever" for her. On the basis of this testimony, the jury reasonably could have found that Simon's representations to the plaintiff constituted a clear and definite promise that her position with Cendant would not be affected adversely if her husband were to secure employment with a competing firm.

Relying primarily on our decision in *D'Ulisse-Cupo,* Cendant contends that, under our law of promissory estoppel, all promises in the employer-employee context, to be actionable, must contain the standard material terms of a contract of employment and clearly reflect an intent by the promisor to undertake conventional contractual liability. In other words, Cendant contends that any such promise must contain all of the elements of an offer to enter into a contract. We conclude that our holding in *D'Ulisse-Cupo* is not so broad.

In *D'Ulisse-Cupo,* the plaintiff, Maria D'Ulisse-Cupo, brought an action against the board of directors (board) and principal of Notre Dame High School (school) in West Haven. The board declined to offer D'Ulisse-Cupo a new contract after her prior contract to teach at the school had expired. D'Ulisse-Cupo alleged that authorized representatives of the board had made certain representations to her prior to the expiration of her teaching contract that suggested that she would be offered a new contract. D'Ulisse-Cupo alleged further that she relied on those representations to her detriment.

We concluded that the "representations [did] not invoke a cause of action for promissory estoppel because they [were] neither sufficiently promissory nor sufficiently definite to support contractual liability." We explained that the "representations manifested no present intention on the part of the [board] to undertake immediate contractual obligations to [D'Ulisse-Cupo]"; and that "none of the representations contained any of the material terms that would be essential to an employment contract, such as terms regarding the duration and conditions of [D'Ulisse-Cupo's] employment . . . and her salary and fringe benefits." Finally, we concluded that, "[a]t most, the [board] made representations to [D'Ulisse-Cupo] concerning the expectation of a future contract, but . . . stopped short of making [D'Ulisse-Cupo] a definite promise of employment on which she could reasonably have relied."

Although we acknowledge that certain language in *D'Ulisse-Cupo* might suggest that, for purposes of a claim of promissory estoppel, the promise upon which the promisee relies must be no less specific and definite than an offer to enter into a contract, we reject Cendant's claim urging that interpretation. Our observations in *D'Ulisse-Cupo* that the representations did not contain the material terms of a new employment contract and otherwise did not reflect an intent by the board to undertake immediate contractual liability were necessary to our determination of whether, in circumstances involving an alleged promise to rehire a employee under contract, the representations constituted a promise to commit or mere expressions of a future intent to enter into a contract. In other words, because D'Ulisse-Cupo alleged that she had been promised a contract of employment, our consideration of whether the contract terms were part of that purported promise and whether the representations reflected an intention to bind the board to a future contract was central to our resolution of D'Ulisse-Cupo's claim that those representations were sufficiently clear and definite such that her reliance on them was reasonable. Thus, when *D'Ulisse-Cupo* is viewed in the context of the particular claim addressed in that case, it is apparent that the language upon which Cendant relies is properly understood as explaining why the representations regarding a future employment contract were insufficiently promissory and definite to be actionable, and not properly understood as indicating that, for purposes of the doctrine of promissory estoppel, any promise relating to employment must be the equivalent of an offer to enter into a contract.

Finally, the present case is readily distinguishable from *D'Ulisse-Cupo.* Although Simon's representations related to the plaintiff's employment, they were far more limited in scope than the representations at issue in *D'Ulisse-Cupo.* Simon promised the plaintiff only that her employment would not be affected adversely by her husband's future employment with a competitor of Cendant. The plaintiff otherwise remained an at-will employee subject to termination at Cendant's sole discretion. Consequently, the issue of whether Simon's representations were sufficiently clear and definite to constitute a promise upon which the plaintiff reasonably could have relied is significantly narrower than the issue that was presented in *D'Ulisse-Cupo,* namely, whether the representations of the representatives of the school board constituted a promise of an entirely new employment contract even when those representations did not contain terms and conditions that necessarily comprise any such contractual arrangement. . . .

The defendant next claims that the evidence was insufficient to establish that the plaintiff detrimentally relied on Simon's representations. We also reject this claim.

The following additional facts are necessary to our disposition of this claim. As we previously have noted, the plaintiff testified on direct examination that she had approached Simon because she wanted to know whether, in light of her husband's likely future employment with a competing relocation services firm, she should stay at Cendant or seek other opportunities within the industry. After Simon assured her that she would suffer no adverse consequences in the event that her husband were to accept employment with a competitor, the plaintiff decided to remain at Cendant and "did not pursue other employment opportunities. . . ." The plaintiff testified during cross-examination, however, that, if Simon had told her that her husband's employment with another relocation services firm would pose a problem, she was not sure "what [she] would have done." The plaintiff also testified that when Simon made his representations to her, she was not investigating other employment opportunities. Additionally, the plaintiff acknowledged that she was an at-will employee and, therefore, subject to discharge at any time.

The plaintiff also adduced evidence that she was one of a relatively small number of highly talented salespeople in the relocation services industry. Indeed, Kelleher testified that the plaintiff would be regarded as a "valued asset" both within Cendant and in the industry on the basis of her productivity. Simon testified that such salespeople have no difficulty finding employment in the relocation services field. According to Simon, salespeople with the plaintiff's credentials "can walk in virtually anywhere" and receive a job offer.

In addition, offers to top performers in the relocation services industry typically include a signing bonus equivalent to some or all of the value of the employee's "pipeline," the industry term for the estimated total commissions due a salesperson, at a specific point in time, on the basis of consummated sales for which the company has not yet been paid in full. Because salespeople do not receive pipeline commissions if they leave a company to join a competitor before the company is paid by the client, signing bonuses are used as a recruitment tool by relocation service companies to induce salespeople employed by other companies to forgo their pipeline commissions and join the recruiting company. Although there are numerous salespeople who, like the plaintiff, do not receive accrued but uncollected commissions, those salespeople, in contrast to salespeople who are recruited by a competitor, are not sufficiently marketable to command a signing bonus. Finally, evidence adduced at trial established that the approximate value of the plaintiff's pipeline when she allegedly was terminated was $812,700, a sum that she never was paid.

To succeed on a claim of promissory estoppel, the party seeking to invoke the doctrine must have relied on the other party's promise. That reliance, of course, may take the form of action or forbearance. Nevertheless, the asserted reliance, regardless of its form, must result in a detrimental change in the plaintiff's position. Thus, "[t]o 'rely,' in the law of promissory estoppel, is not merely to do something in response to the inducement offered by the promise. There must be a cost to the promisee of doing it." Cosgrove v. Bartolotta, 150 F.3d 729, 733 (7th Cir. 1998).

Moreover, "[i]f the claimed reliance consists of the promisee's forbearance rather than an affirmative action, proof that this forbearance was induced by the promise requires a showing that the promisee *could have* acted." (Emphasis added.) 1 E. Farnsworth, supra, at § 2.19, p. 164. Implicit in this principle is the requirement of proof that the plaintiff actually *would have acted* in the absence of the promise.

In the present case, the plaintiff claimed that she relied on Simon's representations by forgoing other employment opportunities that would have resulted in a signing bonus approximately equivalent to her pipeline. Cendant contends that the plaintiff failed to adduce sufficient evidence to establish that she: (1) could have obtained such other employment; (2) would have sought employment elsewhere if Simon had told her that her position at Cendant would be affected adversely if her husband accepted a position with a competing firm; and (3) was not harmed by continuing as an employee of Cendant even if she did so in reliance on Simon's representations. We disagree with each of these contentions.

First, with respect to Cendant's claim that the evidence was inadequate to establish that the plaintiff could have secured a sales position with another relocation services firm, Simon testified that talented salespeople in the relocation services industry—and it was undisputed that the plaintiff was such a salesperson—frequently obtained such positions. Although, as Cendant notes, the plaintiff, herself, testified that she was unaware that any of those positions were available at the time she would have been seeking such a position, the jury nevertheless reasonably could have found, on the basis of Simon's testimony, that the plaintiff likely could have secured such a position if she had sought to do so.

With respect to the issue of whether the plaintiff *would* have departed Cendant if she had not received Simon's assurances, the plaintiff testified that she approached Simon about her husband's likely future employment with a competitor because she needed to decide whether to stay with Cendant or to look for a position elsewhere. The plaintiff also indicated that she elected to stay at Cendant rather than to seek other employment because of Simon's representations that her position at Cendant would not be affected negatively in the event that her husband secured employment with a competing firm. Although the plaintiff also testified that she was unsure what she would have done if Simon had not made those assurances, it was within the province of the jury to resolve any possible inconsistencies in the plaintiff's testimony in a manner favorable to the plaintiff. Thus, the jury reasonably could have found that the plaintiff would have left Cendant if Simon had not assured her as he did.

Finally, Cendant contends that the plaintiff suffered no harm by opting not to seek employment elsewhere after she had spoken with Simon about her husband's likely future employment with a competitor. We disagree. In remaining at Cendant, the plaintiff not only abandoned any opportunity to secure a position with another relocation services company, she also forwent a signing bonus that the jury reasonably could have found approximated the value of her pipeline. Accordingly, we conclude that the evidence was sufficient to warrant the jury's finding that the plaintiff reasonably relied on Simon's representations to her financial detriment.

The judgment is affirmed. . . .

———

NOTE: RELIANCE ON CONTRACT ADJUSTMENTS

Many promissory estoppel cases arise after a contractual relationship typically has been established, and the rendering of performance has begun. One of the parties then promises to modify or eliminate a term of the contract, or, perhaps, to discharge the contract altogether. The rub is that the promise is unsupported by consideration, for, as we shall see, it is hornbook law that modifications of a valid agreement, to be enforceable, must be supported by consideration or a common-law substitute.

The case of Fried v. Fisher, 328 Pa. 497, 196 A. 39 (1938), provides an example. In late 1932, Fried entered into a four-year lease of a building to Fisher and Brill, partners in a florist business. About a year into the lease, Fisher decided to dissolve his partnership with Brill and get out of the florist business, in order to open a restaurant in another city. This was acceptable to Brill, who agreed to take over the lease. Fisher sought out Fried on two occasions, each time telling Fried of his plans and making clear his desire to be released from all obligation under the lease. Fried replied that he "was perfectly satisfied if they [Brill and his son] assumed the balance of the lease, . . . just forget about it," and that "I am satisfied to have Mr. Brill assume the lease, and if it is going to help you any to get started in business, I release you." Thereupon Fisher dissolved the partnership with Brill and opened a restaurant, and Brill continued the florist business on the leased premises. Brill defaulted about a year and a half later, and Fried commenced suit against both Fisher and Brill to enforce the lease. A jury verdict for Fisher was affirmed on appeal, the court holding that Fried's promise to release Fisher was fully enforceable and a complete defense. The court said:

> It is beyond the pale of argument that a promise by a creditor to release one of the partners of a debtor firm from liability for an obligation is, in the absence of qualifying facts, legally unenforceable for want of consideration. . . . The necessity of consideration to support a contract . . . still remains firmly entrenched as one of the fundamental principles of the common law. See opinion by Cardozo, C.J., in Allegheny College v. National Chautauqua County Bank, 246 N.Y. 369, 159 N.E. 173. But just as the law has consistently upheld the doctrine that, under given circumstances, a person may be estopped by his conduct, his statements, or even his silence, if another has thereby been induced to act to his detriment, so from the earliest times there was recognized the principle that an estoppel might similarly arise from the making of a promise, even though without consideration, if it was intended that the promise be relied upon and in fact it was relied upon, and a refusal to enforce it would be virtually to sanction the perpetration of fraud or result in other injustice. . . . In recent years there has been adopted the phrase "promissory estoppel," [which by its language] indicat[es] that the basis of the doctrine is not so much one of contract, with a substitute

for consideration, as an application of the general principle of estoppel to certain situations. . . .

Illustrative cases abound in the reports. . . . Its most frequent application has been to cases in which a person announces his intention of abandoning an existing right, and thereby leads another, relying thereon, to some action or forbearance. Such cases have sometimes been referred to as well-recognized exceptions to the general proposition that, in order to give rise to an estoppel, a representation must relate to an existing fact and not be merely an expression of opinion or a promise of future performance. . . .

The facts in the present case constitute a situation to which [promissory estoppel] peculiarly applies, because they involve the announcement by plaintiff of the intended abandonment of his right to enforce Fisher's liability for the rent, knowing that such announcement would be relied upon by him to the extent of his embarking upon a new business venture. All the safeguarding features thrown around the doctrine of promissory estoppel to prevent its too loose application—that the promise be one likely to induce action, that such action be of a definite and substantial character, that the circumstances be such that injustice can be avoided only by the enforcement of the promise—are here present. Plaintiff contends that it was not shown that Fisher suffered a loss in the restaurant business, but he did substantially change his position by entering into that business upon the faith of plaintiff's promise, and when, at the trial of the case, Fisher was questioned by his counsel on this point for the purpose of proving the consequences of his reliance upon plaintiff's promise, counsel for plaintiff objected, and his objections were—in our opinion improperly—sustained by the court. Having succeeded in ruling out this testimony, plaintiff cannot now contend that proof of the facts thus barred was vital to Fisher's defense.

In the passages last quoted, the court indicated that it would have been proper to receive evidence "for the purpose of proving the consequences of [Fisher's] reliance." If Fried had introduced evidence that Fisher's restaurant was an outstanding success, likely to make Fisher wealthy, should the promise to release Fisher have been enforced? More precisely, if detrimental reliance is an essential element of promissory estoppel, what happens when reliance does not work to the actor's detriment but is in fact beneficial?

In light of the multiple theories at work in the preceding materials (i.e., the different ways of defining the reliance principle), it seems only natural to ask whether Fried v. Fisher might have been decided on another ground. Was promissory estoppel the only doctrine available to the court? Consider the *Mahban* digest below, which also involves contract adjustments or modifications.

————

Mahban v. MGM Grand Hotels, Inc.
100 Nev. 593, 691 P.2d 421 (1984)

Defendant leased space in its hotel to plaintiff, who operated a retail shop in the hotel's "arcade" area. The lease contained a clause permitting either party to terminate if "the leased premises are damaged or destroyed to such an extent that they cannot be put into tenantable condition by Lessor within 180 days after such damage or destruction." On November 21, a fire damaged the hotel; either party could have invoked the destruction-of-premises provision. About ten weeks later, on January 30, plaintiff received from defendant's arcade manager a letter which read in part:

> I would like to let you know additionally, that sometime late in February, our target date to re-open should be finalized. I hope to be able to notify you at that time when you will be able to begin remodeling within the arcade area. All plans for reconstruction must be submitted for approval, in advance of any work beginning, to me at my office.

Plaintiff says he relied on this letter by ordering merchandise for restocking his shop. Then, on March 17, plaintiff received a second letter from defendant, notifying of defendant's termination of the lease pursuant to the destruction-of-premises clause. Plaintiff sued for damages for breach, urging that defendant had lost the contractual power to terminate. The trial court awarded defendant summary judgment, concluding that plaintiff "could not have reasonably relied on the [January 30th letter because it] contained no misrepresentation as to whether defendant intended to waive its contractual rights." *Held*, summary judgment was inappropriate. It appears the trial court relied solely on "waiver," which is "the intentional relinquishment of a known right," but plaintiff also asserts equitable estoppel. In some situations, "there is a potential" for both theories to afford relief; "[r]ights may themselves be waived by a lessor, or he may by his conduct become estopped to assert them." Here, defendant's letter "allows an inference of an intent . . . not to exercise its termination right." Further, the letter instructs plaintiff concerning reconstruction plans. "[Construction plans] are generally acquired only at a substantial expense to one who obtains them. Although the record is unclear as to whether plaintiff actually invested in plans, the letter can be read to have encouraged acts or evidenced intent inconsistent with termination of the lease." Accordingly, there are material questions of fact on both waiver and estoppel issues. Defendant's contention that equitable estoppel "is a defense, not a cause of action for money damages," is of no avail. "[T]he underlying action [here] sought damages for breach of the lease agreement. . . . [E]quitable estoppel has been raised as a bar to defendant's assertion of its [contract] right to terminate. . . . As applied here, estoppel is, therefore, essentially a defense to a defense, rather than a claim for relief." [The court's opinion makes no mention of promissory estoppel.]

———

Kolkman v. Roth

Supreme Court of Iowa, 2003.
656 N.W.2d 148.

CADY, JUSTICE . . . Corrine Roth inherited 800 acres of farmland located in Des Moines County from her father following his death in December 1995. At the time, Dean Kolkman farmed the land pursuant to an oral crop-share lease. The lease term was year-to-year, with profits shared on a fifty-fifty basis between Kolkman and Roth's father. Roth also worked for her father on the farm over the years until approximately two years prior to his death. She was primarily involved in her father's livestock operation. Kolkman was also involved in the livestock operation, especially during the two years prior to the time Roth inherited the farm. During these two years, Kolkman ran the cattle operation under an arrangement similar to the grain operation.

In the spring of 1996, Roth asked Kolkman if he would continue to farm the ground and raise the cattle as he did for her father. Roth and Kolkman agreed that Kolkman would continue in the farming operation. They also agreed Kolkman and his wife would reside in one of the houses on the farm rent-free. Unfortunately, this agreement, and any additional terms, was not reduced to writing.

Kolkman and his wife moved to the farm in June 1996, and Kolkman successfully operated the farm, without incident, until 1999. During this time, Kolkman raised cattle, cultivated and harvested crops, and improved and cared for the land by fixing buildings and removing debris and manure. The farm was generally run down at the time it was inherited by Roth, and Kolkman improved its condition by performing work not typically done by a tenant farmer.

In 1999 Roth sought to charge Kolkman rent for the farmhouse in which he was residing in the amount of $550 a month. Roth also proposed a written farm lease between them that would terminate in 2000. Kolkman refused to execute the written proposals, and Roth sought to terminate the tenancy.

Kolkman responded by filing an action against Roth for breach of contract. He claimed the 1996 oral agreement with Roth included a term permitting him to live in the house rent free and remain the tenant on a fifty-fifty basis until he "retired or couldn't work any more." Kolkman further claimed he relied on this promise in several ways, including selling his former residence and moving to the farm, purchasing various farm equipment, and improving the land by making repairs and removing debris.

Roth denied any term regarding the length of their lease, and sought summary judgment. She claimed the statute of frauds prevented Kolkman from establishing an oral contract between the parties. The district court denied summary judgment and the case proceeded to trial. At trial, the district court, after finding Kolkman established the elements of promissory estoppel, determined the statute of frauds did not bar oral evidence of a lease. The jury then found the parties entered into a contract, supported by consideration, based on the terms asserted by Kolkman. It found Roth breached this contract and awarded Kolkman damages of $154,429. . . .

Under our statute of frauds, evidence of certain types of contracts is inadmissible, unless it is "in writing and signed by the party" sought to be charged. Iowa Code § 622.32 (1999). One type of contract included within the statute is a contract creating or transferring an interest in real estate other than leases for a term less than one year. . . .

Like most other rules, exceptions have been created to the statute of frauds. Iowa Code § 622.33 creates one such exception for contracts that fall within the real estate category. This section removes such oral agreements from the domain of the statute under two circumstances. The first circumstance is where the vendor of a real estate contract has received "the purchase money, or any portion thereof, . . . or when the vendee, with the actual or implied consent of the vendor, has taken and held possession of the premises under and by virtue of the contract." This language codifies the ancient doctrine of part performance, and permits the statute of frauds to be avoided where a party has rendered the type of part performance described in the statute. The rationale for the part performance exception actually lies in the principles of estoppel and fraud. The part performance exception exists to prevent the type of fraud that would occur "if the defendant were permitted to escape performance of his or her part of the oral agreement after permitting the plaintiff to perform in reliance upon the agreement." 73 Am. Jur. 2d Statute of Frauds § 313, at 13. Accordingly, part performance is not a substitute for evidence of a written contract, but is grounded in the theory that the defendant is estopped to assert the statute of frauds as a defense.

The second circumstance that will remove an oral real estate contract from the statute of frauds is derived from the concluding language of section 622.33, which makes the statute inapplicable under "any other circumstance which, by the law heretofore in force, would have taken the case out of the statute of frauds." Iowa Code § 622.33. We have interpreted this language to mean that the doctrine of promissory estoppel is available to remove an oral real estate contract from the statute of frauds. . . .

Promissory estoppel developed as a doctrine in the law in response to the strict traditional requirements for the formation of a contract, especially the requirement that all enforceable contracts be supported by consideration. . . . Thus, the theory behind promissory estoppel was to make parties "liable for their promises despite [the] absence of" consideration required under contract law. Schoff v. Combined Insurance Co., 604 N.W.2d 43, 48 (Iowa 1999). For this reason, we have viewed the effect of promissory estoppel to imply a contract in law based on detrimental reliance. However, other principles of contract law can conflict with the doctrine of promissory estoppel, such as the requirement of a writing for some types of contracts under the statute of frauds. . . . Thus, promissory estoppel is not only a substitute for consideration, but is also recognized as an exception to the statute of frauds even in cases where the promise may be supported by consideration.

Roth acknowledges both exceptions to the statute of frauds, but argues they must not be expanded so far as to apply to leases claimed to be in excess of one year. Roth points out we have refused to apply the part performance exception to oral leases for a term of more than one year, and, as a compatible doctrine, should similarly restrict promissory estoppel under the same circumstances.

We recognize part performance and promissory estoppel to be compatible doctrines as exceptions to the statute of frauds. They are both based on reliance and exist to prevent fraud, and are compatible because they share common goals. However, under section 622.33, the part performance exception is defined in relationship to a contract for the sale or purchase of real estate, not leases. Thus, it describes one type of circumstance that justifies avoidance of the statute of frauds to prevent it from working the same type of fraud it was designed to prevent. The doctrine of promissory estoppel has the same goal, but accomplishes it in other ways. The two exceptions are compatible, yet can embrace distinct circumstances. . . .

Promissory estoppel is broader than part performance and ultimately utilizes special standards to determine whether injustice can be avoided by enforcing a promise otherwise unenforceable under the statute of frauds.

Despite the broad development of the promissory estoppel doctrine over the years, Roth argues we have previously restricted its use as an exception to the statute of frauds to oral leases in a case decided over a century ago. See Powell v. Crampton, 102 Iowa 364, 71 N.W. 579 (1897). Roth argues we are obligated to recognize this early restriction today, especially in light of the language of section 622.33 that limits the second exception to circumstances where "the law heretofore in force" permitted the statute of frauds to be avoided.

In *Powell*, a tenant sought specific performance of an oral lease claimed to be for a term of five years. We held that the statute of frauds prevented proof of the lease, and the exceptions to the statute asserted by the tenant did not apply. However, the tenant did not raise promissory estoppel as an exception and we did not address the question whether promissory estoppel could be used as an exception to the statute of frauds. Instead, the tenant asserted the case fell outside of the statute of frauds based on part performance and based on the landlord's own testimony establishing the oral lease. Based on these arguments, the tenant claimed the landlord was "estopped from denying an oral contract to lease." We determined the part performance exception under the statute did not apply to leases and that the landlord's testimony was insufficient to constitute an admission of all of the lease terms. Although we concluded estoppel was not established, the decision did not consider the specific claim of promissory estoppel. Instead, it simply recognized, as we have since, that the estoppel doctrine lies at the heart of the exceptions to the statute of frauds, and the effect of establishing an exception to the statute is to estop the other party from asserting the statute of frauds to render oral proof of a contract incompetent. Consequently, *Powell* is not inconsistent with our development of the doctrine of promissory estoppel as a circumstance to establish an exception under section 622.33. Moreover, we have never rejected promissory estoppel as an exception in cases involving leases in excess of one year.

Finally, Roth claims that such unbridled use of the promissory estoppel exception will essentially swallow the statute of frauds rule when applied to real estate leases because a tenant will always be able to claim the existence of an oral lease in excess of one year. Roth claims this result is incongruous to the purposes behind the statute of frauds and the specific statutory exclusion for leases with a term less than one year. She argues our legislature would not have excluded oral leases for a term less than one year from the category of real estate cases covered under the statute of frauds, and then establish an exception to avoid the statute of frauds for leases in excess of one year.

We recognize other courts have been cautious to use promissory estoppel to overcome the statute of frauds. The argument advanced by Roth that the promissory estoppel doctrine essentially engulfs the statute of frauds is also commonly used by courts in those states that have been slow to apply promissory estoppel as an exception to the statute of frauds. Nevertheless, we find the argument insufficient to alter what we find to be our longstanding use of promissory estoppel as an exception to the statute of frauds.

The doctrine of promissory estoppel does not eviscerate the statute of frauds, but only applies to circumvent the statute when necessary to prevent an injustice. It requires the party asserting it as a means to avoid the statute of frauds to prove:

> (1) a clear and definite promise; (2) the promise was made with the promissor's clear understanding that the promisee was seeking assurance upon which the promisee could rely and without which he would not act; (3) the promisee acted to his or her substantial detriment in reasonable reliance on the promise; and (4) injustice can be avoided only by enforcement of the promise.

Schoff, 604 N.W.2d at 49. We require strict proof of all the elements. This includes strict proof of a promise that justifies reliance by the promisee. It also requires strict proof that the reliance inflicted injustice that requires enforcement of the promise. Clearly, much more than mere nonperformance of a promise must be shown to obtain the benefits of promissory estoppel. Thus, the strict standards we follow in applying promissory estoppel as a means to avoid the statute of frauds ameliorate the concerns presented by Roth and prevent the statute of frauds from being used to create an unjust result. Additionally, we observe that the majority of courts take a similar approach in applying the doctrine of promissory estoppel to the statute of frauds.

We also observe those jurisdictions that limit the use of promissory estoppel often point out the anomaly created by utilizing promissory estoppel to remove an oral promise from the statute of frauds when the very promise relied upon under promissory estoppel is the same promise declared unenforceable under the statute of frauds. Yet, even these jurisdictions seem to acknowledge that compelling circumstances have been encountered to justify the occasional use of promissory estoppel to avoid the statute of frauds. Thus, it is not really the use of the doctrine of promissory estoppel that is objectionable, and properly limited, promissory estoppel does serve the needed function of preventing the same fraud sought to be avoided by the statute of frauds itself. There is simply no strong reason to restrict the doctrine itself from any particular type of a contract included in the statute of frauds, as long as the doctrine is carefully applied.

Lastly, we perceive no inconsistency between permitting the promissory estoppel exception to the statute of frauds to be used in cases involving leases in excess of one year under a statutory scheme such as ours that excludes leases less than one year from the domain of the statute of frauds. To the contrary, it would be inconsistent to include certain types of leases within the real estate category of cases covered by the statute of frauds, then refuse to apply a broad exception for real estate cases, established to prevent fraudulent use of the statute of frauds, to such leases. . . .

––––––

Stearns v. Emery–Waterhouse Co.

596 A.2d 72 (Maine 1991)

Emery–Waterhouse was a Portland hardware wholesaler that also franchised "Trustworthy" hardware stores throughout the Northeast and owns several such stores. In December, 1984 the Employer's president, Charles Hildreth, met with Stearns in Massachusetts to discuss hiring him to run the Employer's retail stores. Stearns was managing a Sears, Roebuck & Co. Store in Massachusetts, had done retail marketing for Sears for twenty-seven years, and was then fifty years old. He was earning approximately $99,000 per year, owned his home in Massachusetts, and also owned property in Maine. Stearns had some dissatisfactions with Sears but was concerned about retaining his Sears job security and was aware that his age would make it hard to find another marketing job. After the initial meeting Stearns came to Maine, inspected some stores, and met with Hildreth in Portland. The substance of this second meeting was disputed, but the jury found that Hildreth gave Stearns an oral contract of employment to age fifty-five at a guaranteed salary of $85,000 per year. This contract was never reduced to writing.

Stearns resigned from Sears, moved to Maine, and became Emery–Waterhouse's director of retail sales. [He was] retained in this position at $85,000 for nearly two years. In December, 1986 Hildreth advised Stearns that he was being removed, but Stearns was given a different job as the national accounts manager the next day. Stearns remained in this new position at an annual salary of $68,000 for six months. Hildreth then succeeded in his efforts to acquire a national marketing firm, eliminated Stearns's position as a result, and terminated his employment before he reached age fifty-five.

Stearns contended that he could avoid the statute of frauds under the promissory estoppel theory of § 139 of the [Rest.2d]. The Court held that "equitable estoppel, based upon a promisor's fraudulent conduct, can avoid application of the statute of frauds and that this principle applies to a fraudulent promise of employment," but it declined "to accept *promissory* estoppel as permitting avoidance of the statute in employment contracts that require longer than one year to perform. Although § 139 of the Restatement may promote justice in other situations, in the employment context it contravenes the policy of the statute to prevent fraud. It is too easy for a disgruntled former employee to allege reliance on a promise, but difficult factually to distinguish such reliance from the ordinary preparations that attend any new employment. Thus, such pre-employment actions of reliance do not properly serve the evidentiary function of the writing required by the statute."

The court also rejected the part performance doctrine as an avenue for avoidance of the statute of frauds in the employment context. "We have recognized in other circumstances that a promisor's acceptance of partial performance may estop a defense under the statute on the ground of equitable fraud. [351 A.2d 845, 855 (Me.1976)]. . . . Under this doctrine, too, our focus has been upon the conduct of the promisor. Moreover, an employee's preparations to begin a new assignment generally convey no direct benefit to an employer so it is particularly inappropriate to remove from an employer the protections of the statute. An employee can recover for services actually performed in quantum meruit. But to enforce a multi-year employment contract an employee must produce a writing that satisfies the statute of frauds or must prove fraud on the part of the employer."

———————

COMMENT: PROMISSORY ESTOPPEL AND THE STATUTE OF FRAUDS

As *Stearns* suggests, some courts remain reluctant to use the estoppel doctrines to avoid the statute of frauds or diminish its domain, especially in employment cases. E.g., Brown v. Branch, 758 N.E.2d 48 (Ind.2001) (proof of promissory estoppel's elements not enough; party asserting the doctrine to counter statute of frauds "carries heavy burden" of showing reliance resulting in "infliction of unjust and unconscionable injury and loss"); Consolidation Services v. KeyBank Nat'l Ass'n, 185 F.3d 817 (7th Cir.1999) ("since promissory estoppel merely provides alternative to consideration as basis for enforcing a promise as a contract, it would be anomalous to use it to take an oral promise out of the statute of frauds"). Nonetheless, one can safely say at this point that law-equity distinctions have become blurred as estoppel to plead the statute of frauds—equitable or promissory, and often a lumping of the two—expands in both coverage and remedial consequences. It seems worth noting that the "evidentiary" test commonly applied in the equity part-performance cases (e.g., *Seavey*) is expressly made a factor bearing on Restatement (Second) § 139's ultimate question of whether enforcement is required to "avoid injustice." One might ask whether the various application of § 90, including the power to dispense with a statute conferred by § 139, are intended to portray promissory estoppel as a doctrine primarily "equitable" in nature.

SECTION 5. PRECONTRACTUAL OBLIGATION

The preceding section opened up for study the reliance principle in its classic form. But there is more of the developing story of reliance on a promise, an important part of which must be told before we turn, in the next chapter, to contract formation and matters of offer and acceptance. The main event here is the problem of "precontractual" obligation, sometimes spoken of as the "reinforcement" of offers. As we shall see, longstanding common law doctrine says that a simple offer—a proposal of an exchange, no consideration having been given for the proposal—ordinarily is revocable by its maker until the offer is accepted. An offer is something more than a promise, though a promise is usually involved. It has been said that an offer may "start the trouble," typically in the form of reliance. And this trouble requires an inquiry into the obligations that may exist even before a contract is formed.

Thomason v. Bescher

Supreme Court of North Carolina, 1918.
176 N.C. 622, 97 S.E. 654.

[On June 18, 1917, defendants J.C. and W.M. Bescher, tenants in common of land, signed and executed a writing under seal in which they promised "in consideration of the sum of one dollar to us in hand paid by C.E. Thomason, the receipt of which is hereby acknowledged," to sell and convey to Thomason a described tract of timber on land "known as the John S. Bescher Place," provided that Thomason demand a deed and tender $6,000 in cash on or before August 18, 1917. A few days after execution of the writing, Thomason notified one of the Beschers that he would take the timber and promised to pay the $6,000 price the following week. A day or so later, on June 23, before an actual tender of the $6,000 by Thomason, defendants notified him that the "option" given by them on June 18 was withdrawn and "we will not convey the timber." Thomason sued for specific performance. In response to a special interrogatory submitted by the trial judge, the jury replied that the $1 recited in the instrument as paid by Thomason had not in fact been paid. The jury also found that Thomason was "at all times able and willing to pay the purchase price of $6,000." On the basis of the jury's verdict, the trial court gave Thomason a decree of specific performance. Defendants appealed. (This use of a jury in an equitable action is explained by the fact that North Carolina, at the time, was one of a small group of states in which jury trial, with most of its usual features, was standard practice in equity cases.)]

HOKE, J. It is the accepted principle of the common law that instruments under seal require no consideration.... Whether this should rest on the position that a seal conclusively imports a consideration or that the solemnity of the act imports such reflection and care that a consideration is regarded as unnecessary, such instruments are held to be binding agreements enforceable in all actions before the common-law courts....

While there is much diversity of opinion on the subject, we think it the better position and sustained by the weight of authority that the principle should prevail in reference to these unilateral contracts or options when, as in this case, they take the form of solemn written covenants under seal, and its proper application is to render them binding agreements, irrevocable within the time designated, and that the stipulations may be enforced and made effective by appropriate remedies when such time is reasonable and there is nothing oppressive and unconscionable in the terms of the principal contract....

We are not unmindful of the position that, in equity causes, [distinguished from actions at law,] the Court looks beyond the form and will usually refuse to exert its powers in aid of a sealed instrument, its collection and enforcement, except when there is a valuable consideration.* In our own Court, the case of Woodall v. Prevatt, 45 N.C. 199, being an apt illustration of the principle. But these options containing a continuing offer to sell and constituting a contract, binding on the parties because in the form of a covenant under seal, serve their purpose in keeping the offer open for the time specified and preventing a withdrawal by the vendor. On acceptance and offer to perform within the time, a bilateral contract is then constituted which, on breach, is enforceable by appropriate remedies, legal or equitable. And in case of action for specific performance, the consideration is not restricted to the seal or the nominal amount usually present in these bargains, but extends to and includes the purchase price agreed upon. This position is recognized with us in Ward v. Albertson, 165 N.C. 218, 222, 81 S.E. 168....

The verdict having established that, before any attempted withdrawal by defendants, plaintiff had notified one of the parties of acceptance, would in any event be entitled to judgment as to that interest. And it further appearing that plaintiff has been at all times ready and able to comply, tendering the entire purchase money, at latest, by August 7th, that defendants refused to accept the same and deny any and all obligations under the al-

---

* [Equity's historical "position" is summarized in the first Restatement of Contracts § 366: "A contract that is binding solely by reason of its being under seal, or in writing, or having a nominal consideration will not be specifically enforced...." This view prevails even today, save for option contracts on fair terms. Rest.2d § 364, comment b.—Eds.]

leged contract, plaintiff, as held in Ward v. Albertson and other cases of like import, is entitled to have specific performance as to both interests, and the judgment to that effect is affirmed. . . .

NOTE

As Thomason v. Bescher suggests, there is much authority in equity decisions, coming from the period when the seal was in its heyday, to the effect that a seal would not make a promise enforceable in equity even though it had that effect at law. The earlier North Carolina case of Woodall v. Prevatt, cited in *Thomason*, was an action in equity to collect money promised through an instrument under seal which, it was alleged, the defendant promisor had fraudulently procured from plaintiff's wife and then destroyed. The court noted the absence of any allegation that there had been consideration for the sealed promise and dismissed the bill, saying:

> To affect the conscience and entitle the party to the aid of a Court of Equity, there must be an allegation of consideration. If I give a man a horse, or give him money, the thing is done, and the right of property vested. But if I promise to give a man a horse or to pay him money, and afterwards see proper not to do so, this is no matter which affects conscience unless there be a consideration. It is in the language of the civil law, nudum pactum. . . . A Court of Equity addresses itself to the conscience of the parties, and of course pays no respect to forms, and disregards even the solemn act of sealing and delivering, and looks behind all forms to see if there be a consideration binding the conscience of the parties.

This kind of talk has appeared in enough equity decisions to induce a group of states (a minority) to "look behind the seal" even in cases of sealed options, and to reach a result opposite to that in the *Thomason* case. A recent example can be found in Knott v. Racicot, 442 Mass. 314, 812 N.E.2d 1207 (2004), in which the court observed, "[w]hatever the merits of upholding the common-law sealed contract doctrine may have been [in the past], they seem far less apparent today, when option contracts are often an important part of business, professional, employment, and investment transactions. Questions concerning the validity of option contracts are simply too important to our highly literate, highly mobile society to be decided by formalities that have lost all practical utility. As the Legislature has recognized, the written signature has replaced the wax impression as the natural formality authenticating a document. Thus we require no showing of injustice to conclude that the giving of consideration, a necessary element of ordinary (simple or informal) contracts, should be required for option contracts that happen either to be impressed with a seal or to recite a talismanic formula importing a seal." In states that have "abolished" the seal, it is clear that results like that in Thomason v. Bescher would not be reached. The same is true in those states whose statutes make the seal merely "prima facie evidence" of consideration.

QUESTION

Suppose that in *Thomason* the plaintiff had tendered the $1 for the option, but defendants declined it, saying: "That's all right. You keep it. It doesn't mean anything anyway." If the seal would not make the option irrevocable, must the case come out differently?

———

Marsh v. Lott

8 Cal.App. 384, 97 P. 163 (1908)

On February 25, 1905, defendant in writing gave plaintiff an option to buy land for $100,000, payable $30,000 in cash and the balance in four years. The writing acknowledged defendant's receipt of 25 cents "in hand paid" by plaintiff and provided that the option would expire June 1, 1905, "with privilege of 30 days extension." On June 1, plaintiff notified defendant in writing of his election to extend the option for 30 days. On June 2, defendant revoked the option and withdrew the property from sale. On June 29, plaintiff exercised the option in writing and tendered the $30,000 down payment, which defendant refused. Plaintiff's suit for specific performance was denied by the trial court on the ground that the 25 cents paid was "inadequate and insufficient consideration." *Held*, this ruling was error, despite § 3391 of the California Civil Code stating that specific performance "cannot be enforced against a party to a contract . . . if he has not received an adequate consideration for the contract." This statute is merely a codification of "equitable principles that have existed from time immemorial." It refers to the price that is to be paid for an exchange and does not apply to the consideration for the option. Here, the price fixed for the land seems entirely adequate. "In our judgment, any money consideration, however small, paid and received for an option to purchase property at its adequate value is binding upon the seller thereof for the time specified therein." Defendant's attempted revocation was therefore ineffective.

———

Smith v. Wheeler

233 Ga. 166, 210 S.E.2d 702 (1974)

"The [optionor contends] that the option contract was unilateral in nature and since [he] withdrew his offer prior to the tender and payment of the one dollar recited as consideration for the option agreement, the option is a nullity and has no legal force and effect. We do not agree. . . . The majority of cases from other jurisdictions hold that the offeror may prove that the consideration had not been paid and that no other consideration had taken its place. . . . However, the [rule] we consider to be the best view, is that even if it is shown that the dollar was not paid it does not void the contract. We have held many times that the recital of the one dollar consideration gives rise to an implied promise to pay which can be enforced by the other party. . . . It was therefore error for the trial to [rule] that there was a failure of consideration."

[Some courts have arrived at the Smith v. Wheeler result on yet another ground—that an optionor who, in writing, acknowledges receipt of $1 consideration for an option, is "estopped to deny" the statement. E.g., Real Estate Co. of Pittsburgh v. Rudolph, 301 Pa. 502, 153 A. 438 (1930) (if a seal had been used it would have imported a consideration that could not have been contradicted, and thus "it would be neither logical nor consistent to hold that the intentional insertion of an actual consideration may be overthrown"). Is it ordinarily the case that a recital in a written agreement that a stated consideration has been given cannot be contradicted by evidence that no such consideration was given or expected?]

————

RESTATEMENT OF CONTRACTS, SECOND

Section 87. Option Contract

(1) An offer is binding as an option contract if it

(a) is in writing and signed by the offeror, recites a purported consideration for the making of the offer, and proposes an exchange on fair terms within a reasonable time; or

(b) is made irrevocable by statute.

NOTE

Section 87(1) of the Restatement, Second provides an alternative avenue to enforcement when traditional consideration is lacking. Observe that § 87(1) does not require that the "purported consideration" for an offer actually be delivered. The ALI Reporter responsible for the drafting of the section has said that it provides for "nominal consideration." Braucher, Freedom of Contract and the Second Restatement, 78 Yale L.J. 598, 605 (1969). What is it in § 87(1) that gives effect to "nominal consideration?" See, e.g., Knott v. Racicot, noted supra p. 269, where the Massachusetts high court added to its holding (that the giving of consideration was required for sealed option contracts) the further statement that "[w]e henceforth adopt the Restatement (Second) Contracts § 87(1)." At least one court (only one, it appears) has rejected § 87(1) outright, characterizing it as a "minority position." Lewis v. Fletcher, 101 Idaho 530, 617 P.2d 834 (1980). As to false recitals of consideration for an option, it is fair to say that the cases preceding the Second Restatement's § 87(1) were in fact divided. No such division is to be found, however, when consideration, whether or not nominal, is in fact given (look again at Marsh v. Lott). Courts, free to examine the parties' entire dealings in search of consideration for an option, often find a promise, even one dependent on parol evidence. E.g., Matter of Estate of Jorstad, 447 N.W.2d 283 (N.D.1989) (son's oral promise to stay and work parents' farm, made on eve of execution of writing giving son option to purchase farm, constitutes consideration for option).

Statutes providing for irrevocable offers not limited to the purchase or sale of goods were already in place in a number of states prior to the widespread adoption of the UCC and § 2–205. Again, the common pattern was to substitute for consideration the giving of a signed writing which, by its terms, stated assurances of irrevocability. For example, a "firm offer" statute was enacted in New York in 1941; it remains relatively unchanged today, as § 5–1109 of the General Obligations Law, except for language acknowledging the reach of UCC 2–205:

> Written Irrevocable Offer. Except as otherwise provided in [UCC] 2–205 with respect to an offer by a merchant to buy or sell goods, when an offer to enter into a contract is made in a writing signed by the offeror, . . . which states that the offer is irrevocable during a period set forth or until a time fixed, the offer shall not be revocable during

such period or until such time because of the absence of consideration for the assurance of irrevocability. When such a writing states that the offer is irrevocable but does not state any period or time of irrevocability, it shall be construed to state that the offer is irrevocable for a reasonable time.

There are other examples of statutory firm offers, including legislation barring a bidder for government work from withdrawing a bid after the appropriate officials have opened the bids.

James Baird Co. v. Gimbel Bros.

United States Court of Appeals, Second Circuit, 1933.
64 F.2d 344.

L. HAND, CIRCUIT JUDGE. The plaintiff sued the defendant for breach of a contract to deliver linoleum under a contract of sale; the defendant denied the making of the contract; the parties tried the case to the judge under a written stipulation and he directed judgment for the defendant. The facts . . . were as follows: The defendant, a New York merchant knew that the Dep't of Highways in Pennsylvania had asked for bids for the construction of a public building. It sent an employee to the office of a contractor in Philadelphia, who had possession of the specifications, and the employee there computed the amount of the linoleum which would be required on the job, underestimating the total yardage by about one-half the proper amount. In ignorance of this mistake, on December twenty-fourth the defendant sent to some twenty or thirty contractors, likely to bid on the job, an offer to supply all the linoleum required by the specifications at two different lump sums, depending upon the quality used. These offers concluded[:] "If successful in being awarded this contract, it will be absolutely guaranteed, . . . [and] we are offering these prices for reasonable" (sic), "prompt acceptance after the general contract has been awarded." The plaintiff, a contractor in Washington, got one of these on the twenty-eighth, and on the same day the defendant learned its mistake and telegraphed all the contractors to whom it had sent the offer, that it withdrew it and would substitute a new one at about double the amount of the old. This withdrawal reached the plaintiff at Washington on the afternoon of the same day [the twenty-eighth], but not until after it had put in a bid at Harrisburg at a lump sum, based as to linoleum upon the prices quoted by the defendant. The public authorities accepted the plaintiff's bid on December thirtieth, the defendant having meanwhile written a letter of confirmation of its withdrawal, received on the thirty-first. The plaintiff formally accepted [defendant's] offer on January second, and, as the defendant persisted in declining to recognize the existence of a contract, sued it for damages on a breach.

Unless there are circumstances to take it out of the ordinary doctrine, since the offer was withdrawn before it was accepted, the acceptance was too late. Restatement of Contracts, § 35. To meet this, the plaintiff argues as follows: It was a reasonable implication from the defendant's offer that it should be irrevocable in case the plaintiff acted upon it, that is to say, used the prices quoted in making its bid, thus putting itself in a position from which it could not withdraw without great loss. While it might have withdrawn its bid after receiving the revocation, the time had passed to submit another, and as the item of linoleum was a very trifling part of the cost of the whole building, it would have been an unreasonable hardship to expect it to lose the contract on that account, and probably forfeit its deposit. While it is true that the plaintiff might in advance have secured a contract conditional upon the success of its bid, this was not what the defendant suggested. It understood that the contractors would use its offer in their bids, and would thus in fact commit themselves to supplying the linoleum at the proposed prices. The inevitable implication from all this was that when the contractors acted upon it, they accepted the offer and promised to pay for the linoleum, in case their bid were accepted.

It was of course possible for the parties to make such a contract, and the question is merely as to what they meant; that is, what is to be imputed to the words they used. Whatever plausibility there is in the argument, is in the fact that the defendant must have known the predicament in which the contractors would be put if it withdrew its offer after the bids went in. However, it seems entirely clear that the contractors did not suppose that they accepted the offer merely by putting in their bids. If, for example, the successful one had repudiated the contract with the public authorities after it had been awarded to him, certainly the defendant could not have sued him for a breach. If he had become bankrupt, the defendant could not prove against his estate. It seems plain therefore that there was no contract between them. And if there be any doubt as to this, the language of the offer sets it at rest. The phrase, "if successful in being awarded this contract," is scarcely met by the mere use of the prices in the bids. Surely such a use was not an "award" of the contract to the defendant. Again, the phrase, "we are offering these prices for . . . prompt acceptance after the general contract has been awarded," looks to the usual communication of an acceptance, and precludes the idea that the use of the offer in the bidding shall be the equivalent. It may indeed be argued that this last language contemplated no more than an early notice that the offer had been accepted, the actual acceptance being the bid, but that would wrench its natural meaning too far, especially in the light of the preceding phrase. The contractors had a ready escape from their difficulty by insisting upon a contract before they used the figures; and in commercial transactions it does not in the end promote justice to seek strained interpretations in aid of those who do not protect themselves.

But the plaintiff says that even though no bilateral contract was made, the defendant should be held under the doctrine of "promissory estoppel." This is to be chiefly found in those cases where persons subscribe to a venture, usually charitable, and are held to their promises after it has been completed. It has been applied much more broadly, however, and has now been generalized in § 90, of the Restatement of Contracts. We may arguendo accept it as it there reads, for it does not apply to the case at bar. Offers are ordinarily made in exchange for a consideration, either a counter-promise or some other act which the promisor wishes to secure. In such cases they propose bargains; they presuppose that each promise or performance is an inducement to the other. . . . But a man may make a promise without expecting an equivalent; a donative promise, conditional or absolute. The common law provided for such by sealed instruments, and it is unfortunate that these are no longer generally available. The doctrine of "promissory estoppel" is to avoid the harsh results of allowing the promisor in such a case to repudiate, when the promisee has acted in reliance upon the promise. Siegel v. Spear & Co., 234 N.Y. 479, 138 N.E. 414. Cf. Allegheny College v. National Bank, 246 N.Y. 369, 159 N.E. 173. But an offer for an exchange is not meant to become a promise until a consideration has been received, either a counter-promise or whatever else is stipulated. To extend it would be to hold the offeror regardless of the stipulated condition of his offer. In the case at bar the defendant offered to deliver the linoleum in exchange for the plaintiff's acceptance, not for its bid, which was a matter of indifference to it. That offer could become a promise to deliver only when the equivalent was received; that is, when the plaintiff promised to take and pay for it. There is no room in such a situation for the doctrine of "promissory estoppel."

LEARNED HAND
1872–1961

Nor can the offer be regarded as of an option, giving the plaintiff the right seasonably to accept the linoleum at the quoted prices if its bid was accepted, but not binding it to take and pay, if it could get a better bargain elsewhere. There is not the least reason to suppose that the defendant meant to subject itself to such a one-sided obligation. True, if so construed, the doctrine of "promissory estoppel" might apply, the plaintiff having acted in reliance upon it, though, so far as we have found, the decisions are otherwise. Ganss v. Guffey Petroleum Co., 125 App.Div. 760, 110 N.Y.S. 176; Comstock v. North, 88 Miss. 754, 41 So. 374. As to that, however, we need not declare ourselves.

Judgment affirmed.

Drennan v. Star Paving Co.

Supreme Court of California, 1958.
51 Cal.2d 409, 333 P.2d 757.

TRAYNOR, J. Defendant appeals from a judgment for plaintiff in an action to recover damages caused by defendant's refusal to perform certain paving work according to a bid it submitted to plaintiff.

On July 28, 1955, plaintiff, a licensed general contractor, was preparing a bid on the "Monte Vista School Job" in the Lancaster school district. Bids had to be submitted before 8:00 p.m. Plaintiff testified that it was customary in that area for general contractors to receive the bids of subcontractors by telephone on the day set for bidding and to rely on them in computing their own bids. Thus on that day plaintiff's secretary, Mrs. Johnson, received by telephone between fifty and seventy-five subcontractors' bids for various parts of the school job. As each bid came in, she wrote it on a special form, which she brought into plaintiff's office. He then posted it on a master cost sheet setting forth the names and bids of all subcontractors. His own bid had to include the names of subcontractors who were to perform one-half of one per cent or more of the construction work, and he had also to provide a bidder's bond of ten per cent of his total bid of $317,385 as a guarantee that he would enter the contract if awarded the work.

Late in the afternoon, Mrs. Johnson had a telephone conversation with Kenneth Hoon, an estimator for defendant. He gave his name and telephone number and stated that he was bidding for defendant for the paving work at the Monte Vista School according to plans and specifications and that his bid was $7,131.60. At Mrs. Johnson's request he repeated his bid. Plaintiff listened to the bid over an extension telephone in his office and posted it on the master sheet after receiving the bid form from Mrs. Johnson. Defendant's was the lowest bid for the paving. Plaintiff computed his own bid accordingly and submitted it with the name of defendant as the subcontractor for the paving. When the bids were opened on July 28th, plaintiff's proved to be the lowest, and he was awarded the contract.

On his way to Los Angeles the next morning plaintiff stopped at defendant's office. The first person he met was defendant's construction engineer, Mr. Oppenheimer. Plaintiff testified: "I introduced myself and he immediately told me that they had made a mistake in their bid to me the night before, they couldn't do it for the price they had bid, and I told him I would expect him to carry through with their original bid because I had used it in compiling my bid and the job was being awarded them. And I would have to go and do the job according to my bid and I would expect them to do the same."

Defendant refused to do the paving work for less than $15,000. Plaintiff testified that he "got figures from other people" and after trying for several months to get as low a bid as possible engaged L & H Paving Co. to do the work for $10,948.60.

Moulin Archives, San Francisco

ROGER J. TRAYNOR
1900-1983

The trial court found on substantial evidence that defendant made a definite offer to do the paving on the Monte Vista job according to the plans and specifications for $7,131.60, and that plaintiff relied on defendant's bid in computing his own bid for the school job and naming defendant therein as the subcontractor for the paving work. Accordingly, it entered judgment for plaintiff in the amount of $3,817.00 (the difference between defendant's bid and the cost of the paving to plaintiff) plus costs.

reliance

Defendant contends that there was no enforceable contract between the parties [since] it made a revocable offer and revoked it before plaintiff communicated his acceptance to defendant.

There is no evidence that defendant offered to make its bid irrevocable in exchange for plaintiff's use of its figures in computing his bid. Nor is there evidence that would warrant interpreting plaintiff's use of defendant's bid as the acceptance thereof, binding plaintiff, on condition he received the main contract, to award the subcontract to defendant. In sum, there was neither an option supported by consideration nor a bilateral contract binding on both parties.

Plaintiff contends, however, that he relied to his detriment on defendant's offer and that defendant must therefore answer in damages for its refusal to perform. . . . Did plaintiff's reliance make defendant's offer irrevocable?

Section 90 of the Restatement of Contracts states: "A promise which the promisor should reasonably expect to induce action or forbearance of a definite and substantial character on the part of the promisee and which does induce such action or forbearance is binding if injustice can be avoided only by enforcement of the promise." This rule applies in this state. . . .

Defendant's offer constituted a promise to perform on such conditions as were stated expressly or by implication therein or annexed thereto by operation of law. (See 1 Williston, Contracts [3rd ed.], [§§ 24A, 61].) Defendant had reason to expect that if its bid proved the lowest it would be used by plaintiff. It induced "action . . . of a definite and substantial character on the part of the promisee."

Had defendant's bid expressly stated or clearly implied that it was revocable at any time before acceptance we would treat it accordingly. It was silent on revocation, however, and we must therefore determine whether there are conditions to the right of revocation imposed by law or reasonably inferable in fact. In the analogous problem of an offer for a unilateral contract, the theory is now obsolete that the offer is revocable at any time before complete performance. Thus § 45 of the Restatement provides: "If an offer for a unilateral contract is made, and part of the consideration requested in the offer is given or tendered by the offeree in response thereto, the offeror is bound by a contract, the duty of immediate performance of which is conditional on the full consideration being given or tendered within the time stated in the offer, or, if no time is stated therein, within a reasonable time." In explanation, comment *b* states that the "main offer includes as a subsidiary promise, necessarily implied, that if part of the requested performance is given, the offeror will not revoke his offer, and that if tender is made it will be accepted. Part performance or tender may thus furnish consideration for the subsidiary promise. Moreover, merely acting in justifiable reliance on an offer may in some cases serve as sufficient reason for making a promise binding (see § 90)."

[handwritten margin note: past performance = revokability of unilateral contracts]

Whether implied in fact or law, the subsidiary promise serves to preclude the injustice that would result if the offer could be revoked after the offeree had acted in detrimental reliance thereon. Reasonable reliance resulting in a foreseeable prejudicial change in position affords a compelling basis also for implying a subsidiary promise not to revoke an offer for a bilateral contract.

The absence of consideration is not fatal to the enforcement of such a promise. It is true that in the case of unilateral contracts the Restatement finds consideration for the implied subsidiary promise in the part performance of the bargained for exchange, but its reference to § 90 makes clear that consideration for such a promise is not always necessary. The very purpose of § 90 is to make a promise binding even though there was no consideration "in the sense of something that is bargained for and given in exchange." (1 Corbin, Contracts 634 et seq.) Reasonable reliance serves to hold the offeror in lieu of the consideration ordinarily required to make the offer binding. In a case involving similar facts the Supreme Court of South Dakota stated that "we believe that reason and justice demand that the doctrine [of § 90] be applied to the present facts. . . . [T]he defendants in executing the agreement [which was not supported by consideration] made a promise which they should have reasonably expected would induce the plaintiff to submit a bid based thereon to the Government, that such promise did induce this action, and that injustice can be avoided only by enforcement of the promise." Northwestern Eng'g Co. v. Ellerman, 69 S.D. 397, 408, 10 N.W.2d 879, 884; . . . cf. James Baird Co. v. Gimbel Bros., 2 Cir., 64 F.2d 344.

When plaintiff used defendant's offer in computing his own bid, he bound himself to perform in reliance on defendant's terms. Though defendant did not bargain for this use of its bid neither did defendant make it idly, indifferent to whether it would be used or not. On the contrary, it is reasonable to suppose that defendant submitted its bid to obtain the subcontract. It was bound to realize the substantial possibility that its bid would be the lowest, and that it would be included by plaintiff in his bid. It was to its own interest that the contractor be awarded the general contract; the lower the subcontract bid, the lower the general contractor's bid was likely to be and the greater its chance of acceptance and hence the greater defendant's chance of getting the paving subcontract. Defendant had reason not only to expect plaintiff to rely on its bid but to want him to. Clearly defendant had a stake in plaintiff's reliance on its bid. Given this interest and the fact that plaintiff is bound by his own bid, it is only fair that plaintiff should have at least an opportunity to accept defendant's bid after the general contract has been awarded to him.

It bears noting that a general contractor is not free to delay acceptance after he has been awarded the general contract in the hope of getting a better price. Nor can he reopen bargaining with the subcontractor and at the same time claim a continuing right to accept the original offer. See, R.J. Daum Constr. Co. v. Child, Utah, 247 P.2d 817. [Here,] plaintiff promptly informed defendant that plaintiff was being awarded the job and that the subcontract was being awarded to defendant.

Defendant contends, however, that its bid was the result of mistake and that it was therefore entitled to revoke it. . . . Plaintiff, however, had no reason to know that defendant had made a mistake in submitting its bid, since there was usually a variance of 160 percent between the highest and lowest bids for paving in the desert around Lancaster. He committed himself to performing the main contract in reliance on defendant's figures. Under these circumstances defendant's mistake, far from relieving it of its obligation, constitutes an additional reason for enforcing it, for it misled plaintiff as to the cost of doing the paving. Even had it been clearly understood that defendant's offer was revocable until accepted, it would not necessarily follow that defendant had no duty to exercise reasonable care in preparing its bid. It presented its bid with knowledge of the substantial possibility that it would be used by plaintiff; it could foresee the harm that would ensue from an erroneous underestimate of the cost. Moreover, it was motivated by its own business interest. Whether or not these considerations alone would justify recovery for negligence had the case been tried on that theory (see Biakanja v. Irving, 49 Cal.2d 647, 320 P.2d 16), they are persuasive that defendant's mistake should not defeat recovery under the rule of § 90. . . . As between the subcontractor who made the bid and the general contractor who reasonably relied on it, the loss resulting from the mistake should fall on the party who caused it. . . .

The judgment is affirmed.

RESTATEMENT OF CONTRACTS, SECOND

Section 87. Option Contract

(2) An offer which the offeror should reasonably expect to induce action or forbearance of a substantial character on the part of the offeree before acceptance and which does induce such action or forbearance is binding as an option contract to the extent necessary to avoid injustice.

Dynalectric Co., Inc. v. Clark & Sullivan Constructors, Inc.

Supreme Court of Nevada, 2011.
255 P.3d 286.

PER CURIAM. In this appeal, we address the measure of damages applicable to promissory estoppel claims. We adopt a flexible approach as suggested in the Restatement (Second) of Contracts and apply the same factors that bear on promissory estoppel relief to the remedy afforded by the breach. The determination of the appropriate measure of damages in any given case turns on considerations of what justice requires and the foreseeability and certainty of the particular damages award sought. We further conclude that the presumptive measure of damages for a general contractor that reasonably relies upon a subcontractor's unfulfilled promise is the difference between the nonperforming subcontractor's original bid and the cost of the replacement subcontractor's performance. . . .

This appeal arises from a dispute between appellant Dynalectric Company of Nevada, Inc., a subcontractor, and respondent Clark and Sullivan Constructors, Inc. (C & S), a general contractor, concerning a public works project (the Project). The Project involved the expansion of the University Medical Center (UMC) in Las Vegas. In 2004, UMC solicited bids for the Project. C & S, interested in serving as the general contractor for the Project, sought bids from subcontractors. Dynalectric submitted a bid to C & S to perform the electrical work for the Project and repeatedly assured C & S of the accuracy of its bid. C & S incorporated Dynalectric's bid into its bid to UMC for the general contract (Prime Contract). C & S was the low bidder, and UMC awarded it the Prime Contract. C & S notified Dynalectric. Subsequently, Dynalectric repudiated its obligations to C & S and refused to negotiate with C & S. C & S therefore contracted with three replacement subcontractors to complete the electrical work for the Project.

C & S then sued Dynalectric in district court under various theories of liability . . . .

Following a 12-day bench trial, the district court entered a judgment for C & S on its promissory estoppel claim and rejected each of Dynalectric's counterclaims. The district court awarded C & S $2,501,615 in damages, which represents the difference between Dynalectric's bid ($7,808,983) and the amount C & S paid the three replacement contractors to complete the work ($10,310,598). Dynalectric appealed. . . .

Dynalectric contends that the district court applied the incorrect measure of damages. Specifically, it asserts that the district court should not have awarded C & S expectation damages. We disagree.

Broadly speaking, Nevada follows the doctrine of promissory estoppel articulated in the Restatement (Second) of Contracts. . . .

[U]nder the Restatement, an award of expectation damages is often an appropriate remedy for promissory estoppel claims. But, in other instances, reliance damages or restitutionary damages may be more suitable.

Following the lead of the Restatement, we hold that the district court may award expectation, reliance, or restitutionary damages for promissory estoppel claims. . . . [N]o single measure of damages will apply to each and every promissory estoppel claim; instead, to determine the appropriate measure of damages for promissory estoppel claims, the district court should consider the measure of damages that justice requires and that comports with the Restatement's general requirements that damages be foreseeable and reasonably certain.

We now consider whether the district court used the appropriate measure of damages when it awarded C & S promissory estoppel damages representing the difference between Dynalectric's bid and the amount that the three replacement contractors charged C & S to complete the same work. . . .

In the decades since *Drennan*, courts have consistently and uniformly applied the same measure of damages for promissory estoppel claims arising from a subcontractor's repudiation of its obligations to a general contractor. We see no reason to depart from the well-established measure of damages used in *Drennan*.

Interestingly, despite the consensus that the measure of damages adopted in *Drennan* is appropriate in the type of situation presented here, courts have not definitively labeled this measure "expectation" or "reliance" damages. Scholars appear to agree, however, that the *Drennan* measure of damages is, in fact, expectation damages.

As previously noted, Dynalectric's bid was for $7,808,983. C & S was forced to pay $10,310,598 to three replacement subcontractors to complete the work that Dynalectric refused to perform. Thus, the district court awarded C & S $2,501,615, the difference between Dynalectric's bid and the amount C & S paid to the replacement subcontractors. This measure of damages placed C & S in the same position that it would have occupied if Dynalectric had performed as it promised, and thus, it constitutes expectation damages.

It is plain that justice required this measure of damages and that the damages the district court awarded were foreseeable and reasonably certain. As the district court found, Dynalectric made an unequivocal promise by submitting a bid to C & S for the electrical subcontracting of the Project.

Dynalectric thereafter repeatedly assured C & S of the accuracy of the bid that it had submitted. The record demonstrates that Dynalectric fully anticipated that C & S would rely on its bid by incorporating it into its own bid for the Prime Contract. The record also shows that Dynalectric is an experienced and sophisticated subcontractor that could readily anticipate that C & S would be forced to use replacement electrical subcontractors at a higher cost to complete the work that it refused to perform. Finally, the damages that the district court awarded were reasonably certain because C & S presented detailed evidence showing that $2,501,615 represented the difference between Dynalectric's original bid and the amount that the three replacement subcontractors charged. . . .

————

COMMENT: PROMISSORY ESTOPPEL DAMAGES

Consider whether the theory underlying promissory estoppel naturally leads to the award of expectation damages. Comment d to § 90 of the Restatement, Second, offers the following:

> A promise binding under this section is a contract, and full-scale enforcement by normal remedies is often appropriate. But the same factors which bear on whether any relief should be granted also bear on the character and extent of the remedy. . . . Unless there is unjust enrichment of the promisor, damages should not put the promisee in a better position than performance of the promise would have put him. In the case of a promise to make a gift it would rarely be proper to award consequential damages which would place a greater burden on the promisor than performance would have imposed.

The case of Osborn v. Commanche Cattle Indus., 545 P.2d 827 (Okla.Ct.App.1975), involved a three-year contract for services, terminable by either party "at any time by giving 30 days advance notice." In a suit on the contract for lost profits, not in promissory estoppel, the court said:

> [The expectation] interest is given legal protection to achieve the paramount objective of putting the promisee injured by the breach in the position in which he would have been had the contract been performed. . . . But [the promisee] may not recover more than the amount he might have gained by full performance. We think that the only legally protectible expectation interest in the party to a contract terminable by either party upon notice is the prospect of profit over the length of the notice period. Since his assurance of performance never extends beyond the length of the notice period, neither does his prospect of net gain. And allowing him under such circumstances to recover the profit he purportedly could have gained over the maximum life of the contract would be contrary to the whole purpose of permitting recovery of lost profits. Accordingly, [plaintiff was entitled only] to an instruction permitting recovery of lost profits for the length of the notice period—or thirty days from [defendant's] breach.

One question, surely, is whether standard contract notions, such as the differences between, and the respective limitations on, expectation and reliance damages, should be taken into account in measuring relief under promissory estoppel. That doctrine, classified traditionally as contractual, provides none-theless an alternative basis to consideration for the enforcement of a promise. And, as noted, the promissory estoppel claim is undeniably "equitable" in nature, whatever the relief sought (it could be solely an injunction) or the context in which it appears in any particular case.

In 1926, during the extensive discussion by the American Law Institute of the original § 90 of the Restatement of Contracts, there was much attention paid to a hypothetical case put by Professor Williston, the Reporter of the Restatement: Johnny says to his uncle, "I want to buy a Buick car"; Uncle says, "Well, I will give you $1000." The question was asked by Mr. Frederick Coudert whether, if Johnny then proceeded to buy a car for $500, Uncle would be liable for $1,000.

> *Mr. Williston*: If Johnny had done what he was expected to do, or is acting within the limits of his uncle's expectation, I think the uncle would be liable for $1000; but not otherwise.

> *Mr. Coudert*: In other words, substantial justice would require that uncle should be penalized in the sum of $500.

> *Mr. Williston*: Why do you say "penalized"? . . .

> *Mr. Coudert*: Because substantial justice there would require, it seems to me, that Johnny get his money for his car, but should he get his car and $500 more? I don't see. . . .

> *Mr. Williston*: Either the promise is binding or it is not. If the promise is binding it has to be enforced as it is made. As I said to Mr. Coudert, I could leave this whole thing to the subject of quasi contracts so that the promisee under the circumstances shall never recover on the promise but he shall recover such an amount as will fairly compensate him for any injury incurred; but it seems to me you have to take one leg or the other. You have either to say the promise is binding or you have to go on the theory of restoring the status quo. 4 A.L.I.Proc. 98–99, 103–104 (App.1926).

These comments should be read against the further statement of Professor Williston, the Reporter (4 A.L.I.Proc. 91 (App.1926)):

> The qualification is necessary, if injustice can be avoided only by enforcement of the promise. . . . In some cases, in many cases perhaps, it will be possible for the promisee, if he is induced to do some act or pay some money, to recover back what he has given or the value of what he has done. If the court can get out of the difficulty by restoring the status quo, there is no necessity of enforcing the promise, but if detriment has been incurred by the promisee of a definite and substantial character and the status quo cannot be restored, then the proposition is that the court should enforce the promise.

We shall see more of the issue of the appropriate measure of damages for reliance-based liabilities. At this stage, it is clear that there exists an abundance of remedial theories for invoking the factor of detrimental reliance in contract settings. Promissory estoppel, a contract doctrine, seems to be very much like—and to overlap with; indeed, descend from—equitable estoppel, a doctrine derived from tort. The distinguishing feature of equitable estoppel is a misrepresentation, factual and material (again, equitable estoppel is said not to create an "independent" cause of action, but to raise an "affirmative defense"). Yet, if the element of carelessness by the speaker is added, an action in tort for negligent misrepresentation will lie, and if the misrepresentation is intentional ("scienter") or made recklessly, an expanded tort of fraud covers much of the same territory. (W. Keeton, et al., Prosser & Keeton on the Law of Torts 725–770 (5th ed. 1984), contains a helpful sketch of these tort doctrines.) It is, it seems, not at all difficult to portray a single transaction as a breach of some type of contract and as a tort (to say nothing of unjust enrichment and restitution).

A question still debated is whether promissory estoppel, which § 90 defines as a contract (a "promise" is "binding" in stated circumstances), is to be treated as a tort doctrine for purposes of damages. If it is (and a fair number of courts have said as much), it seems only natural to limit any recovery to actual losses suffered in reliance—i.e., restore the injured party to the position it would have occupied had the promise not been made. The permissive language of the Restatement, Second revision of § 90 ("may be limited") quite clearly introduces into the damages decision a large dose of trial-court discretion. In exercising discretion, is it a good idea to separate gift promises from promises made in bargain settings?

A number of cases are examined in Becker, Promissory Estoppel Damages, 16 Hofstra L.Rev. 131 (1987), where the author concludes that, under promissory estoppel, expectation damages are generally available in both donative and commercial settings, and that, in most cases, the measure of relief (full enforcement or reliance loss) can be understood on the basis of traditional contract principles. The thesis that expectancy is in fact the routine measure of relief under § 90—because judges actually enforce promises rather than protect reliance in such cases—is argued in Yorio & Thel, The Promissory Basis of Section 90, 101 Yale L.J. 111 (1991). See also Farber & Matheson, Beyond Promissory Estoppel: Contract Law and the "Invisible Handshake," 52 U.Chi.L.Rev. 903 (1985) (study of § 90 cases over decade 1975–1985, reporting only one-sixth of courts addressing extent of relief limited recovery to reliance damages). In a word, despite § 90's specially-written grant of power to award relief "as justice requires," courts remain divided on the recovery of expectation damages on a claim for promissory estoppel—especially, it seems, when the claim is for lost-profits damages. E.g., Creative Demos, Inc. v. Wal–Mart Stores, Inc., 142 F.3d 367, 369 (7th Cir.1998) (declaring that "in most states" promissory estoppel does not support a claim for profits lost). Part of the difficulty in determining whether § 90 brings its own measure of damages comes from the familiar phenomenon that we explored in Chapter 1—that expectation damages and reliance damages are often proxies for one another and that often the best way to measure one is to use the other.

———

Goodman v. Dicker

United States Court of Appeals, District of Columbia Circuit, 1948.
169 F.2d 684.

PROCTOR, J. This appeal is from a judgment of the District Court in a suit by appellees for breach of contract.

Appellants are local distributors for Emerson Radio & Phonograph Corp. in the District of Columbia. Appellees, with the knowledge and encouragement of appellants, applied for a "dealer franchise" to sell Emerson's products. The trial court found that appellants by their representations and conduct induced appellees to incur expenses in preparing to do business under the franchise, including employment of salesmen and solicitation of orders for radios. Among other things, appellants represented that the application had been accepted; that the franchise would be granted, and that appellees would receive an initial delivery of thirty to forty radios. Yet, no radios were delivered, and notice was finally given that the franchise would not be granted.

The case was tried without a jury. The court held that a contract had not been proven but that appellants were estopped from denying the same by reason of their statements and conduct upon which appellees relied to their detriment. Judgment was entered for $1500, covering cash outlays of $1150 and loss of $350, anticipated profits on sale of thirty radios.

The main contention of appellants is that no liability would have arisen under the dealer franchise had it been granted because, as understood by appellees, it would have been terminable at will and would have imposed no duty upon the manufacturer to sell or appellees to buy any fixed number of radios. From this it is argued that the franchise agreement would not have been enforceable (except as to acts performed thereunder) and cancellation by the manufacturer would have created no liability for expenses incurred by the dealer in preparing to do business. Further, it is argued that as the dealer franchise would have been unenforceable for failure of the manufacturer to supply radios appellants would not be liable to fulfill their assurance that radios would be supplied.

We think these contentions miss the real point of this case. We are not concerned directly with the terms of the franchise. We are dealing with a promise by appellants that a franchise would be granted and radios supplied, on the faith of which appellees with the knowledge and encouragement of appellants incurred expenses in making preparations to do business. Under these circumstances we think that appellants cannot now advance any defense inconsistent with their assurance that the franchise would be granted. Justice and fair dealing require that one who acts to his detriment on the faith of conduct of the kind revealed here should be protected by estopping the party who has brought about the situation from alleging anything in opposition to the natural consequences of his own course of conduct. Dair v. United States, 1872, 16 Wall. 1, 4. In Dickerson v. Colgrove, 100 U.S. 578, 580, the Supreme Court, in speaking of equitable estoppel, said: ". . . The vital principle is that he who by his language or conduct leads another to do what he would not otherwise have done, shall not subject such person to loss or injury by disappointing the expectations upon which he acted. . . . This remedy is always so applied as to promote the ends of justice." . . .

In our opinion the trial court was correct in holding defendants liable for moneys which appellees expended in preparing to do business under the promised dealer franchise. These items aggregated $1150. We think, though, the court erred in adding the item of $350 for loss of profits on radios promised under an initial order. The true measure of damage is the loss sustained by expenditures made in reliance upon the assurance of a dealer franchise. As thus modified, the judgment is [a]ffirmed.

————

American Nat'l Bank v. A.G. Sommerville, Inc.
191 Cal. 364, 216 P. 376 (1923)

Sommerville Co. sold two automobiles to Tomlinson for $3,900 each. Tomlinson signed two contracts, each of which described one of the automobiles and recited that Tomlinson "hereby acknowledges receipt of said property." Each contract also provided that if Sommerville, the seller, assigned to a third party the right to the money promised, Tomlinson "shall be precluded from in any manner attacking the validity of this contract on the ground of fraud, duress, mistake, want of consideration, or failure of consideration, or upon any other ground, and all moneys payable under this contract . . . shall be paid to such assignee or holder without recoupment, setoff or counterclaim of any sort whatsoever." Sommerville promptly assigned its rights under the two contracts to an investment company, which in turn assigned to plaintiff Bank. When plaintiff sued to collect the unpaid balances on the contracts, Tomlinson pleaded that he had never received either of the two automobiles and that neither of them was or ever had been in existence. At trial, Tomlinson tried to testify that he had not received the automobiles, but the court ruled his testimony inadmissible by reason of the quoted provisions of the two contracts. On Tomlinson's appeal, the California Supreme Court stated that the recitals in the contract could not of their own force preclude him from showing either that there was no consideration or that the consideration promised him had not been given; and this was equally true as to an assignee of Sommerville. The court then said that Tomlinson could be precluded through estoppel *in pais* from showing the falsity of a statement of fact on which another had relied. The statements in the contracts were made for the purpose of being acted on. If they were acted on by plaintiff, an estoppel *in pais* would arise, but plaintiff must prove this and the case should be remanded for a determination of this issue of fact.

[handwritten margin note: contracts cannot block lack of consideration.]

[handwritten margin note: in pais?]

————

D'Ulisse–Cupo v. Board of Directors of Notre Dame High School
202 Conn. 206, 520 A.2d 217, 221–223 (1987)

A school board did not rehire a teacher despite representations that she would be given a new contract. The teacher sued for damages, resting on a contract claim of promissory estoppel and a tort claim of negligent misrepresentation. The reviewing court said: "We agree [that the representations plaintiff alleges] do not invoke a cause of action for promissory estoppel because they are neither sufficiently promissory nor sufficiently definite to support contractual liability. . . . We disagree [that the representations are] insufficient to sustain a cause of action for negligent misrepresentation. . . . [E]ven an innocent misrepresentation of fact 'may be actionable if the declarant has the means of knowing, ought to know, or has the duty of knowing the truth.' . . . The governing principles are set forth [in] § 552 of the Rest.2d of Torts: 'One who, in the course of his business, profession or employment . . . supplies false information for the guidance of others in their business transactions, is subject to liability for pecuniary loss caused to them by their justifiable reliance upon the information, if he fails to exercise reasonable care or competence in obtaining or communicating the information.' [D]efendants argue that if they cannot be held liable in contract for their representations based on promissory estoppel, they likewise cannot be held liable in tort for negligent misrepresentation. For purposes of a cause of action for negligent misrepresentation, however, the plaintiff need not prove that the representations made by the defendants were promissory. It is sufficient to allege that the representations contained false information [and that] defendants did not exercise reasonable care in communicating with plaintiff about her prospects for reemployment." [Observe that plaintiff made no claim that defendants' representations were knowingly deceptive, that is, fraudulent. Observe also that the court is clear on the point that the "contractual" remedy of promissory estoppel is wholly independent of a tort remedy for negligent misrepresentation.]

QUESTION

There is reason to think that liability in Goodman v. Dicker could have been based on the tort of negligent misrepresentation. Does that possibility lend support to, or undercut, the court's decision to rest on "estoppel"?

Hoffman v. Red Owl Stores, Inc.

Supreme Court of Wisconsin, 1965.
26 Wis.2d 683, 133 N.W.2d 267.

[Hoffman and his spouse, the plaintiffs, owned and operated a bakery in Wautoma. In 1959, Hoffman began discussions with representatives of Red Owl, which owned and operated a number of grocery supermarkets and franchised "agency stores" owned by others, about opening a Red Owl store. Hoffman mentioned that he had only $18,000 capital; he was "repeatedly assured" by Red Owl representatives that that amount would be sufficient to set him up in a Red Owl agency store. Relying on Red Owl's assurances, in 1961 Hoffman bought the fixtures and inventory of a small grocery store in Wautoma and leased the building in which it was operated, in order to gain experience in the grocery business. After the Hoffmans had run the store profitably for three months, Hoffman, on Red Owl's advice, sold the fixtures and inventory in June 1961, receiving Red Owl's assurance that he would be set up in business in another location by fall. Red Owl selected a site for a new store in Chilton and, on Red Owl's suggestion, Hoffman obtained an option on the site, paying down $1,000 of the $6,000 purchase price. With continuing assurances from Red Owl that "everything is ready to go" and that he should get his capital together, the Hoffmans sold their bakery building. They rented a house in Chilton, paid one month's rent, and, pending the opening of the Chilton store, moved to Neenah where defendant had suggested that Hoffman might gain valuable experience by working in a Red Owl store.

Although the Hoffmans' capital was understood from the beginning to be limited to $18,000, Red Owl raised the required amount to $24,100 after the Hoffmans had sold their grocery store and made the down payment on the Chilton lot. In November 1961, the required sum was increased to $26,100. In February 1962, Red Owl presented another proposal that

Hoffman interpreted to require of him a total of $34,000, of which $13,000 was to come from his father-in-law as a gift. Hoffman thereupon told Red Owl he could not go along with this proposal and this "terminated the negotiations between the parties."]

The case was submitted to the jury on a special verdict with the first two questions answered by the court. This verdict, as returned by the jury, was as follows:

"Question No. 1: Did the Red Owl Stores, Inc. and Joseph Hoffman on or about mid-May of 1961 initiate negotiations looking to the establishment of Joseph Hoffman as a franchise operator of a Red Owl Store in Chilton? Answer: Yes. (Answered by the Court.)

"Question No. 2: Did the parties mutually agree on all of the details of the proposal so as to reach a final agreement thereon? Answer: No. (Answered by the Court.)

"Question No. 3: Did the Red Owl Stores, Inc., in the course of said negotiations, make representations to Joseph Hoffman that if he fulfilled certain conditions that they would establish him as a franchise operator of a Red Owl Store in Chilton? Answer: Yes.

"Question No. 4: If you have answered Question No. 3 'Yes,' then answer this question: Did Joseph Hoffman rely on said representations and was he induced to act thereon? Answer: Yes.

"Question No. 5: If you have answered Question No. 4 'Yes,' then answer this question: Ought Joseph Hoffman, in the exercise of ordinary care, to have relied on said representations? Answer: Yes.

"Question No. 6: If you have answered Question No. 3 'Yes,' then answer this question: Did Joseph Hoffman fulfill all the conditions he was required to fulfill by the terms of the negotiations between the parties up to January 26, 1962? Answer: Yes.

"Question No. 7: What sum of money will reasonably compensate the plaintiffs for such damages as they sustained by reason of:

"(a) The sale of the Wautoma store fixtures and inventory?

"Answer: $16,735.00.

"(b) The sale of the bakery building?

"Answer: $2,000.00.

"(c) Taking up the option on the Chilton lot?

"Answer: $1,000.00.

"(d) Expenses of moving his family to Neenah?

"Answer: $140.00.

"(e) House rental in Chilton?

"Answer: $125.00."

Plaintiffs moved for judgment on the verdict while defendants moved to change the answers to Questions 3, 4, 5, and 6 from "Yes" to "No," and in the alternative for relief from the answers to the subdivisions of Question 7 or a new trial. On March 31, 1964, the circuit court entered the following order:

"IT IS ORDERED in accordance with said decision on motions after verdict hereby incorporated herein by reference:

"1. That the answer of the jury to Question No. 7(a) be and the same is hereby vacated and set aside and that a new trial be had on the sole issue of the damages for loss, if any, on the sale of the Wautoma store, fixtures and inventory.

"2. That all other portions of the verdict of the jury be and hereby are approved and confirmed and all after-verdict motions of the parties inconsistent with this order are hereby denied."

Defendants have appealed from this order and plaintiffs have cross-appealed from paragraph 1, thereof.

CURRIE, C.J. The [appeals] present these questions: (1) Whether [we] should recognize causes of action grounded on promissory estoppel as exemplified by [Restatement] § 90? (2) Do the facts in this case make out a cause of action for promissory estoppel? (3) Are the jury's findings with respect to damages sustained by the evidence?

. . . Since 1933, the closest approach this court has made to adopting the rule of [§ 90] occurred in the recent case of Lazarus v. American Motors Corp. (1963), 21 Wis.2d 76, 123 N.W.2d 548, wherein the court stated: "We recognize that upon different facts it would be possible for a seller of steel to have altered his position so as to effectuate the equitable considerations inherent in § 90."

While it was not necessary [in *Lazarus*] to adopt the promissory estoppel rule of the Restatement, we are squarely faced [here] with that issue. Not only did the trial court frame the special verdict on the theory of [§] 90, . . . but no other possible theory has been presented [which] would permit plaintiffs to recover. Of other remedies considered, that of an action for fraud and deceit seemed to be the most comparable. An action at law for fraud, however, cannot be predicated on unfulfilled promises unless the promisor possessed the present intent not to perform. Suskey v. Davidoff (1958), 2 Wis.2d 503, 87 N.W.2d 306. . . . Here, there is no evidence that would support a finding that Lukowitz [Red Owl's agent] made any of the promises, upon which plaintiffs' complaint is predicated, in bad faith with any present intent that they would not be fulfilled by Red Owl. . . .

Because we deem the [§ 90] doctrine of promissory estoppel . . . [to supply] a needed tool which courts may employ in a proper case to prevent injustice, we endorse and adopt it. The record here discloses a number of promises and assurances given to Hoffman by Lukowitz in behalf of Red Owl upon which plaintiffs relied and acted upon to their detriment.

Foremost were the promises that for the sum of $18,000 Red Owl would establish Hoffman in a store. After Hoffman had sold his grocery store and paid the $1,000 on the Chilton lot, the $18,000 figure was changed to $24,100. Then in November, 1961, Hoffman was assured that if the $24,100 figure were increased by $2,000 the deal would go through. Hoffman was induced to sell his grocery store fixtures and inventory in June, 1961, on the promise that he would be in his new store by fall. In November, plaintiffs sold their bakery building on the urging of defendants and on the assurance that this was the last step necessary to have the deal with Red Owl go through.

. . . [T]here was ample evidence to sustain the answers of the jury to the questions of the verdict with respect to the promissory representations made by Red Owl, Hoffman's reliance thereon in the exercise of ordinary care, and his fulfillment of the conditions required of him by the terms of the negotiations had with Red Owl.

There remains ... the question of law raised by defendants that agreement was never reached on essential factors necessary to establish a contract between Hoffman and Red Owl. Among these were the size, cost, design, and layout of the store building; and the terms of the lease with respect to rent, maintenance, renewal, and purchase options. This poses the question of whether the promise necessary to sustain a cause of action for promissory estoppel must embrace all essential details of a proposed transaction[,] so as to be the equivalent of an offer that would result in a binding contract between the parties if the promisee were to accept the same.

Originally the doctrine of promissory estoppel was invoked as a substitute for consideration rendering a gratuitous promise enforceable as a contract. ... [T]he acts of reliance by the promisee to his detriment provided a substitute for consideration. If promissory estoppel were to be limited to only those situations where the promise giving rise to the cause of action must be so definite with respect to all details that a contract would result were the promise supported by consideration, then the defendants' instant promises to Hoffman would not meet this test. However, § 90 ... does not impose the requirement that the promise giving rise to the cause of action must be so comprehensive in scope as to meet the requirements of an offer that would ripen into a contract if accepted by the promisee. Rather the conditions imposed are:

(1) Was the promise one which the promisor should reasonably expect to induce action or forbearance of a definite and substantial character on the part of the promisee? (2) Did the promise induce such action or forbearance? (3) Can injustice be avoided only by enforcement of the promise?

We deem it would be a mistake to regard an action grounded on promissory estoppel as the equivalent of a breach of contract action. ... [I]t is desirable that fluidity in the application of the concept be maintained. While the first two of the above listed three requirements of promissory estoppel present issues of fact which ordinarily will be resolved by a jury, the third requirement, that the remedy can only be invoked where necessary to avoid injustice, is one that involves a policy decision by the court. Such a policy decision necessarily embraces an element of discretion.

We conclude that injustice would result here if plaintiffs were not granted some relief. ...

Defendants attack all the items of damages awarded by the jury.

The bakery building at Wautoma was sold at defendants' instigation in order that Hoffman might have the net proceeds available as part of the cash capital he was to invest in the Chilton store venture. ... [I]t was sold at a loss of $2,000. Defendants contend that half of this loss was sustained by Mrs. Hoffman because title stood in joint tenancy. They point out that no dealings took place between her and defendants. ... Ordinarily only the promisee and not third persons are entitled to enforce the remedy of promissory estoppel against the promisor. However, if the promisor actually foresees, or has reason to foresee, action by a third person in reliance on the promise, it may be quite unjust to refuse to perform the promise. 1A Corbin, Contracts, [§] 200. Here not only did defendants foresee that it would be necessary for Mrs. Hoffman to sell her joint interest in the bakery building, but defendants actually requested that this be done. We approve the jury's award of $2,000 damages for the loss incurred by both plaintiffs in this sale.

Defendants attack on two grounds the $1,000 awarded because of Hoffman's payment of that amount on the purchase price of the Chilton lot. The first is that this $1,000 had already been lost at the time the final negotiations with Red Owl fell through in January, 1962, because the remaining $5,000 of purchase price had been due on October 15, 1961. The record does not disclose that the lot owner had foreclosed Hoffman's interest in the lot for failure to pay this $5,000. The $1,000 was not paid for the option, but had been paid as part of the purchase price at the time Hoffman elected to exercise the option. This gave him an equity in the lot which could not be legally foreclosed without affording Hoffman an opportunity to pay the balance. The second ground of attack is that the lot may have had a fair market value of $6,000, and Hoffman should have paid the remaining $5,000 of purchase price. [But] it would be unreasonable to require Hoffman to have invested an additional $5,000 in order to protect the $1,000 he had paid. Therefore, we find no merit to defendants' attack upon this item of damages.

We also determine it was reasonable for Hoffman to have paid $125 for one month's rent of a home in Chilton after defendants assured him everything would be set when plaintiff sold the bakery building. This was a proper item of damage.

Plaintiffs never moved to Chilton because defendants suggested that Hoffman get some experience by working in a Red Owl store in the Fox River Valley. Plaintiffs, therefore, moved to Neenah instead of Chilton. After moving, Hoffman worked at night in an Appleton bakery but held himself available for work in a Red Owl store. The $140 moving expense would not have been incurred if plaintiffs had not sold their bakery building in Wautoma in reliance upon defendants' promises. We consider the $140 moving expense to be a proper item of damage.

We turn now to the damage item with respect to which the trial court granted a new trial, i.e., that arising from the sale of the Wautoma grocery store fixtures and inventory for which the jury awarded $16,735. The trial court ruled that Hoffman could not recover for any loss of future profits for the summer months following the sale on June 6, 1961, but that damages would be limited to the difference between the sales price received and the fair market value of the assets sold, giving consideration to any goodwill attaching thereto by reason of the transfer of a going business. There is no direct evidence presented as to what this fair market value was on June 6, 1961. The evidence did disclose that Hoffman paid $9,000 for the inventory, added $1,500 to it and sold it for $10,000 or a loss of $500. His 1961 federal income tax return showed that the grocery equipment had been purchased for $7,000 and sold for $7,955.96. Plaintiffs introduced evidence of the buyer that during the first eleven weeks of operation of the grocery store his gross sales were $44,000 and his profit was $6,000 or roughly 15 percent. On cross-examination he admitted that this was gross and not net profit. Plaintiffs contend that in a breach of contract action damages may include loss of profits. However, this is not a breach of contract action.

The only relevancy of evidence relating to profits would be with respect to proving the element of goodwill in establishing the fair market value of the grocery inventory and fixtures sold. Therefore, evidence of profits would be admissible to afford a foundation for expert opinion as to fair market value.

Where damages are awarded in promissory estoppel instead of specifically enforcing the promisor's promise, they should be only such as in the opinion of the court are necessary to prevent injustice. Mechanical or rule of thumb approaches to the damage problem should be avoided. . . . "The wrong is not primarily in depriving the plaintiff of the promised reward but in causing the plaintiff to change position to his detriment. It would follow that the damages should not exceed the loss caused by the change of position, which would never be more in amount, but might be less, than the promised reward." Seavey, Reliance on Gratuitous Promises or Other Conduct, 64 Harv.L.Rev. (1951), 913, 926. . . .

At the time Hoffman bought the equipment and inventory of the small grocery store at Wautoma he did so in order to gain experience in the grocery store business. At that time discussion had already been had with Red Owl representatives that Wautoma might be too small for a Red Owl operation and that a larger city might be more desirable. Thus Hoffman made this purchase more or less as a temporary experiment. Justice does not require that the damages awarded him, because of selling these assets at the behest of defendants, should exceed any actual loss sustained measured by the difference between the sales price and the fair market value.

Since the evidence does not sustain the large award of damages arising from the sale of the Wautoma grocery business, the trial court properly ordered a new trial on this issue. Order affirmed.

NOTE

Hoffman involves an extended interaction between parties who never entered into a formal contract with one another. Scholars continue to use the facts as set out in the record in *Hoffman* as a vehicle to analyze the circumstances under which the conduct of parties during these negotiations should give rise to legal liability. For contrasting approaches, compare Whitford & Macaulay, *Hoffman v. Red Owl Stores*: The Rest of the Story, 61 Hastings L.J. 801 (2010), with Scott, *Hoffman v. Red Owl Stores* and the Limits of Legal Method, 61 Hastings L.J. 859 (2010).

To what extent is the idea of promissory estoppel a useful way to ensure that parties negotiate with each other in good faith before they actually enter into a contract? What are the alternatives? Should one require that the parties explicitly agree to negotiate with each other in good faith before liability will attach? For a discussion of the emerging line of cases dealing with liability arising out of precontractual negotiations and its relationship with § 90, see Schwartz & Scott, Precontractual Liability and Preliminary Agreements, 120 Harv. L. Rev. 661 (2007).

CHAPTER 3

WHEN (AND HOW) PROMISES BECOME ENFORCEABLE

SECTION 1. MUTUAL ASSENT

INTRODUCTORY NOTE

The aim of this chapter is to examine the rules, doctrines, and techniques employed by courts in determining whether agreement has been achieved to such an extent that legal consequences should follow. To be sure, the problem of "communication" permeates the law's search for binding commitment. Agreement may be manifested wholly or partly by words, written or spoken, by acts, or even by a failure to act. Yet a casual glance through any dictionary is a sufficient reminder of the risk that one person's intention will not be revealed fully or accurately to another. A meaning intended by one party may be understood quite differently by the other. Moreover, doubts about the existence of any moment of real agreement between the parties can arise from any number of steps, or turns, in a negotiation. We have seen enough already to know that the inquiry made by legal agencies, when enforcement of an alleged agreement is demanded, is conducted through a complex procedure with restrictive rules of evidence; it cannot be equated with a psychologist's probe in depth.

Nevertheless, contract obligation is voluntarily assumed, resting on the assent of each party to the proposed exchange. The lawyer who demands or resists judicial enforcement is required to think and talk about the sort of agreement that initiates a contract, and to use the analytical tools and working rules by which this minimum initiating-agreement is determined.

An additional aim of this chapter is to suggest the difficulties encountered when one attempts to define in general terms the elements of agreement. The difficulties arise in large part from the range of human experience to which legal doctrines must apply. Consider the types of transactions in the cases that follow. Consider also the fact that these various consensual arrangements are discussed by the courts with a common vocabulary, and they are perceived as presenting a common problem—has sufficient agreement been achieved to justify enforcement in court? Is it too much to expect that problems appearing in such diverse forms will have enough common elements that a general theory can be made to include them all?

Raffles v. Wichelhaus

Court of Exchequer, 1864.
2 Hurlstone & Coltman 906.

Declaration. For that it was agreed between the plaintiff and the defendants, to wit, at Liverpool, that the plaintiff should sell to the defendants, and the defendants buy of the plaintiff, certain goods, to wit, 125 bales of Surat cotton, guaranteed middling fair merchant's Dhollorah, to arrive ex "Peerless" from Bombay; and that the cotton should be taken from the quay, and that the defendants would pay the plaintiff for the same at a certain rate, to wit, at the rate of 17¼ d. per pound, within a certain time then agreed upon after the arrival of the said goods in England.—Averments: that the said goods did arrive by the said ship from Bombay in England, to wit, at Liverpool, and the plaintiff was then and there ready and willing and offered to deliver the said goods to the defendants, etc. Breach: that the defendants refused to accept the said goods or pay the plaintiff for them.

Plea. That the said ship mentioned in the said agreement was meant and intended by the defendants to be the ship called the "Peerless," which sailed from Bombay, to wit, in October; and that the plaintiff was not ready and willing and did not offer to deliver to the defendants any bales of cotton which arrived by the last-mentioned ship, but instead thereof was only ready and willing, and offered to deliver to the defendants 125 bales of Surat cotton which arrived by another and different ship, which was also called the "Peerless," and which sailed from Bombay, to wit, in December.

Demurrer, and joinder therein.

Milward, in support of the demurrer.—The contract was for the sale of a number of bales of cotton of a particular description, which the plaintiff was ready to deliver. It is immaterial by what ship the cotton was to arrive, so that it was a ship called the "Peerless." The words "to arrive ex 'Peerless,'" only mean that if the vessel is lost on the voyage, the contract is to be at an end. [Pollock, C.B.—It would be a question for the jury whether both parties meant the same ship called the "Peerless."] That would be so if the contract was for the sale of a ship called the "Peerless;" but it is for the sale of cotton on board a ship of that name. [Pollock, C.B.—The defendant only bought that cotton which was to arrive by a particular ship. It may as well be said, that if there is a contract for the purchase of certain goods in warehouse A, that is satisfied by the delivery of goods of the same description in warehouse B.] In that case there would be goods in both warehouses; here it does not appear that the plaintiff had any goods on board the other "Peerless." [Martin, B.—It is imposing on the defendant a contract different from that which he entered into. Pollock, C.B.—It is like a contract for the purchase of wine coming from a particular estate in France or Spain, where there are two estates of that name.] The defendant has no right to contradict by parol evidence a written contract good upon the face of it. He does not impute misrepresentation or fraud, but only says that he fancied the ship was a different one. Intention is of no avail, unless stated at the time of the contract. [Pollock, C.B.—One vessel sailed in October and the other in December.] The time of sailing is no part of the contract.

Mellish (Cohen with him), in support of the plea.—There is nothing on the face of the contract to shew that any particular ship called the "Peerless" was meant; but the moment it appears that two ships called the "Peerless" were about to sail from Bombay there is a latent ambiguity, and parol evidence may be given for the purpose of shewing that the defendant meant one "Peerless" and the plaintiff another. That being so, there was no consensus ad idem, and therefore no binding contract.—He was then stopped by the Court.

[Per Curiam]—There must be judgment for the defendants.

[It has been reported that there were at least eleven ships called "Peerless" sailing the seven seas in 1863, including the two British vessels in question in Raffles v. Wichelhaus, both registered at the port of Liverpool. It is possible that, by specifying the ship in the contract, parties were able to lock in a fixed supply of cotton at a later date, something that was arguably important when the price of cotton was volatile and supplies uncertain, as it was during the American Civil War. In other words, these contracts were an early version of futures contracts. For a discussion of these issues, see Simpson, Contracts for Cotton to Arrive: The Case of the Two Ships *Peerless*, 11 Cardozo L.Rev. 287, 295 (1989).]

QUESTIONS

(1) Is Chief Baron Pollock's two-warehouse example distinguishable from the case of the two wine estates? Which is more like the principal case?

(2) Would the result be different if both parties had known there were two ships named Peerless sailing regularly from Bombay?

(3) What if both parties had known that there were two ships named Peerless sailing regularly from Bombay and both had understood the contract to refer to the same ship, sailing in October?

———

Flower City Painting Contractors v. Gumina Constr. Co.
591 F.2d 162 (2d Cir.1979)

During performance of a painting subcontract, Flower, the sub, insisted that it was required to paint only interior walls of individual units within the apartment project, not exteriors. This reading of the subcontract depended upon a finding that the building plans and specifications had not been incorporated into the subcontract by reference. When Flower held to its interpretation by demanding additional compensation before proceeding with any exterior work, Gumina, the general contractor, cancelled the subcontract and removed Flower from the job. Flower sued for damages. The trial court adopted Gumina's interpretation of the subcontract and dismissed the complaint on the ground that Flower's "asking for extra pay for work it was obligated to do under its contract" was the equivalent of a repudiation, justifying cancellation. On appeal, the court preferred to bypass the "thorny problem" of repudiation presented by these facts. *Held*, judgment of dismissal affirmed under the rule of the *Peerless* case; no contract ever came into existence for lack of a "meeting of the minds in the first instance." Given the ambiguity created by multiple contract documents, two different understandings of the subject matter embraced by the contract are both possible and plausible. Yet the ambiguity might be resolved (in favor of Gumina) by construing the contract as incorporating the customary practice of the construction industry in the Rochester area, that painting subcontracts are awarded on "an entire project basis." But proof of a trade usage is not enough to establish the meaning of a contract, for a party is bound by usage only if "he either knows or has reason to know of its existence and nature." The proofs make clear that Flower <u>did not know of the usage</u>; hence the issue is whether it "had reason to know" of it. Flower was "a neophyte . . . painting contractor. This was its first substantial subcontract on a construction job. It would be unrealistic to hold it strictly to a 'reason to know' standard." Accordingly, "we cannot say that either party acted so unreasonably as to justify construing the ambiguity [against it]. Each party . . . held a different and reasonable view of the undertaking, Flower on the basis of its literal reading of the word 'units' and Gumina because of its supposition concerning trade practice. . . . Though the setting is new, the problem is old."

———

NOTE

In Konic Int'l Corp. v. Spokane Computer Services, Inc., 109 Idaho 527, 708 P.2d 932 (Ct.App.1985), the seller had responded to the buyer's inquiry as to the price of certain computer equipment by saying "fifty-six twenty." The seller had meant $5,620; the buyer thought the asking price was $56.20; the misunderstanding was discovered not long after the equipment had been installed. The court, finding the parties equally at fault and bypassing other legal doctrines, treated the case as governed by the *Peerless* rule.

The *Konic* decision is noted in Colfax Envelope Corp. v. Local No. 458–3M, Chicago Graphic Communications Int'l Union, 20 F.3d 750 (7th Cir.1994) (Posner, J.):

> The premise—that a "meeting of the minds" is required for a binding contract—obviously is strained. . . . Most contract disputes arise because the parties did not foresee and provide for some contingency that has now materialized—so there was no meeting of minds on the matter at issue—yet such disputes are treated as disputes over contractual meaning, not as grounds for rescinding the contract and thus putting the parties back where they were before they signed it. So a literal meeting of the minds is not required for an enforceable contract. . . . [A] contract ought to be terminable without liability and the parties thus allowed to go their own ways when there is "no sensible basis for choosing between conflicting understandings" of the contractual language, as the court said in an American *Raffles*-like case, Oswald v. Allen, 417 F.2d 43, 45 (2d Cir.1969). . . .

> If neither party can be assigned the greater blame for the misunderstanding, there is no nonarbitrary basis for deciding which party's understanding to enforce, so the parties are allowed to abandon the contract without liability. . . . These are not cases in which one party's understanding is more reasonable than the other's. Compare Restatement, supra, § 20(2)(b). If rescission were permitted in *that* kind of case, the enforcement of every contract would be at the mercy of a jury, which might be persuaded that one of the parties had genuinely held an idiosyncratic idea of its meaning, so that there had been, in fact, no meeting of the minds. . . . Intersubjectivity is not the test of an enforceable contract.

The clearest cases for rescission on the ground that there was "no meeting of the minds" (or, better, that there was a "latent ambiguity" in the sense that neither party knew that the contract was ambiguous) are ones in which an offer is garbled in transmission, [if] "transmission" is broadly construed.... [C]onsider *Konic International Corp.*[,] [where] both were equally at fault, being careless in their utterance and interpretation, respectively, of an ambiguous oral formula....

It is common for contracting parties to agree—that is, to *signify* agreement—to a term to which each party attaches a different meaning. It is just a gamble on a favorable interpretation by the authorized tribunal should a dispute arise. Parties often prefer to gamble in this way rather than to take the time to try to iron out all their possible disagreements, most of which may never have any consequence.... When parties agree to a patently ambiguous term, they submit to have any dispute over it resolved by interpretation. That is what courts are *for* in contract cases—to resolve interpretive questions founded on ambiguity. It is when parties agree to terms that reasonably appear to each of them to be unequivocal but are not, cases like that of the ship *Peerless* where the ambiguity is buried, that the possibility of rescission on grounds of mutual misunderstanding, or, the term we prefer, latent ambiguity, arises.

———

Dickey v. Hurd

33 F.2d 415 (1st Cir.1929)

Dickey, resident of Georgia, wrote to Hurd in Massachusetts asking the price for which Hurd would sell land he owned in Georgia. On July 8, 1926, Hurd replied "$15 per acre cash," adding, "I will give you till July 18, 1926 including that day to accept this offer." In two letters, written July 12 and July 15, Dickey expressed great interest in Hurd's land, stating that he would give his "answer" within the time limit. On July 17, Dickey telegraphed an acceptance and promised to send a down payment in a few days. The telegram reached Hurd the same day. Hurd contended that the acceptance was ineffective because the offer called for the whole cash price to be paid by July 18. Bingham, J., said that the original offer was ambiguous, but Dickey's two letters indicated to Hurd that he believed only an "answer" was needed by July 18. When Hurd learned how Dickey interpreted the offer, it was Hurd's duty to inform him that the offer called for payment rather than a promise of payment. "It was not open to him to lie quietly by" until the time limit had expired, and then assert that full cash payment was required.

———

QUESTION

What if the plaintiff in Raffles v. Wichelhaus had known of the existence of both ships Peerless but defendant knew only the October Peerless?

———

RESTATEMENT OF CONTRACTS, SECOND

Section 20. Effect of Misunderstanding ☆

(1) There is no manifestation of mutual assent to an exchange if the parties attach materially different meanings to their manifestations and

(a) neither party knows or has reason to know the meaning attached by the other; or

(b) each party knows or each party has reason to know the meaning attached by the other.

(2) The manifestations of the parties are operative in accordance with the meaning attached to them by one of the parties if

(a) that party does not know of any different meaning attached by the other, and the other knows the meaning attached by the first party; or

(b) that party has no reason to know of any different meaning attached by the other, and the other has reason to know the meaning attached by the first party.

NOTE

When Reporter Robert Braucher presented § 20 to the annual meeting of the American Law Institute in 1964, he explained that it was a "new construction" of the problem of the *Peerless* case—a problem he described as "general to the whole concept of mutual assent." Reporter Braucher added (41 A.L.I. Proc. 319–320 (1965)):

> I tried to straighten it out and get it into a form where I could understand it. . . . In my thinking about [mutual assent], this [§ 20] is a fairly fundamental proposition, and I refer back to it continually because it doesn't just deal with things that go to the heart of the transaction; . . . it also goes to understanding all kinds of incidental terms in a contract. The standard of interpretation may depend upon what one party understood and the other party knew he understood. I am anticipating here [the principles for determining rights and duties under a contract, where formation is not an issue], but it seemed to me you had to, in order to define mutual assent.

The *Peerless* decision has generated a considerable literature. See, e.g., Simpson, Contracts for Cotton to Arrive: The Case of the Two Ships *Peerless*, 11 Cardozo L.Rev. 287 (1989); Birmingham, Holmes on "Peerless": *Raffles v. Wichelhaus* and the Objective Theory of Contract, 47 U.Pitt.L.Rev. 183 (1985); G. Gilmore, The Death of Contract 35–44 (1974).

Some of the first readers of *Raffles* understood it to stand for the proposition that a contract came into being only if there were a subjective meeting of the minds. Oliver Wendell Holmes rejected this view. He believed that *Raffles* was consistent with an objective approach to determining the intent of the parties to enter into a contract. For him, the case turned on the accepted convention for proper names. Each of us is entitled to rely on the link that we make between a name and the person or object we associate with it. I can talk about someone I know by name and expect you to know to whom I am referring. If you are not sure, you need to ask. In this case, Raffles and Wichelhaus were objectively speaking of two different ships, as each was entitled to use "Peerless" to refer to the only ship each knew by that name. The same convention does not apply to ordinary nouns. I cannot use the word "pepper" when I mean "salt," and then later argue that there was never a meeting of the minds. If a merchant enters into a contract for "pepper," while genuinely thinking "salt," she will still be bound to deliver pepper. The words she actually spoke, as defined in the relevant lexicon, bind her regardless of what she was thinking. People communicate through a common language, and commerce depends upon the use of this common language. Merchants need to be able to take what they say to each other at face value. When you say "salt," I am entitled to hold you responsible for salt, regardless of what you subjectively intended.

Holmes's objectivist account of *Raffles* may not be the only or even the best reading of the case, but it has taken hold in large part because it comports so well with how lawyers and judges approach such problems. Indeed, as the noted legal historian Brian Simpson pointed out, it was a practicing lawyer who introduced *Raffles* to the canon, and his account of the case is, in large measure, an objective one. Judah P. Benjamin was a prominent leader of the Confederacy who reinvented himself as an English barrister after he was forced into exile. His treatise on sales has the first discussion of *Raffles*. He summarized the principle in this fashion:

> If *A* and *B* contract for the sale of the cargo per ship Peerless, and there be two ships of that name, and *A* mean one ship and *B* intend the other ship, there is no contract. But if there be but one ship Peerless, and *A* sell the cargo of that ship to *B*, the latter would not be permitted to excuse himself on the ground that he had in his mind the ship Peeress, and intended to contract for a cargo by this last-named ship. Men can only bargain by mutual communication, and if *A*'s proposal were unmistakable, as if it were made in writing, and *B*'s answer an unequivocal and unconditional acceptance, *B* would be bound, however clearly he might afterwards make it appear that he was thinking of a different vessel. For the rule of law is general, that whatever a man's real intention may be, if he manifests an intention to another party, so as to induce that other party to act upon it, he will be estopped from denying that the intention as manifested was his real intention.

See Judah P. Benjamin, A Treatise on the Law of Sale of Personal Property; Reference to the American Decisions and to the French Code and Civil Law 347–48 (J. Perkins ed., first American edition 1875).

Learned Hand captured the objective approach to mutual assent in a vivid metaphor some years later:

> A contract has, strictly speaking, nothing to do with the personal, or individual, intent of the parties. A contract is an obligation attached by the mere force of law to certain acts of the parties, usually words, which ordinarily accompany and represent a known intent. If, however, it were proved by twenty bishops that either party, when he used the words, intended something else than the usual meaning which the law imposes upon them, he would still be held. . . .

Hotchkiss v. National City Bank of New York, 200 F. 287, 293 (S.D.N.Y.1911). Everyone from Judah P. Benjamin to Holmes to Learned Hand can agree with the idea that parties to contracts adopt the formalities inherently associated with language. "Men can only bargain by mutual communication." If there is one ship Peerless and the contract unambiguously calls for cotton on the ship "Peerless," you cannot get off the hook by proving that you had the ship "Peeress" in mind when you entered into the deal. Everyone is both an objectivist and a formalist to at least this extent.

From the perspective of the practicing lawyer, however, the difference between a subjective and objective approach to the creation of the legally enforceable obligation may not in fact prove large. Even were a subjective test to apply, parties would still have to introduce evidence that persuades a jury of their subjective intent. Twenty bishops are likely to be available to testify as to my subjective intentions only when these intentions were objectively manifest. Similarly, if an objective test controlled, my subjective intent provides indirect evidence. Ordinarily, someone who subjectively intends to sell salt will appear objectively to want to sell salt. My subjective intention to sell salt (evidenced perhaps by telling my friends about the deal) is probative of my objective conduct (what I actually told you). See Kabil Developments Corp. v. Mignot, 279 Or. 151, 566 P.2d 505 (Or. 1977).

A commitment to an objective approach does have consequences, however. When an objective benchmark is used to assess meaning, cases like *Raffles* tend to appear only in the rare cases when each party is entitled to use her own lexicon (such as when each refers to a proper noun). Parties are usually held to speak the same language. In these cases, when disputes arise, everyone agrees that there is a contract. The dispute is over the meaning of the agreement. Both parties agree that a single objective test determines what each said, but they disagree about what this test is. We shall return to this issue when we confront the problem of interpreting contracts in Chapter 4.

———

Embry v. Hargadine–McKittrick Dry Goods Co.

Court of Appeals, Missouri, 1907.
127 Mo.App. 383, 105 S.W. 777.

GOODE, J. . . . The appellant was an employee of the respondent company under a written contract to expire December 15, 1903, at a salary of $2,000 per annum. His duties were to attend to the sample department[,] of which he was given complete charge. It was his business to select samples for the traveling salesmen of the company, which is a wholesale dry goods concern, to use in selling goods to retail merchants. Appellant contends that on December 23, 1903, he was re-engaged by respondent, through its president, Thos. H. McKittrick, for another year at the same compensation and for the same duties stipulated in his previous written contract. On March 1, 1904, he was discharged, having been notified in February that, on account of the necessity of retrenching expenses, his services and that of some other employees would no longer be required. The respondent contends that its president never re-employed appellant after the termination of his written contract, and hence that it had a right to discharge him when it chose. The point with which we are concerned requires an epitome of the testimony of appellant and the counter testimony of McKittrick, [in] reference to the alleged re-employment. Appellant testified: That several times prior to the termination of his written contract on December 15, he had endeavored to get an understanding with McKittrick for another year, but had been put off from time to time. That on December 23d, eight days after the expiration of said contract, he called on McKittrick, in the latter's office, and said to him that as appellant's written employment had lapsed eight days before, and as there were only a few days between then and the 1st of January in which to seek employment with other firms, if respondent wished to retain his services longer he must have a contract for another year, or he would quit respondent's service then and there. That he had been put off twice before and wanted an understanding or contract at once so that he could go ahead without worry. That McKittrick asked him how he was getting along in his department, and appellant said he was very busy, as they were in the height of the season getting men out—had about 110 salesmen on the line and others in preparation. That McKittrick then said: "Go ahead, you're all right. Get your men out, and don't let that worry you." That appellant took McKittrick at his word and worked until February 15th without any question in his mind. It was on February 15th that he was notified his services would be discontinued on March 1st. McKittrick denied this conversation as related by appellant, and said that, when accosted by the latter on December 23d, he (McKittrick) was working on his books in order to get out a report for a stockholders' meeting, and, when appellant said if he did not get a contract he would leave, that he (McKittrick) said: "Mr. Embry, I am just getting ready for the stockholders' meeting tomorrow. I have no time to take it up now. I have told you before I would not take it up until I had these matters out of the way. You will have to see me at a later time. I said: 'Go back upstairs and get your men out on the road.' I may have asked him one or two other questions relative to the department, I don't remember. The whole conversation did not take more than a minute."

Embry also swore that, when he was notified he would be discharged, he complained to McKittrick about it, as being a violation of their contract, and McKittrick said it was due to the action of the board of directors, and not to any personal action of his, and that others would suffer by what the board had done as well as Embry. Appellant requested an instruction to the jury setting out, in substance, the conversation between him and McKittrick according to his version, and declaring that those facts, if found to be true, constituted a contract between the parties that defendant would pay plaintiff the sum of $2,000 for another year, provided the jury believed from the evidence that plaintiff commenced said work believing he was to have $2,000 for the year's work. This instruction was refused, but the court gave another embodying in substance appellant's version of the conversation, and declaring it made a contract "if you (the jury) find both parties thereby intended and did contract with each other for plaintiff's employment for one year from and including December 23, at a salary of $2,000 per annum." Embry swore that, on several occasions when he spoke to McKittrick about employment for the ensuing year, he asked for a renewal of his former contract, and that on December 23d, the date of the alleged renewal, he went into Mr. McKittrick's office and told him his contract had expired, and he wanted to renew it for a year, having always worked under year contracts. Neither the refused instruction nor the one given by the court embodied facts quite as strong as appellant's testimony, because neither referred to appellant's alleged statement to McKittrick that unless he was re-employed he would stop work for respondent then and there.

It is assigned for error that the court required the jury, in order to return a verdict for appellant, not only to find the conversation occurred as appellant swore, but that both parties intended by such conversation to contract with each other for plaintiff's employment for the year from December, 1903. . . . [T]o put the question more precisely: Did what was said constitute a contract of re-employment on the previous terms irrespective of the intention or purpose of McKittrick?

Judicial opinion and elementary treatises abound in statements of the rule that to constitute a contract there must be a meeting of the minds of the parties, and both must agree to the same thing in the same sense. Generally speaking, this may be true; but it is not literally or universally true. That is to say, the inner intention of parties to a conversation subsequently alleged to create a contract cannot either make a contract of what transpired, or prevent one from arising, if the words used were sufficient to constitute a contract. In so far as their intention is an influential element, it is only such intention as the words or acts of the parties indicate. . . . In 9 Cyc. 245, we find the following text: "The law imputes to a person an intention corresponding to the reasonable meaning of his words and acts. It judges his intention by his outward expressions and excludes all questions in regard to his unexpressed intention. If his words or acts, judged by a reasonable standard, manifest an intention to agree in regard to the matter in question, that agreement is established, and it is immaterial what may be the real, but unexpressed, state of his mind on the subject." . . . In view of those authorities, we hold that, though McKittrick may not have intended to employ Embry by what transpired between them according to the latter's testimony, yet if what McKittrick said would have been taken by a reasonable man to be an employment, and Embry so understood it, it constituted a valid contract of employment for the ensuing year.

The next question is whether or not the language used was of that character, namely, was such that Embry, as a reasonable man, might consider he was re-employed for the ensuing year on the previous terms, and act accordingly. We do not say that in every instance it would be for the court to pronounce on this question, because, peradventure, instances might arise in which there would be such an ambiguity in the language relied on to show an assent by the obligor to the proposal of the obligee that it would be for the jury to say whether a reasonable mind would take it to signify acceptance of the proposal. . . . The general rule is that it is for the court to construe the effect of writings relied on to make a contract, and also the effect of unambiguous oral words. . . . However, if the words are in dispute, the question of whether they were used or not is for the jury. . . .

With these rules of law in mind, let us recur to the conversation of December 23d between Embry and McKittrick as related by the former. Embry was demanding a renewal of his contract, saying he had been put off from time to time, and that he had only a few days before the end of the year in which to seek employment from other houses, and that he would quit then and there unless he was reemployed. McKittrick inquired how he was getting along with the department, and Embry said they, i.e., the employés of the department, were very busy getting out salesmen. Whereupon McKittrick said: "Go ahead, you are all right. Get your men out, and do not let that worry you." We think no reasonable man would construe that answer to Embry's demand that he be employed for another year, otherwise than as an assent to the demand, and that Embry had the right to rely on it as an assent. The natural inference is, though we do not find it testified to, that Embry was at work getting samples ready for the salesmen to use during the ensuing season. Now, when he was complaining of the worry and mental distress he was under because of his uncertainty about the future, and his urgent need, either of an immediate contract with respondent, or a refusal by it to make one, leaving him free to seek employment elsewhere, McKittrick must have answered as he did for the purpose of assuring appellant that any apprehension was needless, as appellant's services would be retained by the respondent. The answer was unambiguous, and we rule that if the conversation was according to appellant's version, and he understood he was employed, it constituted in law a valid contract of re-employment, and the court erred in making the formation of a contract depend on a finding that both parties intended to make one. It was only necessary that Embry, as a reasonable man, had a right to and did so understand. . . .

The judgment is reversed, and the cause remanded.

––––––––––

New York Trust Co. v. Island Oil & Transport Corp.
34 F.2d 655 (2d Cir.1929)

Island Oil, in order to circumvent restrictions on its owning and exploiting oil-bearing lands within 50 kilometers of the Mexican coast, organized several Mexican subsidiary corporations to appear as owners and operators. Island Oil held virtually all of the stock in the subsidiaries and in fact operated the oil fields; no significant role was played by the Mexican officers of the subsidiaries. Nevertheless, in compliance with Mexican law, accounts were kept that showed substantial sales of oil from the subsidiaries to Island Oil and balances due. Island Oil mortgaged its stock in the subsidiaries, and these shares were later sold in a foreclosure. In an equity receivership of Island Oil, a proceeding similar in purpose to a bankruptcy reorganization, the new owners of one of the subsidiaries filed a claim against the receiver of Island Oil for the balances. *Held*, decree dismissing the claim affirmed. The apparent sales of oil and the substantial balances due were shams. Judge Learned Hand, speaking for the Court:

"However, the form of utterance chosen is never final; it is always possible to show that the parties did not intend to perform what they said they would, as, for example, that the transaction was a joke. . . . It is quite true that contracts depend upon the meaning which the law imputes to the utterances, not upon what the parties actually intended; but, in ascertaining what meaning to impute, the circumstances in which the words are used are always relevant and usually indispensable. The standard is what a normally constituted person would have understood them to mean, when used in their actual setting. In the case at bar it is abundantly clear that no such person, making the records here in question in such a background, would have supposed that they represented actual sales of oil; that is, commercial transactions. They were made for quite other purposes, formally to conform with, and, if one chooses, to evade, the [law]. They were a sham, which nobody did, and nobody advised could, understand as intended to be more. . . .

"The question then becomes whether legal obligations shall be attached to utterances which would otherwise not create them, because they were part of a plan to deceive third persons. We are to distinguish between such a situation and one in which the person deceived has acted in reliance upon the truth of the utterances, and bases his rights upon them, for here we are only concerned with the existence of obligations between parties equally implicated. We cannot see why their common fault should so change the relations between them. Indeed, if we were asked to intervene between them, and give relief based upon the sham transaction, we might refuse; 'in pari delicto potior est conditio possidentis.' Here we must raise an obligation where none would otherwise exist, because by hypothesis both were concerned in a fraud upon a third. As compensation, this would be fruitless; as punishment, it would be capricious; as law, it would create an obligation ex turpi causa."

[Judge Hand, writing seven years later, said: "[W]hatever the formal documentary evidence, it is no objection that [the parties' understanding that a purported contract was not to bind them] contradicts the writing; a writing is conclusive only so far as the parties intend it to be the authoritative memorial of the transaction. Whatever the presumptions, their actual understanding may always be shown except so far as expressly or implicitly they have agreed that the writing alone shall control." In re H. Hicks & Son, 82 F.2d 277, 279 (2d Cir.1936).]

————

Robbins v. Lynch

836 F.2d 330, 332 (7th Cir.1988)

"References in cases to the importance of 'intent to be bound' are misleading if taken literally. As so frequently in law, 'intent' is a conclusion rather than a fact. A signatory to a contract is bound by its ordinary meaning even if he gave it an idiosyncratic one; private intent counts only if it is conveyed to the other party and shared. You can't escape contractual obligation by signing with your fingers crossed behind your back. . . . The parties are free to sign hortatory as well as binding documents; 'intent' is important in the sense that if the parties agree on a hortatory instrument the court may not convert it into a different kind. This sense of 'intent' denotes agreement between the parties and is not a license to allow undisclosed intent to dominate. Even statutes, widely said to follow the 'intent of the legislature,' draw meaning only from the visible indicators such as their structure, the nature of the problem at hand, and public statements (as in committee reports). Private intent is irrelevant."

————

SECTION 2. OFFER AND ACCEPTANCE

Morrison v. Thoelke

District Court of Appeal of Florida, 1963.
155 So.2d 889.

ALLEN, ACTING CHIEF JUDGE. Appellants, defendants and counter-plaintiffs in the lower court, appeal a summary final decree for appellees, plaintiffs and counter-defendants below. The appellees, owners of certain realty, sued to quiet title, specifically requesting that appellants be enjoined from making any claim under a recorded contract for the sale of the subject realty. [A]ppellants counterclaimed, seeking specific performance of the same contract and conveyance of the subject property to them. . . .

A number of undisputed facts were established[:] that appellees are the owners of the property, located in Orange County; that on November 26, 1957, appellants, as purchasers, executed a contract for the sale and purchase of the property and mailed the contract to appellees who were in Texas; that on November 27, appellees executed the contract and placed it in the mails addressed to appellants' attorney in Florida[;] [and] that after mailing said contract, but prior to its receipt in Florida, appellees called appellants' attorney and cancelled and repudiated the execution and contract. Nonetheless, appellants, upon receipt of the contract caused the same to be recorded. . . .

The basis of [the lower court's] decision [for appellees] was[:] . . . "[T]he contract executed by the parties hereto . . . [was] cancelled and repudiated by Plaintiffs prior to its receipt by Defendants . . . and [thus] there was no legal contract binding on the parties."

. . . [W]e are confronted with a question apparently of first impression in this jurisdiction[,] whether a contract is complete and binding when a letter of acceptance is mailed, thus barring repudiation prior to delivery to the offeror, or when the letter of acceptance is received, thus permitting repudiation prior to receipt. . . .

The appellant, in arguing that the lower court erred in giving effect to the repudiation of the mailed acceptance, contends that this case is controlled by the general rule that insofar as the mail is an acceptable medium of communication, a contract is complete and binding upon posting of the letter of acceptance. . . . Appellees, on the other hand, argue that the right to recall mail makes the Post Office Department the agent of the sender, and that such right coupled with communication of a renunciation prior to receipt of the acceptance voids the acceptance. In short, appellees argue that acceptance is complete only upon receipt of the mailed acceptance. . . .

[The court quoted at length from Williston on Contracts and other authority.]

A second leading treatise[,] Corbin, Contracts §§ 78, 80 (1950 Supp.1961), also [discusses] the "rule" urged by appellants. Corbin writes: "Where the parties are negotiating at a distance from each other, the most common method of making an offer is by sending it by mail; and more often than not the offeror has specified no particular mode of acceptance. In such a case, it is now the prevailing rule that the offeree has power to accept and close the contract by mailing a letter of acceptance, properly stamped and addressed, within a reasonable time. The contract is regarded as made at the time and place that the letter of acceptance is put into the possession of the post office department."

Like the editor of Williston, Corbin negates the effect of the offeree's power to recall his letter:

"The postal regulations have for a long period made it possible for the sender of a letter to intercept it and prevent its delivery to the addressee. This has caused some doubt . . . as to whether an acceptance can ever be operative upon the mere mailing of the letter. . . .

"It is believed that no such doubt should exist. . . . [T]he fact that a letter can be lawfully intercepted by the sender should not prevent the acceptance from being operative on mailing. If the offer was made under such circumstances that the offeror should know that the offeree might reasonably regard this as a proper method of closing the deal, and the offeree does so regard it, and makes use of it, the contract is consummated even though the letter of acceptance is intercepted and not delivered."

Significantly, Corbin distinguishes cases involving bank drafts or bills of exchange from cases involving bilateral contracts[:] "It should be borne in mind that whenever the receipt of the letter is necessary to produce some legal effect, the interception, and resulting nondelivery of the letter will prevent that effect. For almost all purposes, other than the acceptance of an offer, the mere mailing of a letter is not enough to attain the purpose. Unless it is clearly otherwise agreed, the mailing of a letter is not a sufficient notice to quit a tenancy, it is not actual payment of money that is inclosed, it does not transfer title to a check or other document. . . ."

A [case] cited by appellee, Dick v. United States, 82 F.Supp. 326, 113 Ct.Cl. 94 (1949), involved mistaken acceptance of an offer evidenced by a government purchase order. The appellant, after mailing his acceptance wired a repudiation of the acceptance. The repudiation was received prior to the acceptance. Although remanding the cause for proofs, the court inferred that the fact of a mailed acceptance did not, as a matter of law, bar subsequent repudiation. . . . [T]he court, over a vigorous dissent, concluded that the Post Office was the sender's [offeree's] agent and that "delivery" was incomplete so long as the acceptance had not been received.

The same court, in Rhode Island Tool Co. v. United States, 128 F.Supp. 417, 130 Ct.Cl. 698 (1955), extended the principle that a contract was made only upon receipt of the acceptance to permit revocation of an offer after an acceptance [mistakingly stating too low a price] had been posted but prior to its receipt. Again predicating its decision on the postal regulations, the court concluded [that] "the [Post Office] becomes, in effect, the agency of the sender until actual delivery." . . .

The rule that a contract is complete upon deposit of the acceptance in the mails, [hereinbefore referred to as "deposited acceptance rule"] had its origin . . . in Adams v. Lindsell, 1 Barn. & Ald. 681, 106 Eng.Rep. 250 (K.B.1818). In that case, the defendants had sent an offer to plaintiffs on September 2nd, indicating that they expected an answer "in course of post." The offer was misdirected and was not received and accepted until the 5th, the acceptance being mailed that day and received by defendant-offerors on the 9th. However, the defendants, who had expected to receive the acceptance on or before the 7th, sold the goods offered on the 8th of September. It was conceded that the delay had been occasioned by the fault of the defendants in initially misdirecting the offer.

Defendants contended that no contract had been made until receipt of the offer on the 9th. ". . . They relied on Payne v. Cave, 3 T.R. 148, and more particularly on Cooke v. Oxley, [ibid., 653]. In that case Oxley, who had proposed to sell goods to Cooke, and given him a certain time at his request, to determine whether he would buy them or not, was held not liable to the performance of the contract, even though Cooke, within the specified time, had determined to buy them, and given Oxley notice to that effect. So here the defendants who have proposed by letter to sell this wool, are not to be held liable, even though it be now admitted that the answer did come back in due course of post. Till the plaintiffs' answer was actually received there could be no binding contract between the parties; and before then the defendants had retracted their offer by selling the wool to other persons.

"But the court said that if that were so, no contract could ever be completed by the post. For if the defendants were not bound by their offer when accepted by the plaintiffs till the answer was received, then the plaintiffs ought not to be bound till after they had received the notification that the defendants had received their answer and assented to it. And so it might go on ad infinitum. The defendants must be considered in law as making, during every instant of the time their letter was traveling, the same identical offer to the plaintiffs, and then the contract is completed by the acceptance of it by the latter. Then as to the delay in notifying the acceptance, that arises entirely from the mistake of the defendants, and it therefore must be taken as against them that the plaintiffs' answer was received in course of post."

Examination of [Adams v. Lindsell] reveals three distinct factors deserving consideration. The first and most significant is the court's obvious concern with the necessity of drawing a line, with establishing some point at which a contract is deemed complete and their equally obvious concern with the thought that if communication of each party's assent were necessary, the negotiations would be interminable. A second factor, again a practical one, was the court's apparent desire to limit but not overrule the decision in Cooke v. Oxley, 3 T.R. 653 [1790], that an offer was revocable at any time prior to acceptance. In application to contracts negotiated by mail, this latter rule would permit revocation even after unqualified assent unless the assent was deemed effective upon posting. Finally, having chosen a point at which negotiations would terminate and having effectively circumvented the inequities of Cooke v. Oxley, the court, apparently constrained to offer some theoretical justification for its decision, designated a mailed offer as "continuing" and found a meeting of the minds upon the instant of posting assent. Significantly, the factor of the offeree's loss of control of his acceptance is not mentioned. . . .

[I]t would seem clear that in attempting to provide additional justification for the "deposited acceptance" rule, the courts, in fact, served only to confuse and weaken the essential validity of the rule. Thus, the observation that the offeror having chosen to utilize the mails should bear the risk of delay occasioned thereby was extended by subsequent cases to a point wherein the validity of the contract was made to turn on a theory of communication to an agent. . . . [T]his fictitious agency theory cannot withstand criticism. 1 Corbin, Contracts, § 78 (1950). . . .

Similarly, the "loss of control" theory, having its origin in the observation that under general contract principles an acceptance is manifest only when the offeree loses the power to suppress the manifestation, has, by a process of extension, come to be urged as a factor of primary legal significance. Yet . . . the "loss of control" was not deemed controlling in the earliest cases. Nor is the general principle that a manifestation of assent must be beyond the party's control to be effective any more sacred than the general rule that assent in contract must be communicated. Yet the latter is obviously qualified in the "deposited acceptance" rule and in many instances of unilateral contract. Why then should the "loss of control" principle not also be—or have been—qualified? . . .

The justification for the "deposited acceptance" rule proceeds from the uncontested premise of Adams v. Lindsell that there must be, both in practical and conceptual terms, a point in time when a contract is complete. In the formation of contracts inter praesentes this point is readily reached upon expressions of assent instantaneously communicated. In the formation of contracts inter absentes by post, however, delay in communication prevents concurrent knowledge of assents and some point must be chosen as legally significant. The problem raised by the impossibility of concurrent knowledge of manifest assent is discussed [in] Corbin, Contracts § 78 (1950).

A better explanation of the existing rule seems to be that the mailing of a letter has long been a customary and expected way of accepting the offer. It is ordinary business usage. More than this, however, is needed to explain why the letter is operative on mailing rather than on receipt. . . . Even though it is business usage to send an offer by mail, it creates no power of acceptance until it is received. Indeed, most notices sent by mail are not operative unless actually received.

The additional reasons for holding that a different rule applies to an acceptance and that it is operative on mailing may be suggested as follows: When an offer is by mail and the acceptance also is by mail, the contract must date either from the mailing of the acceptance or from its receipt. In either case, one of the parties will be bound by the contract without being actually aware of that fact. If we hold the offeror bound on the mailing of the acceptance, he may change his position in ignorance of the acceptance. . . . Therefore this rule is going to cause loss and inconvenience to the offeror in some cases. But if we adopt the alternative rule that the letter of acceptance is not operative until receipt, it is the offeree who is subjected to the danger of loss and inconvenience. He can not know that his letter has been received and that he is bound by contract until a new communication is received by him. His letter of acceptance may never have been received and so no letter of notification is sent to him; or it may have been received, and the letter of notification may be delayed or entirely lost in the mails. One of the parties must carry the risk of loss and inconvenience. We need a definite and uniform rule as to this. . . . The business community could no doubt adjust itself to either rule; but the rule throwing the risk on the offeror has the merit of closing the deal more quickly and enabling performance more promptly. It must be remembered that in the vast majority of cases the acceptance is neither lost nor delayed. . . . Also it is the offeror who has invited the acceptance.

. . . As Corbin indicated, there must be a choice made, and such choice may, by the nature of things, seem unjust in some cases. Weighing the arguments with reference not to specific cases but toward a rule of general application and recognizing the general and traditional acceptance of the rule as well as the modern changes in effective long-distance communication, it would seem that the balance tips, whether heavily or near imperceptibly, to continued adherence to the "Rule in Adams v. Lindsell." This rule [is], in our view, in accord with the practical considerations and essential concepts of contract law. See Llewellyn, Our Case Law of Contracts; Offer and Acceptance II, 48 Yale L.J. 779, 795 (1939). . . . [T]raditional rules and concepts should not be abandoned save on compelling ground. . . . [W]e are constrained [to] hold that an acceptance is effective upon mailing and not upon receipt. . . .

[Here,] an unqualified offer was accepted and the acceptance made manifest. Later, the offerees sought to repudiate their initial assent. Had there been a delay in their determination to repudiate permitting the letter to be delivered to appellant, no question as to the invalidity of the repudiation would have been entertained. As it were, the repudiation antedated receipt of the letter. However, adopting the view that the acceptance was effective when the letter of acceptance was deposited in the mails, the repudiation was equally invalid and cannot alone, support the summary decree for appellees.

The summary decree is reversed and the cause remanded for further proceedings.

———

NOTE: REPLIES FROM A DISTANCE

Had plaintiffs not repudiated by a telephone call, but actually recaptured their acceptance letter from the post office, the result no doubt would have been the same. See, e.g., Soldau v. Organon, Inc., 860 F.2d 355 (9th Cir.1988) (offeree's return to post office and persuading employee to open mailbox and retrieve acceptance is "of no legal consequence"). Observe also that the "mailbox rule" of Adams v. Lindsell means that a revocation of an offer is ineffective if received after an acceptance has been properly dispatched. A well-known English case explains why this should be so: "[B]oth legal principles and practical convenience require that a person who has accepted an offer not known . . . to have been revoked shall be in a position safely to act upon the footing" that a binding contract has been formed. Byrne & Co. v. Leon Van Tien Hoven & Co., 5 C.P.D. 344 (1880).

It seems clear that one original purpose of the mailbox rule was to protect offerees against uncommunicated revocations by offerors. But it was not long before the purpose was defined in somewhat broader terms, that of providing the offeree a firmer base for the decision whether to accept and, perhaps, for other action. What then should be done if the letter of acceptance, properly addressed and stamped, is deposited in the mail (or other appropriate medium of communication) and is thereafter abnormally delayed or lost altogether? Commencing as early as 1854 (Vassar v. Camp, 11 N.Y. 441), a series of decisions, still small in number, has extended the rule to such cases of loss or delay in transit. The Restatement (Second) § 63, comment b, approves this extension "in the interest of simplicity and clarity," though it concedes that the justification for the mailbox rule in these cases is less clear than in situations where there has been an attempt to revoke the offer. In applying the effective-upon-dispatch rule, acceptance by telegram is governed by the same tests as acceptance by mail.

Should the reasoning applied to an acceptance be carried over to a rejection of an offer that is lost or delayed in transit? The case of Egger v. Nesbit, 122 Mo. 667, 27 S.W. 385 (1894), involved not a rejection but a purported acceptance that imposed a new term and thus was a counteroffer, which was then lost in the mails and never delivered. The court held that an unconditional acceptance sent 10 days later was ineffective, since the offer had already been terminated. But the Restatement (Second) § 40 gives effect to an acceptance that arrives first, ahead of an intervening outright rejection. Section 40 states:

> Rejection or counter-offer by mail or telegram does not terminate the power of acceptance until received by the offeror, but limits the pow-

er so that a letter or telegram of acceptance started after the sending of an otherwise effective rejection or counter-offer is only a counter-offer unless the acceptance is received by the offeror before he receives the rejection or counter-offer.

Would a court that accepts the mailbox rule, including its extension to cases of loss or delay, commit the grave fault of inconsistency if it gave effect to an overtaking rejection which arrived ahead of an intervening acceptance? Is the refusal of the court to do this in Morrison v. Thoelke made necessary by the need to give offerees a dependable basis for the decision whether to accept? On what basis would such a refusal be justified?

At least one scholar has found the treatment of contracts by correspondence—"an oddity of liability"—to be instructive on our system of contract in general. Sharp, Reflections on Contract, 33 U.Chi.L.Rev. 211, 212–215 (1966). Cases and writings on the dispatch rule are collected in Soldau v. Organon, Inc., supra, and Mansfield v. Smith, 88 Wis.2d 575, 277 N.W.2d 740 (1979). One point to note is that parties who have contracted to permit notice or other action by mail—that is, action not related to contract formation—may be found to have built into their bargain the principle of the common-law mailbox rule. E.g., Schikore v. BankAmerica Supp. Ret. Plan, 269 F.3d 956 (9th Cir.2001) (ERISA plan administrator acted arbitrarily in refusing to apply common law's effective-on-dispatch principle to participant's benefit-election form mailed in accordance with plan procedures); University Emergency Med. Found. v. Rapier Inv., Ltd., 197 F.3d 18 (1st Cir.1999) (common law default rule that notice is effective only on receipt, not mailing, is displaced by "time-honored mailbox rule" when parties contract to permit notice by mail).

Modern technology, including notably the widespread use of e-mail, suggests that an acceptance should be held effective when received, not when transmitted—i.e., the rules that apply when parties are in each other's presence should govern. See Electronic Messaging Services Task Force, The Commercial Use of Electronic Data Interchange—A Report and Model Trading Partner Agreement, 45 Bus.Law. 1645, 1665–1669 (1990). It is also the position indicated by the Restatement (Second) of Contracts § 64 when the parties are not in each other's presence and acceptance is by a "medium of substantially instantaneous two-way communication" (that is, principles applicable where the parties are in the presence of each other govern). There are presently few decisions raising the dispatch-or-receipt question as concerns transmissions other than letter or telegram. The Uniform Computer Information Transfer Act (UCITA), drafted in 1999 and adopted by only a few states, has attracted much criticism—e.g., that it is too complex and difficult to understand, particularly its unfamiliar terms—and various proposals for amendment. That model act, in § 215(a), states that "[r]eceipt of an electronic message is effective when received even if no individual is aware of its receipt."

––––––––

Trinity Homes, LLC v. Fang
63 Va. Cir. 409, 2003 WL 22699791 (Va. Cir. Ct. 2003)

Stewart alleged that he placed the Agreement in his facsimile machine, dialed the number for Nicholson, pushed the button to start the facsimile and then went on an errand. The facsimile machine utilized by Stewart was not a modern version and did not provide any verification that a facsimile was being transmitted and/or that such facsimile was received. There are no phone records relative to the alleged transmission of the facsimile transmission by Stewart. Shortly after the time Stewart alleged he forwarded the facsimile to Nicholson, he received a phone call from Nicholson indicating that Defendants did not wish to sell the property nor enter into a contract with Complainants for that purpose. Transmitting a fax is not a two-way communication within the meaning of Restatement (Second) § 64 and is instead like mailing an acceptance under the Mailbox Rule, where an offer is accepted when it is deposited in the mail. The court concluded that the Mailbox Rule was applicable and thus the issue was one of fact—whether or not the facsimile transmission was actually forwarded or transmitted by Stewart to Nicholson. The burden was on Stewart to prove by preponderance of the evidence that the fax transmission was actually made and accomplished, and the court found the burden not met.

––––––––

RESTATEMENT OF CONTRACTS, SECOND

Section 63. Time When Acceptance Takes Effect

Unless the offer provides otherwise,

(a) an acceptance made in a manner and by a medium invited by an offer is operative and completes the manifestation of mutual assent as soon as put out of the offeree's possession, without regard to whether it ever reaches the offeror; but

(b) an acceptance under an option contract is not operative until received by the offeror.

Comment: . . .

f. *Option contracts.* An option contract provides a dependable basis for decision whether to exercise the option; and removes the primary reason for the rule of Subsection (a). Moreover, there is no objection to speculation at the expense of a party who has irrevocably assumed that risk. Option contracts are commonly subject to a definite time limit, and the usual understanding is that the notification that the option has been exercised must be received by the offeror before that time. Whether or not there is such a time limit, in the absence of a contrary provision in the option contract, the offeree takes the risk of loss or delay in the transmission of the acceptance and remains free to revoke the acceptance until it arrives. Similarly, if there is such a mistake on the part of the offeror as justifies the rescission of his unilateral obligation, the right to rescind is not lost merely because a letter of acceptance is posted.

––––––––

COMMENT: THE EUROPEAN APPROACH

The problems of contract formation in contracts by correspondence have been much discussed in other countries. Numerous solutions have been suggested and several have been tried. Nowhere outside Anglo–American law, however, has there been any strong and consistent support for the Adams v. Lindsell solution, making acceptance effective on dispatch.

The starting point in European discussions has been the proposition that communications should be effective only when received. The courts have thought it entirely appropriate that an offeror should be unaffected by acts of acceptance, such as a mailed letter, of which the offeror has no knowledge. After all, the offeree could retract the acceptance by a telegram that overtook an accepting letter and arrived first; therefore, the offeror should have a similar opportunity to repent. It seems worth noting that this parity rationale might lead to another solution, that of making both acceptance and revocation effective on dispatch. This is the result provided for by statute in a few states in this country.

In any case, the European notion that communications can have no effect until received leaves unanswered the question of how to protect the offeree during the interval required for transmission of the acceptance.

Insofar as the rule of Adams v. Lindsell is deemed to be a device for limiting the offeror's power of revocation, it raises the question whether one should not go further and hold the offeror to the time limits that the offer itself has defined. Consider, for example, the arguments of the first drafting commission that prepared the German Civil Code (Motives, I, pp. 165–166, 1888):

> It is necessary for commerce that the offeror be bound. If any offer is made the offeree must be able to rely on a contract being formed if he on his side notifies the offeror of his acceptance within the time limit. The offeree needs an assured point of departure for the decision he is about to make; he must under some circumstances take immediately the measures that will be necessary if the contract is entered into; he will reject and ignore other offers relating to the subject of the contract and will himself make offers in relation to it. . . . Because of the possible injury, willingness in general to enter into contract negotiations would be reduced and commerce would be burdened and hampered. The binding of the offeror also corresponds to his own intention as reasonably interpreted. This is clearest in cases where the offeror has set a definite time for the acceptance. Such a time limit, according to the conceptions of everyday life, has the meaning not only that the duration of the offer is limited but that the offeror for the time stated binds his own hands. . . . But if it is recognized that he is bound in the case of the express time limit, then it is not apparent why the same should not be true where the time limit is implied. An implied time limit is to be assumed in every offer. For an offer is made for the purpose of inducing acceptance by the offeree; the offeror must therefore intend that the offeree be allowed the time necessary for acceptance. . . . It has been suggested that the injury to which the offeree is exposed through revocation might be prevented by using various legal theories imposing on the revoking offeror a duty to compensate the offeree for what he would have had if the prospect of making the contract had not been presented to him. [But] such a duty to pay damages does not serve the needs of commerce. Commerce requires a smooth and rapid movement of transactions, whereas a recourse to damages, in ordinary experience, leads to lawsuits of a complex kind and uncertain outcome, and would cripple commerce.

It cannot be doubted that some factors militate against binding the offeror. In particular there is the objection, not without weight, that the offeree is placed in a position to use to his own advantage changes in economic conditions that have occurred between the making of the offer and the receipt of his acceptance. He can, as is said, speculate at the expense of the offeror during this interval. But this danger for the offeror is not too great. He can always protect himself by expressly providing that the offer is not binding. If he does not consider such a provision desirable, he can at least reduce the danger by demanding immediate acceptance by the most rapid means of communication available to the offeree.

For such reasons as these, legislation in Europe—and in numerous other systems that have copied from Europe—has attacked the problem by providing that offers are irrevocable unless a power of revocation is expressly reserved. Nussbaum, Comparative Aspects of the Anglo–American Offer–And–Acceptance Doctrine, 36 Colum.L.Rev. 920 (1936), discusses this loophole left to the offeror. The civil-law result is thought to be precluded in Anglo–American law, in the absence of statute, by the requirement of consideration. But, as noted earlier, in order to bring the requirement of consideration into the picture it was necessary to make the further assumption that offers were a species under the genus of promise, so that an offer could be made irrevocable only by finding a binding promise, express or inferred, not to revoke the offer. The question, of course, is whether this transfer of ideas was necessary.

Moulton v. Kershaw

Supreme Court of Wisconsin, 1884.
59 Wis. 316, 18 N.W. 172.

[On September 19, 1882, defendants, salt dealers in Milwaukee, wrote to plaintiff, a dealer in La Crosse known by defendants to buy salt in large quantities, as follows: "Dear Sir: In consequence of a rupture in the salt trade, we are authorized to offer Michigan fine salt, in full car-load lots of 80 to 95 bbls., delivered at your city, at 85c. per bbl., to be shipped per C. & N.W. R.R. Co. only. At this price it is a bargain, as the price in general remains unchanged. Shall be pleased to receive your order." Plaintiff received the letter on September 20 and the same day wired defendants in reply: "Your letter of yesterday received and noted. You may ship me two thousand (2,000) barrels Michigan fine salt, as offered in your letter. Answer." This wire also was received on the 20th. The following day, the 21st, defendants notified plaintiff of their withdrawal of the September 19 letter. Upon defendants' refusal of a demand for delivery of 2,000 barrels, plaintiff sued to recover $800 damages. Defendants' demurrer to the complaint was overruled below, and defendants appealed.]

TAYLOR, J. The only question presented is whether the appellants' letter, and the telegram sent by the respondent in reply thereto, constitute a contract for the sale of 2,000 barrels of Michigan fine salt. . . . We are very clear that no contract was perfected by the order telegraphed by the respondent in answer to appellants' letter. . . .

[Respondent] claims that the letter [is] an offer to sell to the respondent, on the terms mentioned, any reasonable quantity of Michigan fine salt that he might see fit to order, not less than one car-load. . . . [A]ppellants claim that the letter is not an offer to sell any specific quantity of salt, but simply a letter such as a business man would send out to customers or those with whom he desired to trade, soliciting their patronage. To give the letter . . . the construction claimed for it [by] respondent, would introduce such an element of uncertainty into the contract as would necessarily render its enforcement a matter of difficulty, and in every case the jury trying the case would be called upon to determine whether the quantity ordered was such as the appellants might reasonably expect from the party. This question would necessarily involve an inquiry into the nature and extent of the business of the person to whom the letter was addressed, as well as to the extent of the business of the appellants. . . . And this question would not in any way depend upon the language used in the written contract, but upon proofs to be made outside of the writings. . . . If the letter of the appellants is an offer to sell salt to the respondent on the terms stated, then it must be held to be an offer to sell any quantity at the option of the respondent not less than one car-load. The difficulty and injustice of construing the letter into such an offer is so apparent that the learned counsel for the respondent do not insist upon it, and consequently insist that it ought to be construed as an offer to sell such quantity as the appellants, from their knowledge of the business of the respondent might reasonably expect him to order.

Rather than introduce such an element of uncertainty into the contract, we deem it much more reasonable to construe the letter as a simple notice to those dealing in salt that the appellants were in a condition to supply that article for the prices named, and requested the person to whom it was addressed to deal with them. . . .

We do not wish to be understood as holding that a party may not be bound by an offer to sell personal property, where the amount or quantity is left to be fixed by the person to whom the offer is made, when the offer is accepted and the amount or quantity fixed before the offer is withdrawn. We simply hold that the letter [here] was not such an offer. If the letter had said to the respondent we will sell you all the Michigan fine salt you will order, at the price and on the terms named, then it is undoubtedly the law that the appellants would have been bound to deliver any reasonable amount the respondent might have ordered, possibly any amount, or make good their default in damages. The case [of Keller v. Ybarru, 3 Cal. 147,] was an offer of this kind with an additional limitation. The defendant in that case had a crop of growing grapes, and he offered to pick from the vines and deliver to the plaintiff, at defendant's vineyard, so many grapes then growing in said vineyard as the plaintiff should wish to take during the present year at ten cents per pound on delivery. The plaintiff, within the time and before the offer was withdrawn, notified the defendant that he wished to take 1,900 pounds of his grapes on the terms stated. The court held there was a contract to deliver the 1,900 pounds. In this case the fixing of the quantity was left to the person to whom the offer was made, but the amount which the defendant offered, beyond which he could not be bound, was also fixed by the amount of grapes he might have in his vineyard in that year. The case is quite different in its facts from the case at bar.

. . . [We] place our opinion upon the language of the letter of the appellants, and hold that it cannot be fairly construed into an offer. . . . The language is not such as a business man would use in making an offer to sell to an individual a definite amount of property. The word "sell" is not used. . . .

They do not say, we offer to sell to you. They use general language proper to be addressed generally to those who were interested in the salt trade. It is clearly in the nature of an advertisement or business circular, to attract the attention of those interested in that business to the fact that good bargains in salt could be had by applying to them. . . . [T]he demurrer should have been sustained.

QUESTION

What if the seller's September 19 letter had been preceded by a wire from the buyer to the seller on September 17, saying: "Please advise us the best price you can make us on our order of 2,000 barrels of Michigan fine salt, either delivered here or f.o.b. cars your place, as you prefer"?

———

Sharp, Promissory Liability (pt. 1)
7 U.Chi.L.Rev. 1, 3–4 (1939)

"It is the offer which may start the trouble. A salt buyer receives a communication from a salt seller addressed to him personally, reading 'we are authorized to offer' salt at a specified price in unspecified quantities. There is a reference to 'rupture in the salt trade.' The buyer orders two thousand barrels, an amount the seller might reasonably anticipate. It has been held that there is no offer and so no contract. . . .

"After negotiations about the sale of land, in which uncertainties about the vendor's wife's willingness to release her dower interest have appeared, and $50,000 has been mentioned by the vendor, the purchaser writes the vendor 'will you and your wife accept $49,000?' The vendor replies, 'I will not sell for less than $56,000.' The purchaser wires 'I will accept.' It has been held that there is no offer and hence no contract.

"What is it that a sensible businessman is looking for in such a series of communications? We say an offer as distinguished from a mere statement of intention or invitation to deal, and we find that when we examine the matter further, we begin to talk naturally about promises. The offer which may be significant in these situations is also a promise."

———

Petterson v. Pattberg

Court of Appeals of New York, 1928.
248 N.Y. 86, 161 N.E. 428.

KELLOGG, J. . . . John Petterson, of whose last will and testament the plaintiff is executrix, was the owner of a parcel of real estate in Brooklyn, known as 5301 Sixth Avenue. The defendant was the owner of a bond executed by Petterson, which was secured by a third mortgage upon the parcel. On April 4th, 1924, there remained unpaid upon the principal the sum of $5,450. This amount was payable in installments of $250 on April 25th, 1924, and upon a like monthly date every three months thereafter. Thus the bond and mortgage had more than five years to run before the entire sum became due. Under date of the 4th of April, 1924, the defendant wrote

Petterson as follows: "I hereby agree to accept cash for the mortgage which I hold against premises 5301 6th Ave., Brooklyn, N.Y. It is understood and agreed as a consideration I will allow you $780 providing said mortgage is paid on or before May 31, 1924, and the regular quarterly payment due April 25, 1924, is paid when due." On April 25, Petterson paid the defendant the installment of principal due on that date. Subsequently, on a day in the latter part of May, Petterson presented himself at the defendant's home, and knocked at the door. The defendant demanded the name of his caller. Petterson replied: "It is Mr. Petterson. I have come to pay off the mortgage." The defendant answered that he had sold the mortgage. Petterson stated that he would like to talk with the defendant, so the defendant partly opened the door. Thereupon Petterson exhibited the cash and said he was ready to pay off the mortgage according to the agreement. The defendant refused to take the money. Prior to this conversation Petterson had made a contract to sell the land to a third person free and clear of the mortgage to the defendant. Meanwhile, also, the defendant had sold the bond and mortgage to a third party. It, therefore, became necessary for Petterson to pay to such person the full amount of the bond and mortgage. It is claimed that he thereby sustained a loss of $780, the sum which the defendant agreed to allow upon the bond and mortgage if payment in full of principal, less that sum, was made on or before May 31st. The plaintiff has had a recovery for the sum thus claimed, with interest.

Clearly the defendant's letter proposed to Petterson the making of a unilateral contract, . . . a promise in exchange for the performance of an act. The thing conditionally promised by the defendant was the reduction of the mortgage debt. The act requested to be done, in consideration of the offered promise, was payment in full of the reduced principal of the debt prior to the due date thereof. "If an act is requested, that very act and no other must be given." (Williston on Contracts, § 73.) . . . It is elementary that any offer to enter into a unilateral contract may be withdrawn before the act requested to be done has been performed. (Williston on Contracts, § 60); . . . A bidder at a sheriff's sale may revoke his bid at any time before the property is struck down to him. . . . The offer of a reward in consideration of an act to be performed is revocable before the very act requested has been done. Shuey v. United States, 92 U.S. 73. . . .

An interesting question arises when, as here, the offeree approaches the offeror with the intention of proffering performance and, before actual tender is made, the offer is withdrawn. Of such a case Williston says: "The offeror may see the approach of the offeree and know that an acceptance is contemplated. If the offeror can say 'I revoke' before the offeree accepts, however brief the interval of time between the two acts, there is no escape from the conclusion that the offer is terminated." (Williston on Contracts, § 60–b.) In this instance Petterson, standing at the door of the defendant's house, stated to the defendant that he had come to pay off the mortgage. Before a tender of the necessary moneys had been made the defendant informed Petterson that he had sold the mortgage. That was a definite notice to Petterson that the defendant could not perform his offered promise and that a tender to the defendant, who was no longer the creditor, would be ineffective to satisfy the debt. "An offer to sell property may be withdrawn before acceptance without any formal notice to the person to whom the offer is made. It is sufficient if that person has actual knowledge that the person who made the offer has done some act inconsistent with the continuance of the offer, such as selling the property to a third person." Dickinson v. Dodds, 2 Ch.Div. 463. . . . Thus, it clearly appears that the defendant's offer was withdrawn before its acceptance had been tendered. It is unnecessary to determine, therefore, what the legal situation might have been had tender been made before withdrawal. It is the individual view of the writer that the same result would follow. This would be so, for the act requested to be performed was the completed act of payment, a thing incapable of performance unless assented to by the person to be paid. (Williston on Contracts, § 60–b.) Clearly an offering party has the right to name the precise act performance of which would convert his offer into a binding promise. Whatever the act may be until it is performed the offer must be revocable. However, the supposed case is not before us for decision. We think that in this particular instance the offer of the defendant was withdrawn before it became a binding promise, and, therefore, that no contract was ever made. . . .

The judgment of the Appellate Division and that of the Trial Term should be reversed and the complaint dismissed, with costs in all courts.

LEHMAN, J. (dissenting). The defendant's letter to Petterson constituted a promise on his part to accept payment at a discount of the mortgage he held, provided the mortgage is paid on or before May 31st, 1924. Doubtless by the terms of the promise itself, the defendant made payment of the mortgage by the plaintiff, before the stipulated time, a condition precedent to performance by the defendant of his promise to accept payment at a discount. If the condition precedent has not been performed, it is because the defendant made performance impossible by refusing to accept payment. . . . "It is a principle of fundamental justice that if a promisor is himself the cause of the failure of performance either of an obligation due him or of a condition upon which his own liability depends, he cannot take advantage of the failure." (Williston on Contracts, § 677.) The question in this case is . . . whether at the time the defendant refused the offer of payment, he had assumed any binding obligation, even though subject to condition.

The promise made by the defendant lacked consideration at the time it was made. Nevertheless the promise was not made as a gift or mere gratuity to the plaintiff. It was made for the purpose of obtaining from the [plaintiff] something which the [defendant] desired. It constituted an offer which was to become binding whenever the plaintiff should give . . . exactly the consideration which the defendant requested.

Here the defendant requested no counter promise from the plaintiff[,] [but] some act to be performed by the plaintiff. Until the act requested was performed, the defendant might undoubtedly revoke his offer. Our problem is to determine . . . what act the defendant requested as consideration for his promise.

The defendant undoubtedly made his offer as an inducement to the plaintiff to "pay" the mortgage before it was due. Therefore, it is said that "the act requested to be performed was the completed act of payment, a thing incapable of performance unless assented to by the person to be paid." In unmistakable terms the defendant agreed to accept payment, yet we are told that the defendant intended, and the plaintiff should have understood, that the act requested by the defendant, as consideration for his promise to accept payment, included performance by the defendant himself of the very promise for which the act was to be consideration. . . . So construed, the defendant's promise or offer, though intended to induce action by the plaintiff, is but a snare and delusion. The plaintiff could not reasonably suppose that the defendant was asking him to procure the performance by the defendant of the very act which the defendant promised to do, yet we are told that even after the plaintiff had done all else which the de-fendant requested, the defendant's promise was still not binding because the defendant chose not to perform.

I cannot believe that a result so extraordinary could have been intend-ed when the defendant wrote the letter. "The thought behind the phrase proclaims itself misread when the outcome of the reading is injustice or ab-surdity." See Cardozo, Ch.J., in Surace v. Danna, 248 N.Y. 18, 161 N.E. 315. If the defendant intended to induce payment by the plaintiff and yet reserve the right to refuse payment when offered he should have used a phrase better calculated to express his meaning than the words: "I agree to accept." A promise to accept payment, by its very terms, must necessarily become binding, if at all, not later than when a present offer to pay is made.

I recognize that in this case only an offer of payment, and not a formal tender of payment, was made before the defendant withdrew his offer to accept payment. Even the plaintiff's part in the act of payment was then not technically complete. Even so, under a fair construction of the words of the letter I think the plaintiff had done the act which the defendant re-quested as consideration for his promise. The plaintiff offered to pay with present intention and ability to make that payment. A formal tender is sel-dom made in business transactions, except to lay the foundation for subse-quent assertion in a court of justice of rights which spring from a refusal of the tender. If the defendant acted in good faith in making his offer to accept payment, he could not well have intended to draw a distinction in the act requested of the plaintiff in return, between an offer which unless refused would ripen into completed payment, and a formal tender. Certainly the defendant could not have expected or intended that the plaintiff would make a formal tender of payment without first stating that he had come to make payment. We should not read into the language of the defendant's offer a meaning which would prevent enforcement of the defendant's prom-ise after it had been accepted by the plaintiff in the very way which the de-fendant must have intended it should be accepted, if he acted in good faith.

The judgment should be affirmed.

CARDOZO, C.J., POUND, CRANE and O'BRIEN, JJ., concur with KELLOGG, J.; LEHMAN, J., dissents in opinion, in which ANDREWS, J., concurs.

NOTE

The record in the case indicates that when Petterson called at Pattberg's home to pay off the mortgage, he took with him his spouse and a real estate broker who had assisted in Petterson's sale of the property to the third party. The broker testified that he was asked to go as a notary "to acknowledge Mr. Pattberg's signature" on a satisfaction of the mortgage. In order to record a dis-charge, it was necessary to have either such a notarized acknowledgement or the testimony of a subscribing witness (N.Y.—McKinney's Real Property Law, §§ 291, 304, 321). At trial, Pattberg tried to testify that he had mailed a letter to Petterson on May 3, revoking the offer of April 4, but this testimony was ex-cluded by the trial court under the New York dead man's statute. (Petterson had died before the trial.) A jury having been waived, the trial judge gave judgment for the plaintiff. Do these circumstances give support for the majori-ty's conclusion?

There is further information concerning Petterson v. Pattberg. In 1937, on the recommendation of the state's Law Revision Commission, New York enacted § 15–503 of the General Obligations Law. That statute, titled "Offer of Accord Followed by Tender," now reads as follows:

> (1) An offer in writing, signed by the offeror or by his agent, to accept a performance therein designated in satisfaction or discharge in whole or in part of any claim, cause of action, contract, obligation, or lease, or any mortgage or other security interest in personal or real property, followed by tender of such performance by the offeree or by his agent before revocation of the offer, shall not be denied effect as a defense or as a basis of an action or counterclaim by reason of the fact that such tender was not accepted by the offeror or by his agent. . . .

You might consider whether § 15–503 alters the outcome of the *Petterson* decision.

————

Wormser, The True Conception of Unilateral Contracts
26 Yale L.J. 136–139 (1916)

Suppose A says to B, "I will give you $100 if you walk across the Brooklyn Bridge," and B walks—is there a contract? It is clear that A is not asking B for B's promise to walk across the Brooklyn Bridge. What A wants from B is the act of walking across the bridge. When B has walked across the bridge there is a contract, and A is then bound to pay B $100. At that moment there arises a unilateral contract. . . .

When an act is thus wanted in return for a promise, a unilateral contract is created when the act is done. It is clear that only one party is bound. B is not bound to walk across the Brooklyn Bridge, but A is bound to pay B $100 if B does so. Thus, in unilateral contracts, on one side we find merely an act, on the other side a promise. . . . [I]n bilateral contracts, A barters away his volition in return for another promise. . . . [B]oth parties, A and B, are bound from the moment that their promises are exchanged. . . .

act on one side, promise on other

Let us suppose that B starts to walk across the Brooklyn Bridge and has gone about one-half of the way across. At that moment A overtakes B and says to him, "I withdraw my offer." Has B then any rights against A? Again, let us suppose that after A has said "I withdraw by offer," B continues to walk across the Brooklyn Bridge and completes the act of crossing. Under these circumstances, has B any rights against A?

In the first of the cases just suggested, A withdrew his offer before B had walked across the bridge. What A wanted from B, what A asked for, was the act of walking across the bridge. Until that was done, B had not given to A what A had requested. The acceptance by B of A's offer could be nothing but the act of B's part of crossing the bridge. It is elementary that an offeror may withdraw his offer until it has been accepted. It follows logically that A is perfectly within his rights in withdrawing his offer before B has accepted it by walking across the bridge—the act contemplated by the offeror and the offeree as the acceptance of the offer. . . .

The objection is made, however, that it is very "hard" upon B that he should have walked half-way across the Brooklyn Bridge and should get no compensation. This suggestion, invariably advanced, might be dismissed with the remark that "hard" cases should not make bad law. . . . If B is not bound to continue to cross the bridge, if B is will-free, why should not A also be will-free? Suppose that after B has crossed half the bridge he gets tired and tells A that he refuses to continue crossing. B, concededly, would be perfectly within his rights in so speaking and acting. A would have no cause of action against B for damages. If B has a locus poenitentiae, so has A. They each have, and should have, the opportunity to reconsider and withdraw. . . . To the writer's mind, the doctrine of unilateral contract is thus as just and equitable as it is logical. . . .

Suppose, reverting to the second case, that B completes the act of crossing the bridge after A has told him that the offer is withdrawn. Here too, B has no rights against A, since B had not accepted the offer until after A had duly communicated to B its revocation. An offer cannot be accepted after it has been revoked. B is laboring under an unrelievable error of law in proceeding to accept an offer which . . . had ceased to exist.

COMMENT: THE UNILATERAL CONTRACT

The unilateral contract came first in English law: "If you will shoe my horse, I will pay you two shillings." Later, the main center of attention for lawyers shifted to the bilateral contract, initiated by an exchange of promises. The theory of the unilateral contract, as we find it expounded by Professor Wormser, cannot claim the hallmark of antiquity, however; it was the creation of academic minds and law school classrooms in the latter part of the nineteenth century.

If one accepts Professor Wormser's premises, his argument may appear unassailable. The starting point is the proposition already encountered: every offer is revocable until accepted, in the absence of consideration or perhaps a seal. If the offer can be construed as calling for a promise and the promise is duly given, a contract is made and the hazards attendant upon the offeror's power to revoke an unaccepted offer are ended. But if the offer calls for an act, those hazards remain until the act, exactly as requested, is completed. Thus, simply stated, the theory may not seem particularly objectionable if the word "act" comprehends only conduct of the utmost simplicity, completed in a moment, such as handing over a lost wallet which the finder has just picked up from the street. We would rarely feel that real injustice was done if the offeror effectively revoked the offer just before this act was done, thereby depriving the finder of a reward.

Once the theory of the unilateral contract was formulated, however, it showed a tendency to reach out for a wide range of cases in which the conduct regarded as the acceptance required long or expensive preparation, or was in truth a series of acts extending over an appreciable period of time. Why was a theory which does no appreciable harm where the acceptance is a simple, unified act extended to situations where it would seem to compel results so obviously contrary to common sense and elementary decency? A part of the explanation may be found in a peculiar insensitivity of the legal mind, beguiled by the symmetry of a system, to the fact that all acts are not alike, that they vary in complexity, difficulty, and expense. Further explanation may be found, as Professor Llewellyn has argued (Our Case Law of Contract: Offer and Acceptance, 48 Yale L.J. 1, 779 (1938, 1939)), in a shift to the unilateral contract of requirements and assumptions built up around the bilateral contract, whose essence is present exchange of assurances—present agreement. When the offeror asks for present assurance of future action, the offeror may well be the "master of the offer," invested with a power to revoke until that assurance is given. Still, when the offeror has requested extended, difficult, or expensive action, but no commitment by the offeree in advance of the action, must it follow that the offeror is wholly free of responsibility unless and until the performance sought is received—exactly and completely?

Professor Wormser subsequently returned to the unilateral contract, saying: "Since that time I have repented, so that now, clad in sackcloth, I state frankly that my point of view has changed. I agree, at this time, with the rule set forth in the Restatement of Contracts of the American Law Institute, sec. 45." 3 J.Legal Educ. 146 (1950).

————

RESTATEMENT OF CONTRACTS, SECOND

Section 45. Option Contract Created by Part Performance or Tender

(1) Where an offer invites an offeree to accept by rendering a performance and does not invite a promissory acceptance, an option contract is created when the offeree tenders or begins the invited performance or tenders a beginning of it.

(2) The offeror's duty of performance under any option contract so created is conditional on completion or tender of the invited performance in accordance with the terms of the offer.

Comment: . . .

f. *Preparations for Performance.* What is begun or tendered must be part of the actual performance invited in order to preclude revocation under this Section. Beginning preparations, though they may be essential to carrying out the contract or to accepting the offer, is not enough. Preparations to perform may, however, constitute justifiable reliance sufficient to make the offeror's promise binding under § 87(2). In many cases what is invited depends on what is a reasonable mode of acceptance. . . .

Illustration: . . .

9. A makes a written promise to pay $5000 to B, a hospital, "to aid B in its humanitarian work." Relying upon this and other like promises, B proceeds in its humanitarian work, expending large sums of money and incurring large liabilities. Performance by B has begun, and A's offer is irrevocable.

NOTE

The Second Restatement preserves the theory and the effects, though not the language, of the first § 45. The obligation created by part performance is now called an "option contract," not a unilateral contract. This revision of terms follows the restaters' overall decision not to use the words "unilateral contract" in the Restatement, Second, but to speak descriptively of the different types of contracts which in common usage have been classified as unilateral. As might have been expected, this dropping of the term "unilateral contract" does not appear to have attracted followers in the courts or in the literature of contract law. Nor has it altered the fundamentals of the traditional unilateral contract; under a bargain for performance, the waiving of formal acceptance simply merges the essential elements of performance (consideration) and acceptance.

Carlill v. Carbolic Smoke Ball Co.

Court of Appeal, 1892.
[1893] 1 Q. B. 256.

The defendants, who were the proprietors and vendors of a medical preparation called "The Carbolic Smoke Ball," inserted in the Pall Mall Gazette of November 13, 1891, and in other newspapers, the following advertisement:

> £100 reward will be paid by the Carbolic Smoke Ball Company to any person who contracts the increasing epidemic influenza, colds, or any disease caused by taking cold, after having used the ball three times daily for two weeks according to the printed directions supplied with each ball. £1000 is deposited with the Alliance Bank, Regent Street, shewing our sincerity in the matter.

> During the last epidemic of influenza many thousand carbolic smoke balls were sold as preventives against this disease, and in no ascertained case was the disease contracted by those using the carbolic smoke ball.

> One carbolic smoke ball will last a family several months, making it the cheapest remedy in the world at the price, 10s., post free. The ball can be refilled at a cost of 5s. Address, Carbolic Smoke Ball Company, 27, Princes Street, Hanover Square, London.

The plaintiff, a lady, on the faith of this advertisement, bought one of the balls at a chemist's, and used it as directed, three times a day, from November 20, 1891, to January 17, 1892, when she was attacked by influenza. Hawkins, J., held that she was entitled to recover the £100. The defendants appealed. . . .

LINDLEY, L.J. . . . We must first consider whether this was intended to be a promise at all, or whether it was a mere puff which meant nothing. Was it a mere puff? My answer to that question is "No," and I base my answer upon this passage: "£1000 is deposited with the Alliance Bank, shewing our sincerity in the matter." Now, for what was that money deposited or that statement made except to negative the suggestion that this was a mere puff and meant nothing at all? The deposit is called in aid by the advertiser as proof of his sincerity in the matter—that is, the sincerity of his promise to pay this £100 in the event which he has specified. [T]here is the promise, as plain as words can make it.

Then it is contended that it is not binding. [First,] it is said that it is not made with anybody in particular. Now that point is common to the words of this advertisement and to the words of all other advertisements offering rewards. They are offers to anybody who performs the conditions named in the advertisement, and anybody who does perform the condition accepts the offer. In point of law this advertisement is an offer to pay £100 to anybody who will perform these conditions, and the performance of the conditions is the acceptance of the offer. . . .

But then it is said, "Supposing that the performance of the conditions is an acceptance of the offer, that acceptance ought to have been notified." Unquestionably, as a general proposition, when an offer is made, it is necessary in order to make a binding contract, not only that it should be accepted, but that the acceptance should be notified. But is that so in cases of this kind? I apprehend that they are an exception to that rule, or, if not an exception, they are open to the observation that the notification of the acceptance need not precede the performance. This offer is a continuing offer. It was never revoked, and if notice of acceptance is required—which I doubt very much, . . . the person who makes the offer gets the notice of acceptance contemporaneously with his notice of the performance of the condition. If he gets notice of the acceptance before his offer is revoked, that in principle is all you want. I, however, think that the true view, in a case of this kind, is that the person who makes the offer shews by his language and from the nature of the transaction that he does not expect and does not require notice of the acceptance apart from notice of the performance.

We, therefore, find here all the elements which are necessary to form a binding contract enforceable in point of law. . . . [T]he true construction of this advertisement is that £100 will be paid to anybody who uses this smoke ball three times daily for two weeks according to the printed directions, and who gets the influenza or cold or other diseases caused by taking cold within a reasonable time after so using it; and if that is the true construction, it is enough for the plaintiff.

I come now to the last point which I think requires attention—that is, the consideration. It has been argued that this is nudum pactum—that there is no consideration. We must apply to that argument the usual legal tests. Let us see whether there is no advantage to the defendants. It is said that the use of the ball is no advantage to them, and that what benefits them is the sale; and the case is put that a lot of these balls might be stolen, and that it would be no advantage to the defendants if the thief or other people used them. The answer to that, I think, is as follows. It is quite obvious that in the view of the advertisers a use by the public of their remedy, if they can only get the public to have confidence enough to use it, will react and produce a sale which is directly beneficial to them. Therefore, the advertisers get out of the use an advantage which is enough to constitute a consideration.

But there is another view. Does not the person who acts upon this advertisement and accepts the offer put himself to some inconvenience at the request of the defendants? Is it nothing to use this ball three times daily for two weeks according to the directions at the request of the advertiser? Is that to go for nothing? It appears to me that there is a distinct inconvenience, not to say a detriment, to any person who so uses the smoke ball. I am of opinion, therefore, that there is ample consideration for the promise. . . .

It appears to me, therefore, that the defendants must perform their promise, and, if they have been so unwary as to expose themselves to a great many actions, so much the worse for them.

BOWEN, L.J. I am of the same opinion. We were asked to say that this document was a contract too vague to be enforced. . . . It seems to me that in order to arrive at a right conclusion we must read this advertisement in its plain meaning, as the public would understand it. It was intended to be issued to the public and to be read by the public. How would an ordinary person reading this document construe it? It was intended unquestionably to have some effect, and I think the effect which it was intended to have, was to make people use the smoke ball, because the suggestions and allegations which it contains are directed immediately to the use of the smoke ball as distinct from the purchase of it. It did not follow that the smoke ball was to be purchased from the defendants directly, or even from agents of theirs directly. The intention was that the circulation of the smoke ball should be promoted, and that the use of it should be increased. . . .

Then it was said that there was no notification of the acceptance of the contract. One cannot doubt that, as an ordinary rule of law, an acceptance of an offer made ought to be notified to the person who makes the offer, in order that the two minds may come together. Unless this is done . . . there is not that consensus which is necessary according to the English law—I say nothing about the laws of other countries—to make a contract. But there is this clear gloss to be made upon that doctrine, that as notification of acceptance is required for the benefit of the person who makes the offer, the person who makes the offer may dispense with notice to himself if he thinks it desirable to do so, and I suppose there can be no doubt that where a person in an offer made by him to another person, expressly or impliedly intimates a particular mode of acceptance as sufficient to make the bargain binding, it is only necessary for the other person to whom such offer is made to follow the indicated method of acceptance; and if the person making the offer, expressly or impliedly intimates in his offer that it will be sufficient to act on the proposal without communicating acceptance of it to himself, performance of the condition is a sufficient acceptance without notification. . . .

Now, if that is the law, how are we to find out whether the person who makes the offer does intimate that notification of acceptance will not be necessary in order to constitute a binding bargain? In many cases you look to the offer itself. [Y]ou extract from the character of the transaction that notification is not required, and in the advertisement cases it seems to me to follow as an inference to be drawn from the transaction itself that a person is not to notify his acceptance of the offer before he performs the condition, but that if he performs the condition notification is dispensed with. . . . If I advertise to the world that my dog is lost, and that anybody who brings the dog to a particular place will be paid some money, are all the police or other persons whose business it is to find lost dogs to be expected to sit down and write me a note saying that they have accepted my proposal? Why, of course, they at once look after the dog, and as soon as they find the dog they have performed the condition. The essence of the transaction is that the dog should be found. . . . It follows from the nature of the thing that the performance of the condition is sufficient acceptance without the notification of it, and a person who makes an offer in an advertisement of that kind makes an offer which must be read by the light of that common sense reflection. He does, therefore, in his offer impliedly indicate that he does not require notification of the acceptance of the offer. . . .

Appeal dismissed.

[For a description of the smoke ball, and the manufacturer's directions for its use, see Simpson, Quackery and Contract Law: The Case of the Carbolic Smoke Ball, 14 J.Leg.Stud. 345, 348–352 (1985). The defendant responded to the decision with another advertisement, which is reproduced below. Notice the fine print.]

PROBLEMS

(1) Defendant published the following advertisement in a newspaper: "Saturday 9 A.M. Sharp, 3 Brand New Fur Coats Worth to $100.00, First Come First Served, $1 Each." One week later it published in the same newspaper this advertisement: "Saturday 9 A.M., 2 Brand New Pastel Mink 3–Skin Scarfs Selling for $89.50, Out They Go Saturday. Each . . . $1.00. 1 Black Lapin Stole, Beautiful, Worth $139.50 . . . $1.00. First Come First Served." On each Saturday following the publication of these ads, plaintiff was the first person to present himself at the appropriate counter in defendant's store and to demand the advertised coat and stole, respectively, at the prices of $1.00 each. Defendant refused to sell to plaintiff, stating on the first occasion that a "house rule" limited the sales to women only and on the second that plaintiff knew the defendant's house rules. Even though advertisements of goods ordinarily do not constitute offers to sell, the Minnesota high court found an offer, and thus a contract formed by plaintiff, on each occasion. What is there here to justify a result not commonly reached in the advertising cases? The test, said the court, is "whether the facts show that some performance was promised in positive terms for something requested." Here, the ads were "clear, definite, and explicit, and left nothing open for negotiation." Defendant had also urged that its "house

rule" precluded any liability, but the court rejected this, saying "an advertiser does not have the right, after acceptance, to impose new or arbitrary conditions not contained in the published offer." Was the court right on the house-rule point? See Lefkowitz v. Great Minneapolis Surplus Store, 251 Minn. 188, 86 N.W.2d 689 (1957).

See also Mesaros v. United States, 845 F.2d 1576 (Fed.Cir.1988) (U.S. Mint advertisements for commemorative Statue of Liberty coins generated 756,000 orders of varying quantities); Izadi v. Machado (Gus) Ford, 550 So.2d 1135 (Fla.Dist.Ct.App.1989) (car dealer's advertisement of blanket $3,000 trade-in allowance governed by line of authority that "binding offer may be implied from very fact that deliberately misleading advertising intentionally leads the reader to the conclusion that one exists"); Ford Motor Credit Co. v. Russell, 519 N.W.2d 460 (Minn.Ct.App.1994) (unreasonable for public to believe advertisement of 1988 Ford Escort at $7,826, "11% A.P.R.," constitutes offer, since not everyone qualifies for such financing and all must know dealer does not have unlimited number of Escorts). For an illustration of the various statutes arguably reaching disputed advertisements, see Zanakis–Pico v. Cutter Dodge, Inc., 98 Hawaii 309, 47 P.3d 1222 (2002).

(2) Supermarkets place food on open shelves and give customers free access to the shelves. Is a contract formed when a shopper picks up a box of sugar and places it in a shopping basket? See McQuiston v. K–Mart Corp., 796 F.2d 1346 (11th Cir.1986); Pharmaceutical Society v. Boots Cash Chemists, [1953] 1 Q.B. 401. Self-service shoppers injured by bottles exploding before reaching the check-out station have enjoyed some success in establishing a contract. Why do you suppose the rules of offer and acceptance are manipulated so as to produce such results? See, e.g., Barker v. Allied Supermarket, 596 P.2d 870 (Okl.1979).

The advertisement cases are collected, and the customary approach challenged, in Feinman & Brill, Is an Advertisement an Offer? Why It Is, and Why It Matters, 58 Hastings L.J. 61 (2006).

Cobaugh v. Klick–Lewis, Inc.

Superior Court of Pennsylvania, 1989.
385 Pa.Super. 587, 561 A.2d 1248.

WIEAND, J. On May 17, 1987, Amos Cobaugh was playing in the East End Open Golf Tournament on the Fairview Golf Course in Cornwall, Lebanon County. When he arrived at the ninth tee he found a new Chevrolet Beretta, together with signs which proclaimed: "HOLE–IN–ONE Wins this 1988 Chevrolet Beretta GT Courtesy of KLICK–LEWIS Buick Chevy Pontiac $49.00 OVER FACTORY INVOICE in Palmyra." Cobaugh aced the ninth hole and attempted to claim his prize. Klick–Lewis refused to deliver the car. It had offered the car as a prize for a charity golf tournament sponsored by the Hershey–Palmyra Sertoma Club two days earlier, on May 15, 1987, and had neglected to remove the car and posted signs prior to Cobaugh's hole-in-one. After Cobaugh sued to compel delivery of the car, the parties entered a stipulation regarding the facts and then moved for summary judgment. The trial court granted Cobaugh's motion, and Klick–Lewis appealed. . . .

An offer is a manifestation of willingness to enter into a bargain, so made as to justify another person in understanding that his assent to that bargain is invited and will conclude it. [Rest.2d] of Contracts § 24. . . . Consistent with traditional principles of contract law pertaining to unilateral contracts, it has generally been held that "[t]he promoter of [a prize-winning] contest, by making public the conditions and rules of the contest, makes an offer, and if before the offer is withdrawn another person acts upon it, the promoter is bound to perform his promise." Annot., 87 A.L.R.2d 649, 661. The only acceptance of the offer that is necessary is the performance of the act requested to win the prize. . . .

Appellant argues that it did nothing more than propose a contingent gift and that a proposal to make a gift is without consideration and unenforceable. . . . We cannot accept this argument. Here, the offer specified the performance which was the price or consideration to be given. By its signs, Klick–Lewis offered to award the car as a prize to anyone who made a hole-in-one at the ninth hole. A person reading the signs would reasonably understand that he or she could accept the offer and win the car by performing the feat of shooting a hole-in-one. There was thus an offer which was accepted when appellee shot a hole-in-one. Accord: Champagne Chrysler–Plymouth, Inc. v. Giles, 388 So.2d 1343 (Fla.Dist.Ct.App.1980) (bowling contest). . . .

The contract does not fail for lack of consideration. The requirement of consideration as an essential element of a contract is nothing more than a requirement that there be a bargained for exchange. . . . Consideration confers a benefit upon the promisor or causes a detriment to the promisee. . . . By making an offer to award one of its cars as a prize for shooting a hole-in-one at the ninth hole of the Fairview Golf Course, Klick–Lewis benefited from the publicity typically generated by such promotional advertising. In order to win the car, Cobaugh was required to perform an act which he was under no legal duty to perform. The car was to be given in exchange for the feat of making a hole-in-one. This was adequate consideration to support the contract. See, e.g.: Las Vegas Hacienda, Inc. v. Gibson, 77 Nev. 25, 359 P.2d 85 (1961) (paying fifty cents and shooting hole-in-one was consideration for prize). . . .[1]

There is no basis for believing that Cobaugh was aware that the Chevrolet automobile had been intended as a prize only for an earlier tourna-

---

[1] The issue of an illegal contract . . . was not raised by appellant in the trial court or on appeal. . . .

Even if, as the dissent contends, this Court may act sua sponte to refuse enforcement of an illegal contract, it should not do so unless the illegality is clear. It is not clear in this case that to offer an automobile as a prize for a hole-in-one during a charity golf tournament was to introduce illegal gambling to the tournament. Courts of other jurisdictions have found similar offers legal and enforceable. See: Las Vegas Hacienda, Inc. v. Gibson, supra (contest to award prize to golfer who, having paid fee, scored a hole-in-one was not gambling and, therefore, created valid and enforceable contract). . . .

Finally, there was no evidence in this case that an element of chance was the dominant factor in shooting the hole-in-one. See: Commonwealth v. Laniewski, 173 Pa.Super. 245, 98 A.2d 215 (1953) (chance must be dominant factor). Even if this Court could legitimately consider the "facts" which the dissent introduces from a popular magazine, those statistics demonstrate that a professional golfer is generally twice as likely to shoot a hole-in-one as an amateur golfer. Under these circumstances, it cannot be said that skill is "almost an irrelevant factor." See: Las Vegas Hacienda, Inc. v. Gibson, supra, 77 Nev. at 29–30, 359 P.2d at 87 (where expert testified that "a skilled player will get it (the ball) in the area where luck will take over more often than an unskilled player," there was sufficient evidence to sustain a finding that the shooting of a hole-in-one was a feat of skill). [This footnote is relocated; other footnotes are omitted.—Eds.]

ment. The posted signs did not reveal such an intent by Klick–Lewis, and the stipulated facts do not suggest that appellee had knowledge greater than that acquired by reading the posted signs. Therefore, we also reject appellant's final argument that the contract to award the prize to appellee was voidable because of mutual mistake. . . .

In Champagne Chrysler–Plymouth, Inc. v. Giles, supra, a mistake similar to that made in the instant case had been made. There, a car dealer had advertised that it would give away a new car to any bowler who rolled a perfect "300" game during a televised show. The dealer's intent was that the offer would continue only during the television show which the dealer sponsored and on which its ads were displayed. However, the dealer also distributed flyers containing its offer and posted signs advertising the offer at the bowling alley. He neglected to remove from the alley the signs offering a car to anyone bowling a "300" game, and approximately one month later, while the signs were still posted, plaintiff appeared on a different episode of the television show and bowled a perfect game. The dealer refused to award the car. A Florida court held that if plaintiff reasonably believed that the offer was still outstanding when he rolled his perfect game, he would be entitled to receive the car. . . .

It is the manifested intent of the offeror and not his subjective intent which determines the persons having the power to accept the offer. [Rest.2d] of Contracts § 29. In this case the offeror's manifested intent, as it appeared from signs posted at the ninth tee, was that a hole-in-one would win the car. The offer was not limited to any prior tournament. The mistake upon which appellant relies was made possible only because of its failure to (1) limit its offer to the Hershey–Palmyra Sertoma Club Tournament and/or (2) remove promptly the signs making the offer after the Sertoma Tournament had been completed. It seems clear, therefore, that the mistake in this case was [not mutual but] unilateral and was the product of the offeror's failure to exercise due care. Such a mistake does not permit appellant to avoid its contract.

Affirmed.

POPOVICH, J. (dissenting). . . . [G]olf—as demonstrated by the vast majority of its practitioners who never have and never will score a round at par—is a sport requiring precise skills.

Making a hole-in-one, however, is such a fortuitous event that skill is almost an irrelevant factor. Because of that fact (an element of chance), combined with the payment of an entry fee to the East End Golf Tournament (consideration) and the automobile prize (reward), my view is that the necessary elements of gambling are present thus rendering the contract *sub judice* unenforceable as violating the Commonwealth's policy against gambling.[1] . . . I raise this issue *sua sponte* since we have no jurisdiction to enforce a contract in violation of public policy. . . .

By couching this transaction in terms of a unilateral contract, the majority seems to opine that scoring a hole-in-one is an act of skill which a golfer can choose to undertake. The truth is quite the opposite. . . . So few in fact [ever experience the thrill of a hole-in-one] that "aceing" a hole is

---

[1] Under Pennsylvania law, the three elements of gambling are consideration, a reward and an element of chance. Commonwealth v. Weisman, 331 Pa.Super. 31, 479 A.2d 1063 (1984). . . . Illegal lotteries, gambling and bookmaking are strictly prohibited as delineated in 18 Pa.C.S.A. §§ 5512 (lotteries), 5513 (gaming devices, gambling) and 5514 (pool selling, bookmaking).

truly an act of "luck" not skill. Consider the following statistics: In 1988, approximately 21.7 million golfers played 434 million rounds of golf with only 34,469 holes-in-one being reported to the United States Golf Association. *Golf Digest*, using figures amassed since 1952, estimates that a golfer of average ability playing a par–3 hole of average difficulty has a mere 1 in 20,000 chance of aceing the hole. While the chances increase [to 1 in 10,000] for a professional golfer, the possibility of a hole-in-one, even for the world's best players, is still remote. . . . [E]ven at 10,000 to 1, the professional's chances of aceing a hole are more akin to an act of God than a demonstration of skill. Clearly, the possibility of a hole-in-one is sufficiently remote to qualify as the necessary gambling requirement of an element of chance.

Since all of the elements of gambling are present, . . . I would find that an unenforceable contract was created. While I recognize that there are a variety of socially acceptable forms of gambling indulged in by the public for the most charitable of purposes and the worthiest of causes, they are nonetheless illicit under Pennsylvania law. Dollar raffle tickets for the benefit of a hospital or a Little League Baseball Ass'n are bought and sold innocuously and routinely, and, yet, raffles constitute unsanctioned gambling. Only recently, under strict control, has bingo, a popular and social form of gambling, been legalized. 10 Pa.C.S.A. § 301 et seq. See also 4 Pa.C.S.A. § 325.101 et seq. (horse racing); 72 Pa.C.S.A. § 3761–1 et seq. (state lottery). Millions of citizens spend billions of dollars each year on sports betting in office pools or with the local bookmaker. However, only in one state, Nevada, is it legal so to do.

Thus, when such a rare case as this comes into court, it may be difficult to re-assert a public policy which everyday is violated by common experience. . . . Nevertheless, we cannot usurp the role of the legislature or turn our heads away from the fundamental substance of this transaction: it is a contract, a contract covering the context of gambling. Hence, it is unenforceable no matter how much condoned or indulged.

———

NOTE: UNKNOWN OFFERS OF REWARDS

Suppose Cobaugh, intent on his game, had failed to notice either the Beretta or the signs at the ninth tee. Knowledge of an offer typically becomes an issue in situations where, as in Cobaugh v. Klick–Lewis, the offeror bargains for a performance, not a return promise, but unlike that case, the performance is rendered in total ignorance of the offer. The common illustration is an advertised reward for specified action (e.g., the giving of information leading to the arrest and conviction of the person guilty of a certain crime), and an informant provides the information before learning that the offer has been made. In one such case, Glover v. Jewish War Veterans of United States, Post No. 58, 68 A.2d 233 (D.C.Mun.Ct.App. 1949), the court reviewed the authorities and concluded:

> While there is some conflict in the decided cases on the subject of rewards, most of such conflict has to do with rewards offered by governmental officers and agencies. So far as rewards offered by private individuals and organizations are concerned, there is little conflict on the rule that questions regarding such rewards are to be based upon the law of contracts.

Since it is clear that the question is one of contract law, it follows that, at least so far as private rewards are concerned, there can be no contract unless the claimant when giving the desired information knew of the offer of the reward and acted with the intention of accepting such offer; otherwise the claimant gives the information not in the expectation of receiving a reward but rather out of a sense of public duty or other motive unconnected with the reward. "In the nature of the case," according to Professor Williston, "it is impossible for an offeree actually to assent to an offer unless he knows of its existence."

Observe that *Glover* requires that an offeree know of the reward offer and "act with the intention of accepting" it. What do you understand the quoted phrase to mean? Does it rest on an "assent" principle? A "bargain" principle? Recall that an act can be consideration for another's promise even though it is only "partially" induced or motivated by the promise.

———

COMMENT: *"MASTER OF THE OFFER"*

There is a long tradition of speaking of the offeror as "the master of the offer." The phrase simply recognizes that an offeror has the power to determine not only the substance of the exchange and the identity of the offeree (that is, the person or persons in whom a power of acceptance is created), but such "procedural" matters as the time, place, and form or mode of acceptance. Thus, as *Cobaugh v. Klick–Lewis* illustrates, an offeror may waive formal acceptance (a communicated promise); it is enough that the offeree performs as specified in the offer. Our concern here is whether the offering party, by specifying requirements or limitations, has fixed a course for entry into a contract.

The case of *Caldwell v. Cline*, 109 W.Va. 553, 156 S.E. 55 (1930), provides a well-known example. On January 29, Cline dated and addressed a letter to Caldwell, proposing to exchange land on specified terms. The letter said "will give you eight days in which" to accept or reject. Caldwell received the letter on February 2; six days later, on February 8, Caldwell wired Cline: "Land deal is made. Prepare deed to me." This telegram reached Cline on February 9. Upon Cline's refusal to proceed with the deal, Caldwell brought a bill in equity for specific performance. The trial court, believing that Caldwell's acceptance was untimely, dismissed the suit on demurrer.

On appeal, Caldwell's allegations were held sufficient to withstand a demurrer. Cline was wrong in urging that the eight-day limitation ran from January 29, the date of the letter, for "when a person uses the post to make an offer, the offer is not made when it is posted but when it is received." It followed that Cline's words had no "legal existence" until his letter was received by Caldwell on February 2, and thus the acceptance reaching Cline on the 9th was timely. Moreover, the "eight-days" language "is, without more, conclusive of the offeror's intention" to date the time limit from the moment the letter was put in Caldwell's hands.

Suppose Cline's letter of the 29th had been delayed in the mails and had not reached Caldwell until March 2. Could Caldwell have made a contract by accepting on March 10?

Suppose Amos Cobaugh had hit the hole-in-one on June 15 (with the car and the sign still on the ninth tee), a full month after the charity golf tournament in which Klick–Lewis had put up the Beretta GT as a prize. At what point does Cobaugh no longer have a power of acceptance?

That issue was present in the further example provided by Textron, Inc. v. Froelich, 223 Pa.Super. 506, 302 A.2d 426 (1973). During a telephone conversation with a broker of steel products, seller offered the broker two different lots of steel rods at stated prices. The conversation ended with the broker saying that he thought he wanted the rods, but that he also wanted time to check with his customers before accepting the offer. Nothing was said about a time limit on the offer. Some five weeks later, the broker called back and agreed to buy one lot of the rods at the offered price; two days thereafter, the broker telephoned again to purchase the other lot, also on the terms previously discussed. The seller replied to both phone calls by saying, "Fine, thank you."

The rods were not delivered, and a lawsuit resulted in which the broker was nonsuited on his claim of breach of contract. The trial judge, relying on the often-repeated proposition that "an oral offer ordinarily terminates with the end of the conversation," concluded that no contract was formed by virtue of lapse of the offer. A reviewing court disagreed, stating the rule to be that if no time for expiration of a power of acceptance is specified in the offer, the power terminates at the end of a reasonable time. " 'What is a reasonable time is a question of fact, depending on the nature of the contract proposed, the usages of business and other circumstances of the case which the offeree . . . either knows or has a reason to know.' . . . There may be times when a judge could find as a matter of law that an oral offer made in the course of a conversation terminates with [the conversation]. If there is any doubt as to what is a reasonable interpretation, the decision should be left to the jury. [Here,] it is possible that a jury could have found that the oral offer continued beyond the end of the conversation. We need not, however, decide this appeal on that issue." As the sentence last quoted indicates, the court ultimately rested its reversal and remand for trial on an alternative ground. What might that ground have been?

————

Pine River State Bank v. Mettille
333 N.W.2d 622 (Minn.1983)

Confronting the question whether an employer's power to discharge an at-will employee had been limited by disciplinary procedures contained in a personnel handbook, the court said: "If the handbook language constitutes an offer, and the offer has been communicated by dissemination of the handbook to the employee, the next question is whether there has been an acceptance of the offer and consideration furnished. . . . [W]here an at-will employee retains employment with knowledge of new or changed conditions, the new or changed conditions may become a contractual obligation. In this manner, an original employment contract may be modified or replaced by a subsequent unilateral contract. The employee's retention of employment constitutes acceptance. . . . [B]y continuing to stay on the job, although free to leave, the employee supplies the necessary consideration. . . . An employer's offer of a unilateral contract may very well appear in a personnel handbook as the employer's response to the practical problem of transaction costs. . . . [A]n employer, such as the bank here, may prefer not to write a separate contract with each individual employee.... [W]e do not think that applying the unilateral contract doctrine to personnel handbooks unduly circumscribes the employer's discretion.... [Nor do we believe that] handbook provisions relating to job security require special treatment [or] are an exception to the general rule just discussed."

NOTE: ALTERING THE TERMS OF AT–WILL EMPLOYMENT

The unilateral contract has been used in disputes growing out of at-will employment, as a basis for affording employees both job security and economic benefits. This is, of course, but one dimension of the general erosion of the doctrine of at-will employment currently taking place. Still, it seems that the personnel handbook has spurred something of a rebirth of the unilateral contract. (Examples of the unilateral contract expanding liabilities and redefining relationships in other areas, some nontraditional, are examined in Pettit, Modern Unilateral Contracts, 63 B.U.L.Rev. 551 (1983).) One matter to watch in the employment context is the test of "bargain" that is to be applied. Some courts have openly approved departures from traditional "bargain theory" in the employee-handbook cases. See, e.g., Anderson v. Douglas & Lomason Co., 540 N.W.2d 277 (Iowa 1995) (employee suing to enforce promise in handbook need not show knowledge of promise, else those who read handbook would be treated differently from those who did not).

The *Pine River State Bank* analysis, which conceptualizes at-will employment as a unilateral contract that is accepted by the employee's continuing to work, is seen often in the employment cases. It was central to the decision in Torosyan v. Boehringer Ingelheim Pharmaceuticals, Inc., 234 Conn. 1, 662 A.2d 89 (1995), where the court sustained a finding of an "implied contract" providing that an at-will employee could be terminated only "for cause." The court, in a remarkably elaborate exposition of the usual theory, made these points, among others: (1) All employer-employee relationships not governed by express contracts necessarily involve some type of "implied contract"—there is "a bargain of some kind." (2) The typical implied contract of employment includes terms specifying wages, working hours, job responsibilities and the like; because it is for an indefinite term—does not limit the terminability of employment—the default rule is employment at will. But a term so supplied, like any other contract term, can be modified by the parties' agreement. (3) The contents of any particular implied contract of employment are to be determined by examining the factual circumstances of the parties' relationship "in light of legal rules governing unilateral contracts." (4) In order to find an implied contract incorporating specific representations orally made by the employer or contained in provisions in an employee manual, the trier of fact must find that the representations or issuance of a manual or handbook to the employee was an "offer"—i.e., a promise that, if the employee worked for the company, his or her employment would thereafter be governed by the oral or written statements. If an offer is found, it is then necessary to find the employee's "acceptance" of the offer. (5) Subsequent oral representations or the issuance of subsequent handbooks must be evaluated by the same criteria—an offer to modify preexisting employment terms and acceptance of the proposed modifications, resulting in the "substitution of a new implied contract for the old." (6) When an employer issues a manual that confers greater rights than an employee previously had, the employee's continued work ordinarily demonstrates acceptance of the offer of new rights. This is a logical conclusion because the employer's likely motive for increasing job security is to encourage continued employment. (7) Conversely, when an employer issues a manual that "substantially interferes with an employee's legitimate expectations about the terms of employment," the employee's continued work after notice of those terms cannot be taken as conclusive evidence of consent to the terms. Continued work is admissible evidence of consent to the new contract, but cannot itself mandate a finding of consent. This must be so else an employee with a termination-for-cause contract would have no way to insist on its contractual rights; the only choices would be to resign or continue working, either of which would result in the loss of the very right at issue.

The principle that promises made in an employee handbook may be binding on an employer is no doubt accepted by most courts. Yet there are disagreements both as to the theory of liability and the circumstances justifying a finding of handbook-based obligation. For example, suppose the handbook, in conspicuous terms, reserves to the employer the right to modify unilaterally the handbook's terms. Should it follow that any offer made in issuing the handbook is illusory? Any reliance by an employee unreasonable? Does the *Embry* approach have anything to contribute here?

There is also the question whether a disclaimer, included originally or added later, is a complete defense to a suit based on an employee handbook, whether the claim is for breach of contract or of promissory estoppel. Presumably, any promisor is free by clear and forthright disclaimer to deny legally binding effect to the promise. The fighting issue, of course, is whether, by virtue of packaging and presentation, the disclaimer's meaning or intended effect is put in doubt. Since employment at will is the norm in this country (at least the *legal* norm), should it be enough that a handbook states that it is "not a contract" or "gives no legal rights"? It seems at least some courts require that the handbook state in addition that the employee can be terminated at the will of the employer. E.g., Russell v. Board of County Comm'rs, 952 P.2d 492 (Okla.1997).

Allied Steel & Conveyors, Inc. v. Ford Motor Co.

United States Court of Appeals, Sixth Circuit, 1960.
277 F.2d 907.

MILLER, DISTRICT JUDGE. The question [is] whether a provision in certain written agreements between appellant and appellee purporting to indemnify appellee against damages resulting from its own acts of negligence was binding upon the parties at the time the damages were sustained. . . .

[In 1955, Ford contracted to purchase from Allied numerous items of machinery which were to be installed on Ford's premises by Ford's own employees. On July 26, 1956, Ford submitted to Allied another offer (Amendment No. 2) to purchase additional machinery to be installed on Ford's premises by Allied. This offer provided:

"This purchase order agreement is not binding until accepted. Acceptance should be executed on acknowledgement copy which should be returned to buyer."

Attached to Amendment No. 2 and made a part thereof was a printed Form 3618 containing a broad indemnity provision, requiring Allied to assume responsibility not only for the fault or negligence of its own employees but also for that of Ford's employees arising out of, or in connection with, Allied's work in installing the machinery.

The acknowledgment copy of Amendment No. 2 was executed by Allied about November 10, 1956, and was received by Ford on November 12. Some time prior to these dates, however, Allied had begun the installation of the machinery covered by Amendment No. 2. On September 5, 1956, in connection with that work, Hankins, an Allied employee, was injured as a result of the negligence of Ford employees. Hankins sued Ford to recover damages for his injuries. Ford brought in Allied as a third-party defendant, relying on the indemnity provision in Form 3618 and demanding judgment against Allied for any sums judged to be due Hankins. After a jury trial, judgments were entered, each in the amount of $12,500, in favor of Hankins against Ford and in favor of Ford against Allied. Allied appealed.]

[Allied insists] that the agreement evidenced by Amendment No. 2 which was signed and returned to Ford on November 10, 1956, was not in effect on September 5, when Hankins was injured; and further, that, in any event, it was the intention of the parties to void the broad indemnity provision in Form 3618 attached to Amendment No. 2, thus leaving in effect Item 15 contained in the original Purchase Order which made Allied liable only for its own negligence. Although the agreements contained in Amendment No. 2 were fully performed by the parties and Allied received full payment for its goods and services, the point made by Allied is that it did not become bound by the provisions of such amendment until November 1956, when it actually signed and returned to Ford the acknowledgment copy of Amendment No. 2. It argues that it was under no contractual obligation on . . . the date of Hankins' injury, to indemnify Ford against Ford's negligent acts.

Allied first . . . argues that a binding acceptance of the amendment could be effected only by Allied's execution of the acknowledgment copy of the amendment and its return to Ford.

. . . [W]e cannot agree. It is true that an offeror may prescribe the manner in which acceptance shall be indicated by the offeree, and an acceptance of the offer in the manner prescribed will bind the offeror. And it has been held that if the offeror prescribes an exclusive manner of acceptance, an attempt on the part of the offeree to accept the offer in a different manner does not bind the offeror *in the absence of a meeting of the minds on the altered type of acceptance.* Venters v. Stewart, 261 S.W.2d 444 (Ky.App.1953). . . . On the other hand, if an offeror merely suggests a permitted method of acceptance, other methods of acceptance are not precluded. Restatement, Contracts, § 61; Williston on Contracts, Third Ed. §§ 70, 76. . . .

Applying these principles[,] [we conclude], first, that execution and return of the acknowledgment copy of Amendment No. 2 was merely a suggested method of acceptance and did not preclude acceptance by some other method; and, second, that the offer was accepted and a binding contract effected when Allied, with Ford's knowledge, consent and acquiescence, undertook performance of the work called for by the amendment. The only significant provision, as we view the amendment, was that it would not be binding until it was accepted by Allied. This provision was obviously for the protection of Ford, . . . and its import was that Ford would not be bound by the amendment unless Allied agreed to all of the conditions specified therein. The provision for execution and return of the acknowledgment copy, as we construe the language used, was not to set forth an exclusive method of acceptance but was merely to provide a simple and convenient method by which the assent of Allied to the contractual provisions of the amendment could be indicated. The primary object of Ford was to have the work performed by Allied upon the terms prescribed in the amendment, and the mere signing and return of an acknowledgment copy of the amendment before actually undertaking the work itself cannot be regarded as an essential condition to completion of a binding contract. . . .

[Allied argues], by way of analogy, that Ford could have revoked the order when [it] began installing the machinery without first having executed its written acceptance. If this point should be conceded, cf. Venters v. Stewart, supra, it would avail Allied nothing. For, after Allied began performance by installing the machinery called for, and Ford acquiesced [and] accepted the benefits of the performance, Ford was estopped to object and could not thereafter be heard to complain that there was no contract. Sparks v. Mauk, 170 Cal. 122, 148 P. 926. . . .

The judgment of the District Court is [a]ffirmed.

———

Panhandle Eastern Pipe Line Co. v. Smith
637 P.2d 1020, 1022 (Wyo.1981)

"The offeror is master of the offer, but we think fairness demands that when there is a dispute concerning mode of acceptance, the offer itself must clearly and definitely express an exclusive [mode]. There must be no question that the offeror would accept the prescribed mode and only the prescribed mode. Corbin comments, 'The more unreasonable the method appears, the less likely it will be that a court will interpret [the] offer as requiring [a specific mode of acceptance].' 1 Corbin on Contracts, § 88. The only motivation we could surmise for the requirement that no handwriting be added to the paper, regardless of content, would be that the offeror had an inordinate fondness for tidy sheets of paper. The requirement strikes us as unreasonable, and strikes out as a prescribed mode of acceptance. . . . Had [this offeror, who told the offeree to 'just sign the letter and not add anything,'] seriously been proposing an exclusive mode of acceptance calling for the absence of anything on the paper other than signatures, the letter should have explicitly demanded that."

———

NOTE

An illustration attached to Rest.2d, Contracts § 58 provides:

8. A offers to pay B $100 for plowing Flodden field, and states that acceptance is to be made only by posting a letter before beginning work and before the next Monday noon. Before Monday noon B completes the requested plowing and mails to A a letter stating that the work is complete. There is no contract.

Is the answer given by the second restaters reconcilable with the answer given by the court in *Allied Steel*, which also involved an offeree's beginning of performance?

As we shall see, the Second Restatement, following the lead of the UCC, speaks directly to disputes over the use of the wrong mode of acceptance, especially the beginning of performance. The key Code provision, § 2–206(1)(a), declares: "Unless otherwise unambiguously indicated by language or circumstances (a) an offer to make a contract shall be construed as inviting acceptance in any manner and by any medium reasonable in the circumstances[.]" Section 2–206(2) then treats the exceptional case where performance is an acceptable means of signaling assent but the offeror is not likely to learn of the offeree's performance ("exceptional" because a performance not coming to the offeror's attention in the normal course is probably not a "reasonable-in-the-circumstances" means of acceptance). In such a situation, an offeree's failure to give timely notice of acceptance operates as the nonoccurrence of a "condition"—i.e., the offeror may treat the offer as having lapsed before acceptance. Similar principles are adopted in Rest.2d § 54.

———

Davis v. Jacoby

Supreme Court of California, 1934.
1 Cal.2d 370, 34 P.2d 1026.

THE COURT–Plaintiffs appeal from a judgment refusing to grant specific performance of an alleged contract to make a will. The facts are not in dispute. . . .

The plaintiff Caro Davis was the niece of Blanche Whitehead who was married to Rupert Whitehead. Prior to her marriage in 1913 to her coplaintiff Frank Davis, Caro lived for a considerable time at the home of the Whiteheads, in Piedmont, California. The Whiteheads were childless and extremely fond of Caro. The record is replete with uncontradicted testimony of the close and loving relationship that existed between Caro and her aunt and uncle. During the period that Caro lived with the Whiteheads she was treated as and often referred to by the Whiteheads as their daughter. In 1913, when Caro was married to Frank Davis the marriage was arranged at the Whitehead home and a reception held there. After the marriage Mr. and Mrs. Davis went to Mr. Davis' home in Canada, where they have resided ever since. During the period 1913 to 1931 Caro made many visits to the Whiteheads, several of them being of long duration. The Whiteheads visited Mr. and Mrs. Davis in Canada on several occasions. After the marriage and continuing down to 1931 the closest and most friendly relationship at all times existed between these two families. They corresponded frequently, the record being replete with letters showing the loving relationship.

By the year 1930 Mrs. Whitehead had become seriously ill. She had suffered several strokes and her mind was failing. Early in 1931 Mr. Whitehead had her removed to a private hospital. The doctors in attendance had informed him that she might die at any time or she might linger for many months. Mr. Whitehead had suffered severe financial reverses. He had had several sieges of sickness and was in poor health. The record shows that during the early part of 1931 he was desperately in need of assistance with his wife and in his business affairs, and that he did not trust his friends in Piedmont. On March 18, he wrote to Mrs. Davis telling her of Mrs. Whitehead's condition and added that Mrs. Whitehead was very wistful. "Today I endeavored to find out what she wanted. I finally asked her if she wanted to see you. She burst out crying and we had great difficulty in getting her to stop. Evidently, that is what is on her mind. It is a very difficult matter to decide. If you come it will mean that you will have to leave again, and then things may be serious. I am going to see the doctor, and get his candid opinion and will then write you again. . . . Since writing the above, I have seen the doctor, and he thinks it will help considerably if you come." Shortly thereafter, Mr. Whitehead wrote to Caro Davis further explaining the physical condition of Mrs. Whitehead and himself. On March 24, Mr. Davis, at the request of his wife, telegraphed to Mr. Whitehead as follows: "Your letter received. Sorry to hear Blanche not so well. Hope you are feeling better yourself. If you wish Caro to go to you can arrange for her to leave in about two weeks. Please wire me if you think it advisable for her to go."

On March 30, 1931, Mr. Whitehead wrote a long letter to Mr. Davis, in which he explained in detail the condition of Mrs. Whitehead's health and also referred to his own health. He pointed out that he had lost a considerable portion of his cash assets but still owned considerable realty, that he needed someone to help him with his wife and some friend he could trust to help him with his business affairs and suggested that perhaps Mr. Davis might come to California. He then pointed out that all his property was community property; that under his will all the property was to go to Mrs. Whitehead; that he believed that under Mrs. Whitehead's will practically everything was to go to Caro. Mr. Whitehead again wrote to Mr. Davis under date of April 9, pointing out how badly he needed someone he could trust to assist him, and giving it as his belief that if properly handled he could still save about $150,000. He then stated: "Having you [Mr. Davis] here to depend on and to help me regain my mind and courage would be a big thing." Three days later, on April 12, Mr. Whitehead again wrote, addressing his letter to "Dear Frank and Caro", and in this letter made the definite offer, which offer it is claimed was accepted and is the basis of this action. In this letter he first pointed out that Blanche, his wife, was in a private hospital and that "she cannot last much longer . . . my affairs are not as bad as I supposed at first. Cutting everything down I figure 150,000 can be saved from the wreck." He then enumerated the values placed upon his various properties and then continued "my trouble was caused by my friends taking advantage of my illness and my position to skin me."

"Now if Frank could come out here and be with me and look after my affairs, we could easily save the balance I mentioned, provided I dont get into another panic and do some more foolish things.

"The next attack will be my end, I am 65 and my health has been bad for years, so, the Drs. dont give me much longer to live. So if you can come, Caro will inherit everything and you will make our lives happier and see Blanche is provided for to the end.

"My eyesight has gone back on me, I cant read only for a few lines at a time. I am at the house alone with Stanley [the chauffeur] who does everything for me and is a fine fellow. Now, what I want is some one who will take charge of my affairs and see I dont lose any more. Frank can do it, if he will and cut out the booze.

"Will you let me hear from you as soon as possible, I know it will be a sacrifice but times are still bad and likely to be, so by settling down you can help me and Blanche and gain in the end. If I had you here my mind would get better and my courage return, and we could work things out."

This letter was received by Mr. Davis at his office in Windsor, Canada, about 9:30 A.M. April 14. After reading the letter to Mrs. Davis over the telephone, and after getting her belief that they must go to California, Mr. Davis immediately wrote Mr. Whitehead a letter, which, after reading it to his wife, he sent by air mail. This letter was lost, but there is no doubt that it was sent by Davis and received by Whitehead, in fact, the trial court expressly so found. Mr. Davis testified in substance as to the contents of this letter. After acknowledging receipt of the letter of April 12, Mr. Davis unequivocally stated that he and Mrs. Davis accepted the proposition of Mr. Whitehead and both would leave Windsor to go to him on April 25th. This letter of acceptance also contained the information that the reason they could not leave prior to April 25th was that Mr. Davis had to appear in court on April 22d as one of the executors of his mother's estate. The testimony is uncontradicted and ample to support the trial court's finding that this letter was sent by Davis and received by Whitehead. In fact under date of April 15, Mr. Whitehead again wrote to Mr. Davis and stated "Your letter by air mail received this a.m. Now, I am wondering if I have put you to unnecessary trouble and expense, if you are making any money dont leave it, as things are bad here. . . . You know your business and I dont and I am half crazy in the bargain, but I dont want to hurt you or Caro."

"Then on the other hand if I could get some one to trust and keep me straight I can save a good deal, about what I told you in my former letter."

This letter was received by Mr. Davis on April 17, and the same day Mr. Davis telegraphed to Mr. Whitehead "Cheer up—we will soon be there, we will wire you from the train."

Between April 14, 1931, the date the letter of acceptance was sent by Mr. Davis, and April 22d, Mr. Davis was engaged in closing out his business affairs, and Mrs. Davis in closing up their home and in making other arrangements to leave. On April 22, Mr. Whitehead committed suicide. Mr. and Mrs. Davis were immediately notified and they at once came to California. From almost the moment of her arrival Mrs. Davis devoted herself to the care and comfort of her aunt, and gave her aunt constant attention and care until Mrs. Whitehead's death on May 30, 1931. . . . In fact the record shows that after their arrival in California Mr. and Mrs. Davis fully performed their side of the agreement.

After the death of Mrs. Whitehead, it was discovered that the information contained in Mr. Whitehead's letter of March 30, 1931, in reference to the contents of his and Mrs. Whitehead's wills was incorrect. By a duly witnessed will dated February 28, 1931, Mr. Whitehead, after making several specific bequests, had bequeathed all of the balance of his estate to his wife for life, and upon her death to respondents Geoff Doubble and Rupert Ross Whitehead, his nephews. Neither appellant was mentioned in his will. It was also discovered that Mrs. Whitehead by a will dated December 17, 1927, had devised all of her estate to her husband. The evidence is clear [that] the relationship existing between Whitehead and his two nephews, respondents herein, was not nearly as close and confidential as that existing between Whitehead and appellants.

After the discovery of the manner in which the property had been devised was made, this action was commenced upon the theory that Rupert Whitehead had assumed a contractual obligation to make a will whereby "Caro Davis would inherit everything"; that he had failed to do so; that plaintiffs had fully performed their part of the contract; that damages being insufficient, quasi specific performance should be granted in order to remedy the alleged wrong, upon the equitable principle that equity regards that done which ought to have been done. The requested relief is that the beneficiaries under the will of Rupert Whitehead, respondents herein, be declared to be involuntary trustees for plaintiffs of Whitehead's estate.

It should also be added that the evidence shows that as a result of Frank Davis leaving his business in Canada he forfeited not only all insurance business he might have written if he had remained, but also forfeited all renewal commissions earned on past business. According to his testimony this loss was over $8,000.

The trial court found that the relationship between Mr. and Mrs. Davis and the Whiteheads was substantially as above recounted and that the other facts above stated were true. . . .

The theory of the trial court and of respondents on this appeal is that the letter of April 12th was an offer to contract, but that such offer could only be accepted by performance and could not be accepted by a promise to perform, and that said offer was revoked by the death of Mr. Whitehead before performance.* In other words, it is contended that the offer was an offer to enter into a unilateral contract, and that the purported acceptance of April 14th was of no legal effect.

The distinction between unilateral and bilateral contracts is well settled in the law. . . . "A unilateral contract is one in which no promisor receives a promise as consideration for his promise. A bilateral contract is one in which there are mutual promises between two parties to the contract; each party being both a promisor and a promisee." [Restatement, Contracts § 12]. . . .

Although the legal distinction between unilateral and bilateral contracts is thus well settled, the difficulty in any particular case is to determine whether the particular offer is one to enter into a bilateral or unilateral contract. Some cases are quite clear cut. Thus an offer to sell which is accepted is clearly a bilateral contract, while an offer of a reward is a clear-cut offer of a unilateral contract which cannot be accepted by a promise to perform but only by performance. Berthiaume v. Doe, 22 Cal.App. 78, 133 P. 515. Between these two extremes is a vague field where the particular contract may be unilateral or bilateral depending upon the intent of the offerer and the facts and circumstances of each case. The offer to contract involved in this case falls within this category. By the provisions of the [Restatement] it is expressly provided that there is a presumption that the offer is to enter into a bilateral contract. Section 31 provides: "In case of doubt it is presumed that an offer invites the formation of a bilateral contract by an acceptance amounting in effect to a promise by the offeree to perform what the offer requests, rather than the formation of one or more unilateral contracts by actual performance on the part of the offeree." . . .

In the comment following Restatement § 31 the reason for such presumption is stated as follows: "It is not always easy to determine whether an offerer requests an act or a promise to do the act. As a bilateral contract immediately and fully protects both parties, the interpretation is favored that a bilateral contract is proposed."

While the California cases have never expressly held that a presumption in favor of bilateral contracts exists, the cases clearly indicate a ten-

* [This theory, you may recall, was urged by Judge Kellogg in his dissent in Allegheny College v. National Chautauqua County Bank, p. 247.—Eds.]

dency to treat offers as offers of bilateral rather than of unilateral contracts. Roth v. Moeller, 185 Cal. 415, 197 P. 62; . . . see, also, Wood v. Lucy, Lady Duff–Gordon, 222 N.Y. 88, 118 N.E. 214.

Keeping these principles in mind we are of the opinion that the offer of April 12th was an offer to enter into a bilateral as distinguished from a unilateral contract. Respondents argue that Mr. Whitehead had the right as offerer to designate his offer as either unilateral or bilateral. That is undoubtedly the law. It is then argued that from all the facts and circumstances it must be implied that what Whitehead wanted was performance and not a mere promise to perform. We think this is a non sequitur, in fact the surrounding circumstances lead to just the opposite conclusion. These parties were not dealing at arm's length. Not only were they related, but a very close and intimate friendship existed between them. The record indisputably demonstrates that Mr. Whitehead had confidence in Mr. and Mrs. Davis, in fact that he had lost all confidence in everyone else. The record amply shows that by an accumulation of occurrences Mr. Whitehead had become desperate and that what he wanted was the promise of appellants that he could look to them for assistance. He knew from his past relationship with appellants that if they gave their promise to perform he could rely upon them. The correspondence between them indicates how desperately he desired this assurance. Under these circumstances he wrote his offer of April 12th, above quoted, in which he stated[:] "Will you let me hear from you as soon as possible—I know it will be a sacrifice but times are still bad and likely to be, so by settling down you can help me and Blanche and gain in the end." By thus specifically requesting an immediate reply Whitehead expressly indicated the nature of acceptance desired by him—namely, appellants' promise that they would come to California and do the things requested by him. This promise was immediately sent by appellants upon receipt of the offer, and was received by Whitehead. It is elementary that when an offer has indicated the mode and means of acceptance an acceptance in accordance with that mode or means is binding on the offerer.

Another factor which indicates that Whitehead must have contemplated a bilateral rather than a unilateral contract, is that the contract required Mr. and Mrs. Davis to perform services until the death of both Mr. and Mrs. Whitehead. It is obvious that if Mr. Whitehead died first some of these services were to be performed after his death, so that he would have to rely on the promise of appellants to perform these services. It is also of some evidentiary force that Whitehead received the letter of acceptance and acquiesced in that means of acceptance.

For the foregoing reasons we are of the opinion that the offer of April 12 was an offer to enter into a bilateral contract which was accepted by the letter of April 14. Subsequently appellants fully performed their part of the contract. Under such circumstances it is well settled that damages are insufficient and specific performance will be granted. Wolf v. Donahue, 206 Cal. 213, 273 P. 547. . . .

[The judgment appealed from is reversed. Rehearing denied.]

QUESTION

Assume that after writing the letter of April 14, Frank Davis had written again on April 18, as follows: "Further reflection has led Caro and me regretfully to the conclusion that we should not make the move." Contract?

———————

NOTE

The presumption stated in § 31 of the first Restatement of Contracts has been modified in Restatement, Second § 32, as follows: "In case of doubt an offer is interpreted as inviting the offeree to accept either by promising to perform what the offer requests or by rendering the performance, as the offeree chooses." Would this reformulation have affected the outcome in Davis v. Jacoby? We will return later to the legal implications of the revised § 32.

————

Jordan v. Dobbins
122 Mass. 168 (1877)

Plaintiff Jordan had sold goods to Moore on credit, relying on Dobbins' earlier agreement in writing to guarantee payment of any sums not paid by Moore. But Dobbins had died before the sales in question were made, and Jordan, on the strength of the guaranty agreement, had made the advances of credit in ignorance of Dobbins' death. When Moore failed to pay for his purchases, Jordan sued Dobbins' estate to enforce the guaranty agreement. *Held*, judgment for the estate. No consideration passed to Dobbins at the time he executed the writing to become guarantor for Moore. Yet, the writing by its terms invited Jordan to advance goods on credit: "The agreement which the guarantor makes with the person receiving the guaranty is not that I now become liable to you for anything, but that if you sell goods to a third person, I will then become liable to pay for them if such third person does not. . . . Thus such a guaranty is revocable by the guarantor at anytime before it is acted upon. . . . Such being the nature of a guaranty, . . . the death of the guarantor operates as a revocation of it, and [the person holding it cannot recover] for goods sold after the death. [Death] revokes any authority or license [the deceased] may have given, if it has not been executed or acted upon. His estate . . . is not held for a liability which is created after his death, by the exercise of a power . . . which he might at any time revoke. . . . We are not impressed by the plaintiff's argument that it is inequitable to throw the loss upon them." [You should know that the rule that death (or incapacity) of either offeror or offeree terminates the power of acceptance remains generally in effect today. Do you have trouble explaining the rule's survival, given the prevailing objective theory of contract?]

————

RESTATEMENT OF CONTRACTS, SECOND

Section 36. Methods of Termination of the Power of Acceptance

(1) An offeree's power of acceptance may be terminated by

(a) rejection or counter-offer by the offeree, or

(b) lapse of time, or

(c) revocation by the offeror, or

(d) death or incapacity of the offeror or offeree.

(2) In addition, an offeree's power of acceptance is terminated by the nonoccurrence of any condition of acceptance under the terms of the offer.

————

Brackenbury v. Hodgkin

Supreme Judicial Court of Maine, 1917.
116 Me. 399, 102 A. 106.

CORNISH, C.J. The defendant, Mrs. Sarah D.P. Hodgkin, on the eighth day of February, 1915, was the owner of certain real estate, her home farm, situated in the outskirts of Lewiston. She was a widow and was living alone. She was the mother of six adult children, five sons, one of whom, Walter, is a co-defendant, and one daughter, who is the co-plaintiff. The plaintiffs were then residing in Independence, Missouri. Many letters had passed between mother and daughter concerning the daughter and her husband returning to the old home and taking care of the mother, and finally, on February 8, 1915, the mother sent a letter to the daughter and her husband which is the foundation of this bill in equity. In this letter she made a definite proposal, the substance of which was that if the Brackenburys would move to Lewiston, and maintain and care for Mrs. Hodgkin on the home place during her life, and pay the moving expenses, they were to have the use and income of the premises, together with the use of the household goods, with certain exceptions, Mrs. Hodgkin to have what rooms she might need. The letter closed, by way of postscript, with the words: "you to have the place when I have passed away."

Relying upon this offer, [and] in acceptance thereof, the plaintiffs moved from Missouri to Maine late in April, 1915, went upon the premises described and entered upon the performance of the contract. Trouble developed after a few weeks and the relations between the parties grew most disagreeable. The mother brought two suits against her son-in-law on trifling matters and finally ordered the plaintiffs from the place but they refused to leave. Then on November 7, 1916, she executed and delivered to her son, Walter C. Hodgkin, a deed of the premises, reserving a life estate in herself. Walter, however, was not a bona fide purchaser for value without notice but took the deed with full knowledge of the agreement between the parties and for the sole purpose of evicting the plaintiffs. On the very day the deed was executed he served a notice to quit upon Mr. Brackenbury, as preliminary to an action of forcible entry and detainer which was brought on November 13, 1916. This bill in equity was brought by the plaintiffs to secure a reconveyance of the farm from Walter to his mother, to restrain and enjoin Walter from further prosecuting his action of forcible entry and detainer and to obtain an adjudication that the mother holds the legal title impressed with a trust in favor of the plaintiffs in accordance with their contract.

The sitting Justice made an elaborate and carefully considered finding of facts and signed a decree, sustaining the bill with costs against Walter C. Hodgkin and granting the relief prayed for. The case is before the [court] on the defendants' appeal from this decree. [A number of] main issues are raised.

1. As to the completion and existence of a valid contract.

A legal and binding contract is clearly proven. The offer on the part of the mother was in writing and its terms cannot successfully be disputed.

There was no need that it be accepted in words nor that a counter promise on the part of the plaintiffs be made. The offer was the basis, not of a bilateral contract, requiring a reciprocal promise, a promise for a promise, but of a unilateral contract requiring an act for a promise. "In the latter case the only acceptance of the offer that is necessary is the performance of the act. . . . [T]he promise becomes binding when the act is performed." 6 R.C.L., 607. This is elementary law.

The plaintiffs here accepted the offer by moving from Missouri to the mother's farm in Lewiston and entering upon the performance of the specified acts, and they have continued performance since that time so far as they have been permitted by the mother to do so. The existence of a completed and valid contract is clear.

2. The creation of an equitable interest.

This contract between the parties, the performance of which was entered upon by the plaintiffs, created an equitable interest in the land described in the bill in favor of the plaintiffs. The letter of February 8, signed by the mother, answered the statutory requirement that "there can be no trust concerning lands, except trusts arising or resulting by implication of law, unless created or declared by some writing signed by the party or his attorney." R.S. (1903) Chap. 75, Sec. 14. No particular formality need be observed; a letter or other memorandum is sufficient to establish a trust provided its terms and the relations of the parties to it appear with reasonable certainty. Bates v. Hurd, 65 Maine at 181. . . . The equitable interest of the plaintiffs in these premises is obvious and they are entitled to have that interest protected.

3. Alleged breach of duty on the part of the plaintiffs.

The defendants contend that, granting an equitable estate has been established, the plaintiffs have failed of performance because of their improper and unkind treatment of Mrs. Hodgkin, and therefore have forfeited the right to equitable relief which they might otherwise be entitled to. The sitting Justice decided this question of fact in favor of the plaintiffs and his finding is fully warranted by the evidence. Mrs. Hodgkin's temperament and disposition, not only as described in the testimony of others but as revealed in her own attitude, conduct and testimony as a witness, as they stand out on the printed record, mark her as the provoking cause in the various family difficulties. She was "the one primarily at fault." . . .

The plaintiffs are entitled to the remedy here sought and the entry must be, appeal dismissed.

QUESTION

What if plaintiffs, after securing the trial court's decree, went back home to Missouri? Are §§ 32 and 62 of the Restatement, Second, the subject of the Note which follows, relevant?

―――――

NOTE: DOUBT AS TO THE FORM OF ACCEPTANCE

As was noted after Davis v. Jacoby, the Restatement, Second § 32 changes the earlier formulation to provide that when the nature of the acceptance invited by the offer is "in doubt," the offer should be interpreted as inviting acceptance either by a promise to perform or by rendering the performance, as the offeree chooses. The apparent effect of the revision is to expand an offeree's power to conclude a contract. The point worth noting, however, is that this expanded protection for the offeree involves little loss of the offeror's control over contract formation. The notion that the offeror is master of the offer appears to have survived the revision of § 32, since the offeree's choice between acceptance by promise and acceptance by performance is grounded explicitly in the intention of the offeror. There is a power to choose only "in case of doubt" as to what is called for by the offer. The offeror may act to eliminate any doubt by requiring acceptance to be made in a particular way; cases such as Davis v. Jacoby, Petterson v. Pattberg, and Brackenbury v. Hodgkin will therefore continue to present nice questions of interpretation of the offer to determine whether the offeror has limited acceptance to a particular mode.

The significance of revised § 32, then, is its introduction of a presumption of offeror-indifference when the form of acceptance is not made clear. Should cases such as Allied Steel & Conveyors v. Ford Motor Co., supra p. 333, be read as demonstrating the soundness of the assumption that an offeror who fails to specify a mode of acceptance is relatively indifferent as to how acceptance occurs? It would be useful to look again at UCC 2–206, which, in tandem with § 2–204, was instrumental in developing the second Restatement's approach to formation issues in general, including § 32. The Official Comment to UCC 2–206 includes an explicit rejection of "the artificial theory that only a single mode of acceptance is normally envisaged by an offer."

What is the nature of the contract that results when the offeror is indifferent about the mode of acceptance and the offeree chooses to accept by beginning performance? It seems only natural to view the contract as unilateral, with the principle of § 45 operating to protect the offeree once performance has begun. But does not the conventional option arrangement—the offer is irrevocable but the offeree is under no obligation to carry through—seem anomalous when considered in the light of the probable needs and expectations of most commercial bargainers who, by virtue of the turns of the agreement process, find themselves in the position of offeror? Need we look any further than Sarah Hodgkin?

The Restatement, Second attempts to deal with the anomaly in this way:

> Section 62. Effect of Performance by Offeree Where Offer Invites Either Performance or Promise
>
> (1) Where an offer invites an offeree to choose between acceptance by promise and acceptance by performance, the tender or beginning of the invited performance or a tender of a beginning of it is an acceptance by performance.
>
> (2) Such an acceptance operates as a promise to render complete performance.

What happens to the rule of § 62 when the offer clearly contemplates an option contract (invites acceptance by performance only)?

———

COMMENT: THE REMEDY PROBLEM IN BRACKENBURY

Relief of the kind awarded in Brackenbury v. Hodgkin has been given in other states where contracts to devise land have been breached by a conveyance of the land to a transferee with notice. To the declaration that during the promisor's lifetime the land is held "in trust" for the promisee is sometimes added an injunction against transferring or encumbering the land. See, e.g., Turley v. Adams, 14 Ariz.App. 515, 484 P.2d 668 (1971); Wright v. Dudley, 189 Va. 448, 53 S.E.2d 29 (1949).

One objection often raised in these cases is that any action for specific performance brought in the promisor's lifetime is premature, since performance is not due until the promisor's death. Jesse v. O'Neal, 364 Mo. 333, 261 S.W.2d 88 (1953). To this objection the court in Van Duyne v. Vreeland, 12 N.J.Eq. 142 (1858), answered: "If this court does not interfere now for the protection of the complainant, and secure this property at the death of Vreeland, it may have passed into the hands of a bona fide purchaser, and the complainant then be remediless. A bill *quia timet* is to accomplish the ends of precautionary justice. The party seeks the aid of a court of equity *because he fears* some probable future injury to his rights or interests. They are applied to prevent wrongs or anticipated mischiefs, and not merely to redress them when done." Similarly, in Matheson v. Gullickson, 222 Minn. 369, 24 N.W.2d 704 (1946), the court conceded that plaintiff's rights had "not fully accrued" but concluded that, "in the meantime," it was necessary "to bring justice to the plaintiff" where his claim was "altogether and throughout equitable." The promisor's death will of course remove these standard objections to specific performance. E.g., Story v. Hargrave, 235 Va. 563, 369 S.E.2d 669 (1988); Mutz v. Wallace, 214 Cal.App.2d 100, 29 Cal.Rptr. 170 (Cal.Dist.Ct.App.1963).

A more serious problem in such cases is that of ensuring the promisee's own performance. In Davison v. Davison, 13 N.J.Eq. 246 (1861), the court had this to say:

> It is eminently desirable that this controversy should be amicably adjusted, and the court repeats the hope expressed on the argument, that a settlement may be effected between the parties without further action on the part of the court. The father is entitled to the enjoyment of the farm during his life. No present decree for the specific performance of the contract can be made. The complainant is entitled to the farm only upon the death of his father. By the terms of the contract, [he] is to have the management of the farm and to provide for his father during his life. If the father refuses to accept the services of the complainant, and no amicable adjustment can be made, further directions will be given for the management of the farm and the support of the father during his life.

In White v. Massee, 202 Iowa 1304, 211 N.W. 839 (1927), the court pointed out that because of the controversy that had arisen between father and daughter, the father might find it "morally impossible" to return to the daughter's home, but that the court "in imposing conditions to the granting of equitable relief, is not restrained by the strict legal rights of the parties, but may impose such terms as are demanded by justice and regard for righteous conduct." The court therefore inserted as a condition to the grant of an injunction that the plaintiff pay the clerk of the court $800 a year as rent for the premises, to be paid over to the father. But in O'Brien v. O'Brien, 197 Cal. 577, 241 P. 861

(1925), a husband who gave up a prosperous medical practice in order to marry and help his wealthy wife manage her property, was denied specific performance of her promise to devise property to him by will, since there were no means to compel him to perform on his side. The court said that the husband's remedy was damages for the "detriment" he had suffered in giving up his medical practice, but since he had failed to show his age, his earnings from the practice he surrendered, and the maximum amount he could earn by resuming practice, there was no basis on which such damages could be awarded.

On many occasions, courts have been slow to exercise equity jurisdiction because of the element of personal services in these cases. E.g., Gage v. Wimberley, 476 S.W.2d 724 (Tex.Civ.App.1972); Martin v. Martin, 230 S.W.2d 547 (Tex.Civ.App.1950) ("a court could not require the promisee to be kind and thoughtful and considerate of the promisor"); Hall v. Milham, 225 Ark. 597, 284 S.W.2d 108 (1955) ("there is no method by which a decree could be enforced"). In the case last cited, relief was limited to a money award for the value of improvements made to the land. As one would expect, the restitution remedy is seen often when property has been improved. See Nott v. Howell, 560 So.2d 410 (Fla.Dist.Ct.App.1990); Zvonik v. Zvonik, 291 Pa.Super. 309, 435 A.2d 1236 (1981). When equitable relief is denied altogether, a plaintiff who has performed in full usually recovers the value of the breached promise to devise land or to pay in property. The damage cases are reviewed in Owens v. Church, 675 S.W.2d 178 (Tenn.Ct.App.1984), where it is noted that some states restrict recovery to quantum meruit (the "value of the services" rule). It is probably not necessary to mention that Fitzpatrick v. Michael, supra p. 177, has a good deal to say on the subject of available remedies in *Brackenbury*-type cases.

We are informed that, after the decree in the principal case, Sarah Hodgkin and the Brackenburys continued to live together until the mother's death (of pneumonia) in January 1921, and that "relations were unpleasant to the end." Our informant learned from Mr. Brackenbury that he had secured a transcript of the record in the equity case and "would, from time to time, read from it to the old lady." There is other evidence indicating that Brackenbury was far from an ideal son-in-law to Sarah Hodgkin. After her death in 1921, the Brackenburys immediately sold the farm in Maine and returned to Missouri. We understand that Mrs. Brackenbury moved on to California to live with her son and his family, following Mr. Brackenbury's death. We know nothing about how that worked out. Our last report indicates that in late 1958, Mrs. Brackenbury, then about 94, had returned to Missouri and entered a retirement home.

NOTE: THE OFFER AS "OPTION CONTRACT" REVISITED

Again, "it is the offer which may start the trouble." That was surely true in Brackenbury v. Hodgkin. It was also true in the offer cases examined in Chapter 2—e.g., Thomason v. Bescher, Marsh v. Lott, James Baird Co. v. Gimbel Bros., Drennan v. Star Paving Co. There, it will be recalled, classic doctrines of consideration and reliance provided the basis for talk of a "firm offer" or "option contract" as devices for addressing the revocation problem.

An offeror most certainly has at hand the means for regulating the formation of a contract. The offeree alone may possess the power to close the contract, but that power is taken subject to any specifications laid down by the creator of the power. Not even compliance with the offeror's requirements suffices to ensure that the power of acceptance will be intact when the offeree gets around to using it. The offeror, it will be remembered, retains the power to revoke a simple offer until the very moment of acceptance—even without an explicit reservation of authority to do so. One need only recall Petterson v. Pattberg, where a highly respected court declared—albeit in dictum—that an offer could be revoked even after acceptance had been tendered.

But what if the offeror includes a statement (indeed, a promise) that the offer will remain available for a stated period? An opportunity to answer this question was presented in 1876 by the landmark case of Dickinson v. Dodds (Court of Appeal, Chancery Division), 2 Ch.D. 463. On Wednesday, June 10, 1874, defendant Dodds delivered to Dickinson a written offer to sell a parcel of land, with buildings, on specified terms. The offer provided that it would "be left over until" 9:00 a.m. on Friday, June 12. On Thursday, however, Dodds signed a contract to sell the property to one Allan. On the same day, Dickinson was informed by a person named Berry that Dodds had been "offering or agreeing" to sell to Allan. On Thursday evening, Dickinson left a written acceptance with Dodds' mother-in-law, with whom Dodds was then staying, but she failed to give it to him. On Friday morning about seven o'clock, first Berry, acting as Dickinson's agent, and then Dickinson himself, found Dodds at the local railway station and handed him duplicates of the acceptance. In each instance, Dodds replied that the acceptance was too late as he had sold the property. On defendant's appeal, a decree for specific performance was reversed. The court held that Dickinson's power to accept the offer had ended when, on Thursday, he received Berry's report that Dodds had sold the property to Allan. Dickinson then knew that Dodds "was no longer minded to sell the property to him as plainly and clearly as if Dodds had told him in so many words 'I withdraw the offer.'"

Nor did Dodds' assurance ("this offer to be left over until Friday") alter the result, because "[t]hat [language] shows it was only an offer. There was no consideration given for the undertaking or promise. . . . [It] being a mere *nudum pactum* was not binding, and . . . any moment before a complete acceptance by Dickinson of the offer, Dodds was as free as Dickinson himself."

The English court's first point laid the foundation for the principle of indirect communication of a revocation. Though still valid, this principle usually has been restricted to facts reasonably close to those of Dickinson v. Dodds. The following is a conventional formulation of the principle: "Where an offer is for the sale of an interest in land or in other things, if the offeror, after making the offer, sells or contracts to sell the interest to another person, and the offeree acquires reliable information of that fact, before he has exercised his power of creating a contract by acceptance of the offer, the offer is revoked." Berryman v. Kmoch, 221 Kan. 304, 310, 559 P.2d 790, 795 (1977). Why should the rule be so circumscribed? Why should it not extend to any offer and to any reliable information about what the offeror has been up to since making the original offer?

The second point of interest in the Dickinson v. Dodds analysis was that even the offeror's specification of a life span for the offer did not prevent its termination. There are at least two lines of explanation for this clearly remarkable proposition. One is rooted in the extreme subjectivism that occupied the minds of judges and contract theorists well toward the end of the nineteenth century. Consider Christopher Columbus Langdell's statement in 1880: "An offer is merely one of the elements of a contract; and it is indispensable to the making of a contract that the wills of the contracting parties do, in legal contemplation, concur at the moment of making it. An offer, therefore, which the party making it has no power to revoke, is a legal impossibility." (Law of Contracts § 78 (2d ed. 1880)). You will recognize, of course, that even when Langdell wrote, English law had already loosened, if not broken, the grip of subjectivism. Dickinson v. Dodds itself is proof of that, for there was no suggestion that Dodds' sale to Allan would itself have been enough to terminate Dickinson's power of acceptance before he learned of the sale.

Another possible explanation can be found in the power of legal classifications. Recall that the document Dodds gave Dickinson was called an offer, but the court immediately put it in the broad category of "undertaking or promise." This classification seemed naturally to lead to a search for those factors recognized as identifiers of the enforceable promise. Unable to find any, the court was impelled to conclude that Dodds was free to back away from his "undertaking or promise" before Dickinson's acceptance. Would it not have been entirely rational to say simply that an offer is not a promise, it is an offer? Such a classification might have invoked the basic premise of an offeror's control, with the result that an offer would be effective and immune to revocation to the extent defined in the offer itself. This is the approach adopted in German law and by some modern statutes in this country.

The principal result of these dual influences—subjectivism and the dictates of an unnecessary classification—was a need for devices to "reinforce" the power of acceptance so as to keep the subject of the offer off the market during the period the offeror has given the offeree for deliberation. What followed is a familiar story, most notably the carrying over to offers of principles generalized in the Second Restatement's §§ 87(1) and (2), supra pp. 271 and 279.

SECTION 3. LIMITED AND INDEFINITE PROMISES

INTRODUCTORY COMMENT

A number of the cases to this point have involved promises given in exchange for acts (or abstentions from action) or promises that induced reliance, again in the form of acts or abstentions. Attention has not been called, as it now must be, to the special problems that may arise where nothing more than an exchange of promises has occurred—the so-called "bilateral contract." Applying the tests of consideration, is it enough that each party has made a promise to the other? Does the form or content of the promise make a difference?

It is worth noting again that problems with a bilateral contract could not arise so long as the action of debt was the common law's chosen instrument for the enforcement of informal promises. Consider, for example, an agreement made in the year 1450 and involving an exchange of oral promises—150 bushels of wheat for £10. On the original exchange of promises, no obligation in debt arose; that action would lie only if the wheat had been actually delivered, or at least a "property" in the wheat transferred to the buyer. One or the other was essential to provide the quid pro quo on which the obligation in debt depended. In modern terminology, though the transaction may have begun as bilateral, it would have to become "unilateral" through performance on one side if the action of debt was to lie. Even after 1500, when special assumpsit began to expand as a remedy on promises, the great bulk of the cases involved plaintiffs who had already performed.

When actions on executory, bilateral transactions began to appear, they encountered no difficulty from the evolving doctrine of consideration. As early as 1555 (Pecke v. Redman, 2 Dyer 113a), the enforceability of an exchange of promises was taken for granted without discussion. In the sixteenth century, when lawyers began to search for some limits to liabilities arising from promises, the status of bilateral contracts seemed simple enough. When doubts were raised, for example, in Strangborough v. Warner, 4 Leon. 3 (1589), they were laid to rest with the flat statement that "a promise against a promise will maintain an action on the case."

It was in the nineteenth century effort to systematize and rationalize the doctrine of consideration that this simple affirmation came to seem inadequate, and new difficulties were manufactured. With attention focused on the concept of "detriment," which already had become the principal analytical tool, the question was asked: Where is the detriment in making a promise that enables it to serve as the consideration for a counter-promise? The answer first suggested was that the detriment lay in the promisor's legal obligation created by the promise. Critics pointed out that this response rested on circular reasoning. Legal obligation would result only if A's promise would be enforced by a court, and that would happen only if there were a consideration for it. One must therefore look at B's promise, and if it will provide consideration only if it in turn is legally enforceable, we are called upon to assume the very conclusion we set out to establish. Some participants in the debate argued that the way to get off this merry-go-round was to find the required detriment in A's mere act of promising. This, too, proved too much, for if A supplied consideration by merely mouthing words of promise, it would seem to be neither necessary nor proper to inquire into the content of A's apparent assurances or their legal consequences. Moreover, while it is possible to find that a party bargained wholly and exclusively for the other's statement of certain words, this is not the ordinary meaning or purpose of transactions in which "promises" are exchanged. Corbin observed long ago that the proposer of a bargain seeks both words of promise and the actual performance promised. 1 A. Corbin, Contracts § 142.

We need not pursue further the course of these nineteenth century debates on which so much ingenuity was expended. It is sufficient to point out that while they were taking place it was generally assumed that bilateral contracts—promise for promise—were here to stay, and that most of them were enforceable. We should add a small caveat, however. If for some reason a performance would not provide consideration if actually rendered, the same reason would presumably have the same effect if the performance were postponed and made the subject of a promise. If, for example, the legal-duty rule applied and the act to be performed consisted of nothing more than performance of some already-existing duty, the fact that it was promised would not help. The converse is equally true. It is a working rule, more than 99 percent reliable, that a promise is consideration if the performance promised, either act or forbearance, or both, would be consideration if it alone were bargained for.

Even with this limitation, however, the bilateral contract presents a cluster of problems that makes it inadequate merely to repeat the simple affirmation of 1589—"a promise against a promise" can be enough to create a contract. These problems arise because of the desire of at least one of the promisors to retain some measure of flexibility in confronting an uncertain and changing world. How much freedom may a promisor retain without impairing the basis for binding the other party? Consider the problems presented by the two digested cases that follow.

————

Davis v. General Foods Corp.
21 F.Supp. 445 (S.D.N.Y.1937)

Plaintiff wrote defendant saying that she had an idea and recipe for a new food product. Defendant wrote back, acknowledging receipt of plaintiff's letter and adding: "We shall be glad to examine your idea, but only with the understanding that the use to be made of it by us, and the compensation, if any, to be paid therefor, are matters resting solely in our discretion." After disclosing her recipe plaintiff sued in contract and quantum meruit, alleging that defendant had used her recipe in its business but had refused to compensate her. *Held*, defense motion for judgment on the pleadings granted. Defendant's letter cannot give rise to a binding agreement. " 'One of the commonest kind of promises too indefinite for legal enforcement is where the promisor retains an unlimited right to decide later the nature or extent of his performance. This unlimited choice . . . makes [the promise] merely illusory.' " Nor can there be recovery in quantum meruit. It is true that the law will presume a promise to pay reasonable value where a party has acted in reliance on an alleged contract, the terms of which are too indefinite for enforcement. But "where the form or character of the promise leads to the conclusion that the plaintiff did not rely upon it as a contractual obligation but trusted the fairness and liberality of the defendant, there is not only no contract but no misreliance upon a supposed contract, and consequently no legal obligation whatever."

————

Nat Nal Service Stations v. Wolf
304 N.Y. 332, 107 N.E.2d 473 (1952)

Plaintiff, operator of a service station, sued defendant wholesalers to recover a discount on over 900,000 gallons of gasoline purchases. The complaint alleged an oral agreement that "so long as plaintiff purchased [its gas requirements] through defendants and [they] accepted the same," defendants would pay plaintiff a discount on each gallon purchased. According to plaintiff, the promise of a discount was made when "the defendants desired to increase the volume of their orders for gasoline [with Socony and Standard Oil, their suppliers], and hence came to me with the proposition that if I would give my orders for gasoline through them, thereby increasing their volume, they would pay to me an amount equal to the discount received by them from the oil companies upon whatever orders I gave to them, and if they accepted my orders. I did give the defendants orders which they accepted and then transmitted in their name to the oil companies, under which they received a discount of at least one cent a gallon." The Appellate Division, reversing Special Term, granted defendants' motion for summary judgment and dismissed the complaint, on the ground that the agreement could not, by its terms, "be performed within one year from the making thereof." On further appeal, *held*, reversed; there is nothing in the terms of the oral agreement to bring it within the statute of frauds. Conway, J., explained:

"The agreement alleged here was clearly one at will and for no definite or specific time and thus by its terms did not of necessity extend beyond one year from the time of its making. . . . [N]either party obligated itself to do anything. Unless and until plaintiff had offered to place an order for gasoline and the defendants had accepted such offer and filled the order, only then did there come into existence a legal obligation, viz., the obligation of defendants to pay the agreed discount. . . . The plaintiff could have purchased the same gasoline through someone other than defendants. On the other hand if the plaintiff placed an order the defendant was under no obligation to accept it. Neither party was obligated to deal with the other. Each time the plaintiff offered to buy gasoline from defendants and the defendants accepted the offer and sold gasoline, there was concluded a separate contract and there became due from defendants the discount specified, but neither party was ever obligated to enter into another such contract. . . . [D]efendants were free at any and all times to discontinue payment of a discount either by refusing to accept an order or by notification to plaintiff that thenceforth no discounts would be paid. Plaintiff was at all times free to place all its orders for gasoline elsewhere or to notify defendants that no further orders would be offered to them for acceptance. We are confronted with an alleged contract by the terms of which neither party was bound to do anything at any time."

————

PROBLEMS

Clauses making the contract terminable by one or both parties on short notice are common. For example, in Laclede Gas Co. v. Amoco Oil Co., 522 F.2d 33 (8th Cir.1975), the court, finding that a power to cancel given only the buyer did not render the buyer's side of the contract illusory, said: "There is no necessity that for each stipulation in a contract binding one party there must be a corresponding stipulation binding the other. . . . [A] cancellation clause will invalidate a contract only if its exercise is *unrestricted*."

(1) Suppose a contract for the sale of 500 wool sweaters to be delivered by Seller in installments of 100 a month, with a provision for payment by Buyer for each installment at the rate of $30 a sweater, within 60 days after delivery. Would the contract be enforceable by either party if it contained any one of the following clauses:

(A) "Seller reserves the right to cancel this contract immediately in the event of any default in payment by Buyer";

(B) "Seller reserves the right to cancel this contract on 10 days' notice";

(C) "Seller reserves the right to cancel this contract on the giving of notice"?

(2) Suppose further that Seller had signed the contract but Buyer had not. Then Buyer repudiated after taking delivery of the first 100 sweaters shipped by Seller. Suppose also that the contract included this clause: "Seller reserves the right to cancel this agreement at any time without notice." Could Seller recover damages for Buyer's refusal to take the full 500 sweaters? Recover the

agreed price for the 100 sweaters Buyer accepted? Consult UCC 2–201; 2–607(1).

————

COMMENT: MUTUALITY OF OBLIGATION

The business of promoting contract "mutuality" came into our case law not much more than a century ago. To have consideration, it was said, "both parties must be bound or neither will be." There is, to be sure, an apparent evenhandedness in such a maxim. Talk of a requirement of "mutuality"—of some degree of balance in obligations—is encountered frequently enough in the cases, even today, that we must pause to consider its general reliability.

Suppose a contract that is defective for some reason, such as fraud perpetrated by one party. A promises to sell B a car, B promises to pay A the agreed price, but during negotiations A misrepresents the year, mileage, and condition of the car. If B's reliance on the misrepresentations is justified ("reasonable" in the circumstances), quite clearly B will have an election to rescind the transaction when the fraud is discovered. Does this mean that B's promise is so lacking in binding effect that B cannot enforce A's promise? B may decide after all to "affirm" the transaction and take the car with an allowance in damages for its defective condition. A moment's reflection will indicate how undesirable it is to allow A to escape liability by setting up his own fraud. The same sort of problem would arise if A used duress—let us say, pointed a gun at B to make B sign. Or suppose that B is mentally incapable or an infant. Insane persons and infants can avoid liability on their promises, which are usually described as "voidable." Professor Williston argued (1 S. Williston, Contracts § 105) that the promise of an infant or insane person means no more than "I promise to perform if I choose"; that such a promise if expressed in words would be illusory; and that any doctrine finding consideration in such a promise "must be regarded as an exception to the general principles of consideration." But if one is concerned less with preserving the symmetry of legal doctrine than with examining the purposes that doctrine must serve, the problem takes on a different aspect. There is indeed an apparent injustice in binding the adult or the mentally-competent party, while escape is left open for the infant or the mentally incapacitated. On the other hand, the power of avoidance given to the infant or the mentally ill is intended as protection against disadvantageous agreements. Is this larger purpose served by holding such persons incapable of making advantageous agreements in bilateral form, i.e., through an exchange of promises? Or, phrased another way, the question is whether infants, the insane, or other seriously handicapped persons must be required always to perform first in order to be able to enforce promises made to them by other people. It is not altogether surprising to find that so far as consideration doctrines in law actions are concerned, the answer is "no."

A similar problem arises with the statute of frauds, which usually requires a memorandum signed by "the party to be charged" where the promise in question comes within the statutory classes. What if one party has signed, but the other has not? Again, there is the inequality noted above; the signer is bound even though that party would have no means of compelling performance of any return promise by the other party had the latter breached. In effect, the nonsigner is given a kind of unintended option. Before condemning this result, however, one should ask whether it is necessary, or wise, to go beyond the statutory provision, which requires safeguards only for "the party to be charged." The conclusion generally is that we should not, that an oral promise rendered unenforceable by the statute of frauds is still a promise and that it provides consideration for a written counterpromise.

The Restatement of Contracts, Second § 78 deals with these miscellaneous situations inclusively, as follows: "The fact that a rule of law renders a promise voidable or unenforceable does not prevent it from being consideration."

This principle, coupled with the examples already given, leaves little doubt that the maxim that "both must be bound or neither will be," in the broad sweep of its language, will not stand scrutiny. But what should be the law's approach where the avenue of escape is provided not by a rule of law but by the terms of the promise itself? Are there special problems of fairness in contracts framed as bilateral? Is there some recognized principle compelling the conclusion that a promise of limited commitment, one that reserves to the promisor an option or alternative in some form, is fatally defective and cannot render a return promise enforceable? If there is, the question then must be whether it is an independent principle of general contract law, an offshoot or byproduct of consideration doctrine, or possibly something else.

Our present concern is "mutuality of obligation." The use of mutuality as a factor influencing the grant or refusal of specific performance in equity ("mutuality of remedy") has some distinctive features and will come up later.

Wood v. Lucy, Lady Duff–Gordon

Court of Appeals of New York, 1917.
222 N.Y. 88, 118 N.E. 214.

Cᴀʀᴅᴏᴢᴏ, J. The defendant styles herself "a creator of fashions." Her favor helps a sale. Manufacturers of dresses, millinery and like articles are glad to pay for a certificate of her approval. The things which she designs, fabrics, parasols and what not, have a new value in the public mind when issued in her name. She employed the plaintiff to help her to turn this vogue into money. He was to have the exclusive right, subject always to her approval, to place her indorsements on the designs of others. He was also to have the exclusive right to place her own designs on sale, or to license others to market them. In return, she was to have one-half of "all profits and revenues" derived from any contracts he might make. The exclusive right was to last at least one year from April 1, 1915, and thereafter from year to year unless terminated by notice of ninety days. The plaintiff says that he kept the contract on his part, and that the defendant broke it. She placed her indorsement on fabrics, dresses and millinery without his knowledge, and withheld the profits. He sues her for the damages and the case comes here on demurrer.

The agreement of employment is signed by both parties. It has a wealth of recitals. The defendant insists, however, that it lacks the elements of a contract. She says that the plaintiff does not bind himself to anything. It is true that he does not promise in so many words that he will use reasonable efforts to place the defendant's indorsements and market her designs. We think, however, that such a promise is fairly to be implied. The law has outgrown its primitive stage of formalism when the precise word was the sovereign talisman, and every slip was fatal. It takes a broader view today. A promise may be lacking, and yet the whole writing may be "instinct with an obligation," imperfectly expressed, Scott, J., in McCall Co. v. Wright, 133 App.Div. 62, 117 N.Y.S. 775. . . . If that is so, there is a contract.

Lady Duff-Gordon
Of the English nobility, who employs psychology in designing clothes for women

Good Housekeeping Magazine

LADY DUFF-GORDON
Of the English nobility who employs psychology
in designing clothes for women

The implication of a promise here finds support in many circumstances. The defendant gave an *exclusive* privilege. She was to have no right for at least a year to place her own indorsements or market her own designs except through the agency of the plaintiff. The acceptance of the exclusive agency was an assumption of its duties. . . . We are not to suppose that one party was to be placed at the mercy of the other. Hearn v. Stevens & Bro., 111 App.Div. 101, 97 N.Y.S. 566. . . . Many other terms of the agreement point the same way. We are told at the outset by way of recital that "the said Otis F. Wood possesses a business organization adapted to the placing of such indorsements as the said Lucy, Lady Duff–Gordon has approved." The implication is that the plaintiff's business organization will be used for the purpose for which it is adapted. But the terms of the defendant's compensation are even more significant. Her sole compensation for the grant of an exclusive agency is to be one-half of all the profits resulting from the plaintiff's efforts. Unless he gave his efforts, she could never get anything. Without an implied promise, the transaction cannot have such business "efficacy as both parties must have intended that at all events it should have." Bowen, L.J., in The Moorcock, 14 P.D. 64, 68. But the contract does not stop there. The plaintiff goes on to promise that he will account monthly for all moneys received by him, and that he will take out all such patents and copyrights and trademarks as may in his judgment be necessary to protect the rights and articles affected by the agreement. It is true, of course, as the Appellate Division has said, that if he was under no duty to try to market designs or to place certificates of indorsement, his promise to account for profits or take out copyrights would be valueless. But in determining the intention of the parties, the promise *has* a value. It helps to enforce the conclusion that the plaintiff *had* some duties. His promise to pay the defendant one-half of the profits and revenues resulting from the exclusive agency and to render accounts monthly, was a promise to use reasonable efforts to bring profits and revenues into existence. For this conclusion, the authorities are ample. . . .

The judgment of the Appellate Division should be reversed, and the order of the Special Term affirmed. . . . [The vote in the Court of Appeals was 4 to 3.]

NOTE

The source of Cardozo's gap-filling implication seems clear enough. Even though Lady Duff–Gordon sold endorsements and not goods, if the case arose today presumably UCC 2–306(2) would not hinder the interpretive move Cardozo made.

It is reported that Lucy brought Wood's lawsuit upon herself by arranging with Sears, Roebuck and Co. to sell her dresses through its catalogues. This move was apparently heralded as a stunning marketing tactic for the times, placing Lucy at the forefront of commercial practice. A trade journal commented that the announcement of the agreement with Sears threw "a bomb into the camp of rival mail-order houses." Pratt, American Contract Law at the Turn of the Century, 39 S.Car.L.Rev. 415, 439 (1988).

But the suit brought by Wood was not Lady Duff–Gordon's only encounter with the legal system. In April 1919, a judgment of $1,500 was entered against her in a suit brought by Muriel Ridley, a dancer, for breach of contract. Although Lady Duff–Gordon had asserted that she was unable to pay the $1,500 judgment, it is reported that her lawyer quickly sent Ridley a check in full payment when the contents of Duff–Gordon's Park Avenue (New York) apartment were attached. The whole affair apparently turned Lady Duff–Gordon sour on America, for, when asked by the judge in these proceedings whether she had purchased any Liberty Bonds, she replied: "Why should I buy any? This country means nothing to me. I have had nothing but trouble over here. It is an awful country." N.Y.Times, April 13, 1919, at 22, col. 2.

It seems Lady Duff–Gordon's troubles continued. Her exclusive dress firm, Lucile Ltd., with boutiques in New York, Chicago, London, and Paris, subsequently went into bankruptcy proceedings; she was accused by some of contributing to the failure of the company by her "unjustifiable extravagance." N.Y.Times, April 19, 1923, at 23, col. 3. Although Lady Duff–Gordon was highly regarded as a dress designer (she is said to have coined the term "chic"), her fame was not without its costs—including injury to her standing in the English nobility. Because of her business activities, her name was stricken from the list of persons admitted at Court. N.Y.Times, April 22, 1935, at 17, col. 1.

Lady Duff–Gordon's most notorious court appearance by far came earlier, as a result of the 1912 trip with her husband, Sir Cosmo, on the ill-fated liner Titanic. The couple escaped death, but not the taint of scandal. As the story unfolded in a British Court of Inquiry, the Duff–Gordons had managed to escape in a lifeboat that was less than one-third filled with survivors. It was alleged that Sir Cosmo, afraid that the boat would be swamped, had dissuaded the crew of the lifeboat from turning back to pick up more people. (There was evidence that, after the tragedy, Sir Cosmo had sent to each crew member a gift of £5.) His actions attracted further attention when it was revealed that two witnesses testifying at the inquiry had been "coached" on their testimony by an attorney sent on behalf of the Duff–Gordons. Perhaps that is why Lady Duff–Gordon was described as leaving the inquiry's witness box "white to the lips." N.Y.Times, May 21, 1912, at 4, col. 3.

Harold Spencer of the New York Daily News was among those who showed compassion for Sir Cosmo. Spencer asked in his column: "Who shall throw the first stone? Who shall say how he would have acted if faced with the sudden and unexpected figure of death on that cold, dark Atlantic?" (quoted in the N.Y.Times, May 18, 1912, at 4, col. 1). Something close to that view prevailed in the end, for the British court exonerated the Duff–Gordons of all charges of improper conduct.

Lady Duff–Gordon died in 1935, at the age of 72.

———

Omni Group, Inc. v. Seattle–First Nat'l Bank

Court of Appeals of Washington, 1982.
32 Wash.App. 22, 645 P.2d 727.

JAMES, J. Plaintiff Omni Group, Inc. (Omni), a real estate development corporation, appeals entry of a judgment in favor of John B. Clark, individually, and as executor of the estate of his late wife, in Omni's action to enforce an earnest money agreement for the purchase of realty owned by the Clarks.[1] We reverse.

———

[1] Following Mr. Clark's death, Seattle–First Nat'l Bank, as executor of his estate, was substituted as respondent in this appeal.

In December 1977, Mr. and Mrs. Clark executed an exclusive agency listing agreement with the Royal Realty Co. (Royal) for the sale of approximately 59 acres of property. The list price was $3,000 per acre.

In early May, Royal offered the Clark property to Omni. On May 17, following conversations with a Royal broker, Omni signed an earnest money agreement offering $2,000 per acre. Two Royal brokers delivered the earnest money agreement to the Clarks. The Clarks signed the agreement dated May 19, but directed the brokers to obtain further consideration in the nature of Omni's agreement to make certain improvements on adjacent land not being offered for sale. Neither broker communicated these additional terms to Omni. In pertinent part, the earnest money agreement provides:

> This transaction is subject to purchaser receiving an engineer's and architect's feasibility report prepared by an engineer and architect of the purchaser's choice. Purchaser agrees to pay all costs of said report. If said report is satisfactory to purchaser, purchaser shall so notify seller in writing within fifteen (15) days of seller's acceptance of this offer. If no such notice is sent to seller, this transaction shall be considered null and void.

Exhibit A, ¶ 6. Omni's purpose was to determine, prior to actual purchase, if the property was suitable for development.

On June 2, an Omni employee personally delivered to the Clarks a letter advising that Omni had decided to forgo a feasibility study. They were further advised that a survey had revealed that the property consisted of only 50.3 acres. The Clarks agreed that if such were the case, they would accept Omni's offer of $2,000 per acre but with a minimum of 52 acres ($104,000). At this meeting, the Clarks' other terms (which had not been disclosed by Royal nor included in the earnest money agreement signed by the Clarks) were discussed. By a letter of June 8, Omni agreed to accept each of the Clarks' additional terms. The Clarks, however, refused to proceed with the sale after consulting an attorney.

The Clarks argued and the trial judge agreed, that by making its obligations subject to a satisfactory "engineer's and architect's feasibility report," Omni rendered its promise to buy the property illusory. Omni responds that paragraph 6 created only a condition precedent to Omni's duty to buy, and because the condition was for its benefit, Omni could waive the condition and enforce the agreement as written. We conclude Omni's promise was not illusory.

A promise for a promise is sufficient consideration to support a contract. . . . If, however, a promise is illusory, there is no consideration and therefore no enforceable contract between the parties. . . . Consequently, a party cannot create an enforceable contract by waiving the condition which renders his promise illusory. But that a promise given for a promise is dependent upon a condition does not necessarily render it illusory or affect its validity as consideration. In re Estate of Tveekrem, 169 Wash. 468, 14 P.2d 3 (1932). . . . Furthermore,

> a contractor can, by the use of clear and appropriate words, make his own duty expressly conditional upon his own personal satisfaction with the quality of the performance for which he has bargained and in return for which his promise is given. Such a limitation on his own duty does not invalidate the contract as long as

the limitation is not so great as to make his own promise illusory.

3A A. Corbin, Contracts, § 644 at 78–79 (1960).

Paragraph 6 may be analyzed as creating two conditions precedent to Omni's duty to buy the Clarks' property. First, Omni must receive an "engineer's and architect's feasibility report." Undisputed evidence was presented to show that such "feasibility reports" are common in the real estate development field and pertain to the physical suitability of the property for development purposes. Such a condition is analogous to a requirement that a purchaser of real property obtain financing, which imposes upon the purchaser a duty to make a good faith effort to secure financing. See Highlands Plaza, Inc. v. Viking Inv. Corp., 2 Wash.App. 192, 467 P.2d 378 (1970). In essence, this initial language requires Omni to attempt, in good faith, to obtain an "engineer's and architect's feasibility report" of a type recognized in the real estate trade.

The second condition precedent to Omni's duty to buy [the] property is that the feasibility report must be "satisfactory" to Omni. A condition precedent to the promisor's duty that the promisor be "satisfied" may require performance personally satisfactory to the promisor or it may require performance acceptable to a reasonable person. Whether the promisor was actually satisfied or should reasonably have been satisfied is a question of fact. In neither case is the promisor's promise rendered illusory. 3A A. Corbin, Contracts § 644 (1960).

In Mattei v. Hopper, 51 Cal.2d 119, 330 P.2d 625 (1958), plaintiff real estate developer contracted to buy property for a shopping center " '[s]ubject to Coldwell Banker & Co. obtaining leases satisfactory to the purchaser.' " Plaintiff had 120 days to consummate the purchase, including arrangement of satisfactory leases for shopping center buildings, before he was committed to purchase the property. The trial judge found the agreement "illusory." The California Supreme Court reversed[,] [saying]:

> [I]t would seem that the factors involved in determining whether a lease is satisfactory to the lessor are too numerous and varied to permit the application of a reasonable man standard as envisioned by this line of cases. Illustrative of some of the factors which would have to be considered in this case are the duration of the leases, their provisions for renewal options, if any, their covenants and restrictions, the amounts of the rentals, the financial responsibility of the lessees, and the character of the lessees' businesses.

Comparable factors doubtless determine whether an "engineer's and architect's feasibility report" is satisfactory. But

> [t]his multiplicity of factors which must be considered in evaluating a lease shows that this case more appropriately falls within the second line of authorities dealing with "satisfaction" clauses, being those involving fancy, taste, or judgment. Where the question is one of judgment, the promisor's determination that he is not satisfied, when made in good faith, has been held to be a defense to an action on the contract. . . . [T]he promisor's duty to exercise his judgment in good faith is an adequate consideration to support the contract. . . .

Further,

[e]ven though the "satisfaction" clauses discussed in the above-cited cases dealt with performances to be received as parts of the agreed exchanges, the fact that the leases here which determined plaintiff's satisfaction were not part of the performance to be rendered is not material. The standard of evaluating plaintiff's satisfaction—good faith—applies with equal vigor to this type of condition and prevents it from nullifying the consideration otherwise present in the promises exchanged.

Mattei v. Hopper, at 123–24, 330 P.2d 625. Thus, even the fact that "[i]t was satisfaction with the leases that [the purchaser] was himself to obtain" was immaterial. 3A A. Corbin, Contracts § 644 at 84. Accord, Western Hills, Oregon, Ltd. v. Pfau, 265 Or. 137, 508 P.2d 201 (1973) (purchaser was to obtain necessary permits for a development " 'satisfactory' to the parties"); Hendrix v. Sidney M. Thom & Co., 271 Ark. 378, 609 S.W.2d 98 (Ct.App.1980) (loan commitment contract requiring lender's "satisfaction" with site upon which borrower's project was to be constructed). We conclude that the condition precedent to Omni's duty to buy requiring receipt of a "satisfactory" feasibility report does not render Omni's promise to buy the property illusory.

Paragraph 6 further provides, "If said report is satisfactory to purchaser, purchaser shall so notify seller in writing within fifteen (15) days of seller's acceptance of this offer"; otherwise, the transaction "shall be considered null and void." We read this language to mean that Omni is required ("shall") to notify the Clarks of its acceptance if the feasibility report was "satisfactory." As we have stated, this determination is not a matter within Omni's unfettered discretion.

Omni has, by the quoted language, reserved to itself a power to cancel or terminate the contract. . . . Such provisions are valid and do not render the promisor's promise illusory, where the option can be exercised upon the occurrence of specified conditions. Benard v. Walkup, 272 Cal. App.2d 595, 77 Cal.Rptr. 544 (1969) (fee agreement permitting counsel to withdraw "if 'in his opinion' " investigation of the client's claim indicated no liability of the defendant or contributory negligence of the plaintiff); Wroten v. Mobil Oil Corp., 315 A.2d 728 (Del.1973) (lease permitting prospective tenant to terminate if licenses and permits "in manner and form acceptable to tenant" were not obtained). Here, Omni can cancel by failing to give notice only if the feasibility report is not "satisfactory." Otherwise, Omni is bound to give notice and purchase the property. Accordingly, we conclude paragraph 6 does not render Omni's promise illusory. . . .

The judgment is reversed and remanded with instructions to enter a decree ordering specific performance of the earnest money agreement.

[A recent decision, Chodos v. West Publishing Co., 292 F.3d 992 (9th Cir.2002), also cited the Mattei v. Hopper line of authority approvingly, concluding: "The implied covenant of good faith finds particular application in situations where one party is invested with a discretionary power affecting the rights of another. [Here,] the agreement imposes numerous obligations on the author but gives the publisher 'the right in its discretion to terminate' the relationship after receiving the [author's] manuscript and determining that it is unacceptable. However, the contract is not illusory because West's exercise of its discretion is limited (citing Lady Duff–Gordon). . . . [B]ecause [the agreement] obligates the publisher to make a judgment as to the quality of the author's work . . . it must make that judgment in good faith, and cannot reject a manuscript for other, unrelated reasons."]

––––––––

COMMENT: *FLEXIBLE BUSINESS ARRANGEMENTS*

The preceding cases involved sellers' or buyers' options in one form or another. They can be viewed as attempts by the contracting parties to limit or to shift the risks involved in extended time-span transactions, to reserve by contract sufficient freedom to make adjustments when circumstances change. The question now before us is how much flexibility of this kind is permissible in contracts adopting the bilateral form, no matter how clearly "bargained for."

A party's desire for protection against swings in the market may lead to contractual reservations, not as an escape from all obligation, but as to price. This type of hedge presents problems which we shall encounter again, though in different terms. Then the talk will be of "definiteness" or "certainty," not lack of consideration or mutuality, and the question will be whether the contract wholly fails for lack of assent. Thus, legal doctrines defining the requirements of certainty of terms may overlap with other doctrines having to do with consideration or mutuality.

Numerous devices have been incorporated in contracts to achieve flexibility in pricing through sliding scales. In long-term leases of land, for example, the need for flexibility brought, as early as the 1930s, a frequent resort to the so-called "percentage lease" by which the rent is made dependent on the volume of business or the profit of the tenant. Collective bargaining agreements often provide for automatic adjustments in wages geared to price indices—usually some form of cost-of-living index. In construction contracts, it is common to have a cost-plus provision instead of a fixed price, and sellers of goods also have found this device a useful protection against increases in labor or material costs. While economists have raised questions as to the effects of such arrangements in accelerating inflation and extending the swings of the business cycle, these arrangements are unlikely to encounter difficulties from the law of contract, either through requirements of assent or consideration. Pricing techniques that assure a supplier of goods or services that revenues will cover costs, as well as return a percentage of those costs as profit, may reduce or eliminate the seller's incentive to control or reduce costs. So far as contract law is concerned, however, if the elements of variable cost are sufficiently identified—that is, if the standard employed does not project courts and juries too far into accounting difficulties—such provisions are quite sure to be enforceable. The sliding of the price along the scale of costs will depend on factors beyond the control or influence of the seller-promisor, so that no effective option is reserved and "mutuality" tests are satisfied.

When a party wishes to secure the other as a market for sales, or a source of supply, yet preserve flexibility respecting the quantities of an item to be sold or purchased, a path commonly taken is provision for "output" or "requirements" measures of obligation. This legal category is now governed by UCC 2–306(1), the focus of the cases coming next. It can be assumed that most contracts falling within the output or requirements classification will involve goods.

––––––––

Lima Locomotive & Mach. Co. v. National Steel Castings Co.
155 F. 77 (6th Cir.1907)

The dispute arose out of a written agreement, signed by both parties, which read in part: "We make the following proposition for furnishing all your requirements in steel castings for the remainder of the present year at the prices mentioned below. . . . You agree to furnish us on or before the 15th of each month the tonnage that you wish to order during the following month. We agree to fill your orders as specified to the amount of this tonnage, and to make such deliveries as you require." On appeal, the court upheld the contract against the claim that it was void for lack of mutuality, saying: "The [buyer] was engaged in an established manufacturing business which required a large amount of steel castings. This was well known to the [seller], and the proposition made and accepted was made with reference to the 'requirements' of that well-established business. The [seller] was not proposing to make castings beyond the current requirements of that business. . . . [T]he [buyer] was obligated to take from the [seller] all castings which [its] business should require. . . . Thus read, there is no ground for doubting that the words 'the tonnage you wish to order,' and 'such deliveries as you may require,' have reference to the established 'requirements' of the business. . . . 'A contract to buy all that one shall require for one's own use in a particular manufacturing business is a very different thing from a promise to buy all that one may desire, or all that one may order. The promise to take all that one can consume would be broken by buying from another, and it is this obligation to take the entire supply of an established business which saves the mutual character of the promise.' "

[On the issue of reciprocal obligation (a commitment on each side), another court has said: "The contracts do not expressly obligate the [seller] to supply the [two buyers] with their requirements for milk. But such an obligation can be implicit as well as express, . . . and the inference would be compelling if the contracts forbade the [buyers] to turn elsewhere for milk. A buyer would be unlikely to commit to take all his requirements for some good from the seller if the seller had no reciprocal obligation to supply those requirements. That would put the buyer at the seller's mercy. Contract law, in inferring an obligation to sell in these circumstances, would be performing its frequent office of interpolating a contractual term . . . closely resembl[ing] the best-efforts obligation that is read into exclusive-dealing contracts (see, e.g., *Wood v. Duff–Gordon*)[.]" In re Modern Dairy of Champaign, Inc., 171 F.3d 1106 (7th Cir.1999).]

Feld v. Henry S. Levy & Sons, Inc.

Court of Appeals of New York, 1975.
37 N.Y.2d 466, 373 N.Y.S.2d 102, 335 N.E.2d 320.

COOKE, J. Plaintiff operates a business known as the Crushed Toast Co. and defendant is engaged in the wholesale bread baking business. They entered into a written contract, as of June 19, 1968, in which defendant agreed to sell and plaintiff to purchase "all bread crumbs produced by the Seller in its factory at 115 Thames Street, Brooklyn, during the period commencing June 19, 1968, and terminating June 18, 1969," the agreement to "be deemed automatically renewed thereafter for successive renewal periods of one year" with the right to either party to cancel by giving not less than six months notice to the other by certified mail. No notice of cancellation was served. Additionally, pursuant to a contract stipulation, a faithful performance bond was delivered by plaintiff at the inception of the contractual relationship, and a bond continuation certificate was later submitted for the yearly term commencing June 19, 1969.

Interestingly, the term "bread crumbs" does not refer to crumbs that may flake off bread; rather, they are a manufactured item, starting with stale or imperfectly appearing loaves and followed by removal of labels, processing through two grinders, the second of which effects a finer granulation, insertion into a drum in an oven for toasting and, finally, bagging of the finished product.

Subsequent to the making of the agreement, a substantial quantity of bread crumbs, said to be over 250 tons, were sold by defendant to plaintiff but defendant stopped crumb production on about May 15, 1969. There was proof by defendant's comptroller that the oven was too large to accommodate the drum, that it was stated that the operation was "very uneconomical," but after said date of cessation no steps were taken to obtain more economical equipment. The toasting oven was intentionally broken down, then partially rebuilt, then completely dismantled in the summer of 1969 and, thereafter, defendant used the space for a computer room. It appears, without dispute, that defendant indicated to plaintiff at different times that the former would resume bread crumb production if the contract price of 6 cents per pound be changed to 7 cents, and also that, after the crumb making machinery was dismantled, defendant sold the raw materials used in making crumbs to animal food manufacturers.

Special Term denied plaintiff's motion for summary judgment on the issue of liability and turned down defendant's counter-request for a summary judgment of dismissal. From the Appellate Division's order of affirmance, by a divided court, both parties appeal.

Defendant contends that the contract did not require defendant to manufacture bread crumbs, but merely to sell those it did, and, since none were produced after the demise of the oven, there was no duty to then deliver and, consequently from then on, no liability on its part. Agreements to sell all the goods or services a party may produce or perform to another party are commonly referred to as "output" contracts and they usually serve a useful commercial purpose in minimizing the burdens of product marketing (see 1 Williston, Contracts [3d ed.], § 104A). The [UCC] rejects the ideas that an output contract is lacking in mutuality or that it is unenforceable because of indefiniteness in that a quantity for the term is not specified. . . . Official Comment 2 to [UCC] 2–306 states in part: "Under this Article, a contract for output . . . is not too indefinite since it is held to mean the actual good faith output . . . of the particular party. Nor does such a contract lack mutuality of obligation since, under this section, the party who will determine quantity is required to operate his plant or conduct his business in good faith and according to commercial standards of fair dealing in the trade so that his output . . . will proximate a reasonably foreseeable figure."

The real issue in this case is whether the agreement carries with it an implication that defendant was obligated to continue to manufacture bread crumbs for the full term. Section 2–306 of the [UCC], entitled "Output, Requirements and Exclusive Dealings" provides:

"(1) A term which measures the quantity by the output of the seller or the requirements of the buyer means such actual output or requirements as may occur in good faith, except that no quantity unreasonably disproportionate to any stated estimate or in the absence of a stated estimate to any normal or otherwise comparable prior output or requirements may be tendered or demanded.

"(2) *A lawful agreement* by either the seller or the buyer *for exclusive dealing* in the kind of goods concerned *imposes* unless otherwise agreed an obligation *by the seller to use best efforts to supply the goods and by the buyer to use best efforts to promote their sale.*" (Emphasis supplied.)

[handwritten: best effort required]

The Official Comment thereunder reads in part: "Subsection (2), on exclusive dealing, makes explicit the commercial rule embodied in this Act under which the parties to such contracts are held to have impliedly, even when not expressly, bound themselves to use reasonable diligence as well as good faith in their performance of the contract. . . . An exclusive dealing agreement brings into play all of the good faith aspects of the output and requirement problems of subsection (1). It also raises questions of insecurity and right to adequate assurance under this Article."

Section 2–306 is consistent with prior New York case law. . . . Every contract of this type imposes an obligation of good faith in its performance ([UCC], § 1–203). . . . Under the [UCC], the commercial background and intent must be read into the language of any agreement and good faith is demanded in the performance of that agreement . . ., and, under the decisions relating to output contracts, it is clearly the general rule that good faith cessation of production terminates any further obligations thereunder and excuses further performance by the party discontinuing production. . . .

This is not a situation where defendant ceased its main operation of bread baking. . . . Rather, defendant contends in a conclusory fashion that it was "uneconomical" or "economically not feasible" for it to continue to make bread crumbs. Although plaintiff observed in his motion papers that defendant claimed it was not economically feasible to make the crumbs, plaintiff did not admit that as a fact. In any event, "economic feasibility," an expression subject to many interpretations, would not be a precise or reliable test.

[handwritten: not reliable]

There are present here intertwined questions of fact, whether defendant performed in good faith and whether it stopped its manufacture of bread crumbs in good faith, neither of which can be resolved properly on this record. The seller's duty to remain in crumb production is a matter calling for a close scrutiny of its motives (1 Hawkland, A Transactional Guide to the Uniform Commercial Code, p. [48], 52), confined here by the papers to financial reasons. It is undisputed that defendant leveled its crumb making machinery only after plaintiff refused to agree to a price higher than that specified in the agreement and that it then sold the raw materials to manufacturers of animal food. There are before us no componential figures indicating the actual cost of the finished bread crumbs to defendant, statements as to the profits derived or the losses sustained, or data specifying the net or gross return realized from the animal food transactions.

The parties by their contract gave the right of cancellation to either by providing for a six months' notice to the other. The apparent purpose of such a stipulation was to provide an opportunity to either the seller or buyer to conclude their dealings in the event that the transactions were not as

[handwritten: right of cancellation]

profitable or advantageous as desired or expected, or for any other reason. Correspondingly, such a notice would also furnish the receiver of it a chance to secure another outlet or source of supply, as the case might be. Short of such a cancellation, defendant was expected to continue to perform in good faith and could cease production of the bread crumbs, a single facet of its operation, only in good faith. Obviously, a bankruptcy or genuine imperiling of the very existence of its entire business caused by the production of the crumbs would warrant cessation of production of that item; the yield of less profit from its sale than expected would not. Since bread crumbs were but a part of defendant's enterprise and since there was a contractual right of cancellation, good faith required continued production until cancellation, even if there be no profit. In circumstances such as these and without more, defendant would be justified, in good faith, in ceasing production of the single item prior to cancellation only if its losses from continuance would be more than trivial, which, overall, is a question of fact.

The order of the Appellate Division should be affirmed, without costs.

NOTE

The *Feld* court quoted portions of the Official Comment on UCC 2–306. That comment includes two sentences not mentioned in the *Feld* opinion: "Reasonable elasticity in the requirements is expressly envisioned by this section and good faith variations from prior requirements are permitted even when the variation may be such as to result in discontinuance. A shut-down by a requirements buyer for lack of orders might be permissible when a shut-down merely to curtail losses would not." When the case goes back for trial, which party—seller or buyer—will want to be sure that the court knows of this language?

Corenswet, Inc. v. Amana Refrigeration, Inc.
594 F.2d 129 (5th Cir.1979)

Corenswet sued to enjoin termination of an exclusive wholesale distributorship in Amana appliances, claiming that Amana's attempted termination of the relationship was "arbitrary and capricious." The distributorship agreement was of indefinite duration, but terminable by either party "at any time for any reason" on ten days' notice to the other party. After seven years of a generally successful relationship, Amana gave notice of its decision to terminate in order to give the distributorship to another company. The District Court found that the termination was arbitrary and thus enjoinable as a breach of both the distributorship agreement and the UCC's general obligation of "good faith." The Court of Appeals reversed and vacated the injunction, holding that the termination, even if "arbitrary and without cause," was permissible under both the contract and Iowa's Commercial Code. The contract expressly permitted Amana to terminate without a justification grounded in Corenswet's conduct. Even conceding that Amana needed "some reason" to end the relationship, the reason was supplied by its evident desire to give the distributorship to another company. As to whether the Code's obligation of good faith bars enforcement of contract clauses permitting termination without cause, Judge Wisdom spoke for the court:

As courts and scholars have become increasingly aware of the special problems faced by distributors and franchisees, and of the inadequacy of traditional contract and sales law doctrines to the task of protecting the reasonable expectations of distributors and franchisees, commentators have debated the utility of the Code's general good faith obligation as a tool for curbing abuse of the termination power. See, e.g., E. Gellhorn, Limitations on Contract Termination Rights—Franchise Cancellations, 1967 Duke L.J. 465; Hewitt, Good Faith or Unconscionability—Franchisee Remedies for Termination, 29 Bus.Law 227 (1973).

The courts of late have begun to read a good faith limitation into termination clauses of distributorship contracts that permit termination without cause. . . . Of the cited cases, however, only [one] case relies squarely on the Code. . . . [O]ther courts have held that agency or distributorship contracts of indefinite duration are terminable by either party with or without cause. . . . Those courts have relied on [UCC 2–309(2)], which states:

> Where the contract provides for successive performances but is indefinite in duration it is valid for a reasonable time but unless otherwise agreed may be terminated at any time by either party.

. . . The division in the authorities then, is between those courts that hold that the Code's general good faith obligation overrides the specific rule of § 2–309(2) as applied to distributorship or franchise agreements, and those that give precedence to § 2–309. . . .

The Iowa case law on this question is pre-Code and follows the common law rule, which is essentially the rule of § 2–309 as applied to distributorship contracts. In Des Moines Blue Ribbon Distribs. v. Drewrys Ltd., 1964, 256 Iowa 899, 129 N.W.2d 731, the Iowa Supreme Court held that an exclusive distributorship contract of indefinite duration may be terminated without cause only upon reasonable notice. . . . [T]he court's treatment of the issues raised makes it clear that the requirement of reasonable notice was thought by the court to be the only restriction on the manufacturer's right to cancel the agreement.[1] . . .

[I]n an area such as this, where considerations of *stare decisis* are of importance, we should hesitate to depart from established case authority absent fair assurance that the state's courts would interpret the [UCC] to forbid "bad faith" or "arbitrary" terminations of distributorship contracts. . . .

We are not persuaded that the adoption of the Code has effected any change in Iowa law with regard to distributorship termina-

---

[1] At one point in its opinion the *Drewrys* court seemed to add another limitation: that the agreement must continue in force for a reasonable time. 129 N.W.2d at 736. This is the so-called "Missouri doctrine," a hardship rule of agency law designed to give an agent a reasonable time in which to recoup his original investment in the agency. . . . The *Drewrys* court did not face a claim based on insufficient duration, so its "adoption" of the Missouri doctrine is dictum. Even assuming that the doctrine is indeed law in Iowa, it has no application to this case. The reasonable duration envisioned by the doctrine is quite short. . . . [Some of Judge Wisdom's footnotes are omitted; those retained are renumbered.—Eds.]

tions. We do not agree with Corenswet that the § 1–203 good faith obligation, like the Code's unconscionability provision, can properly be used to override or strike express contract terms. . . . When a contract contains a provision expressly sanctioning termination without cause there is no room for implying a term that bars such a termination. In the face of such a term there can be, at best, an expectation that a party will decline to exercise his rights.[2]

As a tool for policing distributorship terminations, moreover, the good faith test is erratic at best. . . . The better approach . . . is to test the disputed contract clause for unconscionability under § 2–302 of the Code. The question these cases present is whether public policy forbids enforcement of a contract clause permitting unilateral termination without cause. Since a termination without cause will almost always be characterizable as a "bad faith" termination, focus on the terminating party's state of mind will always result in the invalidation of unrestricted termination clauses. We seriously doubt, however, that public policy frowns on any and all contract clauses permitting termination without cause. Such clauses can have the salutary effect of permitting parties to end a soured relationship without consequent litigation. Indeed when, as here, the power of unilateral termination without cause is granted to both parties, the clause gives the distributor an easy way to cut the knot should he be presented with an opportunity to secure a better distributorship from another manufacturer. What public policy does abhor is economic overreaching—the use of superior bargaining power to secure grossly unfair advantage. That is the precise focus of the Code's unconscionability doctrine; it is not at all the concern of the Code's good faith performance provision. . . .

Corenswet's rights with respect to termination extend only to a right to notice. The Amana contract permits termination on ten days' notice. Under the Code, § 2–309(3), and under the *Drewrys* case, however, a distributor is entitled to reasonable notice. Section 2–309(3) states that "an agreement dispensing with notification is invalid if its operation would be unconscionable." But any claim that Corenswet might have based on inadequate notice would not entitle Corenswet to injunctive relief, for it appears from the *Drewrys* case . . . that the manufacturer's failure to give proper notice is adequately remediable at law.

NOTE

Corenswet has been cited widely, especially the court's expression of doubt that "public policy frowns on" termination-without-cause provisions in franchise or dealership agreements. There is, in fact, scant authority holding such

---

[2] Furthermore, the proposition that the Code's good faith obligation cannot be disclaimed must be qualified. Section 1–102(3) of the Code, which provides that the obligation of good faith is not disclaimable, goes on to state that "the parties may by agreement determine the standards by which the performance of such obligation is to be measured if such standards are not manifestly unreasonable." It could be argued that even if arbitrary termination of a distributorship under an agreement silent as to grounds for termination would be in "bad faith," § 1–102(3) nevertheless permits the parties to the contract to stipulate that termination "without cause" or "for any reason" is not in bad faith.

clauses "unconscionable" in franchise settings (this, of course, was the line of attack *Corenswet* left open). See, e.g., General Aviation, Inc. v. Cessna Aircraft Co., 703 F.Supp. 637 (W.D.Mich.1988), aff'd in part, rev'd in part, 915 F.2d 1038 (6th Cir.1990). Is this surprising?

We shall see more of "public policy," "good faith," and "unconscionability" later, including application of these doctrines to disputes over franchise termination. For the moment, it is enough to note that the *Corenswet* court was neither prepared to promote "mutuality" on the basis of these concepts nor inclined to intervene by means of conventional contract doctrines. Indeed, even those jurisdictions recognizing an implied covenant of "good faith and fair dealing" in special circumstances have been unwilling to extend the covenant to the franchisor-franchisee relationship. E.g., United Airlines v. Good Taste, Inc., 982 P.2d 1259 (Alaska 1999); Eichman v. Fotomat Corp., 880 F.2d 149 (9th Cir.1989). Are you satisfied that techniques such as those employed in Wood v. Lucy, Lady Duff–Gordon are properly abandoned in the franchise-cancellation cases?

Sun Printing & Publishing Ass'n v. Remington Paper & Power Co., Inc.

Court of Appeals of New York, 1923.
235 N.Y. 338, 139 N.E. 470.

CARDOZO, J. Plaintiff agreed to buy and defendant to sell 1,000 tons of paper per month during the months of September, 1919, to December, 1920, inclusive, 16,000 tons in all. Sizes and quality were adequately described. Payment was to be made on the 20th of each month for all paper shipped the previous month. The price for shipments in September, 1919, was to be $3.73¾ per 100 pounds, and for shipments in October, November, and December, 1919, $4 per 100 pounds. "For the balance of the period of this agreement the price of the paper and length of terms for which such price shall apply shall be agreed upon by and between the parties hereto fifteen days prior to the expiration of each period for which the price and length of term thereof have been previously agreed upon, said price in no event to be higher than the contract price for news print charged by the Canadian Export Paper Co. to the large consumers, the seller to receive the benefit of any differentials in freight rates."

Between September, 1919, and December of that year, inclusive, shipments were made and paid for as required by the contract. The time then arrived when there was to be an agreement upon a new price and upon the term of its duration. The defendant in advance of that time gave notice that the contract was imperfect, and disclaimed for the future an obligation to deliver. Upon this the plaintiff took the ground that the price was to be ascertained by resort to an established standard. It made demand that during each month of 1920 the defendant deliver 1,000 tons of paper at the contract price for news print charged by the Canadian Export Paper Co. to the large consumers, the defendant to receive the benefit of any differentials in freight rates. The demand was renewed month by month till the expiration of the year. This action has been brought to recover the ensuing damage.

Seller and buyer left two subjects to be settled in the middle of December and at unstated intervals thereafter. One was the price to be paid. The other was the length of time during which such price was to govern. Agreement as to the one was insufficient without agreement as to the other. If price and nothing more had been left open for adjustment, there might be force in the contention that the buyer would be viewed, in the light of later provisions, as the holder of an option. This would mean that, in default of an agreement for a lower price, the plaintiff would have the privilege of calling for delivery in accordance with a price established as a maximum. The price to be agreed upon might be less, but could not be more, than "the contract price for news print charged by the Canadian Export Paper Co. to the large consumers." The difficulty is, however, that ascertainment of this price does not dispense with the necessity for agreement in respect of the term during which the price is to apply. Agreement upon a maximum payable this month or today is not the same as an agreement that it shall continue to be payable next month or tomorrow. Seller and buyer understood that the price to be fixed in December for a term to be agreed upon would not be more than the price then charged by the Canadian Export Paper Co. to the large consumers. They did not understand that, if during the term so established the price charged by the Canadian Export Paper Co. was changed, the price payable to the seller would fluctuate accordingly. This was conceded by plaintiff's counsel on the argument before us. The seller was to receive no more during the running of the prescribed term, though the Canadian Maximum was raised. The buyer was to pay no less during that term, though the maximum was lowered. In the brief, the standard was to be applied at the beginning of the successive terms, but once applied was to be maintained until the term should have expired. While the term was unknown, the contract was inchoate.

The argument is made that there was no need of an agreement as to time unless the price to be paid was lower than the maximum. We find no evidence of this intention in the language of the contract. The result would then be that the defendant would never know where it stood. The plaintiff was under no duty to accept the Canadian standard. It does not assert that it was. What it asserts is that the contract amounted to the concession of an option. Without an agreement as to time, however, there would be not one option, but a dozen. The Canadian price today might be less than the Canadian price tomorrow. Election by the buyer to proceed with performance at the price prevailing in one month would not bind it to proceed at the price prevailing in another. Successive options to be exercised every month would thus be read into the contract. Nothing in the wording discloses the intention of the seller to place itself to that extent at the mercy of the buyer. Even if, however, we were to interpolate the restriction that the option, if exercised at all, must be exercised only once, and for the entire quantity permitted, the difficulty would not be ended. Market prices in 1920 happened to rise. The importance of the time element becomes apparent when we ask ourselves what the seller's position would be if they had happened to fall. Without an agreement as to time, the maximum would be lowered from one shipment to another with every reduction of the standard. With such an agreement, on the other hand, there would be stability and certainty. The parties attempted to guard against the contingency of failing to come together as to price. They did not guard against the contingency of failing to come together as to time. Very likely they thought the latter contingency so remote that it could safely be disregarded. In any event, whether through design or through inadvertence, they left the gap unfilled. The result was nothing more than "an agreement to agree." Defendant [had the right to insist that, to be legally enforceable,] there was need of something more. The right is not affected by our appraisal of the motive.

We are told that the defendant was under a duty, in default of an agreement, to accept a term that would be reasonable in view of the nature of the transaction and the practice of the business. To hold it to such a standard is to make the contract over. The defendant reserved the privilege of doing its business in its own way, and did not undertake to conform to the practice and beliefs of others. We are told again that there was a duty, in default of other agreement, to act as if the successive terms were to expire every month. The contract says they are to expire at such intervals as the agreement may prescribe. There is need, it is true, of no high degree of ingenuity to show how the parties, with little change of language, could have framed a form of contract to which obligation would attach. The difficulty is that they framed another. We are not at liberty to revise while professing to construe.

We do not ignore the allegation of the complaint that the contract price charged by the Canadian Export Paper Co. to the large consumers "constituted a definite and well-defined standard of price that was readily ascertainable." The suggestion is made by members of the court that the price so charged may have been known to be one established for the year, so that fluctuation would be impossible. If that was its character, the complaint should so allege. The writing signed by the parties calls for an agreement as to time. The complaint concedes that no such agreement has been made. The result, prima facie, is the failure of the contract. In that situation the pleader has the burden of setting forth the extrinsic circumstances, if there are any, that make agreement unimportant. There is significance, moreover, in the attitude of counsel. No point is made in brief or in argument that the Canadian price, when once established, is constant through the year. On the contrary, there is at least a tacit assumption that it varies with the market. The buyer acted on the same assumption when it renewed the demand from month to month, making tender of performance at the prices then prevailing. If we misconceive the course of dealing, the plaintiff by amendment of its pleading can correct our misconception. The complaint as it comes before us leaves no escape from the conclusion that agreement in respect of time is as essential to a completed contract as agreement in respect of price. The agreement was not reached, and the defendant is not bound.

The question is not here whether the defendant would have failed in the fulfillment of its duty by an arbitrary refusal to reach any agreement as to time after notice from the plaintiff that it might make division of the terms in any way it pleased. No such notice was given, so far as the complaint discloses. The action is not based upon a refusal to treat with the defendant and attempt to arrive at an agreement. Whether any such theory of liability would be tenable we need not now inquire. Even if the plaintiff might have stood upon the defendant's denial of obligation as amounting to such a refusal, it did not elect to do so. Instead, it gave its own construction to the contract, fixed for itself the length of the successive terms, and thereby coupled its demand with a condition which there was no duty to accept. We find no allegation of readiness, and offer to proceed on any other basis. The condition being untenable, the failure to comply with it cannot give a cause of action. . . .

CRANE, J. (dissenting). I cannot take the view of this contract that has been adopted by the majority. . . .

Surely these parties must have had in mind that some binding agreement was made for the sale and delivery of 16,000 tons rolls of paper, and that the instrument contained all the elements necessary to make a binding contract. . . . If this be so, the court should spell out a binding contract, if it be possible. I not only think it possible, but think the paper itself clearly states a contract recognized under all the rules at law. It is said that the one essential element of price is lacking; that the provision above quoted is an agreement to agree to a price, and that the defendant had the privilege of agreeing or not, as it pleased; that, if it failed to agree to a price, there was no standard by which to measure the amount the plaintiff would have to pay. The contract does state, however, just this very thing. Fifteen days before the 1st of January, 1920, the parties were to agree upon the price of the paper to be delivered thereafter, and the length of the period for which such price should apply. However, the price to be fixed was not "to be higher than the contract price for news print charged by the Canadian Export Paper Co. to large consumers." Here, surely, was something definite. The 15th day of December arrived. The defendant refused to deliver. At that time there was a price for news print charged by the Canadian Export Paper Co. If the plaintiff offered to pay this price, which was the highest price the defendant could demand, the defendant was bound to deliver. This seems to be very clear.

But, while all agree that the price on the 15th day of December could be fixed, the further objection is made that the period during which that price should continue was not agreed upon. There are many answers to this.

We have reason to believe that the parties supposed they were making a binding contract; that they had fixed the terms by which one was required to take and the other to deliver; that the Canadian Export Paper Co. price was to be the highest that could be charged in any event. These things being so, the court should be very reluctant to permit a defendant to avoid its contract.

On the 15th of the fourth month, the time when the price was to be fixed for subsequent deliveries, there was a price charged by the Canadian Export Paper Co. to large consumers. As the defendant failed to agree upon a price, made no attempt to agree upon a price, and deliberately broke its contract, it could readily be held to deliver the rest of the paper, 1,000 rolls a month, at this Canadian price. There is nothing in the complaint which indicates that this is a fluctuating price, or that the price of paper as it was on December 15th was not the same for the remaining 12 months. Or we can deal with this contract month by month. The deliveries were to be made 1,000 tons per month. On December 15th 1,000 tons could have been demanded. The price charged by the Canadian Export Paper Co. on the 15th of each month on and after December 15, 1919, would be the price for the 1,000–ton delivery for that month. Or, again, the word as used in the miscellaneous provision quoted is not "price," but "contract price"—"in no event to be higher than the contract price." Contract implies a term or period, and, if the evidence should show that the Canadian contract price was for a certain period of weeks or months, then this period could be applied to the contract in question. Failing any other alternative, the law should do here what it has done in so many other cases—apply the rule of reason and compel parties to contract in the light of fair dealing. It could hold this defendant to deliver its paper as it agreed to do, and take for a price the Canadian Export Paper Co. contract price for a period which is reasonable under all the circumstances and conditions as applied in the paper trade.

To let this defendant escape from its formal obligations when any one of these rulings as applied to this contract would give a practical and just result is to give the sanction of law to a deliberate breach. . . .

HISCOCK, C. J., and POUND, MCLAUGHLIN, and ANDREWS, JJ., concur with CARDOZO, J. CRANE, J., reads dissenting opinion with which HOGAN, J., concurs.

RESTATEMENT OF CONTRACTS, SECOND

Section 33. Certainty

(1) Even though a manifestation of intention is intended to be understood as an offer, it cannot be accepted so as to form a contract unless the terms of the contract are reasonably certain.

(2) The terms of a contract are reasonably certain if they provide a basis for determining the existence of a breach and for giving an appropriate remedy.

(3) The fact that one or more terms of a proposed bargain are left open or uncertain may show that a manifestation of intention is not intended to be understood as an offer or as an acceptance.

Comment: . . .

b. Certainty in basis for remedy. The rule stated in Subsection (2) reflects the fundamental policy that contracts should be made by the parties, not by the courts, and hence that remedies for breach of contract must have a basis in the agreement of the parties. Where the parties have intended to make a contract and there is a reasonably certain basis for granting a remedy, the same policy supports the granting of the remedy. . . . See [UCC] § 2–204(3) and Comment. Thus the degree of certainty required may be affected by the dispute which arises and by the remedy sought. Courts decide the disputes before them, not other hypothetical disputes which might have arisen. . . .

Illustrations:

1. A agrees to sell and B to buy goods for $2,000, $1,000 in cash and the "balance on installment terms over a period of two years," with a provision for liquidated damages. If it it found that both parties manifested an intent to conclude a binding agreement, the indefiniteness of the quoted language does not prevent the award of the liquidated damages.

2. A agrees to sell and B to buy a specific tract of land for $10,000, $4,000 in cash and $6,000 on mortgage. A agrees to obtain the mortgage loan for B or, if unable to do so, to lend B the amount, but the terms of loan are not stated, although both parties manifest an intent to conclude a binding agreement. The contract is too indefinite to support a decree of specific performance against B, but B may obtain such a decree if he offers to pay the full price in cash. . . .

e. Indefinite price. Where the parties manifest an intention not to be bound unless the amount of money to be paid by one of them is fixed or agreed and it is not fixed or agreed there is no contract. [UCC] § 2–305(4). Where they intend to conclude a contract for the sale of goods, however, and the price is not settled, the price is a reasonable price at the time of delivery [in the circumstances stated in UCC 2–305(1)]. . . . Similar principles apply to contracts for the rendition of service. . . .

Illustrations:

7. A promises to sell and B to buy goods "at cost plus a nice profit." The quoted words strongly indicate that the parties have not yet concluded a bargain.

8. A promises to do a specified piece of work and B promises to pay a price to be thereafter mutually agreed. The provision for future agreement as to price strongly indicates that the parties do not intend to be bound. If they manifest an intent to be bound, the price is a reasonable price at the time for doing the work.

––––––––

Southwest Eng'g Co. v. Martin Tractor Co.
205 Kan. 684, 473 P.2d 18 (1970)

"It is obvious the parties reached no agreement on [the terms of payment for the generator]. However, a failure . . . to agree on terms of payment would not, of itself, defeat an otherwise valid agreement reached by them. [UCC 2–204(3)] reads: 'Even though one or more terms are left open a contract for sale does not fail for indefiniteness if the parties have intended to make a contract and there is a reasonably certain basis for giving an appropriate remedy.' The official U.C.C. Comment is enlightening:

> Subsection (3) states the principle as to "open terms" underlying later sections of [Article 2]. If the parties intend to enter into a binding agreement, this subsection recognizes that agreement as valid in law, despite missing terms, if there is any reasonable certain basis for granting a remedy. The test is not certainty as to what the parties were to do nor as to the exact amount of damages due the plaintiff. Nor is the fact that one or more terms are left to be agreed upon enough of itself to defeat an otherwise adequate agreement. Rather, commercial standards on the point of "indefiniteness" are intended to be applied, this Act making provision elsewhere for missing terms needed for performance, open price, remedies and the like. The more terms the parties leave open, the less likely it is that they have intended to conclude a binding agreement, but their actions may be frequently conclusive on the matter despite the omissions.

"So far as [this] case is concerned, [UCC 2–310(a)] supplies the omitted term. . . . Considered together, we take the two sections [2–204(3) and 2–310(a)] to mean that where parties have reached an enforceable agreement for the sale of goods, but omit therefrom the terms of payment, the law will imply, as part of the agreement, that payment is to be made at time of delivery. In this respect the law does not greatly differ from the rule this court laid down years ago. . . .

"We do not mean to infer that terms of payment are not of importance under many circumstances, or that parties may not condition an agreement on their being included. However, the facts [here] hardly indicate that [either party] considered the terms of payment to be significant, or of more than passing interest. . . . [O]nly a brief and casual conversation ensued as to payment."

———

Vohs v. Donovan

Court of Appeals of Wisconsin, 2009.
322 Wis.2d 721, 777 N.W.2d 915.

VERGERONT, J. . . . On February 18, 2007, Paul and Teresa Donovan signed an offer to purchase the home of Terry and Vicki Vohs for the sum of $550,000. The offer included a contingency providing that the "offer is subject to sellers obtaining home of their choice on or before Feb. 20, 2007." The Vohses accepted the offer to purchase on the same date.

According to the Vohses' unrebutted submissions, as of February 18, 2007, they had a pending counteroffer to purchase another home. That counteroffer contained a provision that it had to be accepted on or before February 19, 2007. On February 19, the counteroffer was accepted and the Vohses' broker communicated this to the Donovans. For reasons not disclosed in the record, the Donovans did not follow through with the purchase of the Vohses' home. The Vohses subsequently sold this home to another buyer for less money.

The Vohses filed this lawsuit alleging the Donovans had breached their contract and requesting judgment in the amount of $50,000, plus costs and attorney fees. The Donovans' filed a motion for summary judgment on the grounds that the contingency made the contract indefinite and illusory and therefore unenforceable. The Vohses opposed the motion. The circuit court granted summary judgment in favor of the Donovans, apparently concluding that the contingency made the contract unenforceable. . . .

On appeal the Vohses contend the circuit court erred in granting summary judgment because the evidence of the surrounding circumstances makes the contingency definite and prevents their promise from being illusory. The Donovans respond that the language "obtaining" and "home of their choice" makes the contingency indefinite and renders the contract illusory. . . .

We begin by summarizing the case law on indefinite contract terms and illusory promises and explaining the distinction between the two concepts. A contract is not enforceable if an essential term is indefinite. Management Computer Servs., Inc. v. Hawkins, Ash, Baptie & Co., 206 Wis.2d 158, 178, 557 N.W.2d 67 (1996). Definiteness requires that there be a mutual assent by the parties, which we determine according to an objective standard. This means that we "examine[ ] both the wording of the contract as well as the surrounding circumstances" to determine if there was mutual assent to a sufficiently definite meaning of the term. Metropolitan Ventures, 291 Wis.2d 393, ¶24, 717 N.W.2d 58. When there is evidence that two parties intended to enter into a contract, "the [court or] trier of fact should not frustrate their intentions, but rather should attach a 'sufficiently definite meaning' to the contract language if possible." Id., ¶25 (quoting Management Computer Services, 206 Wis.2d at 179, 557 N.W.2d 67).

Like a contract with an indefinite essential term, an illusory promise is unenforceable, but for different reasons. An illusory promise—"one that its maker can keep without subjecting him[self] or herself to any detriment or restriction"—does not constitute consideration. When performance by a promisor is "conditional on some fact or event that is wholly under the promisor's control and his [or her] bringing it about is left wholly to his [or her] own will and discretion," then the promise to perform is illusory. Metropolitan Ventures, 291 Wis.2d 393, ¶33, 717 N.W.2d 58. In such a situation, assuming no other consideration is given for a return promise, there is no contract.

In summary, while both indefiniteness and illusoriness affect the enforceability of a contract, they are distinct concepts. If an essential term is indefinite, thereby rendering the contract unenforceable, the analysis ends there. If, on the other hand, the challenged contract term is determined to be definite and the party attacking the contract also asserts the term constitutes an illusory promise, the issue of illusoriness must then be resolved using a distinct analysis. In other words, a contract term may be definite but nonetheless constitute an illusory promise.

Turning to the arguments in this case, we consider first the question whether the contingency that the "offer is subject to sellers obtaining home of their choice on or before Feb. 20, 2007" is indefinite.

This clause creates a condition precedent to the sellers' performance. A significant aspect of the clause is that the condition must occur *two days* from the date on which both parties signed the document. Viewed objectively, this extremely short time period implies that the Vohses are already involved in a transaction to purchase a particular house and they expect a resolution within two days. It is illogical to infer that the Vohses are asking for two days to find a house of their choice and complete the transaction to "obtain" it.

While the specific transaction is not referred to in the clause, the Vohses have submitted an affidavit with attached documents showing they were engaged in negotiations to purchase a particular house. The submission shows that February 19, 2007, is the date by which the owners of the other house had to respond to the Vohses' counteroffer. Thus, the Vohses were agreeing that, if their counteroffer was accepted by February 20, they would be obligated under the contract with the Donovans. The Donovans have not submitted any factual materials disputing that this was the transaction upon which the contingency was based. On these facts, it is reasonable to infer that the Donovans agreed to the two-day contingency, knowing its purpose.

We recognize that the Vohses' knowledge of the pending transaction is not in itself sufficient to make the contingency clause definite. See Gerruth Realty Co. v. Pire, 17 Wis.2d 89, 92-94, 115 N.W.2d 557 (1962) (contingency based "upon the purchaser obtaining the proper amount of financing" was indefinite where there was no evidence the purchaser communicated his views on what the proper amount was, no evidence of the seller's understanding, and no evidence providing a reasonable inference that the parties contracted in light of current practices in the community). But, as we have explained, the undisputed facts support a reasonable inference that the Donovans did know of the pending transaction.

The Donovans argue that the word "obtain" is "unclear on its face" because the acceptance of the Vohses' counteroffer to purchase contained conditions and therefore the other house was not "conclusively obtained." The Donovans suggest that the word "obtain" could also mean either after the closing or after physical occupancy. This is an argument that the language is ambiguous—that is, reasonably susceptible to more than one construction. See Management Computer Services, 206 Wis.2d at 177, 557 N.W.2d 67. Ambiguity is not the same as indefiniteness. Id. at 178, 557 N.W.2d 67. An indefinite term is one that is not susceptible to any reasonable construction, even after considering the surrounding circumstances. See id. at 178-182, 557 N.W.2d 67. Thus, the fact that "obtain" is ambiguous—and we agree that it is—does not make the clause indefinite and therefore unenforceable.[4]

The Donovans also argue that the phrase "home of their choice" is indefinite because it can mean whatever the Vohses want it to mean. They find support for this position in *Nodolf*, in which we concluded that a financing clause making the buyers obligation to perform contingent on obtaining financing by [a certain date] lacked sufficient definiteness for a court to be able to determine the terms of financing and therefore rendered the entire contract unenforceable. [Nodolf v. Nelson, 103 Wis.2d 656, 658-59, 309 N.W.2d 397 (App. 1981)].

Nodolf does not support the Donovans' position. Although the clause there contained a date by which financing had to be obtained, we did not address whether that date, in context, implied a reference to circumstances further defining the condition; and we cannot read from the opinion any suggestion that the date did have that meaning. In addition, in *Nodolf* there was no extrinsic evidence supporting a reasonable inference that the parties shared the same definite understanding of the contingency. Instead, in *Nodolf* the buyer's position was that the fact that he subsequently obtained financing, by itself, made the terms more definite, and that is the proposition we rejected.

We conclude there is a reasonable inference from the record that the Donovans were aware of the Vohses' pending transaction to purchase another house. That transaction provides definiteness to the meaning of the condition that the Vohses "obtain[ ][a] home of their choice by February 20, 2007." Accordingly, the Donovans are not entitled to summary judgment on their defense that this clause is indefinite and makes the contract unenforceable.

Because the contingency clause is sufficiently definite under a reasonable view of the record, we turn to the issue whether that clause makes the Vohses' promise to perform illusory. The Donovans' argument that the Vohses' promise is illusory, like their argument on the indefiniteness of the "home of their choice" language, is based on *Nodolf*. In *Nodolf*, we rejected the buyer's argument that he made the financing contingency definite by obtaining financing by the prescribed date, explaining:

---

[4] While indefiniteness and ambiguity are distinct concepts, they are closely related. If an ambiguity is capable of being resolved through principles of contract construction, it necessarily means that the term is sufficiently definite and does not render the contract unenforceable. Similarly, the determination that a term is sufficiently definite may also resolve an ambiguity in the term. As an example, if the extrinsic evidence in this case establishes that the contingency is sufficiently definite, that same evidence would appear to resolve the ambiguity in the meaning of "obtain."

If the buyer could breathe enforceability into the contract by claiming that the financing condition has been met, the buyer would have an unfettered right to decide whether the condition has been fulfilled. This is true because only the buyer and no court [because of the indefiniteness of the clause] can determine the terms of the financing. That right would render [the] buyer's promise to purchase illusory.

Nodolf, 103 Wis.2d at 659, 309 N.W.2d 397.

The Donovans' reliance on *Nodolf* for their argument on illusoriness has the same deficiency as does their *Nodolf* argument on indefiniteness. They ignore the February 20, 2007, date and the extrinsic evidence of the pending transaction with an acceptance date of February 19, 2007. When the extrinsic evidence is considered, there is a reasonable inference that whether the Vohses' counteroffer will be accepted by the deadline is not "wholly under [their] control" or "left wholly to [their] own will and discretion." Metropolitan Ventures, 291 Wis.2d 393, ¶33, 717 N.W.2d 58 (citing Nodolf, 103 Wis.2d at 660, 309 N.W.2d 397). The Donovans do not provide an argument to the contrary.

We conclude, therefore, that the Donovans are not entitled to summary judgment on their defense that the Vohses' promise to perform is illusory. . . .

———

NOTE

The doctrine of "indefiniteness" may be linked to the other core ideas of classical contract doctrine. Requiring definiteness gives every legally enforceable promise a yes/no, on/off character. Recall the facts of *Embry*. If you believe conduct is insufficient to form a contract, then the boss is free to fire the worker several months after their conversation, even if the worker has given up the chance to move elsewhere. But if you think there is a contract, the boss is liable the second after the conversation takes place to the full extent of expectation damages, regardless of whether the worker has relied in any way.

Someone sympathetic to the idea of promissory estoppel might take a different view of indefiniteness. The liability of one person to another should not turn sharply on a single, discontinuous moment. There should not be a single moment at which something someone said shifted from being utterly unenforceable to being enforceable to the full value of the promise. It makes far more sense to hold people to their words to the extent that others reasonably rely on them. The question of liability should not turn on whether the promise was sufficiently definite. We should assess the conduct of the parties and establish relative culpability as we do with other sorts of injury. The more definite the promise, the more one can reasonably rely on it, but the definitiveness of the promise is not itself a touchstone. Consider this line of thought in reading the next case.

———

Blinn v. Beatrice Community Hosp. and Health Center, Inc.

Supreme Court of Nebraska, 2006.
270 Neb. 809, 708 N.W.2d 235.

GERRARD, J. . . . Robert Blinn . . . was fired by his employer, Beatrice Community Hospital and Health Center, Inc. (Beatrice). Blinn sued Beatrice for breach of contract and promissory estoppel. . . .

Blinn testified that in June 2002, he had received a job offer from a Kansas hospital. The Kansas job would have been at a larger hospital and would have offered more responsibility and income potential than Blinn's job of executive director, medical staff development, at Beatrice. It was Blinn's understanding that the Kansas offer was for a position that Blinn could keep until he retired. Blinn was 67 years old at the time he received the offer. Blinn then went to the Beatrice administrator, Larry Emerson, seeking assurances about the permanency of Blinn's position with Beatrice, and drafted a resignation letter he intended to submit to Beatrice unless he received full assurances that Beatrice wanted him to stay. Blinn said:

> Well, I went in and asked him if I could visit, and I shut the door in his office and handed him this letter, and he read it, and he told me that he did not want me to leave. He assured me that I was doing a good job, and most importantly, he said, "Bob, we've got at least five more years of work to do." And I left his office feeling fully assured and fully confident that he had no negatives, 'cause I gave him total opportunity here to tell me.

> I left his office feeling he wanted me there, that he wanted me to stay there and that I should stay there and that we had plenty of work to do and that I could get the job done.

Blinn also asked for Emerson's permission to talk to the chairman of Beatrice's board of directors to seek similar assurances. Blinn testified that the chairman of the board said: "We want you to stay," and I said, "Well, it's really important to me, because whether I stay here or whether I go to [the Kansas hospital], I want it to be the last job I ever have," and [the chairman] assured me he wanted me to stay there and I could stay there until I retired.

However, Blinn was asked to resign by Beatrice in January 2003, and his employment with Beatrice was terminated in February. . . .

We turn first to Blinn's breach of contract claim, which rests on Blinn's contention that the representations made to him by his superiors were sufficient to modify his status as an at-will employee. When employment is not for a definite term and there are no contractual, statutory, or constitutional restrictions upon the right of discharge, an employer may lawfully discharge an employee whenever and for whatever cause it chooses. Oral representations may, standing alone, constitute a promise sufficient to create contractual terms which can modify the at-will status of an employee. However, the burden of proving the existence of an employment contract and all the facts essential to the cause of action is upon the person who asserts the contract.

The question is whether the assurances allegedly given to Blinn were sufficiently definite in form to constitute an offer of a unilateral contract. The language which forms the basis of an alleged employment contract, whether oral or written, must constitute an offer definite in form which is communicated to the employee, and the offer must be accepted and consideration furnished for its enforceability. Under those circumstances, the employee's retention of employment constitutes acceptance of the offer of a unilateral contract because by continuing to stay on the job although free to leave, the employee supplies the necessary consideration for the job.

The question under such circumstances is whether the employer manifests a clear intent to make a promise as an offer of employment other than employment at will, and to be bound by it, so as to justify an employee in understanding that a commitment has been made. Whether a proposal is meant to be an offer for a unilateral contract is determined by the outward manifestations of the parties, not by their subjective intentions. There must be a meeting of the minds or a binding mutual understanding between the parties to the contract.

Here, even viewed in the light most favorable to Blinn, the assurances offered to him were not sufficiently definite in form to constitute an offer of a unilateral contract. The statement that "we've got at least five more years of work to do" is not a clear offer of definite employment and does not manifest an intent to create a unilateral contract. . . .

An employee's subjective understanding of job security is insufficient to establish an implied contract of employment to that effect, and the record here does not establish sufficient evidence to conclude that any employee of Beatrice intended to offer a contract of employment on terms other than employment at will.

For that reason, the Court of Appeals erred in concluding that there was a genuine issue of material fact with respect to Blinn's breach of contract claim. . . .

Recovery on a theory of promissory estoppel is based upon the principle that injustice can be avoided only by enforcement of a promise. Under the doctrine of promissory estoppel, a promise which the promisor should reasonably expect to induce action or forbearance is binding if injustice can be avoided only by enforcement of the promise.

Under Nebraska law, the doctrine of promissory estoppel does not require that the promise giving rise to the cause of action must meet the requirements of an offer that would ripen into a contract if accepted by the promisee. Simply stated, there is no requirement of "definiteness" in an action based upon promissory estoppel. Instead of requiring reasonable definiteness, promissory estoppel requires only that reliance be reasonable and foreseeable.

Here, we agree with the determination made by the Court of Appeals that there is a genuine issue of material fact with respect to Blinn's promissory estoppel claim. While the statements allegedly made by Blinn's superiors were insufficiently definite to offer a contract of employment on terms other than employment at will, there is a genuine issue of material fact as to whether Blinn was promised terms of employment that could reasonably have been expected to induce Blinn to forgo the job opportunity in Kansas of which he had informed Beatrice. Under the circumstances, when considering the lesser requirement that Nebraska law imposes on a promise that forms the basis of a promissory estoppel cause of action, we conclude that the district court erred in not finding a genuine issue of material fact. . . .

Under the *Restatement* view, a "promise" for purposes of promissory estoppel must meet the same requirements as a "promise" for purposes of contract formation. Generally speaking, under the *Restatement*, when a promise is made, but a contract is not formed because of a lack of consideration, reasonable reliance by the promisee can still render the promisor liable for breach of the promise. In short, analysis of the promise is the same as that for a contract, except that the promisee's reliance on the promise replaces the missing consideration.

But in Nebraska, we have rejected that view. As noted earlier, we have held that there is no requirement of "definiteness" in an action based upon promissory estoppel. Rosnick v. Dinsmore, 235 Neb. 738, 457 N.W.2d 793 (1990). In *Rosnick*, we departed from the Restatement view that a promise for estoppel purposes requires the same definiteness as a promise for contract purposes. In Whorley v. First Westside Bank, 240 Neb. 975, 485 N.W.2d 578 (1992), we expressly considered the Restatement view, cited conflicting authority, and reaffirmed our holding in *Rosnick*. Contrary to the Restatement view, the law in Nebraska is that a promissory estoppel action may be based on an alleged promise that is insufficiently definite to form a contract, but upon which the promisee's reliance is reasonable and foreseeable. The difference between contract and promissory estoppel, then, is that a contract requires that the promisor intend to make a binding promise—a binding mutual understanding or "meeting of the minds"—while promissory estoppel requires only that the promisee's reliance on the promise be reasonable and foreseeable, even if the promisor did not intend to be bound. A promisor need not intend a promise to be binding in order to foresee that a promisee may reasonably rely on it.

. . . Because promissory estoppel does not require definiteness, an employer need not intend to contractually modify an employee's at-will employment in order for an employee to reasonably and foreseeably believe that his or her terms of employment have been changed and, therefore, act in reliance on that belief. Here, there is insufficient evidence to conclude that Beatrice intended to offer Blinn a unilateral contract. But there is sufficient evidence, if believed by the trier of fact, to conclude that Blinn reasonably and foreseeably relied on Beatrice's assurances of a fixed term of employment, and Beatrice breached that promise. There is a genuine issue of material fact to be decided. . . .

NOTE ON AGREEMENTS TO AGREE

The doctrine of indefiniteness is often invoked in cases in which the parties have reached agreement on the general terms of their transaction, but have yet to sign a formal contract. Instead, "they sign a document, captioned 'agreement in principle' or 'letter of intent,' memorializing these terms but anticipating further negotiations and decisions—an appraisal of the assets, the clearing of a title, the list is endless. One of these terms proves divisive, and the deal collapses. The party that perceives itself the loser then claims that the preliminary document has legal force independent of the definitive contract." Empro Mfg. Co. v. Ball–Co Mfg., 870 F.2d 423, 424 (7th Cir. 1989). Letters of intent and agreements in principle set the stage for negotiations on details. Sometimes the details can be ironed out; sometimes they cannot. A letter of intent or other preliminary agreement might show that the parties agreed to bind themselves to some extent immediately, but what exactly does this mean?

Consider the approach of the court in Adjustrite Systems, Inc. v. GAB Business Services, Inc., 145 F.3d 543 (2d Cir.1998):

A framework under New York law for analyzing the issue of whether a preliminary agreement is a binding contract or an unenforceable agreement to agree was articulated by Judge Leval in Teachers Insurance & Annuity Ass'n v. Tribune Co., 670 F.Supp. 491 (S.D.N.Y.1987), and applied by this Court in Arcadian Phosphates, Inc. v. Arcadian Corp., 884 F.2d 69, 71–72 (2d Cir.1989).

Ordinarily, where the parties contemplate further negotiations and the execution of a formal instrument, a preliminary agreement does not create a binding contract. In some circumstances, however, preliminary agreements can create binding obligations. Usually, binding preliminary agreements fall into one of two categories.

The first is a fully binding preliminary agreement, which is created when the parties agree on all the points that require negotiation (including whether to be bound) but agree to memorialize their agreement in a more formal document. Such an agreement is fully binding; it is "preliminary only in form—only in the sense that the parties desire a more elaborate formalization of the agreement." Tribune, 670 F.Supp. at 498. A binding preliminary agreement binds both sides to their ultimate contractual objective in recognition that, "despite the anticipation of further formalities," a contract has been reached. Id. Accordingly, a party may demand performance of the transaction even though the parties fail to produce the "more elaborate formalization of the agreement." Id.

The second type of preliminary agreement, dubbed a "binding preliminary commitment" by Judge Leval, is binding only to a certain degree. It is created when the parties agree on certain major terms, but leave other terms open for further negotiation. The parties "accept a mutual commitment to negotiate together in good faith in an effort to reach final agreement." Tribune, 670 F.Supp. at 498. In contrast to a fully binding preliminary agreement, a "binding preliminary commitment" "does not commit the parties to their ultimate contractual objective but rather to the obligation to negotiate the open issues in good faith in an attempt to reach the . . . objective within the agreed framework." Id. A party to such a binding preliminary commitment has no right to demand performance of the transaction. Indeed, if a final contract is not agreed upon, the parties may abandon the transaction as long as they have made a good faith effort to close the deal and have not insisted on conditions that do not conform to the preliminary writing. Id.

Hence, if a preliminary agreement is of the first type, the parties are fully bound to carry out the terms of the agreement even if the formal instrument is never executed. If a preliminary agreement is of the second type, the parties are bound only to make a good faith effort to negotiate and agree upon the open terms and a final agreement; if they fail to reach such a final agreement after making a good faith effort to do so, there is no further obligation. Finally, however, if the preliminary writing was not intended to be binding on the parties at all, the writing is a mere proposal, and neither party has an obligation to negotiate further.

Courts . . . must keep two competing interests in mind. First, courts must be wary of "trapping parties in surprise contractual obligations that they never intended" to undertake. Tribune, 670 F.Supp. at 497; accord Arcadian, 884 F.2d at 72. Second, "courts [must] enforce and preserve agreements that were intended [to be] binding, despite a need for further documentation or further negotiation," for it is "the aim of contract law to gratify, not to defeat, expectations." Tribune, 670 F.Supp. at 498.

The key, of course, is the intent of the parties: whether the parties intended to be bound, and if so, to what extent. . . .

––––––––

CHAPTER 4

IDENTIFYING THE BARGAIN

SECTION 1. THE EFFECTS OF ADOPTING A WRITING

INTRODUCTORY NOTE

A writing is essential to the full enforceability of some types of agreements. The most familiar are the classes of agreements included in the statute of frauds (see Appendix, p. 885). For them, a note or memorandum is needed. In other situations, statutes expand the writing requirement by making it necessary to put the "contract" itself in writing—for example, agreements to submit disputes to arbitration and, in many states, such "consumer" transactions as home-improvement and automotive-repair contracts. Still, it remains true that many important bargains are entirely exempt from any form of writing requirement. There are, of course, good reasons for putting agreements in written form. A document provides guidance during performance, and evidence of the scope of obligation should disputes arise; it also signals, through the act of signing, the moment when contractual relations begin. When the agreement is reduced to writing, the parties may encounter a number of problems (and legal doctrines) peculiarly associated with written undertakings.

One group of problems is dealt with under the rubric "parol evidence rule," which purports to restrict the use of evidence of negotiating history to vary the terms of a written agreement intended to be the final expression of the parties' deal. But the name (PER) is deceiving for a number of reasons, as you will soon realize. It is not easy to state a single, authoritative "parol evidence rule," largely because it is not "a rule" at all but a whole body of more or less discrete doctrines, about which are clustered overlapping and connected rules and concepts (e.g., "extrinsic evidence," "plain meaning," "four corners"), which, taken together, also function as devices for preferring writings over oral statements or promises. The materials in this section present a number of these rules and doctrines (including those for the "interpretation" of agreements reduced to writing), many of which go to show what the parol evidence rule is *not*—that is to say, they define situations where the rule is not applicable, so-called "exceptions." We defer the exceptions until we have examined the basic doctrine of "integration," sometimes called "merger."

———

Mitchill v. Lath
Court of Appeals of New York, 1928.
247 N.Y. 377, 160 N.E. 646.

ANDREWS, J. In the fall of 1923 the Laths owned a farm. This they wished to sell. Across the road, on land belonging to Lieutenant–Governor Lunn, they had an ice house which they might remove. Mrs. Mitchill looked over the land with a view to its purchase. She found the ice house objectionable. Thereupon "the defendants orally promised and agreed, for and in consideration of the purchase of their farm by the plaintiff, to remove the said ice house in the spring of 1924." Relying upon this promise, she made a written contract to buy the property for $8,400. . . . Later receiving a deed, she entered into possession and has spent considerable sums in improving the property for use as a summer residence. The defendants have not fulfilled their promise as to the ice house and do not intend to do so. We are not dealing, however, with their moral delinquencies. The question before us is whether their oral agreement may be enforced in a court of equity.

This requires a discussion of the parol evidence rule—a rule of law which defines the limits of the contract to be construed. . . . It is more than a rule of evidence and oral testimony even if admitted will not control the written contract, unless admitted without objection. Brady v. Nally, 151 N.Y. 258, 45 N.E. 547. It applies, however, to attempts to modify such a contract by parol. It does not affect a parol collateral contract distinct from and independent of the written agreement. It is, at times, troublesome to draw the line. Williston, in his work on Contracts (§ 637) points out the difficulty. "Two entirely distinct contracts," he says, "each for a separate consideration may be made at the same time and will be distinct legally. Where, however, one agreement is entered into wholly or partly in consideration of the simultaneous agreement to enter into another, the transactions are necessarily bound together. . . . Then if one of the agreements is oral and the other is written, the problem arises whether the bond is sufficiently close to prevent proof of the oral agreement." That is the situation here. It is claimed that the defendants are called upon to do more than is required by their written contract in connection with the sale as to which it deals.

The principle may be clear, but it can be given effect by no mechanical rule. As so often happens, it is a matter of degree, for as Professor Williston also says where a contract contains several promises on each side it is not difficult to put any one of them in the form of a collateral agreement. If this were enough written contracts might always be modified by parol. Not form, but substance, is the test.

In applying this test the policy of our courts is to be considered. We have believed that the purpose behind the rule was a wise one not easily to be abandoned. Notwithstanding injustice here and there, on the whole it works for good. . . . New York has been less open to arguments that would modify this particular rule, than some jurisdictions elsewhere. Thus in Eighmie v. Taylor, 98 N.Y. 288, it was held that a parol warranty might not be shown although no warranties were contained in the writing.

Under our decisions before such an oral agreement as the present is received to vary the written contract at least three conditions must exist, (1) the agreement must in form be a collateral one; (2) it must not contradict express or implied provisions of the written contract; (3) it must be one that parties would not ordinarily be expected to embody in the writing; or put in another way, an inspection of the written contract, read in the light of surrounding circumstances must not indicate that the writing appears "to contain the engagement of the parties, and to define the object and measure the extent of such engagement." Or again, it must not be so clearly connected with the principal transaction as to be part and parcel of it.

THE ICE HOUSE

The respondent does not satisfy the third of these requirements. It may be, not the second. We have a written contract for the purchase and sale of land. The buyer is to pay $8,400 in the way described. She is also to pay her portion of any rents, interest on mortgages, insurance premiums and water meter charges. She may have a survey made of the premises. On their part the sellers are to give a full covenant deed of the premises as described[;] . . . they sell the personal property on the farm and represent they own it; they agree that all amounts paid them on the contract and the expense of examining the title shall be a lien on the property; they assume the risk of loss or damage by fire until the deed is delivered; and they agree to pay the broker his commissions. Are they to do more? Or is such a claim inconsistent with these precise provisions? It could not be shown that the plaintiff was to pay $500 additional. Is it also implied that the defendants are not to do anything unexpressed in the writing?

That we need not decide. At least, however, an inspection of this contract shows a full and complete agreement, setting forth in detail the obligations of each party. On reading it one would conclude that the reciprocal obligations of the parties were fully detailed. Nor would his opinion alter if he knew the surrounding circumstances. The presence of the ice house, even the knowledge that Mrs. Mitchill thought it objectionable would not lead to the belief that a separate agreement existed with regard to it. Were such an agreement made it would seem most natural that the inquirer should find it in the contract. Collateral in form it is found to be, but it is closely related to the subject dealt with in the written agreement—so closely that we hold it may not be proved.

Where the line between the competent and the incompetent is narrow the citation of authorities is of slight use. Each represents the judgment of the court on the precise facts before it. How closely bound to the contract is the supposed collateral agreement is the decisive factor in each case. . . .

[T]he judgment of the Appellate Division and that of the Special Term should be reversed and the complaint dismissed, with costs in all courts.

LEHMAN, J. (dissenting). I accept the general rule as formulated by Judge Andrews. I differ with him only as to its application to the facts shown in the record. . . . I concede at the outset that parol evidence to show additional conditions and terms of the conveyance would be inadmissible. There is a conclusive presumption that the parties intended to integrate in that written contract every agreement relating to the nature or extent of the property to be conveyed, the contents of the deed to be delivered, the consideration to be paid as a condition precedent to the delivery of the deeds, and indeed all the rights of the parties in connection with the land. The conveyance of that land was the subject-matter of the written contract and the contract completely covers that subject.

The parol agreement which the court below found the parties had made was collateral to, yet connected with, the agreement of purchase and sale. It has been found that the defendants induced the plaintiff to agree to purchase the land by a promise to remove an ice house from land not covered by the agreement of purchase and sale. No independent consideration passed to the defendants for the parol promise. To that extent the written contract and the alleged oral contract are bound together. . . .

Judge Andrews has formulated a standard to measure the closeness of the bond. Three conditions, at least, must exist before an oral agreement may be proven to increase the obligation imposed by the written agreement. I think we agree that the first condition that the agreement "must in form be a collateral one" is met by the evidence. I concede that this condition is met in most cases. . . . The difficulty here, as in most cases, arises in connection with the two other conditions.

The second condition is that the "parol agreement must not contradict express or implied provisions of the written contract." Judge Andrews voices doubt whether this condition is satisfied. The written contract has been carried out. . . . By the oral agreement the plaintiff seeks to hold the defendants to other obligations to be performed by them thereafter upon land which was not conveyed to the plaintiff. The assertion of such further obligation is not inconsistent with the written contract unless the written contract contains a provision, express or implied, that the defendants are not to do anything not expressed in the writing. Concededly there is no such express provision in the contract, and such a provision may be implied, if at all, only if the asserted additional obligation is "so clearly connected with the principal transactions as to be part and parcel of it," and is not "one that the parties would not ordinarily be expected to embody in the writing." . . . In this case, therefore, the problem reduces itself to the one question whether or not the oral agreement meets the third condition.

THE MITCHILL RESIDENCE

I have conceded that upon inspection the contract is complete. . . . That engagement was on the one side to convey land; on the other to pay the price. The plaintiff asserts further agreement based on the same consideration to be performed by the defendants after the conveyance was complete, and directly affecting only other land. It is true, as Judge Andrews points out, that "the presence of the ice house, even the knowledge that Mrs. Mitchill thought it objectionable, would not lead to the belief that a separate agreement existed with regard to it;" but the question we must decide is whether or not, assuming an agreement was made for the removal of an unsightly ice house from one parcel of land as an inducement for the purchase of another parcel, the parties would ordinarily or naturally be expected to embody the agreement for the removal of the ice house from one parcel in the written agreement to convey the other parcel. Exclusion of proof of the oral agreement on the ground that it varies the contract embodied in the writing may be based only upon a finding or presumption that the written contract was intended to cover the oral negotiations for the removal of the ice house which lead up to the contract of purchase and sale. To determine what the writing was intended to cover "the document alone will not suffice. What it was intended to cover cannot be known till we know what there was to cover. The question being whether certain subjects of negotiation were intended to be covered, we must compare the writing and the negotiations before we can determine whether they were in fact covered." (Wigmore on Evidence [2d ed.], § 2430.)

The subject-matter of the written contract was the conveyance of land. The contract was so complete on its face that the conclusion is inevitable that the parties intended to embody in the writing all the negotiations covering at least the conveyance. The promise by the defendants to remove the ice house from other land was not connected with their obligation to convey, except that one agreement would not have been made unless the other was also made. The plaintiff's assertion of a parol agreement by the defendants to remove the ice house was completely established by the great weight of evidence. It must prevail unless that agreement was part of the agreement to convey and the entire agreement was embodied in the writing.

The fact that in this case the parol agreement is established by the overwhelming weight of evidence is, of course, not a factor which may be considered in determining the competency or legal effect of the evidence. Hardship in the particular case would not justify the court in disregarding or emasculating the general rule. It merely accentuates the outlines of our problem. The assumption that the parol agreement was made is no longer obscured by any doubts. The problem then is clearly whether the parties are presumed to have intended to render that parol agreement legally ineffective and non-existent by failure to embody it in the writing. Though we are driven to say that nothing in the written contract which fixed the terms and conditions of the stipulated conveyance suggests the existence of any further parol agreement, an inspection of the contract, though it is complete on its face in regard to the subject of the conveyance, does not, I think, show that it was intended to embody negotiations or agreements, if any, in regard to a matter so loosely bound to the conveyance as the removal of an ice house from land not conveyed.

The rule of integration undoubtedly frequently prevents the assertion of fraudulent claims. Parties who take the precaution of embodying their oral agreements in a writing should be protected against the assertion that other terms of the same agreement were not integrated in the writing. The limits of the integration are determined by the writing, read in the light of the surrounding circumstances. A written contract, however complete, yet covers only a limited field. I do not think that in the written contract for the conveyance of land here under consideration we can find an intention to cover a field so broad as to include prior agreements, if any such were made, to do other acts on other property after the stipulated conveyance was made. . . .

CARDOZO, C.J., POUND, KELLOGG and O'BRIEN, JJ., concur with ANDREWS, J.; LEHMAN, J., dissents in opinion in which CRANE, J., concurs.

NOTE: BELIEVABILITY AND "NATURALNESS"

Plaintiff had sued for specific performance. On December 20, 1926, the trial court issued a decree ordering defendants to remove the ice house by December 25, or, alternatively, pay plaintiff $8,000 in damages. Among the findings on which the decree was based were the following (Record, p. 9):

> In the fall of 1923, the defendants orally promised and agreed, for and in consideration of the purchase of their farm by the plaintiff, to remove the said ice house by the spring of 1924. That the plaintiff relied upon the said promise and agreement of the defendants and was induced by the representations made, to and did purchase the farm by deed of conveyance delivered December 19, 1923.

That thereafter the plaintiff took immediate possession of the premises and made extensive repairs and improvements to the house and grounds, costing over $23,000, during the course of some of which the defendants were employed. . . . That the presence of the ice house and the operation of the ice business therein, injuriously affects the value of plaintiff's property and decreases the value in about the sum of $8,000.

Judge Lehman, hearing the appeal in *Mitchill*, made note of these findings. Yet his dissent included this statement: "The fact that in this case the parol agreement is established by the overwhelming weight of evidence is, of course, not a factor which may be considered in determining the competency or legal effect of the evidence." Should this statement be accepted as sound judicial practice in applying the parol evidence rule? The trial judge presumably makes the application, that is, the first cut respecting the admissibility of extrinsic evidence. Is it likely to matter whether the judge, after considering all the parties' evidence, believes that the alleged oral agreement was: (a) most surely made; (b) probably made; (c) probably not made; or (d) most surely not made (a whopper of an untruth)?

Consider also whether Judge Lehman's assertion is connected in any way to the third "condition" or test of admissibility announced by Judge Andrews— i.e., was the oral agreement one the parties "would not ordinarily be expected to embody in the writing"? This test represents standard Restatement (First) doctrine; § 240(1)(b) states that an oral agreement is not superseded by a later writing if it is not inconsistent with the writing and is "such an agreement as might naturally be made as a separate agreement by parties situated as were the parties to the written contract." Corbin has written of this provision (3 A. Corbin, Contracts § 584):

> [It] requires the court to determine what would be "natural" and what would not. The party offering the parol evidence always asserts . . . that [the parties] in fact made the "oral agreement." Should he not always be allowed to show that what they in fact did was "natural"? Even if it was not "natural," the evidence is offered to prove that the parties in fact made the oral agreement and that they did not execute the writing as a complete "integration." The parol evidence rule purports only to exclude evidence in case there is an "integration" that the evidence is offered to contradict or vary. The proof of a provision that is merely "additional" neither contradicts nor varies the writing. . . . Whether or not it was "natural" for the parties to do as they did bears only on the credibility of the evidence offered. This form of language makes the admissibility of an added but not inconsistent term practically discretionary with the court.

The next case, Hatley v. Stafford, is offered as a companion to Mitchill v. Lath. It has more to say on "credibility" and "naturalness."

———————

Hatley v. Stafford

Supreme Court of Oregon, 1978.
284 Or. 523, 588 P.2d 603.

HOWELL, J. Plaintiff, lessee, filed this action for trespass against defendants, lessors. The property involved is a 52–acre farm in Lane County. The defendants contended they were entitled under the lease agreement to terminate the lease and recover possession. The following is the entire written agreement of the parties[:]

"Oct. 16, 1974

"Stafford Farm agrees to rent to Mike Hatley, Rt. 1 Box 83, Halsey, Ore. approximately 52 acres till Sept. 1st 1975 for the purpose of growing wheat with the follow[ing] condition:—Stafford Farm shall have the right to buy out Mr. Mike Hatley at a figure of his cost per acre but not to exceed $70 per acre. This buy out is for the express purpose of developing a Mobile Home Park.

"Terms shall be $1800 paid on or before Jan. 20th 1975 balance due Sept. 20, 1975. The Rent figure shall be $50 per acre.

"Stafford Farm

"By /s/ Robert R. Stafford Mgr.   /s/ Mike Hatley"

Plaintiff Hatley alleged that between June 8 and June 11, 1975, defendants trespassed on the property by taking possession of the farm and cutting the immature wheat crop. The defendants [answered] that they exercised their right to terminate the lease in order to build a mobile home park and that they offered to pay plaintiff his cost per acre but not to exceed $70 per acre. Plaintiff demanded $400 per acre, the fair market value of the wheat crop. [Plaintiff's reply] alleged that the written agreement was not the entire integrated agreement of the parties, and that the parties orally agreed the buy out provision of the lease would apply only for a period of 30 to 60 days after the execution of the lease.

The trial court allowed plaintiff to introduce evidence concerning the alleged oral agreement. . . . The jury returned a verdict for plaintiff. . . . The only error asserted on [defendants'] appeal is that the trial court erred in allowing admission of the parol evidence relating to the time limit on the buy out agreement.

The parol evidence rule[1] applies only to those aspects of a bargain that the parties intend to memorialize in the writing. . . . The fact that a writing exists does not bring the rule into play if the parties do not intend the writing to embody their final agreement. . . . Neither does the rule apply when the parties intended the writing to contain only part of their agreement. . . .

---

[1] ORS § 41.740 states, in pertinent part:

"When the terms of an agreement have been reduced to writing by the parties, it is to be considered as containing all those terms, and therefore there can be, between the parties and their representatives or successors in interest, no evidence of the terms of the agreement, other than the contents of the writing. . . ."

Concededly, a literal reading of this statute would exclude any parol evidence of the terms of an agreement once that agreement had been reduced to writing. . . . This court, however, has never read the statute in such a manner, but instead has treated the statute as a codification of the common law parol evidence rule. . . . Although [our] decisions may be inconsistent with a literal reading of the statute, which has been in effect since 1862, they can be justified under the general rule that statutes codifying the common law are to be construed in a manner consistent with the common law. . . .

[The] plaintiff sought to show that the written lease was a "partial integration," i.e., that the written contract included some, but not all, of the terms of the actual agreement. Defendants contend that such a showing could be made only if the oral agreement was "not inconsistent" with the writing and was "an agreement as might naturally be made as a separate agreement." . . . Plaintiff argues that these limitations apply only after it has been demonstrated that the writing is a complete integration, that whether a writing was intended to be a complete integration is a question of fact, and that the jury may consider any relevant evidence in deciding this question of fact. Both parties find support for their positions in past opinions by this court. . . .

The inconsistency in our prior decisions reflects a long-standing disagreement among courts and commentators generally as to the applicability of the parol evidence rule. . . . The rule apparently was an outgrowth of the law governing contracts under seal. Because the King's word was indisputable, the King's seal on a document made the document uncontestable. 9 J. Wigmore, Evidence 83, § 2426 (3d ed. 1940). The status of writings was further enhanced by the enactment of the Statute of Wills and the Statute of Frauds, both of which made certain transactions legally unenforceable unless they were in writing. This theory was gradually applied to contracts generally, until finally the writing came to be regarded as the agreement itself, rather than merely as evidence of the agreement. Id. at 91.

Modernly, the parol evidence rule has often been justified on grounds of commercial certainty. If parol evidence were allowed to be offered in contradiction of writings, it has been feared that the likelihood of perjury would increase. . . . It is also believed that the rule is needed to ensure that juries will not decide cases on the "equities," the theory being that the economic underdog will most often be the party seeking to vary the terms of the writing by parol evidence. . . . On the other hand, it has been observed that in a modern society where much of business is transacted over the telephone, contracts that are partly oral and partly written have become increasingly common. . . . Moreover, in an era of adhesion contracts and unequal bargaining power, the extent to which many writings actually embody the agreement of the parties is debatable. . . . Finally, it is doubtful that the rule discourages perjury, since the rule can be avoided by fabricating an oral agreement subsequent to the execution of the writing. . . .

The rule does, however, serve an important function. If the parties *in fact* have assented to the writing as the embodiment of their entire agreement, each should be able to rely on the terms of the writing as conclusive evidence of what they have agreed to. . . .

The difficulty arises when one of the parties asserts . . . that the writing does not contain all the terms of the actual agreement. Because the parol evidence rule applies only to complete and final integrations, and because the existence of an integration depends on the intent of the parties, it has been argued that any relevant evidence of the parties' intent should be admissible and that the actual intent of the parties should be a factual question for the jury. As we observed in De Vore v. Weyerhaeuser Co., [265 Or. 388, 508 P.2d 220 (1973), cert. denied, 415 U.S. 913 (1974)], however, a rule allowing the jury to consider any relevant evidence in deciding whether the writing was intended to be a complete integration "without any limitations, would emasculate, if not 'repeal,' the parol evidence rule, which is a rule adopted by statute in Oregon. . . ." 265 Or. at 401. Consequently, we have recognized the criteria of § 240 of the [first] Restatement of Contracts as imposing limitations on the admissibility of evidence in cases involving the partial integration doctrine. We believe these limitations remain appropriate, despite our occasional statements to the contrary.

On the other hand, the Restatement criteria are not to be applied mechanically or formalistically. . . . [T]he purpose of the parol evidence rule is to give special effect to writings only in those cases where the parties intended the writing to be a final and complete statement of their agreement. . . .

. . . [M]ention should be made of the functions of court and jury in cases involving the parol evidence rule. Both plaintiff and defendants appear to have assumed that the jury decides whether or not the parties intended their writing to be a final and complete integration. Such is not the law. As McCormick notes, "The question [of whether the parties intended their writing to be a complete integration] is one for the court, for it relates to the admission or rejection of evidence." [McCormick, Handbook of the Law of Evidence 437, § 215 (1954).] In deciding that the parties did not intend the writing to be an integration, however, the court does not decide that the alleged oral terms actually were agreed upon. That determination is left to the jury. The court's decision is one of admissibility, not probity.[2]

[Here,] the trial court decided that the [parties'] written agreement was not a complete integration of their actual agreement, and permitted plaintiff to introduce evidence that the buy out provision in the written lease was subject to an oral time limitation. No contention is made that the oral agreement was supported by separate consideration, so the trial court's ruling can be upheld only if the agreement: (1) was "not inconsistent" with the written lease and (2) was "such an agreement as might naturally be made as a separate agreement *by parties situated as were parties to the written contract*." DeVore v. Weyerhaeuser Co., supra, . . . (emphasis added).

Defendant argues that the oral time limitation is "clearly inconsistent" with the terms of the written lease, reasoning that a buy out provision with no time limitation in a lease for a fixed term must be read to run for the entire term of the lease. We do not define the term "inconsistent" so broadly. To be "inconsistent" within the meaning of the partial integration doctrine, the oral term must contradict an *express provision* in the writing. As the court observed in Hunt Foods & Indus. v. Doliner, 26 App.Div.2d 41, 270 N.Y.S.2d 937 (1966): "In a sense any oral provision which would prevent the ripening of the obligations of a writing is inconsistent with the writing. But that obviously is not the sense in which the word is used. . . . To be inconsistent the term must contradict or negate *a term of the writing*. A term or condition which has a lesser effect is provable." 270 N.Y.S.2d at 940 (emphasis added). . . .

---

[2] Wigmore explains the procedure thusly: ". . . There is a preliminary question for the judge to decide as to the intent of the parties, and upon this he hears evidence on both sides; his decision here, *pro* or *con*, concerns merely this question preliminary to the ruling of law. If he decides that the transaction was covered by the writing, he does not decide that the excluded negotiations did not take place, but merely that *if* they did take place they are nevertheless legally immaterial. If he decides that the transaction was not intended to be covered by the writing, he does not decide that the negotiations did take place, but merely that *if* they did, they are legally effective, and he then leaves to the jury the determination of fact whether they did take place." 9 J. Wigmore, Evidence 98 § 2430 (3d ed. 1940).

In [this] case, nothing is contained in the writing with respect to the duration of the buy out provision. Therefore, the oral time limitation is "not inconsistent" with the terms of the writing.

Defendants argue that even if the oral term is not inconsistent with the terms of the writing, the parol evidence should have been excluded because the oral term "naturally" would have been included in the writing. We disagree.

In determining whether or not an oral term is one that "naturally" would have been included in the writing, the trial court is not limited to a consideration of the face of the document. "[T]he surrounding circumstances, as well as the written contract, may be considered." Blehm v. Ringering, 260 Or. 46, 50, 488 P.2d 798 (1971). When considering the surrounding circumstances, the trial court should be aware of the fact that parties with business experience are more likely to reduce their entire agreement to writing than parties without such experience[,] . . . and that this is especially true when the parties are represented by counsel on both sides. . . . The relative bargaining strength of the parties also should be considered, since a transaction not negotiated at arm's length may result in a writing that omits essential terms. . . . And, of course, the apparent completeness and detail of the writing itself may lead the court to conclude the parties intended the writing to be a complete integration. . . .

This is not to say, however, that the trial court should readily admit parol evidence whenever one of the parties claims a writing does not include all the terms of an agreement. The court should presume that the writing was intended to be a complete integration, at least when the writing is complete on its face, and should admit evidence of consistent additional terms only if there is substantial evidence that the parties did not intend the writing to embody the entire agreement. . . .

[T]here are a number of facts [here] that could have led the trial court to conclude that it was natural for the parties, "situated as were parties to the written contract," to have omitted the time limitation on the buy out provision from the written lease. First, this was not a sophisticated business transaction in which the parties could be expected to include all the terms of their agreement in the writing. . . . The lease was a handwritten document that hardly shows the kind of careful preparation that accompanies a formal integration. . . . Moreover, the agreement was concluded by the parties themselves, without counsel to advise them of the consequences of the writing. This case is therefore analogous to the leading case of Masterson v. Sine, 68 Cal.2d 222, 65 Cal.Rptr. 545, 436 P.2d 561 (1968), where the court, per Chief Justice Traynor, stated: "There is nothing in the record to indicate that the parties to this family transaction, through experience in land transactions or otherwise, had any warning of the disadvantages of failing to put the whole agreement in the deed. This case is one, therefore, in which it can be said that a collateral agreement such as that alleged 'might naturally be made as a separate agreement.'" 65 Cal.Rptr. at 549, 436 P.2d at 565.

Finally, the trial court was entitled to consider the fact that a literal reading of the written contract would have led to an unreasonable result. Plaintiff was contending the wheat crop he had planted would be worth $400 per acre at harvest. The written agreement, standing alone, would have allowed the defendants to exercise the buy out provision the day before harvest and pay plaintiff $70 per acre for wheat worth $400 per acre. While the mere fact that a contract is one-sided does not by itself justify a

[handwritten margin note: imbalance suggests intension of additional provisions in agreement]

conclusion that the writing does not embody the entire agreement of the parties, the trial court may consider that fact in deciding whether the parties intended additional provisions to be included in the agreement. . . .

For these reasons, we hold that there was sufficient evidence to justify the trial court's decision to admit the parol evidence. . . . [T]he question of whether the parties actually agreed to the time limitation was properly left to the jury.

[One judge dissented, arguing that the majority had rewritten the statute on parol evidence, rendering it "meaningless."]

NOTE

The *Hatley* court identified a "number of facts" which it thought supported a conclusion that the parties' omission of the oral agreement from the writing was "natural" in the circumstances. In Lee v. Joseph E. Seagram & Sons, Inc., 552 F.2d 447 (2d Cir.1977), a federal court applying New York law on the integration question covered similar ground, with the same outcome. It said in part: "[I]ntegration is most easily inferred in the case of real estate contracts for the sale of land [citing Mitchill v. Lath] or leases. . . . In more complex situations, in which customary business practice may be more varied, an oral agreement can be treated as separate and independent of the written agreement even though the written contract contains a strong integration clause." The case involved a written agreement for the sale of business assets; the seller was permitted to introduce proofs of an oral agreement by the purchaser to relocate persons associated with the seller in a business in a different city. Since the written agreement dealt only with the sale of assets, the oral agreement did not "vary or contradict" the writing.

Masterson v. Sine, the case deemed "analogous" by the *Hatley* majority, involved a brother's conveyance of a ranch to a sister and her husband, the deed reserving to the grantors (Masterson and his wife) an option to repurchase the property on stated terms. Later, the grantor-brother was adjudged bankrupt, and the trustee in bankruptcy sued to enforce the option on behalf of creditors. The Masterson family resisted the suit by offering extrinsic evidence that the parties had wanted the ranch kept in the family and that the option was therefore understood to be "personal" to the grantors and not assignable or otherwise available to third persons. The California court (5 to 2), reversing the trial judge, found it "natural" for the parties to have kept their agreement of nontransferability separate from the deed. In addition to the passage quoted in *Hatley*, Chief Justice Traynor said: "The option clause in the deed . . . does not explicitly provide that it contains the complete agreement, and the deed is silent on the question of assignability. Moreover, the difficulty of accommodating the formalized structure of a deed to the insertion of collateral agreements makes it less likely that all the terms of such an agreement were included."

Note also *Hatley*'s test of an "inconsistent" term, a test derived from the often-cited *Hunt Foods* decision. The materials that follow will reveal differing views on the appropriate definition of "contradiction" or "inconsistency" when the task is to determine whether a writing is or is not an integrated agreement, completely or only partially. It may be helpful to look at illustration 2 accompanying Rest.2d § 213 (ahead, p. 396). Is the problem of oral-written conflict presented there like, or unlike, that posed by *Hatley*? Like that detected by the court in Hayden v. Hoadley, immediately below?

Hayden v. Hoadley
94 Vt. 345, 111 A. 343 (1920)

The parties agreed to exchange properties. As part of the consideration for plaintiffs' conveyance of a farm, defendants promised in writing to make certain repairs upon the village house and barn they were to (and did) convey to plaintiffs, namely: "[T]o straighten up and shingle the barn on said premises; to straighten up the house; repair and paint the roof, and paint the same back of said house; [and] to repair the cellar wall[.]" In plaintiffs' action to recover damages for nonperformance, defendants offered to show that at the time the writing was signed it was orally agreed that they should have "until October 1, 1919, in which to make the repairs, that only $60 need be expended therefor, and that No. 2 shingles were to be used on the barn." The offered evidence was excluded. On appeal, *held*, these rulings were correct. "The legal effect of the contract before us—it being silent as to the time of performance—was to require the repairs specified to be completed within a reasonable time." This provision, though "implied by the law," is as binding as any express term of the writing; the contract is just as it would be if the writing had actually said "within a reasonable time." Necessarily, then, "[t]o admit the testimony offered by defendants to the effect that the parties agreed upon October 1 as the [time limit] for repairs would be to allow the plain legal effect of the written contract to be controlled by oral evidence. That is not permissible. . . . The contract before us is unequivocal and complete, and to say that parol evidence can be received to fix the time of performance, on the ground the contract is incomplete, is wholly illogical and wrong." For the same reason, the evidence as to the amount of money to be spent and "the kind of a wall that should be made" was properly excluded. But nothing said herein is intended to suggest that we "question the proposition that an incomplete writing may be supplemented by parol, for this is a rule of unquestioned soundness." Also, since "[t]he evidence under discussion was not offered on the ground that it was admissible on the question of what was a reasonable time under the circumstances, [we] give that question no attention." [Is there a misfire in the court's reasoning?]

The preceding materials illustrate the difficulties in determining whether a writing is a complete or partial integration, and whether a prior agreement is consistent with the writing or within its scope. The excerpts from the Restatement, Second reproduced below summarize the established rules for addressing these difficulties; they provide a roadmap for working out the legal consequences of reducing precontractual discussions and agreements to writing. A point worth noting is the role of a "merger" or "integration" clause, a term of the writing which itself excludes agreements not found in the writing. Courts have divided over the weight to be given such clauses, some holding them conclusive on the parties' intention respecting integration, others deeming a merger provision to be a factor only, perhaps at best presumptive evidence of an intention to completely integrate. Observe what the restaters, in comment on Rest.2d § 216 (p. 397), have to say on the matter. Might "context"—say, unequal bargaining

should prior oral agreements have influence

power between the parties, or concerns about public policy—contribute to the law's uncertain state concerning the effect to be given a merger clause?

RESTATEMENT OF CONTRACTS, SECOND

Section 209. Integrated Agreements

(1) An integrated agreement is a writing or writings constituting a final expression of one or more terms of an agreement.

(2) Whether there is an integrated agreement is to be determined by the court as a question preliminary to determination of a question of interpretation or to application of the parol evidence rule.

(3) Where the parties reduce an agreement to a writing which in view of its completeness and specificity reasonably appears to be a complete agreement, it is taken to be an integrated agreement unless it is established by other evidence that the writing did not constitute a final expression.

Section 213. Effect of Integrated Agreement on Prior Agreements (Parol Evidence Rule)

(1) A binding integrated agreement discharges prior agreements to the extent that it is inconsistent with them.

(2) A binding completely integrated agreement discharges prior agreements to the extent that they are within its scope. . . .

Comment: . . .

b. Inconsistent terms. Whether a binding agreement is completely integrated or partially integrated, it supersedes inconsistent terms of prior agreements. To apply this rule, the court must make preliminary determinations that there is an integrated agreement and that it is inconsistent with the terms in question. See § 209. Those determinations are made in accordance with all relevant evidence, and require interpretation both of the integrated agreement and of the prior agreement. . . . [T]he integrated agreement must be given a meaning to which its language is reasonably susceptible when read in the light of all the circumstances.

Illustrations: . . .

2. A orally agrees to sell a city lot to B. The city is installing a sidewalk in front of the lot, and A orally agrees to pay the cost to be assessed by the city in an amount not exceeding $45. B then retains a lawyer to draw up a written agreement, and A and B execute it, A without reading it. The agreement provides that A will pay all costs of the installation of the sidewalk, but does not mention any dollar limit. If the written agreement is a binding integrated agreement, any agreement for a $45 limit is discharged.

Section 214. Evidence of Prior or Contemporaneous Agreements and Negotiations

Agreements and negotiations prior to or contemporaneous with the adoption of a writing are admissible in evidence to establish

(a) that the writing is or is not an integrated agreement;

(b) that the integrated agreement, if any, is completely or partially integrated;

(c) the meaning of the writing, whether or not integrated;

(d) illegality, fraud, duress, mistake, lack of consideration, or other invalidating cause;

(e) ground for granting or denying rescission, reformation, specific performance, or other remedy.

Section 216. Consistent Additional Terms

(1) Evidence of a consistent additional term is admissible to supplement an integrated agreement unless the court finds that the agreement was completely integrated.

(2) An agreement is not completely integrated if the writing omits a consistent additional agreed term which is

(a) agreed to for separate consideration, or

(b) such a term as in the circumstances might naturally be omitted from the writing.

Comment: . . .

b. Consistency. . . . The determination whether an alleged additional term is consistent or inconsistent with the integrated agreement requires interpretation of the writing in the light of all the circumstances, including the evidence of the additional term. For this purpose, the meaning of the writing includes not only the terms explicitly stated but also those fairly implied as part of the bargain of the parties in fact. It does not include a term supplied by a rule of law designed to fill gaps where the parties have not agreed otherwise, unless it can be inferred that the parties contracted with reference to the rule of law. . . .

e. Written term excluding oral terms ("merger" clause). Written agreements often contain clauses stating that there are no representations, promises or agreements between the parties except those found in the writing. Such a clause . . . if agreed to is likely to conclude the issue whether the agreement is completely integrated. Consistent additional terms may then be excluded even though their omission would have been natural in the absence of such a clause. But such a clause does not control the question whether the writing was assented to as an integrated agreement. . . .

————

Interform Co. v. Mitchell
575 F.2d 1270, 1275–1277 (9th Cir.1978)

The court observed that: "One view is to treat the writing as having a unique and quite compelling force. . . . The writing becomes the focus of attention and the judge by assuming the function of a reasonable person determines whether the writing did supersede all previous undertakings and, if so, its meaning to a reasonable person situated as [were the parties to the writing.] Williston §§ 616–17. An integrated writing clear in meaning to the reasonable person constitutes the contract between the parties. In this manner the judge can fix the legal relations of the parties without aid of a jury and provide a measure of security to written agreements. . . .

"Another, and opposing view, imparts to the writing no unique or compelling force. A writing is integrated when the parties intend it to be and it means what they intended it to mean. Corbin on Contracts § 581 at 442, § 582 at 448–57, § 583 at 485 (1960). . . . In theory, therefore, integration may be lacking even if the additional terms ordinarily and naturally would have been included in the writing and an integrated writing can have a meaning to which a reasonably intelligent person, situated as described above, could not subscribe. Corbin § 544 at 145–46. Again, in theory, this view accords the jury, when the trial employs one, a potentially larger role in the process of fixing contractual relations and provides somewhat less security to written agreements. . . .

"It is unlikely that any jurisdiction will inflexibly adopt one approach to the exclusion of the other; each is likely to influence the conduct of judges and the disposition of cases. However, it must be acknowledged that the influence of Corbin's way is stronger now, . . . than when he and Williston grappled during the drafting of the American Law Institute's first Restatement of Contracts. . . .

"Moreover, [the UCC 2–202] reflects Corbin's influence. It precludes contradiction of 'confirmatory memoranda' by prior or contemporaneous oral agreements when the writing was '*intended* by the parties as a final expression of their agreement' and permits the introduction of consistent additional terms 'unless the court finds the writing to have been *intended* also as a complete and exclusive statement of the terms of the agreement.' (Italics added). The focus plainly is on the intention of the parties, not the integration practices of reasonable persons acting normally and naturally."

————

COMMENT: *THE UCC'S PAROL EVIDENCE RULE*

As Judge Sneed noted in Interform Co. v. Mitchell, it is widely believed that the UCC's formulation of the parol evidence rule reflects Corbin's view that the integration issue is essentially a matter of "intention"—that is, a writing finalizes only what the parties intend it to finalize. Section 2–202 provides:

> Terms with respect to which the confirmatory memoranda of the parties agree or which are otherwise set forth in a writing intended by the parties as a final expression of their agreement with respect to such terms as are included therein may not be contradicted by evidence of any prior agreement or of a contemporaneous oral agreement but may be explained or supplemented
>
> (a) by course of dealing or usage of trade (Section 1–205) or by course of performance (Section 2–208); and
>
> (b) by evidence of consistent additional terms unless the court finds the writing to have been intended also as a complete and exclusive statement of the terms of the agreement.

One assertion commonly heard is that § 2–202 reverses the presumption of general contract law that a writing apparently complete on its face is to be deemed a fully integrated agreement. E.g., Century Ready–Mix Co. v. Lower & Co., 770 P.2d 692, 697 (Wyo.1989) ("the [UCC] parol evidence rule is intended to liberalize the rigidity of the common law and to eliminate the presumption that a written contract is a total integration"). Does the text of 2–202 support that assertion? If it is true that this statute generally lowers barriers to proof of the parties' bargain in fact, it becomes important to know whether the section retains any narrowing tests or concepts. The *Luria Bros.* decision, digested below, speaks to that issue.

As we will see, UCC 2–202 can be raised in a great variety of transactions, including dealings between consumers and merchants. Sales practices in the merchandising of consumer goods usually involve the giving of "assurances" concerning the quality and performance of the goods and the responsibility of the seller for nonperformance. There may even be express promises or representations of fact. The purchaser who decides to buy on credit is typically asked to sign a standardized installment-sales contract and, perhaps, a detachable, negotiable promissory note. The contract commonly contains a "disclaimer" clause (stating that no warranties have been made other than those that appear in the written agreement) and an "integration" clause (stating that the writing embraces the parties' entire agreement). An example of such a transaction (and of the readiness of courts to protect consumer-buyers from a seller's untrue or fraudulent misrepresentations) is provided in Hull–Dobbs, Inc. v. Mallicoat, 57 Tenn.App. 100, 415 S.W.2d 344 (1966). Also, it should be stressed that the presence of a merger clause—generally, and in goods cases falling under the Code—is not conclusive on whether the parties intended an integration, "especially when the contract is a preprinted form drawn by a sophisticated seller and presented to the buyer without any real negotiation." Sierra Diesel Injection Service, Inc. v. Burroughs Corp., 890 F.2d 108, 112 (9th Cir.1989). If, however, the parties are experienced business people, or if they have put the terms of a complex transaction in a detailed writing, the effect given a merger clause in resolving the integration question may well be different. E.g., Bushendorf v. Freightliner Corp., 13 F.3d 1024 (7th Cir.1993) (dealer's oral express warranty that "a 425 engine is 425 horsepower" for a semitractor truck costing $67,000, given in precontractual negotiations but not repeated in written agreement which contained integration clause, is extinguished by UCC 2–202, even though engine produced only 315 horsepower).

There is reason to believe that the UCC alters the consumer's disadvantage and makes it easier for the buyer to show in court the oral representations or promises that led to the purchase. Can you identify anything in the language of § 2–202 pointing in this direction? Travel Craft v. Wilhelm Mende GmbH & Co., 552 N.E.2d 443 (Ind.1990), is representative of one line of attack ("when parties create a complete and exclusive statement on *limited terms,* parol evidence [respecting those terms] is still admissible if it is explanatory or supplemental"). See also Webcor Electronics v. Home Electronics, 231 Mont. 377, 754 P.2d 491 (1988) (seller's employee "made promises far beyond what purchase order was ever intended to address and writing was obviously not intended to be final expression of the agreement"). The approach in Husky Spray Service, Inc. v. Patzer, 471 N.W.2d 146 (S.D.1991), is perhaps even more representative:

> [T]he fact that the written agreement contains a disclaimer of warranties does not preclude evidence of an oral warranty. Where the express representations made by the seller are claimed to be inconsistent with the form language of the contract, parol evidence may be admitted to determine whether the written contract is a fi-

nal expression of the parties' agreement and whether the warranty, or disclaimer thereof, was part of the bargain explicitly negotiated between the parties. See [UCC 2–202]. . . . [T]he essential [legal] inquiry, i.e., whether the disclaimer was explicitly negotiated between the parties, requires that extrinsic evidence be admitted to determine the validity of an attempted disclaimer of warranties under [UCC 2–316]. In this case, the trial court [correctly] found that the exclusion of express warranties was never expressly bargained for and the language used in the contract failed to state with particularity the specific qualities and characteristics of the [product] that were being disclaimed.

On consumer-product warranty law generally, including the contributions of the federal Magnuson–Moss Warranty Act of 1975 (15 U.S.C. §§ 2301–2312), see Braucher, An Informal Resolution Model of Consumer Product Warranty Law, 1985 Wis.L.Rev. 1405. Magnuson–Moss imposes on suppliers who give a "written warranty" various substantive obligations ranging from disclosure to remedies (e.g., clear and unmistakable language, and a replacement or a refund remedy for continuing defects under a "full warranty"). The Act, similar in some respects to state "lemon laws" covering new automobiles, can be avoided altogether by not providing a warranty in writing. That is the point to be stressed: Magnusson–Moss does not require manufacturers—or anyone else in the chain of production and distribution—to issue warranties. But if they do so, in writing, they must meet the Act's requirements. See generally, DiCintio v. DaimlerChrysler Corp., 97 N.Y.2d 463, 768 N.E.2d 1121 (N.Y.2002).

———————

Luria Bros. & Co. v. Pielet Bros. Scrap Iron & Metal, Inc.
600 F.2d 103 (7th Cir.1979)

Through conversations and an exchange of confirming forms, Pielet contracted to sell a large quantity of scrap steel to Luria. Pielet wholly failed to perform and Luria sued for damages, recovering a judgment for $600,000 in the trial court. Pielet defended the suit by urging that the contract was expressly conditioned upon its obtaining the scrap metal from a particular supplier. In an offer of proof at trial, Pielet's vice-president testified that in his first conversation with Luria's vice-president he had said, "I was doing business with people that I had never heard of, that they were fly-by-night people, that I was worried about shipment and if I didn't get shipment, I didn't want any big hassle, but if I got the scrap, [Luria] would get it." The trial court ruled this evidence inadmissible under UCC 2–202. *Held*, this ruling was correct; judgment affirmed. Pielet's own confirmation form, stating "[t]his order constitutes the entire agreement between the parties," brings § 2–202 into play. "Having found § 2–202 applicable, the next question is whether the excluded evidence contradicts or is inconsistent with the terms of the writings. Pielet argues that the offered testimony did not 'contradict' but instead 'explained or supplemented' the writings with 'consistent additional terms.'" For this contention, Pielet relies upon Hunt Foods & Indus., Inc. v. Doliner, 26 A.D.2d 41, 270 N.Y.S.2d 937 (1966). . . . *Hunt* held that evidence of an oral condition precedent did not contradict the terms of a written stock option which was unconditional on its face. Therefore evidence of the condition precedent should not have been barred by § 2–202. . . . "To be inconsistent the term must 'contradict or negate a term of the writing.' Id. at 43, 270 N.Y.S.2d at 940. This reasoning in *Hunt* was followed in Michael Schiavone & Sons, Inc. v. Securalloy Co., 312 F.Supp. 801 (D.Conn.1970)[,] [where] the court found that parol evidence that the quantity in a sales contract was 'understood to be up to 500 tons' cannot be said to be inconsistent with the terms of the written contract which specified the quantity of 500 Gross Ton."

"The narrow view of inconsistency espoused in these two cases has been criticized. In Snyder v. Herbert Greenbaum & Assoc., Inc., 38 Md.App. 144, 380 A.2d 618 (1977), the court held that parol evidence of a contractual right to unilateral rescission was inconsistent with a written agreement for the sale and installation of carpeting. The court defined 'inconsistency' as used in § 2–202(b) as 'the absence of reasonable harmony in terms of the language *and* respective obligations of the parties.' Id. at 623. . . .

"We adopt this latter view of inconsistency and reject the view expressed in *Hunt*. Where writings intended by the parties to be final expression of their agreement call for an unconditional sale of goods, parol evidence that the seller's obligations are conditioned upon receiving the goods from a particular supplier is inconsistent and must be excluded. Had there been some additional reference such as 'per our conversation' on the written confirmation indicating that oral agreements were meant to be incorporated into the writing, the result might have been different. . . .

"We also note that Comment 3 of the Official Comment to § 2–202 provides, among other things: 'If the additional terms are such that, if agreed upon, they would certainly have been included in the document in the view of the court, then evidence of their alleged making must be kept from the trier of fact.' Pielet makes much of the fact that this transaction was an unusual one due to the size and the amount of scrap involved. Surely a term relieving Pielet of its obligations under the contract in the event its supplier failed it would have been included in the Pielet sales confirmation."

Long Island Trust Co. v. International Inst. for Packaging Educ., Ltd.

Court of Appeals of New York, 1976.
38 N.Y.2d 493, 381 N.Y.S.2d 445, 344 N.E.2d 377.

JASEN, J. In this action on a promissory note, [the question] is whether the appellants, individual guarantors of a corporate obligation, may interpose as a defense on the guarantee an alleged oral agreement that the guarantee would not become effective until the payee procured the guarantee of other specific persons as coguarantors. . . . [P]laintiff bank, the holder of the note and the one in whose favor the guarantee ran, argues that the appellants produced no evidence which, if fully accepted, would establish conditional delivery of the endorsed note in suit, but, in any event, asserts that the defense of conditional delivery is not available, as a matter of law, to the appellants.

Special Term granted the bank summary judgment on the grounds that the alleged conditional statement was insufficient notice to the bank and that even if it were sufficient notice, "public policy estops the defendants from showing that a note made payable and delivered to a bank was not to be enforced unless there was compliance with certain oral conditions." The Appellate Division, two Justices dissenting, affirmed.

On March 4, 1970, the bank loaned to defendant International Institute $25,000 for a period of 90 days. A promissory note delivered to the bank for this loan was endorsed by five guarantors, Raymond D'Onofrio, defendants James W. Feeney and Robert Goldberg, and appellants Marty Rochman and Sidney Horowitz. At the time of the making of the loan, Rochman claims that he discussed with George Dean, an officer of the bank, the conditions upon which he would endorse the note and procure Horowitz' endorsement. It was agreed, claims Rochman, that the note would be endorsed by the five aforementioned persons and that any renewal of the note would also require the endorsement of the same five individuals. On June 2, 1970, the bank agreed to renew the loan for another 30 days and to loan an additional $10,000. Rochman delivered a new note, which he and Horowitz had both endorsed, to William Lambui, an officer of the bank, and allegedly told him "to make sure that all the endorsements were on the Note." Although the note was also endorsed by Feeney and Goldberg, D'Onofrio never endorsed it. Nevertheless, the bank extended the loan for 30 days and advanced to the International Institute the additional $10,000. When the loan was not repaid, the bank instituted this action against International Institute and the four guarantors, Rochman, Horowitz, Feeney and Goldberg.

On this appeal Horowitz and Rochman contend that, by virtue of the agreement they made with bank officer Dean, their delivery of the June 2 note was conditional upon the procurement of the endorsement by D'Onofrio, and that, since this endorsement was not obtained by the bank, the note is unenforceable as to them. As we view it, this case involves the questions of whether Horowitz and Rochman may attempt to prove such an agreement by resort to parol evidence, and, if so, whether this agreement, if proved, would bar enforcement of the note as to them. Since we would answer both questions affirmatively, we would reverse the order of the Appellate Division and deny the motion for summary judgment.

[In an omitted passage, the court observed that Article 3 of the UCC, §§ 3–305 and 3–306 dealing with commercial paper, had carried forward the defense of "conditional delivery" and made it available against a bank in the circumstances present here.]

Even before the enactment of the [UCC], it had long been the rule that where the terms of the conditional delivery have not been complied with, the instrument is unenforceable and parol evidence is admissible to show that the delivery of the instrument to the payee was a conditional delivery. . . . Among the conditions precedent which may be proved by parol evidence is that the instrument was not to take effect until the payee had procured other signatures. . . . Thus, an agreement that any renewal notes would be endorsed by all of the original endorsers is provable by use of parol evidence, and, if proved, would make the note unenforceable against the guarantors whose delivery was conditional upon the procurement of all such endorsements.

In granting summary judgment to the bank, Special Term [stated] that "public policy estops the defendants from showing that a note made payable and delivered to a bank was not to be enforced unless there was compliance with certain oral conditions. (Mount Vernon Trust Co. v. Bergoff, 272 N.Y. 192, 196 [5 N.E.2d 196, 197])." While *Mount Vernon Trust Co.* did express a public policy concern that bank examiners might be deceived by an unenforceable note which appears on its face to be an asset of a bank, that case involved a totally fictitious note which was never intended to be enforced. . . . Special Term's reliance on *Mount Vernon Trust Co.* could be read as supporting a view that the public policy expressed therein would prevent the maker or guarantor of a note held by a bank from ever raising any defenses to that note. This, of course, is not what was intended in that case, and it would be completely contrary to law. ([UCC], § 3–306.)

Nor does Meadow Brook Nat. Bank v. Bzura, 20 A.D.2d 287, 246 N.Y.S.2d 787, suggest a different result. At first blush, that case seems nearly identical to this. There a guarantor unsuccessfully sought to defeat a motion for summary judgment by claiming that he signed the guarantee only after he was promised by a bank officer that the guarantee would not become effective unless and until a primary guarantee was first obtained from two other persons. Of vital significance in that case was the nature of the guarantee upon which the lender sought to recover. The Appellate Division described a portion of the guarantee as follows: "The guarantee provided that the guarantor 'unconditionally guarantees to the Bank' the payment of indebtedness incurred by the company" (p. 288, 246 N.Y.S.2d p. 788). Thus, the alleged condition precedent in that case contradicted the express terms of the written agreement, and could therefore not be proved by parol evidence. (Hicks v. Bush, 10 N.Y.2d 488, 225 N.Y.S.2d 34, 180 N.E.2d 425.) What distinguishes *Meadow Brook Nat. Bank* from this case is that the guarantee here is not unconditional. The condition precedent which is alleged here, namely, the procurance of other endorsements, in no way contradicts the express terms of the written agreement and, therefore, it may be proved by parol evidence. We agree with our dissenting colleague that we should not misunderstand and misapply the parol evidence rule so as to "undermine the rules of commercial and banking conduct." Likewise, we share his concern that we should not permit the exceptions to the parol evidence rule to become "the haven of either the devious or the negligent." However, such concerns do not warrant a different result here. Our holding today does not sanction the use of "devious devices of the untrustworthy who can always conceive a less than flat contradiction to avoid their written obligations." There is no basis in the record for characterizing the appellants as "untrustworthy," "devious," or "negligent." Had the bank here merely insisted that appellant "unconditionally guarantee" repayment of the loan, as was done in *Meadow Brook Nat. Bank*, then there would be no room for the "untrustworthy" or even the trustworthy to assert a "less than flat contradiction" of the express terms of the agreement. Our task is not to assist lending institutions in their collection matters by rewriting their agreements so as to remedy the omissions made by their draftsmen.

Accordingly, we would reverse the order of the Appellate Division and deny the motion for summary judgment.

BREITEL, C.J. (dissenting). I would affirm [the] Appellate Division, thus precluding defendants from establishing by oral testimony that they are not bound by their written endorsement and guarantee. . . .

The ultimate principle is a simple one, namely, that an integrated written obligation may not be avoided by the tender of parol, usually oral, evidence which contradicts or varies the written obligation. The great and hoary exception is that a party is always free to establish by parol evidence that the written undertaking by which he is apparently bound, never came into existence because of an agreed precondition that it not take effect unless and until the extraneous precondition has come to pass. The great and hoary exception has its own exception, namely, that it is inapplicable if the proffered parol evidence itself contradicts or varies the terms of the written undertaking sought to be avoided. In short, the precondition must be consistent with the written undertaking.

Illustratively, if one agrees to guarantee a debt unconditionally, it is not an admissible precondition that the guarantee was indeed not unconditional but depended upon some extraneous event or undertaking by another. . . . Sometimes, as in the *Meadow Brook* case, the inconsistency will be a flat contradiction; other times it will be that the inconsistency would be a variance, as in Metropolitan Bank of Syracuse v. Brennan, 48 A.D.2d 254, 368 N.Y.S.2d 914. It is to ignore the principle and the appendant rules to assume that only explicitly contradictory oral preconditions are precluded.

The principle and the appendant rules are parallel and indeed share an analytical genesis with the parol evidence rule, a rule of substantive law and not of evidence (Restatement, Contracts, § 237, comment *a*). To misunderstand them and therefore to misapply them is to undermine the rules of commercial and banking conduct, and to suffer the devious devices of the untrustworthy who can always conceive a less than flat contradiction to avoid their written obligations.

In the *Metropolitan Bank* case (supra), a twin to this one, Mr. Justice Simons . . . applied with clarity the distinctions, in striking down the alleged oral preconditions to effective delivery of the defendant's guarantee. Thus he said (48 A.D.2d 254, at 256–257, 368 N.Y.S.2d at 916): . . .

"Manifestly, the note became a binding obligation as between the bank and the corporation. Defendants do not deny that they signed it—what they really suggest is that notwithstanding those facts and conceding the parties' performance on the instrument, they may still vary the terms of their personal obligation by parol evidence. The rule is stated in Hicks v. Bush, supra 10 N.Y.2d 488, 491[:] 'Parol testimony is admissible to prove a condition precedent to the legal effectiveness of a written agreement . . . if the condition does not contradict the express terms of such written agreement. . . . A certain disparity is inevitable, of course, whenever a written promise is, by oral agreement of the parties, made conditional upon an event not expressed in the writing. Quite obviously, though, the parol evidence rule does not bar proof of every orally established condition precedent, but only of those which in a real sense contradict the terms of the written agreement. (See, e.g., Illustration to Restatement, Contracts, § 241.)'. . . ."

Never has there been a failure, when the rules are properly analyzed, to preclude varying as well as explicitly contradictory preconditions to effective delivery of the written obligation.

In determining whether the varying condition is precluded it is essential to determine the completeness of the written undertaking. . . . Key to the analysis is not whether the oral precondition is explicitly contradictory of a term of the integrated written obligation, but whether "in a real sense" it contradicts (and thus varies) the terms of the obligation. . . . [In this case, the] endorsement and guarantee clauses to which defendant endorsers appended their signatures read as follows:

"FOR VALUE RECEIVED, the undersigned and each of the undersigned in addition to the obligations imposed by endorsement and waiving of notice of every character and nature, hereby become a party to, adopt, agree to, accept, guarantee and assume all the terms, conditions and waivers contained in the note on the reverse side hereof, and guarantee the payment of said note when due and consent without notice of any kind to any and all extensions of time made by the holder of said note.

"Nothing except cash payment to the Trust Company and/or the holder of said note shall release the undersigned or any of the undersigned."

It is not necessary to emphasize how "contradictory" defendants' present contentions and proffered oral evidence are to the terms of the endorsement and guarantee, especially the second paragraph, set forth above. . . .

[Two judges joined in the dissent; the vote was 4 to 3.]

QUESTION

Is the defense of "conditional delivery" distinguishable in principle from the sham-transaction defense used successfully in New York Trust Co. v. Island Oil & Transport Corp., supra p. 303?

———

NOTE: ORAL CONDITIONS

A classic statement of "conditional delivery" can be found in White Showers v. Fischer, 278 Mich. 32, 270 N.W. 205 (1936):

> It is sometimes difficult to make a clear distinction between an attempt to alter, vary, contradict, or add to a written agreement by parol, and a showing by oral testimony that a writing was never intended to bind the parties unless a condition precedent was fulfilled. No attempt was made [here] to alter, vary, contradict, or add to the writing, but oral testimony was offered in support of the proposition that there never was a contract. The distinction is real and not merely academic. [Here] there was manual delivery of a writing which embraced all the provisions of the agreement, if there was a contract; but [defendant says] that whether the contract was to come into being . . . depended upon the fulfillment of a condition precedent. The written stipulation of the order which states "this covers all agreements" presupposes a binding contract inasmuch as only a binding contract could give life to the stipulation. Without such a contract, there is nothing to which the stipulation could be attached. . . . It cannot be used to give life to something which had not as yet come into being.

Suppose a buyer of goods, planning to open a retail store, signs a purchase order with a supplier, depositing $10,000 on the $50,000 of inventory the supplier is to deliver 90 days later. The agreement provides: "This order is NOT subject to cancellation. If Buyer fails to perform as specified herein, the amount paid with this order may be retained by Seller and credited to any damages sustained by it by reason of such default." Assume further that the buyer, unable to finance the planned venture after considerable effort, cancels the purchase order and sues to recover the $10,000 paid down, offering to prove that at the time of signing it was orally agreed that buyer's procurement of an SBA-approved loan in the amount of $75,000 was a "condition of the purchase order's becoming effective as a contract."

Given the opinions in *Long Island Trust Co.*, is it likely Chief Judge Breitel would admit this evidence? Would Judge Jasen find it to be a forbidden "contradiction" of the writing? More to the point, should the outcome depend on whether the offered oral evidence is found to be a condition of the purchase order's effectiveness or a condition of the buyer's duty to go forward with the deal?

Long ago, Corbin wrote the following (3 A. Corbin § 589):

> It has often been said that there is a distinction between a "conditional delivery" of a written contract and a contract that is itself conditional; that oral proof of the conditional delivery is admissible, but oral proof that the contract itself was agreed to be conditional is not admissible. This difference is an illusion. To deliver a written contract subject to a parol condition has identically the same meaning and effect as to deliver unconditionally a written contract that by its own terms makes the promises therein subject to the same condition.

What is the basis for Corbin's assertion that the conventional distinction "is an illusion"? It seems necessary to ask whether there is something special or unusual about oral "conditions"—whether, in this context, there is reason to discard the working notion that a consistent additional term naturally omitted from a writing is provable in court.

————

THE FRAUD EXCEPTION—TORT AND CONTRACT

We have seen something of the overlap of tort and contract—e.g., attempts to establish tort liability for nonperformance of a contract. The concern now is the special tort of fraud (called "deceit" at common law). The case of Hargrave v. Oki Nursery, Inc., 636 F.2d 897 (2d Cir. 1980), is representative of the way in which the fraud issue arises in bargaining transactions. Plaintiffs, operators of a vineyard, brought suit against Oki, a seller of grape vines. The complaint alleged that Oki had represented to plaintiffs that the vines it sold would be healthy, free of disease, and suitable for producing wine grapes; that plaintiffs had relied on these representations in purchasing vines from Oki; that the representations were knowingly false; and that the vines sold to plaintiffs were in fact diseased and incapable of bearing fruit of adequate quality or quantity for plaintiffs' commercial wine production.

In defending a judgment of dismissal entered below, Oki argued that the complaint failed to allege any "tortious act" since plaintiffs, by invoking the fraud label, may not convert what is essentially a claim for breach of a contractual representation into a tort claim. Oki's argument elicited this response from the reviewing court:

> The law of torts and the law of contracts are said to protect different interests. . . . A plaintiff may recover in contract because the defendant has made an agreement, and the law thinks it desirable that he be held to that agreement. Tort liability is imposed on the basis of some social policy that disapproves the infliction of a specific kind of harm irrespective of any agreement. Specifically, the law of

fraud seeks to protect against injury those who rely to their detriment on the deliberately dishonest statements of another.

Thus, it does not follow that because acts constitute a breach of contract they cannot also give rise to liability in tort. Where the conduct alleged breaches a legal duty which exists "independent of contractual relations between the parties" a plaintiff may sue in tort. . . . If the only interest at stake is that of holding the defendant to a promise, the courts have said that the plaintiff may not transmogrify the contract claim into one for tort. [Citing cases.] But if in addition there is an interest in protecting the plaintiff from other kinds of harm, the plaintiff may recover in tort whether or not he has a valid claim for breach of contract.

In the present case the complaint sets forth all the elements of an action in tort for fraudulent representations, namely, "representation of a material existing fact, falsity, scienter, deception and injury." . . . [I]f Oki indeed made the fraudulent representations "it is subject to liability *in tort* whether the agreement is enforceable or not."

As the *Hargrave* court suggests, it is customary to equate fraud with misrepresentation, and probably most frauds involve misrepresentation. Still, the means for deceiving or cheating another can involve conduct other than deliberately false or misleading statements of fact. So "fraud" is a generic term, broader than misrepresentation, its typical core element. Similarly, as we shall see, the tort of misrepresentation is broader than the tort of fraudulent misrepresentation. Sometimes—such as when one party owes a fiduciary duty to another or has a special relationship with another—the misrepresentation tort encompasses statements that are made negligently, even innocently.

The case below, Lipsit v. Leonard, opens up the difficulties encountered when fraud is "promissory" in nature and the defendant raises a contractual defense to the tort action. It may be helpful to recall some territory already visited—the promise-misrepresentation distinction in the context of the "reliance issue" (Goodman v. Dicker and accompanying materials, pp. 283–285) and the element of the antecedent lie, found missing from the representations in Hoffman v. Red Owl Stores (p. 286). It is also necessary to stress that fraud in the sense of deliberate deceit has come to occupy in our law a classification higher on the scale of wrongdoing than simple breach of contract, a classification perhaps just short of criminal activity. Hence it has been customary to impose a higher evidentiary standard for claims of fraud, usually "clear and convincing" proofs.

Lipsit v. Leonard

Supreme Court of New Jersey, 1974.
64 N.J. 276, 315 A.2d 25.

PER CURIAM. This case derives from an employment relationship from September 1961 to January 1969 between plaintiff as employee and defendants as employer. (The individual defendant Leonard, as sole proprietor of a New York business, was the employer between 1961 and the end of

1967, at which time the business was incorporated in New York, the individual defendant owning all the stock, and the corporate defendant became the employer.) The employment arrangement consisted of a series of annual letter agreements.

Plaintiff's claim is that these agreements were accompanied by specific oral promises of the individual defendant, first made to induce him to leave his former employment and enter into the first agreement and renewed thereafter as an inducement to continue his employment, that he would be given an equity interest in the business in consideration of past and future services. The written agreements go no further than to say, in the language of the most explicit of them (covering the year 1964), that "it is understood and agreed that if the relationship between Lipsit and Leonard is mutually satisfactory, a more permanent relationship involving partial ownership, profit sharing, or other incentive plan shall be developed, on a mutually acceptable basis, and put into effect at the end of this contract (Dec. 31, 1964) or sooner; if deemed desirable to do so." Nothing was done by the employer to further this expression of intent until 1968 when a proposal was made to plaintiff which, after some negotiation, he found unacceptable as fiscally impossible from his standpoint. His services were thereafter terminated at the beginning of 1969.

Plaintiff's theories of action, presumably in the alternative although not so stated, are that there resulted a breach of contract based on the oral promises giving rise to a cause of action therefor, as well as a tort claim based on fraud. The latter is spelled out in the complaint in this fashion: "[I]t is clear that Defendant's design from the beginning was to misrepresent and fraudulently obtain the services of Plaintiff through promises of equity and ownership and then attempted to give Plaintiff the equity ownership under a situation that made it impossible for Plaintiff to accept same." In other words, the fraud charge is that Leonard never intended to keep the oral promises at the time he made them, which amounted to a misrepresentation of an existing fact, and therefore there was fraud in the inducement to enter into the several employment agreements.

The rather inartistic complaint . . . seeks relief on both contract and tort theories. For breach of contract, money damages are sought to the amount of 10% of the assets of the business to be valued by an independent appraiser plus "further reasonable damages for Defendant's arbitrary breach of agreement in failing to give Plaintiff what Defendant had agreed to do." In tort, "reasonable damages" are asked "for the fraud and misrepresentations of the Defendant." Punitive as well as compensatory damages are asked for. . . .

Defendants moved for summary judgment upon the entire complaint. . . This meant that they, although denying any oral promises in the answers, took the position that, assuming for purposes of the motion that everything plaintiff alleged and asserted was true and that therefore there was no issue as to any material fact, . . . they were entitled to judgment as a matter of law.

Both sides correctly agreed that New York substantive law governed the case, both on the contract and tort theories. . . . The employment agreements related to a New York business, they, as well as the alleged oral promises, were made and to be performed there and that state certainly was the "center of gravity" of the matter. The suit happened to be brought in New Jersey because both plaintiff and the individual defendant resided here. . . .

The Law Division judge granted defendants' motion, resulting in a dismissal of the entire complaint, in a thorough letter opinion, which judgment the Appellate Division affirmed in an unreported *per curiam* for the reasons expressed below. . . .

The trial court, relying on New York law throughout, was so clearly correct in giving judgment for defendants on the contract cause of action and the miscellaneous claims that any extended discussion is not required. It held in effect that the previously referred to language of intent in the various employment agreements with respect to an equity interest in the business did not reach the level of a contract and constituted at best only an unenforceable agreement to consider and negotiate. It further held that the alleged oral promises were inadmissible under the parol evidence rule (actually a rule of substantive law in the present context) and so that plaintiff could not establish any contract or breach thereof based thereon. . . .

As to the tort cause of action in fraud, the trial judge found it also to be barred under New York law by the parol evidence rule, for the expressed reason that otherwise the rule would be emasculated by simply sounding an action in fraud, when recovery could not be had in breach of contract action on the same facts in which the rule would prevent the admission in evidence of the necessary oral proofs to establish the contract sought to be enforced. The trial court erred here, perhaps because there was apparently not presented to it the New York rule on the available relief and proper measure of damages in an action grounded upon fraud in the inducement for a contract.

. . . [T]he rule is well established that, as Dean Prosser puts it: "A promise, which carries an implied representation that there is a present intention to carry it out, is recognized everywhere as a proper basis for reliance. . . . All but a few courts regard a misstatement of a present intention as a misrepresentation of a material fact; and a promise without the intent to perform it is held to be a sufficient basis for an action of deceit or for restitution or other equitable relief. Prosser, Torts (4th ed. 1971) § 109, pp. 728–729." There is no doubt that New York recognizes such a basis for a cause of action in fraud. Sabo v. Delman, 3 N.Y.2d 155, 164 N.Y.S.2d 714, 143 N.E.2d 906 (1957). . . .

The question is, of course, whether the action can be maintained when the promise itself cannot be enforced, "as where it is without consideration, is illegal, is barred by the statute of frauds, or the statute of limitations, or [as here] falls within the parol evidence rule, or a disclaimer of representations." Prosser, supra, pp. 729–730. As to the effect of the parol evidence rule, New York allows such an action to be maintained and parol evidence to be introduced where the relief sought is rescission or restitution, i.e., repudiation or avoidance of the contract as distinct from affirmation and enforcement of it. [Sabo v. Delman, supra.]

More pertinent to the instant case, New York clearly further allows, in line with the majority of states, an action in tort for money damages, as distinct from one grounded in breach of contract, based upon oral fraudulent promises and misrepresentations which induced the written agreement and permits parol evidence to establish the same. The parol evidence rule is no bar. [See e.g.,] Danann Realty Corp. v. Harris, 5 N.Y.2d 317, 184 N.Y.S.2d 599, 157 N.E.2d 597 (1959); Hanlon v. Macfadden Publications, Inc., 302 N.Y. 502, 99 N.E.2d 546 (1951). . . .

But New York has long adhered to the view that in actions for money damages for fraud in the inducement, the measure of damages is indemnity for the actual pecuniary loss sustained as a direct result of the wrong—the "out of pocket" rule—as distinct from the "loss or benefit of the bargain" rule employed by many jurisdictions in the same situation which is akin to the measure allowed if the action were for breach of the contract. In other words, the contract, with the addition of the oral promises or representations, cannot be enforced in a tort action in fraud for money damages. . . .

Hanlon v. Macfadden Publications, [supra], is particularly analogous to the situation at bar. There plaintiff employee was induced to accept a lower rate of compensation (commissions) for his services on the basis of fraudulent representations made by the defendant employer. The Court of Appeals said:

> The measure of damages in an action for deceit is firmly established. Plaintiff is entitled to indemnity for the actual pecuniary loss sustained as a direct result of the wrong. . . . The instant case, while unusual on its facts, clearly calls for the application of this general rule. Plaintiff, of course, was not induced to part with any tangible object such as land, chattels or money as in the typical case of deceit. Instead, he parted with personal services. He was induced to render those services for a price fraudulently lowered. In the ordinary case of deceit, the measure of damage would be "the difference between the value of the thing bought, sold or exchanged and its purchase price or the value of the thing exchanged for it." (Restatement, Torts, § 549.) The only distinction in the present case is that the jury was required to calculate the value of the plaintiff's services instead of the value of the "thing bought, sold or exchanged." The true measure of damages here is the difference between the value of the plaintiff's services and the price he was actually paid for them by reason of defendant's deceit. . . . (99 N.E.2d at 551).

Defendants apparently agree . . . that the above accurately represents the state of New York law, but say that plaintiff throughout has not sought such damages but rather an amount equal to the value of 10% of the assets of the business—a measure they say would be allowable only under the benefit of the bargain rule. While this appears to be true, the fact that plaintiff may have proceeded under a mistaken view as to the proper measure of damages is not a fatal defect. . . . The complaint and the prayer for damages on the fraud claim are sufficiently broad to permit the proper theory to be advanced. While plaintiff may well have a difficult time not only in establishing out of pocket damages specifically enough, but also in proving sufficiently precise oral promises of equity ownership in the business, in the light of the recitals of mere expectation in the written employment agreements which he signed, he is entitled to try if he wishes. . . .

The trial court therefore should not have granted defendants summary judgment on the tort cause of action in fraud. [Judgment modified and case remanded.]

Bank of America Nat. Trust & Sav. Ass'n v. Pendergrass
4 Cal.2d 258, 48 P.2d 659 (1935)

A bank brought an action on a promissory note for $4,750, signed by defendants and payable "on demand." Defendants' counsel offered to prove that the note and a chattel mortgage securing its payment were signed only after the bank's representatives had promised that, during the year 1932, defendants would be allowed to operate the ranch on which they grew lettuce seed, without interference; that this promise was fraudulently made without intent to perform it; and that "within a short time" after the note was signed the bank seized the property covered by the chattel mortgage. *Held*, the proof offered was inadmissible. Its effect would be to "extend or postpone" for one year the unconditional obligation, expressed in the note, to pay "on demand." Parol evidence of fraud to establish the invalidity of the instrument is admissible where it relates to some independent fact, "some fraud in the procurement of the instrument or some breach of confidence concerning its use." But parol evidence is not admissible where, as here, it would prove "a promise directly at variance with the promise of the writing." [rule]

NOTE: CONFINING PROMISSORY FRAUD

It is commonly said that claims of fraud in the inducement are not barred by the parol evidence rule. At the same time, writings in general are deemed to supersede oral statements, and it is understood that the parol evidence rule's principal purpose is to block attempts to vary the terms of a written contract. Does Bank of America v. Pendergrass look like a case in which one party, through oral testimony, is seeking to rewrite the contract? The California court apparently thought so.

The distinction applied in *Pendergrass* is often put in terms of an "extrinsic" representation or promise ("independent" in the court's language) versus something "intrinsic" ("directly at variance with the writing," says *Pendergrass*). Some courts speak of "extraneous to the contract" and "interwoven with the breach of contract." The purpose of the distinction, quite obviously, is to contain the fraud exception to the parol evidence rule. Duncan v. McCaffrey Group, Inc., 200 Cal.App.4th 346, 133 Cal.Rptr.3d 280, 296-97 (2011). In the words of another California court, the *Pendergrass* approach is "very defensible" since an unlimited doctrine of promissory fraud "allow[s] parties to litigate disputes over the meaning of contract terms armed with an arsenal of tort remedies inappropriate to the resolution of commercial disputes." Banco Do Brasil, S.A. v. Latian, Inc., 234 Cal.App.3d 973, 285 Cal.Rptr. 870 (1991). Nonetheless, a promise that is fraudulent is actionable as a tort in most states; courts employing the "direct variance" limitation—apparently originating in California—are said to be in the clear minority. They are also frequently criticized. See, e.g., Sherrodd, Inc. v. Morrison–Knudsen Co., 249 Mont. 282, 815 P.2d 1135 (1991) (Trieweiler, J., dissenting) (to hold the fraud exception inapplicable when there is a contradiction "totally defeats the purpose for which the exception was provided"); Sweet, Promissory Fraud and the Parol Evidence Rule, 49 Cal.L.Rev. 877 (1961). In deciding whether the criticism is warranted, you might consider what a court following *Pendergrass* is to do about a merger or integration clause in the contract (e.g., this agreement "supersedes any and all previous promises, representations, and agreements"). Are all claims of fraud in the inducement now "intrinsic"?

While most (but not all) states recognize a doctrine of promissory fraud, a few—most notably Illinois—have sought to limit its operation in another way, that is, by requiring the plaintiff to show that the misrepresentation of the promisor's state of mind was part of a "scheme" to defraud. In effect, fraud grounded in an unfulfilled promise, to be actionable, must be one element of an overall pattern of fraudulent acts. See, e.g., Steinberg v. Chicago Medical School, 69 Ill.2d 320, 371 N.E.2d 634 (1977). Presumably a series of unfulfilled promises would provide an evidentiary base for triggering this exception, the scope of which, to be sure, depends on the elusive definition of a "scheme."

Courts sometimes extend the reasoning underlying *Pendergrass* to contract law's other formal requirements, such as the statute of frauds. E.g., Marion Prod. Credit Ass'n v. Cochran, 40 Ohio St.3d 265, 533 N.E.2d 325 (1988) (statute of frauds defense not overcome unless proof of fraudulent inducement is "premised upon matters wholly extrinsic to the writing").

QUESTION

As the court observed in Lipsit v. Leonard, New York, in line with a substantial number of states, measures damages in fraud or deceit under the "out-of-pocket" rule, not the "loss-of-bargain" rule applied in other jurisdictions. Is the out-of-pocket measure a better match with the theory underlying an award of damages for fraud, especially when the fraud is making a promise intending not to keep it?

Sabo v. Delman

3 N.Y.2d 155, 164 N.Y.S.2d 714, 143 N.E.2d 906 (1957)

Plaintiff's complaint alleged that he had entered into a written contract providing for an assignment to defendant of plaintiff's patents on a shoe-cutting machine and providing also for a sharing of the proceeds from its use; that defendant, before the signing of the contract, had represented that he would finance the manufacture of the machine and would use his best efforts to promote its sale; that defendant made only two machines; and that defendant never intended to perform these promises and had made them "fraudulently, falsely and deceitfully." Plaintiff asked for cancellation of the contract. *Held*, it was error to dismiss the complaint. The parol evidence rule forbids proof of extrinsic evidence to contradict or vary the terms of a written instrument, so that an action in contract "to *enforce* an oral representation or promise relating to the subject matter of the contract" must fail. But here plaintiff seeks to set aside the parties' arrangements on the ground of fraud; the complaint neither asserts a breach of contract nor attempts to enforce any promise. If a promise is made with a preconceived and undisclosed intention not to perform it, there is a misrepresentation of a "material existing fact" which justifies rescission. A so-called "merger clause" in the contract, that "[n]o verbal understanding or conditions, not herein specified, shall be binding on either party," merely "furnishes another reason for applying the parol evidence rule," and, just as that rule does not block proof of fraud, a clause of this type is likewise ineffective. Otherwise, it would be possible "to perpetrate a fraud with immunity, depriving the victim of all redress," if a defendant has "the foresight to include a merger clause in the agreement." Of course, such a result, by virtue of a printed clause, is not the law.

———

LaFazia v. Howe

Supreme Court of Rhode Island, 1990.
575 A.2d 182.

FAY, C.J. This matter [is here] on the defendants' appeal from [an] order granting the plaintiff's motion for summary judgment. We affirm. . . .

The defendants, James and Theresa Howe (the Howes), entered into a contract with plaintiffs, Arthur LaFazia and Dennis Gasrow, to purchase Oaklawn Fruit & Produce (Oaklawn), a delicatessen, on July 6, 1987. . . . The Howes had no experience in the business of running a delicatessen, although they had owned a jewelry business for over twenty years.

The Howes met with plaintiffs to discuss the sale for the first time in the middle of June 1987. At that time it had been represented to them that it was an extremely profitable business, that plaintiffs had operated it for eight years, and that they were "burned out." . . . After the first meeting the Howes asked plaintiffs for the tax returns, accounts payable, and other records so they could determine the business's profitability and the amount plaintiffs were spending on inventory. The plaintiffs told the Howes that since they always paid cash and did not keep very good books, there were no records except tax returns, which, they said, did not reflect the true figures. The Howes reviewed the tax returns and had a manager of a sandwich shop with whom they were friendly review the returns as well. Relying on the information they received, they decided that this was not a viable business. The Howes met with plaintiffs again and questioned them regarding the low figures of their tax returns and their previous representation that the business brought in between $450,000 and $500,000 a year. The plaintiffs pointed out to the Howes that they both had fancy cars, lived in fancy houses, and that Dennis Gasrow supported a family with three children. James Howe said he was convinced by their representations that the tax returns did not reflect the true value of the business. . . . In addition Theresa Howe and her brother visited the store a few times before the Howes decided to purchase it and observed what appeared to be a fairly busy sandwich trade.

The Howes agreed to buy the business for $90,000. At the closing the Howes paid plaintiffs $60,000 and signed a promissory note for $30,000. The defendants were represented at the closing by their son, a Providence attorney. Included in the Memorandum of Sale were merger and disclaimer clauses:

"9. The Buyers rely on their own judgment as to the past, present or prospective volume of business or profits of the business of the Seller and does not rely on any representations of the Seller with respect to the same.

"10. No representations or warranties have been made by the Seller, or anyone in its behalf, to the Buyers as to the condition of the assets which are the subject of this sale, and it is understood and agreed that said assets are sold 'as is' at the time of sale. . . .

"12. This agreement constitutes the entire agreement between the parties hereto."

Both [Howes] do not remember reading paragraph 9 or 10 when they signed the documents at the closing. They assumed that their son had reviewed the documents beforehand.

The Howes took over the management of the business the day after the closing. James Howe stated that after approximately one month his business experience told him that "there was a problem." He spoke to plaintiffs, and they told him that in September and October, after the vacation months, business would increase. The promissory note was due in October, and the Howes, who claimed that the business had lost money from the first day, could not make the payment on time. In an attempt to keep his bargain, James Howe said he gave plaintiffs two payments for $10,000, "even though [he] knew [he] had been taken." To make matters worse, the fruit-basket business around the Christmas season did not materialize as plaintiffs had said it would. Consequently the $10,000 outstanding on the promissory note has never been paid. In February 1988 the Howes sold the business for $45,000.

On February 2, 1988, plaintiffs instituted this suit for breach of a promissory note. The Howes counterclaimed that plaintiffs made specific misrepresentations for the purpose of inducing defendants to enter into the contract. [Plaintiffs moved] for summary judgment on the claim and the counterclaim. . . . At the hearing the trial justice addressed defendants:

"I reviewed the contract in this case, and the only action left to you on your counter-claim is to prove that there was deceit; and it seems to me he gave you the tax returns. You came to an opinion that . . . the tax returns didn't justify the asking price. The provisions of the contract clearly indicate that the parties are making their own judgment.

"The contract is complete and regular on its face. I see no ability in the face of that contract for you to show a fraudulent misrepresentation. The contract d[i]sallows any representations. The parties were acting upon their own." . . .

The defendants [contend] that summary judgment was inappropriate because plaintiffs' misrepresentations raised an issue of material fact concerning whether such misrepresentations were intended to induce defendants to purchase a failing business. The defendants argue that plaintiffs' material misrepresentations, even if innocently made, were a basis for rescinding the contract. The plaintiffs [urge that] the specific disclaimer destroys the allegation in defendants' claim that the agreement had been executed in reliance on any oral representations. . . .

The trial justice came to the conclusion that defendants' only recourse on their counterclaim was an action for deceit, yet defendants argue that they are entitled to a rescission of the contract. In McGovern v. Crossley, 477 A.2d 101, 103 (R.I.1984), we stated that a person " 'who has been induced by fraud to enter into a contract may pursue either one of two remedies.' " That person "may rescind the contract or affirm the contract and sue for damages in an action for deceit." The tort claim and the claim for rescission afford alternative sources of relief in which, if one is granted, the other is withheld. . . .

This court has also ruled that the right to rescind a contract must be exercised with "reasonable promptness" after the discovery of the facts that give rise to the right. . . . The Howes attest to the fact that they discovered by October 1987, when the promissory note was due, that they had been "taken." Instead of maintaining an action for abrogation or undoing of the contract, they made $20,000's worth of payments on the contract, and a few months later, in February 1988, they sold the business. . . . [T]he Howes did not declare by word or act that the contract had been rescinded. They elected to affirm the contract instead. Even in the counterclaim . . . defendants never brought up their claim for rescission. Instead they asked for relief in the form of "costs, interest and attorney's fees as well as punitive damages." They also argued the elements of an action for deceit in the counterclaim.

In Halpert v. Rosenthal, 107 R.I. 406, 267 A.2d 730 (1970), we illustrated the difference between a claim for damages for intentional deceit and a claim for rescission. "Deceit is a tort action, and it requires some degree of culpability on the misrepresenter's part." Id. at 412, 267 A.2d at 733. It is fundamental . . . that the party claiming deceit present evidence that shows that he or she was induced to act because of his or her reliance upon the alleged false representations. . . .

We find that there was no issue of material fact and that summary judgment was appropriate because the merger and disclaimer clauses preclude defendants from asserting that plaintiffs made material misrepresentations regarding the profitability of the business. The clauses prevent defendants from successfully claiming reliance on prior representations.

Although we have previously held that fraud vitiates all contracts, Bloomberg v. Pugh Bros. Co., 45 R.I. 360, 121 A. 430 (1923), we emphasized in *Bloomberg* that one could not "by such a provision as is contained in the contract in this case" escape liability for fraudulent misrepresentations. The merger and disclaimer clause in *Bloomberg* was of a general, nonspecific nature:

> The foregoing contains the whole agreement between the parties to this contract and they, and each of them, shall be estopped from asserting, as an inducement to make said contract, any misrepresentation upon the part of either of the parties hereto, or any agent or servant of either of the parties hereto. . . .

The provision in the instant case differs considerably from the one quoted above in that it is not a general but a specific disclaimer. Such a provision, in our view, shall not vitiate the contract if it was read and understood by the party now claiming fraud and the provision itself was not procured by fraud. . . .

[This case is] closely similar to Danann Realty Corp. v. Harris, 5 N.Y.2d 317, 157 N.E.2d 597, 184 N.Y.S.2d 599 (1959), wherein the purchaser initiated an action for damages for fraud because of alleged false representations by the sellers regarding the operating expenses of the building the plaintiff sought to purchase and the profits to be derived from the investment. The following merger and disclaimer language appeared in the contract:

> The Purchaser has examined the premises agreed to be sold and is familiar with the physical condition thereof. The Seller has not made and does not make any representations as to the physical condition, rents, leases, *expenses, operation* or any other matter or thing affecting or related to the aforesaid premises, ex-

cept as herein specifically set forth, and the Purchaser hereby *expressly acknowledges that no such representations have been made, and the Purchaser further acknowledges that it has inspected the premises and agrees to take the premises "as is"* . . . It is understood and agreed that all understandings and agreements heretofore had between the parties hereto are merged in this contract, which alone fully and completely expresses their agreement, *and that the same is entered into after full investigation, neither party relying upon any statement or representation,* not embodied in this contract, made by the other. The Purchaser has inspected the buildings standing on said premises and is thoroughly acquainted with their condition.

The New York Court of Appeals wrote: "Were we dealing solely with a general and vague merger clause, our task would be simple. . . . Here, however, plaintiff has in the plainest language announced and stipulated that it is not relying on any representations as to the very matter as to which it now claims it was defrauded." Id. at 320, 157 N.E.2d at 598–99. The court held that "[s]uch a specific disclaimer destroys the allegations in the complaint that the agreement was executed in reliance upon these contrary oral representations."

. . . [W]e are also confronted with such specific language regarding the very matter concerning which defendants now claim they were defrauded— the profitability of the business. Clause 9 of the Memorandum of Sale declares specifically that the buyers are to rely on their own judgment and not on any representations of the sellers regarding the past, present, or prospective volume of business, or profits of the business. Clause 10 states that no warranties have been made by the sellers regarding the condition of the assets and that the assets are sold "as is" at the time of the sale.

Like the complaint in [*Danann*], defendants' counterclaim contained no allegations that the contract had not been read by the purchaser or that the merger and disclaimer provisions had not been understood or had been procured by fraud. . . . James Howe said he certainly understood the documents when he signed them, although both he and his wife no longer remember seeing the merger and disclaimer clauses. Moreover, at trial it was established that both parties were represented by counsel at the closing. Although plaintiffs' counsel drew up the sales contract, defendants' counsel admitted reviewing the document with his clients and making some initial changes.

For these reasons we find that defendants' asserted reliance on the oral representations of plaintiffs is not justifiable. We agree with the [*Danann*] court when it stated that "[t]o hold otherwise would be to say that it is impossible for two businessmen dealing at arm's length to agree that the buyer is not buying in reliance on any representations of the seller as to a particular fact."

[The order granting summary judgment to plaintiffs is affirmed; defendants' appeal is denied and dismissed.]

NOTE: CONTRACTUAL EXCLUSION OF FRAUD

The *Danann Realty* decision, followed in *LaFazia*, is cited frequently on the effectiveness of "disclaimer" or "nonreliance" clauses. A point worth noting is *Danann*'s assessment of "relative fault." The court said: "[P]laintiff made a representation in the contract that it was not relying on specific representations not embodied in the contract, while, it now asserts, it was in fact relying on such oral representations. Plaintiff admits then that it is guilty of deliberately misrepresenting to the seller its true intention." Later New York decisions have identified this passage ("deliberately misrepresenting [a] true intention") as the basis for *Danann*'s exception to the usual rule that fraud in the inducement taints an entire contract, including a general merger clause. See, e.g., Citibank, N.A. v. Plapinger, 66 N.Y.2d 90, 495 N.Y.S.2d 309, 485 N.E.2d 974 (1985). The cases since *Danann Realty*, in New York and elsewhere, seem generally agreed that "the touchstone is specificity" when a contract clause is urged as a bar to a defense of fraudulent inducement.

Judge Fuld, dissenting in *Danann Realty*, wrote:

> It is said [that] this contract differs from those heretofore considered in that it embodies a specific and deliberate exclusion of a particular subject. The quick answer is that the clause now before us is not of such a sort. On the contrary, instead of being limited, it is all-embracing, encompassing every representation that a seller could possibly make about the property being sold and, instead of representing a special term of a bargain, is essentially "boiler plate." . . . The more elaborate verbiage in the present contract cannot disguise the fact that the language which is said to immunize the defendants from their own fraud is no more specific than the general merger clause in Sabo v. Delman.

On the "boilerplate" point, Judge Easterbrook, in a case holding that a written nonreliance clause precluded any claim of deceit by prior representations, had this answer for Judge Fuld (Rissman v. Rissman, 213 F.3d 381, 385 (7th Cir.2000)):

> [Plaintiff] calls the no-reliance clauses "boilerplate," and they were; transactions lawyers have language of this sort stored up for reuse. But the fact that language has been used before does not make it less binding when used again. Phrases become boilerplate when many parties find that the language serves their ends. That's a reason to enforce the promises, not to disregard them. . . . Contractual language serves its functions only if enforced consistently. This is one of the advantages of boilerplate, which usually has a record of predictable interpretation and application. If as [plaintiff] says the extent of his reliance is a jury question even after he warranted his non-reliance, then the clause has been nullified, and people in [plaintiff's] position will be worse off tomorrow. . . .

There will be more of boilerplate and standardized form contracts in the materials ahead. It is enough for now to focus on the question whether the type of oral evidence offered in court is relevant in applying boilerplate anti-reliance clauses.

There is a firm line of authority opposing the *Danann Realty* analysis (of which see Snyder v. Lovercheck, 992 P.2d 1079 (Wyo.1999)), a line headed by Bates v. Southgate, 308 Mass. 170, 31 N.E.2d 551 (1941), which holds that, for public policy reasons, a party cannot induce a contract by fraudulent misrepresentations and then use contractual clauses to escape liability for its wrongful acts. The *Bates* court said:

As a matter of principle it is necessary to weigh the advantages of certainty in contractual relations against the harm and injustice that result from fraud. . . . The same public policy that in general sanctions the avoidance of a promise obtained by deceit strikes down all attempts to circumvent that policy by means of contractual devices. In the realm of fact it is entirely possible for a party knowingly to agree that no representations have been made to him, while at the same time believing and relying upon representations which in fact have been made and in fact are false but for which he would not have made the agreement. To deny this possibility is to ignore the frequent instances in everyday experience where parties accept, often without critical examination, and act upon agreements containing somewhere within their four corners exculpatory clauses in one form or another, but where they do so, nevertheless, in reliance upon the honesty of supposed friends, the plausible and disarming statements of salesmen, or the customary course of business.

————

Rio Grande Jewelers Supply v. Data General Corp.

101 N.M. 798, 689 P.2d 1269 (1984)

A buyer of a computer system sued the seller in federal court, recovering a judgment of $115,000 on its claim of negligent misrepresentations as to the system's capabilities. On the seller's appeal to the Tenth Circuit, that court certified the following question of state law to the New Mexico Supreme Court: "Whether, in a sale of goods [governed by the state's UCC], a commercial purchaser of a computer system may maintain an action in tort against the seller for pre-contract negligent misrepresentations regarding the system's capacity[,] . . . where the written sales contract contains an effective integration clause, and an effective provision disclaiming all prior representations and all warranties [not] contained in the contract." The New Mexico court answered in the negative. The contract specifically provided that it was to be the "complete and exclusive statement" of the parties' agreement. There was also a disclaimer of warranties that was effective under UCC 2–316. The buyer's claim for negligent misrepresentations "can be nothing more than an attempt to circumvent the [UCC] and to allow the contract to be rewritten under the guise of an alleged tort." Besides, the representations alleged by the buyer are the same representations alleged in its counts for breach of warranties, which are excluded by the contract. One justice dissented, characterizing the majority's result as "condon[ing] unconscionable conduct" by a seller of goods. [There is another view in goods cases, that claims of negligent misrepresentation, which are "based not on principles of contractual obligation but on principles of duty and reasonable conduct," are not lost by virtue of a fully-integrated sales agreement (integrated via a general clause) or a nonreliance clause which, by its terms, fails to "clearly and specifically" disclaim reliance on "all representations made by [the seller] prior to the execution of the contract." Keller v. A.O. Smith Harvestore Products, 819 P.2d 69 (Colo.1991).]

QUESTION

Rio Grande Jewelers again puts the question whether a plaintiff may bring an action arising out of a contract and call it a tort action. If the plaintiffs in *LaFazia* had alleged negligent rather than intentional misrepresentation, should Clause 9 of their Memorandum of Sale bar any claim for damages?

———

Hoffman v. Chapman

Court of Appeals of Maryland, 1943.
182 Md. 208, 34 A.2d 438.

DELAPLAINE, J. This appeal was brought by Joseph Hoffman and wife from a decree . . . reforming their deed for a house and lot in a suburban real estate development at Kensington.

On August 18, 1941, William Chapman and wife, of Gaithersburg, through a real estate agent, agreed to sell to appellants part of Lot 4 in the section known as Homewood on Edgewood Road, the size to be 96 by 150 feet. The purchase price of this part, improved by a bungalow, was $3,600. Before the parcel was surveyed, appellants were given immediate possession. After the survey was made, the real estate agent sent the plat to the Suburban Title Corp. with instructions to examine the title and arrange for settlement. On October 20, 1941, when appellants made final payment in the office of the title company, they clearly understood that they were receiving only a part of Lot 4 containing one dwelling; but the deed actually conveyed the entire lot, which was improved by other dwelling property. When the mistake was discovered some time afterwards, they [appellants] were requested to deed back the unsold part, but they refused to reconvey. The grantors thereupon entered suit in equity to reform the deed on the ground of mistake.

It is a settled principle that a court of equity will reform a written instrument to make it conform to the real intention of the parties, when the evidence is so clear, strong and convincing as to leave no reasonable doubt that a mutual mistake was made in the instrument contrary to their agreement. Gaver v. Gaver, 119 Md. 634, 87 A. 396. . . . It is a general rule of the common law that parol evidence is inadmissible to vary or contradict the terms of a written instrument. . . . But equity refuses to enforce this rule whenever it is alleged that fraud, accident or mistake occurred in the making of the instrument, and will admit parol evidence to reform the instrument, even though it is within the Statute of Frauds. . . . "A court of equity would be of little value," Justice Story said, "if it could suppress only positive frauds, and leave mutual mistakes, innocently made, to work intolerable mischiefs contrary to the intention of parties. It would be to allow an act, originating in innocence, to operate ultimately as a fraud by enabling the party, who receives the benefit of the mistake, to resist the claims of justice under the shelter of a rule framed to promote it. . . . We must, therefore, treat the cases in which equity affords relief, and allows parol evidence to vary and reform written contracts and instruments upon the ground of accident and mistake, as properly forming, like cases of fraud, exceptions to the general rule which excludes parol evidence. . . ." 1 Story, Equity Jurisprudence, 12th Ed., Secs. 155, 156.

It was urged by appellants that there was no meeting of the minds as to the exact location of the parcel sold, and therefore the contract of sale is void. [We] cannot agree. . . . If an agreement is so vague and indefinite that the court finds it impossible to gather from it the full intention of the parties, it must be held void, for the court cannot make an agreement for the parties. De Bearn v. De Bearn, 126 Md. 629, 95 A. 476. Yet the law does not favor, but leans against, the annulment of contracts on the ground of uncertainty. If the intent of the parties can be ascertained from the express terms of the contract or by fair implication, the contract should be sustained. . . . Of course, if the parties to a contract of sale did not understand each other as to the identity of the property, they cannot invoke the aid of equity, for in such a case there was no meeting of the minds. Page v. Higgins, 150 Mass. 27, 22 N.E. 63. However, where there is no mistake as to the identity of the property, but merely an incorrect description, whether in conveying too much property or too little, or referring to property entirely different from that intended to be conveyed, the court will correct the description, except as against *bona fide* purchasers for value without notice. Stoneham Five Cents Savings Bank v. Johnson, 295 Mass. 390, 3 N.E.2d 730. . . .

Equity reforms an instrument . . . simply to enforce the actual agreement of the parties to prevent an injustice which would ensue if this were not done. Chief Justice Alvey warned: "The court will never, by assuming to rectify an instrument, add to it a term or provision which had not been agreed upon. . . ." Stiles v. Willis, 66 Md. 552, 556, 8 A. 353, 354. . . .

Appellants insisted that the mistake in the deed was not due to their fault, but to culpable negligence of the grantors and their agents, and that no relief can be granted because the mistake was unilateral. It is axiomatic that equity aids the vigilant, and will not grant relief to a litigant who has failed to exercise reasonable diligence. In Boyle v. Rider, 136 Md. 286, 110 A. 524, it was stated that people cannot sign papers carelessly and then expect a court to excuse them from their negligence, especially when their action has misled others. But mere inadvertence, or negligence not amounting to a violation of a positive legal duty, does not bar a complainant from relief, especially if the defendant has not been prejudiced thereby. . . . Hence, it is not necessary for the complainant in a suit for a reformation to prove that he exercised diligence to ascertain what the instrument contained at the time he signed it. The term "mistake" conveys the idea of fault, and the mere fact that a mistake was made in the phraseology of an instrument does not establish such negligence as to preclude the right of reformation; for if it did, a court of equity could never grant relief in such a case. . . .

The general rule is accepted in Maryland that a mistake of law in the making of an agreement is not a ground for reformation, and where a mistake, either of law or of fact, is unilateral, equity will not afford relief except by rescinding the agreement on the ground of fraud, duress or other inequitable conduct. . . . The mistake in this case was not unilateral. Here the draftsman of the deed was acting as the agent of the parties. His mistake in the description of the real estate became the mistake of all the parties. . . . Where a deed is intended to carry into execution a written or oral agreement, but fails to express the manifest intention of the parties on account of a mistake of the draftsman, whether from carelessness, forgetfulness or lack of skill, equity will rectify the mistake to make the deed express the real intentions of the parties. . . .

As it is beyond doubt that a mutual mistake was made in the description of [this] property[,] the decree reforming the deed will be affirmed.

NOTE

As *Hoffman* illustrates, a written contract may not reflect the actual agreement of the parties because of mistake. Discrepancy between the written and the actual agreement might also be explained by the parties' intentional acts; they may deliberately omit an agreed term from the writing or insert a sham term, e.g., New York Trust Co. v. Island Oil & Transport Co., supra p. 303. *Hoffman* applies standard equity doctrine to protect the actual agreement in a mistake setting, without hindrance from the parol evidence rule. But where the writing says what the parties intended it to say, even though their agreement was different, reformation to insert omitted terms has been denied by most decisions. Do you see why?

Hoffman v. Chapman indicates clearly enough that the remedy of reformation awarded was conceived to be "equitable," and that the parol evidence rule would have prevented any contradiction or correction of the deed at law. This is the traditional view. As was to be expected, modern procedural reforms raised some new questions. Particularly in a case already in equity for independent reasons, if the facts alleged and proved justify reformation it should be enough that there is a general prayer for relief, as there usually will be. Furthermore, modern notions of fact-pleading would seem to authorize whatever remedy the facts make appropriate, whether the litigant asked for it or not. This much at least would probably be agreed in all the states.

The major question, however, is whether the issue of mistake in expression in a written document (better called "mistake in integration") should be turned over for decision to a jury. Under the older system, the issue of reformation, being equitable, was decided by a judge. The judge could let a jury hear the evidence and render a verdict, but the verdict would be merely advisory and the judge could disregard it altogether. We have the impression that advisory verdicts were and are rarely used in actions for reformation brought, in the usual way, in equity. It has become quite deeply ingrained on courts and lawyers that the issue of reformation, where grounds exist, should be settled by a judge, not a jury.

THE PAROL EVIDENCE RULE AND THE STATUTE OF FRAUDS

The standard clauses of the statute of frauds are examined in greater detail in the Appendix, p. 885. The aim here is to sketch in general terms the relations between that legislation and the parol evidence rule.

(1) The statute of frauds makes certain kinds of contracts unenforceable unless evidenced by a signed memorandum (in sales of goods, part payment or "acceptance and receipt" will suffice). Thus, a writing is required only in the sense that the lack of a writing is a defense to enforcement of a contract. The statute is not a basis for challenging the existence of a contract, for it establishes no requirements for the making of a contract. The parol evidence rule, on the other hand, does not require a writing at all, except in the sense that it can apply only where there is a written document adopted by the parties as the "integration" of their agreement.

(2) The statute of frauds can be satisfied by writings that were never effective, or intended to be, as an "integration" of the agreement. The signed memorandum can consist of a series of letters, a single letter addressed to a third person, a will, a written and signed offer that is later orally accepted, or a memorandum prepared and signed some time after the date of the oral agreement. The memorandum need only be signed by "the party to be charged," and it can be supplied at any time prior to the action brought upon the contract (in some states prior to trial), and this can be done without the knowledge or consent of the other party.

(3) The statute of frauds requires that a memorandum be signed by "the party to be charged," but the parol evidence rule can operate on a document signed by either party; indeed, there is no reason for requiring signature by either, provided the written statement was adopted by agreement of the parties as the expression of the contract.

(4) The statute of frauds is based on a distrust of oral evidence and for this reason requires written evidence. The parol evidence rule, on the other hand, is grossly misnamed; to the extent that it operates, it excludes both written and oral evidence from sources extraneous to the integrated statement.

(5) The parol evidence rule does not prevent a subsequent modification or adjustment by oral agreement. It should be noted, however, that a later oral agreement may itself fall under one of the clauses of the statute of frauds (e.g., if an interest in land is involved, or if not performable within one year.)

POSTSCRIPT

In looking back at the materials on "the effects of adopting a writing," it may be helpful to have in mind the following passage from the Restatement, Second, Contracts, Introductory Note, ch. 9 (1981):

> This Chapter analyzes the process of interpreting and applying agreements, stating separately rules with respect to various aspects of the process. Such a separate statement may convey an erroneous impression of the psychological reality of the judicial process in which many elements are typically combined in a single ruling. Nevertheless, where evidence of an oral term is excluded in an action based on a written agreement with simply the imprecise explanation that "the writing speaks for itself," the ruling, when analyzed, may sum up the following determinations: the contract was integrated (§ 209); the integration was complete (§ 210); the oral term is inconsistent with the written agreement, is within its scope, does not bear on its interpretation, and would not naturally be omitted from the writing (§§ 213–16).

SECTION 2. INTERPRETING THE PROMISE

INTRODUCTORY NOTE

An observer of contract has provided this sketch (Charny, Hypothetical Bargains: The Normative Structure of Contract Interpretation, 89 Mich.L.Rev. 1815, 1819–1820 (1991)):

The law must supply a set of background conditions to interpretation and enforcement of contracts—commonly referred to as
"default rules." Without default rules, *no* contract could have legal
effect. This is the case for two reasons. Most fundamentally, no text
can completely specify its own means of interpretation. A contractual statement that purported to be such a complete specification
would itself have to be interpreted by some set of rules of interpretation. If the text purported to supply those rules, then *those* rules
would have to be interpreted, and so on, ad infinitum. Thus, the default rules must, at a minimum, contain a set of rules about how the
language of contract is to be interpreted.

Second, . . . an important set of practical constraints limits the
completeness of contracts. In almost all transactions, it would be extremely costly to draft a contract that purported explicitly to address
the obligations of the parties for all conceivable future contingencies.
As a practical matter, then, most contracts are quite incomplete.
The law supplies these missing terms. For example, the doctrines of
mistake and impracticability add terms to address low-probability
contingencies; so do doctrines that impose general duties, such as
the duty of good faith. Correlatively, once the parties know that the
law will supply the term, they take that into account when calculating the benefits of drafting an express term.

An examination of the flow of contract litigation passing daily through our
courts indicates that relatively few cases involve serious controversy over principle or doctrine. Rather, it seems that the great majority of cases involve disputes over either (a) the facts (what happened, what the parties said and did)
or (b) the proper meaning to be ascribed to the facts.

Our concern at the moment is with the second type of dispute—the giving
of meaning to words and other conduct. The need to interpret words and actions, as we have seen, is not limited to situations where the parties have stated their agreement in writing. Still, the problems in interpreting written
agreements appear in a form that merits special consideration. If a court concludes that the writing incorporates the parties' entire agreement, or even their
understanding on some part of the transaction, the parol evidence rule operates
to exclude proof of additional, divergent terms. But a fighting issue may remain: Can the words and conduct of the parties leading to the formalization of
the agreement be used to elucidate the terms of the writing? Can testimony
about intentions alter, or substitute for, contractual language? The policies underlying the parol evidence rule—a desire for certainty and predictability, coupled with an interest in reducing litigation and some unease about juries—
would seem to signal caution in allowing contracting parties to testify as to
what they in fact meant their words to mean, particularly when the testimony
is contrary to the apparent meaning of the words in the contract. At the same
time, it seems unrealistic to assume that the parties' meaning in using key
terms will always—or even most of the time—be unquestionably clear from the
face of the writing. And even if a contractual term is clear, other terms in the
contract—perhaps even circumstances outside the contract—may alter its apparent meaning or show that a literal interpretation yields a dubious result.

Even after a court admits proof of surrounding circumstances and all other
indications of the intended meaning of words, ambiguities and apparent incon-

sistencies may remain. Resort may then be had to certain rules of thumb devised by the courts and perhaps grounded in common experience. For example, where words of general import conflict with more specific language, the latter will likely govern. Again, where certain specifics falling into a general class are expressly mentioned and no language of broader inclusion is used, the proper inference may be that other specifics in the same class are to be excluded. No effort will be made here to catalog these ancillary rules of interpretation (sometimes called "canons of construction"), but you should be alert for them as they appear from time to time in the cases. It suffices to observe that their utility is limited. It has been said that they tend to "hunt in pairs," that is, a rule of interpretation pointing toward one meaning may be counterbalanced by another rule of equal respectability, leading to quite a different meaning. For example, the rule favoring specific over general language may, if invoked by an insurance company in a dispute over the meaning of language in the policy, be countered by the "rule" that ambiguity should be resolved against the party responsible for drafting the document. Thus, the "canons" of interpretation become little more than tools of advocacy. Rarely will they be decisive.

There is a further general point, by way of orientation. Since interpretation of a contract depends always on context, it is a "cultural" undertaking. One must bring to the task certain background baggage, as Judge Posner explained in Beanstalk Group, Inc. v. AM General Corp., 283 F.3d 856, 859–862 (7th Cir.2002):

> [The plaintiff] is correct that written contracts are usually enforced in accordance with the ordinary meaning of the language used in them and without recourse to evidence, beyond the contract itself, as to what the parties meant. This presumption simplifies the litigation of contract disputes. . . . It is a strong presumption, motivated by an understandable distrust in the accuracy of litigation to reconstruct contracting parties' intentions, but it is rebuttable—here by two principles of contract interpretation that are closely related in the setting of this suit. The first is that a contract will not be interpreted literally if doing so would produce absurd results, in the sense of results that the parties, presumed to be rational persons pursuing rational ends, are very unlikely to have agreed to seek. . . .

> This is an interpretive principle, not a species of paternalism. "The letters between plaintiff and defendant were from one merchant to another. They are to be read as businessmen would read them, and only as a last resort are to be thrown out altogether as meaningless futilities. . . . If literalness is sheer absurdity, we are to seek some other meaning whereby reason will be instilled and absurdity avoided." Outlet Embroidery Co. v. Derwent Mills, 254 N.Y. 179, 172 N.E. 462, 463 (1930) (Cardozo, C.J.). "There is a long tradition [of] reading contracts sensibly; contracts—certainly business contracts of the kind involved here—are not parlor games but the means of getting the world's work done. . . . True, parties *can* contract for preposterous terms. If contract language is crystal clear or there is independent extrinsic evidence that something silly was actually intended, a party may be held to its bargain, absent some specialized defense." Rhode Island Charities Trust v. Engelhard Corp., 267 F.3d 3, 7 (1st Cir.2001). . . . The second principle is that a contract must be interpreted as a whole. . . . Sentences are not isolated

units of meaning, but take meaning from other sentences in the same document.

The second principle thus is linguistic; the first reflects the fact that interpretation is a cultural as well as a linguistic undertaking. To interpret a contract or other document, it is not enough to have a command of the grammar, syntax, and vocabulary of the language in which the document is written. One must know something about the practical as well as the purely verbal context of the language to be interpreted. In the case of a commercial contract, one must have a general acquaintance with commercial practices. This doesn't mean that judges should have an M.B.A. or have practiced corporate or commercial law, but merely that they be alert citizens of a market-oriented society so that they can recognize absurdity in a business context. A blinkered literalism, a closing of one's eyes to the obvious, can produce nonsensical results. . . .

The cultural background that a judge brings to the decision of a contract case includes as we said a general knowledge of how the world operates, including the commercial world, and this knowledge, precisely because it is general rather than being knowledge of the specific facts of the case ("adjudicative facts"), can show that the literal interpretation of a particular contractual term would be unsound, in which event no evidence need be taken.

The concept of "ambiguity" provides our starting point. Courts commonly say that a written contract that is "clear on its face" may not be altered by testimony about what a party intended the contractual language to mean. That is to say, where the language of the contract is clear and unambiguous, it is to be given effect according to its terms. But may a court—guided initially, and primarily, by the actual words of the contract—nonetheless consider extrinsic evidence for the very purpose of determining whether those words are ambiguous? To what extent must any ambiguity emanate from within, rather than without, the written agreement?

W.W.W. Associates, Inc. v. Giancontieri

Court of Appeals of New York, 1990.
77 N.Y.2d 157, 566 N.E.2d 639, 565 N.Y.S.2d 440.

KAYE, J. In this action for specific performance of a contract to sell real property, the issue is whether an unambiguous reciprocal cancellation provision should be read in light of extrinsic evidence, as a contingency clause for the sole benefit of plaintiff purchaser, subject to its unilateral waiver. Applying the principle that clear, complete writings should generally be enforced according to their terms, we reject plaintiff's reading of the contract and dismiss its complaint.

Defendants, owners of a two-acre parcel in Suffolk County, on October 16, 1986 contracted for the sale of the property to plaintiff, a real estate investor and developer. The purchase price was fixed at $750,000—$25,000 payable on contract execution, $225,000 to be paid in cash on closing (to take place "on or about December 1, 1986"), and the $500,000 balance secured by a purchase-money mortgage payable two years later.

The parties signed a printed form Contract of Sale, supplemented by several of their own paragraphs. Two provisions of the contract have particular relevance to the present dispute—a reciprocal cancellation provision (para. 31) and a merger clause (para. 19). Paragraph 31, one of the provisions the parties added to the contract form, reads: "The parties acknowledge that Sellers have been served with process instituting an action concerned with the real property which is the subject of this agreement. In the event the closing of title is delayed by reason of such litigation it is agreed that closing of title will in a like manner be adjourned until after the conclusion of such litigation provided, *in the event such litigation is not concluded, by or before 6–1–87 either party shall have the right to cancel this contract whereupon the down payment shall be returned and there shall be no further rights hereunder.*" (Emphasis supplied.) Paragraph 19 is the form merger provision, reading: "All prior understandings and agreements between *seller* and *purchaser* are merged in this contract [and it] completely expresses their full agreement. It has been entered into after full investigation, neither party relying upon any statements made by anyone else that are not set forth in this contract."

The Contract of Sale, in other paragraphs the parties added to the printed form, provided that the purchaser alone had the unconditional right to cancel the contract within 10 days of signing (para. 32), and that the purchaser alone had the option to cancel if, at closing, the seller was unable to deliver building permits for 50 senior citizen housing units (para. 29).

The contract in fact did not close on December 1, 1986, as originally contemplated. As June 1, 1987 neared, with the litigation still unresolved, plaintiff on May 13 wrote defendants that it was prepared to close and would appear for closing on May 28; plaintiff also instituted the present action for specific performance. On June 2, 1987, defendants canceled the contract and returned the down payment, which plaintiff refused. Defendants thereafter sought summary judgment dismissing the specific performance action, on the ground that the contract gave them the absolute right to cancel.

Plaintiff's claim to specific performance rests upon its recitation of how paragraph 31 originated. Those facts are set forth in the affidavit of plaintiff's vice-president, submitted in opposition to defendants' summary judgment motion.

As plaintiff explains, during contract negotiations it learned that, as a result of unrelated litigation against defendants, a lis pendens had been filed against the property. Although assured by defendants that the suit was meritless, plaintiff anticipated difficulty obtaining a construction loan (including title insurance for the loan) needed to implement its plans to build senior citizen housing units. According to the affidavit, it was therefore agreed that paragraph 31 would be added for plaintiff's sole benefit, as contract vendee. As it developed, plaintiff's fears proved groundless—the lis pendens did not impede its ability to secure construction financing. However, around March 1987, plaintiff claims it learned from the broker on the transaction that one of the defendants had told him they were doing nothing to defend the litigation, awaiting June 2, 1987 to cancel the contract and suggesting the broker might get a higher price.

Defendants made no response to these factual assertions. Rather, its summary judgment motion rested entirely on the language of the Contract of Sale, which it argued was, under the law, determinative of its right to cancel. . . .

Critical to the success of plaintiff's position is consideration of the extrinsic evidence that paragraph 31 was added to the contract solely for its benefit. . . . In that a party for whose sole benefit a condition is included in a contract may waive the condition prior to expiration of the time period set forth in the contract and accept the subject property "as is," plaintiff's undisputed factual assertions—if material—would defeat defendants' summary judgment motion.

We conclude, however, that the extrinsic evidence tendered by plaintiff is not material. In its reliance on extrinsic evidence to bring itself within the "party benefited" cases, plaintiff ignores a vital first step in the analysis: before looking to evidence of what was in the parties' minds, a court must give due weight to what was in their contract.

A familiar and eminently sensible proposition of law is that, when parties set down their agreement in a clear, complete document, their writing should as a rule be enforced according to its terms. Evidence outside the four corners of the document as to what was really intended but unstated or misstated is generally inadmissible to add to or vary the writing. That rule imparts "stability to commercial transactions by safeguarding against fraudulent claims, perjury, death of witnesses . . . infirmity of memory . . . [and] the fear that the jury will improperly evaluate the extrinsic evidence." (Fisch, New York Evidence § 42, at 22 [2d ed].) Such considerations are all the more compelling in the context of real property transactions, where commercial certainty is a paramount concern.

Whether or not a writing is ambiguous is a question of law to be resolved by the courts. In the present case, the contract, read as a whole to determine its purpose and intent, plainly manifests the intention that defendants, as well as plaintiff, should have the right to cancel after June 1, 1987 if the litigation had not concluded by that date; and it further plainly manifests the intention that all prior understandings be merged into the contract, which expresses the parties' full agreement. Moreover, the face of the contract reveals a "logical reason" for the explicit provision that the cancellation right contained in paragraph 31 should run to the seller as well as the purchaser. A seller taking back a purchase-money mortgage for two thirds of the purchase price might well wish to reserve its option to sell the property for cash on an "as is" basis if third-party litigation affecting the property remained unresolved past a certain date.

Thus, we conclude there is no ambiguity as to the cancellation clause in issue, read in the context of the entire agreement, and that it confers a reciprocal right on both parties to the contract.

The question next raised is whether extrinsic evidence should be considered in order to *create* an ambiguity in the agreement. That question must be answered in the negative. . . .

Plaintiff's rejoinder—that defendants indeed had the specified absolute right to cancel the contract, but it was subject to plaintiff's absolute prior right of waiver—suffers from a logical inconsistency that is evident in a mere statement of the argument. But there is an even greater problem. Here, sophisticated businessmen reduced their negotiations to a clear, complete writing. In the paragraphs immediately surrounding paragraph 31, they expressly bestowed certain options on the purchaser alone, but in paragraph 31 they chose otherwise, explicitly allowing both buyer and seller to cancel in the event the litigation was unresolved by June 1, 1987. By ignoring the plain language of the contract, plaintiff effectively rewrites the bargain that was struck. An analysis that begins with consideration of extrinsic evidence of what the parties meant, instead of looking first to what they said and reaching extrinsic evidence only when required to do so because of some identified ambiguity, unnecessarily denigrates the contract and unsettles the law. . . .

Pacific Gas & Elec. Co. v. G.W. Thomas Drayage & Rigging Co.

Supreme Court of California, 1968.
69 Cal.2d 33, 69 Cal.Rptr. 561, 442 P.2d 641.

TRAYNOR, C.J. Defendant appeals from a judgment for plaintiff in an action for damages for injury to property under an indemnity clause of a contract.

In 1960 defendant entered into a contract with plaintiff to furnish the labor and equipment necessary to remove and replace the upper metal cover of plaintiff's steam turbine. Defendant agreed to perform the work "at [its] own risk and expense" and to "indemnify" plaintiff "against all loss, damage, expense and liability resulting from . . . injury to property, arising out of or in any way connected with the performance of this contract." Defendant also agreed to procure not less than $50,000 insurance to cover liability for injury to property. Plaintiff was to be an additional named insured, but the policy was to contain a cross-liability clause extending the coverage to plaintiff's property.

During the work the cover fell and injured the exposed rotor of the turbine. Plaintiff brought this action to recover $25,144.51, the amount it subsequently spent on repairs. During the trial it dismissed a count based on negligence and thereafter secured judgment on the theory that the indemnity provision covered injury to all property regardless of ownership.

Defendant offered to prove by admissions of plaintiff's agents, by defendant's conduct under similar contracts entered into with plaintiff, and by other proof that in the indemnity clause the parties meant to cover injury to property of third parties only and not to plaintiff's property. Although the trial court observed that the language used was "the classic language for a third party indemnity provision" and that "one could very easily conclude that . . . its whole intendment is to indemnify third parties," it nevertheless held that the "plain language" of the agreement also required defendant to indemnify plaintiff for injuries to plaintiff's property. Having determined that the contract had a plain meaning, the court refused to admit any extrinsic evidence that would contradict its interpretation.

When a court interprets a contract on this basis, it determines the meaning of the instrument in accordance with the "extrinsic evidence of the judge's own linguistic education and experience." (3 Corbin on Contracts (1960 ed.) [§ 579].) The exclusion of testimony that might contradict the linguistic background of the judge reflects a judicial belief in the possibility of perfect verbal expression. (9 Wigmore on Evidence (3d ed. 1940) § 2461.) This belief is a remnant of a primitive faith in the inherent potency and inherent meaning of words.

The test of admissibility of extrinsic evidence to explain the meaning of a written instrument is not whether it appears to the court to be plain and unambiguous on its face, but whether the offered evidence is relevant to prove a meaning to which the language of the instrument is reasonably susceptible. . . .

A rule that would limit the determination of the meaning of a written instrument to its four-corners merely because it seems to the court to be clear and unambiguous, would either deny the relevance of the intention of the parties or presuppose a degree of verbal precision and stability our language has not attained.

Some courts have expressed the opinion that contractual obligations are created by the mere use of certain words, whether or not there was any intention to incur such obligations. Under this view, contractual obligations flow, not from the intention of the parties but from the fact that they used certain magic words. Evidence of the parties' intention therefore becomes irrelevant.

In this state, however, the intention of the parties as expressed in the contract is the source of contractual rights and duties. A court must ascertain and give effect to this intention by determining what the parties meant by the words they used. Accordingly, the exclusion of relevant, extrinsic evidence to explain the meaning of a written instrument could be justified only if it were feasible to determine the meaning the parties gave to the words from the instrument alone.

If words had absolute and constant referents, it might be possible to discover contractual intention in the words themselves and in the manner in which they were arranged. Words, however, do not have absolute and constant referents. "A word is a symbol of thought but has no arbitrary and fixed meaning like a symbol of algebra or chemistry." [54 Cal.2d 184, 5 Cal.Rptr. 553, 353 P.2d 33.] The meaning of particular words or groups of words varies with the "verbal context and surrounding circumstances and purposes in view of the linguistic education and experience of their users and their hearers or readers (not excluding judges). . . . A word has no meaning apart from these factors; much less does it have an objective meaning, one true meaning." (Corbin, The Interpretation of Words and the Parol Evidence Rule (1965) 50 Cornell L.Q. 161, 187.) Accordingly, the meaning of a writing "can only be found by interpretation in the light of all the circumstances that reveal the sense in which the writer used the words. The exclusion of parol evidence regarding such circumstances merely because the words do not appear ambiguous to the reader can easily lead to the attribution to a written instrument of a meaning that was never intended." . . .

Although extrinsic evidence is not admissible to add to, detract from, or vary the terms of a written contract, these terms must first be determined before it can be decided whether or not extrinsic evidence is being offered for a prohibited purpose. The fact that the terms of an instrument appear clear to a judge does not preclude the possibility that the parties chose the language of the instrument to express different terms. That possibility is not limited to contracts whose terms have acquired a particular meaning by trade usage,[1] but exists whenever the parties' understanding of the words used may have differed from the judge's understanding.

---

[1] Extrinsic evidence of trade usage or custom has been admitted to show that the term "United Kingdom" in a motion picture distribution contract included Ireland (Ermolieff v.

Accordingly, rational interpretation requires at least a preliminary consideration of all credible evidence offered to prove the intention of the parties.[2] (Civ.Code, § 1647; Code Civ.Proc. § 1860; see also 9 Wigmore on Evidence, § 2470.) Such evidence includes testimony as to the "circumstances surrounding the making of the agreement . . . including the object, nature and subject matter of the writing" so that the court can "place itself in the same situation in which the parties found themselves at the time of contracting." . . . If the court decides, after considering this evidence, that the language of a contract, in the light of all the circumstances, is "fairly susceptible of either one of the two interpretations contended for," . . . extrinsic evidence relevant to prove either of such meanings is admissible.[3] In the present case the court erroneously refused to consider extrinsic evidence offered to show that the indemnity clause in the contract was not intended to cover injuries to plaintiff's property. Although that evidence was not necessary to show that the indemnity clause was reasonably susceptible of the meaning contended for by defendant, it was nevertheless relevant and admissible on that issue. Moreover, since that clause was reasonably susceptible of that meaning, the offered evidence was also admissible to prove that the clause had that meaning and did not cover injuries to plaintiff's property.[4] Accordingly, the judgment must be reversed. . . .

R.K.O. Radio Pictures (1942) 19 Cal.2d 543, 122 P.2d 3); that the word "ton" in a lease meant a long ton or 2,240 pounds and not the statutory ton of 2,000 pounds (Higgins v. Cal. Petroleum, etc., Co. (1898) 120 Cal. 629, 52 P. 1080); that the word "stubble" in a lease included not only stumps left in the ground but everything "left on the ground after the harvest time" (Callahan v. Stanley (1881) 57 Cal. 476). . . . [Some footnotes have been omitted, the remainder renumbered.—Eds.]

[2] When objection is made to any particular item of evidence offered to prove the intention of the parties, the trial court may not yet be in a position to determine whether in the light of all of the offered evidence, the item objected to will turn out to be admissible as tending to prove a meaning of which the language of the instrument is reasonably susceptible or inadmissible as tending to prove a meaning of which the language is not reasonably susceptible. In such case the court may admit the evidence conditionally by either reserving its ruling on the objection or by admitting the evidence subject to a motion to strike. (See Evid.Code, § 403.)

[3] Extrinsic evidence has often been admitted in such cases on the stated ground that the contract was ambiguous. . . . This statement of the rule is harmless if it is kept in mind that the ambiguity may be exposed by extrinsic evidence that reveals more than one possible meaning.

[4] The court's exclusion of extrinsic evidence in this case would be error even under a rule that excluded such evidence when the instrument appeared to the court to be clear and unambiguous on its face. The controversy centers on the meaning of the word "indemnify" and the phrase "all loss, damage, expense and liability." The trial court's recognition of the language as typical of a third party indemnity clause and the double sense in which the word "indemnify" is used in statutes and defined in dictionaries demonstrate the existence of an ambiguity. [Quoting statutes and dictionaries.]

Plaintiff's assertion that the use of the word "all" to modify "loss, damage, expense and liability" dictates an all inclusive interpretation is not persuasive. If the word "indemnify" encompasses only third-party claims, the word "all" simply refers to all such claims. The use of the words "loss," "damage," and "expense" in addition to the word "liability" is likewise inconclusive. These words do not imply an agreement to reimburse for injury to an indemnitee's property since they are commonly inserted in third-party indemnity clauses, to enable an indemnitee who settles a claim to recover from his indemnitor without proving his liability. (Carpenter Paper Co. v. Kellogg (1952) 114 Cal.App.2d 640, 251 P.2d 40. Civ.Code, § 2778, provides: "1. Upon an indemnity against liability . . . the person indemnified is entitled to recover upon becoming liable; 2. Upon an indemnity against claims, or demands, or damages, or costs . . . the person indemnified is not entitled to recover without payment thereof; . . .")

The provision that defendant perform the work "at his own risk and expense" and the provisions relating to insurance are equally inconclusive. By agreeing to work at its own risk defendant may have released plaintiff from liability for any injuries to defendant's property arising out of the contract's performance, but this provision did not necessarily make defend-

Columbia Nitrogen Corp. v. Royster Co.
451 F.2d 3 (4th Cir.1971)

Royster manufactured and marketed mixed fertilizers, the principal components of which were nitrogen, phosphate and potash. Columbia was primarily a producer of nitrogen, although it manufactured some mixed fertilizer. For several years Royster had been a major purchaser of Columbia's products, but Columbia had never been a significant customer of Royster. In the fall of 1966, Royster constructed a facility which enabled it to produce more phosphate than it needed in its own operations. After extensive negotiations, the companies executed a contract for Royster's sale of a minimum of 31,000 tons of phosphate each year for three years to Columbia, with an option to extend the term. The contract stated the price per ton, subject to an escalation clause dependent on production costs. Phosphate prices soon plunged precipitously. Unable to resell the phosphate at a competitive price, Columbia ordered only part of the scheduled tonnage. At Columbia's request, Royster lowered its price for diammonium phosphate on shipments for three months in 1967, but specified that subsequent shipments would be at the original contract price. Even with this concession, Royster's price was still substantially above the market. As a result, Columbia ordered less than a tenth of the phosphate Royster was to ship in the first contract year. When pressed by Royster, Columbia offered to take the phosphate at the current market price and resell it without brokerage fee. Royster, however, insisted on the contract price. When Columbia refused delivery, Royster sold the unaccepted phosphate for Columbia's account at a price substantially below the contract price. It then sued Columbia for breach.

Columbia defended by offering the testimony of witnesses with long experience in the trade that because of uncertain crop and weather conditions, farming practices, and government agricultural programs, express price and quantity terms in contracts for materials in the mixed-fertilizer industry are mere projections to be adjusted according to market forces. Columbia also offered proof of its business dealings with Royster over the six-year period preceding the phosphate contract. Columbia claimed these proofs evidenced a pattern of repeated and substantial deviation from the stated amount or price. This experience, Columbia wanted to argue to the factfinder, formed the basis of an understanding on which it depended in conducting negotiations with Royster.

Held, Columbia's proffered evidence was improperly excluded. A finding of ambiguity is not necessary for the admission of extrinsic evidence of the usage of the trade or the parties' course of dealing. UCC 2–202 expressly allows evidence of course of dealing or usage of trade to explain or supplement terms intended by the parties as a final expression of their agreement; "the test of admissibility is not whether the contract appears on its face to be complete in every detail, but whether the proffered evidence of course of dealing and trade usage reasonably can be construed as consistent with the express terms of the

---

ant an insurer against injuries to plaintiff's property. Defendant's agreement to procure liability insurance to cover damages to plaintiff's property does not indicate whether the insurance was to cover all injuries or only injuries caused by defendant's negligence.

agreement." Columbia may therefore present evidence that there was "a practice of mutual adjustments so prevalent in the industry and in prior dealings between the parties that it formed a part of the agreement governing this transaction."

––––––––––

Robert Indus. v. Spence
362 Mass. 751, 291 N.E.2d 407 (1973)

"[T]here was no error in the admission of evidence of the facts and circumstances of the transaction, including the situation and relations of the parties, for the purpose of applying the terms of the written contract to the subject matter and removing and explaining any uncertainty or ambiguity which arose from such application. Stoops v. Smith, 100 Mass. 63, 66. A [contract] is to be read in the light of the circumstances of its execution, which may enable the court to see that its words are really ambiguous. . . . When the written agreement, as applied to the subject matter, is in any respect uncertain or equivocal in meaning, all the circumstances of the parties leading to its execution may be shown for the purpose of elucidating, but not of contradicting or changing its terms. . . . Expressions in our cases to the effect that evidence of circumstances can be admitted only after an ambiguity has been found on the face of the written instrument have reference to evidence offered to contradict the written terms. . . . After interpretation has called to its help all those facts which make up the setting in which the words are used, however, the words themselves remain the most important evidence of intention[.]" [Is this court saying that a trial judge may properly hear evidence in aid of interpretation even before deciding whether the written agreement is ambiguous?]

[The authorities indicating "a retreat from the four-corners standard," in favor of a contextual inquiry into ambiguity (the position taken in the Restatement, Second § 212), are collected in C.R. Anthony Co. v. Loretto Mall Partners, 112 N.M. 504, 817 P.2d 238 (1991). Courts employing a "context" approach typically caution that extrinsic evidence is admitted only "for the purpose of aiding in the interpretation of what is in the instrument, and not for the purpose of showing intention independent of the instrument." Berg v. Hudesman, 115 Wash.2d 657, 801 P.2d 222 (1990). Judge Keeting's discussion of procedures for resolving disputes over meaning, in Donoghue v. IBC USA (Publications), Inc., 70 F.3d 206, 214–216 (1st Cir.1995), captures the essence of the ambiguity problem.]

––––––––––

Federal Dep. Ins. Corp. v. W.R. Grace & Co.
877 F.2d 614 (7th Cir.1989)

"Most of the modern cases in the 'four corners' line stand for the unexceptionable proposition that 'language in a contract is not rendered ambiguous simply because the parties do not agree upon its meaning.' . . . The fact that parties to a contract disagree about its meaning does not show that it is ambiguous, for if it did, then putting contracts into writing would provide parties with little or no protection. . . . [T]he words of the contract are not lightly to be ignored. The nature of the offer of proof to show an ambiguity is therefore critical. Although a self-serving statement [that] a party did not understand the contract to mean what it says (or appears to say) will not suffice, an offer to show that anyone who understood the context of the contract would realize it couldn't mean what an untutored reader would suppose it meant will."

QUESTION

In *Pacific Gas*, was the evidence defendant offered of the parties' understanding of the indemnity clause "objective" or "subjective" in nature?

————

NOTE

On the use of extrinsic evidence to aid in the interpretation of a writing, the UCC's Official Comment to § 2–202 rejects "(b) the premise that the language used has the meaning attributable to such language by rules of construction existing in the law rather than the meaning which arises out of the commercial context in which it was used; and (c) the requirement that a condition precedent to the admissibility of [interpretive evidence of a course of dealing or usage of trade or course of performance] is an original determination by the court that the language used is ambiguous." The Comment goes on to say that written agreements "are to be read on the assumption that the course of prior dealings between the parties and the usages of trade[,] [unless carefully negated,] were taken for granted when the document was phrased."

————

Spaulding v. Morse
322 Mass. 149, 76 N.E.2d 137 (1947)

Plaintiff sued in equity to enforce a trust created by defendant and his former wife following their divorce. The critical provision obligated defendant to "pay to the said trustee in trust for his said minor son Richard the sum of twelve hundred dollars ($1,200) per year . . . until the entrance of Richard D. Morse into some college [or] university . . . and thereupon, instead of said payments, amounting to twelve hundred dollars (1200) yearly, he shall and will then pay to the trustee payments in the sum of twenty-two hundred dollars ($2,200) per year for a period of said higher education but not more than four years." The trustee was directed to turn over the payments to Richard's mother, "to be applied by her . . . upon or toward the maintenance and education and benefit of said Richard, so long as she shall maintain and educate said Richard to the satisfaction of said trustee." Richard Morse, the beneficiary, completed high school in 1946 and was immediately inducted into the U.S. Army, where he was when this suit was begun. Defendant ceased making monthly payments to the trustee when Richard finished high school and entered military service. From a decree ordering defendant to pay a sum covering monthly installments not paid and to resume monthly payments until Richard completed college, defendant appealed. *Held*, reversed. "Every instrument in writing is to be interpreted with a view to the material circumstances of the parties at the time of the execution, in the light of the pertinent facts within their knowledge, and in such manner as to give effect to the main end designed to be accomplished." The main purpose of Richard's parents was to provide for his maintenance and education. Since these purposes were achieved or preempted by Richard's military status, "the proper construction of the trust instrument is that the defendant is not required under its terms to perform provisions for the maintenance and education of Richard while he was or is in the armed service of the United States."

NOTE

Is Spaulding v. Morse "interpretation"? Is it simply "common sense"? Consider Judge Learned Hand's reasoning in Readsboro v. Hoosac Tunnel & W.R. Co., 6 F.2d 733 (2d Cir.1925):

> The next question is of the duration of the defendant's obligation, and this necessarily goes back to the original contract. That was in terms unlimited in time, and the plaintiff apparently reasons that the defendant is bound forever to pay one-half of the expenses of maintenance. This seems to us untenable. Had the parties expressed the intention to make a promise for perpetual maintenance, we should, of course, have nothing to say; their words would be conclusive. But they did not, and, as no time is expressly fixed, we must look to the circumstances to learn what they meant. Their purpose is pretty evident. The railroad was to have the use of the bridge, and in using it would help wear it out. It was reasonable, therefore, that it should share the expenses of its upkeep. But, if at any time that use ceased, plainly there was no reason, either in good sense or in justice, that it should continue to pay for what it got no use of, and what it no longer helped destroy. The purpose can hardly have been to supply the town with a bridge forever. This, we think, was the measure of the original covenant.

RESTATEMENT OF CONTRACTS, SECOND

Section 212. Interpretation of Integrated Agreement

(2) A question of interpretation of an integrated agreement is to be determined by the trier of fact if it depends on the credibility of extrinsic evidence or on a choice among reasonable inferences to be drawn from extrinsic evidence. Otherwise a question of interpretation of an integrated agreement is to be determined as a question of law.

Comment: . . .

d. "Question of law." Analytically, what meaning is attached to a word or other symbol by one or more people is a question of fact. But general usage as to the meaning of words . . . is commonly a proper subject for judicial notice without the aid of evidence extrinsic to the writing. Historically, moreover, . . . questions of interpretation of written documents have been treated as questions of law in the sense that they are decided by the trial judge rather than by the jury. Likewise, since an appellate court is commonly in as good a position to decide such questions as the trial judge, they have been treated as questions of law for purposes of appellate review. Such treatment has the effect of limiting the power of the trier of fact to exercise a dispensing power in the guise of a finding of fact, and thus contributes to the stability and predictability of contractual relations. In cases of standardized contracts like insurance policies, it also provides a method of assuring that like cases will be decided alike.

——————

Frigaliment Importing Co. v. B.N.S. International Sales Corp.

United States District Court, Southern District of New York, 1960.
190 F.Supp. 116.

FRIENDLY, J. The issue is what is chicken? Plaintiff says "chicken" means a young chicken, suitable for broiling and frying. Defendant says "chicken" means any bird of that genus that meets contract specifications on weight and quality, including what it calls "stewing chicken" and plaintiff pejoratively terms "fowl." Dictionaries give both meanings, as well as some others not relevant here. To support its, plaintiff sends a number of volleys over the net; defendant essays to return them and adds a few serves of its own. Assuming that both parties were acting in good faith, the case nicely illustrates Holmes' remark "that the making of a contract depends not on the agreement of two minds in one intention, but on the agreement of two sets of external signs—not on the parties' having meant the same thing but on their having said the same thing." The Path of the Law, in Collected Legal Papers, p. 178. I have concluded that plaintiff has not sustained its burden of persuasion that the contract used "chicken" in the narrower sense.

The action is for breach of the warranty that goods sold shall correspond to the description. Two contracts are in suit. In the first, dated May 2, 1957, defendant, a New York sales corporation, confirmed the sale to plaintiff, a Swiss corporation, of

> US Fresh Frozen Chicken, Grade A, Government Inspected, Eviscerated 2½–3 lbs. and 1½–2 lbs. each all chicken individually wrapped in cryovac, packed in secured fiber cartons or wooden boxes, suitable for export
>
> 75,000 lbs. 2½–3 lbs. . . . . . @$33.00
>
> 25,000 lbs. 1½–2 lbs. . . . . . @$36.50
>
> per 100 lbs. FAS New York
>
> scheduled May 10, 1957 pursuant to instructions from Penson & Co., New York.

The second contract, also dated May 2, 1957, was identical save that only 50,000 lbs. of the heavier "chicken" were called for, the price of the smaller birds was $37 per 100 lbs., and shipment was scheduled for May 30. The initial shipment under the first contract was short but the balance was shipped on May 17. When the initial shipment arrived in Switzerland, plaintiff found, on May 28, that the 2½–3 lbs. birds were not young chicken suitable for broiling and frying but stewing chicken or "fowl"; indeed, many of the cartons and bags plainly so indicated. Protests ensued. Nevertheless, shipment under the second contract was made on May 29, the 2½–3 lbs. birds again being stewing chicken. Defendant stopped the transportation of these at Rotterdam. . . .

Since the word "chicken" standing alone is ambiguous, I turn first to see whether the contract itself offers any aid to its interpretation. Plaintiff says the 1½–2 lbs. birds necessarily had to be young chicken since the older birds do not come in that size, hence the 2½–3 lbs. birds must likewise be young. This is unpersuasive—a contract for "apples" of two different sizes could be filled with different kinds of apples even though only one species came in both sizes. Defendant notes that the contract called not simply for chicken but for "US Fresh Frozen Chicken, Grade A, Government Inspected." It says the contract thereby incorporated by reference the Department of Agriculture's regulations, which favor its interpretation; I shall return to this after reviewing plaintiff's other contentions.

The first hinges on an exchange of cablegrams which preceded execution of the formal contracts. The negotiations leading up to the contracts were conducted in New York between defendant's secretary, Ernest R. Bauer, and a Mr. Stovicek, who was in New York for the Czechoslovak government at the World Trade Fair. A few days after meeting Bauer at the fair, Stovicek telephoned and inquired whether defendant would be interested in exporting poultry to Switzerland. Bauer then met with Stovicek, who showed him a cable from plaintiff dated April 26, 1957, announcing that they "are buyer" of 25,000 lbs. of chicken 2½–3 lbs. weight, Cryovac packed, grade A Government inspected, at a price up to 33¢ per pound, for shipment on May 10, to be confirmed by the following morning, and were interested in further offerings. After testing the market for price, Bauer accepted, and Stovicek sent a confirmation that evening. Plaintiff stresses that, although these and subsequent cables between plaintiff and defendant, which laid the basis for the additional quantities under the first and for all of the second contract, were predominantly in German, they used the English word "chicken"; it claims this was done because it understood "chicken" meant young chicken whereas the German word, "Huhn," included both "Brathuhn" (broilers) and "Suppenhuhn" (stewing chicken), and that defendant, whose officers were thoroughly conversant with German, should have realized this. Whatever force this argument might otherwise have is largely drained away by Bauer's testimony that he asked Stovicek what kind of chickens were wanted, received the answer "any kind of chickens," and then, in German, asked whether the cable meant "Huhn" and received an affirmative response. . . .

Plaintiff's next contention is that there was a definite trade usage that "chicken" meant "young chicken." Defendant showed that it was only beginning in the poultry trade in 1957, thereby bringing itself within the principle that "when one of the parties is not a member of the trade or other circle, his acceptance of the standard must be made to appear" by proving either that he had actual knowledge of the usage or that the usage is "so generally known in the community that his actual individual knowledge of it may be inferred." 9 Wigmore, Evidence (3d ed. § 1940) 2464. Here there was no proof of actual knowledge of the alleged usage; indeed, it is quite plain that defendant's belief was to the contrary. In order to meet the alternative requirement, the law of New York demands a showing that "the usage is of so long continuance, so well established, so notorious, so universal and so reasonable in itself, as that the presumption is violent that the parties contracted with reference to it, and made it a part of their agreement." Walls v. Bailey, 1872, 49 N.Y. 464, 472–473.

Plaintiff endeavored to establish such a usage by the testimony of three witnesses and certain other evidence. Strasser, resident buyer in New

York for a large chain of Swiss cooperatives, testified that "on chicken I would definitely understand a broiler." However, the force of this testimony was considerably weakened by the fact that in his own transactions the witness, a careful businessman, protected himself by using "broiler" when that was what he wanted and "fowl" when he wished older birds. . . . [A] witness' consistent failure to rely on the alleged usage deprives his opinion testimony of much of its effect. Niesielowski, an officer of one of the companies that had furnished the stewing chicken to defendant, testified that "chicken" meant "the male species of the poultry industry. That could be a broiler, a fryer or a roaster," but not a stewing chicken; however, he also testified that upon receiving defendant's inquiry for "chickens," he asked whether the desire was for "fowl or frying chickens" and, in fact, supplied fowl, although taking the precaution of asking defendant, a day or two after plaintiff's acceptance of the contracts in suit, to change its confirmation of its order from "chickens," as defendant had originally prepared it, to "stewing chickens." Dates, an employee of Urner–Barry Company, which publishes a daily market report on the poultry trade, gave it as his view that the trade meaning of "chicken" was "broilers and fryers." In addition to this opinion testimony, plaintiff relied on the fact that the Urner–Barry service, the Journal of Commerce, and Weinberg Bros. & Co. of Chicago, a large supplier of poultry, published quotations in a manner which, in one way or another, distinguish between "chicken," comprising broilers, fryers and certain other categories, and "fowl," which, Bauer acknowledged, included stewing chickens. This material would be impressive if there were nothing to the contrary. However, there was, as will now be seen.

Defendant's witness Weininger, who operates a chicken eviscerating plant in New Jersey, testified "Chicken is everything except a goose, a duck, and a turkey. Everything is a chicken, but then you have to say, you have to specify which category you want or that you are talking about." Its witness Fox said that in the trade "chicken" would encompass all the various classifications. Sadina, who conducts a food inspection service, testified that he would consider any bird coming within the classes of "chicken" in the Department of Agriculture's regulations to be a chicken. The specifications approved by the General Services Administration include fowl as well as broilers and fryers under the classification "chickens." Statistics of the Institute of American Poultry Industries use the phrases "Young chickens" and "Mature chickens," under the general heading "Total chickens," and the Department of Agriculture's daily and weekly price reports avoid use of the word "chicken" without specification.

Defendant advances several other points which it claims affirmatively support its construction. Primary among these is the regulation of the Department of Agriculture, 7 C.F.R. § 70.300–70.370, entitled, "Grading and Inspection of Poultry and Edible Products Thereof," and in particular 70.301 which recited:

"Chickens. The following are the various classes of chickens:

(a) Broiler or fryer . . .

(b) Roaster . . .

(c) Capon . . .

(d) Stag . . .

(e) Hen or stewing chicken or fowl . . .

(f) Cock or old rooster . . ."

Defendant argues, as previously noted, that the contract incorporated these regulations by reference. Plaintiff answers that the contract provision related simply to grade and Government inspection and did not incorporate the Government definition of "chicken," and also that the definition in the Regulations is ignored in the trade. However, the latter contention was contradicted by Weininger and Sadina; and there is force in defendant's argument that the contract made the regulations a dictionary, particularly since the reference to Government grading was already in plaintiff's initial cable to Stovicek.

[handwritten margin note: implausibility]

Defendant makes a further argument based on the impossibility of its obtaining broilers and fryers at the 33¢ price offered by plaintiff for the 2½–3 lbs. birds. There is no substantial dispute that, in late April, 1957, the price for 2½–3 lbs. broilers was between 35 and 37¢ per pound, and that when defendant entered into the contracts, it was well aware of this and intended to fill them by supplying fowl in these weights. It claims that plaintiff must likewise have known the market since plaintiff had reserved shipping space on April 23, three days before plaintiff's cable to Stovicek, or, at least, that Stovicek was chargeable with such knowledge. It is scarcely an answer to say, as plaintiff does in its brief, that the 33¢ price offered by the 2½–3 lbs. "chickens" was closer to the prevailing 35¢ price for broilers than to the 30¢ at which defendant procured fowl. Plaintiff must have expected defendant to make some profit—certainly it could not have expected defendant deliberately to incur a loss.

Finally, defendant relies on conduct by the plaintiff after the first shipment had been received. On May 28 plaintiff sent two cables complaining that the larger birds in the first shipment constituted "fowl." Defendant answered with a cable refusing to recognize plaintiff's objection and announcing "We have today ready for shipment 50,000 lbs. chicken 2½–3 lbs. 25,000 lbs. broilers 1½–2 lbs.," these being the goods procured for shipment under the second contract, and asked immediate answer "whether we are to ship this merchandise to you and whether you will accept the merchandise." After several other cable exchanges, plaintiff replied on May 29 "Confirm again that merchandise is to be shipped since resold by us if not enough pursuant to contract chickens are shipped the missing quantity is to be shipped within ten days stop we resold to our customers pursuant to your contract chickens grade A you have to deliver us said merchandise we again state that we shall make you fully responsible for all resulting costs." Defendant argues that if plaintiff was sincere in thinking it was entitled to young chickens, plaintiff would not have allowed the shipment under the second contract to go forward, since the distinction between broilers and chickens drawn in defendant's cablegram must have made it clear that the larger birds would not be broilers. However, plaintiff answers that the cables show plaintiff was insisting on delivery of young chickens and that defendant shipped old ones at its peril. Defendant's point would be highly relevant on another disputed issue—whether if liability were established, the measure of damages should be the difference in market value of broilers and stewing chicken in New York or the larger difference in Europe, but I cannot give it weight on the issue of interpretation. Defendant points out also that plaintiff proceeded to deliver some of the larger birds in Europe, describing them as "poulets"; defendant argues that it was only when plaintiff's customers complained about this that plaintiff developed the idea that "chicken" meant "young chicken." There is little force in this in view of plaintiff's immediate and consistent protests.

When all the evidence is reviewed, it is clear that defendant believed it could comply with the contracts by delivering stewing chicken in the 2½–3 lbs. size. Defendant's subjective intent would not be significant if this did not coincide with an objective meaning of "chicken." Here it did coincide with one of the dictionary meanings, with the definition in the Department of Agriculture Regulations to which the contract made at least oblique reference, with at least some usage in the trade, with the realities of the market, and with what plaintiff's spokesman had said. Plaintiff asserts it to be equally plain that plaintiff's own subjective intent was to obtain broilers and fryers; the only evidence against this is the material as to market prices and this may not have been sufficiently brought home. In any event it is unnecessary to determine that issue. For plaintiff has the burden of showing that "chicken" was used in the narrower rather than in the broader sense, and this it has not sustained.

[handwritten margin note: π has burden]

This opinion constitutes the Court's findings of fact and conclusions of law. Judgment shall be entered dismissing the complaint with costs.

Posner, The Law and Economics of Contract Interpretation
83 Tex. L. Rev. 1581, 1603–1605 (2005)

"Probably more important in the American system of contractual interpretation than either the four corners rule or the parol evidence rule in limiting the scope of the jury and the frequency of trials in contract cases is the tendency of courts—a proclivity, a preference, rather than the dictate of a rule—to resolve contractual ambiguities without recourse to extrinsic evidence and thus without a trial, by making a 'best guess.' I am using 'evidence' here in the standard legal sense of materials that create a contestable issue that requires a trial to resolve. If a contract is not clear on its face, but instead is vague or ambiguous, the judge will have to go outside the contract to decide what it means. But he can go outside it without getting entangled in the sort of factual disagreements that require a trial to untangle—in other words, without taking evidence. He can for example use common sense, which 'is as much a part of contract interpretation as is the dictionary or the arsenal of canons.' . . .

"Suppose the litigants present rival interpretations of their contract to the judge, and it is apparent, without the need for a trial to resolve a factual disagreement, that one of these interpretations would make the contract extremely one-sided. That would be a reason—call it common sense or, if some explicit economic reasoning is employed, the promotion of efficiency—for the judge to choose the other interpretation. '[S]ince most though of course not all contracts involve the exchange of things of commensurate value, an interpretation that makes a contract grossly one-sided is suspect.' 'People usually don't pay a price for a good or service that is wildly in excess of its market value, or sell a good or service . . . for a price hugely less than its market value. . . .' More broadly, 'An interpretation which sacrifices a major interest of one of the parties while furthering only a marginal interest of the other should be rejected in favor of an interpretation which sacrifices marginal interests of both parties in order to protect their major concerns.'

[handwritten margin note: common sense/ efficiency.]

"A closely related principle is that if it is apparent, again without having to conduct a trial to resolve factual disagreements, that one of the rival interpretations proposed does not make commercial sense, the interpretation will be rejected because it probably does not jibe with what the parties understood when they signed the contract. '[A] contract will not be interpreted literally if doing so would produce absurd results, in the sense of results that the parties, presumed to be rational persons pursuing rational ends, are very unlikely to have agreed to seek.' And even if an interpretation makes sense, it will be rejected if the rival interpretation is markedly more sensible. 'Agreements, especially commercial arrangements, are designed to make sense. If one reading produces a plausible result for which parties might be expected to bargain, that reading has a strong presumption in its favor as against another reading producing an unlikely result (e.g., windfall gains, conditions that cannot be satisfied, dubious incentives).'

"[Many interpretative methods]—trying to determine the parties' actual intentions, trying to determine their hypothetical intentions, trying to figure out the efficient resolution of their dispute, and trying to confine interpretation to the words of the contract rather than dumping the interpretive issue in the lap of a jury—tend to merge in practice. It would be one thing to impose the efficient solution in the teeth of the parties' agreement. That would be not only paternalistic but also reckless, because it would be rare that a judge or jury had a better sense of what would be an efficient transaction than the parties themselves had. But often, when the parties' intentions are not readily inferable from the written contract, the best, the most cost-efficient, way to resolve their dispute is not to take testimony and conduct a trial; it is to use commercial or economic common sense to figure out how, in all likelihood, the parties would have provided for the contingency that has arisen had they foreseen it. . . ."

NOTE

Courts are charged with understanding the language, customs, and practices of the parties to a contract. We should be cautious, however, about thinking that courts can readily identify a common language of the trade. Lisa Bernstein has done the foundational work here. See, e.g., Lisa Bernstein, Merchant Law in a Merchant Court: Rethinking the Code's Search for Immanent Business Norms, 144 U. Pa. L. Rev. 1765 (1996). Trade usage may not be clear. It may not be constant across time and place. See Emily Kadens, The Myth of the Customary Law Merchant, 90 Tex. L. Rev. 1153 (2012). And even if it were both clear and constant, a court may not be able to access it. There is also a deeper problem. It is often a mistake to infer legal obligations from the customs and practices of merchants. Merchants may adopt regular practices that are never intended to generate a legal obligation. Hotels commonly allow guests to check in early when rooms are available, but does this mean that they are *legally obliged* to check guests in early if rooms are available? There is another problem. We are trying to extract legal rules from the norms that exist within a merchant community. But these norms arise from regular transactions within a single culture when things are going well. Lawsuits arise only when things have fallen apart. The norms from ordinary times may not be apt. Even if they were, lawsuits frequently involve amateurs or outsiders or people from different commercial cultures. We cannot rely on usage of trade unless we know which usage we are supposed to choose.

Commercial practice arises in a particular context that is often hard for outsiders to divine. A historian in the distant future who knew nothing about the 1960s except a series of amendments to the rules of a country club would see the introduction of all sorts of rules requiring members to wear ties and jackets. She might infer that people's dress became increasingly formal and fastidious during this period. This historian, however, would be making a mistake because she did not understand the context. Such rules were not required at the club until the late 1960s because before then everyone wore a tie and jacket as a matter of course. Rules became necessary only because dress was becoming increasingly casual. The relevant commercial practice in any case is something we have to construct from fragmentary bits of evidence. While most think that courts ought to try to understand the language and the customary practices of merchants in interpreting contracts, these may give us less guidance than we think.

Once the law no longer focuses on the subjective intent of the parties, it is easy to think about rules of interpretation that tend to reduce uncertainty and miscommunication in the first instance. We might want a rule that induces the party with information to disclose it. When a contract has two possible meanings and one party is aware of the ambiguity and the other is not, the rule might provide that it is the party who knows of the ambiguity that must resolve the ambiguity, or be held to the single meaning ascribed to the contract by the other side. The purpose of such a rule is not to try to capture a meeting of minds, but rather to induce parties to be forthcoming when they bargain with one another. The next case provides an example of such an approach.

United Rentals, Inc. v. RAM Holdings, Inc.

Court of Chancery of Delaware, 2007.
937 A.2d 810.

CHANDLER, Chancellor. In classical mythology, it took a demigod to subdue Cerberus, the beastly three-headed dog that guarded the gates of the underworld. In his twelfth and final labor, Heracles journeyed to Hades to battle, tame, and capture the monstrous creature. In this case, plaintiff United Rentals, Inc. journeyed to Delaware to conquer a more modern obstacle that, rather than guards the gates to the afterlife, stands in the way of the consummation of a merger. Nevertheless, like the three heads of the mythological Cerberus, the private equity firm of the same name presents three substantial challenges to plaintiff's case: (1) the language of the Merger Agreement, (2) evidence of the negotiations between the parties, and (3) a doctrine of contract interpretation known as the forthright negotiator principle. In this tale the three heads prove too much to overcome.

First, the language of the Merger Agreement presents a direct conflict between two provisions on remedies, rendering the Agreement ambiguous and defeating plaintiff's motion for summary judgment. Second, the extrinsic evidence of the negotiation process, though ultimately not conclusive, is too muddled to find that plaintiff's interpretation of the Agreement represents the common understanding of the parties. Third, under the forthright negotiator principle, the subjective understanding of one party to a contract may bind the other party when the other party knows or has reason to know of that understanding. Because the evidence in this case shows that defendants understood this Agreement to preclude the remedy of specific performance and that plaintiff knew or should have known of this understanding, I conclude that plaintiff has failed to meet its burden and find in favor of defendants. . . .

On November 19, 2007, plaintiff United Rentals, Inc. ("URI" or the "Company") filed its complaint in this action. Thereafter, on November 29, 2007, URI moved for summary judgment. In its motion for summary judgment, URI sought an order from this Court specifically enforcing the terms of the July 22, 2007 "Agreement and Plan of Merger" (the "Merger Agreement" or the "Agreement") among URI and defendants RAM Holdings, Inc. ("RAM Holdings") and RAM Acquisition Corp. ("RAM Acquisition" and, together with RAM Holdings, "RAM" or the "RAM Entities").[4] . . .

URI is a Delaware corporation with its principal place of business in Greenwich, Connecticut. Founded in 1997, it is a publicly traded company listed on the New York Stock Exchange. URI is the largest equipment rental company in the world based on revenue, earning $3.64 billion in 2006. The Company consists of an integrated network of over 690 rental locations in forty-eight states, ten Canadian provinces, and one location in Mexico. The Company serves construction and industrial customers, utilities, municipalities, homeowners and others. . . .

Throughout the course of negotiation of the Merger Agreement, URI contends that it communicated to RAM's principal attorney contract negotiator, Peter Ehrenberg of Lowenstein Sandler PC ("Lowenstein"), that URI wanted to restrict RAM's ability to breach the Merger Agreement and unilaterally refuse to close the transaction. URI further maintains that URI's counsel, Eric Swedenburg of Simpson Thacher & Bartlett LP ("Simpson"), made clear to Ehrenberg that it was very important to URI that there be "deal certainty" so that RAM could not simply refuse to close if debt financing was available.

On the other side of the negotiation table, the RAM entities argue that Ehrenberg consistently communicated that Cerberus had a $100 million walkway right and that URI knowingly relinquished its right to specific performance under the Merger Agreement. . . .

URI argues that the plain and unambiguous language of the merger agreement allows for specific performance as a remedy for the RAM Entities' breach. Section 9.10 expressly invests URI with a right to seek specific performance to enforce the Merger Agreement and to obtain an order enjoining RAM to (i) make reasonable best efforts to obtain financing and satisfy the Merger Agreement's closing conditions, and (ii) consummate the transactions when financing is available and has not been drawn down by RAM as a result of its breach of the Merger Agreement.

Section 9.10, however, explicitly states that it is "subject in all respects to Section 8.2(e) hereof, which Section shall govern the rights and obligations of the parties . . . under the circumstances provided therein." Section 8.2(e) describes the $100 million Parent Termination Fee payable to URI as the "sole and exclusive" remedy against RAM under the Agreement when there has been a termination of the Merger Agreement by URI. Further, section 8.2(e) provides that

> In no event, whether or not this Agreement has been terminated pursuant to any provision hereof, shall [RAM or Cerberus Partners] . . . be subject to any liability in excess of the Parent Termination Fee for any or all losses or damages relating to or aris-

---

[4] Both because RAM is controlled by Cerberus, as defined below, and because the witnesses' testimony often does not distinguish among these Cerberus-controlled entities, I will sometimes refer to defendants as "Cerberus," though Cerberus is *not* a party to this action; only RAM Holdings and RAM Acquisition are defendants in this case.

ing out of this Agreement or the transactions contemplated by this Agreement, . . . and in no event shall the Company seek equitable relief or seek to recover any money damages in excess of such amount from [RAM or Cerberus Partners]. . . .

Relying heavily on the canon of construction that requires harmonization of seemingly conflicting contract provisions, URI contends that specific performance under section 9.10 remains a viable remedy despite the language of section 8.2(e). URI offers two chief reasons in support of this position. First, section 8.2(e)'s $100 million Parent Termination Fee operates as the "sole and exclusive" remedy only if one of the parties terminates the agreement. Termination is a defined term in the Agreement, however, and it is not equivalent to a breach. URI contends (and RAM does not dispute) that neither party has terminated the agreement pursuant to section 8. Thus, the Termination Fee is not necessarily the "sole and exclusive remedy" in this case. Second, URI submits that the outright prohibition of equitable remedies in the last sentence of section 8.2(e) is limited to equitable remedies that involve monetary compensation like restitution or rescission. The sentence commands that "in no event shall [URI] seek equitable relief or seek to recover any money damages in excess of [the $100 million Termination Fee] from [RAM or Cerberus]." URI argues that the prepositional phrase ("in excess of the" termination fee) modifies *both* "equitable relief" and "money damages." This reading is required, URI says, because otherwise this sentence would render section 9.10 "mere surplusage" devoid of any meaning in violation of longstanding principles of contractual interpretation. Moreover, URI points to the final sentence of section 8.2(a) as proof that the Agreement contemplates a right to specific performance: "The parties acknowledge and agree that, subject to Section 8.2(e), nothing in this Section 8.2 shall be deemed to affect their right to specific performance under Section 9.10." According to URI, section 8.2(a) shows that the parties were aware of the "specific performance" remedy and could have expressly eliminated it. The Merger Agreement does not do so; instead, it explicitly provides that both specific performance and injunctive relief are available remedies.

The RAM Entities counter that URI's interpretation is unreasonable. First, they argue, it is URI's position that would render portions of the Agreement "mere surplusage." If the operation of section 8.2(e) were in fact limited, as URI asserts, to circumstances in which the Merger Agreement had been properly terminated by either party, there would be no need to include a sentence in section 9.10 subjecting the specific performance provisions of section 9.10 to section 8.2(e) because specific performance, by law, would be unavailable in those circumstances; one cannot specifically perform an agreement that has been terminated. Thus, section 8.2(e) must have applicability outside the context of termination. Second, the RAM Entities argue that is unreasonable to limit the phrase "equitable relief" to those equitable remedies that include monetary damages.

Reading the Agreement as a whole and with the aid of the fundamental canons of contract construction, I conclude that URI's interpretation is reasonable. The parties explicitly agreed in section 9.10 that "irreparable damage would occur in the event that any of the provisions of this Agreement were not performed in accordance with their specific terms or were otherwise breached." They further agreed that "the Company shall be entitled to see an injunction or injunctions . . . to enforce compliance." Given this clarion language supporting the existence and availability of specific performance, it is reasonable to read the limitations of section 8.2(e) in the manner URI has championed. RAM's arguments to the contrary are ultimately unpersuasive. Neither party has terminated the Agreement pursuant to the termination provisions of section 8.1, and the context of the final sentence of section 8.2(e) allows one to reasonably conclude that "equitable relief" in that sentence means only equitable relief involving monetary damages. URI's interpretation thus represents a reasonable harmonization of apparently conflicting provisions. . . .

Though defendants fail to demonstrate that plaintiff's interpretation of the Merger Agreement is unreasonable as a matter of law, defendants do succeed in offering a reasonable alternative interpretation. In opposing URI's motion for summary judgment, defendants deny that the provisions of the Merger Agreement conflict so as to require harmonization. The relationship between sections 9.10 and 8.2(e), as set forth in section 9.10 is, defendants contend, clear: section 9.10 is "subject to" section 8.2(e). Section 8.2(e) then provides that "in no event shall [URI] seek equitable relief or seek to recover any money damages in excess of such amount [*i.e.,* the $100 million termination fee] from [RAM or Cerberus]." RAM argues that section 8.2(e) operates to prohibit URI from seeking any form of equitable relief (including specific performance) under all circumstances, relegating URI's relief to only the $100 million termination fee. [D]efendants contend that Delaware law specifically permits the parties to establish supremacy and subservience between provisions such that, where the terms of one provision are expressly stated to be "subject to" the terms of a second provision, the terms of the second provision will control, even if the terms of the second provision conflict with or nullify the first provision. Additionally, RAM argues, unlike plaintiff's interpretation, RAM's interpretation utilizes only the plain meaning of "equitable relief." As described above, plaintiff, in proposing a reconciliation of the section 8.2(e) limitation on equitable relief with the right of specific performance in section 9.10, urges this Court to read the words "equitable relief" and "money damages" as modified by the phrase "in excess of" the termination fee. Defendants' interpretation of this portion of the provision is, however, at least as reasonable as (if not more than) that of plaintiff. The phrase "in excess of" appears, grammatically, to modify only "money damages."

Plaintiff argues that if RAM had wanted to eliminate URI's rights to specific performance in all circumstances, it could have simply stricken out clause (b) of section 9.10. Though the Court has no doubt that this simple (and seemingly obvious) drafting approach would have been superior, on a motion for summary judgment, I cannot look beyond the text of the agreement to inquire into the motivations of the parties or to consider ways in which a particular end may have been more efficiently achieved and more clearly articulated. An interpretation of the Agreement that relies on the parties' addition of hierarchical phrases, instead of the deletion of particular language altogether, is not unreasonable as a matter of law.

Having considered all of plaintiff's arguments, I must conclude that plaintiff has not shown that defendants' interpretation is unreasonable as a matter of law. The contracting parties here chose terms, such as "subject to," that impose a hierarchy among provisions. Defendants' interpretation of those terms and the provisions they affect is not, I conclude, unreasonable. . . .

It is probably unlikely that a single, *unambiguous* agreement can simultaneously affirm and deny the availability of a specific performance remedy. If there is such an unambiguous contract, it is certainly not the contract at issue in this case. Both URI and RAM have proffered reasonable readings of the Merger Agreement, and because "provisions in controversy are fairly susceptible of different interpretations or may have two or more different meanings, there is ambiguity." Thus, plaintiff's and defendants' arguments suffer the same flaw, which is fatal at this stage: each party is unable to demonstrate that its proposed interpretation of the Merger Agreement is the *only* interpretation of the Agreement that is reasonable as a matter of law. In such a case, summary judgment is inappropriate because the court is presented with a genuine issue of material fact: what was the intent of the parties? Therefore, I must consider extrinsic evidence to ascertain the meaning of the Merger Agreement. . . .

The Court heard testimony from seven witnesses over a two-day trial in order to resolve the factual issue of what was the common understanding of the parties with respect to remedies in the Merger Agreement. The Merger Agreement, of course, is a contract, and the Court's goal when interpreting a contract "is to ascertain the shared intention of the parties." . . .

Having determined that the contract is ambiguous on account of its conflicting provisions, the Court permitted the parties to introduce extrinsic evidence of the negotiation process. Such extrinsic evidence may include "overt statements and acts of the parties, the business context, prior dealings between the parties, [and] business custom and usage in the industry." This evidence may lead to "a single 'correct' or single 'objectively reasonable' meaning." Restated, the extrinsic evidence may render an ambiguous contract clear so that an "objectively reasonable party in the position of either bargainer would have understood the nature of the contractual rights and duties to be." In such a case, the Court would enforce the objectively reasonable interpretation that emerges.

The Court must emphasize here that the introduction of extrinsic, parol evidence does not alter or deviate from Delaware's adherence to the objective theory of contracts. As I recently explained to counsel in this case, the private, subjective feelings of the negotiators are irrelevant and unhelpful to the Court's consideration of a contract's meaning, because the meaning of a properly formed contract must be shared or common. That is not to say, however, that a party's subjective understanding is never instructive. On the contrary, in cases where an examination of the extrinsic evidence does not lead to an obvious, objectively reasonable conclusion, the Court may apply the forthright negotiator principle.[120] Under this principle, the Court considers the evidence of what one party *subjectively* "believed the obligation to be, coupled with evidence that the other party knew or should have known of such belief."[121] In other words, the forthright negotiator principle provides that, in cases where the extrinsic evidence does not lead to a single, commonly held understanding of a contract's meaning, a court may consider the subjective understanding of one party that has been objectively manifested and is known or should be known by the other party. It is with these fundamental legal principles in mind that I consider the factual record developed at trial. . . .

The evidence presented at trial conveyed a deeply flawed negotiation in which both sides failed to clearly and consistently communicate their

---

[120] Comrie v. Enterasys Networks, Inc., 837 A.2d 1, 13 (Del. Ch. 2003).

[121] U.S. West, Inc. v. Time Warner, Inc., C.A. No. 14555, 1996 WL 307445 (Del. Ch. June 6, 1996).

client's positions. First, I find that the extrinsic evidence is not clear enough to conclude that there is a single, shared understanding with respect to the availability of specific performance under the Merger Agreement. Second, I employ the forthright negotiator principle to make two additional findings. With respect to URI, I find that even if the Company believed the Agreement preserved a right to specific performance, its attorney Eric Swedenburg categorically failed to communicate that understanding to the defendants during the latter part of the negotiations. Finally, with respect to RAM, although it could have easily avoided this entire dispute by striking section 9.10(b) from the Agreement, I find that its attorney did communicate to URI his understanding that the Agreement precluded any specific performance rights. Consequently, I conclude that URI has failed to meet its burden and determine that the Merger Agreement does not allow a specific performance remedy. . . .

The parties began their negotiations very far apart. URI circulated a draft that included numerous provisions favorable to their side, including several mechanisms by which URI could specifically enforce the merger against Cerberus. RAM responded with a "heavy-handed" mark-up. Early conversations led to no agreement, and URI simply ignored many of the proposed changes that RAM initially made. Although RAM ultimately succeeded in striking many of the provisions entitling URI to specific performance, and although RAM did modify section 8.2(e) to try to limit the availability of equitable relief, section 9.10 in the final agreement continued to speak of the Company's right to specific performance. Testimony revealed that communications between the parties routinely skirted the issue of equitable relief and only addressed it tangentially or implicitly. The defendants put forth some evidence suggesting that by mid to late July Swedenburg had agreed to give up specific performance, but it was not conclusive. Mr. Seitz, URI's attorney, deftly questioned RAM's chief negotiator Ehrenberg about the clarity and wisdom of his curious editing of section 9.10, a provision Ehrenberg also contends he nullified, but this did not uncover "a single 'correct' or single 'objectively reasonable' meaning'" for the Agreement. Indeed, because "a review of the extrinsic evidence does not lead the Court to an 'obvious' conclusion," I must apply the forthright negotiator principle to determine the proper interpretation of this contract. . . .

Based on the evidence presented at trial, I find that the defendants understood the agreement to eliminate any right to specific performance and that URI either knew or should have known of defendants' understanding. Cerberus seems to have come to this transaction halfheartedly and unenthusiastic about committing. It took issue with a great deal of the initial draft agreement URI circulated and failed to submit a bid by the proposed deadline. The defendants offered a go-shop period with a lower break fee to allow URI to shop itself to other bidders without the fear of paying a huge termination fee. Moreover, Cerberus lowered its bid significantly. Cerberus was not acting like an eager buyer and was not willing to do this deal on the terms initially proposed by URI.

Testimony from two of Cerberus's leaders, CEO Stephen Feinberg and managing director Steven Mayer, demonstrated that the firm believed it had the ability to walk away from this agreement relatively unscathed. Indeed, Feinberg, though evidently unsure of what "specific performance" means, did think "very clearly that to the extent we didn't complete the merger, that our—our liability and our—what we'd have to come up with was a hundred million and that we could not be forced to close the deal."

Mayer, who participated more directly in the negotiations and who reviewed the Merger Agreement both in drafts and in final form, testified that he "believe[s] there was an explicit understanding that Cerberus could choose not to close the transaction for any reason or no reason at all and pay a maximum amount of a hundred million dollars." In addition to the Cerberus executives, lawyers for Cerberus testified to and produced contemporaneous notes corroborating their subjective understanding that the $100 million termination fee was the "sole and exclusive" recourse available to URI in the event of a failure to close.

I also find that defendants communicated this understanding to URI in such a way that URI either knew or should have known of their understanding. Initially, Cerberus conveyed its position by means of the drafts and mark-ups it sent to Swedenburg. For example, on June 18, 2007, Ehrenberg sent Simpson his initial mark-ups to the draft circulated by URI. In that mark-up, Ehrenberg wrote, "OUR CLIENT WILL NOT AGREE TO A GUARANTEE." Ehrenberg also removed a provision from section 6.10 "that would have required the buyer to take enforcement actions against the lenders and other persons providing the financing." Finally, Ehrenberg struck portions of section 9.10(b) that would have allowed URI to specifically enforce the Equity Commitment Letter and the Guarantee and to specifically enforce the consummation of the transaction. While discussing these, Swedenburg told Ehrenberg that he would likely not incorporate many of the changes, would send it back, and would expect Cerberus's next mark-up to be "less voluminous."

Nevertheless, Ehrenberg persisted. In a conversation that occurred sometime between June 25 and July 10, Ehrenberg and Swedenburg discussed the extent of the defendants' potential liability. During this conversation, Swedenburg indicated "that it was important for his client to assure that . . . Cerberus and the RAM entities showed up at the closing." Ehrenberg "explained to Mr. Swedenburg that that was a significant problem." At a July 10 meeting of the attorneys, it was decided that the issue of liability needed to be decided by the principals, but that Cerberus would be willing to enter a limited guarantee agreement.

The next important meeting occurred on July 12, 2007. There, via telephone, Mayer represented to the URI team that "Cerberus would not proceed with the negotiations or with the deal unless there was an arrangement where, if the Cerberus parties, to include RAM, failed to close, the obligation would be to pay a fee." Both Ehrenberg and Mayer testified that the URI team agreed to this point on the twelfth.

After this meeting, Ehrenberg and his team returned to the Merger Agreement and made several important revisions. The draft they produced was circulated early in the morning on July 15, 2007 along with new versions of the Equity Commitment Letter and the Limited Guarantee. I find several edits significant in these documents:

　　　1. the Equity Commitment Letter expressly disclaims any third-party beneficiaries and exceptions to allow for suit against the Cerberus entities were removed;

　　　2. the "no recourse" provisions of the Limited Guarantee were expanded to make them farther reaching;

　　　3. section 9.10 was edited to remove references to the Equity Commitment Letter and the final sentence was added to make the provision subservient to section 8.2(e);

    4. section 8.2(e) was substantially rewritten to include a limitation on liability and to provide explicitly that "in no event shall the Company seek equitable relief. . . ."

Although . . . these edits do not provide a perfectly clear expression of RAM's position that the agreement bars specific performance, they are substantial enough that they should have at least put Swedenburg and URI on notice that RAM had a different understanding than URI did. Subsequent communications between the parties go substantively beyond this, and unquestionably convey RAM's position.

Swedenburg made very few changes to this draft. He struck the provision about the Company's ability to "seek equitable relief," but he ultimately did not stand by this revision. When Ehrenberg received Swedenburg's edits, he circulated an agenda for a meeting to discuss the Merger Agreement. On that agenda, Ehrenberg listed "limitation of liability in 8.2(e)" as a topic for discussion, and by this he "intended to address the deletion of the words equity relief." At that meeting, Mr. Swedenburg spent his time lobbying for a higher break-up fee, one that would be "painful," because the potential reputational harm Cerberus would suffer from walking away would not be enough to deter them from doing so. Perhaps more importantly, the RAM attorneys also explained to Swedenburg the importance of the words "equitable relief" that Swedenburg had stricken from the Merger Agreement: "it was important for us that the language that he struck be restored to reflect the agreement that the only remedy available to United Rentals, if Cerberus didn't proceed with the closing, was the break-up fee-reverse break-up fee." Testimony indicated that Swedenburg put up no fight on this issue. He tersely replied, "I get it."

I find this testimony to be credible and I find that it is supported by certain of defendants' exhibits and by Swedenburg's testimony. First, the agenda that Ehrenberg circulated specifically references section 8.2(e). Second, Holt's notes from the July 19 meeting support the proposition that this conversation happened and that Swedenburg assented. Third, Swedenburg essentially capitulated on this point during cross examination. Conceding that he quickly assented to the reinsertion of the language he had removed from section 8.2(e), Swedenburg then testified that he knew "equitable relief included specific performance," that this was "probably why [he] did strike it," admitted that Ehrenberg conveyed how important that provision was to Cerberus, and then concluded by suggesting he knew it would have been a good idea to inquire further about why this provision was so important to Cerberus, but that he failed to so inquire because it "was at the end of an agenda, there was [sic] more negotiations to go, et cetera, et cetera." I find it frankly incredible that Swedenburg could have recognized the import of the language he was striking and that Cerberus considered that language key but manifestly failed to make any further inquiry. Swedenburg, the original architect of this transaction, testified that one lynchpin of his "construct" was the seller's ability to force the sale to close. By the end of this July 19 meeting, Swedenburg either knew or should have known that Cerberus's understanding of the Agreement was fundamentally inconsistent with that construct.

If Swedenburg's faltering on July 19 were not enough to put URI on notice of Cerberus's understanding, the July 21 telephone conversation between the UBS representatives (McNeal and Kochman) and Mayer surely was. On that call, Mayer mentioned something about Cerberus's ability to walk away from the deal. Kochman responded forcefully, declaring that his client, URI, would never agree to this deal if it were merely an option. Mayer reassured him that Cerberus was committed to the deal, but never conceded that the contract amounted to anything other than an option. McNeal and Kochman reported this conversation to Horowitz, and Brad Jacobs, then-CEO/Chairman of URI. Horowitz, who evidently cannot remember much of this deal, failed to raise this issue with Swedenburg, the chief negotiator, or with Ehrenberg. On July 22, the very next day, the Agreement was executed. At that time, I conclude that URI had ample reason to know that Cerberus understood the Agreement to bar the remedy of specific performance. . . .

Although some in the media have discussed this case in the context of Material Adverse Change ("MAC") clauses, the dispute between URI and Cerberus is a good, old-fashioned contract case prompted by buyer's remorse. As with many contract disputes, hindsight affords the Court a perspective from which it is clear that this case could have been avoided: if Cerberus had simply deleted section 9.10(b), the contract would not be ambiguous, and URI would not have filed this suit. The law of contracts, however, does not require parties to choose optimally clear language; in fact, parties often riddle their agreements with a certain amount of ambiguity in order to reach a compromise. Although the language in this Merger Agreement remains ambiguous, the understanding of the parties does not. . . .

One may plausibly upbraid Cerberus for walking away from this deal, for favoring their lenders over their targets, or for suboptimal contract editing, but one cannot reasonably criticize the firm for a failure to represent its understanding of the limitations on remedies provided by this Merger Agreement. From the beginning of the process, Cerberus and its attorneys have aggressively negotiated this contract, and along the way they have communicated their intentions and understandings to URI. Despite the Herculean efforts of its litigation counsel at trial, URI could not overcome the apparent lack of communication of *its* intentions and understandings to defendants. Even if URI's deal attorneys did not affirmatively and explicitly agree to the limitation on specific performance as several witnesses allege they did on multiple occasions, no testimony at trial rebutted the inference that I must reasonably draw from the evidence: by July 22, 2007, URI knew or should have known what Cerberus's understanding of the Merger Agreement was, and if URI disagreed with that understanding, it had an affirmative duty to clarify its position in the face of an ambiguous contract with glaringly conflicting provisions. Because it has failed to meet its burden of demonstrating that the common understanding of the parties permitted specific performance of the Merger Agreement, URI's petition for specific performance is denied. . . .

————

Grandis Family Partnership, Ltd. v. Hess Corp.

United States District Court, Southern District of Florida, 2008.
588 F. Supp. 2d 1319.

ZLOCH, DISTRICT JUDGE. . . . Defendant Hess Corporation (hereinafter "Hess") and Plaintiff Advanced Power Technologies (hereinafter "APT") began working together in 2003, when Hess contracted with APT for it to service and maintain the lighting at many of Hess's retail gas stations in Florida. Hess was pleased with their business relationship, and in June of

2007, Hess expanded its business with APT by purchasing several orders of lighting ballasts.

In the same year, Hess began accepting bids for a major renovation of its gas stations' outdoor lighting. It planned to replace the existing lighting and ballasts with more energy-efficient models. APT's bid was accepted, and in May of that year, the Parties began negotiating the terms of their agreement. When the Parties' formal agreement was memorialized on July 2, 2007, it consisted of an eleven-page written agreement, complete with eighty pages of appendices, schedules, and forms. However, for certain business reasons, APT began its performance on the project in late June of that year.

The first eleven pages of the Parties' contract was a form prepared by Hess's legal department, which it has used for over a decade. At the evidentiary hearing, John Garabino, the Hess representative who negotiated the contract with APT, testified that the eleven-page contract was used as a base for the contractual agreement with APT, while the appendices and schedules attached thereto made up the heart of the Parties' agreement. Despite the contract with its appendices and Schedules being seemingly exhaustive in their breadth and detail, it did not contain an arbitration clause or venue provision. Pertinent to the instant Motion, the contract contained a clause listing the documents that were to be incorporated by reference, an integration clause, and a choice-of-law clause, whereby the Parties agreed that New York law governs any disputes.

After the Parties' agreement was formalized but before the project was completed, the Parties' relationship broke down. APT responded by filing suit in Florida state court, wherein it alleged that Hess was in breach of the contract. Hess timely removed the suit to this Court. With its Answer, it filed a counterclaim for breach of contract and conversion against APT. The factual basis for the counterclaim is immaterial to this Order.

After the case was at issue but before discovery had commenced, Hess filed the instant Motion. In it, Hess argues that any disputes arising from the contract must be referred to arbitration, despite the contract's silence concerning the same. In support of this position, Hess cites the terms and conditions referenced in the thirty-two Purchase Orders it sent APT for work performed under the contract. The face of the Purchase Order references the contract's Schedules and forms in several different areas, including each of the individual projects' start and completion dates, as well as forms APT was to complete with the work it performed. Directly under the Purchase Order's style was the following sentence, in bold:

> THE PURCHASE ORDER TERMS AND CONDITIONS AS WELL AS THE SHIPMENT ROUTING POLICY LOCATED AT http:// www. hess. com/ PO/ Hess MR. htm ARE INCORPO-RATED BY REFERENCE IN THIS PURCHASE ORDER.

By viewing the website listed above, APT would see the additional terms and conditions that it was deemed to assent to by filling the Purchase Order. Among the terms and conditions located on the Hess website, one is of particular importance to this Motion: the arbitration clause. It states, in pertinent part, that "all disputes, claims, questions, or differences shall be finally settled by arbitration." . . .

Hess's principal argument for referring this case to arbitration is that the Hess Purchase Order, complete with its terms and conditions on the Hess website, is incorporated by reference into the contract. New York adheres to the common-law principle that parties are free to incorporate into a contract terms that are contained in a separate, independent document. In order for the separate, referenced document to be incorporated, "it must be clear that the parties to the agreement had knowledge of and assented to the incorporated terms." *Lamb v. Emhart Corp.*, 47 F.3d 551, 558 (2d Cir. 1995). New York courts have expressed the rule as "requir[ing] that the paper to be incorporated into a written instrument by reference must be so referred to and described in the instrument that the paper may be *identified beyond all reasonable doubt." PaineWebber, Inc. v. Bybyk*, 81 F.3d 1193, 1201 (2d. Cir. 1996). For the incorporated terms to be binding "it must be clear that the parties know of and consented to the terms to be incorporated by reference." Creative Waste Management v. Capitol Environmental Services, 429 F. Supp. 2d 582, 602 (S.D.N.Y. 2006) An oblique reference to a separate, non-contemporaneous document is insufficient to incorporate the same into the contract. *Ryan, Beck & Co., LLC v. Fakih*, 268 F. Supp. 2d 210, 223 (E.D.N.Y. 2003). . . .

Hess cites both the language of the contract and APT's prior notice of and dealings with the Purchase Orders to establish that the website's terms are incorporated by reference into the contract. Thus, Hess makes two arguments: one on the four corners of the contract and the other on the Parties' use and understanding of the term "purchase orders." . . .

Hess's primary argument is based on the contract's language: the term "purchase order" is used in Schedule C, and therefore, the Hess Purchase Orders are incorporated by reference into the contract. Schedule C states that "[a]fter receipt of a purchase order for each subproject the Contractor may submit a payment application for 30% of the purchase order value." The next paragraph states: "After receipt of an approved changed [sic] order Contractor may submit a payment application for the remaining value of the purchase order (total revised purchase order value less the 30% of original purchase order value previously paid)." There is no other reference to purchase orders in the 91 pages that make up the Parties' formal agreement.

To bolster its argument that the Purchase Orders are incorporated by reference, Hess introduced the testimony of John Garabino. He testified that he reviewed the contract with APT before entering into it and felt it was clear that the references to purchase orders in Schedule C was to the Purchase Orders used by Hess. He also testified that a sample Hess Purchase Order, complete with the terms and conditions on the website, was provided to APT representatives at a meeting held in late May with APT, Hess, and the supplier of the materials used on the project. In support, Hess introduced as Defendant's Exhibit 1 an email with an agenda of the May 23, 2007, meeting attached. Garabino also testified that Purchase Orders with the bolded language quoted above, directing a reader to the Hess website, were sent to APT when Hess ordered ballasts in June of 2007. Hess also introduced into evidence an email APT sent it commenting on the Purchase Orders Hess sent in June of 2007 regarding the purchase of ballasts.

The precise issue for this Court to determine is whether the language of Schedule C clearly referenced the Hess Purchase Orders to make it clear, beyond a reasonable doubt to APT that the Hess Purchase Order was being incorporated by reference into the contract. Whether an extrinsic document is incorporated by reference is a question of law. As such, the Court looks first to the language of the contract; if its language is ambiguous, then the

Court will look to the "mutual knowledge and understanding on part of both parties [to determine] that reference by implication is clear." *Newton v. Smith Motors, Inc.,* 122 Vt. 409, 175 A.2d 514, 516 (1961).

Looking first to the plain language of the contract, it is clear that the only reference to purchase orders is found in Schedule C. Hess argues that these references refer APT to the Hess Purchase Orders that they were previously provided with, complete with the reference to the Hess website. As noted above, to incorporate the Hess Purchase Orders by reference, Hess must establish that the contract's language both identifies beyond all reasonable doubt the Hess Purchase Orders and makes clear that they are being incorporated by reference into the contract.

In contrast to the high bar set by New York caselaw, Schedule C's references to "purchase orders" speak in a vague and general sense. It does not reference a specific Purchase Order or specific form of purchase order, nor does the contract state that such a Purchase Order is being incorporated by reference. Grammatically, this general rather than specific reference is evidenced by the drafter's choice to refer to purchase orders as a common noun, rather than a proper noun. The latter would evidence a particular purchase order, one that any person reading the contract would either expect to be attached to the contract, or, if not attached, the use of a proper noun would lead APT to expect the purchase order referenced to have a definite form that they are either aware of or should take the time to apprise themselves of. This lack of specificity is confirmed by the drafter's use of the indefinite article "a" when first referring to "purchase orders" in Schedule C, rather than the definite article "the." As it stands, Schedule C's language refers to a generic form, purchase orders, that is common to most industries and does not immediately or clearly denote the specific Hess Purchase Orders, with their particular provisions.

The language of Schedule C does not make a deliberate attempt to alert the reader that the Hess Purchase Orders are being incorporated by reference, or that any purchase orders are being incorporated by reference. . . .

Hess is then, essentially, arguing that the Hess Purchase Orders are incorporated by reference into Schedule C and Schedule C is incorporated by reference into the contract. Nothing in Schedule C, however, indicates with any semblance of intention or clarity that it is incorporating a document by reference. It strains credulity to argue that every common noun referenced in each of the Schedules incorporates by reference a separate nonattached document into the contract.

Reading the contract as a whole and contrasting the purchase order language of Schedule C with the rest of the contract, it is clear that the drafter did not evidence an intent to formally incorporate by reference the Hess Purchase Orders into the contract. Even if the drafter personally intended to incorporate by reference the Hess Purchase Orders, the document's reference to purchase orders was oblique and did not "identif[y] beyond all reasonable doubt" the non-contemporaneous document he sought to incorporate by reference: the Hess Purchase Order. *Bybyk,* 81 F.3d at 1201. The Hess Purchase Orders were not among the items explicitly incorporated by reference in the second provision, they are not referred to as proper nouns, they were not attached to the contract, and the sole reference to "purchase orders" in Schedule C was both oblique and without any indication that it was incorporating a specific document by reference into the contract or Schedule C.

That is not to say that a form being referred to as a proper noun is a necessary condition to have a form incorporated by reference. It is possible that a form could be of such a unique nature that absent being set out with particularity it would be incorporated by reference into the contract because of the mutual knowledge and understanding of the parties. However, with the generic title "purchase order" used in Schedule C, there is nothing that would convey to a person reading the contract a direct and specific indication that a particular document is being incorporated by reference. Purchase orders are a common form in the service industry. Without a definite understanding being set forth for the Parties, knowledge that "purchase orders" in Schedule C refers to the Hess Purchase Orders cannot be imputed to APT. . . .

The language of the contract fails to clearly set forth that the term "purchase order" in Schedule C is meant to incorporate by reference the Hess Purchase Orders; nevertheless, for the benefit of the Parties and any reviewing court, the Court will look to what the Parties clearly understood "purchase orders" in Schedule C to mean, given their dealings in the formation of the contract. In considering parol evidence, Hess's burden remains the same, namely some contract must identify beyond a reasonable doubt that the Hess Purchase Orders are being incorporated by reference. Hess can establish through testimony and documents outside the contract what APT understood the term "purchase orders" in Schedule C to mean. At the hearing, Garabino testified that APT was provided with the Hess Purchase Orders twice before the contract was signed: once at the May 27 meeting and again when Hess purchased ballasts through APT. Hess argues that this May 27 meeting establishes that APT knew precisely what the term "purchase order" in Schedule C referred to, because Hess presented APT with a sample Purchase Order complete with the link to the website that contained the arbitration clause.

At the evidentiary hearing, APT denied having any prior knowledge of the Hess Purchase Orders and the terms and conditions on the website. Several Hess Purchase Orders, complete with the website link, were sent to APT for the ballasts purchased in June of 2007. APT's president Devin Grandis testified that the sale of ballasts was done as a courtesy for Hess, and because of that, he paid no attention to the Purchase Orders that were sent for the ballasts. APT's vice president Freddie Manfretti testified that in the course of APT's dealings with Hess he handled hundreds if not thousands of purchase orders from Hess, and not one of them contained a link to a website containing an arbitration clause. The administrative assistant, Cathy Cole, who dealt with the Purchase Orders for the ballasts also testified that she took no notice of the link to the website, she only paid attention to the fact that the wrong parts number was listed on the order. She mistakenly assumed that those Purchase Orders were like the others that she had processed from Hess.

All of the APT employees testified that in their previous dealings with Hess the purchase orders sent did not resemble those at issue here with the link to the website. This fact is critical because without actual knowledge of these prior Purchase Orders being sent for the ballasts, the term "purchase order" in Schedule C would not carry any significance for APT to know that it incorporated by reference the Hess Purchase Orders with the additional terms. Thus, there was nothing in the prior Purchase Orders for ballasts that would have made APT representatives conscious of the website link and the additional terms contained therein when it signed the contract with Hess.

Additionally, APT's president Devin Grandis testified that neither the Purchase Orders nor the terms and conditions contained on Hess's website were provided to him at the meeting held between APT and Hess on May 27, 2008. Both Manfretti and Cathy Cole testified to this fact. After observing the demeanor of the witnesses for APT, the Court finds their testimony to be credible. In addition, on cross-examination Hess's representative Garabino was not positive that he provided a copy of the Purchase Orders to APT representatives at the meeting; he was only sure that the agenda reflected that they would be discussed. He testified that his assistant Sue Thompson was in charge of handing out the Hess Purchase Order and the terms and conditions on the website. He also believed that because the topics were on the agenda the APT representatives would have received a copy. However, Hess failed to call Sue Thompson, the person who did have actual knowledge of whether a sample Hess Purchase Order was actually distributed to APT. Based on the testimony and evidence, it is not clear whether APT was provided the Purchase Orders with the terms and conditions at the May 23, 2007 meeting, which would have given APT knowledge of what the term "purchase order" in Schedule C was referring to. . . .

New York courts look to many factors, including the form of the contracts, the parties' behavior, and the effect of each contract on the other when determining whether the separate documents should be read together. Here, the contract and the first Purchase Order were executed one week apart. The contract and the Purchase Orders deal with the same subject matter: the relighting of Hess gas stations. The Hess Purchase Orders also reference the contract and various Schedules contained therein. While much of this suggests that the two should be read together, there is nothing that establishes that the intention to read the documents together was mutual.

First, the testimony at the evidentiary hearing and the language of the contract itself do not evidence an intent to read the two documents together. There was no testimony that the contract was not self-executing or somehow dependent on the issuance of Purchase Orders. In fact, Devin Grandis testified that APT began performing under the agreement before a Purchase Order was issued. The contract also had an integration clause evidencing that the document was meant to stand alone. Further, Hess never introduced any evidence that beyond a formal incorporation by reference these documents should be read together by implication.

Second, the divergent evidence produced by both Parties prevents the Court from finding a mutual intent by the Parties to read the two documents together. Hess believed that the Purchase Orders were incorporated by reference, which they were not. Hess's representative did not see the Purchase Orders as a "non-severable package." [Arciniaga v. General Motors Corp., 460 F.3d 231, 236 (2d Cir. 2006).] Garabino testified that he viewed the Purchase Orders as being incorporated by reference, not that they were mutually dependent documents or contracts. The distinction is subtle but important: just because a party desires to have a document incorporated by reference does not necessarily mean that the two documents have a symbiotic relationship that creates a "non-severable package." In this case they surely were not; APT was able to fulfill its duties under the contract without a Purchase Order being issued.

Additionally, APT's representatives testified that the Purchase Orders and terms were never shown to them prior to signing the contract, and that they never assented to the same. Thus, there was never any intent by APT to be bound by the terms and conditions with the Hess Purchase Orders, let alone to have them read together with the contract. . . .

————

Hemenway v. Peabody Coal Co.

United States Court of Appeals, Seventh Circuit, 1998.
159 F.3d 255.

EASTERBROOK, CIRCUIT JUDGE. A mineral lease signed in 1969 requires Peabody Coal Company to pay a royalty based on the coal's "sales price." During the 1970s Congress enacted two excise taxes. One, for the benefit of the Black Lung Disability Trust Fund, is 55¢ per ton of surface-mined coal, with a cap at 4.4% of the coal's selling price. The other, designated a "reclamation fee" by the Surface Mining Control and Reclamation Act of 1977, is 35¢ per ton of surface-mined coal, capped at 10% of "the value of the coal at the mine." In 1983 Peabody began to charge its customers a "mine closing and final reclamation payment" of 25¢ per ton. Peabody's invoices list a per-ton charge for coal, the two taxes, and the mine-closing fee. In an invoice that Peabody calls typical, the charge for coal was $28.635 per ton, and the three additional charges were $1.10 per ton. Peabody paid royalties only on the coal charge, which represented 96.3% of the invoice total.

In this suit under the diversity jurisdiction, plaintiffs (assignees of the original lessors' royalty interests) contend that the two taxes and the mine-closing fee are part of the "sales price" for royalty-calculation purposes. . . .

The lease defines "sales price" unhelpfully as the "average invoice price of coal mined, removed and sold." Are excise taxes part of the "average invoice price"? In one sense this is a trivial question. Of course they are. They appear on the invoice as part of the price the customer must pay. But the idea that a mine operator must pay the mineral owner a royalty on taxes, as opposed to coal, is jarring, and Peabody insists that the parties could not have contemplated this result in 1969. (The "mine closing" charge does not appear to represent an excise tax, but the parties make nothing of this. Like the parties, we treat all three surcharges as excise taxes.)

A tax lowers the demand for coal, and its burden is distributed according to the elasticity of demand. The district court supposed that demand for coal is perfectly inelastic, and if so buyers bear the whole tax and sellers are unaffected. If demand is not perfectly inelastic, then the sellers bear some of the loss, which participants on the seller's side normally would share (or would have so agreed in advance, had they thought about the possibility). But if the excise taxes are included in "sales price," then if elasticity is less than 1 the mineral owners will be better off and Peabody worse off. (If elasticity exceeds 1, both the mineral owners and Peabody can be worse off, because total revenues will fall.)

Consider a simple example. Suppose coal sells for $10 per ton, the royalty paid to the mineral owners is $1 per ton (10% of sales price), and Peabody makes a profit of $1 per ton. Now Congress adds an excise tax of $1 per ton, so that (at first approximation) the price rises to $11. If the tax is part of the "sales price" then the mineral owners' royalty rises to $1.10 per ton and Peabody's profit falls to 90¢ per ton. If because of elastic demand

Peabody cannot raise the price to $11 (or sells fewer tons at that price than at $10) then Peabody's share will be less than 90¢ per ton, it will make that return on fewer tons, or both. Economists believe that many mineral and (other) property taxes fall on the land owner, because real property lacks alternative uses. This implies that if mineral owners and mine operators could bargain in advance they would be likely to assign the economic effects of future taxes to the mineral owners. (The tax is not on any asset specific to coal *extraction*, so operators that can bargain with many mineral owners won't deal with those who seek to shift its incidence to mine operators.) A pact that makes the mineral owner better off, and the mine operator worse off, as a result of a tax makes little economic sense—plaintiffs have not suggested why they would have bargained for this result, or why a mine operator would have agreed to it—and leads to caution in employing a plain-language reading of the text. Especially when plaintiffs agree that a *sales* tax, nominally imposed on the buyer but collected and remitted by the seller, would not be part of the "sales price" under the contract. The choice between a tax formally on the seller (as these two taxes are), and one formally on the buyer is arbitrary; the two have identical economic and practical effects. Yet according to plaintiffs everything turns on this designation.

But it takes more than an economic puzzle to justify giving an unusual spin to contractual language. Contracts allocate risks, and judicial decisions changing those allocations after the fact not only lead to expensive litigation (as each side invests in the pursuit of advantage) but also make the institution of contract less useful *ex ante*. Parties to contracts may prefer simple-minded textualism to costly disputes later on, even knowing that a plain-language reading sometimes goes wrong, and they may make adjustments—in other parts of the contract, or in the royalty rate—to compensate for this possibility. Or perhaps they just made a mistake and now rue the choice. Learned Hand remarked that "in commercial transactions it does not in the end promote justice to seek strained interpretations in aid of those who do not protect themselves," James Baird Co. v. Gimbel Bros., Inc., 64 F.2d 344, 346 (2d Cir. 1933), and Indiana follows this precept by insisting that contracts be implemented as written even if the results are unexpected. Indiana also is of the view that federal excise taxes are part of a product's selling price. Sun Oil Co. v. Gross Income Tax Division, 238 Ind. 111, 149 N.E.2d 115 (1958). Although *Sun Oil* did not involve the interpretation of a contract, the state's understanding of excise taxes as part of a product's price is the norm. To justify excluding from "average invoice price" elements of price that appear on the invoice, Peabody needs more than an observation that the contractual outcome surprises the bench.

One of Peabody's two themes emphasizes "of coal" in the formula "average invoice price of coal." The excise taxes were not part of the price of the coal; they were surcharges. Yet this line of argument proves far too much. It gives Peabody the power to curtail royalties by changing how it designs the invoice. Recall our example, in which coal was $10 per ton. Peabody's position implies that if it broke out the components—coal $3, labor $3, machinery $3, environmental precautions and waste removal $1—it would need to pay a royalty only on the component explicitly identified as "coal." That's not a plausible reading of the contract, especially not given that other taxes (income and payroll taxes, plus the sales and excise taxes Peabody pays on the purchase of equipment) and the costs of satisfying the EPA's environmental regulations are indubitably part of the "average invoice price of coal".

Peabody's other theme is that federal excise taxes on coal were introduced after 1969, which, Peabody insists, necessarily renders the contract ambiguous. How could the parties have resolved the treatment of nonexistent taxes?, Peabody asks. Peabody wants us to deem the treatment of excise taxes an omitted term, on which "the court will admit evidence to show how the parties would have dealt with the contingency had they made specific provision for it." Amoco Oil Co. v. Ashcraft, 791 F.2d 519, 521 (7th Cir. 1986). This in turn, Peabody insists, means that summary judgment is inappropriate.

Yet contracts often handle contingencies. Peabody's own contracts with the utilities that use its coal to make electricity permit it to add excise taxes to the price of coal (which is why the invoices were structured as they were). Many of these were negotiated before 1977, when the first federal excise tax was enacted, so the contention that no contract signed in 1969 can mean anything with respect to excise taxes falls flat. The 1969 contract does not address taxes with the same directness as the sales contracts Peabody negotiated, but plaintiffs insist that this is because it did not have to; the "average invoice price" formula does the necessary work.

What evidence has Peabody to undermine this conclusion? It does not want to argue industry custom or usage of trade; its fundamental position is that there was in 1969 no relevant custom or usage, and anyway the formula "average invoice price" is an unusual one. (A search of online legal databases turned up no references to this formula.) Peabody does not want to offer parol evidence of the negotiations preceding the contract's formation; its position that no one thought about the subject is incompatible with this kind of evidence. Nor does Peabody seek to show how other mineral leases from the 1960s handle taxes, when the parties dealt with that possibility expressly. Such evidence could enable a court to address the question posed in *Amoco Oil*, but it is not on the horizon. (Documents in the record suggest that mineral leases from the 1990s cover excise taxes explicitly; some include the taxes in the royalty base while others do not.) Evidence about the beliefs, wishes, hopes, and fears of its negotiators and managers would be inadmissible, for only objective evidence may be used to elaborate on a contract's meaning.

The sort of objective evidence that Peabody *does* proffer has no bearing on the meaning of a 1969 contract. For example, Peabody wants to argue to a jury that Congress differentiated the excise taxes from the price of coal. Each statute limits the tax to a percentage of the price or value of coal; this supposes, Peabody believes, that the "price" of coal does not include the tax. This evidence would be unhelpful—and not only because federal judges do not hold trials so that jurors may deliberate on the meaning of federal statutes. Congress excluded the tax from "price" to make the formula determinate: a cap of 10% is ambiguous unless we know the denominator—the price of the coal alone, or the price of coal and tax together? Nothing in either 26 U.S.C. § 4121 or 30 U.S.C. § 1232 suggests that the term "sales price" in a private contract must mean the same thing as "price" for the purpose of calculating a maximum tax, let alone that the federal definition of "price" from the 1970s applies retroactively to contracts signed in the 1960s. Many features of the statutes depart from contractual norms. For example, a "ton" in the statutory framework is a ton of dry coal, rather than of coal plus excess moisture (which the contract may permit the seller to deliver). Nothing but grief could come from trying to impress the statutory diction on an older contract that uses the same term in a different context.

In the end, the parties do not dispute any issue of material fact; they just offer different interpretations of their agreement. Whatever meaning the contract conveys must be found within its four corners plus the uncontested economic context (such as the tax provisos in Peabody's sales contracts). That the task of drawing out this meaning is difficult does not transfer the job from a judge to a jury.

Context implies that the phrase "average invoice price" includes excise taxes. These parties gave a good deal of thought to the potential for change in the coal market during the contract's lengthy term. Peabody must pay a royalty of 12¢ per ton, plus 10% of the amount by which the "sales price" exceeds a "base price." The base price was pegged at $2.28 per ton in 1969, but it does not stay there. It rises (or falls) as the cost of mine labor rises (or falls). There is a separate exclusion of 50¢ per ton for coal shipped on barges at the Yankeetown Dock Corporation. That, however, is the end of the list. Higher wages for workers thus yield a higher "base price" (and prevent a change in royalties even if the labor costs are fully passed on to Peabody's customers), but higher costs of heavy earth-moving equipment do not change the base price. If Peabody substitutes capital for labor it must pay greater royalties than if it substitutes labor for capital. Peabody pays many taxes that do not affect the "base price," and which therefore lead to greater royalties for the mineral owners if the taxes affect other firms in the energy business and permit an increase in the price of coal without reducing consumption so much that total income falls. Equally apropos, since 1969 Peabody has been required to follow an increasingly expensive regimen of regulatory constraints designed to make the coal business cleaner and healthier. The Clean Air Act of 1970 and the Clean Water Act of 1970 were but opening salvos. The Surface Mining Control and Reclamation Act of 1977 is only one among many follow-up statutes. CERCLA, SARA, RCRA, and the rest of the alphabet soup of environmental regulation all postdate this contract. Sometimes the federal government levies taxes to fund environmental cleanup, but more often it requires firms in the business to bear these costs directly. Many of the costs of environmental compliance require capital expenditures (or outlays to third-party contractors, such as environmental engineers) and therefore do not affect the "base price" even though they elevate the "sales price." It is safe to say that these costs of environmental compliance and cleanup substantially exceed 35¢ per ton, yet all (other than labor outlays) increase the gap between "base price" and "sales price", and therefore increase plaintiffs' royalties even as they decrease Peabody's profits. We observed above that the choice between an excise tax on the seller and a sales tax on the buyer (but collected by the seller) is arbitrary; the political choice between a tax and additional regulations can be equally arbitrary. But this contract unambiguously includes regulatory costs in the royalty base, which implies that excise taxes in lieu of regulations also are in that base. This contract effectively requires Peabody to pay royalties on its gross billings, less the "base price" and the Yankeetown barge allowance. Excise taxes are omitted from both the "base price" and the barge allowance. It would not have required prescience for parties to subtract taxes as well, had they wanted to do so; even in 1969, death and taxes had a certain inevitability. . . .

Section 3. Contracts Without Bargaining

The tendency of our law for almost a century has been to relax strict rules, perhaps because of growing (though possibly misguided and even sentimental) confidence in the ability of judges and juries to resolve factual questions, with reasonable accuracy and at reasonable cost, by sifting testimony. The legal realists who, led by Karl Llewellyn, drafted the Uniform Commercial Code were leaders in the movement to soften the contours of strict common law rules.

> Posner, J., in Herzog Contracting
> Corp. v. McGowan Corp., 976 F.2d
> 1062, 1070 (7th Cir.1992).

———

Livingstone v. Evans

Supreme Court of Alberta, 1925.
[1925] 4 D.L.R. 769.

Walsh, J. The defendant, T.J. Evans, through his agent, wrote to the plaintiff offering to sell the land in question for $1800 on terms. On the day that he received this offer the plaintiff wired this agent as follows:—"Send lowest cash price. Will give $1600 cash. Wire." The agent replied to this by telegram as follows "Cannot reduce price." Immediately upon the receipt of this telegram the plaintiff wrote accepting the offer. [In the interim, defendant had entered into a contract to sell the land to one Williams, who was joined as a defendant in the present action.] It is admitted by the defendants that this offer and the plaintiff's acceptance of it constitute a contract for the sale of this land to the plaintiff[,] unless the intervening telegrams above set out put an end to his offer so that the plaintiff could not thereafter bind him to it by his acceptance of it.

. . . [W]hen an offer has been rejected it is thereby ended and it cannot be afterwards accepted without the consent of him who made it. The simple question . . . before me is whether the plaintiff's counter-offer was in law a rejection of the defendants' offer which freed them from it. [Hyde v. Wrench (1840), 3 Beav. 334, 49 E.R. 132,] is the authority for the contention that it was. The defendant offered to sell for 1000. The plaintiff met that with an offer to pay 950 and (to quote from the judgment)—"he thereby rejected the offer previously made by the Defendant. . . . [I]t was not competent for him to revive the proposal of the Defendant, by tendering an acceptance of it."

Stevenson v. McLean (1880), 5 Q.B.D. 346, . . . is easily distinguishable from Hyde v. Wrench. . . . Lush, J., who decided it[,] held that the letter there relied upon as constituting a rejection of the offer was not a new proposal "but a mere inquiry, which should have been answered and not treated as a rejection" but the Judge said that if it had contained an offer it would have likened the case to Hyde v. Wrench.

Hyde v. Wrench has stood without question for 85 years. . . . [The case] has firmly established . . . that the making of a counter-offer is a rejection of the original offer.

The plaintiff's telegram was undoubtedly a counter-offer. True, it contained an inquiry as well but that clearly was one which called for an answer only if the counter-offer was rejected. In substance it said: "I will give you $1600 cash. If you won't take that wire your lowest cash price." In my opinion it put an end to the defendants' liability under their offer unless it was revived by the telegram in reply to it.

The real difficulty in the case . . . arises out of the defendants' telegram "cannot reduce price." If this was simply a rejection of the plaintiff's counter-offer it amounts to nothing. If, however, it was a renewal of the original offer it gave the plaintiff the right to bind the defendants to it by his subsequent acceptance of it.

With some doubt I think that it was a renewal of the original offer or at any rate an intimation to the plaintiff that he was still willing to treat on the basis of it. It was, of course, a reply to the counter-offer and to the inquiry in the plaintiff's telegram. But it was more than that. The price referred to in it was unquestionably that mentioned in his letter. His statement that he could not reduce that price strikes me as having but one meaning, namely, that he was still standing by it and, therefore, still open to accept it. . . .

I am, therefore, of the opinion that there was a binding contract for sale of this land to the plaintiff of which he is entitled to specific performance. . . . [Defendant's] subsequent agreement to sell the land to the defendant Williams [is] of no avail as against the plaintiff's contract. . . .

QUESTIONS

(1) Suppose plaintiff's wire reply to defendant's original offer had read: "Your price of $1,800 seems high to me though the terms are o.k. Is your figure firm, or might you talk about $1,600 on the same terms?" Suppose further that defendant wired back: "I accept the deal at $1,600." Contract?

(2) Suppose plaintiff had drawn a line through the $1,800 figure in defendant's original letter, decreased the price to $1,600 (initialing the price change), signed the letter at the bottom, and mailed it back to defendant, who looked at the document but did nothing further. Not hearing from defendant for a week, plaintiff then wrote: "I accept your offer to sell for $1,800." Contract?

COMMENT: THE "DEVIANT ACCEPTANCE" AT COMMON LAW

One of the striking features of the common law governing the formation of a contract is the "deviant acceptance" rule. The introduction of "new" or "variant" terms means that the offer is dead and the process of contract formation must start over again. The rule, however, is alleviated somewhat by a number of qualifying doctrines. For example, immaterial variances between offer and acceptance are usually disregarded. Further, if the offeree's acceptance attempts only to make explicit terms which were already implicit in the offer, or the offeree merely "suggests" a new term without insisting on its inclusion, or an expression of lack of enthusiasm, perhaps even outright dissatisfaction, is appended (the so-called "grumbling acceptance"), the acceptance usually is effective. See, e.g., Massachusetts Hous. Fin. Agency v. Whitney House Assoc., 37 Mass.App.Ct. 238, 638 N.E.2d 1378 (1994); Panhandle Eastern Pipe Line Co. v. Smith, 637 P.2d 1020 (Wyo.1981); Curtis Land & Loan Co. v. Interior Land Co., 137 Wis. 341, 118 N.W. 853 (1908). And it may make a difference whether a party invokes the deviant-acceptance rule "defensively" (e.g., original offeror seeks to avoid offeree's more onerous demand) or "offensively" (e.g., offeree seeks to escape contract formation on basis of its own additional demand). Hollywood Fantasy Corp. v. Gabor, 151 F.3d 203 (5th Cir.1998) (noting reluctance to use offeree's modification as basis for finding no contract when, as here, offeror agrees that those modifications became part of contract).

The fighting issue in the deviant-acceptance cases is of course one of interpretation—whether the offeree's purported acceptance is absolute (with, perhaps, a mere inquiry attached) or conditioned. To give an example, in Ardente v. Horan, 117 R.I. 254, 366 A.2d 162 (1976), the vendor's attorney prepared and forwarded to the vendee a written contract of purchase and sale (an offer, said the court). The vendee's attorney returned three things: (1) the contract properly signed by the vendee; (2) a $20,000 deposit required by the contract; and (3) an accompanying letter which read in part: "My clients are concerned that the following items remain with the real estate:" a) dining room set and tapestry wall covering in dining room; b) fireplace fixtures throughout; c) the sun parlor furniture. I would appreciate your confirming that these items are a part of the transaction, as they would be difficult to replace. Was the acceptance "absolute" or "conditional"? The court said that "an acceptance may be valid despite conditional language if the acceptance is clearly independent of the condition." Does this statement make the decision easier? In the end, the court was of the view that the attorney's letter was "not consistent with an absolute acceptance accompanied by a request for a gratuitous benefit." The purported acceptance was therefore a rejection of the vendor's offer, and no contract resulted.

When the answering communication is held to be qualified, and thus deviant, the analysis typically resumes with an inquiry as to whether the response found to operate as a rejection can also serve as a counteroffer which the original offeror (now an offeree) can in turn accept. If it can, again there must be conformity between the acceptance and the counteroffer, the penalty for nonconformity being that the slate is cleaned to await a resumption of bargaining activity.

The overall impression given by this analysis is that the bargaining process itself is neat and orderly, a series of steps that follow in logical progression—like the stately course of common law pleadings in the golden age of Chitty. The actual process of agreement-making often will not be so orderly, however, for haste and sloppiness, and disregard for lawyerly niceties, commonly attend commercial dealing. Moreover, the widespread use of business forms both produces much transaction-untidiness and, as we shall see, creates loopholes for escape under the traditional analysis. But the difficulty is more serious than this. With transactions that are fairly complex, the process of reaching agreement is likely to be an elaborate one of suggesting, demanding, conceding on some issues but resisting on others, searching out middle grounds, and adopting strategies for eventual compromise. Some discussions may be conducted in face-to-face meetings or by telephone, the balance of negotiations by mail or by exchange of written drafts. If agreement is reached ultimately, it may be next to impossible to identify the offeror, the offer (meaning a definitive proposal on the block for acceptance), or the acceptance. In short, the process of reaching agreement often will not conform to the ideal of orderly progression that conventional analysis assumes, and this becomes more likely as the contemplated transaction becomes more complex and the process of negotiation more costly and time-consuming. The impact of contemporary technology on common law doctrines, such as the now pervasive use of email, must also be taken into account.

Over the last fifty years, orthodox common-law analysis of contract formation has undergone significant rethinking and renovation. The general direction is indicated by the statutory provision encountered earlier, § 2–204 of the Uniform Commercial Code, which authorizes formation of a contract for the sale of goods in any manner sufficient to show agreement and declares unnecessary an actual identification of the offeror, the offeree, and the moment of making the contract. The Restatement, Second takes a similar path in § 22. One consequence, noted earlier, is that, today, there is a greater tolerance of incomplete agreements. And, as we shall see just ahead, the UCC tolerates even contradiction in offer and acceptance, thereby restricting greatly the deviant-acceptance rule of the common law. But it would be a mistake to believe that the courts have discarded the traditional views entirely, or that they are likely to do so any time soon. It remains important for lawyers to understand the theoretical underpinnings and limitations of common law doctrine.

There is need to mention one final aspect of the deviant acceptance at common law—something that was implicit in the option-contract cases considered in the preceding section (e.g., Thomason v. Bescher). Events that ordinarily terminate a power of acceptance, including a deviant acceptance, do not have that effect when the offer that created the power is a binding option. See, e.g., Humble Oil & Refining Co. v. Westside Investment Corp., 428 S.W.2d 92 (Tex.1968) (offeree's counteroffer during option period does not terminate the power of acceptance). Is it difficult to explain why the option contract has such special durability?

PROBLEM

V writes P offering to sell V's farm for $100,000, payment to be $10,000 down and the balance in equal annual installments. The letter adds: "I'm sure you will ultimately decide this is a bargain, so I will hold my offer open for 30 days even though you reject it in the meantime." P promptly replies: "I will give you $88,000 cash for your farm." Not hearing anything from V for a week, P then writes: "I accept your original terms for $100,000 deal." Has a contract been formed?

CONTRACT FORMATION THROUGH EXCHANGE OF PRINTED FORMS

The case that follows provides one of the numerous examples we will encounter of the exchange of printed forms as a method of contract formation. One need not observe modern commercial practice for very long before concluding that merchants—"professionals" says the UCC—do not negotiate the details of every transaction. They prefer instead to exchange forms containing the standard terms on which they conduct business. Attorneys representing each side of recurrent transactions, such as sales and purchases of goods, will have prepared their own forms. Consequently, the chances are pretty good that differences will exist between the seller's "acknowledgment" or "sales order" and the buyer's "purchase order." Such differences—e.g., a limitation of seller's liability for defective quality, an agreement to submit to arbitration all claims arising out of the contract, reservations of power to cancel or to suspend performance on the happening of stated contingencies, etc.—may seem relatively unimportant at the moment the deal is concluded. But they can cause trouble later. When that happens and disputes cannot be resolved, it is safe to predict that one party will then try to impose a term from its form on the other.

At the formation stage, each party may attempt through standardized language to get the other's assent to its own form. Typically this is done by a term requesting that the form be signed and returned, or by a provision declaring that failure to object within a specified time shall constitute assent. In most cases, however, the purchaser's order will be acknowledged by the seller's own form, or vice-versa, with neither party expressly assenting to the other's form and with no effort made to reconcile conflicting terms. Whatever the mechanics of the particular exchange of forms, appropriately dubbed "the battle of the forms," it is obvious that this process of achieving assent differs greatly from that presupposed by orthodox formation doctrine. Instead of discussion and settlement of important details by negotiation, with all (or most) of the terms reflecting the considered judgment of both parties, attention is fixed on only a few key elements. The rest is left to standardized language.

At a later time we shall be interested in whether a party to a contract uses its bargaining position to take advantage of someone else. For present purposes, however, we assume that the bargaining process is not defective in any significant respect and the parties find themselves at the start on a more-or-less level playing field.

In recent decades, discussions of contract formation through exchange of printed forms have focused on the Uniform Commercial Code rules governing sales transactions, most notably § 2–207. We have seen at least two other provisions which reveal important Code policies on formation issues, §§ 2–204 and 2–206. The latter provision gives effect to "any reasonable manner of acceptance," unless the offeror has made quite clear that it will not be acceptable. It also makes either shipment or a promise to ship a proper means of acceptance of an order looking to buy goods for current delivery. It would be useful to review those statutes. It would also be a good idea to consider whether a commercial party who does business by means of preprinted forms, when dealing with another party known by it to do the same, in fact reads—or reasonably can be expected to read—the other's standardized form.

The chief innovation of UCC 2–207 was its abandonment of the very principle of a formal rule of offer and acceptance. In place of a formal rule, the section substitutes a general standard under which the court is to look to the gist of the parties' communications to determine if they have formed a contract. In so doing, the court is to overlook any express terms in those communications that do not fairly reflect the parties' agreement.

Much has been written about § 2–207. Helpful guidance on Code methodology is provided in Brown, Restoring Peace in the Battle of the Forms: A Framework for Making Uniform Commercial Code Section 2–207 Work, 69 N.C.L.Rev. 893 (1991), and von Mehren, The "Battle of the Forms": A Comparative View, 38 Am.J.Comp.L. 265 (1990).

Richardson v. Union Carbide Indus. Gases, Inc.

Superior Court of New Jersey, Appellate Division, 2002.
347 N.J.Super. 524, 790 A.2d 962.

BRAITHWAITE, J. . . . Prior to 1988, Hoeganaes operated furnace 2S, which was used for annealing iron powders. In 1988, Hoeganaes undertook the conversion of furnace 2S to a distalloy furnace. Part of the conversion process required the purchase of a powder transporter system or a "dense phase system" to transport iron powder to the input end of the furnace. Hoeganaes purchased the system from Rage after inquiring from two other possible sellers.

On or about September 26, 1988, Rage proposal number 3313 for a transporter system for iron powder and a transfer system for steel powder was submitted [to] Hoeganaes. Hoeganaes issued purchase order No. 21584 to Rage for that equipment. The transporter system for iron powder, re- ferred to in the Rage proposal as System I, was installed on furnace 2S.

Subsequently, Rage submitted two more proposals to Hoeganaes. Number 3353 was for target boxes and Number 3375 was for control logic panels. Hoeganaes issued purchase order Number 23952 in response to these two proposals. By May 1989, the conversion of furnace 2S was com- pleted.

The proposals issued by Rage were typed in a letter format addressing the items desired by Hoeganaes. At the base of each page of each proposal, the following language in capital letters was typed: "ANY PURCHASE ORDER ISSUED AS A RESULT OF THIS QUOTE IS MADE EXPRESSLY SUBJECT TO THE TERMS AND CONDITIONS ATTACHED HERETO IN LIEU OF ANY CONFLICTING TERMS PROPOSED BY PURCHASER." The terms and conditions attached to Rage's proposals were standard terms that were sent with every proposal and appeared in standard boilerplate format. The terms and conditions were not discussed during Rage's meet- ings with Hoeganaes.

At the top of the terms and conditions was a Limitation of Acceptance which stated:

LIMITATION OF ACCEPTANCE. This sale (including all ser- vices) is limited to and expressly made conditional on Purchas- er's assent to these Terms and Conditions as well as all other provisions contained in any other document to which these Terms and Conditions are attached. Purchaser agrees: (a) These Terms and Conditions . . . shall be deemed to supercede and take precedence over all prior writings, representations or agreements regarding this sale; (b) These Terms and Conditions . . . shall represent our complete agreement; (c) Any inconsistent, conflict- ing or additional terms or conditions proposed by Purchaser in any order, acceptance or other document or form shall be void and without effect unless Seller shall specifically and expressly accept same in writing; (d) No modification of these Terms and Conditions . . . will be affected by Seller's shipment of goods/equipment or the provision of services following receipt of Purchaser's order, acceptance or other document or form contain- ing terms which are inconsistent, conflicting or in addition to these Terms and Conditions . . .; and (e) Any acceptance of goods/equipment or services, or payment constitutes an ac- ceptance by Purchaser of these Terms and Conditions . . .

The Rage terms and conditions also had an indemnity clause, which stated:

> INDEMNITY. Purchaser shall indemnify and hold Seller harmless against and in respect of any loss, claim or damage (including costs of suit and attorneys' fees) or other expense incident to or in connection with: the goods/equipment; the furnishing of design, installation (including site preparation) or other services; processing or use by any person of any goods/equipment or system (including personal injury to the employees of Seller and Purchaser); or Purchaser's violation of any provision of these Terms and Conditions or the provisions of any document to which these Terms and Conditions are attached unless such loss, claim or damage is due solely and directly to the negligence or willful misconduct of Seller.

At the bottom of the purchase orders issued by Hoeganaes the following language in bold face type appeared: "THIS ORDER IS ALSO SUBJECT TO THE TERMS AND CONDITIONS ON THE REVERSE SIDE OF THIS PAGE[.]" The reverse side of the purchase orders included the following section at the top of the boilerplate terms and conditions section:

> 1. Compliance with Terms and Conditions of Order—The terms and conditions set forth below, along with the provisions set forth on the front page hereof, constitute the entire contract of purchase and sale between Buyer and Seller. Any provisions in the Seller's acceptance, acknowledgment or other response to this Order which are different from or in addition to any of the terms and conditions and other provisions of this Order are hereby objected to by Buyer and such different or additional provisions shall not become a part of Buyer's contract of purchase and sale.

Furthermore, the reverse side also contained the following indemnity clause and a clause stating that the purchase order constituted the entire agreement:

> 14. Indemnification—Seller agrees to indemnify and hold harmless and protect Buyer, its affiliated and subsidiary companies, successors, assigns, customers and users of its products from and against all losses, damages, liabilities, claims, demands (including attorneys fees'), and suits at law or equity that arise out of, or are alleged to have arisen out of, directly or indirectly, any act of omission or commission, negligent or otherwise, of Seller, its sub-contractors, their employees, workmen, servants or agents, or otherwise out of the performance or attempted performance by Seller of this purchase order.

> 16. This purchase order contains the entire agreement between the parties and the provisions hereof or rights hereunder may be modified or waived only in writing by Buyer's authorized officials. All matters in connection herewith shall be determined under the laws of New Jersey.

Thus, both Rage and Hoeganaes exchanged documents, pertinent here, with conflicting indemnity clauses. Other than as expressed in the boilerplate language, neither side objected to the language in the documents and the contract was performed.

Plaintiff Jeffrey Richardson was an employee of Hoeganaes when he was injured by the explosion of furnace 2S on May 13, 1992. On September 15, 1994, plaintiff filed suit against numerous defendants including Hoeganaes and Rage. Plaintiff alleged that Rage "did design, manufacture, maintain, assemble, inspect, test, sell and/or distribute the systems and facilities design and/or its component parts" for the furnace which caused his injuries. Plaintiff alleged breaches of the Products Liability Act, N.J.S.A. 2A:58–1 to –11, implied and express warranties and negligence. In its answer, Rage cross-claimed against Hoeganaes seeking contractual indemnification. Hoeganaes, in its answer to the cross-claim, denied any right to indemnification arising out of the contract. . . .

The relevant statutory provision is 2–207, which provides as follows:

Additional Terms in Acceptance or Confirmation.

(1) A definite and seasonable expression of acceptance or a written confirmation which is sent within a reasonable time operates as an acceptance even though it states terms additional to or different from those offered or agreed upon, unless acceptance is expressly made conditional on assent to the additional or different terms.

(2) The additional terms are to be construed as proposals for addition to the contract. Between merchants such terms become part of the contract unless:

(a) the offer expressly limits acceptance to the terms of the offer;

(b) they materially alter it; or

(c) notification of objection to them has already been given or is given within a reasonable time after notice of them is received.

(3) Conduct by both parties which recognizes the existence of a contract is sufficient to establish a contract for sale although the writings of the parties do not otherwise establish a contract. In such case the terms of the particular contract consist of those terms on which the writings of the parties agree, together with any supplementary terms incorporated under any other provisions of this Act.

. . . We note that 2–207 addresses "additional terms in acceptance" and also uses the language "different" terms [in 2–207(1)]. In 2–207(2), however, where the standard to determine whether additional terms become part of the parties' contract, the word "different" is not employed.

Section 2–207 is silent on the question of whether "additional or different terms" mean the same thing. There is seemingly no agreement on that question. Northrop v. Litronic Indus., 29 F.3d 1173, 1175 (7th Cir.1994). It is unclear whether the reference to "different" terms in the acceptance, 2–207(1), means that the drafters intended "different" to be treated like "additional" terms under 2–207(2).

Comment three of 2–207 suggests that both additional and different terms are governed by 2–207(2). However, comment six of 2–207 advances the proposition that conflicting terms in exchanged writing must be assumed to be mutually objected to by each party with the result of a mutual "knock-out" of the conflicting terms.

Scholars differ on this subject. One commentator supports the view that the drafting history of the provision indicates that the word "different" was intentionally deleted from the final draft of 2–207(2) so that different terms would not be treated under that subsection. . . . Others, however, believe that different equates to additional and assert that the drafting history indicates that the omission of "or different" from 2–207(2) was a drafting error. . . .

There are, however, three recognized approaches by the courts to the issue of conflicting terms in contracts under circumstances such as here. . . . The majority view is that the conflicting terms fall out and, if necessary, are replaced by suitable UCC gap-filler provisions. . . .

The minority view is that the offeror's terms control because the offeree's different terms cannot be saved by 2–207(2), because that section applies only to additional terms. . . .

The third view assimilates "different" to "additional" so that the terms of the offer prevail over the different terms in the acceptance only if the latter are materially different. This is the least adopted approach. . . .

We conclude that the majority approach, the "knock-out" rule, is preferable and should be adopted in New Jersey. We reach this conclusion because the other approaches are inequitable and unjust and run counter to the policy behind 2–207, which addresses a concern that existed at common law.

At common law, there could be no meeting of the minds and thus no contract, unless there was agreement on all the terms of the contract. This was the "mirror-image" rule, which Article 2 of the UCC jettisoned by recognizing the existence of a contract even though certain terms remain in conflict or are unresolved. This change was meant to facilitate the completion of large-scale business transactions and practically is a necessity, in light of the way the American economy functions today. . . .

Section 2–207 was enacted to reform the common law mirror-image rule and reject the last-shot doctrine which accorded undue advantage to the mere order in which forms were sent. . . . Our adoption of the "knock-out" rule advances the goal of reformation of the common law mirror-image rule.

The motion judge recognized that each party created its own forms with its own terms that conflicted, yet still proceeded to transact business without objection. The judge noted:

> The truth is, and this really is the truth, what's happening is some little person some place writing these little—trying to plan it out, trying to conflict these things out, but the business people are out there delivering and taking money. And if the people really want to really get into all of this, then they should have taken their stuff away and they should have said, ooh, you know, we—you know, this is real here and, sorry, I'm not going to be able to take your check and, sorry, you're not going to be able to keep the stuff, but they're not doing that. They're just playing a little game with forms.

In granting the motion for summary judgment, the judge implicitly adopted the "knock-out" rule. An approach other than the knock-out rule for conflicting terms would result in Rage, or any offeror, always prevailing on its terms solely because it sent the first form. That is not a desirable result, particularly when the parties have not negotiated for the challenged clause.

Now we address Rage's [assertion] that the motion judge erred in analyzing the matter under 2–207(3) rather than 2–207(2). We are satisfied that under either analysis the result is the same and, therefore, summary judgment was properly granted to Hoeganaes.

Section 2–207(2) sets forth the standard to determine if additional terms of an acceptance become part of the contract. . . .

Applying this section here leads inescapably to the conclusion that Rage's indemnity clause did not become part of the contract. Although Rage's offer specifically limited acceptance to the terms of its offer, Hoeganaes' acceptance materially altered Rage's offer with respect to the issue of indemnification. Additionally, Hoeganaes' acceptance objected to any terms or conditions of the Rage offer that were different from or in addition to any of the terms of its own acceptance.

Moreover, comment six to 2–207, which expresses the "knock-out" rule that we addressed earlier in this opinion, supports the conclusion that Rage's indemnity clause did not become part of the contract. Thus, 2–207(2) offers no support for Rage's position.

Applying 2–207(3) leads to the same result. Here, the contested provision addressed indemnity and only became relevant after plaintiff was injured, some three years after the conversion of the furnace was completed. Pursuant to 2–207(3), the conduct of the parties recognizes the existence of a contract and the "terms of the particular contract consist of those terms on which the writings of the parties *agree*, together with any supplementary terms incorporated under any other provisions of this Act." (Emphasis added). Because the parties' writings disagree on indemnity, that term did not become part of the contract.

Affirmed.

————

The *Richardson* Court shows how alternative paths through § 2–207 leave the parties where they would have been had they signed a contract that omitted any mention of the disputed term. Whatever the path taken, this outcome is found in many cases decided under § 2–207. See Baird & Weisberg, Rules, Standards, and the Battle of the Forms: A Reassessment of § 2–207, 68 Va.L.Rev. 1217 (1982). Courts end up treating the battle of the forms in the same way that they would treat an exchange of forms in which certain elements of the contract are left unaddressed by the parties. In doing this, they act in a way that parallels the Code's general solution to incompleteness problems, contained in § 2–204(3). If § 2–204(3) applies, the court will supply the missing terms by referring to certain "off-the-rack" terms of the Code, which themselves are generally open-ended standards rather than rules, or by referring to the custom and usage of the parties or their trade. Thus, under § 2–204(3), the incompleteness of the exchanged forms is no bar to finding a bargain.

————

NOTE: THE QUALIFIED OR CONDITIONAL ACCEPTANCE TODAY

The first Restatement of Contracts was firmly committed to the requirement of a matching or "mirror-image" acceptance, § 60 providing: "A reply to an offer, though purporting to accept it, which adds qualifications or requires performance of conditions, is not an acceptance but is a counter-offer." The revised version, Restatement, Second § 59, appears to reflect a somewhat different view: "A reply to an offer which purports to accept it but is conditional on the offeror's assent to terms additional to or different from those offered is not an acceptance but is a counter-offer." The official comment to the revised § 59 states that a "qualified or conditional acceptance proposes an exchange different from that proposed by the original offeror. . . . [It] is a counter-offer and ordinarily terminates the power of acceptance of the original offeree." If the adjective "qualified" in this sentence embraces the same substance as the term "adds qualifications" in the original § 60, the revision would not seem to point to any departure from the matching-acceptance rule. The new official comment immediately adds, however, that "a definite and seasonable expression of acceptance is operative despite the statement of additional or different terms if the acceptance is not made to depend on assent to the additional or different terms."

The second Restatement clearly illustrates the effect of the Sales Article of the UCC on the general law of contracts in the second half of the last century. Equally clear is the quasi-legislative impact the drafters of the second Restatement were seeking. Though originally conceived as a systematic "restatement" of established common law rules, with innovation or choice among rules deemed limited to situations in which case authority was lacking or sharply divided, the Restatement, Second appears to have adopted a more activist, reforming posture. The rewritten Restatement § 59 clearly reflects the influence of the Code's § 2–207. Even now, however, it is unclear whether the courts, in applying acceptance doctrines, have carried that influence over to nongoods cases. See, e.g., Logan Ranch v. Farm Credit Bank of Omaha, 238 Neb. 814, 472 N.W.2d 704 (1991); Okemo Mountain, Inc. v. Okemo Trailside Condominiums, Inc., 139 Vt. 433, 431 A.2d 457 (1981); Grossman v. McLeish Ranch, 291 N.W.2d 427 (N.D.1980).

———

ProCD, Inc. v. Zeidenberg

United States Court of Appeals, Seventh Circuit, 1996.
86 F.3d 1447.

EASTERBROOK, CIRCUIT JUDGE. Must buyers of computer software obey the terms of shrinkwrap licenses? The district court held not, [concluding that] they are not contracts because the licenses are inside the box rather than printed on the outside. . . . [W]e disagree. . . . Shrinkwrap licenses are enforceable unless their terms are objectionable on grounds applicable to contracts in general (for example, if they are unconscionable). . . . Because no one argues that the terms of the license at issue here are troublesome, we remand with instructions to enter judgment for the plaintiff.

ProCD, the plaintiff, has compiled information from more than 3,000 telephone directories into a computer database. We may assume that this database cannot be copyrighted. . . . ProCD sells a version of the database, called SelectPhone, on CD–ROM discs. (CD–ROM means "compact disc—read only memory." The "shrinkwrap license" gets its name from the fact that retail software packages are covered in plastic or cellophane "shrinkwrap," and some vendors, though not ProCD, have written licenses that become effective as soon as the customer tears the wrapping from the package. Vendors prefer "end user license," but we use the more common term.) . . . Customers [use] the data with the aid of an application program that ProCD has written. This program, which is copyrighted, searches the database in response to users' criteria (such as "find all people named Tatum in Tennessee, plus all firms with 'Door Systems' in the corporate name"). The resulting lists . . . can be read and manipulated by other software, such as word processing programs.

The database in SelectPhone cost more than $10 million to compile and is expensive to keep current. It is much more valuable to some users than to others. The combination of names, addresses, and SIC codes enables manufacturers to compile lists of potential customers. Manufacturers and retailers pay high prices to specialized information intermediaries for such mailing lists; ProCD offers a potentially cheaper alternative. People with nothing to sell could use the database as a substitute for calling long distance information, or as a way to look up old friends who have moved to unknown towns, or just as an electronic substitute for the local phone book. ProCD decided to engage in price discrimination, selling its database to the general public for personal use at a low price (approximately $150 for the set of five discs) while selling information to the trade for a higher price. It has adopted some intermediate strategies too: access to the SelectPhone database is available via the America Online service for the price America Online charges to its clients (approximately $3 per hour), but this service has been tailored to be useful only to the general public. . . .

To make price discrimination work, however, the seller must be able to control arbitrage. An air carrier sells tickets for less to vacationers than to business travelers, using advance purchase and Saturday-night-stay requirements to distinguish the categories. A producer of movies segments the market by time, releasing first to theaters, then to pay-per-view services, next to the videotape and laserdisc market, and finally to cable and commercial tv. Vendors of computer software have a harder task. Anyone can walk into a retail store and buy a box. Customers do not wear tags saying "commercial user" or "consumer user." Anyway, even a commercial-user-detector at the door would not work, because a consumer could buy the software and resell to a commercial user. That arbitrage would break down the price discrimination and drive up the minimum price at which ProCD would sell to anyone.

Instead of tinkering with the product and letting users sort themselves—for example, furnishing current data at a high price that would be attractive only to commercial customers, and two-year-old data at a low price—ProCD turned to the institution of contract. Every box containing its consumer product declares that the software comes with restrictions stated in an enclosed license. This license, which is encoded on the CD–ROM disks as well as printed in the manual, and which appears on a user's screen every time the software runs, limits use of the application program and listings to noncommercial purposes.

Matthew Zeidenberg bought a consumer package of SelectPhone in 1994 from a retail outlet in Madison, Wisconsin, but decided to ignore the license. He formed Silken Mountain Web Services, Inc., to resell the information in the SelectPhone database. The corporation makes the database available on the Internet to anyone willing to pay its price—which, needless to say, is less than ProCD charges its commercial customers. . . . ProCD filed this suit seeking an injunction against further dissemination that exceeds the rights specified in the licenses (identical in each of the three packages Zeidenberg purchased). The district court held the licenses ineffectual because their terms do not appear on the outside of the packages. The court added that . . . a purchaser does not agree to—and cannot be bound by—terms that were secret at the time of purchase. 908 F.Supp. at 654.

Following the district court, we treat the licenses as ordinary contracts accompanying the sale of products, and therefore as governed by the common law of contracts and the [UCC]. Whether there are legal differences between "contracts" and "licenses" (which may matter under the copyright doctrine of first sale) is a subject for another day. . . . Zeidenberg [urges,] and the district court held, that placing the package of software on the shelf is an "offer," which the customer "accepts" by paying the asking price and leaving the store with the goods. Peeters v. State, 154 Wis. 111, 142 N.W. 181 (1913). In Wisconsin, as elsewhere, a contract includes only the terms on which the parties have agreed. . . . So far, so good—but one of the terms to which Zeidenberg agreed by purchasing the software is that the transaction was subject to a license. Zeidenberg's position therefore must be that the printed terms on the outside of a box are the parties' contract—except for printed terms that refer to or incorporate other terms. But why would Wisconsin fetter the parties' choice in this way? Vendors can put the entire terms of a contract on the outside of a box only by using microscopic type, removing other information that buyers might find more useful (such as what the software does, and on which computers it works), or both. The "Read Me" file included with most software, describing system requirements and potential incompatibilities, may be equivalent to ten pages of type; warranties and license restrictions take still more space. Notice on the outside, terms on the inside, and a right to return the software for a refund if the terms are unacceptable (a right that the license expressly extends), may be a means of doing business valuable to buyers and sellers alike. [See] Restatement (2d) of Contracts § 211 comment a (1981) ("Standardization of agreements serves many of the same functions as standardization of goods and services. . . .").

Transactions in which the exchange of money precedes the communication of detailed terms are common. Consider the purchase of insurance. The buyer goes to an agent, who explains the essentials (amount of coverage, number of years) and remits the premium to the home office, which sends back a policy. On the district judge's understanding, the terms of the policy are irrelevant because the insured paid before receiving them. Yet the device of payment, often with a "binder" (so that the insurance takes effect immediately even though the home office reserves the right to withdraw coverage later), in advance of the policy, serves buyers' interests by accelerating effectiveness and reducing transactions costs. Or consider the purchase of an airline ticket. The traveler calls the carrier or an agent, is quoted a price, reserves a seat, pays, and gets a ticket, in that order. The ticket contains elaborate terms, which the traveler can reject by canceling the reservation. To use the ticket is to accept the terms, even terms that in retrospect are disadvantageous. See Carnival Cruise Lines, Inc. v. Shute, 499 U.S. 585 (1991). . . . Just so with a ticket to a concert. The back of the ticket states that the patron promises not to record the concert; to attend is to agree. A theater that detects a violation will confiscate the tape and escort the violator to the exit. One *could* arrange things so that every concertgoer signs this promise before forking over the money, but that cumbersome way of doing things not only would lengthen queues and raise prices but also would scotch the sale of tickets by phone or electronic data service.

Consumer goods work the same way. Someone who wants to buy a radio set visits a store, pays, and walks out with a box. Inside the box is a leaflet containing some terms, the most important of which usually is the warranty, read for the first time in the comfort of home. By Zeidenberg's lights, the warranty in the box is irrelevant; every consumer gets the standard warranty implied by the UCC in the event the contract is silent; yet so far as we are aware no state disregards warranties furnished with consumer products. Drugs come with a list of ingredients on the outside and an elaborate package insert on the inside. The package insert describes drug interactions, contraindications, and other vital information—but, if Zeidenberg is right, the purchaser need not read the package insert, because it is not part of the contract.

Next consider the software industry itself. Only a minority of sales take place over the counter, where there are boxes to peruse. A customer may place an order by phone in response to a line item in a catalog or a review in a magazine. Much software is ordered over the Internet by purchasers who have never seen a box. Increasingly software arrives by wire. There is no box; there is only a stream of electrons, a collection of information that includes data, an application program, instructions, many limitations ("MegaPixel 3.14159 cannot be used with BytePusher 2.718"), and the terms of sale. The user purchases a serial number, which activates the software's features. On Zeidenberg's arguments, these unboxed sales are unfettered by terms—so the seller has made a broad warranty and must pay consequential damages for any shortfalls in performance, two "promises" that if taken seriously would drive prices through the ceiling or return transactions to the horse-and-buggy age.

According to the district court, the UCC does not countenance the sequence of money now, terms later. . . . One of the court's reasons—that by proposing as part of the draft Article 2B a new UCC 2–2203 that would explicitly validate standard-form user licenses, the American Law Institute and the National Conference of Commissioners on Uniform Laws have conceded the invalidity of shrinkwrap licenses under current law, see 908 F.Supp. at 655–56—depends on a faulty inference. To propose a change in a law's *text* is not necessarily to propose a change in the law's *effect*. New words may be designed to fortify the current rule with a more precise text that curtails uncertainty. To judge by the flux of law review articles discussing shrinkwrap licenses, uncertainty is much in need of reduction—although businesses seem to feel less uncertainty than do scholars, for only three cases (other than ours) touch on the subject and none directly addresses it. . . .

What then does the current version of the UCC have to say? We think that the place to start is § 2–204(1). . . . A vendor, as master of the offer may invite acceptance by conduct, and may propose limitations on the kind of conduct that constitutes acceptance. A buyer may accept by performing the acts the vendor proposes to treat as acceptance. And that is what happened. ProCD proposed a contact that a buyer would accept by *using* the software after having an opportunity to read the license at leisure. This Zeidenberg did. He had no choice, because the software splashed the license on the screen and would not let him proceed without indicating acceptance. So although the district judge was right to say that a contract can be, and often is, formed simply by paying the price and walking out of the store, the UCC permits contracts to be formed in other ways. ProCD proposed such a different way, and without protest Zeidenberg agreed. Ours is not a case in which a consumer opens a package to find an insert saying "you owe us an extra $10,000" and the seller files suit to collect. Any buyer finding such a demand can prevent formation of the contract by returning the package, as can any consumer who concludes that the terms of the license make the software worth less than the purchase price. . . .

Section 2–606, which defines "acceptance of goods," reinforces this understanding. A buyer accepts goods under § 2–606(1)(b) when, after an opportunity to inspect, he fails to make an effective rejection under § 2–602(1). ProCD extended an opportunity to reject if a buyer should find the license terms unsatisfactory; Zeidenberg inspected the package, tried out the software, learned of the license, and did not reject the goods. We refer to § 2–606 only to show that the opportunity to return goods can be important; acceptance of an offer differs from acceptance of goods after delivery, see Gillen v. Atalanta Systems, Inc., 997 F.2d 280, 284 n. 1 (7th Cir.1993); but the UCC consistently permits the parties to structure their relations so that the buyer has a chance to make a final decision after a detailed review.

Some portions of the UCC impose additional requirements on the way parties agree on terms. A disclaimer of the implied warranty of merchantability must be "conspicuous." UCC 2–316(2), incorporating UCC 1–201(10). Promises to make firm offers, or to negate oral modifications, must be "separately signed." UCC §§ 2–205, 2–209(2). These special provisos reinforce the impression that, so far as the UCC is concerned, other terms may be as inconspicuous as the forum-selection clause on the back of the cruise ship ticket in *Carnival Lines*. Zeidenberg has not located any Wisconsin case—for that matter, any case in any state—holding that under the UCC the ordinary terms found in shrinkwrap licenses require any special prominence, or otherwise are to be undercut rather than enforced. In the end, the terms of the license are conceptually identical to the contents of the package. . . . [S]o, we believe, Wisconsin would not let the buyer pick and choose among terms. Terms of use are no less a part of "the product" than are the size of the database and the speed with which the software compiles listings. Competition among vendors, not judicial revision of a package's contents, is how consumers are protected in a market economy. . . .

Reversed and remanded.

––––––––

Hill v. Gateway 2000, Inc.

105 F.3d 1147 (7th Cir.1997)

Judge Easterbrook revisited contract-formation issues raised in *ProCD*, and wrote: "A customer picks up the phone, orders a computer, and gives a credit card number. Presently a box arrives, containing the computer and a list of terms, said to govern unless the customer returns the computer within 30 days. Are these terms effective as the parties' contract, or is the contract term-free because the order-taker did not read any terms over the phone and elicit the customer's assent?

"One of the terms in the box containing a Gateway 2000 system was an arbitration clause. Rich and Enza Hill, the customers, kept the computer more than 30 days before complaining about its components and performance. They filed suit in federal court. . . . Gateway asked the district court to enforce the arbitration clause; the judge refused, [finding no valid agreement to arbitrate].

"The Hills say that the arbitration clause did not stand out; they concede noticing the statement of terms but deny reading it closely enough to discover the agreement to arbitrate, and they ask us to conclude that they therefore may go to court. Yet an agreement to arbitrate must be enforced 'save upon such grounds as exist at law or in equity for the revocation of any contract.' 9 U.S.C. § 2. . . . A contract need not be read to be effective. . . . Terms inside Gateway's box stand or fall together. If they constitute the parties' contract because the Hills had an opportunity to return the computer after reading them, then all must be enforced.

"*ProCD* holds that terms inside a box of software bind consumers who use the software after an opportunity to read the terms and to reject them by returning the product. Likewise, Carnival Cruise Lines, Inc. v. Shute, 499 U.S. 585 (1991), enforces a forum-selection clause that was included among three pages of terms attached to a cruise ship ticket. *ProCD* and *Carnival Cruise Lines* exemplify the many commercial transactions in which people pay for products with terms to follow. . . . Gateway shipped computers with the same sort of accept-or-return offer *ProCD* made to users of its software. . . .

"Plaintiffs ask us to limit *ProCD* to software, but where's the sense in that? *ProCD* is about the law of contract, not the law of software. Payment preceding the revelation of full terms is common for [many] endeavors. Practical considerations support allowing vendors to enclose the full legal terms with their products. Cashiers cannot be expected to read legal documents to customers before ringing up sales. If the staff at the other end of the phone for direct-sales operations such as Gateway's had to read the four-page statement of terms before taking the buyer's credit card number, the droning voice would anesthetize rather than enlighten many potential buyers. Others would hang up in a rage over the waste of their time. And oral recitation would not avoid customers' assertions (whether true or feigned) that the clerk did not read term X to them, or that they did not remember or understand it. Writing provides benefits for both sides of commercial transactions. Customers as a group are better off when vendors skip costly and ineffectual steps such as telephonic recitation, and use instead a simple approve-or-return device. Competent adults are bound by such documents, read or unread. . . .

"For their second sally, the Hills contend that ProCD should be limited to executory contracts (to licenses in particular), and therefore does not apply because both parties' performance of this contract was complete when the box arrived at their home. This is legally and factually wrong: legally because the question at hand concerns the *formation* of the contract rather than its *performance*, and factually because both contracts were incompletely performed. *ProCD* did not depend on the fact that the seller characterized the transaction as a license rather than as a contract; we treated it as a contract for the sale of goods and reserved the question whether for other purposes a 'license' characterization might be preferable. 86 F.3d at 1450. All debates about characterization to one side, the transaction in *ProCD* was no more executory than the one here: Zeidenberg paid for the software and walked out of the store with a box under his arm, so if arrival of the box with the product ends the time for revelation of contractual terms, then the time ended in *ProCD* before Zeidenberg opened the box. But of course ProCD had not completed performance with delivery of the box, and neither had Gateway. One element of the transaction was the warranty, which obliges sellers to fix defects in their products. The Hills have invoked Gateway's warranty and are not satisfied with its response, so they are not well positioned to say that Gateway's obligations were fulfilled when the motor carrier unloaded the box. What is more, both ProCD and Gateway promised to help customers to use their products. Long-term service and information obligations are common in the computer business, on both hardware and software sides. Gateway offers 'lifetime service' and has a round-the-clock telephone hotline to fulfil this promise. . . . The document in Gateway's box includes promises of future performance that some consumers value highly; these promises bind Gateway just as the arbitration clause binds the Hills. . . .

"At oral argument the Hills propounded still another distinction: the box containing ProCD's software displayed a notice that additional terms were within, while the box containing Gateway's computer did not. The difference is functional, not legal. Consumers browsing the aisles of a store can look at the box, and if they are unwilling to deal with the prospect of additional terms can leave the box alone, avoiding the transactions costs of returning the package after reviewing its contents. Gateway's box, by contrast, is just a shipping carton; it is not on display anywhere. Its function is to protect the product during transit, and the information on its sides is for the use of handlers ('Fragile!' 'This side Up!') rather than would-be purchasers.

"Perhaps the Hills would have had a better argument if they were first alerted to the bundling of hardware and legal-ware after opening the box and wanted to return the computer in order to avoid disagreeable terms, but were dissuaded by the expense of shipping. What the remedy would be in such a case—could it exceed the shipping charges?—is an interesting question, but one that need not detain us because the Hills knew before they ordered the computer that the carton would include *some* important terms, and they did not seek to discover these in advance. Gateway's ads state that their products come with limited warranties and lifetime support. How limited was the warranty—30 days, with service contingent on shipping the computer back, or five years, with free onsite service? What sort of support was offered? Shoppers have three principal ways to discover these things. First, they can ask the vendor to send a copy before deciding whether to buy. The Magnuson–Moss Warranty Act requires firms to distribute their warranty terms on request, 15 U.S.C. § 2302(b)(1)(A); the Hills do not contend that Gateway would have refused to enclose the remaining terms too. Concealment would be bad for business, scaring some customers away and leading to excess returns from others. Second, shoppers can consult public sources (computer magazines, the Web sites of vendors) that may contain this information. Third, they may inspect the documents after the product's delivery. Like Zeidenberg, the Hills took the third option. By keeping the computer beyond 30 days, the Hills accepted Gateway's offer, including the arbitration clause. . . . [They must] submit their dispute arbitration."

———

Klocek v. Gateway, Inc.
104 F.Supp.2d 1332 (D.Kan. 2000)

A computer purchaser sued Gateway, whose practice was to include a copy of its "Standard Terms" in the box containing the computer cables and instruction manuals. Gateway, invoking the arbitration clause in its Standard Terms, urged the court to follow *Hill* and *ProCD*. The court declined, on this reasoning: The Seventh Circuit provided no explanation for its conclusion that "the vendor is the master of the offer." Indeed, in typical consumer transactions, the purchaser is the offeror, and the vendor is the offeree. While it is possible for the vendor to be the offeror, Gateway provided no factual evidence which would support such a finding in this case. It can therefore be assumed for purposes of the motion to dismiss that plaintiff offered to purchase the computer (either in person or through catalog order) and that Gateway accepted plaintiff's offer (either by completing the sales transaction in person or by agreeing to ship and/or shipping the computer to plaintiff).

Under § 2–207, the Standard Terms constitute either an expression of acceptance or written confirmation. As an expression of acceptance, the Standard Terms would constitute a counteroffer only if Gateway expressly made its acceptance conditional on plaintiff's assent to the additional or different terms. Gateway provided no evidence that at the time of the sales transaction it had informed plaintiff that the transaction was conditioned on plaintiff's acceptance of the Standard Terms. Moreover, the mere fact that Gateway shipped the goods with the terms attached did not communicate to plaintiff any unwillingness to proceed without plaintiff's agreement to the Standard Terms.

Because plaintiff was not a merchant, additional or different terms contained in the Standard Terms did not become part of the parties' agreement unless plaintiff expressly agreed to them. Gateway's argument that plaintiff demonstrated acceptance of the arbitration provision by keeping the computer more than five days after the date of delivery must fail. Gateway stated only that it enclosed the Standard Terms inside the computer box for plaintiff to read afterwards. It provided no evidence that it had informed plaintiff of the five-day review-and-return period as a condition of the sales transaction, or that the parties contemplated additional terms to the agreement. The act of keeping the computer past five days was not itself sufficient to demonstrate that plaintiff expressly agreed to the Standard Terms. Nor was there evidence sufficient to support a finding under Kansas or Missouri law that plaintiff agreed to the arbitration provision. Gateway's motion to dismiss must therefore be overruled.

NOTE

A number of courts have accepted Judge Easterbrook's analysis, but as *Klocek* suggests, other courts and a number of commentators have rejected it, sometimes harshly. Richard Epstein examines both the Seventh Circuit opinion and the District Court opinion it reversed in *ProCD v. Zeidenberg*: Do Doctrine and Function Mix?, in Contract Stories 94 (2007). These two opinions capture the contours of a debate that has gone on ever since. Epstein praises both, and observes, "The two contrasting opinions reflect a profound difference in the role economic analysis plays in influencing the legal analysis. That difference is encapsulated in the distinction between doctrine versus function: Judge Crabb is the faithful doctrinalist and Judge Easterbrook the ardent functionalist." Id.

at 95. Does this explain the difference in the approaches or is more likely something else at work?

———

Specht v. Netscape Communications Corp.

United States Court of Appeals for the Second Circuit, 2002.
306 F.3d 17.

SOTOMAYOR, CIRCUIT JUDGE. [W]e are asked to determine whether plaintiffs-appellees ("plaintiffs"), by acting upon defendants' invitation to download free software made available on defendants' webpage, agreed to be bound by the software's license terms (which included the arbitration clause at issue), even though plaintiffs could not have learned of the existence of those terms unless, prior to executing the download, they had scrolled down the webpage to a screen located below the download button. We agree with the district court that a reasonably prudent Internet user in circumstances such as these would not have known or learned of the existence of the license terms before responding to defendants' invitation to download the free software, and that defendants therefore did not provide reasonable notice of the license terms. In consequence, plaintiffs' bare act of downloading the software did not unambiguously manifest assent to the arbitration provision contained in the license terms. . . .

In three related putative class actions, plaintiffs alleged that, unknown to them, their use of SmartDownload transmitted to defendants private information about plaintiffs' downloading of files from the Internet, thereby effecting an electronic surveillance of their online activities in violation of two federal statutes, the Electronic Communications Privacy Act and the Computer Fraud and Abuse Act.

Specifically, plaintiffs alleged that when they first used Netscape's Communicator—a software program that permits Internet browsing—the program created and stored on each of their computer hard drives a small text file known as a "cookie" that functioned "as a kind of electronic identification tag for future communications" between their computers and Netscape. Plaintiffs further alleged that when they installed SmartDownload—a separate software "plug-in" that served to enhance Communicator's browsing capabilities—SmartDownload created and stored on their computer hard drives another string of characters, known as a "Key," which similarly functioned as an identification tag in future communications with Netscape. According to the complaints in this case, each time a computer user employed Communicator to download a file from the Internet, SmartDownload "assume[d] from Communicator the task of downloading" the file and transmitted to Netscape the address of the file being downloaded together with the cookie created by Communicator and the Key created by SmartDownload. These processes, plaintiffs claim, constituted unlawful "eavesdropping" on users of Netscape's software products as well as on Internet websites from which users employing SmartDownload downloaded files.

In the time period relevant to this litigation, Netscape offered on its website various software programs, including Communicator and SmartDownload, which visitors to the site were invited to obtain free of charge. It is undisputed that five of the six named plaintiffs—Michael Fagan, John Gibson, Mark Gruber, Sean Kelly, and Sherry Weindorf—

downloaded Communicator from the Netscape website. These plaintiffs acknowledge that when they proceeded to initiate installation of Communicator, they were automatically shown a scrollable text of that program's license agreement and were not permitted to complete the installation until they had clicked on a "Yes" button to indicate that they accepted all the license terms. If a user attempted to install Communicator without clicking "Yes," the installation would be aborted. All five named user plaintiffs expressly agreed to Communicator's license terms by clicking "Yes." The Communicator license agreement that these plaintiffs saw made no mention of SmartDownload or other plug-in programs, and stated that "[t]hese terms apply to Netscape Communicator and Netscape Navigator" and that "all disputes relating to this Agreement (excepting any dispute relating to intellectual property rights)" are subject to "binding arbitration in Santa Clara County, California."

Although Communicator could be obtained independently of SmartDownload, all the named user plaintiffs, except Fagan, downloaded and installed Communicator in connection with downloading SmartDownload. Each of these plaintiffs allegedly arrived at a Netscape webpage captioned "SmartDownload Communicator" that urged them to "Download With Confidence Using SmartDownload!" At or near the bottom of the screen facing plaintiffs was the prompt "Start Download" and a tinted button labeled "Download." By clicking on the button, plaintiffs initiated the download of SmartDownload. Once that process was complete, SmartDownload, as its first plug-in task, permitted plaintiffs to proceed with downloading and installing Communicator, an operation that was accompanied by the clickwrap display of Communicator's license terms described above.

The signal difference between downloading Communicator and downloading SmartDownload was that no clickwrap presentation accompanied the latter operation. Instead, once plaintiffs Gibson, Gruber, Kelly, and Weindorf had clicked on the "Download" button located at or near the bottom of their screen, and the downloading of SmartDownload was complete, these plaintiffs encountered no further information about the plug-in program or the existence of license terms governing its use. The sole reference to SmartDownload's license terms on the "SmartDownload Communicator" webpage was located in text that would have become visible to plaintiffs only if they had scrolled down to the next screen.

Had plaintiffs scrolled down instead of acting on defendants' invitation to click on the "Download" button, they would have encountered the following invitation: "Please review and agree to the terms of the *Netscape SmartDownload software license agreement* before downloading and using the software." Plaintiffs Gibson, Gruber, Kelly, and Weindorf averred in their affidavits that they never saw this reference to the SmartDownload license agreement when they clicked on the "Download" button. They also testified during depositions that they saw no reference to license terms when they clicked to download SmartDownload, although under questioning by defendants' counsel, some plaintiffs added that they could not "remember" or be "sure" whether the screen shots of the SmartDownload page attached to their affidavits reflected precisely what they had seen on their computer screens when they downloaded SmartDownload.

In sum, plaintiffs Gibson, Gruber, Kelly, and Weindorf allege that the process of obtaining SmartDownload contrasted sharply with that of obtaining Communicator. Having selected SmartDownload, they were required neither to express unambiguous assent to that program's license agreement nor even to view the license terms or become aware of their existence before proceeding with the invited download of the free plug-in program. Moreover, once these plaintiffs had initiated the download, the existence of SmartDownload's license terms was not mentioned while the software was running or at any later point in plaintiffs' experience of the product.

Even for a user who, unlike plaintiffs, did happen to scroll down past the download button, SmartDownload's license terms would not have been immediately displayed in the manner of Communicator's clickwrapped terms. Instead, if such a user had seen the notice of SmartDownload's terms and then clicked on the underlined invitation to review and agree to the terms, a hypertext link would have taken the user to a separate webpage entitled "License & Support Agreements." The first paragraph on this page read, in pertinent part:

> The use of each Netscape software product is governed by a license agreement. You must read and agree to the license agreement terms BEFORE acquiring a product. Please click on the appropriate link below to review the current license agreement for the product of interest to you before acquisition. For products available for download, you must read and agree to the license agreement terms BEFORE you install the software. If you do not agree to the license terms, do not download, install or use the software.

Below this paragraph appeared a list of license agreements, the first of which was "*License Agreement for Netscape Navigator and Netscape Communicator Product Family* (Netscape Navigator, Netscape Communicator and Netscape SmartDownload)." If the user clicked on that link, he or she would be taken to yet another webpage that contained the full text of a license agreement that was identical in every respect to the Communicator license agreement except that it stated that its "terms apply to Netscape Communicator, Netscape Navigator, and Netscape SmartDownload." The license agreement granted the user a nonexclusive license to use and reproduce the software, subject to certain terms:

> BY CLICKING THE ACCEPTANCE BUTTON OR INSTALLING OR USING NETSCAPE COMMUNICATOR, NETSCAPE NAVIGATOR, OR NETSCAPE SMART-DOWNLOAD SOFTWARE (THE "PRODUCT"), THE INDIVIDUAL OR ENTITY LICENSING THE PRODUCT ("LICENSEE") IS CONSENTING TO BE BOUND BY AND IS BECOMING A PARTY TO THIS AGREEMENT. IF LICENSEE DOES NOT AGREE TO ALL OF THE TERMS OF THIS AGREEMENT, THE BUTTON INDICATING NON-ACCEPTANCE MUST BE SELECTED, AND LICENSEE MUST NOT INSTALL OR USE THE SOFTWARE.

Among the license terms was a provision requiring virtually all disputes relating to the agreement to be submitted to arbitration:

> Unless otherwise agreed in writing, all disputes relating to this Agreement (excepting any dispute relating to intellectual property rights) shall be subject to final and binding arbitration in Santa Clara County, California, under the auspices of

JAMS/EndDispute, with the losing party paying all costs of arbitration.

. . . Mutual manifestation of assent, whether by written or spoken word or by conduct, is the touchstone of contract. Although an onlooker observing the disputed transactions in this case would have seen each of the user plaintiffs click on the SmartDownload "Download" button, a consumer's clicking on a download button does not communicate assent to contractual terms if the offer did not make clear to the consumer that clicking on the download button would signify assent to those terms. California's common law is clear that "an offeree, regardless of apparent manifestation of his consent, is not bound by inconspicuous contractual provisions of which he is unaware, contained in a document whose contractual nature is not obvious." [Windsor Mills, Inc. v. Collins & Aikman Corp., 25 Cal. App. 3d 987, 992, 101 Cal. Rptr. 347, 351 (1972).]

Arbitration agreements are no exception to the requirement of manifestation of assent. . . . Clarity and conspicuousness of arbitration terms are important in securing informed assent. "If a party wishes to bind in writing another to an agreement to arbitrate future disputes, such purpose should be accomplished in a way that each party to the arrangement will fully and clearly comprehend that the agreement to arbitrate exists and binds the parties thereto." Commercial Factors Corp. v. Kurtzman Bros., 131 Cal. App. 2d 133, 134-35, 280 P.2d 146, 147-48 (1955). Thus, California contract law measures assent by an objective standard that takes into account both what the offeree said, wrote, or did and the transactional context in which the offeree verbalized or acted. . . .

Defendants argue that plaintiffs must be held to a standard of reasonable prudence and that, because notice of the existence of SmartDownload license terms was on the next scrollable screen, plaintiffs were on "inquiry notice" of those terms. We disagree with the proposition that a reasonably prudent offeree in plaintiffs' position would necessarily have known or learned of the existence of the SmartDownload license agreement prior to acting, so that plaintiffs may be held to have assented to that agreement with constructive notice of its terms. It is true that "[a] party cannot avoid the terms of a contract on the ground that he or she failed to read it before signing." Marin Storage & Trucking, Inc. v. Benco Contracting and Engineering, Inc., 89 Cal. App. 4th 1042, 1049, 107 Cal. Rptr. 2d 645, 651 (2001). But courts are quick to add: "An exception to this general rule exists when the writing does not appear to be a contract and the terms are not called to the attention of the recipient. In such a case, no contract is formed with respect to the undisclosed term." *Id.*

Most of the cases cited by defendants in support of their inquiry-notice argument are drawn from the world of paper contracting.

[R]eceipt of a physical document containing contract terms or notice thereof is frequently deemed, in the world of paper transactions, a sufficient circumstance to place the offeree on inquiry notice of those terms. "Every person who has actual notice of circumstances sufficient to put a prudent man upon inquiry as to a particular fact, has constructive notice of the fact itself in all cases in which, by prosecuting such inquiry, he might have learned such fact." Cal. Civ. Code § 19. These principles apply equally to the emergent world of online product delivery, pop-up screens, hyperlinked pages, clickwrap licensing, scrollable documents, and urgent admonitions to "Download Now!". What plaintiffs saw when they were being invited by defendants to download this fast, free plug-in called

SmartDownload was a screen containing praise for the product and, at the very bottom of the screen, a "Download" button. Defendants argue that under the principles set forth in the cases cited above, a "fair and prudent person using ordinary care" would have been on inquiry notice of SmartDownload's license terms.

We are not persuaded that a reasonably prudent offeree in these circumstances would have known of the existence of license terms. Plaintiffs were responding to an offer that did not carry an immediately visible notice of the existence of license terms or require unambiguous manifestation of assent to those terms. Thus, plaintiffs' "apparent manifestation of . . . consent" was to terms "contained in a document whose contractual nature [was] not obvious." *Windsor Mills,* 25 Cal. App. 3d at 992, 101 Cal. Rptr. at 351. Moreover, the fact that, given the position of the scroll bar on their computer screens, plaintiffs may have been aware that an unexplored portion of the Netscape webpage remained below the download button does not mean that they reasonably should have concluded that this portion contained a notice of license terms. In their deposition testimony, plaintiffs variously stated that they used the scroll bar "[o]nly if there is something that I feel I need to see that is on—that is off the page," or that the elevated position of the scroll bar suggested the presence of "mere[ ] formalities, standard lower banner links" or "that the page is bigger than what I can see." Plaintiffs testified, and defendants did not refute, that plaintiffs were in fact unaware that defendants intended to attach license terms to the use of SmartDownload.

We conclude that in circumstances such as these, where consumers are urged to download free software at the immediate click of a button, a reference to the existence of license terms on a submerged screen is not sufficient to place consumers on inquiry or constructive notice of those terms. The SmartDownload webpage screen was "printed in such a manner that it tended to conceal the fact that it was an express acceptance of [Netscape's] rules and regulations." [Larrus v. First Nat. Bank of San Mateo County, 122 Cal. App. 2d 884, 889, 266 P.2d 143, 147 (1954).] Internet users may have, as defendants put it, "as much time as they need[ ]" to scroll through multiple screens on a webpage, but there is no reason to assume that viewers will scroll down to subsequent screens simply because screens are there. When products are "free" and users are invited to download them in the absence of reasonably conspicuous notice that they are about to bind themselves to contract terms, the transactional circumstances cannot be fully analogized to those in the paper world of arm's-length bargaining. . . .

Defendants cite certain well-known cases involving shrinkwrap licensing and related commercial practices in support of their contention that plaintiffs became bound by the SmartDownload license terms by virtue of inquiry notice. For example, in Hill v. Gateway 2000, Inc., 105 F.3d 1147 (7th Cir. 1997), the Seventh Circuit held that where a purchaser had ordered a computer over the telephone, received the order in a shipped box containing the computer along with printed contract terms, and did not return the computer within the thirty days required by the terms, the purchaser was bound by the contract. In *ProCD, Inc. v. Zeidenberg,* the same court held that where an individual purchased software in a box containing license terms which were displayed on the computer screen every time the user executed the software program, the user had sufficient opportunity to review the terms and to return the software, and so was contractually bound after retaining the product.

These cases do not help defendants. To the extent that they hold that the purchaser of a computer or tangible software is contractually bound after failing to object to printed license terms provided with the product, *Hill* and *Brower* do not differ markedly from the cases involving traditional paper contracting discussed in the previous section. Insofar as the purchaser in *ProCD* was confronted with conspicuous, mandatory license terms every time he ran the software on his computer, that case actually undermines defendants' contention that downloading in the absence of conspicuous terms is an act that binds plaintiffs to those terms. . . .

After reviewing the California common law and other relevant legal authority, we conclude that under the circumstances here, plaintiffs' downloading of SmartDownload did not constitute acceptance of defendants' license terms. Reasonably conspicuous notice of the existence of contract terms and unambiguous manifestation of assent to those terms by consumers are essential if electronic bargaining is to have integrity and credibility. We hold that a reasonably prudent offeree in plaintiffs' position would not have known or learned, prior to acting on the invitation to download, of the reference to SmartDownload's license terms hidden below the "Download" button on the next screen. We affirm the district court's conclusion that the user plaintiffs, including Fagan, are not bound by the arbitration clause contained in those terms. . . .

Grosvenor v. Qwest Corp.

United States District Court, District of Colorado, 2012.
854 F. Supp. 2d 1021.

KRIEGER, DISTRICT JUDGE. . . . The key facts in this action are not in dispute. At bottom, Mr. Grosvenor alleges that Defendant Qwest solicited him to purchase internet service through a "Price for Life Guarantee," under which the monthly cost of such service would remain the same as long as Mr. Grosvenor remained a customer. He alleges that Qwest breached its contractual promise to provide service at a fixed price by subsequently raising the rate it charged him for internet service. Mr. Grosvenor's Complaint alleges claims for breach of contract, promissory estoppel, unjust enrichment, and a claim under the Colorado Consumer Protection Act, ostensibly on behalf of a putative class of Qwest internet customers.

However, the instant dispute focuses on a more narrow question. Qwest provides internet service pursuant to a Subscriber Agreement that, among other things, requires the parties to arbitrate disputes arising under it and prohibits the maintenance of class actions in cases alleging breach of the agreement. Shortly after this action was filed, Qwest moved to compel arbitration of Mr. Grosvenor's claims. . . .

This motion presents the most fundamental of contract law questions—when is a contractual agreement formed. The parties appear to agree that the matter is governed by Colorado law. That law provides that a contract is formed "when one party makes an offer and the other party accepts it, and the agreement is supported by consideration." Sumerel v. Goodyear Tire & Rubber Co., 232 P.3d 128, 133 (Colo. App. 2009). For a contract to arise, both parties must mutually assent to all essential element of the agreement. The terms of the offer must be sufficiently definite such that the promises and performances required of each party are reasonably certain. If the parties agree as to some issues, but fail to reach a meeting of the minds as to other material issues, the contract is not sufficiently formed. Whether a term is "essential" or "material"—such that there meeting of the minds by the parties as to that term's requirements—or whether the term is inessential to questions of contract formation is a matter that "must be determined from the intention of the parties as disclosed upon consideration of all surrounding facts and circumstances." American Min. Co. v. Himrod–Kimball Mines Co., 124 Colo. 186, 235 P.2d 804, 807 (1951).

This matter involves contract formation questions attendant to a party manifesting its agreement to a contract's terms by "clicking" on a button during installation of a software program. Numerous courts have considered the contractual effect of such "clickwrap" or "click-through" agreements. Perhaps the most detailed analysis of the unique issues presented in these circumstances is Specht v. Netscape Communications Corp., 306 F. 3d 17 (2d Cir. 2002). . . .

Colorado contract law bears some similarity to the California law assessed in *Specht*. For example, Colorado law also determines whether an offeree has accepted an offer by an objective standard—whether the offeree's words or conduct, objectively-viewed, manifests an intent to accept. Although the Court has not located Colorado authority for the proposition that objective indicia of assent can be overcome where the terms of the agreement were inconspicuous or concealed from the offeree, that proposition is not particularly remarkable. When a party is unaware of a term of a contract because it was hidden or obscured, there can be no presumption that there was a meeting of the minds as to such term. Thus, the Court is inclined to assess the contact formation issues here according to the same standard as *Specht*—that is, ascertaining whether the contractual terms were "reasonably conspicuous" and whether Mr. Grosvenor's alleged assent to them was "unambiguous."

Accordingly, the Court turns to the parties' evidence. In large part, the underlying facts are not in significant dispute. Mr. Grosvenor first subscribed to Qwest internet service in mid–2006. Qwest sent him a disc containing certain software to install to activate the service. When first opened, the install window contains the title "Legal Agreements" and states "Please read the terms *including arbitration and limits on Qwest liability* at *www.quest.com/legal* ("Qwest Agreement") that governs your use and Qwest's provision of the service(s) and equipment you ordered from the list below." (Emphasis in original.) Among the listed services is "Qwest High–Speed Internet Service," the product Mr. Grosvenor had ordered. The text then continues, stating "Please also read the (1) information on term and early termination fee, and (2) disclaimers and the end use license agreement related to the installation and software you receive during in ("Install Agreements") in the scroll box below."

Below that text is a box entitled "Important, Binding Legal Information." The box displays six lines of text, and contains a scroll bar that allows the user to scroll through additional text. As initially displayed, the first six lines of text read:

> Your click below on "I Accept" is an electronic signature and acknowledges: (1) you agree the Qwest Agreement contains the terms under which service and equipment are provided to you, (2) you understand and agree to such terms, (even if you don't read them), and (3) you understand and agree to the Install Agreements. Federal and some state laws provide for certain dis-

closures and the relevant language from the federal act is in this scroll box or at *www.qwest.com/legal/electronicsignatures.html.* You may get a paper copy of the agreements free of charge by printing from this page and *www.qwest.com/legal.* Qwest does not otherwise provide you with a paper copy. A standard connection to the Internet/World Wide Web, a device that sends and accepts standard email, and a software program that[3]

Below the box, text reads "Your click on 'I Accept' is an electronic signature to the agreements and contracts set out herein. Please review the material in the above box for important, binding legal information." The user may then click on a button that says "I Accept" or a button that says "Cancel." The software installation will not proceed unless the user clicks on the "I Accept" button.

Before delving further, the Court pauses at this point to assess what a reasonable user would understand from this information. From the upper portion of the installation window, the user would be aware that there are "terms [of service] including arbitration and limits on Qwest's liability" that accompany the user's use of the internet service. The user would also reasonably understand that those terms are not being presented in the window itself; rather, the user would understand that those terms—collectively referred to as the "Qwest Agreement"—must be viewed at the web address of *www.qwest.com/legal.* In addition, the user would recognize that there are additional agreements—referred to as the "Install Agreement"—as reflected in the scroll box. Both the immediately-visible terms of the Install Agreement as well as information found below the scroll box indicate to the user that clicking on the "I Accept" button manifests the user's acceptance of both the Qwest Agreement and the Install Agreement.

Mr. Grosvenor contends, and Qwest apparently does not dispute, that a user who navigated to *www.qwest.com/legal* on or about the 2006 installation date would have found that the main body of the page consisted of several paragraphs of various legal notices that are unrelated to the issues presented here. On the left side of the page, however, are a list of links to other pages, as set forth below:

- Legal Notices
- Customer Proprietary Network Information Sharing
- Acceptable Use Policy
- Service Level Agreement
- CPE
- Regulatory Documents
- Arizona Consumers
- Washington Consumers
- Colorado Consumers
- Network Disclosures

---

[3] Mr. Grosvenor states that the remaining material contained in the scroll box comprises approximately 10 pages of text. Most of that material is irrelevant to the issues presented here. However, section 7.2 of the material in the scroll box describes "Remedies and Legal Actions." Section 7.2(b) states that "Any dispute with SupportSoft, Inc. [apparently the author of the installation software] regarding the agreement" will be litigated in California. Section 7.2(c) states that "All other dispute regarding this Agreement" shall be litigated in courts in Colorado. As best the Court can see, the text in the scroll box makes no mention whatsoever of arbitration.

- High–Speed Internet Subscriber Agreement
- Qwest Choice TV & Online Legal Notices
- North America IP Network Peering Policy [etc.]

If the user clicked on the link for "High–Speed Internet Subscriber Agreement," it would be taken to another page that contains the arbitration agreement, class action limitation, and other terms relevant to the claims here.

To summarize, a user activating Qwest internet service would become aware of the terms of the agreement (and manifest assent) through the following steps: (i) the installation software directs the user to "Please read the terms . . . at *www.qwest.com/legal* . . . that governs . . . the service(s) and equipment you ordered."; (ii) the user would navigate to the linked page (the "legal" page); (iii) the user, installing Qwest high-speed internet service, would then click on the "High–Speed Internet Subscriber Agreement" link on that page, thus being taken to yet another page; (iv) the user would review that subscriber agreement; and (v) the user would return to the installation software and manifest assent to the subscriber agreement by clicking "I Accept." The question, then, is whether these facts constitute "reasonably conspicuous notice" of the agreement's terms.

Specht is too factually distinct from this case to offer meaningful guidance. There, the users were attempting to download a free product, not install a service they were subscribing to; they were first faced with "a screen containing praise for the product" and no immediate mention of contractual terms, rather than an installation window expressly directing the user to terms governing the use of the service; and users in *Specht* were not asked to expressly manifest their assent to such terms, whereas Qwest required Mr. Grosvenor to affirmatively express his assent to license terms in order to complete the installation.

The other cases cited by Mr. Grosvenor in his summary judgment response are equally inapplicable. [A]ll involved users who were not required to manifest their assent to stated terms and conditions before obtaining the services they sought. . . . Thus, these cases are not persuasive in demonstrating that a user who affirmatively expresses assent to terms whose *existence* is conspicuously disclosed but whose *contents* can only be discovered with additional navigation prevents formation of a contract.

Several cases have concluded that where, during a software installation, the user is presented with the text of an agreement in a scroll box and required the click [of] a button expressing assent to those terms before installation continues, a contract is formed. Rarer are cases in which, rather than presenting the terms of the agreement in a scroll box, the installation software directs the user to the terms of the agreement through a link to a different location. Nevertheless, the reasoning in "scroll box" cases applies with equal force where, rather than scrolling through an agreement's terms in a text box, the user can review the license terms by following the tendered link.

There are two facts that are unique to this scenario. First, Mr. Grosvenor could not review Qwest's terms of service simply by clicking on the link *www.qwest.com/legal*; doing so would have only taken him to a page where he would have to continue to search for a link to the applicable contractual terms. The Court cannot say that, as a matter of law, requiring a user to navigate through two links in order to review the terms of an offer prevents any contractual formation, each additional step required of the user tips against a finding that the terms were sufficiently conspicuous. Second, and perhaps more importantly, the fact that a user must navigate to a web page in order to ascertain terms of an offer is particularly difficult where the software being installed is the means by which the internet can be accessed. In the absence of some other means of accessing the internet, Qwest's program did not allow Mr. Grosvenor to go to *www.qwest.com/legal* or review the applicable documents. The record does not reflect whether Mr. Grosvenor had other operative internet service when he began installation of Qwest's software. In the absence of other operative internet service, Mr. Grosvenor had no way of assessing the terms of Qwest's agreements until he completed installation of the software, and completion of the software installation would not occur until Mr. Grosvenor manifested his acceptance of the terms or the agreement. Under these circumstances, . . . there is no assurance that a user could view the operative terms prior to agreeing to them. Thus, despite the representations made as to the effect of pressing the "I Accept" button, the Court has some doubt that doing so created an enforceable contract.

Second, it is undisputed that on July 24, 2006, Qwest followed up Mr. Grosvenor's activation of his internet service by sending a "Welcome Letter." That letter—which Mr. Grosvenor does not dispute receiving although he professes no specific recollection of it—includes a paragraph reading "Please review the important information about service and terms for use . . . on the back of this letter." The back of the letter contains the following text:

> Qwest High–Speed Internet Service and related products are offered under the Subscriber Agreement terms, which are located at *www.qwest.com/legal* (may also be enclosed). Please review the terms, which include arbitration and limits on Qwest liability. If you do not agree, call Qwest to cancel your service within 30 days.

The Welcome Letter alleviates some of the issues noted above. First, it eliminates some of the confusion in the software's reference to the "Qwest Agreement." The Welcome Letter, specifically directs Mr. Grosvenor to the "Subscriber Agreement" on the qwest.com/legal page as being the document containing terms of service, "includ[ing] arbitration and limits on Qwest liability." Although the "legal" page does not immediately display the Subscriber Agreement, users navigating to that page can readily locate the Subscriber Agreement, because there is only one link on the "legal" page referring to a "Subscriber Agreement." The Welcome Letter, having arrived after internet service software was installed, also addresses the user's potential difficulty in accessing the terms of Qwest's offer in the absence of internet service. Finally, the letter provides time in which to consider the terms of the Subscriber Agreement without the inherent urgency associated with installing the software. It instructs users who do not agree to the terms of the offer to "cancel your service" within 30 days, and thus, a user who does not cancel service is assumed by Qwest to have assented to the agreement's terms. Mr. Grosvenor did not cancel his Qwest internet service.

Taking the circumstances as a whole, the Court finds that on the undisputed facts presented here, Mr. Grosvenor's conduct constitutes an objective manifestation of assent to the contractual terms. Although the presentation of the terms is hardly a model of clarity, the Court nevertheless finds that they were sufficiently conspicuous as to permit a reasonable user the opportunity to review them and either agree to them or to cancel the internet service. Among other things, the installation software conspicuously warned users of the *existence* of contractual terms that accompanied the service, specifically mentioning arbitration as one of the issues addressed. The software provided users with a link by which a reasonable user could locate—albeit with some effort—the relevant contractual language, and required that the user affirmatively express its acceptance of Qwest's terms. To the extent that presentation of the terms via the installation software can be said to be impractical or unclear, the Welcome Letter would be sufficient to cure a reasonable user's confusion. That letter expressly identified arbitration as one of the important terms to be reviewed by the user, sufficiently identified the particular link on the "legal" page that contained the agreement, and arrived at a time when the user would certainly be able to access the internet to view the identified terms. The letter provided that the user's continued use of the service after 30 days effectively manifested assent to the agreement's terms. Although the Court declines to opine as to whether either presentation of the terms—the software installation and the Welcome Letter—would, of itself, be sufficient, it finds that the combination of the two presentations rendered the contractual terms specifically clear that a reasonable user would be deemed to have understood the terms and assented to them. Accordingly, the Court finds that Mr. Grosvenor entered into a contractual agreement with Qwest in July 2006, in which he agreed to arbitrate disputes over his purchase of internet service. . . .

Mr. Grosvenor moves for summary judgment, arguing that any agreement to arbitrate that he may have entered into is illusory and thus unenforceable because Qwest reserved the unilateral right to change terms of the agreement. Mr. Grosvenor points out that Section 4 of the Subscriber Agreement provides that "Qwest may . . . modify the Service and/or any of the terms and conditions of this Agreement." This, Mr. Grosvenor argues renders the agreement illusory under *Dumais v. American Golf Corp.*, 299 F.3d 1216 (10th Cir. 2002). In *Dumais*, the 10th Circuit explained that "an arbitration agreement allowing one party the unfettered right to alter the arbitration agreement's existence or its scope is illusory." Id. at 1219. . . .

Qwest . . . argues that there is no evidence of record establishing that it has changed the arbitration terms. This is true, but irrelevant. The court in *Dumais* gave no indication that the employer had to have altered the terms of the arbitration agreement in order for it to be illusory. To the contrary, it recognized that it was the unilateral power of one party to change the arbitration terms that rendered the arbitration provisions illusory.

The Court finds that *Dumais* controls the outcome of Mr. Grosvenor's motion. Because Qwest retained an unfettered ability to modify the existence, terms and scope of the arbitration clause, it is illusory and unenforceable . . . .

————

NOTE

In a part of the opinion omitted here, the court discussed whether the validity of the arbitration agreement is something that itself is for an arbitrator to decide rather than the court. The threshold question of whether the parties agreed to arbitration is often in dispute. See *Schnabel v. Trilegiant Corp.*, 697 F.3d 110 (2d. Cir. 2012). The Supreme Court has confronted this issue in *Rent-A-Center v. Jackson*, and we examine its opinion below at p. 703.

In reflecting on the question of the enforceability of clauses set out on web pages that require multiple clicks to access, consider how much the law should take into account the behavior of the typical consumer. *Specht* and *Grosvenor* put forward tests suggesting that the test of consent should turn on whether terms were "reasonably conspicuous." This approach implies that the "reasonably prudent" consumer pays at least some attention to such terms. Everyday experience suggests that is not the case. Few of us bother to read any terms that can be accessed only by scrolling down or clicking a hyperlink. To the extent that the legal rule finds the various terms binding because the typical reader will be aware of them, it is completely out of touch.

Some have suggested that the failure of most to read is not itself troubling. They reason that, as long as large enough informed minority reads the terms, sellers need to provide attractive ones in order not to lose customers. Hence, sellers will offer terms to which typical consumers would agree if they had read them. See, e.g., Alan Schwartz & Louis Wilde, Intervening in Alan Schwartz & Louis Wilde, Intervening in Markets on the Basis of Imperfect Information: A Legal and Economic Analysis, 127 U. Pa. L. Rev. 630 (1979). The relevant test therefore should not be whether the typical consumer reads the terms, but rather whether a large enough minority do. Recent empirical work, however, calls into doubt even this line of thought. A study that tracked the Internet browsing behavior of over forty thousand households found that only one or two out of every thousand retail software shoppers chooses to access the license agreement, and those few that do spend too little time, on average, to have read more than a small portion of the license text. See Bakos, Yannis, Marotta-Wurgler, Florencia and Trossen, Does Anyone Read the Fine Print? Testing a Law and Economics Approach to Standard Form Contracts (October 6, 2009). CELS 2009 4th Annual Conference on Empirical Legal Studies Paper; NYU Law and Economics Research Paper No. 09-40. Available at SSRN: http://ssrn.com/abstract=1443256 or http://dx.doi.org/10.2139/ssrn.1443256. If not even an informed minority is reading the contract terms, what is the basis for enforcing them? We shall return to this question in Chapter 5, when we examine standardized fine print terms and the doctrine of unconscionability.

The facts of *ProCD* and *Netscape* raise an additional issue. By the time cases work their way through the legal system, the underlying contracting environment may change significantly. These remain the leading cases, even though shrinkwrap licenses no longer exist and the Netscape browser has long disappeared from the scene. The way consumers acquire new software has completely changed. App stores did not exist at the time either case was decided. How applicable is the reasoning of these cases to a world that has already changed and continues to change?

_____

CONDUCT AS ASSENT: THE IMPLIED CONTRACT

The assent required for the formation of a contract can be inferred from many things. A failure to object, viewed against a given background, may be enough. At the same time, it is necessary to recall a maxim underlying the rules of contract formation: "The offeror is master of the offer." The power to specify an acceptable exchange, in form and in content, surely includes the power to designate the response that will constitute a valid acceptance. Yet, as we have seen, the offeror's power to set the bargain's terms often will be exercised only in part, not in full, perhaps even not at all. So it is not in the least unusual to find commercial dealings lacking formal structure or documentation (recall, for example, *Nat Nal Serv. Stations*, p. 350). If an express contract is established, it will of course bar claims of implied undertakings on matters within its scope—unless the express contract has itself been modified by the parties' conduct.

The main event as concerns activity lacking explicit bargaining is just ahead (Martin v. Little, Brown & Co. and accompanying cases, in particular Collins v. Lewis). But first there is need to take a brief look at two problems lurking in the implied-contract cases. One is the effect of failing to reply to an offer (so-called "silence as acceptance"). The other is the limits, if any, on an offerer's power to bring about a contract by declaring that another's failure to reply or act constitutes acceptance. The governing principles are assembled in Restatement, Second § 69, which is reproduced below. In examining the classifications made by the section, it seems a good idea to keep in mind some concepts traditionally associated with "implied contract" (indeed, with contract in general)—restitution, reliance, estoppel, request, bargain.

RESTATEMENT OF CONTRACTS, SECOND

Section 69. Acceptance by Silence or Exercise of Dominion

(1) Where an offeree fails to reply to an offer, his silence and inaction operate as an acceptance in the following cases only:

(a) Where an offeree takes the benefit of offered services with reasonable opportunity to reject them and reason to know that they were offered with the expectation of compensation.

(b) Where the offeror has stated or given the offeree reason to understand that assent may be manifested by silence or inaction, and the offeree in remaining silent and inactive intends to accept the offer.

(c) Where because of previous dealings or otherwise, it is reasonable that the offeree should notify the offeror if he does not intend to accept.

(2) An offeree who does any act inconsistent with the offeror's ownership of offered property is bound in accordance with the offered terms unless they are manifestly unreasonable. But if the act is wrongful as against the offeror it is an acceptance only if ratified by him.

QUESTION

Look once more at Prescott v. Jones, p. 241, where defendants, by letter, promised to renew plaintiff's insurance policy "unless notified to the contrary," and plaintiff, relying on the letter and believing that his buildings were insured for another year, made no reply. If Rest.2d § 69 applies to such a case (does it?), should the plaintiff lose again?

————

Hobbs v. Massasoit Whip Co.

Supreme Judicial Court of Massachusetts, 1893.
158 Mass. 194, 33 N.E. 495.

HOLMES, J. This is an action for the price of eel skins sent by the plaintiff to the defendant, and kept by the defendant some months, until they were destroyed. It must be taken that the plaintiff received no notice that the defendant declined to accept the skins. The case comes before us on exceptions to an instruction to the jury, that, whether there was any prior contract or not, if skins are sent to the defendant, and it sees fit, whether it has agreed to take them or not, to lie back, and to say nothing, having reason to suppose that the man who has sent them believes that it is taking them, since it says nothing about it, then, if it fails to notify, the jury would be warranted in finding for the plaintiff.

Standing alone, and unexplained, this proposition might seem to imply that one stranger may impose a duty upon another, and make him a purchaser, in spite of himself, by sending goods to him, unless he will take the trouble, and be at the expense, of notifying the sender that he will not buy. The case was argued for the defendant on that interpretation. But, in view of the evidence, we do not understand that to have been the meaning of the judge, and we do not think that the jury can have understood that to have been his meaning. The plaintiff was not a stranger to the defendant, even if there was no contract between them. He had sent eel skins in the same way four or five times before, and they had been accepted and paid for. On the defendant's testimony, it is fair to assume that, if it had admitted the eel skins to be over twenty-two inches in length, and fit for its business, as the plaintiff testified, and the jury found that they were, it would have accepted them; that this was understood by the plaintiff; and, indeed, that there was a standing offer to him for such skins. In such a condition of things, the plaintiff was warranted in sending the defendant skins conforming to the requirements, and even if the offer was not such that the contract was made as soon as skins corresponding to its terms were sent, sending them did impose on the defendant a duty to act about them; and silence on its part, coupled with a retention of the skins for an unreasonable time, might be found by the jury to warrant the plaintiff in assuming that they were accepted, and thus to amount to an acceptance. . . . Taylor v. Dexter Engine Co., 146 Mass. 613, 16 N.E. 462. The proposition stands on the general principle that conduct which imports acceptance or assent is acceptance or assent in the view of the law, whatever may have been the actual state of mind of the party,—a principle sometimes lost sight of in the cases. O'Donnell v. Clinton, 145 Mass. 461, 14 N.E. 747.

Exceptions overruled.

————

COMMENT: THE PRIVILEGE OF SILENCE

Courts typically say that "silence will not constitute acceptance of an offer in the absence of a duty to speak." If such assertions are to be believed, it is essential to determine the kinds of circumstances in which such a "duty" will be found.

One formulation intended to accommodate the duty-to-speak cases can be found in § 69(1)(c) of the Restatement, Second. An illustration of the legal effects of "previous dealings or otherwise" is provided by Ammons v. Wilson & Co., Ammons v. Wilson & Co., 176 Miss. 645, 170 So. 227 (1936), a case much like Hobbs v. Massasoit Whip Co. Plaintiff, a wholesale grocer, was visited on August 23 and 24 by defendant's sales representative, to whom plaintiff gave a large order for shortening. In early September, plaintiff inquired when shipment would be made; on September 4, defendant gave notice that the order had been rejected. During the preceding eight months, a number of orders submitted by plaintiff through the same salesperson had been accepted and shipped by defendant not more than one week from the time they were given. The court held that it was for the jury to say whether defendant's delay and silence for 12 days implied an acceptance of plaintiff's order. The court made no mention of a "duty to speak." Rather, in the language of the Restatement (First) of Contracts § 72(1)(c) (now § 69 in the Rest.2d), it applied the test of whether "the offeree has given the offeror reason to understand that the silence or inaction is intended by the offeree as a manifestation of assent." The legal concept of a duty to speak was thus replaced by a standard of "reasonable understanding," applied by the jury in the light of the full context in which the parties dealt. Is this what Justice Holmes had in mind in *Hobbs*, when he spoke of conduct "warrant[ing] the plaintiff in assuming" an acceptance had occurred?

Does a similar standard of reasonable understanding explain the fate of "additional" terms under § 2–207(2) of the Uniform Commercial Code? You will recall that "between merchants," additional, nonmaterial terms in an accepting form become part of the contract unless timely notice of objection is given. The Official Comment to the section reasons that if there is a failure to respond to such proposals, "it is both fair and commercially sound to assume that their inclusion has been assented to." Given the *Hobbs* analysis and result, as well as the principle stated in § 69(1)(c), it should be clear that even though an offeree's new term is a "material alteration" under UCC 2–207(2), prior dealings between the parties may provide a basis for concluding that the offeree was reasonable in inferring assent to the term from the offeror's failure to object to it. See, e.g., Union Carbide Corp. v. Oscar Mayer Foods Corp., 947 F.2d 1333 (7th Cir.1991).

As for the first category of silence-is-acceptance cases sketched by Restatement § 69 ("the offeree takes the benefit of offered services"), a classic example is the unobjecting owner of the cows in Collins v. Lewis (p. 497). Again, it is not enough that the actor expected to be paid; it must be shown that the party to be charged in some manner "assented." A further example is provided by Moore v. Kuehn, 602 S.W.2d 713 (Mo.Ct.App.1980), where defendant had asked plaintiff for a list of repairs needed to restore a building. After plaintiff provided such a list, with prices, defendant told plaintiff to proceed with one item on the list. Plaintiff did not stop after completing that work, but continued on with the other items, completing the entire list. Defendant was at all times aware of plaintiff's activities but said nothing. As you no doubt have guessed, defendant's silence in circumstances where he might easily have applied the brakes to plaintiff resulted in a contract to pay for the benefits received at the listed prices.

In applying the principle stated in § 69(1)(a), the fighting issue often will be whether the offeree had the requisite "reason to know." That was the situation in McGurn v. Bell Microproducts, Inc., 284 F.3d 86 (1st Cir.2002), where Bell mailed McGurn a signed offer of employment stating that if he was terminated within the first twelve months of employment, he would be given a severance package worth $120,000. In signing and returning the offer letter, McGurn crossed out the word "twelve" and replaced it with "twenty-four," initialing his alteration but otherwise not calling it to Bell's attention. Bell's Human Resources department received the returned letter, filing it without examining its contents. Bell terminated McGurn thirteen months later and refused to pay him the severance package, claiming that the twelve-month period stipulated in the offer letter had passed, and that McGurn's alteration was a counteroffer which Bell had never accepted. A federal district court thought otherwise, granting summary judgment to McGurn for the reason that "a presumably sophisticated employer who receives a signed letter of engagement from a prospective employee and fails to read the letter, does so at its peril." A divided reviewing court was unable to agree that Bell's silence, as a matter of law, constituted acceptance of McGurn's counteroffer. A trial must be had on whether the modification "should have been noticed" (i.e., whether, in circumstances, Bell should be expected to re-read the returned offer).

The applicant for insurance is usually characterized as an offeror. What if the risk that the applicant sought to cover materializes before the insurance company has taken any action on the application? An insurance company surely is entitled to a reasonable opportunity to assess the information in the application and to determine what it wants to do. Unless the insurer, by its mode of doing business, has departed from the usual practice and has itself made the offer, or entered into a contract of "temporary insurance" (e.g., Smith v. Westland Life Ins. Co., 15 Cal.3d 111, 123 Cal.Rptr. 649, 539 P.2d 433 (1975)), or, through language in the application itself, has contracted to act in a timely manner, there is no basis for holding that it has underwritten the risk from the time the person wanting insurance has submitted an application.

But what if the insurance company takes no action promptly, remaining wholly silent for a lengthy period after receiving the application? A number of courts have found in the insurer's silence an "implied" acceptance and have grounded liability in the insurance contract, especially where an unreasonable delay is coupled with retention of an initial premium paid at the time of the application. E.g., St. Paul Fire & Marine Ins. Co. v. Ingall, 228 Mich.App. 101, 577 N.W.2d 188 (1998); Mardirosian v. Lincoln National Life Ins. Co., 739 F.2d 474 (9th Cir.1984) (silence respecting efforts to reinstate lapsed policy amounts to "waiver" of right to refuse reinstatement); Dibble v. Security of America Life Ins. Co., 404 Pa.Super. 205, 590 A.2d 352 (1991). Other courts have accorded the applicant protection on a tort basis. The usual rationale is that the insurer, acting under a franchise from and under the regulation of the state, is under a duty to provide insurance to all qualified applicants and, to this end, the insurer is under a duty to act with reasonable promptness in processing the application and notifying the applicant of the action taken. See, e.g., Kukuska v. Home Mut. Hail–Tornado Ins. Co., 204 Wis. 166, 235 N.W. 403 (1931). The measure of recovery appears to be the same whether a contract or tort theory is used. The cases are collected in Hill v. Chubb Life American Ins. Co., 182 Ariz. 158, 894 P.2d 701 (1995) ("courts and commentators have struggled with whether liability for delay in processing an insurance application sounds in tort or in contract").

The cases on implied contracts through silence are collected and discussed in Grosse, Silence as Acceptance, 9 S.U.L.Rev. 81 (1982).

———

Austin v. Burge

156 Mo.App. 286, 137 S.W. 618 (1911)

Defendant's father-in-law paid for a two-year subscription to plaintiff's newspaper, directing that it be sent to defendant. After the subscription had run out, plaintiff continued to send the paper for several years. Twice defendant paid bills submitted by plaintiff for the subscription price, each time directing that the paper be stopped. Plaintiff still sent the paper and defendant regularly took it home from the post office and read it. On plaintiff's suit for the subscription price, judgment for defendant reversed. "The law in respect to contractual indebtedness for a newspaper is not different from that relating to other things that have not been made the subject of an express agreement. Thus one may not have ordered supplies for his table, or other household necessities, yet if he continue to receive and use them, under circumstances where he had no right to suppose they were a gratuity, he will be held to have agreed by implication, to pay their value."

NOTE: UNSOLICITED MERCHANDISE

Senders of unsolicited goods have aroused a legislative response. Congress and nearly all state legislatures have enacted "unsolicited goods" statutes, the most common provisions of which authorize the recipient to treat unordered merchandise as a gift. An example at the state level is provided by the Michigan Unlawful Trade Practices Act (Mich.Comp.Laws Ann. § 445.131), which provides: ". . . The receipt of any such unsolicited goods shall be deemed for all purposes an unconditional gift to the recipient[,] [who] may refuse to accept delivery of the goods, is not bound to return them to the sender, and may use or dispose of them in any manner he sees fit without any obligation [to] the sender."

The federal act, a provision of the Postal Reorganization Act of 1970, Pub.L. No. 91–375, 84 Stat. 749, appears in 39 U.S.C. § 3009. It provides:

(a) Except for (1) free samples clearly and conspicuously marked as such, and (2) merchandise mailed by a charitable organization soliciting contributions, the mailing of unordered merchandise or of communications prohibited by subsection (c) of this section constitutes an unfair method of competition and an unfair trade practice. . . .

(b) Any merchandise mailed in violation of subsection (a) of this section, or within the exceptions contained therein, may be treated as a gift by the recipient, who shall have the right to retain, use, discard, or dispose of it in any manner he sees fit without any obligation whatsoever to the sender. . . .

(c) No mailer of any merchandise mailed in violation of subsection (a) of this section, or within the exceptions contained therein, shall mail to any recipient of such merchandise a bill for such merchandise or any dunning communications.

This statute presumably alters the Restatement's "exercise-of-dominion" provision, § 69(2), as would similar state legislation. So-called "negative-option" plans, typically used by book clubs, are distinguishable in that the consumer subscribes in advance (a contract). Such plans are regulated by a rule of the Federal Trade Commission (16 C.F.R. § 425.1).

Martin v. Little, Brown & Co.

Superior Court of Pennsylvania, 1981.
304 Pa.Super. 424, 450 A.2d 984.

WIEAND, J. This appeal was taken from an order sustaining preliminary objections in the nature of a demurrer to appellant's pro se complaint in assumpsit. The trial court held that a contract had not been made and that there could be no recovery on quantum meruit where appellant had volunteered information which enabled appellee, a publisher of books, to effect a recovery against a third person for copyright infringement. We agree and, accordingly, affirm.

. . . [O]n September 28, 1976, the appellant, James L. Martin, directed a letter to Bantam Books in which he advised the addressee that portions of a paperback publication entitled "How to Buy Stocks" had been plagiarized by the authors of a later book entitled "Planning Your Financial Future." Appellant's letter offered to provide a copy of the book, in which appellant had highlighted the plagiarized passages, with marginal references to the pages and paragraphs of the book from which the passages had been copied. By letter dated October 21, 1976 and signed by Robin Paris, Editorial Assistant, the appellee, Little, Brown & Co., invited appellant to send his copy of "Planning Your Financial Future." This was done, and appellee acknowledged receipt thereof in writing. Thereafter, appellant made inquiries about appellee's investigation but received no response. Appellant was persistent, however, and upon learning that appellee . . . was pursuing a claim of copyright infringement, he demanded compensation for his services. Appellee denied that it had contracted with appellant or was otherwise obligated to compensate appellant for his work or for his calling the infringement to the publisher's attention. Nevertheless, appellee offered an honorarium in the form of a check for two hundred dollars, which appellant retained but did not cash. Instead, he filed suit to recover one-third of the recovery effected by appellee.

These facts and all reasonable inferences therefrom have been admitted by appellee's demurrer. . . . [W]e are guided by the rule that a demurrer may be sustained only in clear cases, and all doubts must be resolved in favor of the sufficiency of the complaint. . . .

The facts alleged . . . are insufficient to establish a contractual relationship between appellant and appellee. Appellant's initial letter did not expressly or by implication suggest a desire to negotiate. Neither did appellee's letter of October 21, 1976, which invited appellant to send his copy of the offending publication, constitute an offer to enter a unilateral contract [an exchange of appellant's performance for appellee's promise]. It was no more than a response to an initial letter by appellant in which he notified appellee of a copyright infringement and expressed a willingness to forward a copy of the infringing work in which he had highlighted copied portions and cited pages of appellee's work which had been copied. Appellant's letter did not suggest that he intended to be paid, and appellee's response did not contain an offer to pay appellant if he forwarded his copy of the infringing work. In brief, payment to appellant was not discussed in any of the correspondence which preceded the forwarding of appellant's work to appellee.

"A contract, implied in fact, is an actual contract which arises where the parties agree upon the obligations to be incurred, but their intention, instead of being expressed in words, is inferred from their acts in the light of the surrounding circumstances." [In re Home Protection Bldg. & Loan Ass'n, 143 Pa.Super. 96, 17 A.2d 755 (1941).] An implied contract is an agreement which legitimately can be inferred from the intention of the parties as evidenced by the circumstances and "the ordinary course of dealing and the common understanding of men." Hertzog v. Hertzog, 29 Pa. 465 (1857). "Generally, there is an implication of a promise to pay for valuable services rendered with the knowledge and approval of the recipient, in the absence of a showing to the contrary. A promise to pay the reasonable value of the service is implied where one performs for another, with the other's knowledge, a useful service of a character that is usually charged for, and the latter expresses no dissent or avails himself of the service. A promise to pay for services can, however, only be implied when they are rendered in such circumstances as authorized the party performing to entertain a reasonable expectation of their payment by the party benefited. The service or other benefit must not be given as a gratuity or without expectation of payment, and the person benefited must do something from which his promise to pay may be fairly inferred." Home Protection Bldg. & Loan Ass'n, supra. . . . When a person requests another to perform services, it is ordinarily inferred that he intends to pay for them, unless the circumstances indicate otherwise. Restatement Restitution § 107(2) (1937).* However, where the circumstances evidence that one's work effort has been voluntarily given to another, an intention to pay therefor cannot be inferred. [Here,] the facts alleged . . . disclose a submission of information from appellant to appellee without any discussion pertaining to appellee's payment therefor. Clearly, there was no basis upon which to infer the existence of a unilateral contract.

Similarly, there is no factual premise to support a finding that appellee is entitled to recover in quasi-contract for the information supplied by appellant. Where one person has been unjustly enriched at the expense of another he or she must make restitution to the other. DeGasperi v. Valicenti, 198 Pa.Super. 455, 181 A.2d 862 (1962). However, unjust enrichment is the key to an action for restitution. . . . The vehicle for achieving restitution is a quasi-contract, or contract implied in law. "Unlike true contracts, quasi-contracts are not based on the apparent intention of the parties to undertake the performances in question, nor are they promises. They are obligations created by law for reasons of justice." Schott v. Westinghouse Elec. Corp., 436 Pa. 279, 290, 259 A.2d 443, 449 (1969). . . . "Quasi-contracts may be found in the absence of any expression of assent by the

---

* [Section 107(2) provides: "In the absence of circumstances indicating otherwise, it is inferred that a person who requests another to perform services for him or to transfer property to him thereby bargains to pay therefor."—Eds.]

party to be charged and may indeed be found in spite of the party's contrary intention." [Schott v. Westinghouse], at 290–91, 259 A.2d at 449. To sustain a claim of unjust enrichment, it must be shown by the facts pleaded that a person wrongly secured or passively received a benefit that it would be unconscionable to retain. . . .

As a general rule, volunteers have no right to restitution. Reiver v. Safeguard Precision Prods., 240 Pa.Super. 572, 361 A.2d 371 (1976). . . . Appellant was a volunteer. It was he who made the unsolicited suggestion that he would be willing to submit to appellee his copy of "Planning Your Financial Future" with notations to show which portions had been purloined from "How to Buy Stocks." His offer to do so was not conditioned upon payment of any kind. He did not suggest, either expressly or by implication, that he expected to be paid for this information or for time spent in reducing the same to writing. Thus, . . . he was purely a volunteer and cannot properly be reimbursed for unjust enrichment.[1]

Finally, appellant's complaint contains a count in trespass for intentional infliction of mental distress.[*] The basis of this claim is an alleged statement by appellee's counsel that if appellant instituted suit, a counterclaim would be filed for abuse of process.

The Restatement (Second) of Torts § 46, provides: "One who by extreme and outrageous conduct intentionally or recklessly causes severe emotional distress to another is subject to liability for such emotional distress." Under this rule, "[l]iability has been found only where the conduct has been *so outrageous in character, and so extreme in degree, as to go beyond all possible bounds of decency, and to be regarded as atrocious, and utterly intolerable in a civilized community.* Generally, the case is one in which the recitation of the facts to an average member of the community would arouse his resentment against the actor, and lead him to exclaim, 'Outrageous.'" Jones v. Nissenbaum, Rudolph & Seidner, 244 Pa.Super. 377, 383, 368 A.2d 770, 773 (1976). . . .

The mere threat of a legal counterclaim, even if entirely lacking in merit, will not generally satisfy the strict standard required to make out a case of outrageous conduct. The adversary nature of litigation invariably involves a turbulent contest of wills. Appellant, a law student who threatened to avail himself of the judicial process to assert a claim, cannot properly complain when his adversary threatens to file a counterclaim. This did not give rise to an action for the emotional distress, if any, which appellant suffered when he learned that a new dimension would be added to the litigation. The claim was properly dismissed.

---

[1] The parties have not briefed and our decision makes it unnecessary that we consider the damages which appellant would otherwise be entitled to recover. It is clear, however, that such damages are measured by the reasonable value of services rendered and not by a percentage of the recovery achieved by appellee as a result of the copyright infringement first observed by appellant. . . . [This footnote is renumbered; the court's other footnotes are omitted.—Eds.]

[*] [Recall the discussion of this tort in the Note accompanying Valentine v. General American Credit, supra p. 90.—Eds.]

Collins v. Lewis

111 Conn. 299, 149 A. 668 (1930)

Plaintiff, a deputy sheriff, attached and took away cows found in the possession of one Kinne. Plaintiff later learned that the cows belonged to defendant and that Kinne held them under a conditional-sale contract. A few days later, plaintiff returned the cows to Kinne's farm but Kinne refused to take them. Subsequently, plaintiff offered to return the cows to defendant but was told that defendant had no place for them at that time. Plaintiff's attorney then informed defendant that the cows were being kept for him and that he would be held for the cost of their keep. After being boarded by plaintiff for thirty-eight days, the cows were sold by defendant and taken away by the new purchaser. The court said: "It is to be noted that during this period he [defendant] knew from the letter which had been sent to him by counsel for the plaintiff, that the plaintiff was holding the cows for him with the expectation of being paid for their care and keep. By selling the cows and taking possession of them, he thus appropriated the benefit of the thirty-eight days' care and keep which had been bestowed upon them by the plaintiff. It was under these established facts that the trial court held there was an implied contract created by law, that the defendant would pay the plaintiff."

"A true implied contract can only exist where there is no express one. It is one which is inferred from the conduct of the parties though not expressed in words. Such a contract arises where a plaintiff, without being requested to do so, renders services under circumstances indicating that he expects to be paid therefor, and the defendant, knowing such circumstances, avails himself of the benefit of those services. In such a case, the law implies from the circumstances, a promise by the defendant to pay the plaintiff what those services are reasonably worth. . . . 'One may . . . be required to compensate another for the benefits conferred by the other's labor and services, either accepted by or necessarily accruing to the beneficiary, when, having reasonable ground to believe that the labor is being done or service performed in the expectation of compensation, he stands silently by and permits the labor or service to continue.' Chesebro v. Lockwood, 88 Conn. 219, 224, 91 A. 188. Upon this record as it stands, therefore, we sustain the conclusion of the trial court that there was an implied contract, that this defendant would pay the reasonable cost of the care and keep of these cows."

———

Seaview Ass'n of Fire Island, N.Y., Inc. v. Williams

69 N.Y.2d 987, 517 N.Y.S.2d 709, 510 N.E.2d 793 (1987)

Plaintiff, a homeowners' association, owned and maintained the streets, walkways, and beaches of Seaview, an unincorporated community of some 330 homes used largely for summer recreation. Plaintiff provided many community services, including recreational facilities. Each Seaview property owner was assessed a share of plaintiff's annual operating expenses; the assessment policy was generally known in the community (the forms of notice included posted signs). Defendants, year-round residents active in the real estate business, owned seven houses in Seaview (their first purchase was in 1963), but refused to pay any assessments, contending that nonmembers of the association and nonusers of the recreational facilities cannot be charged. In plaintiff's suit to recover assessments against defendants for an eight-year period, the trial court, finding an "implied contract" to pay assessments, awarded judgment for plaintiff. *Held*, there is ample evidence to support the trial court's findings. Defendants had "actual or constructive knowledge" of the nature of the community and plaintiff's activities for the benefit of residents. Their purchases impliedly accepted "the conditions accompanying ownership of property" in Seaview. "The resulting implied-in-fact contract includes the obligation to pay a proportionate share of the full cost of maintaining [plaintiff's] facilities and services, not merely the reasonable value of those actually used by any particular resident."

Martin v. Campanaro
156 F.2d 127 (2d Cir.1946)

"The claimants are entitled to recover on a quantum meruit basis. But 'quantum meruit' is ambiguous; it may mean (1) that there is a contract 'implied in fact' to pay the reasonable value of the services, or (2) that, to prevent unjust enrichment, the claimant can recover on a quasi-contract (an 'as if' contract) for that reasonable value. . . . The confusion involved in the use of the old phrase 'implied contracts' to label both those 'implied in fact' and 'implied in law' (now called 'quasi-contracts') has not been entirely obliterated. Nor is it easy to eradicate. Thus it is said that a quasi-contract is 'imposed by law . . . irrespective of, and sometimes in violation of, . . . intention' and therefore not a 'true' contract, while a 'true' contract, (including a contract 'implied in fact') arises from 'intent.' Williston, sec. 3; Woodward, The Law of Quasi Contracts (1913), sec. 4."

[As noted (the Comment on the Common Counts, p. 111), the phrase "quantum meruit" can be (and is) used to describe liabilities resting in either contract or quasi-contract. Some courts have attempted to limit it to contract implied-in-fact, in order to distinguish the action for "unjust enrichment" applicable when contract principles are unavailable. E.g., Paffhausen v. Balano, 708 A.2d 269 (Me.1998). Nevertheless, the phrase probably is used most often to mean quasi-contract, something different from a contract implied in fact, which depends on the parties' intentions. One court's statement is fairly representative of this usage: "The whole point of quantum meruit recovery is to compensate plaintiffs who have provided a benefit to defendants but who do *not* have a contract—express or implied—with those defendants." In re De Laurentiis Entertainment Group Inc., 963 F.2d 1269 (9th Cir.1992).]

QUESTIONS

(1) What do you suppose would have happened in Collins v. Lewis if the defendant had not sold the cows and kept the money proceeds, but had refused altogether to have anything more to do with the cows?

(2) Suppose the defendant in Collins v. Lewis, when told by plaintiff's attorney that he would be held for the expenses of keeping the cows, had replied that he would pay plaintiff nothing. Suppose also that 38 days later defendant

recovered the cows through judicial proceedings (e.g., a replevin action) and sold them to a third party. Is defendant liable for plaintiff's expenses?

(3) Both Martin v. Little, Brown & Co. and Collins v. Lewis limit any recovery to the reasonable value of services rendered. If the plaintiff establishes a restitution claim in such cases, why shouldn't the measure of recovery be the defendant's net gain?

———

Morone v. Morone

Court of Appeals of New York, 1980.
50 N.Y.2d 481, 429 N.Y.S.2d 592, 413 N.E.2d 1154.

MEYER, J. Presented [here] are the questions whether a contract as to earnings and assets may be implied in fact from the relationship of an unmarried couple living together and whether an express contract of such a couple on those subjects is enforceable. Finding an implied contract such as was recognized in Marvin v. Marvin, 18 Cal.3d 660, 134 Cal.Rptr. 815, 557 P.2d 106, to be conceptually so amorphous as practically to defy equitable enforcement, and inconsistent with the legislative policy enunciated in 1933 when common-law marriages were abolished in New York, we decline to follow the *Marvin* lead. Consistent [with] Matter of Gorden, 8 N.Y.2d 71, 202 N.Y.S.2d 1, 168 N.E.2d 239, however, we conclude that the express contract of such a couple is enforceable. Accordingly, the order of the Appellate Division dismissing the complaint should be modified to dismiss only the first (implied contract) cause of action and as so modified should be affirmed. . . .

On a motion to dismiss a complaint we accept the facts alleged as true [and determine] simply whether the facts alleged fit within any cognizable legal theory. . . .

Plaintiff alleges that she and defendant have lived together and held themselves out to the community as husband and wife since 1952 and that defendant acknowledges that the two children born of the relationship are his. Her first cause of action alleges the existence of this long-continued relationship and that since its inception she has performed domestic duties and business services at the request of defendant with the expectation that she would receive full compensation for them, and that defendant has always accepted her services knowing that she expected compensation for them. Plaintiff suggests that defendant has recognized that their economic fortunes are united, for she alleges that they have filed joint tax returns "over the past several years." She seeks judgment [of] $250,000.

The second cause of action begins with the reallegation of all of the allegations of the first cause of action. Plaintiff then alleges that in 1952 she and the defendant entered into a partnership agreement by which they orally agreed that she would furnish domestic services[1] and defendant was to have full charge of business transactions, that defendant "would support, maintain and provide for plaintiff in accordance with his earning capacity and that defendant further agreed [to] take care of the plaintiff and do right by her," and that the net profits from the partnership were to be used

---

[1] Paragraph 9, one of the realleged allegations, avers that "plaintiff performed work, labor and services for the defendant in the nature of domestic duties *and business services* at the request of the defendant" (emphasis supplied).

for and applied to the equal benefit of plaintiff and defendant. Plaintiff avers that defendant commanded that she not obtain employment or he would leave her, and that since 1952 the defendant has collected large sums of money "from various companies and business dealings." Finally, plaintiff states that since December 1975 defendant has dishonored the agreement, has failed to provide support or maintenance, and has refused her demands for an accounting. She asks that defendant be directed to account for moneys received by him during the partnership.

Special Term dismissed the complaint, concluding that no matter how liberally it was construed it sought recovery for "housewifely" duties within a marital-type arrangement for which no recovery could be had. The Appellate Division affirmed because the first cause of action did not assert an express agreement and the second cause of action, though asserting an express partnership agreement, was based upon the same arrangement which was alleged in the first and was therefore "contextually inadequate." . . .

Development of legal rules governing unmarried couples has quickened in recent years with the relaxation of social customs. . . . It has not, however, been a development free of difficult problems: Is the length of time the relationship has continued a factor? Do the principles apply only to accumulated personal property or do they encompass earnings as well? If earnings are to be included how are the services of the homemaker to be valued? Should services which are generally regarded as amenities of cohabitation be included? Is there unfairness in compensating an unmarried renderer of domestic services but failing to accord the same rights to the legally married homemaker? Are the varying types of remedies allowed mutually exclusive or cumulative? . . .

New York courts have long accepted the concept that an express agreement between unmarried persons living together[2] is as enforceable as though they were not living together (Rhodes v. Stone, 63 Hun. 624, 17 N.Y.S. 561; Vincent v. Moriarty, 31 App.Div. 484, 52 N.Y.S. 519), provided only that illicit sexual relations were not "part of the consideration of the contract" (Rhodes v. Stone, at 17 N.Y.S., p. 562, quoted in Matter of Gorden, 8 N.Y.2d 71, 75). The theory of these cases is that while cohabitation without marriage does not give rise to the property and financial rights which normally attend the marital relation, neither does cohabitation disable the parties from making an agreement within the normal rules of contract law. . . .

Even an express contract presents problems of proof, however, as Matter of Gorden illustrates. . . . We reversed [in that case], because the evidence was not of the clear and convincing character required to establish a claim against a decedent's estate, but expressly adopted the rationale of Rhodes v. Stone that the unmarried state of the couple did not bar an express contract between them. Ironically, part of the basis for holding the evidence less than clear and convincing was that "If she had been working as an employee instead of a *de facto* wife, she would not have labored from 8 o'clock in the morning until after midnight without demanding pay or without being paid" [8 N.Y.2d at p. 75].

---

[2] Much of the case law speaks of such a relationship as "meretricious." Defined as "[o]f or pertaining to a prostitute; having a harlot's traits" (Webster's Third New International Dictionary Unabridged, p. 1413), that word's pejorative sense makes it no longer, if it ever was, descriptive of the relationship under consideration. . . .

While accepting *Gorden's* concept that an unmarried couple living together are free to contract with each other in relation to personal services, including domestic or "housewifely" services, we reject the suggestion, implicit in the sentence quoted above, that there is any presumption that services of any type are more likely the result of a personal, rather than a contractual, bond, or that it is reasonable to infer simply because the compensation contracted for may not be payable in periodic installments that there was no such contract.

Changing social custom has increased greatly the number of persons living together without solemnized ceremony and consequently without benefit of the rules of law that govern property and financial matters between married couples. The difficulties attendant upon establishing property and financial rights between unmarried couples under available theories of law other than contract . . . warrant application of *Gorden's* recognition of express contract even though the services rendered be limited to those generally characterized as "housewifely." . . . There is, moreover, no statutory requirement that such a contract as plaintiff here alleges be in writing (cf. General Obligations Law, § 5–701, subd. a, pars. 1, 3). The second cause of action is, therefore, sustained.[3]

The first cause of action was, however, properly dismissed. Historically, we have required the explicit and structured understanding of an express contract and have declined to recognize a contract which is implied from the rendition and acceptance of services [Rhodes v. Stone, supra]. The major difficulty with implying a contract from the rendition of services for one another by persons living together is that it is not reasonable to infer an agreement to pay for the services rendered when the relationship of the parties makes it natural that the services were rendered gratuitously. . . . As a matter of human experience personal services will frequently be rendered by two people living together because they value each other's company or because they find it a convenient or rewarding thing to do [see Marvin v. Marvin, 18 Cal.3d 660, 675–676, n. 11, supra]. For courts to attempt through hindsight to sort out the intentions of the parties and affix jural significance to conduct carried out within an essentially private and generally noncontractual relationship runs too great a risk of error. Absent an express agreement, there is no frame of reference against which to compare the testimony presented and the character of the evidence that can be presented becomes more evanescent. There is, therefore, substantially greater risk of emotion-laden afterthought, not to mention fraud, in attempting to ascertain by implication what services, if any, were rendered gratuitously and what compensation, if any, the parties intended to be paid.

Similar considerations were involved in the Legislature's abolition [Laws of 1933, ch. 606] of common-law marriages in our State. . . . [It] was the unanimous opinion of the members of the Commission to Investigate Defects in the Law of Estates that the concept of common-law marriage

---

[3] We have not overlooked the holding of Dombrowski v. Somers, 41 N.Y.2d 858, 859, 393 N.Y.S.2d 706, 362 N.E.2d 257, that the words "take care of" are too vague to spell out a meaningful promise. In the instant complaint we regard those words as surplusage in light of the further allegation that the profits of the partnership were to be used and applied for the equal benefit of both plaintiff and defendant. Nor can we accept the . . . concept that there need necessarily be "profits" from the domestic services. Plaintiff alleges an express agreement of partnership under which she was to contribute services in return for which she was to share in the profits from the business conducted by defendant; more is not required to make defendant accountable for profits of the partnership.

should be abolished because attempts to collect funds from decedents' estates were a fruitful source of litigation. . . . [The legislature's] purpose was to prevent fraudulent claims against estates. . . . The consensus was that while the doctrine of common-law marriage could work substantial justice in certain cases, there was no built-in method for distinguishing between valid and specious claims and, thus, that the doctrine served the State poorly.

The notion of an implied contract between an unmarried couple living together is, thus, contrary to both New York decisional law and the implication arising from our Legislature's abolition of common-law marriage. The same conclusion has been reached by a significant number of States other than our own which have refused to allow recovery in implied contract (see Ann., 94 A.L.R.3d 552, 559). Until the Legislature determines otherwise, therefore, we decline to recognize an action based upon an implied contract for personal services between unmarried persons living together. . . .

NOTE

What if plaintiff had added a third cause of action that realleged the allegations of the first cause of action but was labeled "quantum meruit"? Even if the restitution remedy is available as concerns arrangements between unmarried cohabitants, claimants in such cases have often been unsuccessful in court. Why might that be so? Consider the story told in Shold v. Goro, 449 N.W.2d 372 (Iowa 1989), where plaintiff was awarded judgment for monies she had advanced defendant as "loans." Because the sums in question had "retained their character as loans," and the benefit received "was not based on the parties' relationship" and did not represent "accumulated property of cohabitat[ion]," the court concluded that "it does not violate public policy to grant relief against a [cohabiting] party unjustly enriched." On further appeal, the Iowa court clarified its ruling, distinguishing "loans" from "gifts or other advances which merely reflected [plaintiff's] contribution to shared expenses," and holding that plaintiff could recover all amounts advanced with an understanding—express or implied—that she would be reimbursed (i.e., "loans"). The court underscored the importance of the burden of proof of "expected repayment," concluding that in "these special circumstances" the plaintiff "made out a prima facie case" upon showing an advance of money, at which point "the burden of going forward then shifts to [defendant] to show no repayment of the advance was contemplated." Shold v. Goro, 480 N.W.2d 892 (Iowa 1992).

――――――

Sharon v. City of Newton
437 Mass. 99, 769 N.E.2d 738 (2002)

In November 1995, Merav Sharon, then 16, was injured during cheerleading practice at school. Three months prior to the injury, Merav and her father had signed a document entitled "Parental Consent, Release from Liability and Indemnity Agreement," in which both father and daughter released defendant from "any and all claims" for personal injuries resulting from Merav's participating in cheerleading. In November 1998, Merav, now 19 and no longer under the age of majority, sued the city of Newton for damages, alleging negligence. The city, raising the signed release in defense, was awarded summary judgment. Merav, appealing, contended summary judgment was inappropriate because of factual issues respecting the validity of the release—specifically, that neither she nor her father realized they were waiving future claims against the school, and their understanding of what they signed was a factual issue for a jury. *Held*, summary judgment was proper as a matter of law. Merav and her father both signed the front of the release, indicating it was for "cheerleading." They also filled out the back of the document calling for Merav's medical history and providing for the purchase of optional student-accident insurance through the school (an option they explicitly declined on the form). And her father signed the back of the release giving parental consent to a physical exam of Merav. "In these respects, the circumstances differ substantially from the so-called 'baggage check' or 'ticket' cases[,] [where] the 'type of document the patron receives and the circumstances under which he receives it are not such that a person of ordinary intelligence would assume that the ticket limits the proprietor's liability unless the patron becomes aware of that limitation.' [So] in those cases actual notice of the limitation of liability may be a question of fact properly [given] the jury." But this is not such a case. A person of ordinary intelligence, reviewing a "clearly labeled" document known to be for the purpose of ensuring a child's participation in a school's extracurricular activity, is not likely to be misled "as to whether a limitation of liability might be included in the type of document being executed." Nor is there any dispute about the signers' opportunity to review and understand the release. As for the argument that a jury should consider whether the release was signed "under duress" (Merav's refusal to sign would have barred her participation in cheerleading), the failure to urge the point before the trial judge means it is waived. But there is Massachusetts case law enforcing a "take it or leave it" release required as a condition of voluntary participation in an offered activity.

Section 4. Mistake, Misrepresentation, Warranty, and Nondisclosure

Introductory Note

The story that is told here (indeed, in the balance of this chapter) involves more than "defective" bargains. A dispute may arise because of something that was said, or something not mentioned at all, in an agreement reduced to writing. Or, since commercial dealings require communication between bargainers, a party's affirmative statements made in getting to an agreement, or its silence on a particular matter, may be offered as the basis for a legal claim, perhaps a demand to be let out of the contract. We know at this stage that filling "gaps" in contracts—i.e., allocating risks the parties have not themselves assigned—is standard judicial work. A point to look for now is how legal categories seem to overlap, how, for example, a single fact or event (say, a simple, declarative sentence) can be recast as either a tort or some form of contract, perhaps both.

We begin with two cases, at both ends of the spectrum, that set the background for what follows. In the first case, two parties dealing at arm's length enter a bargain when one possesses information the other does not. The Supreme Court found no duty to disclose on the part of the party possessed with superior knowledge. In the second case, a duty to disclose is found when the two parties are not strangers, but rather brother and sister. The challenge the law faces is one of sensibly resolving disputes that fall between sophisticated merchants in the marketplace and close relatives.

————

Laidlaw v. Organ
Supreme Court of the United States, 1817.
15 U.S. 178.

[Plaintiff Organ] filed his petition . . . in the court below, stating, that on the 18th day of February, 1815, he purchased of [defendant Laidlaw] 111 hogsheads of tobacco, as appeared by the copy of a bill of parcels annexed, and that the same were delivered to him by the said Laidlaw & Co., and that he was in the lawful and quiet possession of the said tobacco, when, on the 20th day of the said month, the said Laidlaw & Co., by force, and of their own wrong, took possession of the same, and unlawfully withheld the same from the petitioner, notwithstanding he was at all times, and still was, ready to do and perform all things on his part stipulated to be done and performed in relation to said purchase, and had actually tendered to the said Laidlaw & Co. bills of exchange for the amount of the purchase money, agreeably to the said contract. . . . Wherefore the petition prayed that the said Laidlaw & Co. might be cited to appear and answer to his plaint, and that judgment might be rendered against them for his damages, & c. . . .

[T]he cause was tried by a jury, who returned the following verdict, to wit: "The jury find for [the buyer Organ], for the tobacco named in the petition, without damages, payable as per contract." Whereupon the court rendered judgment "that [Organ] recover of [Laidlaw] the said 111 hogsheads of tobacco . . . and ordered, that the marshal deliver the said tobacco to [Organ], and that he have execution for his costs aforesaid, upon [Organ's] depositing in this court his bills of exchange for the amount of the purchase money. . . ."

[Laidlaw] filed the following bill of exceptions, to wit: . . . [O]n the night of the 18th of February, 1815, Messrs. Livingston, White, and Shepherd brought from the British fleet the news that a treaty of peace had been signed at Ghent by the American and British commissioners, contained in a letter from Lord Bathurst to the Lord Mayor of London, published in the British newspapers, and that Mr. White caused the same to be made public in a handbill on Sunday morning, 8 o'clock, the 19th of February, 1815, and that the brother of Mr. Shepherd, one of these gentlemen, and who was interested in one-third of the profits of the purchase set forth in [Organ's] petition, had, on Sunday morning, the 19th of February, 1815, communicated said news to [Organ]; that [Organ], on receiving said news, called on Francis Girault, (with whom he had been bargaining for the tobacco mentioned in the petition, the evening previous,) said Francis Girault being one of the said house of trade of Peter Laidlaw & Co., soon after sunrise on the morning of Sunday, the 19th of February, 1815, before he had heard said news. Said Girault asked if there was any news which was calculated to enhance the price or value of the article about to be purchased; and that the said purchase was then and there made, and the bill of parcels annexed to the plaintiff's petition delivered to [Organ] between 8 and 9 o'clock in the morning of that day; and that in consequence of said news the value of said article had risen from 30 to 50 per cent. There being no evidence that the [Organ] had asserted or suggested any thing to the said Girault, calculated to impose upon him with respect to said news, and to induce him to think or believe that it did not exist; and it appearing that the said Girault, when applied to, on the next day, Monday, the 20th of February, 1815, on behalf of [Organ], for an invoice of said tobacco, did not then object to the said sale, but promised to deliver the invoice to [Organ] in the course of the forenoon of that day; the court charged the jury to find for [Organ]. . . .

MARSHALL, C.J. The question in this case is, whether the intelligence of extrinsic circumstances, which might influence the price of the commodity, and which was exclusively within the knowledge of the vendee, ought to have been communicated by him to the vendor? The court is of opinion that he was not bound to communicate it. It would be difficult to circumscribe the contrary doctrine within proper limits, where the means of intelligence are equally accessible to both parties. But at the same time, each party must take care not to say or do any thing tending to impose upon the other. The court thinks that the absolute instruction of the judge was erroneous, and that the question, whether any imposition was practised by the vendee upon the vendor ought to have been submitted to the jury. For these reasons the judgment must be reversed. . . .

————

NOTE: NONDISCLOSURE AND CONCEALMENT

When Chief Justice Marshall says that those in Organ's position must take care not "to impose upon the other," he is using the word "impose" as it was used in the eighteenth century (by Thomas Paine and others) to mean "to cheat or deceive by false representations." He means that, even though there is no affirmative duty to disclose, there needs to be a jury trial to determine whether Organ's conduct was deceptive. The jury needs to decide whether Organ's reaction when asked whether he had news that would affect the price was, in the words of Laidlaw's lawyer, "equivalent to a false answer, and as much calculated to deceive as the communication of the most fabulous intelligence."

Even after we settle upon how much needs to be disclosed in any context, we still need a way to understand what counts as a misrepresentation. Misrepresentations include not only outright lying, but also behavior and actions that are misleading. In some environments, an answer that is technically speaking completely accurate may nevertheless constitute a misrepresentation. Consider the apocryphal advertising slogan promoting tuna in the face of strong demand for salmon, "Guaranteed not to turn pink in the can." This is a misrepresentation to the extent it would lead a reasonable person to believe that salmon turns pink only after it is canned.

The most common misrepresentation case arises when someone says something that, while true on its own terms, is misleading in light of what has come before. In the words of *Restatement of Torts*, one is required to disclose "matters known to him that he knows to be necessary to prevent his partial or ambiguous statement of the facts from being misleading." Restatement (Second) of Torts § 551. One is also required to disclose "subsequently acquired information that he knows will make untrue or misleading a previous representation that when made was true or believed to be so."

Some jurisdictions in recent years have also required disclosure when one party to the transaction knows that disclosure "would correct a mistake of the other party as to a basic assumption on which that party is making the contract and if nondisclosure of the fact amounts to a failure to act in good faith and in accordance with reasonable standards of fair dealing." See Restatement (Second) of Contracts § 161(b). The owner of a building brings in a second contractor to repair the mistakes of a previous one and fails to disclose a number of defects that are not readily observable that will make the job much more costly than first appears. Los Angeles Unified School Dist. v. Great American Ins. Co., 234 P.3d 490 (Cal. 2010). I have a storeroom by the ocean that I have converted to an amusement center containing a number of different concessions with pinball machines and other devices that might or might not be legal. I sell my amusement center to you knowing that the police plan to raid the establishment and close down many parts of it. Dyke v. Zaiser, 182 P.2d 344 (Cal. App. 1947). I own a rubbish collection business and sell it to you knowing that there is a strong possibility that the city will let a contract for the rubbish collection and render the business superfluous. Jappe v. Mandt, 278 P.2d 940 (Cal. App. 1955). Courts have not decided these cases uniformly, but the difficulties they raise in identifying what counts as a misrepresentation complicate the blackletter doctrine of *Laidlaw* considerably. See Kim Lane Scheppelle, Legal Secrets: Equality and Efficiency in the Common Law 269–98 (1988).

A most illuminating effort to sort out the pieces of the problem is made in Wonnell, The Structure of a General Theory of Nondisclosure, 41 Case W. Res.L.Rev. 329 (1991). Consider the guidance provided by the passages taken from the following opinions:

(a) Matthews v. Kincaid, 746 P.2d 470 (Alaska 1987): The Restatement (Second) Torts [§ 551(2)] suggests that a duty to disclose [arises in situations involving] facts that are concealed or unlikely to be discovered because of the special relationship between the parties, the course of their dealings, or the nature of the fact itself. A duty to disclose is rarely imposed where the parties deal at arm's length and where the information is the type which the buyer would be expected to discover by ordinary inspection and inquiry.... [Here,] the lack of off-street parking [for the four-plex] is an obvious fact which the ordinary purchaser [of the apartment building] would be expected to discover, before she bought the property.

(b) Federal Dep. Ins. Corp. v. W.R. Grace & Co., 877 F.2d 614 (7th Cir.1989): An omission can of course be actionable as a fraud.... But not every failure by a seller (or borrower, or employee, etc.) to disclose information to the buyer (or lender, or employer, etc.) that would cause the latter to reassess the deal is actionable. A general duty of disclosure would turn every bargaining relationship into a fiduciary one.... [But the seller] must disclose that the house he is trying to sell is infested with termites.... [The distinction] is illustrated [by a case] where the failure to disclose an assessor's valuation was held not to be actionable, since the valuation was a matter of public record and therefore ascertainable by the buyer at reasonable cost.... [But if] you go to a bank for a loan on your house, and the bank tentatively agrees to make it, and on the day before the loan papers are to be signed the house is destroyed by a flood and you don't disclose the fact at the signing, then we suppose ...

that you are guilty of fraud even if you made no representation that the house was still in existence.

(c) Hill v. Jones, 151 Ariz. 81, 725 P.2d 1115 (Ct.App.1986): Suffice it to say that [caveat emptor's] vitality has waned during the latter half of the twentieth century.... The modern view is that a vendor has an affirmative duty to disclose material facts where: 1. Disclosure is necessary to prevent a previous assertion from being a misrepresentation or from being fraudulent or material; 2. Disclosure would correct a mistake of the other party as to a basic assumption on which that party is making the contract and if nondisclosure amounts to a failure to act in good faith and in accordance with reasonable standards of fair dealing; 3. Disclosure would correct a mistake of the other party as to the contents or effect of a writing . . .; 4. The other person is entitled to know the fact because of a relationship of trust and confidence between them. [Rest.2d Contracts § 161; see Rest.2d Torts § 551.] . . . The doctrine imposing a duty to disclose is akin to [rules] pertaining to relief [for] mistake. Although the law of contracts supports the finality of transactions, over the years courts have recognized that under [certain] circumstances it is unjust to strictly enforce the policy favoring finality. Thus, e.g., even a unilateral mistake . . . may justify rescission. There is also a judicial policy promoting honesty and fair dealing in business relationships. This policy is expressed in the law of fraudulent and negligent misrepresentations. Where a misrepresentation is fraudulent or where a negligent misrepresentation is one of material fact, the policy of finality rightly gives way to the policy of promoting honest dealings.... Thus, nondisclosure may be equated with . . . fraud and misrepresentation.... [This is especially so where] nondisclosure of material facts affect[s] the value of property, [and the facts] are not reasonably capable of being known to the buyer.

Again, various statutes dealing with "deceptive" and "unfair" trade practices—many limited to specified consumer transactions, some applying to commercial parties as well—may encompass the full range of the misrepresentation cases, including nondisclosure. A useful discussion of the statutory approach can be found in Shell, Substituting Ethical Standards for Common Law Rules in Commercial Cases: An Emerging Statutory Trend, 82 Nw.L.Rev. 1198 (1988). As concerns residential real estate, a number of states have enacted statutes governing disclosures in the transfer of such property. See, e.g., Amyot v. Luchini, 932 P.2d 244 (Alaska 1997) (statute requiring "good faith" disclosure of house's defects bars purchaser's theory of innocent misrepresentation respecting matters covered in mandatory disclosure form).

Chief Justice Marshall asserts that Laidlaw took advantage of information "equally accessible" to both parties. This turns out not to be true. This aspect of the case is set out in Joshua Kaye, Disclosure, Information, The Law of Contracts, and the Mistaken Use of Laidlaw v. Organ, 79 Mississippi L.J. 577 (2010). Organ learned that the war was over before anyone else, not because of special diligence on his part, but through the brother of his business partner who was the aide-de-camp to the commander of naval defenses in New Orleans. The brother had been among those whom Andrew Jackson sent to negotiate the exchange of prisoners and the return of escaped slaves. There he learned the treaty had been signed and that the war was over from the British, and he sought to profit from it on his return. This information was conveyed to Organ, who then tried to make money for them both. Far from acquiring "equally accessible" information through careful diligence, Organ acquired knowledge of the war's end through his private contacts with government officials. Should trading on such knowledge be prohibited?

As you read the next case, consider the extent to which disclosure obligations must take into account not merely what is spoken, but also the relationship between the contracting parties.

————

Jackson v. Seymour

Supreme Court of Appeals of Virginia, 1952.
193 Va. 735, 71 S.E.2d 181.

EGGLESTON, J. In May, 1950, Lucy S. Jackson filed her bill of complaint [seeking] rescission of a deed dated February 18, 1947, and recorded the next day, whereby she had conveyed to her brother, Benjamin J. Seymour, a tract of thirty-one acres of land. . . . [S]he alleged that she had been induced by her brother to convey the land to him for the sum of $275, through his representations to her that it was "of no value except for a pasture" and that [$275] was "a good price therefor;" that relying upon the representations of her brother, in whom she reposed complete confidence with respect to his management of her property and business affairs, and being unfamiliar with the land and unaware that there was merchantable timber growing thereon she had conveyed it to him at that price; that about two and one-half years later she discovered for the first time that . . . there was on the land considerable merchantable timber, of the stumpage value of from $3,200 to $5,000, and that subsequent to his acquisition of the land her brother had cut and sold the timber at a price unknown to her, but with considerable profit to himself.

She further alleged that the statements and representations made to her by her brother, through which she had been induced to sell him the land, were "false and were fraudulently made;" that she had offered to restore to him the [$275] he had paid for the property, with interest, upon the condition that he would rescind the transaction, and that he had rejected this offer. The prayer of the bill was that the deed be canceled and that the defendant be required to account to her for all moneys which he may have realized from the sale of the timber taken from the land. . . .

In his answer the defendant . . . denied that he had made any representations to her that [$275] was the fair value of the land or that it "had no value except for a pasture." He alleged that he had purchased the property from her at her urgent request and for her accommodation, and that, at the time he had no knowledge "of the existence of merchantable timber upon said land." [He] further denied all charges of fraud or misrepresentations[,] [but] admitted that since he had acquired the property he had cut and marketed from this and an adjoining tract of land 148,055 feet of timber, from which he had realized the sum of $2,353.42. He denied the plaintiff's right to have the deed rescinded or to have an accounting by him. . . . Inasmuch as the trial court's findings of fact are binding on us the evidence will be summarized from the viewpoint most favorable to the defendant.

Since 1931 Mrs. Jackson had been the owner of a farm of 166 acres in Brunswick county which adjoined lands owned by her brother. . . . After the death of her husband (the date of which is not shown) Mrs. Jackson sought and obtained the assistance of her brother, who is a successful farmer and business man, in renting the farm for her. He rented the tillable portions of the farm, collected the rents, and made settlements with her which she never questioned. . . . [T]hey were devoted to each other and she had, as she says, "the utmost confidence in him."

In 1946 Tazewell Wilkins approached Seymour about the purchase of a tract of Seymour's land containing 30.46 acres for a pasture. He also wanted to buy the adjoining tract of 31 acres, which was a part of the land owned by Mrs. Jackson. Seymour told Wilkins that while he was willing to take $275 for his (Seymour's) land, he did not own the 31–acre tract and suggested that Wilkins see Mrs. Jackson about buying it. While Seymour also conveyed this information to Mrs. Jackson the record discloses no negotiations between Wilkins and Mrs. Jackson for the purchase of her land.

In February, 1947, Mrs. Jackson approached her brother, saying that she was in need of funds and was anxious to sell the 31–acre tract in which Wilkins had shown interest. Seymour did not want to buy the property, but because of his sister's need for money he agreed to purchase it at $275, which was the price which had been mentioned in his negotiations with Wilkins. The brother was then unaware that there was valuable timber on the land and contemplated using it for a pasture. Seymour gave his sister a check for $275 and she signed a receipt therefor. On the next day Mrs. Jackson executed and delivered a deed conveying the property to her brother. The deed was prepared by a local attorney at Seymour's request and expense.

A short while after Seymour had acquired the property it came to his attention that some trees had been cut from the tract. Upon investigation he discovered for the first time that there was valuable timber on the land. The evidence does not disclose the exact quantity and value of this timber. It shows that in 1948 Seymour cut from the land which he had purchased from his sister and from adjoining lands owned by him, 148,055 feet of lumber and that the greater portion of this came from the Jackson tract. This timber had a stumpage value of approximately $20 per 1,000 feet.

The land in controversy is located in an isolated section and it is undisputed that Mrs. Jackson had never been on it and knew nothing of its character. While Seymour had hunted in the vicinity and been within sight of the property he had never actually been on the land. To use his own words, "I was positive that it was just naked land" and worth $8 or $9 an acre. Thus, neither vendor nor vendee knew that there was valuable timber growing on the land. On cross-examination Seymour admitted that the presence of timber on the land "was not within the contemplation" of him and his sister at the time the sale was consummated. He testified that if he had known of this timber he would not have bought the property from her for $275. . . .

Upon the conclusion of the evidence the lower court dictated from the bench an opinion holding that the plaintiff's allegations of *actual* fraud had not been sustained by the evidence. . . It took under advisement whether under the allegations of the bill the plaintiff was entitled to relief on the ground of *constructive* fraud because of the "confidential relationship" of the parties and the "gross inadequacy in price."

While the court had the matter under consideration the plaintiff tendered an amendment to her bill which in substance charged that she was unfamiliar with the character of the land, was unaware that there was any merchantable timber on it, that she had sold it "under an honest and material mistake of fact with reference to the subject matter of the contract," and that to permit the deed to stand "would operate as a fraud" upon her rights. There was no allegation that the vendee . . . was likewise mistaken as to the existence of timber on the land at the time the sale was consummated. Thus the amendment fell short of alleging a mutual mistake. . . .

About sixty days after the amendment had been tendered the lower court rejected it on the ground that it had been "tendered too late. . . ." It further held that since the plaintiff had grounded her case on actual fraud, and since [she] had failed to sustain that charge or make out a case within the scope of the bill, she was not entitled to the relief prayed for. . . . [T]he plaintiff has appealed.

Under our view of the case it is unnecessary that we deal with the [rejection of] the amendment to the bill. We are of opinion that . . . the plaintiff is entitled to equitable relief on the ground of constructive fraud, and that such relief is within the scope of the allegations of the original bill of complaint.

. . . [S]hortly after the defendant had acquired this tract of land[,] he cut and marketed therefrom timber valued at approximately ten times what he had paid for the property. A mere statement of the matter shows the gross and shocking inadequacy of the price paid.

This is not the ordinary case in which the parties dealt at arm's length and the shrewd trader was entitled to the fruits of his bargain. The parties were brother and sister. He was a successful business man and she a widow in need of money and forced by circumstances . . . to sell a part of the lands which she had inherited. Because of their friendly and intimate relations she entrusted to him and he assumed the management and renting of a portion of this very land. . . . [Moreover,] neither of the parties knew of the timber on the land and we have from the defendant's own lips the admission that as it turned out "afterwards" he had paid a grossly inadequate price for the property and that he would not have bought it from her for the small amount paid if he had then known of the true situation. . . .

The controlling principles were thus stated in Planters Nat. Bank v. Heflin Co., 166 Va. 166, 184 S.E. 216: "Mere failure of consideration or want of consideration will not ordinarily invalidate an executed contract. The owner of the historic estate of 'Blackacre' can give it away, and he can sell it for a peppercorn. Courts, though they have long arms, cannot relieve one of the consequences of a contract merely because it was unwise. . . . [B]ut where inadequacy of price is such as to shock their conscience equity is alert to seize upon the slightest circumstance indicative of fraud, either actual or constructive." . . .

Clearly, the inadequacy of consideration here meets that definition. In addition to the gross inadequacy of consideration we have the confidential relation of the parties, the pecuniary distress of the vendor, and the mutual mistake of the parties as to the subject matter of the contract. . . . [T]o permit the transaction to stand would result in constructive fraud upon the rights of the plaintiff. Hence, she is entitled to relief in equity. . . . While the bill alleges actual fraud, it also contains allegations of these constituent elements of constructive fraud: The confidential relation of the parties; the reliance by the plaintiff upon the advice and judgment of the defendant in her business affairs; the gross inadequacy of the price paid; her offer to restore the purchase price and rescind the transaction, and his rejection of the offer.

In Moore v. Gregory, 146 Va. 504, 131 S.E. 692, we [said]: "'Constructive fraud is a breach of legal or equitable duty which, irrespective of the moral guilt of the fraud feasor, the law declares fraudulent because of its tendency to deceive others, to violate public or private confidence, or to injure public interests. Neither actual dishonesty of purpose nor intent to deceive is an essential element of constructive fraud. . . .' Constructive fraud may be inferred from the intrinsic nature and subject of the bargain itself." 146 Va., at 523, 527,131 S.E., at 697–698.

. . . [T]he lower court should have entered a decree granting the plaintiff's prayer for a rescission of the conveyance and restoring the parties to the *status quo* in so far as practicable. By way of incidental relief the plaintiff is entitled to recover of the defendant the fair stumpage value of the timber removed by the latter from the land, with interest from the date of such removal, and the fair rental value of the property during the time the defendant was in possession. The defendant is entitled to a return of the purchase price paid by him, with interest from the date that the plaintiff offered to rescind the transaction, and taxes paid by him on the land since the date of the conveyance, with interest.

The decree appealed from is reversed and the cause remanded for further proceedings in conformity with the views here expressed.

————

COMMENT: *FIDUCIARY DUTIES*

The doctrines expressed in Jackson v. Seymour owe much of their currency in this country to Justice Story, who, in 1842, wrote (1 Equity Jurisprudence 256–258 (3d ed.)):

> Mere inadequacy of price, or any other inequality in the bargain, is not, however, to be understood as constituting, per se, a ground to avoid a bargain in Equity. For Courts of Equity, as well as Courts of Law, act upon the ground, that every person who is not, from his peculiar condition or circumstances, under disability, is entitled to dispose of his property in such manner . . . as he chooses; and whether his bargains are wise and discreet, or profitable or unprofitable, or otherwise, are considerations, not for Courts of Justice, but for the party himself to deliberate upon. . . .
>
> Still, however, there may be such an unconscionableness or inadequacy in a bargain, as to demonstrate some gross imposition or undue influence; and in such cases Courts of Equity ought to interfere upon the satisfactory ground of fraud. But then such unconscionableness or such inadequacy should be made out, as would (to use an expressive phrase) shock the conscience and amount in itself to conclusive and decisive evidence of fraud. And where there are other ingredients in the case of a suspicious nature, or peculiar relations between the parties, gross inadequacy of price must necessarily furnish the most vehement presumption of fraud.

One large and important area for the application of these ideas, in particular constructive fraud ("constructive" because based on the inadequacy of the consideration), is the group of relationships usually described as "confidential" and "fiduciary." Both are terms of broad reach, and their outer limits are ill-defined. A "fiduciary" relationship is one whose successful functioning requires a high degree of candor and reliability between the participants. As one court has said, "[a] fiduciary, unlike an ordinary contract promisor, undertakes to treat the affairs of the promisee as if they were the promisor's own affairs." Olympia Hotels Corp. v. Johnson Wax Dev. Corp., 908 F.2d 1363 (7th Cir.1990). Illustrations are the relations of trustee and beneficiary of an express trust, principal and agent, attorney and client, business partners, guardian and minor ward, even directors of a corporation and its stockholders. In addition to categories of relations, fiduciary duties are sometimes imposed on an ad hoc basis. The key is again one person's ascendancy over another, achieved through the placing of trust and confidence on one side and the assumption of a position of influence on the other. The standards of disclosure and disinterestedness are not the same in all fiduciary relationships, and often the requirements are one-sided in the sense that higher standards are imposed on one participant than on the other.

A "confidential" relationship, on the other hand, is not so much the product of a legal status as it is the result of unusual trust or confidence reposed in fact (e.g., Von Hake v. Thomas, infra p. 604, which speaks of one party exercising "extraordinary influence over the other"). Blood relationship or marriage will be the most common examples, though the list of "confidential relations" extends far beyond those sources. Intimate personal friendship between such persons as physician and patient, minister and parishioner, or next-door neighbors is commonly enough. All that is required is proof that in fact the parties did not deal on equal terms, that there was a high degree of confidence reposed in the honesty and good faith of the other party. Then, too, the categories of "confidential" and "fiduciary" relationship are not mutually exclusive; both presumably exist, for example, when an attorney undertakes representation of a client. The mere willingness to enter into a "fiduciary" relationship often will be a mark of confidence reposed, sufficient for the relationship to be "confidential" as well.

In neither type of relationship is bargaining between the participants wholly excluded. The principal requirement is one of full disclosure of all of the elements that have a bearing on the transaction or the terms of the bargain made. This means, however, that any transfer or exchange between the parties, either by way of gift or bargain, will be examined closely to be sure that there was full disclosure and no unfair advantage taken. The technique chiefly used is framed as a procedural handicap: the party in whom trust or confidence is reposed, and who seems to have profited, is forced to assume the burden of showing that the transaction was in every way fair and beyond suspicion. This burden is often difficult to carry; for many courts, the starting premise will be that the transaction is "prima facie voidable." If the burden is not sustained, the transaction will be set aside or its enforcement denied. Though these high standards originated primarily in equity, there is no reason today why they would not be applied at law where a legal remedy is appropriate, by way of either defense or affirmative action aiming at rescission.

Did a lack of full disclosure by Seymour explain the discrepancy in values in Jackson v. Seymour?

————

Sherwood v. Walker

Supreme Court of Michigan, 1887.
66 Mich. 568, 33 N.W. 919.

MORSE, J. Replevin for a cow. Suit commenced in justice's court. Judgment for plaintiff. Appealed to circuit court of Wayne county, and verdict and judgment for plaintiff. . . . The defendants bring error. . . .

The main controversy depends upon the construction of a contract for the sale of the cow. The plaintiff claims that the title passed, and bases his action upon such claim. The defendants contend that the contract was executory, and by its terms no title to the animal was acquired by plaintiff.

The defendants reside at Detroit, but are in business at Walkerville, Ontario, and have a farm at Greenfield, in Wayne County, upon which were some blooded cattle supposed to be barren as breeders. The Walkers are importers and breeders of polled Angus cattle.

The plaintiff is a banker living at Plymouth, in Wayne County. He called upon the defendants at Walkerville for the purchase of some of their stock, but found none there that suited him. Meeting one of the defendants afterwards, he was informed that they had a few head upon their Greenfield farm. He was asked to go out and look at them, with the statement at the time that they were probably barren, and would not breed. May 5, 1886, plaintiff went out to Greenfield and saw the cattle. A few days thereafter, he called upon one of the defendants with the view of purchasing a cow, known as "Rose 2d of Aberlone." After considerable talk, it was agreed that defendants would telephone Sherwood at his home in Plymouth in reference to the price. The second morning after this talk he was called up by telephone, and the terms of the sale were finally agreed upon. He was to pay five and one-half cents per pound, live weight, fifty pounds shrinkage. He was asked how he intended to take the cow home, and replied that he might ship her from King's cattle-yard. He requested defendants to confirm the sale in writing, which they did by sending him the following letter [dated May 15, 1886]: "T.C. SHERWOOD, *Dear Sir*: We confirm sale to you of the cow Rose 2d of Aberlone, lot 56 of our catalogue, at five and a half cents per pound, less fifty pounds shrink. We inclose herewith order on Mr. Graham for the cow. You might leave check with him, or mail to us here, as you prefer. Yours truly, HIRAM WALKER & SONS."

The order upon Graham inclosed in the letter read as follows: "May 15, 1886. *George Graham*: You will please deliver at King's cattle-yard to Mr. T.C. Sherwood, Plymouth, the cow Rose 2d of Aberlone, lot 56 of our catalogue. Send halter with cow, and have her weighed. Yours truly, HIRAM WALKER & SONS."

On [May 21] the plaintiff went to defendants' farm at Greenfield, and presented the order and letter to Graham, who informed him that the defendants had instructed him not to deliver the cow. Soon after, the plaintiff tendered [$80] to Hiram Walker[,] demand[ing] the cow. Walker refused to take the money or deliver the cow. The plaintiff then instituted this suit.

After he had secured possession of the cow under the writ of replevin, the plaintiff caused her to be weighed by the constable who served the writ. . . . She weighed 1,420 pounds. . . .

HIRAM WALKER
1816-1898

The defendants [at trial] introduced evidence tending to show that at the time of the alleged sale it was believed by both the plaintiff and themselves that the cow was barren and would not breed; that she cost $850, and if not barren would be worth from $750 to $1,000; that after the date of the letter, and the order to Graham, the defendants were informed by said Graham that in his judgment the cow was with calf, and therefore they instructed him not to deliver her to plaintiff, and on the twentieth of May, 1886, telegraphed to the plaintiff what Graham thought about the cow being with calf, and that consequently they could not sell her. The cow had a calf in the month of October following. . . .

It appears from the record that both parties supposed this cow was barren and would not breed, and she was sold by the pound for an insignificant sum as compared with her real value if a breeder. She was evidently sold and purchased on the relation of her value for beef, unless the plaintiff had learned of her true condition, and concealed such knowledge from the defendants. . . . The circuit judge ruled that [the sale could not be avoided], and it made no difference whether she was barren or not. I am of the opinion that the court erred in this. . . . [I]t must be considered as well settled that a party who has given an apparent consent to a contract of sale may refuse to execute it, or he may avoid it after it has been completed, if the assent was founded, or the contract made, upon the mistake of a material fact,—such as the subject-matter of the sale, the price, or some collateral fact materially inducing the agreement; and this can be done when the mistake is mutual. . . .

If there is a difference or misapprehension as to the substance of the thing bargained for, if the thing actually delivered or received is different in substance from the thing bargained for and intended to be sold, then there is no contract; but if it be only a difference in some quality or accident, even though the mistake may have been the actuating motive to the purchaser or seller, or both of them, yet the contract remains binding. . . .

It seems to me, however, that [here] the mistake or misapprehension of the parties went to the whole substance of the agreement ["the root of the matter"]. If the cow was a breeder, she was worth at least $750; if barren, she was worth not over $80. The parties would not have made the contract of sale except upon the understanding and belief that she was incapable of breeding, and of no use as a cow. It is true she is now the identical animal that they thought her to be when the contract was made; there is no mistake as to the identity of the creature. Yet the mistake was not of the mere quality of the animal, but went to the very nature of the thing. A barren cow is substantially a different creature than a breeding one. There is as much difference between them for all purposes of use as there is between an ox and a cow that is capable of breeding and giving milk. If the mutual mistake had simply related to the fact whether she was with calf or not for one season, then it might have been a good sale; but the mistake affected the character of the animal for all time, and for her present and ultimate use. She was not in fact the animal, or the kind of animal, the defendants intended to sell or the plaintiff to buy. She was not a barren cow, and, if this fact had been known, there would have been no contract. The mistake affected the substance of the whole consideration, and it must be considered that there was no contract to sell or sale of the cow as she actually was. . . .

The court should have instructed the jury that if they found that the cow was sold, or contracted to be sold, upon the understanding of both parties that she was barren, and useless for the purpose of breeding, and that in fact she was not barren, but capable of breeding, then the defendants had a right to rescind . . . and the verdict should be in their favor.

The judgment of the court below must be reversed, and a new trial granted. . . .

BLACK ANGUS IN PENSIVE MOOD

SHERWOOD, J. (dissenting). . . . [T]he record shows that the plaintiff is
a banker and farmer as well, carrying on a farm, and raising the best
breeds of stock, and lived in Plymouth, in the county of Wayne, 23 miles
from Detroit; that the defendants lived in Detroit, and were also dealers in
stock of the higher grades; that they had a farm at Walkerville, in Canada,
and also one in Greenfield in said county of Wayne, and upon these farms
the defendants kept their stock. The Greenfield farm was about 15 miles
from the plaintiff's. In the spring of 1886 the plaintiff, learning that the
defendants had some "polled Angus cattle" for sale, was desirous of purchasing some of that breed, and meeting the defendants, or some of them,
at Walkerville, inquired about them, and was informed that they had none
at Walkerville, "but had a few head left on their farm in Greenfield, and

asked the plaintiff to go and see them, stating that in all probability they were sterile and would not breed." In accordance with said request, the plaintiff, on the fifth day of May, went out and looked at the defendants' cattle at Greenfield, and found one called "Rose, Second," which he wished to purchase, and the terms were finally agreed upon at five and a half cents per pound. . . . The sale was in writing, and the defendants gave an order to the plaintiff directing the man in charge of the Greenfield farm to deliver the cow to plaintiff. This was done on the fifteenth of May. On the twenty-first of May plaintiff went to get his cow, and the defendants refused to let him have her; claiming at the time that the man in charge at the farm thought the cow was with calf, and, if such was the case, they would not sell her for the price agreed upon. The record further shows that the defendants, when they sold the cow, believed the cow was not with calf, and barren; that from what the plaintiff had been told by defendants (for it does not appear he had any other knowledge or facts from which he could form an opinion) he believed the cow was farrow, but still thought she could be made to breed. The foregoing shows the entire interview and treaty between the parties as to the sterility and qualities of the cow sold to the plaintiff. The cow had a calf in the month of October. There is no question but that the defendants sold the cow representing her of the breed and quality they believed the cow to be, and that the purchaser so understood it. And the buyer purchased her believing her to be of the breed represented by the sellers, and possessing all the qualities stated, and even more. He believed she would breed. There is no pretense that the plaintiff bought the cow for beef, and there is nothing in the record indicating that he would have bought her at all only that he thought she might be made to breed. Under the foregoing facts,—and these are all that are contained in the record material to the contract,—it is held that because it turned out that the plaintiff was more correct in his judgment as to one quality of the cow than the defendants, and a quality, too, which could not by any possibility be positively known at the time by either party to exist, the contract may be annulled by the defendants at their pleasure. I know of no law, and have not been referred to any, which will justify any such holding. . . .

In this case neither party knew the actual quality and condition of this cow at the time of the sale. The defendants say, or rather said to the plaintiff, "they had a few head left on their farm in Greenfield, and asked plaintiff to go and see them, stating to plaintiff that in all probability they were sterile and would not breed." Plaintiff did go as requested, and found there three cows, including the one purchased, with a bull. The cow had been exposed, but neither knew she was with calf or whether she would breed. The defendants thought she would not, but the plaintiff says that he thought she could be made to breed, but believed she was not with calf. The defendants sold the cow for what they believed her to be, and the plaintiff bought her as he believed she was. . . . I know of no authority by which this Court can alter the contract thus made by these parties in writing. . . .

. . . There was no mistake of any such material fact by either of the parties. . . . There was no difference between the parties, nor misapprehension, as to the substance of the thing bargained for, which was a cow supposed to be barren by one party, and believed not to be by the other. As to the quality of the animal, subsequently developed, both parties were equally ignorant, and as to this each party took his chances. If this were not the law, there would be no safety in purchasing this kind of stock. . . . [I]f either party had superior knowledge as to the qualities of this animal to the other, certainly the defendants had such advantage.

I understand the law to be well settled that "there is no breach of any implied confidence that one party will not profit by his superior knowledge as to facts and circumstances" equally within the knowledge of both, because neither party reposes in any such confidence unless it be specially tendered or required, and that a general sale does not imply warranty of any quality, or the absence of any; and if the seller represents to the purchaser what he himself believes as to the qualities of an animal, and the purchaser buys relying upon his own judgment as to such qualities, there is no warranty in the case, and neither has a cause of action against the other if he finds himself to have been mistaken in judgment. . . . The judgment should be affirmed.

————

Aluminum Co. of America v. Essex Group

499 F.Supp. 53 (W.D.P.A.1980)

"Is it enough that one party is indifferent to avoid a mutual mistake? The court thinks not. . . . [In Sherwood v. Walker], as here, the buyer was indifferent to the unknown fact; he would have been pleased to keep the unexpected profit. But he understood the bargain rested on a presumed state of facts. The court let the seller avoid the contract because of mutual mistake."

————

Beachcomber Coins, Inc. v. Boskett

166 N.J.Super. 442, 400 A.2d 78 (1979)

Plaintiff, a retail dealer in coins, purchased from defendant, a part-time coin dealer, a dime purportedly minted in 1916 in Denver, for a price of $500. Defendant had paid $450 for the coin, which was understood to be a rarity because Denver-minted. At the time of plaintiff's purchase, defendant stated that he would not sell for less than $500; plaintiff closely examined the coin for 15 to 45 minutes. Soon after the purchase, plaintiff received an offer of $700 for the coin, subject to a certification of genuineness by the American Numismatic Society. That organization declared the coin a counterfeit. Plaintiff thereupon sued his seller for rescission on the ground of mutual mistake. The trial court held for defendant, ruling that "customary coin-dealing procedures" require a dealer purchasing a coin to make his own investigation of genuineness and to "assume the risk" if that investigation is faulty. *Held*, reversed; this is "a classic case of rescission for mutual mistake." Both believed the coin was Denver-minted and genuine; the price asked and paid was based on that "essential fact." Defendant's contention that plaintiff assumed the risk of the coin's value is wrong on these facts. The governing rule is stated in Restatement § 502: " 'Where the parties know that there is doubt in regard to a certain matter and contract on that assumption, the contract is not rendered voidable because one is disappointed in the hope that the facts accord with his wishes. The risk of the existence of the doubtful fact is then assumed as one of the elements of the bargain.' " But the parties must be conscious of the uncertainty of the "pertinent fact" for this rule to apply. Here, both were certain the coin was genuine; they so testified. It would be a different case "if the seller were uncertain either of the genuineness of the coin or its value if genuine, and had accepted the expert buyer's judgment on these matters." Nor is rescission barred because, as the trial court implied, plaintiff may have been negligent in inspecting the coin. Where, as here, the parties can be restored to the status quo, a negligent failure to discover a mistake such as this does not preclude rescission.

_____

QUESTIONS

The American Law Institute, through various Restatements, has offered the following illustrations (among others) of the rules and principles applicable to mistake:

(1) A contracts to sell and B to buy a tract of land, the value of which has depended mainly on the timber on it. Both A and B believe that the timber is still there, but in fact it has been destroyed by fire. The contract is voidable by B. [Restatement (Second) of Contracts § 152 comment b, illustration 1 (1981).]

(2) A contracts to sell and B to buy a tract of land. A and B both believe that A has good title, but neither has made a title search. The contract provides that A will convey only such title as he has, and A makes no representation with respect to title. In fact, A's title is defective. The contract is not voidable by B. . . . [(Second) of Contracts § 154 comment b, illustration 1 (1981).]

(3) Twelve-year-old Collector examines a baseball card offered for sale by Dealer. A price label on the item reads "1200." Collector asks the sales clerk to confirm the price of the card; the clerk, a temporary employee alone in the shop, surmises that it must be $12.00. Collector pays $12.00 and takes the card. Collector is aware that the market price of this card is approximately $1200 and that Dealer is presumably offering it for sale at this price. The transaction between the parties did not result in a valid sale. Dealer is entitled to recover the card on tender of $12.00. [Restatement (Third) of Restitution Tentative Draft No. 3 § 34 comment e, illustration 23 (2004).]

(4) A enters a second-hand bookstore where, among books offered for sale at one dollar each, he discovers a rare book having, as A knows, a market value of not less than $50. He hands this [book] to the proprietor with one dollar. The proprietor, reading the name of the book and the price tag, keeps the dollar and hands the book to A. The book dealer is not entitled to restitution. . . . [Restatement of Restitution § 12 comment c, illustration 9 (1937).]

Which of these illustrations is most nearly like Sherwood v. Walker as seen by the majority? As seen by the dissenter?

_____

NOTE: STILL MORE ON SHERWOOD V. WALKER

1. The Replevin Remedy

Had there been no issue of mistake in the cow case, would Sherwood have been granted the remedy he sought—replevin? Apparently so, as there was evidence to sustain a finding by the jury that the parties had intended "title" to Rose to pass to Sherwood before delivery was to occur. Today, the buyer's remedy of replevin no longer depends upon this common-law idea of passage of "title" or "property." Section 2–716(3) of the UCC provides in part: "The buyer has a right of replevin for goods identified to the contract if after reasonable effort he is unable to effect cover for such goods or the circumstances reasonably indicate that such effort will be unavailing[.]" With mutual mistake removed from the case, how would Sherwood have fared under this statute?

2. Reformulating *Sherwood*

In Lenawee County Bd. of Health v. Messerly, 417 Mich. 17, 331 N.W.2d 203 (1982), decided nearly a full century after Sherwood v. Walker, the Supreme Court of Michigan condemned the distinction between mistakes "running to value" and those "touching the substance of the consideration," declaring that the distinction was "inexact and confusing" and served "only as an impediment to a clear and helpful analysis" of the mistake cases. The case involved a seller and a purchaser who had believed that the small, three-unit apartment building that was the subject of the sale could be used to generate rental income. Problems with the building's septic system were discovered a week after the transaction was closed. These sewage problems led local health authorities to condemn the property and enjoin habitation of the premises. The ensuing litigation established that the septic system could not be remedied within the confines of the 600–square–foot parcel. Nor was it feasible to pump and haul the sewage. The property, for which the purchaser had paid $25,500, was therefore valueless (worse yet, it had a negative value).

Was this a mistake merely as to quality or value, and thus not "material" but only "collateral" to the agreement? The court, indicating that *Sherwood* should be "limited to [its] facts," stated its new approach this way:

> [W]e think the better-reasoned approach is a case-by-case analysis whereby rescission is indicated when the mistaken belief relates to a basic assumption of the parties upon which the contract is made, and which materially affects the agreed performance of the parties. . . . Restatement, Contracts, 2d § 152. Rescission is not available, however, to relieve a party who has assumed the risk of loss in connection with the mistake.

Is this test much different from the analysis employed in Sherwood v. Walker? The *Lenawee County* court apparently thought it was announcing a different test, for it indicated that the result in *Sherwood* "might have been different" had the court engaged in the sort of risk-of-loss analysis that the Michigan court was now embracing. Look again at the opinions in Sherwood v. Walker. Was there no inquiry into which of the parties should assume the risk of loss? How does one answer the question of "essences" or "roots" without making some judgment about the customary allocation of risks between sellers and buyers? Again, a court must "gap-fill" by drawing an inference as to risk allocation. That ordinarily is done by asking what the parties were contemplating (in one court's words, whether "the post-contract discovery comes out of left field") and whether one was more at fault than the other.

It is necessary to add that the ultimate result in *Lenawee County* was placed on a ground not available in *Sherwood*. Despite the court's conclusions that the parties' beliefs as to the suitability of the premises constituted a "[mutual] mistake as to a basic assumption," and that the agreed exchange had been "materially affect[ed]," rescission was nevertheless denied because the contract itself allocated to the purchaser the risk of habitability, in the form of a clause which read:

> Purchaser has examined this property and agrees to accept same in its present condition. There are no other or additional written or oral understandings.

This clause, the court said, is a "persuasive indication" that the parties wished to assign to the purchaser all risks as to the condition of the property. Unless the "as is" clause applied to unknown defects, it would have no meaning. But such a clause would not preclude a purchaser from alleging fraud or misrepresentation as a basis for rescission.

––––––––

Kull, Mistake, Frustration, and the Windfall Principle of Contract Remedies
43 Hastings L.J. 1, 2, 5–6 (1991)

"A substantial body of case law supports an important but unacknowledged rule of contract doctrine: that the proper legal response to certain problems resulting from contracts that are 'incomplete' or 'not fully specified' is to leave the parties alone. Such a rule stands in sharp contrast to the usual prescription of modern commentary, which recommends that 'gaps' in contracts be 'filled' by judicial intervention to serve a variety of social ends. . . . [T]he characteristic and traditional response of our legal system to cases of mistaken and frustrated contracts is neither to relieve the disadvantaged party nor to assign the loss to the superior risk bearer, but to leave things alone. The party who has balked at performing will not be forced to proceed, but the completed exchange will not be recalled. Walker will not be forced to deliver to Sherwood a breeding cow sold for the price of beef; but neither will [the seller] be allowed to recover the yellow diamond, already delivered, unwittingly sold to the buyer for the price of a topaz. . . .

"The principle of inertia that frequently seems to guide the remedies for mistake and frustration . . . is neither arbitrary nor illogical. Disparities between anticipation and realization in contractual exchange, the risk of which has not been allocated by the parties, are in the nature of 'windfalls' (including those, carrying adverse consequences, that might more properly be described as 'casualties'). The law will not act to enforce such windfalls—to compel an exchange on terms that were not bargained for—because its objective is limited to giving effect to the parties' agreement. But if the parties have not allocated the risk of a particular windfall or casualty to one of them, neither have they allocated it to the other. There is thus no basis in their bargain on which to justify a court's intervention to shift windfall benefits and burdens in either direction. . . . [E]xcluding for the moment considerations of fairness, it will ordinarily be a matter of indifference [to society] whether the windfall cost or benefit,

once realized, falls to A or B. Reallocation after the event thus invokes significant administrative costs while achieving no social advantage. The judicial disposition to let windfalls lie—to answer the claim of mistake or frustration by
confirming the status-quo—[therefore raises the question] whether the traditional rule [the 'windfall principle'] may not serve ['gap-filling'] ends with equal
or greater efficiency."

———————

Tracy v. Morell

Court of Appeals of Indiana, 2011.
948 N.E.2d 855.

NAJAM, JUDGE. . . . In 2002, Morell sold Tracy a used Ford New Holland tractor for $12,500. Tracy signed a promissory note in which he agreed
to pay Morell $500 down and $500 per month with no interest until the
note was paid in full. Tracy initially made monthly payments totaling
$8,500, but stopped making payments in June 2003.

In September 2003, the State charged Morell with four counts of receiving stolen property, namely, tractors and other farm equipment. After
Tracy heard about the charges, he contacted the Orange County Sheriff's
Department and asked that the Department investigate whether the tractor he had purchased from Morell was stolen property. Accordingly, Detective Lieutenant Michael Dixon, with the assistance of the Indiana State
Police, inspected Tracy's tractor and found that its identification number
had been altered. Detective Dixon impounded Tracy's tractor pending further investigation. . . .

Morell ultimately pleaded guilty to four counts of receiving stolen
property, as Class D felonies. At least one of the items that Morell admitted
to having stolen had a missing identification number, and another of the
stolen items displayed an identification number that belonged to another
machine. Detective Dixon suspected that the tractor Morell had sold to
Tracy was also stolen because of the altered identification number. But Detective Dixon's efforts to confirm that suspicion were inconclusive. A man
whose Ford New Holland tractor had been stolen came to look at Tracy's
tractor to see if he could identify it, but he was unable to determine whether it was his because of a lack of identifying marks. And, after Detective
Dixon learned that the cost would be prohibitive to dismantle the tractor to
find the valid identification number located inside the engine, he and the
prosecuting attorney abandoned the investigation.

On December 11, 2003, Tracy filed a complaint against Morell alleging
fraud. In particular, Tracy asserted that Morell knowingly misrepresented
that he owned the tractor when he sold it to Tracy and that the tractor had
been seized by law enforcement officials as stolen property. Tracy sought
treble damages and attorney's fees under the Crime Victim's Relief Act.
Morell filed a counterclaim alleging that Tracy had defaulted on the promissory note and seeking the unpaid balance of $4000, attorney's fees, and
court costs.

The trial court held a bench trial on June 21, 2010. Kelly Minton, Orange County Prosecuting Attorney, testified regarding Morell's convictions.
And Minton testified that he and Detective Dixon "obviously" suspected
that Morell had stolen the tractor he sold to Tracy, but that Minton decided

not to expend the resources necessary to prove theft. Detective Dixon also testified that he strongly suspected that Morell had stolen the tractor. And he testified that a technician from the Indiana State Police Auto Theft Squad had discovered that the identification number on Tracy's tractor had been "ground out and filled in with putty" and painted over. The technician "tried to [use] acid to bring the numbers back, but it was ground too deep and they couldn't be recovered." Detective Dixon then testified regarding how difficult it would have been to ascertain the tractor's identification number. . . .

To prove fraud, Tracy was required to show that Morell made a material misrepresentation of past or existing facts made with knowledge or reckless ignorance of its falsity, and the misrepresentation caused reliance to the detriment of Tracy. The evidence presented at trial shows that both the Orange County Prosecuting Attorney and Detective Dixon suspected that Morell had stolen the tractor he sold to Tracy or that Morell knew that the tractor was stolen when he sold it to him. Detective Dixon took steps to prove that suspicion, but he and the prosecuting attorney agreed that it would be too expensive to pursue the evidence needed to support a criminal charge against Morell. Further, Morell testified that he had pleaded guilty to receiving stolen property with respect to two other tractors and other farm equipment, some of which had altered or destroyed identification numbers, and that that conduct occurred at around the same time that Morell had sold the tractor to Tracy. . . .

At trial, Morell testified that he did not know that the identification number had been ground out, filled in with putty, and painted over. Thus, crediting his testimony as we must on appeal, the trial court did not err when it found, in effect, that Morell lacked the necessary culpability, that is, that he either "recklessly, knowingly, or intentionally" dealt in altered property, in violation of Indiana Code Section 35–43–4–2.3, and Morell also avoided a civil judgment for violation of Indiana's Crime Victim's Relief Act, Indiana Code Section 34–24–3–1. . . . Our consideration of Morell's counterclaim presents a much different question. In his counterclaim, Morell asked the trial court to enforce the promissory note and order Tracy to pay the $4000 unpaid balance. The trial court found that Tracy was the equitable owner of the tractor and that Tracy owed Morell $4000. We cannot agree.

The trial court concluded that Morell had "an enforceable promissory note signed by Mr. Tracy." However, mutual assent is a prerequisite to the creation of a contract. Where both parties share a common assumption about a vital fact upon which they based their bargain, and that assumption is false, the transaction may be avoided if because of the mistake a quite different exchange of values occurs from the exchange of values contemplated by the parties. There is no contract, because the minds of the parties have in fact never met.

In the landmark case of Sherwood v. Walker, 66 Mich. 568, 33 N.W. 919 (1887), at the time of sale both the seller and purchaser of a cow believed that the cow was barren and would not breed. Accordingly, the parties agreed on a purchase price of approximately $80. However, immediately prior to delivery, the seller discovered that the cow was bearing a calf, which increased its value to approximately $750 to $1000. On appeal, the court held that the transaction was voidable because the mistake of the parties "was not of the mere quality of the animal, but went to the very nature of the thing. A barren cow is substantially a different creature than a breeding one. . . . She was not a barren cow, and, if this fact had been known, there would have been no contract." Id. at 923.

Here, as in *Sherwood*, the undisputed evidence shows that the sale was based upon a common, mistaken assumption about a vital fact regarding "the very nature of the thing." Both Tracy and Morell testified that they did not know that the tractor's identification number had been altered. If Morell was ignorant that the tractor's identification number had been altered, then he, like Tracy, was also mistaken about the tractor's value. When the deal was struck, Morell agreed to sell and Tracy agreed to buy the tractor, free and clear of liens and encumbrances, for the sum of $12,500. Instead, both as a matter of fact and a matter of law, the tractor was altered property and was not marketable in any legitimate farm equipment market. The essential terms, including both the sale and the sale price, were based on a mutual mistake about a vital fact that Morell had good title and lawful authority to sell the tractor to Tracy free and clear. But a tractor with an altered identification number has no bona fide fair market value because it cannot be knowingly or intentionally sold without committing a crime. For that reason, Tracy has recourse against Morell without regard to fraud. There was a mutual mistake of fact between them that went to the heart of the bargain, to the substance of the whole contract, and, as such, there was no contract, as a matter of law. . . .

A rescission requires that we adjust the equities and return the parties to the status quo ante. See Smith v. Brown, 778 N.E.2d 490, 497 (Ind. Ct. App. 2002). As Judge Posner recently observed in an Indiana case before the Seventh Circuit, when a rescission occurs, the parties are put back, so far as possible, in the positions they would have occupied had the contract never been made in the first place. Scheiber v. Dolby Laboratories, Inc., 293 F.3d 1014, 1022 (7th Cir. 2002). Here, in order to implement a rescission, we hold that Morell is the owner and is entitled to possession of the tractor, subject to any impoundment and storage charges, that the promissory note is null and void, and that Tracy is entitled to recover the amount he has paid on the promissory note. . . .

———

Gartner v. Eikill

319 N.W.2d 397 (Minn.1982)

"[A]ll parties assumed the property conveyed to be property that could be developed. The mistake, as in *Sherwood*, was not of *monetary* value of the land, but 'went to the very nature' of the property. In *Sherwood*, neither party had any way of discovering whether the cow was in fact barren. [These sellers] argue that [the purchaser] could have gone to City Hall and inquired about the zoning and that because he did not do so, he is not entitled to rescind the transaction. The failure of a party to investigate, however, will not always preclude rescission. . . . Here, [the purchaser] does not appear to have been negligent at all. He inquired [of sellers' realtor] regarding the zoning of the property and was assured that it was zoned M–1 and was suitable for commercial use. . . . [A]lthough he had purchased real estate on several previous occasions, he had never before found it necessary to go to City Hall to determine whether additional zoning restrictions existed. He had no reason to suspect that any such restriction prohibited the development of [this] property. His reliance on [sellers'] agent's statements was reasonable; we do not believe that he had any duty to inquire further. . . . [The sellers] thought that they were selling property suitable for commercial use; [the purchaser] thought he was buying property suitable for commercial use. . . . [A] mutual mistake of fact occurred that entitled [the purchaser] to a rescission of the conveyance."

———————

Elsinore Union Elementary School Dist. v. Kastorff

Supreme Court of California, 1960.
54 Cal.2d 380, 6 Cal.Rptr. 1, 353 P.2d 713.

SCHAUER, J. Defendants, a building contractor and his surety, appeal from an adverse judgment in this action by plaintiff school district to recover damages allegedly resulting when defendant Kastorff, the contractor, refused to execute a building contract pursuant to his previously submitted bid to make certain additions to plaintiff's school buildings. . . . [B]ecause of an honest clerical error in the bid and defendant's subsequent prompt rescission he was not obliged to execute the contract[;] the judgment should therefore be reversed.

Pursuant to plaintiff's call for bids, defendant Kastorff secured a copy of the [construction] plans and specifications and proceeded to prepare a bid to be submitted by the deadline of 8 p.m., August 12, 1952, at Elsinore, California. Kastorff testified that in preparing his bid he employed worksheets upon which he entered bids of various subcontractors for such portions of the work as they were to do, and that to reach the final total of his own bid for the work he carried into the right-hand column of the worksheets the amounts of the respective sub bids which he intended to accept and then added those amounts to the cost of the work which he would do himself[;] that there is "a custom among subs [to] delay giving . . . their bids until the very last moment"; that the first sub bid for plumbing was in the amount of $9,285 and he had received it "the afternoon of the bid-opening," but later that afternoon when "the time was drawing close for me to get my bids together and get over to Elsinore" (from his home in San Juan Capistrano) he received a $6,500 bid for the plumbing. Erroneously thinking he had entered the $9,285 plumbing bid in his total column and had included that sum in his total bid and realizing that the second plumbing bid was nearly $3,000 less than the first, Kastorff then deducted $3,000 from the total amount of his bid and entered the resulting total of $89,994 on the bid form as his bid for the school construction. Thus the total included no allowance whatsoever for the plumbing work.

Kastorff then proceeded to Elsinore and deposited his bid with plaintiff. When the bids were opened shortly after 8 p.m. that evening, it was discovered that of the five bids submitted that of Kastorff was some $11,306 less than the next lowest bid. The school superintendent and board members present thereupon asked Kastorff whether he was sure his figures were correct, Kastorff stepped out into the hall to check with the person who had assisted in doing the clerical work on the bid, and a few minutes later returned and stated that the figures were correct. He testified that he did not have his worksheets or other papers with him to check against at the time. The board thereupon, on August 12, voted to award Kastorff the contract. . . .

[The next morning, August 13, Kastorff checked his worksheets with the School District's architect, who supported Kastorff's claim that he had failed to carry over the plumbing figure of $9,285 so that it was not included in the "total" column in arriving at the bid of $89,994. On August 13, the architect informed the school superintendent of the mistake by telephone; on August 14, Kastorff wrote the school board to describe his error, asking in both instances to be released from his bid. On August 15, the board voted at a special meeting not to release him; on August 28, it notified him in writing that he had been awarded the contract. When a written contract was sent to Kastorff, he returned it and again asked to be released. Plaintiff then let the contract to the next lowest bidder, in the amount of $102,900. Plaintiff sued to recover from Kastorff the $12,906 difference between this figure and Kastorff's $89,994 bid, and to recover $4,999.60 from the surety on the bond posted by Kastorff.

The trial court found that Kastorff's worksheet showed he had not carried over from the left-hand column the figure for the plumbing subcontractor's bid, but found no evidence that the right-hand column had been used in calculating the total bid. The trial court also found that the School District did not know of Kastorff's withdrawal of his bid when it requested him to sign the contract; hence, the court concluded that it would not be inequitable or unjust to require Kastorff to perform at a price of $89,994, since this was the price that he intended to bid. The trial court gave judgment for plaintiff in the amounts sued for.]

In reliance upon M.F. Kemper Constr. Co. v. City of Los Angeles (1951), 37 Cal.2d 696, 235 P.2d 7, and Lemoge Elec. v. County of San Mateo (1956), 46 Cal.2d 659, 297 P.2d 638, defendants urged that where, as [here], a contractor makes a clerical error in computing a bid on a public work he is entitled to rescind.

In the *Kemper* case one item on a worksheet in the amount of $301,769 was inadvertently omitted by the contractor from the final tabulation sheet and was overlooked in computing the total amount of a bid. . . . The error was caused by the fact that the men preparing the bid were exhausted after working long hours under pressure. When the bids were opened it was found that plaintiff's bid was $780,305, and the next lowest bid was $1,049,592. Plaintiff discovered its error several hours later and immediately notified defendant's board of public works of its mistake in omitting one item [from] its bid. Two days later it explained its mistake to the board and withdrew its bid. A few days later it submitted to the board evidence which showed the unintentional omission of the $301,769 item. The board nevertheless passed a resolution accepting plaintiff's erroneous bid of $780,305, and plaintiff refused to enter into a written contract at that figure. The board then awarded the contract to the next lowest bidder, the city demanded forfeiture of plaintiff's bid bond, and plaintiff [sued] to cancel its bid and obtain discharge of the bond. The trial court found that the bid had been submitted as the result of an excusable and honest mistake of a material and fundamental character, that plaintiff company had not been negligent in preparing the proposal, that it had acted promptly to notify the board of the mistake and to rescind the bid, and that the board had accepted the bid with knowledge of the error. The court further found and concluded that it would be unconscionable to require the company to perform for the amount of the bid, that no intervening rights had accrued, and that the city had suffered no damage or prejudice. . . . [T]his court affirmed. . . .

[The Supreme Court in *Kemper* had pointed out that, by statute, a bid filed with the governmental agency on a publicly-financed project, when opened and declared, acquired "the status of an irrevocable option, a contract right of which the city could not be deprived without its consent un-less the requirements for rescission were satisfied." Nevertheless, as the court emphasized, the city had actual notice of the error before it attempted to accept the bid. The omission of $301,769, when the next lowest bid was $1,049,592, was clearly a material mistake. Any carelessness of the bidder did not rise to the level of "neglect of legal duty," and the city would lose nothing except "the benefit of an inequitable bargain."]

In the *Lemoge* case, supra, the facts were similar to *Kemper*, except that plaintiff Lemoge did not attempt to rescind but instead, after discover-ing and informing defendant of inadvertent clerical error in the bid, entered into a formal contract with defendant on the terms specified in the errone-ous bid, performed the required work, and then sued for reformation. . . . Although this court affirmed the trial court's determination that plaintiff was not, under the circumstances, entitled to have the contract reformed, we also reaffirmed [a contractor's] right to rescind [in such situations].

[In *Lemoge*, the plaintiff had submitted a bid of $172,421; the next lowest bid was $197,500. A clerk on plaintiff's staff had listed the cost of certain materials as $104.52 when the correct figure was $10,452; with sales tax and other markups, the total bid was understated by $11,744.39. The complaint seeking reformation was dismissed on demurrer, without leave to amend, even though the complaint had alleged that defendant knew the amount of the mistake and its cause before it accepted plaintiff's bid. The court said that the defendant never agreed to pay more than $172,421, the amount of plaintiff's bid, and that the purpose of reformation is to make the writing express the agreed intent of the parties.]

The rules stated [in] *Kemper* and *Lemoge* would appear to entitle de-fendant to relief here, were it not for the findings of the trial court adverse to defendant. However, certain of such findings are clearly not supported by the evidence and others are immaterial to the point at issue. The finding that it is not true that the right-hand column of figures on the bid sheet was totaled for the purpose of arriving at the total bid, and that it cannot be ascertained from the evidence for what purpose either the bid sheets or the right-hand column total thereon were used in arriving at the total bid, is without evidentiary support in the face of the worksheets which were introduced in evidence and of the uncontradicted testimony not alone of defendant Kastorff, but also of plaintiff's own architect and witness Rendon, explaining the purpose of the worksheets and the nature of the error which had been made. [These sheets] plainly show the entry of the sums of $9,285 and of $6,500 in the left-hand columns as the two plumbing sub bids which were received by defendant, and the omission from the right-hand totals column of any sum whatever for plumbing.

The same is true of the finding that although "on or about August 15" plaintiff received Kastorff's letter of August 14 explaining the error in his bid, it was not true that plaintiff knew at any time that the bid was intend-ed to be other than as submitted. Again, it was shown by the testimony of plaintiff's architect, its school superintendent, and one of its board mem-bers, all produced as plaintiff's witnesses, that the board was informed of the error and despite such information voted at its meeting of August 15 not to grant defendant's request to withdraw his bid.

Further, we are persuaded that the trial court's view, as expressed in the finding set forth in the margin,[1] that "Kastorff had ample time and opportunity after receiving his last subcontractor's bid" to complete and check his final bid, does not convict Kastorff of that "neglect of legal duty" which would preclude his being relieved from the inadvertent clerical error of omitting from his bid the cost of the plumbing. (See Civ.Code, § 1577; *Kemper*, supra.) Neither should he be denied relief from an unfair, inequitable, and unintended bargain simply because, in response to inquiry from the board when his bid was discovered to be much the lowest submitted, he informed the board, after checking with his clerical assistant, that the bid was correct. He did not have his worksheets present to inspect at that time, he did thereafter inspect them at what would appear to have been the earliest practicable moment, and thereupon promptly notified plaintiff and rescinded his bid. [Further,] Kastorff's bid agreement, as provided by plaintiff's own bid form, was to execute a formal written contract only after receiving written notification of acceptance of his bid, and such notice was not given to him until some two weeks following his rescission.

If the situations of the parties were reversed and plaintiff and Kastorff had even executed a formal written contract (by contrast with the preliminary bid offer and acceptance) calling for a fixed sum payment to Kastorff large enough to include a reasonable charge for plumbing but inadvertently through the *district's* clerical error omitting a mutually-intended provision requiring Kastorff to furnish and install plumbing, we have no doubt but that the district would demand and expect reformation or rescission. [Here,] the district expected Kastorff to furnish and install plumbing; surely it must also have understood that he intended to, and that his bid did, include a charge for such plumbing. The omission of any such charge was as unexpected by the board as it was unintended by Kastorff. Under the circumstances the "bargain" for which the board presses (which action we, of course, assume to be impelled by advice of counsel and a strict concept of official duty) appears too sharp for law and equity to sustain.

Plaintiff suggests that in any event the amount of the plumbing bid omitted from the total was immaterial. The bid as submitted was in the sum of $89,994, and whether the sum for the omitted plumbing was $6,500 or $9,285 (the two sub bids), the omission of such a sum is plainly material to the total. In *Lemoge*, . . . the error which it was declared would have entitled plaintiff to rescind was the listing of the cost of certain materials as $104.52, rather than $10,452, in a total bid of $172,421. Thus the percentage of error here was larger than in *Lemoge*, and was plainly material.

The judgment is reversed.

----

[1] Other findings are that Kastorff "in the company of his wife and another couple left San Juan Capistrano for Elsinore . . . at 6:00 P.M. on August 12, 1952, a distance of 34 miles. . . . Kastorff had ample time and opportunity after receiving his last subcontractor's bid to extend the figures on his bid sheet from one column to the other, to check and recheck his bid sheet figures and to take his papers to Elsinore and to check them there prior to close of receipt of bids at 8:00 P.M."

S.T.S. Transport Serv., Inc. v. Volvo White Truck Corp.
766 F.2d 1089 (7th Cir.1985)

Judge Cudahy writing: "[T]he cases have also avoided contracts—though more reluctantly—where only one party is mistaken as to the facts. In the typical case of this sort, a seller or contractor will miscalculate in adding up a list of items. . . . It is true that [if] the mistake result[s] from a miscalculation as to the economic climate, to undo the contract would fly in the face of the very reason for having contracts in the first place. . . . But that problem is solved by excluding miscalculations of judgment. . . . The mistake in this case relates to the price, which must be conceded to be material. The mistake must also have occurred in spite of the exercise of reasonable care. Although reasonable care is as difficult to be precise about in this sort of case as it is elsewhere, there are some fairly clear groupings of mistake cases that can serve as guideposts. Most helpful is the knowledge that courts will generally grant relief for errors which are 'clerical or mathematical.'

"The reason for the special treatment for such errors, of course, is that they are difficult to prevent, and that no useful social purpose is served by enforcing the mistaken term. No incentives exist to make such mistakes; all the existing incentives work, in fact, in the opposite direction. There is every reason for a contractor to use ordinary care. . . . Naturally there are cases of extreme negligence to which this presumption [of rescission rather than enforcement] should not apply; and there is an exception of sorts where the contract has been relied upon[,] [for reliance, in this context,] is no different from the question whether the parties can be put into the position they were in at the time the contract was signed. . . . Although it would be wrong to suppose that 'merely' mathematical or clerical errors are easily distinguished from other errors such as those of judgment[,] the distinction is clear enough for ordinary purposes. A merely mathematical or clerical error occurs when some term is either one-tenth or ten times as large as it should be; when a term is added in the wrong column; when it is added rather than subtracted; when it is overlooked."

———

COMMENT: UNILATERAL MISTAKE

1. The Grounds for Rescission

When only one of the contracting parties was mistaken, we have a case of unilateral rather than mutual mistake. Unilateral mistake, we are told (recall Cobaugh v. Klick–Lewis, p. 326), is generally not a ground for rescinding a contract—or reforming one, says California's *Lemoge* decision. But exceptions have appeared, as *Elsinore* suggests. Not surprisingly, the "exceptional" case awarding relief usually has involved a party who knew of and, saying nothing, claimed the benefit of, another's mistake. This, of course, is but another way of recasting basic objective theory—that is to say, the recipient of an incorrectly worded or transmitted offer may not always make a contract by accepting it. For example, long ago the California court indicated that a seller's price quotation, erroneously transcribed and delivered by a telegraph company, could contractually bind the seller to the incorrect price—provided the buyer had no reason to suspect that a mistake had been made. Germain Fruit Co. v. Western Union Telegraph, 137 Cal. 598, 70 P. 658 (1902). To be sure, if a party reasonably and detrimentally relied on the mistaken expression of the party seeking rescission, cases such as Drennan v. Star Paving Co. tell why the exceptions are inapplicable.

In any event, a question raised by *Elsinore* is the content, and the scope, of the defense of unilateral mistake.

The California court returned to such matters in Donovan v. RRL Corp., 26 Cal.4th 261, 109 Cal.Rptr.2d 807, 27 P.3d 702 (2001), where, because of typographical and proofreading errors by a local newspaper, defendant auto dealer's advertisement of a 1995 Jaguar XJ6 erroneously listed the price at $25,995, not the intended $37,995. Plaintiff read the advertisement, examined and test drove the vehicle, and said to defendant's salesperson: "Okay. We will take it at your price of $25,995." When there was no reply, plaintiff produced the ad; the salesperson immediately said, "That's a mistake." Defendant's sales manager was summoned and, confirming the mistake and refusing to sell at the advertised price, the manager apologized and offered to reimburse plaintiff for his fuel, time, and effort expended in traveling to the dealership. The manager, when pressed by plaintiff for a selling price, offered to let him take it for $37,016. Plaintiff, insisting on a deal at the advertised price, then brought a lawsuit for breach of contract.

The trial court, finding that plaintiff had no reason to suspect the mistake, nevertheless entered judgment for defendant, holding that the advertisement was not a valid offer because defendant's "unilateral mistake of fact" vitiated contractual intent. An intermediate court of appeal rejected that view, finding that any defects in contract formation were cured by a California statute making it unlawful for an auto dealer to refuse to sell a motor vehicle at the advertised price (i.e., the statute "tips the scale in favor of construing" the ad as an offer that, in the circumstances, reasonably invited plaintiff's acceptance by the act of tendering the advertised price.) On further appeal, the California Supreme Court agreed that a contract was made by plaintiff's tender of the advertised price. Nonetheless, defendant had a complete defense of rescission for unilateral mistake, on this reasoning:

> The court of appeal erred in crediting plaintiff's contention that unilateral mistake affords grounds for rescission only where the other party is—or should have been—aware of the mistake. *Kemper* and *Elsinore* establish that relief for mistake is not so limited, but is authorized where "enforcement of the contract would be unconscionable." This additional ground is now recognized generally in Rest.2d Contracts, § 153, which is based in part on *Elsinore*. Here, there was a material mistake regarding a basic assumption upon which defendant contracted. Even assuming defendant's failure to review the work of the newspaper's advertising staff constituted negligence, such an omission does not amount to "neglect of a legal duty" sufficient to preclude equitable relief for mistake. Moreover, enforcing the contract with the mistaken price would give defendant $12,000 less than the intended price, an error of 32 percent. That defendant subsequently sold the car for $38,399 is proof of its actual market value. And since defendant had paid $35,000 for the vehicle and incurred additional costs in preparing it for sale, a forced sale at the advertised price would result in defendant losing more than $9,000 of its original investment. Plaintiff, in contrast, would obtain a

$12,000 "windfall," simply for coming to the dealership and stating a willingness to pay the advertised price. As in *Elsinore*, a party who is promptly informed of the other's discovery of an honest mistake that results in an "unfair, one-sided" contract should not be permitted to demand enforcement. That decision, where there was no procedural unconscionability (indeed, the mistaken contractor was afforded an opportunity to verify accuracy of price before acceptance), settles the point that "overly harsh results" are alone enough to warrant rescission for unilateral mistake.

2. Information and Mistake

Cases like *Elsinore* suggest that there are circumstances in which a mistake can be inferred from the price stated in the offer. In fact, relief is routinely given in the mistaken-bid cases if the bidder-offeror's error reasonably should have been known by the offeree before acceptance. By one count, in 109 of 187 construction-bidding cases of all types decided between 1969 and 1977, the mistaken bidder was awarded some form of relief. Jones, The Law of Mistaken Bids, 48 Cinn. L. Rev. 43 (1979).

The refusal to permit the offeree with superior information to enjoy the advantage of the mistaken bid stands in contrast to the results in the standard cases where there is an imbalance in the parties' information and the less-informed party may have been greatly disadvantaged by that imbalance. In some situations, of course, as where a fiduciary or confidential relation gives rise to a duty to disclose, the knowledgeable party is required to share information—"required" in the sense of putting at risk the right to enforce the agreement if disclosure is not made. But if the parties stand in an arm's-length relationship, courts have been reluctant to impose a duty of disclosure that would erase the knowledgeable party's advantage. Can this attitude be reconciled with the courts' routine refusal to permit an offeree to "snap up" an offer which the offeree has reason to know is based on incomplete or erroneous information?

One answer from an economic perspective has been offered by Kronman, Mistake, Disclosure, Information, and the Law of Contracts, 7 J. Legal Stud. 1 (1978). According to the author, the risk of mistake represents a cost to both society and the contracting parties, because a mistake entails a misallocation, or waste, of resources. Since information prevents mistakes, a court concerned with economic efficiency should assign the risk of mistake—where the parties themselves have not done so—to the better (lower-cost) information-gatherer, thereby promoting the discovery of information at the least cost (and reducing the transaction costs of contracting). Thus, where the mistake in a bid is known or reasonably should have been known to the offeree, the risk should be assigned to that party. At that stage, the offeree can more cheaply rectify the error. To explain the apparent conflict between the mistaken-bidder cases and the cases sanctioning nondisclosure, Kronman distinguishes "casually acquired" information from that which is "deliberately acquired." Information which has been deliberately acquired through research or by expertise necessarily involves a discovery cost to its possessor, which must be offset by some benefit if the search or development is to be worthwhile. A rule of nondisclosure therefore promotes efficiency by encouraging the deliberate search for socially-useful information. On the other hand, casually-acquired information—for example, knowledge of a mistaken bid gathered by reviewing a group of bids—is discovered by happenstance and is, therefore, cost-free. Denying its possessors the benefits of such chanced-upon information, Kronman argues, will have no effect on the amount of information generated because there are no expenses which must be compensated.

Kronman recognizes, however, that high administration costs prohibit a case-by-case scrutiny to determine whether specific information has been acquired deliberately or casually. An alternative approach, he suggests, would be for the courts to adopt blanket rules for categories of cases, with the categories determined on the basis of whether a type of information (e.g., information about defects in goods or realty offered for sale) is, in general, more likely to be generated by chance or by deliberate search. "The greater the likelihood that such information will be deliberately produced rather than casually discovered, the more plausible the assumption becomes that a blanket rule permitting nondisclosure will have benefits that outweigh its costs."

Is it clear that the mistaken-bid cases can be explained in the manner Professor Kronman suggests? If it is recognized that there are difficulties in applying the deliberate-casual distinction to offerees of construction bids, what is one to think about the soundness of the distinction in other situations?

————

THE WARRANTY ALTERNATIVE

A claim of rescission for mistake does not necessarily depend on statements passing between contracting parties (yes, what is said in the contract, or in negotiations, is relevant on whether the party seeking relief bears the risk of mistake). Nonetheless, the mistake cases, commonly arising from sales of things, most often property, also commonly involve affirmative statements by the seller of the thing. Such statements may be challenged as deliberate or careless misrepresentations amounting to fraud or some similar tort (e.g., Hargrave v. Oki Nursery, p. 406; LaFazia v. Howe, p. 413). Or a seller's representations may be interpreted as a warranty of performance. The point is that the legal landscape changes with misstatements of fact in the picture. To see how the UCC handles warranties in the sale of goods, turn again to § 2–313 on "express" warranties. Then look once more at the "implied" warranties of merchantability and fitness defined in §§ 2–314 and 2–315. Attempts to disclaim warranty liability are regulated by § 2–316, and § 2–714(2) deals with relief for breach of warranty. A much-litigated question is whether a seller's statement is interpretable as a warranty of performance (it may be puffing, mere opinion). Another is whether the law will read into a contract an off-the-rack warranty. Consider the two cases that come next.

————

Tribe v. Peterson

Supreme Court of Wyoming, 1998.
964 P.2d 1238.

TAYLOR, J. Appellant, Steve Tribe, purchased his first horse, Moccasin Badger, from appellees, [the] Petersons. Asserting that the sellers had expressly guaranteed that the horse would never buck, Tribe brought suit against the Petersons for breach of warranty when Moccasin Badger unceremoniously ejected [him] from the saddle, shattering his left wrist. After the district court denied Tribe's motion for summary judgment on the issue of express warranty, the subsequent trial resulted in the jury's rejection of [his] claims and a "no buck" verdict. [He] then moved for judgment as a matter of law, or in the alternative, a new trial. Both motions were denied. Finding that the jury acted reasonably, we affirm. . . .

The known history of Moccasin Badger (Badger) begins with his purchase in August 1994 by Larry Painter, a rancher who had bought and sold horses "[a]ll [his] life." When Painter bought and owned Badger, the horse was "plumb gentle. . . ." Mr. Painter brought Badger to his Uncle Oliver's in Rapid City, South Dakota in January 1995, describing him at that time: "Well, he was real gentle. And as far as we was concerned anybody could ride him that had any experience at all riding." Oliver Painter was not called as a witness at trial, but the parties read into the record the stipulation [that] "if he did testify, he would [say] that Moccasin Badger was calm and gentle while he was around him[,] [and he] did not have any experiences where he bucked."

In February 1995, Oliver Painter advertised the sale of Badger, and the Petersons responded. After Mrs. Peterson rode Badger and found him to be very calm and gentle, and a second visit revealed the same disposition, they purchased him for $2,200. During the first month the Petersons owned Badger, they rode him "two to three times a week." "[N]eeding a little money," the Petersons decided to sell Badger at the "Leo Perino sale," which attracts buyers from all over the world.

To ensure that Badger was sound and ready for sale, the Petersons twice brought Badger to Dr. Margie Jones, a board certified horse veterinarian from Sturgis, South Dakota, and Mr. Peterson trained Badger every day for a month prior to the sale. Dr. Jones testified that she found Badger to be "sound," and after performing an extensive physical examination and riding Badger, she concluded that Badger "was gentle and kind and he did what I asked him to."

The Leo Perino sale was held in Newcastle, Wyoming on June 3, 1995. Tribe and his wife attended the sale, accompanied by Steve Stoddard. The Tribes had moved to Wyoming in 1993 after selling Mr. Tribe's car dealership in northern California and purchasing a 12,000 acre ranch near Colony. The Tribes leased all but 400 acres to Stoddard, who they asked to assist them in recommending a place to purchase a horse which would be gentle enough for very inexperienced riders. Stoddard recommended the Leo Perino sale. . . .

Badger's description in the sale brochure represented him as a "quiet . . . and extra gentle gelding easy to catch, haul and shoe," and "overly kind which makes him a definite kids prospect. . . ." Stoddard initially noticed Badger while Mr. Peterson was roping with [the horse] in the arena. Stoddard spoke with Mr. Peterson, [who] told him that Badger "was five years old and that he was really gentle." Later, Stoddard approached the Petersons to get a better look at Badger, at which time Stoddard and Mrs. Tribe rode Badger. Stoddard found the horse to be "very gentle and very well-broke to ride." According to Stoddard, he asked Mr. Peterson if the horse "had any buck in him" to which Peterson responded, "No." Peterson told Stoddard that the horse had never bucked with him or any of its previous owners. The testimony conflicts, however, as to whether Mr. Peterson "guaranteed" the horse would never buck in the future. Stoddard stated he got a "guarantee" from both Petersons, while the Petersons denied they made such a guarantee, insisting it would be impossible to guarantee that any horse would not buck in the future.

Nonetheless, Tribe purchased Badger on his belief that he had been guaranteed that this horse would never buck. Upon returning to the ranch, Mrs. Tribe rode Badger without incident. The third time [she] rode Badger, however, she was thrown. Ten days later, after riding Badger, Mrs. Tribe asked Mr. Tribe if he wanted to ride. When he said he did, she resaddled the horse[,] Tribe got on [and] almost immediately was thrown to the ground, shattering his wrist. Some time later, Tribe contacted the Petersons to inform them of the injury, tape recording one conversation with Mr. Peterson. . . .

Tribe contends that, as a matter of law, the written description in the sale brochure and verbal representations of the Petersons created an express warranty that Badger was a calm and gentle horse which would never buck. "An express warranty is created by any affirmation of fact made by the seller to the buyer which relates to the goods and becomes a part of the basis of the bargain." Garriffa v. Taylor, 675 P.2d 1284, 1286 (Wyo.1984), see also Wyo. Stat. [UCC] § 34.1–2–313(a)(ii) (1997) ("Any description of the goods which is made part of the basis of the bargain creates an express warranty that the goods shall conform to the description [.]"). "In order for an express warranty to exist, there must be some positive and unequivocal statement concerning the thing sold which is relied on by the buyer and which is understood to be an assertion concerning the items sold and not an opinion." Garriffa, 675 P.2d at 1286. A representation which expresses the seller's opinion, belief, judgment or estimate does not constitute an express warranty. . . . [W]hether there was an affirmation of fact which amounted to an express warranty [depends on a] consideration of all the circumstances surrounding a sale and should be made by the trier of fact.

The verdict form at trial asked only: "Are defendants liable to the plaintiff for damages for breach of an express warranty?" We therefore do not know if the jury determined there was no express warranty or whether a warranty was given but not breached. Either way, the jury's conclusion could reasonably be reached on the evidence presented at trial.

We begin by examining the description of Badger in the sales brochure. Tribe insists that this description guaranteed a gentle horse, and that the fact that he and his wife were thrown establishes that Badger was not gentle or calm. The testimony of all the witnesses, however, reveals that Badger was calm and gentle with everyone but the Tribes. . . .

Moreover, Mrs. Tribe telephoned Mrs. Peterson within four or five days after the sale to say: "I want you to know I'm really getting along well with Badger. I just love him. Do you have anymore like him that we could buy?" Finally, evidence was presented which established that the disposition of a horse may be affected by the rider, the equipment, the type of feed, or a new environment. Mr. Perino affirmed that "even gentle horses" may buck. Clearly, there was evidence to support a finding that the description of Badger in the brochure was the Peterson's well-founded opinion regarding Badger's disposition. Further, even if the brochure constituted an express warranty that Badger was calm and gentle, the evidence supports the conclusion that the warranty was not breached.

We next examine Tribe's contention that he was given a guarantee that Badger would never buck. . . . It appears a "no buck" warranty is a hard sell to a Wyoming jury. Obviously, the record supports the jury's conclusion that representations regarding Badger's past behavior were true, and no express warranty was given as to Badger's future behavior.

Tribe's claim to judgment as a matter of law on the theory of negligent misrepresentation is equally without merit. There is overwhelming evidence that the information provided by the Petersons did not misrepresent Badger's disposition. . . . We also note that Tribe's reliance on his alleged naivete is contradicted by the fact that Stoddard, who accompanied Tribe and advised him in the purchase of the horse, was "knowledgeable about horses." It is undisputed that all discussions allegedly relating to a "guarantee" were with Stoddard, not Tribe. . . .

The jury reached a patently reasonable verdict, and therefore we affirm. . . .

QUESTION

What would have happened had Tribe, alleging mistake, sued to recover not damages but the price paid for Moccasin Badger?

Johnson v. Healy

Supreme Court of Connecticut, 1978.
176 Conn. 97, 405 A.2d 54.

PETERS, J. This case arises out of the sale of a new one-family house by its builder, the defendant John J. Healy, to the plaintiff, Ronald K. Johnson. The plaintiff bought the house, located in Naugatuck, in 1965, for $17,000. Between 1968 and 1971, the house settled in such a way as to cause major displacements in various foundation walls, and substantial damage to the sewer lines. In 1971, the plaintiff instituted this law suit alleging misrepresentation and negligence on the part of the defendant builder-vendor. The court below found for the plaintiff on the claims of misrepresentation, for the defendant on the claims of negligence, and assessed damages. Both parties have appealed. . . .

The claims of misrepresentation are based on [facts] amply supported by the evidence below. As part of the negotiations leading to the contract of sale of the house, the plaintiff inquired about the quality of its construction. The defendant replied that the house was made of the best material, that he had built it, and that there was nothing wrong with it. These representations were relied upon by the plaintiff. . . . The damage which the house sustained because of its uneven settlement was due to improper fill which had been placed on the lot beneath the building at some time before the defendant bought the lot, as a building lot, in 1963. On the basis of these findings, the trial court concluded that the defendant had made an express warranty coextensive with the doctrine of implied warranty of workmanship and habitability in cases involving the sale of new homes by a builder. . . .

The defendant assigns as error the trial court's conclusion that defendant bore responsibility for a condition of which he had no knowledge, actual or constructive. The trial court found that defendant's representations, although innocent, amounted to an express warranty of workmanlike construction and fitness for habitation. Since those representations reasonably induced reliance in the purchase of the house, the defendant was held liable despite the absence of written warranties concerning the fitness or condition of the home in the contract of sale or the deed of conveyance.

The scope of liability for innocent misrepresentation has varied with time and with context, in American law generally and in this court. Traditionally, no cause of action lay in contract for damages for innocent misrepresentation; if the plaintiff could establish reliance on a material innocent misstatement, he could sue for rescission, and avoid the contract, but he could not get affirmative relief. . . . In tort, the basis of responsibility, although at first undifferentiated, was narrowed, at the end of the nineteenth century, to intentional misconduct, and only gradually expanded, in this century, to permit recovery in damages for negligent misstatements. Prosser, Torts (4th Ed.1971) § 107. At the same time, liability in warranty, that curious hybrid of tort and contract law, became firmly established. . . . In contracts for the sale of tangible chattels, express warranty encompasses material representations which are false, without regard to the state of mind or the due care of the person making the representation. For breach of express warranty, the injured plaintiff has always been entitled to choose between rescission and damages. Although the description of warranty liability has undergone clarification in the [UCC], which supersedes the Uniform Sales Act, these basic remedial principles remain unaffected. At the same time, liability in tort, even for misrepresentations which are innocent, has come to be the emergent rule for transactions that involve a commercial exchange. See Restatement (Second), Torts § 524A (1958); Prosser, Torts (4th Ed.1971) § 107.

In Connecticut law, strict liability for innocent misrepresentation in the sale of goods is well established. As long ago as Bartholomew v. Bushnell, 20 Conn. 271 (1850), this court held that "[i]f a man sell a horse to another, and expressly warrant him to be sound, the contract is broken, if the horse prove otherwise. The purchaser, in such case, relies *upon the contract*; and it is immaterial to him, whether the vendor did, or did not, know of the unsoundness of the horse. In either case, he is entitled to recover all the damages, which he has sustained." For similar reasons, strict liability for innocent misrepresentation was imposed in a construction contract in E. & F. Constr. Co. v. Stamford, 114 Conn. 250, 158 A. 551 (1932). In *Stamford*, the defendant's erroneous description of subsurface conditions materially affected the plaintiff's excavation costs. This court held the misrepresentation to be actionable, even though there was no allegation of fraud or bad faith, because it was false and misleading, "in analogy to the right of a vendee to elect to retain goods which are not as warranted, and to recover damages for the breach of warranty." Id., 258, 158 A. 553. *Stamford* quotes [from] 3 Williston, Contracts § 1512 (1920): " 'If a man makes a statement in regard to a matter upon which his hearer may reasonably suppose he has the means of information, . . . and the statement is made as part of a business transaction, or to induce action from which the speaker expects to gain an advantage, he should be held liable for the consequences of reliance upon his misstatement.' " Id., 259, 158 A. 554. *Bartholomew* and *Stamford* together make it clear that liability for innocent misrepresentation is not a novelty in this state, that such liability is based on principles of warranty, and that such warranty law is not confined to contracts for the sale of goods.

Extension of warranty liability for innocent misrepresentation to a builder-vendor who sells a new home is, as a matter of policy, consistent with the developing law of vendor and purchaser generally. In the not too distant past, it is true, *caveat emptor* dominated the law of real estate. . . . In this state, however, *caveat emptor* has not been allowed to stand in the way of imposition of liability for negligent misrepresentations. See Warman v. Delaney, 148 Conn. 469, 172 A.2d 188 (1961). . . . Furthermore, Scribner v. O'Brien, Inc., 169 Conn. 389, 363 A.2d 160 (1975), recognized the propriety of claims for negligence, express warranty, and, in dictum, implied warranty, and thus effectively and explicitly ended the role of *caveat emptor* in sales of new homes by builder-vendors.

[Here], as the trial court concluded, liability for innocent misrepresentation is entirely appropriate. Although the defendant vendor had built no houses other than this one, this information was not disclosed to the buyer until the sale had been concluded; the defendant had been otherwise engaged in the real estate business for about thirty years. Although indefinite, the defendant's statement that there was "nothing wrong" with the house could reasonably have been heard by the plaintiff as an assertion that the defendant had sufficient factual information to justify his general opinion about the quality of the house. In context, this statement of opinion could reasonably have induced reliance. . . .

The claims for negligence in construction depend upon a showing by plaintiff that defendant knew, or should have known, that the subsurface conditions of the building were substandard, and thus required special plans for the footings and the foundation of the house that he was building. The trial court found that defendant had no actual knowledge of the soil defects, a finding which plaintiff does not directly attack. The issue therefore is the defendant's constructive notice of the lot's instability despite its apparent content of standard bank run gravel. It is significant that the building inspector, who approved the construction plans, was found to have had no notice. At the time of this building project, test borings to determine soil suitability were not customary for residential construction. Although there was testimony which might have supported a different finding, the trial court was not bound to accept as persuasive even testimony that was not directly contradicted. . . . Its conclusion of absence of notice is amply supported by other evidence and must therefore stand. Without notice, the claims for negligence are unsustainable. . . .

The assessment of damages in the trial court was an award in the amount of $5000 for breach of warranties and not for negligence. The plaintiff attacks this award as inadequate, since it does not measure damages by the cost of repairs. The defendant attacks the award as excessive because it does not measure the difference between the value of the property as warranted and as sold.

The plaintiff's claim for damages was twofold: $882.50 for sewer repairs occasioned by the settling of the foundation which damaged the sewer line, and $27,150 as an estimate, procured in 1971, for the cost of constructing a new foundation. The court specifically found that the cost of replacing the foundation would in all likelihood exceed the value of the house, originally purchased for $17,000.

Apart from the sewer repair costs, plaintiff incurred, from 1965 to 1970, additional expenditures of $5112 in connection with the house. These expenses were largely, but not exclusively, incurred in making repairs. The trial court concluded that, since a substantial part of the $5112 was for repairs attributable to the faulty settlement of the house, he would allocate to damages an amount which, when added to the $882.50 sewer costs, would produce a total recovery of $5000. The court noted that, in late 1971, when plaintiff first complained to defendant about problems with the house, defendant offered to repurchase the property for the purchase price of $17,000 and the expense of repairs then represented by plaintiff to approximate $5000.

The general rule for measurement of damages upon breach of warranty is to award the prevailing party such compensation as will place him in the same position as he would have enjoyed had the property been as warranted. This is the general rule of contract law, and was discussed extensively, and applied to the sale of a new residential house, in Levesque v. D & M Builders, Inc., 170 Conn. 177, 365 A.2d 1216 (1976). *Levesque* involved a buyer who wanted to relocate a house misplaced on a building lot. This court refused to permit relocation costs of $10,800 to be awarded for breach of contract and warranty, when the original contract price had been $22,600. *Levesque* adopts a rule that limits damages to the diminished value of the building whenever the cost of repairs is dramatically larger than is the difference in value. Although the costs of repair may more precisely place the injured party in the same physical position as full performance, policy dictates limitation to diminution of value to avoid unreasonable economic waste. It is clear that *Levesque* forbids recovery of the costs of a new foundation in the case before us, since the price discrepancy between reconstruction cost and contract price is even larger than it was in *Levesque*. Moreover, *Levesque* involved a defendant whose default could hardly be characterized as innocent. Contract restraints are particularly appropriate when damages are awarded, as in this case, for misrepresentations which, though actionable, are totally innocent. See Hill, "Damages for Innocent Misrepresentation," 73 Colum.L.Rev. 679 (1973), and Hill, "Breach of Contract as a Tort," 74 Colum.L.Rev. 40 (1974). The trial court was therefore correct in refusing to measure damages by the $27,150 estimated to be required to replace the foundation.

The proper test for damages was the difference in value between the property had it been as represented and the property as it actually was. This standard is notoriously more difficult to apply than to state. Reasonable costs of repair may therefore sometimes furnish a reasonable approximation of diminished value. Richard v. A. Waldman & Sons, Inc., 155 Conn. 343, 232 A.2d 307 (1967). . . . Reliance expenses often serve as a surrogate for damages otherwise inaccessible to proof. See the classic articles, Fuller & Perdue, "The Reliance Interest in Contract Damages: 1," 46 Yale L.J. 52 (1936–1937), and Fuller & Perdue, "The Reliance Interest in Contract Damages: 2," 46 Yale L.J. 373 (1936–1937). The trial court's reference to the $5112 expended by plaintiff with regard to the house would have been an acceptable resource for the inquiry into diminution of value, if only the $5112 list had accurately distinguished between expenses for repairs and expenses for improvements. To the extent that reliance expenses are probative of losses incurred because of breach, they must be expenses demonstrably incident to breach. The tender of a particular sum by the defendant in negotiation of an aborted settlement is no more dispositive than is the plaintiff's unwillingness to agree to a rescission and to insist, as he had a right to do, on affirmative relief in damages.

Under these circumstances, the court's award of damages was in error, the judgment is set aside, and the case is remanded with direction to render judgment for the plaintiff to recover such damages as he may prove on a new trial limited to the issue of damages.

QUESTION

Suppose defendant knew of the "improper fill" but made no representations of any kind respecting the house or subsurface conditions and plaintiff asked no questions. Would defendant have a duty to disclose the soil defects?

––––––––––

NOTE: CLASSIFYING MISREPRESENTATION

It is commonly understood that the tort of misrepresentation takes three forms—intentional ("deceit" at common law), negligent, and innocent. In Johnson v. Healy, the focus was on innocent misrepresentation, a representation made in blameless ignorance of its falsity. (Some courts speak of "equitable fraud," to make clear that proof that a statement was knowingly false is not required.) Nevertheless, the court's opinion included this statement: "In tort, the basis of responsibility, although at first undifferentiated, was narrowed, at the end of the nineteenth century, to intentional misconduct, and only gradually expanded, in this century, to permit recovery in damages for negligent misstatements." Considerable history underlies that statement. The main point is that there occurred a major relaxation of the element of scienter ("evil mind," intent to defraud) which was central to the common law action of deceit. For example, the absence of honest belief which is involved when a statement is made in complete ignorance of its truth or falsity (at the least, a "reckless" statement, because made with no concern about truth or falsity), was treated in many courts as equivalent to actual knowledge of falsity. Also, courts came to find fraud in a statement made as of one's own knowledge when that knowledge did not exist; such a representor was deemed to misstate the state of his knowledge as to the fact misrepresented. The element of the speaker's knowledge of the falsity was therefore allowed to substitute for the element of intent to defraud.

The result was that it became possible to award damages in what was called a deceit action where the representor's fault consisted essentially of negligence (perhaps even innocent ignorance of falsity). Emphasis on negligence or on mere falsity removed the need to show specific intent to defraud. The term "fraud" therefore could be used to describe both intentional and negligent misrepresentation, even though liability for the latter is understood to exist alongside and independently of the traditional liability in deceit. The problem of classification that developed in the first half of the twentieth century was not helped by the murkiness of language found in the decisions. The court in Florenzano v. Olson, 387 N.W.2d 168 (Minn.1986), sought to sort out at least the major outlines of the problem:

> Because fraud, in its broadest form, can be understood to encompass actions that result from both deceit and negligence, the line between the two theories of culpability can sometimes disappear.... [A]n actionable misrepresentation requires proof either that the misrepresenter acted dishonestly or in bad faith, i.e., with fraudulent intent, or, alternatively, that the misrepresenter was negligent.... Fraud is distinguished from negligence by the element of scienter required. Fraud is an intentional tort and scienter is an essential element.... We have stated that a representation is made with fraudulent intent when it is known to be false or, in the alter-

native, when it is asserted as of the represser's own knowledge
when he or she does not in fact know whether it is true or false. . . .
This formula can be ambiguous. . . . The language of [the] cases, if
read out of context, could blur the meaning of the term "fraudulent
intent" such that it is indistinguishable from the failure to use reasonable care required to prove liability in negligence. . . .

A misrepresentation is made negligently when the
misrepresenter has not discovered or communicated certain information that the ordinary person in his or her position would have
discovered or communicated. Proof of the subjective state of the
misrepresenter's mind, whether by direct evidence or by inference, is
not needed to prove negligence. [This] is proved by measuring one's
conduct against an objective standard of reasonable care or competence. In [this state], one making representations is held to this duty
of care only when supplying information, either for the guidance of
others in the course of a transaction in which one has a pecuniary
interest, or in the course of one's business, profession, or employment. [We thus] adopt the [Rest.2d Torts § 552] definition of negligent misrepresentation.

As the reference to § 552 of the Rest.2d of Torts indicates, liability for negligent misrepresentation is usually more restricted—narrower in scope—than
that for fraudulent misrepresentation. Also, in many courts, a plaintiff's proofs
of negligent misrepresentation are measured by the usual standard applied in
civil actions (a preponderance of the evidence), not the heightened standard of
proof ("clear and convincing") typically found in fraud actions.

Hinson v. Jefferson

Supreme Court of North Carolina, 1975.
287 N.C. 422, 215 S.E.2d 102.

[Plaintiff sued to recover the purchase price of a parcel of land sold
and conveyed by defendants to plaintiff in 1971, and to cancel the deed. The
facts were stipulated. The land, measuring 200 by 300 feet, was conveyed
by a deed that restricted use to residential purposes and provided that no
residence should be constructed at a cost of less than $25,000, or without
the defendants' approval of the plans. The deed also forbade the carrying on
of any "noxious or offensive trade," the erection of signs or billboards, and
the storage of trade inventories, trucks, or tractors. As defendants knew,
plaintiff planned to build a residence, and since the land was not served by
a municipal sewage-disposal system, it would require for the contemplated
use a septic tank or an on-site sewage system. When plaintiff was ready to
begin construction, county and federal health officials carried out evalua-
tions of the land and determined that it was only 2.6 feet above the water
level of Black Swamp, and was subject to flooding. The severe drainage
problem could only be solved by channel improvements to Black Swamp
and Little Contentnea Creek—at an estimated cost of several hundred
thousand dollars. These conditions led county authorities to deny plaintiff a
permit for a septic system. While all of the described conditions of the land
existed at the time of the sale to plaintiff, neither she nor defendants knew
that the land would not support a septic system. Plaintiff's suit did not al-

lege any fraud or misrepresentation by defendants. Their deed to plaintiff contained no covenant or warranty that the land was suitable for the construction of a residence.

The trial court concluded as a matter of law that plaintiff was not entitled to relief. The Court of Appeals reversed, granting rescission and restitution.]

COPELAND, J. . . . [Plaintiff] relies on the following legal points in support of her exception to the [trial court's] judgment:

"1. That the stipulated facts show that there was a mutual mistake of an existing material fact, common to both parties, and by reason thereof each has done what neither intended, coupled with a failure of consideration.

"2. That in a conveyance of land by deed containing restrictions therein which restrict the use of the property for a certain purpose, the grantor thereby warrants that the property so conveyed and restricted can be used for the specific purpose to which its use is restricted by the deed of conveyance."

. . . [T]he Court of Appeals held that plaintiff was entitled to rescind the contract on the grounds of "mutual mistake of material fact" coupled with a "total failure of consideration." . . . Assuming, *arguendo*, . . . that this is a true mistake case, then it is one that must necessarily involve a mistaken *assumption* of the parties in the formation of the contract of purchase. In these mistaken assumption cases, unlike other kinds of mistake cases, . . . [d]ifficulties subsequently arise because at least one of the parties has, either consciously or unconsciously, mistaken beliefs concerning facts that make the sale appear more attractive to him than it actually is. . . .

In [determining] whether the aggrieved party is entitled to some kind of relief in these mistaken assumption cases, courts and commentators have suggested a number of factors as relevant. E.g., was the mistake bilateral or unilateral; was it palpable or impalpable; was one of the parties unjustly enriched; was the other party unjustly impoverished; was the risk assumed by one of the parties (i.e., subjective ignorance); was the mistake fundamental or collateral; was the mistake related to present facts or to future expectations; etc. . . . Our research has failed to disclose a prior North Carolina case applying the doctrine of mutual mistake pertaining to a physical condition of real property as a ground for rescission. . . . However, we have found a few cases from other jurisdictions.

In Blythe v. Coney, 228 Ark. 824, 310 S.W.2d 485 (1958), the court allowed rescission where the vendor and purchaser of a residence were mistaken as to the adequacy of water pressure. . . . [T]he water meter in the home was unconnected at the time it was shown to the purchasers so that neither party was aware of the water shortage until after the sale. Likewise, in Davey v. Brownson, 3 Wash.App. 820, 478 P.2d 258 (1970), cert. denied, 78 Wash.2d 997 (1971), the court relied on the doctrine of mutual mistake of a material fact in rescinding the sale of, inter alia, a 26–unit motel that, unknown to either party at the time of signing the contract, was infested with termites, a condition that could only be corrected by substantial structural repair. . . . One court has held that there were sufficient grounds for rescission of a sale of realty where both the vendor and the vendee were mistaken as to the suitability of the soil or the terrain for agricultural purposes. See, e.g., Binkholder v. Carpenter, 260 Iowa 1297, 152

N.W.2d 593 (1967). . . . Suffice it to say, all [these] decisions appear to be contra to the traditional doctrine of *caveat emptor*.

The closest mistaken assumption case to our fact situation is A & M Land Dev. Co. v. Miller, 354 Mich. 681, 94 N.W.2d 197 (1959)[,] [which] held that the trial judge was correct in refusing to rescind the sale of 42 building lots slated for subdivision and development, because of mutual mistake regarding the poor absorptive qualities of the soil that resulted in a *tentative* refusal of septic tank permits to the subdivider. The court concluded that assuming there was a mutual mistake, to grant rescission would be improper since the purchaser received the property for which he contracted, notwithstanding that it was less attractive and less valuable to him than he had anticipated.

There are, however, several important distinguishing factors between the *Miller* case and our case. First, the purchaser in *Miller* was a developer-speculator; in our case the purchaser is a consumer-widow. Second, the property in *Miller* was not rendered valueless for its intended use, but only rendered less valuable because it could not be developed as densely as originally anticipated; in our case the property was rendered totally valueless for the intended use.

In our view, the difficulty with the above listed factors and with the decisions we have examined is that in any given case several factors are likely to be present, and each may point toward a different result. For example, in *Miller*, supra, the mistake appears to have been mutual and it also appears to have been induced by misrepresentations of the vendor (i.e., vendor furnished reports of engineers and sanitation officials indicating that the character of the soil was suitable for the use of individual septic tank systems). Yet, the court held that rescission would be improper since the purchaser received the property for which he had contracted. Perhaps the court felt that since the vendee was a developer-speculator he assumed the risk of soil defects. In short, the relation of one factor to another is not clear. . . . In any event, because of the uncertainty surrounding the law of mistake we are extremely hesitant to apply [it] to a case involving the completed sale and transfer of real property. Its application to this type of situation might well create an unwarranted instability with respect to North Carolina real estate transactions and lead to the filing of many non-meritorious actions. Hence, we expressly reject this theory as a basis for plaintiff's rescission.

Is plaintiff therefore without a remedy? Did plaintiff buy this property "at the end of the halter" (an expression of horse traders)? At this moment, plaintiff has naked legal title to a tract of real estate whose use to her is limited by the restrictive covenants and by the facts as stipulated to what she calls "the dubious pleasure of viewing the same." On the other hand, defendants have $3,500 of plaintiff's money. [The parties] never contemplated this particular use of the subject property. In fact, the deed, by its very terms, makes it clear that the intended use was for the construction of a single-family residence, strictly limited as to costs and as to design. [Also,] both prior to and at the time of the conveyance neither defendants nor plaintiff knew that the property would not support a septic tank or on-site sewage disposal system.

In the face of these uncontroverted facts, defendants rely upon the doctrine of *caveat emptor*. . . . The common law doctrine of *caveat emptor* historically applied to sales of both real and personal property. Its application to personal property sales, however, has been restricted by the [UCC]. See

G.S. § 25–2–314 et seq. Over the years, as to real property, the number of cases that strictly apply the rule of *caveat emptor* appears to be diminishing, while there is a distinct tendency to depart therefrom, either by way of interpretation, or exception, or by simply refusing to adhere to the rule where it would work injustice. . . . In recent years the rule of *caveat emptor* has suffered severe inroads in sales of houses to be built or in the course of construction. . . . Today, it appears that a majority of the states imply some form of warranty in the purchase of a new home by a first purchaser from a builder-vendor. . . .

During the course of [the present] litigation, and subsequent to the oral arguments of this case in the Court of Appeals, this Court decided the case of Hartley v. Ballou, 286 N.C. 51, 209 S.E.2d 776 (1974)[,] [wherein we] approved the "relaxation of the rule of *caveat emptor*" in respect of defects of which the purchaser of a recently completed or partially completed dwelling was unaware and could not discover by a reasonable inspection, and substituted therefore, for the first time in this State, an implied warranty defined as follows:

"[I]n every contract for the sale of a recently completed dwelling, and in every contract for the sale of a dwelling then under construction, the vendor, if he be in the business of building such dwellings, shall be held to impliedly warrant to the initial vendee that, at the time of the passing of the deed or the taking of possession by the initial vendee (whichever first occurs), the dwelling, together with all its fixtures, is sufficiently free from major structural defects, and is constructed in a workmanlike manner, so as to meet the standard of workmanlike quality then prevailing at the time and place of construction; and that this implied warranty in the contract of sale survives the passing of the deed or the taking of possession by the initial vendee." Id. at 62, 209 S.E.2d at 783. At the same time, *Hartley* made it clear that such implied warranty falls short of "an absolute guarantee." "An implied warranty cannot be held to extend to defects which are visible or should be visible to a reasonable man." . . .

We believe that many of the mutual mistake cases discussed supra were in fact embryo implied warranty cases. For example in Davey v. Brownson, the purchaser obtained rescission because of termites on the ground of mutual mistake. Although the court denied its decision was based on implied warranty, it is difficult to understand the application of the mutual mistake doctrine. . . . In this context, *Hartley* could easily be classified as a mutual mistake case, i.e., both parties assumed that the basement wall was sufficiently free from structural defects so as to prevent any water leakage. But, in *Hartley* we recognized the implied warranty as a limited exception to the general rule of *caveat emptor*; if we had elected to totally abolish the doctrine, then perhaps application of the mutual mistake theory would have been appropriate. *Hartley* is not an abrogation of the doctrine of *caveat emptor*; on the contrary it is only a well-reasoned exception.

Concededly, this is not the *Hartley* fact situation. *Hartley* involved a builder-vendor of new homes and a consumer-vendee. Nonetheless, we believe that *Hartley* provides the legal precedent for deciding this case. The [decision] is a recognition that in some situations the rigid common law maxim of *caveat emptor* is inequitable. We believe this is one of those situations. . . . [W]e hold that where a grantor conveys land subject to restrictive covenants that limit its use to the construction of a single-family dwelling, and, due to subsequent disclosures, both unknown to and not reasonably discoverable by the grantee before or at the time of conveyance, the property cannot be used by the grantee, or by any subsequent grantees[,] . . . for the specific purpose to which its use is limited by the restrictive covenants, the grantor breaches an implied warranty arising out of said restrictive covenants.

Defendant contends that if plaintiff is permitted to rescind, then any contract or conveyance can be set aside under a set of circumstances rendering the land no longer attractive to a purchaser. If we applied the mutual mistake doctrine, then there might be some merit to this argument. But, under the rule we have announced, a purchaser is bound by patent defects or by facts a reasonable investigation would normally disclose. [Here,] it is clear that a reasonable inspection by the grantee either before or at the time of conveyance would not have disclosed that the property could not support a septic tank or on-site sewage disposal system.

. . . [W]e hold that defendant grantors have breached the implied warranty, as set out above, and that plaintiff, by timely notice of the defect, once it was discovered, is entitled to full restitution of the purchase price; provided that she execute and deliver a deed reconveying the subject lot to defendants. The judgment of the Court of Appeals, as modified herein, is thus affirmed.

———

COMMENT: MISTAKE OR IMPLIED WARRANTY?

What are the implications of a court's preference for implied warranty, not mistake, as the basis for decision in situations such as that presented by *Hinson*?

In considering this question, you should know of at least one court's reaction to the rule of Hinson v. Jefferson. Cook v. Salishan Properties, Inc., 279 Or. 333, 569 P.2d 1033 (1977), saw the Oregon Supreme Court refuse to imply a warranty of fitness in a case involving a long-term lease (99 years, with renewal rights) of an unimproved lot situated in a seashore residential development. The lessees had paid $14,950 for the leasehold and nearly $35,000 to build a residence on the lot, only to find their investment in peril from soil erosion. They sued the lessor (subdivider-developer) to recover damages for the diminished value of the house and lot, relying in part on the claim that the developer's acts of offering and entering into the leases amounted to an implied warranty that the lots were fit for residential construction and use. Plaintiffs' warranty allegations were stricken by the trial court, and the jury returned a verdict for the defendant on the other issues in the case (claims of misrepresentation and negligence). On appeal, then, the only remaining question was remarkably reminiscent of *Hinson*: "Whether a commercial seller or lessor who has not made false representations and who has not been negligent either in failing to discover defects in the land or in failing to warn prospective purchasers of known defects will, nevertheless, be held liable if the land turns out to be unsuitable for the purposes for which it was sold or leased."

Three years earlier the Oregon Supreme Court, like the North Carolina court in Hartley v. Ballou, had held that a warranty of workmanlike construction and fitness for habitation was implied in the sale of a new home by a builder-vendor. Yepsen v. Burgess, 269 Or. 635, 525 P.2d 1019 (1974). Recognizing that it was following a course set by other jurisdictions, the *Yepsen* court offered the following justification:

> These cases, reflecting a change in the morals of the market place, [rest] their holdings on the ground that the underlying theory of caveat emptor, predicating an arm's length transaction between seller and buyer of comparable skill and experience, is unrealistic as applied to the sale of new houses. The courts of this persuasion recognize that the essence of the transaction is an implicit engagement upon the part of the seller to transfer a house suitable for habitation. It is also recognized that the purchaser is not in an equal bargaining position with the builder-seller of a new house and is forced to rely upon the latter's skill and knowledge with respect to the ingredients of an adequately constructed dwelling house. It is further explained that, although a house becomes a part of the realty according to the technical law of accession, the purchaser sees the transaction primarily as the purchase of a house with the land only as an incident thereto. Looked at in this light, there is no substantial difference between the sale of a house and the sale of goods and it follows, therefore, that the implied warranties of fitness for use attendant upon a sale of personal property should attach to a sale of a house. [269 Or. at 639–640, 525 P.2d at 1021–1022.]

The scope of the warranty implied in *Yepsen* was left to await more precise definition in later cases. Should it now be extended to the sale or lease of unimproved land in a subdivision?

The Oregon Court concluded in Cook v. Salishan Properties, Inc. that it should not:

> Purchasers of subdivided land from commercial developers undoubtedly are justified in expecting that land to have been chosen for development and laid out into lots with reasonable care and professional skill. We are, however, unaware of any general expectation on the part of such purchasers, or the public at large, that a land developer will provide a lot which is free of all defects, including those which could not reasonably have been discovered prior to the sale. Even those who hold themselves out as "highly skilled and competent" land developers, as is alleged [here], are not, so far as we are aware, expected to guarantee that the land is without any flaws, even though undetectable, which might render it unfit for use in the future.

> Moreover, while it is true that the ordinary purchaser of subdivided land relies . . . on the expertise of the developer, the degree of the purchaser's necessary reliance is not as great as that of the purchaser of a home. Land is accessible for inspection before it is purchased. Although we do not suggest that the prospective purchaser's opportunity to inspect, or the expertise which he or she brings to that inspection, is equal to that of the developer, nevertheless the situation is not comparable to that involving a completed house, where many of the crucial details, such as wiring and structural materials, are placed beyond the purchaser's power to inspect by the construction process itself. . . .

If this problem requires attention[,] . . . the legislature is capable of correcting the situation. We have found only one reported case in which the court has implied a warranty like the one the plaintiffs urge us to adopt. Hinson v. Jefferson, 287 N.C. 422, 215 S.E.2d 102 (1975). . . . Whether or not we would approve the result in *Hinson* in a suit for rescission on comparable facts, we decline to adopt its theoretical basis to support an action for damages. If both parties are free from fault, as we must assume for purposes of this analysis, there is no compelling reason to require the seller (or lessor) rather than the purchaser (or lessee) to bear fortuitous losses. We must assume that the defendant neither knew nor should have known that plaintiff's lot would be susceptible to erosion. [279 Or. at 338–341, 569 P.2d at 1035–1037.]

Most courts that have addressed the question presented in *Cook* have shown the same reluctance to imply a warranty of suitability in the sale of raw land, on largely the same reasoning.

As the *Cook* analysis makes clear, the subdivider-developer was "free from fault"—without knowledge or reason to know of the problem and guilty of no negligence in failing to discover. Would it be surprising to find that "reason to know" or "lack of due care" has resulted in the imposition of an implied warranty of habitability on a professional seller of land? One court's answer is given in Jordan v. Talaga, 532 N.E.2d 1174 (Ind.Ct.App.1989) (not implying a warranty means that "unscrupulous developers would be vested with impunity to develop marginal and unsuitable land" and "homeowners would be left without a remedy for latent undisclosed defects in real estate not chargeable to the builder"). The sale of land may of course be subject to a state's Unfair Trade Practices Act; some of our states have added to the judicially-implied warranties in new construction legislation in the form of a New Home Warranties Act. See, e.g. Tessmann v. Tiger Lee Constr. Co., 228 Conn. 42, 634 A.2d 870 (1993).

Cushman v. Kirby

Supreme Court of Vermont, 1987.
148 Vt. 571, 536 A.2d 550.

DOOLEY, J. This is an appeal by the defendants-sellers of a home from a judgment entered, after a jury verdict in favor of the plaintiffs-buyers, in a suit for misrepresentation. We affirm.

In the spring of 1984, the plaintiffs, Lynn and Julie Cushman, entered into negotiations with the defendants, Gregory and Elizabeth Kirby, for the purchase of a single-family home in the Town of Waltham. After viewing the premises on two occasions, and agreeing on a purchase price of $102,500, the parties executed a purchase and sale agreement in April, 1984[,] [and the] property was conveyed [on] June 12, 1984.

Two months later, plaintiffs [sued] for misrepresentation claiming defendants had, during the course of negotiations, represented that there was good quality well water available on the land suitable for all household uses, when in fact the available well water was not of good quality. Trial by jury resulted in a verdict for plaintiffs of $6,600. Defendants now appeal the judgment entered on the verdict. . . . [They] raise [these] claims[:] (1)

the trial court erred in not granting their motions for directed verdicts because the evidence showed that no actionable misrepresentations were made by defendants; [and (2)] the court's charge on the issue of damages was incorrect as a matter of law.

. . . Through a realtor, plaintiffs briefly viewed the property once in the summer of 1983, and again in March of 1984. During the second visit, which was a much more thorough tour of the house, they discovered an apparatus for a water treatment system in the basement. Since the apparatus was labelled "water conditioner," plaintiffs inquired [of] defendants: "What kind of water do you have?" Mrs. Kirby answered: "It's good. It's fine. It's a little hard, but the system downstairs takes care of it." Mr. Kirby, who was present during this exchange, remained silent. Satisfied with the representation that the water was simply hard, plaintiffs inquired no further about water quality.

While moving into the home after closing, plaintiffs first discovered that the well water was in fact sulfur water that smelled strongly of rotten eggs. Dismayed by this discovery, plaintiffs contacted Mrs. Kirby, who responded by stating that she forgot to tell plaintiffs that the basement water treatment system needed "Clorox." She said that when the "Clorox" level is too low, the water smells and tastes bad.

Following Mrs. Kirby's instruction, plaintiffs added "Clorox" to the system. Rather than solving the problem, the "Clorox" made the water taste like sulfur and chlorine. They then consulted a plumber, who confirmed that they had sulfur water, and explained that sulfur water is not the same as hard water. The plumber testified that hard water is a condition caused by calcium, which does not require treatment for drinking, or cause foul taste or smell, as does sulfur water. The plumber also informed plaintiffs that it would cost at least $1,000 to rehabilitate the existing system—exclusive of labor, regular maintenance, and repair costs. He also testified that even with a properly operating system, the end result would be treated sulfur water, which even defendants testified would bring the water only to a "tolerable level of drinkability."

Based on advice from their plumber, as well as information received from other people who were not satisfied with similar sulfur filtration systems, plaintiffs determined that the most cost-effective, long-term solution to their sulfur water problem was to join with two other neighbors and hookup to the Vergennes city water supply. Thereafter, they accomplished the hookup for a cost of approximately $5,000, plus annual water bills.

Defendants' first argument is that, because of the absence of any evidence that either defendant made any affirmative misrepresentation to plaintiffs concerning water quality, the trial court erroneously denied their motions for directed verdicts. The premise of this argument is that the legal standard applicable to their conduct requires that they must have made intentional misrepresentations of existing fact before either of them could be held liable for fraud. We disagree.

This Court stated in Crompton v. Beedle, 83 Vt. 287, 75 A. 331 (1910)[:]

> Where one has full information and represents that he has, if he discloses a part of his information only, and by words or conduct leads the one with whom he contracts to believe that he has made a full disclosure and does this with intent to deceive and overreach and to prevent investigation, he is guilty of fraud

against which equity will relieve, if his words and conduct in consequence of reliance upon them bring about the result which he desires.

We think that, regardless of whether Mrs. Kirby's statement was actually false, and known by her to be false when it was made, the standard of conduct applicable to her was that stated in *Crompton*. . . .

Mrs. Kirby testified that at the time of the sale to the Cushmans, she was aware that the well water on the property contained sulfur to an extent requiring treatment to make it of tolerable quality. It was also uncontroverted that, despite her knowledge[,] Mrs. Kirby represented to the Cushmans, in response to inquiries about water quality, that the water on the property was "a little hard," but that the water treatment equipment in the basement would take care of it. There was no evidence that either defendant ever disclosed the presence of sulfur in the water. The plaintiffs testified that they relied on the truth of Mrs. Kirby's statements about the extent of the water problem when they decided to buy the house.

This evidence makes out a case of actionable fraud, under the [*Crompton*] standard, sufficient to carry the case to the jury. . . . [I]t was not error to deny Mrs. Kirby's motion for directed verdict.

A somewhat different standard of conduct applies to Mr. Kirby, since he made no affirmative representations to plaintiffs about the quality of water. The claim for fraud against him was based exclusively on his silence while in the company of plaintiffs and Mrs. Kirby when she made the statements about water quality.

"Silence alone is insufficient to constitute fraud unless there is a duty to speak." Cheever v. Albro, 138 Vt. 566, 421 A.2d 1287 (1980). . . . In *Cheever*, we concluded that the party sued for fraud had such a duty to speak based on "superior knowledge and means of knowledge" over the plaintiff, as well as certain contract language relevant to the disputed transaction. . . . Although *Cheever* involved the sale of a corporation, rather than real estate, we think that a duty to speak based on the superior knowledge of a seller is equally present where the relationship of the parties is that of vendor and purchaser of real estate. As stated by one court:

> Where material facts are accessible to the vendor only, and he knows them not to be within the reach of the diligent attention, observation and judgment of the purchaser, the vendor [of real estate] is bound to disclose such facts and make them known to the purchaser.

Lawson v. Citizens & Southern Nat'l Bank, 259 S.C. 477, 193 S.E.2d 124 (1972); see also Posner v. Davis, 76 Ill.App.3d 638, 395 N.E.2d 133 (1979) ("used-home seller [may be] liable for failing to disclose material defects of which he was aware at the time of sale."); Obde v. Schlemeyer, 56 Wash.2d 449, 353 P.2d 672 (1960) (home sellers have duty to disclose material defects [here, termite damage] known at time of sale). . . .

Mr. Kirby testified that he was aware of the sulfur in the water at the time of the sale. He also testified that he had assisted in maintaining the water treatment system, that he had a working knowledge of the system, and that he understood the system was designed to treat sulfur in the water. Thus, Mr. Kirby was fully cognizant of the quality of the water, and no question of fact existed as to his state of mind regarding this issue. Mr. Kirby further testified that he heard Mrs. Kirby represent to the plaintiffs that the water equipment took care of the "hard water" problem. As such,

[margin handwriting: relationship.]

the only question of fact at issue with respect to Mr. Kirby's liability was whether his wife's representation constituted fraud [under *Crompton*]. This is because if Mrs. Kirby's statement amounted to an inadequate disclosure constituting a misrepresentation, then, Mr. Kirby, based on his own knowledge, and his position as a seller of the property, had an affirmative duty to speak. . . The jury found Mrs. Kirby's statement to be a misrepresentation. Given the resolution of this sole factual issue, in conjunction with his own testimony, Mr. Kirby had a duty to speak, yet he remained silent. . . . [T]his silence constituted a misrepresentation.

Mr. Kirby's liability hinged on the determination of the factual issue of whether Mrs. Kirby's representation to the plaintiffs amounted to a misrepresentation, which was a question clearly within the province of the jury. Therefore, the trial court correctly denied Mr. Kirby's motion for directed verdict. . . .

Defendants' remaining argument is that the court's instruction on damages was erroneous. Defendants requested that the court instruct that plaintiffs were entitled to recover at most the cost of repairs to the treatment system. Instead, the court charged that it is a jury question whether repairs to the treatment system would fully and adequately accomplish the goal of placing plaintiffs in the same position in which they would have been had the property been sold as represented—with good quality water. If so, the court charged, the measure of damages suggested by defendants would be the maximum recovery. If not, the proper measure of damages is the difference in value of the property as represented and the value of the property as it actually existed.

In general, a party seeking damages for fraud is entitled to "recover such damages . . . as will compensate him for the loss or injury actually sustained and place him in the same position that he would have occupied had he not been defrauded." Larochelle v. Komery, 128 Vt. 262, 261 A.2d 29 (1969). The precise measure of damages that will provide the defrauded party with the benefit of his bargain, however, depends on "the facts and circumstances surrounding the fraud, and the nature and extent of the injury suffered by the defrauded party." Conover v. Baker, 134 Vt. 466, 365 A.2d 264 (1976) (citing Bean v. Sears, Roebuck & Co., 129 Vt. 278, 276 A.2d 613 (1971)).

We expressed more fully how the nature and extent of the injury suffered by a defrauded party affects the determination of the appropriate damage award in *Bean*, 129 Vt. at 282, 276 A.2d at 616:

> If the injury is temporary in the sense that restoration can cure the harm, the reasonable cost of repair may serve the need and provide adequate and fair compensation. If the damage is permanent and beyond full repair, the variance in value of the property before and after the injury often affords the better guide to a just award. It all depends upon the character of the property and the nature and extent of the injury.

The court's charge appropriately tracked [this] rule. Furthermore, there was ample evidence in the record to support the jury's conclusion that the fraud in this case could not be adequately remedied by repair of the water treatment system. . . . [The] damage award must stand.

————

Eytan v. Bach
374 A.2d 879 (D.C.App.1977)

The purchasers of three paintings brought an action to recover the price of $157.50 paid to defendant, a retailer of antiques and second-hand furniture. The three paintings—the purchasers learned subsequently—were not original productions of unknown nineteenth-century artists, but were recent reproductions that had been placed in old frames (we are not told by whom). Plaintiffs had "inspected and touched" several paintings displayed in defendant's Georgetown shop, ultimately selecting the three in question, "because the brittleness of the material, cracks in the paint, discoloration, grease stains on the back, and punctures in the frame . . . led them to believe these particular items were old." It was conceded that defendant had made no express representation, either that the paintings were "originals or ancient." At trial, defendant insisted that the paintings, even though reproductions, were worth "considerably more" than plaintiffs had paid; he said that he had cut his prices in order to make the sale. The trial judge summarily dismissed the complaint upon finding "no controverted issues of material fact." Based on a "general knowledge of the economics of the locality," the average price paid for each of the paintings—approximately $50—was "a sufficiently small amount to put any purchaser on notice that he was not buying a legitimate antique original work of art." Plaintiffs appealed, urging that "because [they] had, in the course of their inspection, displayed such interest in indicia of age, it became the legal duty of the dealer to disclose the true facts before the sale was completed." *Held*, dismissal affirmed. "[I]n certain circumstances, concealment of a 'material fact is as fraudulent as a positive direct misrepresentation.'" But this issue is not raised by the record here. "What the [lower] court [held] was that a purchaser who bought artificially aged copies of primitive paintings for the low unit prices upon which he and the dealer ultimately agreed, could not credibly assign as fraud the fact that the articles purchased turned out not to be vastly more valuable. . . . [T]he customer not having inquired as to whether the canvases were originals[,] we perceive no duty upon the part of the vendor to inform him of the obvious. If a customer went into a jewelry store and bought for $50 an item which looked like a diamond pendant set with pearls, it would plainly not be incumbent upon the sales clerk to warn the customer that what he had selected was a piece of costume jewelry with synthetic gems."

SECTION 5. CHANGED CIRCUMSTANCES JUSTIFYING NONPERFORMANCE

No doubt we have gone far since Paradine v. Jane, Aleyn, 26 [1647], but a promise still involves risks that the promisor may find burdensome or even impossible to meet. . . . Its very purpose is to give assurance to the promisee against the hazards of the future. The promisor, by undertaking these pro tanto relieves the promisee, and it is in the end a question of how unexpected at the time was the event which prevented performance.

Learned Hand, Circuit Judge, in
Companhia De Navegacao Lloyd
Brasileiro v. C.G. Blake Co.,
34 F.2d 616, 619 (2d Cir.1929).

INTRODUCTORY NOTE

As Judge Hand notes, our common law has "gone far" since the time of Paradine v. Jane, the mid 1600s, when contracts were read "literally" and excuses based on changed circumstances had to be written into the contract. How "far"—that is, the extent to which the accepted maxim of *pacta sunt servanda*, agreements are to be kept, still governs—is the focus of this section. At some point along the way courts came to recognize that commercial parties cannot be expected to anticipate every contingency that might arise in the performance of their contract. One dimension of the law's evolution centered on the meaning of the term "impossibility."

Consider a leading American case from early in the last century, Mineral Park Land Co. v. Howard, 172 Cal. 289, 156 P. 458 (1916). Defendants had a contract with public authorities to build a concrete bridge across a ravine. Plaintiff, owner of land in the ravine, entered into a written contract with defendants by which plaintiff granted to defendants the right to haul gravel and earth from plaintiff's land, and defendants agreed to take all the gravel and earth required for the construction of the bridge, and to pay five cents a cubic yard for the gravel and earth taken. After defendants had taken 50,131 cubic yards from plaintiff's land, they procured the balance of their requirements (50,869 cubic yards) from another source. When sued, defendants proved that the remainder of the gravel and earth on plaintiff's land lay below water level, could only be taken by a steam dredger, and would have to be dried before use, so that the total cost would have been 10 to 12 times the usual cost per yard.

Plaintiff therefore could not have damages for defendants' failure to take the remainder of the gravel they required. Where performance depends on the existence of a given thing, as here ("the requisite quantity, available for use"), it is excused if the thing ceases to exist or turns out to be nonexistent. There was gravel on plaintiff's land, but defendants could take it only at a prohibitive cost. "To all fair intents, it was impossible for defendants to take it." A thing is "impossible," said the court, when it is "not practicable," and it is impracticable when it can be done only "at an excessive and unreasonable cost." This does not mean that these defendants could excuse themselves by showing that performance would be more expensive than anticipated, or entail a loss. But where the difference in cost is as great as it is here, making performance "impracticable," the situation is the same as one where there is a total absence of earth and gravel.

Might it be useful to think of this case as presenting nothing more than a question of what the parties' deal was, their presuppositions? If so, does the court's approach look familiar?

Observe further Judge Hand's point, in *C.G. Blake Co.*, that a promise is a means of providing insurance in the contract itself, insurance against "the hazards of the future." For example, the buyer in *Mineral Park Land Co.* might have promised to take its gravel requirements from the seller "come Hell or high water." Such an explicit undertaking presumably would have assigned the risk of the contingency that arose. The question now before us is what to do when the parties are not so explicit, when they likely never thought about the thing that happened. How much risk does the ordinary promisor assume?

————

Taylor v. Caldwell

King's Bench, 1863.
3 Best & S. 826.

BLACKBURN, J. . . . [P]laintiff and defendants had, on the 27th May, 1861, entered into a contract by which the defendants agreed to let the plaintiffs have the use of The Surrey Gardens and Music Hall on four days then to come, viz., the 17th June, 15th July, 5th August and 19th August, for the purpose of giving a series of four grand concerts, and day and night fetes at the Gardens and Hall on those days respectively; and the plaintiffs agreed to take the Gardens and Hall on those days, and pay £100 for each day.

The parties inaccurately call this a "letting," and the money to be paid a "rent;" but the whole agreement is such as to shew that the defendants were to retain the possession of the Hall and Gardens so that there was to be no demise of them, and that the contract was merely to give the plaintiffs the use of them on those days. Nothing however . . . depends on this. The agreement then proceeds to set out various stipulations between the parties as to what each was to supply for these concerts and entertainments, and as to the manner in which they should be carried on. The effect of the whole is to shew that the existence of the Music Hall in the Surrey Gardens in a state fit for a concert was essential for the fulfilment of the contract. . . .

After the making of the agreement, and before the first day on which a concert was to be given, the Hall was destroyed by fire. This destruction . . . was without the fault of either party, and was so complete that in consequence the concerts could not be given as intended. And the question we have to decide is whether . . . the loss which the plaintiffs have sustained is to fall upon the defendants. The parties when framing their agreement evidently had not present to their minds the possibility of such a disaster, and have made no express stipulation with reference to it, so that the answer to the question must depend upon the general rules of law applicable to such a contract.

There seems no doubt that where there is a positive contract to do a thing, not in itself unlawful, the contractor must perform it or pay damages for not doing it, although in consequence of unforeseen accidents, the performance of his contract has become unexpectedly burthensome or even impossible. The law is so laid down in 1 Roll.Abr. 450 [and the] case of Hall v. Wright, E.B. & E. 746. But this rule is only applicable when the contract is positive and absolute, and not subject to any condition either express or implied; and there are authorities which . . . establish the principle that where, from the nature of the contract, it appears that the parties must from the beginning have known that it could not be fulfilled unless when the time for the fulfillment of the contract arrived some particular specified thing continued to exist, so that, when entering into the contract, they must have contemplated such continuing existence as the foundation of what was to be done; there, in the absence of any express or implied warranty that the thing shall exist, the contract is not to be construed as a positive contract, but as subject to an implied condition that the parties shall be excused in case, before breach, performance becomes impossible from the perishing of the thing without default of the contractor.

. . . [T]his implication tends to further the great object of making the legal construction such as to fulfil the intention of those who entered into the contract. For in the course of affairs men in making such contracts in general would, if it were brought to their minds, say that there should be such a condition. . . .

There is a class of contracts in which a person binds himself to do something which requires to be performed by him in person; and such promises, e.g. promises to marry, or promises to serve for a certain time, are never in practice qualified by an express exception of the death of the party; and therefore in such cases the contract is in terms broken if the promisor dies before fulfillment. Yet it was very early determined that, if the performance is personal, the executors are not liable; Hyde v. The Dean of Windsor, Cro.Eliz. 552, 553. See 2 Wms.Exors. 1560, 5th ed., where a very apt illustration is given. "Thus," says the learned author, "if an author undertakes to compose a work, and dies before completing it, his executors are discharged from this contract: for the undertaking is merely personal in its nature, and, by the intervention of the contractor's death, has become impossible to be performed." . . . In Hall v. Wright, E.B. & E. 746, 749, Crompton J., puts another case. "Where a contract depends upon personal skill, and the act of God renders it impossible, as, for instance, in the case of a painter employed to paint a picture who is struck blind, it may be that the performance might be excused."

It seems that in those cases the only ground on which the parties or their executors, can be excused from the consequences of the breach of the contract is, that from the nature of the contract there is an implied condition of the continued existence of the life of the contractor, and perhaps in the case of the painter of his eyesight. In the instances just given, the person, the continued existence of whose life is necessary to the fulfilment of the contract, is himself the contractor, but that does not seem in itself to be necessary to the application of the principle. . . . In the ordinary form of an apprentice deed the apprentice binds himself in unqualified terms to "serve until the full end and term of seven years to be fully complete and ended," during which term it is covenanted that the apprentice his master "faithfully shall serve," and the father of the apprentice in equally unqualified terms binds himself for the performance by the apprentice of all and every covenant on his part. (See the form, 2 Chitty on Pleading, 370, 7th ed. by Greening.) It is undeniable that if the apprentice dies within the seven years, the covenant of the father that he shall perform his covenant to serve for seven years is not fulfilled, yet surely it cannot be that an action would lie against the father? Yet the only reason why it would not is that he is excused because of the apprentice's death.

These are instances where the implied condition is of the life of a human being, but there are others in which the same implication is made as to the continued existence of a thing. For example, where a contract of sale is made[,] transferring presently the property in specific chattels, which are to be delivered by the vendor at a future day; there, if the chattels, without the fault of the vendor, perish in the interval, the purchaser must pay the price and the vendor is excused from performing his contract to deliver, which has thus become impossible.

[This rule] is established by the case of Rugg v. Minett, 11 East, 210, where the article that perished before delivery was turpentine, and it was decided that the vendor was bound to refund the price of all those lots in which the property had not passed; but was entitled to retain without deduction the price of those lots in which the property had passed, though they were not delivered, and though in the conditions of sale, which are set out in the report, there was no express qualification of the promise to deliver on payment. It seems in that case rather to have been taken for granted than decided that the destruction of the thing sold before delivery excused the vendor from fulfilling his contract to deliver on payment. . . .

It may, we think, be safely asserted to be now English law, that in all contracts of loan of chattels or bailments if the performance of the promise of the borrower or bailee to return the things lent or bailed, becomes impossible because it has perished, this impossibility (if not arising from the fault of the borrower or bailee from some risk which he has taken upon himself) excuses the borrower or bailee from the performance of his promise to redeliver the chattel.

The great case of Coggs v. Bernard, 1 Smith's L.C. 171, 5th ed.; 2 L.Raym. 909, is now the leading case on the law of bailments, and Lord Holt, in that case, referred so much to the Civil law that it might perhaps be thought that this principle was there derived direct from the civilians, and was not generally applicable in English law except in the case of bailments; [but] the same law had been already adopted by the English law as early as The Book of Assises. The principle seems to us to be that, in contracts in which the performance depends on the continued existence of a given person or thing, a condition is implied that the impossibility of performance arising from the perishing of the person or thing shall excuse the performance.

In none of these cases is the promise in words other than positive, nor is there any express stipulation that the destruction of the person or thing shall excuse the performance; but that excuse is by law implied, because from the nature of the contract it is apparent that the parties contracted on the basis of the continued existence of the particular person or chattel. . . . [L]ooking at the whole contract [here], we find that the parties contracted on the basis of the continued existence of the Music Hall at the time when the concerts were to be given. . . . [T]herefore, the Hall having ceased to exist, without fault of either party, both parties are excused, the plaintiffs from taking the gardens and paying the money, the defendants from performing their promise to give the use of the Hall and Gardens and other things. Consequently the rule must be absolute to enter the verdict for the defendants.

QUESTION

Is there conflict between Blackburn's statement that the "parties when framing their agreement evidently had not present to their minds the possibility of such a disaster" and the later assertion that "they must have contemplated such continuing existence [of the music hall] as the foundation of what was to be done"?

———

Roberts v. Lynn Ice Co.

187 Mass. 402, 73 N.E. 523 (1905)

By written instrument, Roberts "let" to defendant ice company "his ice business and privileges in [Lynn, at Flax Pond,] with the use and benefit of his ice-houses" for a period of 9½ months, which was later extended by agreement for another three years. Before the extended term had expired, the ice houses burned to the ground. Roberts sued to recover rent for the period after the fire. Whether rent was due, the court said, depended on whether the parties' agreement was a lease or merely a license. If it was a lease, the ice houses were the property of defendant for the term specified and the loss through fire was defendant's loss. Such questions have usually arisen in contracts for the use of specified rooms in a building, and the answer must depend on whether the occupant had been given "exclusive possession of the premises against the world, including the owner," for the period of time stated. The instrument in this case should be read as having this effect; it was a lease and a judgment for plaintiff for the stipulated rent was affirmed.

––––––––

Harrison v. Conlan

92 Mass. 85 (1865)

Plaintiff brought an action against the administratrix of a Roman Catholic priest to recover for his services as organist in the decedent's church. Plaintiff was employed by decedent on January 1, 1862, for a period of three months at a salary of $50. He performed until the priest's death on February 1, 1862, and thereafter remained ready to play. After the priest's death, no successor was appointed by the bishop and the church was closed except for the priest's funeral. Judgment for plaintiff for the full $50 was reversed. The court declared that in Catholic churches the organist is furnished by the pastor and the organist's services are "rendered to him personally as conductor of the worship of the church." Upon the priest's death, therefore, the contract was ended since further performance under it was impossible. Plaintiff was entitled to only $16.67 for one month's services, plus $5 for playing the organ at the priest's funeral. [This case has been cited for the proposition that "contracts [which can only be performed personally by the promisor] terminate when death renders the personal performance impossible." Kowal v. Sportswear by Revere, Inc., 351 Mass. 541, 222 N.E.2d 778 (1967). Was it "impossible" for plaintiff to play the church organ?]

QUESTION

Suppose on January 15 the organist, without speaking to anyone at the church, delegated his duties under the three-month agreement to a friend and left town. Must the priest allow "the friend" to play the organ?

––––––––

Tompkins v. Dudley

Court of Appeals of New York, 1862.
25 N.Y. 272.

Appeal from the Supreme Court. The plaintiffs sued as trustees of a school district for money advanced by them upon a contract to build a school-house, and for damages from the non-performance of the contract. There was a verdict and judgment for the defendants, which having been affirmed at general term[,] the plaintiffs appealed to this court. . . .

DAVIES, J. On the 31st of August, 1857, Cornelius Chambers, by a written contract, agreed to make, erect, build and furnish for the plaintiffs, a school-house, according to certain plans and specifications, and to furnish the materials for the sum of $678.50. The school-house was to be completed on the 1st day of October, 1857. The defendants guaranteed the performance of the contract on the part of the builder. The building was not completed on the 1st day of October, and it was burned down on the night of the 5th of October. The judge who tried the cause found [that] the contract was substantially performed by Chambers, but that the building was not entirely completed according to the specifications, there remaining to be done a small amount of painting and the hanging of the window blinds, and that the same had not been formally accepted nor the key delivered on the 5th of October. This action is brought to recover the money paid on account to Chambers as the building progressed, and for the damages which the plaintiffs have sustained by reason of the non-completion of the contract, the fulfillment of which was guaranteed by the defendants. It is undeniable that the school-house was not completed, nor delivered and accepted by the plaintiffs at the time of its destruction. . . . A substantial compliance with the terms of the contract will not answer when the contractor, as [here], concedes that the work was incomplete; he was still in possession, engaged in its completion. . . . [A]bout $60 was yet to be expended on the building. Had the builder completed the building and complied with his contract at the time of the destruction of the school-house? [He] had not. He was . . . to deliver it over to the plaintiffs thus finished, or offer to deliver it, before his whole duty was performed. . . .

The [court] in Adams v. Nichols (19 Pick., 275), a case quite like the present, [states]: "It is not very material to consider whose property the house was before its destruction. The principal defendant had contracted to build and finish a house on the plaintiff's land. After the conflagration, he might have proceeded, under the contract, and if he had completed a house according to the terms of his agreement the plaintiff would have been bound to perform his part of the stipulations. So if in any stage of its progress he had seen fit to remove any part of the materials, and substitute others, the plaintiff could not complain. They must, therefore, be deemed to be at his risk. And if he had not intended to incur this risk, he should otherwise have stipulated in his agreement. Had the article to be made been a chattel, or a coach, or a vessel, it is clear that the materials in the first place, and the article itself, in every stage of its manufacture, from its inception to its completion, would have been at the risk of the builder. . . ."

The builder [here], by his own contract, created a liability and incurred a duty, which the defendants guaranteed he should perform, and which he has not performed. In justification of such non-performance, he alleges the destruction of the building by fire and inevitable accident, without any fault on his part. The law is well settled, that this is no legal justification for the non-performance of the contract. . . . [W]hen a party is prevented by the act of God from discharging a duty created by the law, he is excused; but when he engages unconditionally, by express contract, to do an act, performance is not excused by inevitable accident or other unforeseen contingency not within his control. . . .

The only additional case needful to refer to, is that of School Trustees of Trenton v. Bennett (3 Dutcher [N.J.], 514). . . . [T]he court very justly says: "No matter how harsh and apparently unjust in its operation the rule may occasionally be, it cannot be denied that it has its foundation in good sense and in inflexible honesty. The party that agrees to do an act should *do it*, unless absolutely impossible. He should provide against contingencies in his contract. When one of two innocent persons must sustain a loss, the law casts it upon him who has agreed to sustain it, or, rather, the law leaves it where the agreement of the parties has put it. . . ."

. . . [The] defence interposed by the defendants constitutes no justification to Chambers, the builder, for the non-performance of his contract with the plaintiffs and that, having guaranteed for an adequate consideration, expressed therein, its performance, they are liable to respond to the plaintiffs for the damages which they have sustained by reason of such non-performance. . . .

Judgment reversed, and new trial ordered.

Garman v. Hoover

95 Pa.Super. 203 (1928)

Plaintiffs agreed to build a house on defendants' land, for a price of $8,300. Plaintiffs had constructed the house to the point that it was under roof, and had received from defendants some $5,600 in progress payments, when the building was completely destroyed by fire. Defendants had taken out insurance on the building in their own names, in the amount of $8,000, and after the fire collected $5,600 on the insurance policy. Plaintiffs built another similar house on the land, supplying materials worth $7,968, and then sued to recover the contract price without deducting the $5,600 progress payments they had received for the work done before the fire. Plaintiffs contended that by their work on the destroyed building they had earned the progress payments, that as to these sums the transactions were closed, and they could keep the sums thus earned. *Held*, the installment payments were not agreed equivalents for the successive stages of construction, but were merely advance payments for an entire performance, the construction of a completed house. Plaintiffs were obligated to complete their contract even though the house, when partially completed, had been destroyed by fire. If plaintiffs had not rebuilt they would have been liable in damages. Nor did the plaintiffs have any claim on the insurance proceeds received by defendants. The fact these proceeds reimbursed defendants for the $5,600 in progress payments does "not put plaintiffs in a position of reaping the fruits of defendants' prudence" in taking out insurance, at least where the insurance received does not exceed the owner's investment in the building. If plaintiffs wished insurance protection, they should have insured their own interest.

[handwritten margin note: Π's responsibility to provide house for $. Having to start over does not change that.]

NOTE

The infrequency today of cases like *Tompkins* and *Garmon Bros.* is no doubt explained by the presence of insurance covering the builder's losses from fire, theft, and other hazards. Standard forms used in the construction industry regularly require the project owner to purchase worksite property insurance protecting the owner, contractor, and subcontractors, "as the parties' interests may appear" (the so-called "builder's risk" policy). See, e.g., American Institute of Architects, General Conditions of the Contract for Construction §§ 11.3.1, 11.3.3 (1976). Another technique for mitigating the impact of the rule of absolute contractor liability (that is, shifting risk to owners) is to find the contract specifications given the contractor both faulty—defective, at least inadequate—and the responsibility of someone other than the contractor. The case immediately below suggests one more way to avoid the *Tompkins* rule.

Carroll v. Bowersock

Supreme Court of Kansas, 1917.
100 Kan. 270, 164 P. 143.

[Plaintiff agreed to construct a reinforced concrete floor in defendant's warehouse. After removing the old floor, plaintiff put in concrete footings, built wooden forms for concrete pillars to support the floor, and installed reinforcing rods in these column forms. The warehouse was then totally destroyed by fire, without the fault of either party. Plaintiff sued to recover for his performance prior to the fire, prevailing in the trial court. Defendant appealed.]

BURCH, J. . . . It is apparent that the [trial] court permitted recovery for substantially what the plaintiff had done by way of performance of the contract before the fire.

The contract was to place the floor in a specific warehouse. Destruction of the warehouse without fault of either party put an end to construction of a floor in that warehouse. No warehouse except the one destroyed having been contemplated or contracted about, the defendant could not be charged with delinquency for not building another. . . . If continued existence of the particular warehouse to which the contract related were not taken for granted by both parties, the plaintiff would be bound by his contract and could not recover at all, no concrete floor having been constructed.

It was not material that the defendant collected insurance on the warehouse, purchased before the contract was made. The insurance covered nothing but property of the defendant. He paid for the insurance and was entitled to it, just as the plaintiff would have been entitled to insurance on his property had he seen fit to insure. If any part of the plaintiff's labor and material was incorporated into the insured building, so that the insurance covered it as substance of the structure, the plaintiff can recover, if at all, not because of the insurance, but because of the incorporation.

If a contractor should engage to furnish all labor and material and build a house, and the house should burn before completion, the loss falls on him. If a contractor should engage to refloor two rooms of a house already in existence, and should complete one room before the house burned, he ought to be paid something. So far the authorities are in substantial agreement.

The principle upon which the contractor may recover in [the reflooring] case [is that] [p]erformance was prevented without fault of either party, and the true rule is that neither party can be charged with delinquency because the contract cannot be fulfilled.

The contractor cannot give and the owner cannot obtain that which they contracted about. . . . [T]he law must deal with the new situation of the parties created by the fire. The owner cannot be called on to reimburse the contractor merely because the contractor has been to expense in taking steps tending to performance. A contractor may have purchased special material to be used in repairing a house, and may have had much mill work done upon it. If the material remain in the mill and the house burn, there can be no recovery. If the milled material be delivered at the house ready for use, and the house burn, there can be no recovery. It takes something more to make the owner liable for what the contractor has done toward performance. The owner must be benefited. . . . The only basis on which the law can raise an obligation on the part of the owner is the consideration he has received by way of benefit, advantage, or value to him.

The question whether or not the owner has been benefited frequently presents difficulties. Sometimes the question is answered by the owner's own conduct, as when by taking possession, or by insuring as his own property, or by other act, he evinces a purpose to appropriate the contractor's material and labor. Sometimes the circumstances are such that the owner is precluded from rejecting the fruits of the contractor's efforts if he would, as when one room is finished under a contract to refloor two. In such cases it merely confuses the matter to bring in the terms "acceptance," "assent," and similar expressions indicative of the owner's attitude. If he should pay, it is not because assent or acceptance of benefit is "implied," or because he is "regarded as accepting benefit," but because of the fact that he has been benefited.

The test of benefit received has been variously stated. Sometimes it is said that benefit accrues whenever the contractor's material and labor, furnished and performed according to the contract, have become attached to the owner's realty. The facts of particular cases suggest different forms of expression. . . . [We are] inclined to approve the form adopted [in] Young v. Chicopee, 186 Mass. 518, 72 N.E. 63. . . . The action was one for labor and material furnished to repair a bridge destroyed by fire while the work was proceeding. The contract required at least half of the material to be "upon the job" before work commenced. The contractor complied with this condition, and distributed material "all along the bridge" and on the river bank. A portion of the material thus distributed but not wrought into the structure was destroyed by fire. Liability for work done upon and material wrought into the structure was not disputed, but the contractor sought to make good his entire loss. The [Massachusetts] court said: "[I]t would seem that the liability of the owner in a case like this should be measured by the amount of the contract work done which, at the time of the destruction of the structure, had become so far identified with it as that but for the destruction it would have inured to him as contemplated by the contract." 186 Mass. 546, 72 N.E. 64.

Applying the test stated[,] it is clear that the plaintiff should recover for the work done in cutting the old floor away from the wall and in removing such part of the old floor as was necessary. The warehouse was improved to that extent by labor, the benefit of which had inured to the defendant when the fire occurred. If the fire had not occurred, the undesirable floor would have been out of the way, precisely as the contract contemplated. Likewise, the contractor should recover for the completed concrete footings.

The contractor should not recover for material furnished or labor performed in the construction of either column or floor forms. They were temporary devices, employed to give form to the structure which was to be produced. They were not themselves wrought into the warehouse, were to be removed when the work was completed, and inured to nobody's benefit but that of the contractor. The contractor should not recover for either upright or floor rods, or for the labor of putting them in place. While the rods were wired together, they were not attached to the building and would not have been wrought into the structure until the concrete was poured. If the fire had not occurred the contractor could have removed the rods without dismembering or defacing the warehouse, and the defendant could not have held the rods as amalgamated into the fabric of his structure. There should be no recovery for superintendence and use of tools, except as regards that part of the work done which had become identified with the warehouse itself. Other items sued for should be allowed or disallowed by application of the principle indicated. . . .

The defendant says . . . that cutting away the old floor from the walls of the building and concrete footings for a floor which was never laid were of no value to him. The test is whether or not the work would have inured to his benefit as contemplated by the contract if the fire had not occurred. The cutting away of the old floor was done according to the contract, and the defendant had the benefit of that work as soon as it was finished. . . . [P]utting in the concrete footings was the next step in the construction. . . . Those footings would have inured to his benefit [if] the fire had not occurred. They became a part of his warehouse. . . . [H]e was benefited by them at the time of their incorporation into his structure. Test of a completed concrete floor was one of the things rendered impossible by the fire. . . .

The judgment of the district court is reversed, and the cause is remanded with direction to take such additional evidence as may be necessary and determine the rights of the parties according to the views which have been expressed.

JOHNSTON, C.J. (dissenting, joined by DAWSON, J.). I am of the opinion that the upright rods set up and tied together were a part of the building, and a recovery for them should be allowed.

———

Lincoln Welding Works v. Ramirez

98 Nev. 342, 647 P.2d 381 (1982)

Defendant, general contractor for a sewage-lagoon project undertaken by a sanitation district, subcontracted the sheet-piling work to plaintiff, who completed the work and was paid in full the agreed price of $54,000. A month later, a flood caused extensive damage to the work plaintiff had performed. Defendant asked plaintiff to make the necessary repairs; plaintiff did so, believing that he would be compensated for the additional work. But defendant refused to pay plaintiff the cost of the repairs, $19,000, contending that their subcontract had incorporated by reference the prime contract and that the latter obligated all subs on the project to bear the risk of loss for their respective portions of the job until the entire project was formally accepted by the sanitation district. The project was not accepted by the district until a month or so after the flood damage had been repaired. *Held*, summary judgment for defendant affirmed. The parties' agreement, considered in its totality, indicates that the subcontract was made with reference to the prime contract, which contemplates that plaintiff would bear the risk of loss to its work until formal acceptance of the project. Moreover, plaintiff agreed in the subcontract to do all work "to the entire satisfaction of the owner, contractor, and architect," and the subcontract states that final payment to plaintiff is conditioned on "completion of his work to the full satisfaction of said contractor, owner, and architect." In addition, the subcontract does not contain a risk-shifting provision absolving plaintiff from bearing the risk of loss.

NOTE: TRANSFERRING RISK BY CONTRACT

The *Ramirez* case is the ordinary business of contracting out of a default rule, here the transfer to a subcontractor of a risk that party would not have borne under the principle applied in Carroll v. Bowersock. One question that has arisen in the building cases is whether an owner's contractual undertaking to insure operates to shift the risk of loss during construction from the builder to the owner. In United States Fid. & Guar. Co. v. Parsons, 147 Miss. 335, 112 So. 469 (1927), a fire destroyed an almost-completed house; the builder had been paid nearly all of the contract price of $9,265. When the builder refused to rebuild, the owner contracted with another person who built the house for just over $13,000. The original contract contained a provision: "The owner is to carry fire insurance on the building and the contractor is to pay his pro rata share of the cost." The owner had taken out fire insurance in the amount of $12,500. The builder contended that the contract's insurance clause placed the risk of loss on the owner and relieved the builder of any duty to rebuild, especially where, as here, the owner had in fact taken out sufficient insurance. The court, in line with prevailing authority, rejected that claim and held that the risk of loss was unchanged. Do you see why? The court's analysis included this: "[T]o our minds, the fact that the parties agreed to insure the house is an additional reason for saying that [they] contemplated a completed building, and a rebuilding of said house in case of its destruction by fire."

Suppose the contract had required the builder, not the owner, to maintain fire insurance. Could it be said that the parties had modified the usual allocation of risk by substituting insurance for the builder's liability under general law?

COMMENT: RISK AND INSURANCE IN LAND PURCHASES

Contracting parties are free to make provision for intervening casualties, and many do. But when the contract is silent, and no statute covers the matter, courts apply a judge-made rule. In a majority of jurisdictions in this country (a bare majority, it seems), the doctrine of "equitable conversion" operates to place on the vendee the risk of loss from fortuitous casualties occurring after entry into the contract of sale and prior to its closing. The land vendee's longstanding right to specific performance means that the contract itself, from its first moment, creates "equitable ownership" in the vendee. Corbin put it this way: "The contract [gives] to the purchaser the substantial control of the premises and the principal valuable elements of 'property' therein." 3A A. Corbin § 667. Once the theory of equitable ownership was in place, there was no obvious reason not to apply it to risk of loss of a building or other improvements. After all, most—if not all—of the incidents of ownership were believed to accrue to the equitable owner, and, to be sure, the vendee had become the "owner" before the casualty occurred.

But what if the vendor carried insurance on the property that was damaged (which, presumably, would be the usual case)? With insurance in the picture, the issue most likely to be raised is whether the vendee is entitled to enforce the contract of sale with an "abatement" of the purchase price in the amount of the insurance proceeds. It is the view in most American jurisdictions that the vendee may have specific performance with a price abatement. E.g., Skelly Oil Co. v. Ashmore, 365 S.W.2d 582 (Mo.1963). A Pennsylvania court's analysis is typical: "Because the vendee [bears the risk of harm to the property and] must pay the full contract price whatever the condition of the property, our case law has long held that, although a vendor is legally entitled to recover the proceeds of his insurance policy[,] . . . the vendor's equitable entitlement to the proceeds extends only to the unpaid balance of the purchase price; any excess is deemed to be held 'in trust' for the vendee." Partrick & Wilkins Co. v. Reliance Ins. Co., 500 Pa. 399, 456 A.2d 1348 (1983). Corbin is quite specific about why it is that the vendor is required to credit the vendee with insurance money (3A A. Corbin § 670):

> If the vendee is held to have "equitable ownership," and for that reason to bear the risk of loss by destruction, the vendor's interest in the premises is only a security for payment. If the insurance policy is solely for the personal indemnity of the vendor, the only risk that remains to be carried by the insurer is the risk of nonpayment of the price. Actual payment by the vendee in accordance with the majority rule, prevents loss and leaves nothing to be paid by the insurer. In such case, money paid to [the vendor] by the insurer appears to be money to which he has no right; it was not paid to him as a gift. The best solution seems to be to apply it on the purchase price.

As is indicated by the reference above to a "bare majority" of states, the use of equitable conversion to assign the interim risk of casualty loss in the land-contract context has many critics. One small group of states rejects it altogether, following instead the rule that passage of the risk of loss to the vendee must await actual transfer of title. In contrast, a substantial and apparently growing number of jurisdictions deem the right to possession of the property at the time of the casualty to be the decisive factor. A version of this view is found in the Uniform Vendor and Purchaser Risk Act § 1, which was promulgated in 1968 and has been adopted in a substantial minority of states, including California and New York. Under that legislation, absent contrary agreement the risk of intervening casualty is determined by transfer of either legal title or possession. If neither has been transferred, the risk of loss is on the vendor ("the vendor cannot enforce the contract, and the purchaser is entitled to recover any portion of the price paid"). But if either legal title or possession of the premises has been transferred, "the purchaser is not relieved from a duty to pay . . . nor entitled to [restitution] of any portion [of the price paid]." Like the standard explanation for the distinction between building and repair contracts, the Uniform Risk Act can be read as suggesting that "control" counts for something, and that, in the event of a sale, it follows possession or title. (Similarly, as you will discover in the Sales or Commercial Law courses, the UCC, in §§ 2–509 and 2–510, states rules that by and large put the risk of loss on the party that controls the goods.) If there has been no change in possession or formal title, is it sound policy to let the loss remain with the vendor? A court not operating under the Uniform Risk Act, but favoring a rule turning on the right of possession, has given this answer (Brush Grocery Kart, Inc. v. Sure Fine Market, 47 P.3d 680, 685 (Colo.2002)):

> As a matter of both logic and equity, the obligation to maintain property in its physical condition follows the right to have actual

possession and control rather than a legal right to force conveyance of the property through specific performance at some future date. . . . The equitable conversion theory is literally stood on its head by imposing on a vendee, solely because of his right to specific performance, the risk that the vendor will be unable to [perform] when the time comes because of an accidental casualty loss. It is counterintuitive . . . that merely contracting for the sale of real property should not only relieve the vendor of his responsibility to maintain the property until execution but also impose a duty on the vendee to perform despite the intervention of a material, no-fault casualty loss preventing him from ever receiving the benefit of his bargain. Such an extension of equitable conversion to casualty loss . . . is [not] justified solely for the sake of consistency [of theory].

The Uniform Risk Act quite clearly opts for a policy of judicial inertia: absent a change in title or possession, a loss is to remain where it falls (on the property's owner), not to be shifted to another person.

It should be noted that the Uniform Risk Act is silent on the vendee's standard remedy of specific performance with price abatement. Is such silence to be read as a preclusion of this widely-recognized (and judicially-created) remedy? Probably not, since, as the New York court has put it, the Uniform Act is "addressed to risk and not to remedy." Lucenti v. Cayuga Apartments, Inc., 48 N.Y.2d 530, 423 N.Y.S.2d 886, 399 N.E.2d 918 (1979). More specifically, when the risk of loss remains with the vendor at the time of the intervening casualty, the Uniform Act says that "the purchaser is entitled to recover any portion of the price paid." That sounds like rescission. Is there a problem with saying that, as concerns casualty loss, partial specific performance with price abatement should be generally available as an alternative to the remedy of rescission?

RESTATEMENT OF CONTRACTS, SECOND

Section 264. Prevention by Government Regulation or Order

If the performance of a duty is made impracticable by having to comply with a domestic or foreign governmental regulation or order, that regulation or order is an event the non-occurrence of which was a basic assumption on which the contract was made.

Comment:

a. Rationale. . . . It is "a basic assumption on which the contract was made" that the law will not directly intervene to make performance impracticable when it is due. . . . With the trend toward greater governmental regulation, however, parties are increasingly aware of such risks, and a party may undertake a duty that is not discharged by such supervening [actions], as where governmental approval is required for his performance and he assumes the risk that approval will be denied. Such an agreement is usually interpreted as one to pay damages if performance is prevented rather than one to render a performance in violation of law. . . .

Louisville & Nashville R.R. Co. v. Crowe

156 Ky. 27, 160 S.W. 759 (1913)

On April 2, 1898, plaintiff conveyed to defendant's predecessor a strip of land through his farm for use as a right of way, in consideration of a promise to issue plaintiff, during his life, an annual pass on the railroad between Scottsville, Kentucky and Gallatin, Tennessee. Defendant and its predecessor issued such passes until 1911, when defendant recalled plaintiff's pass in reliance on a federal statute which the Supreme Court of the United States interpreted as forbidding such passes in interstate commerce. Defendant offered to issue plaintiff a pass between Scottsville and the Tennessee line, but denied any further liability. Plaintiff sued for specific performance of the contract; if such relief could not be granted, money damages were sought. In affirming a judgment for plaintiff for $200, the court declared that a contract which is lawful when made is terminated by a later governmental regulation or order which renders its performance unlawful, but that a party who has received a performance under such an agreement should not be permitted to retain it without payment. "In this case, it would not be equitable to restore to appellee the land taken and retained; nor could this now be done, the rights of the public having intervened. The equitable way to adjust the matter is to require [defendant] to pay to [plaintiff], a reasonable sum, based, not on the probable value of what he would have received thereunder for the remainder of his life, nor upon a breach of the contract; but for the right of way so taken and necessarily retained; taking into consideration, of course, what [plaintiff] has already received under the contract."

The Isle of Mull

278 F. 131 (4th Cir.1921)

On May 19, 1913, the Isles Steamship Co., a British corporation, chartered the steamship Isle of Mull to plaintiff Gans Steamship Line, a New York corporation. The charter contract provided for a term of "about five years" and a rental of £1,370 a month. The ship began service under the charter on January 7, 1914. On June 10, 1915, the ship was requisitioned by the British Admiralty, which assumed control two days later and retained control for more than the five-year period of the charter contract. The British government fixed as compensation to the owner £2,361 and 15 shillings a month, i.e., £991 and 15 shillings a month more than the rental specified in plaintiff's charter contract. Plaintiff then sued for damages measured by the difference between the market value of the use of the ship, alleged to be £5,110 a month, and the rent plaintiff had agreed to pay. The trial court held that the charter contract had not been frustrated and that plaintiff was entitled to the difference between the contract rate and the greater price paid by the British government. On appeal, this decree was reversed and plaintiff's suit dismissed. The legal authority of the British government to requisition the vessel could not be questioned in American courts. At the time the ship was requisitioned it was impossible to forecast the duration of the war, but the enormous resources mobilized on both sides and the urgent need of Britain to employ its full sea power made it unlikely that the Isle of Mull would be released before the end of the five-year period of the charter. Plaintiff argued that defendant owner would be unjustly enriched by retaining the excess paid by the British government. But defendant argued for a definite rule discharging both parties at once, permitting them promptly to readjust their affairs, and operating independently of the gains or losses of either party. This was the view adopted by the English courts where, as here, the frustration was or probably would be total. Under this view, if compensation paid for the requisitioned asset exceeded the contract rate, this was the owner's gain, just as inadequate compensation would be the owner's loss. The court, adopting, in effect, the English rule, concluded that the contract was wholly discharged and defendant was not required to account for the profit it had received.

———

Kel Kim Corp. v. Central Markets, Inc.

Court of Appeals of New York, 1987.
70 N.Y.2d 900, 524 N.Y.S.2d 384, 519 N.E.2d 295.

MEMORANDUM. . . . In early 1980, plaintiff Kel Kim Corp. leased a vacant supermarket in Clifton Park from defendants. The lease was for an initial term of 10 years with two 5–year renewal options. The understanding [was] that plaintiff would use the property as a roller skating rink open to the general public, although the lease did not limit use of the premises to a roller rink.

The lease required Kel Kim to "procure and maintain in full force and effect a public liability insurance policy or policies in a solvent and responsible company . . . of not less than Five Hundred Thousand Dollars . . . to any single person and in the aggregate of not less than One Million Dollars . . . on account of any single accident." Kel Kim obtained the required insurance and for six years operated the facility without incident. In November 1985 its insurance carrier gave notice that the policy would expire on January 6, 1986 and would not be renewed due to uncertainty about the financial condition of the reinsurer, which was then under the management of a court-appointed administrator. Kel Kim [gave] this information to defendants and, it asserts, thereafter made every effort to procure the requisite insurance elsewhere but was unable to do so on account of the liability insurance crisis. Plaintiff ultimately succeeded in obtaining a policy in the aggregate amount of $500,000 effective March 1, 1986 and contends that no insurer would write a policy in excess of that amount on any roller skating rink. As of August 1987, plaintiff procured the requisite coverage.

On January 7, 1986, when plaintiff's initial policy expired and it remained uninsured, defendants sent a notice of default, directing that it cure within 30 days or vacate the premises. Kel Kim and the individual guarantors of the lease then began this declaratory judgment action, urging that they should be excused from compliance with the insurance provision either because performance was impossible or because the inability to procure insurance was within the lease's *force majeure* clause.* Special Term granted defendants' motion for summary judgment, nullified the lease, and

---

* The clause reads: "If either party to this Lease shall be delayed or prevented from the performance of any obligation through no fault of their own by reason of labor disputes, inability to procure materials, failure of utility service, restrictive governmental laws or regulations, riots, insurrection, war, adverse weather, Acts of God, or other similar causes beyond the control of such party, the performance of such obligation shall be excused for the period of the delay."

directed Kel Kim to vacate the premises. A divided Appellate Division affirmed. [We affirm.]

Generally, once a party to a contract has made a promise, that party must perform or respond in damages for its failure, even when unforeseen circumstances make performance burdensome; until the late nineteenth century even impossibility of performance ordinarily did not provide a defense. . . . While such defenses have been recognized in the common law, they have been applied narrowly, due in part to judicial recognition that the purpose of contract law is to allocate the risks that might affect performance and that performance should be excused only in extreme circumstances. . . . Impossibility excuses a party's performance only when the destruction of the subject matter of the contract or the means of performance makes performance objectively impossible. Moreover, the impossibility must be produced by an unanticipated event that could not have been foreseen or guarded against in the contract (see, 407 E. 61st Garage v. Savoy Fifth Ave. Corp., 23 N.Y.2d 275, 296 N.Y.S.2d 338, 244 N.E.2d 37 . . .).

Applying these principles, we conclude that plaintiff's predicament is not within the embrace of the doctrine of impossibility. Kel Kim's inability to procure and maintain requisite coverage could have been foreseen and guarded against when it specifically undertook that obligation in the lease. . . .

For much the same underlying reason, contractual *force majeure* clauses—or clauses excusing nonperformance due to circumstances beyond the control of the parties—under the common law provide a similarly narrow defense. Ordinarily, only if the *force majeure* clause specifically includes the event that actually prevents a party's performance will that party be excused. (See, e.g., . . . Squillante & Congalton, Force Majeure, 80 Com.L.J. 4 [1975].) Here, of course, the contractual provision does not specifically include plaintiff's inability to procure and maintain insurance. Nor does this inability fall within the catchall "or other similar causes beyond the control of such party." The principle of interpretation applicable to such clauses is that the general words are . . . confined to things of the same kind or nature as the particular matters mentioned (see, 18 Williston, Contracts § 1968 [3d ed. 1978]).

We agree with the [majority below] that the events listed in the *force majeure* clause here are different in kind and nature from Kel Kim's inability to procure and maintain public liability insurance. The recited events pertain to a party's ability to conduct day-to-day commercial operations on the premises. While Kel Kim urges that the same may be said of a failure to procure and maintain insurance, such an event is materially different. The requirement that specified amounts of public liability insurance at all times be maintained goes not to frustrated expectations in day-to-day commercial operations on the premises—such as interruptions in the availability of labor, materials and utility services—but to the bargained-for protection of the landlord's unrelated economic interests where the tenant chooses to continue operating a public roller skating rink on the premises.

NOTE

Consider the position that Kel Kim would been in had it prevailed. Although it points to its inability to obtain insurance as falling within the doctrine of impossibility, Kel Kim is not seeking to call off the contract. It wants to continue to enjoy the benefits of the lease, but without the obligation to obtain insurance. The extent to which the existence of an excuse calls off the contract as a whole or merely relieves one party of its own obligation is an issue to which we return in Chapter 6. In all these cases, however, you should consider what consequences should follow if excuse were to be found. To the extent that something unexpected has happened, it is almost always the case that there is a new cost that *someone* will have to bear, one way or the other.

If the contract explicitly assigns a particular risk, there is no occasion to apply the general body of excuse doctrine. The fighting issue is likely to be whether the contract, read in context, reveals an implicit allocation, that is, whether a promise unconditional on its face was in fact "conditioned" on some person or thing. Where resort to surrounding circumstances includes evidence of negotiating history, we have seen that the parol evidence rule is an obstacle for the party seeking to qualify an undertaking. Take for example Luria Bros. & Co. v. Pielet Bros. Scrap Iron & Metal, supra p. 400, where, it was concluded, a term relieving the seller of its obligations in the event its supplier failed is an "inconsistent" term which, if intended to be part of the deal, "surely would have been included" in the written sales confirmation. Whatever the basis for determining that the risk of a contingency's occurrence has been assumed (perhaps an amalgam of commercial context, custom, and the terms of the agreement), presumably the general aim is to place the risk on the party who can best bear it.

Posner & Rosenfield, Impossibility and Related Doctrines in Contract Law: An Economic Analysis, 6 J. Legal Stud. 83 (1977), suggest that risk be assigned by the courts to the "superior risk bearer," unless the contract has clearly allocated it to one of the parties. A party is a superior risk bearer, in their view, because of an ability either to prevent the risk from materializing or to insure against it at a lower cost. Determining which party is the cheaper insurer involves such factors as the costs of assessing the probability that the risk will materialize and its magnitude if it does materialize (risk-appraisal costs), and the costs of eliminating or minimizing the risk through pooling it with other uncertain events (transaction costs).

Applying this analysis to contracts for the supply of agricultural products, the authors generally approve as economically efficient the tendency in the cases to discharge the promisor, after weather or other natural phenomena have created difficulty in performance, where the promisor-supplier is a grower but not where the promisor is a wholesaler or dealer. While no party could prevent the risk from materializing, the dealer is identifiable as the cheaper insurer—and thus the superior risk-bearer—because of an ability to diversify purchases geographically and thereby reduce the risks from unfavorable weather.

If the Posner & Rosenfield analysis is applied to the case that follows, involving disruption of a transportation contract between a ship's owner and hirer, would the outcome be different? It should be noted that the authors themselves conceded the many difficulties in identifying "superior risk bearers," whether case-by-case or by classes of commercial parties or activity.

————

American Trading & Prod. Corp. v. Shell Int'l Marine, Ltd.

United States Court of Appeals, Second Circuit, 1972.
453 F.2d 939.

MULLIGAN, CIRCUIT JUDGE. This is an appeal by American Trading & Prod. Corp. ("owner") from a judgment . . . dismissing its claim against Shell Int'l Marine Ltd. ("charterer") for additional compensation of $131,978.44 for the transportation of cargo from Texas to India via the Cape of Good Hope as a result of the closing of the Suez Canal in June, 1967. . . . The action was tried on stipulated facts and without a jury. . . . We affirm.

The owner is a Maryland corporation doing business in New York and the charterer is a United Kingdom corporation. On March 23, 1967 the parties entered into a contract of voyage charter in New York City which provided that the charterer would hire the owner's tank vessel, WASHINGTON TRADER, for a voyage with a full cargo of lube oil from Beaumont/Smiths Bluff, Texas to Bombay, India. The charter party provided that the freight rate would be in accordance with the then prevailing American Tanker Rate Schedule (ATRS), $14.25 per long ton of cargo, plus seventy-five percent (75%), and in addition there was a charge of $.85 per long ton for passage through the Suez Canal. On May 15, 1967 the WASHINGTON TRADER departed from Beaumont with a cargo of 16,183.32 long tons of lube oil. The charterer paid the freight at the invoiced sum of $417,327.36 on May 26, 1967. On May 29th, 1967 the owner advised the WASHINGTON TRADER by radio to take additional bunkers at Ceuta due to possible diversion because of the Suez Canal crisis. The vessel arrived at Ceuta, Spanish Morocco on May 30, bunkered and sailed on May 31st, 1967. On June 5th the owner cabled the ship's master advising him of various reports of trouble in the Canal and suggested delay in entering it pending clarification. On that very day, the Suez Canal was closed due to the state of war which had developed in the Middle East. The owner then communicated with the charterer on June 5th[,] requesting approval for the diversion of the WASHINGTON TRADER which then had proceeded to a point about 84 miles northwest of Port Said, the entrance to the Canal. On June 6th the charterer responded that under the circumstances it was "for owner to decide whether to continue to wait or make the alternative passage via the Cape since Charter Party Obliges them to deliver cargo without qualification." In response the owner replied on the same day that in view of the closing of the Suez, the WASHINGTON TRADER would proceed to Bombay via the Cape of Good Hope and "[w]e [are] reserving all rights for extra compensation." The vessel proceeded westward, back through the Straits of Gibraltar and around the Cape and eventually arrived in Bombay on July 15th (some 30 days later than initially expected), traveling a total of 18,055 miles instead of the 9,709 miles which it would have sailed had the Canal been open. The owner billed $131,978.44 as extra compensation which the charterer has refused to pay.

. . . [T]he owner argues that transit of the Suez Canal was the agreed specific means of performance of the voyage charter and that the supervening destruction of this means rendered the contract legally impossible to perform and therefore discharged the owner's unperformed obligation (Restatement of Contracts § 460 (1932)). Consequently, when the WASHINGTON TRADER eventually delivered the oil after journeying around the Cape of Good Hope, a benefit was conferred upon the charterer for which it should respond in *quantum meruit*. The validity of this proposition depends upon a finding that the parties contemplated or agreed that the Suez passage was to be the exclusive method of performance. . . . We cannot construe the agreement in such a fashion. The parties contracted for the shipment of the cargo from Texas to India at an agreed rate and the charter party makes absolutely no reference to any fixed route. It is urged that the Suez passage was a condition of performance because the ATRS rate was based on a Suez Canal passage, the invoice contained a specific Suez Canal toll charge and the vessel actually did proceed to a point 84 miles northwest of Port Said. In our view all that this establishes is that both parties contemplated that the Canal would be the probable route. It was the cheapest and shortest, and therefore it was in the interest of both that it be utilized. However, this is not at all equivalent to an agreement that it be the exclusive method of performance. The charter party does not so provide and it seems to have been well understood in the shipping industry that the Cape route is an acceptable alternative in voyages of this character.

The District of Columbia Circuit decided a closely analogous case, Transatlantic Financing Corp. v. United States, 124 U.S.App.D.C. 183, 363 F.2d 312 (1966). There the plaintiff had entered into a voyage charter with defendant in which it agreed to transport a full cargo of wheat on the CHRISTOS from a United States port to Iran. The parties clearly contemplated a Suez passage, but on November 2, 1956 the vessel reduced speed when war blocked the Suez Canal. The vessel changed its course in the Atlantic and eventually delivered its cargo in Iran after proceeding by way of the Cape of Good Hope. In an exhaustive opinion Judge Skelly Wright reviewed the English cases which had considered the same problem and concluded that "the Cape route is generally regarded as an alternative means of performance. So the implied expectation that the route would be via Suez is hardly adequate proof of an allocation to the promisee of the risk of closure. In some cases, even an express expectation may not amount to a condition of performance." [*Transatlantic*], 363 F.2d at 317.

Appellant argues that *Transatlantic* is distinguishable since there was an agreed upon flat rate in that case unlike the instant case where the rate was based on Suez passage. This does not distinguish the case in our view. . . . [T]he only ATRS rate published at the time of the agreement from Beaumont to Bombay was the one utilized as a basis for the negotiated rate ultimately agreed upon. This rate was escalated by 75% to reflect whatever existing market conditions the parties contemplated. These conditions are not stipulated. Had a Cape route rate been requested, which was not the case, it is agreed that the point from which the parties would have bargained would be $17.35 per long ton of cargo as against $14.25 per long ton.

Actually, in *Transatlantic* it was argued that certain provisions in the P. & I. Bunker Deviation Clause referring to the direct and/or customary route required, by implication, a voyage through the Suez Canal. The court responded "[a]ctually they prove only what we are willing to accept—that the parties expected the usual and customary route would be used. The provisions in no way condition performance upon non-occurrence of this contingency." [*Transatlantic*], 363 F.2d at 317 n. 8. We hold that all that the ATRS rate establishes is that the parties obviously expected a Suez passage but there is no indication at all in the instrument or *dehors* that it was a condition of performance.

This leaves us with the question whether the owner was excused from performance on the theory of commercial impracticability (Restatement of Contracts § 454 (1932)). Even though the owner is not excused because of strict impossibility, it is urged that American law recognizes that performance is rendered impossible if it can only be accomplished with extreme and unreasonable difficulty, expense, injury or loss. There is no extreme or unreasonable difficulty apparent here. The alternate route taken was well recognized, and there is no claim that the vessel or the crew or the nature of the cargo made the route actually taken unreasonably difficult, dangerous or onerous. The owner's case here essentially rests upon the element of the additional expense involved—$131,978.44. This represents an increase of less than one third over the agreed upon $417,327.36. We find that this increase in expense is not sufficient to constitute commercial impracticability under either American or English authority. Mere increase in cost alone is not a sufficient excuse for nonperformance (Restatement of Contracts § 467 (1932)). It must be an "extreme and unreasonable" expense (Restatement of Contracts § 454 (1932)).*...

Appellant further seeks to distinguish *Transatlantic* because in that case the change in course was in the mid-Atlantic and added some 300 miles to the voyage while in this case the WASHINGTON TRADER had traversed most of the Mediterranean and thus had added some 9000 miles to the contemplated voyage. It should be noted that although both the time and the length of the altered passage here exceeded those in *Transatlantic*, the additional compensation sought here is just under one third of the contract price. Aside from this however, it is a fact that the master of the WASHINGTON TRADER was alerted by radio on May 29th, 1967 of a "possible diversion because of Suez Canal crisis," but nevertheless two days later he had left Ceuta (opposite Gibraltar) and proceeded across the Mediterranean. While we may not speculate about the foreseeability of a Suez crisis at the time the contract was entered, there does not seem to be any question but that the master here had been actually put on notice before traversing the Mediterranean that diversion was possible. Had the WASHINGTON TRADER then changed course, the time and cost of the Mediterranean trip could reasonably have been avoided, thereby reducing the amount now claimed. (Restatement of Contracts § 336, Comment *d* to subsection (1) (1932))....

Matters involving impossibility or impracticability of performance of contract are concededly vexing and difficult. One is even urged on the allocation of such risks to pray for the "wisdom of Solomon." 6 A. Corbin, Contracts § 1333 (1962). On the basis of all of the facts, the pertinent authority and a further belief in the efficacy of prayer, we affirm.

[The *American Trading* court quotes from, and follows, the "closely analogous" *Transatlantic* decision. There, Judge Wright said: "The surrounding circumstances [such as awareness that the canal might become a dangerous area] do indicate, however, a willingness by [shipowner and carrier] Transatlantic to assume abnormal risks, and this fact [causes] us to

---

* Both parties take solace in the [UCC] which in comment 4 to § 2–615 states that the rise in cost must "alter the essential nature of the performance." This is clearly not the case here. The owner relies on a further sentence in the comment which refers to a severe shortage of raw materials or of supplies due to "war, embargo, local crop failure, unforeseen shutdown of major sources of supply or the like, which either causes a marked increase in cost. . . ." Since this is not a case involving the sale of goods but transportation of a cargo where there was an alternative which was a commercially reasonable substitute (see [UCC] § 2–614(1)) the owner's reliance is misplaced. [The court's other footnotes have been omitted.—Eds.]

judge the impracticability of performance by an alternative route in stricter terms than we would were the contingency unforeseen." Turning to the impracticability issue, which, like *American Trading*, was urged solely on the basis of added expense, Judge Wright observed: "Transatlantic was no less able than the United States [the cargo shipper] to purchase insurance to cover the contingency's occurrence. If anything, it is more reasonable to expect owner-operators of vessels to insure against the hazards of war. They are in the best position to calculate the cost of performance by alternative routes (and therefore to estimate the amount of insurance required), and are undoubtedly sensitive to international troubles which uniquely affect the demand for and cost of their services."]

––––––––

YPI 180 N. LaSalle Owner, LLC v. 180 N. LaSalle II, LLC

Appellate Court of Illinois, 2010.
403 Ill. App. 3d 1, 933 N.E.2d 860.

HALL, J. . . . On August 12, 2008, defendant-appellee, 180 N. LaSalle II, LLC (LaSalle), as seller, and Younan Properties, Inc. (Younan), as purchaser, entered into a purchase agreement (contract), for the sale and purchase of commercial property located at 180 North LaSalle Street, Chicago, Illinois. The purchase price was $124 million. The purchase price (less earnest money) was to be deposited with an escrow agent two business days prior to closing. Pursuant to the contract, Younan deposited initial earnest money of $2.5 million into an escrow account.

Between August 29, 2008, and September 30, 2008, LaSalle and Younan executed three amendments to the contract. The first amendment extended the time in which Younan could evaluate and then terminate the contract if it decided to do so. In the second amendment, LaSalle and Younan acknowledged that the time to terminate the contract had expired, and as a result, Younan deposited an additional $2.5 million in earnest money with the escrow agent.

In the third amendment, LaSalle provided Younan with a $500,000 credit against the purchase price, and Younan deposited an additional $1 million in earnest money with the escrow agent. LaSalle and Younan also directed the escrow agent to release $1 million of the earnest money to LaSalle and agreed that the released earnest money would be credited against the purchase price at closing but was "hereby deemed earned by Seller and shall be non-refundable to Purchaser for any reason whatsoever except in the event of a default by Seller of Seller's obligations to close the sale or a failure of a condition to Purchaser's obligation to close the sale."

On October 9, 2008, Younan assigned all of its rights, title, and interest in the contract to plaintiff-appellant, YPI 180 N. LaSalle Owner, LLC (YPI). The assignment provided that Younan remained liable under the contract.

In early October 2008, Younan received notice that one of its lenders, Allied Irish Bank, had pulled out of the financing arrangement on the ground that economic conditions in Ireland beyond the bank's control or anticipation had forced it to withdraw from the credit markets.

Between October 15, 2008, and December 9, 2008, LaSalle, and this time YPI, executed additional amendments to the contract. On October 15, 2008, pursuant to the fourth amendment to the contract, LaSalle and YPI directed the escrow agent to release the remaining earnest money to LaSalle and also agreed that the earnest money would be credited at closing and was deemed earned by seller and non-refundable, except in the event of default by seller of seller's obligations to close the sale. In return, the parties extended the closing date to December 17, 2008.

Also in the fourth amendment, LaSalle and YPI acknowledged the assignment and agreed that Younan would be jointly and severally liable with YPI for buyer's obligations under the contract. Younan joined in execution of the fourth amendment.

On November 20, 2008, LaSalle and YPI executed a fifth amendment to the contract. Under this amendment, LaSalle agreed to reduce the purchase price by $4 million, and YPI waived the option to extend the closing date beyond December 17, 2008. Younan joined in execution of the fifth amendment.

On December 9, 2008, LaSalle and YPI executed a sixth and final amendment to the contract. Under this amendment, the parties agreed to extend the closing date to no later than February 18, 2009. Younan also joined in execution of this sixth amendment.

When Younan failed to close on purchase of the commercial property, LaSalle terminated the contract and retained the deposited earnest money as its sole remedy for breach of the contract. Shortly thereafter, YPI filed the underlying complaint against LaSalle seeking to rescind the contract and recover $6 million in earnest money retained by LaSalle.

YPI argued that pursuant to the contract-law doctrine of impossibility of performance, it was excused from performing under the contract due to the 2008 global credit crisis which it claimed prevented it and Younan from obtaining the commercially-practical financing contemplated when the contract was originally formed.

Following a hearing, the trial court granted LaSalle's . . . motion to dismiss, striking YPI's complaint with prejudice and without leave to amend. This timely appeal followed. . . .

Impossibility of performance as a ground for rescission of a contract refers to those factual situations where the purposes for which the contract was made have, on one side, become impossible to perform. The doctrine of impossibility of performance in contract was recognized by our supreme court in Leonard v. Autocar Sales & Service Co., 392 Ill. 182, 187, 64 N.E.2d 477 (1945).

The doctrine excuses performance where performance is rendered objectively impossible due to destruction of the subject matter of the contract or by operation of law. This doctrine has been narrowly applied "due in part to judicial recognition that the purpose of contract law is to allocate the risks that might affect performance and that performance should be excused only in extreme circumstances." Kel Kim Corp. v. Central Markets, Inc., 70 N.Y.2d 900, 902, 519 N.E.2d 295, 296, 524 N.Y.S.2d 384, 386 (1987).

The party advancing the doctrine must show that the events or circumstances which he claims rendered his performance impossible were not reasonably foreseeable at the time of contracting. Where a contingency that causes the impossibility might have been anticipated or guarded against in the contract, it must be provided for by the terms of the contract or else impossibility does not excuse performance.

In this case, YPI argues that its performance under the contract was made impossible due to the 2008 global credit crisis, which it claimed prevented it and Younan from obtaining the commercially-practical financing contemplated when the contract was originally made. YPI's argument is misplaced.

Even if the global credit crisis made it difficult, to nearly impossible, to procure the sought-after commercial financing, this is not the relevant issue. The primary issue is whether it was foreseeable that a commercial lender might not provide Younan and YPI with the financing they sought. Even without the global credit crisis of 2008, it was foreseeable that a commercial lender might not provide Younan and YPI with the financing they sought.

foreseeability

The potential inability to obtain commercial financing is generally considered a foreseeable risk that can be readily guarded against by inclusion in the contract of financing contingency provisions. If the inability to obtain commercial financing, standing alone, were sufficient to excuse performance under the doctrine of impossibility of performance, then the law binding contractual parties to their agreements would be of no consequence.

In addition, the doctrine of impossibility of performance does not apply to excuse performance "as long as it lies within the power of the promisor to remove the obstacle to performance." Felbinger & Co. v. Traiforos, 76 Ill.App.3d 725, 733, 31 Ill.Dec. 906, 394 N.E.2d 1283 (1979). The underlying complaint alleged that Younan's current assets exceeded $1.6 billion. Nothing in the record indicates that Younan lacked sufficient assets or equity to pay the contract purchase price. To the extent its resources were not liquid, nothing in the record suggests it would have been impossible for Younan to convert its nonliquid assets to liquid assets in order to pay the contract purchase price.

We find that under the facts and circumstances of this case, as a matter of law, Younan's and YPI's failure to obtain the commercially-practical financing they sought was not an adequate ground to rescind the contract under the doctrine of impossibility of performance. . . .

———

Dawson, Judicial Revision of Frustrated Contracts: The United States
64 Boston U.L.Rev. 1, 25–26, 37–38 (1984)

"Miscalculation by a supplier reached a new scale of magnitude in the contracts of Westinghouse Electric to supply 49 nuclear power plants with their requirements of uranium. The 27 utilities that owned the sites where these plants were projected wanted assurances before making the necessary huge investment in nuclear plant and equipment, of which Westinghouse was a major supplier. The assurances they received took the form of contracts, mostly made in the early 1970s, for Westinghouse to supply the requirements of uranium for these plants when in operation, at fixed prices—$8 or $10 (up to $12) a pound. . . . [T]he market price of uranium began to rise sharply in 1974. In September, 1975, when Westinghouse announced that it could not and would not perform further, the market price approached $40 a pound and later went higher. The guesses as to how much Westinghouse would lose if it performed all its contracts for their full terms (on the doubtful assumption they could procure the supplies) started from a base of two billion dollars and went considerably higher. In actions for damages by thirteen power companies, consolidated in a trial that lasted six months, the conclusion reached by the trial judge was that Westinghouse had no sufficient excuse and was liable full scale for expectancy damages. [Since this decision has not been reported, the main events have been described only in newspaper reports. The 13 actions for damages brought in different parts of the country were consolidated for trial in Virginia, in In re Westinghouse Elec. Corp. Uranium Contracts Litig., 405 F.Supp. 316 (J.P.M.D.L1975). . . . An excellent account of the economic and legal background and of the astonishing lack of foresight shown by the Westinghouse management is given by Joskow, Commercial Impossibility, The Uranium Market and the Westinghouse Case, 6 J.Legal Stud. 119, 143–50 (1977).] Unfortunately for posterity a reasoned opinion was not filed but this may have been just as well for Westinghouse, since its damage-claim creditors, motivated presumably by their own self-interest in preserving it as a fully functioning enterprise, agreed to settlements that were vastly more lenient than any that a court would have been bold enough to propose. [Extremely lenient terms in the settlements that Westinghouse was able to secure assisted it greatly in wiping out the effects of this potentially fatal episode. N.Y.Times, March 15, 1981, § 3, at 1.]

"So the question becomes whether, as the interests at stake rise higher on a scale of magnitude and the complexities of the performances multiply, these are reasons for judges to intervene and impose new terms that to them will seem more workable and fair. . . .

"The first reason that I have urged (for me it is a sufficient reason) for judges to abstain from rewriting the contracts of other people is that they are not qualified for such tasks. Nothing in their prior training as lawyers or their experience in directing litigation and giving coherence to its results will qualify them to invent viable new designs for disrupted enterprises, now gone awry, that the persons most concerned had tried to construct but without success. . . . The second reason, however, is important enough to be stated first for it raises an issue that I regard as a major issue of civil liberty. The question that I have repeatedly raised but have not tried to answer is the question—when an unforeseen event has so drastically altered a contract that the parties to it are fully excused from its further performance, from what source does any court derive the power to impose on them a new contract without the free assent of both? Where rescission is awarded on any of the other standard grounds— fraud, mistake,* substantial breach, defective capacity, duress—no one has even

---

* If one could imagine, as I cannot, that an expected rise in energy costs occurring nine years after the contract was a mistake of present fact, it would have to be described . . . as a mistake in a "basic assumption." For this the standard remedies, if any were to be granted, would all require rescission of the contract. How far-fetched the notion of court-ordered revision would have seemed in such a case can be illustrated by imagining a variation on a time-worn relic of our contract law, the sale of the fertile cow. Sherwood v. Walker, 66 Mich. 568, 33 N.W. 919 (1887). The cow was Rose of Aberlone, of distinguished Scottish lineage, who was believed by its owner to be sterile and was sold to a local banker for a price that was calculated to be her value as beef. She was in fact pregnant at the time of the sale and therefore worth about ten times the price agreed. Should the seller be told that he could not keep the cow, as the court allowed him to do in the original case, and that he must deliver her to the buyer, but that he would be given judgment for the value of a well-bred pregnant cow[,] an amount that

suggested that such a power lay hidden somewhere. For myself, I do not propose to spend time looking for the source of the power. I am convinced that it does not exist."

———————

Krell v. Henry

Court of Appeal, 1903.
[1903] 2 K.B. 740.

Appeal from a decision of Darling, J. The plaintiff, Paul Krell, sued the defendant, C.S. Henry for £50, being the balance of a sum of £75, for which the defendant had agreed to hire a flat at 56A, Pall Mall on the days of June 26 and 27, for the purpose of viewing the processions to be held in connection with the coronation of His Majesty [Edward VII]. The defendant denied his liability, and counterclaimed for the return of the sum of £25, which had been paid as a deposit, on the ground that, the processions not having taken place owing to the serious illness of the King, there had been a total failure of consideration for the contract. . . .

The facts [were undisputed]. The plaintiff on leaving the country in March, 1902, left instructions with his solicitor to let his suite of chambers at 56A, Pall Mall on such terms and for such period (not exceeding six months) as he thought proper. On June 17, 1902, the defendant noticed an announcement in the windows of the plaintiff's flat to the effect that windows to view the coronation processions were to be let. The defendant interviewed the housekeeper on the subject, when it was pointed out to him what a good view of the processions could be obtained from the premises, and he eventually agreed with the housekeeper to take the suite for the two days in question for a sum of £75.

On June 20, the defendant wrote the following letter to the plaintiff's solicitor: "I am in receipt of yours of the 18th instant, inclosing form of agreement for the suite of chambers on the third floor at 56A, Pall Mall, which I have agreed to take for the two days the 26th and 27th instant, for the sum of £75. For reasons given you I cannot enter into the agreement, but as arranged over the telephone I inclose herewith cheque for £25, as deposit, and will thank you to confirm to me that I shall have the entire use of these rooms during the days (not the nights) of the 26th and 27th instant. You may rely that every care will be taken of the premises and their contents. On the 24th inst. I will pay the balance, viz., £50, to complete the £75 agreed upon."

On the same day the defendant received the following reply from the plaintiff's solicitor: "I am in receipt of your letter of today's date inclosing cheque for £25 deposit on your agreeing to take Mr. Krell's chambers on the third floor at 56A, Pall Mall for the two days, the 26th and 27th June, and I confirm the agreement that you are to have the entire use of these rooms during the days (but not the nights), the balance, £50, to be paid to me on Tuesday next the 24th instant."

———————

the court would fix with perhaps the help of a jury? If the buyer then protested that he did not want the cow if he had to pay for it a sum possibly ten times as much as he had agreed to pay, there would not be much comfort in the only justification that a judge could give—that being a banker he could afford it.

The processions not having taken place [on] June 26 and 27, the defendant declined to pay the balance of £50. . . . Hence the present action. Darling J., held, upon the authority of Taylor v. Caldwell, 3 B. & S. 826, and The Moorcock, (1889) 14 P.D. 64, that there was an implied condition in the contract that the procession should take place, and gave judgment for the defendant on the claim and counter-claim. The plaintiff appealed.

VAUGHAN WILLIAMS, L.J. The real question [here] is the extent of the application in English law of the principle of the Roman law which has been adopted and acted on in many English decisions, and notably in the case of Taylor v. Caldwell, 3 B. & S. 826. That case at least makes it clear that "where, from the nature of the contract, it appears that the parties must from the beginning have known that it could not be fulfilled unless. . . . some particular specified thing continued to exist, so that when entering into the contract they must have contemplated such continued existence as the foundation of what was to be done; there, [absent] any express or implied warranty that the thing shall exist, the contract is not to be considered a positive contract, but as subject to an implied condition that the parties shall be excused in case, before breach, performance becomes impossible from the perishing of the thing without default of the contractor." Thus far it is clear that the principle of the Roman law has been introduced into the English law. . . .

I do not think that [the principle] is limited to cases in which the event causing the impossibility of performance is the destruction or nonexistence of some thing which is the subject-matter of the contract or of some condition or state of things expressly specified as a condition of it. I think that you first have to ascertain, not necessarily from the terms of the contract, but, if required, from necessary inferences, drawn from surrounding circumstances[,] what is the substance of the contract, and then to ask the question whether that substantial contract needs for its foundation the assumption of the existence of a particular state of things. If it does, this will limit the operation of the general words, and [if] the contract becomes impossible of performance by reason of the nonexistence of the state of things assumed by both contracting parties as the foundation of the contract, there will be no breach of the contract thus limited.

Now what are the facts of the present case? The contract is contained in [the] two letters of June 20. . . . These letters do not mention the coronation, but speak merely of the taking of Mr. Krell's chambers, or, rather, of the use of them. . . . [T]he plaintiff [had] exhibited on his premises, third floor, 56A, Pall Mall, an announcement to the effect that windows to view the Royal coronation procession were to be let, and [defendant] was induced by that announcement to apply to the housekeeper on the premises, who said that the owner was willing to let the suite of rooms for the purpose of seeing the Royal procession for both days, but not nights, of June 26 and 27. . . . [T]he use of the rooms was . . . for the purpose of seeing the Royal procession. It was not a demise of the rooms, or even an agreement to let and take the rooms. It is a license to use rooms for a particular purpose and none other. [And] the taking place of those processions on the days proclaimed along the proclaimed route, which passed 56A, Pall Mall, was regarded by both contracting parties as the foundation of the contract; and I think that it cannot reasonably be supposed to have been in the contemplation of the contracting parties, when the contract was made, that the coronation would not be held on the proclaimed days, or the processions not take place on those days along the proclaimed route. . . .

It was suggested in the course of the argument that if the occurrence, on the proclaimed days, of the coronation and the procession in this case were the foundation of the contract, and if the general words are thereby limited or qualified, so that in the event of the nonoccurrence of the coronation and procession along the proclaimed route they would discharge both parties from further performance of the contract, it would follow that if a cabman was engaged to take some one to Epsom on Derby Day at a suitable enhanced price for such a journey, say £10, both parties to the contract would be discharged in the contingency of the race at Epsom for some reason becoming impossible; but I do not think this follows, for I do not think that in the cab case the happening of the race would be the foundation of the contract. No doubt the purpose of the engager would be to go to see the Derby, and the price would be proportionately high; but the cab had no special qualifications for the purpose which led to the selection of the cab for this particular occasion. Any other cab would have done as well. Moreover, under the cab contract, the hirer, even if the race went off, could have said, "Drive me to Epsom; I will pay you the agreed sum; you have nothing to do with the purpose for which I hired the cab," and if the cabman refused he would have been guilty of a breach of contract, there being nothing to qualify his promise to drive the hirer to Epsom on a particular day. Whereas in the case of the coronation, there is not merely the purpose of the hirer to see the coronation procession, but it is the coronation procession and the relative position of the rooms which is the basis of the contract as much for the lessor as the hirer; and I think that if the King, before the coronation day and after the contract, had died, the hirer could not have insisted on having the rooms on the days named. It could not in the cab case be reasonably said that seeing the Derby race was the foundation of the contract. . . . Whereas in the present case, where the rooms were offered and taken, by reason of their peculiar suitability from the position of the rooms for a view of the coronation procession, surely the view of the coronation procession was the foundation of the contract, which is a very different thing from the purpose of the man who engaged the cab—namely, to see the race—being held to be the foundation of the contract. Each case must be judged by its own circumstances. In each case one must ask oneself first, what, having regard to all the circumstances, was the foundation of the contract? Secondly, was the performance of the contract prevented? Thirdly, was the event which prevented the performance of the contract of such a character that it cannot reasonably be said to have been in the contemplation of the parties at the date of the contract? If all these questions are answered in the affirmative (as I think they should be in this case), both parties are discharged from further performance of the contract. . . . [T]he coronation procession was the foundation of this contract, and the non-happening of it prevented the performance of the contract. . . . The test seems to be whether the event which causes the impossibility was or might have been anticipated and guarded against. It seems difficult to say, in a case where both parties anticipate the happening of an event, which anticipation is the foundation of the contract, that either party must be taken to have anticipated, and ought to have guarded against, the event which prevented the performance of the contract. . . .

[Here,] where we have to ask ourselves whether the object of the contract was frustrated by the non-happening of the coronation procession[,] parol evidence is admissible to shew that the subject of the contract was rooms to view the coronation procession. . . . When once this is established, I see no difficulty whatever in the case. It is not essential to the application of the principle of Taylor v. Caldwell that the direct subject of the contract should perish or fail to be in existence at the date of performance of the contract. It is sufficient if a state of things or condition expressed in the contract and essential to its performance perishes or fails to be in existence at that time. . . . This disposes of the plaintiff's claim for £50 unpaid balance of the price agreed. . . . The defendant at one time set up a cross-claim for the return of the £25 he paid at the date of the contract. As that claim is now withdrawn it is unnecessary to say anything about it. I have only to add that the facts of this case do not bring it within the principle laid down in Stubbs v. Holywell Ry. Co., L.R., 2 Ex. 311, that in the case of contracts falling directly within the rule of Taylor v. Caldwell the subsequent impossibility does not affect rights already acquired, because the defendant had the whole of June 24 to pay the balance, and the public announcement that the coronation and processions would not take place on the proclaimed days was made early on the morning of the 24th, and no cause of action could accrue till the end of that day. . . .

Appeal dismissed.

COMMENT: RELIEF FOLLOWING DISCHARGE

In Krell v. Henry, as the court pointed out, defendant had abandoned his counterclaim for restitution of the £25 sent in with his letter of June 20. The court therefore did not have to face the question whether money already paid on the contract must be restored. Also, since the £50 sued for by the plaintiff was not due until the end of the day on which the illness of the king was announced, June 24, the court did not have to face another question—what if the £50 was already due (say on June 22) and unpaid, so that plaintiff's right to that sum was "already acquired"?

Both of these questions were raised the next year in Chandler v. Webster, [1904] 1 K.B. 493, where the Court of Appeal held on very similar facts that (1) money paid down before the king's illness was announced could not be recovered, and (2) money due before the frustrating event must be paid by the hirer of the unused room. The court put it that "the law leaves the parties where they were, and relieves them both from further performance of the contract." It would have been more accurate to say that the parties were to be left at the point where they *contracted* to be at the moment when the unexpected event occurred. The court admitted that this result was "to some extent an arbitrary one," but justified it by saying: "Time has elapsed and the position of both parties may have been more or less altered, and it is impossible to adjust or ascertain the rights of both parties with exactitude." The absurdity of this solution is at once apparent. The parties were left suspended at the point where they had planned to be when the unforeseen event occurred, despite the conclusion already reached by the court that their contractual plan had been so shattered that the contract could not be enforced.

This solution—suspension in midair, leaving in place obligations already matured—has been rejected by almost all American courts, and was rejected in England in the *Fibrosa* case in 1943 (Fibrosa Spolka Akcyjna v. Fairbairn L.C.B., Ltd., [1943] A.C. 32). But the *Fibrosa* case brought to the surface the problem that evidently made the judge in Chandler v. Webster so uneasy—what if one of the parties, before the supervening event, had made expenditures in preparing to perform? For example, what if the owner of the hired space in Krell v. Henry had erected stands for the onlookers in conformity with the terms of the hiring agreement and these stands were useless for any other purpose? In the *Fibrosa* case, an English manufacturer had agreed to manufacture, deliver, and install, in Poland, textile machinery ordered by Fibrosa, a Polish company. Delivery and installation of the machinery became impossible after the German invasion of Poland and Britain's declaration of war. Of the contract price of £4800, Fibrosa had paid £1000. When Fibrosa demanded return of the £1000, the seller refused to return it on the ground that "considerable work had been done on the machines." Fibrosa's action for restitution ultimately succeeded in the House of Lords; the full £1000 was recovered without any deduction for the seller's loss in work done on this special order. The common law, the judges concluded, "does not attempt to apportion a prepaid sum in such circumstances" and any remedy would have to come from the legislature.

Parliament did respond with the Law Reform (Frustrated Contracts) Act, 1943 (6 & 7 Geo. VI, c. 40). The effect of this statute is to allow restitution of money paid, and of the value of any "benefit" conferred through part performance of a frustrated contract, but, if the court "considers it just to do so," it may allow deduction of expenses incurred by the receiver of the benefit if these expenses were incurred before the supervening event and were "in, or for the purpose of, the performance of the contract." Thus, a compromise is struck. Reliance losses are deductible from restitution claims, and they are collectible to the extent of any payment or performance that was due from the opposite party before the supervening event occurred. But the effect of the statute, if it had been in force at the time of the *Fibrosa* contract, would have been that if the buyer had paid or owed nothing to the seller at the time Poland was invaded by Hitler's army, there would have been no recovery by the seller for its reliance losses, since there would be no restitution claim from which a deduction could be made.

In American decisions, which generally allow restitution of the value of performances already rendered in impossibility or frustration cases (recall, for example, Louisville & Nashville R.R. Co. v. Crowe, supra p. 564, and see J & M Constr., Inc. v. Southam, 722 P.2d 779 (Utah 1986)), the concept of "benefit" often becomes so attenuated as to give disguised protection to the reliance interest. This is particularly clear in cases like Carroll v. Bowersock, supra p. 558, where recovery is allowed for labor and materials contributed to a structure and the structure is then totally destroyed. The test of "incorporation" into the structure, which reflects the compromise usually adopted in such cases, is stretched quite far at times. For example, in Angus v. Scully, 176 Mass. 357, 57 N.E. 674 (1900), recovery was allowed for the value of services rendered in moving a house, when the house was totally destroyed by an accidental fire after being moved half way to its destination. This case was relied on in Albre Marble & Tile Co. v. John Bowen Co., 338 Mass. 394, 155 N.E.2d 437 (1959), to justify recovery by a subcontractor for the fair value of work and labor in preparing "samples, shop drawings, tests and affidavits" for the tile and marble to be placed in a hospital. The subcontractor's work on the plans was wasted and no tile or marble was ever "incorporated" in the hospital, because the state cancelled its contract for the construction of the hospital. One interesting feature of the court's opinion was its suggestion that degrees of fault could be taken into account. The state's cancellation of the hospital contract had occurred because the general contractor had not complied with statutory requirements in preparing its bid. The Massachusetts court had already held that defendant was not liable in damages, since the state's cancellation made his performance impossible. But since defendant had been involved in "creating" the impossibility and plaintiff, the sub, had not, the court concluded that plaintiff should be reimbursed for its wasted expenditure.

There continues to be limited case authority explicitly awarding reliance expenditures in impossibility and frustration situations. (The departure from restitution's "wrought into" principle in *Albre Marble & Tile*, noted above, was accompanied by a disclaimer of any intention to lay down a "broader principle" than the "peculiar" facts of the case warranted.) Over the years, however, arguments for apportionment or splitting of reliance losses in such cases have appeared in the literature. E.g., Note, Apportioning Loss After Discharge of a Burdensome Contract: A Statutory Solution, 69 Yale L.J. 1054 (1960). The Restatement of Contracts, Second § 272, comment b, takes the position that recovery in impossibility and frustration cases "may go beyond mere restitution and include elements of reliance by the claimant even though they have not benefitted the other party."

————————

PROBLEM

Grand Hotel and Pride Sports Club, unrelated businesses, entered into a five-year contract under which Grand was to pay Pride $3,000 a month for making its exercise facilities and programs available to Grand's hotel guests free of charge to them. A year into the contract, Grand Hotel was totally destroyed by a fire of accidental origin and ceased operations altogether (rebuilding was not economically feasible). When Grand refused to make further payments under the contract, Pride brought suit for breach. (1) Does Grand have the defense of discharge? (2) Had the fire destroyed Pride Sports Club, not the hotel, would Pride be liable to Grand for breach of contract?

————————

Lloyd v. Murphy
25 Cal.2d 48, 153 P.2d 47 (1944)

TRAYNOR, J., writing: "The courts have required a promisor seeking to excuse himself from performance to prove that the risk of the frustrating event was not reasonably foreseeable and that the value of counterperformance is totally or nearly totally destroyed, for frustration is no defense if it was foreseeable or controllable by the promisor, or if counterperformance remains valuable. . . . Thus laws or other governmental acts that make performance unprofitable or more difficult or expensive do not excuse the duty to perform a contractual obligation. . . .

"At the time [this] lease was executed the National Defense Act, approved June 28, 1940, authorizing the President to allocate materials and mobilize industry for national defense, had been law for more than a year. The automotive industry was in the process of conversion to supply the needs of our growing mechanized army and to meet lend-lease commitments. Iceland and Greenland had been occupied by the army. Automobile sales were soaring because the public anticipated that production would soon be restricted. These facts

were commonly known and it cannot be said that the risk of war and its consequences necessitating restriction of the production and sale of automobiles was
so remote a contingency that its risk could not be foreseen by [the lessee], an
experienced automobile dealer. Indeed, the conditions prevailing at the time
the lease was executed, and the absence of any provision in the lease contracting against the effect of war, gives rise to the inference that the risk was assumed. Defendant has therefore failed to prove that the possibility of war and
its consequences on the production and sale of new automobiles was an unanticipated circumstance wholly outside the contemplation of the parties. Nor has
defendant sustained the burden of proving that the value of the lease has been
destroyed. The sale of automobiles was not made impossible or illegal but merely restricted and if governmental regulation does not entirely prohibit the business to be carried on in the leased premises but only limits or restricts it,
thereby making it less profitable and more difficult to continue, the lease is not
terminated or the lessee excused from further performance. . . ."

Weyerhaeuser Real Estate Co. v. Stoneway Concrete, Inc.
96 Wash.2d 558, 637 P.2d 647 (1981)

Plaintiff landowner and defendant Stoneway entered into a nine-year
mineral lease for the strip mining of sand and gravel, anticipating no more
than a wait of two years before obtaining the state and local permits needed to
begin operations. But a large public outcry over the environmental impact of
the proposed project and strip mining in general stymied the approval process.
After five years of applications, hearings, and litigation, Stoneway, anticipating
further delays and costs with no guarantee of ever obtaining the permits,
abandoned the project. Plaintiff sued to recover the minimum rentals called for
by the contract ($10,000 a year for two years, $25,000 for each year thereafter),
relying on the following provision: "This basic minimum annual rental shall be
due and payable irrespective of whether Lessee produces any minerals from the
leasehold." The agreement also included a term granting Stoneway the option
to terminate the lease, by giving one-year's notice at the end of any contract
year, if in Stoneway's "reasonable judgment the mining operations contemplated hereby have become uneconomical." The trial court ruled for Stoneway but
was reversed by an intermediate appellate court, which rejected Stoneway's
defense of commercial frustration because (1) the parties had agreed upon a
remedy in the event the project became economically unfeasible, and (2) the
payment of rent was not conditioned on Stoneway's success in the venture.
Held, reversed and remanded for entry of the trial court's judgment for
Stoneway. All must agree that there was frustration of purpose and that
Stoneway was without fault. The only question is whether the supervening
event was contemplated and its risk allocated by the contract. Even though the
parties were mindful of a lengthy permit-application process, they "simply did
not anticipate the flood of environmental legislation and litigation that ensued
. . . and which motivated environmentalists to adamant opposition to projects of
this type. . . . [T]here is no indication that they could, or did, anticipate the response of the public." Nor did the parties allocate the risk of such public opposition by the minimum annual-rental clause, which was intended merely to "discourage idleness and procrastination when it was permissible to mine." One
justice dissented, saying: "[T]he majority holds that, although the parties clear-

ly understood the permits might be *difficult* to obtain, they were unable to foresee that the venture might prove *impossible* because of hostile public reaction and legal opposition. This is specious reasoning. . . . It is well known that public sentiment is both fluid and changeable."

Chase Precast Corp. v. John J. Paonessa Co.

Supreme Judicial Court of Massachusetts, 1991.
409 Mass. 371, 566 N.E.2d 603.

LYNCH, J. . . . The claim of the plaintiff, Chase Precast Corp. (Chase), arises from the cancellation of its contracts with [defendant] Paonessa to supply median barriers in a highway reconstruction project of the Commonwealth. Chase brought an action to recover its anticipated profit on the amount of median barriers called for by its supply contracts with Paonessa but not produced. Paonessa brought a cross action against the Commonwealth for indemnification in the event it should be held liable to Chase. After a jury-waived trial, [the] judge ruled for Paonessa on the basis of impossibility of performance.[1] Chase and Paonessa cross appealed. The Appeals Court affirmed, noting that the doctrine of frustration of purpose more accurately described the basis of the trial judge's decision than the doctrine of impossibility. [28 Mass.App.Ct. 639, 554 N.E.2d 868 (1990).] We agree [and] we now affirm.

. . . In 1982, the Commonwealth, through the Department of Public Works (department), entered into two contracts with Paonessa for resurfacing and improvements to two stretches of Route 128. Part of each contract called for replacing a grass median strip between the north and southbound lanes with concrete surfacing and precast concrete median barriers. Paonessa entered into two contracts with Chase under which Chase was to supply, in the aggregate, 25,800 linear feet of concrete median barriers according to the [department's] specifications for highway construction. . . .

The highway reconstruction began in the spring of 1983. By late May, the department was receiving protests from angry residents who objected to use of the concrete median barriers and removal of the grass median strip. Paonessa and Chase became aware of the protest around June 1. On June 6, a group of 100 citizens filed [a suit] to stop installation of the concrete median barriers and other aspects of the work. On June 7, anticipating modification by the department, Paonessa notified Chase by letter to stop producing concrete barriers for the projects. Chase did so upon receipt of the letter the following day. On June 17, the department and the citizens' group entered into a settlement which provided, in part, that no additional concrete median barriers would be installed. On June 23, the department deleted the permanent concrete median barriers item from its contracts with Paonessa.

---

[1] The judge also ruled that the Department of Public Works had the right to cancel the order for median barriers under its general contracts with Paonessa, particularly under subsection 4.06 of those contracts. See note 3, infra.

[The court's footnotes are renumbered; some are omitted.—Eds.]

Before stopping production on June 8, Chase had produced approximately one-half of the median barriers called for by its contracts with Paonessa, and had delivered most of them to the construction sites. Paonessa paid Chase for all that it had produced, at the contract price. Chase suffered no out-of-pocket expense as a result of cancellation of the remaining portion of barriers.

This court has long recognized and applied the doctrine of impossibility. . . . See, e.g., Boston Plate & Window Glass Co. v. John Bowen Co., 335 Mass. 697, 141 N.E.2d 715 (1957). . . . On the other hand, although we have referred to the doctrine of frustration of purpose[,] we have never clearly defined it. See Mishara Constr. Co. v. Transit–Mixed Concrete Corp., 365 Mass. 122, 310 N.E.2d 363 (1974). . . . Other jurisdictions have explained the doctrine as follows: when an event neither anticipated nor caused by either party, the risk of which was not allocated by the contract, destroys the object or purpose of the contract, thus destroying the value of performance, the parties are excused from further performance. [See] Lloyd v. Murphy, 25 Cal.2d 48, 153 P.2d 47 (1944).

In *Mishara Constr. Co.*, we called frustration of purpose a "companion rule" to the doctrine of impossibility.[2] . . . [A] definition of frustration of purpose is found in the Restatement (Second) of Contracts § 265 (1981):

> Where, after a contract is made, a party's principal purpose is substantially frustrated without his fault by the occurrence of an event the non-occurrence of which was a basic assumption on which the contract was made, his remaining duties to render performance are discharged, unless the language or the circumstances indicate the contrary.

This definition is nearly identical to the defense of "commercial impracticability," found in the [UCC], G.L. c. 106, § 2–615, which this court, in *Mishara*[,] held to be consistent with the common law of contracts regarding impossibility of performance. . . .

Paonessa bore no responsibility for the department's elimination of the median barriers from the projects. Therefore, whether it can rely on the defense of frustration turns on whether elimination of the barriers was a risk allocated by the contracts to Paonessa. *Mishara*, 365 Mass. at 129, articulates the relevant test:

> The question is, given the commercial circumstances in which the parties dealt: Was the contingency which developed one which the parties could reasonably be thought to have foreseen as a real possibility which could affect performance? Was it one of that variety of risks which the parties were tacitly assigning to the promisor by their failure to provide for it explicitly? If it was, performance will be required. If it could not be so considered, performance is excused.

---

[2] Clearly frustration of purpose is a more accurate label for the defense argued in this case[,] since "[p]erformance was not literally impossible. Nothing prevented Paonessa from honoring its contract to purchase the remaining sections of median barrier, whether or not the [department] would approve their use in the road construction." 28 Mass.App.Ct. 639, 644 n. 5, 554 N.E.2d 868 (1990).

. . . Paonessa's contracts with the department contained a standard provision allowing the department to eliminate items or portions of work found unnecessary.[3] The purchase order agreements between Chase and Paonessa[,] [which were prepared by Chase,] do not contain a similar provision. This difference in the contracts does not mandate the conclusion that Paonessa assumed the risk of reduction in the quantity of the barriers. It is implicit in the judge's findings that Chase knew the barriers were for department projects [and] that Chase was aware of the department's power to decrease quantities of contract items. . . . Chase had been a supplier of median barriers to the department in the past. The provision giving the department the power to eliminate items or portions thereof was standard in its contracts. . . . The judge found that Chase had furnished materials under and was familiar with the so-called "Unit Price Philosophy" in the construction industry, whereby contract items are paid for at the contract unit price for the quantity of work actually accepted. Finally, the judge's finding that "[a]ll parties were well aware that lost profits were not an element of damage in either of the public works projects in issue" further supports the conclusion that Chase was aware of the department's power to decrease quantities, since the term prohibiting claims for anticipated profit is part of the same sentence in the standard provision as that allowing the engineer to eliminate items or portions of work.

In *Mishara*, we held that, although labor disputes in general cannot be considered extraordinary, whether the parties in a particular case intended performance to be carried out, even in the face of a labor difficulty, depends on the facts known to the parties at the time of contracting with respect to the history of and prospects for labor difficulties. [Here,] even if the parties were aware generally of the department's power to eliminate contract items, the judge could reasonably have concluded that they did not contemplate the cancellation for a major portion of the project of such a widely used item as concrete median barriers, and did not allocate the risk of such cancellation.[4]

Our opinion in Chicopee Concrete Serv. v. Hart Eng'g Co., 398 Mass. 476, 498 N.E.2d 121 (1986), does not lead to a different conclusion. Although we held there that a provision of a prime contract requiring city approval of subcontractors was not incorporated by reference into the subcontract, we nevertheless stated that, if the record had supported the conclusion that the subcontractor knew, or at least had notice of, the approval

---

[3] The contracts contained the following provision:

"4.06 Increased or Decreased Contract Quantities.

"When the accepted quantities of work vary from the quantities in the bid schedule, the Contractor shall accept as payment in full, so far as contract items are concerned, payment at the original contract unit prices for the accepted quantities of work done.

"The Engineer may order omitted from the work any items or portions of work found unnecessary to the improvement and such omission shall not operate as a waiver of any condition of the Contract nor invalidate any of the provisions thereof, nor shall the Contractor have any claim for anticipated profit.

"No allowance will be made for any increased expenses, loss of expected reimbursement therefor or from any other cause."

[4] The judge did not explicitly find that cancellation of the barriers was not contemplated and that the risk of their elimination was not allocated by the contracts. However, the judge's decision imports every finding essential to sustain it if there is evidence to support it. . . .

clause, the result might have been different. Id. at 478–479, 498 N.E.2d 121.[5] . . . Judgment affirmed.

————

[5] This court held in John Soley & Sons v. Jones, 208 Mass. 561, 95 N.E. 94 (1911), that, where by its terms the prime contract could be cancelled if the defendant was not making sufficient progress on the work, and the plaintiff knew of the article of cancellation, nevertheless, even if it was mutually understood that the defendant did not intend to perform unless the prime contract remained in force, the defendant was not relieved from performance on the ground of impossibility where it failed to provide for the risk of cancellation in its contract with the plaintiff. To the extent that holding is contrary to our decision in this case, we decline to follow it, and refer to our adoption in *Mishara*, 365 Mass. at 130, 310 N.E.2d 363, of the following statement: "Rather than mechanically apply any fixed rule of law, where the parties themselves have not allocated responsibility, justice is better served by appraising all of the circumstances, the part the various parties played, and thereon determining liability," quoting [138 F.Supp. 595, 607 (S.D.N.Y.1955), aff'd, 245 F.2d 903 (2d Cir.1957)]. See West Los Angeles Inst. v. Mayer, 366 F.2d 220 (9th Cir.1966), cert. denied, 385 U.S. 1010 (1967) ("foreseeability of the frustrating event is not alone enough to bar rescission if it appears that the parties did not intend the promisor to assume the risk of its occurrence").

CHAPTER 5

POLICING THE BARGAIN

INTRODUCTORY NOTE

The basic theme of this chapter, that courts "police" the bargains made by private parties, has been implicit in many of the decisions already encountered. Even though the law's formal requirements for enforceability of a contract have been met, a court may nonetheless intervene because of an abuse in bargaining or a defect in the substance of the bargain (say, violation of a positive rule of law). Yet there is a fundamental tension between the regulatory function and certain premises of our political-economic tradition—e.g., "freedom of contract," "private autonomy," "security of transactions." These concepts, of course, have their corollaries in judicial attitudes; judges, over many years, have said that it is the function of courts to enforce the parties' agreement, not to make a new agreement for them or shelter one party from obligations that have proved burdensome. To be sure, the traditional attitudes have not been superseded or abandoned; their influence remains pervasive. Nevertheless, it is a fact that a "policing" function emerged in the middle of the last century (the most visible legislative contribution is undoubtedly UCC 2–302), and there can be little doubt that modern courts are equipped with an array of regulatory rules, doctrines, and standards. Some of the familiar techniques and approaches were observed in Chapter 4, where attention was focused on the element of assent. Others, of still-indeterminate sweep (e.g., "unconscionability"), assign to courts an explicit role in avoiding injustices that result from market forces. The body of regulation examined in this chapter serves as a reminder that the law of contract enjoys no immunity from the large and puzzling issues of political, economic, and judicial philosophy.

SECTION 1. COMPETENCY AND OTHER LIMITS

Halbman v. Lemke

Supreme Court of Wisconsin, 1980.
99 Wis.2d 241, 298 N.W.2d 562.

CALLOW, J. . . . On or about July 13, 1973, James Halbman, Jr., a minor, entered into an agreement with Michael Lemke whereby Lemke agreed to sell Halbman a 1968 Oldsmobile for the sum of $1,250. Lemke was the manager of L & M Standard Station in Greenfield, and Halbman was an employee at L & M. . . . Halbman paid Lemke $1,000 cash and took possession of the car. Arrangements were made for Halbman to pay $25 per week until the balance was paid, at which time title would be transferred. About five weeks after the purchase agreement, and after Halbman had paid a total of $1,100 of the purchase price, a connecting rod on the vehicle's engine broke. Lemke, while denying any obligation, offered to assist Halbman in installing a used engine in the vehicle if Halbman, at his expense, could secure one. Halbman declined the offer and in September took the vehicle to a garage where it was repaired at a cost of $637.40. Halbman did not pay the repair bill.

In October of 1973 Lemke endorsed the vehicle's title over to Halbman, although the full purchase price had not been paid by Halbman, in an effort to avoid any liability for the operation, maintenance, or use of the vehicle. On October 15, Halbman returned the title to Lemke by letter which disaffirmed the purchase contract and demanded the return of all money theretofore paid by Halbman. Lemke did not return the money. . . .

The repair bill remained unpaid, and the vehicle remained in the garage where the repairs had been made. In the spring of 1974, in satisfaction of a garageman's lien for the outstanding amount, the garage elected to remove the vehicle's engine and transmission and then towed the vehicle to the residence of James Halbman, Sr., the father of the plaintiff minor. Lemke was asked several times to remove the vehicle from the senior Halbman's home, but he declined to do so, claiming he was under no legal obligation to remove it. During the period when the vehicle was at the garage and then subsequently at the home of the plaintiff's father, it was subjected to vandalism, making it unsalvageable.

Halbman [sued for] return of the $1,100 he had paid toward the purchase [and] Lemke counterclaimed for $150, the amount still owing on the contract. . . . [T]he trial court granted judgment [to] Halbman, concluding that when a minor disaffirms a contract for the purchase of an item, he need only offer to return the property remaining in his hands without making restitution for any use or depreciation. . . . [T]he court also allowed interest to the plaintiff dating from the disaffirmance of the contract. . . . The appellate court affirmed. . . .

The sole issue [is] whether a minor, having disaffirmed a contract for the purchase of an item which is not a necessity and having tendered the property back to the vendor, must make restitution to the vendor for damage to the property prior to the disaffirmance. Lemke argues that he should be entitled to recover for the damage to the vehicle up to the time of disaffirmance, which he claims equals the amount of the repair bill.

Neither party challenges the absolute right of a minor to disaffirm a contract for the purchase of items which are not necessities. . . . [T]he doctrine of incapacity or the "infancy doctrine," is one of the oldest and most venerable of our common law traditions. . . . [I]ts purpose is the protection of minors from foolishly squandering their wealth through improvident contracts with crafty adults who would take advantage of them in the marketplace. . . . Thus[,] a contract of a minor for items which are not necessities is void or voidable at the minor's option. . . .

Once there has been a disaffirmance, however, [problems] arise regarding the rights and responsibilities of the parties relative to the disposition of the consideration exchanged on the contract. As a general rule a minor who disaffirms a contract is entitled to recover all consideration he has conferred incident to the transaction. . . . In return the minor is expected to restore as much of the consideration as, at the time of disaffirmance, remains in the minor's possession. . . . Restatement of Restitution, § 62, comment b, (1937); Restatement (Second) of Contracts, [§ 14], comment c. . . . The minor's right to disaffirm is not contingent upon the return of the property, however, as disaffirmance is permitted even where such return cannot be made. Olson v. Veum, 197 Wis. 342, 222 N.W. 233 (1928). . . . [But here we] have a situation where the property cannot be returned to the vendor in its entirety because it has been damaged and therefore diminished in value, and the vendor seeks to recover the depreciation. . . .

The law regarding . . . the consideration exchanged on a disaffirmed contract is characterized by confusion, inconsistency, and a general lack of uniformity as jurisdictions attempt to reach a fair application of the infancy doctrine in today's marketplace. [See] Navin, The Contracts of Minors Viewed from the Perspective of Fair Exchange, 50 N.C.L.Rev. 517 (1972); Note, Restitution in Minors' Contracts in California, 19 Hastings L.Rev. 1199 (1968). . . . That both parties rely on this court's decision in Olson v. Veum, supra, is symptomatic of the problem.

In *Olson* a minor, with his brother, an adult, purchased farm implements and materials, paying by signing notes payable at a future date. Prior to the maturity of the first note, the brothers ceased their joint farming business, and the minor abandoned his interest in the material purchased by leaving it with his brother. The vendor initiated an action against the minor to recover on the note, and the minor (who had by then reached majority) disaffirmed. . . . [We held] that the contract of a minor for the purchase of items which are not necessities may be disaffirmed even when the minor cannot make restitution. Lemke calls our attention to the following language in that decision:

> [There is a] substantial distinction between a mere denial by an infant of contract liability where the other party is seeking to enforce it and those cases where he who was the minor not only disaffirms such contract but seeks the aid of the court to restore to him that with which he has parted at the making of the contract. In the one case he is using his infancy merely as a shield, in the other also as a sword. 197 Wis. at 344, 222 N.W. 233.

From this Lemke infers that when a minor, as a plaintiff, seeks to disaffirm a contract and recover his consideration, different rules should apply than if the minor is defending against an action on the contract by the other party. . . .

Additionally, Lemke [argues] that a disaffirming minor's obligation to make restitution turns upon his ability to do so[,] [and that the obligation is excused] only when restitution is not possible. Here Lemke holds Halbman's $1,100, and accordingly there is no question as to Halbman's ability to make restitution.

Halbman argues in response that, while the "sword-shield" dichotomy may apply where the minor has misrepresented his age to induce the contract, that did not occur here and he may avoid the contract without making restitution notwithstanding his ability to do so.

The principal problem is the use of the word "restitution" in *Olson*. A minor, as we have stated, is under an enforceable duty to return to the vendor, upon disaffirmance, as much of the consideration as remains in his possession. When the contract is disaffirmed, title to that part of the purchased property which is retained by the minor revests in the vendor; it no longer belongs to the minor. See, e.g., Restatement (Second) of Contracts, [§ 14], comment c. . . . The rationale for the rule is plain: a minor who disaffirms a purchase and recovers his purchase price should not also be permitted to profit by retaining the property purchased. The infancy doctrine is designed to protect the minor, sometimes at the expense of an innocent vendor, but it is not to be used to bilk merchants out of property as well as proceeds of the sale. Consequently, it is clear that, when the minor no longer possesses the property which was the subject matter of the contract, the rule requiring the return of property does not apply.[1] The minor will not be required to give up what he does not have. . . . *Olson* does no more than set forth the foregoing rationale[;] the word "restitution" as it is used in that opinion is limited to the return of the property to the vendor. . . .

Here Lemke seeks restitution of the value of the depreciation by virtue of the damage to the vehicle prior to disaffirmance. Such a recovery would require Halbman to return more than that remaining in his possession. It seeks compensatory value for that which he cannot return. Where there is misrepresentation by a minor or willful destruction of property, the vendor may be able to recover damages in tort. . . . But absent these factors, as [here], to require a disaffirming minor to make restitution for diminished value is, in effect, to bind the minor to a part of the obligation which by law he is privileged to avoid. . . . The cases upon which the petitioner relies for the proposition that a disaffirming minor must make restitution for loss and depreciation would at some point force the minor to bear the cost of the very improvidence from which the infancy doctrine is supposed to protect him; we cannot follow them.

. . . [M]odifications of the rules governing the capacity of infants to contract are best left to the legislature. Until such changes are forthcoming, however, we . . . believe [our] result is consistent with the purpose of the infancy doctrine.

The decision of the court of appeals is affirmed.

[Courts applying the *Halbman* rule often register doubts about "the wisdom of this approach," inviting legislative intervention. E.g., Swalberg v. Hannegan, 883 P.2d 931 (Utah Ct.App.1994). Since, historically, the typical disaffirmance case has involved a minor's purchase of a car, is that surprising?]

———

Webster Street Partnership v. Sheridan
220 Neb. 9, 368 N.W.2d 439 (1985)

Two minors (ages 17 and 18), unable to pay the agreed rent, disaffirmed a lease for an apartment after only a short period of occupancy. They had paid the landlord a total of $500 in rent and a security deposit, which sum they demanded be returned. The landlord refused this demand and brought suit seeking an additional $630 for accrued rent and expenses. *Held*, judgment of $500 restitution for the minors. A disaffirming infant is liable only for the value of "necessaries" supplied under the contract. That term is flexible and varies with the facts of each case; it is not confined to things that are required for bare sub-

---

[1] Although we are not presented with the question here, we recognize there is considerable disagreement . . . on whether a minor who disposes of the property should be made to restore the vendor with something in its stead. The general rule appears to limit the minor's responsibility for restoration to specie only. . . . But see: Boyce v. Doyle, 113 N.J.Super. 240, 273 A.2d 408 (1971), adopting a "status quo" theory which requires the minor to restore the precontract status quo, even if it means returning proceeds or other value; Fisher v. Taylor Motor Co., 249 N.C. 617, 107 S.E.2d 94 (1959), requiring the minor to restore only the property remaining in the hands of the minor, " 'or account for so much of its value as may have been invested in other property which he has in hand or owns and controls.' " Finally, some attention is given to the "New Hampshire Rule" or benefits theory, which requires the disaffirming minor to pay for the contract to the extent he benefited from it. Hall v. Butterfield, 59 N.H. 354 (1879). . . .

sistence, but "depends on the social position and situation in life of the infant, as well as upon his own fortune and that of his parents." However, goods or other items of property are not necessaries if the infant has a parent or guardian who is willing and able to supply them. Here, neither minor "was in need of shelter but, rather, [both] had chosen to voluntarily leave home, with the understanding that they could return whenever they desired." One may "at first blush" believe that such a disaffirmance rule is unfair. "Yet, on further consideration, the wisdom of the rule is apparent. If, indeed, landlords may not contract with minors, except at their peril, they may refuse to do so. In that event, minors who voluntarily leave home but who are free to return will be compelled to return to their parents' home—a result which is desirable." Because the facts of this case make clear that the apartment was not a necessary, neither the minors nor their parents are liable, and the landlord's claim of emancipation is of no moment.

NOTE: LIMITS ON DISAFFIRMANCE

As *Halbman* and *Webster Street Partnership* indicate, at common law a minor who attempts to disaffirm a contract for "necessaries" does not escape liability. The explanation usually given rests on quasi-contractual principles. See, e.g., State, University of Cincinnati Hosp. v. Cohen, 57 Ohio App.3d 30, 566 N.E.2d 187 (1989) (benefit received from antecedent transaction involving necessaries results in an unjustly-retained enrichment for which the law implies a promise of "reasonable value"). For the doctrine of necessaries to apply, however, it must be shown that the minor entered into a contract—express or implied in fact—for the goods or services in question. Stated differently, a minor is not liable for necessaries furnished on someone else's credit. Why such a rule? If a minor has received but not contracted for necessaries, is anyone liable? One or both of the minor's parents? On what reasoning?

Incidentally, a minor's right to disaffirm survives for a "reasonable time" after reaching the age of majority (in most places in this country, and for most purposes, lowered from 21 to 18 beginning in the 1970s). A state legislature may of course alter an infant's common-law rights, as by a statute conferring upon infants, through a parent's consent binding the infant, the right to make enforceable agreements respecting certain matters. Litigation under such statutes is likely to involve child models, actors, or athletes. E.g., Shields v. Gross, 58 N.Y.2d 338, 448 N.E.2d 108 (1983).

The question of the validity of a contract signed by the minor's parent arose in Sharon v. City of Newton, supra p. 502. There, the defendant, conceding that minors may ratify or disaffirm their own contracts on reaching majority, nevertheless prevailed on the theory that Merav's father could effectively waive her claim for negligence against the city by signing the release in dispute. Among Merav's contentions was the argument that allowing the parent to do what the minor cannot do violates public policy. The Massachusetts high court thought otherwise:

> While the common-law rule has been narrowed somewhat by statute,[1] it remains our law that the contract of a minor is generally

---

[1] See, e.g., G.L. c. 167E, § 10 (student under eighteen admitted to institution of higher learning has full legal capacity to act on her own behalf in contracts and other transactions regarding financing of education); G.L. c. 175 § 128 (certain contracts for life or endowment insurance may not be voided by minor over fifteen years of age); G.L. c. 175 § 113K (minor

voidable when she reaches the age of majority. Merav unequivocally repudiated the release (to the extent it might be deemed a contract executed by her) by filing suit against the city. . . .

The purpose of the policy permitting minors to void their contracts is "to afford protection to minors from their own improvidence and want of sound judgment." Frye v. Yasi, 327 Mass. 724, 728, 101 N.E.2d 128 (1951). This purpose comports with common sense and experience and is not defeated by permitting parents to exercise their own providence and sound judgment on behalf of their minor children. Parham v. J.R. 442 U.S. 584, 602 (1979) ("The law's concept of the family rests on a presumption that parents possess what a child lacks in maturity, experience, and capacity for judgment required for making life's difficult decisions."). . . . Moreover, our law presumes that fit parents act in furtherance of the welfare and best interests of their children . . . and with respect to matters relating to their care, custody, and upbringing have a fundamental right to make those decisions for them. . . .

Merav's father signed the release in his capacity as parent because he wanted his child to benefit from participating in cheerleading. . . . He made an important family decision cognizant of the risk of physical injury to his child and the financial risk to the family as a whole. In the circumstances of a voluntary, nonessential activity, we will not disturb this parental judgment. This comports with the fundamental liberty interest of parents in the rearing of their children, and is not inconsistent with the purpose behind our public policy permitting minors to void their contracts. . . .

Our views with respect to the . . . enforceability of releases signed by parents on behalf of their children for [the] purposes [involved here] are also consistent with and further the public policy of encouraging athletic programs for the Commonwealth's youth. To hold that releases of [this] type are unenforceable would expose public schools, who offer many of the extracurricular sports opportunities available to children, to financial costs and risks that will inevitably lead to the reduction of those programs.

Should one be surprised to learn that courts in many places do not subscribe to the public policy views expressed in *Sharon*? For a roundup of this line of cases, see Cooper v. Aspen Skiing Co., 48 P.3d 1229 (Colo.2002) ("Colorado's public policy [reflected in many special statutes] affords minors significant protections which preclude parents from releasing a minor's own prospective claim for negligence"; "in the tort context especially, a minor should be [protected from both his own improvidence as well as] from unwise decisions made on his behalf by parents who are routinely asked to release their child's claims for liability" and whose actions "may as a practical matter leave the minor in an

---

over sixteen permitted to contract for motor vehicle liability insurance); G.L. c. 112, § 12E (minor over twelve found to be drug dependent may consent to treatment for dependency); G.L. c. 112, § 12F (minor may consent to medical or dental treatment if she meets criteria outlined in statute). [This footnote has been renumbered.—Eds.]

unacceptably precarious position with no recourse, no parental support, and no method to support or care for himself").

MENTAL COMPETENCE

For a considerable time, the view prevailed that mental incompetency of one of the parties made a contract entirely void. An emphatic and much-quoted statement to this effect was made by the United States Supreme Court in 1872 (Dexter v. Hall, 82 U.S. (15 Wall.) 9, 20), with a logic that, as framed, seems irresistible:

> The fundamental idea of a contract is that it requires the assent of two minds. But a lunatic, or a person *non compos mentis*, has nothing which the law recognizes as a mind, and it would seem, therefore, upon principle, that he cannot make a contract that will have any efficacy as such.

This consequence—total nullity—is still called for by statute in a few states. Elsewhere it has become standard to describe transactions entered into by persons shown to have been mentally incompetent at the time as merely "voidable." It thus becomes possible for the party suffering under such disability to enforce a transaction that has proved advantageous. At the same time, means are usually provided for protecting the interests of others who in dealing with the disabled person were unaware of the disability.

There may be special complications where a court previously has entered a formal decree declaring the individual in question to be incompetent. Surely the legal effect of such a decree should depend on its purpose. If its purpose is to appoint a guardian to care for and preserve the estate of the handicapped person, some statutes authorizing such proceedings have been read as prescribing that, until the adjudication has been reversed in a later proceeding, all of the incompetent's commercial transactions are void. The effect of such a reading is to establish incapacity as a "status." An argument supporting such a view is that otherwise the guardian's management and control of the incompetent's affairs may be nullified or, at the least, hampered. But mental or emotional disorder may be cured or remissions may occur, with no interested party having enough incentive to apply for termination of the guardianship by the court that decreed it. Several state courts have concluded that a guardianship order does not have this conclusive, status-creating effect and is only one of numerous admissible facts that may show a person's incompetence for the purpose of voiding a contract. Still less should a previous court order for involuntary commitment to a hospital for medical or custodial care have the effect of invalidating transactions by the hospitalized individual. The court order, or a diagnosis by a hospital's medical or psychiatric staff, would of course be admissible as evidence, but the need for hospital care and treatment can arise from such a diversity of causes that, on the difficult legal issue as to whether capacity to enter the particular transaction had been impaired, a record of hospitalization should have, and nowadays would have, very little weight. Of course, the timing of the hospitalization in relation to the transaction in question will count for something.

As for the substantive tests of mental incompetency, the *Ortelere* decision just ahead celebrates the "candid approach" of Faber v. Sweet Style Mfg. Corp.,

40 Misc.2d 212, 242 N.Y.S.2d 763 (N.Y.Supp.Ct.1963), an earlier New York landmark. In that case, a rapidly-moving plaintiff, found to be in the depressed phase of a manic-depressive illness, entered into a contract to purchase land for a commercial venture. Despite the absence of a finding of the transaction's unfairness, the court declared the contract rescinded. Justice Meyer said:

> The standards by which competence to contract is measured were, apparently, developed without relation to the effects of particular mental diseases or disorders and prior to recognition of manic-depressive psychosis as a distinct form of mental illness. . . . Primarily they are concerned with capacity to understand: Aldrich v. Bailey, 132 N.Y. 85, 87–88, 30 N.E. 264—"so deprived of his mental faculties as to be wholly, absolutely, and completely unable to understand or comprehend the nature of the transaction;" Paine v. Aldrich, 133 N.Y. 544, 546, 30 N.E. 725—"such mental capacity at the time of the execution of the deed that he could collect in his mind without prompting all the elements of the transaction, and retain them for a sufficient length of time to perceive their obvious relations to each other, and to form a rational judgment in regard to them;" Matter of Delinousha v. National Biscuit Co., 248 N.Y. 93, 95, 161 N.E. 431, 432—"A contract may be avoided only if a party is so affected as to be unable to see things in their true relations and to form correct conclusions in regard thereto." . . . If cognitive capacity is the sole criterion used, the manic must be held competent, [for] manic-depressive psychosis affects motivation rather than ability to understand.
>
> The law does, however, recognize stages of incompetence other than total lack of understanding. Thus it will invalidate a transaction when a contracting party is suffering from delusions if there is "some such connection between the insane delusions and the making of the deed as will compel the inference that the insanity induced the grantor to perform an act the purport and effect of which he could not understand, and which he would not have performed if thoroughly sane." . . . Moreover, it holds that understanding of the physical nature and consequences of an act of suicide does not render the suicide voluntary within the meaning of a life insurance contract if the insured "acted under the control of an insane impulse caused by disease, and derangement of his intellect, which deprived him of the capacity of governing his own conduct in accordance with reason." Newton v. Mut. Benefit Life Ins. Co., 76 N.Y. 426, 429. . . . Finally, Paine v. Aldrich, supra, and the *Delinousha* case consider not only ability to understand but also capacity to form "a rational judgment" or "correct conclusions." Thus, capacity to understand is not, in fact, the sole criterion. Incompetence to contract also exists when a contract is entered into under the compulsion of a mental disease or disorder but for which the contract would not have been made.

The second restaters, in writing and explaining the Restatement section that follows, acknowledged the contributions of the *Faber–Ortelere* "motivational" approach.

————

RESTATEMENT OF CONTRACTS, SECOND

Section 15. Mental Illness or Defect

(1) A person incurs only voidable contractual duties by entering into a transaction if by reason of mental illness or defect

(a) he is unable to understand in a reasonable manner the nature and consequences of the transaction, or

(b) he is unable to act in a reasonable manner in relation to the transaction and the other party has reason to know of his condition.

(2) Where the contract is made on fair terms and the other party is without knowledge of the mental illness or defect, the power of avoidance under Subsection (1) terminates to the extent that the contract has been so performed in whole or in part or the circumstances have so changed that avoidance would be unjust. In such a case a court may grant relief as justice requires.

Comment:

a. Rationale. A contract made by a person who is mentally incompetent requires the reconciliation of two conflicting policies: the protection of justifiable expectations and of the security of transactions, and the protection of persons unable to protect themselves against imposition. . . . [I]t has been asserted that mental incompetency has no effect on a contract unless other grounds of avoidance are present, such as fraud, undue influence, or gross inadequacy of consideration; it is now widely believed that such a rule gives inadequate protection to the incompetent and his family, particularly where the contract is entirely executory. . . .

d. Operative effect of incompetency. Where no guardian has been appointed, the effect on executory contracts of incompetency by reason of mental illness or defect is very much like that of infancy. Regardless of the other party's knowledge or good faith and regardless of the fairness of the terms, the incompetent person on regaining full capacity may affirm or disaffirm the contract, or the power to affirm or disaffirm may be exercised on his behalf by his guardian or after his death by his personal representative. . . .

e. Effect of performance. Where the contract has been performed in whole or in part, avoidance is permitted only on equitable terms. In the traditional action at law, the doing of equity by or on behalf of the incompetent was accomplished by a tender before suit, but in equity or under modern merged procedure it is provided for in the decree. Any benefits still retained by the incompetent must be restored or paid for, and restitution must be made for any necessaries furnished under the contract. . . . If the other party knew of the incompetency at the time of contracting, or if he took unfair advantage of the incompetent, consideration not received by the incompetent or dissipated without benefit to him need not be restored.

———————

Ortelere v. Teachers' Retirement Bd.

25 N.Y.2d 196, 303 N.Y.S.2d 362, 250 N.E.2d 460 (1969)

Grace Ortelere, a 60–year–old teacher who had taught in the New York City schools since 1924, had a "nervous breakdown" in March 1964. In July of that year, a psychiatrist diagnosed her condition as a psychosis, involutional melancholia. Electroshock and tranquilizer treatments, given for six weeks, were discontinued when it was suspected that she had cerebral arteriosclerosis; this diagnosis was later confirmed. The psychiatrist continued to see her until March 1965, when she had a cerebral thrombosis which caused her death on April 7, 1965. Not quite two months earlier, on February 11, she had applied to the Teachers' Retirement Board for retirement, electing to have all her retirement benefits paid to her "without option." The effect of this election was to give her, for her life, the maximum payments permitted ($450 a month) and to leave no reserve after her death, from which payments could be made to her husband (she also had two children). Some ten years earlier she had filed with the Board an election to take smaller allowances in her own lifetime (at the rate of $375 a month), and thus leave a reserve for payments to her husband, with whom she had at the time of her death been "happily married for 38 years" (the court's characterization). The husband, an electrician, had given up his $222–a–week job in order to stay at home to care for his wife when she became severely depressed. The couple owned their home and had $8,000 in savings, but without the husband's income they would be almost entirely dependent on the income from the wife's retirement benefits.

The psychiatrist who had seen Grace Ortelere monthly from July 1964 until March 1965, described her condition as follows: "At no time since she was under my care was she ever mentally competent"; that "[m]entally she couldn't make a decision of any kind, actually, of any kind, small or large." He also described how involutional melancholia affects the judgment processes of those afflicted: "They can't think rationally, no matter what the situation is. They will even tell you, 'I used to be able to think of anything and make any decision. Now,' they say, 'even getting up, I don't know whether I should get up or whether I should stay in bed.' Or, 'I don't even know how to make a slice of toast any more.' Everything is impossible to decide, and everything is too great an effort to even think of doing. They just don't have the effort, actually, because their nervous breakdown drains them of all their physical energies."

In an action brought by Ortelere's husband (also executor) to set aside her application for retirement "without options," the trial court found that she had been mentally incompetent when she made the application and declared it "null and void and of no legal effect." The Appellate Division reversed by a divided vote, holding the proofs of mental incompetency insufficient. The Court of Appeals, 4 to 2, reversed the Appellate Division.

Judge Breitel spoke for the majority: "[The] traditional standards governing competency to contract were formulated when psychiatric knowledge was quite primitive. They fail to account for one who by reason of mental illness is unable to control his conduct even though his cognitive ability seems unimpaired. . . . Hence, because the cognitive rules are, for the most part, too restrictive and rest on a false factual basis they must be re-examined. Once it is understood that, accepting plaintiff's proof, Mrs. Ortelere was psychotic and because of that psychosis could have been incapable of making a voluntary selection of her retirement system benefits, there is an issue that a modern jurisprudence should not exclude, merely because her mind could pass a 'cognition' test based on nineteenth century psychology. . . ."

Judge Breitel then pointed out that the Retirement Board was or should have been aware of Grace Ortelere's condition, since it, or the Board of Education, knew that she was on leave of absence for medical reasons and had consulted the staff psychiatrist of the Board of Education, at the Board's request. Also, there were no significant changes of position by the Board other than some changes in its actuarial computations. The choice she made "while under psychiatric care, ill with cerebral arteriosclerosis, aged 60, and with a family in which she had always manifested concern, was so unwise and foolhardy that a factfinder might conclude that it was explainable only as a product of psychosis."

There was a vigorous dissent by Jasen, J., summarized as follows:

(1) The evidence established conclusively that Ortelere understood that she had selected the maximum payment during her lifetime.

(2) Her letter of inquiry sent to the Board three days before her election was made showed a mind "fully in command" of the salient features of the retirement system.

(3) Her retirement pay had become the family's only source of income, since both spouses had retired; so securing a $75 a month increase in income (from $375 to $450) was a necessity for them and a rational decision for her.

(4) The present state of knowledge does not enable psychiatry to give a fixed rule for each type of mental disorder. The legal rules determining mental capacity are general enough to encompass all types of incapacity, and they are phrased in such a manner that they can be understood and applied by juries of lay people. The generally accepted test—capacity to understand the nature and consequences of the transaction—represents a balance struck between the security of transactions and protection to the mentally handicapped. It is workable in practice and fair in result. To minimize injustices, "the line should be drawn as clearly as possible." Any benefit "to those who understand what they are doing, but are unable to exercise self-discipline, will be outweighed by frivolous claims which will burden our courts and undermine the security of contracts."

––––––

Sparrow v. Demonico

461 Mass. 322, 960 N.E.2d 296 (Mass. 2012)

Sparrow filed a complaint alleging she was entitled to a one-half interest in the family home against her sister Susan. The parties and the attorneys who were representing them participated in mediation that resulted in a settlement. When Sparrow sought an order enforcing the agreement, alleging that the Demonicos reneged on their obligations under it, the Demonicos claimed that the agreement was unenforceable because Susan had, in their view, experienced a mental breakdown during the mediation and thus lacked the capacity to authorize settlement.

It has been long established that a contract is voidable by a person who, due to mental illness or defect, lacked the capacity to contract at the time of entering into the agreement. As Justice Holmes observed, it is a question of fact whether a person was competent to enter into a transaction—that is, whether the person suffered from "insanity" or "was of unsound mind, and incapable of understanding and deciding upon the terms of the contract." See Wright v. Wright, 139 Mass. 177, 182, 29 N.E. 380 (1885). Over time, however, the traditional test for contractual incapacity evolved to incorporate an increased understanding of the nature of mental illness in its various forms. Based on this understanding, courts in Massachusetts and elsewhere have adopted a second, alternative test for incapacity. There may be circumstances when, although a party claiming incapacity has some, or sufficient, understanding of the nature and consequences of the transaction, the contract would still be voidable where, by reason of mental illness or defect, the person is unable to act in a reasonable manner in relation to the transaction and the other party has reason to know of his condition. This modern test—also described as an "affective" or "volitional" test—recognizes that competence can be lost, not only through cognitive disorders, but through affective disorders that encompass motivation or exercise of will.

Under this modern, affective test, where a person has some understanding of a particular transaction which is affected by mental illness or defect, the controlling consideration is whether the transaction in its result is one which a reasonably competent person might have made. The evidence required to support a finding of incapacity to contract, whether considered under the traditional or modern standard, need not in all cases demonstrate that a party suffers from a mental illness or defect that is permanent, degenerative, progressive, or of significant duration. Although such incapacity has historically been established by evidence of a long-standing mental illness, nothing requires such evidence. The inquiry as to the capacity to contract focuses on a party's understanding or conduct only at the time of the disputed transaction.

The defendants contended that the evidence established Susan's incapacity without showing a permanent, degenerative, progressive, or long-standing mental illness. Susan's asserted mental impairment arose and was limited to the period of the mediation session. The defendants argued that this evidence was sufficient to support a conclusion of incapacity, despite the lack of medical evidence or expert testimony as to the nature of Susan's mental impairment and its effect on her decision-making ability.

The court concluded, however, that medical evidence is necessary to establish that a person lacked the capacity to contract due to the existence of a mental condition. There was lay evidence that Susan's speech was "slurr[ed]," that she was in a state of uncontrollable crying, and that she had experienced an inability to focus or "think rationally" throughout the day of the mediation. Susan testified also that she had recently discontinued taking the prescribed medication Zoloft. However, she presented no medical evidence regarding a diagnosis that would have required her to take the medication, or the effect, if any, that ceasing to take the medication would have had on her medical or mental condition. There was also no evidence that Susan's condition at the mediation was related to or caused by her discontinuing the medication. There was no expert or medical testimony to explain the effect of Susan's experiences or behavior on her ability to understand the agreement, to appreciate what was happening, or to comprehend the reasonableness of the settlement terms or the consequences to her of authorizing the settlement. Without such medical evidence, there was no basis to conclude that Susan lacked the capacity to contract. Under the modern test to establish Susan's incapacity, the evidence was insufficient. There was no evidence that the settlement agreement was unreasonable, or that a reasonably competent person would not have entered into it.

___

COMMENT: "UNDERSTANDING" THE TRANSACTION

The tests of mental incompetency originally formulated by the courts were expressed in ordinary language and did not purport to reproduce the findings of medical science, which for a long time could contribute little in any event. Cognition tests were central, but they were embellished with so many qualifying adjectives that one diligent reader of court opinions described the net result as "ambiguous, self-contradictory and practically meaningless." Green, Judicial Tests of Mental Incompetency, 6 Mo.L.Rev. 141 (1941). The tests showed little or no recognition of the enduring difficulties that advances in modern psychiatry have illuminated by disclosing both the variety of forms that mental defect and disorder can take and the vast differences among them. It is difficult indeed to adhere consistently to a single all-encompassing test when mental and emotional disturbances show as much diversity as in the small group of examples given here.

The workings of private litigation in struggling for answers to the question of sufficient understanding, and the wide range of inquiry required, are described in a valuable early study by Green, Proof of Mental Incompetency and the Unexpressed Major Premise, 53 Yale L.J. 271, 298–311 (1944). Of particular interest is the "inarticulate premise" Professor Green found implicit in most decisions: that transactions under scrutiny should be tested also by their own terms, the degree of "abnormality" they show. If they are gifts—many are— experience will supply a basis for judging whether the bounty to the particular recipient shows such eccentricity as to call for explanation. If the dealings purport to be an exchange transaction, do the terms, including the fairness of the exchange, show rational calculation, that is, a result which a reasonably competent person might have made?

___

Kelly v. Provident Life & Accident Insurance Co.

United States District Court, Southern District of California, 2010.
734 F. Supp. 2d 1085.

HAYES, DISTRICT JUDGE. ... Defendant issued Plaintiff two own-occupation disability insurance policies in the early 1980s which provided a combined benefit of $5,500 per month. At the time he purchased the policies, Plaintiff sold insurance as a General Agent for General American Life Insurance Company. Pursuant to the disability policies, Plaintiff could claim total disability if he was unable "to perform the substantial and material duties of his occupation" and was "under the care and attendance of a Physician." In May of 1986, Plaintiff began seeing psychologist Russell Gold, Ph.D., who diagnosed Plaintiff with depression, dysthymic disorder, and schizoid personality disorder. Dr. Gold attributed Plaintiff's condition to stress from contentious divorce proceedings. Plaintiff filed a claim for complete disability in September of 1986. Defendant accepted the claim and began paying benefits. Plaintiff continued to see Dr. Gold for the thirteen-year period he received disability benefits from Defendant.

In addition to paying benefits of $5,500 per month, in 1986 and 1987, Defendant paid Plaintiff's business expenses, such as rent for his office, salaries of employees, utilities, and accounting services.

While Plaintiff was on disability benefits, various insurance companies terminated their relationship with Plaintiff as an agent. . . .

Over the course of Plaintiff's disability claim, Defendant investigated Plaintiff's medical condition and whether Plaintiff had returned to work on multiple occasions. . . .

During the investigation, Blochl contacted the San Diego District Attorney's Office, the United States' Attorney's Office, and the FBI to report insurance fraud. A deputy district attorney informed Blochl that "Mr. Kelly should be asked if he in fact has sold policies after his date of disability and whether or not he has an office. Very specific questions about sales, marketing, and prospecting should be asked" and warned Blochl that "the questions on the Insured's Supplementary Statement of Claim form were vague." Defendants never asked Plaintiff these questions. The deputy district attorney also "suggested that the Insured should be examined under oath by Provident attorneys regarding this claim. She indicated that very specific questions about the insured[']s alleged disability and possible insurance related activity should be explored." Defendant never conducted such an interview. In his deposition, Blochl testified that when he investigated Plaintiff and contacted various law enforcement agencies, he was unaware that Plaintiff had ever informed Defendant that he was continuing to provide some services to existing clients, that he was unaware that Plaintiff's attorney had provided Plaintiff's business records to Defendant in 1990, and that he was unaware that Plaintiff had informed Defendant that Plaintiff had initiated some new policies. Blochl testified in his deposition that this information would have affected his determination of whether fraud had been committed and that this information was the reason the FBI declined to pursue the case after a preliminary investigation.[5] . . .

On August 18, 1999, Defendant sent Plaintiff a letter notifying him that it was terminating his benefits, although it would provide him with benefits through August 16, 1999, which was the date it concluded Plaintiff was not disabled. The letter informed Plaintiff that he was required to pay his premiums in order to continue coverage under his policies. Plaintiff sent a series of letters to Defendant after the termination and Dr. Gold also wrote to Defendant on Plaintiff's behalf. In April of 2000, Defendant stated it was reviewing Plaintiff's submissions and would get back to him. However, Defendant never responded.

In November of 2000, Plaintiff was served with process in *Provident Life and Accident Insurance Co. v. Kelly,* the prior litigation before this Court. Defendant Provident, as a plaintiff in that suit, alleged claims for fraud, conspiracy to defraud, breach of the covenant of good faith and fair dealing, rescission, and restitution against Kelly. Defendant Provident also sued Kelly Insurance Services, Inc. and Wobegone Enterprises, Inc., alleging a cause of action for conspiracy to defraud.

---

[5] Although Plaintiff was never charged criminally in connection with the alleged insurance fraud, he was convicted of tax evasion in 2004.

Plaintiff attempted to retain his former attorney, Steinberg, to represent him and the companies [but] Steinberg told Plaintiff that he did not handle defense cases and advised Plaintiff to hire another attorney. Plaintiff attempted to hire an attorney, but could not afford the fees and could not find an attorney who would take his case on a contingency basis because he was a defendant. Plaintiff contacted Defendant, seeking a settlement, because Defendant had previously offered Plaintiff $330,000 to surrender the policies. Defendant's attorney, Gregory Scarlett, told Plaintiff that he would put the lawsuit on hold while he looked into a settlement.

On April 11, 2001, Plaintiff learned that a clerk's default had been entered against him and the companies and that Defendant was moving for default judgment. Plaintiff, proceeding *pro se,* wrote a letter to Judge Huff explaining that he had not responded to the lawsuit because of his conversation with Defendant's attorney. Plaintiff stated he believed the litigation was on hold. In the letter, Plaintiff also stated that he did not own either of the corporate defendants, rather his wife Anna did. At this time, Plaintiff was still under investigation by the FBI, which he found "tremendously upsetting. . . ." Plaintiff did not understand how he could be accused of fraud because "Provident never asked for any additional information" about his "limited work" after Steinberg sent Defendant his work records in 1990. Plaintiff states "I did not understand how I could lie about something I was never asked about."

Because Plaintiff was not an attorney, he could not file an answer or oppose default judgment on behalf of the corporate defendants, and Defendant obtained a default judgment. Although Plaintiff's wife, not Plaintiff, was the registered agent for service of process, she was never served. Plaintiff's wife states in a declaration that the default judgment

> put a tremendous financial strain on Richard and I. With Richard unable to work, I needed to make money to support us both. I counted on the income from my insurance sales, including the residual commissions flowing through Wobegone, in order to make ends meet. When Provident entered default against my company, it took away this source of income entirely.

After the default judgment, Plaintiff began drinking heavily. Plaintiff's wife states that his condition worsened after Defendant cut off Plaintiff's disability benefits and during the lawsuit and that at one point, she discovered he had been researching suicide. On July 2, 2001 and July 5, 2001, Plaintiff and Defendant's attorney attended an early neutral evaluation conference before the magistrate judge. Plaintiff settled his case with Defendant, giving up his claim for disability benefits in exchange for Defendant agreeing to dismiss the lawsuit and "giving up its judgment against Anna's company." The settlement agreement was signed by both parties on November 21, 2001. Plaintiff states he signed the settlement agreement "because I did not have the mental or emotional capacity to engage in the conflictual situation that Provident had created. I did not sign the agreement because it was what I wanted to do, but because I could not resist Provident's pressure."

Plaintiff submitted the declaration of Dr. Lynn Ponton, M.D., a Professor of Clinical Psychiatry at the University of California, San Francisco, who reviewed Plaintiff's medical records and the records of the three [independent medical examinations] with Defendant's selected doctors. Based on her review of the records, Dr. Ponton offers her opinion that Plaintiff suffers from Avoidant Personality Disorder with schizoid features. Dr. Ponton states "Avoidant Personality Disorder is often characterized by shifts in the level of avoidant behavior depending on the level of conflict associated with certain interpersonal relationships." Dr. Ponton states that Plaintiff's condition creates "undue susceptibility to [ ] pressure," such as the pressure that Defendant's investigations, the prior lawsuit, and the investigations of alleged insurance fraud by various law enforcement agencies would create. Under this pressure, given Plaintiff's diagnosis, "[h]is depression and social avoidance would have been at an all-time high" at the time of the settlement. . .

[Under] California Civil Code § 1575,

Undue influence consists:

> 1. In the use, by one in whom a confidence is reposed by another, or who holds a real or apparent authority over him, of such confidence or authority for the purpose of obtaining an unfair advantage over him;

> 2. In taking an unfair advantage of another's weakness of mind; or,

> 3. In taking a grossly oppressive and unfair advantage of another's necessities or distress.

A seminal California appellate case defined undue influence as follows:

> "[u]ndue influence . . . is a shorthand legal phrase used to describe persuasion which tends to be coercive in nature, persuasion which overcomes the will without convincing the judgment. The hallmarks of such persuasion is high pressure, a pressure which works on mental, moral, or emotional weakness to such an extent that it approaches the boundaries of coercion. In this sense, undue influence has been called overpersuasion."

[Odorizzi v. Bloomfield School Dist., 246 Cal. App. 2d 123, 130, 54 Cal. Rptr. 533 (1966).] If the party seeking to rescind a contract is a "person of subnormal capacities," even subjecting them to "ordinary force" may constitute undue influence.

Odorizzi lists seven factors which "generally accompany" overpersuasion:

> (1) discussion of the transaction at an unusual or inappropriate time, (2) consummation of the transaction in an unusual place, (3) insistent demand that the business be finished at once, (4) extreme emphasis on untoward consequences of delay, (5) the use of multiple persuaders by the dominant side against a single servient party, (6) absence of third-party advisers to the servient party, (7) statements that there is no time to consult financial advisers or attorneys. If a number of these elements are simultaneously present, the persuasion may be characterized as excessive.

[Id. at 133.] Although *Odorizzi* states these factors are generally present, the Ninth Circuit's previous ruling in this case states "[t]he *Odorizzi* list was not described as exhaustive. Some contracts might be formed through undue influence even if most or all of the *Odorizzi* factors are absent." In Keithley v. Civil Service Bd. of the City of Oakland, 11 Cal. App. 3d 443, 451, 89 Cal. Rptr. 809 (1970), a California Court of Appeals made the same point: "[i]ndeed, there are no fixed definitions or inflexible formulas. Rather, we are concerned with whether from the entire context it appears that one's will was overborne and he was induced to do or forbear to do an act which he would not do, or would do, if left to act freely." The same opinion notes "direct evidence of undue influence is rarely obtainable and, thus the court is normally relegated to determination by inference from the totality of facts and circumstances."

At least one California appellate decision addresses mental illness as a form of "weakness of the mind." See Smalley v. Baker, 262 Cal. App. 2d 824, 834, 69 Cal. Rptr. 521 (1968). In *Smalley*, the court held that a manic depressive man was competent to enter a contract, but that his mental illness was a "weakness of the mind" pursuant to California Civil Code § 1575(2) because his "judgment was affected." Id. at 836, 69 Cal.Rptr. 521. The court explained that "the lesser weakness of the mind [which does not render a party incompetent] referred to in section 1575 need not be long lasting or wholly incapacitating, but may consist of such factors as a lack of vigor due to age, physical condition, emotional anguish, or a combination of such factors." Id. at 835, 69 Cal.Rptr. 521. However, Smalley ultimately lost because there was "no claim or showing that Baker knew or was aware of Smalley's mental illness, or that he took advantage of such illness so as to bring Civil Code section 1575 into play." Id. at 836, 69 Cal.Rptr. 521.

Plaintiff's statements, Plaintiff's wife's statements, the records of a long period of psychological counseling . . . and the fact that Defendant paid Plaintiff disability benefits for thirteen years could lead a reasonable jury to conclude that Plaintiff was suffering from mental illness which amounts to "weakness of the mind" under California law. Although Defendant disputes Plaintiff's diagnosis, viewed in the light most favorable to Plaintiff, this evidence could lead a reasonable jury to conclude that Defendant knew that Plaintiff was unusually susceptible to pressure.

The Court must next examine whether there is evidence that could lead a reasonable jury to determine that Defendant took unfair advantage of Plaintiff's weakened state of mind. Although Defendant contends the Court should only consider the settlement negotiations, the Court finds that the appropriate inquiry is broader. The ultimate question is "whether from the *entire context* it appears that [Plaintiff's] will was overborne." *See* Keithley, 11 Cal.App.3d at 451, 89 Cal.Rptr. 809 (emphasis added). In this case, the "entire context" of the settlement agreement includes Defendant's investigation of Plaintiff's claim, Defendant's termination of Plaintiff's benefits, Defendant reporting that Plaintiff had committed insurance fraud to various law enforcement agencies, and Defendant suing Plaintiff. The Court must determine whether there is sufficient evidence in the record, viewed in the light most favorable to Plaintiff, that a jury could find that Defendant acted in bad faith in its investigation and subsequent termination of Plaintiff's benefits and by suing Plaintiff in order to take advantage of Plaintiff's weakened state of mind. This determination requires an examination of California law on own occupation disability insurance policies and bad faith termination.

Under California law, own occupation insurance policies define total disability not as " 'an absolute state of helplessness but means such disability as renders the insured unable to perform the substantial and material acts necessary to the prosecution of a business or occupation in the usual or customary way.' " Hangarter v. Provident Life and Accident Ins. Co., 373 F.3d 998, 1006 (9th Cir. 2004) (quoting Erreca v. Western States Life Ins. Co., 19 Cal.2d 388, 121 P.2d 689 (1942)). Regardless of the definition of "total disability" in an own occupation insurance policy, "California law *re-*

quires courts to deviate from the explicit policy definition of 'total disability' in the occupational policy context." Hangarter, 373 F.3d at 1006.

Under California law, "[t]he fact that the insured may do some work or transact some business duties during the time for which he claims indemnity for total disability or even the fact that he may be physically able to do so is not conclusive evidence that his disability is not total, if reasonable care and prudence require that he desist." Id. at 1007. If an insured can perform the duties of his occupation intermittently, but cannot do so in a "continuous, normal" way, the insured is totally disabled under California law. An insured's income is irrelevant to the disability determination. "[T]he magnitude of [the insured's] enterprise and his income therefrom . . . have *no proper place* in the determination of whether [the insured] is totally disabled [because such insurance] *does not insure against loss of income.*" Id. at 1009.

In determining whether an insurer acted in bad faith by denying coverage, the fact-finder must determine whether the denial was reasonable. . . .

There is evidence in the record which, viewed in the light most favorable to Plaintiff, could lead a jury to conclude that, despite knowing that Plaintiff was mentally ill, Defendant terminated Plaintiff's coverage in bad faith after conducting a biased investigation, contacted law enforcement agencies to instigate an investigation of Plaintiff for the purposes of harassment and sued Plaintiff for the return of all benefits without a valid basis for doing so in order to take unfair advantage of Plaintiff's weakness of mind. Although Defendant points out that none of the *Odorizzi* factors are present, this is not dispositive, as the Ninth Circuit previously ruled. The *Odorizzi* list of factors is not exclusive, and under California law, all of the circumstances surrounding contract negotiations should be examined to determine whether a party to a contract engaged in "overpersuasion." Keithley, 11 Cal. App. 3d at 451, 89 Cal. Rptr. 809. If a jury determined that Defendant took these actions in bad faith in order to pressure Plaintiff to surrender his benefits via a settlement agreement, it could find that Defendant "took unfair advantage of [Plaintiff's] weakness of mind," allowing rescission of the settlement agreement for undue influence. Defendant's motion for summary judgment on Plaintiff's rescission claim is denied. . . .

———

Von Hake v. Thomas
705 P.2d 766 (Utah 1985)

"A confidential relationship [where one party, having gained the trust and confidence of another, exercises extraordinary influence over the other,] is a prerequisite to proving constructive fraud. . . . The law presumes that one ordinarily makes his or her own judgments, however imperfect, and acts on them; it does not readily assume that one's will has been overborne by another. Therefore, the law does not lightly recognize the existence of a confidential relationship. . . . [Here,] the evidence is insufficient to establish that [such] a relationship arose between Von Hake and Thomas. Although Von Hake was 82 years old and distressed over the imminent [foreclosure] sale of the ranch he had owned for forty years, and Thomas clearly induced Von Hake to believe that he was interested in 'saving' the ranch, those facts alone did not require Thomas to act as a fiduciary toward Von Hake. No evidence suggests that Von

Hake so trusted Thomas that Thomas was able to substitute his will for Von Hake's. . . . The parties had no long-established relationship of trust[,] . . . nor was Thomas's relationship to Von Hake one that traditionally imposes a fiduciary duty, such as an attorney/client relationship. . . . And while Von Hake was elderly, there is no evidence that he was feeble or not in full possession of his faculties. Von Hake at all times was aware that he could and should consult his own attorney about the deal he was making, although admittedly [Thomas] talked him out of doing so. It is true that Thomas worked hard to ingratiate himself with Von Hake and to gain his confidence, but that is likely to be true of anyone who defrauds another. There is no evidence that at any time Von Hake relinquished control over his own decision making. Rather, these facts present something of a 'garden variety' fraud case, in which one party intentionally or recklessly misrepresents a presently existing material fact, thereby inducing another to reasonably rely and act upon that falsehood to the other's detriment."

NOTE

While it is possible to isolate a pure issue of legal capacity in the cases (think of *Ortelere*), impaired capacity more typically figures into the broader inquiries that are opened up by claims of undue influence and breach of confidential or fiduciary obligation, where the question is whether undue advantage has been taken of physical or emotional weakness, or dependency, or of trust and confidence reposed. Should an effort be made to distinguish the standards of competency applied in these two contexts?

––––––––––

Even when individuals are competent to contract, the state may declare some matters off limits. Gambling contracts, for example, are typically not enforceable, as are contracts involving activities that are illegal. The refusal to enforce the promise follows from the law's attitude towards the underlying activity. As the case coming next shows, however, the state sometimes removes matters from the domain of contract even when the activity itself is permitted.

––––––––––

In re Baby M
Supreme Court of New Jersey, 1988.
109 N.J. 396, 537 A.2d 1227.

WILENTZ, C.J. [We are] asked to determine the validity of a contract that purports to provide a new way of bringing children into a family. For a fee of $10,000, a woman agrees to be artificially inseminated with the semen of another woman's husband; she is to conceive a child, carry it to term, and after its birth surrender it to the natural father and his wife. The intent of the contract is that the child's natural mother will thereafter be forever separated from her child. The wife is to adopt the child, and she and the natural father are to be regarded as its parents for all purposes. The contract providing for this is called a "surrogacy contract," the natural mother inappropriately called the "surrogate mother." . . .

We find no offense to our present laws where a woman voluntarily and without payment agrees to act as a "surrogate" mother, provided that she is not subject to a binding agreement to surrender her child. Moreover, our holding today does not preclude the Legislature from altering the current statutory scheme, within constitutional limits, so as to permit surrogacy contracts. Under current law, however, the surrogacy agreement before us is illegal and invalid. . . .

In February 1985, William Stern and Mary Beth Whitehead entered into a surrogacy contract. It recited that Stern's wife, Elizabeth, was infertile, that they wanted a child, and that Mrs. Whitehead was willing to provide that child as the mother with Mr. Stern as the father.

The contract provided that through artificial insemination using Mr. Stern's sperm, Mrs. Whitehead would become pregnant, carry the child to term, bear it, deliver it to the Sterns, and thereafter do whatever was necessary to terminate her maternal rights so that Mrs. Stern could thereafter adopt the child. Mrs. Whitehead's husband, Richard,[1] was also a party to the contract; Mrs. Stern was not. Mr. Whitehead promised to do all acts necessary to rebut the presumption of paternity under the Parentage Act. Although Mrs. Stern was not a party to the surrogacy agreement, the contract gave her sole custody of the child in the event of Mr. Stern's death. Mrs. Stern's status as a nonparty to the surrogate parenting agreement presumably was to avoid the application of the baby-selling statute to this arrangement.

Mr. Stern, on his part, agreed to attempt the artificial insemination and to pay Mrs. Whitehead $10,000 after the child's birth, on its delivery to him. In a separate contract, Mr. Stern agreed to pay $7,500 to the Infertility Center of New York ("ICNY"). The Center's advertising campaigns solicit surrogate mothers and encourage infertile couples to consider surrogacy. ICNY arranged for the surrogacy contract by bringing the parties together, explaining the process to them, furnishing the contractual form, and providing legal counsel.

The history of the parties' involvement in this arrangement suggests their good faith. William and Elizabeth Stern were married in July 1974, having met at the University of Michigan, where both were Ph.D. candidates. Due to financial considerations and Mrs. Stern's pursuit of a medical degree and residency, they decided to defer starting a family until 1981. Before then, however, Mrs. Stern learned that she might have multiple sclerosis and that the disease in some cases renders pregnancy a serious health risk. Her anxiety appears to have exceeded the actual risk, which current medical authorities assess as minimal. Nonetheless that anxiety was evidently quite real, Mrs. Stern fearing that pregnancy might precipitate blindness, paraplegia, or other forms of debilitation. Based on the perceived risk, the Sterns decided to forego having their own children. The decision had special significance for Mr. Stern. Most of his family had been destroyed in the Holocaust. As the family's only survivor, he very much wanted to continue his bloodline.

Initially the Sterns considered adoption, but were discouraged by the substantial delay apparently involved and by the potential problem they saw arising from their age and their differing religious backgrounds. . . .

---

[1] Subsequent to the trial court proceedings, Mr. and Mrs. Whitehead were divorced, and soon thereafter Mrs. Whitehead remarried. Nevertheless, in the course of this opinion we will make reference almost exclusively to the facts as they existed at the time of trial, the facts on which the decision we now review was reached. We note moreover that Mr. Whitehead remains a party to this dispute. For these reasons, we continue to refer to appellants as Mr. and Mrs. Whitehead.

The paths of Mrs. Whitehead and the Sterns to surrogacy were similar. Both responded to advertising by ICNY. The Sterns' response, following their inquiries into adoption, was the result of their long-standing decision to have a child. Mrs. Whitehead's response apparently resulted from her sympathy with family members and others who could have no children (she stated that she wanted to give another couple the "gift of life"); she also wanted the $10,000 to help her family. . . .

Mrs. Whitehead had reached her decision concerning surrogacy before the Sterns, and had actually been involved as a potential surrogate mother with another couple. After numerous unsuccessful artificial inseminations, that effort was abandoned. Thereafter, the Sterns learned of the Infertility Center, the possibilities of surrogacy, and of Mary Beth Whitehead. The two couples met to discuss the surrogacy arrangement and decided to go forward. On February 6, 1985, Mr. Stern and Mr. and Mrs. Whitehead executed the surrogate parenting agreement. After several artificial inseminations over a period of months, Mrs. Whitehead became pregnant. The pregnancy was uneventful and on March 27, 1986, Baby M was born. . . .

Her birth certificate indicated her name to be Sara Elizabeth Whitehead and her father to be Richard Whitehead. In accordance with Mrs. Whitehead's request, the Sterns visited the hospital unobtrusively to see the newborn child.

Mrs. Whitehead realized, almost from the moment of birth, that she could not part with this child. She had felt a bond with it even during pregnancy. Some indication of the attachment was conveyed to the Sterns at the hospital when they told Mrs. Whitehead what they were going to name the baby. She apparently broke into tears and indicated that she did not know if she could give up the child. She talked about how the baby looked like her other daughter, and made it clear that she was experiencing great difficulty with the decision.

Nonetheless, Mrs. Whitehead was, for the moment, true to her word. Despite powerful inclinations to the contrary, she turned her child over to the Sterns on March 30 at the Whiteheads' home.

The Sterns were thrilled with their new child [who they named Melissa]. They had planned extensively for its arrival, far beyond the practical furnishing of a room for her. It was a time of joyful celebration—not just for them but for their friends as well. . . .

Later in the evening of March 30, Mrs. Whitehead became deeply disturbed, disconsolate, stricken with unbearable sadness. She had to have her child. She could not eat, sleep, or concentrate on anything other than her need for her baby. The next day she went to the Sterns' home and told them how much she was suffering.

The depth of Mrs. Whitehead's despair surprised and frightened the Sterns. She told them that she could not live without her baby, that she must have her, even if only for one week, that thereafter she would surrender her child. The Sterns, concerned that Mrs. Whitehead might indeed commit suicide, not wanting under any circumstances to risk that, and in any event believing that Mrs. Whitehead would keep her word, turned the child over to her. It was not until four months later, after a series of attempts to regain possession of the child, that Melissa was returned to the Sterns, having been forcibly removed from the home where she was then living with Mr. and Mrs. Whitehead, the home in Florida owned by Mary Beth Whitehead's parents.

The struggle over Baby M began when it became apparent that Mrs. Whitehead could not return the child to Mr. Stern. . . . Mr. Stern filed a complaint seeking enforcement of the surrogacy contract. He alleged, accurately, that Mrs. Whitehead had not only refused to comply with the surrogacy contract but had threatened to flee from New Jersey with the child in order to avoid even the possibility of his obtaining custody. The court papers asserted that if Mrs. Whitehead were to be given notice of the application for an order requiring her to relinquish custody, she would, prior to the hearing, leave the state with the baby. And that is precisely what she did. After the order was entered, *ex parte*, the process server, aided by the police, in the presence of the Sterns, entered Mrs. Whitehead's home to execute the order. Mr. Whitehead fled with the child, who had been handed to him through a window while those who came to enforce the order were thrown off balance by a dispute over the child's current name.

The Whiteheads immediately fled to Florida with Baby M. They stayed initially with Mrs. Whitehead's parents. . . . For the next three months, the Whiteheads and Melissa lived at roughly twenty different hotels, motels, and homes in order to avoid apprehension. From time to time Mrs. Whitehead would call Mr. Stern to discuss the matter; the conversations, recorded by Mr. Stern on advice of counsel, show an escalating dispute about rights, morality, and power, accompanied by threats of Mrs. Whitehead to kill herself, to kill the child, and falsely to accuse Mr. Stern of sexually molesting Mrs. Whitehead's other daughter.

Eventually the Sterns discovered where the Whiteheads were staying, commenced supplementary proceedings in Florida, and obtained an order requiring the Whiteheads to turn over the child. Police in Florida enforced the order, forcibly removing the child from her grandparents' home. She was soon thereafter brought to New Jersey and turned over to the Sterns. The prior order of the court, issued *ex parte*, awarding custody of the child to the Sterns *pendente lite*, was reaffirmed by the trial court after consideration of the certified representations of the parties (both represented by counsel) concerning the unusual sequence of events that had unfolded. Pending final judgment, Mrs. Whitehead was awarded limited visitation with Baby M.

The Sterns' complaint, in addition to seeking possession and ultimately custody of the child, sought enforcement of the surrogacy contract. Pursuant to the contract, it asked that the child be permanently placed in their custody, that Mrs. Whitehead's parental rights be terminated, and that Mrs. Stern be allowed to adopt the child, *i.e.*, that, for all purposes, Melissa become the Sterns' child.

The trial took thirty-two days over a period of more than two months. [T]he bulk of the testimony was devoted to determining the parenting arrangement most compatible with the child's best interests. [The trial court] held that the surrogacy contract was valid; ordered that Mrs. Whitehead's parental rights be terminated and that sole custody of the child be granted to Mr. Stern; and . . . immediately entered an order allowing the adoption of Melissa by Mrs. Stern, all in accordance with the surrogacy contract. Pending the outcome of the appeal, we granted a continuation of visitation to Mrs. Whitehead, although slightly more limited than the visitation allowed during the trial.

Although clearly expressing its view that the surrogacy contract was valid, the trial court devoted the major portion of its opinion to the question of the baby's best interests. The inconsistency is apparent. The surrogacy contract calls for the surrender of the child to the Sterns, permanent and sole custody in the Sterns, and termination of Mrs. Whitehead's parental rights, all without qualification, all regardless of any evaluation of the best interests of the child. As a matter of fact the contract recites (even before the child was conceived) that it is in the best interests of the child to be placed with Mr. Stern. In effect, the trial court awarded custody to Mr. Stern, the natural father, based on the same kind of evidence and analysis as might be expected had no surrogacy contract existed. Its rationalization, however, was that while the surrogacy contract was valid, specific performance would not be granted unless that remedy was in the best interests of the child. The factual issues confronted and decided by the trial court were the same as if Mr. Stern and Mrs. Whitehead had had the child out of wedlock, intended or unintended, and then disagreed about custody. The trial court's awareness of the irrelevance of the contract in the court's determination of custody is suggested by its remark that beyond the question of the child's best interests, "[a]ll other concerns raised by counsel constitute commentary."

On the question of best interests—and we agree, but for different reasons, that custody was the critical issue—the court's analysis of the testimony was perceptive, demonstrating both its understanding of the case and its considerable experience in these matters. We agree substantially with both its analysis and conclusions on the matter of custody.

The court's review and analysis of the surrogacy contract, however, is not at all in accord with ours. . . .

We have concluded that this surrogacy contract is invalid. Our conclusion has two bases: direct conflict with existing statutes and conflict with the public policies of this State, as expressed in its statutory and decisional law.

One of the surrogacy contract's basic purposes, to achieve the adoption of a child through private placement, though permitted in New Jersey "is very much disfavored." Its use of money for this purpose—and we have no doubt whatsoever that the money is being paid to obtain an adoption and not, as the Sterns argue, for the personal services of Mary Beth Whitehead—is illegal and perhaps criminal. In addition to the inducement of money, there is the coercion of contract: the natural mother's irrevocable agreement, prior to birth, even prior to conception, to surrender the child to the adoptive couple. Such an agreement is totally unenforceable in private placement adoption. Even where the adoption is through an approved agency, the formal agreement to surrender occurs only *after* birth . . ., and then, by regulation, only after the birth mother has been offered counseling. Integral to these invalid provisions of the surrogacy contract is the related agreement, equally invalid, on the part of the natural mother to cooperate with, and not to contest, proceedings to terminate her parental rights, as well as her contractual concession, in aid of the adoption, that the child's best interests would be served by awarding custody to the natural father and his wife—all of this before she has even conceived, and, in some cases, before she has the slightest idea of what the natural father and adoptive mother are like.

The foregoing provisions not only directly conflict with New Jersey statutes, but also offend long-established State policies. These critical terms, which are at the heart of the contract, are invalid and unenforceable; the conclusion therefore follows, without more, that the entire contract is unenforceable. . . .

Our law prohibits paying or accepting money in connection with any placement of a child for adoption. Violation is a high misdemeanor. Excepted are fees of an approved agency (which must be a non-profit entity) and certain expenses in connection with childbirth.

Considerable care was taken in this case to structure the surrogacy arrangement so as not to violate this prohibition[:] . . . the adopting parent, Mrs. Stern, was not a party to the surrogacy contract; the money paid to Mrs. Whitehead was stated to be for her services—not for the adoption; the sole purpose of the contract was stated as being that "of giving a child to William Stern, its natural and biological father"; the money was purported to be "compensation for services and expenses and in no way . . . a fee for termination of parental rights or a payment in exchange for consent to surrender a child for adoption"; the fee to the Infertility Center ($7,500) was stated to be for legal representation, advice, administrative work, and other "services." Nevertheless, it seems clear that the money was paid and accepted in connection with an adoption.

The Infertility Center's major role was first as a "finder" of the surrogate mother whose child was to be adopted, and second as the arranger of all proceedings that led to the adoption. Its role as adoption finder is demonstrated by the provision requiring Mr. Stern to pay another $7,500 if he uses Mary Beth Whitehead again as a surrogate, and by ICNY's agreement to "coordinate arrangements for the adoption of the child by the wife." The surrogacy agreement requires Mrs. Whitehead to surrender Baby M for the purposes of adoption. The agreement notes that Mr. *and Mrs.* Stern wanted to have a child, and provides that the child be "placed" with Mrs. Stern in the event Mr. Stern dies before the child is born. The payment of the $10,000 occurs only on surrender of custody of the child and "completion of the duties and obligations" of Mrs. Whitehead, including termination of her parental rights to facilitate adoption by Mrs. Stern. As for the contention that the Sterns are paying only for services and not for an adoption, we need note only that they would pay nothing in the event the child died before the fourth month of pregnancy, and only $1,000 if the child were stillborn, even though the "services" had been fully rendered. Additionally, one of Mrs. Whitehead's estimated costs, to be assumed by Mr. Stern, was an "Adoption Fee," presumably for Mrs. Whitehead's incidental costs in connection with the adoption.

Mr. Stern knew he was paying for the adoption of a child; Mrs. Whitehead knew she was accepting money so that a child might be adopted; the Infertility Center knew that it was being paid for assisting in the adoption of a child. The actions of all three worked to frustrate the goals of the statute. It strains credulity to claim that these arrangements, touted by those in the surrogacy business as an attractive alternative to the usual route leading to an adoption, really amount to something other than a private placement adoption for money.

The prohibition of our statute is strong. Violation constitutes a high misdemeanor, a third-degree crime, carrying a penalty of three to five years imprisonment. The evils inherent in baby-bartering are loathsome for a myriad of reasons. The child is sold without regard for whether the purchasers will be suitable parents. The natural mother does not receive the benefit of counseling and guidance to assist her in making a decision that may affect her for a lifetime. In fact, the monetary incentive to sell her child may, depending on her financial circumstances, make her decision less voluntary. Furthermore, the adoptive parents[2] may not be fully informed of the natural parents' medical history.

Baby-selling potentially results in the exploitation of all parties involved. Conversely, adoption statutes seek to further humanitarian goals, foremost among them the best interests of the child. The negative consequences of baby-buying are potentially present in the surrogacy context, especially the potential for placing and adopting a child without regard to the interest of the child or the natural mother.

The termination of Mrs. Whitehead's parental rights, called for by the surrogacy contract and actually ordered by the court fails to comply with the stringent requirements of New Jersey law. Our law, recognizing the finality of any termination of parental rights, provides for such termination only where there has been a voluntary surrender of a child to an approved agency or to the Division of Youth and Family Services ("DYFS"), accompanied by a formal document acknowledging termination of parental rights, or where there has been a showing of parental abandonment or unfitness. A termination may ordinarily take one of three forms: an action by an approved agency, an action by DYFS, or an action in connection with a private placement adoption. . . .

In this case a termination of parental rights was obtained not by proving the statutory prerequisites but by claiming the benefit of contractual provisions. [I]t is clear that a contractual agreement to abandon one's parental rights, or not to contest a termination action, will not be enforced in our courts. The Legislature would not have so carefully, so consistently, and so substantially restricted termination of parental rights if it had intended to allow termination to be achieved by one short sentence in a contract.

Since the termination was invalid, it follows, as noted above, that adoption of Melissa by Mrs. Stern could not properly be granted. . . .

It is clear that the Legislature so carefully circumscribed all aspects of a consent to surrender custody—its form and substance, its manner of execution, and the agency or agencies to which it may be made—in order to provide the basis for irrevocability. It seems most unlikely that the Legislature intended that a consent not complying with these requirements would also be irrevocable, especially where, as here, that consent falls radically short of compliance. . . .

Contractual surrender of parental rights is not provided for in our statutes as now written. Indeed, in the Parentage Act, there is a specific provision invalidating any agreement "between an alleged or presumed father and the mother of the child" to bar an action brought for the purpose of determining paternity "[r]egardless of [the contract's] terms." Even a settlement agreement concerning parentage reached in a judicially-mandated consent conference is not valid unless the proposed settlement is approved beforehand by the court. There is no doubt that a contractual provision purporting to constitute an irrevocable agreement to surrender custody of a child for adoption is invalid. . . .

The surrogacy contract's invalidity, resulting from its direct conflict with the above statutory provisions, is further underlined when its goals and means are measured against New Jersey's public policy. The contract's

---

[2] Of course, here there are no "adoptive parents," but rather the natural father and his wife, the only adoptive parent. As noted, however, many of the dangers of using money in connection with adoption may exist in surrogacy situations.

basic premise, that the natural parents can decide in advance of birth which one is to have custody of the child, bears no relationship to the settled law that the child's best interests shall determine custody. The fact that the trial court remedied that aspect of the contract through the "best interests" phase does not make the contractual provision any less offensive to the public policy of this State. . . .

The point is made that Mrs. Whitehead *agreed* to the surrogacy arrangement, supposedly fully understanding the consequences. Putting aside the issue of how compelling her need for money may have been, and how significant her understanding of the consequences, we suggest that her consent is irrelevant. There are, in a civilized society, some things that money cannot buy. In America, we decided long ago that merely because conduct purchased by money was "voluntary" did not mean that it was good or beyond regulation and prohibition. Employers can no longer buy labor at the lowest price they can bargain for, even though that labor is "voluntary," or buy women's labor for less money than paid to men for the same job, or purchase the agreement of children to perform oppressive labor, or purchase the agreement of workers to subject themselves to unsafe or unhealthful working conditions. There are, in short, values that society deems more important than granting to wealth whatever it can buy, be it labor, love, or life. Whether this principle recommends prohibition of surrogacy, which presumably sometimes results in great satisfaction to all of the parties, is not for us to say. We note here only that, under existing law, the fact that Mrs. Whitehead "agreed" to the arrangement is not dispositive. . . .

In sum, the harmful consequences of this surrogacy arrangement appear to us all too palpable. In New Jersey the surrogate mother's agreement to sell her child is void. Its irrevocability infects the entire contract, as does the money that purports to buy it. . . .

Having decided that the surrogacy contract is illegal and unenforceable, we now must decide the custody question without regard to the provisions of the surrogacy contract that would give Mr. Stern sole and permanent custody. (That does not mean that the existence of the contract and the circumstances under which it was entered may not be considered to the extent deemed relevant to the child's best interests.) With the surrogacy contract disposed of, the legal framework becomes a dispute between two couples over the custody of a child produced by the artificial insemination of one couple's wife by the other's husband. Under the Parentage Act the claims of the natural father and the natural mother are entitled to equal weight, *i.e.*, one is not preferred over the other solely because he or she is the father or the mother. The applicable rule given these circumstances is clear: the child's best interests determine custody. . . .

Based on all of this we have concluded, independent of the trial court's identical conclusion, that Melissa's best interests call for custody in the Sterns. . . .

. . . Our reversal of the trial court's order, however, requires delineation of Mrs. Whitehead's rights to visitation. It is apparent to us that this factually sensitive issue, which was never addressed below, should not be determined *de novo* by this Court. We therefore remand the visitation issue to the trial court. . . .

NOTE

Professor Carol Sanger has offered the following observations about the case (Sanger, In the Matter of Baby M, in Contract Stories 127, 157 (2007)):

> In removing surrogacy from the realm of permissible commercial activity in New Jersey, Justice Wilentz focused on what he saw as the pernicious role of the middleman. By taking money out of the equation, entrepreneurs would have to go elsewhere to extract surplus from trades like this, and that is certainly what happened. Surrogacy brokers decamped to jurisdictions where surrogacy was permitted or to those still in legal limbo, as New Jersey had been. But *Baby M* had revealed surrogacy's potential for heartbreak—or, as many contended, heartbreak's inevitability—and many state legislatures took note. Some banned commercial surrogacy outright; others were content to make surrogacy contracts legal but unenforceable. And in many jurisdictions, brokers have come in for special mention. Some states, such as Colorado, ban payment to the mothers but permit it to the broker. Others, such as the United Kingdom, permit payment to the mother but completely ban the broker. It is an offense in the United Kingdom to negotiate a commercial deal or even to advertise for a volunteer surrogate. Where surrogacy is legal, as in California, it appears to thrive. With this array of options, couples can now decide whether to follow the law of their own state or country, or to forum shop in the global market of reproductive tourism.

SECTION 2. DURESS AND COERCIVE RENEGOTIATION

Batsakis v. Demotsis

Court of Civil Appeals of Texas, 1949.
226 S.W.2d 673.

McGILL, J. This is an appeal from a judgment of the [district court]. Appellant was plaintiff and appellee was defendant in the trial court.... Plaintiff sued defendant to recover $2,000 with interest at the rate of 8% per annum from April 2, 1942, alleged to be due on the following instrument, being a translation from the original, which is written in the Greek language:

"Peiraeus
April 2, 1942

"Mr. George Batsakis
Konstantinou Diadohou #7
Peiraeus

"Mr. Batsakis:

"I state by my present (letter) that I received today from you the amount of two thousand dollars ($2,000) of United States of America money, which I borrowed from you for the support of my family during these difficult days and because it is impossible for me to transfer dollars of my own from America.

"The above amount I accept with the expressed promise that I will return to you again in American dollars either at the end of the present war or even before in the event that you might be able to find a way to collect them (dollars) from my representative in America to whom I shall write and give him an order relative to this. You understand until the final execution (payment) to the above amount an eight per cent interest will be added and paid together with the principal. I thank you and I remain yours with respects.

"The recipient,

(Signed) Eugenia The. Demotsis."

Trial to the court . . . resulted in a judgment in favor of plaintiff for $750 principal, and interest at the rate of 8% per annum from April 2, 1942 to the date of judgment, totaling $1163.83, with interest thereon at the rate of 8% per annum until paid. Plaintiff [appeals].

The court sustained certain special exceptions of plaintiff to defendant's first amended original answer on which the case was tried, and struck therefrom paragraphs II, III and V. Defendant excepted to such action of the court, but has not cross-assigned error here. The answer, stripped of such paragraphs, consisted of a general denial contained in paragraph I thereof, and of paragraph IV, which is as follows:

"IV. That under the circumstances alleged in Paragraph II of this answer, the consideration upon which said written instrument sued upon by plaintiff herein is founded, is wanting and has failed to the extent of $1975, and defendant pleads specially under the verification hereinafter made the want and failure of consideration stated, and now tenders, as defendant has heretofore tendered to plaintiff, $25 as the value of the loan of money received by defendant from plaintiff, together with interest thereon.

"Further, in connection with this plea of want and failure of consideration defendant alleges that she at no time received from plaintiff himself or from anyone for plaintiff any money or thing of value other than, as hereinbefore alleged, the original loan of 500,000 drachmae. That at the time of the loan by plaintiff to defendant of said 500,000 drachmae the value of 500,000 drachmae [in] Greece in dollars of money of the United States of America, was $25, and also at said time the value of 500,000 drachmae of Greek money in the [United States] in dollars was $25. . . . The plea of want and failure of consideration is verified by defendant as follows."

The allegations in paragraph II which were stricken, referred to in paragraph IV, were that the instrument sued on was signed and delivered in Greece on or about April 2, 1942, at which time both plaintiff and defendant were residents of and residing in Greece, and

"[Defendant] avers that on or about April 2, 1942 she owned money and property and had credit in the United States of America, but was then and there in Greece in straitened financial circumstances due to the conditions produced by World War II and could not make use of her money and property and credit existing in the [United States]. That in the circumstances the plaintiff agreed to and did lend to defendant the sum of 500,000 drachmae, which at that time, on or about April 2, 1942, had the value of $25 in money of the [United States]. That the said plaintiff, knowing defendant's financial distress and desire to return to [America], exacted of her the written instrument plaintiff sues upon, which was a promise by her to pay to him the sum of $2,000 of United States of America money."

Plaintiff specially excepted to paragraph IV because the allegations thereof were insufficient to allege either want of consideration or failure of consideration, in that it affirmatively appears therefrom that defendant received what was agreed to be delivered to her, and that plaintiff breached no agreement. The court overruled this exception, and such action is assigned as error. Error is also assigned because of the court's failure to enter judgment for the whole unpaid balance of the principal of the instrument with interest as therein provided.

Defendant testified that she did receive 500,000 drachmas from plaintiff. It is not clear whether she received all the 500,000 drachmas or only a portion of them before she signed the instrument in question. Her testimony clearly shows that the understanding of the parties was that plaintiff would give her the 500,000 drachmas if she would sign the instrument. She testified:

"Q. [W]ho suggested the figure of $2,000?

"A. That was how he asked me from the beginning. He said he will give me five hundred thousand drachmas provided I signed that I would pay him $2,000 American money."

The transaction amounted to a sale by plaintiff of the 500,000 drachmas in consideration of the execution of the instrument sued on, by defendant. It is not contended that the drachmas had no value. Indeed, the judgment indicates that the trial court placed a value of $750 on them or on the other consideration which plaintiff gave defendant for the instrument if he believed plaintiff's testimony. Therefore the plea of want of consideration was unavailing. A plea of want of consideration amounts to a contention that the instrument never became a valid obligation in the first place. National Bank of Commerce v. Williams, 125 Tex. 619, 84 S.W.2d 691.

Mere inadequacy of consideration will not void a contract. 10 Tex.Jur., Contracts, Sec. 89, p. 150; Chastain v. Texas Christian Missionary Society, Tex.Civ.App., 78 S.W.2d 728.

Nor was the plea of failure of consideration availing. Defendant got exactly what she contracted for according to her own testimony. The court should have rendered judgment in favor of plaintiff against defendant for the principal sum of $2,000 evidenced by the instrument sued on, with interest as therein provided. We construe the provision relating to interest as providing for interest at the rate of 8% per annum. The judgment is reformed so as to award appellant a recovery against appellee of $2,000 with interest thereon at the rate of 8% per annum from April 2, 1942. Such judgment will bear interest at the rate of 8% per annum until paid on $2,000 thereof and on the balance interest at the rate of 6% per annum. As so reformed, the judgment is affirmed.

NOTE: GREECE IN 1942

The promise of Eugenia Demotsis was given not quite one year after the German armies had invaded Greece. The invasion occurred on April 6, 1941, and despite bitter resistance by the Greeks, soldiers and civilians, the main forces of the Greek armies surrendered to the Nazis on April 23, 1941. The devastation from the fighting itself was enormous, and continued after the surrender as a result of reprisals ordered by the Nazis for Greek resistance. Large numbers of country people fled to the cities, a very large portion to Athens and its adjoining port city, Peiraeus. The disruption that resulted for all forms of economic activity was magnified by a galloping inflation of the currency.

Greece before the war had long been deficient in agricultural products; only one-fifth of its land was arable. It was necessary even in normal times to import about half its food supplies, especially cereals. The German and Italian forces, during the occupation, confiscated large stocks of food. Imports were almost entirely cut off, on the West by an Allied blockade and to the North by continuing military operations. It was later estimated that in 1941 the average daily diet for all Greeks was about 900 calories per person, and until the end of the occupation (October 1944) the intake never rose above an average of 1,400 calories per person, well below normal requirements of 2,500 to 3,000. There is no way of knowing how many thousands died of malnutrition, most of them in the cities. Some estimates for the country as a whole ran into the hundreds of thousands. Finally, as accounts of this vast tragedy reached the outside world, the leading belligerents agreed to grant safe passage to shipments of food and medical supplies under the direction of Swiss and Swedish Red Cross officials. The shipments began to arrive in the last six months of 1942 and attained a substantial volume in 1943. (There is a brief account of these events in B. Sweet–Escott, Greece, A Political and Economic Survey, 1939–1953, 93–96 (1954).)

Embola v. Tuppela

127 Wash. 285, 220 P. 789 (1923)

Tuppela prospected for gold in Alaska, acquired a gold mine worth $500,000, but was then adjudged insane and committed to an asylum in Oregon. On his release after four years' confinement, Tuppela learned that his Alaska mine had been sold by his guardian. He searched but found no one willing to advance him funds for use in recovering the property. Then, destitute and without work, Tuppela encountered the plaintiff, a "close friend" of 30 years, who gave him shelter and money for support. Tuppela later said to plaintiff: "You have already let me have $270. If you will give me $50 more so I can go to Alaska and get my property back, I will pay you ten thousand dollars when I win my property." Plaintiff at once gave him $50, Tuppela went to Alaska and, after litigation lasting three years, won back his gold mine. Remembering his agreement, Tuppela asked "his trustee" (apparently, in the interim, Tuppela had again become incompetent) to pay plaintiff $10,000. The trustee refused, claiming that the contract was "unconscionable," not supported by adequate consideration, and in violation of usury laws. Plaintiff sued the trustee, recovering judgment for the $10,000 Tuppela had promised. Affirming, the Supreme Court agreed that all objections to the contract must fail. Tuppela's mind was "sound" when he gave his promise, and he considered the exchange "fair and to his advantage." It was unlikely he would ever recover his property, as an attorney had told him. "The risk of losing the money advanced was as great [as it would be] under a grubstake contract." A contingency that may never occur makes a transaction such as this "an investment and not a loan"; usury is not a concern. The uncertain event conditioning Tuppela's promise also "supports the finding that the consideration was not inadequate."

Cᴏᴍᴍᴇɴᴛ: "AᴅᴇQᴜᴀᴄʏ" ᴏꜰ Cᴏɴꜱɪᴅᴇʀᴀᴛɪᴏɴ

In Chapter 2, we encountered talk of "nominal" consideration in connection with purported bargains that in fact involved a great disparity in values. There is perhaps no more accepted proposition in Anglo–American contract law than the one requiring but a single line of space in Batsakis v. Demotsis: "Mere inadequacy of consideration will not void a contract." The same can be said of the corollary principle, that "ordinarily the courts will not inquire into the adequacy of consideration."

The failure of the early common law to review the "adequacy" of consideration is quite understandable. We have seen that developments in the sixteenth and seventeenth centuries were mainly procedural, and thus technical, in nature (should assumpsit be extended to particular types of informal promises?). Because the emphasis was on the harm suffered by the promisee, it was inevitable that attention was drawn to the question whether enforcement was called for. The emerging test of consideration, cabined by the assumpsit remedy, was not seen as an occasion for raising challenges to unequal bargains. The Chancellor, of course, was available to entertain claims of hardship, claims for revision or cancellation of obligations that, for any number of reasons, had become onerous (see Chapter 1, supra pp. 166–170). Later, in the eighteenth and nineteenth centuries, the reluctance of courts to take up "adequacy" directly was put on other grounds. The Arkansas case of Buckner v. McIlroy, 31 Ark. 631 (1877), provides an example:

> While it is true a right of action does not arise on a mere naked promise, yet, if there be any legal consideration for the promise, the court will not inquire into its adequacy,—"The law having no means of deciding upon this matter, and it being considered unwise to interfere with the facility of contracting, and the free exercise of the judgment and will of the parties, by not allowing them to be the judges of the benefits to be derived from their bargains, provided there be no incompetency to contract, and the agreement violate no rule of law. It is, indeed, necessary that the consideration be of some value, but it is sufficient if it be of slight value only. [E.g.,] the compromise or abandonment of a doubtful right is a sufficient consideration for a contract, even when it turns out that the point given up was in truth against the promisee." 1 Chitty on Contracts (11 Ed.) 29.

Modern views of the social gains realized through private exchange transactions remain rooted in these nineteenth century ideas about economic individualism and enlightened self-interest. You will note that the Restatement, Second § 71 (supra p. 213) uses only the term "consideration," dropping all reference to the *Buckner* court's talk of "sufficient consideration." One puzzle over the years has been the historical distinction between "sufficiency" of consideration and "adequacy" of consideration; the former was said to be required while an inquiry into the latter was deemed inappropriate.

Still, a brief word of caution is necessary. One should not conclude that the broad prohibition against review of "adequacy" has meant that the fairness of an exchange is not a legal concern. In fact, there exists a vast body of doctrine and special rules—both judicially-declared and legislative in origin, much of it developed in equity—which courts invoke regularly in passing on the fairness of bargains, including the problem of equivalence. We shall see once again in this chapter that refusing enforcement of a contract is by no means an uncommon event. All we have observed to this point is that the requirement of consideration, standing alone, is not a front-line insurer of fair exchanges. It is another question whether, as one court has asserted, the inadequacy of consideration is "more properly construed as a factor relevant in the application of other rules." Oh v. Wilson, 112 Nev. 38, 910 P.2d 276 (1996).

One finds in the writings on contract, including judicial opinions, statements much like the following: (1) "In many contracts, especially those requiring alternating performances over time, the need for adjustments, perhaps even major modifications, will be commonplace." (2) "Given the delay, uncertainty, and expense of court proceedings, it is unlikely that legal remedies for breach of contract will give the promisee the full equivalent of the promisor's actual performance." (3) "At times, a promisee will be well advised to offer a benefit to a promisor who is refusing to honor a contract, in order to induce performance."

Do these statements appear to be unexceptional, perhaps rooted in everyday experience? The cases coming next ask whether generalizations such as these require significant qualification or elaboration. It should be noted that we have already seen something of the law's policy favoring compromises and settlements (recall, e.g., Military College Co. v. Brooks, p. 217). Yet modifications of rights and duties, resulting from bargaining advantages gained by virtue of an existing contract, present troublesome issues as to what is "proper" conduct.

Alaska Packers' Ass'n v. Domenico

United States Court of Appeals, Ninth Circuit, 1902.
117 F. 99.

ROSS, CIRCUIT JUDGE. The libel in this case was based upon a contract alleged to have been entered into between the libelants and the appellant corporation on the 22d day of May, 1900, at Pyramid Harbor, Alaska, by which it is claimed the appellant promised to pay each of the libelants, among other things, the sum of $100 for services rendered and to be rendered. . . .

The evidence shows that on March 26, 1900, [in] San Francisco, the libelants entered into a written contract with the appellant, whereby they agreed to go from San Francisco to Pyramid Harbor, Alaska, and return, on board such vessel as might be designated by the appellant, and to work for the appellant during the fishing season of 1900, at Pyramid Harbor, as sailors and fishermen, agreeing to do "regular ship's duty, both up and down, discharging and loading; and to do any other work whatsoever when requested to do so by the captain or agent of the Alaska Packers' Ass'n." By the terms of this agreement, the appellant was to pay each of the libelants $50 for the season, and two cents for each red salmon in the catching of which he took part.

On the 15th day of April, 1900, 21 of the libelants signed shipping articles by which they shipped as seamen on the Two Brothers, a vessel chartered by the appellant for the voyage between San Francisco and Pyramid

Harbor, and also bound themselves to perform the same work for the appellant provided for by the previous contract of March 26th; the appellant agreeing to pay them therefor the sum of $60 for the season, and two cents each for each red salmon in the catching of which they should respectively take part. Under these contracts, the libelants sailed on board the Two Brothers for Pyramid Harbor, where the appellant had about $150,000 invested in a salmon cannery. The libelants arrived there early in April of the year mentioned, and began to unload the vessel and fit up the cannery. A few days thereafter, to wit, May 19th, they stopped work in a body, and demanded of the company's superintendent there in charge $100 for services in operating the vessel to and from Pyramid Harbor, instead of the sums stipulated for in and by the contracts; stating that unless they were paid this additional wage they would stop work entirely, and return to San Francisco. The evidence showed, and the court below found, that it was impossible for the appellant to get other men to take the places of the libelants, the place being remote, the season short and just opening; so that, after endeavoring for several days without success to induce the libelants to proceed with their work in accordance with their contracts, the company's superintendent, on the 22d day of May, so far yielded to their demands as to instruct his clerk to copy the contracts executed in San Francisco, substituting, for the $50 and $60 payments, respectively, of those contracts, the sum of $100, which document, so prepared, was signed by the libelants before a shipping commissioner whom they had requested to be brought from Northeast Point; the superintendent, however, testifying that he at the time told the libelants that he was without authority to enter into any such contract, or to in any way alter the contracts made between them and the company in San Francisco. Upon the return of the libelants to San Francisco at the close of the fishing season, they demanded pay in accordance with the terms of the alleged contract of May 22d, when the company denied its validity, and refused to pay other than as provided for by the contracts of March 26th and April 5th, respectively. . . .

Duress

. . . [T]he libelants undertook to show [at trial] that the fishing nets provided by the respondent were defective, and that it was on that account that they demanded increased wages. On that point, the evidence was substantially conflicting, and the finding of the court was against the libelants. . . . The evidence being sharply conflicting in respect to these facts, the conclusions of the court, who heard and saw the witnesses, will not be disturbed. . . .

The real questions [here are] questions of law, and [it] will be necessary to consider but one of those. Assuming that the appellant's superintendent at Pyramid Harbor was authorized to make the alleged contract of May 22d, . . . was it supported by a sufficient consideration? . . . [T]he libelants agreed in writing, for certain stated compensation, to render their services to the appellant in remote waters . . .; and, after having entered upon the discharge of their contract, and at a time when it was impossible for the appellant to secure other men in their places, the libelants, without any valid cause, absolutely refused to continue the services they were under contract to perform unless the appellant would consent to pay them more money. Consent to such a demand, under such circumstances, if given, was, in our opinion, without a consideration, for the reason that it was based solely upon the libelants' agreement to render the exact services, and none other, that they were already under contract to render. . . . [T]hey willfully and arbitrarily broke that obligation. As a matter of course, they were liable to the appellant in damages, and it is quite probable, as suggested by the court below[,] that they may have been unable to respond in damages. But we are unable to agree with the conclusions there drawn, from these facts, in these words:

"Under such circumstances, it would be strange, indeed, if the law would not permit the defendant to waive the damages caused by the libelants' breach, and enter into the contract sued upon,—a contract mutually beneficial to all the parties thereto, in that it gave to the libelants reasonable compensation for their labor, and enabled the defendant to employ to advantage the large capital it had invested in its canning and fishing plant."

Certainly, it cannot be justly held [that] there was any voluntary waiver on the part of the appellant of the breach of the original contract. The company itself knew nothing of such breach until the expedition returned to San Francisco, and the testimony is uncontradicted that its superintendent at Pyramid Harbor . . . distinctly informed the libelants that he had no power to alter the original or to make a new contract; and it would, of course, follow that, if he had no power to change the original, he would have no authority to waive any rights thereunder. The circumstances of the present case bring it, we think, directly within the sound and just observations [made in] [King v. Duluth, M & N Railway Co., 61 Minn. 482, 63 N.W. 1105]:

"No astute reasoning can change the plain fact that the party who refuses to perform, and thereby coerces a promise from the other party to the contract to pay him an increased compensation for doing that which he is legally bound to do, takes an unjustifiable advantage of the necessities of the other party. Surely it would be a travesty on justice to hold that the party so making the promise for extra pay was estopped from asserting that the promise was without consideration. A party cannot lay the foundation of an estoppel by his own wrong, where the promise is simply a repetition of a subsisting legal promise. . . ."

[The court then referred to Lingenfelder v. Wainwright Brewing Co., 103 Mo. 578, 15 S.W. 844 (1891), where an architect, Jungenfeld, was employed by Wainwright to draw plans for a refrigerator plant. Jungenfeld was also president of the Empire Refrigerator Co., manufacturer of refrigerating equipment, and "was largely interested therein." Over Jungenfeld's protest, Wainwright awarded a contract for refrigerating equipment to a competitor of Jungenfeld's company. Jungenfeld then took away his plans and refused to perform further. Wainwright "was in great haste to have its brewery completed for divers reasons," and to secure a new architect and new plans would take much time. Wainwright thereupon agreed to pay Jungenfeld five percent of the price of the refrigerating equipment it had purchased from the competitor if Jungenfeld would continue his work as supervising architect. The court in the principal case proceeded to quote from the opinion of the Missouri court, which refused to allow recovery of the five percent promised to Jungenfeld:]

"It is urged upon us by respondents that this was a new contract. New in what? Jungenfeld was bound by his contract to design and supervise this building. Under the new promise, he was not to do anything more or anything different. What benefit was to accrue to Wainwright? He was to receive the same service from Jungenfeld under the new, that Jungenfeld was bound to tender under the original, contract. What loss, trouble, or inconvenience could result to Jungenfeld that he had not already assumed? No amount of metaphysical reasoning can change the plain fact that

Jungenfeld took advantage of Wainwright's necessities, and extorted the promise of five per cent on the refrigerator plant as the condition of his complying with his contract already entered into. . . . To permit plaintiff to recover under such circumstances would be to offer a premium upon bad faith, and invite men to violate their most sacred contracts that they may profit by their own wrong. That a promise to pay a man for doing that which he is already under contract to do is without consideration is conceded by respondents. . . . But it is 'carrying coals to Newcastle' to add authorities on a proposition so universally accepted, and so inherently just and right in itself. . . . [R]espondents do not controvert the general proposition. Their contention is, and the circuit court agreed that, when Jungenfeld declined to go further on his contract, the defendant then had the right to sue for damages, and not having elected to sue Jungenfeld, but having acceded to his demand for the additional compensation, defendant cannot now be heard to say his promise is without consideration. While it is true Jungenfeld became liable in damages for the obvious breach of his contract, we do not think it follows that defendant is estopped from showing its promise was made without consideration. . . . [W]hen a party merely does what he has already obligated himself to do, he cannot demand an additional compensation therefor; and although, by taking advantage of the necessities of his adversary, he obtains a promise for more, the law will regard it as nudum pactum, and will not lend its process to aid in the wrong." . . .

It results from the views above expressed that the judgment must be reversed, and the cause remanded, with directions to the court below to enter judgment for the respondent, with costs. It is so ordered.

NOTE

In Selmer Co. v. Blakeslee–Midwest Co., 704 F.2d 924, 927 (7th Cir.1983), Judge Posner analyzed *Alaska Packers* and observed, "Although the technical ground of decision was the absence of fresh consideration for the modified agreement, it seems apparent . . . that the court's underlying concern was that the modified agreement had been procured by duress in the form of the threat to break the original contract." In his view, the vice at which the law should aim are attempts "to exploit the contract promisee's lack of an adequate legal remedy."

Austin Instrument, Inc. v. Loral Corp.

Court of Appeals of New York, 1971.
29 N.Y.2d 124, 324 N.Y.S.2d 22, 272 N.E.2d 533.

FULD, C.J. The defendant, Loral Corp., seeks to recover payment for goods delivered under a contract which it had with the plaintiff Austin Instrument, on the ground that the evidence establishes, as a matter of law, that it was forced to agree to an increase in price on the items in question under circumstances amounting to economic duress.

In July of 1965, Loral was awarded a $6,000,000 contract by the Navy for the production of radar sets. The contract contained a schedule of deliveries, a liquidated damages clause applying to late deliveries and a cancellation clause in case of default by Loral. The latter thereupon solicited bids for some 40 precision gear components needed to produce the radar sets, and awarded Austin a subcontract to supply 23 such parts[;] [Austin] commenced delivery in early 1966.

In May 1966, Loral was awarded a second Navy contract for the production of more radar sets and again went about soliciting bids. Austin bid on all 40 gear components but, on July 15, a [Loral] representative informed Austin's president, Krauss, that his company would be awarded the subcontract only for those items on which it was low bidder. The Austin officer refused to accept an order for less than all 40 of the gear parts and on the next day he told Loral that Austin would cease deliveries of the parts due under the existing subcontract unless Loral consented to substantial increases in the prices provided for by that agreement—both retroactively for parts already delivered and prospectively on those not yet shipped—and placed with Austin the order for all 40 parts needed under Loral's second Navy contract. Shortly thereafter, Austin did, indeed, stop delivery. After contacting 10 manufacturers of precision gears and finding none who could produce the parts in time to meet its commitments to the Navy,[1] Loral acceded to Austins demands; in a letter dated July 22, Loral wrote to Austin that "We have feverishly surveyed other sources of supply and find that because of the prevailing military exigencies, were they to start from scratch as would have to be the case, they could not even remotely begin to deliver on time to meet the delivery requirements established by the Government. . . . Accordingly, we are left with no choice or alternative but to meet your conditions."

Loral thereupon consented to the price increases insisted upon by Austin under the first subcontract and the latter was awarded a second subcontract making it the supplier of all 40 gear parts for Loral's second contract with the Navy. Although Austin was granted until September to resume deliveries, Loral did, in fact, receive parts in August and was able to produce the radar sets in time to meet its commitments to the Navy on both contracts. After Austin's last delivery under the second subcontract in July, 1967, Loral notified it of its intention to seek recovery of the price increases.

On September 15, 1967, Austin instituted this action against Loral to recover an amount in excess of $17,750 which was still due on the second subcontract. On the same day, Loral commenced an action against Austin claiming damages of some $22,250—the aggregate of the price increases under the first subcontract—on the ground of economic duress. [Loral made no claim on the second subcontract.] The two actions were consolidated and, following a trial, Austin was awarded the sum it requested and Loral's complaint against Austin was dismissed on the ground that it was not shown that "it could not have obtained the items in question from other sources in time to meet its commitment to the Navy under the first contract." A closely divided Appellate Division affirmed (35 A.D.2d 387, 316 N.Y.S.2d 528, 532). . . .

The applicable law is clear. . . . A contract is voidable on the ground of duress when it is established that the party making the claim was forced to agree to it by means of a wrongful threat precluding the exercise of his free will. . . . The existence of economic duress or business compulsion is demonstrated by proof that "immediate possession of needful goods is threatened"

---

[1] The best reply Loral received was from a vendor who stated he could commence deliveries some time in October. [Other footnotes have been omitted.—Eds.]

[or,] more particularly, in cases such as the one before us, by proof that one party to a contract has threatened to breach the agreement by withholding goods unless the other party agrees to some further demand. However, a mere threat by one party to breach the contract by not delivering the required items, though wrongful, does not in itself constitute economic duress. It must also appear that the threatened party could not obtain the goods from another source of supply and that the ordinary remedy of an action for breach of contract would not be adequate.

RULE

We find without any support in the record the conclusion reached by the courts below that Loral failed to establish that it was the victim of economic duress. On the contrary, the evidence makes out a classic case, as a matter of law, of such duress.

duress

It is manifest that Austin's threat—to stop deliveries unless the prices were increased—deprived Loral of its free will. . . . Loral's relationship with the Government is most significant. . . . [I]ts contract called for staggered monthly deliveries of the radar assets, with clauses calling for liquidated damages and possible cancellation on default. Because of its production schedule, Loral was, in July, 1966, concerned with meeting its delivery requirements in September, October and November, and it was for the sets to be delivered in those months that the withheld gears were needed. Loral had to plan ahead, and the substantial liquidated damages for which it would be liable, plus the threat of default, were genuine possibilities. Moreover, Loral did a substantial portion of its business with the Government, and it feared that a failure to deliver as agreed upon would jeopardize its chances for future contracts. . . . It was perfectly reasonable for Loral, or any other party similarly placed, to consider itself in an emergency, duress situation.

. . . [T]he parts necessary for production of the radar sets to be delivered in September were delivered to Loral on September 1, and the parts needed for the October schedule were delivered in late August and early September. Even so, Loral had to "work [around] the clock" to meet its commitments. Considering that the best offer Loral received from the other vendors it contacted was commencement of delivery sometime in October, which, as the record shows, would have made it late in its deliveries to the Navy in both September and October, Loral's claim that it had no choice but to accede to Austin's demands is conclusively demonstrated.

We find unconvincing Austin's contention that Loral, in order to meet its burden, should have contacted the Government and asked for an extension of its delivery dates so as to enable it to purchase the parts from another vendor. Aside from the consideration that Loral was anxious to perform well in the Government's eyes, it could not be sure when it would obtain enough parts from a substitute vendor to meet its commitments. The only promise which it received from the companies it contacted was for *commencement* of deliveries, not full supply, and, with vendor delay common in this field, it would have been nearly impossible to know the length of the extension it should request. It must be remembered that Loral was producing a needed item of military hardware. Moreover, there is authority for Loral's position that nonperformance by a subcontractor is not an excuse for default in the main contract. (See, e.g., McBride & Wachtel, Government Contracts, § 35.10, [11].) . . .

Loral also had the burden of demonstrating that it could not obtain the parts elsewhere within a reasonable time, and there can be no doubt that it met this burden. The 10 manufacturers whom Loral contacted comprised its entire list of "approved vendors" for precision gears, and none was able to commence delivery soon enough. As Loral was producing a highly sophisticated item of military machinery requiring parts made to the strictest engineering standards, it would be unreasonable to hold that Loral should have gone to other vendors, with whom it was either unfamiliar or dissatisfied, to procure the needed parts. . . .

It is hardly necessary to add that Loral's normal legal remedy of accepting Austin's breach of the contract and then suing for damages would have been inadequate under the circumstances, as Loral would still have had to obtain the gears elsewhere with all the concomitant consequences mentioned above. In other words, Loral actually had no choice, when the prices were raised by Austin, except to take the gears at the "coerced" prices and then sue to get the excess back.

Austin's final argument is that Loral, even if it did enter into the contract under duress, lost any rights it had to a refund of money by waiting until July, 1967, long after the termination date of the contract, to disaffirm it. It is true that one who would recover moneys allegedly paid under duress must act promptly to make his claim known. . . . In this case, Loral delayed making its demand for a refund until three days after Austin's last delivery on the second subcontract. Loral's reason—for waiting until that time—is that it feared another stoppage of deliveries which would again put it in an untenable situation. Considering Austin's conduct in the past, this was perfectly reasonable. . . .

In sum, the record before us demonstrates that Loral agreed to the price increases in consequence of the economic duress employed by Austin. Accordingly, the matter should be remanded to the trial court for a computation of its damages. The order appealed from should be modified, by reversing so much thereof as affirms the dismissal of [Loral's] claim and, except as so modified, affirmed.

The order [is] affirmed. [The majority prevailed by a vote of 4 to 3; a dissenting opinion argued that Loral's failure to seek out alternative suppliers other than those it had used in the past raised an issue of fact as to whether Loral had acted reasonably.]

Smithwick v. Whitley

152 N.C. 369, 67 S.E. 913 (1910)

Plaintiff contracted in writing to purchase from defendant a tract of land containing not quite 14 acres, for $35 an acre, went into possession (without getting a deed) and began clearing it. Three years later defendant informed plaintiff that the deal was off. Shortly thereafter, plaintiff went to see defendant, who told him he could have the land for a price of $50 an acre. "After considerable talk," plaintiff paid the sum demanded "rather than lose the land," which he had worked for three years, ditching, fencing, and getting it into tillable condition. Defendant gave him a deed in return for the payment. In an action brought to recover the overpayment, *held*, a nonsuit ordered by the trial court was proper. The payment made to secure a deed was "voluntary." Duress exists only where the unlawful act of another has deprived one of free will. Plaintiff could have sued in equity for specific performance when defendant demanded a higher price. [Is there anything here suggesting that plaintiff would have been hard-pressed to make effective use of its legal remedies against breach, or that defendant knew that to be the case? Compare an illustration given by Rest.2d, Contracts § 175: "A, with whom B has left a machine for repairs, makes an improper threat to refuse to deliver the machine to B, although B has paid for the repairs, unless B agrees to make a contract to have additional repair work done. B can replevy the machine, but because he is in urgent need of it and delay would cause him heavy financial loss, he is induced by A's threat to make the contract. B has no reasonable alternative, A's threat amounts to duress, and the contract is voidable by B."]

———————

Wolf v. Marlton Corp.

57 N.J.Super. 278, 154 A.2d 625 (1959)

The Wolfs, husband and wife, contracted to buy land in a subdivision that Marlton was developing and to pay $24,500 for a house to be built by Marlton on the land. Marlton's plan for developing the subdivision was to combine the sale of lots and the building of houses. The Wolfs made a down payment of $2,450. Another $2,450 was to be paid when their house was "closed in," but by that time marital difficulties led them to request a cancellation of their contract and repayment of the $2,450 they had paid. Marlton's agent proposed to return only $1,450; Mr. Wolf demanded $2,000. According to Marlton's agent, Wolf stated that unless this was agreed to he would go through with the purchase and then resell to "an undesirable purchaser," so that this "will be the last tract that you will ever build in New Jersey and it will be the last house that you will sell in this tract." Marlton eventually sold the house to another person. In an action by the Wolfs to recover their full $2,450 deposit, *held*, it was error for the trial court to hold Marlton in default for its refusal to go forward with the contract in face of this threat. There was no physical violence exerted or threatened by Wolf, but a distinction depending on the kind of pressure exerted carries little weight. "Duress is tested, not by the nature of the threats, but rather by the state of mind induced thereby in the victim." It is true that once plaintiffs bought the house they had a legal right to sell to whomever they wished, but "where a party for purely malicious and unconscionable motives threatens to sell such a home to a purchaser, specially selected because he would be undesirable, for the sole purpose of injuring the builder's business, fundamental fairness requires the conclusion that his conduct in making this threat be deemed 'wrongful' as the term is used in the law of duress." The case was remanded for the trial judge to determine whether the threat was made, whether Marlton's manager believed it would be carried out, and whether his will was thereby overborne.

———————

NOTE: AN "IMPROPER" THREAT

The *Marlton* court said that the Wolfs had a "legal right" to sell to whomever they wished, yet, in the end, their conduct was deemed "wrongful." Statements to the effect that "it is not a breach of contract to threaten to do something you have a right to do" are seen often. In a contractor's suit to declare a settlement agreement null and void, Stewart M. Muller Constr. Co. v. New

York Tel. Co., 40 N.Y.2d 955, 390 N.Y.S.2d 817, 359 N.E.2d 328 (1976), the court said:

> The order of the Appellate Division should be affirmed. A contract may be voided on the ground of economic duress where the complaining party was compelled to agree to its terms by means of a wrongful threat which precluded the exercise of its free will. [Citing Austin Instrument v. Loral Corp.] Here, plaintiff alleged that the settlement agreement was induced by defendant's threat to terminate their earlier contract. The amended complaint and the affidavit in opposition to the motion to dismiss fail to allege that the defendant was not within its contractual rights in threatening to exercise the termination clause contained in the contract. Rather, it appears that the defendant, in the context of contractual dispute, preserved its rights by following the letter of the termination clause, while at the same time seeking an accommodation with the financially hardpressed plaintiff. In view of the explicit provisions of the termination clause, which gave defendant the right to cancel the contract upon an architect's certificate of substantial breach, there is no possibility that the plaintiff could present evidence which would establish that the defendant's threatened cancellation was in excess of its contractual rights and, hence, was wrongful. The only reasonable inference that can be drawn from the complaint and the affidavits is that the plaintiff is unable to prevail.

Consider also the following passage from Dawson, Economic Duress—An Essay in Perspective, 45 Mich.L.Rev. 253, 283–288 (1947):

> If it can be assumed that the object of relief for duress is to cancel out advantages secured by superior bargaining power, the whole group of duress cases takes on a new perspective. The objective of ensuring the freedom of the individual will, so frequently proposed in the nineteenth century cases, becomes on this analysis an incidental or at most a subsidiary objective. More important, the concentration of the modern cases on the distinction between legal and illegal means seems misdirected, a survival from an earlier period in which duress doctrines were merely an adjunct of the law of crime and tort.

> It is indeed this concentration on distinctions between legal and illegal means which has chiefly arrested the modern development of the law of duress. No single formula has achieved so wide a circulation in the duress cases as the statement that "It is not duress to threaten to do what there is a legal right to do." Certainly no other formula is anything like so misleading. Its vice lies in the half-truth it contains. For an enormous range of conduct is included in the class of acts that there is a "right" to do (and therefore, under this formula, to threaten). At one extreme are various types of severe injury and oppression that narrowly escape the sanctions of the law of crime and tort. At the opposite extreme are the types of pressure that are specifically provided by organized legal agencies, for the very purpose for which they are used (e.g., the remedies of civil litigation). Somewhere between these extremes must be classed all those multiplied forms of economic pressure by which the exchange

of goods and services is accomplished in an individualist society. Without doubt such forms of pressure are normally permissible, and it is the essence of economic individualism to subject their use to a minimum of external regulation. From this it by no means follows that the effects of pressure exerted in particular cases will always escape judicial scrutiny. Doctrines of duress are intended to raise precisely the question whether it is "rightful" to use particular types of pressure for the purpose of extracting an excessive or disproportionate return. Over the whole range of conduct to which this question applies, it is plain that the tests of the criminal law or a damage remedy can no longer determine the limits of relief for unjust enrichment. The insight of Holmes cut through to the central distinction: "When it comes to the collateral question of obtaining a contract by threats, it does not follow that, because you cannot be made to answer for the act, you may use the threat."

A typical case of duress in early law was a deed of land executed by a grantor to secure release from imprisonment or to forestall a threat of serious bodily harm. In the eighteenth century, the concept was extended to include the kind of economic duress that consisted of a wrongful seizure or detention of personal property. This extension began with Astley v. Reynolds, 2 Strange 915 (1732), which is cited and distinguished in Hackley v. Headley, infra p. 639. "Duress of goods" is now well established as a ground for rescission and restitution. Another type of relievable duress, developed in the nineteenth century, is the refusal of a public utility, endowed by law with a monopoly of a service (transportation, gas, electric power), to supply the service unless paid a sum exceeding the authorized rate. Both duress of goods and refusal of service by public utilities have the same feature that helped to open up remedies in cases of violence to the person: the conduct, actual or threatened, is independently wrongful by the law of tort. For a collection of the early American cases on duress by physical compulsion distinguished from duress by threat, see United States for Use of Trane Co. v. Bond, 322 Md. 170, 586 A.2d 734 (1991).

The Chancery had for some time given relief analogous to that provided by the law courts through the doctrine of duress. Undue influence, a notion developed originally in equity, involved not economic pressure but, as we have seen, personal ascendancy over individuals weakened by age, illness, or mental deficiency. The Chancery's solution was rescission of the transaction procured through undue influence, with restitution of any gains thereby secured. There was, and is, considerable overlap between undue influence and abuse of "confidential" relations, in which the securing of unfair advantages by one party from the other is often called "constructive fraud" (see Jackson v. Seymour, supra p. 508). With the fusion of law and equity, the barriers between common law duress and the various equity doctrines have been broken down. The ultimate result of this intermixture is still uncertain.

The legal system faces the challenge of policing misbehavior without at the same time thwarting contract renegotiations that are mutually beneficial and on which parties may subsequently rely. The material that follows examine some of the doctrines that have emerged. The first case begins with the legal duty rule, the idea that contract modifications need to be supported by consideration to be enforceable.

————

Levine v. Blumenthal

Supreme Court of New Jersey, 1936.
117 N.J.L. 23, 186 A. 457.

HEHER, J. By an indenture dated April 16th, 1931, plaintiff leased to defendants, for the retail merchandising of women's wearing apparel, store premises situate in the principal business district of the city of Paterson. The term was two years, to commence on May 1st next ensuing, with an option of renewal for the further period of three years; and the rent reserved was $2,100 for the first year, and $2,400 for the second year, payable in equal monthly installments in advance.

. . . [D]efendants adduced evidence tending to show that, in the month of April, 1932, before the expiration of the first year of the term, they advised plaintiff that "it was absolutely impossible for them to pay any increase in rent; that their business had so fallen down that they had great difficulty in meeting the present rent of $175 per month; that if the plaintiff insisted upon the increase called for in the lease, they would be forced to remove from the premises or perhaps go out of business altogether;" and that plaintiff "agreed to allow them to remain under the same rental 'until business improved.'" While conceding that defendants informed him that "they could not pay the increase called for in the lease because of adverse business conditions," plaintiff, on the other hand, testified that he "agreed to accept the payment of $175 each month, on account." For eleven months of the second year of the term rent was paid by defendants, and accepted by plaintiff, at the rate of $175 per month. The option of renewal was not exercised; and defendants surrendered the premises at the expiration of the term, leaving the last month's rent unpaid. This action was brought to recover the unpaid balance of the rent reserved by the lease for the second year—$25 per month for eleven months, and $200 for the last month.

The District Court found, as a fact, that "a subsequent oral agreement had been made to change and alter the terms of the written lease, with respect to the rent paid," but that it was not supported by "a lawful consideration," and therefore was wholly ineffective.

The insistence is that the current trade depression had disabled the lessees in respect of the payment of the full rent reserved, and a consideration sufficient to support the secondary agreement arose out of these special circumstances; and that, in any event, the execution of the substituted performance therein provided is a defense at law, notwithstanding the want of consideration. The principle invoked is applied in Long v. Hartwell, 34 N.J.L. 116. . . . It is said also that, "in so far as the oral agreement has become executed as to the payments which had fallen due and had been paid and accepted in full as per the oral agreement," the remission of the balance of the rent is sustainable on the theory of gift, if not of accord and satisfaction. . . .

It is not suggested that the primary contract under consideration was of a class which may not lawfully be modified by parol. . . . The point made by respondent is that the subsequent oral agreement to reduce the rent is *nudum pactum*, and therefore created no binding obligation.

It is elementary that the subsequent agreement, to impose the obligation of a contract, must rest upon a new and independent consideration. The rule was laid down in very early times that even though a part of a matured liquidated debt or demand has been given and received in full satisfaction thereof, the creditor may yet recover the remainder. The payment of a part was not regarded in law as a satisfaction of the whole, unless it was in virtue of an agreement supported by a consideration. Pinnel's Case, 5 Coke 117a; 77 Eng.Rep. 237; Fitch v. Sutton, 5 East. 230; Foakes v. Beer, 9 App.Cas. 605.... The principle is firmly imbedded in our jurisprudence that a promise to do what the promisor is already legally bound to do is an unreal consideration.... It has been criticized, at least in some of its special applications, as "mediaeval" and wholly artificial—one that operates to defeat the "reasonable bargains of business men."... But these strictures are not well grounded. They reject the basic principle that a consideration, to support a contract, consists either of a benefit to the promisor or a detriment to the promisee—a doctrine that has always been fundamental.... It is a principle, almost universally accepted, that an act or forbearance required by a legal duty owing to the promisor that is neither doubtful nor the subject of honest and reasonable dispute is not a sufficient consideration....

Yet any consideration for the new undertaking, however insignificant, satisfies this rule. Coast Nat'l Bank v. Bloom, 113 N.J.L. 597, 174 A. 576. For instance, an undertaking to pay part of the debt before maturity, or at a place other than where the obligor was legally bound to pay, or to pay in property, regardless of its value, or to effect a composition with creditors by the payment of less than the sum due, has been held to constitute a consideration sufficient in law. The test is whether there is an additional consideration adequate to support an ordinary contract, and consists of something which the debtor was not legally bound to do or give....

The cases to the contrary either create arbitrary exceptions to the rule, or profess to find a consideration in the form of a new undertaking which in essence was not a tangible new obligation or a duty not imposed by the lease, or, in any event, was not the price "bargained for as the exchange for the promise," and therefore do violence to the fundamental principle. They exhibit the modern tendency, especially in the matter of rent reductions, to depart from the strictness of the basic common law rule and give effect to what has been termed a "reasonable" modification of the primary contract....

So tested, the secondary agreement at issue is not supported by a valid consideration; and it therefore created no legal obligation. General economic adversity, however disastrous it may be in its individual consequences, is never a warrant for judicial abrogation of this primary principle of the law of contracts.

It remains to consider the second contention that, in so far as the agreement has been executed by the payment and acceptance of rent at the reduced rate, the substituted performance stands, regardless of the want of consideration. This is likewise untenable. Ordinarily, the actual performance of that which one is legally bound to do stands on the same footing as his promise to do that which he is legally compellable to do.... This is a corollary of the basic principle. Of course, a different rule prevails where *bona fide* disputes have arisen respecting the relative rights and duties of the parties to a contract, or the debt or demand is unliquidated, or the contract is wholly executory on both sides. Anson on Contracts (Turck Ed.) 240, 241.

It is settled in this jurisdiction that, as in the case of other contracts, a consideration is essential to the validity of an accord and satisfaction. . . . Judgment affirmed, with costs.

———

McDevitt v. Stokes
174 Ky. 515, 192 S.W. 681 (1917)

Plaintiff's petition alleged that he, "a driver of great skill and experience," was employed by Shaw, owner of the mare Grace, to drive Grace in the Kentucky Futurity, one of the most noted races in the United States for trotting horses, that was to occur in 1910 in Lexington, Kentucky. The petition alleged that defendant Stokes owned a large stock farm near Lexington on which he bred horses, and that Stokes owned the sire, dam, and two brothers of Grace, so that her winning the race would entitle him to $300 from the purse for the race and would greatly increase the value of these four relatives of Grace. The petition then alleged that Stokes promised plaintiff $1,000 if he would drive Grace to victory in the Futurity, that plaintiff did so, and that Stokes had paid him only $200 and owed him an $800 balance, for which plaintiff sued. The court held that the defendant's demurrer was properly sustained. Plaintiff was already legally and morally bound by his contract with Shaw to perform the service called for by defendant's promise. To hold that he would not have won the race with Grace, if Stokes had not promised to pay him the $1,000, would be to say that he would have been recreant to his duty, an inference that the petition does not justify. Plaintiff incurred no detriment and the benefit to Stokes was purely incidental, one to which he was already entitled.

———

COMMENT: THE LEGAL–DUTY RULE

The view of the *Blumenthal* court was stated as long ago as 1602, when Coke reported a dictum (it was no more than this) in Pinnel's Case, 5 Coke Rep. 117a: "It was resolved by the whole court, that payment of a lesser sum on the day in satisfaction of a greater, cannot be satisfaction for the whole, because it appears to the judges that by no possibility, a lesser sum can be a satisfaction to the plaintiff for a greater sum: but the gift of a horse, hawk, robe, etc., in satisfaction is good. For it shall be intended that a horse, hawk, robe, etc., might be more beneficial to the plaintiff than the money, in respect of some circumstance, or otherwise the plaintiff would not have accepted it in satisfaction." But Coke, serving as a judge 12 years later, quoted himself—again in strong dicta—to precisely the opposite effect, and the King's Bench before that had found consideration in a benefit to the creditor in securing the payment without court action. Reynolds v. Pinhowe, Cro.Eliz., 429 (1595). The inability of the parties to discharge a money debt through part payment was not finally settled in England until the House of Lords decision in Foakes v. Beer, L.R. 9 A.C. 605 (1884). Altogether, then, although it was a distinct reversal of much earlier authority, during the nineteenth century it came to be widely accepted in this country that consideration doctrines preclude an effective accord and satisfaction through part payment of "matured and liquidated" money debts.

The sweeping effect of this limitation on contract modifications is summarized in J. Dawson, Gifts and Promises 210 (1980):

> After the House of Lords had spoken in 1884, the generalization swept all before it and became an immutable principle of the common law, engraved on a tablet. Any performance that was already due under an existing obligation was erased—deleted—as a permissible subject of new agreement. . . . Thus, within the limits of the obligation their agreement had created, the parties had destroyed their own power to contract.

The legal-duty rule—often described as the doctrine of Foakes v. Beer—extends far beyond money debts for which part payment is made or promised. We shall see more of it in the materials ahead, including the problem of contract adjustments prompted by unexpected or changed circumstances. The court's account in Levine v. Blumenthal reflects standard solutions, both as to the effects of the rule where it does apply and as to the means by which it can be escaped. Prepayment, payment at a different place, or probably payment to a different person are variations from the preexisting duty that would alter the result. Payment in whole or in part with something other than money would do the same—e.g., if Levine had been willing to take a coat or a dress from Blumenthal's stock. And what if Blumenthal could show an "honest" dispute with Levine as to how much rent was due?

Section § 89 of the Restatement, Second, states:

> A promise modifying a duty under a contract not fully performed on either side is binding
>
> > (a) if the modification is fair and equitable in view of circumstances not anticipated by the parties when the contract was made; or
> >
> > (b) to the extent provided by statute; or
> >
> > (c) to the extent that justice requires enforcement in view of material change of position in reliance on the promise.

How would *Blumenthal* come out if § 89 applied? One court embraced § 89 as "the proper rule" because it "not only prohibits modifications obtained by coercion, duress, or extortion but also fulfills society's expectation that agreements entered into voluntarily will be enforced." Angel v. Murray, 113 R.I. 482, 322 A.2d 630 (1974).

Statutes modifying the doctrine found in the principal case are fairly common, which is to say that the subject has generated a substantial history of legislative intervention. The most important development by far is § 2–209(1) of the UCC, which provides: "An agreement modifying a contract within this Article needs no consideration to be binding." While the Official Comment indicates that this sweeping language is intended to free all "necessary and desirable modifications" from the "technicalities which at present hamper" them, it goes on to declare that modifications must meet the test of good faith imposed by the Code. You should study the Comment for the guidance it provides on the meaning of "good faith" in this context.

Is there a parallel between the approaches taken in Restatement, Second § 89 and UCC 2–209(1)? In Roth Steel Products v. Sharon Steel Corp., 705 F.2d 134 (6th Cir.1983), an often-cited decision applying 2–209(1) in a modification setting, it was observed that the Code's general obligation of "good faith" requires inquiries into (1) the parties' "subjective honesty" and (2) the "justification" for the decision to seek a modification. In applying these tests, will it matter if the reason for a party's requesting a modification rests in circumstances the party should have "anticipated" when the contract was made? Had the Code applied in *Levine* (a lease of real estate, not a sale of goods), is there much doubt about the outcome under § 2–209(1)?

As to "modifying" transactions outside the reach of the UCC, the statutory solutions vary somewhat. Some representative examples are provided below.

California Civil Code § 1524 (West 2007). "Part performance of an obligation, either before or after a breach thereof, when expressly accepted by the creditor in writing, in satisfaction, or rendered in pursuance of an agreement in writing for that purpose, though without any new consideration, extinguishes the obligation." [This provision is copied in Montana (Code Ann. § 28–1–1403 (2003)); North Dakota (Cent.Code § 9–13–07 (2005)); and South Dakota (Codified Laws Ann. § 20–7–4 (1995)).]

Michigan Comp.Laws § 566.1 (1996). "An agreement hereafter made to change or modify, or to discharge in whole or in part, any contract, obligation, or lease, or any mortgage or other security interest in personal or real property, shall not be invalid because of the absence of consideration: Provided, That the agreement changing, modifying, or discharging such contract, obligation, lease, mortgage or security interest shall not be valid or binding unless it shall be in writing and signed by the party against whom it is sought to enforce the change, modification, or discharge." [Written agreements for "receipts, releases and discharges" are effective without other consideration in Alabama (Code § 12–21–109 (1995)), and Tennessee (Code Ann. § 24–7–106 (2000)).]

Virginia Code Ann. § 11–12 (2001). "Part performance of an obligation, promise or undertaking, either before or after a breach thereof, when expressly accepted by the creditor in satisfaction and rendered in pursuance of an agreement for that purpose, though without any new consideration, shall extinguish such obligation, promise, or undertaking." [Does this differ significantly from the California provision quoted above? Substantially the same result as in Virginia is reached, with wide variations in language, in Georgia (Code Ann. § 13–4–103 (1982)), Maine (Rev.Stat.Ann. tit. 14 § 155 (2003)), and North Carolina (Gen.Stat. § 1–540 (2000)).]

———

Schwartzreich v. Bauman–Basch, Inc.
231 N.Y. 196, 131 N.E. 887 (1921)

In August 1917, Bauman–Basch and Schwartzreich signed a contract by which Bauman agreed to employ Schwartzreich, and he agreed to work full-time, as a designer of coats and wraps, at a salary of $90 a week for one year starting November 22, 1917. Schwartzreich testified that he told Bauman in October that he had received an offer of $110 a week from another firm, and said: "Will you advise me as a friendly matter what to do?" Schwartzreich stated that Bauman said nothing at the time but the next day came to him and said: "I will give you $100 a week and I want you to stay with me." Bauman's version of the conversation was that Schwartzreich said he wanted to leave, since he had been offered $115 a week, and that Bauman replied: "I cannot get a designer now, and, in view of the fact that I have to send my sample line out on the road, I will give you a hundred dollars a week rather than to let you go." On October 17, Bauman and Schwartzreich signed a new employment contract providing a wage of $100 a week. Schwartzreich surrendered to Bauman his copy of the original contract with the signatures torn off. Schwartzreich worked for Bauman–Basch until December, when he was discharged. *Held*, judgment for plaintiff Schwartzreich for damages affirmed. The parties to a contract can rescind it by mutual consent. They can then proceed to make a new contract in which their mutual promises are consideration for each other. "The same effect follows . . . from a new contract entered into at the same time the old one is destroyed and rescinded by mutual consent. . . . [T]he time of rescission, whether a moment before or at the same time as the making of the new contract, is unimportant. . . . There is no reason that we can see [why] both transactions [cannot] take place at the same time."

QUESTIONS

(1) The authorities leave no doubt that the *Schwartzreich* court correctly stated the premise from which it proceeded, that the parties to a bilateral contract neither has performed may rescind it by mutual agreement. Still, if consideration is required for the modification or discharge of a contract, how is it that the agreement to rescind is effective?

(2) The Restatement, Second, in comment accompanying § 89, approves the result in *Schwartzreich* but not the court's reasoning. Why can't two things the parties are perfectly free to do—rescind an old agreement and make a new one—"take place at the same time"?

One court has given this answer: "[W]here an alleged rescission is coupled with a simultaneous re-entry into a new contract and the terms of that new contract are more favorable to only one of the parties, doubt is created as to the mutuality of the agreement to rescind the original contract. . . . Moreover, this exception [to the new-consideration requirement] is based on circular logic because the validity of the new agreement depends upon the rescission while the rescission depends upon the new agreement." McCallum Highlands v. Washington Capital Dus, Inc., 66 F.3d 89 (5th Cir.1995).

Universal Builders, Inc. v. Moon Motor Lodge, Inc.

Supreme Court of Pennsylvania, 1968.
430 Pa. 550, 244 A.2d 10.

EAGEN, J. This appeal is from a final decree of the [trial court] sitting in equity. Plaintiff asked the court to set aside a real estate conveyance as a violation of the Fraudulent Conveyance Act, 39 P.S. §§ 351–363, to declare void a supplemental agreement allegedly induced by fraud, and to grant plaintiff a money decree for work done under both the supplemental agreement and the basic contract as well as for loss of profits and punitive damages. Defendant denied that there was fraud involved in either the real estate conveyance or the supplemental agreement, denied that it owed plaintiff any sum under the basic contract and supplemental agreement, claimed a set-off for uncompleted work and counterclaimed for delay damages. The court below refused the request for a reconveyance under the Fraudulent Conveyance Act, refused to declare the supplemental agreement void, dismissed plaintiff's claims for lost profits and punitive damages, denied defendant a set-off for uncompleted work, dismissed the counterclaim for delay damages and decreed that defendant should pay plaintiff $127,759.54 (the balance due on the basic contract price together with extras) plus interest. Defendant appeals.

. . . On August 16, 1961, the plaintiff, Universal Builders, entered into a written contract with the defendant, Moon Motor Lodge, for the construction of a motel and restaurant in Allegheny County. The contract provides, inter alia, that all change orders must be in writing and signed by Moon and/or the Architect and that all requests for extension of time must be made in writing to the Architect. The contract specifications also required that a certain proportion of a re-inforcing substance be used in the building walls. The masonry sub-contractor failed to use the specified proportion. When this defect was discovered, Moon magnified its importance, withheld from Universal a progress payment to which [it] was entitled, threatened to expel Universal from the job and thereby induced Universal to enter into the supplemental agreement. The supplemental agreement, dated March 27, 1962, provides that Universal will pay Moon $5000 as damages for the absence of the re-inforcing material, that Universal will perform certain additional work at no additional cost to Moon, that the date for completion of the project is extended from April 1, 1962, to July 1, 1962, and that liquidated damages at a specified rate per day will be assessed for delay.

Universal substantially completed performance on September 1, 1962, and left the construction site on October 1. After filing this suit, Universal went into bankruptcy. The trustee prosecuted this action and won a final decree in the lower court. . . .

First Moon submits that the chancellor erred in not enforcing the contract provision that extras would not be paid for unless done pursuant to a written, signed change order.

Unless a contract is for the sale of goods, see the [UCC] § 2–209(3), as amended, 12A P.S. § 2–209(2), it appears undisputed that the contract can be modified orally although it provides that it can be modified only in writing. . . . Construction contracts typically provide that the builder will not be paid for extra work unless it is done pursuant to a written change order, yet courts frequently hold that owners must pay for extra work done at their oral direction. See generally Annot., 2 A.L.R.3d 620 (1965). This liability can be based on several theories. For example, the extra work may be said to have been done under an oral agreement separate from the written contract and not containing the requirement of a written authorization. 3A Corbin on Contracts, § 756 (1960). The requirement of a written authorization may also be considered a condition which has been waived. 5 Williston on Contracts § 689 (3d ed. 1961).

On either of the above theories, the chancellor correctly held Moon liable to pay for the extras in spite of the lack of written change orders. The evidence indicates that William Berger, the agent of Moon, requested many changes, was informed that they would involve extra cost, and promised to pay for them. In addition, Berger frequently was on the construction site and saw at least some of the extra work in progress. . . . [H]e was a keen observer with an extraordinary knowledge of the project in general and the contract requirements in particular. Thus it is not unreasonable to infer that he was aware that extra work was being done without proper authorization, yet he stood by without protesting while the extras were incorporated into the project. Under these circumstances there also was an implied promise to pay for the extras.

C.I.T. Corp. v. Jonnet, 419 Pa. 435, 214 A.2d 620 (1965), does suggest that such non-written modifications are ineffective unless the contract provision requiring modifications to be in writing was first waived. That case, however, is misleading. Although it involved a contract for the sale of movable bar and restaurant equipment, which is a contract for the sale of "goods" controlled by the [UCC], it overlooks that legislation, in particular § 2–209, which provides:

["(1) An agreement modifying a contract within this Article needs no consideration to be binding.]

"(2) A signed agreement which excludes modification or rescission except by a signed writing cannot be otherwise modified or rescinded but except as between merchants such a requirement on a form supplied by the merchant must be separately signed by the other party.

"(3) The requirement of the Statute of Frauds section of this Article (Section 2–201) must be satisfied if the contract as modified is within its provisions.

"(4) Although an attempt at modification or rescission does not satisfy the requirements of subsection (2) or (3) it can operate as a waiver.

"(5) A party who has made a waiver affecting an executory portion of the contract may retract the waiver by reasonable notification received by the other party that strict performance will be required of any term waived, unless the retraction would be unjust in view of a material change of position in reliance on the waiver."

From subsection (5) it can be inferred that a provision in a contract for [goods] that the contract can be modified only in writing is waived, just as such a provision in a construction contract is waived, under the circumstances described by Restatement of Contracts § 224 (1932), which provides:

"The performance of a condition qualifying a promise in a contract within the Statute [of Frauds or in a contract containing a provision requiring modifications to be in writing (§ 407)] may be excused by an oral agreement or permission of the promisor that the condition need not be performed, if the agreement or permission is given while the performance of the condition is possible, and in reliance on the agreement or permission, while it is unrevoked, the promisee materially changes his position."

Obviously a condition is considered waived when its enforcement would result in something approaching fraud. 5 Williston on Contracts § 689 (3d ed. 1961). Thus the effectiveness of a non-written modification in spite of a contract condition that modifications must be written depends upon whether enforcement of the condition is or is not barred by equitable considerations, not upon the technicality of whether the condition was or was not expressly and separately waived before the non-written modification.

In view of these equitable considerations underlying waiver, it should be obvious that when an owner requests a builder to do extra work, promises to pay for it and watches it performed knowing that it is not authorized in writing, he cannot refuse to pay on the ground that there was no written change order. Focht v. Rosenbaum, 176 Pa. 14, 34 A. 1001 (1876). When

Moon directed Universal to "go ahead" and promised to pay for the extras, performance of the condition requiring change orders to be in writing was excused by implication. It would be manifestly unjust to allow Moon, which misled Universal into doing extra work without a written authorization, to benefit from nonperformance of that condition. . . . [T]here was sufficient evidence to establish the amount of Universal's claim for extras and that there was not sufficient evidence to establish Moon's set-off claim for uncompleted work. The decree of the lower court therefore was correct, except insofar as it failed to allow Moon's counterclaim for delay damages, as before indicated, for the period from July 1, 1962, to September 1, 1962.

3A A. Corbin, Contracts § 753

"[W]e have seen that a promise can become enforceable by reason of other factors than a bargained-for exchange. . . . We need not be surprised, therefore, to find that a promisor can sometimes turn his conditional duty into an unconditional one by a 'waiver' of the condition, without any consideration therefor. . . . A condition of a promisor's duty can be eliminated by a mere voluntary expression of his willingness to waive it, if its performance does not constitute a material part of the agreed equivalent of the promise and its nonperformance does not materially affect the value received by the promisor. . . .

"In order to illustrate the kind of condition that [cannot] be voluntarily waived, let us suppose the following case: A contracts to erect a building for B, and the latter promises to pay $10,000 therefor after completion. . . . [The] completion of the building, substantially according to plans and specifications, is by construction of law a condition of B's duty to pay the price. Suppose that B should, without consideration, agree to waive this condition and to pay $10,000 to A without getting any building whatever. It is believed that no court would enforce this promise of B to pay $10,000 for nothing. A promise to make a gift of $10,000 would not be enforced, if no antecedent building contract had been made. One can not 'waive' himself into a duty to make a gift of the money. And the fact that a building contract had formerly been made is not a good reason for reaching a different result, when the waiver eliminates the building and causes the new promise to be, in substantial part at least, the promise of a gift." [This passage is taken from Corbin's discussion of "waiver of conditions," a subject addressed in Chapter 6. As Corbin noted many times (e.g., 3A A. Corbin § 752), "if the question is asked whether a 'waiver' can be legally effective if it is not accompanied by a 'consideration,' it cannot be answered without knowing what it is that is being 'waived' and what is the mode in which the 'waiver' is being attempted."]

Nassau Trust Co. v. Montrose Concrete Prod. Corp.
56 N.Y.2d 175, 451 N.Y.S.2d 663, 436 N.E.2d 1265 (1982)

"The [court below] erred in failing to distinguish between an oral agreement that purports to modify the terms of a prior written agreement and an oral waiver by one party to a written agreement of a right to require of the other party certain performance in compliance with that agreement. . . . Modification of the terms of a [contract] requires consideration except when a statute . . . dispenses with the need for consideration when a writing [exists]. Neither waiver [nor estoppel] rests upon consideration or agreement. A modification, because it is an agreement based upon consideration, is binding according to its terms and may only be withdrawn by agreement. . . . While estoppel requires detriment to the party claiming to have been misled, waiver requires no more than the voluntary and intentional abandonment of a known right which, but for the waiver, would have been enforceable. . . . A waiver, to the extent that it has been executed, cannot be expunged or recalled[,] . . . but, not being a binding agreement, can, to the extent that it is executory, be withdrawn, provided the party whose performance has been waived is given notice of withdrawal and a reasonable time after notice within which to perform[.]"

Cole Taylor Bank v. Truck Ins. Exch.

51 F.3d 736 (7th Cir.1995)

"Unlike modification of a contract, the efficacy of a waiver of a contractual right is generally not thought to require special tokens of reliability, such as a writing, consideration, reliance, judicial screening, or a heightened standard of proof. . . . What is more, a waiver of contractual rights can be implied as well as express—implied from words or actions inconsistent with the assertion of those rights. . . . Yet all that waiver means, when it is carefully defined, is the intentional relinquishment of a right. . . . [T]he courts have not been indifferent to the danger of [one party's] self-serving testimony that the other party to the contract waived a right that the contract had conferred on him. In some cases they have required proof of reliance on the alleged waiver, in effect converting the doctrine of waiver into the harder-to-prove doctrine of estoppel. . . . [Other courts] require[ ] that an alleged waiver either have induced reliance or that it be *clearly* inferable from the circumstances. . . . The fact that the courts have not converged on a blanket general requirement of reliance, consideration, a writing, a heightened standard of proof, or other means of assuring the reliability of questionable evidence may reflect the inherent implausibility of offers to prove 'bare' waiver in a contractual setting. Unless the right waived is a minor one . . ., why would someone give it up in exchange for nothing? If something is given in return, there is consideration."

Quigley v. Wilson

474 N.W.2d 277 (Iowa Ct.App.1991)

In 1980, Quigley sold his farm "on contract" to the Wilsons, husband and wife, who made the annual installment payment of $7,000 plus interest until 1985, when they assigned the contract to Hatfield. Sometime prior to February 1986, Hatfield returned the farm to the Wilsons, informing them that he could not make the payments. The Wilsons then met with Quigley, telling him that they, too, were unable to make the yearly payments, another of which was due March 1. After negotiations, Quigley agreed to change a number of the contract's original terms, including a reduction of the price from $210,000 to $120,500 and the annual payments from $7,000 to $1,562, plus interest. These changes were written up in a new contract prepared by Quigley's lawyer and signed by Quigley and the Wilsons on March 7, 1986. The Wilsons thereafter made all payments due under the 1986 contract. In 1988, Quigley who had been in a nursing home since 1985, established a voluntary conservatorship appointing his two children as "co-conservators" for him. The co-conservators then filed suit against the Wilsons seeking a declaratory judgment that they were in default under the 1980 contract, because the 1986 contract was unenforceable for lack of consideration, Quigley's lack of mental competency, fraud, and undue influence. The trial court found for the Wilsons on all plaintiffs' claims (some of which were tried separately before a jury) and ruled the 1986 contract enforceable. This judgment was affirmed on appeal.

The trial judge had stated that the 1986 contract "appeared to constitute a waiver" within the meaning of an earlier Iowa case, In re Guardianship of Collins, 327 N.W.2d 230 (Iowa 1982). In *Collins*, the seller under a land contract, despite advice not to alter the bargain, agreed to eliminate the interest requirement altogether and to reduce the period of the buyer's payments from 24 to 12 years. A conservator of the seller, appointed after execution of the new agreement, sued to declare that agreement unenforceable for lack of consideration (mental incompetence was also alleged, but not proved). The Iowa Supreme Court found the agreement to be a "valid waiver," saying: "[W]e have long held that contract rights can be waived. . . . The essential elements [of a waiver] are the existence of a right, actual or constructive knowledge of it, and an intention to give it up. No consideration is required. Nor is prejudice necessary."

After quoting this language from *Collins*, the *Quigley* appellate court said: "The distinguishing factor [in *Collins* is that] the vendor simply made a unilateral decision to waive her right to interest so each payment made by the buyer went entirely toward principal, whereas Quigley and the Wilsons renegotiated a new price and payment schedule. . . . [I]t could be said that Quigley waived the $89,500 difference between the original price of $210,000 and the amended price of $120,500. However, it is difficult to describe the changing of a payment schedule providing for annual payments of $7,000 plus interest to one providing for annual payments of $1,562 plus interest, along with the changing of the due date for a balloon payment from March 1, 1988, to March 1, 1996, as simply a waiver of payments. Additionally, the amendment provides for changes in the insurance requirements and allows for sale of the mobile home on the property.

"These changes constitute more than the seller abandoning a contractual right arising from a contract. They create new and different obligations to be performed by the buyer. We therefore limit waiver to situations where a party to a contract abandons a right that party has under a contract. We categorize situations where contracting parties incur different duties and obligations from those in their original contract as modifications.

"Therefore, we do not find [a waiver here], but rather a modification which normally require[s] consideration. . . . We [further] find [this] case an appropriate circumstance for the adoption of the Restatement's position [on modifications resting on circumstances not anticipated, § 89]. The unanticipated circumstances were the drastic decrease in the value of the land* coupled with the seller's concern about tax repercussions from reacquiring the land and the fact

---

* [There occurred a dramatic fall in the market value of midwestern farm land during the first half of the 1980s, 40 to 50 percent in some places.—Eds.]

the Wilsons had not received any income from the farm for the previous year. Additionally, the new agreement followed negotiations lasting over a period of time, the document was written by the seller's attorney, the trial court found the reduced price was roughly the fair market value of the property at the time the re-negotiations occurred, and the buyers had already paid $58,000 toward principal on the original contract and the balance of the new contract price was $62,500. Additionally, we find it significant that the jury found Quigley was competent when he entered the 1986 agreement and the trial court found no undue influence or fraudulent misrepresentation involved in the agreement. These factors lead us to find this is a situation where it is appropriate to find the modification fair and equitable and does not require proof of additional consideration." [This decision was affirmed per curiam by the Iowa Supreme Court, 474 N.W.2d 277 (1991).]

––––––

FINALIZING CONTRACT DISPUTES

Sometimes an agreement to modify a contract is made midstream, at a time when neither party has done what the bargain requires. At other times, trouble arises only after the party who was required to perform first—typically a provider of services or goods—has completed performance. The "trouble" usually takes the form of disagreement over the amount the "paying party" owes the "performing party." Such disputes more often than not end in a settlement agreement. The question now before us is what happens when the settlement is challenged or otherwise becomes derailed. Again, a settlement agreement, like a modifying agreement, is itself a contract, subject to the ordinary contract defenses.

––––––

Hackley v. Headley

Supreme Court of Michigan, 1881.
45 Mich. 569, 8 N.W. 511.

COOLEY, J. Headley sued Hackley & McGordon to recover compensation for cutting, hauling and delivering in the Muskegon River a quantity of logs. . . . The contract was in writing, and date[d] August 20, 1874. Headley agreed thereby to cut on specified lands and deliver in the Muskegon river the next spring 8,000,000 feet of logs[,] [which] were to be measured or scaled by a competent person to be selected by Hackley & McGordon, "and in accordance with the standard rules or scales in general use on Muskegon lake and river," and the expense of scaling was to be mutually borne by the parties.

[Two issues were in dispute. One related to the food supplied the scaler. The court rejected evidence offered by Hackley that it was the custom "on the Muskegon river" for jobbers like Headley to assume the whole cost of maintaining scalers, concluding that the scaler's board was to be shared equally by the parties. The other dispute related to the scale that would be used to measure logs. The "Scribner rule" was the scale generally used at the time the contract was made, but by the time the logs were cut and delivered the scale in general use was the "Doyle scale," by which the amount Headley would be entitled to would be reduced by some $2,000. The court concluded that the scale contemplated must have been that in common use when the scaling was done, because the scalers would be third parties whom they would expect to use whatever scale was standard at that time.]

The question of duress[,] in obtaining the discharge, remains. The paper [the defendants claim was given in settlement] reads as follows:

Muskegon, Mich., August 3, 1875.

Received from Hackley & McGordon their note for four thousand dollars, payable in thirty days, at First National Bank, Grand Rapids, which is in full for all claims of every kind and nature which I have against said Hackley & McGordon.

Witness: Thomas Hume.   John Headley.

Headley's account of the circumstances under which this receipt was given is [this:] On August 3, 1875, he went to Muskegon . . . from his home in Kent county, for the purpose of collecting the balance which he claimed was due him under the contract. The amount he claimed was upwards of $6200, estimating the logs by the Scribner scale. He had an interview with Hackley in the morning, who insisted that the estimate should be according to the Doyle scale, and who also claimed that he had made payments to others amounting to some $1400 which Headley should allow. Headley did not admit these payments, and denied his liability for them if they had been made. Hackley told Headley to come in again in the afternoon, and when he did so Hackley said to him: "My figures show there is 4260 and odd dollars in round numbers your due, and I will give you $4000. I will give you our note for $4000." To this Headley replied: "I cannot take that: it is not right, and you know it. There is over $2000 besides that belongs to me, and you know it." Hackley replied: "That is the best I will do with you." Headley said: "I cannot take that, Mr. Hackley," and Hackley replied, "You do the next best thing you are a mind to. You can sue me if you please." Headley then said: "I cannot afford to sue you, because I have got to have the money, and I cannot wait for it. If I fail to get the money today, I shall probably be ruined financially, because I have made no other arrangements to get the money only on this particular matter." Finally he took the note and gave the receipt, because at the time he could do nothing better, and in the belief that he would be financially ruined unless he had immediately the money that was offered him, or paper by means of which the money might be obtained.

If this statement is correct, the defendants not only took a most unjust advantage of Headley, but they obtained a receipt which, to the extent that it assumed to discharge anything not honestly in dispute between the parties, and known by them to be owing to Headley beyond the sum received, was without consideration and ineffectual. But was it a receipt obtained by duress? That is the question. . . . The circuit judge was of opinion that if the jury believed the statement of Headley they would be justified in finding that duress existed. . . .

Duress exists when one by the unlawful act of another is induced to make a contract or perform some act under circumstances which deprive him of the exercise of free will. It is commonly said to be of either the person or the goods of the party. . . . It is not pretended that duress of the person existed in this case; it is if anything duress of goods, or at least of that nature, and properly enough classed with duress of goods. Duress of goods may exist when one is compelled to submit to an illegal exaction in order to obtain them from one who has them in possession but refuses to surrender them unless the exaction is submitted to.

The leading case involving duress of goods is Astley v. Reynolds, 2 Strange, 915. The plaintiff had pledged goods for £20, and when he offered to redeem them, the pawnbroker refused to surrender them unless he was paid £10 for interest. The plaintiff submitted to the exaction, but was held entitled to recover back all that had been unlawfully demanded and taken. This, say the court, "is a payment by compulsion: the plaintiff might have such an immediate want of his goods that an action of trover would not do his business. . . ." The principle of this case was approved [in] Ashmole v. Wainwright, 2 Q.B. 837[,] [which] was a suit to recover back excessive charges paid to common carriers who refused until payment was made to deliver the goods for the carriage of which the charges were made. There has never been any doubt but recovery could be had under such circumstances. Harmony v. Bingham, 12 N.Y. 99. . . . So if illegal tolls are demanded, for passing a raft of lumber, and the owner pays them to liberate his raft, he may recover back what he pays. Chase v. Dwinal, 7 Me. 134. . . .

But where the party threatens nothing which he has not a legal right to perform, there is no duress. . . . When therefore a judgment creditor threatens to levy his execution on the debtor's goods, and under fear of the levy the debtor executes and delivers a note for the amount, with sureties, the note cannot be avoided for duress. Wilcox v. Howland, 23 Pick. 167. . . .

In what did the alleged duress consist in the present case? Merely in this: that the debtors refused to pay on demand a debt already due, though the plaintiff was in great need of the money and might be financially ruined in case he failed to obtain it. It is not pretended that Hackley & McGordon had done anything to bring Headley to the condition which made this money so important to him at this very time, or that they were in any manner responsible for his pecuniary embarrassment. . . . The duress, then, is to be found exclusively in their failure to meet promptly their pecuniary obligation. But this, according to the plaintiff's claim, would have constituted no duress whatever if he had not happened to be in pecuniary straits; and the validity of negotiations, according to this claim, must be determined, not by the defendants' conduct, but by the plaintiff's necessities. The same contract which would be valid if made with a man easy in his circumstances, becomes invalid when the contracting party is pressed with the necessity of immediately meeting his bank paper. But this would be a most dangerous, as well as a most unequal doctrine; and if accepted, no one could well know when he would be safe in dealing on the ordinary terms of negotiation with a party who professed to be in great need. . . .

These views render a reversal of the judgment necessary, and the case will be remanded for a new trial. . . .

[Headley prevailed before a jury in the new trial following remand, and the case was again taken to the Supreme Court of Michigan. This time Headley did not urge duress, but "took the ground that [the payment of the $4,000 and the giving of the receipt] operated to prove that there was no [binding] compromise at all," because defendant "well knew his firm was indebted in a much larger sum and acted in bad faith and set up claims which he knew were unfounded," all of which resulted in the giving of a receipt which was "without valid consideration." The court agreed, saying: "[W]hen one of the parties to a transaction sets it up against the other as an effective compromise, the latter may hinder it from operating in that sense and with that force by showing that his opponent acted unfairly or oppressively and asserted claims which he knew to be void of right with the design of getting the terms which were nominally assented to." 50 Mich. 43, 14 N.W. 693 (1883).]

––––––––

Capps v. Georgia Pacific Corp.
253 Or. 248, 453 P.2d 935 (1969)

The complaint alleged that, with defendant's approval, plaintiff had searched for and found a lessee of industrial property owned by defendant, that defendant signed with this lessee a 20–year lease of the property for a total rent of $3,040,000, and that defendant therefore owed plaintiff a commission of five percent of this sum, plus one-half of one month's rent, or a total commission of $157,000, but that defendant had paid him only $5,000, leaving a balance owed of $152,000. Defendant filed a general denial and, as an affirmative defense, submitted to the court a release given by plaintiff in return for the $5,000 payment. Plaintiff's reply alleged that, when he had requested payment of his commission, defendant knew that because of his adverse financial situation plaintiff was in danger of losing his home immediately by mortgage foreclosure, and of losing other personal property by repossession, and that defendant also knew that plaintiff had no other source of funds. Plaintiff further alleged that defendant's agent informed him that, even though he was entitled to the sums he demanded, he would receive nothing unless he signed the release, since defendant had "extensive resources and powerful and brilliant attorneys," who could and would prevent him from recovering more in any later legal proceeding. Plaintiff then alleged that he was deprived of the free exercise of his will and was forced to sign a release of his valid claim for $157,000 for "the grossly inadequate sum" of $5,000. Defendant's demurrer to this reply was sustained by the court.

Held, reversed. Defendant's answer setting up the signed release was defective for failing to allege that the claim released was "either unliquidated or otherwise in dispute." As to duress, in early decisions, of which Hackley v. Headley was a leading example, dire financial circumstances, of which the other party took advantage, were held to provide no basis for a finding of duress. More recent cases, though often conflicting, seem to take a different view. "[W]e conclude that the better rule is one which allows the statement of a duress cause or defense such as plaintiff has pleaded here to be tried on its facts."

Denecke, J., concurred only in the result. Though conceding that "[t]his seems to be as strong a case [for] economic duress as can be made," he nevertheless urged that it would be "judicially unwise" to hold these allegations to constitute duress. "[A] substantial number of business transactions today have these same basic ingredients." A majority of the business community, while not approving such conduct, do not believe it to be enough to avoid an otherwise binding legal obligation, especially because the party asserting duress "will usually be an unfortunate and unsuccessful party opposing a fortunate and successful party." This could "cause the trier of fact to find the facts to fit the result." Other grounds for relief are available and more desirable. On these facts, it would be much better to rest the result on the recognized doctrine that a release given for payment of a sum less than the amount acknowledged to be owing fails for a "lack of consideration."

NOTE

Duress can take many forms, ranging from old-fashioned violence to the person to threats of criminal prosecution or a simple lawsuit for damages. The question raised by Hackley v. Headley (and by Capps v. Georgia Pacific Corp.) is whether the withholding of a performance due under an existing contract can constitute duress where the opposite party is in need, and is known to be in need, of the performance. If one simply were to tabulate the decisions involving a withheld performance on one side and the pressure of circumstances—usually financial—on the other, it is quite probable that the views expressed in Hackley v. Headley still would be found to represent the prevailing view. Financial difficulty by itself will not justify setting aside a settlement. What is it about standard tests of duress that produce such results? One court has said: "The adverse effect on the finality of settlements and hence on the willingness of parties to settle their contract disputes without litigation would be great if the cash needs of one party were alone enough to entitle him to a trial on the validity of the settlement." Selmer Co. v. Blakeslee–Midwest Co., 704 F.2d 924 (7th Cir.1983).

LEGAL DUTY APART FROM CONTRACT

On occasion, a promise of compensation is made to a public official, who, by virtue of the position held, already owes a duty to the general public (and thus the promisor) to perform the acts or services that are the reason for the promise. It is agreed everywhere that a bargain by a public official to obtain additional benefits for performing regular duties is unenforceable as against public policy. Still, the scope of a legal duty that is noncontractual in origin may be uncertain (consider the "legal" duties of public utilities, fiduciaries, spouses, or citizens generally). Is the legal duty in fact owed to the promisor? If it is not, performance of the duty is presumably consideration for a promise, even though concerns about public policy remain.

Denney v. Reppert

Court of Appeals of Kentucky, 1968.
432 S.W.2d 647.

MYRE, SPECIAL COMMISSIONER. The question [is] which of several claimants is entitled to an award for information leading to the apprehension and conviction of certain bank robbers. Since the learned judge of the Pulaski Circuit Court correctly set out the facts and the law[,] we are affirming the judgment entered in accordance thereto and are adopting, in substance, the written opinion of the circuit judge as the opinion of this court.

On June 12th or 13th, 1963, three armed men entered the First State Bank, Eubank, Kentucky, and with a display of arms and threats robbed the bank of over $30,000. Later in the day they were apprehended by State Policemen Garret Godby, Johnny Simms and Tilford Reppert, placed under arrest, and the entire loot was recovered. Later all of the prisoners were convicted and Garret Godby, Johnny Simms and Tilford Reppert appeared as witnesses at the trial.

The First State Bank of Eubank was a member of the Kentucky Bankers Ass'n which provided and advertised a reward of $500 for the arrest and conviction of each bank robber. Hence the outstanding reward for the three bank robbers was $1,500. Many became claimants for the reward and the Kentucky State Bankers Ass'n being unable to determine the merits of the claims asked the circuit court to determine . . . who was entitled to receive the reward or share in it. All of the claimants were made defendants in the action.

At the time of the robbery the claimants Murrell Denney, Joyce Buis, Rebecca McCollum and Jewell Snyder were employees of the First State Bank and came out of the grueling situation with great credit and glory. Each one of them deserves approbation and an accolade. They were vigilant in disclosing to the public and the peace officers the details of the crime, and in describing the culprits, and giving all the information that they possessed that would be useful in capturing the robbers. Undoubtedly, they performed a great service. . . .

The first question [is] whether the employees of the robbed bank are eligible to receive or share in the reward? The great weight of authority answers in the negative. In re Waggoner, 47 S.D. 401, 199 N.W. 244 (1924) states the rule thusly: "To the general rule that, when a reward is offered to the general public for the performance of some specified act, such reward may be claimed by any person who performs such act, is the exception of agents, employés and public officials who are acting within the scope of their employment or official duties." . . .

In Stacy v. State Bank of Ill., 4 Scam., Ill., 91 (1842), it was held that a director of a bank was not entitled to share in the reward offered by the bank for the arrest of a robber because it was his duty as a director to further the best interests of the bank, and apprehending one who had robbed the bank was in the best interest of the bank. . . .

At the time of the robbery the claimants Murrell Denney, Joyce Buis, Rebecca McCollum, and Jewell Snyder were employees of the First State Bank. They were under duty to protect and conserve the resources and moneys of the bank, and safeguard every interest of the institution furnishing them employment. Each of these employees exhibited great courage, and cool bravery, in a time of stress and danger. The community and the county have recompensed them in commendation, admiration and high praise, and the world looks on them as heroes. But in making known the robbery and assisting in acquainting the public and the officers with details of the crime and with identification of the robbers, they performed a duty to the bank and the public, for which they cannot claim a reward.

The claims of Corbin Reynolds, Julia Reynolds, Alvie Reynolds and Gene Reynolds also must fail. . . . [T]hey gave valuable information to the arresting officers[,] [but] they did not follow the procedure as set forth in the offer of reward in that they never filed a claim with the Kentucky Bankers Ass'n. . . . A claimant of a reward must comply with the terms and conditions of the offer of reward. Miles v. Booth, 287 Ky. 246, 152 S.W.2d 577 (1941).

State Policemen Garret Godby, Johnny Simms and Tilford Reppert made the arrest of the bank robbers and captured the stolen money. All participated in the prosecution. At the time of the arrest, it was the duty of the state policemen to apprehend the criminals. Under the law they cannot claim or share in the reward and they are interposing no claim to it.

This leaves the defendant, Tilford Reppert the sole eligible claimant. The record shows that at the time of the arrest he was a deputy sheriff in Rockcastle County, but the arrest and recovery of the stolen money took place in Pulaski County. He was out of his jurisdiction, and was thus under no legal duty to make the arrest, and is thus eligible to claim and receive the reward. In Kentucky Bankers Ass'n v. Cassady, 264 Ky. 351, 94 S.W.2d 622, it was said: "It is . . . well established that a public officer within the authority of the law to make an arrest may accept an offer of reward or compensation for acts or services performed outside of his bailiwick or not within the scope of his official duties."

The claimant Tilford Reppert was present with Garret Godby and Johnny Simms at the time of the arrest and all cooperated in its consummation. The claimant Tilford Reppert personally recovered the stolen money. He recovered $2,000 more than the bank records show was stolen. This record does not reveal what became of the $2,000 excess.

It is manifest from the record that Tilford Reppert is the only claimant qualified and eligible to receive the reward. . . . [H]e is entitled to receive payment of the $1,500 reward now deposited with the Clerk of this Court.

The judgment is affirmed.

————

Board of Comm'rs of Montgomery County v. Johnson
126 Kan. 36, 266 P. 749 (1928)

Everett Bible killed a man in Kansas and fled the state, a fugitive from justice. Montgomery County, Kansas, and the State of Kansas had offered rewards for the arrest of Bible, totaling $500. Four months later, Bible drove up to a diner operated by Johnson in Tulsa, Oklahoma, purchased lunch, and drove away without paying for it. Johnson armed himself, chased and caught up with Bible, who shot at Johnson; Johnson returned the fire; they clinched, scuffled, and fell to the ground. Both had hold of Johnson's gun; Bible, partly on top of Johnson, was trying to bend Johnson's arm around so that when the gun discharged it would shoot Johnson. At that point, Crabaugh and Hamilton, constables in the district, and Hopkins, a special deputy sheriff, drove up, separated, and arrested the two wrestlers. If they had not intervened, Johnson would probably have been killed or severely injured. The $500 reward was paid into court to await the outcome of a suit brought to determine who was entitled to the rewards. The lower court concluded that all four claimants, Johnson and the three officers, were entitled, each to receive one-fourth. *Held*, affirmed. There was no law in Oklahoma requiring constables or deputy sheriffs to arrest fugitives from justice from other states. (The court did not comment on Johnson's assertion that, at the time of the arrest, the officers did not know Bible was a fugitive.) Johnson tackled Bible first, but if the other three had not intervened his arrest would not have occurred.

————

In re Estate of Lord

93 N.M. 543, 602 P.2d 1030 (1979)

In 1974, the decedent, a widow then 64 and suffering from cancer, lived alone on a ranch. According to Lord, a claimant against her estate, in October 1974 the decedent entered into an oral agreement with Lord whereby she agreed to devise to him her entire estate, if he would agree to marry her and to "be a loyal, faithful husband" and "take care of her like a husband would" until her death. Lord and the decedent were married on November 21, 1974. The following day, the decedent executed a will devising $10,000 to Lord and the bulk of her estate to her sister, Hughes, the plaintiff. Lord contends that he fulfilled his part of the oral agreement by caring for decedent until her death in 1977. Plaintiff Hughes sought formal probate of decedent's will; Lord urged specific performance of the oral agreement. *Held*, the oral agreement is void as against public policy; there was no error in excluding all evidence of it. This court adheres to the view that "a contract whereby one spouse agrees to pay the other spouse for his or her care, which is part of the other's duties as a spouse, is against public policy and void." It is the state's policy "to protect the marriage institution" by "not encourag[ing] spouses to marry for money." Lord's contention that this agreement is distinguishable because of "extraordinary services, far beyond the normal duties any spouse owes to the other," is unconvincing. There is nothing exceptional or extraordinary about one spouse utilizing his or her particular skills or aptitudes to assist the other spouse in times of trouble. (No mention was made of lack of consideration.)

[A year later, the New Mexico court found no breach of a reconciliation contract when a husband failed to keep promises—"to refrain from infidelity, be a faithful and providing husband, and to submit to counselling"—given in return for his wife's promise to forbear prosecution of a divorce action she had commenced. The court said: "[A] promise to do what a party is already obligated by contract or law to do is not consideration for a promise made in return. . . . [Here,] appellee promised to do no more than what he was already obligated to do as a husband. There was no mutuality of contract and therefore no breach. Further, we [have] previously held that nuptial contracts which attempt to alter the legal relations of the parties [are] 'void for want of consideration, or against public policy.' . . . It is the policy of this State to foster and protect the marital institution. See In re Estate of Lord, 93 N.M. at 544, 602 P.2d at 1031." Hurley v. Hurley, 94 N.M. 641, 615 P.2d 256 (1980).]

SECTION 3. SCRUTINY OF LIMITED COMMITMENT

INTRODUCTORY NOTE

In a number of environments—franchising and employment among the most conspicuous—the parties enjoy a long-term relationship and often plan on it continuing, even though the duration of the contract itself may be unspecified, even quite limited. For example, in the employment setting the background common-law rule in this country is a contract at will: In the absence of agreement to the contrary, the employer or the worker can end the relationship unilaterally—for any reason or no reason at all. In recent decades, however, we have seen legislative (and sometimes judicial) interventions into the employment relationship as well as others in which the parties have long-term relationships but only limited legal commitments to each other. In reading the materials that follow, you should consider the extent to which it makes sense to have legal obligations that are so out of step with the ordinary expectations of the parties (e.g., studies show that vast numbers of employees working under indefinite-term contracts do not understand the full meaning of "at will") and whether it makes sense to develop doctrines—such as implied duties of good faith or fair dealing—to bring the two more in alignment with each other.

COMMENT: THE FRANCHISED DEALER AND THE LAW

The problem of termination-without-cause provisions in franchise or dealership agreements first appeared in Chapter 3 (recall Judge Wisdom's analysis in *Corenswet*, p. 364). Nearly 40 years earlier, in Bushwick–Decatur Motors v. Ford Motor Co., 116 F.2d 675 (2d Cir.1940), another federal court rejected a terminated dealer's claim in a suit involving an equally broad termination clause ("at any time at the will of either party by written notice to the other"). Judge Clark explained why the automobile manufacturer, by giving notice, had ended its obligations under the contract:

> With a power of termination at will here so unmistakably expressed, we certainly cannot assert that a limitation of good faith was anything the parties had in mind. Such a limitation can be read into the agreement only as an overriding requirement of public policy. This seems an extreme step for judges to take. The onerous nature of the contract for the successful dealer and the hardship which cancellation may bring him have caused some writers to advocate it, however; and an occasional case has seized upon elements of overreaching to come to such a result on particular facts. . . . But, generally speaking, the situation arises from the strong bargaining position which economic factors give the great automobile manufacturing companies: the dealers are not misled or imposed upon, but accept as nonetheless advantageous an agreement in form bilateral, in fact one-sided. To attempt to redress this balance by judicial action without legislative authority appears to us a doubtful policy. We have not proper facilities to weigh economic factors, nor have we before us a showing of the supposed needs which may lead the manufacturers to require these seemingly harsh bargains.

Judge Clark in 1940, like Judge Wisdom in 1979, was not prepared to promote "mutuality" by the means made available by conventional contract doctrines. The point to be stressed is that courts, especially federal courts, can no longer follow the course of abstention recommended by these judges. That is because courts today are called upon to apply a considerable body of legislation, state and federal, involving various aspects of the franchise system, including general antitrust and unfair trade practices statutes.

It is in the automobile industry that the dealer-franchise has been most widely used and most extensively studied, but of course its importance reaches far beyond that industry. In the early years of franchising autos, it soon became clear that the formal separation between franchisor and franchisee achieved in legal analysis did not correspond with the interdependence that existed in fact. The franchisor's interests would ordinarily lead it to press its retailers to expand sales. But the facilities of the particular franchisee might be limited, and expansion might be costly or beyond the franchisee's means. Not surprisingly, clauses reserving an unlimited power of cancellation became common. They were reinforced by clauses requiring the franchised dealer to provide "satisfactory sales performance" or "best efforts," either of which would be tested by the franchisor's "satisfaction." Since the impact of such controls was for the most part one-sided, tensions and conflict arose.

Efforts began in the 1930s to provide controls through state legislation. By 1964, statutes had been passed in 40 states, most commonly requiring both manufacturers and retailers to be licensed to sell automobiles within the state, setting up administrative procedures for mediation of disputes, and authorizing cancellation of licenses of manufacturers found to have acted unfairly or to have used undue coercion. In some states, sanctions enforced by courts were provided, perhaps even injunctions. By 1980, only a few states lacked legislation focusing directly upon the automobile manufacturer-dealer relationship. A provision found in many states (e.g., Delaware, Massachusetts, Rhode Island) simply declares that "it shall be unlawful directly or indirectly to impose unreasonable restrictions" on the motor vehicle dealer or franchisee respecting a wide range of matters, including "right to renew" and "termination." The various provisions, including restrictions on franchise termination, are collected in Note, State Motor Vehicle Franchise Legislation: A Survey and Due Process Challenge to Board Composition, 33 Vand.L.Rev. 385 (1980). See also Briley, Franchise Termination Litigation: A Comparative Analysis, 16 U.Tol.L.Rev. 891 (1985).

After extensive public hearings, Congress in 1956 passed the Automobile Dealers' Day in Court Act, which provided a damage remedy for losses sustained by an automobile dealer through the failure of a manufacturer to act in "good faith" in performing or in terminating (including not renewing) the dealer's franchise. "Good faith" was defined as acting "in a fair and equitable manner toward each other so as to guarantee the one party freedom from coercion or intimidation by the other party." A proviso was then added that "recommendation, endorsement, exposition, persuasion, urging or argument" would not constitute lack of good faith.

How wide was the range of inquiry that courts were directed to undertake under tests so open-ended as "good faith" and "a fair and equitable manner," and on what sources could courts draw to give these phrases content? Take an imaginary example—a successful dealer, who for 25 years has shown superior salesmanship, is served with a notice of cancellation in order to make room for the child of a high company executive. The displaced franchisee may (or may not) be able to salvage some of its considerable investment in quite specialized facilities. Is the termination in "good faith"? Look back to the key words quoted in the last paragraph and underline "*so as to*" after "fair and equitable manner." The legislative history of the Day in Court Act has much in it to show that this phrasing was chosen deliberately. At any rate, it is now just about settled (after some hesitation) that in the conduct that can amount to "bad faith" for the purposes of the federal damage remedy, coercion or intimidation will be an essential element. Would you have it otherwise?

Legislative efforts, both state and federal, were of course not limited to the automobile industry. There developed a wide assortment of state enactments designed to regulate both franchise relationships in general and franchising in specific types of goods—e.g., petroleum products, beer and wine. These statutes impose a variety of restraints on franchisors, which are collected and discussed in Annot., 67 A.L.R.3d 1299 (1975). An example of parallel action at the federal level is the Petroleum Marketing Practices Act 15 U.S.C. § 2801), which Congress enacted in 1978 in order to balance the perceived unequal bargaining power between oil companies and their dealers. More generally, in 1987 the National Conference of Commissioners on Uniform State Laws drafted and recommended for adoption the Uniform Franchise and Business Opportunities Act (7A U.L.A. 77), which mainly imposes on the parties a duty of "good faith" in the performance and enforcement of the franchise agreement. It does not call for a "good cause" rule on terminations.

In short, courts are now cabined by statutes in resolving franchise disputes. The whole subject has become quite specialized, prompting separate courses in the law schools. For the typical franchise litigation, see The Original Great American Chocolate Chip Cookie Co., Inc. v. River Valley Cookies Ltd., 970 F.2d 273 (7th Cir.1992), involving claims under both a federal act and the Illinois Franchise Disclosure Act. To be sure, there remain some painful questions as to how far the courts should go, and by what means, in enforcing the legislative mandate. But one point seems settled. The mandate under the typical franchise act is that franchisors deal with their franchisees in "good faith." What does that mean when the contract states that "either party may terminate this Agreement upon 90 days' written notice"? Again, a party may always stand on rights given by the contract. When the contract is unquestionably terminable at will, it is not easy to find that a general duty of good faith read into every franchise arrangement authorizes a judicial inquiry into the motives for exercising the contractual right. So the duty of good faith created by a franchise act seems no more powerful as a trumping device than the common law and UCC versions of the good faith duty. Something more, perhaps opportunistic or otherwise improper efforts to escape contractual obligation, is likely required.

Sheets v. Teddy's Frosted Foods, Inc.

Supreme Court of Connecticut, 1980.
179 Conn. 471, 427 A.2d 385.

PETERS, J. [The issue] is whether an employer has a completely unlimited right to terminate the services of an employee whom it has hired for an indefinite term. The plaintiff, Emard H. Sheets, filed a complaint that as amended alleged that he had been wrongfully discharged from his employment as quality control director and operations manager of the defendant, [who] responded with a motion to strike the complaint as legally [in]sufficient. The plaintiff declined to plead further when that motion was granted. . . .

Since this appeal is before us pursuant to a motion to strike, we must take the facts to be those alleged in the plaintiff's complaint as amended, and must construe the complaint in the manner most favorable to the pleader. . . . The complaint alleges that for a four-year period, from November 1973 to November 1977, plaintiff was employed by defendant, a producer of frozen food products, as its quality control director and subsequently also as operations manager. . . . [He] received periodic raises and bonuses. In his capacity as quality control director and operations manager, plaintiff began to notice deviations from the specifications contained in defendant's standards and labels, in that some vegetables were substandard and some meat components underweight. These deviations meant that defendant's products violated the express representations contained in [its] labeling; false or misleading labels in turn violate the provisions of Gen. Stat. § 19–222, the Conn. Uniform Food, Drug and Cosmetic Act. In May of 1977, plaintiff communicated in writing to defendant concerning the use of substandard raw materials and underweight components in defendant's finished products. His recommendations for more selective purchasing and conforming components were ignored. On November 3, 1977, his employment [was] terminated. Although the stated reason for his discharge was unsatisfactory performance of his duties, he was actually dismissed in retaliation for his efforts to ensure that defendant's products would comply with the applicable law relating to labeling and licensing.

The plaintiff's complaint alleges that his dismissal was wrongful in three respects. He claims that there was a violation of an implied contract of employment, a violation of public policy, and a malicious discharge. . . . [T]he claim of malice has not been separately pursued, and we are asked to consider only whether he has stated a cause of action for breach of contract or for intentionally tortious conduct. On oral argument, it was the tort claim that was most vigorously pressed, and it is upon the basis of tort that we have concluded that the motion to strike was granted in error.

The issue before us is whether to recognize an exception to the traditional rules governing employment at will so as to permit a cause of action for wrongful discharge where the discharge contravenes a clear mandate of public policy. In addressing that claim, we must clarify what is not at stake in this litigation. The plaintiff does not challenge the general proposition that contracts of permanent employment, or for an indefinite term, are terminable at will. . . . Nor does he argue that contracts terminable at will permit termination only upon a showing of just cause for dismissal. Some statutes, such as the Conn. Franchise Act, Gen. Stat. §§ 42–133e through 42–133h, do impose limitations of just cause upon the power to terminate some contracts; see § 42–133f; but the legislature has recently refused to interpolate such a requirement into contracts of employment. See H.B. No. 5179, 1974 Sess.[1] There is a significant distinction between a criterion of just cause and what the plaintiff is seeking. "Just cause" substantially limits employer discretion to terminate, by requiring the employer, in all instances, to proffer a proper reason for dismissal, by forbidding the employer to act arbitrarily or capriciously. See Pierce v. Ortho Pharm. Corp., 166 N.J.Super. 335, 399 A.2d 1023, 1026 (1979). By contrast, the plaintiff asks only that the employer be responsible for damages if the former employee can prove a demonstrably *improper* reason for dismissal, a reason whose impropriety is derived from some important violation of public policy.

The argument that contract rights which are inherently legitimate may yet give rise to liability in tort if they are exercised improperly is not a novel one. Although private persons have the right not to enter into contracts, failure to contract under circumstances in which others are seriously misled gives rise to a variety of claims sounding in tort. See Kessler & Fine, "Culpa in Contrahendo," Kessler & Fine, "Culpa in Contrahendo," 77

---

[1] Some statutes of course expressly forbid retaliatory discharge. See, e.g., Public Acts 1979, No. 79–599, and 29 U.S.C. § 660(c)(1) (1976), which is discussed in Marshall v. Whirlpool Corp., 593 F.2d 715 (6th Cir.1979), cert. granted, 444 U.S. 823 (on other grounds). [Some footnotes have been omitted and those retained are renumbered.—Eds.]

Harv.L.Rev. 401 (1964). The development of liability in contract for action induced by reliance upon a promise, despite the absence of common-law consideration normally required to bind a promisor; see Restatement (Second), Contracts § 90 (1973); rests upon principles derived at least in part from the law of tort. See Gilmore, The Death of Contract 8–90 (1974). By way of analogy, we have long recognized abuse of process as a cause of action in tort whose gravamen is the misuse or misapplication of process, its use "in an improper manner or to accomplish a purpose for which it was not designed." Varga v. Pareles, 137 Conn. 663, 667, 81 A.2d 112, 115 (1951). . . .

It would be difficult to maintain that the right to discharge an employee hired at will is so fundamentally different from other contract rights that its exercise is never subject to judicial scrutiny regardless of how outrageous, how violative of public policy, the employer's conduct may be. Cf. Gen. Stat. § 31–126 (unfair employment practices). The defendant does not seriously contest the propriety of cases in other jurisdictions that have found wrongful and actionable a discharge in retaliation for the exercise of an employee's right to: (1) refuse to commit perjury; . . . (2) file a workmen's compensation claim; . . . (3) engage in union activity; . . . (4) perform jury duty. . . . While it may be true that these cases are supported by mandates of public policy derived directly from the applicable state statutes and constitutions, it is equally true that they serve at a minimum to establish the principle that public policy imposes some limits on unbridled discretion to terminate the employment of someone hired at will. See Blades, "Employment at Will vs. Individual Freedom: On Limiting the Abusive Exercise of Employer Power," 67 Colum.L.Rev. 1404 (1967). . . . No case has been called to our attention in which, despite egregiously outrageous circumstances, the employer's contract rights have been permitted to override competing claims of public policy, although there are numerous cases in which the facts were found not to support the employee's claim. . . .

The issue then becomes the familiar common-law problem of deciding where and how to draw the line between claims that genuinely involve the mandates of public policy and are actionable, and ordinary disputes between employee and employer that are not. We are mindful that courts should not lightly intervene to impair the exercise of managerial discretion or to foment unwarranted litigation. We are, however, equally mindful that the myriad of employees without the bargaining power to command employment contracts for a definite term are entitled to a modicum of judicial protection when their conduct as good citizens is punished by their employers.

The central allegation of the plaintiff's complaint is that he was discharged because of his conduct in calling to his employer's attention repeated violations of the Conn. Uniform Food, Drug and Cosmetic Act. This act prohibits the sale of mislabeled food. . . . The act, in § 19–215, imposes criminal penalties upon anyone who violates § 19–213; subsection (b) of § 19–215 makes it clear that criminal sanctions do not depend upon proof of intent to defraud or mislead, since special sanctions are imposed for intentional misconduct. The plaintiff's position as quality control director and operations manager might have exposed him to the possibility of criminal prosecution under this act. The act was intended to "safeguard the public health and promote the public welfare by protecting the consuming public from injury by product use and the purchasing public from injury by merchandising deceit. . . ."

It is useful to compare the factual allegations of this complaint with those of other recent cases in which recovery was sought for retaliatory discharge. In Geary v. United States Steel Corp., [456 Pa. 171, 319 A.2d 174 (1974)], in which the plaintiff had disputed the safety of tubular steel casings, he was denied recovery because, as a company salesman, he had neither the expertise nor the corporate responsibility to "exercise independent, expert judgment in matters of product safety." By contrast, this plaintiff . . . did have responsibility for product quality control. Three other recent cases in which the plaintiff's claim survived demurrer closely approximate the claim before us. In Trombetta v. Detroit, Toledo & Ironton R. Co., 81 Mich.App. 489, 265 N.W.2d 385 (1978), a cause of action was stated when an employee alleged that he had been discharged in retaliation for his refusal to manipulate and alter sampling results for pollution control reports required by Michigan law. There as here falsified reports would have violated state law. In Harless v. First Nat'l Bank in Fairmont, 246 S.E.2d 270 (W.Va.1978), an employee stated a cause of action when he alleged that he had been discharged in retaliation for his efforts to ensure his employer's compliance with state and federal consumer credit protection laws. There as here the legislature had established a public policy of consumer protection. In Pierce v. Ortho Pharm.Corp., 166 N.J.Super. 335, 399 A.2d 1023 (1979), the plaintiff was entitled to a trial to determine whether she had been wrongfully discharged for refusing to pursue clinical testing of a new drug containing a high level of saccharin; the court noted that the plaintiff's status as a physician entitled her to invoke the Hippocratic Oath as well as state statutory provisions governing the licensing and the conduct of physicians. There as here the case might have been dismissed as a conflict in judgment.

In the light of these recent cases, which evidence a growing judicial receptivity to the recognition of a tort claim for wrongful discharge, the trial court was in error in granting defendant's motion to strike. The plaintiff alleged that he had been dismissed in retaliation for his insistence that defendant comply with the requirements of a state statute, . . . We need not decide whether violation of a state statute is invariably a prerequisite to the conclusion that a challenged discharge violates public policy. Certainly when there is a relevant state statute we should not ignore the statement of public policy that it represents. For today, it is enough to decide that an employee should not be put to an election whether to risk criminal sanction or to jeopardize his continued employment.

There is error and the case is remanded for further proceedings.

COTTER, C.J. (dissenting). I cannot agree that, on the factual situation presented to us, we should abandon the well-established principle that an indefinite general hiring may be terminated at the will of either party without liability to the other. . . . The majority by seeking to extend a "modicum" of judicial protection to shield employees from retaliatory discharges instead offers them a sword with which to coerce employers to retain them in their employ. In recognizing an exception to the traditional rules governing employment at will[,] . . . the majority is necessarily led to the creation of an overly broad new cause of action whose nuisance value alone may impair employers' ability to hire and retain employees who are best suited to their requirements. Other jurisdictions which have recognized a cause of action for retaliatory discharge have done so on the basis of a much clearer and more direct contravention of a mandate of public policy. . . .

In contrast, the purposes of the statute the majority would rely on . . . can only be considered as, at most, marginally affected by an allegedly retaliatory discharge of an employee who observed the supposed sale of shortweight frozen entrées and the use of [substandard] vegetables. A retaliatory discharge in the present case would not necessarily thwart or inhibit [the Act's] purpose of protecting the consumer. The plaintiff, if he desired to protect the consumer, could have communicated [his concerns], even anonymously, to the commissioner of consumer affairs. . . . [T]he plaintiff need not have jeopardized his continued employment. There is no indication that the plaintiff has either, before or after his discharge, informed or even attempted to inform the commissioner of consumer protection of violations the plaintiff claims. . . . Unlike those cases where an employer allegedly discharged employees for engaging in union activities or filing workmen's compensation claims and the discharge itself contravened a statutory mandate, [here] the discharge itself at most only indirectly impinged on the statutory mandate.

Consequently, the majority seemingly invites the unrestricted use of an allegation of almost any statutory or even regulatory violation by an employer as the basis for a cause of action by a discharged employee hired for an indefinite term. . . . [T]he majority is creating an open-ended arena for judicial policy making and the usurpation of legislative functions. To base this new cause of action on a decision as to whether an alleged reason for discharge "is derived from some important violation of public policy" is not to create adequate and carefully circumscribed standards for this new cause of action but is to invite the opening of a Pandora's box of unwarranted litigation. . . .

Moreover, this is policy making that the Connecticut legislature recently declined to undertake. In 1974, the General Assembly considered and rejected a bill which would have provided that "[a]ny employee [including private sector employees] hired for an indefinite term, may be dismissed only for just cause or because of the employer's reduction in work force for business reasons." H.B. No. 5179, 1974 Sess. [T]he bill's sponsor gave examples of the kind of discharges he intended the bill to cover: discharges for overlooking violations of building codes or for campaigning for the wrong political party. . . . Thus, "just cause" in the overwhelmingly rejected 1974 bill was meant to encompass the kinds of retaliatory discharge that the majority approves as a new cause of action. Furthermore, the most recent legislature enacted a statute protecting "whistle blowing" state employees; Public Acts 1979, No. 79–599; and in Public Acts 1979, No. 153, addressed the problem of retaliatory dismissals of building officials. The legislature is thus adopting appropriate remedies for certain types of retaliatory discharges at its own considered pace. . . . In these circumstances, this court should consider itself precluded from substituting its own ideas of what might be wise policy. . . .

Finally, it should be reiterated that the minority of jurisdictions which have created a cause of action for retaliatory discharges have done so with caution. . . . It is because the majority abandons that caution and for the reason that the factual situation before us does not demonstrate a "wrongful discharge where the discharge contravenes a clear mandate of public policy" that I feel compelled to dissent.

[Another justice joined the dissent; the vote was 3 to 2.]

QUESTION

Suppose, at a trial after remand, plaintiff requested the following jury instruction: "As a matter of law, if you find for the plaintiff, Emard Sheets, you may award him such damages as are attributable to the amount of salary and fringe benefits he would have made had he continued to work at Teddy's Frosted Foods, minus any amounts which Mr. Sheets earned during the period from the date of discharge until the date of this trial. You may, in addition, compensate Mr. Sheets for his complete injury by awarding him such damages as are attributable to any mental distress caused by the termination of his employment." Would the court commit reversible error by giving this instruction?

Price v. Carmack Datsun, Inc.
109 Ill.2d 65, 485 N.E.2d 359 (1985)

Defendant, an auto dealer, had a group health-insurance plan for employees. Plaintiff, a sales representative for defendant, was hospitalized following an automobile accident which left him with serious injuries and $7,000 in medical expenses. When plaintiff returned to work three months later, defendant asked whether he intended to submit a claim under the health-insurance plan and sought to discourage him from doing so. Three days later, plaintiff told defendant of his intention to file a claim. Defendant then discharged plaintiff, who brought suit alleging that the health-insurance provisions of the Illinois Insurance Code reflect a "public policy" against the discharge of employees for filing such claims. A jury found for plaintiff and awarded him $5,525 in compensatory damages and $2,762 in punitive damages. *Held*, plaintiff failed to state a cause of action in tort for retaliatory discharge. An exception to the at-will doctrine is made in Illinois only when the discharge violates a "clearly mandated public policy." While that term is imprecise, a survey of cases elsewhere shows that "a matter must strike at the heart of a citizen's social rights, duties, and responsibilities before the tort will be allowed." This court has approved a cause of action for a discharge in retaliation for filing a workers' compensation claim and for furnishing police with information regarding possible criminal conduct of a fellow employee. But here "the matter is one of private and individual grievance rather than one affecting our society," and plaintiff's reliance on the health-care provisions of the Insurance Code is unavailing. "The entire insurance industry . . . is a regulated industry. The Insurance Code regulates all types of insurance and all policies issued are required to have State approval. It should be noted, too, that the Code was designed to govern operations of insurance companies, not insureds, such as defendant. The filing of a claim under a policy of insurance is pursuant to an individual contract between the insurer and the insured. We consider that the discharge of an employee for filing a claim under a policy in which he is a beneficiary does not violate a clearly mandated public policy."

NOTE: THE PUBLIC'S POLICY

What is the "public policy" rule of the *Sheets* and *Price* cases designed to protect? It is clear that a great majority of states have adopted the public-policy "exception" to the at-will doctrine, and that a recurring theme in the cases is the "public-private" dichotomy observed in Price v. Carmack Datsun. Still, in most places the exception is viewed as "narrow" or "limited." Discharged at-will employees suing for tort damages in California must show that the public interests they seek to vindicate are "tethered to fundamental policies delineated in constitutional or statutory provisions." Gantt v. Sentry Ins., 1 Cal.4th 1083, 4 Cal.Rptr.2d 874, 824 P.2d 680 (1992). The Connecticut court, in later applications of *Sheets*, has stressed that, absent unusual circumstances, "we will interfere with a personnel decision only if it implicates an explicit statutory or constitutional provision, or judicially conceived notion of public policy." Daley v. Aetna Life & Cas. Co., 249 Conn. 766, 734 A.2d 112 (1999). In Illinois, as *Price* suggests, absent a firing for refusing to violate a statute or to act illegally, courts are likely to find the requisite "mandate of public policy" in only two settings: a discharge stemming from an employee's pursuit of a worker's compensation claim or from an employee's reporting of unlawful or improper conduct. Russ v. Pension Consultants Co., 182 Ill.App.3d 769, 538 N.E.2d 693 (1989). Separating a "private" concern from a matter of "public policy" is perhaps most difficult in the latter situation, where, as in *Sheets*, the basis for the discharge is alleged to be "whistleblowing" in some form. Should such cases turn on the entity to whom plaintiff reported workplace activity (firm management rather than public or law-enforcement officials), or on a characterization of what plaintiff reported (actual criminal activity distinguished from co-workers' shoddy performance or questionable practices)? See, e.g., Belline v. K–Mart Corp., 940 F.2d 184 (7th Cir.1991), where a dissenter complained that "[i]t is easy for a jury to mistake a pest, a busybody, for a champion of the law." Is that a persuasive reason for narrowing the exception?

New York's highest court, in Murphy v. American Home Products Corp., 58 N.Y.2d 293, 461 N.Y.S.2d 232, 448 N.E.2d 86 (1983), refused to recognize either a common-law tort theory based on abusive or wrongful discharge ("the Legislature has infinitely greater resources and procedural means to discern the public will") or the implied covenant of "good faith" that perhaps seven or eight states have carried over to the at-will cases. In rejecting plaintiff's urging of an implied covenant of "good faith" in employment contracts, the court reaffirmed but distinguished Wood v. Lucy, Lady Duff–Gordon, stressing that the implied obligation in that case was "in aid and furtherance of other terms of the agreement." A dissenter, invoking Feld v. Henry S. Levy & Sons, p. 361, argued that the "same reasoning that reads into an output contract the requirement that the manufacturing plant continue to perform in good faith" requires reading the good-faith obligation into employment contracts which are only "impliedly," not expressly, terminable at will.

A useful survey of common law doctrines used to erode the at-will rule can be found in Note, Implied Contract Rights to Job Security, 26 Stan.L.Rev. 335 (1974). Although both tort and contract theories have provided a basis for judicially-created exceptions, the most successful technique appears to be the tort claim that a discharge violates some "mandate of public policy."

————

McDonald v. Mobil Coal Producing, Inc.

Supreme Court of Wyoming, 1991.
820 P.2d 986.

GOLDEN, J. This employment termination case comes before the court on appellee Mobil Coal Producing's motion for rehearing. In our previous decision, McDonald v. Mobil Coal Producing, Inc., 789 P.2d 866 (Wyo.1990) (*McDonald I*), we ruled that summary judgment in favor of the appellees must be reversed and the case remanded for further proceedings. The five justices of this court rendered a total of four opinions, including a special concurrence and two separate dissents. Following our decision, we granted Mobil's petition for rehearing to review and clarify our earlier decision.

The relevant facts are more fully set out in *McDonald I.* [In brief, McDonald worked at Mobil's Caballo Rojo mine as a technician in the preparation plant, from August 1987 until June 1988, when he "resigned" his position following rumors that he had sexually harassed a female coworker. McDonald contended that his resignation in fact was a "dismissal," resulting from a meeting with three company officials including the mine superintendent, who told him he had "the choice of either resigning or being fired." McDonald's suit challenging his dismissal named Mobil Coal and the three company officials as defendants.]

After the trial court granted summary judgment against him, [McDonald] appealed to this court, claiming breach of contract based on the terms of his employee handbook. . . . A plurality of this court rejected the [claim] that Mobil's handbook constituted a valid contract sufficient to modify the terms of McDonald's at-will employment. . . . However, a different plurality reversed summary judgment and remanded for a determination of whether the principle of promissory estoppel applied to the facts of this case.

Justice Golden, specially concurring, rejected the application of promissory estoppel, stating that he would have remanded to resolve the ambiguity in the effect of the disclaimer contained in Mobil's employee handbook. Justice Cardine, dissenting, found the disclaimer effective to assure there was not an employment contract. . . . Justice Thomas, also dissenting, agreed with Justice Cardine, noting that he could see no difference between [viewing] the handbook as creating a contract and finding it to be a binding promise under the doctrine of promissory estoppel.

We reaffirm our earlier decision reversing summary judgment and remanding this case for further proceedings. We hold that a question of material fact exists concerning whether the employee handbook and Mobil's course of dealing with appellant modified the terms of appellant's at-will employment.

. . . Mobil claims that it effectively disclaimed any employment relationship other than at-will. McDonald argues Mobil objectively manifested its intent to modify the initial at-will contract with the employment manual and by its course of dealing. We examine both [claims].

The Federal District Court of Wyoming explored the issue of effective contract disclaimers in Jimenez v. Colorado Interstate Gas Co., 690 F.Supp. 977 (D.Wyo.1988). The plaintiff's employer had adopted standard operating procedures relating to cause for termination. The employer had inserted a disclaimer in these procedures to the effect that they did not constitute terms of a contract. The court stated that for a disclaimer to be effective it must be conspicuous and whether it was conspicuous was a matter of law.

Where the disclaimer was not set off in any way, was placed under a general subheading, was not capitalized, and contained the same type size as another provision on the same page, it was not conspicuous.

We adopt the rule in *Jiminez* that disclaimers must be conspicuous to be effective against employees and that conspicuousness is a matter of law. The trial court erred in its statement that there was no requirement that the disclaimers be conspicuous. We examine the disclaimers in this case to see whether they were sufficiently conspicuous to be binding on appellant.

The application form which Craig McDonald signed on July 20, 1987, contained the following disclaimer:

READ CAREFULLY BEFORE SIGNING

I agree that any offer of employment, and acceptance thereof, does not constitute a binding contract of any length, and that such employment is terminable at the will of either party, subject to appropriate state and/or federal laws.

The MCPI Employee Handbook which he received [after starting work at the mine] contained the following disclaimer, located on its first page, which we reproduce in full to show the context in which [it] was made:

WELCOME

Mobil Coal Producing Inc., Caballo Rojo Mine, is proud to welcome you as an employee. We believe you will find safety, opportunity and satisfaction while making your contribution to Mobil's growth as a major supplier of coal. This handbook is intended to be used as a guide for our nonexempt mine technicians and salaried support personnel, to help you understand and explain to you Mobil's policies and procedures. It is not a comprehensive policies and procedures manual, nor an employment contract. More detailed policies and procedures are maintained by the Employee Relations supervisor and your supervisor. While we intend to continue policies, benefits and rules contained in this handbook, changes or improvements may be made from time to time by the company. If you have any questions, please feel free to discuss them with your supervisor, a member of our Employee Relations staff, and/or any member of Caballo Rojo's Management. We urge you to read your handbook carefully and keep it in a safe and readily available place for future reference. Sections will be revised as conditions affecting your employment or benefits change.

Sincerely,   R.J. Kovacich

                                                                  Mine Manager

/s/   Caballo Rojo Mine

The circumstances surrounding this disclaimer are nearly identical to those of the *Jiminez* case. [It] was not set off by a border or larger print, was not capitalized, and was contained in a general welcoming section of the handbook.

Additionally, the disclaimer was unclear as to its effect on the employment relationship. For persons untutored in contract law, such clarity is essential, as stated [by the] New Jersey Supreme Court[:]

It would be unfair to allow an employer to distribute a policy manual that makes the workforce believe that certain promises have been made and then to allow the employer to renege on those promises. What is sought here is basic honesty: if the employer, for whatever reason, does not want the manual to be capable of being construed by the court as a binding contract, there are simple ways to attain that goal. All that need be done is the inclusion in a very prominent position of an appropriate statement *that there is no promise of any kind by the employer contained in the manual; that regardless of what the manual says or provides, the employer promises nothing and remains free to change wages and all other working conditions without having to consult anyone and without anyone's agreement; and that the employer continues to have the absolute power to fire anyone with or without good cause.*

Woolley v. Hoffmann–La Roche, Inc., 99 N.J. 284, 309, 491 A.2d 1257, 1271 (1985), [modified,] 101 N.J. 10, 499 A.2d 515 (1985). No explanation was given in the disclaimer that Mobil did not consider itself bound by the terms of the handbook. Instead, McDonald would have been led to draw inferences from the handbook language: that it was intended to be a guide, and that Mobil intended to continue the policies, benefits and rules contained in the handbook. The same paragraph which disclaimed a contract also informed McDonald that he could discuss "any questions" he might have with his supervisor, employee relations staff and management and urged him to read the handbook carefully and to keep it in a safe and readily available place.

The trial court erred in finding that the disclaimer was conspicuous. We hold that the attempted disclaimers in the employee handbook and in the employment application were insufficiently conspicuous to be binding on McDonald.

In our earlier opinion, [we] stated:

Following [Mobil Coal Producing, Inc. v. Parks, 704 P.2d 702 (Wyo.1985)], Mobil revised its handbook. The most significant revision was the addition of a statement that the handbook was not an employment contract. A contract exists when there is a meeting of the minds. Mobil's express disclaimer demonstrates that it had no intention to form a contract.

McDonald I, 789 P.2d at 869.

The above quotation could be interpreted as importing an unduly subjective element into contract analysis. See Pine River State Bank v. Mettille, 333 N.W.2d 622, 630 n. 6 (Minn.1983). However, we did not mean to say that a contract could not be formed where one party somehow lacked "subjective intent" but nevertheless proceeded as if there were a contract.

Under the "objective theory" of contract formation, contractual obligation is imposed not on the basis of the subjective intent of the parties, but rather upon the outward manifestations of a party's assent sufficient to create reasonable reliance by the other party. . . That Mobil did not subjectively "intend" that a contract be formed is irrelevant, provided that Mobil made sufficient intentional, objective manifestations of contractual assent to create reasonable reliance by McDonald. . . .

We must determine whether there is a genuine issue of material fact concerning Mobil's objective manifestations of assent to contract. The disclaimers figure in this analysis, as do the remainder of the handbook provisions and Mobil's course of dealing with McDonald.

The handbook informed McDonald that "individual consideration on employee-supervisor matters provides the best method for satisfying the employees' and the Company's needs" which could not be improved on by union representation. Mobil stated that it planned to provide, inter alia, "free and open communications" and stated that "on those rare occasions when differences cannot be resolved, we have a Fair Treatment Procedure that affords an employee the opportunity to be heard, without fear of reprisal." Union representation, the handbook stated, is unnecessary for employees to enjoy job security or consistent treatment.

The manual stated that Mobil recognized a "fundamental obligation" to its employees to "give helpful consideration when an employee makes a mistake or has a personal problem with which we are asked to help." The handbook outlined a procedure for presenting a problem or complaint which an employee might have. The manual also set forth a progressive discipline schedule for cases in which the employee broke the company rules or failed to meet a reasonable standard of conduct and work performance. This five-step schedule could be disregarded by the company at its discretion.

The "welcoming" section, quoted above, stated that Mobil intended to continue policies, benefits and rules contained in the handbook and that changes or improvements could be made from time to time by the company. The inference favorable to McDonald is that Mobil would follow the rules unless changed, and that since they had not been changed, Mobil was bound by them.

When McDonald went to his supervisor over the rumors that he had heard, he was told that he should "just do his job and not worry about what had been said." McDonald alleges that Mobil's course of conduct led him to believe that Mobil would follow the handbook procedures concerning the complaint of his co-employee.

Examining the handbook provisions cited above and Mobil's course of dealing with McDonald on the rumor of accusation and his termination, we find ambiguity as to whether Mobil manifested intent to modify the at-will employment to an employment which could be terminated only for cause. Mobil made numerous statements which could be construed as promises to McDonald concerning communication with him and Mobil's disciplinary procedures. Mobil's handbook stated that individual consideration and open communication would be an effective substitute for unionization. All of these manifestations could suggest to a reasonable person that Mobil intended to make legally-binding promises. . . .

The meaning and effect of this employment contract, a mixed question of law and fact, remains unresolved. Therefore, we must reverse summary judgment on the contract issue. The case is remanded to the trial court for determination of whether the employee handbook and Mobil's course of dealing with McDonald modified the employment relationship from one terminable at will to one terminable only for cause.

MACY, J. (concurring). I specially concur. In *McDonald I*, we stated that genuine issues of material fact existed as to the effect, if any, the representations made by Mobil in its handbook had upon an otherwise at-will employment relationship. The Court went on to state in *McDonald I* that those issues were (1) whether Mobil should have expected McDonald's reliance upon the procedures outlined in the handbook, (2) whether McDonald's reliance was reasonable, and (3) whether Mobil's termination procedures should have been enforced to avoid injustice.

. . . Even if the employment handbook was ambiguous, Mobil's course of conduct clearly demonstrated that Mobil intended to make legally binding promises concerning Mobil's employment termination procedures and that Mobil certainly led McDonald to rely upon the termination procedures outlined in the handbook. [Thus,] the only question which should be resolved on remand is whether Mobil's termination procedures should have been enforced to avoid an injustice; i.e., whether Mobil should have been estopped from firing McDonald without cause.

THOMAS, J. (dissenting). I persist in my vote to affirm the trial court in this case. Like Justice Cardine, in whose dissent I join, I am at a loss to understand what more Mobil Coal Producing, Inc. could do to make it clear to an employee that he was entering into an employment-at-will arrangement. I am satisfied that this was an employment-at-will. That relationship was not modified by the handbook. . . .

. . . [T]he fact of that specific employment-at-will arrangement serves to distinguish this case from [*Jimenez*]. There are other distinguishing facts. The employee handbook, in this instance, was not adopted and issued after the time that McDonald was employed. It is difficult for me to understand how it could amend, or could in some manner have changed, the clear employment-at-will that was documented. In *Jimenez*, there was no separate document articulating an employment-at-will, and the court was dealing only with the factors of employment plus the existence of a handbook. While it might be appropriate to emphasize in an employee's handbook, that was issued without a separate document articulating the employment arrangement, the caveat explaining that the handbook is not an employment contract, that requirement is far less imperative when one recognizes that the handbook was generally available to [Mobil's] employees. After the handbook already had been published and issued, McDonald signed a document that provided that the "employment is terminable at will." Under these circumstances, the subsequent delivery of the handbook simply did not make any difference.

In my opinion, this case strikes the death knell for employment-at-will in Wyoming. It says, in effect, that even though there is a clear statement by the employee that the relationship with the employer is an employment-at-will, after the employment commences, the employer cannot engage in any dialogue with the employee about the conditions and circumstances of the employment. If any such dialogue occurs, it will be considered to have amended the arrangement in such a way that the question of employment must be submitted to a jury. I lack the imagination to visualize any situation in which dialogue about the conditions and circumstances of the employment would not occur and, consequently, it is hereafter impossible to have an employment-at-will in Wyoming.

CARDINE, J. (dissenting, with whom Thomas, J., joins). I continue my dissent . . . for the reasons previously stated. *McDonald I*, 789 P.2d 866, 871 (Wyo.1990) (Cardine, C.J., dissenting). This opinion after rehearing merely informs Mobil of additional requirements for effective disclaimer. If Mobil should in the future satisfy these requirements, can it assume that this court will give effect to its disclaimer—or should Mobil eliminate its employee handbook? Perhaps the answer will only come with more litigation.

In *McDonald I*, the court reversed summary judgment on the basis of promissory estoppel. Despite the disclaimer in the handbook, the court said McDonald could recover if he could demonstrate that it was reasonable to rely upon the promises contained in the handbook and if enforcement of the promises was the only way to avoid an injustice. 789 P.2d at 870. The court held that no contract was formed because there was no meeting of the minds in forming a contract. . . . Now, upon rehearing, the court holds that if it was reasonable to rely upon promises in the handbook, then a contract was formed. This opinion states a contract is formed by "outward manifestations of a party's assent sufficient to create reasonable reliance by the other party." . . . A promise is not a contract. But this court now says the making of a promise alone reasonably relied upon by another creates an enforceable contract.

. . . It is clear from the disclaimer that Mobil never intended to make a contract. There was never a meeting of the minds nor was there a valid consideration. There was no contract. That is why this court in *McDonald I* rested its decision to reverse upon the doctrine of promissory estoppel. I would affirm the decision of the trial court.

Kari v. General Motors Corp.

79 Mich.App. 93, 261 N.W.2d 222 (1977)

Plaintiff, an engineer employed by defendant from 1955–1972, was "separated" from the company when he attempted to return to work following an extended leave of absence. Plaintiff brought suit to recover separation pay allegedly guaranteed by defendant's employee handbook. The handbook, entitled "Working with General Motors," had been issued to plaintiff at the time of his initial employment. A section termed "Separation Allowance" read in part:

> A Separation Allowance Plan has been established for the benefit of salaried employe[e]s laid off or separated from the payroll under certain circumstances. The primary purpose of this Plan is to provide a source of income to eligible employe[e]s beyond the date of their layoff or separation. The inclusion of a schedule of separation allowances in this booklet, together with the conditions governing their payment, however, is not intended nor is it to be interpreted to establish a contractual relationship with the employe[e]. . . .

Additional language appeared on the last page of the handbook, italicized and outlined in red:

> The contents of this handbook are presented as a matter of information only. While General Motors believes wholeheartedly in the plans, policies and procedures described here, they are not conditions of employment. General Motors reserves the right to modify, revoke, suspend, terminate, or change any or all such plans, policies, or procedures, in whole or in part, at any time, with or without notice. The language used in this handbook is not intended to create, nor is it to be construed to constitute, a contract between General Motors and any one or all of its employe[e]s.

Plaintiff contended that the handbook's separation-allowance provision constituted an offer which he had accepted by working for defendant. *Held*, summary judgment for defendant affirmed; as a matter of law, no contract existed. The theory that an employer's communications to employees may constitute an offer to contract is sound. But the offer must contain a promise, "communicated in such a manner . . . that [the promisee] may justly expect performance and may reasonably rely thereon." This is not a situation where an employer adopts a policy of severance payments as a part of a drive to attract employees. Here, the handbook "clearly evinced an intention *not* to create an offer capable of acceptance"; the communication was "couched in disclaimers." It is difficult to imagine what defendant could have done, short of not mentioning the severance plan, to prevent it from being read as an offer. "An employee reading this language . . . should realize that further negotiations . . . are necessary to create a contract for severance pay."

————

Dore v. Arnold Worldwide, Inc.

Supreme Court of California, 2006.
39 Cal.4th 384, 139 P.3d 56, 46 Cal.Rptr.3d 668.

WERDEGAR, J. . . . Plaintiff Brook Dore was employed with an advertising agency in Colorado as a regional account director specializing in automobile accounts. In late 1998, Dore discussed with his employer the possibility of relocating to the employer's Los Angeles office.

In 1999, Dore learned that a management supervisor position was available in the Los Angeles office of defendant Arnold Worldwide, Inc., formerly known as Arnold Communications, Inc., (hereafter AWI). Dore interviewed with several AWI officers and employees. According to Dore, he was never told during the interview process that his employment would be terminable without cause or "at will." Dore alleges he was told that AWI had landed a new automobile account and needed someone to handle it on a long-term basis. He also was told that, if hired, he would "play a critical role in growing the agency," that AWI was looking for "a long-term fix, not a Band–Aid," and that AWI employees were treated like family. Dore alleges he learned that the two people previously holding the position for which he was being considered had been terminated for cause—one for committing financial indiscretions, the other because his work had not satisfied a client. Dore states that AWI offered him the management supervisor position by telephone in April 1999, and he orally accepted.

Later that same month, Dore received a three-page letter from Sharon McCabe, senior vice-president of AWI, dated April 6, 1999 (AWI's letter), purporting to "confirm our offer to join us as Management Supervisor in our Los Angeles office" and to state "[t]he terms of this offer." AWI's letter then listed, in bullet-pointed sections, a commencement date, compensation details, and various benefits (including reimbursement of relocation expenses, parking at the AWI offices, various types of insurance, expense reimbursement, and vacation).

AWI's letter also stated: "You will have a 90 day assessment with your supervisor at which time you will receive initial performance feedback. This assessment will also be the time that you will work with your supervisor to set objectives against which you will be evaluated at the time of your annual review. After your assessment is complete, you and your supervisor will have the opportunity to discuss consideration for being named an officer of Arnold Communications."

In a separate paragraph central to the present dispute, AWI's letter stated: "Brook, please know that as with all of our company employees, your employment with Arnold Communications, Inc. is at will. This simply means that Arnold Communications has the right to terminate your employment at any time just as you have the right to terminate your employment with Arnold Communications, Inc. at any time."

AWI's letter requested that Dore sign and return the letter signifying his acceptance of these employment terms. Dore read and signed the letter.

AWI terminated Dore's employment in August 2001. Thereafter, Dore sued AWI and a related entity, Arnold Worldwide Partners (AWP). . . .

Dore alleges that AWI, by various oral representations, conduct, and documents, led him reasonably to understand there existed between AWI and himself an implied-in-fact contract that provided he would not be discharged from his employment except for cause. AWI contends that its oral representations, conduct, and documents could not reasonably have raised any such understanding in Dore. . . .

Dore acknowledges that a clear and unambiguous at-will provision in a written employment contract, signed by the employee, cannot be overcome by evidence of a prior or contemporaneous implied-in-fact contract requiring good cause for termination. But he contends this rule cannot govern here because AWI's letter neither constitutes nor contains a clear and unambiguous agreement that his employment would be terminable without cause. . . .

The Court of Appeal below agreed with Dore that AWI's letter, signed by Dore, was not clear and unambiguous with respect to cause for termination. Notwithstanding the letter's statement that "your employment with Arnold Communications, Inc. is at will," the court reasoned, by going on to define the term "at will" to mean that AWI had the right to terminate Dore's employment "at any time," AWI impliedly relinquished the right to terminate Dore without cause. We disagree. . . .

We disagree with Dore that the verbal formulation "at any time" in the termination clause of an employment contract is per se ambiguous merely because it does not expressly speak to whether cause is required. As a matter of simple logic, rather, such a formulation ordinarily entails the notion of "with or without cause." . . .

That the phrase "at any time" is not in itself ambiguous with respect to cause for termination does not preclude the possibility that AWI's letter, when considered as a whole, contains ambiguity on the topic. . . .

In this case, the trial court recognized that the presumption of at-will employment . . . can be overcome by an express or implied agreement to the contrary. Nevertheless, the court ruled that because the express written contract—i.e., AWI's letter—controls, it need not consider whether Dore's proffered extrinsic evidence establishes the existence of an earlier implied agreement to terminate only for cause.

The Court of Appeal, in reaching the contrary conclusion, relied primarily on the fact that AWI's letter, after stating that Dore's employment is "at will," defines "at will" in a manner that refers expressly only to the duration of the contract (i.e., as meaning "that Arnold Communications has the right to terminate your employment at any time") and does not state explicitly whether cause is required. The Court of Appeal also relied on evidence extrinsic to the letter, in particular, that AWI required Dore to sign a post-employment noncompetition and nondisclosure agreement.

The trial court's ruling was correct. The language of the parties' written agreement is unambiguous. AWI's letter plainly states that Dore's employment with AWI was at will. Indeed, as the trial court observed, Dore admitted as much and further admitted that he "read, signed, understood and did not disagree with the terms of the letter." Even the Court of Appeal acknowledged that the term "at will" when used in an employment contract normally conveys an intent employment may be ended by either party "at any time without cause." Although AWI's letter also states that AWI would provide Dore a "90 day assessment" and "annual review," these provisions, in describing AWI's employee evaluation schedule, neither expressly nor impliedly conferred on Dore the right to be terminated only for cause.

That AWI's letter went on to define at-will employment as employment that may be terminated at any time did not introduce ambiguity rendering the letter susceptible of being interpreted as allowing for an implied agreement that Dore could be terminated only for cause. In defining at-will employment, AWI used language similar to the language the Legislature used in our statutory provision. Labor Code section 2922 says that an "employment, *having no specified term*, may be terminated at the will of either party on notice to the other." (Italics added.)

. . . For the parties to specify—indeed to emphasize—that Dore's employment was at will (explaining that it could be terminated at any time) would make no sense if their true meaning was that his employment could be terminated only for cause. Thus, even though AWI's letter defined "at will" as meaning "at any time," without specifying it also meant without cause or for any or no reason, the letter's meaning was clear.

Nor did Dore's proffered extrinsic evidence render AWI's letter ambiguous concerning whether he could be terminated only for cause. As noted, Dore declared that he was told his role would be "critical" because AWI "needed a long-term fix" of certain problems and wanted Dore to "build a relationship" with an important new client. He also testified that he learned in interviews that some people at AWI had been employed there for long periods and he was assured the company had a family atmosphere. Even if credited, such evidence would not support an inference that Dore reasonably understood AWI's letter as consistent with a promise not to terminate him without cause. "When a dispute arises over the meaning of contract language, the first question to be decided is whether the language is 'reasonably susceptible' to the interpretation urged by the party. If it is not, the case is over." Southern Cal. Edison Co. v. Superior Court (1995) 37 Cal.App.4th 839, 847, 44 Cal.Rptr.2d 227.

We conclude, in sum, that AWI's letter contained no ambiguity, patent or latent, in its termination provisions. Accordingly, we agree with the trial court that no triable issues of fact exist with respect to Dore's causes of action for breach of contract and breach of the implied covenant of good faith and fair dealing. . . .

SECTION 4. STANDARDIZED TERMS, UNCONSCIONABLE INEQUALITY, AND GOOD FAITH

INTRODUCTORY NOTE

We have seen a number of instances in which one or more printed forms entered into the making of a contract. The classic use of preprinted writings is of course the "battle of the forms," where a form is sent by one party to the other and answered by the other's own form. Our concern now is not an exchange of forms (and the problems addressed through UCC 2–207), but the situation where one party simply signs, or acquiesces in, the standard form prepared and presented by the other—the much-maligned "contract of adhesion" that is infected with a take it or leave it quality. Most transactions between businesses and consumers fall into this pattern, as do a great many contracts between businesses. Accordingly, the recurring question is whether a party should be prevented from enforcing a term of a contract because the term is "buried in the fine print" and was not "freely negotiated."

Although our principal interest remains the "assent" analysis of traditional contract law, we will see that the talk in the cases in this section shifts often to "unconscionability" and "public policy." This is not surprising, since it is difficult to isolate the "assent problem" from the larger "fairness problem" that results from an imbalance of some sort, including boilerplate one-sidedness.

The starting point in the interpretation of fine-print terms in form contracts is the common law "duty to read." A Florida case, Allied Van Lines, Inc. v. Bratton, 351 So.2d 344 (Fla.1977), illustrates the reasoning commonly employed:

> May an interstate shipper avoid the legal consequences of a limitation of liability contained in a Bill of Lading issued by a carrier and signed by the shipper, on the ground that the shipper did not read the document and therefore did not assent to its provisions? . . . It has long been held in Florida that one is bound by his contract. Unless one can show facts and circumstances to demonstrate that he was prevented from reading the contract, or that he was induced by statements of the other party to refrain from reading the contract, it is binding. No party to a written contract in this state can defend against its enforcement on the sole ground that he signed it without reading it. . . . [Here, we are not] dealing with a situation where a shipper signed a Bill of Lading under the mistaken belief that it was not a contractual document at all. . . . In the [two cases] before us, there is no evidence of misrepresentation as to the character of the documents signed. Both shippers knew they were signing a contract. [One] simply did not read the documents furnished or even ask questions about the Bill of Lading. [The other's] situation is different, however, for she sought information, was misled by the carrier's agent as to available [insurance] coverage, and was prevented from exercising her right to choose adequate coverage. . . . [T]he legal consequences of the contract [she signed] may be avoided.

Observe that the "duty to read," like the "duty to speak" encountered earlier, appears rooted in the idea that action or inaction "with reason to know" results in a preclusion of sorts, a foregoing or waiver of the privilege of objecting to legal consequences. A good discussion of the formal approach indicated by the traditional rule can be found in Calamari, Duty to Read—A Changing Concept, 43 Fordham L.Rev. 341 (1974).

Yet the duty to read, like most legal generalizations, depends ultimately on circumstances; the duty may be raised or lowered, even extinguished. Take, for example, the ordinary transaction litigated in Agricultural Ins. Co. v. Constantine, 144 Ohio St. 275, 58 N.E.2d 658 (1944).

Bova parked her car on defendant's parking lot one morning, left her keys in the ignition as the attendant instructed her, and was given a "ticket." When Bova returned about 3 p.m., defendant could not locate the car on the lot. It was found by the police three days later, in a damaged condition, and returned to Bova. Plaintiff, having insured the car, paid $155 for the repairs and sued defendant to recover that amount. Defendant's answer alleged that the car had been removed from the lot by an unknown person, without the knowledge or consent of defendant's employees, and that on the ticket given to Bova was "printed in clear, legible type" the following:

> No attendant on duty after regular closing time. Cars left after closing hour at owner's risk. This station will endeavor to protect the property of its patrons, but it is agreed that it will not be liable for loss or damage of cars, accessories or contents, from whatever cause arising.

Plaintiff's evidence showed that Bova had parked her car on defendant's lot an average of twice a week for a period of five to six years, that she had always left the keys in the ignition as instructed, and, though given a ticket in the form described by defendant, she had never read it. At the conclusion of plaintiff's evidence, the trial court directed a verdict for defendant on the basis of the "not-liable-for-loss" provision on the ticket. This judgment was reversed by the court of appeals, and defendant appealed. Ohio's highest court agreed that the trial court's judgment was properly reversed. In considering the legal relations of Bova and the defendant, that court concluded:

(1) Since the attendant assumed control over and custody of the Bova automobile, defendant became a bailee rather than a mere lessor of a parking space.

(2) Under the "great weight of authority," a ticket like that given Bova was "a mere token for identification," and the terms on it limiting liability did not become a part of the bailment contract, "at least in the absence of anything to indicate that the bailor assented to the conditions before delivering the property to the bailee." There was no evidence of Bova's assent. Her mere retention of the ticket was not enough, since she had no knowledge of the conditions on the ticket. Defendant should have called her attention to the printed terms.

(3) Even if Bova had assented to the exculpation clause, she would not have been bound by it since an attempt by a bailee for hire to relieve itself of liability for its negligence, "in the course of a general dealing with the public," is "contrary to law and against public policy."

Does it appear that defendant was attempting to take advantage of the special vulnerabilities of people like Bova (i.e., operating at the edges of fraud)? One court has noted that "perhaps most of us are blind when confronted by a parking receipt with disclaimers of liability on the back." Northwestern Nat'l Ins. Co. v. Donovan, 916 F.2d 372, 378 (7th Cir.1990).

The *Constantine* analysis provides an opportunity to recall Sharon v. City of Newton, supra, p. 502, where, in upholding a release of liability signed by a father and his cheerleader daughter, the Massachusetts high court explicitly distinguished the "baggage check" or "ticket" line of cases.

Weisz v. Parke–Bernet Galleries, Inc.
67 Misc.2d 1077, 325 N.Y.S.2d 576 (N.Y.Civ.Ct.1971)

At auctions conducted by defendant in May of 1962, Dr. Weisz purchased, for $3,348, a painting listed in the auction catalog as the work of "Raoul Dufy," and David and Irene Schwartz paid $9,360 for a painting also listed as Dufy's work. Later, as a result of a district attorney's investigation, all parties learned that the paintings in question were forgeries, of little value. When defendant denied any legal responsibility, Weisz and the Schwartzes sued to recover the prices paid for the paintings, alleging that defendant's catalog presentation constituted an express warranty of authenticity. Defendant relied on a "disclaimer" set forth in its catalog:

> The Galleries has endeavored to catalogue and describe the property correctly, but all property is sold "as is" and neither the Galleries nor its consignor warrants or represents, and they shall in no event be responsible for, the correctness of description, genuineness, authorship, . . . or condition of the property, and no statement contained in the catalogue or made orally at the sale or elsewhere shall be deemed to be such a warranty or representation, or an assumption of liability.

This disclaimer was positioned on a preliminary page of the catalog, entitled "Conditions of Sale" in large print, under which appeared 15 paragraphs running a page and a half in length (the disclaimer was paragraph 2), in print somewhat smaller in size than that used in most of the catalog. Following the "Conditions" pages came an index of the works to be auctioned, listed alphabetically by the name of the artist, with catalog numbers provided. The balance of the catalog consisted of over 80 pages setting forth a black-and-white reproduction of each painting and descriptive material about the artist and the work. At both auctions, the procedure followed by defendant was simply to announce at the outset that "the auction is subject to the conditions of sale"; no reference to the disclaimer or other "conditions" was made.

A jury having been waived, the trial judge first concluded that Dr. Weisz had no knowledge of the "conditions of sale." Nor could he be charged with knowledge, since, in the circumstances, a reasonable bidder on defendant's impressive premises would not expect that a catalog "overwhelmingly devoted to descriptions of works of art" would also disclaim liability for the accuracy of the very information provided. To bind Dr. Weisz, defendant must do "considerably more" by way of notice. The Schwartzes, on the other hand, knew of the disclaimer; the question, then, is whether "the language of disclaimer relied upon as a bar to the action should be deemed effective for that purpose." The judge ruled the disclaimer ineffective, saying:

> Parke–Bernet expected that bidders at its auctions would rely
> upon the accuracy of its descriptions, and intended that they should.

[It] is an exceedingly well-known gallery, linked in the minds of people with the handling, exhibition, and sale of valuable artistic works and invested with an aura of expertness and reliability. The very fact that Parke–Bernet was offering a work of art for sale would inspire confidence that it was genuine. . . .

The wording of the catalogue was clearly designed to emphasize the genuineness of the works to be offered. . . . After reassuring the reader that Parke–Bernet endeavored to catalogue the works of art correctly, there follow highly technical and legalistic words of disclaimer in a situation in which plain and emphatic words are required. And this provision, in light of the critical importance to the buyer of a warning that he may not rely on the fact that a work attributed to an artist was in fact his creation, is in no way given the special prominence that it clearly requires. The language used, the understated manner of its presentation, the failure to refer to it explicitly in the preliminary oral announcement at the auction, all lead to the conclusion that Parke–Bernet did not expect the bidders to take the disclaimer too seriously or to be too concerned about it. I am convinced that the average reader of this provision would view it as some kind of technicality that should in no way derogate from the certainty that he was buying genuine artistic works, and that this was precisely the impression intended to be conveyed.

[The judgments for the plaintiffs in the *Weisz* case were reversed by the Appellate Term of the New York Supreme Court, in part on the ground that defendant's catalog "gave [a] leading and prominent place, in its prefatory terms of sale, [to] a clear, unequivocal disclaimer of any express or implied warranty or representation of genuineness of any paintings." In addition, the situation itself—a public auction of paintings whose value depended upon "the degree of certainty with which they could be authenticated"—required that plaintiffs act "with the caution of one in circumstances abounding with signals of *caveat emptor*." 77 Misc.2d 80, 351 N.Y.S.2d 911 (1974).]

COMMENT: FORM "CONTRACTS"

It has been observed that ours is not an economy "in which the terms of every transaction, or even of most transactions, are individually dickered; even when they are, standard clauses are commonly incorporated in the final contract, without separate negotiation of each of them." Northwestern Nat'l Ins. Co. v. Donovan, 916 F.2d 372, 377 (7th Cir.1990). Many of the same ideas reappear in the following discussion by Karl Llewellyn, The Common Law Tradition 362–363 (1960), including the impulse to economize in carrying out repetitive transactions:

I know of few "private" law problems which remotely rival the importance, economic, governmental, or "law"-legal, of the form-pad agreement, and I know of none which has been either more disturbing to life or more baffling to lawyers.

The impetus to the form-pad is clear, for any business unit: by standardizing terms, and by standardizing even the spot on the form where any individually dickered term appears, one saves all the time and skill otherwise needed to dig out and record the meaning of variant language; one makes check-up, totaling, follow-through, etc., into routine operations; one has duplicates (in many colors) available for the administration of a multidepartment business; and so on more. The content of the standardized terms accumulates experience, it avoids or reduces legal risks and also confers all kinds of operating leeways and advantages, all without need of either consulting counsel from instance to instance or of bargaining with the other parties. Not to be overlooked, either, is the tailoring of the crude misfitting hand-me-down pattern of the "general law" "in the absence of agreement" to the particular detailed working needs of your own line of business—whether apartment rentals, stock brokerage, international grain trade, installment selling of appliances, flour milling, sugar beet raising, or insurance. It would be a heart-warming scene, a triumph of private attention to what is essentially private self-government in the lesser transactions of life or in those areas too specialized for the blunt, slow tools of the legislature—if only all businessmen and all their lawyers would be reasonable.

> But power, like greed, if it does not always corrupt, goes easily to the head. So that the form-agreements tend either at once or over the years, and often by whole lines of trade, into a massive and almost terrifying jug-handled character; the one party lays his head into the mouth of a lion—either, and mostly, without reading the fine print, or occasionally in hope and expectation (not infrequently solid) that it will be a sweet and gentle lion.

After giving some of the reasons why standardized forms may have terms that seem one-sided, Llewellyn added that it was no less vital to note that:

> [W]here, as with the overseas grain contracts or the Pacific Coast dried fruit contracts or the Worth Street Rules on textiles, two-fisted bargainers on either side have worked out in the form a balanced code to govern the particular line or trade or industry, there is every reason for a court to assume both fairness and wisdom in the terms, and to seek in first instance to learn, understand, and fit both its own thinking and its action into the whole design. Contracts of this kind (so long as reasonable in the net) are a road to better than official-legal regulation of our economic life; indeed, they tend to lead into the setting up of their own quick, cheap, expert tribunals.

Llewellyn then described the methods by which courts, when troubled by unfairly one-sided terms, "construed" language to mean the opposite of what it obviously was saying, to find inconsistencies so that troublesome clauses could be treated as cancelled out, even to reject particular clauses as counter to the purposes of the transactions they served. He criticized such techniques for providing invitations to form-writers to "recur to the attack" and try again, as failing to give guidance by marking out the minimum decencies for particular transaction-types, and (being "tools of intentional and creative misconstruction") as seriously embarrassing efforts to find the true meaning of wholly legitimate clauses. "Covert tools are never reliable tools." Llewellyn then discussed the possibilities of finding statutory solutions (especially through provisions like UCC 2–302), but concluded that in our system an approach through statute was dubious, uncertain, likely to be awkward and spotty in its results. The "true answer," he said, was obvious.

The answer, I suggest, is this: Instead of thinking about "assent" to boiler-plate clauses, we can recognize that so far as concerns the specific, there is no assent at all. What has in fact been assented to, specifically, are the few dickered terms, and the broad type of the transaction, and but one thing more. That one thing more is a blanket assent (not a specific assent) to any not unreasonable or indecent terms the seller may have on his form, which do not alter or eviscerate the reasonable meaning of the dickered terms. The fine print which has not been read has no business to cut under the reasonable meaning of those dickered terms which constitute the dominant and only real expression of agreement. . . .

The queer thing is that where the transaction occurs without the fine print present, courts do not find this general line of approach too hard to understand; . . . nor can I see a court having trouble, where a short memo agrees in due course to sign "our standard contract," in rejecting an outrageous form as not being fairly within the reasonable meaning of the term. The clearest case to see is the handing over of a blank check: no court, judging as between the parties, would fail to reach for the circumstances, in determining whether the amount filled in had gone beyond the reasonable.

Why, then, can we not face the fact where boiler-plate is present? There has been an arm's-length deal, with dickered terms. There has been accompanying that basic deal another which, if not on any fiduciary basis, at least involves a plain expression of confidence, asked and accepted, with a corresponding limit on the powers granted: the boiler-plate is assented to en bloc, "unsight, unseen," on the implicit assumption and to the full extent that (1) it does not alter or impair the fair meaning of the dickered terms when read alone, and (2) that its terms are neither in the particular nor in the net manifestly unreasonable and unfair. Such is the reality, and I see nothing in the way of a court's operating on that basis, to truly effectuate the only intention which can in reason be worked out as common to the two parties, granted good faith. And if the boiler-plate party is not playing in good faith, there is law enough to bar that fact from benefiting it. We had a hundred years of sales law in which any sales transaction with explicit words resulted in two several contracts for the one consideration: that of sale, and the collateral one of warranty. The idea is applicable here, for better reason: any contract with boiler-plate results in *two* several contracts: the *dickered* deal, and the collateral one of *supplementary* boiler-plate.

Rooted in sense, history, and simplicity, it is an answer which could occur to anyone.

Karl N. Llewellyn was a dominant and flamboyant figure in twentieth century American jurisprudence. Regarded by many as the leading "legal realist" of the 1930s, he taught law at Yale, Columbia, and Chicago for a period of nearly four decades. Llewellyn's fields were sales law and contracts, and his work included the position of principal draftsman and Chief Reporter for the

Uniform Commercial Code. An account of Llewellyn and his contributions can be found in W. Twining, Karl Llewellyn and the Realist Movement (1973). For a critique of Llewellyn's "assent" or "true answer" analysis of standard-form contracts (the passages quoted above), see Rakoff, Contracts of Adhesion: An Essay in Reconstruction, 96 Harv.L.Rev. 1174, 1198–1206 (1983) (arguing generally that form terms in contracts of adhesion ought to be deemed presumptively unenforceable).

KARL N. LLEWELLYN
1893–1962

Is it possible that, because of our training as lawyers, we attach too much importance to having a dickered bargain? Consider the following line of argument. The warranty that comes with your laptop computer is one of its many product attributes. The laptop has a screen of a particular size. Its microprocessors work at a particular speed, and the battery lasts a given amount of time between recharging. The hard drive has a certain capacity and mean time to failure. There is an instruction manual, online technical support (or lack thereof), and software. Then there are the warranties that the seller makes (or does not make) that are also part of the bundle. Just as you know the size of the screen, but nothing about the speed of the microprocessor, you know about only some of the warranty terms that come with the computer and remain wholly ignorant of others.

With respect to some product attributes, the seller will give buyers a choice of options. For a higher price, you can buy a computer with a larger screen. But with respect to others, there is no choice. A seller may offer laptop computers with only one type of battery. So too with the attributes that are legal terms. A seller may give you a choice. For example, you can buy a service contract that extends the warranty. Other times, there will be no choice, as when the seller specifies that Delaware law governs any contract dispute that may arise in the future. Similarly, some product attributes are readily apparent to everyone, such as the size of the screen and the availability of an expensive service contract. Other product attributes, like the speed of the microprocessor and the forum selection clause, are apparent only to those who spend time and energy looking for them.

To say that a product comes with boilerplate is to say that one of its attributes, along with many others, is partially hidden and is one over which there is no choice on the part of the buyer. But why should any of this raise special concern? The legislature can regulate microprocessor speeds or not. So too with boilerplate. But why is boilerplate any different? Legal scholars have long assumed that standardized contract terms in fine print are suspect, but is it obvious why they should be, given how readily we accept so much else about products that are standardized and hard to observe?

Buyers often have little choice over the way that a particular seller bundles a product. You could buy Henry Ford's Model T in any color you wanted as long as it was black. There was no choice about any product feature. The inability to choose is a by-product of mass production. Goods are cheaper, but there is more uniformity. Moreover, the costs are not spread evenly. Those who care about color are worse off; the price-conscious are better off. But again, these trade-offs are inevitable in a world of mass production. The warranty that came with the Model T was just like its color. You could have any promises you wanted as long as they were Ford's.

When product attributes are hidden, the buyer is flying blind with respect to them. At some cost, of course, she can read the fine print or disassemble the product or ask the seller to make an explicit representation about the warranty term or the magneto coils. But in many cases, the benefit to the buyer is too small to justify the expense. The costs include not only obtaining the information, but gaining enough expertise to make sensible judgments. The buyer who discovered that the Model T had a magneto radically different from that in any other car still needed to figure out whether it was better or worse than a more conventional design. The typical buyer had no way of doing this.

The typical buyer cannot rely on her own expertise or her ability to dicker with her seller. When the market works effectively, however, each benefits from the presence of other, more sophisticated buyers. A seller in a mass market cannot distinguish among its buyers. To make a profit, the seller cannot focus exclusively on the unsophisticated if there are enough knowledgeable buyers who are indistinguishable from the ignorant. When the seller decides on the microprocessor to use in a new computer, she may have to worry about making a choice that suits not only the buyers who do not know about microprocessors, but also those who do. It is possible that enough sophisticated buyers are aware of the importance of having the right microprocessor, and their knowledge—and the seller's inability to distinguish them from everyone else—forces the seller to choose well. So too with warranties and other terms largely invisible to average buyers. The sophisticated buyer provides protection for those that are entirely ignorant.

This logic, however, depends crucially on the existence of a well-functioning competitive market with a sufficient number of sophisticated buyers. While reading the cases that follow, consider how often this is in fact the case.

———

Henningsen v. Bloomfield Motors, Inc.

Supreme Court of New Jersey, 1960.
32 N.J. 358, 161 A.2d 69.

[Claus Henningsen purchased from Bloomfield Motors a new Plymouth automobile manufactured by the Chrysler Corp. Ten days after the car was delivered, while his wife was driving it, the steering wheel spun in her hands and the car veered sharply and crashed into a highway sign and brick wall. The car, with 468 miles on the odometer, was deemed a total loss by the collision-insurance carrier. The damage was so extensive that it was impossible to determine whether the steering mechanism was defective prior to the accident. Henningsen's wife sued both Bloomfield Motors and Chrysler to recover damages for her personal injuries; her husband joined in the action, seeking recovery of consequential losses. Both claims were based on an alleged breach of an implied warranty of merchantability imposed by the Uniform Sales Act. The defense relied on a contractual disclaimer of the warranty, which the Sales Act would permit. The disclaimer in question appeared on the back of the sales contract, among 8½ inches of fine type, consisting of 10 separate paragraphs and 65 lines. It purported to limit liability for breach of any warranty to replacement of defective parts within 90 days of the sale or before the car had been driven 4,000 miles, whichever period was shorter.

The sales contract was a one-page printed form, front and back. Most of the print on the front was twelve-point type. Near the bottom of the front, above the signature lines, the type became smaller, different in style, and more difficult to read. The following paragraphs appeared there:

> The front and back of this Order comprise the entire agreement affecting this purchase and no other agreement or understanding of any nature concerning same has been made or entered into, or will be recognized. . . .

> I have read the matter printed on the back hereof and agree to it as a part of this order the same as if it were printed above my signature. I certify that I am 21 years of age, or older, and hereby acknowledge receipt of a copy of this Order.

Henningsen testified that he did not read these two paragraphs or any of the printed material on the back of the form. This evidence was not contradicted and defendants did not contend that any of these provisions were called to Henningsen's attention.

From a judgment for plaintiffs, the defendants appealed. The opinion of Justice Francis fills 60 pages in the official report; it has been severely edited here.]

FRANCIS, J. . . . The terms of the warranty are a sad commentary upon the automobile manufacturers' marketing practices. Warranties developed in the law . . . to protect the ordinary consumer who cannot be expected to have the knowledge or capacity or even the opportunity to make adequate inspection of mechanical instrumentalities, like automobiles, and to decide for himself whether they are reasonably fit for the designed purpose. . . . But the ingenuity of the Automobile Manufacturers Association [AMA], by means of its standardized form, has metamorphosed the warranty into a device to limit the maker's liability. . . .

[W]hat effect should be given to the express warranty in question which seeks to limit the manufacturer's liability to replacement of defective parts, and which disclaims all other warranties, express or implied? . . . [W]e must keep in mind the general principle that, in the absence of fraud, one who does not choose to read a contract before signing it, cannot later relieve himself of its burdens. . . . And in applying that principle, the basic tenet of freedom of competent parties to contract is a factor of importance. But in the framework of modern commercial life and business practices, such rules cannot be applied on a strict, doctrinal basis. The conflicting interests of the buyer and seller must be evaluated realistically and justly, giving due weight to the social policy evinced by the Uniform Sales Act, the progressive decisions of the courts engaged in administering it, the mass production methods of manufacture and distribution to the public, and the bargaining position occupied by the ordinary consumer in such an economy. This history of the law shows that legal doctrines, as first expounded, often prove to be inadequate under the impact of later experience. . . .

The traditional contract is the result of free bargaining of parties who are brought together by the play of the market, and who meet each other on a footing of approximate economic equality. In such a society there is no danger that freedom of contract will be a threat to the social order as a whole. But in present-day commercial life the standardized mass contract has appeared. It is used primarily by enterprises with strong bargaining power and position. "The weaker party, in need of the goods or services, is frequently not in a position to shop around for better terms, either because the author of the standard contract has a monopoly (natural or artificial) or because all competitors use the same clauses. His contractual intention is but a subjection more or less voluntary to terms dictated by the stronger party, terms whose consequences are often understood in a vague way, if at all." Kessler, "Contracts of Adhesion—Some Thoughts About Freedom of Contract," 43 Colum.L.Rev. 629, 632 (1943). . . .

The warranty before us is a standardized form designed for mass use. It is imposed upon the automobile consumer. He takes it or leaves it, and he must take it to buy an automobile. No bargaining is engaged in with respect to it. In fact, the dealer through whom it comes to the buyer is without authority to alter it; his function is ministerial—simply to deliver it. The form warranty is not only standard with Chrysler, but, as mentioned above, it is the uniform warranty of the [AMA]. . . .

The gross inequality of bargaining position occupied by the consumer in the automobile industry is thus apparent. There is no competition among the car makers in the area of the express warranty. Where can the buyer go to negotiate for better protection? Such control and limitation of his remedies are inimical to the public welfare and, at the very least, call for great care by the courts to avoid injustice through application of strict common-law principles of freedom of contract. Because there is no competition among the motor vehicle manufacturers with respect to the scope of protection guaranteed to the buyer, there is no incentive on their part to stimulate good will in that field of public relations. Thus, there is lacking a factor existing in more competitive fields, one which tends to guarantee the safe construction of the article sold. . . .

Although the courts, with few exceptions, have been most sensitive to problems presented by contracts resulting from gross disparity in buyer-seller bargaining positions, they have not articulated a general principle condemning, as opposed to public policy, the imposition on the buyer of a skeleton warranty as a means of limiting the responsibility of the manufacturer. They have endeavored thus far to avoid a drastic departure from age-old tenets of freedom of contract by adopting doctrines of strict construction, and notice and knowledgeable assent by the buyer to the attempted exculpation of the seller. . . . Accordingly to be found in the cases are statements that disclaimers and the consequent limitation of liability will not be given effect if "unfairly procured"; . . . if not brought to the buyer's attention and he was not made understandingly aware of it; . . . or if not clear and explicit. . . .

The rigid scrutiny which the courts give to attempted limitations of warranties and of the liability that would normally flow from a transaction is not limited to the field of sales of goods. Clauses on baggage checks restricting the liability of common carriers for loss or damage in transit are not enforceable unless the limitation is fairly and honestly negotiated and understandingly entered into. If not called specifically to the patron's attention, it is not binding. It is not enough merely to show the form of a contract; it must appear also that the agreement was understandingly made. . . . The same holds true in cases of such limitations on parcel check room tickets, . . . and on storage warehouse receipts; . . . on automobile parking lot or garage tickets or claim checks; . . . as to exculpatory clauses in leases releasing a landlord of apartments in a multiple dwelling house from all liability for negligence where inequality of bargaining exists, see Annot., 175 A.L.R. 8 (1948). . . .

It is true that the rule governing [many of] the limitation of liability cases . . . is generally applied in situations said to involve services of a public or semi-public nature. Typical, of course, are the public carrier or storage or parking lot cases. . . . But in recent times the books have not been barren of instances of its application in private contract controversies. . . . Basically, the reason a contracting party offering services of a public or *quasi*-public nature has been held to the requirements of fair dealing, and, when it attempts to limit its liability, of securing the understanding consent of the patron or consumer, is because members of the public generally have no other means of fulfilling the specific need represented by the contract. Having in mind the situation in the automobile industry as detailed above, . . . there would appear to be no just reason why the principles of all of the cases set forth should not chart the course to be taken here.

It is undisputed that [the dealer] with whom Henningsen dealt did not specifically call attention to the warranty on the back of the purchase order. The form and the arrangement of its face, as described above, certainly would cause the minds of reasonable men to differ as to whether notice of a yielding of basic rights stemming from the relationship with the manufacturer was adequately given. The words "warranty" or "limited warranty" did not even appear in the fine print above the place for signature. . . .

But there is more than this. Assuming that a jury might find that the fine print referred to reasonably served the objective of directing a buyer's attention to the warranty on the reverse side, and, therefore, that he should be charged with awareness of its language, can it be said that an ordinary layman would realize what he was relinquishing in return for what he was being granted? Under the law, breach of warranty against defective parts or workmanship which caused personal injuries would entitle a buyer to damages even if due care were used in the manufacturing process. Because of the great potential for harm if the vehicle was defective, that right is the most important and fundamental one arising from the relationship. Difficulties so frequently encountered in establishing negligence in manufacture in the ordinary case, make this manifest. . . . Any ordinary layman of reasonable intelligence, looking at the phraseology, might well conclude that Chrysler was agreeing to replace defective parts and perhaps replace anything that went wrong because of defective workmanship during the first 90 days or 4,000 miles of operation, but that he would not be entitled to a new car. It is not unreasonable to believe that the entire scheme being conveyed was a proposed remedy for physical deficiencies in the car. *In the context* of this warranty, only the abandonment of all sense of justice would permit us to hold that, as a matter of law, the phrase "its obligation under this warranty being limited to making good at its factory any part or parts thereof" signifies to an ordinary reasonable person that he is relinquishing any personal injury claim that might flow from the use of a defective automobile. Such claims are nowhere mentioned. . . .

The task of the judiciary is to administer the spirit as well as the letter of the law. . . . [P]art of that burden is to protect the ordinary man against the loss of important rights through what, in effect, is the unilateral act of the manufacturer. . . . From the standpoint of the purchaser, there can be no arms length negotiating on the subject [of warranties]. Because his capacity for bargaining is so grossly unequal, the inexorable conclusion which follows is that he is not permitted to bargain at all. . . .

Public policy is a term not easily defined. Its significance varies as the habits and needs of a people may vary. It is not static and the field of application is an ever increasing one. A contract, or a particular provision therein, valid in one era may be wholly opposed to the public policy of another. . . . Public policy at a given time finds expression in the Constitution, the statutory law and in judicial decisions. In the area of sale of goods, the legislative will has imposed an implied warranty of merchantability as a general incident of sale of an automobile by description. The warranty does not depend upon the affirmative intention of the parties. It is a child of the law; it annexes itself to the contract because of the very nature of the transaction. . . . The judicial process has recognized a right to recover damages for personal injuries arising from a breach of that warranty. The disclaimer of the implied warranty and exclusion of all obligations except those specifically assumed by the express warranty signify a studied effort to frustrate that protection. True, the Sales Act authorizes agreements between buyer and seller qualifying the warranty obligations. But quite obviously the Legislature contemplated lawful stipulations (which are determined by the circumstances of a particular case) arrived at freely by parties of relatively equal bargaining strength. The lawmakers did not authorize the automobile manufacturer to use its grossly disproportionate bargaining power to relieve itself from liability and to impose on the ordinary buyer, who in effect has no real freedom of choice, the grave danger of injury to himself and others that attends the sale of such a dangerous instrumentality as a defectively made automobile. . . . [W]e are of the opinion that Chrysler's attempted disclaimer of an implied warranty of merchantability and of the obligations arising therefrom is so inimical to the public good as to compel an adjudication of its invalidity. . . . The principles that have been expounded as to the obligation of the manufacturer apply with equal force to the separate express warranty of the dealer. . . .

[W]e conclude that the disclaimer of an implied warranty of merchantability by the dealer, as well as the attempted elimination of all obligations other than replacement of defective parts, are violative of public policy and void. . . . [T]he judgments in favor of the plaintiffs and against the defendants are affirmed.

NOTE

At the time of *Henningsen*, three manufacturers made substantially all of the cars sold in the United States, and they entered an explicit agreement to provide the same warranty and to require their dealers to do the same. Indeed, the minutes survive from the meeting in which this agreement was discussed and voted upon. The 4,000–mile warranty that was to persist until the 1960s was put in place in the 1930s. See Fed. Trade Comm'n, Report on the Motor Vehicle Industry at 56–57 (1939). Does the existence of an agreement among the manufacturers to limit the warranties they offered change the way you look at the case?

The UCC replaced the Sales Act in New Jersey some three years after *Henningsen* (most of our state legislatures did the same by the 1960s). Hence, today, and nearly everywhere, considerable "public policy" relating to the sale of goods, including warranty creations and disclaimers and limitations on remedies, is to be found in the UCC. Take a look at §§ 2–314, 2–315, 2–316, 2–719, and 2–302. In the excerpt immediately below, Professor Grant Gilmore provides some broad outlines of the story as it was unfolding in the middle of the last century. The seller's warranty liability was only a part of a larger story. The major tort development he notes, the move to strict liability for personal injuries caused by an allegedly defective product, was in fact accelerated shortly after *Henningsen* was decided. See Restatement of Torts, Second § 402A.

The full picture of the overlap between warranty and tort law, and the question whether one is preemptive of the other, must await courses in Commercial Law and Products Liability. The summary of Superwood Corp. v. Siempelkamp Corp., below, suggests a principal means of ensuring that the UCC governs ordinary commercial disputes. Much depends on the type of loss asserted—personal injury, property damage (the product itself, or other property), or business harms (contract interests). Observe that the UCC attempts to take account of such differences, e.g., §§ 2–318, 2–715(2), 2–719(3). On the "conspicuousness" of warranty exclusion in form contracts, a representative application of § 2–316 can be found in Sierra Diesel Injection Serv. v. Burroughs Corp., 890 F.2d 108 (9th Cir.1989).

––––––––

Grant Gilmore, Law, Logic and Experience
3 How.L.J. 26, 40–41 (1957)

"In most social or economic relationships there is an active party and a passive party, an enterprising party and a party who merely receives—which is, we are told on authority, less blessed. Over the past hundred years—to go no further back—we have experienced a curious shift of attitude toward the relative merits of action and passivity. Our forefathers were, on the whole, tender toward the party who acted: it was better to do than to do nothing; action should be encouraged; and, since action is dangerous, the actor should be protected from the incidentally harmful consequences of his socially useful activity. The risks, therefore, should fall on the passive party. We have, even in our own generation, made great strides toward reversing that position. Ethically, we feel, the weak should be protected against the strong, and the full consequences of his actions should be visited on the head of whoever dares to act.

"In politics and government—if a private law man may poach for a moment on the public law domain—we may see an illustration of what we are saying in the downfall of laissez-faire and the rise of the welfare state, not to mention our current passion for security—political, economic and social. We seek protection and stability and status—which means, in an overliteral sense to be sure, the right to stand still wherever we are. . . .

"It has been a commonplace of legal scholarship that one of the great ground-swells of movement in the nineteenth century was from status to contract—from the protection of rights of property and ownership to the protection of rights of contract. It is easy to see how this should have happened as wealth multiplied and an aristocratic society gave way to its pushing, aggressive, dynamic successor. I suggest that the ground-swell carried an undercurrent with it and that, as the great wave recedes, we are being caught in the undertow. The next half century may well record a reverse movement.

"In the crucial business of allocating commercial and social risks we have already gone a long way toward reversing the nineteenth century. In tort we follow a banner which bears the strange device: liability without fault—although we soften the impact on the innocent tortfeasor by various schemes of insurance and compensation. In contract we have broken decisively with the nineteenth century theory that breach of contract was not very serious and not very reprehensible—as Justice Holmes once put it: every man is 'free to break his contract if he chooses'—from which it followed that damages for breach should be held to a minimum. Today we look on breach of contract as a very serious and immoral thing indeed: never, I dare say, in our history have the remedies for breach been so easily available to the victim, or the sanctions for breach so heavy against the violator—who will be, in most cases, the active or enterprising party. The continuing increase in seller's warranty liability is merely one illustration of what has been going on all along the contract front.

"I assume—although I will not attempt to prove, if indeed I could—that what has been going on, alike in our public law theories of the state and in the obscure and dusty corner of the private law attic which we have visited this afternoon [the obligation imposed on a seller of goods for their quality], reflects a great swing in our fundamental ethical concepts—a swing which, at a still further remove, reflects, if it did not inspire, the later stages of the industrial, economic and technological revolution of the past two hundred years. As I suggested, nothing can ever be explained—but the perspective is a spacious one."

————

Superwood Corp. v. Siempelkamp Corp.

311 N.W.2d 159 (Minn.1981)

A press plaintiff had purchased from defendant failed and could not be repaired. Plaintiff sued in a federal district court, alleging claims in negligence, strict tort, breach of warranty, and breach of contract, and asking for $600,000 in damages for lost profits and damage to the press itself. After ruling that the contract and warranty claims were barred by the statute of limitations, the federal court certified questions of "uncertain" state law to the Supreme Court of Minnesota: "1. Is the manufacturer of defective equipment (a press) . . . liable in negligence to the user of the equipment damaged in its property and business? 2. Is the manufacturer of defective equipment (a press) strictly liable in tort to the user of the equipment damaged in its property and business by the product defect?" The Minnesota court answered both questions in the negative, saying: "The U.C.C. clarifies the rights and remedies of parties to commercial transactions. For example, there are specific provisions covering warranties, [§ 2–314]; warranty disclaimers, [§ 2–316]; liability limitations, [§ 2–719]; and notice provisions, [§ 2–607]. The recognition of tort actions in the instant case would create a theory of redress not envisioned by the legislature when it enacted the U.C.C. Furthermore, tort theories of recovery would be totally unrestrained by legislative liability limitations, warranty disclaimers and notice provisions. To allow tort liability in commercial transactions would totally emasculate these provisions of the U.C.C. . . . We, however, do not [believe] that the U.C.C. was intended to preempt the entire area of products liability. Strict products liability developed in large part to fill gaps in the law of sales with respect to consumer purchasers. . . . Limiting the application of strict products liability to consumers' actions or actions involving personal injury will allow the U.C.C. to satisfy the needs of the commercial sector and still protect the legitimate expectations of consumers. . . . [W]e hold that economic losses that arise out of commercial transactions, except those involving personal injury or damage to other property, are not recoverable under the tort theories of negligence or strict product liability."

[Observe that the court's distinction between physical harms to person or property and commercial harms is based on the traditional thinking that separates contract from tort (contract liability rests on obligations undertaken by bargain, tort liability on duties imposed by law). The function of the "economic loss" doctrine, a judicially-created rule of case law, is to confine remedies for contract-type losses—the "inadequate value" that results from a failure of performance—to the well-developed remedies of contract law featured in this book. The problems, and divisions, in applying the doctrine are collected in Fox & Loftus, Riding the Choppy Waters of East River: Economic Loss Doctrine Ten Years Later, 64 Def. Couns. J. 260 (1997).]

————

Richards v. Richards

Supreme Court of Wisconsin, 1994.
181 Wis.2d 1007, 513 N.W.2d 118.

ABRAHAMSON, J. . . . The circuit court granted summary judgment to Monkem Co., the defendant, dismissing the complaint with prejudice. It held that the form signed by Jerilyn Richards, the plaintiff, was an exculpatory contract that was not void or unenforceable as contrary to public policy. It further held that the plaintiff's claim for injuries suffered while riding as a passenger in a truck operated by Leo Richards, her husband, and owned by Monkem Co., her husband's employer, was clearly within the contemplation of the parties at the time the exculpatory contract was executed. The circuit court thus foreclosed the plaintiff's claim as a matter of law [and the] court of appeals affirmed. . . . [We reverse].

. . . An examination of the principles underlying the determination of the validity of exculpatory contracts leads us to the conclusion that the form is an unenforceable exculpatory contract due to a combination of three factors. None of these factors alone would necessarily invalidate the release; however, taken together . . . the contract is void as against public policy. . . .

In February 1990, Leo Richards was hired by Monkem Co. as an over-the-road truck driver. Shortly thereafter, the plaintiff and her husband discussed the possibility of her riding as a passenger with him. Before the plaintiff could accompany her husband, however, Monkem required that she sign a form entitled "Passenger Authorization," and she did so on or about May 22, 1990.

The "Passenger Authorization" form used by Monkem appears to have two purposes. First, it served as the Company's authorization to the passenger to ride in a company truck. Second, it serves as a passenger's general release of all claims against the Company. The language of release attempts to transform the "Passenger Authorization" form into an exculpatory contract relieving Monkem and all of its affiliated companies, partnerships, individuals and corporations (as well as others) from any and all liability for harm to the person signing the form. . . . The form reads as follows:

Passenger Authorization

Date: 5/22/90

Full and final release covering all claims or rights of action of every description past, present or future.

I/we being of lawful age, for myself/ourselves, my/our heirs, administrators, executors, successors, and assigns, hereby fully and forever release an[d] discharge the said Monkem Co., Inc., and all affiliated, associated, or subsidiary companies, partnerships, individuals or corporations and all other person, firms, and corporations, and their heirs, administrators, executors, successors, and assigns from any and all actions, causes of actions, claim and demands of whatsoever kind or nature on account of any and all known and unknown injuries, losses, and damages by me/us or my/our property sustained or received while a passenger in any and all equipment, vehicles, or while located on any/all Monkem Co., Inc./Joplin Hiway, Inc. property.

It is expressly understood and agreed that this release is intended to cover and does cover not only all now known injuries, losses and damages, but any future injuries, losses and damages not now known or anticipated, but which may later develop or be discovered, including all the effects and consequences thereof.

Permission is granted by Monkem Co., Inc. for *Jerilyn Richards* to be a passenger in Monkem Co., Inc./Joplin Hiway Inc./Burlington Motor carrier leasing vehicle unit number *42424* for a period starting *6/1/90* and ending 9/1/90. This permission is given only upon full understanding of the above release and is accepted and executed and acknowledged by signature of the person below:

Absolutely no driving privileges

Signed /s/ L. J. Richards
    Driver Signature

Signed /s/ Jerilyn Richards
    Passenger Signature

/s/ C. L. McCarley

C.L. McCarley, Director of Risk Mgt.

On June 14, 1990, plaintiff accompanied her husband on one of his scheduled trips. When the truck, negotiating a left curve, overturned, plaintiff was pinned inside the vehicle. The injuries she sustained as a result of this accident are the basis for the current lawsuit.

The principles applicable to the determination of the validity of exculpatory contracts were recently set forth in Dobratz v. Thomson, 161 Wis.2d 502, 468 N.W.2d 654 (1991), which incorporated, explained, and elaborated on the principles set forth in several earlier cases. See, e.g., Discount Fabric House v. Wisconsin Tel. Co., 117 Wis.2d 587, 345 N.W.2d 417 (1984) (contract releasing liability of telephone company for negligent omission of ad from yellow pages); Arnold v. Shawano Co. Agr. Socy., 111 Wis.2d 203, 330 N.W.2d 773 (1983) (contract releasing liability of race track to driver), overruled on other grounds; Merten v. Nathan, 108 Wis.2d 205, 321 N.W.2d 173 (1982) (contract releasing liability of horseback riding school to pupil); and College Mobile Home Park & Sales v. Hoffmann, 72 Wis.2d 514, 241 N.W.2d 174 (1976) (contract releasing liability of landlord to tenant).

. . . Exculpatory contracts are not favored by the law because they tend to allow conduct below the acceptable standard of care applicable to the activity. Exculpatory contracts are not, however, automatically void and unenforceable as contrary to public policy. . . . Rather, a court closely examines whether such agreements violate public policy and construes them strictly against the party seeking to rely on them. [*Merten*],108 Wis.2d 205.

In determining whether an exculpatory agreement [is] void, courts recognize that public policy is not an easily defined concept. The concept embodies the common sense and common conscience of the community. Public policy is that principle of law under which "freedom of contract is restricted by law for the good of the community." [*Merten*, 108 Wis. 2d at 213.] In [*Dobratz*,] 161 Wis.2d 502, 520, a unanimous court, striking down an overly broad release, stated that "this court will not favor an exculpatory contract that is broad and general in its terms."

In reviewing an exculpatory agreement for violation of public policy, a court attempts to accommodate the tension between the principles of contract and tort law that are inherent in such an agreement. The law of contract is based on the principle of freedom of contract; people should be able to manage their own affairs without government interference. Freedom of contract is premised on a bargain freely and voluntarily made through a bargaining process that has integrity. Contract law protects justifiable expectations and the security of transactions. The law of torts is directed toward compensation of individuals for injuries resulting from the unreasonable conduct of another. Tort law also serves the "prophylactic" purpose of preventing future harm; tort law seeks to deter certain conduct by imposing liability for conduct below the acceptable standard of care. . . .

Applying these principles[,] we conclude that the exculpatory contract at issue is void as against public policy. In this case, the public policy "of imposing liability on persons whose conduct creates an unreasonable risk of harm" outweighs the public policy of "freedom of contract." [*Merten*], 108 Wis.2d at 215. Accordingly we conclude that it would be contrary to public policy to enforce the exculpatory language in Monkem Co.'s "Passenger Authorization" form. A combination of three factors in this case leads us to this conclusion.

First, the contract serves two purposes, not clearly identified or distinguished[:] . . . (1) the Company authorizes the passenger to ride in a Company truck, and (2) the passenger releases the Company and others from liability. This dual function, however, is not made clear in the title of the contract; the form is designated merely as a "Passenger Authorization." The written terms clearly state that the document is a release of liability. A person signing a document has a duty to read it and know the contents of the writing. . . . Nevertheless it is not reasonably clear to the signer of a form entitled "Passenger Authorization" that the document would in reality be the passenger's agreement to release the Company (and others) from liability. Rather the title "Passenger Authorization" implies that only the Company is making the concessions and only the Company is bound. We conclude that [this] release should have been conspicuously labelled as such to put the person signing the form on notice. Moreover, to prevent confusion under these circumstances, the passenger's release of the Company from liability should have been carefully identified and distinguished from the Company's authorization for a passenger to ride along. Identifying and distinguishing clearly between those two contractual arrangements could have provided important protection against a signatory's inadvertent agreement to the release.

Second, the release is extremely broad and all-inclusive. It purports to excuse intentional, reckless, and negligent conduct not only by the Company but by another entity (Joplin Hiway, Inc.) and by all affiliated, associated, or subsidiary companies, partnerships, individuals, or corporations, and all other persons, firms or corporations. Further, although the passenger's release is combined with the Company's authorization to the plaintiff to ride in a specified Company vehicle during a specified period, the release does not refer to an injury the plaintiff may sustain while riding as a passenger in the specified Company vehicle during the specified time period. It purports to release the Company from liability for any and all injury to the plaintiff while the plaintiff is a passenger in any vehicle (not necessarily one owned by the Company) at any time and while the plaintiff is on any and all Company property at any time. The release, unlike the authorization, is not limited to a specified vehicle or to a specified time period. Had the Company intended that it be released from liability to the plaintiff while she was riding with her husband in the Company truck during the period the Company authorized, that is not what the release says. The very breadth of the release raises questions about its meaning and demonstrates its one-sidedness; it is unreasonably favorable to the Company, the drafter of the contract. . . .

Third, this contract is a standardized agreement on the Company's printed form which offers little or no opportunity for negotiation or free and voluntary bargaining. . . . [W]hen the Company forwarded the form to plaintiff its cover letter did not advise her that the document was a release of all claims and did not advise her of the legal significance attached to her signing of the document. The employee handbook advised employees that Company authorization was needed for a passenger to ride along but did not advise employees that the passenger would have to release all claims against the Company.

The fact that a release is printed in a standardized form is not, by itself, enough to invalidate it. However, the plaintiff's lack of an opportunity for discussing and negotiating the contract is significant when considered with the breadth of the release. If her plans to ride with her husband were to go forward, the plaintiff simply had to adhere to the terms of the written form. While the Company had the time and resources to draft the provisions and plan their effect, the plaintiff did not. Had the plaintiff been afforded the opportunity to negotiate a release, she might have declined to release the Company from liability for intentional or reckless actions or the driver's negligence, or from liability for its defective equipment. Because the Company probably derives some benefit from allowing family members to join drivers on the road, such as improving employee morale, the Company might not necessarily have rejected such proposals out of hand.

As we have said, none of these factors alone would necessarily have warranted invalidation of the exculpatory contract. [But here] a combination of these factors demonstrate that adherence to the principle of freedom of contract is not heavily favored. The principle of tort law, to compensate persons for injuries resulting from unreasonable conduct of another, prevails. Accordingly, . . . the document contravenes public policy and is void and unenforceable. The decision of the court of appeals is reversed and the cause remanded for proceedings not inconsistent with this opinion.

[The vote was 4 to 3. The dissenters disagreed with each of the reasons given by the majority, as well as their application "in combination."]

NOTE

As *Richards* illustrates, it is not unusual for courts to associate form contracts with inequality of bargaining power. We shall see more of this. For now, it should be enough simply to direct attention to some of the main issues. The overriding question would seem to be whether excessive one-sidedness built into fine-print forms raises problems that, on balance, are a mismatch for the assent doctrines of general contract law. Even if it were feasible for courts to conduct evidentiary hearings on issues of relative market power and overall bargaining fairness, case-by-case and form-by-form, the finding of imbalance does not itself dictate a conclusion of impaired assent. Persons and firms no doubt sign form contracts for any number of reasons, including a desire to act quickly and inexpensively and a wish to be unburdened by a mass of detail (mainly nonperformance terms) that probably will never come up. Perhaps the test of fine-print terms should be "externalized," that is, turned away from the parties themselves, at least to the extent of viewing superior bargaining power as primarily a matter to be observed, and taken note of, not probed. Look again at the court's approach in *Richards*. Has conventional "assent analysis" been removed altogether?

———

Woollums v. Horsley

Court of Appeals of Kentucky, 1892.
93 Ky. 582, 20 S.W. 781.

HOLT, C.J. In August, 1887, the appellant, John Woollums, was living upon his mountain farm of 200 acres in Bell County. He was then about 60 years old, uneducated, afflicted with disease disabling him from work, owned no other land, and very little personal property. He knew but little of what was going on in the business world. . . . He moved in a small circle.

At this time the appellee, W.J. Horsley, who was then a man of large and varied experience in business; who was then buying mineral rights in that locality by the thousands of acres, and who was evidently familiar with all that was then going on and near at hand in the way of business and development in that section, through his agent entered into a contract with the appellant, which was signed by the latter only, by which he sold to Horsley all the oils, gases and minerals in his land, with customary mining privileges, for 40 cents per acre, and obligated himself to convey the same by general warranty deed, free of dower claim or other incumbrance, when the purchase money was paid, to-wit; one-half in three months and the balance in four months from the first payment, or as soon as the deed should be made, three dollars of it, however, being then paid.

It is suggestive upon the question of the then value of the purchase, and as regarded by Horsley, that his agent, who made it, was to get $80 for his pay, or as much as Woollums was to receive for all he sold. . . .

The purchase money was not paid as stipulated, but the reason given is that it was a sale of the minerals by the acre, and the quantity of land was not known and Woollums refused to survey it. Nothing appears to have transpired between the parties until the summer after the trade, when Horsley demanded a deed. He says he sent his agent to do so before that time, but it does not appear he did so.

In December, 1888, this suit was brought for a specific performance of the contract. The main defense is that it was procured through undue advantage, and under such circumstances that, in equity, its performance should not be decreed. . . . The specific execution of the contract was ordered. Considering all the circumstances, and the rule applicable in such a case, the judgment should not be upheld.

There is a distinction between the case of a plaintiff asking a specific performance of a contract in equity, and that of a defendant resisting such a performance. Its specific execution is not a matter of absolute right[,] but of sound discretion in the court. It requires less strength of case on the side of the defendant to resist the bill, than it does upon the part of the plaintiff to enforce it. If the court refuses to enforce specifically, the party is left to his remedy at law.

Thus a hard or unconscionable bargain will not be specifically enforced, nor, if the decree will produce injustice or under all the circumstances be inequitable, will it be rendered. In other words, a court of equity will not exercise its power . . . to enforce a claim which is not, under all the circumstances, just as between the parties, and it will allow a defendant to resist a decree, where the plaintiff will not always be allowed relief upon the same evidence.

A contract ought not to be carried into specific performance unless it be just and fair in all respects. When this relief is sought ethics are considered, and a court of equity will sometimes refuse to set aside a contract, and yet refuse its specific performance. Story says: "Courts of equity will not proceed to decree a specific performance where the contract is founded in fraud, imposition, mistake, undue advantage, or gross misapprehension; or where, from a change of circumstances or otherwise, it would be unconscientious to enforce it." (2 Story's Equity, § 750a.). . . .

The appellee testifies that he did not know anything as to the mineral value of this land when the contract was made; but it is evident he had a thorough knowledge of the value of lands generally in that section, and of the developments then in progress or near at hand. All this was unknown to the appellant. . . . [H]is land was valuable almost altogether in a mineral point of view. While it is not shown what it was worth at the date of the contract, yet it is proven to have been worth in April, 1889, $15 an acre, and that this value arises almost altogether from its mineral worth; and yet the appellee is asking the enforcement of a contract by means of which he seeks to obtain all the oil, gas, and minerals, and the virtual control of the land, at 40 cents an acre. The interest he claims under the contract is substantially the value of the land. Equity should not help out such a harsh bargain.

The appellee shows pretty plainly, by his own testimony, that when the contract was made he was advised of the probability of the building of a railroad in that locality in the near future. His agent, when the trade was made, assured the appellant that he would never be bothered by the contract during his life time. He was lulled in the belief that the Rip Van Winkle sleep of that locality in former days was to continue; and the grossly inadequate price of this purchase can only be accounted for upon the ground that the appellant was misled and acted under gross misapprehension.

The contract was not equitable or reasonable, or grounded upon sufficient consideration, and no interest has arisen in any third party. A court of equity should, therefore, refuse its specific enforcement but the [appellee] should have what was in fact paid, with its interest; and when this is done his petition should be dismissed.

Judgment reversed, and cause remanded for proceedings consistent with this opinion.

QUESTION

It appears that John Woollums was not much of a traveler, so that any suit against him for damages would probably have to be brought in Kentucky, in the county of his residence. Would you have advised Horsley to bring such an action?

———

Kleinberg v. Ratett
252 N.Y. 236, 169 N.E. 289 (1929)

Plaintiffs contracted to buy a lot in the village of Mt. Kisko, paying down $2,000. The contract called for a deed warranting the title to be free of all encumbrances, except a specified mortgage. At closing, plaintiffs refused to perform on the ground that a stream of water, contained in a 24–inch pipe laid four feet underground, crossed the lot from south to north. One block to the south it was "a living stream of water" across open fields; after crossing the lot that plaintiffs had contracted to buy, it passed through a culvert under a village street and resumed its flow as an open brook. There was no evidence that the stream's course in crossing defendant's lot, encased in pipe, had been altered, lowered, or lifted in any way following the making of the contract. The court concluded that such a subterranean water course was not an encumbrance, since nature was responsible for it, though the owners of land above and below had the right to have the stream continue with an undiminished flow. Plaintiffs proved that they were unaware of the existence of the stream at the time of the contract and that defendant was silent on the subject. Plaintiffs sued for restitution of their $2,000 down payment; defendant, by answer, prayed for specific performance. *Held*, since there was no showing of fraud, plaintiffs could not have rescission. But since they were ignorant of the underground water course, and defendant was well aware of it, great hardship would result through specific performance. While the court could not grant rescission, it would "stay its hand" and refuse specific performance.

NOTE

What factors distinguish Kleinberg v. Ratett from Jackson v. Seymour, supra p. 508, where, you will recall, a vendor who had failed to establish her claim of fraud was nevertheless granted rescission?

The Court of Appeals of New York reads the *Kleinberg* decision as establishing that "the rules of law governing mistake as related to specific performance differ from those governing rescission for mistake." Da Silva v. Musso, 53 N.Y.2d 543, 444 N.Y.S.2d 50, 428 N.E.2d 382 (1981). Do you understand what the court means by this statement? The question of rescission for unilateral mistake was presented in the *Elsinore* case, p. 525, where it was concluded: "Under the circumstances, the 'bargain' for which the board presses . . . appears too sharp for law and equity to sustain." It is quite common for the courts in such cases to ask whether enforcement of the agreement would be "unconscionable." Is it surprising to find the same question asked where a defense of unilateral mistake is made in a suit for specific performance? The cases suggest not. E.g., Bailey v. Musumeci, 134 N.H. 280, 591 A.2d 1316 (1991).

The tactic of discretionary refusal of specific performance goes far back in New York legal history. As early as 1824, Chief Justice Savage, urging such a refusal in his dissenting opinion in Seymour v. Delancy, 3 Cow.(N.Y.) 445, provided a most candid statement of what was behind this evasive device: A court of equity granting specific performance "must act *ex rigore*, and cannot weigh the equities of the parties; whereas a jury, in a Court of law, can mitigate the damages according to equity and good conscience. It seems, indeed, paradoxical, to send parties from a Court of Equity to a Court of Law, to obtain equity; but it arises from the peculiar construction and practice of the Courts."

————

COMMENT: DENIAL OF EQUITABLE RELIEF

1. The "Cleanup" Principle

In a well-known American decision, Marks v. Gates, 154 F. 481 (9th Cir.1907), a written agreement made in 1903 provided that defendant Gates would convey to plaintiff a 20 percent interest in any property Gates might thereafter acquire in Alaska. The agreement was under seal and recited that Gates had received $1 "in consideration." Two years later, plaintiff sued for specific performance of the agreement, alleging that in fact $1,000 cash and the cancellation of a debt of $11,225 had been given as consideration for the promise and that defendant, since signing the agreement, had acquired Alaska holdings worth $750,000 (mainly mining claims), all of which entitled plaintiff to a decree ordering defendant to transfer property having a value of at least $150,000. The trial court sustained a demurrer to the complaint, on the ground the contract sued on was too "unjust and inequitable" to warrant the relief sought. This decree was affirmed on appeal. The court said:

> A contract may be valid in law and not subject to cancellation in equity, and yet the terms thereof, the attendant circumstances, and in some cases the subsequent events, may be such as to require the court to deny its specific performance. . . . The contract [here] had, when it was made, no reference to any property then owned by the contracting parties, or even to property then in existence. It did not obligate Gates ever to go to Alaska or to acquire property there. It bound him during his lifetime to transfer to the appellant a one-fifth interest in all property of every description that he might acquire in Alaska by whatever means, . . . property of which neither party could know even approximately the value. It was a bargain made in the dark. . . .

> Courts of equity have often decreed specific performance where the consideration was inadequate. . . . But where the consideration is so grossly inadequate as it is in the present case, and the contract is made without any knowledge at the time of its making . . . of the nature of the property to be affected thereby, or of its value, no equitable principle is violated if specific performance is denied, and the parties are left to their legal remedies, if any they have. . . .

> The facts presented [here] are not such as to entitle the court to retain the case for the assessment of such damages as the appellant may have sustained for breach of the contract. A court of equity will not grant pecuniary compensation in lieu of specific performance unless the case presented is one for equitable interposition such as would entitle the plaintiff to performance but for intervening facts, such as the destruction of the property [or] the conveyance of the same to an innocent third person.

The possibility mentioned in Marks v. Gates, of retaining the case for assessment of damages after refusal of specific performance, rests on the so-called "cleanup" principle, sometimes called the principle of "completeness." This is an idea that goes far back in Chancery history and has much to recommend it still. The usual statement of the principle is that when an equity court acquires jurisdiction of a case, it will proceed to give whatever remedies are needed for a complete and final disposition of the issues raised. The clearest case for invoking the principle is one in which equitable relief is awarded and decision of the equity issues compels the court to receive evidence, and decide disputed issues, as to claims that would be clearly "legal" by historical tests. E.g., Turley v. Ball Associates Ltd., 641 P.2d 286 (Colo.Ct.App.1981). In a suit for specific performance of a contract, the defendant's breach may already have caused damage; in an injunction action against trespass or nuisance, the past tort may have caused injuries that will not be indemnified merely by enjoining defendant's wrongful acts for the future. The arguments for awarding damages in the equity suit may not be so clear where, for some reason especially appealing in an "equity" context, all equitable relief is refused. Yet there is abundant authority for giving damages *in lieu of* equitable relief, instead of as a supplement to such relief. See, e.g., Ferguson v. Green, 266 Ark. 556, 587 S.W.2d 18 (1979); Fran Realty, Inc. v. Thomas, 30 Md.App. 362, 354 A.2d 196 (1976); Charles County Broadcasting Co., Inc. v. Meares, 270 Md. 321, 311 A.2d 27 (1973). The same reasons of convenience, the same desire to save time, money, and duplicated effort, can operate in this latter situation, if to decide the equity case it has been necessary to receive most of the evidence and consider most of the issues that can arise in awarding damages.

In all of these situations, the main obstacle to awarding damages in the equity suit will be the constitutional guarantees of jury trial. See, e.g., Bourne & Lynch, Merger of Law & Equity Under the Revised Maryland Rules: Does it Threaten Trial by Jury? 14 U.Balt.L.Rev. 1 (1984). It is assumed that the award of damages will be by the equity judge, without the aid of a jury. This is essential if the main purpose of avoiding duplicated effort is to be served, since the judge in the equity case will normally have heard the case with no jury present. Still, the constitutional guarantees of jury trial are not a conclusive deterrent to complete relief in equity. They presuppose a historical test, and use of the cleanup principle goes far back in time, before our American constitutions were adopted, even thought of. It can therefore be argued that the right to jury trial guaranteed by our constitutions was always qualified by the power of equity courts to administer legal relief as an incident to, or in lieu of, equitable relief, in cases properly brought in equity. Then, too, it has long been true that a trial court has considerable discretion to try legal and equitable issues separately, despite connections between the two, thereby safeguarding rights to a jury on legal issues. Quigley v. Wilson, 474 N.W.2d 277 (Iowa Ct.App.1991).

The cleanup principle presents a peculiar dilemma in the cases just considered. Indeed, it is the defendant who is in a dilemma, proving a wide disparity of values to defeat specific performance and then, if sued at law, forced to prove the opposite in order to reduce any liability in damages. Levin, Equitable Cleanup and the Jury, 100 U.Pa.L.Rev. 320 (1951), discusses these and related questions. The case of Medtronic, Inc. v. Intermedics, Inc., 725 F.2d 440 (7th Cir.1984), is also helpful on the limitations of the cleanup principle.

On the whole, the federal cases have been conservative in their use of the cleanup principle, in order to preserve rights to jury trial. There is other authority, not only in federal but in state decisions, employing the test stated in Marks v. Gates—was the obstacle to specific performance some fact intervening since the transaction took place, or even since the bill in the case was filed? This approach is most likely explained by the broader rule that a plaintiff, in order to get any legal relief from an equity court, must first show a good case in equity (else one could bypass the law court and litigate a purely legal claim in equity).

2. The Effects of Withholding Equitable Relief

The requirements of good faith and fairness found in the specific performance cases are applied in a great variety of equitable actions. They derive from the premise, historically accurate, that equitable remedies are exceptional and supplementary, so that denying equitable relief in a particular case does not necessarily, or entirely, defeat the claim asserted. History also played a part in creating a large deposit of "good conscience" and morality in the standard doctrines of equity, even in those areas where, like the express trust, equitable remedies are not merely a supplement to common law remedies but are for practical purposes exclusive.

We shall not have much to do with such special equity doctrines as "unclean hands" or "laches." Both lead to a denial of equitable relief without purporting to outlaw the transaction for the purposes of legal remedies. "Unclean hands" is an extension of illegality and operates on equity plaintiffs who have engaged in criminal, immoral, or unfair conduct in the transaction in question. Laches is a law-French term best translated as "laxness." It describes a delay in suing or in asserting rights, often a delay far short of the statutory period of limitation. It is usually close to estoppel in the sense that the delay has induced reliance and prejudice to an opponent, though the reliance factor is not indispensable if the delay has been prolonged.

There are, of course, other doctrines that lead to a denial of equitable relief, without any attempt to preclude a remedy at law. The technique of discretionary refusal of equitable remedies is, in short, well known and widely used. In most situations where the technique is used the same question arises—how effective is it?

An early study by Frank & Endicott, Defenses in Equity and "Legal Rights," 14 La.L.Rev. 380 (1954), produced an interesting conclusion. The authors took 350 reported cases in which equitable relief was refused, not for adequacy of the legal remedy, but for some reason of "conscience," hardship, soiled hands, or laches. The cases covered a wide range of tort and contract claims. The authors then wrote to the lawyers for the unsuccessful litigants to find out what had happened next. They received 56 responses, none of which reported success in a later action at law. In only two cases were later law actions even brought. In the authors' words, "in every instance equitable defeat was total defeat." The most multifarious reasons made plaintiffs' counsel decide against a second try. In some cases, the reasons for dismissal of the equity suit were phrased in the special vocabulary of equity, but counsel considered the risk too great that "unclean hands" might prove to be illegality, or equitable fraud might be legal fraud—in other words, that law and equity might in fact coincide in their results despite different formulations. In one case it was held that the dismissal in equity was res judicata, a bar to a later action at law. It should be noted in passing that the risk from res judicata is increased by the cleanup principle, which makes it proper for the equity court to retain the case for legal relief. If "cleanup" is proper, a decree of dismissal which fails to specify the grounds of dismissal can often be interpreted as an adjudication of both legal and equitable issues.

From a sample of only 56 cases, no firm conclusions could be drawn, as the authors conceded. But they raised some further questions. They suggested, first, that the finality of the dismissals from equity had the virtue in all but two of the cases studied of settling the issues without further litigation. They then suggested that there may be "judicial self-deception" in denying an equitable remedy in the belief that a legal remedy remains; "if without that mistaken belief [the judge] might have given judgment for the plaintiff, then serious injustice is done." The authors also suggested that if the special equity defenses were "bodily and overtly taken out of the cloud of conscience and transferred to law," plaintiffs in equity would not lose anything substantial and "the conscious responsibility" of judges might thereby be increased. Instead of a "bodily transfer" of these special equity doctrines to courts of law, would it be better if the equity doctrines themselves were eliminated or reduced in scope?

Waters v. Min Ltd.

Supreme Judicial Court of Massachusetts, 1992.
412 Mass. 64, 587 N.E.2d 231.

LYNCH, J. This case arises from a contract between Gail A. Waters (plaintiff) and "the DeVito defendants"[1] (defendants), whereby the plaintiff was to assign her annuity policy having a cash value of $189,000 to the defendants in exchange for $50,000. The plaintiff brought suit to rescind the contract on the ground of unconscionability. Defendant Min Ltd. counterclaimed seeking declaratory relief and specific enforcement of the contract. [The trial] judge, sitting without a jury, found for the plaintiff, ordered that the annuity be returned to the plaintiff on repayment of $18,000 with interest, and dismissed the counterclaim of Min Ltd. . . . We now affirm.

. . . The plaintiff was injured in an accident when she was twelve years old. At the age of eighteen, she settled her claim and, with the proceeds, purchased the annuity contract in question from the defendant Commercial Union Ins. Co. When the plaintiff was twenty-one, she became romantically involved with the defendant Thomas Beauchemin, an ex-convict, who introduced her to drugs. Beauchemin suggested that she sell her annuity contract, introduced her to one of the defendants, and represented her in the contract negotiations. She was naive, insecure, vulnerable in contract matters, and unduly influenced by Beauchemin. The defendants drafted the contract documents with the assistance of legal counsel, but the plaintiff had no such representation. At least some portions of the contract were executed in unusual circumstances: i.e., part of the contract was signed on the hood of an automobile in a parking lot, part was signed in a restaurant. The defendants agreed to pay $50,000 for the annuity policy which would return to them as owners of the policy $694,000 over its guaranteed term of

---

[1] The judge referred to the defendants Min Ltd., Cube Ltd., David A. DeVito, Robert A. DeVito, and Michael D. Steamer, collectively as "the DeVito defendants" because their identities and roles were not made clear at trial. The plaintiff originally agreed to assign her rights and interest in a certain annuity policy to Cube Ltd., which later transferred all its interest in the annuity to Min Ltd. David A. DeVito is president of Cube Ltd. Michael D. Steamer is business manager of Min Ltd. Robert A. DeVito conducted negotiations with the plaintiff regarding the annuity policy.

twenty-five years, and which had a cash value at the time the contract was executed of $189,000.

Beauchemin acted for himself and as agent of the defendants. For example, the defendants forgave a $100 debt of Beauchemin as deposit for the purchase of the annuity policy. From a subsequent $25,000 payment, the defendants deducted $7,000 that Beauchemin owed them.

Based on the foregoing, the judge found the contract unconscionable. . . . The defendants argue that the evidence does not support the finding that the contract was unconscionable or that they assumed no risks and therefore that the contract was oppressive. . . . The doctrine of unconscionability has long been recognized by common law courts in this country and in England. . . . "Historically, a [contract] was considered unconscionable if it was 'such as no man in his senses and not under delusion would make on the one hand, and as no honest and fair man would accept on the other.' Hume v. United States, 132 U.S. 406[, 411,] (1889), quoting Earl of Chesterfield v. Janssen, 38 Eng.Rep. 82, 100 (Ch. 1750). Later, a contract was determined unenforceable because unconscionable when 'the sum total of its provisions drives too hard a bargain for a court of conscience to assist.' Campbell Soup Co. v. Wentz, 172 F.2d 80 (3d Cir.1948)." . . .

The doctrine of unconscionability has also been codified in the [UCC], G.L. c. 106, § 2–302,[2] and, by analogy, it has been applied in situations outside the ambit of the code. See, e.g., Zapatha v. Dairy Mart, 381 Mass. 284, 408 N.E.2d 1370 (1980) (termination clause in franchise agreement not considered unconscionable); Commonwealth v. DeCotis, 366 Mass. 234, 316 N.E.2d 748 (1974) (extraction of resale fees for no rendered services deemed unfair act or practice under G.L. c. 93A, § 2[a]). . . . As explained in Bronstein v. Prudential Ins. Co., 390 Mass. 701, 459 N.E.2d 772 (1984), "[in *Zapatha*] the court applied statutory policy to common law contract issues, which, for centuries have been within the province of this court." Accordingly, although we are not here concerned with a sale of goods or a commercial transaction, *Zapatha* is instructive on the principles to be applied in testing this transaction for unconscionability.

unconscionability

Unconscionability must be determined on a case-by-case basis, with particular attention to whether the challenged provision could result in oppression and unfair surprise to the disadvantaged party and not to allocation of risk because of "superior bargaining power." *Zapatha*, 381 Mass. at 292–293, 408 N.E.2d 1370. Courts have identified other elements of the unconscionable contract. For example, gross disparity in the consideration alone "may be sufficient to sustain [a finding that the contract is unconscionable]," since the disparity "itself leads inevitably to the felt conclusion

---

[2] General Laws c. 106, § 2–302, reads as follows:

"§ 2–302. Unconscionable Contract or Clause.

"(1) If the court as a matter of law finds the contract or any clause of the contract to have been unconscionable at the time it was made the court may refuse to enforce the contract, or it may enforce the remainder of the contract without the unconscionable clause, or it may so limit the application of any unconscionable clause as to avoid any unconscionable result.

"(2) When it is claimed or appears to the court that the contract or any clause thereof may be unconscionable the parties shall be afforded a reasonable opportunity to present evidence as to its commercial setting, purpose, and effect to aid the court in making the determination."

The standards of determining a contract unconscionable set forth in G.L. c. 106, § 2–302, are the same standards expressed in Restatement (Second) of Contracts § 208 (1981). "The issue is one of law for the court, and the test is to be made as of the time the contract was made." Zapatha v. Dairy Mart, Inc., 381 Mass. 284, 408 N.E.2d 1370 (1980).

that knowing advantage was taken of [one party]." Jones v. Star Credit Corp., 59 Misc.2d 189, 298 N.Y.S.2d 264 (N.Y.Sup.Ct.1969). . . . High pressure sales tactics and misrepresentation have been recognized as factors rendering a contract unconscionable. . . . If the sum total of the provisions of a contract drive too hard a bargain, a court of conscience will not assist its enforcement. *Campbell Soup Co.*, supra at 84.

The judge found that Beauchemin introduced the plaintiff to drugs, exhausted her credit card accounts to the sum of $6,000, unduly influenced her, suggested that the plaintiff sell her annuity contract, initiated the contract negotiations, was the agent of the defendants, and benefited from the contract between the plaintiff and the defendants.[3] The defendants were represented by legal counsel; the plaintiff was not. . . . The cash value of the annuity policy at the time the contract was executed was approximately four times greater than the price to be paid by the defendants. For payment of not more than $50,000 the defendants were to receive an asset that could be immediately exchanged for $189,000, or they could elect to hold it for its guaranteed term and receive $694,000. . . . [T]he judge could correctly conclude the contract was unconscionable.

The defendants assumed no risk and the plaintiff gained no advantage. Gross disparity in the values exchanged is an important factor to be considered in determining whether a contract is unconscionable. "[C]ourts [may] avoid enforcement of a bargain that is shown to be unconscionable by reason of gross inadequacy of consideration accompanied by other relevant factors." 1 A. Corbin, Contracts § 128, at 551. . . . See In re Estate of Vought, 76 Misc.2d 755, 351 N.Y.S.2d 816 (N.Y.Sur.Ct.1973) (assignment of interest in spendthrift trust for $66,000 under provisions which guaranteed assignees ultimate return of $1,100,000). We are satisfied that the disparity of interests in this contract is "so gross that the court cannot resist the inference that it was improperly obtained and is unconscionable." In re Estate of Vought, at 760, 351 N.Y.S.2d 816.

The defendants also argue that the judge erred in failing to require the plaintiff to return the full amount paid by them for the annuity.[4] The judges order was consistent with his findings that Beauchemin was the agent of the defendants, and that the plaintiff only received $18,000 for her interest in the annuity.

QUESTION

If the plaintiff in *Waters* had not mentioned unconscionability, but relied exclusively on the tort of fraud, would the result have been any different?

––––––––––

[3] These latter two findings were grounds enough for the judge to rescind the contract. See 1 H.C. Black, Rescission of Contracts § 32 (2d ed. 1929), and cases cited. The plaintiff relied on Beauchemin to represent her in the contract negotiations. Accordingly, he was obligated to act on her behalf and in her interest. Instead, he acted in his own self-interest and caused benefits to inure to himself by having his debts forgiven and requiring he be named beneficiary of the annuity policy.

[4] The defendants paid $18,000 cash after deducting $7,000 for a debt which was owed to them by Beauchemin. The remaining $25,000 due on the contract was never paid.

Williams v. Walker–Thomas Furniture Co.

United States Court of Appeals, District of Columbia Circuit, 1965.
350 F.2d 445.

WRIGHT, CIRCUIT JUDGE. Appellee, Walker–Thomas Furniture Co., operates a retail furniture store in the District of Columbia. During the period from 1957 to 1962 each appellant in these cases purchased a number of household items from Walker–Thomas, for which payment was to be made in installments. The terms of each purchase were contained in a printed form contract which set forth the value of the purchased item and purported to lease the item to appellant for a stipulated monthly rent payment. The contract then provided, in substance, that title would remain in Walker–Thomas until the total of all the monthly payments made equalled the stated value of the item, at which time appellants could take title. In the event of a default in the payment of any monthly installment, Walker–Thomas could repossess the item.

The contract further provided that "the amount of each periodical installment payment to be made by (purchaser) to the Company under this present lease shall be inclusive of and not in addition to the amount of each installment payment to be made by (purchaser) under such prior leases, bills or accounts; and all payments now and hereafter made by (purchaser) shall be credited pro rata on all outstanding leases, bills and accounts due the Company by (purchaser) at the time each such payment is made." The effect of this rather obscure provision was to keep a balance due on every item purchased until the balance due on all items, whenever purchased, was liquidated. As a result, the debt incurred at the time of purchase of each item was secured by the right to repossess all the items previously purchased by the same purchaser, and each new item purchased automatically became subject to a security interest arising out of the previous dealings.

On May 12, 1962, appellant Thorne purchased an item described as a Daveno, three tables, and two lamps, having total stated value of $391.10. Shortly thereafter, he defaulted on his monthly payments and appellee sought to replevy all the items purchased since the first transaction in 1958. Similarly, on April 17, 1962, appellant Williams bought a stereo set of stated value of $514.95.[1] She too defaulted shortly thereafter, and appellee sought to replevy all the items purchased since December, 1957. The Court of General Sessions granted judgment for appellee. The [D.C.] Court of Appeals affirmed, and we granted appellants' motion for leave to appeal to this court.

Appellants' principal contention, rejected by both the trial and the appellate courts below, is that these contracts, or at least some of them, are unconscionable and, hence, not enforceable.... [T]he [D.C.] Court of Appeals explained its rejection of this contention as follows:

> Appellant's second argument presents a more serious question. The record reveals that prior to the last purchase appellant had reduced the balance in her account to $164. The last purchase, a stereo set, raised the balance due to $678. Significantly, at the time of this and the preceding purchases, appellee was

---

[1] At the time of this purchase her account showed a balance of $164 still owing from her prior purchases. The total of all the purchases made over the years in question came to $1,800. The total payments amounted to $1,400.

aware of appellant's financial position. The reverse side of the stereo contract listed the name of appellant's social worker and her $218 monthly stipend from the government. Nevertheless, with full knowledge that appellant had to feed, clothe and support both herself and seven children on this amount, appellee sold her a $514 stereo set.

We cannot condemn too strongly appellee's conduct. It raises serious questions of sharp practice and irresponsible business dealings. A review of the legislation in the District of Columbia affecting retail sales and the pertinent decisions of the highest court in this jurisdiction disclose, however, no ground upon which this court can declare the contracts in question contrary to public policy. We note that were the Maryland Retail Installment Sales Act, Art. 83 §§ 128–153, or its equivalent, in force in the District of Columbia, we could grant appellant appropriate relief. We think Congress should consider corrective legislation to protect the public from such exploitive contracts as were utilized in the case at bar.

We do not agree that the court lacked the power to refuse enforcement to contracts found to be unconscionable. In other jurisdictions, it has been held as a matter of common law that unconscionable contracts are not enforceable. While no decision of this court so holding has been found, the notion that an unconscionable bargain should not be given full enforcement is by no means novel. In Scott v. United States, 79 U.S. (12 Wall.) 443, 445, 20 L.Ed. 438 (1870), the Supreme Court stated:

> . . . If a contract be unreasonable and unconscionable, but not void for fraud, a court of law will give to the party who sues for its breach damages, not according to its letter, but only such as he is equitably entitled to. . . .

Since we have never adopted or rejected such a rule, the question here presented is actually one of first impression.

Congress has recently enacted the Uniform Commercial Code, which specifically provides that the court may refuse to enforce a contract which it finds to be unconscionable at the time it was made. The enactment of this section, which occurred subsequent to the contracts here in suit, does not mean that the common law of the District of Columbia was otherwise at the time of enactment, nor does it preclude the court from adopting a similar rule in the exercise of its powers to develop the common law for the District. . . . In fact, in view of the absence of prior authority on the point, we consider the congressional adoption of § 2–302 persuasive authority for following the rationale of the cases from which the section is explicitly derived. Accordingly, we hold that where the element of unconscionability is present at the time a contract is made, the contract should not be enforced.

Unconscionability has generally been recognized to include an absence of meaningful choice on the part of one of the parties together with contract terms which are unreasonably favorable to the other party. Whether a meaningful choice is present in a particular case can only be determined by consideration of all the circumstances surrounding the transaction. In many cases the meaningfulness of the choice is negated by a gross inequality of bargaining power.[2] The manner in which the contract was entered is

---

[2] Inquiry into the relative bargaining power of the two parties is not an inquiry wholly divorced from the general question of unconscionability, since a one-sided bargain is itself evi-

also relevant to this consideration. Did each party to the contract, considering his obvious education or lack of it, have a reasonable opportunity to understand the terms of the contract, or were the important terms hidden in a maze of fine print and minimized by deceptive sales practices? Ordinarily, one who signs an agreement without full knowledge of its terms might be held to assume the risk that he has entered a one-sided bargain. But when a party of little bargaining power, and hence little real choice, signs a commercially unreasonable contract with little or no knowledge of its terms, it is hardly likely that his consent, or even an objective manifestation of his consent, was ever given to all the terms. In such a case the usual rule that the terms of the agreement are not to be questioned should be abandoned and the court should consider whether the terms of the contract are so unfair that enforcement should be withheld.

In determining reasonableness or fairness, the primary concern must be with the terms of the contract considered in light of the circumstances existing when the contract was made. The test is not simple, nor can it be mechanically applied. The terms are to be considered "in the light of the general commercial background and the commercial needs of the particular trade or case." Corbin suggests the test as being whether the terms are "so extreme as to appear unconscionable according to the mores and business practices of the time and place." 1 Corbin, Contracts § 128 (1963). We think this formulation correctly states the test to be applied in those cases where no meaningful choice was exercised upon entering the contract.

Because the trial court and the appellate court did not feel that enforcement could be refused, no findings were made on the possible unconscionability of the contracts in these cases. Since the record is not sufficient for our deciding the issue as a matter of law, the cases must be remanded to the trial court for further proceedings.

So ordered.

DANAHER, CIRCUIT JUDGE (dissenting). The [D.C.] Court of Appeals obviously was as unhappy about the situation here presented as any of us can possibly be. [It] concludes: "We think Congress should consider corrective legislation to protect the public from such exploitive contracts as were utilized in the case at bar."

My view is thus summed up by an able court which made no finding that there had actually been sharp practice. Rather the appellant seems to have known precisely where she stood.

There are many aspects of public policy here involved. What is a luxury to some may seem an outright necessity to others. Is public oversight to be required of the expenditures of relief funds? A washing machine, e.g., in the hands of a relief client might become a fruitful source of income. Many relief clients may well need credit, and certain business establishments will take long chances on the sale of items, expecting their pricing policies will

---

dence of the inequality of the bargaining parties. This fact was vaguely recognized in the common law doctrine of intrinsic fraud, that is, fraud which can be presumed from the grossly unfair nature of the terms of the contract. See the oft-quoted statement of Lord Hardwicke in Earl of Chesterfield v. Janssen, 28 Eng. Rep. 82, 100 (1751):

> [Fraud] may be apparent from the intrinsic nature and subject of the bargain itself; such as no man in his senses and not under delusion would make. . . .

And cf. Hume v. United States, 132 U.S. at 413, 10 S.Ct. at 137, where the Court characterized the English cases as "cases in which one party took advantage of the other's ignorance of arithmetic to impose upon him, and the fraud was apparent from the face of the contracts."

afford a degree of protection commensurate with the risk. Perhaps a remedy when necessary will be found within the provisions of the "Loan Shark" law, D.C.Code §§ 26–601 et seq. (1961).

I mention such matters only to emphasize the desirability of a cautious approach to any such problem, particularly since the law for so long has allowed parties such great latitude in making their own contracts. I dare say there must annually be thousands upon thousands of installment credit transactions in this jurisdiction, and one can only speculate as to the effect the decision in these cases will have. . . .

[It is reported that the case was settled following remand, with Walker–Thomas dropping all claims and paying Williams the fair value of the items it had taken from her. Dostert, Appellate Restatement of Unconscionability: Civil Legal Aid at Work, 54 A.B.A.J. 1183 (1968).]

NOTE

The cross-collateralization clause in the contract Williams signed gave Walker–Thomas a security interest in the stereo and all the other furniture she bought from it over the years. To understand the case, one has to understand the work the clause is doing. Some readers of the case are left with the impression that the clause gives Walker–Thomas the right to keep all of the property in the event of default even if its value exceeds what it is owed. This is wrong. A secured creditor has no right to keep collateral in the event of default. As long as the debtor insists, the seller is obliged to sell the property and return any surplus of the sale proceeds to the debtor. So something else must be at work in such clauses.

A distinctive feature of debtor-creditor law suggests a reason for the cross-collateralization clause. Those in the position of Walker–Thomas—those who are owed money and who have sued and reduced their claim to judgment—can reach most of a debtor's property without relying on any particular term in the contract. A cross-collaterization clause does nothing to increase the pool of assets available to satisfy the debt. Some property, however, is sufficiently important to the debtor that the law puts it presumptively beyond the reach of creditors. Such assets are "exempt" from creditor levy. Creditors can reach them only if the debtor grants a security interest in them at the time he or she borrows. Williams's household furniture was such "exempt" property. The cross-collateralization clause therefore enabled Walker–Thomas to reach assets that it otherwise could not.[*] Does this clause make the use of fine print especially suspect? Once the law protects certain assets from the reach of creditors, it would seem to follow that the debtor's waiver of such a right ought to be deliberate and knowing.

One can take this argument a step further. How can we ever be confident that the waiver is a deliberate and knowing one? Can there ever be a fully informed waiver on the floor of an inner-city furniture store? In a mass market, credit transactions are so routine that requiring that a cross-collateralization be disclosed conspicuously, or made the subject of explicit negotiation, may not

---

[*] A secured creditor also has a right to repossess in the event of a default without first going to court, provided the repossession can be done without a breach of the peace. As "breach of the peace" includes any unauthorized entry into a private home, this right, while relevant when the collateral is a car parked on the street, has little relevance when the collateral is household furniture.

be enough. Such logic is a justification for making cross-collateralization clauses, such as the one in cases such as *Walker–Thomas*, an unfair credit practice.
This was done in the 1980s. See 16 C.F.R. §§ 444.1–444.5.

————

Shapiro, Courts, Legislatures, and Paternalism
74 Va.L.Rev. 519, 534–538 (1988)

"In the sphere of contract, the judicial decisions most likely to be paternalist in their motivation, at least in substantial part, are those in which a contract term is imposed or invalidated despite the contrary intention of the parties. Even these outcomes may be substantially induced by a desire to achieve a
greater measure of efficiency or a fairer distribution of resources. But I agree
with those who find the notions of unfair overreaching and unequal bargaining
power in these cases (and to a lesser extent, some uses of the notions of coercion
and duress) proxies for the idea that one of the contracting parties simply did
not know what was in his own best interest. . . .

"For present purposes, the important point is that in a wide range of human activity—even those touching sensitive moral nerves—the courts are reluctant to invoke common law principles to invalidate private choice. And despite the charter granted to the courts by the Uniform Commercial Code's
unconscionability provision [§ 2–302], such decisions remain especially rare in
the realm of commercial and consumer sales. The landmark decisions declining
enforcement of written provisions—decisions like Henningsen v. Bloomfield
Motors, Inc., and Williams v. Walker–Thomas Furniture Co.—are beginning to
stand out in the casebooks as curiosities. . . .

"Indeed, the *Williams* case, which cast doubt on the validity of a particularly troublesome credit arrangement in an installment sale of consumer goods
to a person on welfare, was far from clear about the basis of the holding: was it
the procedural irregularities suggested by the record, the unfairness of the arrangement, or some combination of both? To the extent that procedural irregularities (such as lack of adequate notice of the nature and impact of the arrangement) lay at the root of the holding, it can hardly be classified as paternalist. To the extent that the court's true goal was substantive but was dressed
in procedural clothing, the decision may underscore even reformist judges' unwillingness to take an openly paternalist stance. Finally, to the extent that the
opinion reveals a paternalist readiness to invalidate a credit arrangement that
a consumer was willing to enter in order to get the goods she wanted, that readiness has not met with universal approval. . . .

"For the most part, then, courts are still reluctant—at least when acting
without legislative guidance or mandate—to interfere with sales agreements
that people apparently regard as in their interests, even though if the world
were a better and fairer place, they might not have to enter such bargains.*

---

* It might be argued that some basic contract doctrines, like consideration and the unen-
forceability of certain oral agreements, as well as certain remedial rules like that against punitive damage clauses, are paternalist to the extent that they interfere with private prefer-
ences. While not denying the presence of a paternalist ingredient in the mix, I believe that the
primary explanation for these doctrines lies elsewhere, and that the heavy going that some of
them have encountered in recent years may be due to an effort to rid them of their paternalist
aura.

Outside the realm of sales transactions, there are some significant developments that may have paternalist roots—for example, the judicial imposition of limitations on employment at will in employment contracts, and of a warranty of habitability in landlord-tenant relations. To the extent that employment at will contracts and warranty of habitability provisions involve the filling of gaps that the parties have left open, and are free to change, these developments can perhaps best be explained as prompted by motives of efficiency and redistribution. To the extent that the judicially imposed limitations are not subject to waiver, the paternalist explanation seems more natural, though not inevitable. Yet it is significant that the spread of limitations on employment at will has not been unrestrained, and that the warranty of habitability is widely reinforced by housing code provisions that impose criminal penalties on landlords who fail to meet minimum standards. . . .

"The problem of analyzing the degree to which paternalist ideas have affected the common-law doctrines governing private agreement is complicated by the inroads that tort law has made on areas traditionally reserved for contract. But these inroads do not in the main appear to be the result of paternalist prompting. The most dramatic change in tort law in this century—the emergence of strict product liability—is supported by powerful arguments for economic efficiency. Moreover, even in the midst of all this change, courts remain reluctant to override a clearly expressed intention to sell a product 'as is,' warts and all, or to hold a manufacturer liable for dangers that the buyer should have understood when he bought the product."

———

Dawson, Unconscionable Coercion: The German Version
89 Harv.L.Rev. 1041, 1042–1044 (1976)

"All will agree that by any test § 2–302 is a general clause. Instead of 'good morals' or 'good faith,' . . . the standard proposed—again the only standard—is 'conscience'; courts are authorized to refuse enforcement to any contract or clause that offends it. If the draftsmen of the U.C.C. had any particular limitations or targets in mind, no clues can be found in the Official Comment. . . . It is idle to parse this [language] or to seek guidance from the illustrations [given]. It is clear that the notion of unconscionability extends far beyond setting limits to self-exculpation. If the draftsmen of the U.C.C. had in mind other objectives or limitations on the scope of § 2–302, they did not express them in the one way that counts, in the language of the Code. So it is only a slight exaggeration to say that § 2–302, as it appeared in the Code at the outset had no meaning, and most of the meanings it is to have will be discovered in the course of its application. This is a characteristic feature of general clauses. . . .

———

The statute of frauds, for example, has been riddled with exceptions designed to permit enforcement of agreements when the evidentiary hazards are reduced by such events as part performance. The [UCC] has gone so far as to take an agreement for the sale of goods outside the statute if its existence is admitted in litigation (voluntarily or under compulsion). See U.C.C. § 2–201(3)(b) (1978). As for the doctrine of consideration, I think it reflects the view that in the vast majority of cases, the unbargained-for promise is not a reliable indicator of the promisor's intent to tie himself to the mast. After all, a promisor can find the necessary rope by transferring property outright, or even by a declaration of trust. [Other footnotes have been omitted.—Eds.]

"Nevertheless, to insert such a clause deliberately in a comprehensive scheme of legislation is in effect to concede that the norms expressed in the legislation are incomplete in ways that have not been identified, so that some means are needed for discovering and incorporating additional elements not yet formulated or foreseen. . . . [T]he initial leadership is clearly cast on judges, not only because the need for new departures will ordinarily be disclosed through litigation but because judges have the first opportunity, through the reasons they give, to provide a good start in perceiving and defining the new elements. . . . The aims [of this] enterprise are obviously to scale down the apparently unlimited mandate of the general clause, to restructure it into distinct subordinate norms that become intelligible and manageable through their narrowed scope and function."

————

Brower v. Gateway 2000, Inc.

Supreme Court of New York, Appellate Division, 1998.
246 A.D.2d 246, 676 N.Y.S.2d 569.

MILONAS, J. Appellants are among the many consumers who purchased computers and software products from defendant Gateway 2000 through a direct-sales system, by mail or telephone order. As of July 3, 1995, it was Gateway's practice to include with the materials shipped to the purchaser along with the merchandise a copy of its "Standard Terms and Conditions Agreement" and any relevant warranties for the products in the shipment. The Agreement begins with a "NOTE TO CUSTOMER," which provides, in slightly larger print than the remainder of the document, in a box that spans the width of the page: "This document contains Gateway 2000's Standard Terms and Conditions. By keeping your Gateway 2000 computer system beyond thirty (30) days after the date of delivery, you accept these Terms and Conditions." The document consists of 16 paragraphs[;] paragraph 10 of the agreement, entitled "DISPUTE RESOLUTION," reads as follows:

> Any dispute or controversy arising out of or relating to this Agreement or its interpretation shall be settled exclusively and finally by arbitration. The arbitration shall be conducted in accordance with the Rules of Conciliation and Arbitration of the International Chamber of Commerce. The arbitration shall be conducted in Chicago, Illinois, U.S.A. before a sole arbitrator. Any award rendered in any such arbitration proceeding shall be final and binding on each of the parties, and judgment may be entered thereon in a court of competent jurisdiction.

Plaintiffs commenced this action on behalf of themselves and others similarly situated for compensatory and punitive damages, alleging deceptive sales practices in seven causes of action, including breach of warranty, breach of contract, fraud and unfair trade practices. In particular, the allegations focused on Gateway's representations and advertising that promised "service when you need it," including around-the-clock free technical support, free software technical support and certain on-site services. According to plaintiffs, not only were they unable to avail themselves of this offer because it was virtually impossible to get through to a technician, but also Gateway continued to advertise this claim notwithstanding numerous complaints and reports about the problem.

. . . Gateway moved to dismiss the complaint based on the arbitration clause in the Agreement. Appellants argued that the arbitration clause is invalid under UCC 2–207, unconscionable under UCC 2–302 and an unenforceable contract of adhesion. Specifically, they claimed that the provision was obscure; that a customer could not reasonably be expected to appreciate or investigate its meaning and effect; that the Int'l Chamber of Commerce ("ICC") was not a forum commonly used for consumer matters; and that because ICC headquarters were in France, it was particularly difficult to locate the organization and its rules. To illustrate just how inaccessible the forum was, appellants advised the court that the ICC was not registered with the Secretary of State, that efforts to locate and contact the ICC had been unsuccessful and that apparently the only way to attempt to contact the ICC was through the United States Council for Int'l Business, with which the ICC maintained some sort of relationship.

In support of their arguments, appellants submitted a copy of the ICC's Rules of Conciliation and Arbitration and contended that the cost of ICC arbitration was prohibitive, particularly given the amount of the typical consumer claim involved. For example, a claim of less than $50,000 required advance fees of $4,000 (more than the cost of most Gateway products), of which the $2,000 registration fee was nonrefundable even if the consumer prevailed at the arbitration. Consumers would also incur travel expenses disproportionate to the damages sought, which appellants' counsel estimated would not exceed $1,000 per customer in this action, as well as bear the cost of Gateway's legal fees if the consumer did not prevail at the arbitration; in this respect, the ICC rules follow the "loser pays" rule used in England. Also, although Chicago was designated as the site of the actual arbitration, all correspondence must be sent to ICC headquarters in France.

The IAS court dismissed the complaint based on the arbitration clause. . . . We agree with the court's decision and reasoning in all respects but for the issue of the unconscionability of the designation of the ICC as the arbitration body.

First, the court properly rejected appellants' argument that the arbitration clause was invalid under UCC 2–207. . . . [A]s the court correctly concluded, the clause was not a "material alteration" of an oral agreement [under UCC 2–207(2),] but, rather, simply one provision of the sole contract that existed between the parties. That contract, the court explained, was formed and acceptance was manifested not when the order was placed but only with the retention of the merchandise beyond the 30 days specified in the Agreement enclosed in the shipment of merchandise. Accordingly, the contract was outside the scope of UCC 2–207.

[In omitted passages, this conclusion was rested on the rationale of ProCD, Inc. v. Zeidenberg and Hill v. Gateway 2000, Inc., supra pp. 469–475. The court, addressing "the realities of conducting business in today's world," including the "cash now, terms later" transaction, approved in full the lower court's embrace of the contract-formation analysis found in those decisions. Hence there was no "battle of the forms" here, only a sole contract "proposed" and "effectual" as a whole.]

Second, with respect to appellants' claim that the arbitration clause is unenforceable as a contract of adhesion, in that it involved no choice or negotiation on the part of the consumer but was a "take it or leave it" proposition[,] we find that this argument, too, was properly rejected. Although the parties clearly do not possess equal bargaining power, this factor alone does not invalidate the contract as one of adhesion. . . . [W]ith the ability to make the purchase elsewhere and the express option to return the goods, the consumer is not in a "take it or leave it" position at all; if any term of the agreement is unacceptable to the consumer, he or she can easily buy a competitor's product instead—either from a retailer or directly from the manufacturer—and reject Gateway's agreement by returning the merchandise (see, e.g. Carnival Cruise Lines v. Shute, 499 U.S. 585, 593–594 . . .). The consumer has 30 days to make that decision. Within that time, the consumer can inspect the goods and examine and seek clarification of the terms of the agreement; until those 30 days have elapsed, the consumer has the unqualified right to return the merchandise, because the goods or terms are unsatisfactory or for no reason at all.

While returning the goods to avoid the formation of the contract entails affirmative action on the part of the consumer, and even some expense, this may be seen as a trade-off for the convenience and savings for which the consumer presumably opted when he or she chose to make a purchase of such consequence by phone or mail as an alternative to on-site retail shopping. That a consumer does not read the agreement or thereafter claims he or she failed to understand or appreciate some term therein does not invalidate the contract any more than such claim would undo a contract formed under other circumstances. . . . We further note that appellants' claim of adhesion is identical to that made and rejected in Filias v. Gateway 2000, Inc., an unreported case brought to our attention by both parties that interprets the same Gateway agreement (No. 97C 2523 [N.D.Ill., January 15, 1998]). . . .

Finally, we turn to appellants' argument that the IAS court should have declared the contract unenforceable, pursuant to UCC 2–302, on the ground that the arbitration clause is unconscionable due to the unduly burdensome procedure and cost for the individual consumer. The IAS court found that while a class-action lawsuit, such as the one herein, may be a less costly alternative to arbitration (which is generally less costly than litigation), that does not alter the binding effect of the valid arbitration clause contained in the agreement. . . .

As a general matter, under New York law, unconscionability requires a showing that a contract is "both procedurally and substantively unconscionable when made" (Gillman v. Chase Manhattan Bank, 73 N.Y.2d 1, 10, 537 N.Y.S.2d 787, 534 N.E.2d 824). That is, there must be "some showing of 'an absence of meaningful choice on the part of one of the parties together with contract terms which are unreasonably favorable to the other party' [citation omitted]" (Matter of State of New York v. Avco Fin. Serv., 50 N.Y.2d 383, 389–390, 429 N.Y.S.2d 181, 406 (N.E.2d 1075)). The Avco court took pains to note, however, that the purpose of this doctrine is not to redress the inequality between the parties but simply to ensure that the more powerful party cannot "surprise" the other party with some overly oppressive term.

As to the procedural element, a court will look to the contract formation process to determine if in fact one party lacked any meaningful choice in entering into the contract, taking into consideration such factors as the setting of the transaction, the experience and education of the party claiming unconscionability, whether the contract contained "fine print," whether the seller used "high-pressured tactics" and any disparity in the parties' bargaining power (Gillman, at 10–11, 537 N.Y.S.2d 787, 534 N.E.2d 824). None of these factors supports appellants' claim here. Any purchaser has 30 days within which to thoroughly examine the contents of their shipment, including the terms of the Agreement, and seek clarification of any term therein. The Agreement itself, which is entitled in large print "STANDARD TERMS AND CONDITIONS AGREEMENT," consists of only three pages and 16 paragraphs, all of which appear in the same size print. Moreover, despite appellants' claims to the contrary, the arbitration clause is in no way "hidden" or "tucked away" within a complex document of inordinate length, nor is the option of returning the merchandise, to avoid the contract, somehow a "precarious" one. . . .

With respect to the substantive element, . . . we do not find that the possible inconvenience of the chosen site (Chicago) alone rises to the level of unconscionability. We do find, however, that the excessive cost factor that is necessarily entailed in arbitrating before the ICC is unreasonable and surely serves to deter the individual consumer from invoking the process. . . . Barred from resorting to the courts by the arbitration clause in the first instance, the designation of a financially prohibitive forum effectively bars consumers from this forum as well; consumers are thus left with no forum at all in which to resolve a dispute. In this regard, we note that this particular claim is not mentioned in the *Hill* decision, which upheld the clause as part of an enforceable contract.

While it is true that, under New York law, unconscionability is generally predicated on the presence of both the procedural and substantive elements, the substantive element alone may be sufficient to render the terms of the provision at issue unenforceable. . . . Excessive fees, such as those incurred under the ICC procedure, have been grounds for finding an arbitration provision unenforceable or commercially unreasonable. . . .

In the *Filias* case previously mentioned, the [court] stated that it was "inclined to agree" with the argument that selection of the ICC rendered the clause unconscionable, but concluded that the issue was moot because Gateway had agreed to arbitrate before the American Arbitration Association ("AAA") and sought court appointment of the AAA pursuant to Federal Arbitration Act (9 U.S.C. § 5). The court accordingly granted Gateway's motion to compel arbitration and appointed the AAA in lieu of the ICC. Plaintiffs in that action (who are represented by counsel for appellants before us) contend that costs associated with the AAA process are also excessive, given the amount of the individual consumer's damages, and their motion for reconsideration of the court's decision has not yet been decided. While the AAA rules and costs are not part of the record before us, the parties agree that there is a minimum, non-refundable filing fee of $500, and appellants claim each consumer could spend in excess of $1,000 to arbitrate in this forum.

Gateway's agreement to the substitution of the AAA is not limited to the *Filias* plaintiffs. Gateway's brief includes the text of a new arbitration agreement that it claims has been extended to all customers, past, present and future (apparently through publication in a quarterly magazine sent to anyone who has ever purchased a Gateway product). The new arbitration agreement provides for the consumer's choice of the AAA or the ICC as the arbitral body and the designation of any location for the arbitration by agreement of the parties which "shall not be unreasonably withheld." It also provides telephone numbers at which the AAA and the ICC may be reached for information regarding the "organizations and their procedures."

As noted, however, appellants complain that the AAA fees are also excessive and thus in no way have they accepted defendant's offer (see, UCC

2–209); because they make the same claim as to the AAA as they did with respect to the ICC, the issue of unconscionability is not rendered moot, as defendant suggests. We cannot determine on this record whether the AAA process and costs would be so "egregiously oppressive" that they, too, would be unconscionable. . . . Thus, we modify the order on appeal to the extent of finding that portion of the arbitration provision requiring arbitration before the ICC to be unconscionable and[,] [vacating that portion of the arbitration agreement,] remand to Supreme Court so that the parties have the opportunity to seek appropriate substitution of an arbitrator pursuant to the Federal Arbitration Act (9 U.S.C. § 1 et seq.), which provides for such court designation of an arbitrator upon application of either party, where, for whatever reason, one is not otherwise designated. . . .

All concur.

————

Rent-A-Center v. Jackson

Supreme Court of the United States, 2010.
130 S. Ct. 2772.

SCALIA, J. . . . On February 1, 2007, the respondent here, Antonio Jackson, filed an employment-discrimination suit . . . against his former employer in the United States District Court for the District of Nevada. The defendant and petitioner here, Rent–A–Center, West, Inc., filed a motion under the [Federal Arbitration Act] to dismiss or stay the proceedings, and to compel arbitration. Rent–A–Center argued that the Mutual Agreement to Arbitrate Claims (Agreement), which Jackson signed on February 24, 2003 as a condition of his employment there, precluded Jackson from pursuing his claims in court. The Agreement provided for arbitration of all "past, present or future" disputes arising out of Jackson's employment with Rent–A–Center, including "claims for discrimination" and "claims for violation of any federal . . . law." It also provided that "[t]he Arbitrator, and not any federal, state, or local court or agency, shall have exclusive authority to resolve any dispute relating to the interpretation, applicability, enforceability or formation of this Agreement including, but not limited to any claim that all or any part of this Agreement is void or voidable."

Jackson opposed the motion on the ground that "the arbitration agreement in question is clearly unenforceable in that it is unconscionable" under Nevada law. Rent–A–Center responded that Jackson's unconscionability claim was not properly before the court because Jackson had expressly agreed that the arbitrator would have exclusive authority to resolve any dispute about the enforceability of the Agreement. It also disputed the merits of Jackson's unconscionability claims. . . .

The FAA reflects the fundamental principle that arbitration is a matter of contract. Section 2, the "primary substantive provision of the Act," Moses H. Cone Memorial Hospital v. Mercury Constr. Corp., 460 U.S. 1, 24, 103 S.Ct. 927, 74 L.Ed.2d 765 (1983), provides:

> A written provision in . . . a contract evidencing a transaction involving commerce to settle by arbitration a controversy thereafter arising out of such contract . . . shall be valid, irrevocable, and enforceable, save upon such grounds as exist at law or in equity for the revocation of any contract. 9 U.S.C. § 2.

The FAA thereby places arbitration agreements on an equal footing with other contracts, and requires courts to enforce them according to their terms. Like other contracts, however, they may be invalidated by "generally applicable contract defenses, such as fraud, duress, or unconscionability."

The Act also establishes procedures by which federal courts implement § 2's substantive rule. Under § 3, a party may apply to a federal court for a stay of the trial of an action "upon any issue referable to arbitration under an agreement in writing for such arbitration." Under § 4, a party "aggrieved" by the failure of another party "to arbitrate under a written agreement for arbitration" may petition a federal court "for an order directing that such arbitration proceed in the manner provided for in such agreement." The court "shall" order arbitration "upon being satisfied that the making of the agreement for arbitration or the failure to comply therewith is not in issue." *Ibid.*

The Agreement here contains multiple "written provision[s]" to "settle by arbitration a controversy," § 2. Two are relevant to our discussion. First, the section titled "Claims Covered By The Agreement" provides for arbitration of all "past, present or future" disputes arising out of Jackson's employment with Rent–A–Center. Second, the section titled "Arbitration Procedures" provides that "[t]he Arbitrator . . . shall have exclusive authority to resolve any dispute relating to the . . . enforceability . . . of this Agreement including, but not limited to any claim that all or any part of this Agreement is void or voidable." The current "controversy" between the parties is whether the Agreement is unconscionable. It is the second provision, which delegates resolution of that controversy to the arbitrator, that Rent–A–Center seeks to enforce. Adopting the terminology used by the parties, we will refer to it as the delegation provision.

The delegation provision is an agreement to arbitrate threshold issues concerning the arbitration agreement. We have recognized that parties can agree to arbitrate "gateway" questions of "arbitrability," such as whether the parties have agreed to arbitrate or whether their agreement covers a particular controversy. This line of cases merely reflects the principle that arbitration is a matter of contract. An agreement to arbitrate a gateway issue is simply an additional, antecedent agreement the party seeking arbitration asks the federal court to enforce, and the FAA operates on this additional arbitration agreement just as it does on any other. The additional agreement is valid under § 2 "save upon such grounds as exist at law or in equity for the revocation of any contract," and federal courts can enforce the agreement by staying federal litigation under § 3 and compelling arbitration under § 4. The question before us, then, is whether the delegation provision is valid under § 2.

There are two types of validity challenges under § 2: "One type challenges specifically the validity of the agreement to arbitrate," and "[t]he other challenges the contract as a whole, either on a ground that directly affects the entire agreement (*e.g.,* the agreement was fraudulently induced), or on the ground that the illegality of one of the contract's provisions renders the whole contract invalid." *Buckeye,* 546 U.S., at 444, 126 S.Ct. 1204. In a line of cases neither party has asked us to overrule, we held that only the first type of challenge is relevant to a court's determination whether the arbitration agreement at issue is enforceable. See Prima Paint Corp. v. Flood & Conklin Mfg. Co., 388 U.S. 395, 403–404, 87 S.Ct. 1801, 18 L.Ed.2d 1270 (1967). That is because § 2 states that a "written provision" "to settle by arbitration a controversy" is "valid, irrevocable, and enforceable" *without mention* of the validity of the contract in which it is contained. Thus, a party's challenge to another provision of the contract, or to the contract as a whole, does not prevent a court from enforcing a specific agreement to arbitrate. "[A]s a matter of substantive federal arbitration law, an arbitration provision is severable from the remainder of the contract." *Buckeye,* 546 U.S., at 445, 126 S.Ct. 1204; see also *id.,* at 447, 126 S.Ct. 1204 (the severability rule is based on § 2).

But that agreements to arbitrate are severable does not mean that they are unassailable. If a party challenges the validity under § 2 of the precise agreement to arbitrate at issue, the federal court must consider the challenge before ordering compliance with that agreement under § 4. In *Prima Paint,* for example, if the claim had been "fraud in the inducement of the arbitration clause itself," then the court would have considered it. 388 U.S., at 403–404, 87 S.Ct. 1801. "To immunize an arbitration agreement from judicial challenge on the ground of fraud in the inducement would be to elevate it over other forms of contract," *id.,* at 404, n. 12, 87 S.Ct. 1801. In some cases the claimed basis of invalidity for the contract as a whole will be much easier to establish than the same basis as applied only to the severable agreement to arbitrate. Thus, in an employment contract many elements of alleged unconscionability applicable to the entire contract (outrageously low wages, for example) would not affect the agreement to arbitrate alone. But even where that is not the case—as in *Prima Paint* itself, where the alleged fraud that induced the whole contract equally induced the agreement to arbitrate which was part of that contract—we nonetheless require the basis of challenge to be directed specifically to the agreement to arbitrate before the court will intervene.

Here, the "written provision . . . to settle by arbitration a controversy," 9 U.S.C. § 2, that Rent–A–Center asks us to enforce is the delegation provision—the provision that gave the arbitrator "exclusive authority to resolve any dispute relating to the . . . enforceability . . . of this Agreement." The "remainder of the contract," *Buckeye, supra,* at 445, 126 S.Ct. 1204, is the rest of the agreement to arbitrate claims arising out of Jackson's employment with Rent–A–Center. To be sure this case differs from *Prima Paint, Buckeye,* and *Preston,* in that the arbitration provisions sought to be enforced in those cases were contained in contracts unrelated to arbitration—contracts for consulting services, check-cashing services, and "personal management" or "talent agent" services. In this case, the underlying contract is itself an arbitration agreement. But that makes no difference. Application of the severability rule does not depend on the substance of the remainder of the contract. Section 2 operates on the specific "written provision" to "settle by arbitration a controversy" that the party seeks to enforce. Accordingly, unless Jackson challenged the delegation provision specifically, we must treat it as valid under § 2, and must enforce it under §§ 3 and 4, leaving any challenge to the validity of the Agreement as a whole for the arbitrator. . . .

The District Court correctly concluded that Jackson challenged only the validity of the contract as a whole. Nowhere in his opposition to Rent–A–Center's motion to compel arbitration did he even mention the delegation provision. Rent–A–Center noted this fact in its reply: "[Jackson's response] fails to rebut or otherwise address in any way [Rent–A–Center's] argument that the Arbitrator must decide [Jackson's] challenge to the enforceability of the Agreement. *Thus, [Rent–A–Center's] argument is uncontested.*"

The arguments Jackson made in his response to Rent–A–Center's motion to compel arbitration support this conclusion. Jackson stated that "the *entire agreement* seems drawn to provide [Rent–A–Center] with undue advantages should an employment-related dispute arise." (emphasis added). At one point, he argued that the limitations on discovery "further suppor[t] [his] contention that the *arbitration agreement as a whole* is substantively unconscionable." (emphasis added). And before this Court, Jackson describes his challenge in the District Court as follows: He "opposed the motion to compel on the ground that the *entire arbitration agreement,* including the delegation clause, was unconscionable." (emphasis added). That is an accurate description of his filings.

As required to make out a claim of unconscionability under Nevada law, he contended that the Agreement was both procedurally and substantively unconscionable. It was procedurally unconscionable, he argued, because it "was imposed as a condition of employment and was non-negotiable." But we need not consider that claim because none of Jackson's substantive unconscionability challenges was specific to the delegation provision. First, he argued that the Agreement's coverage was one sided in that it required arbitration of claims an employee was likely to bring—contract, tort, discrimination, and statutory claims—but did not require arbitration of claims Rent–A–Center was likely to bring—intellectual property, unfair competition, and trade secrets claims. This one-sided-coverage argument clearly did not go to the validity of the delegation provision.

Jackson's other two substantive unconscionability arguments assailed arbitration procedures called for by the contract—the fee-splitting arrangement and the limitations on discovery—procedures that were to be used during arbitration under *both* the agreement to arbitrate employment-related disputes *and* the delegation provision. It may be that had Jackson challenged the delegation provision by arguing that these common procedures *as applied* to the delegation provision rendered *that provision* unconscionable, the challenge should have been considered by the court. To make such a claim based on the discovery procedures, Jackson would have had to argue that the limitation upon the number of depositions causes the arbitration of his claim that the Agreement is unenforceable to be unconscionable. That would be, of course, a much more difficult argument to sustain than the argument that the same limitation renders arbitration of his factbound employment-discrimination claim unconscionable. Likewise, the unfairness of the fee-splitting arrangement may be more difficult to establish for the arbitration of enforceability than for arbitration of more complex and fact-related aspects of the alleged employment discrimination. Jackson, however, did not make any arguments specific to the delegation provision; he argued that the fee-sharing and discovery procedures rendered the *entire* Agreement invalid.

Jackson's appeal to the Ninth Circuit confirms that he did not contest the validity of the delegation provision in particular. His brief noted the existence of the delegation provision, but his unconscionability arguments made no mention of it. He also repeated the arguments he had made before the District Court, that the "entire agreement" favors Rent–A–Center and that the limitations on discovery further his "contention that the arbitration agreement as a whole is substantively unconscionable." Finally, he repeated the argument made in his District Court filings, that under state law the unconscionable clauses could not be severed from the arbitration agreement. The point of this argument, of course, is that the Agreement *as a whole* is unconscionable under state law.

Jackson repeated that argument before this Court. At oral argument, counsel stated: "There are certain elements of the arbitration agreement that are unconscionable and, under Nevada law, which would render the *entire arbitration agreement* unconscionable." And again, he stated, "we've got both certain provisions that are unconscionable, that under Nevada law render the *entire agreement* unconscionable . . ., and that's what the Court is to rely on." . . .

We reverse the judgment of the Court of Appeals for the Ninth Circuit.

————

Grosvenor v. Qwest Corp.

854 F.Supp.2d 1021 (D. Colo. 2012)

The plaintiff argued that any agreement to arbitrate that he may have entered into was illusory and thus unenforceable because Qwest reserved the unilateral right to change terms of the agreement. Citing *Rent-A-Center*, Qwest contended that challenges to the enforceability of the contract as a whole (rather than challenges to the enforceability of the arbitration clause) are questions that are reserved to the arbitrator, not the courts. The court rejected this argument, reasoning that the plaintiff was making "an attack on the arbitration provision, rather than an attack on the illusory nature of the Subscriber Agreement as a whole." The plaintiff "is not contending that the entirety of his agreement with Qwest was illusory; indeed, he seeks to enforce the agreement (particularly the 'Price for Life' program). Because Mr. Grosvenor is attacking only the validity of the arbitration clause, cases like *Prima Paint* and *Rent–A–Center* instruct that it is the obligation of the Court, rather than the arbitrator, to determine whether the arbitration clause is illusory."

————

NOTE: CONTEMPORARY UNCONSCIONABILITY

It seems in order to return for a moment to *Henningsen*, where the court barely mentioned unconscionability and spoke mainly of "public policy." Nonetheless, courts and commentators often say that *Henningsen* illustrates "the unconscionability analysis." In light of what you have seen to this point, is that an accurate statement?

The case law makes clear that we have come to divide the doctrine of unconscionability into two aspects, one intended to prevent unfair surprise and the other intended to prevent oppression. More precisely, two categories of factors must ordinarily coalesce. One court's discussion of the linkage between the two branches of unconscionability includes this statement (Resource Mgmt. Co. v. Weston Ranch & Livestock Co., 706 P.2d 1028, 1043 (Utah 1985)):

> Whatever the particular formulation, the standard for determining unconscionability is high, even if not precise. . . . While it is conceivable that a contract might be unconscionable on the theory of unfair surprise without any substantive imbalance in the obligations of the parties to the contract, that would be rare. . . . Where only

procedural irregularities are involved, the judicial doctrines of fraud, misrepresentation, duress, and mistake may provide superior tools for analyzing the validity of contracts.

The *Brower* court also has something to say on whether the absence of procedural irregularities bars any attempt to avoid liability for substantive unfairness. Moreover, in support of its conclusion that plaintiffs were not in a "take-it-or-leave-it position," the *Brower* court cites Carnival Cruise Lines v. Shute, 499 U.S. 585 (1991). In that case, a passenger was injured on a cruise ship and brought suit. The cruise line sought to dismiss the suit on the basis of a forum-selection clause printed on the passenger's ticket. Even though the passenger had had no knowledge of the clause until the transaction was complete (the ticket was mailed after its purchase), the passenger failed to raise before the Supreme Court any claim of insufficient notice. The Court, finding the clause otherwise "reasonable" in the circumstances, added this sentence: "Finally, respondents have conceded that they were given notice of the forum provision and, therefore, presumably retained the option of rejecting the contract with impunity."

There is a further dimension of unconscionability today. As noted, every jurisdiction in this country, spurred by the "consumer movement" of the 1960s and 1970s, now has some form of unfair and deceptive trade practices or consumer protection act. The various types of statutes, a fair number of which were inspired by the Federal Trade Commission Act (15 U.S.C. § 45(a)–(m) (1982)), are collected and examined in Comment, Consumer Protection: The Practical Effectiveness of State Deceptive Trade Practices Legislation, 59 Tul.L.Rev. 427 (1984), and Leaffer & Lipson, Consumer Actions Against Unfair or Deceptive Acts or Practices: The Private Uses of Federal Trade Commission Jurisprudence, 48 Geo.Wash.L.Rev. 521 (1980). Perhaps as many as 15 to 20 of the state acts specifically include "unconscionable" practices or contract provisions among the "fraudulent or illegal" activities reached by the legislation. The telling feature of a number of these statutes is the alternative to private litigation that is added—a suit by a public agency, upon a consumer complaint, to obtain injunctive relief against objectionable business practices. See, e.g., State v. Avco Fin.Serv. of New York, 50 N.Y.2d 383, 429 N.Y.S.2d 181, 406 N.E.2d 1075 (1980), which was quoted approvingly in *Brower*. The main point here is that common law and UCC approaches to unconscionability have been expanded, and that, in general, much of the law of consumer protection is currently the work of statutes and not common law doctrines. These developments, and the issues they raise, are usually treated in courses in Commercial and Consumer Law.

JOINING UNCONSCIONABILITY AND "GOOD FAITH"

It is standard practice to join a claim of unconscionability with a claim of breach of the duty of good faith. The classic instance of such a dual attack against one-sidedness is to be found in lawsuits growing out of the yanking of a franchise. A decision encountered earlier, Corenswet v. Amana Refrigeration, supra p. 364, illustrates both the practice and the usual outcome when exercise of a contractual power is challenged as abusive. Why was it that Judge Wisdom, in the termination-without-cause setting of *Corenswet*, was content to allow the doctrine of unconscionability preemptive force, trumping any test of good faith? In the words of another court, when a claim of bad faith rests solely upon a party's basis, or lack thereof, for ending a contract that is terminable at the will of either party, "motivation is immaterial." Smith v. Price's Creameries, 98 N.M. 541, 650 P.2d 825 (1982).

Is there a blanket duty of good faith in the sense of a source of "independent" obligation? Is "reasonableness" the test of whether conduct crosses over into "bad faith"? Consider the illustration given in The Original Great Am. Chocolate Chip Cookie Co. v. River Valley Cookies, Ltd., 970 F.2d 273, 280 (7th Cir.1992):

> Suppose A hires B to paint his portrait to his satisfaction, and B paints it and A in fact is satisfied but says he is not in the hope of chivvying down the agreed-upon price because the portrait may be unsaleable to anyone else. [This] would be bad faith, not because any provision of the contract was unreasonable and had to be reformed but because a provision had been invoked dishonestly to achieve a purpose contrary to that for which the contract had been made.

And, in sizing up contract law's obligation of good faith, what is one to make of the standard view that the doctrine of unconscionability, like such common law doctrines as fraud and duress, is designed primarily to prevent overreaching at the contract-formation stage?

————

RESTATEMENT OF CONTRACTS, SECOND

Section 205. Duty of Good Faith and Fair Dealing

Every contract imposes upon each party a duty of good faith and fair dealing in its performance and its enforcement.

Comment:

a. Meanings of "Good Faith." . . . The phrase "good faith" is used in a variety of contexts, and its meaning varies somewhat with the context. [Here the phrase] emphasizes faithfulness to an agreed common purpose and consistency with the justified expectations of the other party; it excludes a variety of types of conduct characterized as involving "bad faith" because they violate community standards of decency, fairness, or reasonableness. The appropriate remedy for a breach of the duty of good faith varies with the circumstances. . . .

d. Good Faith Performance. . . . [T]he obligation [of good faith in performance] goes further than [subterfuges and evasions]: bad faith may be overt or may consist of inaction, and fair dealing may require more than honesty. . . . [T]he following types [of bad faith] are among those which have been recognized in judicial decisions: evasion of the spirit of the bargain, lack of diligence and slacking off, willful rendering of imperfect performance, abuse of a power to specify terms, and interference with or failure to cooperate in the other party's performance.

[When this section was before the annual meeting of the ALI in 1970, Robert Braucher, the Reporter, said: "I don't think you can find a case in the whole history of the common law in which a court says that good faith is not required in the performance of a contract or in enforcement of a contract. Now, the trouble with this section, of course, is that it's very general, very abstract. . . . Anyway, the principle is to be found in judicial opinions. I haven't invented it." 47 A.L.I.Proc.489–491 (1970).]

Market Street Associates Ltd. Partnership v. Frey

United States Court of Appeals, Seventh Circuit, 1991.
941 F.2d 588.

POSNER, CIRCUIT JUDGE. . . . In 1968, J.C. Penney Co., the retail chain, entered into a sale and leaseback arrangement with General Electric Pension Trust in order to finance Penney's growth. Under the arrangement Penney sold properties to the pension trust which the trust then leased back to Penney for a term of 25 years. Paragraph 34 of the lease entitles the lessee to "request Lessor [the pension trust] to finance the costs and expenses of construction of additional Improvements upon the Premises," provided the amount of the costs and expenses is at least $250,000. Upon receiving the request, the pension trust "agrees to give reasonable consideration to providing the financing of such additional Improvements and Lessor and Lessee shall negotiate in good faith concerning the construction of such Improvements and the financing by Lessor of such costs and expenses." Paragraph 34 goes on to provide that, should the negotiations fail, the lessee shall be entitled to repurchase the property at a price roughly equal to the price at which Penney sold it to the pension trust in the first place, plus 6 percent a year for each year since the original purchase. So if the average annual appreciation in the property exceeded 6 percent, a breakdown in negotiations over the financing of improvements would entitle Penney to buy back the property for less than its market value (assuming it had sold the property to the pension trust in the first place at its then market value).

One of these leases was for a shopping center in Milwaukee. In 1987 Penney assigned this lease to Market Street Associates, which the following year received an inquiry from a drugstore chain that wanted to open a store in the shopping center, provided (as is customary) that Market Street Associates built the store for it. Whether Market Street Associates was pessimistic about obtaining financing from the pension trust, still the lessor of the shopping center, or for other reasons, it initially sought financing for the project from other sources. But they were unwilling to lend the necessary funds without a mortgage on the shopping center, which Market Street Associates could not give because it was not the owner but only the lessee. It decided therefore to try to buy the property back from the pension trust. Market Street Associates' general partner, Orenstein, tried to call David Erb of the pension trust, who was responsible for the property in question. Erb did not return his calls, so Orenstein wrote him, expressing an interest in buying the property and asking him to "review your file on this matter and call me so that we can discuss it further." At first, Erb did not reply. Eventually Orenstein did reach Erb, who promised to review the file and get back to him. A few days later an associate of Erb called Orenstein and indicated an interest in selling the property for $3 million, which Orenstein considered much too high.

That was in June of 1988. On July 28, Market Street Associates wrote a letter to the pension trust formally requesting funding for $2 million in improvements to the shopping center. The letter made no reference to paragraph 34 of the lease; indeed, it did not mention the lease. The letter asked Erb to call Orenstein to discuss the matter. Erb, in what was becoming a habit of unresponsiveness, did not call. On August 16, Orenstein sent a second letter—certified mail, return receipt requested—again requesting financing and this time referring to the lease, though not expressly to paragraph 34. The heart of the letter is the following two sentences: "The purpose of this letter is to ask again that you advise us immediately if you are willing to provide the financing pursuant to the lease. If you are willing, we propose to enter into negotiation to amend the ground lease appropriately." The very next day, Market Street Associates received from Erb a letter, dated August 10, turning down the original request for financing on the ground that it did not "meet our current investment criteria": the pension trust was not interested in making loans for less than $7 million. On August 22, Orenstein replied to Erb by letter, noting that his letter of August 10 and Erb's letter of August 16 had evidently crossed in the mails, expressing disappointment at the turn-down, and stating that Market Street Associates would seek financing elsewhere. That was the last contact between the parties until September 27, when Orenstein sent Erb a letter stating that Market Street Associates was exercising the option granted it by paragraph 34 to purchase the property upon the terms specified in that paragraph in the event that negotiations over financing broke down.

The pension trust refused to sell, and this suit to compel specific performance followed. Apparently the price computed by the formula in paragraph 34 is only $1 million. The market value must be higher, or Market Street Associates wouldn't be trying to coerce conveyance at the paragraph 34 price; whether it is as high as $3 million, however, the record does not reveal.

The district judge granted summary judgment for the pension trust on two grounds that he believed to be separate although closely related. The first was that, by failing in its correspondence with the pension trust to mention paragraph 34 of the lease, Market Street Associates had prevented the negotiations over financing that are a condition precedent to the lessee's exercise of the purchase option from taking place. Second, this same failure violated the duty of good faith, which the common law of Wisconsin, as of other states, reads into every contract. In support of both grounds the judge emphasized a statement by Orenstein in his deposition that it had occurred to him that Erb mightn't know about paragraph 34, though this was unlikely (Orenstein testified) because Erb or someone else at the pension trust would probably check the file and discover the paragraph and realize that if the trust refused to negotiate over the request for financing, Market Street Associates, as Penney's assignee, would be entitled to walk off with the property for (perhaps) a song. The judge inferred that Market Street Associates didn't want financing from the pension trust—that it just wanted an opportunity to buy the property at a bargain price and hoped that the pension trust wouldn't realize the implications of turning down the request for financing. Market Street Associates should, the judge opined, have advised the pension trust that it was requesting financing pursuant to paragraph 34, so that the trust would understand the penalty for refusing to negotiate.

We begin our analysis by setting to one side two extreme contentions by the parties. The pension trust argues that the option to purchase created by paragraph 34 cannot be exercised until negotiations over financing break down; there were no negotiations; therefore they did not break down; therefore Market Street Associates had no right to exercise the option. This argument misreads the contract. Although the option to purchase is indeed contingent, paragraph 34 requires the pension trust, upon demand by the lessee for the financing of improvements worth at least $250,000, "to give reasonable consideration to providing the financing." The lessor who fails to give reasonable consideration and thereby prevents the negotiations from taking place is breaking the contract; and a contracting party cannot be allowed to use his own breach to gain an advantage by impairing the rights that the contract confers on the other party. Often, it is true, if one party breaks the contract, the other can walk away from it without liability, can in other words exercise self-help. But he is not required to follow that course. He can stand on his contract rights.

But what exactly are those rights in this case? The contract entitles the lessee to reasonable consideration of its request for financing, and only if negotiations over the request fail is the lessee entitled to purchase the property at the price computed in accordance with paragraph 34. It might seem therefore that the proper legal remedy for a lessor's breach that consists of failure to give the lessee's request for financing reasonable consideration would not be an order that the lessor sell the property to the lessee at the paragraph 34 price, but an order that the lessor bargain with the lessee in good faith. But we do not understand the pension trust to be arguing that Market Street Associates is seeking the wrong remedy. We understand it to be arguing that Market Street Associates has no possible remedy. That is an untenable position.

Market Street Associates argues, with equal unreason as it seems to us, that it could not have broken the contract because paragraph 34 contains no express requirement that in requesting financing the lessee mention the lease or paragraph 34 or otherwise alert the lessor to the consequences of his failing to give reasonable consideration to granting the request. There is indeed no such requirement (all that the contract requires is a demand). But no one says there is. The pension trust's argument, which the district judge bought, is that either as a matter of simple contract interpretation or under the compulsion of the doctrine of good faith, a provision requiring Market Street Associates to remind the pension trust of paragraph 34 should be read into the lease.

It seems to us that these are one ground rather than two. A court has to have a reason to interpolate a clause into a contract. The only reason that has been suggested here is that it is necessary to prevent Market Street Associates from reaping a reward for what the pension trust believes to have been Market Street's bad faith. So we must consider the meaning of the contract duty of "good faith." The Wisconsin cases are cryptic as to its meaning though emphatic about its existence, so we must cast our net wider. We do so mindful of Learned Hand's warning, that "such words as 'fraud,' 'good faith,' 'whim,' 'caprice,' 'arbitrary action,' and 'legal fraud' . . . obscure the issue." Thompson–Starrett Co. v. La Belle Iron Works, 17 F.2d 536, 541 (2d Cir.1927). Indeed they do. The particular confusion to which the vaguely moralistic overtones of "good faith" give rise is the belief that every contract establishes a fiduciary relationship. A fiduciary is required to treat his principal as if the principal were he, and therefore he may not take advantage of the principal's incapacity, ignorance, inexperience, or even naïveté. If Market Street Associates were the fiduciary of General Electric Pension Trust, then (we may assume) it could not take advantage of Mr. Erb's apparent ignorance of paragraph 34, however exasperating Erb's failure to return Orenstein's phone calls was and however negligent Erb or his associates were in failing to read the lease before turning down Orenstein's request for financing.

But it is unlikely that Wisconsin wishes, in the name of good faith, to make every contract signatory his brother's keeper, especially when the brother is the immense and sophisticated General Electric Pension Trust, whose lofty indifference to small ($\leq$ $7 million) transactions is the signifier of its grandeur. In fact the law contemplates that people frequently will take advantage of the ignorance of those with whom they contract, without thereby incurring liability. The duty of honesty, of good faith even expansively conceived, is not a duty of candor. You can make a binding contract to purchase something you know your seller undervalues. Laidlaw v. Organ, 15 U.S. (2 Wheat.) 178, 181 n. 2, 4 L.Ed. 214 (1817). That of course is a question about formation, not performance, and the particular duty of good faith under examination here relates to the latter rather than to the former. But even after you have signed a contract, you are not obliged to become an altruist toward the other party and relax the terms if he gets into trouble in performing his side of the bargain. Otherwise mere difficulty of performance would excuse a contracting party—which it does not.

But it is one thing to say that you can exploit your superior knowledge of the market—for if you cannot, you will not be able to recoup the investment you made in obtaining that knowledge—or that you are not required to spend money bailing out a contract partner who has gotten into trouble. It is another thing to say that you can take deliberate advantage of an oversight by your contract partner concerning his rights under the contract. Such taking advantage is not the exploitation of superior knowledge or the avoidance of unbargained-for expense; it is sharp dealing. Like theft, it has no social product, and also like theft it induces costly defensive expenditures, in the form of overelaborate disclaimers or investigations into the trustworthiness of a prospective contract partner, just as the prospect of theft induces expenditures on locks.

The form of sharp dealing that we are discussing might or might not be actionable as fraud or deceit. That is a question of tort law and there the rule is that if the information is readily available to both parties the failure of one to disclose it to the other, even if done in the knowledge that the other party is acting on mistaken premises, is not actionable. [Citing cases, including Guyer v. Cities Service Oil Co., 440 F.Supp. 630 (E.D.Wis.1977).] All of these cases, however, with the debatable exception of *Guyer*, involve failure to disclose something in the negotiations leading up to the signing of the contract, rather than failure to disclose after the contract has been signed. (*Guyer* involved failure to disclose during the negotiations leading up to a renewal of the contract.) The distinction is important, as we explained in Maksym v. Loesch, 937 F.2d 1237, 1242 (7th Cir.1991). Before the contract is signed, the parties confront each other with a natural wariness. Neither expects the other to be particularly forthcoming, and therefore there is no deception when one is not. Afterwards the situation is different. The parties are now in a cooperative relationship the costs of which will be considerably reduced by a measure of trust. So each lowers his guard a bit, and now silence is more apt to be deceptive.

Moreover, this is a contract case rather than a tort case, and conduct that might not rise to the level of fraud may nonetheless violate the duty of good faith in dealing with one's contractual partners and thereby give rise to a remedy under contract law. This duty is, as it were, halfway between a fiduciary duty (the duty of *utmost* good faith) and the duty merely to refrain from active fraud. Despite its moralistic overtones it is no more the injection of moral principles into contract law than the fiduciary concept itself is. It would be quixotic as well as presumptuous for judges to undertake through contract law to raise the ethical standards of the nation's business people. The concept of the duty of good faith like the concept of fiduciary duty is a stab at approximating the terms the parties would have negotiated had they foreseen the circumstances that have given rise to their dispute. The parties want to minimize the costs of performance. To the extent that a doctrine of good faith designed to do this by reducing defensive expenditures is a reasonable measure to this end, interpolating it into the contract advances the parties' joint goal.

It is true that an essential function of contracts is to allocate risk, and would be defeated if courts treated the materializing of a bargained-over, allocated risk as a misfortune the burden of which is required to be shared between the parties (as it might be within a family, for example) rather than borne entirely by the party to whom the risk had been allocated by mutual agreement. But contracts do not just allocate risk. They also (or some of them) set in motion a cooperative enterprise, which may to some extent place one party at the other's mercy. "The parties to a contract are embarked on a cooperative venture, and a minimum of cooperativeness in the event unforeseen problems arise at the performance stage is required even if not an explicit duty of the contract." AMPAT/Midwest, Inc. v. Illinois Tool Works Inc., 896 F.2d 1035, 1041 (7th Cir.1990). The office of the doctrine of good faith is to forbid the kinds of opportunistic behavior that a mutually dependent, cooperative relationship might enable in the absence of rule. . . . The contractual duty of good faith is thus not some newfangled bit of welfare-state paternalism or the sediment of an altruistic strain in contract law, and we are therefore not surprised to find the essentials of the modern doctrine well established in nineteenth century cases, a few examples being Bush v. Marshall, 47 U.S. (6 How.) 284, 291, 12 L.Ed. 440 (1848); Chicago, Rock Island & Pac. R.R. v. Howard, 74 U.S. (7 Wall.) 392, 413, 19 L.Ed. 117 (1868); Marsh v. Masterson, 101 N.Y. 401, 410–11, 5 N.E. 59, 63 (1886), and Uhrig v. Williamsburg City Fire Ins. Co., 101 N.Y. 362, 4 N.E. 745 (1886). . . .

We could of course do without the term "good faith," and maybe even without the doctrine. We could, as just suggested, speak instead of implied conditions necessitated by the unpredictability of the future at the time the contract was made. Suppose a party has promised work to the promisee's "satisfaction." As Learned Hand explained, "he may refuse to look at the work, or to exercise any real judgment on it, in which case he has prevented performance and excused the condition." Thompson–Starrett Co. v. La Belle Iron Works, supra, 17 F.2d at 541. That is, it was an implicit condition that the promisee examine the work to the extent necessary to determine whether it was satisfactory; otherwise the performing party would have been placing himself at the complete mercy of the promisee. The parties didn't write this condition into the contract either because they thought such behavior unlikely or failed to foresee it altogether. In just the same way—to switch to another familiar example of the operation of the duty of good faith—parties to a requirements contract surely do not intend that if the price of the product covered by the contract rises, the buyer shall be free to increase his "requirements" so that he can take advantage of the rise in the market price over the contract price to resell the product on the open market at a guaranteed profit. If they fail to insert an express condition to this effect, the court will read it in, confident that the parties would have inserted the condition if they had known what the future held. Of similar character is the implied condition that an exclusive dealer will use his best efforts to promote the supplier's goods, since otherwise the exclusive feature of the dealership contract would place the supplier at the dealer's mercy. Wood v. Duff–Gordon, 222 N.Y. 88, 118 N.E. 214 (1917) (Cardozo, J.).

But whether we say that a contract shall be deemed to contain such implied conditions as are necessary to make sense of the contract, or that a contract obligates the parties to cooperate in its performance in "good faith" to the extent necessary to carry out the purposes of the contract, comes to much the same thing. They are different ways of formulating the overriding purpose of contract law, which is to give the parties what they would have stipulated for expressly if at the time of making the contract they had had complete knowledge of the future and the costs of negotiating and adding provisions to the contract had been zero.

. . . The dispositive question in the present case is simply whether Market Street Associates tried to trick the pension trust and succeeded in doing so. If it did, this would be the type of opportunistic behavior in an ongoing contractual relationship that would violate the duty of good faith performance however the duty is formulated. There is much common sense in Judge Reynolds' conclusion that Market Street Associates did just that. The situation as he saw it was as follows. Market Street Associates didn't want financing from the pension trust (initially it had looked elsewhere, remember), and when it learned it couldn't get the financing without owning the property, it decided to try to buy the property. But the pension trust set a stiff price, so Orenstein decided to trick the pension trust into selling at the bargain price fixed in paragraph 34 by requesting financing and hoping that the pension trust would turn the request down without noticing the paragraph. His preliminary dealings with the pension trust made this hope a realistic one by revealing a sluggish and hidebound bureaucracy unlikely to have retained in its brontosaurus's memory, or to be able at short notice to retrieve, the details of a small lease made twenty years earlier. So by requesting financing without mentioning the lease Market Street Associates might well precipitate a refusal before the pension trust woke up to paragraph 34. It is true that Orenstein's second letter requested financing "pursuant to the lease." But when the next day he received a reply to his first letter indicating that the pension trust was indeed oblivious to paragraph 34, his response was to send a lulling letter designed to convince the pension trust that the matter was closed and could be forgotten. The stage was set for his thunderbolt: the notification the next month that Market Street Associates was taking up the option in paragraph 34. Only then did the pension trust look up the lease and discover that it had been had.

The only problem with this recital is that it construes the facts as favorably to the pension trust as the record will permit, and that of course is not the right standard for summary judgment. The facts must be construed as favorably to the nonmoving party, to Market Street Associates, as the record permits. . . . When that is done, a different picture emerges. On Market Street Associates' construal of the record, $3 million was a grossly excessive price for the property, and while $1 million might be a bargain it would not confer so great a windfall as to warrant an inference that if the pension trust had known about paragraph 34 it never would have turned down Market Street Associates' request for financing cold. And in fact the pension trust may have known about paragraph 34, and either it didn't care or it believed that unless the request mentioned that paragraph the pension trust would incur no liability by turning it down. Market Street Associates may have assumed and have been entitled to assume that in reviewing a request for financing from one of its lessees the pension trust would take the time to read the lease to see whether it bore on the request. Market Street Associates did not desire financing from the pension trust initially—that is undeniable—yet when it discovered that it could not get financing elsewhere unless it had the title to the property it may have realized that it would have to negotiate with the pension trust over financing before it could hope to buy the property at the price specified in the lease.

On this interpretation of the facts there was no bad faith on the part of Market Street Associates. It acted honestly, reasonably, without ulterior motive, in the face of circumstances as they actually and reasonably appeared to it. The fault was the pension trust's incredible inattention, which misled Market Street Associates into believing that the pension trust had no interest in financing the improvements regardless of the purchase option. We do not usually excuse contracting parties from failing to read and understand the contents of their contract; and in the end what this case comes down to—or so at least it can be strongly argued—is that an immensely sophisticated enterprise simply failed to read the contract. On the other hand, such enterprises make mistakes just like the rest of us, and deliberately to take advantage of your contracting partner's mistake during the performance stage (for we are not talking about taking advantage of superior knowledge at the formation stage) is a breach of good faith. To be able to correct your contract partner's mistake at zero cost to yourself, and decide not to do so, is a species of opportunistic behavior that the parties would have expressly forbidden in the contract had they foreseen it. The immensely long term of the lease amplified the possibility of errors but did not license either party to take advantage of them.

The district judge jumped the gun in choosing between these alternative characterizations. The essential issue bearing on Market Street Associates' good faith was Orenstein's state of mind, a type of inquiry that ordinarily cannot be concluded on summary judgment, and could not be here. If Orenstein believed that Erb knew or would surely find out about paragraph 34, it was not dishonest or opportunistic to fail to flag that paragraph, or even to fail to mention the lease, in his correspondence and (rare) conversations with Erb, especially given the uninterest in dealing with Market Street Associates that Erb fairly radiated. To decide what Orenstein believed, a trial is necessary. As for the pension trust's intimation that a bench trial (for remember that this is an equity case, since the only relief sought by the plaintiff is specific performance) will add no illumination beyond what the summary judgment proceeding has done, this overlooks the fact that at trial the judge will for the first time have a chance to see the witnesses whose depositions he has read, to hear their testimony elaborated, and to assess their believability.

The judgment is reversed and the case is remanded for further proceedings consistent with this opinion.

NOTE

Professor Todd Rakoff offers the following critique of Judge Posner's opinion (Good Faith in Contract Performance: Market Street Associates Ltd. Partnership v. Frey, 120 Harv. L. Rev. 1187 (2007)):

> *Market Street Associates* offers what seems to me an excellent examination of the doctrine of good faith. But as to its treatment of the work still needed to reach a decision, I am more doubtful. Judge Posner cited a lot of cases, both from his own circuit and from common law "greats" like Cardozo, Hand, and Friendly. But he did not rely on any prior opinion as a precedent to be directly applied to the facts before him. Nor did he use the cases to build an analytical series covering the remaining middle ground. Rather, he offered us a general approach (which the cases were taken to illustrate) and a specific outcome. . . .
>
> The connection between this general method and [his] specific conclusion seems unclear. Judge Posner's own explanation of why "tried to trick" was the "dispositive" standard was that "this would be the type of opportunistic behavior in an ongoing contractual relationship that would violate the duty of good faith performance however the duty is formulated." But the trial judge did not deny that intentional trickery would be bad faith; what he claimed was that the duty went further, requiring the lessee (regardless of motive) to remind the lessor of paragraph 34 as a precondition to later claiming rights under it. To justify the Seventh Circuit's reversal, it is not enough to allow that the duty of good faith goes as far as Judge Posner specified; one has to show that it goes no further. More is needed.
>
> The only textual support for [Posner's narrow formulation of the duty of good faith] is the statement he made at one point that "[i]t would be quixotic as well as presumptuous for judges to undertake through contract law to raise the ethical standards of the nation's business people." Admittedly, that statement is ambiguous. It might be read simply to say that judges should try to give the parties what they (and not the judges) would have wanted. But it might also be read as evincing a fear that if judges (perhaps especially trial judges) are not restrained, they will not be very good at creating implied terms; even if appellate courts tell them to aim only to give the parties what they would have wanted, judges' natural tendency will be to state a higher standard. Or, to put the matter more particularly, perhaps Judge Posner favored the reading of the obligation of good faith nearest to intentional tort—the outlaw-tricky-behavior reading—because he thought it would yield the best results overall when implemented by the courts.
>
> The point is not simply that Judge Posner may have generalized, that he might have been concerned with the proper scope of good faith in the run of cases and not just in the particular instance he faced. The claim that business people do not expect from each other actions that facilitate each other's required performances, and only expect their partners not to be "tricky," is not always wrong,

but in the view recognized by many prior cases it is wrong often enough that we ought not ground a doctrine on it.

Rather, the point is that Judge Posner's statement might rest on the proposition that policing really smelly behavior is the most that judges can reliably and usefully do—on an assessment, that is, of judicial capabilities rather than of actual commercial practice. That claim, in turn, might come from a belief that, all things considered, trial judges are usually better at understanding interpersonal human relations than they are at decoding the workings of commercial relationships, so that their creation of implied terms in the latter situations will be unreliable. Or it might come from a belief that it is better to set the default rule of good faith at a minimal level in order to put pressure on commercial parties to specify their expectations up front, rather than to have them rely on the judges after the fact, because even if the judges are competent, the parties are more competent. Or it might come from both of these beliefs. These claims would support the result in *Market Street Associates*, although whether Judge Posner, or the panel, thought about them must remain a matter of speculation. . . .

————

COMMENT: REGULATION OF UNFAIR TERMS

Development by the courts of more potent tools for dealing with oppression, accomplished typically through the use of printed-form contracts, parallels the efforts of legislatures and, to some extent, of private associations, to reach the same goal. Several of the techniques developed merit brief mention.

(1) **Compulsory contracts.** The capacity for coercion by a supplier of essential goods and services is obviously increased if the supplier has available the option not to deal at all. That option was surely implicit in general common law principles of contract. In a number of areas, however, modern statutes eliminate or greatly restrict it. Utility companies—deemed "quasi-public" in character, like common carriers—are required to provide service on a nondiscriminatory basis to all who request it. Insurance companies writing types of insurance that consumers are legally required to carry (for example, automobile liability coverage) may be required to underwrite any standard risk and to share with other insurers the underwriting of high-risk applicants. Modern civil rights legislation, applicable to enterprises ranging from restaurants to landlords, has also expanded the scope of compulsory contracts.

Of course, compulsion of the more powerful party to deal is of limited benefit to the weaker party if the substantive terms of the required contract may be determined in the sole discretion of the former. This fact has led in a number of instances to substantial legal control over the terms of the contracts themselves. To cite one example, the Restatement (Second) of Torts, § 763 declares that utilities are under a duty to contract "on proper terms" with those who seek service. This flexible standard of fair terms, derived from decisional law, is buttressed by modern statutory schemes of regulation. The utility company is assured a reasonable rate of return on its investment, but a public regulatory commission must approve the rates the utility charges to realize that return. Even insurance companies that are under no legal duty to make contracts are commonly required to use, in policies they do issue, provisions set wholly or in substantial part by statute or administrative regulation. We shall see such terms in Chapter 6.

(2) **Prohibited terms.** Despite the basic theme of "freedom of contract," we have encountered numerous judicially-developed restraints on what the parties may agree to, or, at the least, on what courts will enforce. In some instances, proscriptions will have been developed with sufficient certainty to take on the appearance of firm legal rules—for example, the distinction between valid liquidated damages clauses and unenforceable penalties. In others, the denial of legal effect to a clause may be grounded on a judicially-perceived "public policy." The cases cover a vast range of consensual activity, from the gambling question in *Cobaugh* (p. 326) to the exculpation question in *Richards* (p. 680) to surrogacy in *Baby M* (p. 605). In the end, this ill-defined and thus highly pliable defense, when successful, amounts to a judicial determination that private choice should be overridden by social ends. Moreover, contract terms that are unenforceable because "against public policy" merge imperceptibly into terms deemed "illegal." Illegality is a complex concept, applied case-by-case and often with scant guidance as to its scope. We cannot explore it fully here, but must rest on a caution that illegality is a basis for invalidating entire contracts or only selected provisions, and that the standard may be created by the legislature, the courts, or possibly administrative authorities. Furthermore, illegality can have a variety of legal effects, particularly on the question of relief in restitution.

(3) **Requirements of form.** Even if a contract provision is not prohibited or denied legal effect, it may have such severe and perhaps unanticipated consequences for one of the parties that special care is warranted to assure that the term is brought to the attention of the party who would be disadvantaged. We saw in Chapter 3 that at least some of the doctrines on mutual assent impose requirements of form, by denying legal effect to clauses or terms that would escape the notice of normally-attentive readers. Such requirements may achieve much greater specificity and inflexibility in statutes. For example, UCC 2–316 requires that if the implied warranty of merchantability is to be excluded or modified, the language must mention "merchantability" and, if written, must be "conspicuous."

(4) **Balancing the standard form.** One of the most attractive techniques for preserving the advantages of printed forms, while avoiding their potential for misleading and oppressing, involves private, not official, action. Parties regularly operating in a particular trade or business, perhaps organized in a trade association, may devise standard forms that fairly balance the interests of all the parties. A good example from commercial history is the Worth Street Rules, which were developed by a number of associations representing all interests in the cotton industry. Another is the standard agreement between an owner and a general contractor developed by the American Institute of Architects. The mere fact that a trade association has developed the form does not, of course, assure its fairness. A standard listing agreement prepared by a board of realtors may serve only to aggregate tendencies toward over-reaching. The best assurance of fairness and balance arises when the process that gave rise to the form itself is itself unbiased. This can happen when there is negotiation or bargaining between the groups whose transactions will be structured by the form, when an impartial third group whose interests are not centrally involved in the

transaction prepares the form, or when the parties to the negotiations are equally likely to be on either side of the transaction.

———

CHAPTER 6

THE MATURING AND BREACH OF CONTRACT DUTIES

SECTION 1. THE INTERDEPENDENCE OF PROMISES

Nichols v. Raynbred

Court of King's Bench, 1615.
Hobart, 88.

Nichols brought an assumpsit against Raynbred, declaring that in consideration that Nichols promised to deliver the defendant to his own use a cow, the defendant promised to deliver him 50 shillings: adjudged for the plaintiff in both courts, that the plaintiff need not aver the delivery of the cow, because it is promise for promise. Note here the promises must be at one instant, for else they will both be nuda pacta.

COMMENT: THE DEPENDENCY OF PROMISES

Nichols v. Raynbred illustrates early attitudes toward what is now described as "the dependency of mutual promises." Is this not a strange way to look at an agreement consisting of promises—by their terms, unqualified and unconditional—to exchange goods or services for a stated price? Again, some historical perspective is needed.

The problem of "dependency" had not been particularly troublesome before the time of this case. For those informal promises enforced through the action of debt, the requirement of *quid pro quo* meant that the performance for which the money was promised must have been already rendered—i.e., the plaintiff's half of the exchange would have had to be completed. When special assumpsit became available in the sixteenth century, the whole emphasis was on what we now call the unilateral contract, where the defendant-promisor who had not performed was again protected through having secured the other party's performance. In other words, the experience of the early common law (say, before 1600) was very heavily focused on the unilateral type of obligation, while the assumption here is that "dependency" is almost entirely a problem of bilateral contracts.

The issue of "dependency" could arise, of course, in connection with agreements under seal. It was entirely possible for two persons, in the same sealed instrument, to make "covenants" to each other, looking forward ultimately to an exchange of performances. The question then would be whether one covenantee could sue the other without having given or tendered performance. The answer provided by Chief Justice Fineux in a Year Book case in 1500 was this:

[handwritten margin note: Q. Who must peform first?]

721

If one covenant with me to serve me for a year, and I covenant with him to give him £20, if I do not say "for the same cause," he shall have an action for the £20, although he never serves me; otherwise, if I say he shall have £20 "for the same cause." So if I covenant with a man that I will marry his daughter, and he covenants with me to make an estate to me and his daughter, and to the heirs of our two bodies begotten; though I afterwards marry another woman, or his daughter marry another man; yet I shall have an action of covenant against him, to compel him to make this estate; but if the covenant be that he will make the estate to us "for the same cause," then he shall not make the estate until we are married.

The report concludes that "such was the opinion of the court," and Rede, J., said "it is so without doubt." Y.B. 15 Henry VII, fol. 10b, pl. 17 (1500). You will note that there is in this passage a notion of "dependency" in rudimentary form; the insertion of the small phrase "for the same cause" would suffice to tie the two performances together in each of the cases supposed. This is probably as far as one could expect construction to be carried by common lawyers at this stage.

Nichols v. Raynbred indicates that literalism was transferred from sealed instruments to informal promises enforced through assumpsit, during the early period when assumpsit was expanding. Indeed, there is much evidence to suggest that the same attitudes persisted and were even extended during the next 150 years. An illustration is the King's Bench decision in 1669, Pordage v. Cole, 1 Wms. Saunders 319, which became notorious for various reasons. In this case, a vendor of land sued the vendee at law, relying on an instrument under seal in which the vendee promised £775 for the lands in question, to be paid before a particular day which had passed by the time of the action. The vendor did not expressly promise to convey the lands; there was merely the statement that the vendee promised the vendor £775 "for all his lands," but with this phrase it would seem that even the requirements of Fineux, J., back in 1500, had been satisfied. The defendant demurred to the vendor's declaration, relying mainly on the ground that "the plaintiff in his declaration has not averred that he had conveyed the lands, or at least tendered a conveyance of them; for the defendant has no remedy to obtain the lands, and therefore the plaintiff ought to have conveyed them, or tendered a conveyance of them, before he brought his action for the money." But the demurrer was overruled. The court stated that the language of the instrument "amounted" to a promise by the vendor to convey the land and the defendant therefore had a remedy of covenant for damages if the vendor did not convey. The only qualification was the admission that "it might be otherwise" if no promise by the vendor to convey could be extracted from the language of the instrument.

There were in this period some expressions of dissatisfaction with results like that of Pordage v. Cole. The best known complaint is that of Willes, C.J., (reported in Willes, 496) who, in 1744, referred to his dislike of "those cases, though they are too many to be now overruled, where it is determined that the breach of one covenant, though plainly relative to the other, cannot be pleaded in bar to an action brought for the breach of the other, but the other party must be left to bring his action for the breach of the other; as where there are two covenants in a deed, the one for repairing and the other for finding timber for the reparations; this notion plainly tending to make two actions instead of one, and to a circuity of action and multiplying actions, both which the law so much abhors." Willes suggested that the defendant should at least be permitted to plead the plaintiff's failure to render the performance promised, though he (Willes) would not impose on the plaintiff the burden of pleading and proving performance affirmatively. Willes concluded, however, that "this has been so often determined otherwise, that it is too late now to alter the law in this respect." He evidently did not foresee the towering Scot, Lord Mansfield.

In the procedures criticized by Willes, is the only objection circuity and multiplication of actions? Doesn't the central problem look familiar, though we now see it through a different telescope? Recall, again, that the typical contract has a performing party and a paying party, and that, because each acts separately, the party who is required by the contract to perform first is in need of protection against a failure by the other.

Before leaving the pre-Mansfield history, we should note that Pordage v. Cole achieved immortality by a strange kind of transmigration. After Mansfield had done his work and retired from the bench, Serjeant Williams, a prominent lawyer and law reporter, sought to summarize the results of Mansfield's innovations through a statement of "rules" appended as a note to Pordage v. Cole. The publication did not occur until 1791, long after the whole structure of common law doctrine on which Pordage v. Cole (decided in 1669) rested had been undermined. The result was a confusing picture for later generations. Serjeant Williams' "rules" have been much quoted and we will see something of them. But first a look at Lord Mansfield and the decision which set in motion the modern machinery of the bilateral contract.

Kingston v. Preston

Court of King's Bench, 1773.
2 Doug. 689.

This was an action of debt, for nonperformance of covenants contained in certain articles of agreement between the plaintiff and the defendant. The declaration stated;—That, by articles made the 24th of March 1770, the plaintiff, for the considerations thereinafter mentioned, covenanted, with the defendant, to serve him for one year and a quarter next ensuing, as a covenant-servant, in his trade of a silk-mercer at £200 a year, and in consideration of the premises, the defendant covenanted, that at the end of the year and a quarter, he would give up his business of a mercer to the plaintiff, and a nephew of the defendant, or some other person to be nominated by the defendant, and give up to them his stock in trade, at a fair valuation; and that, between the young traders, deeds of partnership should be executed for 14 years, and, from and immediately after the execution of the said deeds, the defendant would permit the said young traders to carry on the said business in the defendant's house.—Then the declaration stated a covenant by the plaintiff, that he would accept the business and stock in trade, at a fair valuation, with the defendant's nephew, or such other person, etc. and execute such deeds of partnership, and, further, that the plaintiff should, and would, at, and before the sealing and delivery of the deeds, cause and procure good and sufficient security to be given to the defendant, to be approved of by the defendant, for the payment of £250 monthly, to the defendant, in lieu of a moiety of the monthly produce of the stock in trade, until the value of the stock should be reduced to £4000.—

Then the plaintiff averred, that he had performed, and been ready to perform, his covenants, and assigned for breach, on the part of the defendant, that he had refused to surrender and give up his business, at the end of the said year and a quarter.—The defendant pleaded, 1. That the plaintiff did not offer sufficient security; and, 2. That he did not give sufficient security for the payment of the £250 etc.—And the plaintiff demurred generally to both pleas.—On the part of the plaintiff, the case was argued by Mr. Buller, who contended, that the covenants were mutual and independent, and, therefore, a plea of the breach of one of the covenants to be performed by the plaintiff was no bar to an action for a breach by the defendant of one of which he had bound himself to perform, but that the defendant might have his remedy for the breach by the plaintiff, in a separate action. On the other side, Mr. Grose insisted, that the covenants were dependent in their nature, and, therefore, performance must be alleged: The security to be given for the money, was manifestly the chief object of the transaction, and it would be highly unreasonable to construe the agreement, so as to oblige the defendant to give up a beneficial business, and valuable stock in trade, and trust to the plaintiff's personal security, (who might, and indeed was admitted to be worth nothing,) for the performance of his part.—In delivering the judgment of the court, Lord Mansfield expressed himself to the following effect:—There are three kinds of covenants: 1. Such as are called mutual and independent, where either party may recover damages from the other, for the injury he may have received by a breach of the covenants in his favour, and where it is no excuse for the defendant, to allege a breach of the covenants on the part of the plaintiff. 2. There are covenants which are conditions and dependent, in which the performance of one depends on the prior performance of another, and, therefore, till this prior condition is performed, the other party is not liable to an action on his covenant. 3. There is also a third sort of covenants, which are mutual conditions to be performed at the same time; and, in these, if one party was ready, and offered, to perform his part, and the other neglected, or refused to perform his, he who was ready, and offered, has fulfilled his engagement, and may maintain an action for the default of the other; though it is not certain that either is obliged to do the first act.—His Lordship then proceeded to say, that the dependence or independence of covenants was to be collected from the evident sense and meaning of the parties, and, that, however transposed they might be in the deed, their precedency must depend on the order of time in which the intent of the transaction requires their performance. That, in the case before the court, it would be the greatest injustice if the plaintiff should prevail: The essence of the agreement was, that the defendant should not trust to the personal security of the plaintiff, but, before he delivered up his stock and business, should have good security for the payment of the money. The giving such security, therefore, must necessarily be a condition precedent.—Judgment was accordingly given for the defendant, because the part to be performed by the plaintiff was clearly a condition precedent.

National Portrait Gallery, London.

WILLIAM MURRAY, EARL OF MANSFIELD
1705-1793

———

5 S. Williston, Contracts
§ 619 (3d ed.1961)

"Since an express condition, like a condition implied in fact, depends for its validity on the manifested intention of the parties, it has the same sanctity as the promise itself. Though the court may regret the harshness of such a condition, as it may regret the harshness of a promise, it must, nevertheless, generally enforce the will of the parties unless to do so would violate public policy. Where, however, the law itself has ['constructively'] imposed the condition, in absence of or irrespective of the manifested intention of the parties, it can deal with its creation as it pleases, shaping the boundaries of the constructive condition in such a way as to do justice and avoid hardship."

RESTATEMENT OF CONTRACTS, SECOND

Section 234. Order of Performances

(1) Where all or part of the performances to be exchanged under an exchange of promises can be rendered simultaneously, they are to that extent due simultaneously, unless the language or the circumstances indicate the contrary.

Comment: . . .

b. When simultaneous performance possible under agreement. . . . Cases in which simultaneous performance is possible under the terms of the contract can be grouped into five categories: (1) where the same time is fixed for the performance of each party; (2) where a time is fixed for the performance of one of the parties and no time is fixed for the other; (3) where no time is fixed for the performance of either party; (4) where the same period is fixed within which each party is to perform; (5) where different periods are fixed within which each party is to perform. The requirement of simultaneous performance applies to the first four categories. . . .

Section 238. Effect on Other Party's Duties of a Failure to Offer Performance

Where all or part of the performances to be exchanged under an exchange of promises are due simultaneously, it is a condition of each party's duties to render such performance that the other party either render or, with manifested present ability to do so, offer performance of his part of the simultaneous exchange.

Price v. Van Lint

Supreme Court of New Mexico, 1941.
46 N.M. 58, 120 P.2d 611.

SADLER, J. . . . [T]he district court had before it for construction the following agreement in writing, signed by the plaintiff and by the defendant, for claimed breach of which the former sought damages, to-wit:

"Cimarron, N.M. 12–23–1939

"This agreement, entered into by V.J. Van Lint party of the first part and C.S. Price, party of the second part,

"First party agrees to deposit the sum of fifteen hundred on or before the first day of February, A.D. 1940 for which security said party of the second part agrees to give mortgage-deed and insurance for the full sum of fifteen hundred dollards and agrres to use the above named amount for erecting a building on the land purchased from the Maxwell Land Grant Co. for which a warranty-deed will be executed and delivered. Party of the second part agrees to keep all taxes and insurance paid up to date on the above described property.

"Party of the second part   Party of the first part

"(Sgd.) C.S. Price   (Sgd.) V.J. Van Lint."

    This inartificially drawn contract resulted from the joint efforts of the parties thereto, the plaintiff having contributed its phraseology in seemingly extemporaneous dictation to the defendant who furnished the mechanical skill of reducing it to form on the typewriter.

    The parties [both] resided at Cimarron. . . . The defendant was local agent for Maxwell Land Grant Co. . . . but without authority to execute a deed on its behalf. The plaintiff, desiring to purchase a small tract of land near Cimarron and to construct a building thereon in which to conduct a business, negotiated with the defendant touching the matter. The contract in question resulted. [It] reflects the plaintiff's plan for financing both the purchase of the site and the construction of the building.

    Anticipatory of the loan mentioned in the writing, the defendant advanced for the plaintiff's account the sum of $134, the agreed sale price of the tract being purchased as a site, repayable from the proceeds of the loan. This sum, along with a deed prepared by the defendant, in due course was dispatched to Amsterdam in the [Netherlands]. Likewise and in due course, said deed was returned from Amsterdam, apparently the residence of officials of the grantor with authority to act in this connection, and duly delivered to the plaintiff in the early part of March, 1940. Both parties were aware of the necessity of these steps being taken to consummate the purchase and that a considerable time would necessarily elapse before the deed could be delivered to the plaintiff.

    In the meantime, the plaintiff seemed anxious to proceed with the construction of the proposed building. The defendant had left Cimarron in late December for a sojourn of more than two months at Corpus Christi, Texas. Apparently, meeting with disappointment in realizing funds from which to make the agreed loan, the defendant sought release from the contract. . . . This is shown by the correspondence passing between the parties. Indeed, the tenor of defendant's letters to him was such that the plaintiff very well might have elected to claim an anticipatory breach of the agreement. But he did not do so. On the contrary, he refused to release defendant from the contract and on January 16, 1940, caused his attorney to make telegraphic demand on defendant for performance, declaring: "Your contract has not been canceled and Price (the plaintiff) will hold you liable to any actual damages which may result to him by your failure to comply with agreement. . . . If money agreed to be loaned not here by February first you will be held liable for actual damages. . . ."

    The trial court made the following additional findings: . . . "That the plaintiff has never tendered to the defendant any mortgage deed; that the defendant has never offered to or been willing to advance to the plaintiff the balance of the agreed loan prior to the receiving from the plaintiff of a valid mortgage deed on said premises; that the plaintiff has never repaid to the defendant the sum of $134.00 advanced to him by the defendant or any part thereof or any interest thereon." . . .

    The court [also] found that the loan was to be for a period of two years; that the loan was to bear interest at the rate of 10% per annum; that the mortgage was to cover the land being purchased by the plaintiff from Maxwell Land Grant Co.; and that the "deposit" was to be made at First National Bank in Raton.

It further found that prior to his departure for Corpus Christi, the defendant informed Lorenzo Rosso[,] . . . doing business as Cimarron Mercantile Co., and R.E. Adams of Springer, New Mexico, doing business as R.E. Adams Lumber Co., of his agreement to make a loan of $1,500 to the plaintiff; that on January 9, 1940, the defendant [wrote] to said Lorenzo Rosso . . . stating that the contemplated loan to plaintiff was not going through due to unforeseen difficulties met with by the defendant; that a similar notice was given by defendant to R.E. Adams Lumber Co.; and "that some time thereafter both Cimarron Mercantile Co. and R.E. Adams Lumber Co. refused to extend any substantial further credit to the plaintiff."

It was also found that because of defendant's refusal to advance the amount of the loan to plaintiff on or before February 1, 1940, the plaintiff was compelled to suspend construction work on his building; that but for said refusal, the building would have been ready for use and occupancy by February 10, 1940, instead of April 27, 1940.

The trial court concluded: "That the written agreement . . . required the defendant to deposit the balance of the agreed loan on or before February 1, 1940, and that the amount so deposited should be immediately paid to the plaintiff, whether or not the plaintiff should at that time have received a deed to the real estate, and whether or not the plaintiff should at that time be the legal owner or the record owner of said real estate, and whether or not the plaintiff at that immediate time should be able to give a valid mortgage, and whether or not the real estate at that time should be free from liens and encumbrances; that the defendant, in refusing to deposit said balance for the plaintiff's immediate use on or before February 1, breached said agreement, and the defendant is liable to the plaintiff for the damages resulting therefrom."

Having thus concluded, the court rendered judgment in plaintiff's favor for $543.55 being the aggregate amount of plaintiff's damage[,] . . . after deducting therefrom $134 advanced by defendant to cover the purchase price of the real estate with accrued interest thereon.

. . . The [trial] court held in substance [that] the written agreement, interpreted in the light of the unchallenged findings, imposed upon the defendant the obligation to deposit to the plaintiff's credit in the bank named the amount of the loan, notwithstanding the fact that because of the delayed delivery of the deed, the plaintiff could not then deliver to the defendant the mortgage which was to furnish the security for the loan.

The correctness of the trial court's ruling on this question . . . involves the determination whether the plaintiff's promise to give a mortgage to secure the promised loan and the defendant's promise to make the loan are dependent or independent covenants of the contract. If the former, then the plaintiff's failure to allege performance denies him the right of recovery. If the latter, the defendant was under obligation to perform his covenant and look to his remedy for any breach of performance on the plaintiff's part. . . .

The rule of decision is not to construe promises as independent unless the nature of the contract or the surrounding circumstances compel a contrary inference. In other words, interpretation favors the conclusion of an agreed exchange of performance as the true intent of the parties unless such a construction does violence to the language employed in the light of known facts and circumstances. . . .

In Glaser v. Dannelley [23 N.M. 593, 170 P. 63], our holding [was]: "Where a contract contains mutual promises to pay money or perform some other act, and the time for performance for one party is to, or may, arrive before the time for performance by the other, the latter promise is an independent obligation, and nonperformance thereof merely raises a cause of action in the promisee, and does not defeat the right of the party making it to recover for a breach of the promise made to him."

This holding is but an application of the first portion of Rule 1 of the well known Sergeant Williams' Rules, annexed as a note to Pordage v. Cole, 1 Wm.Saund. 319 "1" . . . While certain of Sergeant Williams' rules are the subject of critical comment[,] . . . we find nothing [critical] of that portion of Rule 1 approved by us in Glaser v. Dannelley. We think it is decisive of the question presented. When we apply it to [this] situation . . . we are compelled to hold with the trial court that the mutual covenants are independent of each other.

We are not unfamiliar with the rule that where the mutual covenants go to the entire consideration on both sides, they are considered mutual conditions and dependent unless there are clear indications to the contrary. 17 C.J.S., Contracts § 344. We seek, then, in the findings, something to support the trial court's conclusion that the covenants are independent. The contract in question was made on December 23, 1939. It obligated the defendant to deposit in First National Bank in Raton the amount of the loan on or before February 1, 1940. It obligated the plaintiff to give as security a mortgage on the land he was purchasing from Maxwell Land Grant Co. It was well known to both parties that the deed must go to . . . the Netherlands for execution by proper officers of the corporate grantor and that a considerable period would "necessarily elapse before said deed could be delivered to the plaintiff." While it may be said to have been within the contemplation of the parties that by expedient passage and return, a delivery could occur before the defendant was called upon to perform by depositing the loan in the bank agreed upon; nevertheless, and necessarily, the parties must have known that the day for performance by defendant might arrive before the plaintiff would be in a position to give the promised mortgage following delivery of his deed upon its return from abroad. This brings the case squarely within the test applied in Glaser v. Dannelley, supra.

It is the general rule that a breach of contract to loan money, standing alone, imposes no liability to damages. But this rule does not apply where there are extraordinary circumstances, as in this case, which result in injury. The defendant knew that the plaintiff was preparing to erect a building on the lot he had purchased, and to assist the plaintiff in securing material for the erection of such building, he notified certain material dealers that he had agreed to make the loan for the intended purpose. This caused the dealers to furnish to plaintiff a portion of the materials necessary for the erection of the building, which was commenced the 20th day of December, [1939]. Thereafter the defendant, knowing the reliance placed upon his agreement by plaintiff and the material dealers, notified the same dealers after considerable material had been furnished, that he would not make the loan. Thereupon, they not only refused to continue furnishing material but filed materialmen's liens against the property to secure that previously supplied. The result was that the plaintiff was unable to secure a substitute loan until the 12th day of April, 1940, by reason of which the building was not ready for occupancy until the 27th of April, two months and seventeen days after it would have been completed had the loan been made by defendant as provided in the contract.

These extraordinary circumstances resulted in injury to the plaintiff, and defendant is liable for the consequential damages. . . . "Damages for breach of a contract to lend money are measured by the cost of obtaining the use of money during the agreed period of credit, less interest at the rate provided in the contract, plus compensation for other unavoidable harm that the defendant had reason to foresee when the contract was made." Restatement of the Law, "Contracts" § 343. . . .

The item of $35 paid to Fred C. Stringfellow, attorney for Santa Fe Builders Supply Co. who made the substitute loan to plaintiff, was correctly allowed. This was for examination of the abstract of title and other papers, and for closing the loan. This is an ordinary and usual expense in connection with the loaning of money upon real property and must have been contemplated by the parties. . . .

The court found that the [plaintiff] was entitled to $298.75 damages, "being the net loss to the plaintiff in respect of the profits which the plaintiff would have received from the operation of his business in his new building during the period from February 10, 1940, to April 27, 1940." This was arrived at by the conclusion that the profits would amount to $5 a day for the time mentioned and that there should be deducted therefrom $31.25 which would be the saving of interest for the like period. The evidence upon which this finding was based was that of the plaintiff which was in substance that he intended to operate a night club in the building; that, prior thereto, he had operated a saloon in [Cimarron], and that based upon his knowledge of the saloon business, he estimated that the net profits would be not less than $5 per day.

There is no evidence from which the jury could determine for itself the amount of the lost profits (if any) plaintiff sustained during the two months and 17 days, except the conclusion of the plaintiff himself, that it was $5 a day. Undoubtedly, the plaintiff was entitled to recover his actual loss of profits by reason of the circumstances we have mentioned, if they were capable of legal ascertainment. . . . But we are of the opinion that there was no basis in the evidence for the conclusion of the witness (apparently testifying as an expert) that his profits for the time lost would have been $5 a day. It was purely a speculative estimate unsupported by any substantial testimony. But aside from the considerations stated from the fact that plaintiff was entering into a new business never opened up, any mere estimate as to profits is too remote and speculative to establish damages. . . .

We are of the opinion that item "H" in the sum of $62.50 for rental lost by the plaintiff during the period from February 10 to April 27 was proven by substantial testimony. It establishes a rental value of the restaurant portion of the building, thereafter rented at $25 a month.

The item allowed by the court of $173.40 for necessary travel expenses incurred by the plaintiff in attempting to secure another loan was proved by substantial evidence and correctly allowed by the court. . . .

We find that the trial court allowed the damages in the sum of $420.05 erroneously, in that there was no substantial evidence to support the several items aggregating that sum. That there was substantial evidence to support items of damage aggregating $270.90. If the appellee will enter a remittitur in this court in the sum of $420.05, the judgment will be affirmed for the balance and the costs of the appeal will be divided equally between the parties, failing which the judgment will be reversed and the cause remanded with instructions to the district court to grant a new trial, said costs to be charged to appellee. The appellant's counterclaim, properly allowed, is taken care of in the remittitur authorized.

QUESTIONS

(1) If the deed had arrived from Amsterdam on January 26, could plaintiff have insisted on payment of the $1,500 promised on February 1 without tendering a mortgage?

(2) What if the deed had arrived in early March, but plaintiff, instead of demanding the money promised on February 1, had remained entirely silent and had made no demand on defendant until March 15, after the deed had arrived?

————

Sharp, Promissory Liability (pt. 2)
7 U.Chi.L.Rev. 250, 269–272 (1940)

"As more complicated contracts, at various stages of performance, came before the courts, it became increasingly apparent that it is the absence of conditions which creates the troublesome problems of adjustment when one party to a bilateral contract has not performed, or is likely not to perform, part of his undertakings, and the other party relies on this circumstance, not simply for a cause of action but for an excuse for discontinuing performance on his part. Again, the extent of the risks which parties must be regarded as taking and the unfairness of contracts infected with serious lack of foresight, are the factors to be considered. . . .

"Two extreme and simple treatments of the effect of one party's default on the other's obligations are thinkable. Each might simply have a cross action against the other. . . . At the opposite extreme, every default might be treated as an excuse for the other party, and the defaulting party protected against unfairness resulting from his part performance, by quasi-contractual relief to prevent unjust enrichment or forfeiture or both. . . . Neither of these simple solutions has, of course, been adopted by the courts. After struggling . . . to discover some indication of the parties' expectations about the variety of contingencies which may occur in the course of performance, the courts recognized that they were dealing with a problem which could not be solved by interpretation. As in cases of mistake and impossibility, some attempt was made to distinguish between 'substantial' and other differences. The suggestion that such a word could be used to describe a systematic, metaphysical or scientific test, while comforting, is, of course, illusory. The word may be used to describe the results of a practical judgment; but the difficult necessity of making the practical judgment remains. . . .

"One reminder of the impossibility of solving these questions by resort either to interpretation or to such clear-cut rules as are suggested by the effect of a specified order of performance, appears in the cases dealing with the effect of default on a party who was to perform first. If a party has let the time for the first performance pass, and is then not in a position to perform himself when he calls for performance on the other side, it appears that some principle not dependent on interpretation requires that the other party be excused. This principle, on examination, seems closely related to the principles applicable to mistake and impossibility."

———————

Conley v. Pitney Bowes

United States Court of Appeals, Eighth Circuit, 1994.
34 F.3d 714.

M. ARNOLD, CIRCUIT JUDGE. Conley initiated this action . . . against his employer Pitney Bowes after he had been denied continued disability benefits for a claim arising from injuries suffered in an automobile accident. The company removed the case to the [federal district court] because the suit related to benefits under the Employee Retirement Income Security Act, 29 U.S.C. § 1001 et seq. (ERISA). The district court granted the defendants's motion for summary judgment, 839 F.Supp. 1364, and this appeal followed. At issue is whether a claimant must exhaust administrative procedures when, contrary to the requirements of his plan, the letter denying his benefits does not inform him of appeal procedures.

ERISA does not explicitly require exhaustion of administrative or plan remedies. The doctrine is, in this context, a creature either of contract or judicial invention. We have required exhaustion in ERISA cases only when it was required by the particular plan involved. . . . The appellant concedes that the plan which is the subject of the suit before us does contain, in fact, such a requirement.

The language of the plan requiring exhaustion is complimented . . . by language that requires that any notice of denial of benefits be accompanied by explicit instructions informing the plan participant of the procedures for appeal. Section 7.8(a) of the plan document requires that the plan administrator provide to "any person whose claim for benefits has been denied . . . a written notification of the denial. The written notification shall include . . . an explanation of the claim appeal procedure." This plan language comports with the requirements of 29 C.F.R. § 2560.50:–1(f)(4), which dictates that the "[c]ontent of notice . . . to every claimant who is denied a claim for benefits . . . set[ ] forth . . . [a]ppropriate information as to the steps to be taken if the participant or beneficiary wishes to submit his or her claim for review."

The present case, therefore, may be distilled to one of contract. Two terms of an ERISA plan are the focus of this dispute, namely, an exhaustion clause and a clause requiring notice of appeal procedures. . . .

The terms that are at the center of this dispute are promises that were exchanged as part of a complex agreement. While pension and benefit plans are typically characterized as being unilateral contracts (agreements where an offer is accepted by a performance), the promises in the plan before us are more properly characterized as a bilateral contract (an agreement where promises of future performance are exchanged). See Corbin on Contracts § 21 (one vol. ed. 1962). . . .

One well established rule of contract construction is that "[i]n bilateral contracts for an agreed exchange of performances, . . . where one party's performance is to be rendered prior in time to that of the other, it is a constructive condition precedent to the latter's duty." Simpson, Handbook of the Law of Contracts § 152 (1965). See also Restatement (Second) of Contracts § 237 (1981) ("[I]t is a condition of each party's remaining duties to render performances to be exchanged under an exchange of promises that there be no material failure by the other party to render any such performance due at an earlier time.") . . . Such a "performance is as much a condition precedent to the other's duty as though expressly made so." Simpson, § 152; See also Loud v. Pomona Land & Water Co., 153 U.S. 564, 577 (1894) (agreement to convey land "*after* the making of the payment and full performance" rendered such payment and performance a condition precedent to the duty to convey. (emphasis in original)). . . .

Application of these principles to the case at hand is straightforward. Because appellees were obligated to inform appellant of the appeal procedure at the time they denied him benefits, appellees performance had necessarily to precede exhaustion by the plaintiff. A defense under the exhaustion clause, therefore, may not be asserted absent performance of the notice clause, since they are presumed to be the subject of promises made in exchange for each other.

The appellees maintain that failure to impose the exhaustion requirement would be contrary to the public policy behind such a requirement. We disagree. Exhaustion is a very important concept in our jurisprudence, with deep roots in the principles of federalism and comity. See e.g., Rose v. Lundy, 455 U.S. 509 (1982). . . . We believe, however, that the freedom of contract between autonomous parties is a more important principle than even the very important judicially-created doctrine of exhaustion. Furthermore, where exhaustion is a bargained-for term of a contract, freedom of contract is not necessarily inconsistent with the principles underlying exhaustion requirements.

Requiring plan administrators to provide notice of appeals procedure as required by contract and the Secretary's regulations is not inconsistent with the goals that exhaustion typically furthers. Indeed, such a requirement serves much the same purpose as the exhaustion clause, namely, to avert resort to federal litigation where an administrative procedure is available. In fact, inclusion of such a term serves to avoid not only frivolous suits, but mistakenly filed suits as well. To advance the purposes of the Act, the Secretary's regulations, the contract, and the principles underlying the exhaustion and notice terms, we must construe and enforce the whole contract, including the notice of appeals procedure requirement.

In their motion for summary judgment and their supporting memorandum, the defendants-appellees rely expressly and exclusively upon Conley's failure to exhaust the plan's procedures. They do not allege that Conley had actual knowledge of the plan's procedures, thereby making any breach of the plan's notice requirements immaterial. The district court appears to have felt that the plaintiff-appellant's possession of the summary plan description gave him constructive knowledge of the appeals procedures. The terms of the plan and the requirements of the regulation, however, confer upon a claimant a right to more than just a copy of the summary plan description. He had a contractual right to information on the appeals procedure included with his notice of denial of benefits. On summary judgment, the movant is not entitled to the benefit of a legal rule that the summary plan description gave claimant constructive knowledge of the appeals procedures.

. . . [T]he defendants-appellees further assert that Conley did not deny having actual knowledge of the plan's procedures. This argument, however, puts the cart before the horse. The defendants-appellees never alleged, either in their answer, their motion for summary judgment, or their memorandum in support of their motion, that Conley or his attorney had actual knowledge of the plan's appeals process. We do not think that Conley could be expected to deny something of which he had not been accused. . . .

For the foregoing reasons, we reverse the judgment of the district court, and remand for proceedings consistent with this opinion.

GIBSON, SENIOR CIRCUIT JUDGE, dissenting. . . . I would affirm the judgment of the district court for the reasons articulated in its decision.

Conley's testimony is very clear that after he received the letter denying benefits he turned it over to his lawyer. He felt that he should be getting a pension, disability or something, so retained the lawyer to look after his interests. He let the lawyer handle it and do the work. In addition to the letter, he gave a copy of the benefit plans book to the lawyer. The booklet set forth in clear detail the claim appeal procedure.

The court today elevates form over substance and ignores the factual situation before the district court and on which it ruled. This is not a case where an employee failed to file an application for review because he was not told of the procedures, but rather one where the employee relied on his lawyer, who dropped the ball.

————

Bell v. Elder

782 P.2d 545 (Utah Ct.App.1989)

The Bells' contract to purchase undeveloped land for $25,000 required the Elders, sellers and defendants, to furnish culinary water to the property, for which the Bells, upon acquiring a building permit, were to pay a hook-up and installation fee. A lawsuit for rescission and restitution of the down payment, brought unsuccessfully by the Bells, followed the deal's collapse. The reviewing court said: "[A]lthough the contract contains a promise by the Elders to supply water, as well as a related promise by the Bells to obtain a building permit for the construction of a house to receive the water, no time is specified for performing either promise. . . . The situation at trial consisted of the Bells [asking] to rescind the contract on the grounds that the Elders had breached an obligation to actually furnish water to the property, and [the Elders] insisting that they would supply the required water when the Bells demanded it and performed their obligations. The question thus presented boils down to the order in which these parties must perform. . . . [Since the] contract is silent on the time or times for actually furnishing water and for obtaining a building permit[,] . . . the law implies a covenant and condition that the related obligations be performed concurrently. . . . [N]either party could claim a breach by the other until the party claiming the breach tendered performance of its concurrent obligation. . . . This case demonstrates that the rule requiring tender before claiming breach of a concurrent promise is not a mere formality or trap for the unwary. Here, the claimant's tender would demonstrate the continued practical vitality and purposefulness of the promise owed the claimant. Public policy and common sense oppose the waste of installing a culinary water line to serve land which, for all that appears, will remain unused. The rule requiring tender thus serves, among other purposes, to prevent a claimant from insisting upon a purposeless performance, or from avoiding his own obligations on pretext. Inasmuch as the [Bells'] failure to perform their own obligations precludes recovery on their claims, the judgment of dismissal is affirmed."

———

Wholesale Sand & Gravel, Inc. v. Decker

Supreme Judicial Court of Maine, 1993.
630 A.2d 710.

ROBERTS, J. Wholesale Sand & Gravel appeals from a judgment entered in favor of James Decker on its claim for the breach of their contract. . . . Wholesale contends that the court erred in holding that its conduct constituted an anticipatory repudiation of the contract. . . . Finding no error, we affirm the judgment.

On June 13, 1989, [the parties] entered into a contract whereby Wholesale agreed to perform earth work, including the installation of a gravel driveway, on Decker's property in Bowdoin. The contract contained no provision specifying a completion date for the work. Indeed, the only time reference made in the contract was that payment was to be made within 90 days. Although Carl Goodenow, Wholesale's president, believed the company had 90 days within which to complete the work, he told Decker that the driveway portion of the work would be completed within one week.

Wholesale began work on the driveway on the weekend after the contract was executed and immediately experienced difficulty because of the wetness of the ground. In fact, Wholesale's bulldozer became stuck in the mud and had to be removed with a backhoe. Wholesale returned to the site the following weekend, when it attempted to stabilize the driveway site by hauling out mud and hauling in gravel. Because the ground was too wet to allow Wholesale to perform the work without substantially exceeding the contract price, Goodenow decided to wait for the ground to dry out before proceeding further.

On July 12, 1989, Decker contacted Goodenow concerning the lack of activity at the site and his urgent need to have the driveway completed. Goodenow responded that he would "get right on it." On July 19, Decker telephoned Goodenow to inquire again about the lack of activity and gave him one week in which to finish the driveway. Again, Goodenow said that he would "get right on it." On July 28, Decker called Goodenow for the purpose of terminating the contract. When Goodenow stated that he would be at the site the next day, Decker decided to give him one more chance. Goodenow, however, did not appear at the site and Decker subsequently terminated the contract. At that point Goodenow believed Wholesale still had 45 days to complete the job. Decker, however, hired another contractor to finish the driveway and complete the excavation work.

Wholesale commenced this action. . . . After a jury-waived trial, the court entered a judgment in favor of Decker. Although it found that a reasonable time for completion of performance was 60 days, the court concluded that Wholesale's conduct constituted an anticipatory repudiation of the contract, permitting Decker to terminate the contract during the 60–day period. This appeal followed.

An anticipatory repudiation of a contract is "a definite and unequivocal manifestation of intention on the part of the repudiator that he will not

anticipatory repudiation

render the promised performance when the time fixed for it in the contract arrives." 4 Corbin, Corbin on Contracts § 973 (1951); Restatement (Second) of Contracts § 250 (1979). The manifestation of an intention to repudiate a contract may be made and communicated by either words or conduct. . . . The words or conduct evidencing such refusal or inability to perform, however, must be definite, unequivocal, and absolute. Martell Bros., Inc. v. Donbury Inc., 577 A.2d 334 (Me.1990). Wholesale contends that the court erred in concluding that its conduct constituted an anticipatory repudiation. . . . We disagree. After its second weekend of work at the site, Wholesale removed its equipment and did not return. Moreover, on two occasions Goodenow, responding to Decker's inquiries about the progress of the job, promised to get right to work but did not do so. Indeed, when confronted by the fact that Wholesale would be fired if he did not appear at the job site the following day, Goodenow promised that he would be at the site but did not appear. On this record it was reasonable for Decker to conclude that Wholesale would never complete its performance under the contract. We conclude therefore that the court properly found that Wholesale, through its conduct, manifested an unequivocal and definite inability or unwillingness to perform within a reasonable time. . . .

WATHEN, C.J., with whom CLIFFORD, J., joins, dissenting. . . . [B]oth this Court and the Superior Court misapply the doctrine of anticipatory repudiation. The record is devoid of any words or conduct on the part of plaintiff that distinctly, unequivocally, and absolutely evidence a refusal or inability to perform. . . . There was a disagreement between the parties as to how much time was allowed for performance, but it is clear that plaintiff expected to perform the contract as soon as circumstances permitted. The Superior Court found a repudiation of the contract even though the 60 days it found available for performance had not passed. I would vacate the judgment.

NOTE: BREACH BY ANTICIPATORY REPUDIATION

A "repudiation" is said to occur when a party's statements or actions can fairly be interpreted to mean that the party will not or cannot perform its contractual obligations. Recall, for example, the notice to stop work given the contractor in Rockingham County v. Luten Bridge Co., p. 56. There is, of course, much litigation over the question whether particular words and/or actions constitute a repudiation of the contract. A particularly troublesome problem arises when, in mid-course, one party demands that the other do something not required by their agreement. If such a demand is accompanied by a statement that the demanding party will not perform its contractual duties unless the additional term is met, a finding of anticipatory breach is likely. E.g., Chamberlin v. Puckett Constr., 277 Mont. 198, 921 P.2d 1237 (1996). Again, the standard rule is that a breach occurs when it is reasonably certain that a party is not going to meet its obligations under the contract.

Another cluster of problems centers on the effects of a breach by repudiation, distinguished from a breach by simple nonperformance. A contract plaintiff's standing in court may rest wholly on the good fortune of a finding that the defaulter has also repudiated the contract. The principal effects of the so-called "anticipatory breach" are stated in Restatement, Second § 253:

(1) Where an obligor repudiates a duty before he has committed a breach by non-performance and before he has received all of the agreed exchange for it, his repudiation alone gives rise to a claim for damages for total breach.

(2) Where performances are to be exchanged under an exchange of promises, one party's repudiation of a duty to render performance discharges the other's remaining duties to render performance.

A repudiation may, of course, have an additional consequence: it may excuse the nonoccurrence of a condition.

Many of the remedial problems associated with anticipatory repudiation are familiar at this point. It is now necessary to stress that the doctrine of anticipatory breach is applicable to bilateral contracts which contemplate some future performance by the nonbreaching party. A principal effect of the doctrine is to free that party (the nonrepudiator) of its obligations of future performance.

K & G Constr. Co. v. Harris

Court of Appeals of Maryland, 1960.
223 Md. 305, 164 A.2d 451.

[Plaintiff, owner and general contractor, entered into a contract with defendant subcontractor for the excavating and earth-moving work required in a housing project. The contract contained the following provisions: (1) defendant agreed to perform the work "in a workmanlike manner and in accordance with the best practices," without delay, as called for by plaintiff, it being agreed that "time was of the essence"; (2) plaintiff had the right to terminate the contract and employ a substitute to perform the work in the event of delay by defendant, and defendant agreed to indemnify plaintiff for any loss caused thereby, but nothing in this provision "shall be construed to deprive Contractor [plaintiff] of any rights or remedies it would otherwise have as to damage for delay"; (3) defendant was to submit to plaintiff by the 25th day of each month a requisition for work performed during the preceding month, and plaintiff agreed to pay 90 percent of each requisition by the 10th of the following month; (4) defendant agreed to carry liability insurance against property damage caused in the progress of the work, and plaintiff was not obligated to make payments under the contract until the insurance requirements were met.

Defendant performed work under the contract during July 1958, for which it submitted a requisition on July 25. This requisition would have entitled defendant to a progress payment on August 10. On August 9, however, defendant's bulldozer operator drove his machine too close to a house belonging to plaintiff, causing the collapse of a wall and other damage amounting to $3,400. Both defendant and its insurer denied liability for this damage. Because the damage was not repaired or paid for, plaintiff refused to make the progress payment due defendant on August 10. Defendant continued work until September 12, when it left the job because of plaintiff's refusal to pay the July and August requisitions, notifying plaintiff that it was willing to resume work but only on payment for work already done. Plaintiff continued to refuse to pay, asked defendant to complete the work, and, on defendant's refusal, had the remaining work done by another excavator at a cost increase of $450. It was stipulated that defendant had completed work for which it had not been paid in the amount of $1,484.50, and that if it had completed the remainder of the work under the contract it would have realized a profit on that portion amounting to $1,340.

Plaintiff sued for both the damages caused by the bulldozer, alleging negligence of the operator, and the additional $450 required to have the work completed by another contractor. Defendant counterclaimed for the value of work performed and for the lost profits on the remainder of the job. By agreement of the parties, plaintiff's claim for bulldozer damage was submitted to a jury, which found for plaintiff in the amount of $3,400. The judgment for this sum has been paid by defendant. Plaintiff's other claim and defendant's counterclaims were submitted to the court for determination without a jury. The trial court found for defendant on both counterclaims and plaintiff appealed.]

PRESCOTT, J. . . . Does a contractor, damaged by a subcontractor's failure to perform a portion of his work in a workmanlike manner, have a right, under the circumstances of this case, to withhold, in partial satisfaction of said damages, an installment payment, which, under the terms of the contract, was due the subcontractor, unless the negligent performance of his work excused its payment? . . .

It is immediately apparent that our decision turns upon the respective rights and liabilities of the parties under that portion of their contract whereby the subcontractor agreed to do the excavating and earth-moving work in "a workmanlike manner, and in accordance with the best practices," with time being of the essence of the contract, and the contractor agreed to make progress payments therefor on the 10th day of the months following the performance of the work by the subcontractor. The subcontractor contends, of course, that when the contractor failed to make the payment due on August 10, he breached his contract and thereby released him (the subcontractor) from any further obligation to perform. The contractor, on the other hand, argues that the failure of the subcontractor to perform his work in a workmanlike manner constituted a material breach of the contract, which justified his refusal to make the August 10 payment; and, as there was no breach on his part, the subcontractor had no right to cease performance on September 12, and his refusal to continue work on the project constituted another breach, which rendered him liable to the contractor for damages. . . . Did the contractor have a right, under the circumstances, to refuse to make the progress payment, due on August 10, 1958? . . .

While the courts assume, in deciding the relation of one or more promises in a contract to one or more counter-promises, that the promises are dependent rather than independent, the intention of the parties, as shown by the entire contract as construed in the light of the circumstances of the case, [is] the controlling factor. . . .

Considering the presumption that promises and counter-promises are dependent[,] . . . we have no hesitation in holding that the promise and counter-promise under consideration here were mutually dependent, that is to say, the parties intended performance by one to be conditioned on performance by the other; and the subcontractor's promise was, by the explicit wording of the contract, precedent to the promise of payment, monthly, by the contractor. . . . [I]t is the general rule that where a total price for work is fixed by a contract the work is not rendered divisible by progress payments. It would, indeed, present an unusual situation if we were to hold that a building contractor, who has obtained someone to do work for him and has agreed to pay each month for the work performed in the previous month, has to continue the monthly payments, irrespective of the degree of skill and care displayed in the performance of work, and his only recourse is by way of suit for ill-performance. If this were the law, it is conceivable, in fact, probable, that many contractors would become insolvent before they were able to complete their contracts. As was stated [in] Measures Bros. Ltd. v. Measures, 2 Ch. 248: "Covenants are to be construed as dependent or independent according to the intention of the parties and the good sense of the case."

We hold that when the subcontractor's employee negligently damaged the contractor's wall, this constituted a breach of the subcontractor's promise to perform his work in a "workmanlike manner, and in accordance with the best practices." . . . And there can be little doubt that the breach was material: the damage to the wall amounted to more than double the payment due on August 10. 3A Corbin, Contracts, § 708, says: "The failure of a contractor's [in our case, the subcontractor's] performance to constitute 'substantial' performance may justify the owner [in our case the contractor] in refusing to make a progress payment. . . . If the refusal to pay an installment is justified on the owner's [contractor's] part, the contractor [subcontractor] is not justified in abandoning work by reason of that refusal. His abandonment of the work will itself be a wrongful repudiation that goes to the essence, even if the defects in performance did not." . . . Professor Corbin, in § 954, states further: "The unexcused failure of a contractor to render a promised performance when it is due is always a breach of contract. . . . Such failure may be of such great importance as to constitute what has been called herein a 'total' breach. . . . For a failure of performance constituting such a 'total' breach, an action for remedies that are appropriate thereto is at once maintainable. Yet the injured party is not required to bring such action. He has the option of treating the nonperformance as a 'partial' breach only." . . . In permitting the subcontractor to proceed with work on the project after August 9, the contractor, obviously, treated the breach by the subcontractor as a partial one. As the promises were mutually dependent and the subcontractor had made a material breach in his performance, this justified the contractor in refusing to make the August 10 payment; hence, as the contractor was not in default, the subcontractor again breached the contract when he, on September 12, discontinued work on the project, which rendered him liable (by the express terms of the contract) to the contractor for his increased cost in having the excavating done—a stipulated amount of $450. . . .

The appellees suggest [a minor point] that may be disposed of rather summarily. . . . [They] contend that the contractor had no right to refuse the August 10 payment, because the subcontractor had furnished the insurance against property damage, as called for in the contract. There is little, or no, merit in this suggestion. The subcontractor and his insurance company denied liability. The furnishing of the insurance by him did not constitute a license to perform his work in a careless, negligent, or unworkmanlike manner; and its acceptance by the contractor did not preclude his assertion of a claim for unworkmanlike performance directly against the subcontractor.

Judgment against the appellant reversed; and judgment entered in favor of the appellant against the appellees for $450, the appellees to pay the costs.

———

Stanley Gudyka Sales Co. v. Lacy Forest Products Co.
915 F.2d 273 (7th Cir.1990)

Lacy, a dealer in wood products, contracted for the services of a similar dealer, Gudyka, who was to be compensated by an agreed split of the profits on sales Gudyka made. Their agreement provided for termination by either party for "just cause." Some months after entering into the agreement, Lacy terminated Gudyka on the ground that he had failed to promptly remit to Lacy $3,000 of commissions (Lacy's share) collected from a customer. At the time, Lacy owed Gudyka $46,000 in commissions from all other accounts (this sum was eventually paid). Gudyka filed suit against Lacy, alleging the termination was without "just cause" and therefore a breach of contract. *Held*, judgment for Gudyka affirmed. "The self-help remedy [afforded by the 'doctrine of conditions'] is only available where termination is in proportion to the 'need' for accountability from the breaching party, and where the breach is material rather than 'insignificant.' The district court determined that Lacy's use of the 'self-help remedy' of [termination] was not proportional to its need and that the amount Gudyka owed to Lacy, as compared with the amounts Lacy owed Gudyka, was an 'insignificant' breach. [Also,] the district court found that because Lacy knew how much Gudyka owed it, Lacy was obligated to give Gudyka notice and an opportunity to cure its breach. [If] Gudyka did not cure, Lacy still had the alternative self-help remedy of deducting (as it later did deduct) the [$3,000] from [Gudyka's monthly] commission check. Without having given notice and an opportunity to cure, the district court [properly found that the termination] was without 'just cause.' . . . The 'doctrine of conditions' is not a tool which will 'permit a party to . . . us[e] an insignificant breach as a pretext for avoiding his contractual obligations.' "

NOTE

K & G Constr. and *Gudyka Sales* pursue the ever-present distinction between total and partial breach. And *K & G* tells us something basic about the law of conditions that builds upon that gateway to self-protective measures: If the performing party stops performing, or performs badly, the paying party can stop paying. Yet *Gudyka* is a reminder that not every self-help response to breach on the other side is legitimate, for the law reads into the doctrine of conditions implicit limitations, even obligations (e.g., the familiar duty to give notice and an opportunity to cure a breach). Suppose, in *K & G*, there had been no bulldozer incident; rather, the general, short on cash, simply failed to make the August 10th payment due the sub for the preceding month's work. Suppose further that this breach continued for a period of time. The Restatement, Second § 237, in illustrations 1 and 2, tells of such a story:

> 1. A contracts to build a house for B for $50,000, progress payments to be made monthly in an amount equal to 85% of the price of the work performed during the preceding month, the balance to be paid on the architect's certificate of satisfactory completion of the

house. Without justification B fails to make a $5,000 progress payment. A thereupon stops works on the house and a week goes by. A's failure to continue the work is not a breach and B has no claim against A. B's failure to make the progress payment . . . operates as the non-occurrence of a condition of A's remaining duties of performance. . . . If B offers to make the delayed payment and in all the circumstances it is not too late to cure the material breach, A's duties to continue the work are not discharged. A has a claim against B for damages for partial breach because of the delay.

2. The facts being otherwise as stated in Illustration 1, B fails to make the progress payment or to give any explanation or assurances for one month. If, in all the circumstances, it is now too late for B to cure his material failure of performance . . ., A's duties to continue the work are discharged. Because B's failure to make the progress payment was a breach, A also has a claim against B for total breach of contract.

K & G also includes the point that the injured party is free to treat the other's breach by nonperformance—even a "material" breach—as partial only. If that happens (the injured party, through its actions, continues to live with the contract, perhaps asking the defaulter to do so as well), is it appropriate to speak of such conduct as "waiver"? Waiver of what? A cause of action for damages? We shall see more of these questions ahead.

Ziehen v. Smith

Court of Appeals of New York, 1896.
148 N.Y. 558, 42 N.E. 1080.

O'BRIEN, J. The plaintiff, as vendee, under an executory contract for the sale of real estate, has recovered of the defendant, the vendor, damages for a breach of the contract to convey, to the extent of that part of the purchase money paid at the execution of the contract, and for certain expenses in the examination of the title. The question [is] whether the plaintiff established at the trial such a breach of the contract as entitled him to recover.

By the contract, which bears date August 10th, 1892, the defendant agreed to convey to the plaintiff by good and sufficient deed the lands described therein, being a country hotel with some adjacent land. The plaintiff was to pay for the same the sum of $3,500, as follows: $500 down, which was paid at the time of the execution of the contract, $300 more on the 15th day of September, 1892. He was to assume an existing mortgage on the property of $1,000, and the balance of $1,700 he was to secure by his bond and mortgage on the property, payable, with interest, one year after date. The courts below have assumed that the payment of the $300 by the plaintiff, the execution of the bond and mortgage, and the delivery of the conveyance by the defendant, were intended to be concurrent acts, and, therefore, the day designated by the contract for mutual performance was the 15th of September, 1892. Since no other day is mentioned in the contract for the payment of the money, or the exchange of the papers, we think that this construction was just and reasonable, and, in fact, the only legal inference of which the language of the instrument was capable. It is not alleged or claimed that the plaintiff on that day, or at any other time, offered to perform on his part or demanded performance on the part of the defendant, and this presents the serious question in the case and the only obstacle to the plaintiff's recovery.

It is, no doubt, the general rule that in order to entitle a party to recover damages for the breach of an executory contract of this character he must show performance or tender of performance on his part. He must show in some way that the other party is in default in order to maintain the action, or that performance or tender has been waived. But a tender of performance on the part of the vendee is dispensed with in a case where it appears that the vendor has disabled himself from performance, or that he is on the day fixed by the contract for that purpose, for any reason, unable to perform. The judgment in this case must stand, if at all, upon the ground that on the 15th day of September, 1892, the defendant was unable to give to the plaintiff any title to the property embraced in the contract, and hence any tender of performance on the part of the plaintiff, or demand of performance on his part, was unnecessary, because upon the facts appearing it would be an idle or useless ceremony.

It appeared upon the trial that at the time of the execution of the contract there was another mortgage upon the premises of $1,500, which fact was not disclosed to the plaintiff, and of the existence of which he was then ignorant. That on or prior to the 21st of July, 1892, some twenty days before the contract was entered into, an action was commenced to foreclose this mortgage, and notice of the pendency of the action filed in the county clerk's office. That on the 30th of September following judgment of foreclosure was granted and entered on the 31st of October thereafter, and on the 28th of December the property was sold to a third party by virtue of the judgment, and duly conveyed by deed from the referee. It appears that the defendant was not the maker of this mortgage and was not aware of its existence, but it was made by a former owner, and the defendant's title was subject to it when he contracted to sell the property to the plaintiff.

The decisions on the point involved do not seem to be entirely harmonious. In some of them it is said that the existence, at the date fixed for performance, of liens or incumbrances upon the property is sufficient to sustain an action by the vendee to recover the part of the purchase money paid upon the contract. Morange v. Morris, 3 Keyes 48; Ingalls v. Hahn, 47 Hun. 104. The general rule, however, . . . seems to be that in cases where by the terms of the contract the acts of the parties are to be concurrent, it is the duty of him who seeks to maintain an action for a breach of the contract, either by way of damages for the non-performance, or for the recovery of money paid thereon, not only to be ready and willing to perform on his part, but he must demand performance from the other party. The qualifications to this rule are to be found in cases where the necessity of a formal tender or demand is obviated by the acts of the party sought to be charged as by his express refusal in advance to comply with the terms of the contract in that respect, or where it appears that he has placed himself in a position in which performance is impossible. If the vendor of real estate [is] unable to perform on his part, at the time provided by the contract, a formal tender or demand on the part of the vendee is not necessary in order to enable him to maintain an action to recover the money paid on the contract, or for damages. . . .

In this case there was no proof that the defendant waived tender or demand either by words or conduct. The only difficulty in the way of the performance on his part was the existence of the mortgage which the proof tends to show was given by a former owner and its existence on the day of performance was not known to either party. In order to sustain the judgment we must hold that the defendant on the day of performance was unable to convey to the plaintiff the title which the contract required, simply because of the existence of the incumbrance. We do not think that it can be said . . . that the defendant had placed himself in such a position that he was unable to perform the contract on his part and that his title was destroyed or that it was impossible for him to convey within the meaning of the rule which dispenses with the necessity of tender and demand in order to work a breach of an executory contract for the sale of land. It cannot be affirmed under the circumstances that if the plaintiff had made the tender and demand on the day provided in the contract that he would not have received the title which the defendant had contracted to convey. The contract is not broken by the mere fact of the existence on the day of performance of some lien or incumbrance which it is in the power of the vendor to remove. That is all that was shown in this case. . . .

For this reason the judgment should be reversed and a new trial granted. . . .

QUESTION

After receiving this news from the Court of Appeals, would the plaintiff, by tendering $300 and demanding a deed, be entitled to a conveyance or, alternatively, to damages?

———————

Neves v. Wright

638 P.2d 1195 (Utah 1981)

The court found that the purchasers were not entitled to rescind prior to closing, on the ground that the vendors did not have a good title when the contract was made. The court said: "As early as 1909, this court established the fundamental rule that a seller need not have legal title during the entire executory period of a real estate contract. . . . [The rule] is not designed to favor sellers over buyers; rather, the purpose is to enhance the alienability of real estate by providing necessary flexibility in real estate transactions. Nevertheless, . . . the rule must be carefully applied to avoid unfairness, sharp practice, and outright dishonesty. . . . [The basic test] is whether the defect, by its nature, is one that can be removed, as a practical matter." Justice Oaks, concurring, added: "[T]he variety of circumstances that can arise with a title during the executory period of a real estate contract and the variety of possible explanations that can be given for apparent problems or negative prospects make it imperative that the buyer not act unilaterally in renouncing a contract because of a particular problem or prospect without giving the seller an opportunity and a reasonable time to explain or give assurances. The fact that these buyers renounced the contract without making any inquiry of the sellers as their actual ownership or ability to acquire title to fulfill their contract obligation is therefore critical to my concurrence." [A year later, the Utah court was faced with a case where, because of a deadlock over the need to remove an encumbrance on the vendor's title before proceeding to closing, neither party made a tender of performance on or before the date for closing. In affirming dismissal of the vendee's lawsuit, the court cited Neves v. Wright, adding: "In a case like this, where the executory contract [contemplates simultaneous performance and] contains no declaration that time is of the essence, the contract obligations can continue for some time beyond the agreed closing date. . . . In other words, the party who desires to use legal process [must] put the other party in default." Century 21 All Western Real Estate v. Webb, 645 P.2d 52 (Utah 1982).]

––––––––

6 S. Williston, Contracts § 832 (3d ed.1961)

"Where conditions are concurrent, the allegation of tender need not be of absolute tender. A tender conditional on contemporaneous performance by the defendant is sufficient and necessary. It has sometimes been said that in such a case readiness and willingness on the part of the plaintiff is a sufficient allegation; or even that this is not part of the plaintiff's case, but, though in suits for specific performance a different rule prevails in many jurisdictions, to maintain an action at law the plaintiff must not only be ready and willing but he must have manifested this before bringing his action, by some offer of performance to the defendant, for, otherwise, both parties might be ready and willing and each stay at home waiting for the other to come forward. While the situation is possible of each of two parties having a right to specific performance against the other, it is not possible that each shall have a right to damages for a total breach of the contract.

"It is one of the consequences of concurrent conditions that a situation may arise where no right of action ever arises against either party. Since a conditional tender is necessary to put either party in default, so long as both parties remain inactive, neither is liable and neither has acquired a right of action. Moreover, the possibility of putting either party in default will cease if the delay is too long." [Courts usually find that the tender requirement is satisfied by conduct amounting to the giving of notice of readiness to perform. Also, a demand for the other's performance of a concurrent act is understood to indicate readiness and an offer to perform.]

NOTE

Recall that in Bell v. Elder, p. 734, a vendee who had failed to tender lost a suit for restitution of the part of the price paid at closing (the report of the case does not tell us the amount paid down). In Cleary v. Folger, 84 Cal. 316, 24 P. 280 (1890), neither party had tendered performance, but the vendee, in an action for money had and received, was allowed to recover his down payment minus the vendor's damages resulting from the vendee's failure to perform. The court relied on an express "time-is-of-the-essence" clause and concluded that since the date for performance had passed, "the contract is at an end." If this was a proper conclusion (both parties were discharged from their contract obligations), how could the vendor be awarded "damages" by a deduction from the vendee's recovery?

In a similar vendor-vendee "stalemate" situation (neither had performed and both were denied contract damages), a court awarded the vendee restitution of earnest money deposits of some $15,000 (plus interest and cancellation of a note). An appellate court approved, on this reasoning: The vendee's complaint had asked for "such other and further relief [deemed] just and equitable" in the circumstances. In essence, what the trial court did amounted to "rescission," which is an "equitable remedy" requiring the fashioning of an "equitable solution." There is no abuse of discretion in crafting a solution that returns the parties to their precontract positions. Willener v. Sweeting, 107 Wash.2d 388, 730 P.2d 45 (1986).

Caporale v. Rubine
92 N.J.L. 463, 105 A. 226 (1918)

Caporale and Rubine contracted for an exchange of lands, deeds to be exchanged May 1, 1917. Caporale later sued for damages for breach by Rubine in conveying to a third party the land promised to Caporale. However, it appeared that Caporale had merely a contract right to purchase the land that he was to convey to Rubine, that his land-contract vendor was not under a legal duty to make a conveyance of the legal title until 1926, and was not shown to be willing to convey sooner, and, further, that there were restrictions on the use of the land that might not be removable. In his action for damages, Caporale claimed that he was not obligated to have a good title until the date fixed for closing and that since Rubine had conveyed away his land to a third party, he (Caporale) was relieved from the need to perfect his own title. The court described this contention as "obviously unsound." Rubine's conveyance, disabling him from performing, excused Caporale from making a tender of his own performance. But, to recover damages for Rubine's breach, Caporale must show that "he was able and ready to perform his part of the undertaking" and this "he clearly failed to do." He could not have conveyed the title required by the contract.

NOTE: ESTABLISHING ENTITLEMENT TO RELIEF

Breach by repudiation in advance of the contract's time of performance produces effects we first met in Chapter 1. For example, anticipatory breach by repudiation discharges any remaining duties of the nonbreacher; that party no longer need remain ready and able to perform on the date of performance. In Caporale v. Rubine, of course, the aggrieved party sued to recover damages based on an anticipatory breach. When enforcement is sought, whether by damages or an equity claim for specific performance, it may be necessary to untangle contractual stipulations that operate to condition a party's right to demand the other's performance from a party's obligation to establish, in court, its own entitlement to a remedy.

Another court, confronted with the Caporale v. Rubine problem, also required a plaintiff suing on an anticipatory breach to demonstrate an ability to perform had the breach not occurred. That court declared: "It would be anomalous to allow plaintiff to put itself in a better position by suing immediately on an anticipatory breach and thus avoid the necessity of proving its . . . ability and willingness to perform [at the time] when defendant's performance is due." Yale Dev. Co. v. Aurora Pizza Hut, Inc., 95 Ill.App.3d 523, 420 N.E.2d 823 (1981). The prevailing view that a repudiating party's liability for damages is discharged, if it subsequently appears that there would have been a total failure of performance by the injured party, has been applied in situations where the parties' obligations are not due simultaneously. E.g., Randall v. Peerless

Motor Car Co., 212 Mass. 352, 99 N.E. 221 (1912). These problems of ability to perform (usually financial in nature), including allocation of the burden of proof of ability, are illustrated in DiBella v. Widlitz, 207 Conn. 194, 541 A.2d 91 (1988), and Kanavos v. Hancock Bank & Trust Co., 395 Mass. 199, 479 N.E.2d 168 (1985).

Stewart v. Newbury

Court of Appeals of New York, 1917.
220 N.Y. 379, 115 N.E. 984.

CRANE, J. The defendants are partners in the pipe fitting business under the name of Newbury Mfg. Co. The plaintiff is a contractor and builder residing at Tuxedo, N.Y. The parties had the following correspondence about the erection for the defendants of a concrete mill building at Monroe, N.Y. [Plaintiff Stewart's letter to defendants, dated July 18, 1911, stated:]

"Gentlemen.—With reference to the proposed work on the new foundry building I had hoped to be able to get up and see you this afternoon, but find that impossible and am, in consequence, sending you these prices, which I trust you will find satisfactory.

"I will agree to do all excavation work required at sixty-five ($.65) cents per cubic yard.

"I will put in the concrete work, furnishing labor and forms only, at Two and 05–100 ($2.05) Dollars per cubic yard.

"I will furnish labor to put in reenforcing at Four ($4.00) Dollars per ton.

"I will furnish labor only to set all window and door frames, window sash and doors, including the setting of hardware for One Hundred Twelve ($112) Dollars. As alternative I would be willing to do any or all of the above work for cost plus 10 per cent., furnishing you with first class mechanics and giving the work considerable of my personal time. Hoping to hear favorably from you in this regard, I am,

"Respectfully yours,

"(signed) Alexander Stewart."

[Defendants' reply, dated July 22, 1911, was as follows:]

"Dear Sir.—Confirming the telephone conversation of this morning we accept your bid of July the 18th to do the concrete work on our new building. We trust that you will be able to get at this the early part of next week.

"Yours truly,

"The Newbury Mfg. Co.,

"H.A. Newbury."

Nothing was said in writing about the time or manner of payment. The plaintiff, however, claims that after sending his letter and before receiving that of the defendant he had a telephone communication with Mr. Newbury and said: "I will expect my payments in the usual manner," and Newbury said, "All right, we have got the money to pay for the building." This conversation over the telephone was denied by the defendants. The custom, the plaintiff testified, was to pay 85% every thirty days or at the end of each month, 15% being retained till the work was completed.

In July the plaintiff commenced work and continued until September 29th, at which time he had progressed with the construction as far as the first floor. He then sent a bill for the work done up to that date for $896.35. The defendants refused to pay the bill and work was discontinued. The plaintiff claims that the defendants refused to permit him to perform the rest of his contract, they insisting that the work already done was not in accordance with the specifications. The defendants claimed upon the trial that the plaintiff voluntarily abandoned the work after their refusal to pay his bill.

On October 15, 1911, the defendants wrote the plaintiff a letter [saying]: "Notwithstanding you promised to let us know on Monday whether you would complete the job or throw up the contract, you have not up to this time advised us of your intention. . . . Under the circumstances we are compelled to accept your action as being an abandonment of your contract. . . . As you know, the bill which you sent us and which we declined to pay is not correct, either in items or amount, nor is there anything due you under our contract as we understand it until you have completed your work on our building."

To this letter the plaintiff replied the following day. In it he makes no reference to the telephone communication agreeing, as he testified, to make "the usual payments," but does say this: "There is nothing in our agreement which says that I shall wait until the job is completed before any payment is due, nor can this be reasonably implied. . . . As to having given you positive date as to when I should let you know what I proposed doing, I did not do so; on the contrary I told you that I would not tell you positively what I would do until I had visited the job, and I promised that I would do this at my earliest convenience and up to the present time I have been unable to get up there."

The defendant Herbert Newbury testified that the plaintiff "ran away and left the whole thing." And the defendant F.A. Newbury testified that he was told by Mr. Stewart's man that Stewart was going to abandon the job; that he thereupon telephoned Mr. Stewart, who replied that he would let him know about it the next day, but did not.

In this action, which is brought to recover the amount of the bill presented, as the agreed price and $95.68 damages for breach of contract, the plaintiff had a verdict for the amount stated in the bill, but not for the other damages claimed, and the judgment entered thereon has been affirmed by the Appellate Division.

The appeal to us is upon exceptions to the judge's charge. The court charged the jury as follows: "Plaintiff says that he was excused from completely performing the contract by the defendants' unreasonable failure to pay him for the work he had done during the months of August and September. . . . Was it understood that the payments were to be made monthly? If it was not so understood the defendants' only obligation was to make payments at reasonable periods, in view of the character of the work, the amount of work being done and the value of it. In other words, if there was no agreement between the parties respecting the payments [and no custom], the defendants' obligation was to make payments at reasonable times." . . .

The jury was plainly told that if there were no agreement as to payments, yet the plaintiff would be entitled to part payment at reasonable times as the work progressed, and if such payments were refused he could abandon the work and recover the amount due for the work performed. This is not the law. . . . In fact the law is very well settled to the contrary. This was an entire contract. Ming v. Corbin, 142 N.Y. 334, 37 N.E. 105. Where a contract is made to perform work and no agreement is made as to payment, the work must be substantially performed before payment can be demanded. . . .

This case was also submitted to the jury upon the ground that there may have been a breach of contract by the defendants in their refusal to permit the plaintiff to continue with his work, claiming that he had departed from the specifications, and there was some evidence justifying this view of the case, but it is impossible to say upon which of these two theories the jury arrived at its conclusion. The above errors, therefore, cannot be considered as harmless and immaterial. . . . As the verdict was for the amount of the bill presented and did not include the damages for a breach of contract, which would be the loss of profits, it may well be presumed that the jury adopted the first ground of recovery charged by the court as above quoted and decided that the plaintiff was justified in abandoning work for non-payment of the installment.

The judgment should be reversed, and a new trial ordered, costs to abide the event.

QUESTION

Suppose that the price for the concrete work had been a fixed sum, say $5,000, and that the contract said nothing about time of payment. Nevertheless, Newbury, acting on its own, paid Stewart the $5,000 upon his beginning work. If Stewart then failed to complete performance, would Newbury be entitled to recover the full $5,000 payment?

––––––––

Patterson, Constructive Conditions in Contracts
42 Colum.L.Rev. 903, 918–920 (1942)

"Where one party's promise requires a substantial time for performance, some extension of credit is practically unavoidable. The rule laid down for all such promises, where the other party's performance does not require a substantial time, is that the latter's duty is conditional on performance by the former; the party whose performance requires time is to extend credit to the latter. . . . [O]ne may ask, why should the party whose promised performance takes time be required to extend credit to the one whose performance does not? The typical case falling under this rule . . . is the contract to do work for money. The usual practice in the community to which the rule was applicable was to pay for the work after it was completed. . . . The practice may be ascribed to the influence of employers as a dominant class, and to judicial inertia which allows an outmoded rule to continue unchanged. The dominance of employers as a class is not what it used to be, yet no demand has appeared to require that employees generally be paid their wages or salaries in advance. There may be sufficient reasons for the survival of the rule. Professor Williston suggests two: 1. The normally greater responsibility of the employer; and 2., the fact that the employee cannot be compelled to perform specifically.

"The policy of the law, here as in the tendency to construct concurrent conditions, is to minimize credit risks. If employers usually present less credit risks than employees, the rule of construction effectuates this end. That colleges and theatres ordinarily require payment in advance for the services which they furnish merely exemplifies the operation of the principle. A further justification may be found in the belief that a moderate postponement of reward stimulates productivity of social goods. . . . The rule which makes performance by the employee a condition precedent of the duty of payment by the employer and which thus places the credit risk and the credit strain on the employee, has been mitigated in its severity by statutes requiring that wages be paid at short intervals (weekly or bi-weekly) to certain classes of employees (in the lower income brackets), by provisions making wage claims preferred in the case of bankruptcy of the employer and by a limited relief for unjust enrichment. The order-of-performance test of credit burdens is thus supplemented by custom and by policy."

———

Kelly Constr. Co. v. Hackensack Brick Co.
91 N.J.L. 585, 103 A. 417 (1918)

Plaintiff, who had a contract to build Englewood school, entered into an agreement with defendant for the "furnishing and delivering and stacking on the job all the common hard brick required by the plans [for Englewood school] at $7 per thousand; brick to be delivered as required by [plaintiff] and sufficient brick to be kept on the job so that [plaintiff] will always have approximately [50,000] brick stacked until completion." The agreement said nothing about the time defendant was to be paid for the brick. After making several deliveries, defendant refused to proceed with the contract because plaintiff had not paid for the brick already on the job. Plaintiff then "covered" by making purchases in the market and sued for damages measured by the cost of cover less the contract price. *Held*, directed verdict for plaintiff affirmed. Where the sale is of a specified quantity of goods (here, sufficient brick to construct a building according to agreed plans), "the contract is entire, and a failure to pay when a part delivery has been made does not excuse the seller from completing delivery, no time for payment being stated in the contract." This is so notwithstanding the Uniform Sales Act's provision that "unless otherwise agreed, delivery of the goods and payment of the price are concurrent conditions." This statute does not require payment with each delivery where, as here, deliveries are pursuant to an "entire contract," which, because of the large quantity involved, must necessarily be performed in installments. Being "entire," the contract by its terms does not require any payment until defendant's performance is completed in full.

NOTE

Section 2–307 of the UCC states: "Unless otherwise agreed all goods called for by a contract for sale must be tendered in a single delivery and payment is due only on such tender but where the circumstances give either party the right to make or demand delivery in lots the price if it can be apportioned may be demanded for each lot." Again, a default rule is provided in the absence of agreement—here, where the parties have not specifically agreed whether delivery and payment are to by lots. Does the section address the problem of the *Kelly* case? Comment 4 to § 2–307 states that where the circumstances indicate that the seller is entitled to deliver in lots, "the price may be demanded for each lot if it is apportionable." In effect, circumstances may give rise to an installment contract, defined in § 2–612 as one requiring or authorizing delivery "in separate lots to be separately accepted."

The influence of UCC 2–307 can be seen in § 233 of the Restatement, Second, which states the following rules:

> (1) Where performances are to be exchanged under an exchange of promises, and the whole of one party's performance can be rendered at one time, it is due at one time, unless the language or the circumstances indicate the contrary.

> (2) Where only a part of one party's performance is due at one time under Subsection (1), if the other party's performance can be so apportioned that there is a comparable part that can also be rendered at that time, it is due at that time, unless the language or the circumstances indicate the contrary.

The case that follows was decided long before the writing of Rest.2d § 233. Does it embrace, or reject, the approach of that provision?

Tipton v. Feitner

Court of Appeals of New York, 1859.
20 N.Y. 423.

Appeal from the Supreme Court. Action to recover the price of certain slaughtered hogs, sold by the plaintiffs to the defendant. It was defended on the ground that they were purchased under a special contract with the plaintiffs, which had been violated on their part. The case, according to the finding of the referee, before whom it was tried, was as follows: On February [3], 1855, at the city of New York, the plaintiffs agreed with the defendant, by parol, by one and the same contract, to sell the defendant eighty-eight dressed hogs, then at the slaughter-house of a third person, in the city, at 7 cents per pound; and also certain live hogs of the plaintiffs, which were being driven, and were then on their way from Ohio to New York, at 5¼ cents per pound live weight, the defendant agreeing on his part to buy the dressed and live hogs at these prices. The dressed hogs were to be delivered immediately after the sale, and the live ones on their arrival at the city, where they were expected, and did arrive some days afterwards. The dressed hogs were delivered on the same day, but were not paid for by the defendant. The live hogs arrived five days afterwards; they were not delivered to the defendant, but were slaughtered by the plaintiffs, and by them sold to other parties. The defendant insisted that the plaintiffs could not recover for the dressed hogs, on the ground that they had failed to perform their agreement as to the live ones. The referee however held, that the plaintiffs were entitled to recover the price of the dressed hogs, deducting the damages which the defendant had sustained for the breach of the other branch of the contract. . . . The dressed hogs came to $1,182.57; deducted for defendant's damages, $401, leaving $780.38, for which judgment was given, which was affirmed at a general term. The defendant appealed.

DENIO, J. It is not universally true that a party to a contract who has himself failed to perform some of its provisions is thereby precluded from recovering damages for a breach committed by the other party. The question in such cases is, whether the stipulation which the plaintiff has failed to observe was a condition precedent to the performance by the defendant; and whether it is of that character or not depends upon the general scope and intention of the agreement, to be gathered from its several provisions. If the parties have in terms stipulated that the defendant's performance shall be dependent or conditional upon something to be done by the plaintiff, the case is a plain one. It is equally so where the act to be done by the plaintiff must naturally precede in the order of time what the defendant is called upon to do, and where the former is necessary to be done to enable the defendant to perform; and also where the defendant's performance is the payment or equivalent for something which he is to receive from the plaintiff unless, in the latter case, it is provided that such equivalent is to be rendered in advance of what is to be received on account of it, credit being given for the latter.

In contracts for the purchase of property, real or personal, where there is no stipulation for credit or delay on either side, the delivery of the property (or its conveyance where it is of a nature to pass by grant), and the payment of the price are each conditions of the other, and neither party can sue for a breach without having offered performance on his part. Such was the nature of the contract in this case. The plaintiffs had slaughtered hogs and also live hogs to dispose of, and the defendant agreed to purchase the whole of both kinds, and to pay a certain price per pound, discriminating, however, as to price between the two species of property. There was no agreement for credit for any part of the property for any time; and in the absence of such a stipulation we must consider that it was to be paid for on delivery, and that the delivery of the property and the payment of the price were to be concurrent acts. But a question then arises, whether the contract was entire in the sense that a delivery of the whole—the live hogs as well as the dressed meat—was to precede the payment for the latter; and it is upon the answer to that inquiry, as I think, that this case depends. And I am of the opinion that the bargain respecting the several kinds of property, in regard to the payment for each, is to be taken distributively. The dressed hogs were to be delivered immediately, while those which were alive, and were on their way from Ohio, were to be delivered when they should arrive. It would not be unreasonable for the parties to have agreed that payment for those first delivered should be postponed until the others came to hand, so that there should be one settlement for the whole; but it would be a more probable mode of adjustment for the purchaser to agree to pay for the parcel which he was to receive at once, and for the other when he should receive it. In that way neither of the parties would be called upon to trust the other—and there being nothing in the contract which looked to credit, we cannot, I think, reasonably hold that any was contemplated. The difference in the kind of property, in the price, and in the time of delivery showed such a diversity in the two operations as to preclude any necessary or probable inference that the one first to be consummated by delivery was to be suspended, as to its liquidation, for the period, more or less uncertain, which might elapse before the other would be ready for adjustment. Upon the construction of so peculiar an agreement a precise precedent is not to be expected. But there is a modern case in the Court of King's Bench, which somewhat confirms the opinion to which I have arrived. The defendant contracted in writing, in October, 1829, to supply the plaintiff with wheat straw sufficient for his use as a stable keeper, till the 24th June, 1830, to be delivered at his stables in London, at the sum of 33s. per load, of thirty-six trusses, and to be delivered at the rate of three loads in a fortnight; and the plaintiff agreed to pay the defendant "the sum of 33s. per load for each load of straw so delivered" on his premises, from that day to the 24th June. The action was for not continuing to deliver the straw after it had been furnished under the contract for about three months; and the defendant's excuse was, that the plaintiff had refused to pay down for the last load. The question then was, whether the price was payable on the delivery of each load, and the court held that it was so payable. Lord Tenterden, C.J., said, he had no doubt that by the terms of this agreement the plaintiff was to pay for the loads of straw as they were delivered. If that were not so, he said, the defendant would have been liable to the inconvenience of giving credit for an indefinite length of time; and in case of non-payment, bringing an action for a very large sum of money, which did not appear to have been intended by the contract. Parke, J., said, the defendant clearly did not contemplate giving credit.... (Withers v. Reynolds, 2 Barn. & Adol., 882.)

Assuming that I am right in the construction of the contract, ... the defendant cannot refuse to pay for the dressed hogs delivered, on the ground that the plaintiff has broken his contract respecting the live ones. The only condition upon which the payment for the former depended, was their delivery. The payment might have been required to be made concurrently with the delivery; but that being waived, the plaintiff might have sued immediately afterwards, and before the time for the delivery of the other property had arrived. It is true, that before this action was commenced the plaintiff was in default for not delivering the other parcel of the property; but for that wrong the defendant had his remedy, either by separate action or by a recoupment in the plaintiff's action; and the referee has allowed him the benefit of it in the latter form. The law no doubt intends to discourage [contractors] from breaking their engagements, but this is not generally accomplished by visiting them with a penalty beyond the damages sustained by the party injured. If I am right in my construction of the agreement, there can be no pretence that the delivery of the hogs coming from Ohio was a precedent condition to the payment for the others; and if this were not so when the agreement was made, it did not become so by the facts which afterwards took place.... Judgment affirmed.

RESTATEMENT OF CONTRACTS, SECOND

Section 240. Part Performances as Agreed Equivalents

If the performances to be exchanged under an exchange of promises can be apportioned into corresponding pairs of part performances so that the parts of each pair are properly regarded as agreed equivalents, a party's performance of his part of such a pair has the same effect on the other's duties to render performance of the agreed equivalent as it would have if only that pair of performances had been promised.

Comment: . . .

b. Separate contracts distinguished. When it is proper to regard parts of pairs of corresponding performances under a contract as agreed equivalents, the contract is sometimes loosely said to be "divisible" or "severable." But under the rule stated [here], the pairs of corresponding parts are not treated as if they were separate contracts. If there are two separate contracts, one party's performance under the first and the other party's performance under the second are not to be exchanged under a single exchange of promises, and even a total failure of performance by one party as to the first has no necessary effect on the other party's duty to perform the second. . . . This is not so, however, if there is a single contract under which the parties are to exchange performances, even though it is proper to regard pairs of corresponding parts of those performances as agreed equivalents. . . . [T]he parties are bound by a single contract and not by a series of separate contracts for each pair of corresponding parts. Although the pairs of performances may be regarded as agreed equivalents, the parties exchanged promises for an exchange of their whole performances.

NOTE: "DIVISIBLE" OR "SEVERABLE" CONTRACTS

Tipton v. Feitner presents problems that are commonly grouped under the heading "entire" versus "divisible" contracts. In making the distinction, the search is for pairs of corresponding performances that appear to be rough compensation for each other. One court, citing *Tipton*, puts the "divisible" inquiry this way: "[W]hether, had the parties thought of it, they would be willing to exchange the part performance irrespective of what transpired subsequently. . . ." Trapkus v. Edstrom's Inc., 140 Ill.App.3d 720, 489 N.E.2d 340 (1986). It should be clear that § 240 of the Restatement, Second, set out above, pursues such an inquiry. Moreover, Tipton v. Feitner was drawn upon by the second restaters in formulating the mitigating doctrine of § 240. Appended to that provision are the following illustrations:

1. A contracts to sell and B to buy a quantity of dressed hogs and a quantity of live hogs at stated prices for each quantity. A is to deliver the dressed hogs first and the live hogs 15 days later, and B is to pay for each delivery within 30 days after it is made. A delivers the dressed hogs, but unjustifiably refuses to deliver the live ones. If a court finds that delivery of the dressed hogs and payment of the price stated for them are agreed equivalents, A can recover the stated price for the dressed hogs under the contract. B then has a claim against A for damages for his failure to deliver the live hogs.

2. The facts being otherwise as stated in Illustration 1, A has no right to payment for either the dressed or the live hogs until 30 days after delivery of the live ones, but A unjustifiably refuses to deliver the live hogs until B pays for the dressed ones. If a court finds that delivery of the dressed hogs and the price stated for them are agreed equivalents, A can recover the stated price for the dressed hogs under the contract. . . . B then has a claim against A for damages for failure to deliver the live hogs.

3. The facts being otherwise as stated in Illustration 1, before A delivers the dressed hogs, he repudiates the contract by stating that he will not deliver the live ones. B then refuses to accept the dressed hogs. Even if a court finds that delivery of the dressed hogs and payment of the price stated for them are agreed equivalents, A has

no claim against B. B has a claim against A for damages for total breach of contract. . . .

Observe that a party who has performed part of a divisible contract may recover the agreed equivalent in an action on the contract; the remedy is not off-the-contract restitution. Young v. Tate, 232 Neb. 915, 442 N.W.2d 865 (1989) ("the rule that a party who fails [to perform] cannot recover on the contract for part performance applies only to entire, indivisible contracts, not to severable contracts"). Also, under the doctrine of conditions, substantial performance of one part of a divisible contract has the same effect on the corresponding part as substantial performance of an indivisible duty has on the entire contract. But if the parties have made not one but two contracts, a party's breach of one will not excuse the other party from the performance due the breacher under the second contract—unless of course performance under one contract is conditioned expressly on performance under the other.

SECTION 2. INTERPRETING CONDITIONS

A contract for the sale of a farm includes a provision stating that the property's existing well "shall have the capacity to pump 300 gallons of water per minute." An inspection made following entry into the contract reveals that the well is capable of delivering only 150 gallons of water per minute. The vendee, urging that the well's capacity "goes to the root of the contract," demands rescission of the written deal and a return of the earnest money paid down. Alternatively, the vendee says that the transaction can proceed if the vendor will reduce the contract price by half. In what sense is either party "in default"? What courses of action, through "self-help" or judicial intervention, are open to the party claiming not to be in default? The talk turns quite naturally to the common law's distinction between a "covenant" and a "condition."

Corbin, Conditions in the Law of Contracts
28 Yale L.J. 739, 743, 745–746 (1919)

"The word 'condition' is used in the law of property as well as in the law of contract and it is used with some variation in meaning. . . . In its proper sense the word *'condition' means some operative fact subsequent to acceptance and prior to discharge*, a fact upon which the rights and duties of the parties depend. Such a fact may be an act of one of the two contracting parties, an act of a third party, or any other fact of our physical world. It may be a performance that has been promised or a fact as to which there is no promise.

". . . [A]ny operative fact may with some propriety be said to be a cause or condition of the legal relations that are consequent thereon. . . . An offer is a cause (or condition) of the power in the offeree. An acceptance is a cause (or condition) of contractual rights and duties. Nevertheless in contract law it is not common to speak of these facts as conditions. . . . The term condition is more properly restricted to facts subsequent to acceptance and prior to discharge. . . .

"A promise is always made by the act or acts of one of the parties . . .; a fact can be made to operate as a condition only by the agreement of both parties or by the construction of the law. The purpose of a promise is the creation of a duty or a disability in the promisor; the purpose of constituting some fact as a condition is always the postponement of an instant duty (or other specified legal relation). The fulfilment of a promise discharges a duty; the occurrence of a condition creates a duty. The non-fulfilment of a promise is called a breach of contract, and creates in the other party a . . . right to damages; it is the failure to perform that which was required by a previous duty. The non-occurrence of a condition will prevent the existence of a duty in the other party; but it may not create any [duty to pay damages] at all, and it *will* not unless someone has promised that it shall occur. . . .

ARTHUR LINTON CORBIN
1874-1967

"It may be observed that both a promise and a condition are means that are used to bring about certain desired action by another person. For example, an insurance company desires the payment of premiums. One means of securing this desired object would be to obtain a promise by the insured to pay premiums; on failure to pay them an action would lie. In fact, however, insurance policies seldom contain such a promise; the payment of the premiums is secured in a more effective way than that. The insurance company makes its own duty to pay the amount of the policy expressly conditional upon the payment of premiums. Here is no express promise of the insured creating a duty to pay premiums, but there is an express condition precedent to his right to recover on the policy. Payment by the insured is obtained not by holding a lawsuit over him *in terrorem* but by hanging before him a purse of money to be reached only by climbing the ladder of premiums. Before bilateral contracts became enforceable this was the only contractual way for a promisor to secure his desired object."

Glaholm v. Hays

2 Mann & Granger 257 (1841)

The contract provided that a chartered vessel "shall proceed to Trieste, and there load a complete cargo; that the vessel being so loaded shall therewith proceed" to a port in the United Kingdom; "that the freight shall be paid" in a specified manner; "that forty running days shall be allowed" for the voyage. Then appeared the clause, "the vessel to sail from England on or before the 4th day of February next." Defendants, the freighters, were sued by the shipowner for refusal to accept the vessel and perform the charter. Defendants pleaded that the vessel did not sail by February 4, but remained in England "for a long time thereafter." The plea was held good against a demurrer. Whether a particular clause is a condition which, when not performed, allows a party to abandon the contract, or amounts only to a promise, the breach of which is recompensed by damages, "must depend upon the intention of the parties," to be determined from the language of the entire agreement and the subject matter to which it relates. This clause specifying February 4, compared with the writing's other clauses, "all of which are framed strictly in the language of agreement only," sounds more nearly in the language of condition. There is, accordingly, "reasonable ground for surmising that some distinction must have been intended" by this variation in terms. And looking at the subject matter, "[b]oth parties were aware that the whole success of a mercantile adventure, does, in ordinary cases, depend upon the commencement of the voyage" on time. Construing the words as a condition precedent will therefore effectuate the parties' intention better than finding them merely words of promise, with damages as the remedy. "[N]othing will so effectually insure both dispatch and certainty, as the knowledge that the obligation of the contract itself shall be made to depend upon the actual performance of the stipulation which relates to them." This must be so because "the performance of the stipulation goes to the very root and the whole of the consideration of the contract," as defendant's prompt objection makes manifest.

Howard v. Federal Crop Ins. Corp.

United States Court of Appeals, Fourth Circuit, 1976.
540 F.2d 695.

WIDENER, CIRCUIT JUDGE. Plaintiff-appellants sued to recover for losses to their 1973 tobacco crop due to alleged rain damage. The crops were insured by defendant-appellee, Federal Crop Ins. Corp. (FCIC). Suits were brought in a state court in North Carolina and removed to the United States District Court. The three suits . . . were combined for disposition in the district court and for appeal. The district court granted summary judgment for the defendant and dismissed all three actions. We remand for further proceedings. Since we find for the plaintiffs as to the construction of the policy, we express no opinion on the procedural questions.

[FCIC], an agency of the United States, in 1973, issued three policies to the Howards, insuring their tobacco crops, to be grown on six farms, against weather damage and other hazards.

The Howards (plaintiffs) established production of tobacco on their acreage, and have alleged that their 1973 crop was extensively damaged by heavy rains, resulting in a gross loss to the three plaintiffs in excess of $35,000. The plaintiffs harvested and sold the depleted crop and timely filed notice and proof of loss with FCIC, but, prior to inspection by the adjuster for FCIC, the Howards had either plowed or disked under the tobacco fields in question to prepare the same for sowing a cover crop of rye to preserve the soil. When the FCIC adjuster later inspected the fields, he found the stalks had been largely obscured or obliterated by plowing or disking and denied the claims, apparently on the ground that the plaintiffs had violated a portion of the policy which provides that the stalks on any acreage with respect to which a loss is claimed shall not be destroyed until the corporation makes an inspection.

The holding of the district court is best capsuled in its own words: "The inquiry here is whether compliance by the insureds with this provision of the policy was a condition precedent to the recovery. The court concludes that it was and that the failure of the insureds to comply worked a forfeiture of benefits for the alleged loss."

There is no question but that apparently after notice of loss was given to defendant, but before inspection by the adjuster, plaintiffs plowed under the tobacco stalks and sowed some of the land with a cover crop, rye. The question is whether, under paragraph 5(f) of the tobacco endorsement to the policy of insurance, the act of plowing under the tobacco stalks forfeits the coverage of the policy. Paragraph 5 [is] entitled *Claims*. Pertinent to this case are subparagraphs 5(b) and 5(f), which are as follows:

> "5(b) *It shall be a condition precedent* to the payment of any loss that the insured establish the production of the insured crop on a unit and that such loss has been directly caused by one or more of the hazards insured against during the insurance period for the crop year for which the loss is claimed, and furnish any other information regarding the manner and extent of loss as may be required by the Corporation. (Emphasis added)."

> "5(f) The tobacco stalks on any acreage of tobacco of types 11a, 11b, 12, 13, or 14 with respect to which a loss is claimed *shall not be destroyed until the Corporation makes an inspection.* (Emphasis added)."

The arguments of both parties are predicated upon the same two assumptions. First, if subparagraph 5(f) creates a condition precedent, its violation caused a forfeiture of plaintiffs' coverage. Second, if subparagraph 5(f) creates an obligation (variously called a promise or covenant) upon plaintiffs not to plow under the tobacco stalks, defendant may recover from plaintiffs (either in an original action, or, in this case, by a counterclaim, or as a matter of defense) for whatever damage it sustained because of the elimination of the stalks. However, a violation of subparagraph 5(f) would not, under the second premise, standing alone, cause a forfeiture of the policy.

Generally accepted law provides us with guidelines here. There is a general legal policy opposed to forfeitures. . . . Insurance policies are generally construed most strongly against the insurer. . . . When it is doubtful whether words create a promise or a condition precedent, they will be construed as creating a promise. Harris & Harris Const. Co. v. Crain & Denbo, Inc., 256 N.C. 110, 123 S.E.2d 590 (1962). The provisions of a contract will not be construed as conditions precedent in the absence of language plainly requiring such construction. *Harris*, 123 S.E.2d at 596. . . .

Plaintiffs rely most strongly upon the fact that the term "condition precedent" is included in subparagraph 5(b) but not in subparagraph 5(f). It is true that whether a contract provision is construed as a condition or an obligation does not depend entirely upon whether the word "condition" is expressly used. . . . However, the persuasive force of plaintiffs' argument in this case is found in the use of the term "condition precedent" in subparagraph 5(b) but not in subparagraph 5(f). Thus, it is argued that the ancient maxim to be applied is that the expression of one thing is the exclusion of another.

The defendant places principal reliance upon the decision of this court in Fidelity–Phenix Fire Ins. Co. v. Pilot Freight Carriers, 193 F.2d 812 (4th Cir.1952). Suit there was predicated upon a loss resulting from theft out of a truck covered by defendant's policy protecting plaintiff from such a loss. The insurance company defended upon the grounds that the plaintiff had left the truck unattended without the alarm system being on. The policy contained six paragraphs limiting coverage. Two of those imposed what was called a "condition precedent." They largely related to the installation of specified safety equipment. Several others, including paragraph 5, [began] with the phrase, "It is further warranted." In paragraph 5, the insured warranted that the alarm system would be on whenever the vehicle was left unattended. Paragraph 6 starts with the language: "The assured agrees, by acceptance of this policy, that the foregoing conditions precedent relate to matters material to the acceptance of the risk by the insurer." Plaintiff recovered in the district court, but [the] judgment was reversed because of a breach of warranty of paragraph 5, the truck had been left unattended with the alarm off. In that case, plaintiff relied upon the fact that the words "condition precedent" were used in some of the paragraphs but the word "warranted" was used in the paragraph in issue. In rejecting that contention, this court said that "warranty" and "condition precedent" are often used interchangeably to create a condition of the insured's promise, and "[m]anifestly the terms 'condition precedent' and 'warranty' were intended to have the same meaning and effect." 193 F.2d at 816.

Fidelity–Phenix thus does not support defendant's contention here. . . . Unlike the case at bar, each paragraph in *Fidelity–Phenix* contained either the term "condition precedent" or the term "warranted." We held that, in that situation, the two terms had the same effect in that they both involved forfeiture. That is well established law. . . . In the case at bar, the term "warranty" or "warranted" is in no way involved, either in terms or by way of like language, as it was in *Fidelity–Phenix*. The issue upon which this case turns, then, was not involved in Fidelity–*Phenix*. . . .

The Restatement of the Law of Contracts states:

§ 261. INTERPRETATION OF DOUBTFUL WORDS AS PROMISE OR CONDITION

Where it is doubtful whether words create a promise or an express condition, they are interpreted as creating a promise; but the same words may sometimes mean that one party promises a performance and that the other party's promise is conditional on that performance.

Two illustrations (one involving a promise, the other a condition) are used in the Restatement:

2. A, an insurance company, issues to B a policy of insurance containing promises by A that are in terms conditional on the

happening of certain events. The policy contains this clause: "provided, in case differences shall arise touching any loss, *the matter shall be submitted to impartial arbitrators*, whose award shall be binding on the parties." This is a promise to arbitrate and does not make an award a condition precedent of the insurer's duty to pay.

3. A, an insurance company, issues to B an insurance policy in usual form containing this clause: "In the event of disagreement as to the amount of loss it shall be ascertained by two appraisers and an umpire. The loss shall *not be payable until 60 days after the award of the appraisers when such an appraisal is required.*" This provision is not merely a promise to arbitrate differences but makes an award a condition of the insurer's duty to pay in case of disagreement. (Emphasis added.)

We believe that subparagraph 5(f) in the policy here under consideration fits illustration 2 rather than illustration 3. Illustration 2 specifies something to be done, whereas subparagraph 5(f) specifies something not to be done. Unlike illustration 3, subparagraph 5(f) does not state any conditions under which the insurance shall "not be payable," or use any words of like import. We hold that the district court erroneously held, on the motion for summary judgment, that subparagraph 5(f) established a condition precedent to plaintiffs' recovery which forfeited the coverage.

From our holding that defendant's motion for summary judgment was improperly allowed, it does not follow the plaintiffs' motion for summary judgment should have been granted, for if subparagraph 5(f) be not construed as a condition precedent, there are other questions of fact to be determined. At this point, we merely hold that the district court erred in holding, on the motion for summary judgment, that subparagraph 5(f) constituted a condition precedent with resulting forfeiture.

The explanation defendant makes for including subparagraph 5(f) in the tobacco endorsement is that it is necessary that the stalks remain standing in order for the Corporation to evaluate the extent of loss and to determine whether loss resulted from some cause not covered by the policy. However, was subparagraph 5(f) inserted because without it the Corporation's opportunities for proof would be more difficult, or because they would be impossible? Plaintiffs point out that the Tobacco Endorsement, with subparagraph 5(f), was adopted in 1970, and crop insurance goes back long before that date. Nothing is shown as to the Corporation's prior 1970 practice of evaluating losses. Such a showing might have a bearing upon establishing defendant's intention in including 5(f). Plaintiffs state, and defendant does not deny, that another division of the Department of Agriculture, or the North Carolina Department, urged that tobacco stalks be cut as soon as possible after harvesting as a means of pest control. Such an explanation might refute the idea that plaintiffs plowed under the stalks for any fraudulent purpose. Could these conflicting directives affect the reasonableness of plaintiffs' interpretation of defendant's prohibition upon plowing under the stalks prior to adjustment?

We express no opinion on these questions. . . . Nothing we say here should preclude FCIC from asserting as a defense that the plowing or disking under of the stalks caused damage to FCIC if, for example, the amount of the loss was thereby made more difficult or impossible to ascertain whether the plowing or disking under was done with bad purpose or innocently. To repeat, our narrow holding is that merely plowing or disking under the stalks does not of itself operate to forfeit coverage under the policy.

The case is remanded for further proceedings not inconsistent with this opinion.

———

Merritt Hill Vineyards, Inc. v. Windy Heights Vineyard, Inc.
61 N.Y.2d 106, 472 N.Y.S.2d 592, 460 N.E.2d 1077 (1984)

At the closing of an agreement entered into six months earlier, plaintiff, the purchaser, learned that defendants, the sellers, had failed to secure two things provided for in the agreement—a title insurance policy and a FHA mortgage confirmation statement. Plaintiff thereupon refused to close and demanded return of its $15,000 deposit. When defendants did not return the deposit, plaintiff brought suit asserting two causes of action, one for return of the $15,000 deposit and one for $26,000 in damages alleged to have been suffered as a result of defendants' failure to perform. *Held*, summary judgment for return of plaintiff's deposit affirmed. "A condition [is] 'an event, not certain to occur, which must occur, unless its nonoccurrence is excused, before performance under a contract becomes due.' (Restatement, Contracts 2d § 224). Here, the contract requirements of a title insurance policy and mortgage confirmation . . . are contained in a section of the agreement entitled 'Conditions Precedent to Purchaser's Obligation to Close,' which provides that plaintiff's obligation to pay the purchase price and complete the purchase . . . is 'subject to' fulfillment of those requirements. No words of promise are employed. Defendants' agreement to sell the stock of the vineyard, not those conditions, was the promise by defendants for which plaintiff's promise to pay the purchase price was exchanged." But defendants' failure to fulfill these conditions entitles plaintiff only to a return of its deposit, not to a recovery of damages. "While a party's failure to fulfill a condition excuses performance by the other party whose performance is so conditioned, it is not, without an independent promise to perform the condition, a breach of contract subjecting the nonfulfilling party to liability for damages."

NOTE

In *Merritt Hill*, if there had been no section entitled "Conditions Precedent" and no "subject to" language, and the agreement simply stated that a title insurance policy and FHA mortgage statement "shall be furnished the purchaser on or before closing," should the court have found a promise? The issue, here and in general, is the degree of clarity required to override the law's presumption against conditions. Language alleged to create a condition is to be strictly interpreted; special scrutiny is the rule of thumb.

The opinion in Howard v. FCIC is not entirely clear about the court's basis for choosing between promise and condition, though the court does appear to be influenced by a term's specification of action or inaction ("something to be done" or "something not to be done") and by an explicit statement of consequences if the specified event does not occur. Another court has taken a different approach: "The test for distinguishing promises from conditions calls for inquiry as to whose words undertake the performance of the act. Are they the words of the person who is doing the act? If so, the words are interpreted, unless a contrary intent is plain, as a *promise* by that person to perform that act. If the words purport to be those of a party who is not doing the act, they are interpreted as limiting the promise of that party by making the performance of the act a condition." Mularz v. Greater Park City Co., 623 F.2d 139, 142–143 (10th Cir.1980).

As you study the cases ahead, consider whether any single test is adequate to the task of distinguishing conditions from promises. Consider also Restatement, Second § 226, illustration 6, which purports to show the usual process of "interpretation" at work:

> A contracts to sell and B to buy a house for $50,000. The contract recites that financing is to take the form of "$30,000 mortgage from X Bank" on stated terms and provides that B's duty is "conditional upon B's ability to arrange above described financing." B is unable to get the mortgage from X Bank but A offers to take a $30,000 purchase money mortgage on the stated terms and makes a conditional offer to deliver a deed. B refuses to perform. Although circumstances may show a contrary intention, the quoted language will ordinarily be interpreted so that the condition occurs only if B is able to get the mortgage from X Bank, and not if B is able to get a similar mortgage from A. Under this interpretation, B's refusal is not a breach.

Moore Bros. Co. v. Brown & Root, Inc.

United States Court of Appeals, Fourth Circuit, 2000.
207 F.3d 717.

MURNAGHAN, CIRCUIT JUDGE. This case arises out of the construction of the Dulles Toll Road Extension, a privately owned and operated toll road connecting Dulles Airport and Leesburg, Virginia. Two issues are raised on appeal: first, whether a surety may rely on a "pay when paid" clause in a subcontract as a defense to liability for payment on a bond; and second, whether a general contractor may rely on the non-occurrence of a valid "pay when paid" condition precedent in the subcontract as a defense to liability where the general contractor was partly responsible for the failure of the condition precedent. . . .

The Dulles Toll Road Extension ("DTRE") is a fourteen mile long private toll road between Dulles Airport and Leesburg, Virginia. It was built and is operated by the Toll Road Investors Partnership II ("TRIP"). In 1993, TRIP (the "Owners") awarded the general construction contract to Brown & Root, Inc. In addition to its role as general contractor, Brown & Root was also an equity partner in TRIP.

Brown & Root in turn entered into subcontracts with Moore Brothers Co., Inc. and The Lane Construction Corp., the plaintiffs, to build parts of the road. Highlands Insurance Co. issued a contract payment bond as surety.

The subcontracts between Brown & Root and plaintiffs contain a general "pay when paid" clause:

> Notwithstanding any other provision hereof, payment by Owner to General Contractor is a condition precedent to any ob-

ligation of General Contractor to make payment hereunder; General Contractor shall have no obligation to make payment to Subcontractor for any portion of the Sublet Work for which General Contractor has not received payment from the Owner.

The contract payment bond issued by Highlands states in part:

> The above named Principal [Brown & Root] and Surety [Highlands] hereby jointly and severally agree with the Obligees that every claimant herein defined who has not been paid in full before the expiration of a period of 90 days after the date on which the last of such claimant's work or labor was done or performed, or materials were furnished by such claimant, may sue on the bond for the use of such claimant, prosecute the suit to final judgment for such sum or sums as may be justly due claimant, and have execution thereon.

The prime construction contract contains provisions for additional payment if the Owners order substantial design changes that constitute a "change in scope" of the project, including a provision for binding arbitration. The early drafts of the contract also contained several specific design change illustrations to clarify the type of situation in which Brown & Root would be entitled to additional payment from the Owners.

Changing the thickness of the pavement subbase material was included in the examples of design changes that would warrant additional payment. Changing the thickness of the pavement subbase is a common and costly design change in highway construction, and throughout the development of the DTRE project there was some uncertainty about the adequacy of the initial pavement design and the thickness of the subbase material that would be required by the Virginia Department of Transportation. As early as 1991 the Brown & Root project manager knew that the initial pavement design for the DTRE was on the "marginal end."

The lenders who were financing the highway project, however, wanted to contain the costs of the project and insisted on a "high degree of certainty" in assessing the total project costs. They were hesitant to agree to a contract that contained specific illustrations of design changes that would warrant additional payment. The Owners and Brown & Root, therefore, agreed in July of 1993 to delete the specific illustrations of design changes from the prime contract to placate the lenders. At the same time, the Owners and Brown & Root assured the lenders that no substantial changes in the work, as defined in the base contract, were anticipated.

After deleting the design change illustrations from the prime contract, the Owners and Brown & Root incorporated the illustrations into a "Policy and Procedures" letter, the existence of which was not revealed to the lenders. In essence, the Owners and Brown & Root reached a side agreement concerning additional "change in scope" illustrations and then concealed that agreement from the lenders by placing it in a side letter, while leaving it out of the prime contract. Brown & Root did not tell the subcontractors that the design change illustrations and the potential need for additional "change in scope" work were hidden from, and therefore not adequately funded by, the lenders.

When the need for a thicker pavement subbase became apparent, Brown & Root ordered the subcontractors to proceed with the additional work. Under the terms of the "pay when paid" condition precedent in the subcontract, Brown & Root knew that if payment for the additional work were not forthcoming from TRIP, it was the subcontractors who would assume the bulk of the loss.

After the additional work was completed, both Brown & Root and the subcontractors sought arbitration of their claim for additional payment from the Owners. The arbitrator concluded that the additional work did constitute a "change in scope" and therefore ordered the Owners to make payments beyond the base contract price. The arbitrator ordered TRIP to pay Brown & Root, who was subsequently required to pay the subcontractors.

Because the lenders were not made aware of the significant likelihood that additional work would be necessary, financing was never arranged to cover payment for additional "change in scope" work. TRIP, therefore, did not have the funds to pay Brown & Root the amount of the arbitration award. Brown & Root, as a result, claims that it is not obligated to pay the subcontractors for the additional work because of the "pay when paid" clause contained in the subcontracts.

The DTRE project was completed ahead of schedule in September of 1995. The matter of a bonus for early completion of the project was the subject of extensive negotiations between Brown & Root, TRIP, and the lenders before the prime construction contract was signed and the financing agreements were reached. The Note Agreement, which governed the financing of the project, contained restrictions on the contractor bonus. In essence, payment of the bonus was subordinated to virtually all other project debts, and could not be made until the outstanding balance of the revolving credit loan was zero, which was anticipated to take five to seven years. Brown & Root knew, therefore, that payment of the early completion bonus would be delayed for at least five to seven years. They did not, however, reveal that information to the subcontractors during the negotiations over distribution of the bonus.

The final version of the bonus provision in the primary contract was left somewhat vague. In the subcontracts, however, a change order was added that read:

> Within 30 days of receipt by General Contractor, Subcontractor will receive 31.5% (or equivalent of $13,500.00 per day of earned bonus whichever is greater) of all Incentive Bonus monies paid to General Contractor by Owner for early completion of the General Contractor's Work Scope.... Except as amended herein, all Subcontract terms and conditions shall remain unchanged, in full force and effect.

Regarding the bonus, the district court concluded:

> Plaintiffs did not know when they negotiated and entered into the relevant change orders that the earliest reasonably anticipated pay out was in five to seven years, or that the financial arrangement created a risk that the bonus would not be paid by the Owners at all. Plaintiffs rejected Brown & Root's second contractor bonus proposal, which was designed to reduce the risk of substantial delay or nonpayment by the owner, because information and documents material to these risks had been either concealed or withheld from plaintiffs by Brown & Root.

Brown & Root has not been paid the early completion bonus, nor has it in turn paid a portion of that bonus to the subcontractors.

Plaintiffs filed separate complaints against Brown & Root and its payment bond surety, Highlands, in the U.S. District Court for the Eastern District of Virginia in December of 1996. On April 22, 1997, the district court granted plaintiffs' motion for summary judgment against Highlands. The court rejected Highlands' argument that it was entitled to assert the "pay when paid" defense available to Brown & Root. Because Highlands did not expressly incorporate the "pay when paid" provision into its bond contract, and because the very purpose of a surety bond is to provide payment when the principal is unable to pay, the court held that Highlands was liable to plaintiffs and must pay for the additional work that plaintiffs performed.

On December 30, 1998, the district court issued extensive findings of fact and conclusions of law after a bench trial on the plaintiffs' claims against Brown & Root. The court held that Brown & Root is liable (1) to Lane for $1.4 million plus prejudgment interest for the additional "change in scope" work, (2) to Lane for $2.4 million for the early completion bonus, (3) to Moore for $2.1 million for the additional "change in scope" work, and (4) to Moore for $2.4 million for the early completion bonus. . . .

The district court found that Brown & Root's own actions in connection with the prime contract and the arrangements for financing additional "change in scope" work contributed to the non-occurrence of the condition precedent. The court found that Brown & Root knew that additional "change in scope" work on the DTRE project would likely be necessary to accommodate design changes regarding the thickness of the pavement subbase material. Brown & Root nonetheless assured the lenders that no additional work would be necessary. Brown & Root then acquiesced in the decision to remove the "change in scope" illustrations from the contract to accommodate the lenders' interest in capping costs, while at the same time protecting themselves with the Policy and Procedures Letter which memorialized the change illustrations as a "side agreement."

In short, the district court found that Brown & Root agreed to remove the design change illustrations from the prime construction contract to placate the lenders, placed those illustrations in a side agreement (the existence of which was not revealed to the lenders), and assured the lenders that no additional work or design changes would be necessary. In finding these facts, the district court weighed the credibility of witnesses, the testimony offered during the prior arbitration, and various documents entered into evidence during the trial. Because the district court's findings of fact are consistent with the evidence contained in the record before this court, those findings are not clearly erroneous.

The subcontracts between Brown & Root and the plaintiffs contain a valid "pay when paid" condition precedent. See [Galloway Corp. v. S.B. Ballard Const. Co., 464 S.E.2d 349, 354 (Va. 1995)]. Because the Owners have not paid Brown & Root for the arbitration judgment regarding the additional "change in scope" work, Brown & Root can, as an initial matter, assert the non-occurrence of the condition precedent as a valid defense to plaintiffs' claims.

Having found that by its own actions Brown & Root contributed to the non-occurrence of the condition precedent, however, the district court applied the "prevention doctrine" to waive the condition precedent and held that Brown & Root is liable to the plaintiffs for payment for the additional "change in scope" work notwithstanding the "pay when paid" clause in the subcontract.

The prevention doctrine is a generally recognized principle of contract law according to which if a promisor prevents or hinders fulfillment of a condition to his performance, the condition may be waived or excused. The Supreme Court of Virginia recognized the prevention doctrine in Parrish v. Wightman, 184 Va. 86, 34 S.E.2d 229, 232 (1945).

The prevention doctrine does not require proof that the condition would have occurred "but for" the wrongful conduct of the promisor; instead it only requires that the conduct have "contributed materially" to the non-occurrence of the condition. The Supreme Court of Virginia does not require the plaintiff to prove "but for" causation. Rather, as that court specifically noted, "[i]t is as effective an excuse of performance of a condition that the promisor has hindered performance as that he has actually prevented it." Parrish, 34 S.E.2d at 232.

The district court found that Brown & Root misled the lenders regarding its expectations that potentially costly design changes would occur. By misleading the lenders in this way, Brown & Root made it less likely that the lenders would arrange additional financing to cover the cost of anticipated design changes. We therefore agree with the district court's conclusion that Brown & Root's conduct "hindered" the fulfillment of the condition precedent.

Brown & Root offers an alternative explanation for the failure of the condition precedent. The failure, they contend, was caused by the financial insolvency of the DTRE project, which was a result of lower than projected traffic flow on the DTRE. According to TRIP's Chief Financial Officer, because of the project's financial distress, sometime in December of 1995 the lenders halted all payments to Brown & Root since it was a partner in the DTRE project. Brown & Root concludes, therefore, that the May 1996 arbitration award would not have been paid regardless of whether additional contingency funding had been arranged by the lenders.

We are not persuaded by Brown & Root's argument. The fact that the lenders halted payments to Brown & Root under the circumstances as they existed in December of 1995 is not proof that the lenders would have forbidden TRIP to draw on some other source of funds to pay Brown & Root for the additional work after the arbitration award in May of 1996 under different circumstances. Had the lenders been apprised early on of the strong possibility that the pavement design would change, it is reasonable to infer that appropriate funding would have been arranged and made available for payment to Brown & Root.

The question is essentially a factual inquiry: why did TRIP fail to pay Brown & Root for the additional "change in scope" work? The district court found that TRIP failed to pay, at least in part, because of Brown & Root's misconduct. Because the district court's findings of fact are not clearly erroneous, and given the speculative nature of Brown & Root's alternative explanation, we do not find reversible error in the conclusions reached below as to the additional work claims. We agree that Brown & Root's misrepresentations "contributed materially" to TRIP's failure to pay for the additional "change in scope" work.

Having so concluded, we hold that the prevention doctrine was properly invoked and the performance of the condition precedent was correctly waived as to the additional "change in scope" work. Without the condition precedent as a defense, Brown & Root is liable to the plaintiffs for payment for the additional work. . . .

We next consider whether the district court properly found that Brown & Root is liable to the plaintiffs for payment of the early completion bonus. . . .

At trial, Brown & Root relied on the "pay when paid" condition precedent contained in the base subcontracts and argued that it was not liable to plaintiffs for the early completion bonus because TRIP never paid Brown & Root any bonus monies. The plaintiffs argued that Brown & Root was liable for payment of the bonus because (1) the "pay when paid" clause in the base subcontracts did not apply to the early completion bonus change orders, and alternatively (2) the condition precedent was waived under the prevention doctrine.

The district court agreed with the plaintiffs' first contention. The court examined the language in the change orders without reference to the "pay when paid" clause in the base subcontracts and found that the change orders were "infected with latent ambiguity." After finding that there was no meeting of the minds as to the meaning of the "within 30 days of receipt" language in the change orders, the district court concluded that such language could not be interpreted as a condition precedent. Relying on *Galloway,* the court construed the "within 30 days of receipt" language as merely a time of payment provision, rather than a risk shifting provision.

Whether a contract is ambiguous is a question of law which we review *de novo.* While the change orders, *standing alone,* are arguably ambiguous under the district court's analysis, in the instant case the relevant change orders do not, in fact, stand alone. They very clearly incorporate the terms of the base subcontract to the extent that those terms are not modified by provisions in the change orders. The "within 30 days of receipt" language in the change orders is consistent with and does not modify the "pay when paid" condition in the base subcontracts. Payment of the bonus for early completion of the project was, therefore, subject to the "pay when paid" condition precedent in the base subcontracts.

The question remains whether, regarding the bonus claims, the "pay when paid" condition in the subcontract should be waived under the prevention doctrine. The district court did not reach this issue. To properly apply the prevention doctrine and waive the "pay when paid" condition precedent as to the bonus claims, the district court must determine whether active, wrongful conduct by Brown & Root "prevented or hindered" TRIP's payment of the early completion bonus to Brown & Root. Judgment in plaintiffs' favor on the bonus claims is proper only if plaintiffs have demonstrated that Brown & Root's conduct contributed materially to TRIP's failure to pay Brown & Root the bonus. Since factual questions are properly considered by the district court in the first instance, we remand for further proceedings to consider whether the "pay when paid" condition should be waived as to the bonus claims under the prevention doctrine.

Berry v. Time Insurance Co.

United States District Court, District of South Dakota, 2011.
798 F. Supp. 2d 1015.

SCHREIER, CHIEF JUDGE. . . . Berry purchased a Nursing Home Insurance Policy (the policy) from Time on or about November 1, 1996. Hancock administers the policy. Berry continues to pay premiums and Time continues to provide insurance under this policy. The policy provides for alternate care in lieu of care in a residential nursing home if both parties agree to an alternative care plan.

Since Berry fell in September of 2008, she has required home healthcare assistance to remain in her home. Berry's daughter, Lisa Paulson, contacted Hancock shortly after the fall. Hancock informed her that, with no exceptions, alternate care could only be covered by the policy if it were provided by a licensed home healthcare provider. After this discussion, Berry discovered South Dakota does not license home healthcare providers. Therefore, Berry believed Hancock would not provide alternate care coverage and obtained independently funded home healthcare, services, and equipment so she could remain in her home.

Eighteen months later, Berry's son, Dr. Spencer Berry, M.D., contacted Hancock and, for the first time, Berry was informed of a list of steps that were required before she could receive alternative care benefits. After Berry was evaluated by a registered nurse, she received an insurance-sanctioned plan and a recommended home healthcare provider, who is neither licensed nor certified by the State of South Dakota. Dr. Berry called Hancock to request coverage of Berry's treatment plan, which had been in effect prior to the evaluation, and he provided Hancock with information on Berry's healthcare providers. Hancock refused to cover this care because the home healthcare provider did not meet minimum licensing criteria. The policy does not state that a home health provider must be licensed or certified.

Subsequently, Hancock offered to pay for some equipment and approved some home healthcare expenses. Berry rejected this offer because she desires full coverage of the expenses associated with her chosen home healthcare provider. The policy states that alternative care plans are to be negotiated between the parties, but the parties were unable to reach a final agreement. Berry then brought this suit. . . .

Berry asserts a breach of contract claim. Time and Hancock argue that there is no contractual obligation to provide alternative care because a condition precedent to the contract was not fulfilled and, therefore, there can be no breach of contract claim. Berry responds that the prevention doctrine makes the contract enforceable.

Under South Dakota law, "[t]he elements of a breach of contract are (1) an enforceable promise; (2) a breach of the promise; and, (3) resulting damages." Bowes Constr., Inc. v. S.D. DOT, 793 N.W.2d 36, 43 (S.D.2010). In the insurance context:

> Where the provisions of an insurance policy are fairly susceptible of different interpretations, the interpretation most favorable to the insured should be adopted. This rule of liberal construction in favor of the insured and strictly against the insurer applies only where the language of the insurance contract is ambiguous and susceptible of more than one interpretation. . . . This rule does not mean, however, that the court may seek out a strained or unusual meaning for the benefit of the insured.

Rumpza v. Donalar Enters., 581 N.W.2d 517, 521 (S.D. 1998) (quoting Olson v. U.S. Fidelity and Guar. Co., 549 N.W.2d 199, 200 (S.D. 1996)).

"It is a general principle of contract law that failure of a condition precedent . . . bars enforcement of the contract." Farmers Feed & Seed, Inc. v. Magnum Enterprises, Inc., 344 N.W.2d 699, 701 (S.D. 1984). "A condition precedent is a contract term distinguishable from a normal contractual promise in that it does not create a right or duty, but instead is a limitation on the contractual obligation of the parties." Johnson v. Coss, 667 N.W.2d 701, 705–06 (S.D. 2003).

The prevention doctrine is an exception to the general rule of condition precedent. The South Dakota Supreme Court has adopted the Restatement (Second) of Contracts § 245 cmt. (a) prevention doctrine:

> Where a duty of one party is subject to the occurrence of a condition, the additional duty of good faith and fair dealing imposed on him . . . may require some cooperation on his part, either by refraining from the conduct that will prevent or hinder the occurrence of that condition or by taking affirmative steps to cause its occurrence. . . . Non-performance of that duty when performance is due is a breach. . . . It has the further effect of excusing the non-occurrence of the condition itself, so that performance of the duty that was originally subject to its occurrence can become due in spite of its non-occurrence.

Id. (quoting Restatement (Second) of Contracts § 245cmt. (a)). In other words, "if a party to a contract hinders the occurrence of a condition precedent, that condition is waived." *Id.* The prevention doctrine requires that the conduct preventing the condition precedent have "contributed materially" to the non-occurrence of the condition precedent.

The prevention doctrine is similar to " 'waiver by estoppel' in the context of excuses for nonperformance of contractual duties." *Id.* The party who prevents a condition from occurring is estopped from benefitting from the non-occurrence of the condition precedent, which would have removed the contractual obligation. "To prove waiver by estoppel one need only show that he or she was misled to his or her prejudice by the conduct of the other party into the honest and reasonable belief that the other party was not insisting upon some right." 13 Williston on Contracts § 39:29(4th ed.).

The policy specifies that Berry may receive benefits for alternate care, meaning care provided outside of a nursing facility, in order to facilitate Berry remaining in her home. In order to receive alternate care benefits the policy requires that: (1) Time receive proof that Berry is eligible for nursing facility benefits; (2) Berry would otherwise require care at a nursing facility; and (3) Berry, Time, and Berry's physician mutually agree to the plan. The policy specifies that the alternative care plan "is negotiable."

Berry contends that she provided Time with proof that she is eligible for nursing facility benefits, thereby satisfying the first condition. In addition, Berry asserts that she would otherwise require care at a nursing facility, thereby satisfying the second condition. Viewing the facts in the light most favorable to the nonmoving party, Berry has pleaded sufficient facts to show that she meets these two conditions. All parties are in agreement that the third condition, a mutual agreement on the alternate care plan, has not been fulfilled.

Berry contends that Time and Hancock would not negotiate with her, and, therefore, blocked mutual agreement, ensuring that the condition precedent to coverage would never be fulfilled. Berry further alleges that Hancock did not provide proper information at initial contact. Hancock then denied coverage for Berry without negotiation. Berry believes this denial was unreasonable. Berry complains that Hancock's actions were a breach of contract and constituted bad faith and therefore trigger the prevention doctrine because the contract requires a good-faith negotiation between the parties.

Berry argues that because Time and Hancock purposefully prevented the condition precedent from occurring, the prevention doctrine waives the condition precedent and makes the policy enforceable. Berry relies on two prevention doctrine cases to buttress her argument: Johnson v. Coss, 667 N.W.2d 701 (S.D. 2003) and Weitzel v. Sioux Valley Heart Partners, 714 N.W.2d 884 (S.D. 2006).

In *Johnson,* the plaintiff Johnson owned a Ford Motor Company franchise and planned to sell the franchise to defendant Coss. The contract contained a condition precedent requirement that Ford Motor Company needed to approve the transfer. Ford Motor Company identified its requirements to Coss, who was unable to meet those requirements. The condition precedent was not fulfilled and the contract failed. Johnson claimed that Coss had caused the condition precedent not to occur. Coss claimed that he made sufficient efforts to fulfill the requirements and the failure of the condition precedent barred Johnson from bringing a breach of contract claim. The South Dakota Supreme Court reversed the grant of summary judgment to Johnson and remanded because the "alleged facts were sufficient to create genuine issues of dispute as to whether Coss spent sufficient time, energy, and expense to satisfy the condition precedent."

In *Weitzel,* the South Dakota Supreme Court remanded a breach of contract case with instructions to the lower court to rely on *Johnson* when determining whether the prevention doctrine should apply. As acknowledged by Time and Hancock, "[i]n each case the court ruled that a jury must determine whether the prevention doctrine applied." Contract interpretation is usually a matter of law, but the prevention doctrine and waiver by estoppel are usually questions of fact. "Whether interference by one party to a contract amounts to prevention . . . is a question of fact to be decided by the jury." *Johnson,* 667 N.W.2d at 707.

Berry contends that despite an agreement being necessary to obtain policy coverage, Time and Hancock would not engage in negotiations on an alternate care plan as required by the policy. Berry states that Hancock initially provided inconsistent information, then subsequently imposed licensing restrictions that were not listed in the policy. These facts are sufficient to state a breach of contract claim because Time and Hancock may have acted to prevent the condition from going into effect and thus, the prevention doctrine as recognized in *Johnson* may excuse the condition precedent.

Time and Hancock argue that allowing this claim to move forward means that Berry can file suit anytime an agreement is not reached. Berry pleads that Hancock intentionally engaged in these actions to prevent the condition precedent from being fulfilled. Berry's contentions are sufficient to move the prevention doctrine claims beyond the pleading stage. . . .

The preceding factual allegations, if true, along with the inferences drawn in favor of Berry as the nonmoving party, sufficiently state claims for relief that are plausible on their face with regard to both the breach of contract claim. . . . Thus, Time and Hancock's motion to dismiss under Rule 12(b)(6) for failure to state a claim upon which relief can be granted is denied. . . .

———

RESTATEMENT OF CONTRACTS, SECOND

Section 227. Standards of Preference with Regard to Conditions

(1) In resolving doubts as to whether an event is made a condition of an obligor's duty, and as to the nature of such an event, an interpretation is preferred that will reduce the obligee's risk of forfeiture, unless the event is within the obligee's control or the circumstances indicate that he has assumed the risk.

Illustrations:

> 1. A, a general contractor, contracts with B, a subcontractor, for the plumbing work on a construction project. B is to receive $100,000, "no part of which shall be due until five days after Owner shall have paid Contractor therefor." B does the plumbing work, but the owner becomes insolvent and fails to pay A. A is under a duty to pay B after a reasonable time.
>
> 2. A, a mining company, hires B, an engineer, to help reopen one of its mines for "$10,000 to be payable as soon as the mine is in successful operation." $10,000 is a reasonable compensation for B's service. B performs the required services, but the attempt to reopen the mine is unsuccessful and A abandons it. A is under a duty to pay B $10,000 after the passage of a reasonable time.
>
> 3. A, a mining company, contracts with B, the owner of an untested experimental patented process, to help reopen one of its mines for $5,000 paid in advance and an additional "$15,000 to be payable as soon as the mine is in successful operation." $10,000 is a reasonable compensation for B's services. B performs the required services, but because the process proves to be unsuccessful, A abandons the attempt to reopen the mine. A is under no duty to pay B any additional amount. . . .

NOTE

The result indicated in illustration 1 to Restatement, Second § 227 is widely understood to represent prevailing views on the type of "pay-when-paid" clause found there. Is that surprising? One court embraced this proposition: "If there is no express language to the contrary in the written document (and no extrinsic evidence), . . . where payment is stipulated to occur on an event, the occurrence of the event fixes only a time for payment; it is not . . . a substantive condition of the legal responsibility to pay." Schuler–Haas Elec. Co. v. Aetna Cas. & Sur. Co., 40 N.Y.2d 883, 389 N.Y.S.2d 348, 357 N.E.2d 1003 (1976). Under such a standard, what is one to conclude when the face of the subcontract explicitly makes payment from the owner to the general contractor a "condition precedent" to any payment to the subcontractor? Is this "express language to the contrary"?

————

Ewell v. Landing

199 Md. 68, 85 A.2d 475 (1952)

Landing loaned $550 in cash to Payne, who promised to repay this sum when he had "sold his timber." Payne died without repaying. In an action brought by Landing against Payne's executor, the evidence was inconclusive as to whether Payne's timber had been sold. Judgment for Landing was nevertheless affirmed. An obligation to pay money can clearly be made contingent on the occurrence of a future event. But here Payne's selling of the timber must have constituted merely a convenient time for payment. "[T]here can be no doubt that there was absolute liability, and that payment was merely postponed until timber could be sold." It could not have been the intention of the parties that if the timber were not sold plaintiff could recover nothing. As an earlier case had said: "Such a result would be a mockery of justice."

————

Amies v. Wesnofske

255 N.Y. 156, 174 N.E. 436 (1931)

Amies and Hines, real estate brokers, were hired under an oral agreement by the Wesnofskes as agents for the sale of the Wesnofskes' farm. It was agreed they would be paid $5,000, half on the signing of any contract of sale and half on "closing." Amies and Hines found vendees who, on December 9, 1925, signed a written contract to purchase the farm for $124,000, of which $10,000 was paid down and $30,000 was to be paid April 9, 1926. In April, the vendees found themselves unable to finance the purchase as they had intended. After postponement of closing until June 1, 1926, the vendees declined to proceed further and it was agreed between them and the Wesnofskes that the latter would keep the $10,000 paid and the contract obligations of both parties should cease. Amies and Hines thereafter brought an action for the balance of the agreed commission, $2,500, but a majority of the court denied recovery. The majority said that the words "when," "after," and "as soon as" are just as effective as "if" to create an express condition, with the result that when the event referred to by such a phrase does not occur no duty of performance arises. Active conduct of the conditional promisor, "preventing or hindering the fulfillment of the condition, eliminates it and makes the promise absolute," but from this it does not follow that a vendor of land promises the broker to procure the vendee's performance. "The broker, in placing reliance upon the self-interest of the vendor in procuring performance from the vendee, is ordinarily secure." Where, as here, the vendor is "passive and neutral" there is no prevention or hindrance that will excuse the condition.

————

Royal–Globe Ins. Co. v. Craven

Supreme Judicial Court of Massachusetts, 1992.
411 Mass. 629, 585 N.E.2d 315.

Abrams, J. At issue is the liability under an uninsured motorist policy of Royal–Globe Ins. Co. (Royal–Globe) to its insured, Theresa M. Craven (Craven), for personal injuries suffered by Craven in a hit and run accident.

Royal–Globe sought a declaratory judgment that it was not liable to Craven because Craven's notice to Royal–Globe was not timely. . . . On cross-motions for summary judgment, the [trial] judge entered a summary judgment for Craven, denied Royal–Globe's motion for summary judgment, and ordered that the matter proceed to arbitration. Royal–Globe appealed. . . . We reverse and order that a judgment be entered declaring that Royal–Globe is not liable to Craven because Craven's notice to Royal–Globe was not timely. . . .

. . . In the early morning of September 19, 1979, Craven was injured in a hit and run automobile accident. [She says] an unidentified motor vehicle forced her automobile off the road and into a wall barrier. Craven was taken by ambulance to a hospital, where she was treated for a number of serious injuries. She remained in intensive care for several days and was released from the hospital twenty-three days after the accident.

Craven gave Royal–Globe formal notice of her claim on January 23, 1980. Royal–Globe denied her claim for recovery under her uninsured motorist policy on April 6, 1981.[1] On December 12, 1984, Craven filed a demand for arbitration of her uninsured motorist claim. On March 11, 1985, Royal–Globe filed [suit] seeking a declaration that it had no obligation to submit to arbitration as it was not liable under the policy.[2]

Royal–Globe asks us to reverse the summary judgment for Craven on the ground that Craven did not comply with her contractual obligation to give timely notice of her claim.[3] . . . The uninsured motorist policy in effect at the time of the accident requires notice to both the police and the insurer "[w]ithin [twenty-four] hours . . . if [the insured has] . . . been involved in a hit and run accident." The judge concluded, however, that Craven "was in the intensive care unit during the first twenty-four hours [after the accident]" and could not be expected to notify the police and her insurance company within twenty-four hours. . . . Craven therefore was excused from the twenty-four hour notice requirement. . . . There was no error in that determination.

Royal–Globe [urges] that even if twenty-four hour notice was excused because of disability, the requirement should be reimposed once the disability is removed. Under this interpretation of the policy, disability tolls the running of the twenty-four hour period but does not dispense with it. The judge concluded that in the event that twenty-four hour notice is excused initially by disability, as was the case here, the policy requires prompt notice but not necessarily twenty-four hour notice. We agree. The language of the policy puts a time pressure on the insured to notify the company immediately after the disability is removed.

Royal–Globe contends that based on the undisputed facts in this record, Craven's notification, given more than four months after the accident and more than three months after her release from the hospital, was not prompt. We agree. Royal–Globe argues, and Craven does not dispute, that

---

[1] Royal–Globe paid Craven's claims under her Personal Injury Protection and Medical Payments policies and her claim for property damages. [The court's footnotes have been renumbered; some are omitted.—Eds.]

[2] The arbitration has been stayed pending the outcome of this action.

[3] The standard Massachusetts automobile insurance policy in question instructs the insured what to do "[w]hen [t]here is an [a]ccident or [l]oss." The policy requires that the insured notify both the police and the insurance company within twenty-four hours if the insured has "been involved in a hit and run accident." The policy further requires that, in all events, the insurance company "must be notified *promptly* of the accident or loss" (emphasis added).

Craven was released from the hospital twenty-three days after the accident and that she stopped using medication one week after leaving the hospital. While at home, Craven was able to leave her home to visit doctors and dine out with her family[;] [she] also communicated with her office. Craven returned to work roughly three months after the accident; she did not give notice to Royal–Globe for another month. On this record, we cannot tell precisely when Craven's disability was removed, but it is clear that she did not notify Royal–Globe immediately thereafter.[4]

The burden of proving that she gave her notice promptly was on Craven. . . . Regardless of when her disability is determined to have disappeared, Craven's notice to Royal–Globe was not "performed readily or immediately[; nor was it] given without delay or hesitation." Webster's Third New Int'l Dictionary 1816 (1961). Giving "prompt" its fair meaning, Craven did not notify Royal–Globe promptly as a matter of law.[5]

Craven contends that Royal–Globe is estopped from raising her failure of notice as a basis to deny liability[,] [urging] that from the time she notified Royal–Globe of her claim, the company investigated the claim, communicated with her counsel about the status of the claim, and even informed her counsel of the possibility that liability might be denied because of a failure of proof—all without ever reserving the right to deny the claim based on late notice. The absence of such a reservation of rights, Craven argues, estops the company from denying liability because of her late notice.[6]

"In order to work an estoppel it must appear that one has been induced by the conduct of another to do something different from what otherwise would have been done and which has resulted to his harm. . . ." [389 Mass. 85, 112, 449 N.E.2d 1189 (1983)]. . . . As we have previously noted, "where the denial of liability takes place after the expiration of the period for . . . [giving prompt notice], it cannot be said that the insured has been induced to forego steps to prevent a default under the policy, for the default has already occurred. Consequently, there is no basis for an estoppel." [320 Mass. 719, 722, 71 N.E.2d 232 (1947)]. . . .

Because Craven's notice was not prompt, and because Royal–Globe was not estopped from defending against liability on the basis of Craven's

---

[4] The judge reasoned that, where there is an ambiguous provision in an insurance policy, the court must construe it strictly against the insurer. There was, however, no ambiguity in the policy's use of the term "promptly." . . .

[5] We have said, albeit in dicta, that an insured "did not act with reasonable promptness" when it waited forty-six days after learning of a claim before notifying its insurer. Depot Cafe, Inc. v. Century Indem. Co., 321 Mass. 220, 225, 72 N.E.2d 533 (1947). Similarly, an injured plaintiff who did not notify his insurer of his claim on the policy for two months and six days did not act "with reasonable promptness" and thereby violated the policy's requirement of immediate notice. Wainer v. Weiner, 288 Mass. 250, 252, 192 N.E. 497 (1934). In construing analogous notice provisions, we have held that similar, and even shorter, delays in notifying insurers barred recovery. . . .

[6] Craven also argues that Royal–Globe's payment of her personal injury protection, medical benefits, and collision benefits claims is inconsistent with its denial of benefits under the uninsured motorist policy. Royal–Globe replies, however, that these benefits are recoverable in a one-car accident. Timely notice of these claims is thus not as crucial to the insurance company. Generally in a one-car accident, fault is not an issue. Craven's argument would require litigation as to claims in which there is no controversy, if there are some claims in dispute. We decline to adopt such a rule.

late notice, a judgment declaring that Royal–Globe is not liable to Craven because the notice was not timely should be entered. . . .

———

Semmes v. Hartford Ins. Co.
80 U.S. (13 Wall.) 158 (1871)

Plaintiff, a resident of Mississippi, brought suit on a policy of fire insurance issued by defendant, a Connecticut company. As recounted in the opinion, Plaintiff's loss occurred on January 5, 1860; suit was begun on October 31, 1866. Defendant relied on a provision of the policy to the effect that "no suit . . . should be sustainable in any court unless such suit should be commenced within the term of twelve months next after any loss or damage should occur." The lower court held the suit barred by this provision, notwithstanding plaintiff's contention that the Civil War had prevented commencement of the action within 12 months of the loss. That court reasoned that the 12–month provision was like a statute of limitation, and thus the running of the 12 months was suspended ("tolled") during the period of disability created by the war. Nevertheless, by tacking the time between the date of the loss and the commencement of the war to the time between the close of the war and the commencement of the action, the trial court concluded that plaintiff had waited more than the 12 months allowed by the contract.

Held, reversed and remanded for a new trial. "[T]he period of twelve months . . . does not open and expand itself so as to receive within it three or four years of legal disability . . . and then close together at each end of that period so as to complete itself, as though the war had never occurred. It is true that, in regard to the limitation imposed by statute . . . the time may be so computed, but there the law imposes the limitation and the law imposes the disability. [It is] a necessary legal logic that the one period should be taken from the other. . . . Such is not the case as regards this contract. The defendant has made its own special and hard provision on that subject. . . . The condition is that no suit or action shall be sustainable unless commenced within the *time of twelve months next after the loss shall occur*, and in case such action shall be commenced after the expiration of twelve months *next after such* loss, the lapse of time shall be taken . . . as conclusive evidence against the validity of the claim. . . . [I]f the plaintiff shows any reason which in law rebuts the presumption, which, on the failure to sue within twelve months, is, by the contract, made conclusive against the validity of the claim, that presumption is not revived again by the contract. . . . There is nothing in the contract which does it. . . . Nor does the same evil consequence follow from removing absolutely the bar of the contract that would from removing absolutely the bar of the statute, for when the bar of the contract is removed there still remains the bar of the statute, and though the plaintiff may show by his disability to sue a sufficient answer to the twelve months provided by the contract, he must still bring his suit within the reasonable time fixed by the legislative authority, that is, by the statute of limitations.

"We have no doubt that the disability to sue imposed on the plaintiff by the war relieves him from the consequences of failing to bring suit within twelve months after the loss, because it rendered a compliance with that condition impossible and removes the presumption which that contract says shall be conclusive against the validity of the plaintiff's claim. That part of the contract, therefore, presents no bar to the plaintiff's right to recover."

NOTE

Semmes, like *Royal–Globe*, revisits excuse for "impracticability." Only now the inquiry is about the nonoccurrence of a condition, not the discharge of an underlying duty. Suppose the policy in *Semmes* had made it a condition of defendant's liability that premiums be paid annually, and that plaintiff, contending that the Civil War had rendered him unable to pay the premium for the year in which the loss occurred, nonetheless sued on the policy, tendering in court the overdue premium? New York Life Ins. Co. v. Statham, 93 U.S. (3 Otto) 24 (1876), was a consolidation of three actions brought on life insurance policies issued by defendant before 1860, insuring the lives of Mississippi residents who died after the outbreak of the Civil War. Payment of funds between North and South having been forbidden by both belligerents, premiums were not paid on the policies after the start of hostilities. Each policy contained the clause: "In case the said [insured] shall not pay the said premium on or before the several days hereinbefore mentioned for the payment thereof, then and in every such case the said company shall not be liable to the payment of the sum insured, or in any part thereof, and this policy shall cease and determine." The Court declared that the contract in each case was not merely a contract to insure for a single year, with a privilege of renewal from year to year by paying an annual premium, but that it was an "entire" contract for insurance for life, subject to discontinuance on nonpayment of the premiums stipulated. The Court nevertheless declared, without citing *Semmes*, that prompt payment of premiums was essential to the conduct of the insurance business and the calculation of insurance risks, and that nonpayment of premiums avoided the policies. But since the nonpayment was caused by an act of government without fault of the insured, restitution should be awarded of the "equitable value" of the policies, measured by the premiums paid minus "the value of the assurance enjoyed by [the insured] whilst the policy was in existence." A similar conclusion was reached in Abell v. Penn Mut. Life Ins. Co., 18 W.Va. 400 (1881), though with a different method of measuring restitution, which aimed to prevent retention of any "profit" by the insurance company.

If you are familiar with Civil War history, the opinion in *Semmes* will seem strange, as it reports that the loss took place on January 5, 1860 and Mississippi did not secede from the Union until more than a year later (January 9, 1861), and Fort Sumter surrendered to Confederate forces later still (April 13, 1861). Nineteenth century reports of opinions, however, were at times unreliable, as this report illustrates. The record of the case makes clear that the fire was in fact on January 5, 1861, just a few days before Mississippi seceded. In assessing whether the filing of the claim was timely you should bear in mind that the Civil War came to an end with the surrender at Appomattox Court House on April 9, 1865.

COMMENT: WAIVER OF CONDITIONS

Waiver, like estoppel, is a general doctrine of American law. "Generality" means, of course, that a doctrine may take different forms as bases for application are varied. Courts and commentators commonly say that waiver and estoppel are "distinct but related doctrines," that is, despite distinguishable elements, they overlap in application and, at times, are discussed in words used interchangeably (e.g., a court may ask whether the proofs add up to "waiver by estoppel"). In our most recent encounter with waiver and estoppel (Chapter 5, pp. 633–639), it might be said that the function of these doctrines was to terminate contract rights and discharge contract duties. Corbin would classify the cases in this way, making clear that decisions of the *Globe*-type involve the elimination of express conditions to a promised performance, not the alteration of underlying rights or duties that is normally accomplished through an agreed modification of a promise. 3A A. Corbin, Contracts § 752.

In the insurance cases, waiver and estoppel are in practice almost interchangeable, and a number of courts have said they are fully so. E.g., Hanover Ins. Co. v. Fireman's Fund Ins. Co., 217 Conn. 340, 586 A.2d 567 (1991) ("in certain cases, the conduct claimed to give rise to estoppel may be so clear and unequivocal as to support an inference that a party intentionally relinquished its known right to rely on the one year suit provision"). Whether this is true is a point to watch for in both insurance and noninsurance cases.

For now, it should be stressed that conduct amounting to a waiver typically invites reliance, particularly when the conduct occurs before the time for occurrence of the condition. Absent such reliance, a number of courts have signalled caution in equating waiver and estoppel. An example is Thomason v. Aetna Life Ins. Co., 9 F.3d 645 (7th Cir.1993), where the court was unwilling to extend waiver principles to actions, brought under a federal statute (ERISA), in which it had previously applied estoppel:

> While it is true that the same facts that give rise to a claim of waiver may also support a claim of estoppel, this is not enough to support plaintiff's argument [that waiver is applicable where estoppel would be applied.] Waiver is the "voluntary and intentional relinquishment or abandonment of a known existing right or privilege, which, except for such waiver, would have been enjoyed." . . . An estoppel, on the other hand, "arises when one party has made a misleading representation to another party and the other has reasonably relied to his detriment on that representation." . . . Facts that give rise to an estoppel need not support a finding of waiver, and vice versa. [Moreover,] the requisites to finding a valid waiver of a known right are not as well established as the requisites to finding an equitable estoppel. To find a valid expressed waiver, some courts require that the waiving party has received consideration for the waiver or that the non-waiving party has acted in reasonable reliance on the apparent waiver. . . . Other courts hold, especially in the insurance context, that an implied waiver can be found without any detrimental reliance or exchange of consideration.

> In this case plaintiff concedes that she cannot establish any sort of detrimental reliance on the misleading letters [defendant] sent. Nor did she give [defendant] consideration for the alleged waiver. The waiver that plaintiff seeks, then, is a something-for-nothing kind of waiver whereby [defendant] will be held to the terms of its misleading representations for no reason other than that it made them.

It is another question whether a condition once eliminated by waiver or estoppel can be revived. One continues to find in the cases statements that "[a] waiver once made is irrevocable and cannot be revived." Tri–City Jewish Center v. Blass Riddick Chilcote, 159 Ill.App.3d 436, 512 N.E.2d 363 (1987), appeal denied, 118 Ill.2d 552, 520 N.E.2d 393 (1988). If goods are involved, § 2–209 of the UCC (recall Universal Builders, Inc. v. Moon Motor Lodge, supra p. 633), has something to say on this. What about a land contract with an express condition of installment payments on the first day of each month, and "waiver" by the vendor's acceptance of successive payments 10, 12, and 15 days late; can the vendor reinstate the condition by notice communicated well in advance of the next payment day? A similar question may arise as to insurance premiums accepted late, or accepted through an agent when direct payment to the home office is required. You may expect that many conditions can be revived within certain limits that are not always well defined. Recall, for example, the court's statement about "expunging or recalling" a waiver, in Nassau Trust Co. v. Montrose Concrete Prod., supra p. 636. One of the pervasive questions of this chapter is—what are those limits? Might it count for something that the waiver occurs after the time for occurrence of the condition has passed?

There is need to add a word on the relevance of the consideration requirement in applying the contractual doctrine of waiver. Since consideration is used in our law only in connection with a bargain ("an agreement to exchange"), it was necessary to provide that some promises are binding without consideration. Promises found to constitute a "waiver" by virtue of an obligor's manifested intention to disregard an unfulfilled condition are so classified. The problem is that not all conditions may be dropped from a contract by mere words of promise or waiver, as Clark v. West, just ahead, reveals.

It is usual in treating conditions to postpone to a later point the whole subject of excuse of conditions, i.e., the means by which conditions can be eliminated or suspended. We find this unsatisfactory, because problems concerning the interpretation and the legal effect of conditions are mixed up with problems as to when conditions are or may be excused.

———

Timeliness as an Express Condition

If the parties to a contract wish to make timely performance a material element of their agreement, there is nothing to stop them. Timeliness, like other bargainable items, is mainly a matter of contract and not of law. The question whether a contract must be performed at the exact time specified usually takes the form of an inquiry into whether "time is of the essence." Many written agreements include a time-is-of-the-essence clause. The typical case involves a duty to pay money on a stated date—for example, a land-contract installment of $500 on or before June 15. Is the vendee's payment of $500 no later than June 15 an "express condition" of the vendor's duties under the contract? Whether performance at the specified time is of the essence is most certainly a question of the parties' intent, to be determined, as a matter of fact, from the language of the contract and the circumstances attending its negotiation. Because interpretation always has a context, Professor Corbin's warning about the hazards of boilerplate bears repeating: "It is not desirable to try to achieve [the conditioning of a duty upon a performance on or by a specified time] by merely putting into the contract the words 'time is of the essence of this contract.' " 3A A. Corbin, Contracts § 715.

If time is found to be "of the essence," courts usually say that performance on the designated date is "mandatory." One matter worth special attention is how (and by whom) the question of timely performance is raised—that is, the type of claim or defense brought to court. Another is that in many courts, perhaps most, contract provisions specifying dates for performance are more strictly enforced in actions at law than in suits for equitable relief. Still another is the course-of-performance conduct of the parties in relation to terms specifying dates or schedules for performance. It should be noted that the rule that time ordinarily is not of the essence in transactions involving real property applies to the occurrence of a contractual condition as well as to the performance of a contractual duty. Kakalik v. Bernardo, 184 Conn. 386, 439 A.2d 1016 (1981). In light of what we have seen, might the same be said of building or construction contracts?

———

Sahadi v. Continental Illinois Nat'l Bank & Trust Co. of Chicago
706 F.2d 193 (7th Cir.1983)

"The Bank [urges] that no room for a 'materiality' analysis and its concomitant factual inquiry exists here because the payment of the interest on or before November 15 was an 'express condition' of the Bank's forbearance, and thus its terms were required to be exactly fulfilled. This [argument] suffers from its conclusory assumption of what it seeks to prove—that the payment of the interest on the precise named date rather than payment . . . in a reasonably prompt manner was of threshold importance to the completion of the contract. In short, asking whether a provision is a 'condition' is similar to stating the 'materiality' question: both seek to determine whether its performance was a *sine qua non* of the contract's fulfillment. And that determination may not be made through a mechanical process."

———

Porter v. Harrington
Supreme Judicial Court of Massachusetts, 1928.
262 Mass. 203, 159 N.E. 530.

RUGG, C.J. This is a suit in equity whereby the plaintiff seeks to compel the defendants specifically to perform an agreement to convey land to him. The judge [below] entered a final decree in favor of the plaintiff. . . . The findings of fact are amply supported by the evidence, and must be accepted as true. [I]n 1919, by a written contract, the plaintiff agreed to buy and the defendants to sell two lots of land for a specified sum, of which $60 was the initial payment, the balance being payable at the rate of $10 each month. In February, 1922, the defendants, for the sums already paid, conveyed one of these lots to the plaintiff, the contract remaining in force as to the other lot. On January 1, 1923, the balance charged against the plaintiff upon the books of the defendants was $578.54. The plaintiff made no payments in 1923. In 1924 he paid $60 in instalments, besides the taxes for that year. In 1925 he paid $60 in instalments. On March 25, 1926, he paid

$40 in one sum. This was the last payment made by him. On November 9, 1926, the plaintiff offered to pay $30 upon the contract, but was informed by one of the defendants that they had, on August 1 previous, "exercised the option and decided to close the account." The plaintiff has been ready and before filing this bill offered to pay the entire amount due upon his contract, but the defendants have declined to accept it upon the ground that on August 1, 1926, they exercised their option under the contract to cancel the same for default of the plaintiff in failing to keep up the payments, and claim the right to hold the money paid in by the plaintiff as liquidated damages.

The contract contained these clauses: "It is further mutually agreed and understood [as] follows: . . . Second: That prompt performance and time are the nature and essence of this contract and each of its conditions, and therefore if default of payment is made of any of said installments of said principal sum or interest, and such default shall continue for a period of thirty-one days after it becomes due, or if the party of the second part [the present plaintiff] shall fail to promptly perform any other of the agreements or conditions herein contained, . . . at the option of the party of the first part [the present defendants], all right, title, interest and claim of the party of the second part in and to said described premises shall thereupon cease and this agreement shall become null and void and of no effect, without any notice to the said party of the second part, notice, tender and demand being hereby waived by the party of the second part, and the party of the first part shall thereupon and thereby be released from all obligations hereunder, and all moneys paid thereon previous to said default shall be and become the absolute property of the party of the first part as fixed, ascertained, and liquidated damages for failure to perform this contract[.] . . . Fifth: It is understood and agreed that . . . no waiver of a breach of any term or condition shall be a waiver of any other or subsequent breach of the same or of any other term or condition."

Further findings of the judge are that it appears that, while during the period between the date of the contract and the time when the plaintiff paid for and took title to one of the lots [February 1922], the instalments payments were made with considerable regard for punctuality, since February, 1922, and for about four years, the plaintiff has made payments [which the defendants have during all this period accepted without, so far as appears, making any objection or giving any warning against future delays] at times far behind the dates when according to the contract such payments were due. When the last payment of $40 was made on March 25, 1926, no notice was then given by the defendants of an intention on their part to hold the plaintiff in the future to a more strict compliance with the contract. Until the plaintiff offered in November, 1926, to make another payment upon this contract he was not told by the defendants or notified in any way that they had in August, 1926, undertaken to exercise their option to cancel the contract. The defendants have, by a course of dealings lasting over several years, constantly accepted delayed payments from the plaintiff without objection.

Parties have a right to make a stated time for performance the essence of a contract. Such an agreement, when not waived either by words or conduct, is binding and will be given effect by courts of equity as well as of law. . . . The contract in the case at bar was of that nature.

No principle of law or equity prevents the waiver by parties of such terms of a contract, however explicit may be its phraseology. Waiver may be manifested by acts as well as by words. The defendants, by a course of conduct covering nearly if not quite three years, accepted from the plaintiff payments long overdue. As a consequence, they have taken from him more than one fourth of the entire amount due under the contract. In addition, he has paid some of the taxes on the land, which accrued to the benefit of the defendants. All this the defendants claim as a forfeiture or, to use the words of the contract, as "liquidated damages." There is no finding that the failure of the plaintiff promptly to make payments was intentional or wilful or in any way offensive, or that it has caused any loss to the defendants for which full compensation cannot be made by payment of interest. . . . When a party without objection has accepted overdue payments not made in accordance with the strict terms of the contract, an order of business has been established inconsistent with rigid insistence upon a clause of the contract which in effect is a forfeiture or the enforcement of a penalty. The finding of the trial judge in substance was that the conduct of the defendants was such as to lull the plaintiff into a justifiable assumption that, notwithstanding the terms of the contract, he would be given indulgence in making his payments, and that the conduct of the defendants amounted to a waiver of their right to elect to close out all rights of the plaintiff without notice and without giving him a reasonable opportunity to save his payments already made by paying the balance due on his contract, and that the conduct of the defendants was harsh, oppressive and vindictive. It is usually a question of fact whether there has been a waiver of stipulations of a contract. [That] is the necessary effect of all the findings of the trial judge. . . . Such a finding is not affected by the words of the contract concerning waiver by the plaintiff of the right to such notice. It is difficult to frame a contract so as to foreclose the operation in equity of the doctrine of waiver in order to prevent an injustice. The terms of the present contract did not go far enough to prevent [relief] against a result which does violence to the sense of fairness and good conscience of a court of equity. It would be unconscionable to permit the defendants, in view of their conduct, without notice or warning to insist upon strict performance of the contract and to forfeit all rights of the plaintiff. . . .

Decree affirmed with costs.

QUESTIONS

(1) Suppose a land contract with $1,000 paid down and a promise of the vendee to pay $500 every six months until the total price of $5,000 is paid. The contract includes a time-is-of-the-essence clause and provision for forfeiture by written notice in case of any default by vendee. The first installment due October 1 is paid December 1; the second installment due April 1 is not paid and written notice of forfeiture is given May 1. Can the vendee be evicted?

(2) Suppose the same facts as above, except that the first installment, due October 1, is not paid and the notice of forfeiture is sent by the vendor March 1. Can the vendee be evicted?

Clark v. West

Court of Appeals of New York, 1908.
193 N.Y. 349, 86 N.E. 1.

On February 12th, 1900, the plaintiff and defendant entered into a written contract under which the former was to write and prepare for publication for the latter a series of law books. . . . After the plaintiff had completed a three-volume work known as "Clark & Marshall on Corporations," the parties disagreed. The plaintiff claimed that the defendant had broken the contract by causing the book to be copyrighted in the name of a corporation, which was not a party to the contract, and he brought this action to recover what he claims to be due him, for an accounting and other relief. The defendant demurred to the complaint on the ground that it did not state facts sufficient to constitute a cause of action. The Special Term overruled the demurrer, but upon appeal to the Appellate Division, that decision was reversed and the demurrer sustained.

Those portions of the contract [germane] to the present stage of the controversy are as follows: The plaintiff agreed to write a series of books relating to specified legal subjects; the manuscript furnished by him was to be satisfactory to the defendant; the plaintiff was not to write or edit anything that would interfere with the sale of books to be written by him under the contract and he was not to write any other books unless requested so to do by the defendant, in which latter event he was to be paid $3,000 a year. The contract contained a clause [providing:] "The first party (the plaintiff) agrees to totally abstain from the use of intoxicating liquors during the continuance of this contract, and that the payment to him in accordance with the terms of this contract of any money in excess of $2 per page is dependent on the faithful performance of this as well as the other conditions of this contract." . . .

In a later paragraph it further recited that, "In consideration of the above promises of the first party (the plaintiff), the second party (the defendant) agrees to pay to the first party $2 per page, . . . on each book prepared by the first party under this contract and accepted by the second party, and if said first party abstains from the use of intoxicating liquor and otherwise fulfills his agreements as hereinbefore set forth, he shall be paid an additional $4 per page in manner hereinbefore stated." . . .

The plaintiff [alleges] completion of the work on corporations and publication thereof by the defendant; the sale of many copies thereof from which the defendant received large net receipts; the number of pages it contained (3,469), for which he had been paid at the rate of $2 per page, amounting to $6,938; and that defendant has refused to pay him any sum over and above that amount, or any sum in excess of $2 per page. Full performance of the agreement on plaintiff's part is alleged, except that he "did not totally abstain from the use of intoxicating liquor during the continuance of said contract, but such use by the plaintiff was not excessive and did not prevent or interfere with the due and full performance by the plaintiff of all the other stipulations in said contract." The complaint further alleges a waiver on the part of the defendant of the plaintiff's stipulation to totally abstain from the use of intoxicating liquors. . . .

The [following] questions have been certified to us: 1. Does the complaint herein state facts sufficient to constitute a cause of action? 2. Under the terms of the contract alleged in the complaint, is the plaintiff's total abstinence from the use of intoxicating liquors a condition precedent which can be waived so as to render defendant liable upon the contract notwithstanding plaintiff's use of intoxicating liquors? 3. Does the complaint herein allege facts constituting a valid and effective waiver of plaintiff's nonperformance of such condition precedent?

WERNER, J. . . . [T]he defendant's position is that the stipulation as to plaintiff's total abstinence is the consideration for the payment of the difference between $2 and $6 per page and therefore could not be waived except by a new agreement to that effect based upon a good consideration; that the so-called waiver alleged by the plaintiff is not a waiver but a modification of the contract in respect of its consideration. The plaintiff argues that the stipulation for his total abstinence was merely a condition precedent intended to work a forfeiture of the additional compensation in case of a breach and that it could be waived without any formal agreement to that effect based upon a new consideration.

The subject-matter of the contract was the writing of books by the plaintiff for the defendant. . . . The compensation for the work specified in the contract was to be $6 per page, unless the plaintiff failed to totally abstain from the use of intoxicating liquors during the continuance of the contract, in which event he was to receive only $2 per page. . . . It is not a contract to write books in order that the plaintiff shall keep sober, but a contract containing a stipulation that he shall keep sober so that he may write satisfactory books. . . . [T]he particular stipulation is not the consideration for the contract, but simply one of its conditions which fits in with those relating to time and method of delivery of manuscript, revision of proof, citation of cases, assignment of copyrights, keeping track of new cases and citations for new editions, and other details which might be waived by the defendant, if he saw fit to do so. This is made clear . . . by the provision that, "In consideration of the above promises," the defendant agrees to pay the plaintiff $2 per page on each book prepared by him, and if he "abstains from the use of intoxicating liquor and otherwise fulfills his agreements as hereinbefore set forth, he shall be paid an additional $4 per page in manner hereinbefore stated." . . .

It is obvious that the parties thought that the plaintiff's normal work was worth $6 per page. That was the sum to be paid for the work done by the plaintiff and not for total abstinence. If the plaintiff did not keep to the condition as to total abstinence, he was to lose part of that sum. . . . [I]t follows that the stipulation as to the plaintiff's total abstinence was nothing more nor less than a condition precedent [which] could be waived; and if it was waived the defendant is clearly not in a position to insist upon the forfeiture which his waiver was intended to annihilate. . . . Defendant still has the right to counterclaim for any damages which he may have sustained in consequence of the plaintiff's breach, but he cannot insist upon strict performance. Dunn v. Steubing, 120 N.Y. 232, 24 N.E. 315. . . .

This whole discussion is predicated of course upon the theory of an express waiver. We assume that no waiver could be implied from the defendant's mere acceptance of the books and his payment of the sum of $2 per page without objection. It was the defendant's duty to pay that amount in any event after acceptance of the work. The plaintiff must stand upon his allegation of an express waiver. . . .

The [defendant's] theory . . . is that even if he has represented to the plaintiff that he would not insist upon the condition that the latter should observe total abstinence from intoxicants, he can still refuse to pay the full contract price for his work. The inequity of this position becomes apparent when we consider that this contract was to run for a period of years, during a large portion of which the plaintiff was to be entitled only to the advance payment of $2 per page, the balance being contingent, among other things, upon publication of the books and returns from sales. Upon this theory the defendant might have waived the condition while the first book was in process of production, and yet when the whole work was completed, he would still be in a position to insist upon the forfeiture because there had not been strict performance. Such a situation is possible in a case where the subject of the waiver is the very consideration of a contract, Organ v. Stewart, 60 N.Y. 413, 420, but not where the waiver relates to something that can be waived. [Here,] as we have seen, the waiver is not of the consideration or subject-matter, but of an incident to the method of performance. . . .

The cases which present the most familiar phases of the doctrine of waiver are those which have arisen out of litigation over insurance policies where the defendants have claimed a forfeiture because of the breach of some condition in the contract, . . . but it is a doctrine of general application which is confined to no particular class of cases. A waiver has been defined to be the intentional relinquishment of a known right. It is voluntary and implies an election to dispense with something of value, or forego some advantage which the party waiving it might at its option have demanded or insisted upon. . . . [In] Draper v. Oswego Co. Fire R. Ass'n, 190 N.Y. 12, 16, 82 N.E. 755, Chief Judge Cullen [said]: "While that doctrine and the doctrine of equitable estoppel are often confused in insurance litigation, there is a clear distinction between the two. A waiver is the voluntary abandonment or relinquishment by a party of some right or advantage. As said [in] 150 N.Y. 190, 44 N.E. 698: 'The law of waiver seems to be a technical doctrine, introduced and applied by the court for the purpose of defeating forfeitures. . . . While the principle may not be easily classified, it is well established that if the words and acts of the insurer reasonably justify the conclusion that with full knowledge of all the facts it intended to abandon or not to insist upon the particular defense afterwards relied upon, a verdict or finding to that effect establishes a waiver, which, if it once exists, can never be revoked.' The doctrine of equitable estoppel, or estoppel in pais, is that a party may be precluded by his acts and conduct from asserting a right to the detriment of another party who, entitled to rely on such conduct, has acted upon it." . . .

It remains to be determined whether the plaintiff has alleged facts which, if proven, will be sufficient to establish his claim of an express waiver by the defendant of the plaintiff's breach of the condition to observe total abstinence. In the 12th paragraph of the complaint, the plaintiff alleges facts and circumstances which we think, if established, would prove defendant's waiver of plaintiff's performance of that contract stipulation. These facts and circumstances are that long before the plaintiff had completed the manuscript of the first book undertaken under the contract, the defendant had full knowledge of the plaintiff's non-observance of that stipulation, and that with such knowledge he not only accepted the completed manuscript without objection, but "repeatedly avowed and represented to the plaintiff that he was entitled to and would receive said royalty payments (i.e., the additional $4 per page), and plaintiff believed and relied upon such representations . . . and at all times during the writing of said treatise on corporations, and after as well as before publication thereof, as aforesaid, it was mutually understood, agreed and intended by the parties hereto that notwithstanding plaintiff's said use of intoxicating liquors, he was nevertheless entitled to receive and would receive said royalty as the same accrued under said contract." . . .

The three questions certified should be answered in the affirmative, the order of the Appellate Division reversed, the interlocutory judgment of the Special Term affirmed. . . .

————

Schultz v. Los Angeles Dons, Inc.
107 Cal.App.2d 718, 238 P.2d 73 (1951)

A professional football player brought an action to recover the $7,500 balance of the $8,000 salary under a contract to play for the 1948 season. The contract permitted the Club to terminate the contract during the training season, on payment to the player of his expenses, but one clause stated: "If this contract is terminated by Club by reason of Player's failure to render his services hereunder due to disability resulting directly from injuries sustained in the performance of his services hereunder and written notice of such injury is given by the Player as provided in Regulation 6, Club agrees to pay Player" his full season's salary. Regulation 6 stated that "written notice of any injury sustained by Player in rendering services under his contract, stating the time, place, cause and nature of the injury shall be delivered to Club by Player within 10 days of the sustaining of the injury." During the training season in July 1948, plaintiff, after taking part in two vigorous scrimmages, developed pain in the back of his leg and numbness in his foot, both of which he reported at once, orally, to the head coach and the trainer. During the next few days, the trainer gave plaintiff treatments, with little success, and plaintiff was then examined, under the head coach's orders, by three orthopedic surgeons, who reported that it would be very dangerous for plaintiff to play any more football because of an injury to his back. The trainer made full written reports of plaintiff's injury to the insurance company from which the Club had purchased insurance. *Held*, the Club's termination of plaintiff's contract, by notice given in August, was not justified by plaintiff's failure to give written notice of his injury. "The apparent purpose of the required notice was to make certain that appellant was promptly and fully informed of any such injury so that it could take the necessary steps to have its trainer and doctors treat the injury and protect its investment in respondent [plaintiff]. It may also have had some relation to the insurance carried on respondent by appellant. The evidence clearly establishes that respondent promptly gave appellant, through its trainer and coach, all information in his possession in regard to the injury, and that appellant took full advantage of it by having respondent treated by its trainer and examined and treated by one of its doctors on July 19th and shortly thereafter by two others, and that these doctors made written reports to appellant of their findings. By so doing, appellant waived the requirement of written notice. In addition, the trainer sent the reports about the injury to the insurance company. Appellant was therefore as fully protected as if the required information had been given in writing. A written notice from respondent would have been an idle act." [Is this waiver, estoppel, or "interpretation"? Does it matter what it is called?]

————

NOTE ON TIMELY NOTICE AND INSURANCE POLICIES

Courts are divided on whether an insurer defending on the basis of an insured's failure to give timely notice under the policy is required to show that it suffered actual prejudice. See Aetna Cas. & Sur. Co. v. Murphy, 206 Conn. 409, 538 A.2d 219 (Conn. 1988). Yet there is apparently broad agreement on one point: where a "notice-prejudice" rule in some form is applied to a contractual condition, it will likely be in the area of insurance. If a contract not involving insurance unmistakably establishes an express condition requiring the giving of written notice by a specified date, there is much authority holding that "substantial compliance" (say, the giving of oral notice) will not suffice. Some other basis for excusing the nonoccurrence of the condition must be found. One court has summarized its approach in the notice cases in this way: "Inasmuch as we are not dealing here with a situation where plaintiff stands to suffer forfeiture or undue hardship, we perceive no justification for engaging in a 'materiality-of-the-nonoccurrence' analysis. To do so would simply frustrate the clearly expressed intention of the parties. Freedom of contract prevails in an arm's length transaction between sophisticated parties[,] and in the absence of countervailing public policy concerns there is no reason to relieve them of the consequences of their bargain." Oppenheimer & Co. v. Oppenheim, Appel, Dixon & Co., 86 N.Y.2d 685, 636 N.Y.S.2d 734, 660 N.E.2d 415 (1995).

The Restatement, Second § 229, which focuses attention not on the time a contract is made but on ensuing events, is yet another instance of what courts "may" do in order to avoid forfeiture. Among the diverse examples provided by the restaters to show § 229's discretionary principle at work is the following (illustration 2):

> A, an ocean carrier, carries B's goods under a contract providing that it is a condition of A's liability for damage to cargo that "written notice of claim for loss or damage must be given within 10 days after removal of goods." B's cargo is damaged during carriage and A knows of this. On removal of the goods, B notes in writing on the delivery record that the cargo is damaged, and five days later informs A over the telephone of a claim for that damages and invites A to participate in an inspection within the ten day period. A inspects the goods within the period, but B does not given written notice of its claim until 25 days after removal of the goods. Since the purpose of requiring the condition of written notice is to alert the carrier and enable it to make a prompt investigation, and since this purpose had been served by the written notice of damage and the oral notice of claim, the court may excuse the non-occurrence of the condition to the extent required to allow to recovery by B.

SECTION 3. CONDITIONS OF "SATISFACTION"

Grenier v. Compratt Constr. Co.

Supreme Court of Connecticut, 1983.
189 Conn. 144, 454 A.2d 1289.

PETERS, J. This case concerns the effect of a provision in a construction contract that conditions payment upon a municipal official's certificate of performance. The plaintiffs, Frank Grenier, John Grenier and Eugene

Grenier, brought an action against the defendant, Compratt Constr. Co., to recover $25,500 which the defendant had agreed to pay for blasting work performed in the construction of certain roads. The defendants responded with an answer and a counterclaim seeking to enforce a liquidated damages clause in the contract. After a trial to the court, judgment was rendered for the plaintiffs in the amount of $23,000 together with interest and costs. The defendant has appealed.

. . . After disputes had arisen concerning performance under a subdivision contract negotiated on May 26, 1977, the parties entered into a settlement agreement on May 23, 1978. That settlement agreement, which is the subject matter of this lawsuit, entitled the plaintiffs to $25,500 upon the completion of certain subdivision roads by June 30, 1978. The agreement defined "completion" of the roads as "[any] work necessary, so far as the subdivision roads are concerned, so that a certificate of occupancy can be obtained on any lot in the subdivision as of 5:00 p.m. on June 30, 1978, and the providing to Compratt of a letter signed by the [Danbury] City Engineer, certifying that a certificate of occupancy can be obtained on any lot owned by Compratt Constr. Co. in the subdivision." Although the roads were in fact satisfactorily completed, the plaintiffs were unable to provide the stipulated letter from the city engineer because the city engineer did not ordinarily write such letters. Instead, the assistant city attorney, by letter of July 10, 1978, authorized the building inspector to issue certificates of occupancy for the roads in question. Appropriate certificates of occupancy were thereafter issuable and issued.

The contract of May 23 contained a liquidated damages clause. That clause provided for cumulative weekly penalties to be paid by the plaintiffs to the defendant for failure to complete the roads by 5:00 p.m. on June 30, 1978. The designated amounts were: $1500 at the end of the first week (July 7); an additional $2000 at the end of the second week (July 14); an additional $2500 at the end of the third week (July 21); and an additional $3000 (or daily per diem portion) for each additional week or part thereof. The defendant conceded that accrual of these damages would terminate upon the sworn testimony of the city engineer on September 7, 1978 that the roads in question were approved for the issuance of certificates of occupancy. The amount so cumulated is, according to the defendant's calculations, $26,571.42.

The trial court concluded . . . that the plaintiffs had failed to complete the roads in question on June 30, but found that the city attorney's letter of July 10, 1978, constituted compliance with the contract as of that date. Although the court recognized that the parties had seriously bargained for a letter from the city engineer, the court held that the parties' major concern was not the letter itself but what it represented, to wit, whether the roads were acceptable so that certificates of occupancy could be issued. On this basis, the city attorney's letter constituted adequate compliance with the terms of the contract. Because of the delay between the contract's date of performance, June 30, and the city attorney's letter, July 10, the court found that the defendant had been damaged to some extent, and that such damages were difficult to ascertain. Although the court found the contract's liquidated damages clause as a whole to be invalid as a penalty clause violative of public policy, the court nonetheless awarded the defendant liquidated damages for a delay of one and one-half weeks in accordance with the contractual liquidated damages clause. Accordingly, the court rendered judgment for the plaintiffs in the amount of $25,500 minus $2500, or $23,000 with interest from July 10, 1978. Only the defendant has appealed.

The defendant . . . argues that the trial court erred: (1) in applying a substantial performance test to the settlement agreement; (2) in concluding that the settlement agreement had been substantially performed; (3) in failing to enforce fully the settlement agreement's provision for liquidated damages. Since the first two claims both arise out of the contractual provision requiring a letter from the city engineer, we will consider these claims jointly before we turn to the legality of the liquidated damages clause. . . . [W]e find no error.

The defendant's principal claim of error is that the trial court failed to give full effect to the provision in the settlement agreement that made the defendant's obligation to pay conditional upon a letter from the city engineer certifying that the defendant could obtain needed certificates of occupancy. . . . Drawing upon cases involving architects' or engineers' certificates, the defendant argues that the city engineer's failure to give a written certification precludes recovery by the plaintiffs. The defendant claims that the court erroneously applied a substantial performance test to the defendant's conditional contract obligation. We disagree with the defendant's analysis. . . .

It is of course well established that contracting parties are free to impose conditions upon contractual liability. . . . Frequently, building contracts provide that a third party, an architect or an engineer, acting in good faith and in the exercise of his best judgment, shall decide when one of the contracting parties has fulfilled the requirements of the contract. [I]f the architect or engineer withholds certification, and his decision is not arbitrary or made in bad faith, a court is not authorized to substitute its judgment for that of the designated expert. [Citing cases, including Clover Mfg. Co. v. Austin Co., 101 Conn. 208, 125 A. 646 (1924).]

The regular enforcement of conditions is, however, subject to the competing but equally well established principle that the occurrence of a condition may be excused in the event of impracticability "if the occurrence of the condition is not a material part of the agreed exchange and forfeiture would otherwise result." 2 Restatement (Second), Contracts § 271; 6 Corbin, Contracts § 1362 (1962). . . . Excuse of the condition, in such circumstances, is based upon the presumption that insistence on an impracticable condition was not in the contemplation of the parties when they entered into their contract. 6 Corbin, supra, 499. . . . A prime example of an excused condition, in the context of building contracts, arises upon the death or insanity of the architect or engineer who was to have certified performance. If the work has been properly done, presentation of the unavailable architect's or engineer's certificate is excused. . . . Although this court has not had the occasion to adjudicate a case involving an engineer's death or insanity, we have recognized that enforcement of a condition depends upon a finding of the intent of the parties as evidenced by their agreement[,] . . . and that an agreement for personal services is normally subject to the condition that the person who is to render the services must be able to perform at the appointed time. Wasserman Theatrical Enterprise, Inc. v. Harris, 137 Conn. 371, 77 A.2d 329 (1950). These cases indicate that Connecticut law is consistent with the statement of the law in § 271 of the Restatement.

The facts of the present case fall somewhere between the usual deference to express conditions and the usual inference of excuse for impracticability. The contracting parties have stipulated for the certification of performance by a city engineer who was not obligated, either by contract or by his employment, to furnish such certification. In contradistinction to the ordinary case where a certificate has not been produced, the engineer has not exercised any judgment that the plaintiffs' performance was wanting. Although physically able to produce the desired certification, he has refused to do so. Given these facts, the trial court was warranted in inquiring whether the failure to produce the engineer's certificate was a material part of the agreed exchange in the contract. The court found that it was not, because the defendant's major concern was not the letter itself but what it represented, "to wit, whether the road was acceptable so that a certificate of occupancy could be issued." In making this finding, the trial court did not, as the defendant alleges, apply a substantial performance test. Instead, the court correctly found that the parties' inability to procure the city engineer's certification entirely excused the plaintiffs from their duty to produce it. This case is therefore similar to Clover Mfg. Co. v. Austin Co., supra, where we held that "[t]he parties bargain for some reasonable degree of expert knowledge of the facts and the contract, and an engineer who fails to give the parties what they bargained for . . . may justly be said to have acted in 'bad faith' as regards the performance of his contractual obligations."* If an engineer's certificate is excused where, by his actions, he fails to give the parties "what they bargained for," it must be equally excused where the engineer refuses entirely to exercise any written judgment at all.

The court also found that, except for the delay between June 30 and July 10, the plaintiffs had fully performed the material part of the bargained-for exchange, because the roads were then sufficiently completed so that the city engineer in fact gave his approval and the defendant thereafter was able to obtain its certificates of occupancy. . . . [Defendant] has not challenged this specific factual finding. It is clear that enforcement of the condition would forfeit the plaintiffs' right to the payment which the trial court found it had earned. This case therefore falls within the principles of § 271 of the Restatement. The plaintiffs may recover, not because there has been substantial performance of the contract, but because there has been full performance, the limiting condition having been excused.

The trial court dealt separately with the effect of the delay between the stipulated date of performance, June 30, and the actual date of the letter of the city attorney, July 10. As to this delay, the court awarded the defendant an offset, finding the delay not so substantial as to warrant a finding of breach of the contract as a whole. The fact that a contract states a date for performance does not necessarily make time of the essence. . . . The defendant has made no factual showing of how it was injured by the ten-day delay and relies on its liquidated damages clause to defeat the plaintiffs' recovery. Whatever the validity of the liquidated damages clause, however, that clause cannot in and of itself convert a minor delay into so substantial a breach of contract as totally to foreclose the plaintiffs' recov-

---

* [The court in *Clover Mfg.* also said: "[T]he law requires something more of an engineer to whom such authority is given than the mere negative virtue of not acting dishonestly, fraudulently or in bad faith. By accepting the position of an umpire upon whose decisions the parties agree to rely, an engineer assumes a positive responsibility, and impliedly agrees that in making his decisions he will exercise the care to be expected of his calling to ascertain the facts, and will be governed by the terms of the agreement between the parties. . . . [T]he term 'bad faith' as used in [the certification] cases may be evidenced by conduct falling short of fraud or dishonesty."—Eds.]

ery. The trial court was not in error in affirming the plaintiffs' ability to recover some sum on the contract despite their delay.

The only issue which remains to be addressed is the validity of the liquidated damages clause and the extent of the offset to which the defendant was entitled because of the plaintiffs' partial breach. We agree with the defendant that a contractual provision for liquidated damages is not illegal simply because the clause uses language of "penal" or "penalty." . . . Nor is such a clause necessarily violative of public policy simply because the amount of damages escalates with the period of delay. To the extent that the trial court ruled to the contrary, it was mistaken. The defendant was not, however, injured by the trial court's mistaken disapproval of the liquidated damages clause, because the trial court awarded the defendant an offset that adopted the formula provided by the liquidated damages clauses. The trial court found that the plaintiffs' performance was delayed for ten days and awarded one and one-half weeks of damages according to the contract's provision for the first two weeks' delay. Having found full performance by July 10, the court could not appropriately have awarded greater damages under the liquidated damages clause even had it found that clause fully enforceable.

There is no error.

Loyal Erectors, Inc. v. Hamilton & Son, Inc.
312 A.2d 748 (Me.1973)

"The parties to the instant building contract had dissimilar purposes in mind when they conditioned, upon the architect's certificate of approval, the right to receive both, (1) progress payments at periodic intervals of performance and (2) the final payment of the retainage fund at the end of the construction. Progress payment clauses are inserted in building contracts mostly for the protection of the contractor who is assured of periodic instalments of cash moneys with which he can continue performance of his contract and save himself from the embarrassment of extended credit and the costs thereof. True, the other party may be benefited incidentally by reason of the timely performance of the work, the avoidance of any breaches and the consequential inconveniences arising therefrom. On the other hand, the conditioning of the final payment of the retainage money upon the architect's certificate of approval is solely for the protection of the [owner]; it is a substantial leverage to assure strict performance of the contract in accordance with the agreement, drawings and specifications and to compel correction for material deviations therefrom. . . . The retainage clause . . . induces the contractor to render a performance that conforms in fact to plans and specifications, spurs him to stay with the job and, upon completion, furnishes the main incentive to make conforming corrections."

Second Nat'l Bank v. Pan–American Bridge Co.
183 Fed. 391 (6th Cir.1910)

"The defendant [urged] that plaintiff [contractor] was precluded from recovery by the architect's refusal to accept performance of the contract and to give his certificate thereof. . . . The court instructed the jury that if plaintiff's work and material conformed to the contract recovery could be had, notwithstanding the lack of acceptance or certificate by the architect, provided the jury should find that such certificate was withheld 'unreasonably and unfairly[.]' . . . [T]he trial judge erred in holding that the architect's certificate could be dispensed with if the jury were satisfied that it was 'unreasonably and unfairly' withheld. . . . [T]he certificate of acceptance is a condition precedent to recovery upon the contract in the absence of fraud or of mistake so gross as to imply bad faith; in other words, that the withholding of the certificate must have been in bad faith. . . . The jury could scarcely be expected to understand that the words 'unreasonably and unfairly' meant 'in bad faith[.]' . . . [T]he actual conformity of the work and materials to the plans and specifications [cannot be] made the test of the bad faith which the law requires for setting aside the action of the architect."

————

Maurer v. School Dist. No. 1
186 Mich. 223, 152 N.W. 999 (1915)

"The [question] is whether the court erred in holding that plaintiffs [contractors] could not recover because the terms of the contract were not followed in that they did not procure a certificate from the architects. It is undisputed that from the time plaintiffs entered upon the execution of this work no architects' certificates were asked for or required, but payments were made by defendant on the contract monthly during the continuance of the work upon informal statements made in writing by plaintiffs, certifying the amounts of material and labor which had actually been expended since the last payment, and as to these payments and the amounts thereof there is no dispute in the case.

"There seems also to be no dispute but that the entire contract price of $22,756 has been paid to plaintiffs in this manner, except the balance of $1,205.30, for which suit is brought, and that no such certificates were ever asked for by defendant [the owner] until some time in April, or May, 1913, after the foregoing payments had been made and after the building had been completed for about two months, when the contractors asked one of the architects to furnish a final certificate. This architect, who, under the contract, acted as agent of defendant, testified that he refused to furnish such certificate although the building was completed, because there was a question of liquidated damages arising out of delay in completing the building, which had not been adjusted. The contract gave no authority to the architects to refuse a certificate for that reason. The only condition attached to issuing a certificate is the completion of the work. . . . [I]t is clear that defendant waived the condition in the contract relative to certificates of the architects until the building was completed, and as to the final certificate plaintiffs were not at fault because it was not furnished upon request."

————

Nolan v. Whitney

Court of Appeals of New York, 1882.
88 N.Y. 648.

In July, 1877, Michael Nolan, the plaintiffs' testator, entered into an agreement with the defendant to do the mason work in the erection of two buildings in the city of Brooklyn for the sum of $11,700, to be paid to him by her in installments as the work progressed. The last installment of $2,700 was to be paid thirty days after completion and acceptance of the work. The work was to be performed to the satisfaction and under the direction of M.J. Morrill, architect, to be testified by his certificate, and that was to be obtained before any payment could be required to be made. As the work progressed, all the installments were paid except the last, and Nolan, claiming that he had fully performed his agreement, commenced this action to recover that installment. The defendant defended the action upon the ground that Nolan had not fully performed his agreement according to its terms and requirements, and also upon the ground that he had not obtained the architect's certificate. . . .

Upon the trial the defendant gave evidence tending to show that much of the work was imperfectly done, and that the agreement had not been fully kept and performed [by] Nolan; the latter gave evidence tending to show that the work was properly done, that he had fairly and substantially performed his agreement, and that the architect had refused to give him the certificate, which, by the terms of his agreement, would entitle him to the final payment. The referee found that Nolan completed the mason work required by the agreement according to its terms; that he in good faith intended to comply with, and did substantially comply with, and perform the requirements of his agreement; but that there were trivial defects in the plastering for which a deduction of $200 should be made from the last installment, and he ordered judgment in favor of Nolan for the last installment less $200.

EARL, J. It is a general rule of law that a party must perform his contract before he can claim the consideration due him upon performance; but the performance need not in all cases be literal and exact. It is sufficient if the party bound to perform, acting in good faith, and intending and attempting to perform his contract, does so substantially, and then he may recover for his work, notwithstanding slight or trivial defects in performance, for which compensation may be made by an allowance to the other party. Whether a contract has been substantially performed is a question of fact depending upon all the circumstances of the case. . . . Smith v. Brady, 17 N.Y. 189. . . . [U]pon the facts found by the referee, Nolan was entitled to recover unless he is barred because he failed to get the architect's certificate, which the referee found was unreasonably and improperly refused. But when he had substantially performed his contract, the architect was bound to give him the certificate, and his refusal to give it was unreasonable, and it is held that an unreasonable refusal on the part of an architect in such a case to give the certificate dispenses with its necessity.

Judgment affirmed.

———

Van Iderstine Co. v. Barnet Leather Co.

242 N.Y. 425, 152 N.E. 250 (1926)

In two separate contracts, plaintiff agreed to sell and defendant to buy a total of 21,000 vealskins. Both contracts provided that the skins were to be delivered to Jules Star & Co., a firm of brokers, and were to be "subject to their approval." In an action for damages for alleged wrongful refusal to accept vealskins tendered by plaintiff, the chief issue concerned 6,000 skins which were examined by Jules Star & Co. but rejected by them. The trial court charged the jury that plaintiff could recover if "approval was unreasonably withheld," that Star "must have acted honestly," and "if he [Star] showed an honest judgment the defendant is entitled to a verdict." This instruction was held to be erroneous insofar as it made the test of defendant's liability the reasonableness of the decisions of Jules Star & Co. Cases involving refusal by architects or engineers to approve work done or materials furnished under building contracts could not be used to justify the test employed in this case. It must be remembered that in the building cases the failure to obtain approval has meant that "the benefit of work actually performed and materials actually furnished could be appropriated by the owner without payment." The rule of Nolan v. Whitney may therefore be seen as a natural evolution of the universal view that in building contracts there may be recovery for "substantial performance." But here, the parties agreed to employ a designated expert to pass upon the goods, and the refusal of approval does not enable the buyer to obtain the seller's property without payment. The rule applied to building contracts "should not be extended by analogy where the reason for the rule fails." So, "unless the certificate has been withheld dishonestly and in bad faith," plaintiff cannot recover. It had not made the goods to special order; it could resell them at the market price, in which event only the anticipated profit of the sale would be lost. This risk the plaintiff assumed.

NOTE

The Court of Appeals of New York, like most courts, maintains that the doctrine of substantial performance ordinarily is not applicable to excuse the nonoccurrence of an express condition—at least where plaintiff has conferred no benefit upon defendant. It should be added that the New York court has continued to repeat, and apply, the proposition asserted in *Van Iderstine*: the rule developed in the construction cases "should not be extended by analogy where the reason for the rule fails." E.g., Oppenheimer & Co. v. Oppenheim, Appel, Dixon & Co., 86 N.Y.2d 685, 636 N.Y.S.2d 734, 660 N.E.2d 415 (1995).

Also, New York is known to be strict in its denial of quasi-contractual relief to building contractors who fail to substantially perform their contracts. See, e.g., Steel Storage & Elevator Constr. Co. v. Stock, 225 N.Y. 173, 121 N.E. 786 (1919). At the same time, it is believed that New York has not been strict in its tests for "substantial performance" (some evidence on this point will appear later in this chapter). Does this information shed light on *Nolan* and *Van Iderstine*?

The antiforfeiture principle of the Restatement (Second) of Contracts § 229 states: "To the extent that the non-occurrence of a condition would cause disproportionate forfeiture, a court may excuse the non-occurrence of that condition unless its occurrence was a material part of the agreed exchange." In construction disputes where considerable work has been done but the architect's certificate has been withheld, is the excuse-to-avoid-forfeiture approach preferable to the one taken by the court in Nolan v. Whitney?

Fursmidt v. Hotel Abbey Holding Corp.

Supreme Court of New York, Appellate Division, 1960.
10 A.D.2d 447, 200 N.Y.S.2d 256.

RABIN, J. The plaintiff and his father had been rendering valet and laundry services at the Hotel Abbey for a great many years[,] . . . [in] space in the hotel basement. On February 1, 1958, the plaintiff entered into an agreement in writing with the defendant, the owner of the hotel, which provided for the plaintiff to render such services for an additional three-year period for which the defendant was to receive compensation of $325 per month. This agreement provided in Paragraph "5" thereof as follows:

"It is distinctly understood and agreed that the services to be rendered by the second party [plaintiff] shall meet with the approval of the first party [defendant], who shall be the sole judge of the sufficiency and propriety of the services."

In September, 1958 the defendant informed the plaintiff that he was to discontinue his services as of October 1, 1958. The plaintiff thereafter removed from the premises. . . . Upon such discontinuance the valet and laundry service was resumed by a third party who paid to the defendant the sum of $250 per month as consideration for the concession.

The plaintiff claims that the defendant had no right to terminate the contract. . . . The defendant defends saying that the services did not meet with its approval and were unsatisfactory. It counterclaims for damages which it claims it sustained by reason of plaintiff's breach of the contract in failing to render adequate and proper service.

The defendant takes the position that it had a right to terminate the agreement if it genuinely and honestly felt that the services rendered were unsatisfactory to it and did not meet with its approval, urging that under the contract it was to be the sole judge of the "sufficiency and propriety of the services." Accordingly it urges that it was not for the court or a jury to pass upon the reasonableness of such conclusion if in fact it was a conclusion honestly arrived at by it.

The Trial Court disagreed holding that it was not enough that the defendant be dissatisfied, even though such dissatisfaction be not feigned, but implicit in law was a requirement that such dissatisfaction be reasonably grounded. Consequently, the Court in its charge gave to the jury for resolution not only the question of whether the defendant was in fact dissatisfied but also the question as to whether such dissatisfaction was reasonable. Under the Court's charge therefore even though the jury found the dissatisfaction to be genuine it would be obliged to find for the plaintiff if nonetheless it found that such dissatisfaction had no reasonable basis. In other words the court substituted the judgment of a reasonable man in place of the judgment of the defendant. . . .

Provisions in agreements calling for performance to the satisfaction of a party fall into two general categories. In contracts relating to operative fitness, utility or marketability the provision "is construed as a matter of law as imposing only the requisite of satisfying a reasonable man" (3 Williston, Contracts, § 675A [Rev.Ed.]). For example, such a construction has been given to "satisfaction" provisions where the performance called for was the installation of machinery, . . . and where repairs were to be made to a boiler (Duplex Safety Boiler Co. v. Garden, 101 N.Y. 387, 4 N.E. 749).

On the other hand a literal construction of the "satisfaction" provisions is made where the agreements provide for performance involving "fancy, taste, sensibility, or judgment" of the party for whose benefit it was made (10 N.Y.Jur., Contracts, § 302). Such a result obtains in cases calling for performance to one's satisfaction in the making of a garment, the giving of a course of instruction, the services of an orchestra, the making of recordings by a singer and the painting of a portrait (see cases cited in 2 Clark, N.Y. Law of Contracts, § 928).

The resolution of the issue here presented lies with the determination of whether the instant agreement is one relating to operative fitness, utility or marketability or one involving fancy, taste, sensibility or judgment. We find that it comes within the rules applicable to the latter class. . . .

In reaching this determination we recognize that the performance here called for does not lie at either extreme of the respective categories. However, it is by far closer to the category involving taste or judgment than the one where "satisfaction" is complied with by reasonable performance. Such a conclusion is inescapable when the agreement is examined in the light of its purpose.

This agreement provided that the defendant was to exercise strict control and direction of almost every aspect of the plaintiff's operation. The prices were to be fixed by the defendant; disputes with hotel guests were to be finally resolved by the defendant; the specific hours of service were to be established by the defendant "to conform to the convenience of its guests"; the plaintiff's employees had to be approved by the defendant as were their uniforms; and all the billing was to be done through the defendant as though it were rendering the services to the guests.

Thus, it appears that the primary and overriding objective of the defendant . . . was to ensure to its guests proper, efficient, courteous and reasonable valet and laundry facilities as an integral part of the overall personal services rendered by the hotel to the end that the good will of the guests be retained. It becomes clear therefore that the performance here called for is much removed from that involving mechanical fitness, utility or marketability. In such cases there is a "positive, objective standard" against which the performance may be measured. Wynkoop Hallenbeck Crawford Co. v. Western Union Tel. Co., 268 N.Y. 108, 196 N.E. 760. Contra in cases involving taste and judgment such standards of reasonableness cannot be established. In this case the defendant did not bargain for a particular type of pressing, stitching or laundering but rather for a relationship between the plaintiff's organization and the hotel's guests as would protect and enhance the good will so essential to the operation of the hotel business. No objective standards of reasonableness can be set up by which the effectiveness of the plaintiff's performance in achieving the effect sought can be measured. It is for that reason that in cases of this nature the honest judgment of the party rather than that of a jury is all that is required. . . .

It was therefore error for the Trial Court to give to the jury the question of the reasonableness of the defendant's asserted dissatisfaction. Sufficient that the jury be satisfied that it was a dissatisfaction honestly arrived at. While in determining the question as to the bona fides of the defendant's dissatisfaction, evidence as to the quality of the plaintiff's services may well be admissible as having probative value, the ultimate and only question to be decided by the jury . . . is whether the defendant's dissatisfaction was bona fide or feigned.

It may very well be that the charge of the court is correct for the purpose of determining whether the plaintiff breached the agreement so as to entitle the defendant to damages on its counterclaim as distinguished from its right to terminate the contract. Honest dissatisfaction on the part of the defendant, although entitling it to terminate will not, in and of itself, entitle it to recover damages on its counterclaim. Such determination will depend on the facts surrounding the manner of the plaintiff's performance in relation to what he was obliged to do under the agreement and accordingly we do not pass on that phase of the case at this time.

[Reversed on the law and a new trial ordered.]

––––––––

Haymore v. Levinson

8 Utah 2d 66, 328 P.2d 307 (1958)

Plaintiff builder contracted to sell to defendants, for $36,000, a house that plaintiff had almost completed. The contract provided that $3,000 of the purchase price was to be held in escrow until "satisfactory completion" of a list of items attached to the contract. Defendants moved into the house while plaintiff continued construction. When plaintiff finished the work and requested release of the $3,000 from escrow, defendants refused, asserting that they were not satisfied with certain of the items. After discussion, plaintiff agreed to take care of another list of items which defendants insisted must be completed. When plaintiff and his workers appeared to do this work, however, defendants expressed dissatisfaction with the second list and demanded still further work, but plaintiff would not agree. Defendants then told plaintiff that, unless he agreed to do all the work they had requested and in the manner they required, he could do nothing. On plaintiff's refusal of this demand, he was ordered off the property. Plaintiff recovered judgment for $2,739, that is, the $3,000 escrow less $261 which the trial court found to be the "total value" of certain "minor deficiencies" in plaintiff's performance. *Held*, affirmed. Building contracts generally fall into a class where "taste, fancy or sensibility" is not of predominant importance; therefore, a condition of satisfaction involves an objective standard on such matters as "operative fitness, mechanical utility or structural completion. . . . [T]he party favored by such a provision has no arbitrary privilege of declining to acknowledge satisfaction and [such party] cannot withhold approval unless there is apparent some reasonable justification for doing so." The trial court correctly applied this standard.

––––––––

Breslow v. Gotham Securities Corp.

77 Misc.2d 721, 354 N.Y.S.2d 550 (N.Y.Civ.Ct.1974)

"Where an attorney has fully performed the objectives of a contingent retainer agreement for his client, these tidings of comfort are ordinarily sufficient to warrant payment of the fee in full. In this case the client would press beyond mere comfort and would infuse the lawyer-client relationship with qualities of aesthetic joy. . . . Plaintiff, an experienced law firm in the securities field, was retained by defendant, an underwriter, to render customary legal services in connection with a SEC Regulation A public stock offering. The basic terms of the oral retainer are [undisputed]: if the offering were successfully completed, the underwriter was to receive a $20,000 expense allowance from the proceeds, and of this sum plaintiff was to be entitled to half, or the sum of $10,000. Defendant has paid the sum of $3,500 but resists payment of the balance of $6,500, and plaintiff now moves for summary judgment. Although the offering was fully sold, and defendant received the $20,000 expense allowance, the underwriter asserts . . . that plaintiff's services did not measure up to 'the quality of service rendered to defendant by previous attorneys' and that 'the services rendered did not meet such standards and plaintiff was so advised.'

"It may well be true that defendant had known some giant oaks (albeit anonymous at the present time) in the forest of the bar, and that they cast a long shadow in the underwriting business. So vague a standard, however, given its maximum effect, would amount to nothing more than a condition in the contract that performance be personally satisfactory. The ingredient of personal satisfaction in contractual arrangements, however, is subject to certain well-recognized limitations. . . . Clearly this case, [compared with *Fursmidt*,] falls into the [operative fitness or utility] category as a matter of law. [Defendant's] asserted lack of satisfaction cannot, in the face of conceded full performance, raise an issue of fact for trial, for 'that which the law shall say a contracting party ought in reason to be satisfied with, that the law will say he is satisfied with.'"

Morin Bldg. Prods. Co. v. Baystone Constr., Inc.

717 F.2d 413 (7th Cir.1983)

"[M]ost cases conform to the position stated in § 228 of the Restatement (Second) of Contracts (1979): if 'it is practicable to determine whether a reasonable person in the position of the obligor would be satisfied, an interpretation is preferred under which the condition [that the obligor be satisfied with the obligee's performance] occurs if such a reasonable person in the position of the obligor would be satisfied.' We do not understand the majority position to be paternalistic. . . . The requirement of reasonableness is read into a contract not to protect the weaker party but to approximate what the parties would have expressly provided with respect to a contingency that they did not foresee, if they had foreseen it. Therefore the requirement is not read into every contract, because it is not always a reliable guide to the parties' intentions. In particular, the presumption that the performing party would not have wanted to put himself at the mercy of the paying party's whim is overcome when the nature of the performance contracted for is such that there are no objective standards to guide the court. It cannot be assumed in such a case that the parties would have wanted a court to second-guess the buyer's rejection. So 'the reasonable person standard is employed when the contract involves commercial quality, operative fitness, or mechanical utility which other knowledgeable persons can judge. . . . The standard of good faith is employed when the contract involves personal aesthetics or fancy.'"

SECTION 4. PROTECTING THE EXCHANGE ON BREACH

At the start of this casebook, cases such as *Groves*, *Peevyhouse*, and *Landis* raised the question of how damages should be calculated when the promisor breached and the cost of repairs greatly exceeded their market value. In this section, we face cases that arise out of similar facts, and raise several additional problems. The first problem arises when the promisor breaches and the promisee seeks to walk away from the contract. The issue is the right to terminate before performance is completed, not the amount of damages when promised performance is completed, but proves defective. This issue is the focus of the first case. In the other cases, the breaching party is the one seeking relief. The threshold question, again one that arises before damages are measured, is whether the breaching party has the right to recover in restitution. The next question is whether, as an alternative to recovering under a restitution theory, the breaching party can sue under the contract. Only if this question is answered in the affirmative do we return to the question of how to calculate contract damages. (Damages become relevant again as they must be deducted from the recovery of the breaching party.)

————

Strouth v. Pools by Murphy and Sons, Inc.

Appellate Court of Connecticut, 2003.
79 Conn. App. 55, 829 A.2d 102.

LAVERY, C.J. . . . The plaintiffs, owners of a residence in West Suffield, contacted the defendant in May, 1998, because they were interested in having a swimming pool installed in their yard. Ed Carter, the defendant's salesman at that time, visited the property and met with the plaintiffs on May 19, 1998. After viewing a color brochure depicting various shapes for pools and spas, the plaintiffs decided on a peanut shaped pool with a circular six-foot interior spa. They informed Carter of their choice. Carter drew a contract for the construction of a pool. The contract specified a "custom" shaped pool, forty feet long by twenty feet wide.

Dennis Murphy, the defendant's president, arrived at the property on July 16, 1998, to commence excavation. He showed Caroline Strouth a picture of the kidney shaped pool he planned to dig and laid out staking. She told Murphy that the picture he was showing her did not look like the pool she was expecting. Murphy assured her that the pool would look like she expected it to when completed. The excavation was in the shape of a kidney. After the excavation was complete, a crew arrived to install the steel frame (rebar). An electrician and plumber also did work at the property. The rebars outlined an almond-shaped spa, not a circular spa.

After receiving a bill from the defendant for additional excavation time incurred because the defendant hit ledge on the first day of excavation, Robert Strouth telephoned the defendant to complain about the extra cost. He spoke to Joseph Murphy, the father of Dennis Murphy and an employee of the defendant. After a short, acrimonious conversation, Joseph Murphy abruptly terminated the conversation. Robert Strouth did not have an opportunity to complain that the pool was not excavated in the shape for which he and his wife had contracted.

Four days later, Robert Strouth contacted the defendant and ordered it to discontinue all work at the property. Carter telephoned the plaintiffs several times to try to work out a completion of the pool. On September 20, 1998, the defendant sent a letter to the plaintiffs in which it offered to complete the pool at the property with a circular spa. There was never an offer to reconfigure the pool in a peanut shape. Substantial additional work would have been needed to complete the kidney shaped pool, which was not the pool for which the plaintiffs had contracted. The excavation remained, in a deteriorated condition, in the backyard.

In 1999, the plaintiffs brought the present action. As to the defendant, they claimed damages for breach of contract, unjust enrichment and unfair trade practices in violation of the Connecticut Unfair Trade Practices Act. The defendant filed a counterclaim, alleging breach of contract. The court rendered judgment for the plaintiffs on the breach of contract claim and awarded damages in the amount of $10,618.63. The court rendered judgment for the defendant on the plaintiffs' claims of unjust enrichment and unfair trade practices, and for the plaintiffs on the defendant's counterclaim.

In its memorandum of decision, the court determined that the word "custom," used in the contract to describe the shape of the pool, was ambiguous. It found that the plaintiffs believed they were contracting for a peanut shaped pool and that the defendant subsequently interpreted the contract as calling for a kidney shaped pool. Because "custom" could describe a kidney shaped pool or a peanut-shaped pool, the court determined that the ambiguity should be construed against the party who drew the contract, which was the defendant. The court concluded that "[t]he parties entered into a contract on May 19, 1998, for construction of a peanut shaped pool, forty feet long by twenty feet wide with an interior, circular six-foot spa." The court determined that the kidney shaped pool, begun by the defendant, was a substantial deviation from the pool for which the plaintiffs had contracted. It therefore held that the defendant's failure to build the pool in a peanut shape with a circular interior spa was a material breach of the parties' contract that justified the plaintiffs in terminating additional construction of the kidney-shaped pool. . . .

The defendant first claims that the court improperly determined that the construction of a kidney shaped pool constituted a material breach of the parties' contract. Specifically, the defendant argues that the construction of a kidney-shaped pool would have amounted to substantial performance of the parties' contract and, therefore, the plaintiffs breached the parties' contract when they ordered the defendants to discontinue all work at the property. We are not persuaded.

The issue here is whether the construction of a kidney-shaped pool, when the contract called for a peanut-shaped pool, constituted a material breach of the parties' contract so as to justify the plaintiffs in not performing their remaining duties under the contract. The defendant does not challenge the underlying facts found by the court. . . .

The court, in its memorandum of decision, did not specifically apply the standards of materiality enunciated in § 241 of the Restatement. The court did, however, find that the construction of a kidney-shaped pool would be a substantial deviation from the shape of the pool for which the plaintiffs contracted and that the plaintiffs "were not obliged to have a pool built in their backyard that did not conform to the pool for which they contracted." The court also found that although the defendant had offered to complete the pool with a circular spa, it never offered to reconfigure the pool to a peanut shape. Thus, it would appear that the court, essentially, focused on the criteria set forth in § 241(a) and (d) to reach its conclusion that the construction of a kidney shaped pool constituted a material breach of the parties' contract. Under the circumstances, we cannot say that the court's conclusion was clearly erroneous.

Although the defendant argues that the construction of a kidney-shaped pool would not deprive the plaintiffs of the benefit that they reasonably expected because the pool would still be fit for its intended use, we are not convinced that constructing a pool in the shape of a kidney, when the contract called for a pool in the shape of a peanut, would have constituted substantial performance. We therefore conclude that the court's determination that the defendant materially breached the parties' contract, thereby excusing the plaintiffs from any further performance due under the contract, was not clearly erroneous. . . .

The defendant's next claim is that the court improperly failed to award restitution. Specifically, the defendant claims that it is entitled to "restitution for its costs, labor and expenses in the amount of $5471, which included $2158 for the commission paid to Ed Carter . . . $1000 for the first day of excavation . . . $750 for the second day of excavation . . . $908 for installation of the steel rebar . . . and $505 for installation of plumbing. . . ." We decline to review that claim. . . .

Because the defendant did not raise the issue of restitution in its pleading and because it does not appear that the parties actually litigated that issue, the defendant's claim for restitution was not before the court properly. . . .

———

Plante v. Jacobs

Supreme Court of Wisconsin, 1960.
10 Wis.2d 567, 103 N.W.2d 296.

Suit to establish a lien to recover the unpaid balance of the contract price plus extras of building a house for the defendants, [the] Jacobs, who in their answer allege no substantial performance and breach of the contract by the plaintiff and counterclaim for damages due to faulty workmanship and incomplete construction. . . . After a trial to the court, judgment was entered for the plaintiff in the amount of $4,152.90 plus interest and costs, from which the defendants appealed and the plaintiff petitioned for a review. . . .

The Jacobs, on or about January 6, 1956, entered into a written contract with the plaintiff to furnish the materials and construct a house upon their lot in Brookfield, . . . in accordance with plans and specifications, for the sum of $26,765. During the course of construction the plaintiff was paid $20,000. Disputes arose between the parties, the defendants refused to continue payment, and the plaintiff did not complete the house[,] [but] duly filed his lien.

The trial court found the contract was substantially performed and was modified in respect to lengthening the house two feet and the reasonable value of this extra was $960. The court disallowed extras amounting to $1,748.92 claimed by the plaintiff because they were not agreed upon in writing in accordance with the terms of the agreement. In respect to defective workmanship the court allowed the cost of repairing the following items: $1,550 for the patio wall; $100 for the patio floor; $300 for cracks in the ceiling of the living room and kitchen; and $20.15 credit balance for hardware. The court also found the defendants were not damaged by the misplacement of a wall between the kitchen and the living room, and the other items of defective workmanship and incompleteness were not proven. The amount of these credits allowed the defendants was deducted from the gross amount found owing the plaintiff, and the judgment was entered for the difference and made a lien on the premises. . . .

HALLOWS, J. The defendants argue the plaintiff cannot recover any amount because he has failed to substantially perform the contract. The plaintiff conceded he failed to furnish the kitchen cabinets, gutters and downspouts, sidewalk, closet clothes poles, and entrance seat amounting to $1,601.95. This amount was allowed to the defendants. The defendants claim some 20 other items of incomplete or faulty performance by the plaintiff and no substantial performance because the cost of completing the house in strict compliance with the plans and specifications would amount to 25 or 30 percent of the contract price. The defendants especially stress the misplacing of the wall between the living room and the kitchen, which narrowed the living room in excess of one foot. The cost of tearing down this wall and rebuilding it would be approximately $4,000. The record is not clear why and when this wall was misplaced, but the wall is completely built and the house decorated and the defendants are living therein. Real estate experts testified that the smaller width of the living room would not affect the market price of the house.

The defendants rely on Manitowoc Steam Boiler Works v. Manitowoc Glue Co., 1903, 120 Wis. 1, 97 N.W. 515, for the proposition there can be no recovery on the contract as distinguished from quantum meruit unless there is substantial performance. This is undoubtedly the correct rule at common law. . . . The question here is whether there has been substantial performance. The test of what amounts to substantial performance seems to be whether the performance meets the essential purpose of the contract. In the *Manitowoc* case the contract called for a boiler having a capacity of 150 percent of the existing boiler. The court held there was no substantial performance because the boiler furnished had a capacity of only 82 percent of the old boiler and only approximately one-half of the boiler capacity contemplated by the contract. In Houlahan v. Clark, 1901, 110 Wis. 43, 85 N.W. 676, the contract provided the plaintiff was to drive pilings in the lake and place a boat house thereon parallel and in line with a neighbor's dock. This was not done and the contractor so positioned the boat house that it was practically useless to the owner. Manthey v. Stock, 1907, 133 Wis. 107, 113 N.W. 443, involved a contract to paint a house and to do a good job, including the removal of the old paint where necessary. The plaintiff did not remove the old paint, and blistering and roughness of the new paint resulted. The court held that the plaintiff failed to show substantial performance. . . .

Substantial performance as applied to construction of a house does not mean that every detail must be in strict compliance with the specifications and the plans. Something less than perfection is the test . . . unless all details are made the essence of the contract. This was not done here. There may be situations in which features or details of construction of special or of great personal importance, which if not performed, would prevent a find-

[handwritten margin note: Test for substantial performance.]

ing of substantial performance of the contract. In this case the plan was a stock floor plan. No detailed construction of the house was shown on the plan. There were no blueprints. The specifications were standard printed forms with some modifications and additions written in by the parties. Many of the problems that arose during the construction had to be solved on the basis of practical experience. No mathematical rule relating to the percentage of the price, of cost of completion or of completeness can be laid down to determine substantial performance of a building contract. Although the defendants received a house with which they are dissatisfied in many respects, the trial court was not in error in finding the contract was substantially performed.

The next question is what is the amount of recovery when the plaintiff has substantially, but incompletely, performed. For substantial performance the plaintiff should recover the contract price less the damages caused the defendant by the incomplete performance. Both parties agree. Venzke v. Magdanz, 1943, 243 Wis. 155, 9 N.W.2d 604, states the correct rule for damages due to faulty construction amounting to such incomplete performance, which is the difference between the value of the house as it stands with faulty and incomplete construction and the value of the house if it had been constructed in strict accordance with the plans and specifications. This is the diminished-value rule. The cost of replacement or repair is not the measure of such damage, but is an element to take into consideration in arriving at value under some circumstances. The cost of replacement or the cost to make whole the omissions may equal or be less than the difference in value in some cases and, likewise, the cost to rectify a defect may greatly exceed the added value to the structure as corrected. The defendants argue that under the *Venzke* rule their damages are $10,000. The plaintiff on review argues the defendants' damages are only $650. Both parties agree the trial court applied the wrong rule to the facts.

diminished value rule

The trial court applied the cost-of-repair or replacement rule as to several items, relying on Stern v. Schlafer, 1943, 244 Wis. 183, 11 N.W.2d 640, 12 N.W.2d 678, wherein it was stated that when there are a number of small items of defect or omission which can be remedied without the reconstruction of a substantial part of the building or a great sacrifice of work or material already wrought in the building, the reasonable cost of correcting the defect should be allowed. However, [this] court [has] held [that] when the separation of defects would lead to confusion, the rule of diminished value could apply to all defects.

In this case no such confusion arises in separating the defects. The trial court disallowed certain claimed defects because they were not proven. This finding was not against the great weight and clear preponderance of the evidence and will not be disturbed on appeal. Of the remaining defects claimed by the defendants, the court allowed the cost of replacement or repair except as to the misplacement of the living-room wall. Whether a defect should fall under the cost-of-replacement rule or be considered under the diminished-value rule depends upon the nature and magnitude of the defect. This court has not allowed items of such magnitude under the cost-of-repair rule as the trial court did. Viewing the construction of the house as a whole and its cost we cannot say, however, that the trial court was in error in allowing the cost of repairing the plaster cracks in the ceilings, the cost of mud jacking and repairing the patio floor, and the cost of reconstructing the non-weight-bearing and nonstructural patio wall. Such reconstruction did not involve an unreasonable economic waste.

The item of misplacing the living room wall . . . was clearly under the diminished-value rule. There is no evidence that defendants requested or demanded the replacement of the wall in the place called for by the specifications during the course of construction. To tear down the wall now and rebuild it in its proper place would involve a substantial destruction of the work, if not all of it, which was put into the wall and would cause additional damage to other parts of the house and require replastering and redecorating the walls and ceilings of at least two rooms. Such economic waste is unreasonable and unjustified. The rule of diminished value contemplates the wall is not going to be moved. Expert witnesses for both parties, testifying as to the value of the house, agreed that the misplacement of the wall had no effect on the market price. The trial court properly found that the defendants suffered no legal damage, although the defendants' particular desire for specified room size was not satisfied. For a discussion of these rules of damages for defective or unfinished construction and their application see Restatement, 1 Contracts, § 346(1)(a) and illustrations. . . .

Judgment affirmed.

––––––––––

3A A. Corbin, Contracts § 702

"When we use the term 'substantial performance of a promissory duty,' we always mean something less than full and exact performance of that duty. As so used, therefore, substantial performance is not a complete discharge of duty. It is not a defense in a suit against the building contractor for damages. Judgment will not be prevented from going against him in such a suit by his averring and proving that he performed almost in full, that his deviations have been small, that the owner can live comfortably in the house, or that the value to the owner is very nearly as great as it would have been had exact performance been rendered. . . . One who has rendered substantial performance, but less than full performance, and has already received the agreed price, has a defense in a suit by the owner for the restitution of that price. There has been no such 'failure of consideration' as to create a quasi-contractual duty of restitution. The reason is not merely the fact that the contractor is in possession or that 'possession is nine points' in the law. It is because the contractor had a right to the payment when it was made and could have maintained suit for it."

––––––––––

Jacob & Youngs v. Kent

Court of Appeals of New York, 1921.
230 N.Y. 239, 129 N.E. 889.

CARDOZO, J. The plaintiff built a country residence for the defendant at a cost of upwards of $77,000, and now sues to recover a balance of $3,483.46, remaining unpaid. The work of construction ceased in June, 1914, and the defendant then began to occupy the dwelling. There was no complaint of defective performance until March, 1915. One of the specifications for the plumbing work provides that "all wrought-iron pipe must be well galvanized, lap welded pipe of the grade known as 'standard pipe' of Reading manufacture."

The defendant learned in March, 1915, that some of the pipe, instead of being made in Reading, was the product of other factories. The plaintiff was accordingly directed by the architect to do the work anew. The plumbing was then encased within the walls except in a few places where it had to be exposed. Obedience to the order meant more than the substitution of other pipe. It meant the demolition at great expense of substantial parts of the completed structure. The plaintiff left the work untouched, and asked for a certificate that the final payment was due. Refusal of the certificate was followed by this suit.

The evidence sustains a finding that the omission of the prescribed brand of pipe was neither fraudulent nor willful. It was the result of the oversight and inattention of the plaintiff's subcontractor. Reading pipe is distinguished from Cohoes pipe and other brands only by the name of the manufacturer stamped upon it at intervals of between six and seven feet. Even the defendant's architect, though he inspected the pipe upon arrival, failed to notice the discrepancy. The plaintiff tried to show that the brands installed, though made by other manufacturers, were the same in quality, in appearance, in market value, and in cost as the brand stated in the contract—that they were, indeed, the same thing, though manufactured in another place. The evidence was excluded, and a verdict directed for the defendant. The Appellate Division reversed, and granted a new trial.

We think the evidence, if admitted, would have supplied some basis for the inference that the defect was insignificant in its relation to the project. The courts never say that one who makes a contract fills the measure of his duty by less than full performance. They do say, however, that an omission, both trivial and innocent, will sometimes be atoned for by allowance of the resulting damage, and will not always be the breach of a condition to be followed by a forfeiture. The distinction is akin to that between dependent and independent promises, or between promises and conditions. Some promises are so plainly independent that they can never by fair construction be conditions of one another. Others are so plainly dependent that they must always be conditions. Others, though dependent and thus conditions when there is departure in point of substance, will be viewed as independent and collateral when the departure is insignificant. Considerations partly of justice and partly of presumable intention are to tell us whether this or that promise shall be placed in one class or in another. The simple and the uniform will call for different remedies from the multifarious and the intricate. The margin of departure within the range of normal expectation upon a sale of common chattels will vary from the margin to be expected upon a contract for the construction of a mansion or a "skyscraper." There will be harshness sometimes and oppression in the implication of a condition when the thing upon which labor has been expended is incapable of surrender because united to the land, and equity and reason in the implication of a like condition when the subject-matter, if defective, is in shape to be returned. From the conclusion that promises may not be treated as dependent to the extent of their uttermost minutiae without a sacrifice of justice, the progress is a short one to the conclusion that they may not be so treated without a perversion of intention. Intention not otherwise revealed may be presumed to hold in contemplation the reasonable and probable. If something else is in view, it must not be left to implication. There will be no assumption of a purpose to visit venial faults with oppressive retribution.

Those who think more of symmetry and logic in the development of legal rules than of practical adaptation to the attainment of a just result will be troubled by a classification where the lines of division are so wavering and blurred. Something, doubtless, may be said on the score of consistency and certainty in favor of a stricter standard. The courts have balanced such considerations against those of equity and fairness, and found the latter to be the weightier. The decisions in this state commit us to the liberal view, which is making its way, nowadays, in jurisdictions slow to welcome it. Where the line is to be drawn between the important and the trivial cannot be settled by a formula. "In the nature of the case precise boundaries are impossible." 2 Williston on Contracts, § 841. The same omission may take on one aspect or another according to its setting. Substitution of equivalents may not have the same significance in fields of art on the one side and in those of mere utility on the other. Nowhere will change be tolerated, however, if it is so dominant or pervasive as in any real or substantial measure to frustrate the purpose of the contract. There is no general license to install whatever, in the builder's judgment, may be regarded as "just as good." The question is one of degree, to be answered, if there is doubt, by the triers of the facts, and, if the inferences are certain, by the judges of the law. We must weigh the purpose to be served, the desire to be gratified, the excuse for deviation from the letter, the cruelty of enforced adherence. Then only can we tell whether literal fulfillment is to be implied by law as a condition. This is not to say that the parties are not free by apt and certain words to effectuate a purpose that performance of every term shall be a condition of recovery. That question is not here. This is merely to say that the law will be slow to impute the purpose, in the silence of the parties, where the significance of the default is grievously out of proportion to the oppression of the forfeiture. The willful transgressor must accept the penalty of his transgression. For him there is no occasion to mitigate the rigor of implied conditions. The transgressor whose default is unintentional and trivial may hope for mercy if he will offer atonement for his wrong.

In the circumstances of this case, we think the measure of the allowance is not the cost of replacement, which would be great, but the difference in value, which would be either nominal or nothing. . . . It is true that in most cases the cost of replacement is the measure. The owner is entitled to the money which will permit him to complete, unless the cost of completion is grossly and unfairly out of proportion to the good to be attained. When that is true, the measure is the difference in value. . . . The rule that gives a remedy in cases of substantial performance with compensation for defects of trivial or inappreciable importance has been developed by the courts as an instrument of justice. The measure of the allowance must be shaped to the same end.

The order should be affirmed, and judgment absolute directed in favor of the plaintiff upon the stipulation, with costs in all courts.

NOTE

The record in *Jacob & Youngs* indicates (R. 106) that the contract between the parties contained the following provision, which was not mentioned by the court:

> Any work furnished by the Contractor, the material or work-manship of which is defective or which is not fully in accordance with the drawings and specifications, in every respect, will be reject-ed and is to be immediately torn down, removed and remade or re-

placed in accordance with the drawings and specifications, whenever discovered.

Was Cardozo right in his assertion that the question of intention to make "performance of every term . . . a condition . . . is not here"? Suppose the contract had said: "Payment of Contractor by Owner shall be on condition that no pipe other than that of Reading manufacture has been used in the work"?

––––––

Reynolds v. Armstead

166 Colo. 372, 443 P.2d 990 (1968)

Plaintiff contracted to apply a brick veneer to defendant's house, expressly promising to use "new brick matching as closely as possible the color and appearance of [the] existing brickwork." Although plaintiff failed (for reasons not disclosed in the opinion) to use such brick, the trial court found the veneer was in all other respects of sound construction and entered judgment for plaintiff for the contract price of $535.25, less "damages" in the amount of $267.63 caused defendant by plaintiff's failure to perform fully. *Held*, affirmed. As a matter of law, plaintiff's breach, which damaged the appearance of the house to the extent of half the contract price of the veneer work, was "material." Thus, this failure substantially to perform deprived plaintiff of the right to recover under the "theory" of express contract. But plaintiff is entitled to the judgment entered on a "theory" of quantum meruit. [In assessing what this court did and said, it may be useful to recall and compare Britton v. Turner and Pinches v. Swedish Evangelical Lutheran Church, supra pp. 125–133.]

––––––

NOTE: RESTITUTION FOR THE "WILLFUL" DEFAULTER

The "willful" breach and the issue of restitution for defaulters are familiar subjects at this stage (see, e.g., Chapter 1, pp. 133–134). As Judge Cardozo indicated, things might be different for the willful defaulter, at least as concerns a recovery on the contract. There is need to add only a brief word on whether a party's own nonperformance precludes a restitution remedy.

In Glazer v. Schwartz, 276 Mass. 54, 176 N.E. 613 (1931), plaintiff sought recovery for labor and materials furnished under a contract to construct a house and garage for $14,700, of which $13,000 had been paid. Defendant counterclaimed for damages caused by plaintiff's failure to complete the work in accordance with the specifications. At trial, it was found that plaintiff had substantially performed the contract but that his failure to perform fully was "willful." It was also found that plaintiff had failed to supply materials worth $200 and that the value of the house as built was $500 less than it would have been if plaintiff had performed fully. The Supreme Judicial Court held that recovery on the contract itself required "complete performance." Recovery in quantum meruit, on the other hand, was said to be available in Massachusetts only if the owner obtains "substantially what was called for by the contract" *and* the failure to perform fully is not willful. Plaintiff, therefore, could recover nothing. As for defendant, not only was there no duty to pay the contract balance of $1,700, but defendant was entitled to "affirmative relief" in the form of damages of $200 for materials not supplied *plus* "the cost of making the structure conform

. . . to the contract"—a figure which, on remand, might well turn out to be greater than the $500 already found to represent diminution in value of the premises.

It was surely predictable that the *Glazer* court's treatment of the willful defaulter would again come before the Massachusetts high court. One such occasion, some two decades later, was Ficara v. Belleau, 331 Mass. 80, 117 N.E.2d 287 (1954), where builders had agreed to install a heating and cooling system for $6,200, but "intentionally and willfully" abandoned performance after the owner had paid them $4,200. The owner reasonably paid another contractor $2,361 to finish the work and sued builders for this amount, relying on Glazer v. Schwartz. The lower court gave the owner judgment for only $361, which was affirmed on appeal. Insofar as *Glazer* indicated that the owner in this case could recover $2,361, the Massachusetts court refused to follow it, declaring that the owner was attempting, in effect, to collect exemplary damages and to obtain a $6,200 heating and cooling system for $4,200. The court said: "It is not the policy of our law to award damages which would put a plaintiff in a better position than if the defendant had carried out the contract. . . . The plaintiff is entitled to be made whole and no more. This is true in an action against a defendant for breach of contract, albeit a willful one, even though the same defendant in suing as a plaintiff on the same contract might be barred" by the rule denying both contract and quasi-contract remedies to the willful defaulter.

Massachusetts continues to adhere to the overall view that a contractor's failure to perform in full bars recovery on the contract, but that one who both substantially performs and makes a "good faith" effort to perform fully may recover in quantum meruit. Peabody, N.E., Inc. v. Town of Marshfield, 426 Mass. 436, 689 N.E.2d 774 (1998) (but denying recovery of overhead costs in determining defaulter's quantum meruit award, since such costs—expenses not chargeable to a particular contract or work—"do not directly confer any value or benefit" on defendant). It seems that a principal measure of good faith is the absence of intentional departures from the contract. See, e.g., J.A. Sullivan Corp. v. Commonwealth, 397 Mass. 789, 494 N.E.2d 374 (1986). But, of course, only a few states have fallen in line with Massachusetts on the question of remedies available to a defaulting provider of services. Further clues as to the general common law standing of the "willful" defaulter today are provided by the New York case described immediately below.

Hadden v. Consolidated Edison Co. of New York
34 N.Y.2d 88, 356 N.Y.S.2d 249, 312 N.E.2d 445 (1974)

This case presented the question whether an employee's pension could be revoked when, after the employee's retirement, the employer discovered facts which would have been grounds for discharge "for cause" (and thus a loss of an expected pension) had they been known during employment. The newly-discovered facts were that in the last year or two of his employment, Hadden, then a vice-president of Con Edison, had secretly accepted cash totaling $15,000 and other benefits from contractors doing business with Con Edison. Upon obtaining this information through transcripts of Hadden's testimony in criminal proceedings involving others, Con Edison promptly terminated

Hadden's pension. He sued to compel resumption of his pension benefits, which amounted to nearly $4,000 a month. After holding that the termination was not authorized by any provision of the pension contract, the Court of Appeals turned to the question whether "Hadden's misconduct in the latter years of his employment [excuses] Con Edison from paying his pension benefits."

The court, through Rabin, J., said: "While there is no language in the Plan expressly conditioning pension payments upon the employee's performing honestly and loyally, there is little difficulty in regarding these qualifications as a constructive condition of Con Edison's duty [to] make pension payments. . . . If the party in default has substantially performed, the other party's performance is not excused. . . . This doctrine, familiar in construction contract situations, is not limited to that area, but applies to employment contracts as well. . . . Weighing the factors involved we find that Hadden's performance has been substantial. Con Edison has received the benefit of his 37 years of employment. . . . The value of Hadden's performance to Con Edison over the course of nearly four decades is not substantially impaired by his disloyalty in some of those later years. In so stating we do not condone his actions or disregard the fact that his breach was willful."

At this point, the court's opinion includes the following footnote: "In deciding controversies in the field of construction contracts, it has frequently been said that a 'willful' breach defeats a claim of substantial performance. (See, e.g., Jacob & Youngs v. Kent . . .). Our treating willfulness here as one of several factors to be considered in determining whether Hadden's performance is substantial does not compel a different result in those cases. Weighing willfulness as one of several relevant factors is also supported by authority. . . . Since employment contracts are divisible, the situation presented by an employee's breach in some, but not all, of the years of his employment relationship is somewhat analogous to the problem encountered in installment contracts where there has been a material breach with regard to one of the installments. . . . In the present case, while Hadden's willful misconduct may have been a material breach with regard to a specific term of his employment, it does not impair the value of his nearly four decades of work for the Company."

––––––––

Worcester Heritage Society, Inc. v. Trussell

Court of Appeals of Massachusetts, 1991.
31 Mass.App.Ct. 343, 577 N.E.2d 1009.

ARMSTRONG, J. The plaintiff (the society), a private, non-profit organization dedicated to the preservation of historically significant buildings in Worcester, appeals from a judgment . . . which refused it a rescission of a contract and reconveyance of a house which it had conveyed to the defendant (Trussell) in 1984. The house at that time was vacant and uninhabitable, with no heat, electricity, or plumbing, was in severe disrepair, and had recently been damaged by fire. The sale was for $20,100, Trussell agreeing to abide by historic preservation restrictions and to do a complete historic restoration. The exterior portion was to be completed in one year, failing which the society could, at its option, engage workers to complete the exterior restoration at Trussell's expense. No time limit was specified for interior restoration. There was no requirement that the house be opened to public viewing or that the house be occupied.

Trussell, prior to the conveyance, gave the society, as required, evidence of his financial ability to invest the purchase price plus $45,000, the then estimated cost of the restoration. About a year and a half after the transfer, however, Trussell lost his job, with the result that work on the house, which had proceeded less rapidly than anticipated, was further slowed. The society sued for rescission in 1986 but then agreed, by way of a stipulation, to stay its hand for a further period. The case was not tried until 1989.

The society put in evidence that the exterior work was at that time still uncompleted, particularly on the rear side of the house, where sash was missing on one or two windows and a porch was supported on jacks. Trussell testified that he had scraped forty to fifty percent of the exterior to bare wood; replaced most of the clapboards on the south, sun-exposed side; prime-coated the entire house and finish-coated sixty percent of it; replaced most of the sash (most of the windows were boarded up before the sale); done roof repairs (taking some portions down to the carrying timbers); gutted most of the interior of the house, including all plaster, and carted the materials away. He acknowledged having done no restoration of the interior. The needed work, he estimated, would cost $100,000, far in excess of what had been estimated at the time of the sale. In general, he painted a picture, which the judge accepted, of meticulous, steady progress on the house, primarily by his own work, but hampered by shortage of funds which he hoped would soon be alleviated by settlement of his father's estate. The judge found the exterior work to be sixty-five to seventy-five percent complete. Acting "in [his] discretion," he refused rescission (the only remedy sought in the complaint) and suggested that the society, if it continued to be dissatisfied with the exterior progress, employ the self-help remedy set out in the contract.

There was no error. . . . There is ample authority for refusing rescission where there has been only a breach of contract rather than an utter failure of consideration or a repudiation by the party in breach. "In the absence of fraud, nothing less than conduct that amounts to an abrogation of the contract, or that goes to the essence of it, or takes away its foundation, can be made a ground for rescission of it by the other party." Runkle v. Burrage, 202 Mass. 89, 88 N.E. 573 (1909). "Ordinarily equity will not set aside a contract at the suit of a party thereto on the sole ground of nonperformance by the other party of one of his agreements therein contained, in the absence of an agreement for termination upon breach by such nonperformance, where the breach is not of such a material and substantial nature as to excuse the party suing from proceeding with the contract, but will leave the party suing to his remedy by way of damages." Barry v. Frankini, 287 Mass. 196, 191 N.E. 651 (1934). . . . See 5 Corbin on Contracts (1964) § 1104 ("In the case of a breach by non-performance[,] assuming that there has been no repudiation, the injured party's alternative remedy by way of restitution depends upon the extent of the non-performance by the defendant. . . . The injured party [may] not maintain an action for restitution of what he has given the defendant unless the defendant's non-performance is so material that it is held to go to the 'essence'."). . . . Cases such as Nevins v. Ward, 320 Mass. 70, 67 N.E.2d 673 (1946), discussing "substantial performance" in the context of an action by a construction contractor seeking payment for work done, are not determinative here.

Trussell's actions certainly have not amounted to a repudiation of the contract. . . . There has not been a total failure of consideration, Trussell having paid the purchase price and invested some additional sums and much labor in the restoration work. The visibly uncompleted portions of the exterior restoration are at the rear side of the house, the front appearing quite presentable. The society's concern was focused primarily, as its director testified, on the exterior appearance of the houses it rescued (explaining the cursory treatment of interior renovation in the contract[1] and the absence of a time limit therefor or of any provision for opening the house to public view). The provisions of the purchase and sale agreement that time was of the essence applied to the closing date of the conveyance, not to the restoration provisions.

Courts have traditionally applied discretion in affording relief by way of rescission, as they have with most equitable remedies.... Thus, the judge could properly take into account the "sweat equity" (in the judge's phrase) that Trussell had put into the restoration, which might be forfeit if a rescission were ordered. He could also properly take into account the fact that the contract expressly contemplated the possibility of delay in completion of the exterior work and empowered the society in that circumstance to engage a contractor to complete the exterior work and charge all costs (including architectural fees and attorney's fees) to Trussell. It was not shown that this remedy would be ineffectual.[2]

Judgment affirmed.

QUESTION

What is the basis for the court's statement that the construction-contractor cases litigating the issue of substantial performance "are not determinative here"? Presumably, the court is saying that the question before it is different from the question raised by such cases as Plante v. Jacobs and Jacob & Youngs v. Kent. But is the court saying something more, perhaps something about the legal tests for opening up one remedy but not another?

———

Tichnor Bros. v. Evans

92 Vt. 278, 102 A. 1031 (1918)

Seller sold Buyer a quantity of goods, including sets of post cards; it was agreed that Seller would not sell similar sets to other stores in the town where Buyer did business. In Seller's action for the balance of the price of goods delivered, Buyer, who had not returned or offered to return the postcard sets, asserted as a defense that Seller had sold similar sets to one of Buyer's competitors. *Held*, this was no defense to Seller's action. "It is not every breach that goes to the essence.... Where, as here, the stipulation goes only to a part of the consideration, and may be compensated for in damages, its breach does not relieve the other party from performance. In such cases, the broken promise is an

———

[1] The contract did not speak of "interior restoration" (the parties infer the requirement from the contract's requirement that Trussell "complete a certified historic restoration"). The time limit applied only to the exterior restoration, and it was only with respect to the exterior work that the society imposed restrictions on alterations of architectural form.

[2] Even if the expense should cause Trussell to lose the house, the preservation restrictions, which are recorded, run with the land. Parenthetically, we note that a different case would be presented if the contract contained a specific provision for reconveyance where the society is dissatisfied with the progress of the restoration.

independent undertaking and not a condition precedent." [This case was decided long before passage of the UCC. Is it surprising that the court was unwilling to construct conditions (i.e., the broken promise was "independent")?]

Hathaway v. Sabin

Supreme Court of Vermont, 1891.
63 Vt. 527, 22 A. 633.

MUNSON, J. . . . The contract required the defendant to furnish a hall [the Blanchard Opera House] for the concert, and to pay $75 after the entertainment. The plaintiff alleged readiness to perform on his part, and assigned as the breach the defendant's failure to furnish a hall. The court directed a verdict for the plaintiff for $75 and interest. The defendant insists that, inasmuch as the non-payment of the $75 was not assigned as the breach, and as there was no proof of any loss except in the non-payment of the $75, there was no proof of loss from any breach complained of, and that consequently there could be no recovery. We think it cannot be said that the proof of loss in the non-receipt of the $75 did not apply to the breach declared upon. The plaintiff was ready to give the concert, and on giving it would have been entitled to the $75, but he was prevented from giving it by the defendant's failure to furnish a hall. This failure was properly assigned as the breach from which the plaintiff suffered damage. The plaintiff does not sue for the compensation to which he would have been entitled if the contract had been carried out, but for the damages he has sustained in being compelled to leave the contract unperformed. The breach is not the non-payment of the unearned compensation, but the failure to perform the antecedent stipulation which would have enabled the plaintiff to earn it.

The defendant also contends that he was excused from opening and heating the hall by the apparent impossibility of the musicians' reaching the town. During the 36 hours preceding the evening appointed for the concert a snow-storm of unusual violence prevailed in Montpelier and vicinity, which early on the day of the concert rendered the streets of that village and the roads from the surrounding country practically impassable. The quartette by which the concert was to be given was in Barre,* having gone there from Montpelier the evening before, and trains on the spur from Montpelier to Barre were suspended. Late in the afternoon, however, an irregular train went to Barre, and on this the musicians returned to Montpelier, arriving early in the evening, and going to the hall at the time appointed. It is claimed that the defendant's conduct must be tested by the situation as it was at the time when action on his part became necessary, and that he is saved from liability by the doctrine that, when one party ascertains that the other will not be able to perform what he has undertaken, the party ascertaining this is excused from performing the obligations resting upon him. It is doubtless true that, when one party has put it out of his power to perform, the other party can maintain an action without having tendered performance on his part. But a party who becomes involved in difficulties for which he is not responsible, if ultimately able to perform, is not to be deprived of the benefits of his contract because of an assumption by the other party that the difficulties would prove insurmountable. Here

---

* [For those who may not know northern Vermont, Barre is located about five miles from Montpelier.—Eds.]

the defendant was mistaken in supposing that the plaintiff would not be able to perform, and we know of no rule which permits him to plead reasonable cause to believe so in excuse for the failure on his part. It is apparent, also, that the defendant's course was determined before the time when action on his part became necessary. It was not necessary to commence the heating of the hall until 4 o'clock in the afternoon, but about 10 o'clock in the forenoon the defendant telephoned the manager** that, owing to the condition of the streets in Montpelier, it would be impossible to have the entertainment that evening. It is evident from this that the defendant based his action upon his belief that there would be no audience, rather than upon the supposition that the musicians could not reach the place of entertainment. He did not wait until it was necessary to take action about the hall before deciding that there could be no concert. But, at the time when action on his part became necessary, there was nothing in the situation which could relieve him from liability. The contract contains no provision for his protection from such a misfortune, and the loss must fall on him.

Vermont Historical Society

BLANCHARD OPERA HOUSE

** [The record in this case indicates that "the manager" who received defendant's telephone call at 10 a.m. on the day of the concert was the plaintiff Hathaway, the musicians' representative.—Eds.]

The defendant also insists that upon being held liable he was entitled to have the damages assessed by the jury. We think, however, that the plaintiff was entitled to have this verdict directed. Having incurred all the expense necessary to enable him to give the concert, the plaintiff's damages were necessarily the amount to which he would have been entitled for giving it. It is not for the defendant to say that the damages were less than the amount he had agreed to pay, when the plaintiff had done and incurred everything on his part, and was prevented from earning the compensation agreed upon solely by the defendant's failure. The message sent the manager in the forenoon, even if treated as a sufficient notice to stop performance, did not require any different action as regards the damages. It afforded no ground for an application of the doctrine which forbids the making of expense after receiving notice of the repudiation of a contract; for the expense afterwards incurred by the musicians was only such as was required by the situation in which the notice found them. Neither did the case permit an application of the rule which requires a party who is stopped in the performance of a contract for service to do what he can to lessen the damages by seeking like employment elsewhere. Judgment affirmed.

QUESTIONS

(1) Assume defendant had heated and otherwise readied the hall, and the musicians were in place at 8 p.m. But no audience appeared, and defendant, pointing to an "act of God," canceled the concert? Does defendant owe the musicians $75?

(2) Suppose defendant had employed an event staff and prepared the hall, a full audience appeared, but the musicians, despite extraordinary effort, remained stranded in Barre at 8 p.m. Are the musicians liable in damages to defendant? Can they collect the $75 by bringing a lawsuit?

––––––––

NOTE: A ROADMAP FOR "INSECURITY"

In cases governed by the UCC, § 2–609—titled "Right to Adequate Assurances of Performance" and dating from the 1950s—confers yet another self-help remedy (there was no such right to demand assurances under the common law of most of our states). The methodology for "insecurity" the section prescribes has been hailed for its recognition of "the desirability of providing an opportunity for dialogue to establish whether the parties intend to repudiate or to fulfill their contractual obligations." Conference Ctr. v. TRC—The Research Corp. of New England, 189 Conn. 212, 455 A.2d 857 (1983). Hence it is not surprising that over the years UCC 2–609 came to be seen as a source of general law, and that, in Restatement, Second § 251, reproduced immediately below, its principle has been extended to all contracts. That extension beyond UCC boundaries has, in general, been characterized by courts as "sound," and in keeping with the "traditional common-law developmental method." C.L. Maddox, Inc. v. Coalfield Services, 51 F.3d 76 (7th Cir.1995); Norcon Power Partners v. Niagara Mohawk Power Corp., 92 N.Y.2d 458, 682 N.Y.S.2d 664, 705 N.E.2d 656 (1998). Whether under § 2–609 or Rest.2d § 251, observe that the "assurances" privilege comes into play only when one party believes the other may break the contract when the other's performance comes due. Observe also that a party demanding assurances is calling for something not required by the parties' contract.

———

RESTATEMENT OF CONTRACTS, SECOND

Section 251. When a Failure to Give Assurance May be Treated as a Repudiation

(1) Where reasonable grounds arise to believe that the obligor will commit a breach by non-performance that would of itself give the obligee a claim for damages for total breach . . ., the obligee may demand adequate assurance of due performance and may, if reasonable, suspend any performance for which he has not already received the agreed exchange until he receives such assurance.

(2) The obligee may treat as a repudiation the obligor's failure to provide within a reasonable time such assurance of due performance as is adequate in the circumstances of the particular case.

Comment: . . .

b. Relation to other rules. An obligee who believes, for whatever reason, that the obligor will not or cannot perform without a breach, is always free to act on that belief. . . . If he can prove that his belief would have been confirmed, he is at least shielded from liability even if he has failed to give a performance that is due before that of the obligor or has, by making alternative arrangements, done an act that amounts to a repudiation. . . . If, however, the obligee's belief is incorrect, his own failure to perform or his making of alternate arrangements may subject him to a claim for damages for total breach. This [s]ection affords him an opportunity, in appropriate cases, [to] avoid the uncertainties that would otherwise inhere in acting on his belief.

§ 268. Effect on Other Party's Duties of a Prospective Failure Justified by Impracticability or Frustration

(1) A party's prospective failure of performance may, except as stated in Subsection (2), discharge the other party's duties or allow him to suspend performance under the rules stated in §§ 251(1) and 253(2) even though the failure would be justified under the rules stated in this Chapter.

(2) The rule stated in Subsection (1) does not apply if the other party assumed the risk that he would have to perform in spite of such a failure.

Comment:

a. Relation to other rules. This Restatement adopts the principle "that a continuing sense of reliance and security that the promised performance will be forthcoming when due, is an important feature of the bargain." Comment 1 to Uniform Commercial Code § 2-609; see Comment a to § 251. If there is reason to expect that a party will not perform as promised, the other party has the protection afforded by the rules stated in §§ 250 and 253 if the first party has repudiated, and by the rule stated in § 251 if reasonable grounds for insecurity have arisen with respect to the first party's future performance. However, those sections apply only if such prospective non-performance would amount to a breach. This Section applies when the prospective non-performance would not be a breach because of the rules on impracticability of performance or frustration of purpose stated in this Chapter. Subsection (2) makes it clear that if the other party has assumed the risk that he will have to perform although he receives no return performance, his duties are not discharged. . . .

Illustration:

> 1. *A*, an impresario, contracts with *B*, a singer, for an engagement for three months beginning on January 1. On the preceding November 30, *B* contracts pneumonia, and states to *A* that he will be unable to sing before February 1. *A* employs another singer to fill *B*'s place. On January 1, *B*, having recovered, offers to perform but *A* refuses. Since *B*'s statement would have been a repudiation under the rule stated in § 250 but for the operation of the rules on impracticability of performance stated in §§ 261 and 262, *A*'s duty to employ *B* is discharged, and *A* is not liable to *B* for breach of contract.

c. Failure to give assurances. If reasonable grounds arise to believe that a party will not perform because of impracticability of his performance or frustration of his purpose, the other party cannot demand assurances and treat a failure to give them as a repudiation under the rule stated in § 251, because the prospective non-performance would not be a breach. It therefore gives him no claim for breach of contract. Nevertheless, under the rule stated in this Section, he may in a proper case suspend his own performance and treat a failure to give assurance as discharging any remaining duties that he has to render the agreed exchange.

Illustrations:

> 2. *A*, an impresario, contracts with *B*, a singer, for an engagement for three months beginning on January 1. On the preceding November 30, *B* contracts pneumonia, and *A* is advised by competent medical authority that *B* will not be able to sing before February 1. *A* reasonably demands assurances of due performance by B. B ignores the demand, and A employs another singer to fill *B*'s place. On January 1, B, having recovered, offers to perform, but *A* refuses. Since *B*'s failure to furnish assurance of due performance would have been a repudiation under the rule stated in § 251 but for the operation of the rules on impracticability of performance stated in §§ 261 and 262, *A*'s duty to employ *B* is discharged, and *A* is not liable to *B* for breach of contract.

Printing Center of Texas, Inc. v. Supermind Pub. Co.

Court of Appeals of Texas, 1984.
669 S.W.2d 779.

CANNON, J. Appellee sued appellant for refund of a deposit made under a written contract to print 5000 books entitled "Supermind Supermemory." Appellee alleged that it rightfully rejected the books upon delivery under Tex.Bus. & Com.Code Ann. § 2.601 (Tex. UCC) and that it has a right to cancel the contract and recover the part of the purchase price paid under Tex.Bus. & Com.Code Ann. § 2.711 (Tex. UCC). . . . [In omitted passages, the court noted that the case may have been tried below "on the wrong legal theory." The parties proceeded on the assumption the Texas UCC governed. But the Code is limited to transactions involving the sale of goods, and, said the court, services are "the essence or dominant factor" of this contract for the printing of books. Hence common-law rejection rules, not UCC Article 2, would apply in this case. Nevertheless, appellant, in failing to assign error on the point, was found to have waived it on appeal, the court concluding: "We indulge in the doubtful assumption that [the UCC] governs the [parties'] contract to enable us to adequately consider appellant's points of error."]

Appellant contends in its second point of error that jury finding that the books failed to conform to the contract is so against the great weight and preponderance of the evidence as to be manifestly unjust. This finding is related to whether appellee had a right to reject the books under § 2.601, which states in part: "[I]f the goods or tender of delivery fail in any respect to conform to the contract, the buyer may (1) reject the whole. . . ."

This provision has been called the perfect tender rule because it supposedly allows a buyer to reject whenever the goods are less than perfect. This statement is not quite accurate; under § 2.601 the tender must be perfect only in the sense that the proffered goods must conform to the contract in every respect. Conformity does not mean substantial performance; it means complete performance. The long standing doctrine of sales law that "there is no room in commercial contracts for the doctrine of substantial performance" is carried forward into § 2.601 of the Code. . . . Substantial compliance is not the legal equivalent of conformity with the contract under § 2.601.

In analyzing whether tendered goods are conforming, the contract of the parties must first be determined. "Conform" is defined in § 2.106(b), as "in accordance with the obligations under the contract." The contract of the parties includes more than the words used by the parties. It encompasses "the bargain of the parties in fact as found in their language or by implication from other circumstances including course of dealing or usage of trade or course of performance as provided in the Code." § 1.201(11) and § 1.201(3). Thus, the terms of a contract may be explained and supplemented through trade usage, but it may not be used to contradict an express term. The existence and scope of trade usage must be proved as facts. A buyer has a right to reject goods under § 2.601 if the goods fail to conform to either the express or implied terms of the contract.

Once the contract of the parties has been determined, the evidence must be reviewed to see if the right goods were tendered at the right time and place. If the evidence does establish nonconformity in some respect, the buyer is entitled to reject if he rejects in good faith. [Section] 1.203 provides that, "Every contract or duty within this Act imposes an obligation of good faith in its performance or enforcement." Since the rejection of goods is a matter of performance, the buyer is obligated to act in good faith when he rejects the goods. Where the buyer is a merchant, his standard of good faith rejection requires honesty in fact and observance of reasonable commercial standards of fair dealing in the trade. If the seller alleges that the buyer rejected in bad faith, the seller has the burden of proof on this issue. Evidence of circumstances which indicate that the buyer's motivation in rejecting the goods was to escape the bargain, rather than to avoid acceptance of a tender which in some respect impairs the value of the bargain to him, would support a finding of rejection in bad faith. Thus, evidence of rejection of the goods on account of a minor defect in a falling market would in some instances be sufficient to support a finding that the buyer acted in bad faith when he rejected the goods.

The written contract between the parties which is expressed in a bid proposal dated July 31, 1981 covers only essential terms such as quantity, trim size, and type of paper and cover. The type of paper specified in the contract was thirty pound white newsprint. Appellee's witness testified that he was shown a sample of the newsprint to be used and that the tendered books were not the same color as the sample. The witness stated the pages of the books were gray while the sample was white. This testimony is evidence of nonconformity because any sample which is made part of the basis of the bargain creates an express warranty that the whole of the goods shall conform to the sample. § 2.313(a)(3).

Other nonconformities which appellee alleges and offers proof of are off center cover art, crooked pages, wrinkled pages and inadequate perforation on a pull out page. The contract does not expressly address any of these matters. Although evidence of trade usage may have indicated that these conditions are contrary to the standards of commercial practice within the publishing industry, appellant failed to offer evidence of trade usage to supplement the contract. However, appellant knew that appellee wanted the books printed for sale to the public. In these circumstances, it is implied in the contract that the books be commercially acceptable and appealing to the public. Section 2.314 states that a warranty that the goods shall be merchantable is implied in a contract for their sale and that for goods to be merchantable, they must pass without objection in the trade and be fit for the ordinary purposes for which such goods are used. A jury could reasonably conclude that books with crooked and wrinkled pages, off center cover art, and inadequate perforation are not fit for sale to the public. We find sufficient evidence to support the jury's finding that the books did not conform to the contract.

Appellant contends that if nonconformities exist, they are minor and that appellee rejected the books in bad faith. Appellant has failed to carry its burden to prove that appellee rejected the books in bad faith. First, we do not agree with appellant's contention that the alleged nonconformities should be classified as minor. Second, there is no evidence which indicates that appellee's primary motivation in rejection of the books was to escape a bad bargain. We also note that appellant has waived its defense of rejection in bad faith by its failure to request an issue on this defense, because it has not conclusively established it under the evidence.

Appellant's second point of error is overruled. . . .

———

Prescott & Co. v. J.B. Powles & Co.

113 Wash. 177, 193 P. 680 (1920)

On January 12, 1918, buyer placed with seller, in Seattle, the following order: "Sold to J.B. Powles Co. How ship, Boat. When, March. 300 crates Australian onions, $94 per ton. Cost, freight & insurance Frisco. Acceptance Australia." The parties understood there was but one ship sailing monthly between the Australian port of shipment and San Francisco, and thus a March shipment would be by the S.S. Sonoma. The seller had ready the 300 crates called for, but was allowed to load only 240, the remainder of the Sonoma's space being taken at the last moment by the government of the United States, to ship wheat. The buyer refused to accept the 240 crates shipped. The seller thereupon resold these crates at less than the contract price and sued the buyer to recover the resulting loss, including the expenses of resale. Trial of the case resulted in a judgment against the buyer for the full amount claimed. *Held*, judgment reversed; seller's action dismissed. "[D]elivery of goods [must generally] be of the exact quantity ordered, otherwise the buyer may refuse to receive them. . . . Since the seller [was bound] to deliver the exact quantity ordered, may he be excused from making full delivery because our national government (rightfully as we must assume), as a war measure, commandeered the only available shipping space for its necessities? Much as [we] would like to so hold, the authorities lay down the contrary rule. Had [the seller] been sued for damages for failure to ship the full order, this act by the government might have afforded a defense, but having sued on the contract, it is essential to a recovery that a full performance be shown, and no excuse not provided for in the contract will justify a recovery where the performance is partial only, save only an act of the buyer rendering performance impossible or a waiver by it. . . ."

––––––––

Ramirez v. Autosport
88 N.J. 277, 440 A.2d 1345 (1982)

Pollock, J., writing for the court: "In the nineteenth century, sellers were required to deliver goods that complied exactly with the sales agreement. See Filley v. Pope, 115 U.S. 213 (1885) (buyer not obliged to accept otherwise conforming scrap iron shipped to New Orleans from Leith, rather than Glasgow, Scotland, as required by contract). . . . That rule, known as the 'perfect tender' rule, remained part of the law of sales well into the twentieth century. By the 1920's, the doctrine was so entrenched in the law that Judge Learned Hand declared '[t]here is no room in commercial contracts for the doctrine of substantial performance.' Mitsubishi Goshi Kaisha v. J. Aron & Co., Inc., 16 F.2d 185, 186 (2d Cir.1926). The harshness of the rule led courts to seek to ameliorate its effect and to bring the law of sales in closer harmony with the law of contracts, which allows rescission only for material breaches. . . . Nevertheless, a variation of the perfect tender rule appeared in the Uniform Sales Act. N.J.S.A. 46:30–75 (purchasers permitted to reject goods or rescind contracts for any breach of warranty); N.J.S.A. 46:30–18 to –21 (warranties extended to include all the seller's obligations to the goods). See Honnold, Buyer's Right of Rejection, A Study in the Impact of Codification Upon a Commercial Problem, 97 U.Pa.L.Rev. 457, 460 (1949). The chief objection to the continuation of the perfect tender rule was that buyers in a declining market would reject goods for minor nonconformities and force the loss on surprised sellers. . . . To the extent that a buyer [under § 2–601] can reject goods for any nonconformity, the UCC retains the perfect tender rule. . . . The Code, however, mitigates the harshness of the [rule] and balances the interests of buyer and seller."

[The "perfect tender" rule of § 2–601 is noted by Justice Pollock. It would be a good idea to look also at UCC 2–607(1) and (2), as well as the index of a buyer's Code remedies in general, provided in § 2–711. Note also that § 2–601, by its terms, excludes installment contracts falling within the scope of § 2–612. It would be a good idea to look closely at the three subdivisions of § 2–612. The first point to note is the broad definition of an "installment contract." Observe also the test of "materiality" stated in 2–612 (2) and (3). Why should installment contracts involving goods be subject to a test of "substantial impairment" while a one-shot, unitary sales contract is governed by a rule of "perfect tender" (softened, of course, by § 2–508)?]

————

Beck & Pauli Lithographing Co. v. Colorado Milling & Elevator Co.

52 F. 700 (8th Cir.1892)

Plaintiff was engaged in lithographing and printing at Milwaukee. In June 1889, defendant, a Colorado company engaged in milling, entered into a contract to purchase from plaintiff more than 300,000 copies of engraved letterhead paper, bills, envelopes, and cards, together with some advertising material. The contract provided that plaintiff would prepare designs of defendant's buildings, together with sketches of its trademarks, submit these designs to defendant for approval, execute engravings "in first class style," and furnish the engraved letterhead paper and other material "in the course of the year" 1889. Plaintiff's lithographing process involved the preparation of a sketch which was then transferred to stone, with a separate stone for each color used. The process required from two to three months; the most expensive part was the artists' work and the reproduction on stone. Sketches and proofs were submitted to and approved by defendant, the last proof being approved on November 16, 1889. In December 1889, plaintiff shipped the finished product by rail in five boxes, four of which did not arrive in Denver until the morning of January 1, 1890, and one of which did not arrive until January 4. Plaintiff tendered delivery of all five boxes before January 8, but defendant refused to receive or examine them, asserting that delivery was too late. In an action brought by plaintiff for the contract price, the trial court directed a verdict for defendant. On appeal, this ruling was overturned and the case remanded for further proceedings. The court said that stipulations as to the time of performance are not necessarily of the essence, unless express provisions of the contract or the nature of the subject matter indicates that the parties intended performance on time to be a condition precedent. In the ordinary contracts of merchants for the sale or manufacture of marketable commodities, time clauses should be strictly construed "on account of the frequent and rapid interchange and use of such commodities made necessary by the demands of commerce." But this was a contract for artistic skill and labor, to be bestowed on articles that would not be saleable to any other buyer. There was nothing to indicate that delivery a few days late would be harmful to defendant, but if there was injury, defendant's remedy was in damages for the delay. Its refusal to accept delivery was not justified by this trifling delay. [The Comment that follows considers the applicability of the UCC to facts like those in *Beck & Pauli*.]

————

COMMENT: "GOODS" AND "SERVICES"—THE SCOPE OF THE UCC SALES ARTICLE

Because a more demanding law of performance is commonly applied in sales of goods than in other types of transactions, many contractual disputes will present a troublesome problem of classification. If a contract provides only for a present or future transfer of goods from seller to buyer, no difficulty usually arises and the law of sales set out in Article 2 of the UCC can safely be assumed to govern disputes that may arise. Under the UCC, § 2–105, "goods" are defined as "all things . . . which are movable at the time of identification to the contract for sale." The first phase of any inquiry into the type of contract sued on therefore centers on the nature of particular items at the time of identification to the contract (are they movable and thus "goods" within the scope of the Code?).

An issue as to the applicability of sales law is likely to arise in three common types of transactions.

(a) The contract may provide for the transfer of ownership of goods, as well as incorporeal rights or realty. An example is an agreement to sell a going business—its inventory of movable goods, buildings and fixtures, and good will. If disputes arise, one obvious solution is to apply Article 2 to issues involving "goods" and to decide others under general contract law. This is the course taken by many decisions, e.g., Foster v. Colorado Radio Corp., 381 F.2d 222 (10th Cir.1967), and Kazerouni v. De Satnick, 228 Cal.App.3d 871, 279 Cal.Rptr. 74 (1991), though there is support for a test of "reasonable characterization of the transaction as a whole," that is, scrutiny of the assets to be sold to determine whether the bulk qualifies as "goods" under the Code's definition. Fink v. DeClassis, 745 F.Supp. 509 (N.D.Ill.1990); Advent Systems Ltd. v. Unisys Corp., 925 F.2d 670 (3d Cir.1991), quoting De Filippo v. Ford Motor Co., 516 F.2d 1313 (3d Cir.1975), cert. denied, 423 U.S. 912 (1975) ("[t]o segregate 'goods' assets from 'non-goods' assets . . . would be to make the contract divisible and impossible of performance within the intention of the parties").

(b) The rendition of a service often involves the transfer of ownership of goods. *Beck & Pauli Lithographing*, supra, provides an example of a sale not only of goods but also of services (a "hybrid" transaction). When dealing with such cases, most courts have made the classification (and thus the applicable law) turn on what is found to be the "essence" of the contract, the "main objective" of the parties, or the "dominant aspect" of the transaction—i.e., which aspect of the transaction, the sale of goods or the sale of services, predominates. A popular statement of this general approach to "mixed" goods and service contracts can be found in Bonebrake v. Cox, 499 F.2d 951, 960 (8th Cir.1974): "The [test] is not whether they are mixed, but, granting that they are mixed, whether their predominant factor, their thrust, their purpose, reasonably stated, is the rendition of service, with goods incidentally involved (e.g., contract with artist for painting) or is a transaction of sale, with labor incidentally involved (e.g., installation of a water heater in a bathroom)." Under this test, virtually every jurisdiction that has addressed the question whether a franchise or dealership agreement is predominantly for the sale of goods has concluded that it is. So, too, according to the weight of authority, is the sale of custom computer software. Conversely, agreements to provide specified materials and install a roof for a building (Quality Guaranteed Roofing v. Hoffmann–La Roche, 302 N.J.Super. 163, 694 A.2d 1077 (App.Div.1997)), to supply and install a grain-storage system (Valley Farmers' Elevator v. Lindsay Bros. Co., 398 N.W.2d 553 (Minn.1987)), to supply the structural steel and build a bridge (Schenectady Steel Co. v. Bruno Trimpoli General Constr. Co. Inc., 43 A.D.2d 234, 350 N.Y.S.2d 920 (1974), aff'd, 34 N.Y.2d 939, 359 N.Y.S.2d 560, 316 N.E.2d 875 (1974)), and to give a blood transfusion (Howell v. Spokane & Inland Empire

Blood Bank, 114 Wash.2d 42, 785 P.2d 815 (1990)), have been classified as service contracts to which sales law was not applicable.

If, however, the rendition of services is not central to a mixed contract ("not at the heart" of the contract), there is a general trend to view any transaction weighted towards goods as governed by the UCC. See, e.g, Judge Coffin's discussion in Cambridge Plating Co. v. Napco, Inc., 991 F.2d 21 (1st Cir.1993). See also Micro Data Base Sys. v. Dharma Sys., 148 F.3d 649 (7th Cir.1998) (where sale of goods predominates, but contract price includes a charge for labor in the manufacture of the goods, "we doubt it should even be called a 'hybrid' sale, for this would imply that every sale of goods is actually a hybrid sale, since labor is a service and labor is an input into the manufacture of every good"). Here, too, there is an occasional call for bypassing the "predominant factor" test in favor of severance of a mixed goods-services transaction. For example, in Stephenson v. Frazier, 399 N.E.2d 794 (Ind.App.Ct.1980), the contract called for the sale of a modular home, the construction of a foundation for the home, and the installation of a septic system. The court held only the sale of the modular home ("movable goods") to be governed by the Code; those portions of the contract pertaining to services were left to common law principles. (For a different view in Indiana, and elsewhere, see Baker v. Compton, 455 N.E.2d 382 (Ind.App.1983); In re Trailer & Plumbing Supplies, 133 N.H. 432, 578 A.2d 343 (1990).)

(c) Many persons and businesses elect not to purchase equipment but to lease instead. Should the rights and obligations of the parties depend on whether they are classified as seller-buyer or lessor-lessee? Since § 2–102 defines the applicability of Article 2 in terms of "transactions in goods," it is arguable that this term is more embracing than "contract of sale" and that an agreement for equipment-leasing falls within the technical reach of the Code. There is some authority to this effect, at least to the extent of bringing into play the implied warranty provisions of the Code. See Owens v. Patent Scaffolding Co., 77 Misc.2d 992, 354 N.Y.S.2d 778 (1974), rev'd on other grounds, 50 A.D.2d 866, 376 N.Y.S.2d 948 (1975). Even if the transaction falls technically outside the scope of Article 2, however, sales-law results may be reached because of the view that many leases are closely analogous to, and not economically different from, a sale. Barco Auto Leasing Corp. v. PSI Cosmetics, Inc., 125 Misc.2d 68, 478 N.Y.S.2d 505 (N.Y.Civ.Ct.1984); Xerox Corp. v. Hawkes, 124 N.H. 610, 475 A.2d 7 (1984). The general subject of extension of Code provisions by analogy is examined in Note, Disengaging Sales Law From the Sale Construct: A Proposal to Extend the Scope of Article 2 of the UCC, 96 Harv.L.Rev. 470 (1982). Article 2A on the law of leases, added to the UCC in May 1987, is discussed in Note, Article 2A of the Uniform Commercial Code: An Unnecessary Perpetuation of the Lease–Sale Distinction, 54 Brooklyn L.Rev. 1357 (1989).

On the general issue of extending the UCC by analogy, there is considerable evidence that Code principles will govern breaches of duty to provide services. For example, assume that a court adhering to the "goods supplied" approach to mixed transactions concludes that a particular contract is predominantly for services. The court may nevertheless rule that exclusion from Article 2 does not foreclose the application of Code policies. An example of this can be found in Semler v. Knowling, 325 N.W.2d 395 (Iowa 1982), where an implied warranty of fitness was found in a contract to supply and install sewer pipes and fittings. See also Midwest Dredging Co. v. McAninch Corp., 424 N.W.2d

216 (Iowa 1988), which collects cases extending relief for implied warranty in various nonconstruction contexts.

Plateq Corp. of North Haven v. Machlett Labs., Inc.

Supreme Court of Connecticut, 1983.
189 Conn. 433, 456 A.2d 786.

PETERS, J. In this action by a seller of specially manufactured goods to recover their purchase price from a commercial buyer, the principal issue is whether the buyer accepted the goods before it attempted to cancel the contract of sale. The plaintiff, [Plateq Corp.], sued the defendant, [Machlett Laboratories], to recover damages, measured by the contract price and incidental damages, arising out of defendant's allegedly wrongful cancellation of a written contract for the manufacture and sale of two leadcovered steel tanks and appurtenant stands. The defendant denied liability and counterclaimed for damages. . . . [T]he trial court found for plaintiff both on its complaint and on the defendant's counterclaim. The defendant has appealed.

The trial court . . . found the following facts. On July 9, 1976, defendant ordered from plaintiff two leadcovered steel tanks to be constructed by plaintiff according to specifications supplied by defendant. The parties understood that the tanks were designed for the special purpose of testing x-ray tubes and were required to be radiation-proof within certain federal standards. Accordingly, the contract provided that the tanks would be tested for radiation leaks after their installation on defendant's premises. The plaintiff undertook to correct, at its own cost, any deficiencies that this post-installation test might uncover.[1] The plaintiff had not previously constructed such tanks nor had the defendant previously designed tanks for this purpose. The contract was amended on August 9, 1976, to add construction of two metal stands to hold the tanks. All the goods were to be delivered to the defendant at the plaintiff's place of business.

Although the plaintiff encountered difficulties both in performing according to contract specifications and in completing performance within the time required, the defendant did no more than call these deficiencies to the plaintiff's attention during various inspections in September and early October, 1976. By October 11, 1976, performance was belatedly but substantially completed. On that date, Albert Yannello, the defendant's engineer, noted some remaining deficiencies which the plaintiff promised to remedy by the next day, so that the goods would then be ready for delivery. Yannello gave no indication to the plaintiff that this arrangement was in any way unsatisfactory to the defendant. Not only did Yannello communicate general acquiescence in the plaintiff's proposed tender but he specifically led plaintiff to believe that defendant's truck would pick up the tanks and the stands within a day or two. Instead of sending its truck, defendant sent a notice of total cancellation which plaintiff received on October 14,

---

[1] The contract incorporated precise specifications in the form of detailed drawings. The drawings for the tank and the tank cover contained specific manufacturing instructions as well as provision 6: "Tank with cover will be tested for radiation leaks after installation. Any deficiencies must be corrected by the vendor." [The court's footnotes have been renumbered; some are omitted.—Eds.]

1976. That notice failed to particularize the grounds upon which cancellation was based.[2]

On this factual basis, the trial court, having concluded that the transaction was a contract for the sale of goods falling within the [UCC], General Statutes §§ 42a–2–101 et seq., considered whether defendant had accepted the goods. The court determined that defendant had accepted the tanks, primarily by signifying its willingness to take them despite their nonconformities, in accordance with § 42a–2–606(1)(a), and secondarily by failing to make an effective rejection, in accordance with § 42a–2–606(1)(b). Once the tanks had been accepted, defendant could rightfully revoke its acceptance under § 42a–2–608 only by showing substantial impairment of their value to defendant. In part because the defendant's conduct had foreclosed any post-installation inspection, the court concluded that such impairment had not been proved. Since the tanks were not readily resaleable on the open market, plaintiff was entitled, upon defendant's wrongful revocation of acceptance, to recover their contract price, minus salvage value, plus interest. §§ 42a–2–703; 42a–2–709(1)(b). Accordingly, the trial court awarded the plaintiff damages in the amount of $14,837.92.

. . . [T]he defendant raises four principal claims of error. It maintains that the trial court erred: (1) in invoking the "cure" section, § 42a–2–508, when there had been no tender by the plaintiff seller; (2) in concluding, in accordance with the acceptance section, § 42a–2–606(1), that defendant had "signified" to plaintiff its willingness to take the contract goods; (3) in misconstruing defendant's statutory and contractual rights of inspection; and (4) in refusing to find that defendant's letter of cancellation was occasioned by plaintiff's breach. We find no error.

Upon analysis, all of defendant's claims of error are variations upon one central theme. The defendant claims that on October 11, when its engineer Yannello conducted the last examination on the plaintiff's premises, the tanks were so incomplete and unsatisfactory that defendant was rightfully entitled to conclude that plaintiff would never make a conforming tender. From this scenario, defendant argues that it was justified in cancelling the contract of sale. It denies that the seller's conduct was sufficient to warrant a finding of tender, or its own conduct sufficient to warrant a finding of acceptance. The difficulty with this argument is that it is inconsistent with the underlying facts found by the trial court. . . . There is simply no fit between the defendant's claims and the trial court's finding that, by October 11, 1976, performance was in substantial compliance with the terms of the contract. The trial court further found that on that day defendant was notified that the goods would be ready for tender the following day and that the defendant responded to this notification by promising to send its truck to pick up the tanks in accordance with the contract.

On the trial court's finding of facts, it was warranted in concluding, on two independent grounds, that defendant had accepted the goods it had ordered from plaintiff. Under the [UCC], § 42a–2–606(1), "[a]cceptance of goods occurs when the buyer (a) after a reasonable opportunity to inspect the goods signifies to the seller . . . that he will take . . . them in spite of their nonconformity; or (b) fails to make an effective rejection."

---

[2] The defendant sent the plaintiff a telegram stating: "This order is hereby terminated for your breach, in that you have continuously failed to perform according to your commitment in spite of additional time given you to cure your delinquency. We will hold you liable for all damages incurred [sic] by Machlett including excess cost of reprocurement."

In concluding that defendant had "signified" to plaintiff its willingness to "take" the tanks despite possible remaining minor defects, the trial court necessarily found that defendant had had a reasonable opportunity to inspect the goods. The defendant does not maintain that its engineer, or the other inspectors on previous visits, had inadequate access to the tanks, or inadequate experience to conduct a reasonable examination. It recognizes that inspection of goods when the buyer undertakes to pick up the goods is ordinarily at the seller's place of tender. . . . The defendant argues, however, that its contract, in providing for inspection for radiation leaks after installation of the tanks at its premises, necessarily postponed its inspection rights to that time. The trial court considered this argument and rejected it, and so do we. It was reasonable, in the context of this contract for the special manufacture of goods with which neither party had had prior experience, to limit this clause to adjustments to take place after tender and acceptance. After acceptance, a buyer may still, in appropriate cases, revoke its acceptance, § 42a–2–608, or recover damages for breach of warranty, § 42a–2–714. The trial court reasonably concluded that a post-installation test was intended to safeguard these rights of the defendant as well as to afford the plaintiff a final opportunity to make needed adjustments. The court was therefore justified in concluding that there had been an acceptance within § 42a–2–606(1)(a). A buyer may be found to have accepted goods despite their known nonconformity[,] and despite the absence of actual delivery to the buyer. [Citing cases.]

The trial court's alternate ground for concluding that the tanks had been accepted was the defendant's failure to make an effective rejection. Pursuant to § 42a–2–606(1)(b), an acceptance occurs when, after a reasonable opportunity to inspect, a buyer has failed to make "an effective rejection as provided by subsection (1) of § 42a–2–602." The latter subsection, in turn, makes a rejection "ineffective unless the buyer seasonably notifies the seller."[3] [Section] 42a–2–605(1)(a) goes on to provide that a buyer is precluded from relying, as a basis for rejection, upon unparticularized defects in his notice of rejection, if the defects were such that with seasonable notice, the seller could have cured by making a substituted, conforming tender.[4] The defendant does not question the trial courts determination that its telegram of cancellation failed to comply with the requirement of particularization contained in § 42a–2–605(1). Instead, defendant argues that plaintiff was not entitled to an opportunity to cure, under § 42a–2–508, because plaintiff had never made a tender of the tanks. That argument founders, however, on the trial court's finding that the seller was ready to make a tender on the day following the last inspection by the defendant's engineer and would have done so but for its receipt of defendant's telegram of cancellation. The trial court furthermore found that defendant's unparticularized telegram of cancellation wrongfully interfered with plaintiff's contractual right to cure any remaining post-installation defects. In these circumstances the telegram of cancellation constituted both a wrongful and an ineffective rejection on the part of the defendant. . . .

---

[3] General Statutes § 42a–2–602(1) provides: "MANNER AND EFFECT OF RIGHTFUL REJECTION. (1) Rejection of goods must be within a reasonable time after their delivery or tender. It is ineffective unless the buyer seasonably notifies the seller."

[4] General Statutes § 42a–2–605(1)(a) provides: "WAIVER OF BUYER'S OBJECTIONS BY FAILURE TO PARTICULARIZE. (1) The buyer's failure to state in connection with rejection a particular defect which is ascertainable by reasonable inspection precludes him from relying on the unstated defect to justify rejection or to establish breach (a) where the seller could have cured it if stated seasonably."

Once the conclusion is reached that defendant accepted the tanks, its further rights of cancellation under the contract are limited by the governing provisions of the [UCC]. . . . "After acceptance, the buyer must pay for the goods at the contract rate; § 42a–2–607(1); and bears the burden of establishing their nonconformity. § 42a–2–607(4)." Stelco Industries, Inc. v. Cohen, 182 Conn. 561, 563–64, 438 A.2d 759 (1980). After acceptance, the buyer may only avoid liability for the contract price by invoking the provision which permits revocation of acceptance. That provision, § 42a–2–608(1), requires proof that the "nonconformity [of the goods] substantially impairs [their] value to him." . . . On this question, which is an issue of fact[,] . . . the trial court again found against the defendant. Since the defendant has provided no basis for any argument that the trial court was clearly erroneous in finding that defendant had not met its burden of proof to show that the goods were substantially nonconforming, we can find no error in the conclusion that defendant's cancellation constituted an unauthorized and hence wrongful revocation of acceptance.

Finally, defendant . . . challenges the trial court's conclusion about the remedial consequences of its earlier determinations. Although the trial court might have found plaintiff entitled to recover the contract price because of defendant's acceptance of the goods; §§ 42a–2–703(e) and 42a–2–709(1)(a); the court chose instead to rely on § 42a–2–709(1)(b), which permits a price action for contract goods that cannot, after reasonable effort, be resold at a reasonable price.[5] Since the contract goods in this case were concededly specially manufactured for the defendant, the defendant cannot and does not contest the trial court's finding that any effort to resell them on the open market would have been unavailing. In the light of this finding, defendant can only reiterate its argument, which we have already rejected, that the primary default was that of the plaintiff rather than that of the defendant. The trial court's conclusion to the contrary supports both its award to the plaintiff and its denial of the defendant's counterclaim.

There is no error.

NOTE

The buyer's unparticularized telegram of cancellation was an important aspect of *Plateq*. Prior to the Code, there was some uncertainty over the question whether a promisor refusing to perform on a stated ground could later rely on a different, unstated ground. It would seem on first glance that any defense, breach of promise or nonoccurrence of condition, should be available at trial whether or not formally stated to the opposite party at the time of termination of the contract. Altering one's legal grounds after litigation has begun is of course a different matter. Yet there is a very considerable group of decisions, centered in sales cases but by no means confined to them, which invokes "waiver" (sometimes "estoppel") to preclude the use of unstated objections to the op-

---

[5] . . . It should be noted that § 42a–2–709(1)(b) is not premised on a buyer's acceptance. Instead, it requires a showing that the goods were, before the buyer's cancellation, "identified to the contract." In the circumstances of this case, that precondition was presumably met by their special manufacture and by the defendant's acquiescence in their imminent tender. See White & Summers, Uniform Commercial Code, § 7–5 (2d Ed.1980). The defendant has not, on this appeal, argued the absence of identification.

It should further be noted that § 42a–2–709(1)(b), because it is not premised on acceptance, would have afforded the seller the right to recover the contract price even if the trial court had found the conduct of the buyer to be a wrongful rejection (because of the failure to give the seller an opportunity to cure) rather than a wrongful revocation of acceptance.

posite party's performance, where one or more specific objections have been made. In almost all of these cases, the unstated objections were known and consciously withheld. Even so, there has been much criticism of "waiver" doctrines which require the correct choice of grounds on penalty of losing an otherwise meritorious defense. See 3A A. Corbin, Contracts § 762. Now, of course, UCC 2–605(1) speaks directly to the problem of a buyer who rejects a tender without stating objections. Recall also the rule stated in § 2–606(1)(b), that goods are deemed accepted if the buyer fails, after having had a reasonable amount of time in which to inspect them, to communicate its rejection to the seller. Are these two rules cut from the same cloth?

––––––––

Worldwide RV Sales & Service v. Brooks
534 N.E.2d 1132 (Ind.Ct.App. 1989)

Brooks contracted to purchase a motor home from Worldwide for $39,000, paying $1,500 down. The parties agreed that Brooks would pick up the vehicle three weeks later, at which time the full price was due. Brooks had made clear that he wanted two roof air-conditioning units in the vehicle, one near the front and one near the rear, and Worldwide's letter confirming the contract stated that the motor home was to have "dual roof air conditioning." When Brooks arrived to take delivery, he discovered the vehicle had only one roof air conditioner, positioned in the center of the motor home. Brooks refused to accept the vehicle and demanded return of his down payment. In an effort to save the deal, Worldwide offered to install front and rear units and remove the center air conditioner, recognizing that this alteration would leave a hole in the center of the vehicle's roof. This offer was unacceptable to Brooks. *Held*, judgment for refund of deposit affirmed. The refusal to take the motor home was proper under UCC 2–601. Nor can Worldwide claim the benefit of § 2–508, for it neither made "a conforming delivery" nor substituted "a conforming tender." What it offered the day of the rejection "was inadequate." [What if Worldwide's offer had included a 20 percent reduction of the price?]

––––––––

Fortin v. Ox–Bow Marina, Inc.
408 Mass. 310, 557 N.E.2d 1157 (1990)

Some four months after taking delivery of a 32–foot Bayliner power boat, plaintiffs, the Fortins, notified defendant Ox–Bow, the seller, that they were revoking their acceptance of the Bayliner. Plaintiffs then sued for a refund of the purchase price and recovery of incidental and consequential damages, including the sales tax paid on the boat and the interest paid on a loan taken out to finance the purchase. The Fortins prevailed at trial and on appeal. The court said: "We [conclude] that the judge had evidentiary support for all his findings. The evidence that the starboard engine overheated twice; the bilge pump was defective; there was an array of malfunctioning electrical equipment; and the marine toilet only functioned partially—none of which alone could be characterized as a minor, cosmetic, or insubstantial problem with a power boat—in concert support a finding of substantial impairment of the boat's value.

"The defendant stresses the replacement of the defective starboard engine with a new engine prior to the Fortins' revocation, and the Fortins' use of the boat on some six or seven weekends in the summer of 1985, to assert that the judge clearly erred in finding the boat's value had been substantially impaired. In weighing this issue the trier of fact must decide whether the defects substantially impair the value of the goods to the revoking buyer, § 2–608(1). Most courts read this test as an objective, or common sense, determination that the impaired value of the goods to the buyer was substantial as opposed to trivial, or easily fixed, given his subjective needs. . . . The evaluation is made in light of the 'totality of the circumstances' of each particular case, including the number of deficiencies and type of nonconformity and the time and inconvenience spent in downtime and attempts at repair. . . . Thus, it has been said that, in the proper circumstances, even cosmetic or minor defects that go unrepaired despite a number of complaints or attempts at repair, . . . or remaining minor defects after an earlier, serious problem has been repaired, . . . or defects which do not totally prevent the buyer from using the goods, but circumscribe that use or warrant unusual or excessive maintenance actions in order to use, . . . can substantially impair the goods' value to the buyer. Experiencing in a major investment a series of defects, even if some have been cured and others are curable, can shake a buyer's faith in the goods, at which point 'the item not only loses its real value in the buyer's eyes, but also becomes an article whose integrity has been substantially impaired and whose operation is fraught with apprehension.' . . .

"Under these principles we have no difficulty in concluding that the judge's finding of substantial impairment was not clearly erroneous, despite the fact that the Bayliner's most serious defect, the starboard engine, was rectified before the Fortins revoked acceptance. The judge's unassailed conclusion that the defendants were negligent in inspecting, maintaining, and repairing the Fortins' Bayliner supported the view that the boat's value to its owners was substantially impaired. There was evidence that a number of defects, observed by the Fortins from the moment their Bayliner arrived at Ox–Bow Marina, were never repaired, despite regularly repeated complaints.

". . . [W]hether notice of revocation has been made within a 'reasonable time' is also a question of fact. . . . Many courts have held that any delay on the part of the buyer in notification of revocation of acceptance is justified where the buyer is in constant communication with the seller regarding nonconformity of the goods, and 'the seller makes repeated assurances that the defect or nonconformity will be cured and attempts to do so.' . . . Beginning weeks before they accepted the Bayliner, right up through the time of revocation, the Fortins were in frequent contact with Ox–Bow Marina in an effort to have their boat repaired. . . . It would be anomalous, given the U.C.C.'s purpose to encourage buyers and sellers to reach reasonable accommodations to minimize losses, . . . to penalize buyers like the Fortins for their patience in giving sellers like Ox–Bow the opportunity to rectify nonconformities before revoking acceptance of the goods."

COMMENT: ANTICIPATORY BREACH OF UNILATERAL OBLIGATIONS

There is need to make brief mention of an established limit on the doctrine of anticipatory breach, namely, that the doctrine is usually not extended to unilateral contracts. The same is true of bilateral contracts under which one party has performed fully so that all executory duties are those of the repudiator. Thus, the doctrine ordinarily is not applicable to contracts for the payment of money only. Kelly v. Security Mut. Life Ins. Co., 186 N.Y. 16, 78 N.E. 584 (1906).

So where a payee, having performed in full its side of the contract, is awaiting payments in installments as the contract provides, and the payor repudiates the obligation to pay, the payee ordinarily may not recover a lump-sum judgment for the full amount of the debt. There may, however, be remedial possibilities other than a damage remedy measured by the expectancy—perhaps restitution, a declaratory judgment, a money judgment payable in installments, even relief in equity. See, e.g., Caporali v. Washington Nat'l Ins. Co., 102 Wis.2d 669, 307 N.W.2d 218 (1981) (insured suing on disability income policy awarded future monthly installments, with interest, payable as they become due); Brads v. First Baptist Church of Germantown, 89 OhioApp.3d 328, 624 N.E.2d 737 (Ohio Ct.App.1993) (only equity order against church to specifically perform pension contract for remainder of former pastor's life yields a remedy "absolutely certain" to restore "exact benefit of bargain").

This exception to the rules for anticipatory breach derives from the justification used in Hochster v. De La Tour, 2 El. & Bl. 678 (1853), where modern doctrines concerning anticipatory breach originated. Lord Campbell in that case argued that if an action for damages was not allowed when the repudiation occurred in May, the plaintiff, whose employment as a courier on a continental tour was to commence on June 1, would not be free in the interval to accept other employment, must remain idle, and spend money in preparations that would be useless. Rockingham County v. Luten Bridge Co., supra p. 56, suggests how unfounded that argument was. Nevertheless, later cases derived from it the consequence that a promisee who had fully performed faced no problem of mitigation, and therefore had no need to sue at once, before actual breach had occurred. Does this not treat anticipatory repudiation as primarily a doctrine of self-help, unavailable when the promisee can no longer protect himself in the customary manner—e.g., suspend performance—against the promisor's nonperformance? Is it clear that the doctrine should be so limited, that suing at once for all that is owed should not be an option when the other party states an intention to pay nothing more?

Historically, and even today, a further justification for the exception is offered: that there is a special objection to "accelerating" money debts. An illustration is Huffman v. Martin, 226 Ky. 137, 10 S.W.2d 636 (1928), where plaintiffs sold and conveyed to defendants land for an agreed price of $7,000, of which $3,000 was paid in cash. Defendants gave their promissory note for the balance, the note to mature in ten years with interest payable annually. After taking possession of the land and working it for three years, defendants abandoned the property and moved to another state, declaring that they did not intend to make any further effort to pay plaintiffs' note. In holding that defendants' repudiation gave plaintiffs no right to maintain an action to recover the principal of the debt, the court declared that "where the contract or obligation is purely executory on the part of one of the contractors, and entirely executed as to the other one," the rule of anticipatory breach does not apply. The court continued:

[T]he alleged precipitating abandonment and renunciation by defendants occurred seven years before the due date of the note, and we cannot attribute to them any greater effect than a present indisposition on their part to meet the payments of either interest on, or principal installments of, their note to plaintiffs. Such abandoning acts or conduct may be superinduced by momentary discouragement, and might disappear long before the due date of the obligation. But, whatever reason may exist for the exception to the general rule, it is firmly established in the law, and we have no hesitancy in concluding that the court correctly held that the due date of defendants' note to plaintiffs was not precipitated by the facts relied on for the purpose.

It should be added, of course, that the result in cases like Huffman v. Martin ordinarily can be avoided by including in the purchase contract an "acceleration clause," to the effect that the money debt shall fully and automatically (or, at the creditor's option) become due in the event of the obligor's default. Differing views on the absence of an acceleration clause, a standard and thus well-known means of protection against money-payment defaults, can be found in Carpenter v. Smith, 147 Mich.App. 560, 383 N.W.2d 248 (1985). Yet the analysis of an Illinois court is typical: "Defendant may be in default, but the contract for deed makes no provision for an acceleration of payments. . . . No court can rewrite the contract to suit plaintiff's demand for full payment, but rather, must enforce for both parties the terms as written." Biehl v. Atwood, 151 Ill.App.3d 763, 502 N.E.2d 1234 (1986). See also Rosenfeld v. City Paper Co., 527 So.2d 704 (Ala.1988) (anticipatory repudiation doctrine "will not intercede to rescue the promisee from the consequences of the absence of an acceleration clause"); Johnston v. Austin, 748 P.2d 1084 (Utah 1988) ("only if enforcement would be unconscionable under the circumstances" should a court intervene to alter acceleration provisions in uniform real estate contracts).

Except in a few states, the "unilateral contract" exception to the doctrine of anticipatory breach remains in place in our law, though there has been talk of the need for "reconsideration" of the exception. E.g., Sheet Metal Workers Local No. 76 v. Hufnagle, 295 N.W.2d 259 (Minn.1980). A good illustration of the main route of escape from the completed-performance exception—the finding of some remaining "dependency of obligation" at the time of the repudiation—can be found in Long Island R.R. Co. v. Northville Indus. Corp., 41 N.Y.2d 455, 393 N.Y.S.2d 925, 362 N.E.2d 558 (1977).

———

CHAPTER 7

THE RIGHTS AND DUTIES OF NONPARTIES

SECTION 1. THIRD PARTY BENEFICIARIES

But an abstract notion of "privity" serves no better purpose here than elsewhere in the law. . . . If privity requirements reflected a disinclination to compel a contracting party to meet in litigation a person with whom he had not chosen to do business, they were a reminder of a simple, neighborly society already on the way out, and now long vanquished. . . . The rather confusing patchwork of "exceptions" to (or formulas of evasion of) this court's [prohibitory rule that "a stranger to the consideration cannot sue on the contract"] should be supplanted by the general rule now prevalent, which avoids circuity of action and is calculated to accord with the probable intentions of the contracting parties and to respond to the reasonable reliance of the third party [beneficiary].

> Kaplan, J., in Choate, Hall & Stewart
> v. SCA Services, Inc., 378 Mass. 535,
> 392 N.E.2d 1045 (1979).

Lawrence v. Fox

Court of Appeals of New York, 1859.
20 N.Y. 268.

Appeal from the Superior Court. . . . On the trial [below], it appeared by the evidence of a bystander, that one Holly, in November, 1857, at the request of [Fox], loaned and advanced to him $300, stating at the time that he [Holly] owed that sum to [Lawrence] for money borrowed of him, and had agreed to pay it to him the then next day; that [Fox] in consideration thereof, at the time of receiving the money, promised to pay it to [Lawrence] the then next day. . . . [Fox] moved for a nonsuit, upon [several] grounds, viz.: . . . that the agreement by [Fox] with Holly to pay [Lawrence] was void for want of consideration, and that there was no privity between [Lawrence] and [Fox]. The court overruled the motion, and the [jury] found a verdict for [Lawrence] for the amount of the loan and interest, $344.66, upon which judgment was entered; from which [Fox] appealed to the Superior Court, at general term, where the judgment was affirmed, and [Fox] appealed to this court. . . .

H. GRAY, J. . . . [I]t is claimed that notwithstanding [Fox's] promise was established by competent evidence, it was void for the want of consideration. It is now more than a quarter of a century since it was settled by the Supreme Court of this State . . . that a promise in all material respects like the one under consideration was valid; and the judgment of that court was unanimously affirmed by the Court for the Correction of Errors. Farley v. Cleaveland, 4 Cow., 432; 9 id., 639. In that case one Moon owed Farley and sold to Cleaveland a quantity of hay, in consideration of which Cleaveland promised to pay Moon's debt to Farley; and the decision in favor of Farley's right to recover was placed upon the ground that the hay received by Cleaveland from Moon was a valid consideration for Cleaveland's promise to pay Farley, and that the subsisting liability of Moon to pay Farley was no objection to the recovery.

The fact that the money advanced by Holly to [Fox] was a loan to him for a day, and that it thereby became the property of [Fox], seemed to impress [Fox's] counsel with the idea that because [Fox's] promise was not a trust fund placed by [Lawrence] in [Fox's] hands, out of which he was to realize money as from the sale of a chattel or the collection of a debt, the promise although made for the benefit of [Lawrence] could not enure to his benefit. The hay which [Moon] delivered to [Cleaveland] was not to be paid to Farley, but the debt incurred by Cleaveland for the purchase of the hay, like the debt incurred by [Fox] for money borrowed, was what was to be paid.

That case . . . puts to rest the objection that [Fox's] promise was void for want of consideration. [There,] the promise was not only made to Moon but to the plaintiff Farley. In this case the promise was made to Holly and not expressly to [Lawrence]; and this difference between the two cases presents the question . . . as to the want of privity between [Lawrence and Fox]. As early as 1806 it was announced by the Supreme Court of this State, upon what was then regarded as the settled law of England, "That where one person makes a promise to another for the benefit of a third person, that third person may maintain an action upon it." Schermerhorn v. Vanderheyden (1 John R., 140), has often been re-asserted by our courts and never departed from. . . .

The same principle is adjudged in several cases in Massachusetts. . . In Hall v. Marston [1822, 17 Mass. 575], the court say: "It seems to have been well settled that if A promises B for a valuable consideration to pay C, the latter may maintain assumpsit for the money;" and in [1851, Brewer v. Dyer, 7 Cush. 337, 340,] the recovery was upheld, as the court said, ". . . not upon the ground of any actual or supposed relationship between the parties as some of the earlier cases would seem to indicate, but upon the broader and more satisfactory basis, that the law operating on the act of the parties creates the duty, establishes a privity, and implies the promise and obligation on which the action is founded." . . .

But it is urged that because the defendant was not in any sense a trustee of the property of Holly for the benefit of the plaintiff, the law will not imply a promise. I agree that many of the cases where a promise was implied were cases of trusts, created for the benefit of the promiser. Felton v. Dickinson, 10 Mass. 189, and others that might be cited are of that class; but concede them all to have been cases of trusts, and it proves nothing against the application of the rule to this case. The duty of the trustee to pay the *cestuis que trust*, according to the terms of the trust, implies his promise to the latter to do so. In this case the defendant, upon ample consideration received from Holly, promised Holly to pay his debt to the plaintiff; the consideration received and the promise to Holly made it as plainly his duty to pay the plaintiff as if the money had been remitted to him for that purpose, and as well implied a promise to do so as if he had been made a trustee of property to be converted into cash with which to pay. The fact that a breach of the duty imposed in the one case may be visited, and justly, with more serious consequences than in the other, by no means disproves the payment to be a duty in both. The principle illustrated by the example so frequently quoted (which concisely states the case in hand) "that a promise made to one for the benefit of another, he for whose benefit it is made may bring an action for its breach," has been applied to trust cases, not because it was exclusively applicable to those cases, but because it was a principle of law, and as such applicable to those cases.

It was also insisted that Holly could have discharged the defendant from his promise, though it was intended by both parties for the benefit of the plaintiff, and therefore the plaintiff was not entitled to maintain this suit for the recovery of a demand over which he had no control. It is enough that the plaintiff [Holly?] did not release the defendant from his promise, and whether he could or not is a question not now necessarily involved; but if it was, I think it would be found difficult to maintain the right of Holly to discharge a judgment recovered by the plaintiff upon confession or otherwise, for the breach of the defendant's promise; and if he could not, how could he discharge the suit before judgment, or the promise before suit, made as it was for the plaintiff's benefit and in accordance with legal presumption accepted by him, Berly v. Taylor, 5 Hill 577, until his dissent was shown.

The cases cited, and especially Farley v. Cleaveland, establish the validity of a parol promise; it stands then upon the footing of a written one. Suppose the defendant had given his note in which, for value received of Holly, he had promised to pay the plaintiff and the plaintiff had accepted the promise, retaining Holly's liability. Very clearly Holly could not have discharged that promise, be the right to release the defendant as it may. No one can doubt that he owes the sum of money demanded of him, or that in accordance with his promise it was his duty to have paid it to the plaintiff; nor can it be doubted that whatever may be the diversity of opinion elsewhere, the adjudications in this State, from a very early period . . . have established the defendant's liability; if, therefore, it could be shown that a more strict and technically accurate application of the rules applied, would lead to a different result (which I by no means concede), the effort should not be made in the face of manifest justice.

The judgment should be affirmed.

JOHNSON, C.J., DENIO, SELDEN, ALLEN and STRONG, JJ., concurred. JOHNSON, C.J. and DENIO, J., were of opinion that the promise was to be regarded as made to the plaintiff through the medium of his agent, whose action he could ratify when it came to his knowledge, though taken without his being privy thereto.

COMSTOCK, J. (dissenting). The plaintiff had nothing to do with the promise on which he brought this action. It was not made to him, nor did the consideration proceed from him. If he can maintain the suit, it is because an anomaly has found its way into the law. . . . In general, there must be privity of contract. The party who sues upon a promise must be the promisee, or he must have some legal interest in the undertaking. [Here], it is plain that Holly, who loaned the money to the defendant, and to whom the promise in question was made, could at any time have claimed that it should be performed to himself personally. He had lent the money to the defendant, and at the same time directed the latter to pay the sum to the plaintiff. This direction he could countermand, and if he had done so, manifestly the defendant's promise to pay according to the direction would have ceased to exist. The plaintiff would receive a benefit by a complete execution of the arrangement, but the arrangement itself was between other parties, and was under their exclusive control. If the defendant had paid the money to Holly, his debt would have been discharged thereby. So Holly might have released the demand or assigned it to another person, or the parties might have annulled the promise now in question, and designated some other creditor of Holly as the party to whom the money should be paid. It has never been claimed, that in a case thus situated, the right of a third person to sue upon the promise rested on any sound principle of law. . . .

The cases in which some trust was involved are also frequently referred to as authority for the doctrine now in question, but they do not sustain it. If A delivers money or property to B, which the latter accepts upon a trust for the benefit of C, the latter can enforce the trust by an appropriate action for that purpose. Berly v. Taylor, 5 Hill 577. If the trust be of money, I think the beneficiary may assent to it and bring the action for money had and received to his use. If it be of something else than money, the trustee must account for it according to the terms of the trust, and upon principles of equity. There is some authority even for saying that an express promise founded on the possession of a trust fund may be enforced by an action at law in the name of the beneficiary, although it was made to the creator of the trust. Thus, in Comyn's Digest [B.15], it is laid down that if a man promise a pig of lead to A, and his executor give lead to make a pig to B, who assumes to deliver it to A, an assumpsit lies by A against him. The case of The Delaware & Hudson Canal Co. v. The Westchester County Bank, 4 Denio 97, involved a trust because the defendants had received from a third party a bill of exchange under an agreement that they would endeavor to collect it, and would pay over the proceeds when collected to the plaintiffs. A fund received under such an agreement does not belong to the person who receives it. He must account for it specifically; and perhaps there is no gross violation of principle in permitting the equitable owner of it to sue upon an express promise to pay it over. Having a specific interest in the thing, the undertaking to account for it may be regarded as in some sense made with him through the author of the trust. But further than this we cannot go without violating plain rules of law. In [this] case there was nothing in the nature of a trust or agency. The defendant borrowed the money of Holly and received it as his own. The plaintiff had no right in the fund, legal or equitable. The promise to repay the money created an obligation in favor of the lender to whom it was made and not in favor of any one else. . . . The judgment of the court below should therefore be reversed, and a new trial granted.

GROVER, J., also dissented.

————

COMMENT: THE USES OF LEGAL CATEGORIES

The opinions in this famous case deserve study, not only for the points of view they adopt on the Lawrence–Holly–Fox triangle, but also as samples of nineteenth century legal analysis. To be sure, the debate within the court showed concern for practical problems. Judge Comstock, for example, foresaw serious inconvenience through overlap and conflict between the claims of Lawrence and Holly against Fox. Looming larger than such considerations, however, was the question whether the solution was ordained by some "plain rules of law," ascertainable by reason (at least lawyers' reason) derived from basic premises of the legal order itself. If so, judges might naturally disregard the intentions of the contracting parties or any calculus of social gains and losses. This larger question can be framed by asking whether Judge Comstock's dissent rests on some such "plain rules of law," that is, fundamental conceptual objections to allowing a person who is not a party to a contract to sue under it as a "beneficiary." It was of course a relative novelty for the common law to allow nonparties to enforce a contract.

In fact, as we shall see in Seaver v. Ransom, the next case, the difficulties Comstock identified in permitting an action by Lawrence against Fox made enough impression on his contemporaries that there followed for decades a sharp retreat from the sweeping propositions asserted by the majority in Lawrence v. Fox. Only in the twentieth century did the claims of third party beneficiaries advance again on a broad front.

The great nineteenth century effort to organize and systematize legal doctrine deserves respect, however much it may now seem misdirected in details. Similar efforts were made in Western Europe, for similar reasons and with similar results on lawyers' thinking. Certainly it would be too much to say that these efforts have now been wholly abandoned. Lawyers, like others dealing with large bodies of knowledge, must have the means to organize at ascending levels of generality. Perhaps the major shift of attitudes can best be described by saying that the broad movements of opinion in the twentieth century and beyond have exposed the multiple purposes that a legal order must serve, making the internal consistency of the rules themselves merely one of the values to be measured against many others.

When the claims of third party beneficiaries began to be asserted on a broad scale, they placed a considerable strain on legal categories. There were several modes of analysis that would almost (though not quite) fit the assertion of third-party rights in a contract, as the opinions in Lawrence v. Fox reveal. The labels and classifications that have been used most often are described here, in the form of variations on that case.

(1) Holly takes from his wallet three $100 bills, hands them over to Fox and says, "Take these and use them to pay Lawrence the $300 I owe him." Fox takes the three bills and uses them to make a payment on his own overdue debt at the corner saloon. Is this a misapplication of funds deposited for a special purpose, or something that sounds still more serious, a breach of *trust*? In Lawrence v. Fox, the statement of facts might almost permit one to say so, for the statement was that "at the time of receiving the money, [Fox] promised to pay it to the plaintiff [Lawrence] the next day." If Fox really did undertake to hold "it" (the money) intact and use "it" only for that designated purpose, one would move into the realm of trust where even Judge Comstock evidently would have been at home. Fox, as trustee, would then have a legal title to the money; Lawrence would be the "equitable" owner, and his ownership would be protected by an equity court against any diversion from the trust purpose (the enforceable rights of a trust's beneficiary go far back in the history of equity). It is perfectly possible, of course, to have an express trust of a sum of money, even a small sum. The question would be whether the parties *intended* Fox to be so restricted, i.e., to assume the status of a fiduciary who was bound to spend every penny of the money received for the designated purpose, and possibly be guilty of

embezzlement if he spent it in any other way. In short, had the court employed a trust analysis, there would have been no need to invoke the law of contract at all. Some early decisions did use the conception of trust in situations not unlike Lawrence v. Fox, but this was because it was thought that categorizing the Holly–Fox transaction as a contract and allowing a stranger to enforce it would have opened a path into an enchanted forest where all sorts of weird creatures might be found.

(2) Holly says to his neighbor, Fox: "I owe $300 to Lawrence, a friend who lives over in Lawrenceville (a nearby town), and the money is due tomorrow. I don't have a checking account, I don't want to send money through the mail, and I'd like to stay home tomorrow and do some chores. I know you go through Lawrenceville on your way to work. I will mow your lawn tomorrow after I've done mine if you will promise to take this $300 and pay Lawrence." To this Fox replies, "Sure, I'll be glad to do it." Holly then hands over the money. When Lawrence hears of this arrangement in a telephone call from Holly, he says, "Fine, I'm glad you have worked out a way to pay on time." If Fox does not pay Lawrence the $300, a suit by Lawrence against Fox is likely. Should this suit be heard by Justices Johnson and Denio of the Lawrence v. Fox court, there would be little doubt about either the outcome or the analysis—if they could be persuaded that Holly purported and intended to act as Lawrence's *agent* for the purpose of receiving the promise of Fox to pay Lawrence. It would not matter that, at the time, Holly had no authority to serve Lawrence in this way, for Holly's unauthorized receipt of the promise has been "ratified" by Lawrence (recall their telephone conversation). The acts of the agent, including unauthorized acts subsequently ratified, are in law the acts of the principal. So, miraculously, through talk of *agency*, Lawrence is made the promisee (his agent received the promise) and may directly sue Fox, the promisor. From the statement of facts in Lawrence v. Fox, does it appear that Holly purported and intended to act as agent of Lawrence?

(3) Holly owes Lawrence $300. Fox, having an interest in Holly's affairs, goes directly to Lawrence and offers to sign a note for $300 in return for a release of Holly by Lawrence. Lawrence agrees, and Fox signs and delivers a $300 note payable to Lawrence. This agreement between Lawrence and Fox is often described as a *novation*—a new contract substituted for and displacing the old one. In the usual case of this type, the original debtor (here, Holly) will be a party to the novation, so that the transaction is three-cornered; but this is not essential. The deal can be two-cornered as well. In any event, it is clear that Fox is liable to Lawrence on his note since he has received what he bargained for, the release of Holly. (How would you describe Holly's role in all of this?)

(4) Another possible line of analysis uses the preceding transaction as a runway and takes off on a more uncertain course. Return to Lawrence v. Fox itself, where the only parties that meet are Holly and Fox. When Holly pays cash and buys the promise of Fox to pay Lawrence, the evident purpose as between Holly and Fox is to make Fox the primary debtor. But this purpose cannot be accomplished without the consent of the absent creditor, Lawrence. So why not construe the Holly–Fox deal as an *offer* to Lawrence, an offer of a novation? There is enough substance to this thought that if Lawrence were actually to say at a later date, "Fox's promise is good enough for me; I'll look only to him," a release of Holly would be inferred and, again, would provide consideration for Fox's promise. But if Lawrence merely asks Fox to pay him (as Fox promised Holly to do), or Lawrence starts suit against Fox, is the inference jus-

tified that Lawrence has thereby released Holly and accepted Fox as a substitute debtor? In many cases of this type, it will be clear that the inference of release of the original debtor is drawn in order to avoid entering the enchanted forest—i.e., for the purpose of solving the doctrinal problem that baffled Judge Comstock. One must ask of these cases: Why must a valid claim against the original debtor necessarily be surrendered by Lawrence merely because he pursues the course—asserting a claim against Fox—that both Holly and Fox intended? Why should the creditor be forced to a choice? See, e.g., Vetter v. Security Cont'l Ins. Co., 567 N.W.2d 516 (Minn.1997) (proof of novation requires strong evidence of "clear and definite intention on part of all concerned" to release one obligor and substitute another).

A detailed inquiry into Lawrence v. Fox and the factors that produced the third party beneficiary rule can be found in Waters, The Property in the Promise: A Study of the Third Party Beneficiary Rule, 98 Harv.L.Rev. 1109 (1985). See also the discussion of legal formalism in Hoeflich & Perelmuter, The Anatomy of a Leading Case: Lawrence v. Fox in the Courts, The Casebooks, and the Commentaries, 21 Mich. J.L. Reform 721 (1988).

Seaver v. Ransom

Court of Appeals of New York, 1918.
224 N.Y. 233, 120 N.E. 639.

POUND, J. Judge Beman and his wife were advanced in years. Mrs. Beman was about to die. She had a small estate, consisting of a house and lot in Malone and little else. Judge Beman drew his wife's will according to her instructions. It gave $1,000 to plaintiff, $500 to one sister, plaintiff's mother, and $100 each to another sister and her son, the use of the house to her husband for life, and remainder to the American Society for the Prevention of Cruelty to Animals. She named her husband as residuary legatee and executor. Plaintiff was her niece, 34 years old, in ill health, sometimes a member of the Beman household. When the will was read to Mrs. Beman, she said that it was not as she wanted it. She wanted to leave the house to plaintiff. She had no other objection to the will, but her strength was waning, and, although the judge offered to write another will for her, she said she was afraid she would not hold out long enough to enable her to sign it. So the judge said, if she would sign the will, he would leave plaintiff enough in his will to make up the difference. He avouched the promise by his uplifted hand with all solemnity and his wife then executed the will. When he came to die, it was found that his will made no provision for the plaintiff.

This action was brought, and plaintiff recovered judgment in the trial court, on the theory that Beman had obtained property from his wife and induced her to execute the will in the form prepared by him by his promise to give plaintiff $6,000, the value of the house, and that thereby equity impressed his property with a trust in favor of plaintiff. Where a legatee promises the testator that he will use property given him by the will for a particular purpose, a trust arises. O'Hara v. Dudley, 95 N.Y. 403. . . . Beman received nothing under his wife's will but the use of the house in Malone for life. Equity compels the application of property thus obtained to the purpose of the testator, but equity cannot so impress a trust, except on property obtained by the promise. Beman was bound by his promise, but no property was bound by it; no trust in plaintiff's favor can be spelled out.

An action on the contract for damages, or to make the executors trustees for performance, stands on different ground. . . . The Appellate Division properly passed to the question whether the judgment could stand upon the promise made to the wife, upon a valid consideration, for the sole benefit of plaintiff. The judgment of the trial court was affirmed by a return to the general doctrine laid down in the great case of Lawrence v. Fox, 20 N.Y. 268, which has since been limited as herein indicated.

Contracts for the benefit of third persons have been the prolific source of judicial and academic discussion. . . . The general rule, both in law and equity[,] . . . was that privity between a plaintiff and a defendant is necessary to the maintenance of an action on the contract. The consideration must be furnished by the party to whom the promise was made. The contract cannot be enforced against the third party, and therefore it cannot be enforced by him. On the other hand, the right of the beneficiary to sue on a contract made expressly for his benefit has been fully recognized in many American jurisdictions, either by judicial decision or by legislation and is said to be "the prevailing rule in this country." Hendrick v. Lindsay, 93 U.S. 143. . . . It has been said that "the establishment of this doctrine has been gradual, and is a victory of practical utility over theory, of equity over technical subtlety." Brantly on Contracts (2d Ed.) p. 253. The reasons for this view are that it is just and practical to permit the person for whose benefit the contract is made to enforce it against one whose duty it is to pay. Other jurisdictions still adhere to the present English rule . . . that a contract cannot be enforced by or against a person who is not a party (Exchange Bank v. Rice, 107 Mass. 37). . . .

In New York the right of the beneficiary to sue on contracts made for his benefit is not clearly or simply defined. It is at present confined: First. To cases where there is a pecuniary obligation running from the promisee to the beneficiary, "a legal right founded upon some obligation of the promisee in the third party to adopt and claim the promise as made for his benefit." [Farley v. Cleaveland, 4 Cow., 432; Lawrence v. Fox, supra.] Secondly. To cases where the contract is made for the benefit of the wife . . ., affianced wife, . . . [or child] of a party to the contract. The close relationship cases go back to the early King's Bench case (1677), long since repudiated in England, of Dutton v. Poole, 2 Lev. 211 (s. c., 1 Ventris, 318, 332). . . . The natural and moral duty of the husband or parent to provide for the future of wife or child sustains the action on the contract made for their benefit. "This is the farthest the cases in this state have gone," says Cullen, J., in the marriage settlement case of Borland v. Welch, 162 N.Y. 104, 56 N.E. 556.

The right of the third party is also upheld in, thirdly, the public contract cases, . . . where the municipality seeks to protect its inhabitants by covenants for their benefit; and, fourthly, the cases where, at the request of a party to the contract, the promise runs directly to the beneficiary although he does not furnish the consideration. . . . It may be safely said that a general rule sustaining recovery at the suit of the third party would include but few classes of cases not included in these groups, either categorically or in principle.

The desire of the childless aunt to make provision for a beloved and favorite niece differs imperceptibly in law or in equity from the moral duty of the parent to make testamentary provision for a child. The contract was made for the plaintiff's benefit. She alone is substantially damaged by its breach. The representatives of the wife's estate have no interest in enforcing it specifically. It is said in Buchanan v. Tilden that the common law imposes moral and legal obligations upon the husband and the parent not measured by the necessaries of life. It was, however, the love and affection or the moral sense of the husband and the parent that imposed such obligations in the cases cited, rather than any common-law duty of husband and parent to wife and child. If plaintiff had been a child of Mrs. Beman, legal obligation would have required no testamentary provision for her, yet the child could have enforced a covenant in her favor identical with the covenant of Judge Beman in this case. . . . The constraining power of conscience is not regulated by the degree of relationship alone. The dependent or faithful niece may have a stronger claim than the affluent or unworthy son. No sensible theory of moral obligation denies arbitrarily to the former what would be conceded to the latter. We might consistently either refuse or allow the claim of both, but I cannot reconcile a decision in favor of the wife in Buchanan v. Tilden, based on the moral obligations arising out of near relationship, with a decision against the niece here on the ground that the relationship is too remote for equity's ken. No controlling authority depends upon so absolute a rule. . . . Kellogg, P.J., writing for the court below well said: "The doctrine of Lawrence v. Fox is progressive, not retrograde. The course of the late decisions is to enlarge, not to limit, the effect of that case."

The court in that leading case attempted to adopt the general doctrine that any third person, for whose direct benefit a contract was intended, could sue on it. . . . Finch, J., in Gifford v. Corrigan [117 N.Y. 257, 22 N.E. 756], says that the case rests upon that broad proposition; Edward T. Bartlett, J., in Pond v. New Rochelle Water Co. [183 N.Y. 330, 76 N.E. 211], calls it "the general principle"; but Vrooman v. Turner, supra, confined its application to the facts on which it was decided. "In every case in which an action has been sustained," says Allen, J., "there has been a debt or duty owing by the promisee to the party claiming to sue upon the promise." 69 N.Y. 285. As late as Townsend v. Rackham, 143 N.Y. 516, 38 N.E. 731, we find Peckham, J., saying that, "to maintain the action by the third person, there must be this liability to him on the part of the promisee." Buchanan v. Tilden went further than any case since Lawrence v. Fox in a desire to do justice rather than to apply with technical accuracy strict rules calling for a legal or equitable obligation. . . .

But, on principle, a sound conclusion may be reached. If Mrs. Beman had left her husband the house on condition that he pay the plaintiff $6,000, and he had accepted the devise, he would have become personally liable to pay the legacy, and plaintiff could have recovered in an action at law against him, whatever the value of the house. Gridley v. Gridley, 24 N.Y. 130. . . . That would be because the testatrix had in substance bequeathed the promise to plaintiff, and not because close relationship or moral obligation sustained the contract. The distinction between an implied promise to a testator for the benefit of a third party to pay a legacy and an unqualified promise on a valuable consideration to make provision for the third party by will is discernible, but not obvious. The tendency of American authority is to sustain the gift in all such cases and to permit the donee beneficiary to recover on the contract. . . . The equities are with the plaintiff, and they may be enforced in this action, whether it be regarded as an action for damages or an action for specific performance to convert the defendants into trustees for plaintiff's benefit under the agreement.

The judgment should be affirmed, with costs.

NOTE: OVERLAPPING DUTIES

The person bringing suit in Seaver v. Ransom was the recipient of a "gift promise." Although the judge meant to benefit the niece, she had paid nothing for his promise, nor did it satisfy or discharge any right she had against anyone. In conventional terms, the plaintiff was a "donee beneficiary" in the sense that the contract conferred upon her the benefit of the promised performance. The plaintiff in Lawrence v. Fox, in contrast, is commonly referred to as a "creditor beneficiary," because performance of the promise given would satisfy the promisee's "actual or supposed duty to the beneficiary." The first Restatement of Contracts, in § 133, distinguished between types of beneficiaries in this manner—donees as recipients of gift promises and creditors as recipients of promises to pay the promisee's debt. Yet the point to be underscored is that the promisor under either type of beneficiary contract owes a duty of performance to the promisee as well as to the intended beneficiary (i.e., two people, one a nonparty, have rights to performance and the usual remedies for breach of contract).

Where a damage suit against the promisor is brought not by the donee beneficiary, as was the case in Seaver v. Ransom, but by the promisee of a gift promise, it is customary for courts to say (and to hold) that the promisee may recover only "nominal damages." E.g., Hawkins v. Gilbo, 663 A.2d 9 (Me.1995). Why is the promisee of a donee-beneficiary contract limited to nominal damages? Do the factors which limit a promisee to nominal damages bear on what the parties most interested in the promised performance—the beneficiary and the promisee—might actually do in the event of nonperformance by the promisor?

The transaction in Seaver v. Ransom provides a place to begin. If more is required, the decision in Drewen v. Bank of Manhattan, 31 N.J. 110, 155 A.2d 529 (1959), is worth study. There, a husband and wife, contemplating divorce in 1945, signed an agreement settling their rights in each other's property. The husband executed on the same day a will by which he bequeathed approximately 30–percent shares of his estate to the two children of the marriage. In one clause of the agreement, the husband promised the wife that he would never reduce the quantity or quality of the childrens' shares in his estate. The divorce was granted, and in 1948 the wife died. In 1951, the husband executed a new will revoking the 1945 will and changing the outright gifts to the children to life estates. The new will also contained a clause voiding bequests to any beneficiary under the will who called in question—directly or indirectly, before any tribunal—any devise or gift under the will. The husband died in 1958, with only one of the two children still surviving. Plaintiff, a special administrator of the wife's estate, sought a declaratory judgment that the husband's 1945 agreement was still binding, and an order that the husband's executor distribute the husband's estate in accordance with it. It was held that the action, essentially for specific performance, was proper, on this reasoning: The wife as promisee would have had a right to sue to enforce the husband's promise if she were still alive. Moreover, an action in equity should be available because the promisee's remedy at law is inadequate. This right passed to her estate on her death. The surviving son, beneficiary of the promise, could also sue, but he offered no objection to the present action. No policy, said the court, would be violated by permitting the action. "Indeed, if any policy has a place in our decision it is that policy which favors the enforcement of promises for which valuable consideration has been received."

If the promisee has an economic interest in the promised performance, as in the ordinary creditor-beneficiary case, presumably there will be a clear incentive for the promisee to enforce the contract in the event of the promisor's breach. Of course, both promisee and beneficiary have rights to performance in such cases; also, a breach may damage both in the full amount of the debt. Must it follow that a promisor with essentially the same duty running in different directions is in danger of having to pay twice? With the modern fusion of law and equity, it is widely understood that courts have the means to sort out conflicting claims and to prevent a doubling of liability. The Restatement, Second § 305, illustration 4, summarizes those means, including the power to enjoin enforcement of any judgment which fails to credit the promisor for payments which reduce the promisee's debt. It is standard practice to permit the promisor to join the beneficiary in an action brought by the promisee. The beneficiary may also be joined as a party to a lawsuit brought by the promisee.

RESTATEMENT OF CONTRACTS, SECOND

Section 302. Intended and Incidental Beneficiaries

(1) Unless otherwise agreed between promisor and promisee, a beneficiary of a promise is an intended beneficiary if recognition of a right to performance in the beneficiary is appropriate to effectuate the intention of the parties and either

(a) the performance of the promise will satisfy an obligation of the promisee to pay money to the beneficiary; or

(b) the circumstances indicate that the promisee intends to give the beneficiary the benefit of the promised performance.

(2) An incidental beneficiary is a beneficiary who is not an intended beneficiary.

Comment: . . .

d. Other intended beneficiaries. Either a promise to pay the promisee's debt to a beneficiary or a gift promise involves a manifestation of intention by the promisee and promisor sufficient, in a contractual setting, to make reliance by the beneficiary both reasonable and probable. Other cases may be quite similar in this respect. Examples are a promise to perform a supposed or asserted duty of the promisee, a promise to discharge a lien on the promisee's property, or a promise to satisfy the duty of a third person. In such cases, if the beneficiary would be reasonable in relying on the promise as manifesting an intention to confer a right on him, he is an intended beneficiary. Where there is doubt whether such reliance would be reasonable, considerations of procedural convenience and other factors not strictly dependent on the manifested intention of the parties may affect the question whether under [s]ubsection (1) recognition of a right in the beneficiary is appropriate. In some cases an overriding policy, which may be embodied in a statute, requires recognition of such a right without regard to the intention of the parties.

Illustrations: . . .

> 8. A conveys land to B in consideration of B's promise to pay $15,000 as follows: $5000 to C, A's wife, on whom A wishes to make a settlement, $5000 to D to whom A is indebted in that amount, and $5000 to E, a life insurance company, to purchase an annuity payable to A during his life. C is an intended beneficiary under Subsection (1)(b); D is an intended beneficiary under Subsection (1)(a); E is an incidental beneficiary. . . .

> 10. A, the operator of a chicken processing and fertilizer plant, contracts with B, a municipality, to use B's sewage system. With the purpose of preventing harm to landowners downstream from its system, B obtains from A a promise to remove specified types of waste from its deposits into the system. C, a downstream landowner, is an intended beneficiary under Subsection (1)(b).

> 12. B contracts to build a house for A. Pursuant to the contract, B and his surety S execute a payment bond to A by which they promise A that all of B's debts for labor and materials on the house will be paid. B later employs C as a carpenter and buys lumber from D. C and D are intended beneficiaries of S's promise to A, whether or not they have power to create liens on the house. . . .

> 15. A buys food from B, a grocer, for household use, relying on B's express warranty. C, A's minor child, is injured in person by breach of the warranty. Under Uniform Commercial Code § 2–318, without regard to the intention of A or B, the warranty extends to C. . . .

e. Incidental beneficiaries. Performance of a contract will often benefit a third person. But unless the third person is an intended beneficiary as herein defined, no duty to him is created.

Illustrations:

> 16. B contracts with A to erect an expensive building on A's land. C's adjoining land would be enhanced in value by the performance of the contract. C is an incidental beneficiary. . . .

> 19. A contracts to erect a building for C. B then contracts with A to supply lumber needed for the building. C is an incidental beneficiary of B's promise, and B is an incidental beneficiary of C's promise to pay A for the building.

[The Reporter's Note to § 302 states that "the definition of 'intended beneficiary' is new; it comprehends all those included as 'donee' and 'creditor' beneficiaries in former § 133." It was apparently believed by the restaters that the overall aim of recognizing the parties' power to create rights in a third party, by "manifesting an intention to do so," is obstructed by the use of terms—"donee" and "creditor"—which are not entirely appropriate in some instances and which, in general, carry overtones of doctrinal difficulties now thought to be obsolete. The definitional language of § 302 has been read to mean that "the right to performance in a third party beneficiary is determined both by the intention of the contracting parties and by the intention of one of [them] to benefit the third party." Grigerik v. Sharpe, 247 Conn. 293, 721 A.2d 526 (1998). Is that a fair reading of the section?]

QUESTION

The results in illustration 19 obviously rest on the belief that, in the circumstances stated, recognition of beneficiary rights in B and C would not be appropriate. Why should this be so?

———

Pierce Assocs. v. Nemours Foundation
865 F.2d 530 (3d Cir.1988)

"The intent to confer a third party beneficiary benefit is to be determined from the language of the contract. . . . The language of a contract, however, cannot be divorced from the context in which it is written. Here, we are dealing with a general contract and a subcontract in the construction industry. Typically when major construction is involved an owner has neither the desire nor the ability to negotiate with and supervise the multitude of trades and skills required to complete a project. Consequently, an owner will engage a general contractor[,] [who] will retain, coordinate and supervise subcontractors. The owner looks to the general contractor, not the [subs], both for performance of the total construction project and for any damages or other relief if there is a default in performance. Performance and payment of damages are normally assured by the bond of a surety on which the general contractor is principal and the owner is the obligee. The [general], in turn, who is responsible for the performance of the [subs], has a right of action against any [sub] which defaults. Performance and payment of damages by a [sub] are normally assured by the bond of a surety on which the [sub] is principal and the [general] is the obligee.

"Thus the typical owner is insulated from the [subs] both during the course of construction and during the pursuit of remedies in the event of a default. Conversely, the [subs] are insulated from the owner[,] [who] deals with and, if necessary, sues the [general], and the [general] deals with and, if necessary, sues the [subs]. These typical construction relationships have long been recognized [quoting 4 A. Corbin, Contracts § 779D]. . . . [Courts have] referred to the 'buffer zone' which a general contract creates between the owner and a subcontractor. . . . There is nothing to prevent a departure from the typical pattern, and . . . a contractor and subcontractor may agree to [extinguish the buffer zone by conferring] upon an owner rights which are enforceable directly against the [sub]. However, an intent to do so must be found in the contract documents."

———

Anderson v. Fox Hill Village Homeowners Corp.

Supreme Judicial Court of Massachusetts, 1997.
424 Mass. 365, 676 N.E.2d 821.

LYNCH, J. The plaintiff appeals from summary judgment for the defendant entered in her claim for damages arising from a slip and fall caused by an icy condition on property under the control of the defendant. [We] affirm the judgment.

The following facts are not in dispute. . . . The defendant is a tenant of property used as a retirement community in Westwood. Its lease states in part:

> Tenant agrees to be solely responsible for maintaining the Premises and the Improvements and each and every part thereof in good condition throughout the term of this Lease, reasonable wear and use only excepted and agrees without limitation to:. . . (iv) *promptly remove snow and ice from all driveways and walkways* (emphasis added).

The plaintiff worked at Clark House, a skilled nursing facility, located on the premises. On December 9, 1990, while getting out of her automobile, she slipped and fell on a patch of ice in the Clark House parking lot. The defendant did nothing to remove the ice prior to that morning.

On appeal the plaintiff claims that she was entitled to recover on two theories. First, the plaintiff argues that she was an intended third-party beneficiary of the lease. Alternatively, the plaintiff argues that the defendant assumed a duty greater than that imposed under tort principles to remove the snow and ice promptly, and negligently failed to do so.

The judge correctly ruled that the plaintiff was not an intended third-party beneficiary under the lease. Choate, Hall & Stewart v. SCA Servs., Inc., 378 Mass. 535, 392 N.E.2d 1045 (1979). In order to prevail under this theory the plaintiff must show that the defendant and the lessor intended to give her the benefit of the promised performance. [See Rest.2d,] Contracts § 302 (1981). We look at the language and circumstances of the contract for indicia of intention. *Choate*, at 545–547, 392 N.E.2d 1045. The intent must be clear and definite. . . .

Under the lease the defendant assumed sole responsibility for operation and maintenance of a retirement complex.[1] There is no indication, express or implied, that any obligations were imposed for the benefit of employees of the nursing facility. Compare Rae v. Air–Speed, Inc., 386 Mass. 187, 435 N.E.2d 628 (plaintiff and her decedent intended beneficiary of contract between employer and insurer to obtain insurance); *Choate*, supra (named creditor intended beneficiary of contract with indemnity clause). In these circumstances the plaintiff is no more than an incidental beneficiary and cannot recover under the lease. . . .

Neither can the plaintiff recover in tort. As a general rule, there is no duty by a landowner to remove a natural accumulation of snow or ice. Sullivan v. Brookline, 416 Mass. 825, 626 N.E.2d 870 (1994). . . . However, the plaintiff argues that the defendant assumed a greater duty than that imposed under the common law because the defendant agreed "promptly [to] remove snow and ice from all driveways and walkways."

We have held that a landlord, who agrees in a lease to remove snow and ice and negligently fails to perform that duty, may be liable to his tenant. Falden v. Gordon, 333 Mass. 135, 128 N.E.2d 778 (1955). . . .

We have also concluded that one who assumes a duty under contract "is liable to third persons not parties to the contract who are foreseeably

---

[1] The "Background and Purpose" section of the lease reads, in pertinent part, as follows:

"Whereas, concurrently herewith, Landlord has conveyed to Tenant all of Landlord's right, title and interest in and to the improvements on said parcel, except for the building containing a 70–bed skilled nursing facility and the land under said improvements and building. . . ."

exposed to danger and injured as a result of its negligent failure to carry out that obligation." Parent v. Stone & Webster Eng'g Corp., 408 Mass. 108, 556 N.E.2d 1009 (1990), quoting Banaghan v. Dewey, 340 Mass. 73, 162 N.E.2d 807 (1959). See [Rest.2d,] Torts § 324A (1965). Thus, a defendant who contracted to design and build an electric power plant was liable to a utility company employee injured as a result of the defendant's negligent performance of the contract. Parent v. Stone & Webster Eng'g Corp., supra. Similarly, a defendant who agreed to maintain an elevator in a safe condition was liable to third persons injured as a result of the negligent failure to carry out that obligation. Banaghan v. Dewey, supra. In those cases, the contract created a relationship between the defendant and third parties, by reason of which the law recognized a duty of reasonable care in the performance of the obligation, that supported a tort action.

However, failure to perform a contractual obligation is not a tort in the absence of a duty to act apart from the promise made. . . . See Redgrave v. Boston Symphony Orchestra, Inc., 557 F.Supp. 230 (D.Mass.1983) ("a breach of contract is not, standing alone, a tort as well"). "Although the duty arises out of the contract and is measured by its terms, negligence in the manner of performing that duty as distinguished from mere failure to perform it, causing damage, is a tort." Abrams v. Factory Mut. Liab. Ins. Co., 298 Mass. 141, 10 N.E.2d 82 (1937). This view is endorsed by a leading authority on tort law: "Tort obligations are in general obligations that are imposed by law on policy considerations to avoid some kind of loss to others. They are obligations imposed apart from and independent of promises made and therefore apart from any manifested intention of parties to a contract or other bargaining transaction. Therefore, if the alleged obligation to do or not to do something that was breached could not have existed but for a manifested intent, then contract law should be the only theory upon which liability would be imposed." W. Prosser & W. Keeton, Torts § 92, at 656 (5th ed.1984).

To conclude that tort liability exists solely because the defendant did not perform a contractual duty to remove snow and ice would give rise to a common law duty which we repeatedly have declined to impose on landowners. As we indicated in Sullivan v. Brookline, supra at 827, 626 N.E.2d 870, . . . "under Massachusetts law, landowners are liable only for injuries caused by defects existing on their property and . . . the law does not regard the natural accumulation of snow and ice as an actionable property defect, if it regards such weather conditions as a defect at all."

Judgment affirmed.

H.R. Moch Co. v. Rensselaer Water Co.

Court of Appeals of New York, 1928.
247 N.Y. 160, 159 N.E. 896.

CARDOZO, C.J. The defendant, a water works company[,] made a contract with the city of Rensselaer for the supply of water during a term of years. Water was to be furnished to the city for sewer flushing and street sprinkling; for service to schools and public buildings; and for service at fire hydrants, the latter service at the rate of $42.50 a year for each hydrant. Water was to be furnished to private takers within the city at their homes and factories and other industries at reasonable rates, not exceeding a stated schedule. While this contract was in force, a building caught fire. The flames, spreading to the plaintiff's warehouse near by, destroyed it and its contents. The defendant according to the complaint was promptly notified of the fire, "but omitted and neglected after such notice, to supply or furnish sufficient or adequate quantity of water, with adequate pressure to stay, suppress or extinguish the fire before it reached the warehouse of the plaintiff, although the pressure and supply which the defendant was equipped to supply and furnish, and had agreed by said contract to supply and furnish, was adequate and sufficient to prevent the spread of the fire to and the destruction of the plaintiff's warehouse and its contents." By reason of the failure of the defendant to "fulfill the provisions of the contract between it and the city of Rensselaer," the plaintiff is said to have suffered damage, for which judgment is demanded. A motion, in the nature of a demurrer, to dismiss the complaint, was denied at Special Term. The Appellate Division reversed by a divided court.

. . . The complaint, we are told, is to be viewed as stating: (1) A cause of action for breach of contract within Lawrence v. Fox, 20 N.Y. 268; [and] (2) a cause of action for a common-law tort, within MacPherson v. Buick Motor Co., 217 N.Y. 382, 111 N.E. 1050. . . .

(1) We think the action is not maintainable as one for breach of contract.

No legal duty rests upon a city to supply its inhabitants with protection against fire. Springfield Fire & Marine Ins. Co. v. Village of Keeseville, 148 N.Y. 46, 42 N.E. 405. That being so, a member of the public may not maintain an action under Lawrence v. Fox against one contracting with the city to furnish water at the hydrants, unless an intention appears that the promisor is to be answerable to individual members of the public as well as to the city for any loss ensuing from the failure to fulfill the promise. No such intention is discernible here. On the contrary, the contract is significantly divided into two branches: one a promise to the city for the benefit of the city in its corporate capacity, in which branch is included the service at the hydrants; and the other a promise to the city for the benefit of private takers, in which branch is included the service at their homes and factories. In a broad sense it is true that every city contract, not improvident or wasteful, is for the benefit of the public. More than this, however, must be shown to give a right of action to a member of the public not formally a party. The benefit, as it is sometimes said, must be one that is not merely incidental and secondary. . . . It must be primary and immediate in such a sense and to such a degree as to bespeak the assumption of a duty to make reparation directly to the individual members of the public if the benefit is lost. The field of obligation would be expanded beyond reasonable limits if less than this were to be demanded as a condition of liability. A promisor undertakes to supply fuel for heating a public building. He is not liable for breach of contract to a visitor who finds the building without fuel, and thus contracts a cold. The list of illustrations can be indefinitely extended. The carrier of the mails under contract with the government is not answerable to the merchant who has lost the benefit of a bargain through negligent delay. The householder is without a remedy against manufacturers of hose and engines, though prompt performance of their contracts would have stayed the ravages of fire. "The law does not spread its protection so far." Robins Dry Dock & Repair Co. v. Flint, 275 U.S. 303.

So with the case at hand. By the vast preponderance of authority, a contract between a city and a water company to furnish water at the city hydrants has in view a benefit to the public that is incidental rather than immediate, an assumption of duty to the city and not to its inhabitants.... Such with few exceptions has been the ruling in other jurisdictions.... Page, Contracts, § 2401. An intention to assume an obligation of indefinite extension to every member of the public is seen to be the more improbable when we recall the crushing burden that the obligation would impose.... The consequences invited would bear no reasonable proportion to those attached by law to defaults not greatly different. A wrongdoer who by negligence sets fire to a building is liable in damages to the owner where the fire has its origin, but not to other owners who are injured when it spreads. The rule in our State is settled to that effect, whether wisely or unwisely.... If the plaintiff is to prevail, one who negligently omits to supply sufficient pressure to extinguish a fire started by another, assumes an obligation to pay the ensuing damage, though the whole city is laid low. A promisor will not be deemed to have had in mind the assumption of a risk so overwhelming for any trivial reward.

The cases that have applied the rule of Lawrence v. Fox to contracts made by a city for the benefit of the public are not at war with this conclusion. Through them all there runs as a unifying principle the presence of an intention to compensate the individual members of the public in the event of a default. For example, in Pond v. New Rochelle Water Co., 183 N.Y. 330, 76 N.E. 211, the contract with the city fixed a schedule of rates to be supplied not to public buildings but to private takers at their homes. In Matter of Int'l Ry. Co. v. Rann, 224 N.Y. 83, 120 N.E. 153, the contract was by street railroads to carry passengers for a stated fare. In Smyth v. City of N.Y., 203 N.Y. 106, 96 N.E. 409, and Rigney v. N.Y.C. & H.R.R.R. Co., 217 N.Y. 31, 111 N.E. 226, covenants were made by contractors upon public works, not merely to indemnify the city, but to assume its liabilities. These and like cases come within the third group stated in the comprehensive opinion in Seaver v. Ransom, 224 N.Y. 233, 120 N.E. 639. The municipality was contracting in behalf of its inhabitants by covenants intended to be enforced by any of them severally as occasion should arise.

(2) We think the action is not maintainable as one for a common law tort.

"It is ancient learning that one who assumes to act, even though gratuitously, may thereby become subject to the duty of acting carefully, if he acts at all" (Glanzer v. Shepard, 233 N.Y. 236, 135 N.E. 275).... The plaintiff would bring its case within the orbit of that principle. The hand once set to a task may not always be withdrawn with impunity though liability would fail if it had never been applied at all. A time-honored formula often phrases the distinction as one between misfeasance and nonfeasance. Incomplete the formula is, and so at times misleading. Given a relation involving in its existence a duty of care irrespective of a contract, a tort may result as well from acts of omission as of commission in the fulfillment of the duty thus recognized by law (Pollock, Torts [12th ed.], p. 555; Kelly v. Met. Ry. Co., 1895, 1 Q.B. 944). What we need to know is not so much the conduct to be avoided when the relation and its attendant duty are established as existing. What we need to know is the conduct that engenders the relation. It is here that the formula, however incomplete, has its value and significance. If conduct has gone forward to such a stage that inaction would commonly result, not negatively merely in withholding a benefit, but positively or actively in working an injury, there exists a relation out of which arises a duty to go forward (Bohlen, Studies in the Law of Torts, p.

87). So the surgeon who operates without pay is liable, though his negligence is in the omission to sterilize his instruments (cf. Glanzer v. Shepard, supra); the engineer, though his fault is in the failure to shut off steam (Kelly v. Met. Ry. Co., supra); the maker of automobiles, at the suit of some one other than the buyer, though his negligence is merely in inadequate inspection (MacPherson v. Buick Motor Co., 217 N.Y. 382, 111 N.E. 1050). The query always is whether the putative wrongdoer has advanced to such a point as to have launched a force or instrument of harm, or has stopped where inaction is at most a refusal to become an instrument for good. . . .

The plaintiff would have us hold that the defendant, when once it entered upon the performance of its contract with the city, was brought into such a relation with every one who might potentially be benefited through the supply of water at the hydrants as to give to negligent performance, without reasonable notice of a refusal to continue, the quality of a tort. . . . We are satisfied that liability would be unduly and indeed indefinitely extended by this enlargement of the zone of duty. The dealer in coal who is to supply fuel for a shop must then answer to the customers if fuel is lacking. The manufacturer of goods, who enters upon the performance of his contract, must answer, in that view, not only to the buyer, but to those who to his knowledge are looking to the buyer for their own sources of supply. Every one making a promise having the quality of a contract will be under a duty to the promisee by virtue of the promise, but under another duty, apart from contract, to an indefinite number of potential beneficiaries when performance has begun. The assumption of one relation will mean the involuntary assumption of a series of new relations, inescapably hooked together. . . . "The law does not spread its protection so far" (Robins Dry Dock & Repair Co. v. Flint, supra.) . . . What we are dealing with at this time is a mere negligent omission, unaccompanied by malice or other aggravating elements. The failure in such circumstances to furnish an adequate supply of water is at most the denial of a benefit. It is not the commission of a wrong. . .

The judgment should be affirmed with costs.

––––––––

Doyle v. South Pittsburgh Water Co.

414 Pa. 199, 199 A.2d 875 (1964)

Plaintiffs' complaint alleged that the destruction of their home by fire would have been averted if the local fire department could have obtained water from fire hydrants, of which there were at least five, in the immediate neighborhood of the house. The complaint also alleged that defendant Water Co. had contracted with the city of South Pittsburgh to provide water for these fire hydrants, "for the sole purpose" of fighting fires in the vicinity of plaintiffs' home. The complaint further alleged that defendant had negligently allowed the water in the hydrants to freeze, had failed to inspect the hydrants, had failed to maintain sufficient pressure or repair inoperative valves or notify plaintiffs or the fire department that the hydrants were inoperative. *Held*, the complaint stated a cause of action in negligence. Defendant gained nothing by "the elusive debating dialectic" that it was the fire and not the lack of water that destroyed the house. The case fell squarely within the rule that "where a party to a contract assumes a duty to the other party to the contract, and it is foreseeable that a breach of that duty will cause injury to some third person not a party to the contract, the contracting party owes a duty to all those falling within the foreseeable orbit of risk of harm." As to the opinion of Judge Cardozo in H.R. Moch v. Rensselaer Water Co., "it must be stated, with some regret, that at this point Homer nodded," for Judge Cardozo, "without apparently intending to do so, contradicted what he had said" in MacPherson v. Buick Motor Co., 217 N.Y. 382, 111 N.E. 1050 (1916). Once he recognized that the city was guilty of a "negligent omission," the "breach of duty" required for negligence was conceded.

"The argument that to insure safety to the public would entail great expense is, and should no longer be, a defense where a duty to life, limb and property is inherent. Depressing as the reflection may be, it is true nevertheless that the absence of financial responsibility for negligence is to encourage further negligence. To announce to water companies throughout the Commonwealth that no species of indifference on their part, no negligence, no matter how gross, will call for pecuniary answerability is to invite progressive inattention and indifference to protection against the scourge of flame and incendiary invasion." [The result here is not typical; tort claims against water companies usually fail.]

NOTE

Who should have the right to sue—that is, what remedies should be available—when a contract designed to effectuate a government-initiated program is breached?

The problem of the *Moch* case (and the cases digested above) is dealt with by the Restatement of Contracts, Second, as follows:

Section 313. Government Contracts

(1) The rules [on contract beneficiaries] apply to contracts with a government or governmental agency except to the extent that application would contravene the policy of the law authorizing the contract or prescribing remedies for its breach.

(2) In particular, a promisor who contracts with a government or governmental agency to do an act for or render a service to the public is not subject to contractual liability to a member of the public for consequential damages resulting from performance or failure to perform unless

(a) the terms of the promise provide for such liability; or

(b) the promisee is subject to liability to the member of the public for the damages and a direct action against the promisor is consistent with the terms of the contract and with the policy of the law authorizing the contract and prescribing remedies for its breach.

The situations described in subsection (2) are designed to conform to the classification of beneficiaries in § 302 ("intended" and "incidental," the former comprehending the definitions of donee and creditor beneficiaries in § 133 of the first Restatement). Does subsection (2) adequately bring into focus the policy considerations relevant in determining the existence of enforceable rights in a member of the public? In the view of one court, such determinations are "much like the question whether a particular federal statute creates an implied right of action in favor of its beneficiaries." Price v. Pierce, 823 F.2d 1114 (7th

Cir.1987) (applicants for subsidized housing not third-party beneficiaries of contracts between developers and state housing agency). The Restatement, Second, in a comment accompanying § 313, states that the factors which may make inappropriate a direct action against the promisor include "arrangements for governmental control over the litigation and settlement of claims, the likelihood of impairment of service or of excessive financial burden, and the availability of alternatives such as insurance."

Basic Capital Management, Inc. v. Dynex Commercial, Inc.

Supreme Court of Texas, 2011.
348 S.W.3d 894.

HECHT, J. Basic Capital Management, Inc. managed publicly traded real estate investment trusts in which it also owned stock, including American Realty Trust, Inc. ("ART") and Transcontinental Realty Investors, Inc. ("TCI"). We refer to the three collectively as petitioners. Respondent Dynex Commercial, Inc. provided financing for multi-family and commercial real estate investors.

ART and TCI held investment property through wholly owned "single-asset, bankruptcy-remote entities"—SABREs, for short. A SABRE, as the term for which it stands suggests, is an entity that owns a single asset and whose solvency is independent of affiliates. Lenders like Dynex commonly require a SABRE as a borrower so that in the event of default, the collateral can be recovered more easily than from a debtor with multiple assets and multiple creditors.

After several months of discussions and negotiations, Dynex agreed to loan three TCI-owned SABREs $37 million to acquire and rehabilitate three commercial buildings—one each—in New Orleans if Basic would propose other acceptable SABREs to borrow $160 million over a two-year period. The agreements were eventually formalized in letters. . . .

TCI accepted the agreement as "borrower", although it is not a SABRE. The $160 million commitment ("the Commitment") was between Dynex and Basic. It also stated that each borrower would be a "Single Asset, Bankruptcy Remote Borrowing Entity acceptable to Lender." The SABREs would be owned by ART or TCI. "First and foremost," Dynex stressed, "the two transactions [were] intertwined."

Dynex loaned TCI's three SABREs the money to acquire the New Orleans buildings and funded a $6 million loan presented by Basic under the Commitment. But then market interest rates rose, making the terms of the Commitment unfavorable to Dynex. Dynex refused to provide further funding for improvements to the New Orleans buildings or to make any other loans under the Commitment.

Petitioners sued Dynex for breach of the Commitment, alleging that as a result, transactions that would have qualified for funding were financed elsewhere at higher rates or not at all. Petitioners claimed damages for interest paid in excess of what would have been charged under the Commitment and for lost profits from investments for which financing could not be found. TCI also sued Dynex for breach of the New Orleans Agreement. Dynex counterclaimed against petitioners for fraud.

ART and TCI alleged that they "were intended beneficiaries of the $160 million Commitment because their wholly owned subsidiaries would own the properties and borrow the funds advanced by Dynex Commercial under the commitment." . . .

We consider first whether ART and TCI can recover for breach of the Commitment, and TCI for breach of the New Orleans Agreement, as third-party beneficiaries. . . .

The law governing third-party beneficiaries is relatively settled:

> The fact that a person might receive an incidental benefit from a contract to which he is not a party does not give that person a right of action to enforce the contract. A third party may recover on a contract made between other parties only if the parties intended to secure some benefit to that third party, and only if the contracting parties entered into the contract directly for the third party's benefit. . . .

> In determining whether a third party can enforce a contract, the intention of the contracting parties is controlling. A court will not create a third party beneficiary contract by implication. The intention to contract or confer a direct benefit to a third party must be clearly and fully spelled out or enforcement by the third party must be denied. Consequently, a presumption exists that parties contracted for themselves unless it clearly appears that they intended a third party to benefit from the contract.

MCI Telecomms. Corp. v. Texas Utils. Elec. Co., 995 S.W.2d 647, 651 (Tex. 1999) (citations and internal quotation marks omitted).

And of course, "[w]hen a contract is not ambiguous, the construction of the written instrument is a question of law for the court." Id. at 650.

Dynex knew that the purpose of the Commitment was to secure future financing for ART and TCI, real estate investment trusts that Basic managed and in which it held an ownership interest. Basic was never to be the borrower. On the contrary, the Commitment expressly required that the borrowers be SABREs acceptable to Dynex. Nor was Basic to own the SABREs. Dynex knew that Basic's business was to manage the investment trusts that created and owned the SABREs as part of their investment portfolio. The requirement that all borrowers be SABREs was for Dynex's benefit, to provide more certain recourse to the collateral in the event of default.

As a practical matter, the parties knew that it would likely not be a SABRE that would enforce the Commitment. By its very nature as a single-asset entity, a SABRE would not be created until an investment opportunity presented itself, and without financing, there would be no investment. It would be unreasonable to require ART and TCI to have created SABREs for no business purpose, merely in order that those otherwise inert entities could sue Dynex.

The court of appeals was concerned that the benefit to ART and TCI was indirect in the sense that it flowed through the SABRE-borrowers. We certainly agree that as a general proposition, a corporate parent is not a third-party beneficiary of its subsidiary's contract merely by virtue of their relationship. But here the benefit to each SABRE not only inured to its parent, the transaction was so structured to benefit Dynex. SABRE-borrowers provided a mechanism for ART and TCI to hold investment property directly but in a way that would provide Dynex greater security. If Dynex and Basic did not intend the Commitment to benefit ART and TCI directly, then the Commitment had no purpose whatever.

Dynex and Basic could have prevented any doubt about their intentions by expressly stating in the Commitment that it was to benefit ART and TCI. Perhaps they did not do so because it seemed to go without saying. But we need not speculate. The Commitment "clearly and fully spelled out" the benefit to ART and TCI because their role was basic to Dynex's and Basic's agreement.

Dynex insists that ART's and TCI's failure to request a jury finding on whether they were third-party beneficiaries is fatal to their recovery on that theory. But as we noted above, the proper construction of an unambiguous contract is a matter of law. The Commitment itself, and the undisputed evidence regarding its negotiation and purpose, establish that ART and TCI were third-party beneficiaries.

Dynex argues that the New Orleans Agreement consisted of the promissory notes signed by each of TCI's three SABREs, and that TCI was not a third-party beneficiary of the obligations set out in those notes. But the notes were executed pursuant to a commitment by Dynex that TCI itself signed. As a party to the commitment that provided the New Orleans Agreement financing for its SABREs, TCI was a third-party beneficiary of the Agreement.

Accordingly, we conclude that ART and TCI were entitled to recover for Dynex's breach of the Commitment and the New Orleans Agreement. . . .

––––––––

RESTATEMENT OF CONTRACTS, SECOND

Section 311. Variation of a Duty to a Beneficiary

(1) Discharge or modification of a duty to an intended beneficiary by conduct of the promisee or by a subsequent agreement between promisor and promisee is ineffective if a term of the promise creating the duty so provides.

(2) In the absence of such a term, the promisor and promisee retain power to discharge or modify the duty by subsequent agreement.

(3) Such a power terminates when the beneficiary, before he receives notification of the discharge or modification, materially changes his position in justifiable reliance on the promise or brings suit on it or manifests assent to it at the request of the promisor or promisee.

(4) If the promisee receives consideration for an attempted discharge or modification of the promisor's duty which is ineffective against the beneficiary, the beneficiary can assert a right to the consideration so received. The promisor's duty is discharged to the extent of the amount received by the beneficiary.

NOTE

The first Restatement of Contracts, in §§ 142 and 143, distinguished between creditor and donee beneficiaries as concerns the power of the contracting parties to alter or terminate rights under the beneficiary contract. The rights of the donee beneficiary were deemed to vest at once upon the making of the contract; there was no vesting of creditor beneficiary rights until there was reliance on the contract by that nonparty. The Second Restatement, in § 311 set out above, discards the distinction, treating all intended beneficiaries alike. The Reporter's Note to § 311 states that "[t]he weight of authority is opposed to a distinction between donee beneficiaries and creditor beneficiaries with respect to the power of promisor and promisee to vary" duties owed third parties, and that the authorities support termination of that power "by either assent or reliance by the beneficiary." Accordingly, the power to vary duties is made to turn "primarily on the terms of the promise." Some courts continue to follow the rule that the rights of the donee beneficiary vest indefeasibly at the time of the contract. See, e.g., Biggins v. Shore, 523 Pa. 148, 565 A.2d 737 (1989) ("Restatement (Second) [§ 311] affords no greater freedom of contract than exists [under Pennsylvania's indefeasibility rule]; if [the parties] do not intend to convey an [irretrievable] benefit, they need merely say so in the contract").

SECTION 2. ASSIGNMENT AND DELEGATION

INTRODUCTORY COMMENT

The power of creditors to make effective transfers of rights created by contract developed late in our legal history, and the development has encountered many obstacles. Assignees, like third party beneficiaries, are strangers to the contract. Both have caused lawyers much strain and discomfort, as was almost bound to occur with strangers who arrived late at a supposedly well-organized feast. In theory, the claims of assignees might appear even more troublesome than the claims of third party beneficiaries, for with assignees one cannot use the ready explanation that both contracting parties agreed that the third party was to receive the benefit of the promised performance. The assignee usually steps in without the debtor's consent, often against the debtor's wish. To explain how this can occur requires some basic rethinking of postulates, and basic rethinking is apt to come only after social needs have been clearly demonstrated.

Similar difficulties were encountered in the development of Roman law, where obligations were understood to be intensely personal relations between particular people. Whether obligations arose through consent (i.e., contract) or through delict (tort), their personal nature made it difficult for Roman lawyers to conceive of simple substitution of a different creditor by the unilateral act of an assignor. Yet, as was true in medieval English law, there were certain situations for which it was necessary to make provision. One was the creditor who died leaving an uncollected claim arising from contract. Another was the surety who had paid the principal's debt and then sought an assignment of the rights of the paid-off creditor against the principal debtor. But such scattered instances did not produce a general theory authorizing assignments. The nearest approach to a generalized technique in classical Roman law was that employed for centuries by the English common law—the assignee became an agent (in Roman terms, was given a "mandate") with a power to sue in the assignor's name. But, until very late in Roman law, the agency (mandate) was fully revocable, so that it was most incomplete as a device for the transfer of rights.

The concept used by common lawyers to describe rights created by contract was the French legal phrase "chose in action." This is an essentially negative term, meaning a right enforceable only by action and in no way connected with ownership, custody, or use of an identified physical asset. The term encompasses an enormous diversity of human relationships, and this has been one of the difficulties in constructing an intelligible theory. It includes, for example, tort claims of all kinds. The drag produced by this extensive coverage may be illustrated by the fact that even now claims for personal torts, unconnected with specific property, are generally not assignable. Why should they be? What needs are served by opening up commerce in damage claims for personal injuries or defamation? Might not such commerce cause positive harm in fomenting litigation by persons having no connection with the injured party? Doubts of this kind have operated to restrict the assignability of various kinds of personal claims. Even today, when assignability has become a familiar feature of many types of choses in action, much can depend on the kind of chose in action it is.

It may also be that the early lawyers had difficulty visualizing the process by which rights unconnected with a tangible thing could be effectively transferred. There would be no cow or horse to be handed over, no twig or clod of earth that could be given as a symbol. But, fairly early, lawyers began to develop the notion that an owner out of possession could transfer an ownership interest, a mere right of action, without physical delivery of the asset itself, and surely it was not too great a stretch to extend this notion more broadly. Indeed, the incapacity of early lawyers to corporealize the incorporeal has been greatly over-stressed by modern writers. Medieval lawyers were perfectly capable of imagining ownership of disembodied interests—ownership of an office, the right to appoint a parson to a church, rights to services in homes or in fields, rights to be paid annuities, to collect tolls from passersby, or to occupy a front seat at the King's coronation. The difficulty was that at the point when lawyers were ready to formulate broader theories for explaining transfers of "rights of action," their thinking became confused. They mixed the question of assignments with the problem of fomented litigation, which was dealt with by the rules against "maintenance" and "champerty."

Maintenance in modern law is the supporting or promoting of another's litigation; champerty is the same, plus an agreement to share the proceeds. Both may have been crimes under the early common law; they were certainly made crimes by a series of statutes that began in the fourteenth century. To understand the problem, one must imagine a society in which central governments were weak and power was dispersed through an aristocracy that was often turbulent. The favor and support of powerful persons and their armed retainers were much sought after, especially by those who quarrelled with their neighbors. Maintenance, with or without profit-sharing, was a constant threat to the administration of justice, especially during the civil wars of the fifteenth century. Even after the power of the central government was rebuilt under the Tudors, the problem survived. Coke, in the early seventeenth century, revived memories that were not yet stale when he expressed his approval of the rule that "no possibility, right, title nor thing in action shall be granted or assigned to strangers, for that would be the occasion of multiplying of contentions and suits, of great oppression of the people, and chiefly of terre-tenants, and the subversion of the due and equal execution of justice." Lampet's Case, 10 Coke Rep. 48a, 77 Eng.Rep. 994.

The rules against maintenance and champerty have been greatly modified since the time of Coke, though they have not disappeared. Legal aid societies escape the penalties of maintenance because of their charitable purpose in aiding needy persons. A person who has an interest to assert can conduct litigation on behalf of others, pay all the expenses, and share in the proceeds. But if a person's only interest is in securing an agreed share in the proceeds of a claim belonging to another, the arrangement will ordinarily be illegal; under the law of most states, any purported assignment of a right to sue will be ineffective. Most of the problems of champerty and maintenance now arise in connection with arrangements for lawyers' services. A contingent-fee contract between lawyer and client would probably be valid in every state, even though it gives a share in the proceeds to the lawyer in the event of success. But if the lawyer under a contingent contract agrees, in addition, to pay the costs of litigation, this may well suffice to make the whole contract illegal. Ambulance chasers who actively promote litigation and pay others to bring them business are not only subject to discipline by bar association committees, but are subject independently, in some states at least, to criminal penalties also. Though the sanctions are now much diluted and the scope of the offense much narrowed, there remain some areas in which profit-making through promoting litigation of other persons' claims is still strongly disapproved.

It should be evident that there was some confusion of thought in the identification of assignments with maintenance or champerty. The obvious purpose of an assignment was to create an interest in the assignee, which that person would then assert. The law courts, however, were not consistent in the policies they asserted. Even before the time of Coke, in one large group of cases the courts had admitted that an assignee of a claim for money acquired a power of attorney to sue in the name of the assignor—where the assignment was in settlement of a debt already owed the assignee by the assignor. The assignee in such a case was not charged with maintaining another's quarrel; by taking the assignment for the protection of self-interest, the assignee had become a party to the quarrel. This kind of reasoning could readily have been extended to the case of an outright purchaser who paid cash or other consideration for an assignment of the claim. Indeed, in one isolated case in 1590, a law court so held, using again the theory that the assignee had a power of attorney to sue in the assignor's name. Penson v. Hickbed, Cro.Eliz. 70, 78 Eng.Rep. 427. But this case was not followed until almost a century had elapsed. There were certain exceptions: assignments by and to the Crown, and transfers of contract rights to executors or administrators on the death of a contract creditor. But, on the whole, the common law courts stood their ground until the eighteenth century. Even the concession that an assignee might have a power of attorney was limited to the case of assignment in satisfaction of an antecedent debt.

The date when the Chancery first began to intervene is not clear. Perhaps it responded quite early to the appeals of individual merchants who had purchased mercantile debts. It was not until the seventeenth century, apparently, that the Chancery began regularly to protect the assignee against the assignor's attempts to defeat the assignment. In the eighteenth century, such relief became a standard feature of Chancery jurisdiction, for even after the power-of-attorney technique became broadly available in law actions, it had the major defect of any simple agency theory: the agency was revocable by the death, the bankruptcy, or the repudiation of the principal (assignor), even though revocation might be a breach of the duty the assignor owed to the assignee. It was not until 1787 that the King's Bench achieved the position, already reached by the Chancery, that the bankruptcy of the assignor did not destroy or impair the assignee's right under an assignment made before the bankruptcy. Winch v. Keeley, 1 T.R. 619, 99 Eng.Rep. 1284.

This long-delayed response of the law courts was partly due, no doubt, to a desire to meet the Chancery's competition. But the courts must have been influenced also by the example of free transferability supplied by such mercantile instruments as the bill of exchange and the promissory note. These instruments had been evolved by "the custom of merchants," a body of rules applied in the trading communities of Europe through special courts and through self-regulation by the merchants themselves. The absorption of the custom of merchants into the common law began in the sixteenth century, through decisions that allowed the rules of custom to be proved as facts and then applied as governing norms in common law actions. The process of absorption was gradual and involved much more than the principle of assignability of contract rights. The bill of exchange and promissory note were important devices, much used in trade, and their most prominent feature was that the holder's right was highly transferable. If the promise expressed in the instrument satisfied certain strict requirements of form, a transferee could acquire better rights than the transferor had enjoyed. The instrument, in other words, was "negotiable," and if transferred before maturity, for value, to a "holder in due course" (i.e., a purchaser in good faith), most of the defenses that would be available to the promisor against the promisee-transferor would be excluded as against the good-faith purchaser. As to the bill of exchange (a modern analogue is the bank check), the common law before 1700 had gone a long way in absorbing the rules of negotiability developed by the law merchant. A statute passed in 1704 achieved similar results for promissory notes. The full-scale adoption of the law merchant by the common law owed much to the influence of Lord Mansfield in the second half of the eighteenth century. If so much could be accomplished through negotiable instruments, the lawyers must have seen the anomaly of denying protection to other kinds of assignees.

This section examines contract rights that, through defects of form or for other reasons, are not negotiable under contemporary rules of commercial law. The rules for negotiable instruments form a special and complex subject, now governed by the UCC, that must be postponed to a later course.

Assignees of nonnegotiable choses do receive some aid from statutes, whose popularity began in the nineteenth century, requiring that actions be brought in the name of "the real party in interest." This procedural requirement dispenses with the form of suit by the assignee in the assignor's name.

Langel v. Betz

Court of Appeals of New York, 1928.
250 N.Y. 159, 164 N.E. 890.

POUND, J. Plaintiff, on August 1, 1925, made a contract with Irving W. Hurwitz and Samuel Hollander for the sale [to them] of certain real property. This contract the vendees assigned to Benedict, who in turn assigned it to Isidor Betz, the defendant herein. The assignment contains no delegation to the assignee of the performance of the assignor's duties. The date for performance of the contract was originally set for October 2, 1925. This was extended to October 15, 1925, at the request of the defendant, the last assignee of the vendees. The ground upon which the adjournment was asked for by defendant was that the title company had not completed its search and report on the title to the property. Upon the adjourned date the defendant refused to perform. The vendor plaintiff was ready, able and willing to do so, and was present at the place specified with a deed, ready to tender it to the defendant who did not appear.

The plaintiff as vendor brought this action against the defendant assignee for specific performance of the contract [and] has had judgment therefor.

The question is: "Can the vendor obtain specific performance of a contract for the sale of real estate against the assignee of the vendee, where the assignee merely requests and obtains an extension of time within which to close title?" Here we have no novation, no express assumption of the obligations of the assignor in the assignment and no demand for performance by the assignee.

The mere assignment of a bilateral executory contract may not be interpreted as a promise by the assignee to the assignor to assume the performance of the assignor's duties, so as to have the effect of creating a new liability on the part of the assignee to the other party to the contract assigned. The assignee of the vendee is under no personal engagement to the vendor where there is no privity between them. . . . The assignee may, however, expressly or impliedly, bind himself to perform the assignor's duties. This he may do by contract with the assignor or with the other party to the contract. It has been held, Epstein v. Gluckin, 233 N.Y. 490, 135 N.E. 861, that, where the assignee of the vendee invokes the aid of a court of equity in an action for specific performance, he impliedly binds himself to perform. . . . "He who seeks equity must do equity." The converse of the proposition, that the assignee of the vendee would be bound when the vendor began action, did not follow from the decision in that case. On the contrary, the question was wholly one of remedy rather than right and it was held that mutuality of remedy is important only so far as its presence is essential to the attainment of the ends of justice. This holding was necessary to sustain the decision. No change was made in the . . . rule for the interpretation of an assignment of a contract.

A judgment requiring the assignee of the vendee to perform at the suit of the vendor would operate as the imposition of a new liability on the assignee which would be an act of oppression and injustice, unless the assignee had, expressly or by implication, entered into a personal and binding contract with the assignor or with the vendor to assume the obligations of the assignor.

It has been urged that the probable intention of the assignee is ordinarily to assume duties as well as rights and that the contract should be so interpreted in the absence of circumstances showing a contrary intention. . . . [The] Restatement of Contracts (§ 164) proposes a change in the rule of interpretation of assigned contracts[:] . . .

"(1) Where a party to a bilateral contract which is at the time wholly or partially executory on both sides, purports to assign the whole contract, his action is interpreted, in the absence of circumstances showing a contrary intention, as an assignment of the assignor's rights under the contract and a delegation of the performance of the assignor's duties.

"(2) Acceptance by the assignee of such an assignment is interpreted, in the absence of circumstances showing a contrary intention, as both an assent to become an assignee of the assignor's rights and as a promise *to the assignor to assume the performance of the assignor's duties.*"

This promise to the assignor would then be available to the other party to the contract. Lawrence v. Fox, 20 N.Y. 268. . . . The [Restatement's] proposed change is a complete reversal of our present rule of interpretation as to the probable intention of the parties. It is, perhaps more in harmony with modern ideas of contractual relations than is "the archaic view of a contract as creating a strictly personal obligation between the creditor and debtor," Pollock on Contracts (9th ed.), 232, which prohibited the assignee from suing at law in his own name and which denied a remedy to third party beneficiaries. "The fountains out of which these resolutions issue" have been broken up if not destroyed, Seaver v. Ransom, 224 N.Y. 233, 120 N.E. 639, but the law remains that no promise of the assignee to assume the assignor's duties is to be inferred from the acceptance of an assignment of a bilateral contract, in the absence of circumstances surrounding the assignment itself which indicate a contrary intention.

With this requirement of the interpretation of the intention of the parties controlling, we must turn from the assignment to the dealings between the plaintiff and the defendant to discover whether the defendant entered into relations with the plaintiff whereby he assumed the duty of performance. The assignment did not bring the parties together and the request for a postponement differs materially from the commencement of an action in a court of equity, whereby the plaintiff submits himself to the jurisdiction of the court or from a contractual assumption of the obligations of the assignor. If the substance of the transaction between the vendor and the assignee of the vendee could be regarded as a request on the part of the latter for a postponement of the closing day and a promise on his part to assume the obligations of the vendee if the request were granted, a contractual relation arising from an expression of mutual assent, based on the exchange of a promise for an act might be spelled out of it; but the transaction is at least as consistent with a request for time for deliberation as to the course of condut to be pursued as with an implied promise to assume the assignor's duties if the request were granted. The relation of promisor and promisee was not thereby expressly established and such relation is not a necessary inference from the nature of the transaction. . . .

Plaintiff contends that the request for an adjournment should be construed (time not being the essence of the contract) as an assertion of a right to such adjournment, and, therefore, as a binding act of enforcement, whereby defendant accepted the obligations of the [assignor]. Here again we have an equivocal act. There was no demand for an adjournment as a matter of right. The request may have been made without any intent to assert a right. It cannot be said that by that act alone the assignee assumed the duty of performance. Furthermore, no controlling authority may be found which holds that a mere demand for performance by the vendee's assignee creates a right in the complaining vendor to enforce the contract against him. . . . That question may be reserved until an answer is necessary.

[Judgment] reversed and the complaint dismissed.

———

RESTATEMENT OF CONTRACTS, SECOND

Section 328. Interpretation of Words of Assignment; Effect of Acceptance of Assignment

(1) Unless the language or the circumstances indicate the contrary, as in an assignment for security, an assignment of "the contract" or of "all my rights under the contract" or an assignment in similar general terms is an assignment of the assignor's rights and a delegation of his unperformed duties under the contract.

(2) Unless the language or the circumstances indicate the contrary, the acceptance by an assignee of such an assignment operates as a promise to the assignor to perform the assignor's unperformed duties, and the obligor of the assigned rights is an intended beneficiary of the promise.

Caveat: The Institute expresses no opinion as to whether the rule stated in Subsection (2) applies to an assignment by a purchaser of his rights under a contract for the sale of land.

NOTE

Langel v. Betz purported to reserve decision on the question whether the assignee's "assertion of a right" under the contract could amount to an assumption of the vendee's obligations. In Kunzman v. Thorsen, 303 Or. 600, 740 P.2d 754 (1987), another vendor's suit for specific performance against the vendee's assignee, the court took the view that "a claim of the contract's benefits"—e.g., taking possession of the land, making payments directly to the vendor, and "behaving generally" like a party to the original contract—creates a presumption that the assignee intended to assume the duties the contract imposes. In evaluating such a test, consider whether assignments of land-sale contracts are likely to be broadly worded and whether, in the usual case, the parties' intentions at the time of the assignment are likely to be unclear.

Section 328 of the Restatement, Second follows the phrasing of UCC 2–210(4), which governs when the contract assigned is for the sale of goods. New York, it seems, remains out of line with the position taken in the second Restatement (and the UCC) on the construction of an assignment of simply "the contract." E.g., A.C. Associates v. Metropolitan Steel Indus., 1989 WL 1111034 (S.D.N.Y.1989) (citing *Langel* in support of "settled rule" that, absent contrary indication, "the mere assignment of a contract is an assignment of rights . . . and not of the assignor's duties and liabilities"). The second Restatement's caveat to § 328(2) is based on the views expressed in Langel v. Betz, which, said the restaters in 1981, represents the overwhelming weight of authority in the land-contract cases. If § 328 offers a defensible approach to the interpretation of "assignments" in general, are you satisfied that land contracts should be treated differently? Is the explanation that an assignment by a purchaser (vendee) under a land contract is the practical equivalent of a sale "subject to" any mortgage on the land?

––––––––

Herzog v. Irace

Supreme Judicial Court of Maine, 1991.
594 A.2d 1106.

BRODY, J. Anthony Irace and Donald Lowry appeal from an order entered by the Superior Court affirming a District Court judgment in favor of Dr. John P. Herzog in an action for breach of an assignment to Herzog of personal injury settlement proceeds[1] collected by Irace and Lowry, both attorneys, on behalf of their client, Gary G. Jones. Irace and Lowry contend that the District Court erred in finding that the assignment was valid and enforceable against them. . . .

Gary Jones was injured in a motorcycle accident and retained Irace and Lowry to represent him in a personal injury action. Soon thereafter, Jones dislocated his shoulder, twice, in incidents unrelated to the motorcycle accident. Dr. Herzog examined Jones's shoulder and concluded that he needed surgery. . . Jones was unable to pay for the surgery and in consideration for the performance of [it], he signed a letter dated June 14, 1988, written on Dr. Herzog's letterhead stating:

> I, Gary Jones, request that payment be made directly from settlement of a claim currently pending for an unrelated incident, to John Herzog, D.O., for treatment of a shoulder injury which occurred at a different time.

Dr. Herzog notified Irace and Lowry that Jones had signed an "assignment of benefits" from the motorcycle personal injury action to cover the cost of surgery on his shoulder and was informed by an employee of Irace and Lowry that the assignment was sufficient to allow the firm to pay Herzog's bills at the conclusion of the case. Dr. Herzog performed the surgery and continued to treat Jones for approximately one year.

In May, 1989, Jones received a $20,000 settlement in the motorcycle personal injury action. He instructed Irace and Lowry not to disburse any funds to Dr. Herzog indicating that he would make the payments himself. Irace and Lowry informed Herzog that Jones had revoked his permission to have the bill paid by them directly and indicated that they would follow Jones's directions. Irace and Lowry issued a check to Jones for $10,027 and disbursed the remaining funds to Jones's other creditors. Jones did send a check to Dr. Herzog but the check was returned by the bank for insufficient funds. . . .

Dr. Herzog filed a complaint in District Court against Irace and Lowry seeking to enforce the June 14, 1988 "assignment of benefits." . . . The court entered a judgment in favor of Herzog finding that the June 14, 1988 letter constituted a valid assignment of the settlement proceeds enforceable against Irace and Lowry. Following an unsuccessful appeal to the Superior Court, Irace and Lowry appealed to this court. . . . [W]e will set aside trial court findings based solely upon documentary evidence and stipulated facts only if clearly erroneous. . . .

An assignment is an act or manifestation by the owner of a right (the assignor) indicating his intent to transfer that right to another person (the assignee). Shiro v. Drew, 174 F.Supp. 495, 497 (D.Me.1959). . . . [T]he assignor must make clear his intent to relinquish the right to the assignee and must not retain any control over the right assigned or any power of

---

[1] This case involves the assignment of proceeds from a personal injury action, not an assignment of the cause of action itself.

revocation. The assignment takes effect through the actions of the assignor and assignee and the obligor need not accept the assignment to render it valid. Palmer v. Palmer, 112 Me. 149, 153, 91 A. 281, 282 (1914). Once the obligor has notice of the assignment, the fund is "from that time forward impressed with a trust; it is . . . impounded in the [obligor's] hands, and must be held by him not for the original creditor, the assignor, but for the substituted creditor, the assignee." Id., at 152, 91 A. 281. After receiving notice of the assignment, the obligor cannot lawfully pay the amount assigned either to the assignor or to his other creditors and if the obligor does make such a payment, he does so at his peril because the assignee may enforce his rights against the obligor directly.

Ordinary rights, including future rights, are freely assignable unless the assignment would materially change the duty of the obligor, materially increase the burden or risk imposed upon the obligor by his contract, impair the obligor's chance of obtaining return performance, or materially reduce the value of the return performance to the obligor, and unless the law restricts the assignability of the specific right involved. See Restatement (Second) Contracts § 317(2)(a) (1982). In Maine, the transfer of a future right to *proceeds* from pending litigation has been recognized as a valid and enforceable equitable assignment. McLellan v. Walker, 26 Me. 114, 117–18 (1896). An equitable assignment need not transfer the entire future right but rather may be a partial assignment of that right. *Palmer*, 112 Me. at 152, 91 A.281. . . .

Relying primarily upon the Federal District Court's decision in *Shiro*, 174 F.Supp. 495, a bankruptcy case involving the trustee's power to avoid a preferential transfer by assignment, Irace and Lowry contend that Jones's June 14, 1988 letter is invalid and unenforceable as an assignment because it fails to manifest Jones's intent to permanently relinquish all control over the assigned funds and does nothing more than request payment from a specific fund. We disagree. The June 14 letter gives no indication that Jones attempted to retain any control over the funds he assigned to Dr. Herzog. Taken in context, the use of the word "request" did not give the court reason to question Jones's intent to complete the assignment and, although no specific amount was stated, the parties do not dispute that the services provided by Dr. Herzog and the amounts that he charged for those services were reasonable and necessary to the treatment of the shoulder injury referred to in the June 14 letter. Irace and Lowry had adequate funds to satisfy all of Jones's creditors, including Herzog, with funds left over for disbursement to Jones himself. Thus, this case simply does not present a situation analogous to *Shiro* because Dr. Herzog was given preference over Jones's other creditors by operation of the assignment. Given that Irace and Lowry do not dispute that they had ample notice of the assignment, the court's finding on the validity of the assignment is fully supported by the evidence and will not be disturbed. . . .

———

Dinslage v. Stratman
105 Neb. 274, 180 N.W. 81 (1920)

Frank Stratman lived with, and was in debt to, his mother, Thresa, for loans totaling $1,400, the indebtedness not being evidenced by any note or other writing. A granddaughter, Tracey Dinslage, also lived with Thresa, who very much wanted the young child to remain with her. Thresa told those around her (including Tracey's father) that if Tracey continued to live with her until she reached the age of 18, or until Thresa died, whichever first occurred, Tracey would be given $1,000. Later Thresa, with witnesses present, told her son Frank to pay Tracey $1,000 of the $1,400 debt he owed, when Tracey became of age or at Thresa's death. Upon Thresa's death some five months later, Frank paid $1,000 to John Dinslage, Tracey's father, for her. In an action by the administrator of Thresa's estate to recover the $1,400 debt from Frank, it was held that Thresa had made an effective assignment to Tracey and that the payment by Frank for Tracey's benefit discharged that much of the debt. The court said: "[T]here was no promissory note or other documentary evidence of the $1,400 debt, and, consequently, there was nothing tangible that could be delivered by Thresa Stratman to anyone. The whole thing rested in parol. The only thing that could be done by her was to direct her debtor to pay $1,000 of the money to Tracey, instead of to herself. It is conclusively established by the evidence that she gave that direction. Hence, she did everything that was in her power to divest herself of the title to the chose in action, and invest Tracey with it. . . . To hold otherwise would be to say that there can be no delivery of a chose in action unless it is accompanied by delivery of written evidence of it, and this would be absurd. . . . [I]t is inconceivable that [Thresa] had any other notion than that the gift was absolute[;] her direction to [Frank] settled the matter beyond recall," amounting in law to "a sufficient constructive delivery."

NOTE

One of the attributes of ownership is the power to dispose. If the asset to be transferred is a contract right, cases such as *Herzog* and *Dinslage* raise generally the question whether lack of formality renders the transfer ineffective. After all, an assignment is at bottom a present transfer of a right by the owner to another (distinguished from a contract, which is a promise of future performance). It may be gratuitous or for value. The statement found in Lone Star Cement Corp. v. Swartwout, 93 F.2d 767 (4th Cir.1938), is representative of much authority: "No particular phraseology is required to effect an assignment, and it may be either in oral or written form; but the intent to vest in the assignee a present right in the thing assigned must be manifested by some oral or written word or by some conduct signifying a relinquishment of control by the assignor and an appropriation to the assignee." Yet, as the Restatement provision displayed below suggests (Rest.2d § 332), a gratuitous assignment remains revocable unless the formal requisites of a valid gift are met. We must therefore talk of the common law's traditional tests of "intention" and "delivery," of "stripping the donor of dominion over the thing given." *Dinslage* serves as a reminder of the many problems in applying the time-worn property test of delivery, rooted in gifts of chattels (visible things), to a vast array of intangibles. How would you characterize the test of "delivery" applied in that case?

The Second Restatement, § 324 on the essentials of an assignment, generally adopts the *Lone Star Cement* approach quoted above, but with the qualification that a statute or a contract may alter the requirements for an effective assignment. The statute of immediate importance is of course the UCC, and it preempts much of the law of assignments. Still, the common law of assignment generally remains effective despite a state's adoption of the Code. This means that even though the Code now governs many transactions (in particular assignments of obligations that fall within the definition of, "accounts receivable" within the meaning of Article 9), the common law of assignment continues to apply to transactions outside the scope of the UCC.

————

RESTATEMENT OF CONTRACTS, SECOND

Section 332. Revocability of Gratuitous Assignments

(1) Unless a contrary intention is manifested, a gratuitous assignment is irrevocable if

(a) the assignment is in a writing either signed or under seal that is delivered by the assignor; or

(b) the assignment is accompanied by delivery of a writing of a type customarily accepted as a symbol or as evidence of the right assigned.

(2) Except as stated in this Section, a gratuitous assignment is revocable and the right of the assignee is terminated by the assignor's death or incapacity, by a subsequent assignment by the assignor, or by notification from the assignor received by the assignee or by the obligor.

(3) A gratuitous assignment ceases to be revocable to the extent that before the assignee's right is terminated he obtains

(a) payment or satisfaction of the obligation, or

(b) judgment against the obligor, or

(c) a new contract of the obligor by novation.

(4) A gratuitous assignment is irrevocable to the extent necessary to avoid injustice where the assignor should reasonably expect the assignment to induce action or forbearance by the assignee or a subassignee and the assignment does induce such action or forbearance. . . .

————

Lojo Realty Co. v. Isaac G. Johnson's Estate, Inc.
253 N.Y. 579, 171 N.E. 791 (1930)

This question was certified to the Court of Appeals: "Could plaintiff have specific performance where it is the assignee of the contract and a valid assignment has been executed by plaintiff's assignor when the contract contains no prohibition against assignment, but on the contrary contains the following clause, to wit: 'The stipulations aforesaid are to apply to and bind the heirs, executors, administrators, successors and assigns of the respective parties,' and the contract does not state that the purchaser's bond and mortgage must be delivered at the closing?" The court answered: "We interpret the [question] as propounding an inquiry whether specific performance may be granted to an assignee of such a contract as is pleaded in the complaint if he has failed to tender a bond executed by his assignor. So interpreting it, the answer must be 'no'."

————

P/T Ltd. II v. Friendly Mobile Manor, Inc.
79 Md.App. 227, 556 A.2d 694 (Md.Ct.Spec.App.1989)

"The UCC, [in contrast with the weight of authority at common law,] provides that duties as well as rights pass under the assignment unless there are circumstances or language to the contrary. . . . There is, at least historically, a logical basis for the distinction [made for the sale of goods]. Originally, assignments of contracts were either not permitted or were frowned upon. When A contracts with B, he bargains for B's performance, not C's. But if the contract is one of performance of service by A in exchange for payment of money by B, it is of little consequence to B whether he pays the money to A or to C, provided he gets what he bargained for, A's performance. Correspondingly, so long as he is paid for his work, it little matters to A whether he performs the same duties for the benefit of B or C. Consequently, the law eventually came to accept the notion of assignment of benefits while still rejecting the proposition that one could assign his duties, i.e., foist off on the promisee someone else's work, craftsmanship, reliability, skill, etc., in place of his own. Most contracts for sales of goods, however, involve obligations that can be performed by C just as well as A or B. Unless the goods are unique, they may be supplied by C as well as B; unless A is relying on B's credit, payment by C should be just as satisfactory as payment by B. And if the contract is of such a peculiar nature that substitution of C for B would be prejudicial to A, A may by appropriate contract provision prevent the assignment of either benefits or duties. For example, if the sale is on credit, A may object to B's assignment to C of the duty to pay. Or, if A's obligation is to supply all the goods of a certain type that B needs, A may be very reluctant indeed to permit C, whose needs may be totally different, to be substituted for B. But, here again, the UCC [in § 2–210(2) and (3)] establishes rules to apply in the absence of a manifestation of a contrary intent."

————

Macke Co. v. Pizza of Gaithersburg, Inc.

Court of Appeals of Maryland, 1970.
259 Md. 479, 270 A.2d 645.

SINGLEY, J. The appellees and defendants below, Pizza of Gaithersburg, Inc.; Pizzeria, Inc.; The Pizza Pie Corp., Inc. and Pizza Oven, Inc., four corporations under the common ownership of the same [three] individuals as partners or proprietors (the Pizza Shops) operated at six locations in Montgomery and Prince George's Counties. The appellees had arranged to have installed in each of their locations cold drink vending machines owned by Virginia Coffee Service, Inc., and on 30 December 1966, this arrangement was formalized at five of the locations, by contracts for terms of one year, automatically renewable for a like term in the absence of 30 days' written notice. A similar contract for the sixth location, operated by Pizza of Gaithersburg, Inc., was entered into on 25 July 1967.

On 30 December 1967, Virginia's assets were purchased by The Macke Co. (Macke) and the six contracts were assigned to Macke by Virginia. In January, 1968, the Pizza Shops attempted to terminate the five contracts having the December anniversary date, and in February, the contract which had the July anniversary date.

Macke [sued] each of the Pizza Shops for damages for breach of contract. From judgments for the defendants, Macke has appealed.

The lower court based [its] result on two grounds: first, that the Pizza Shops, when they contracted with Virginia, relied on its skill, judgment and reputation, which made impossible a delegation of Virginia's duties to Macke; and second, that the damages claimed could not be shown with reasonable certainty. These conclusions are challenged by Macke.

In the absence of a contrary provision—and there was none here—rights and duties under an executory bilateral contract may be assigned and delegated, subject to the exception that duties under a contract to provide personal services may never be delegated, nor rights be assigned under a contract where *delectus personae* was an ingredient of the bargain.[1] 4 Corbin on Contracts 865 (1951). . . . Crane Ice Cream Co. v. Terminal Freezing & Heating Co., 147 Md. 588, 128 A. 280 (1925), held that the right of an individual to purchase ice under a contract which by its terms reflected a knowledge of the individual's needs and reliance on his credit and responsibility could not be assigned to the corporation which purchased his business. . .

The six machines were placed on the appellees' premises under a printed "Agreement–Contract" which identified the "customer," gave its place of business, described the vending machine, and then provided:

"TERMS

"1. The Company will install on the Customer's premises the above listed equipment and will maintain the equipment in good operating order and stocked with merchandise.

"2. . . .This equipment shall remain the property of the Company and shall not be moved from the location at which installed, except by the Company. . .

"4. The Customer will exercise every effort to protect this equipment from abuse or damage.

"5. The Company will be responsible for all licenses and taxes on the equipment and sale of products.

"6. This Agreement–Contract is for a term of one (1) year from the date indicated herein and will be automatically renewed for a like period, unless thirty (30) day written notice is given by either party to terminate service.

"7. Commission on monthly sales will be paid by the Company to the Customer at the following rate:. . . ."

The rate provided in each of the agreements was "30% of Gross Receipts to $300 monthly[,] 35% over [$]300," except for the agreement with Pizza of Gaithersburg, Inc., which called for "40% of Gross Receipts."

We cannot regard the agreements as contracts for personal services. They were either a license or concession granted Virginia by the appellees, or a lease of a portion of the appellees' premises, with Virginia agreeing to pay a percentage of gross sales as a license or concession fee or as rent, . . . and were assignable by Virginia unless they imposed on Virginia duties of a personal or unique character which could not be delegated. . . .

---

[1] Like all generalizations, this one is subject to an important exception. [Article 9 of the UCC] makes ineffective a term in any contract prohibiting the assignment of a contract right: i.e., a right to payment. Compare Restatement, Contracts § 151(c) (1932).

The appellees earnestly argue that they had dealt with Macke before and had chosen Virginia because they preferred the way it conducted its business. Specifically, they say that service was more personalized, since the president of Virginia kept the machines in working order, that commissions were paid in cash, and that Virginia permitted them to keep keys to the machines so that minor adjustments could be made when needed. Even if we assume all this to be true, the agreements with Virginia were silent as to the details of the working arrangements and contained only a provision requiring Virginia to "install . . . the above listed equipment and . . . maintain the equipment in good operating order and stocked with merchandise." We think the Supreme Court of California put the problem of personal service in proper focus a century ago when it upheld the assignment of a contract to grade a San Francisco street:

> "All painters do not paint portraits like Sir Joshua Reynolds, . . . nor do all writers write dramas like Shakespeare or fiction like Dickens. Rare genius and extraordinary skill are not transferable, and contracts for their employment are therefore personal, and cannot be assigned. But rare genius and extraordinary skill are not indispensable to the workmanlike digging down of a sand hill or the filling up of a depression to a given level, or the construction of brick sewers with manholes and covers, and contracts for such work are not personal, and may be assigned." Taylor v. Palmer, 31 Cal. 240 at 247–248 (1866).

. . . Moreover, the difference between the service the Pizza Shops happened to be getting from Virginia and what they expected to get from Macke did not mount up to such a material change in the performance of obligations under the agreements as would justify the appellees' refusal to recognize the assignment, Crane Ice Cream Co. v. Terminal Freezing & Heating Co., supra. . . .

We find . . . apposite [a case which was] not cited by the parties. In The British Waggon Co. & The Parkgate Waggon Co. v. Lea & Co., 5 Q.B.D. 149 (1880), a lessor of railway cars, who had agreed to keep the cars "in good and substantial repair and working order," made an assignment of the contract. . . . When [the assignee of the lessor] sued for rent, [the] court held that the lessee remained bound under the lease, because there was no provision making performance of the lessor's duty to keep in repair a duty personal to it or its employees.

. . . Modern authorities [establish] that, absent provision to the contrary, a duty may be delegated, as distinguished from a right which can be assigned, and that the promisee cannot rescind, if the quality of the performance remains materially the same. . . . In cases involving the sale of goods, the Restatement rule respecting delegation of duties has been amplified by [UCC] § 2–210(5), . . . which permits a promisee to demand assurances from the party to whom duties have been delegated. . . .

As we see it, the delegation of duty by Virginia to Macke was entirely permissible under the terms of the agreements. . . .

Having concluded that the Pizza Shops had no right to rescind the agreements, we turn to the question of damages. [The court rejected the lower court's conclusion that damages could not be proved with reasonable certainty.]

Judgment reversed as to liability; judgment entered for appellant for costs, on appeal and below; case remanded for a new trial on the question of damages.

QUESTIONS

Suppose that on March 1, A agrees to sell and B to buy a particular automobile for $15,000, payment, delivery of possession, and transfer of title all to occur on April 1. Would an assignment on March 15, by B to C of the right to receive the automobile, be valid? Would an assignment on March 15, by A to D of A's right to receive $15,000, be valid?

————

Crane Ice Cream Co. v. Terminal Freezing & Heating Co.
147 Md. 588, 128 A. 280 (1925)

Defendant Terminal had supplied ice to Frederick, an ice cream manufacturer, under a three-year contract in which defendant undertook to supply Frederick's requirements of ice up to a total of 250 tons a week. Frederick promised not to buy ice from any other source (except in excess of the 250–ton maximum) and to pay $3.25 a ton on the Tuesday following the week in which ice was delivered. On the expiration of this contract, a new contract for an additional three years (with the same terms) was agreed to by the parties. Less than a year after the new contract was signed, Frederick sold his plant, equipment, good will, "rights" and "contracts" to the Crane Ice Cream Co., a corporation engaged in the ice cream business on a large scale in Pennsylvania and Maryland. The Crane Co. indicated to defendant Terminal its willingness to pay cash for all ice delivered under the contract, but defendant refused to deliver any ice whatever and notified Frederick that the contract was at an end. The trial court's order sustaining a demurrer to Crane's complaint for damages was affirmed by the Court of Appeals. The contract made by defendant Terminal was with an individual whose character, credit, and resources had been tried and tested by defendant. Frederick's requirements of ice were variable, but defendant had learned what they were. Defendant had also acquired confidence in the stability of Frederick's enterprise, his competence in commercial affairs, and his probity, personal judgment, and financial responsibility. The contract called for an extension of credit that might continue for as many as eight days after ice had been delivered. If the Crane Co. found it more profitable to do so, it could supply the plant purchased from Frederick with ice it had purchased in Philadelphia, or it could concentrate its purchases and buy the maximum of 250 tons a week from defendant, thus imposing on defendant a greater obligation than had been anticipated. Moreover, Frederick had evidently attempted to transfer not only his rights but also the performance of his duties, so that the assignment was in itself a repudiation of his duties. Defendant could not be required to accept the performance of a stranger in place of that due from an individual whom it knew and on whom it had relied.

NOTE: DELEGATION UNDER THE UCC

Would the outcome of the *Crane* case now be different under UCC 2–210(2)? Note the Official Comment to that subsection.

Recall that the court in *Macke Co.* stated that the common law rules on delegation of duties have been "amplified" by UCC 2–210(5). That subsection provides that a nonassigning party to a contract for the sale of goods "may treat any assignment which delegates performance as creating reasonable grounds for insecurity and may without prejudice to his rights against the assignor demand assurances from the assignee (§ 2–609)."

Also, the *Macke Co.* court's reference to the "Restatement rule respecting delegation of duties" was based on § 160(3) of the first Restatement, which was phrased in terms of whether a delegee's performance would "vary materially" from the delegor's performance. In the Restatement, Second, the phrasing of the rule on delegation of performance of a duty is somewhat different. Section 318(2) provides: "Unless otherwise agreed, a promise requires performance by a particular person only to the extent that the obligee has a substantial interest in having that person perform or control the acts promised." This is the approach taken in UCC 2–210.

The question of delegation under UCC 2–210 was before the court in *Sally Beauty Co. v. Nexxus Products Co.*, 801 F.2d 1001 (7th Cir.1986), where Nexxus had contracted with Best for the exclusive distribution of its hair products in a specified area. When Best was acquired by and merged into Sally Beauty, a wholly-owned subsidiary of a major Nexxus competitor, Nexxus cancelled the distribution contract. This cancellation was not a breach said the court:

> The UCC recognizes that in many cases an obligor will find it convenient or even necessary to relieve himself of the duty of performance under a contract, see Official Comment 1, UCC 2–210 ("[T]his section recognizes both delegation of performance and assignability as normal and permissible incidents of a contract for the sale of goods."). The Code therefore sanctions delegation except where the delegated performance would be unsatisfactory to the obligee: "A party may perform his duty through a delegate unless otherwise agreed to or unless the other party has a substantial interest in having his original promisor perform or control the acts required by the contract." UCC 2–210(1). Consideration is given to balancing the policies of free alienability of commercial contracts and protecting the obligee from having to accept a bargain he did not contract for. . . .

> In the exclusive distribution agreement before us, Nexxus had contracted for Best's "best efforts" in promoting the sale of Nexxus products. UCC § 2–306(2) states that "[a] lawful agreement by either buyer or seller for exclusive dealing in the kind of goods concerned imposes unless otherwise agreed an obligation by the seller to use best efforts to supply the goods and by the buyer to use best efforts to promote their sale." This implied promise on Best's part was the consideration for Nexxus' promise to refrain from supplying any other distributors within Best's exclusive area. . . . It was this contractual undertaking which Nexxus refused to see performed by Sally. . . .

> [We hold] that the duty of performance under an exclusive distributorship may not be delegated to a competitor in the market place—or the wholly-owned subsidiary of a competitor—without the

obligee's consent. . . . [S]uch a rule is consonant with the policies behind § 2–210, which is concerned with preserving the bargain the obligee has struck. Nexxus should not be required to accept the "best efforts" of Sally Beauty when those efforts are subject to the control of [its competitor.] It is entirely reasonable that Nexxus should conclude that this performance would be a different thing than what it had bargained for.

————

COMMENT: CONTRACTUAL PROHIBITION OF ASSIGNMENT

In Allhusen v. Caristo Constr. Corp., 303 N.Y. 446, 103 N.E.2d 891 (1952), a general contractor's agreement with a painting subcontractor included this prohibitory provision: "The assignment by the [Subcontractor] of this contract or any interest therein, or of any money due or to become due by reason of the terms hereof without the written consent of the [General Contractor] shall be void." The sub, without the general's consent, later assigned to a third party the "right to moneys due and to become due" under the painting contract. The contract itself was not assigned. When the assignee sued to recover monies allegedly due and owing for work done by the sub, the general invoked the anti-assignment clause. The Court of Appeals agreed that the assignee's complaint must be dismissed, saying:

> [W]hile the courts have striven to uphold freedom of assignability, they have not failed to recognize the concept of freedom to contract. . . . We have [here] a clause embodying clear, definite and appropriate language, which may be construed in no other way but that any attempted assignment of either the contract or any rights created thereunder shall be "void" as against the obligor. One would have to do violence to the language here employed to hold that it is merely an agreement by the subcontractor not to assign. . . .

The approach taken in *Allhusen* has many followers, including courts that have explicitly adopted the Second Restatement's formulation, in § 322, of the "ineffective term" principle (prohibition gives "a right to damages for breach [but] does not render the assignment ineffective"). See, e.g., Bel–Ray Co. v. Chemrite Ltd., 181 F.3d 435 (3d Cir.1999).

The language of Justice Holmes in Portuguese–American Bank v. Welles, 242 U.S. 7 (1916), has been quoted often. After stating that a promisor's undertaking ordinarily may be defined as narrowly as the promisor wishes, Holmes said (242 U.S. 11):

> But when [the promisor] has incurred a debt, which is property in the hands of the creditor, it is a different thing to say that as between the creditor and a third person the debtor can restrain his alienation of that, although he could not forbid the sale or pledge of other chattels. When a man sells a horse, what he does, from the point of view of the law, is to transfer a right, and a right being regarded by the law as a thing, even though a res incorporalis, it is not illogical to apply the same rule to a debt that would be applied to a horse.

In the case before Holmes, the obligor (the City of San Francisco) had not objected to the assignment, unlike the obligor defendant, the general contractor, in the *Allhusen* case. The city in Holmes' case was perfectly willing to pay whoever was entitled to the money, and the contest was for priority between two successive assignees. It is generally agreed that a contractual prohibition of assignment by the creditor will seldom have any bearing on this issue, since priority between successive assignees is rarely a matter of concern to the debtor. See I G. Gilmore, Security Interests in Personal Property § 7.8 (1965).

Some of the reasons why debtors might desire to protect themselves by contract provisions that prohibit assignments by their creditors have been explained by Professor Gilmore (vol. I, § 7.6):

> Prohibitions of assignment have their principal commercial use in the case of obligors who have large numbers of creditors to deal with. There are public authorities, federal, state and municipal, dealing with contractors. There are prime or first-tier contractors dealing with subcontractors. There are manufacturers dealing with suppliers of raw materials, component parts or sub-assemblies. There are banks dealing with holders of bank obligations. There are insurance companies dealing with policy holders. It is easy to understand why obligors so situated are loath to be required to recognize claimants other than those they originally dealt with. Where thousands and tens of thousands of claims are involved, the mere bookkeeping, if transfers must be recognized, becomes an expensive item. . . . When many claims are to be paid, it is inevitable that mistakes will be made, and if the obligor pays the wrong person he still owes the money to the rightful claimant. . . . Beyond clerical error and routine mistake, there is the problem of deciding whether an assignment is valid, under the law of some state or of a foreign country. Finally, under the normal rule of assignment law, the obligor will not be able to make set-offs against the assignee on account of claims or defenses against the assignor which arise after the obligor has received notification of the assignment. Quite naturally the obligor would prefer to avoid the fuss, the bother, the certainty of mistake, the duty of deciding difficult and obscure questions of law and the possibility of losing rights to resist payment. He therefore writes into his contract, letter of credit or insurance policy a clause to prohibit assignments made without his consent.

The author then observed that public authorities, especially the federal or a state government, by virtue of legislation can refuse consent to be sued by strangers and are not controlled in this respect by ordinary rules of private law. He found that the *Allhusen* case had been qualified and its effects obscured by later decisions (vol. I, § 7.9), but, in its application to privately-created debts, he rejected the decision in any event (vol. I, § 7.6):

> The position taken here is in favor of the unrestricted and unrestrictable alienability of contract rights. . . . On propositions of so fundamental an order belief is instinctive and irrational, not logical or reasoned. Freedom of contract cuts both ways: to the freedom of a debtor to restrict or prohibit transfer of claims against him may be opposed the freedom of a creditor to transfer rights whose value may be attested by the fact that a transferee is willing to pay for

them or lend money on their security. The social and economic utility of permitting creditors to transfer rights is believed to outweigh the utility of permitting obligors to forbid the transfer. That one utility outweighs the other lies beyond demonstration or proof.

This is pretty clearly the view adopted by the Uniform Commercial Code. See U.C.C. 9–406(c). As the comment notes, "[t]he policies underlying the ineffectiveness of contractual restrictions under this section build on common-law developments that essentially have eliminated legal restrictions on assignments of rights to payment as security and other assignments of rights to payment such as accounts."

The passage previously quoted from Gilmore describes some of the administrative burdens and legal risks of "account debtors" who have many creditors to keep track of. Under traditional common-law rules, debtors are required to pay the assignee, not the original creditor, after notice of the assignment. This means that account debtors must identify assignees correctly—and even decide at their own peril the validity of the assignments asserted. Risks of this kind may be reduced by the requirements of § 9–406, that the notification to the account debtor must "reasonably identify the rights assigned," and that the assignee, if requested by the account debtor, must furnish "reasonable proof" of the assignment (if the proof is not furnished the debtor is left free to pay the assignor).

––––––

THE ASSIGNMENT OF FUTURE RIGHTS

The leading case of Taylor v. Barton–Child Co., 228 Mass. 126, 117 N.E. 43 (1917), provides the common law view on the assignability of rights not yet in existence. At issue in that case was the enforceability of a wholesaler's assignment of "future book accounts," that is, sums to be earned in the future from transactions occurring in the course of business. The court said:

> The crucial question is whether the assignment of book accounts which are to come into existence in the future in connection with an established business, will be enforced [by the assignee] in equity. . . . It is a well recognized principle . . . that a man cannot sell or mortgage property which he does not possess and to which he has no title. . . . There can be no present transfer of property not in existence, or of property not in the possession of the seller to which he has no title. . . .

> There is an exception at the common law to the effect that one may sell that in which he has a potential title although not present actual possession. The present owner might sell the wool to be grown upon his flock, the crop to be harvested from his field or the young to be born of his herd, or assign the wages to be earned under existing employment. . . . That [principle] has never been carried so far as to include the case at bar. The catch of fish expected to be made upon a voyage about to begin cannot be sold. . . . There can be no sale of the wool of sheep, the crop of a field or the increase of herds not owned but to be bought, and there can be no assignment of wages to be earned under a contract of employment to be made in the future. . . . Practical difficulties of no small consequence would

be encountered in the operation of the contrary doctrine. . . . Merchants and manufacturers well might acquire a considerable credit upon the supposed strength of book accounts which later might turn out to have been assigned long before they came into existence. A door would be opened for the accomplishment of fraud in business.

Legislation, most notably Article 9 of the UCC, has reduced dramatically the role of the common law in disputes over the assignment of future claims. As for developments apart from the Code, the treatment of the subject of wages is representative of legislative action in general.

The court in Taylor v. Barton–Child Co. stated that one might "assign the wages to be earned under existing employment," but that "there can be no assignment of wages to be earned under a contract of employment to be made in the future." This was essentially the view at common law: unless wages related to existing employment or an existing contract of employment, they were not assignable. As one court explained it, "an assignment of wages expected to be earned in the future, and not based upon an existing contract, engagement, or employment, is [an attempt] to assign something which exists in expectancy only. In such a case it is apparent that there is nothing to assign. The expectancy may never become a reality." Metcalf v. Kincaid, 87 Iowa 443, 54 N.W. 867 (1893).

Most of our states have enacted statutes regulating the assignment of wages and salary. Policy considerations only vaguely reflected in the common law rules are brought sharply into focus by such acts. A few fairly common provisions in this legislation are worth noting. (1) The statutes frequently distinguish between assignments given to secure small loans and those given for other purposes, the former being more stringently regulated. (2) The assignment is commonly required to be in writing, sometimes in accord with a statutory form, and signed by the assignor personally. (3) If the assignor is married, the spouse may also be required to sign. (4) A valid assignment is commonly limited to only a part of the wages earned—a designated percentage or the amount in excess of a specified nonassignable sum. (5) The assignment is usually limited in duration, the permissible periods varying up to three years. (6) In order to protect the employer against competing claims, prompt notice of the assignment is frequently required. Some states also make wage assignments ineffective unless the employer consents. (7) Recordation of the assignment is sometimes required to give the assignee priority over subsequent, attaching creditors of the assignor.

The court in Taylor v. Barton–Child Co. noted an additional aspect of the problem of enforcing assignments of future rights—the prospect that equity courts might enforce a mortgage of property not yet acquired. In fact, from early times, there is in the equity cases a strong propensity in favor of enforcing contracts to give security interests in identified assets. The case of Holroyd v. Marshall, 10 House of Lords Cases 191, 11 Eng.Rep. 999 (1862), gives an example. It involved an attempted transfer, not of choses in action, but of chattels not yet owned by the owner of a textile factory. Owing a debt of £5,000, the owner transferred, by way of mortgage, machinery and equipment he then owned; he also covenanted to transfer all machinery, implements, and fixtures that he should in the future place in his factory while the mortgage debt was unpaid. Machinery thereafter acquired was attached by one of his creditors, but the House of Lords affirmed an equity decree establishing the priority of the mortgage as to after-acquired assets. Lord Westbury said:

> It is quite true that a deed which professes to convey property which is not in existence at the time is as a conveyance void at law, simply because there is nothing to convey. So in equity a contract which engages to transfer property, which is not in existence, cannot operate as an immediate alienation merely because there is nothing to transfer. But if a vendor or mortgagor agrees to sell or mortgage property, real or personal, of which he is not possessed at the time, and he receives the consideration for the contract, and afterwards becomes possessed of property answering the description in the contract, there is no doubt that a court of equity would compel him to perform the contract, and that the contract would, in equity, transfer the beneficial interest to the mortgagee or purchaser immediately on the property being acquired. This, of course, assumes that the supposed contract is one of that class of which a court of equity would decree the specific performance. If it be so, then immediately on the acquisition of the property described the vendor or mortgagor would hold it in trust for the purchaser or mortgagee, according to the terms of the contract. For if a contract be in other respects good and fit to be performed, and the consideration has been received, incapacity to perform it at the time of its execution will be no answer when the means of doing so are afterward obtained.

To be sure, the relief given in such cases depends on an "equity" that arises as a byproduct of specific performance (that is to say, the contract in question must meet some version of the "inadequacy" test, so that the result can be explained, as *Holroyd* explains it, as specific performance). The question, of course, is whether the doctrine applied in *Holroyd* should be carried over to assignments of nonexistent rights. The doctrine has been so extended by our courts, from an early date. See, e.g., Field v. City of New York, 6 N.Y. 179 (1852), where the equity court recognized the primacy of the claim of the first assignee, as against the assignor and subsequent assignees, under an attempted assignment which covered claims not yet in existence and which therefore had no present effectiveness. The court explained: "There was indeed no present, actual, potential existence of the thing to which the assignment or grant related, and therefore it could not and did not operate *eo instanti* to pass the claim which was expected thereafter to accrue to [the assignor] against the [obligor]; but it did nevertheless create an equity, which would seize upon these claims as they should arise, and would continue so to operate until the object of the [assignment] agreement was accomplished." Some courts gave another explanation that was a clear short-circuit: that the agreement itself creates an "equitable lien."

In many instances, courts must confront a contest between an assignee and other creditors of the assignor. Having an equitable lien does not itself ensure that the assignee will enjoy priority. How exactly the assignee fares in that battle must await a course in secured transactions. In any event, the modern common law's generally favorable attitude toward the assignment of rights to arise in the future is captured in the provisions of Restatement, Second § 321. In a word, the assignee has rights in court against the assignor only to the extent that contractual remedies are available to enforce a promise to assign.

————

Homer v. Shaw

Supreme Judicial Court of Massachusetts, 1912.
212 Mass. 113, 98 N.E. 697.

[Shaw was the general contractor for the construction of a section of the Tremont Street subway in Boston. Lancaster was a subcontractor who agreed to do certain excavating and mason work, as well as the erection and riveting of iron work for this section. Lancaster began work on June 1, 1896, but on June 13, in need of funds, he applied to Homer, plaintiff in this action, for money. Homer advanced $1,010.83 to Lancaster under an agreement that Lancaster would give him half the profits of his work. About June 27, Lancaster gave Homer as security a written assignment of the sums due and to come due to him under his contract with defendant. This assignment was sent to defendant and accepted by him in writing. On July 20, Lancaster wrote defendant: "Owing to my peculiar financial circumstances it will be impossible for me to go on with the iron work on the subway and shall have to give the job up." Defendant met with Lancaster the same day, and it was agreed, at defendant's request, that Lancaster would complete the work he had agreed to do, that defendants would pay debts Lancaster had already incurred for labor and material, would advance the money needed in the future for labor and material, and would pay Lancaster personally $25 a week until the job was done. Defendant testified that his original contract was entirely rescinded and that he assumed entire responsibility for payments for labor and materials, though he did agree that if Lancaster completed the work to defendant's satisfaction, and "got rid of the plaintiff's claim and any other claims and suits," he would pay Lancaster the difference between the cost of completing the job and the contract price of $6 a ton. An auditor to whom the case was referred found that "this new arrangement was in effect a rescission of the original contract and the substitution of a new and radically different one for it, and that the rights of the plaintiff under his assignment did not extend to the sums payable to Lancaster after this date." Plaintiff, alleging that Lancaster had completed the work, asked for rulings that the new contract between defendant and Lancaster was merely a change in the terms of payment, that defendant owed no duty to pay Lancaster's employees, and that after accepting the assignment he (defendant) could not deprive plaintiff of his rights under it. The trial judge refused these rulings and gave judgment for defendant.]

BRALEY, J. The defendant's liability upon acceptance of the assignment depended upon the assignor's performance of his contract to transport, erect and paint the steel work required for a section of a subway which the defendant was building in accordance with the plans and specifications of the transit commissioners. If not fully performed the entire contract price although payable in monthly instalments never became due, or if before completion the assignor by reason of his inability to go on, voluntarily abandoned the work, he could not recover for work and labor already performed and furnished. Homer v. Shaw, 177 Mass. 1, 58 N.E. 160. . . . [A]fter the assignor entered upon the performance of the contract he informed the defendant, that owing to the failure of the plaintiff to advance money, which apparently he had agreed to furnish, he would be unable to complete the work as his workmen had not been paid, and if their wages remained in arrears they would leave his employment. The evidence, if no further action had been taken by the parties, and performance of the work had ceased, would have warranted a finding, that, the assignor having repudiated or abandoned his contract before the first instalment of the contract price became payable, the defendant would not have been indebted to the plaintiff. Homer v. Shaw, 177 Mass. 1, 58 N.E. 160; Bowen v. Kimbell, 203 Mass. 364, 89 N.E. 542. . . . But without any ostensible change the assignor remained in charge of the work until completion, and the plaintiff contends under the substituted declaration, that the money thereafter received should be considered as earned under the original contract. The assignor needed immediate financial assistance, and if the defendant might have advanced the money which the evidence shows he furnished to enable him to pay his employees, yet if he had done so the plaintiff's assignment would have been given priority over the loan. Buttrick Lumber Co. v. Collins, 202 Mass. 413, 89 N.E. 138.

The parties, while they could not modify to his prejudice the terms of the contract assigned without the plaintiff's consent, or by a secret fraudulent arrangement deprive him of the benefit of the assignment, were not precluded from entering into a new agreement if performance by the assignor had become impossible from unforeseen circumstances. Eaton v. Mellus, 7 Gray 566, 572. . . . It consequently was a question of fact upon all the evidence for the presiding judge before whom the case was tried without a jury to decide whether upon facing the exigencies of changed conditions the parties mutually agreed to a cancellation, and thereupon in good faith an independent contract was substituted, by the terms of which the defendant undertook to furnish sufficient funds to pay the workmen the wages then due, and their future wages as they accrued, while the assignor was to receive a weekly salary for his personal services of supervision. The refusal to comply with the plaintiff's request for findings, and the general finding for the defendant manifestly show his conclusion to have been that the first contract was treated as having been rescinded, and the plaintiff had no enforceable claim against the defendant under the assignment. . . . The plaintiff's requests for rulings in so far as they were not given were rightly refused, and the exceptions must be overruled. So ordered.

SECTION 3. TORTIOUS INTERFERENCE WITH CONTRACT

We began this book with Oliver Wendell Holmes' observation that, at common law, a legally enforceable promise gives its maker a choice between keeping the promise or paying a compensatory sum. From this perspective, it would seem the person who induces another to breach a contract could not commit a tort. Doing what the law entitles one to do is not a civil wrong. Advising someone to do it would not seem to be either. (Both may be the acts of Holmesian "bad men," but this is not relevant as far as the law is concerned.) Indeed, from the perspective of Holmes' heir—Richard Posner—there are times when the person who chooses to pay damages is an efficient breacher. Far from being morally reprehensible, the breach is affirmatively desirable; the person who induces the breach of contract is even doing affirmative good.

In the first chapter of the book, however, we saw that there are times when equity intervenes to take away the option not to perform. The paradigm case is Lumley v. Wagner. A performer with extraordinary skills, even if she cannot be forced to keep her promise, can be enjoined from working any place else. So too there are times when a court will allow an action against someone who induces a breach of contract. The leading case again grew out of the contract between Benjamin Lumley and Johanna Wagner. This time the defendant is the impresario who persuaded Wagner to sing at his theater instead.

Lumley v. Gye

Court of Queen's Bench, 1853.
[1843–1860] All ER Rep 208.

CROMPTON, J. [The plaintiff Lumley alleged that Wagner had agreed to sing at his opera house, but the defendant Gye] maliciously procured her to depart out of the employment of [Lumley]; whereby she did depart out of the employment and service of [Lumley]; whereby damage was suffered by [Lumley]. It was said, in support of the demurrer, that it did not appear in the declaration that the relation of master and servant ever subsisted between [Lumley] and Miss Wagner; that Miss Wagner was not averred . . . to have entered upon the service of [Lumley]; and that the engagement of a theatrical performer, even if the performer has entered upon the duties, is not of such a nature as to make the performer a servant within the rule of law which gives an action to the master for the wrongful enticing away of his servant. It was laid down broadly, as a general proposition of law, that no action will lie for procuring a person to break a contract, although such procuring is with a malicious intention and causes great and immediate injury. The law as to enticing servants was said to be contrary to the general rule and principle of law, to be anomalous, and probably to have had its origin from the state of society when serfdom existed and to be founded upon, or upon the equity of, the Statute of Labourers. It was said that it would be dangerous to hold that an action was maintainable for persuading a third party to break a contract unless some boundary or limits could be pointed out; that the remedy for enticing away servants was confined to cases where the relation of master and servant, in a strict sense, subsisted between the parties; and that, in all other cases of contract, the only remedy was against the party breaking the contract.

Whatever may have been the origin or foundation of the law as to enticing of servants, and whether it be, as contended by the plaintiff, an instance and branch of a wider rule, or, as contended by the defendant, an anomaly and an exception from the general rule of law on such subjects, it must now be considered clear law that a person who wrongfully and maliciously, or, which is the same thing, with notice, interrupts the relation subsisting between master and servant by procuring the servant to depart from the master's service, or by harbouring and keeping him as servant after he has quitted it and during the time stipulated for as the period of service, whereby the master is injured, commits a wrongful act for which he is responsible at law. I think that the rule applies wherever the wrongful interruption operates to prevent the service during the time for which the parties have contracted that the service shall continue: and I think that the relation of master and servant subsists, sufficiently for the purpose of such action, during the time for which there is in existence a binding contract of hiring and service between the parties. I think that it is a fanciful and technical and unjust distinction to say that the not having actually entered into the service, or that the service is not actually continuing, can make any difference. The wrong and injury are surely the same whether the wrongdoer entices away the gardener, who has hired himself for a year, the night before he is to go to his work, or after be has planted the first cabbage on the first morning of his service; and I should be sorry to support a distinction so unjust, and so repugnant to common sense. . . .

. . . In deciding this case . . ., I wish by no means to be considered as deciding that . . . in no case except that of master and servant is an action maintainable for maliciously inducing another to break a contract to the injury of the person with whom such contract has been made. It does not appear to me to be a sound answer to say that the [actionable] act in such cases is the act of the party who breaks the contract; for that reason would apply in the acknowledged case of master and servant. Nor is it an answer to say that there is a remedy against the contractor and that the party relies on the contract; for, besides that reason also applying to the case of master and servant, the action on the contract and the action against the malicious wrong-doer may be for a different matter; and the damages payable for such malicious injury might be calculated on a very different principle from the amount of the debt which might be the only sum recoverable on the contract. Suppose a trader, with a malicious intent to ruin a rival trader, goes to a banker or other party who owes money to his rival, and begs him not to pay the money which he owes him, and by that means ruins or greatly prejudices the party: I am by no means prepared to say that an action could not be maintained, and that damages, beyond the amount of the debt if the injury were great, or much less than such amount if the injury were less serious, might not be recovered. . . .

Without however deciding any such more general question, I think that we are justified in applying the principle of the action for enticing away servants to a case where the defendant maliciously procures a party, who is under a valid contract to give her exclusive personal services to the plaintiff for a specified period, to refuse to give such services during the period for which she had so contracted, whereby the plaintiff was injured.

I think, therefore, that our judgment should be for the plaintiff.

NOTE

Lumley v. Gye leaves a number of questions open. While the *Lumley* doctrine grows out of the law governing master and servant, it has been applied in many contexts, perhaps most notably in Pennzoil's multi-billion dollar action against Texaco for interfering with its contract to buy part of Getty Oil See Texaco, Inc. v. Pennzoil, Co., 729 S.W.2d 768 (Tex. App. 1987). But identifying when redress is available has proved elusive. If a party to a contract is free to choose whether to perform or breach and pay damages, then why should it be a tort for someone to persuade that person to exercise one of the choices the law gives? Should this tort be available only if a right of specific performance exists against the breacher of the underlying contract? And what exactly does the *Lumley* court mean when it refers to "malice"? Is it enough that the defendant acted with knowledge of the contract? The next case explores these questions and also examines the way the doctrine has expanded over time to include not only interference with an existing contract, but also situations in which a person deliberately acts to prevent a contract from coming into being in the first instance.

Della Penna v. Toyota Motor Sales, U.S.A., Inc.

Supreme Court of California, 1995.
11 Cal.4th 376, 45 Cal.Rptr.2d 436, 902 P.2d 740.

ARABIAN, J. . . . John Della Penna, an automobile wholesaler doing business as Pacific Motors, brought this action for damages against Toyota Motor Sales, U.S.A., Inc., and its Lexus division, alleging that certain business conduct of defendants both violated provisions of the Cartwright Act, California's state antitrust statute, and constituted an intentional interference with his economic relations. The impetus for Della Penna's suit arose out of the 1989 introduction into the American luxury car market of Toyota's Lexus automobile. Prior to introducing the Lexus, the evidence at trial showed, both the manufacturer, Toyota Motor Corp., and defendant, the American distributor, had been concerned at the possibility that a resale market might develop for the Lexus in Japan. Even though the car was manufactured in Japan, Toyota's marketing strategy was to bar the vehicle's sale on the Japanese domestic market until after the American roll-out; even then, sales in Japan would only be under a different brand name, the "Celsior." Fearing that auto wholesalers in the United States might re-export Lexus models back to Japan for resale, and concerned that, with production and the availability of Lexus models in the American market limited, re-exports would jeopardize its fledgling network of American Lexus dealers, Toyota inserted in its dealership agreements a "no export" clause, providing that the dealer was "authorized to sell [Lexus automobiles] only to customers located in the United States. [Dealer] agrees that it will not sell [Lexus automobiles] for resale or use outside the United States. [Dealer] agrees to abide by any export policy established by [distributor]."

Following the introduction into the American market, it soon became apparent that some domestic Lexus units were being diverted for foreign sales, principally to Japan. To counter this effect, Toyota managers wrote to their retail dealers, reminding them of the "no-export" policy and explaining that exports for foreign resale could jeopardize the supply of Lexus automobiles available for the United States market. In addition, Toyota compiled a list of "offenders"—dealers and others believed by Toyota to be involved heavily in the developing Lexus foreign resale market—which it distributed to Lexus dealers in the United States. American Lexus dealers were also warned that doing business with those whose names appeared on the "offenders" list might lead to a series of graduated sanctions, from reducing a dealer's allocation to possible reevaluation of the dealer's franchise agreement.

During the years 1989 and 1990, plaintiff Della Penna did a profitable business as an auto wholesaler purchasing Lexus automobiles, chiefly from the Lexus of Stevens Creek retail outlet, at near retail price and exporting them to Japan for resale. By late 1990, however, plaintiff's sources began to dry up, primarily as a result of the "offenders list." Stevens Creek ceased selling models to plaintiff; gradually other sources declined to sell to him as well.

In February 1991, plaintiff filed this lawsuit against Toyota Motors, U.S.A., Inc., alleging both state antitrust claims under the Cartwright Act and interference with his economic relationship with Lexus retail dealers. At the close of plaintiff's case-in-chief, the trial court granted Toyota's motion for nonsuit with respect to the remaining Cartwright Act claim (plaintiff had previously abandoned a related claim—unfair competition—prior to trial). The tort cause of action went to the jury, however, under the standard . . . instructions applicable to such claims with one significant exception. At the request of defendant and over plaintiff's objection, the trial judge modified . . . the basic instruction identifying the elements of the tort and indicating the burden of proof[,] to require plaintiff to prove that defendant's alleged interfering conduct was "wrongful."[1]

---

[1] The standard instruction governing "intentional interference with prospective economic advantage," . . . describes the essential elements of the claim as (1) an economic relationship between the plaintiff and another, "containing a probable future economic benefit or advantage to plaintiff," (2) defendant's knowledge of the existence of the relationship, (3) that defendant "intentionally engaged in acts or conduct designed to interfere with or disrupt" the

The jury returned a divided verdict, nine to three, in favor of Toyota. [Della Penna] appealed. In an unpublished disposition, the Court of Appeal unanimously reversed the trial court's judgment, ruling that a plaintiff alleging intentional interference with economic relations is not required to establish "wrongfulness" as an element of its prima facie case, and that it was prejudicial error for the trial court to have read the jury an amended instruction to that effect. The Court of Appeal remanded the case to the trial court for a new trial; we then granted Toyota's petition for review and now reverse.

Although legal historians have traced the origins of the so-called "interference torts" as far back as the Roman law, the proximate historical impetus for their modern development lay in mid–19th century English common law. . . .

The opinion in [Lumley v. Gye] dealt, of course, with conduct intended to induce the *breach* of an *existing* contract, not conduct intended to prevent or persuade others *not to contract* with the plaintiff. That such an interference with *prospective* economic relations might itself be tortious was confirmed by the Queen's Bench over the next 40 years. In Temperton v. Russell, 1 Q.B. 715 (1893), a labor union, embroiled in a dispute with a firm of builders, announced what today would be called a secondary boycott, intended to force a resolution of the union's grievances by pressuring suppliers of the builder to cease furnishing him construction materials. A failure to comply with the union's boycott demands, suppliers were warned, would result in union pressure on those who bought *their* supplies not to deal with *them*.

One such supplier of the builder, Temperton, sued the union's leadership, alleging that his business had been injured by breaches of supply contracts and the refusal of others to do business with him, all as a result of the union's threats. A unanimous Queen's Bench upheld the jury's verdict for the plaintiff, reasoning in part on the authority of *Lumley*, that in the words of Lord Esher, the Master of the Rolls, "the distinction . . . between the claim for inducing persons to break contracts already entered into . . . and . . . inducing persons not to enter into contracts . . . can [not] prevail." (*Temperton*, at p. 728.)

"There was the same wrongful intent in both cases, wrongful because malicious," Lord Esher wrote. "There was the same kind of injury to the plaintiff. It seems rather a fine distinction to say that, where a defendant maliciously induces a person not to carry out a contract already made with the plaintiff and so injures the plaintiff, it is actionable, but where he injures the plaintiff by maliciously preventing a person from entering into a contract with the plaintiff, which he would otherwise have entered into, it is not actionable." (*Temperton*, at p. 728.)

As a number of courts and commentators have observed, the keystone of the liability imposed in *Lumley* and *Temperton* to judge from the opinions of the justices, appears to have been the "malicious" intent of a defendant in enticing an employee to breach her contract with the plaintiff, and

---

relationship, (4) actual disruption, and (5) damage to the plaintiff as a result of defendant's acts. The modification sought by defendant and adopted by the trial court consisted in adding the word "wrongful" in element (3) between the words "in" and "acts." The trial court also read to the jury *plaintiff's* special jury instruction defining the "wrongful acts" required to support liability as conduct "outside the realm of legitimate business transactions. . . . Wrongfulness may lie in the method used or by virtue of an improper motive."

damaging the business of one who refused to cooperate with the union in achieving its bargaining aims. While some have doubted whether the use of the word "malicious" amounted to anything more than an intent to commit an act, knowing it would harm the plaintiff, Dean Keeton, assessing the state of the tort as late as 1984, remarked that "[w]ith intent to interfere as the usual basis of the action, the cases have turned almost entirely upon the defendant's motive or purpose and the means by which he has sought to accomplish it. As in the cases of interference with contract, any manner of intentional invasion of the plaintiff's interests may be sufficient if the purpose is not a proper one." (Prosser & Keeton on Torts (5th ed. 1984) § 130, p. 1009.)

It was, legal historians have suggested, this early accent on the defendant's "intentionality" that was responsible for allying the interference torts with their remote relatives, intentional torts of a quite different order—battery, for example, or false imprisonment. More than one account of the rise of the tort has relied on Lord Bowen's statement in an interference with contract case that "intentionally to do that which is calculated in the ordinary course of events to damage, and which does, in fact, damage another in that person's property or trade, is actionable if done without just cause or excuse." (Mogul Steamship Co. v. McGregor, Gow & Co., 23 Q.B.D. 598, 613 (1889)).

One consequence of this superficial kinship was the assimilation to the interference torts of the pleading and burden of proof requirements of the "true" intentional torts: the requirement that the plaintiff need only allege a so-called "prima facie tort" by showing the defendant's awareness of the economic relation, a deliberate interference with it, and the plaintiff's resulting injury. By this account of the matter—the traditional view of the torts and the one adopted by the first Restatement of Torts—the burden then passed to the defendant to demonstrate that its conduct was *privileged*, that is, "justified" by a recognized defense such as the protection of others or, more likely in this context, the defendant's own competitive business interests.

These and related features of the economic relations tort and the requirements surrounding its proof and defense led, however, to calls for a reexamination and reform as early as the 1920's. . . .

Calls for a reformulation of both the elements and the means of establishing the economic relations tort reached a height around the time the Restatement Second of Torts was being prepared for publication and are reflected in its departures from its predecessor's version. Acknowledging criticism, the American Law Institute discarded the prima facie tort requirement of the first Restatement. A new provision, § 766B, required that the defendant's conduct be "improper," and adopted a multifactor "balancing" approach, identifying seven factors for the trier of fact to weigh in determining a defendant's liability. The Restatement Second of Torts, however, declined to take a position on the issue of which of the parties bore the burden of proof, relying on the "considerable disagreement on who has the burden of pleading and proving certain matters" and the observation that "the law in this area has not fully congealed but is still in a formative stage." (See Rest.2d of Torts (1965 ed.), Introductory Note, ch. 37, pp. 5–6.) In addition, the Restatement Second provided that a defendant might escape liability by showing that his conduct was justifiable and did *not* include the use of "wrongful means." *Id.*, §§ 768–771. . . .

In searching for a means to recast the elements of the economic relations tort and allocate the associated burdens of proof, we are guided by an overmastering concern articulated by high courts of other jurisdictions and legal commentators: The need to draw and enforce a sharpened distinction between claims for the tortious disruption of an *existing* contract and claims that a *prospective* contractual or economic relationship has been interfered with by the defendant. Many of the cases do in fact acknowledge a greater array of justificatory defenses against claims of interference with prospective relations. Still, in our view and that of several other courts and commentators, the notion that the two torts are analytically unitary and derive from a common principle sacrifices practical wisdom to theoretical insight, promoting the idea that the interests invaded are of nearly equal dignity. They are not.

The courts provide a damage remedy against third party conduct intended to disrupt an existing contract precisely because the exchange of promises resulting in such a formally cemented economic relationship is deemed worthy of protection from interference by a stranger to the agreement. Economic relationships short of contractual, however, should stand on a different legal footing as far as the potential for tort liability is reckoned. Because ours is a culture firmly wedded to the social rewards of commercial contests, the law usually takes care to draw lines of legal liability in a way that maximizes areas of competition free of legal penalties.

A doctrine that blurs the analytical line between interference with an existing business contract and interference with commercial relations *less* than contractual is one that invites both uncertainty in conduct and unpredictability of its legal effect. The notion that inducing the breach of an existing contract is simply a subevent of the "more inclusive" class of acts that interfere with economic relations, while perhaps theoretically unobjectionable, has been mischievous as a practical matter. Our courts should, in short, firmly distinguish the two kinds of business contexts, bringing a greater solicitude to those relationships that have ripened into agreements, while recognizing that relationships short of that subsist in a zone where the rewards and risks of competition are dominant.

Beyond that, we need not tread today. It is sufficient to dispose of the issue before us in this case by holding that a plaintiff seeking to recover for alleged interference with prospective economic relations has the burden of pleading and proving that the defendant's interference was wrongful "by some measure beyond the fact of the interference itself." Top Service Body Shop v. Allstate Ins. Co. 582 P.2d 1365, 1371 (1978). It follows that the trial court did not commit error when it . . . require[d] the jury to find that defendant's interference was "wrongful." And because the instruction defining "wrongful conduct" given the jury by the trial court was offered by plaintiff himself, we have no occasion to review its sufficiency in this case. The question of whether additional refinements to the plaintiff's pleading and proof burdens merit adoption by California courts—questions embracing the precise scope of "wrongfulness," or whether a "disinterested malevolence," in Justice Holmes's words, American Bank & Trust Co. v. Federal Reserve Bank 256 U.S. 350, 358 (1921), is an actionable interference in itself, or whether the underlying policy justification for the tort, the efficient allocation of social resources, justifies including as actionable conduct that is recognized as anticompetitive under established state and federal positive law—are matters that can await another day. . . .

We hold that a plaintiff seeking to recover for an alleged interference with prospective contractual or economic relations must plead and prove as part of its case-in-chief that the defendant not only knowingly interfered

with the plaintiff's expectancy, but engaged in conduct that was wrongful by some legal measure other than the fact of interference itself. . . .

J.D. Edwards & Co. v. Podany

United States Court of Appeals, Seventh Circuit, 1999.
168 F.3d 1020.

POSNER, CHIEF JUDGE. A company had a contract to sell computer services. The buyer broke the contract, but the seller's suit, a diversity suit governed, so far as substantive issues are concerned, by the law of Illinois, is not against the buyer; it is against a consulting firm (and a former employee of the firm) that advised the buyer and was responsible for the buyer's decision to break its contract with the seller. The defendants are accused of having committed the tort of deliberately inducing a breach of contract. This is a mysterious tort. It seems to give the victim of a breach of contract two remedies, where one—a suit for breach of contract against the party who broke the contract—ought to suffice. But in some cases, of which this is not one, the contract breaker is insolvent; and in others, the third party could have avoided the breach of contract at a lower cost than the contract breaker. This may be such a case; SNE, the party that broke the contract, did so on the advice of a consultant who purported to be a specialist in the field of business and computer systems.

In any event, whether the provision of a remedy in tort for inducing a breach of contract is wise is not for us to decide. It is a settled part of the law of Illinois. Nor is there any doubt that the plaintiff made out a prima facie case. The only issue is whether the jury was justified in rejecting, en route to awarding the plaintiff $2.3 million in damages, the defense to inducing breach of contract that is called the "consultant's privilege," or more commonly the privilege of "honest advice." This is the privilege of a consultant, or other advisor, to offer good-faith advice to a client without fear of liability should the client act on that advice to the harm of a third person, in this case the plaintiff.

The privilege resembles the rule in defamation law that where there is a duty to speak, a defamatory utterance, if made in good faith and not disseminated any further than necessary, is privileged. A consultant is hired to give advice. Often the advice is painful, because firms frequently turn to consultants when they are in trouble or when they want to do something that hurts and want to spread the blame a bit. The consultant's advice may lead to downsizing, layoffs, outsourcing, and countless other perturbations, including, as here, contractual terminations. It would cast quite a large, dark cloud over the consulting business if consultants could be hauled into court for having given advice that in hindsight could be characterized as having been ill-advised, ill-informed, or otherwise negligent. The consultant's privilege cuts off this possibility. But it is not absolute. It is a qualified privilege, like qualified immunity as distinct from absolute immunity in the law of public officers' torts.

It is qualified in two ways. First, it is limited to advice given within the scope of the consultant's engagement. If a consultant hired to advise the client, a fast-food chain, on selecting a new telephone system suggested that the client terminate its fast-food franchisee in Oshkosh because the franchisee was serving soggy doughnuts, and the suggestion was adopted, the consultant could not set up the consultant's privilege in defense of the franchisee's suit for interference with contract. Not having been hired to advise on the client's franchise system, the consultant would have no contractual duty to render frank and fearless (or indeed any) advice on the subject.

Second, if the consultant does not give honest advice—if he uses his engagement to hurt other people exclusively for his own benefit (or out of dislike of his victim) rather than for the benefit of his client—he forfeits the privilege. If solely to feather his own nest, and without believing that (or caring whether) he is helping his client, he causes the client to break a contract to the detriment of the other party to the contract, he is liable for inducing the breach.

Both limitations on the consultant's privilege, scope and good faith are in issue here. The defendants argue that there was insufficient evidence to justify the jury's rejecting the privilege on either ground. The argument fails, as we can show largely just by recounting the facts, viewed as favorably to the plaintiff, the winner in the district court, as the record will permit.

SNE—the client and contract breaker—manufactures windows. It hired J.D. Edwards & Co., the plaintiff, to supply software for a project that SNE called PBS (for "Primary Business System") and that involved streamlining SNE's business and obtaining the computer support necessary for the streamlining. SNE rejected another company's software called BPCS because BPCS lacked a "configurator," which is a program that facilitates custom manufacturing. While the transition to PBS was under way, there was a reorganization that made SNE one of three divisions of a corporation headed by Gary Massel. Enter the defendants, Randy Podany and Mercer Management Consulting, Inc. Massel knew Podany, an employee of Mercer, and asked him to do what is called in the consulting trade a "sniff test"—a very quick, light review—of PBS. The fee was $10,000. After "sniffing" for a day (concretely, meeting with the PBS managers and reviewing relevant documents), Podany advised Massel that the basic approach that SNE had taken to streamlining its business, that of "reengineering in parallel," and the leading role that it had assigned to J.D. Edwards, were unsound. Reengineering in parallel means defining the company's business needs and *at the same time* obtaining the necessary computer support or other technical support. Podany is not a software expert and neither he nor his company had been retained to select software or offer a critique of the contract with J.D. Edwards. His advice had been sought at the business level. But reengineering in parallel is an example in consultant-speak of a "systems concept" and thus fell within the scope of Podany's (and Mercer's) engagement.

Podany also advised Massel to stop installing J.D. Edwards' software. The plaintiff argues that this advice was outside the terms of the engagement and so outside the protection of the consultant's privilege, but we disagree. If reengineering in parallel was a mistake and (as Podany urged) the definition of SNE's business needs should precede the installation of any software, it followed that the installation should be halted; and making this explicit did not carry the consultant's advice outside the boundaries of the privilege. To hold that it did would simply lead consultants to insist on very broad terms of engagement. That, or make them too timid. If a surgeon discovered a cancerous polyp on the patient's colon while performing an appendectomy, we wouldn't want him to refuse to remove the polyp because he feared exceeding the scope of his engagement. There might be medical reasons for him to decline to remove it; it might be beyond his competence; but if it were within his competence, we would want him to act because the patient if he could be consulted would want him to act. Similarly, if a consultant discovers a problem that is outside the strict terms of his engagement but within the range of his competence, the client would want him to bring the problem to the client's attention without fear of being sued should the solution involve the termination of a contract. So likely is this to be what the client would want that we can assume, just as in the surgical case, that it is an implied term of the engagement.

Podany, however, went further than merely advising Massell to stop installing J.D. Edwards' software. He ordered the SNE executive in charge of implementation of the contract with J.D. Edwards to stop paying Edwards. This went well beyond his original engagement, but the engagement had been enlarged by Massel, who had directed everyone in his company to "have all computer related purchases approved by Randy [Podany]." Podany's stop-payment orders were within the implied scope of this new engagement.

The problem with the defendants' assertion of the consultant's privilege is not that Podany exceeded the scope of their engagement; it is that a reasonable jury could find that he acted in bad faith. Podany knew very little about the software that was being supplied by J.D. Edwards. The only software program he was familiar with was—BPCS. So he maneuvered to replace Edwards' software with BPCS, even though BPCS lacked a configurator, which SNE had wanted. The reason he gave was that the only one of Massel's three divisions that was able to provide Massel with timely and accurate financial data had BPCS, and he ascribed the division's success in this regard to BPCS. But he did not attempt to trade off this advantage against the disadvantage, for SNE, that BPCS lacked a configurator. He arranged things so that BPCS would be selected without a fair comparison with J.D. Edwards' software. And, what is critical—for mistakes do not void the consultant's privilege—he did all this in order to land himself a lucrative job with SNE's parent as director of information services. And having done so he procured further engagements of his former employer, Mercer. During the 18 months that he remained employed by SNE, he earned $370,000 and Mercer billed SNE $1.6 million. But BPCS was a flop; it was never successfully installed in SNE. One reason it was a flop was that it lacked a configurator.

If Podany was simply a fool, and got SNE to replace J.D. Edwards' software with BPCS because he ignorantly believed that the latter really was superior for SNE's needs even though it lacked a configurator, he and his employer would be sheltered from liability by the consultant's privilege. They would be, indeed, securely within the core of the privilege. But if Podany's only object was to enrich himself—and Mercer—the privilege is forfeited. Here we pause to observe that the parties have not tried to distinguish Mercer's liability from Podany's. It has been understood that they sink or swim together. Podany was acting to further Mercer's interests as well as his own, thus making Mercer liable for Podany's intentional tort under the doctrine of respondeat superior.

In pointing to Podany's motives, we do not make the mistake of confusing bad faith with greed. A consultant might be in consulting purely for the money, but as long as he made his money by offering honest advice within the scope of his employment, his private motives would be irrelevant. It is when a consultant decides to make money by rendering dishonest advice (or going outside the terms of his engagement) that he loses the protection of privilege and assumes the usual liabilities.

Podany denied any such ulterior motive. But his credibility was impeached, and the jury was not required to believe him. His lack of credibility, like pretext in a discrimination case, combined with circumstantial evidence to justify the jury in finding bad faith. A plaintiff cannot win just by putting the defendant on the stand and asking the jury to disbelieve him. But if there is other evidence of liability, then unconvincing denials by the defendant can help persuade the jury that the plaintiff's story is true. The other evidence in this case included the fact that, after rejecting the concept of reengineering in parallel and on the basis of that rejection halting the implementation of the contract with J.D. Edwards, Podany had SNE install BPCS on the same basis—that is, in parallel with the specification of SNE's needs. The justification for rigging the software selection process to assure the selection of BPCS—the only software he could work with—that he offered (the success of BPCS in generating prompt and accurate financial information for another division) was inadequate given BPCS's lack of a configurator, which SNE had deemed essential. He misrepresented the relative cost of the two software packages. He pronounced the J.D. Edwards software a "piece of shit" without knowing enough about it to have an opinion. Of course all these things could have been innocent mistakes. But the more, and the more egregious, a consultant's mistakes, the less innocent they are likely to be. And when on top of this the defendants' efforts to show that they were innocent (maybe negligent, but not deliberate) foundered, there was enough to justify a reasonable trier of fact in rejecting the defense of privilege. That doesn't mean that the jury was right in this case. But its decision was not so unreasonable as to warrant reversal.

———

APPENDIX

THE STATUTE OF FRAUDS

General contract law imposes no requirement that an agreement be in writing, or even signed, to be enforceable. But legislation stretching back more than three centuries in Anglo–American history requires that, for certain classes of agreements to be enforceable in court, the party "sought to charged" must have signed a "memorandum" of the parties' agreement. The memorandum need only be evidence of the contract and its essential terms. An ordinary statute of frauds therefore performs an evidentiary function. The defense the statute provides is a means of preventing enforcement of an otherwise perfectly valid contract.

The original English Statute of Frauds, which provided the model for American legislation, became effective in 1677. It contained some 25 provisions, including sections 4 and 17, the sections important for contract law. The other sections of the 1677 statute dealt with a heterogeneous group of problems—the creation and surrender of leaseholds in land, the execution and revocation of testamentary devises of land, the creation and assignment of trust interests in land, the execution of judgments against land, and formalities for the execution and revocation of wills of personalty. The requirement most commonly stated for this mixed collection of provisions was a "writing," but in some cases other formalities were introduced, such as attestation by witnesses or, for revocation of a will, physical burning or destruction.

The original English statute contained no general statement of purpose, except the introductory clause: "For prevention of many fraudulent practices, which are commonly endeavored to be upheld by perjury or subornation of perjury, be it enacted. . . ." It has long been understood that the statute was enacted out of a distrust of the ability of juries to determine the truth of conflicting testimony about the making of a contract. The common law action of assumpsit had of course opened the King's courts to the enforcement of oral promises. And since juries at the time decided cases on their own personal knowledge of the facts, not evidence submitted by others, it is not at all surprising that the statute's introductory clause should speak of "perjury or the subornation of perjury." The jury's discretion was therefore to be limited—at least in the transactions specified—by a requirement of "some memorandum . . . in writing, and signed by the party to be charged."

There has been much speculation as to the reasons for including the various classes of transactions treated in the original statute. The legislation certainly was not concocted hastily. It was formally pending for more than four years before its passage, went through numerous revisions, many of which were substantial, and accumulated new clauses suggested by a variety of legal experts of the time. Despite the time and attention given to its drafting, there are almost no guides to legislative intent on the many problems the legislation has raised. In any event, more than 300 years have intervened and the statute has been overlaid with an immense rubble of judicial interpretations. It is the supreme example of a statute whose framers are treated as dead, beyond hope of reincarnation.

Although the main attitudes toward the general statute have entered into the common law tradition, it remains the case that there is no common law statute of frauds. Each state has its own statute (more accurately, a "general" statute, a UCC statute for sales of goods, and—typically—enactments imposing a writing requirement for specialized transactions, say credit agreements). Variations in statutory detail and in judicial interpretation are frequent, though the main lines of operation are firm. This is so because the general statute found in practically every state has its origins in the 1677 English statute.

Before considering American solutions for the problems raised by the statute, we should note that the British Parliament, by an act effective in 1954, repealed all but two provisions of the original statute, the "land contract" clause and the "suretyship" clause ("promises to answer for the debt, default or miscarriages of another"). 2 & 3 Eliz. 2, c. 34 (1954), discussed in Note, 68 Harv.L.Rev. 383 (1954). It is useful to have in mind the general nature of the criticisms that induced the country that created and exported the statute to abandon most of its provisions. The English Law Reform Committee, in 1953 (CMD, No. 8809, at 3), said of the sections whose repeal was recommended "that they had outlived the conditions which generated and, in some degree, justified them; that they operate in an illogical and often one-sided and haphazard fashion over a field arbitrarily chosen; and that on the whole they promote rather than restrain dishonesty." Similar criticisms have long been heard in this country as well. E.g., Perillo, The Statute of Frauds in the Light of the Functions and Dysfunctions of Form, 43 Fordham L.Rev. 39 (1974).

Still, even though American views remain divided (deeply, in many quarters), there has developed in this country no strong movement for large-scale repeal of the general statute. In the words of one respected authority, "a cautious approach to the Statute of Frauds seems to be in harmony with American professional opinion." Braucher, The Commission and the Law of Contracts, 40 Cornell L.Q. 696, 705 (1955). That opinion, it seems, is that there are good reasons for requiring a writing in some situations, whether or not the approach of the statute is the best way to impose such a requirement.

1. The Original Statute

"AN ACT FOR THE PREVENTION OF FRAUDS AND PERJURIES

"29 Car. 2, c. 3 (1677)

"Section 4. And be it further enacted by the authority aforesaid, That from and after the said four and twentieth day of June no action shall be brought (1) whereby to charge any executor or administrator upon any special promise, to answer damages out of his own estate; (2) or whereby to charge the defendant upon any special promise to answer for the debt, default or miscarriages of another person; (3) or to charge any person upon any agreement made upon consideration of marriage; (4) or upon any contract or sale of lands, tenements, or hereditaments, or any interest in or concerning them; (5) or upon any agreement that is not to be performed within the space of one year from the making thereof; (6) unless the agreement upon which such action shall be brought, or some memorandum or note thereof, shall be in writing, and signed by the party to be charged therewith, or some other person thereunto by him lawfully authorized. . . .

"Section 17. And be it further enacted by the authority aforesaid, that from and after the said four and twentieth day of June no contract for the sale of any goods, wares and merchandizes, for the price of ten pounds sterling or upwards, shall be allowed to be good, except the buyer shall accept part of the goods so sold, and actually receive the same, or give something in earnest to bind the bargain, or in part payment, or that some note or memorandum in writing of the said bargain be made and signed by the parties to be charged by such contract, or their agents thereunto lawfully authorized."

2. Construction of Specific Clauses

a. Contracts for the Sale of Land.

The coverage of the land-contract section was defined inclusively in the original statute, specifically, "lands, tenements or hereditaments or any interest in or concerning them." Modern statutes as a rule speak more tersely, but with equal inclusiveness: "any interest in land." This language has been applied by courts to cover not only the whole range of common law estates in land, but equitable interests such as the interest of a beneficiary of an express trust, the lien of a mortgagee, or the "equity of redemption" of a mortgagor. E.g., Summa Corp. v. Greenspun, 96 Nev. 247, 607 P.2d 569, modified, 98 Nev. 528, 655 P.2d 513 (1982) (oral agreement to remove lien of a deed of trust). One exception typically made by modern statutes is the short-term lease of land, often defined as less than one year (in a few states, less than three years). Such a provision was before the Kentucky court in Boone v. Coe, p. 98. Easements to use the land of another are interests in land for statute-of-frauds purposes. A license to enter or to occupy another's land would ordinarily be revocable and thus too tenuous an interest, but not all licenses are revocable; there may be reliance by the licensee or an agreement to give a license may be enforceable as a bargain. Under the latter circumstances, a license could become an interest "in" land. But see Kitchen v. Kitchen, 465 Mich. 654, 641 N.W.2d 245 (2002) ("irrevocable license" cannot be created by applying doctrine of estoppel to oral promise of use of land, since statute of frauds requires any grant of a "permanent" interest in land to be in writing).

There has been much litigation over substances that are attached to land but are severable (coal, oil, rock, trees, ice, even buildings), and the contract of sale looks forward to severance. At the time of entering into the contract these things are "land," but in the future they will become personalty; classifying them as personalty makes the contract into a sale of goods, governed by a different statute (today, the UCC's 2–201), with requirements different from those of the general statute's sale-of-land section. For example, a state's general statute may require that a writing state the substance of the contract "with reasonable certainty," whereas the UCC statute of frauds does not require that a writing contain the terms of the contract (as we shall see, it is enough to show written corroboration of the alleged oral contract). Whether such "goods-to-be-severed" contracts involve interests in land is much debated. Property and contract ideas intersect, as is made clear in the UCC's treatment of the problem, in § 2–107. Answers can be found in a particular state only by close study of its decisions.

The answers to other problems of coverage are clear, as in the following illustrations.

Case 1. Owner of land orally appoints Broker as agent to sell the land, agreeing to pay Broker a commission of six percent of the sale price if she finds a purchaser who will agree in writing to buy the property for $52,000 or more. Broker finds a purchaser, X, who meets these terms and signs a written contract with Owner.

The only contract to sell land is the contract between Owner and X. The Owner–Broker contract is one to pay money for a service; it is clearly outside the standard clauses of the statute. It should be noted, however, that many states have tacked on to a general statute a provision requiring that promises to pay commissions to real estate brokers be in writing and signed by those who employ them. Case 1 is but an example of the many situations where a sale of land is connected to, but not regulated by, the disputed oral agreement. E.g., Reum v. Brazeau, 1 Mass.App.Ct. 549, 303 N.E.2d 119 (1973) (divorced couple's oral agreement to divide proceeds of sale of home not within statute, because "concerned merely personalty").

Case 2. Vendee, party to a written contract with Vendor for the purchase of land, orally agrees to assign all rights under the contract to X, who orally agrees in return to pay Vendee $8,000.

The oral agreement with X is within the land-contract clause of the statute. A land purchaser's remedy of specific performance has become so predictable that the Vendee here is quite naturally described as the owner of an "equity." This figure of speech has become such a fixture in the vocabulary that it is transferred without hesitation in defining the interests in land covered by the statute of frauds.

Case 3. Vendor, party to a written contract for the sale of land to Vendee, agrees orally with X to assign to X the Vendee's promissory notes for the unpaid balance of the purchase price, and X agrees orally to pay Vendor $8,000.

You may be surprised to learn that this is not a contract to transfer an interest in land, but a contract to assign promissory notes, choses in action. The difficulty with this construction is that the assignment of the notes will almost certainly transfer to X the Vendor's equitable foreclosure remedy which operates against the land itself. (Otherwise, consider where we would be if the assigning Vendor retained a "vendor's lien" on the land to secure the payment of money which is now due X.) The issue involved in Case 3 is usually raised by a mortgagee's oral promise to transfer the secured debt, and the conclusion is the same—the oral promise is not within the statute, even though the mortgage security will "follow" the debt. This is said to result by "operation of law," not by agreement. Nevertheless, the question is close enough that a slight variation in the language of the oral agreement will bring it within the statute. If the Vendor orally promises to transfer not merely the notes signed by the Vendee, but "my interest in the land" or "my title to the land," the promise comes under the land-contract clause and must be in writing to be enforceable. Roti v. Roti, 364 Ill.App.3d 191, 845 N.E.2d 892 (2006).

Case 4. Vendor and Vendee exchange oral promises, Vendor to convey lot 41 on May 1 and Vendee to pay $52,000 for the lot on May 1. Vendor on May 1 tenders a deed, but Vendee rejects it and refuses to pay. Can Vendor recover damages or sue for the price?

Vendee has promised only to pay money; nevertheless, the promise is within the statute and thus unenforceable. Corbin puts it well (2 A. Corbin, Contracts § 397): "A promise to pay money is not, in itself and standing alone, within the statute; but it does not stand alone." A few states reach the opposite result by construing "the party to be charged" as meaning the Vendor only; in still fewer states, the requirement of a signed memorandum is expressly applied by the statute to the Vendor only.

> **Case 5.** Vendor and Vendee exchange oral promises, Vendor to convey lot 41 on April 1 and Vendee to pay $52,000 a month later, on May 1. Vendor conveys lot 41 on April 1, but on May 1 Vendee refuses to pay. Can Vendor collect $52,000 from Vendee? [This is a freak case, for it seems the height of folly for Vendor to convey the title outright in exchange for an oral promise; yet, with facts not quite so extreme, such freaks have occurred.]

Vendor can collect $52,000 on or after May 1, without hindrance from the statute. In light of Case 4 above, this seems at first sight most illogical. In Case 4, it was stated that in most states an executory contract to exchange land for money is within the statute as to both parties to the exchange, Vendee as well as Vendor. How does a contract that was within the statute escape it when one party, here the Vendor, has performed? One must face the startling consequence that unless something is done, Vendee will be able to keep the land without paying for it. One solution would be restitution, with cancellation of Vendor's deed in equity on the ground that Vendee has defaulted on the oral promise of payment. In the converse case, if Vendor has defaulted, Vendee could surely recover any money payments made before the default. But all courts go further on the facts outlined in Case 5 and allow the Vendor to collect the price promised in an action on the oral promise. This is not equity "part performance" (discussed in the Comment in the casebook, pp. 234–238), for the remedy is given only after full performance by the Vendor, and the Vendor's action can be brought at law. The argument usually given for this result is that through Vendor's conveyance the contract has been removed from the statute and has become a simple promise to pay money. Logic gives way to justice, not for the first time.

There is a further dimension of the statute's land clause, raised by the disputed oral promise of a deed in Seavey v. Drake, p. 233. Even though the land-contract clause speaks of a "contract for sale," it is customarily read to cover a promised gift of land. The reasoning provided in Brown v. Branch, 758 N.E.2d 48 (Ind.2001), is typical: A promise to give land implicates a "right of possession" that is itself an "interest" in land, and it is the aim of the statute to require a writing for any promise or undertaking "to convey" an interest in land. So the statute's word "sale" means any form of commitment "to convey"— even, for example, a contract to "devise" land by will. Nonetheless, in many places an oral promise to give land may be removed from the reach of the statute on estoppel grounds—provided the promisee's reliance can be shown to result in serious enough injury or loss.

b. Contracts Not to Be Performed Within One Year.

Why this clause? One thinks at once of the factors inspiring statutes of limitation—the fallibility of memories and the death or disappearance of witnesses, both of which increase the hazards of litigation and the dangers of perjury. Contracts whose performance stretches over long periods of time might therefore need extra safeguards—a documented record offering a bulwark against perjury and a reminder for fading memories. But is this necessarily so? The hazards resulting from delay are present whenever there is this lapse of time between the making of the contract and trial of the dispute. The trial may come soon if the breach occurs early, no matter how long performance was to last. And even where the entire performance of both parties was due very shortly after the date of the contract, no suit may in fact be started until just before the end of the limitation period (say six years from breach) and the trial may be another three or four years later (think of court dockets in large cities). It is not at all clear that the architects of the statute adapted means to ends. The statute's one-year period runs not from a contract's making to its proof in court, but from its making to the completion of performance.

> **Case 6.** Defendant owns a tract of land on which there are trees containing approximately 8,000,000 feet of logs. Plaintiff is an experienced saw-mill operator. Plaintiff and defendant orally agree that plaintiff will cut all of the merchantable logs on defendant's land and deliver them to defendant's lumber yard, defendant agreeing to pay $35 per thousand feet for the logs so delivered. Plaintiff works at the job for three years, cuts 1,700,000 feet of logs in this period, and is paid for the logs as they are delivered. The rate of cutting is the best plaintiff can achieve with his equipment, and defendant does not complain that plaintiff is moving too slowly. Naturally, with more equipment and a larger crew plaintiff could operate at a much faster pace. At the end of three years, defendant repudiates the oral agreement and orders plaintiff off the land.

This contract clearly was not performed in one year. At its inception, it was most improbable that it would be; in fact, both parties must have known that it was realistically impossible for performance to be completed within a year. Is it a contract "not to be" performed within one year? It is not. So plaintiff has a good claim on the oral agreement; the lack of a writing is no bar to enforcement. If you are unconvinced, take a look at W.P. Brown & Sons Lumber Co. v. Rattray, 238 Ala. 406, 192 So. 851 (1939), and the Restatement, Second, Contracts § 130. Much, it seems, depends on whether the contract's express terms specify that performance will extend beyond one year (remember, the key language is "not to be performed within the space of one year from the making thereof").

Consider the alternatives. Case 6 is one of a very large number of cases in which performance within one year from the date of the contract is possible though not probable (often highly improbable). Should we wait to see how long performance actually takes, and hold the promises on both sides unenforceable if performance on either side extends over the deadline? This would mean that one party, by mere delay, could make a contract unenforceable that was previously enforceable. Surely a "wait and see" approach would be the worst escape from the dilemma. Or, alternatively, should we estimate the degrees of probability, attempting to visualize the performance situation as it seemed (or should have seemed) to the parties at the date of the oral agreement? This is a possible approach, and indeed the language of the statute suggests some kind of projection back to the date of the contract. But there are difficulties with this solution. What kind of evidence should we receive in building up a picture of what the parties foresaw but did not speak about? What if the parties foresaw the future differently? What degree of probability should we require? A decision often cited has captured the likely consequences of such pursuits: "Such a collateral inquiry would not only expand the 'destructive force' of the statute by expanding it to contracts not plainly within its terms, but would also inevitably waste judicial resources on the resolution of an issue that has nothing to do with the merits of the case or the attainment of a just outcome." C.R. Klewin, Inc. v. Flagship Properties, Inc., 220 Conn. 569, 583, 600 A.2d 772 (1991).

Still, a word of caution is required. Despite prevailing views, one continues to find courts who are prepared to "look to the circumstances" and bring within the statute oral agreements that might conceivably have been performed within a year. See, e.g., Great Hill Fill & Gravel, Inc. v. Shapleigh, 692 A.2d 928 (Me. 1997), where a course of performance lasting 15 years was made the basis for a finding that the parties "plainly manifested" an intention that their agreement was not to be performed within one year.

> **Case 7.** Walters, a 60–year–old brakeman employed by Decatur Railroad, is severely injured while working on the job. He claims the injury was due to defective equipment supplied by Decatur. In settlement of his claim for damages, Decatur, through an authorized agent, orally promises Walters $500 a month for life. The payments are made to Walters for six years; Decatur then repudiates the settlement agreement, refusing to pay any more.

This case is much like Fitzpatrick v. Michael (supra p. 177), and the answer will be the same as the one given there. Walters might conceivably live another 40 years; it is also possible that he may die the next day. Decatur's promise is therefore outside the statute. In effect, "not to be performed within a year" is read as meaning "not performable within a year." This agreement could be performed in full within a year.

> **Case 8.** Change Case 7 in one respect only: Decatur promises to pay Walters $500 a month for a period of 13 months.

If this promise means what it says, and the money is due even if Walters dies (being payable then to his estate), Decatur's promise is clearly within the statute. By its own terms, it cannot be performed in less than a year; in fact, completion within a year would be inconsistent with the express terms of the contract.

> **Case 9.** Employee orally agrees to serve as Employer's sales manager for three years, and Employer agrees to pay her $2,500 a month for the period. Employee performs satisfactorily for eight months and then dies.

This case is within the statute even though Employee's death produces a so-called "impossibility" of performance and operates to discharge both parties. This is not Case 7, where the promise by its own terms was operative only for Walters' lifetime. The difference may seem formal, but one must consider that contracts can be terminated in a variety of ways—not only by impossibility or frustration through unforeseen change of conditions, but by substantial breach, repudiation, or rescission by mutual agreement. If these possibilities, which are always present, were to make promises "performable" within a year, there would be very little left for the statute to operate on.

For this reason, the standard test is whether the performance called for by the contract must necessarily extend for a year or more under the terms of the contract, disregarding possibilities of discharge through conditions or events not expressly stated in the agreement itself. As Nat Nal Service Stations, Inc. v. Wolf illustrates (p. 350), there have been difficulties and disagreements in applying the standard test to oral arrangements of indefinite or uncertain duration—e.g., agency or franchise agreements and agreements for "lifetime" or "permanent" employment. The approaches and the divisions are shown in Pruitt v. Levi Strauss & Co., 932 F.2d 458 (5th Cir.1991); Hodge v. Evans Fin. Corp., 778 F.2d 794 (D.C.Cir.1985), modified, 823 F.2d 559 (D.C.Cir.1987); and D & N Boening, Inc. v. Kirsch Beverages, Inc., 63 N.Y.2d 449, 483 N.Y.S.2d 164, 472 N.E.2d 992 (1984). Most courts today would likely hold that an oral contract that does not say, in express terms, that performance is to have a specific duration beyond one year is the functional equivalent of a contract of indefinite duration for purposes of the statute of frauds (that is, the oral contract is outside the statute and enforceable). E.g., Kestenbaum v. Pennzoil Co., 108 N.M. 20, 766 P.2d 280 (1988). This characterization, and result, would be unaffected by a showing that, at the time of contracting, performance of the oral agreement within one year was exceedingly unlikely.

Moreover, in keeping with the trend to limit the reach of the one-year provision, courts have found a range of termination provisions, when set forth explicitly, sufficient to keep agreements out of the statute. E.g., Professional Bull Riders, Inc. v. Autozone, Inc., 113 P.3d 757 (Colo.2005) (provision allowing party to be charged option to terminate two-year agreement by giving notice within seven months); Schara v. Commercial Envelope Mfg. Co., 321 F.3d 240 (1st Cir.2003) (provision for payment of salary and bonus to employee in event company sold during first year of contract). The standard analysis is that a termination clause that can fairly be read as a provision for an alternative way of "performing" brings the case within established doctrine—that if any one of a party's alternative performances can be given with the one-year period the contract is not within the statute.

It is clear that the one-year provision is disfavored by courts, and that its application has been limited ("restricted" is probably more accurate). But, again, there will be departures from prevailing views, including the tendency to narrowly construe the one-year clause. An example is McInerney v. Charter Golf, Inc., 176 Ill.2d 482, 680 N.E.2d 1347 (1997), holding, 4 to 3, that a "lifetime" employment contract is essentially one for "permanent" employment and thus, by its terms, "not to be performed" within a year since "a long duration, certainly longer than a year," is anticipated. A writing was therefore required for enforcement.

Case 10. Lender on May 1 orally promises Borrower a loan of $3,000 on May 15; Borrower orally promises repayment in three annual installments of $1,000 each with interest at nine percent.

Now there is the special feature that performance on one side (Lender's) is to be fully rendered within a year; it is only Borrower's performance that stretches beyond a year. This feature will make no difference. Since the promise of one party is not performable within a year, the entire bilateral contract, while still executory, is within the statute. But what if Lender turns over the money to Borrower on May 15? Now we have our earlier Case 5 in another form: one party has fully performed and the other (Borrower) will certainly be enriched if the statute forecloses all remedy. Restitution for Lender would be one way out, but courts go further, as illustrated in Case 5, and enforce the oral promise, which has been "taken out" of the statute by Lender's full performance. An example of this doctrine appears in Mason v. Anderson, 146 Vt. 242, 499 A.2d 783 (1985). It has been explained as simply "a version of equitable estoppel"—the prevention of a fraud or injustice. Fowler v. Fowler, 933 P.2d 502 (Wyo.1997).

c. Contracts in Consideration of Marriage.

This clause is the least important in practice, and there seems to be no good reason why it should be retained. Times have indeed changed. The old English marriage settlement, in which the relatives with their solicitors gathered round to bargain for their contributions to the upkeep of the betrothed, disappeared long ago. But the clause does present a few problems worth mention.

Case 11. John asks Mary, "Will you marry me?" Mary replies, "Yes."

Strangely enough, this agreement is not within the statute. It has been argued that in 1677, when the original English statute was passed, the framers did not know (though it was already true) that mutual promises to marry could create liability for breach by one promisor. It also has been argued that such promises are a prelude to marriage, and that no one has seriously contended that the marriage ceremony itself should be ineffective unless there are memoranda "signed by the party to be charged." It should be noted, parenthetically, that the action for breach of promise to marry has since met with uniform disfavor. Legislation in most American states has abolished damage liability for breach of promises to marry; no one has yet suggested specific performance.

Case 12. Mellon and Tycoon learn that Mellon's son and Tycoon's daughter have decided to marry. Delighted at the prospect of a union between the families, Mellon and Tycoon orally agree that each will give $500,000 to the young people when the marriage ceremony is completed.

This transaction will encounter no trouble from the "consideration of marriage" clause. The marriage is a condition, but not the consideration. The consideration should be easy to find.

Case 13. John and Mary, both wealthy, orally agree to marry and to execute wills by which each shall leave all of his or her estate at death to the survivor. They marry, John makes a will in favor of Mary as agreed, but Mary makes a will in favor of her brother X and dies first with this will in effect.

This agreement appears to be within the statute; a court will so rule if it finds that the other's promise to marry was a motive for each in promising to make a will. The fact that there was an additional consideration for the agreement will make no difference if marriage, or promise of marriage, was part of the total performance "bargained for." But Case 13 provides the opportunity for another caveat. In some states, a promise to dispose of property by will (not only land but any kind of property) must be in writing. This is but one of numerous examples of specific types of promises for which requirements of a writing have been introduced by special legislation, adding to the traditional categories of the statute of frauds.

The courts generally have been unwilling to extend the statute's marriage provision to alleged oral agreements between unmarried, cohabitating persons. The case of Marvin v. Marvin, 18 Cal.3d 660, 134 Cal.Rptr. 815, 557 P.2d 106

(1976), is unequivocal in supplying the standard explanation, that the marriage clause contemplates marriage. In contrast, the Reporter's Note to the Restatement, Second, Contracts § 124, in comment a, states that "both the cautionary and evidentiary functions of the Statute of Frauds would appear to apply even more forcefully to such [nonmarital] relationships than to formal marriages."

d. Promises to Answer for the "Debt, Default or Miscarriage of Another."

Most people who have considered the issue would agree that promises to guarantee another person's debt require some special safeguards. It was noted earlier that the English legislation of 1954, which repealed other clauses of the statute, saved the land-contract and suretyship clauses. European systems that have gone a long way in eliminating requirements of form (e.g., Germany), still require a writing to make promises of sureties enforceable.

There is one feature of the suretyship section that is easy. The enumeration "debt, default or miscarriage of another" is very broadly written and very broadly interpreted.

Case 14. Virgil Vandal, 13, has terrorized the neighborhood for years, mainly by throwing rocks through the windows of nearby houses. His mother discusses the problem with the irate neighbors, orally promising them that if they will not bring court proceedings against Virgil, she will pay the cost of any past or future damage done by Virgil.

The promise comes within the statute's § 4(2); being oral, is unenforceable. No court would have to work very hard to determine whether Virgil's liability should be called a "debt, default or miscarriage." Virgil has clearly breached a tort duty and cannot escape such liability by a privilege of disaffirmance, as he could with his contracts. Nor would it matter that the promise includes an "answering" for future breaches that have not yet occurred. One can go further. "Debt" under § 4(2) includes not only existing debts, matured or unmatured, but also debts to arise in the future through advances, loans, or sales not yet made. The enumeration "debt, default or miscarriage" includes legal obligations or liabilities of any kind, from any source, matured, unmatured or not yet created, provided they are debts "of another person."

Case 15. Virgil Vandal, the neighborhood menace in Case 14, is now in the process of rehabilitation. His mother encourages him to buy a bicycle. Virgil goes down to Ralph's bicycle shop and picks out a bicycle. Ralph knows just enough contract law to telephone Virgil's mother and say: "Your son Virgil is in here and wants to buy a $700 bicycle. Shall I sell it to him?" Virgil's mother says: "Go ahead and sell it to him. I'll see that the bill is paid." Ralph hands over the bicycle to Virgil, who rides away with all guns blazing.

One small point can be disposed of quickly. If this is in fact a sale to Virgil, on Virgil's "credit," most courts would say (there is a minority to the contrary) that the power of disaffirmance possessed by this infant will not take the case out of § 4(2). It would be otherwise if his promise were wholly void, as with promises of married women in earlier times, for then there would be no promise "of another." But an infant's promise is now usually described as merely voidable and, on reaching majority, the infant can ratify it, so that there is a promise "of another" that Mother, in Case 15, can guarantee. Thus, we dismiss the point that Virgil is an infant and move on to the hard part.

The hard question is often phrased as, "To whom did the creditor give credit?" The answer could be that Ralph gave credit to both, being unwilling to accept Virgil's promise alone, but quite willing to accept it when guaranteed by a reliable adult like Mother. If that is the case, we have a transaction within the statute. If you reread the language of the telephone conversation, you will note that it seems to constitute a sale to Virgil, with Mother a guarantor. But would Ralph the Retailer be likely to give any weight to a promise of $700 from a 13–year–old with no visible assets, who is heavily indebted to the neighbors? Would Virgil himself expect to be personally liable (for, among other things, it is necessary to find a contract between Ralph and Virgil if Mother is to be in the subordinate role of guarantor); and could Mother reasonably expect Ralph the Retailer to rely on the promise of a very irresponsible teenager? It would be relevant to inquire how Ralph entered the transaction on his books, but surely an entry of Virgil's name as the buyer is not conclusive against Ralph, any more than an entry of Mother's name will be conclusive in Ralph's favor. These questions have been litigated in many situations. No form of words can decide the essential questions and, as Corbin points out, 2 A. Corbin, Contracts § 353, a great many decisions admit oral evidence that the creditor relied on the oral guaranty, permit this evidence to go to the jury, and the jury does the rest. Mother would be well advised to pay for Virgil's bicycle. See Restatement, Second § 112.

> **Case 16.** Holly owns a car, subject to a security interest (mortgage) in favor of the Lawrence Bank on which a balance of $4,200 is due. Holly and Fox enter into an oral agreement by which Fox agrees to buy the car and to pay the Lawrence Bank the $4,200 balance. The Bank is notified and raises no objection, merely stating that it will continue to hold Holly liable on the mortgage debt. The car is delivered to Fox, who does not pay the next three installments of principal and interest as they fall due. The Bank sues Fox.

One can be reasonably sure that a court would follow Lawrence v. Fox (p. 829) and allow the Bank, as third party beneficiary of the Holly–Fox contract, to recover from Fox. Does the statute of frauds require a signed memorandum of Fox's promise to Holly? The answer is "no," since the promise was made to the debtor, Holly. The language of the statute draws no such distinction. But consider whether the statute should apply if Holly, not the Bank, were suing on the ground that Fox's default in payment damaged Holly and made it likely that he would have to pay the Bank, his creditor. The promisee can always sue the promisor in the Lawrence v. Fox type of case. There is much to be said for the view that § 4(2) has no more bearing on Fox's promise to Holly than if Fox had promised to pay $4,200 directly to Holly instead of the Bank. It would seem equally irrelevant if the money were to be paid to Holly's spouse, the Angel Memorial Hospital, or some other payee chosen by Holly. This, at any rate, is standard construction, and it means that to fall within § 4(2) the promise of the surety must be made *to the creditor*.

> **Case 17.** Assume the same facts as Case 16, except that the officers of the Lawrence Bank know Fox well and are quite content to lend him money. The Bank's cashier says to Holly: "O.K. We'll take Fox's note secured by a mortgage on the car and cancel your note." Holly

and Fox both agree; Fox signs a note payable to the Bank for the $4,200 balance, and Holly's note is cancelled.

This is an unmistakable "novation," with a new promise made by Fox directly to the creditor, the Bank, in consideration of its discharging Holly. This, too, is outside the statute, but for a different reason. Here, the intended effect of the transaction is not to guarantee Holly's debt to the Bank, but to extinguish it. A new debtor, Fox, is substituted and the old debtor, Holly, is completely discharged. In effect, the statute is read as meaning "a promise to answer for the debt, default or miscarriage of another that will continue or arise after the date of the promise." Accordingly, had Fox not signed a note to the bank, but merely promised orally to do so, the statute would not bar enforcement of the promise.

> **Case 18.** Holly, owner of land mortgaged to Lawrence to secure a debt of $8,000, conveys the land to Fox, who takes title "subject to" the mortgage but does not assume it. Payments due on the mortgage are not made, and Lawrence starts foreclosure proceedings. Fox then makes an oral promise to Lawrence to pay the balance due on the mortgage, in consideration of Lawrence's promise to discontinue foreclosure proceedings. Nothing is said between Lawrence and Fox to suggest that Holly is to be discharged of his liability to Lawrence (i.e., there is no novation).

It is clear in almost all states that a vendee's promise to the mortgagee is outside § 4(2). This appears to be a vast hole dug through the statute, and indeed it is. Here, we encounter the "leading object" formula, which applies in Case 18 because Fox's promise is made in order to serve an interest of, or secure an advantage for, the promisor himself. Fox, in our example, is deemed to have acted "to benefit his own pecuniary or business position." Merdes v. Underwood, 742 P.2d 245 (Alaska 1987). The argument is that where the promise is not for the advantage or convenience of a third person (usually the debtor, whose debt is guaranteed), but for the promisor's own interest or advantage, then confirmation of the oral guarantee can be found in external circumstances. This argument overlooks the point that the issue will arise ordinarily in a case where the promisor strenuously denies making the oral promise. The "leading object" formula has been defined in various ways, including an immediate pecuniary interest in the creation or payment of the debt that is guaranteed, the receipt of a new and beneficial consideration, a financial or business purpose of the promisor to be served, etc. The concept clearly means something more than consideration sufficient for the formation of a contract, for in all the cases we have examined under the suretyship section, there was consideration for the surety's promise. In some of them, § 4(2) applies, as we have seen. 2 A. Corbin on Contracts discusses these problems in §§ 366–382.

e. Sales of Goods.

Sales of goods were regulated in the original English statute of frauds in a separate section (§ 17), and by rules that varied in significant ways from those applied to the provisions in § 4. They are now separately regulated by the Uniform Commercial Code. The leading features of the basic statute-of-frauds provision of the UCC, § 2–201, some of which are similar to the displaced sections of the Uniform Sales Act, should be noted.

First, however, there is the problem of determining whether the Sales Article of the UCC is applicable at all.

The Uniform Sales Act included in its statute-of-frauds section both contracts to assign choses in action and contracts to sell goods. This is not true of § 2–201 of the Code, which applies only to "contract[s] for the sale of goods." (There are, however, some other Code provisions requiring formalities, which will be noted later.) For example, Article 2A (Leases) includes § 2A–201(1), a statute-of-frauds provision covering oral leases of goods. But even if "goods" are involved, there may still be a problem of applicability of the Code.

> **Case 19.** Bulge, a young lawyer, enters the Tagend Tailor Shop and selects material for a suit. Bulge's somewhat irregular contours are measured and noted; he selects a style from a book. The clerk states a price of $1,500 for the suit, to be made of the material selected and to be cut to measure by Tagend's own tailor upstairs. Bulge tells the clerk to go ahead and make the suit, and to call him when it is ready for a fitting. Tagend's tailor proceeds to cut the material and has it ready for a first fitting when Bulge informs Tagend's clerk that changes in fashions have eliminated the need for the suit.

We think Bulge is both highly unethical and liable in damages for rejecting the suit. Is this a sale of goods or a contract for services? Clearly, it is both. In some instances of "mixed" contracts, one can be much more certain about the result than here. A person engaged by oral contract to dig a hole in the ground for $150 is not a seller of goods, even though the digger uses gasoline for a backhoe and possibly other materials in the process. A building contractor (or even a specialist, like a plumber) who orally agrees to incorporate materials into a structure on real estate is not ordinarily considered a seller of goods, though the final result of the work will be to transfer ownership of specific chattels to the owner of the land. A lawyer who draws a deed under instructions from the client is not selling goods by virtue of the supplying of the paper on which the deed is written. On the other hand, if classifying the transaction as a sale of goods will serve to make available protective provisions of the Code, such as those relating to warranties, rather than to make nonactionable an oral arrangement, a court might be inclined to accord greater significance to the fact that goods will be used or ownership of them transferred. The Comment in Chapter 6, pp. 818–821, sketches the main attitudes (e.g., the predominant-purpose test) that have emerged on the range of applicability of Article 2 of the Code. If the Code applies to Bulge, § 2–201(3)(a) will no doubt need to be examined.

Even if the transaction is a sale of goods, no writing is required if the purchase price is below a specified figure. Under the UCC, as under the Uniform Sales Act, the cut-off point is $500.

The primary means for satisfying the UCC's version of the statute is a "writing sufficient to indicate that a contract for sale has been made between the parties and signed by the party against whom enforcement is sought or by his authorized agent or broker" (§ 2–201(1)). If this means is relied on, an important issue may be whether the writing is "sufficient." We will consider that issue later. Now, we stress the fact that a writing signed by the party against whom enforcement is sought is the primary, but not the exclusive, means of satisfying the statute of frauds. There are several others.

Case 20. Grocer, anticipating a sharp increase in the price of shortening, telephones Wholesaler and orders 100 cases to be delivered on request. The following day, Wholesaler, in accordance with Wholesaler's business practice, which is well known to Grocer, prepares, signs, and mails to Grocer a "Sales Note" covering fully and clearly the order for shortening. By the time the Sales Note is received, Grocer has developed doubts about the wisdom of the order (shortening prices having started to decline); so Grocer requests no deliveries. After two weeks, Grocer informs Wholesaler that the order for shortening is cancelled.

This case is governed by § 2–201(2) of the Code, and Wholesaler can enforce the oral contract. Grocer's failure to answer the written confirmation of the sale (the Sales Note) within ten days of its receipt is, under 2–201(2), tantamount to a sufficient writing. It is as if the recipient of the other's writing had himself sent the writing. It must be emphasized, however, that this requirement of an objection at the risk of losing the protection of the statute of frauds applies only "between merchants." The theory of the "merchant's exception" seems clearly to be estoppel—an experienced party who does not object to a confirming document sent by the other is denied the statute-of-frauds defense. (The unresponsive merchant can still persuade the trier of fact that no contract for sale was made orally prior to the other's sending of the confirmation.) Thus, in determining whether a writing satisfies 2–201(2), neither explicit words of confirmation nor express references to the parties' prior agreement are ordinarily required—that is to say, 2–201(2) contemplates no more stringent requirement of explicitness than is called for by 2–201(1). It is enough that a writing, whatever its terms, confirms a contract and includes a quantity term. Bazak Int'l Corp. v. Mast Indus., Inc., 73 N.Y.2d 113, 538 N.Y.S.2d 503, 535 N.E.2d 633 (1989).

Case 21. On placing the original telephone order for shortening, Grocer requests immediate delivery of 20 cases. These 20 cases arrive two days later, along with Wholesaler's "Sales Note" confirming the sale of the entire 100 cases. Five days later, Grocer objects to Seller's written confirmation and repudiates the contract.

Grocer's timely objection to the written confirmation makes inapplicable the Code provision that made the contract enforceable in Case 20. But if Grocer deals with the 20 cases delivered in a manner sufficient to constitute "acceptance" under UCC 2–606, Grocer will be liable for the contract price of that amount of shortening. The reverse is also true: If the buyer under an oral agreement for goods pays part of the price, and the payment is accepted by the seller, an enforceable contract results as to a part of the goods proportionate to the part payment. The UCC follows the older law in making "part performance" by either buyer or seller an alternative means of satisfying the statute of frauds. The thinking, quite obviously, is that a person's actual performance, received by another without objection, is pretty solid evidence for inferring a contract. Before the Code, however, the partial-performance exception made enforceable an oral contract for a quantity greater than that already delivered (e.g., a seller who had delivered 10 units could, without hindrance from the writing requirement, sue to enforce a contract for 20 units).

Under § 2–201(3)(c), however, enforceability is limited to the portion of one party's obligation that is proportionate to the other party's part performance.

The argument given in the Official Comment for allowing partial enforcement is that "receipt and acceptance either of goods or of the price constitute an unambiguous overt admission by the parties that a contract exists." Seldom, however, will such actions provide evidence of the terms of the main contract, and, in order to make the apportionment contemplated, it will still be necessary, as it was before, to prove the terms of the oral contract by oral evidence. Nothing is said by the Code or the Official Comment about what should be done if apportionment is not possible. For example, if the contract is for the sale of a 1967 "Silver Shadow" Rolls Royce for $11,400 and $100 has been paid by the buyer, is the buyer entitled to 1/114th of a car? What do you think should be done when the partial performance is not the delivery of some of the goods, but part payment for all the goods? Do such cases present the danger at which § 2–201(3)(c)'s limitation on the partial-performance doctrine is aimed? Look at Lockwood v. Smigel, 18 Cal.App.3d 800, 96 Cal.Rptr. 289 (1971), or Sedmak v. Charlie's Chevrolet, Inc., 622 S.W.2d 694 (Mo.Ct.App.1981), only if you are uncertain about your answers.

> **Case 22.** After making the oral contract to purchase the shortening, Grocer decides not to perform at all and rejects the 20 cases when they are delivered. When sued by Wholesaler, Grocer relies on quality defects in the 20 cases delivered to justify the failure to perform.

The UCC (§ 2–201(3)(b)) opens the possibility that this wholly oral contract may become enforceable, in whole or in part. If Grocer admits in a "pleading, testimony or otherwise in court that a contract for sale was made," the contract, if otherwise valid, becomes enforceable but only to the extent of the quantity of goods admitted. The provision applies whether it is the buyer or the seller who makes the critical admission. 2 A. Corbin, Contracts § 498 discusses the authorities that have been slow to embrace the judicial-admissions escape from the statute. Other summaries can be found in Shedd, The Judicial Admissions Exception to the Statute of Frauds: An Update, 12 Whittier L.Rev. 131 (1991), and Annot., 88 A.L.R.3d 416 (1978). The direction of case authority, which is divided, is indicated in Mitchell v. Barendregt, 120 Idaho 837, 820 P.2d 707 (1991), and Quaney v. Tobyne, 236 Kan. 201, 689 P.2d 844 (1984) (§ 2–201(3)(b) exception satisfied where the "party who has denied the existence of an oral contract in reliance on the statute takes the stand and, without admitting explicitly that a contract was made, testifies as to his statements or his actions which establish the terms of the oral contract claimed by the opposing party").

> **Case 23.** Tool Co. manufactures and sells hand tools, many of which have plastic handles or housings. Toy Co., learning that Tool Co.'s facilities for manufacturing plastic items are not being used to capacity, makes an oral agreement with Tool Co. for the manufacture and sale to it of 5,000 plastic toy telephones. Before Tool Co. has any indication that Toy Co. will not perform, it makes the required molds and manufactures 500 of the toy telephones.

If what the Tool Co. has done is characterized as a "substantial beginning" of the manufacture of the telephones (as to which see Chambers Steel Engraving Corp. v. Tambrands, Inc., 895 F.2d 858 (1st Cir.1990)), it can enforce the contract (§ 2–201(3)(a)). This may seem surprising since, unlike the earlier cases involving exceptions to the statute, no written evidence of the contract exists and the party against whom enforcement is sought has engaged in no post-contract conduct which could provide objective evidence that a contract had been made. But note the aspects of the case that press hard for recognition of an enforceable obligation: (a) the goods are to be specially manufactured for the buyer, (b) in the ordinary course of the seller's business, the goods are not suitable for sale to others, and (c) the seller has made a substantial start on manufacturing the goods. The Official Comment on the Code provides no explanation or justification for the section's abandonment of the writing requirement, or, alternatively, contract-evidencing conduct of the obligor. Perhaps the explanation lies simply in the belief that it is necessary to protect the reliance of the performing party.

3. Sufficiency of the Writing or Memorandum

Under the traditional reading, a memorandum satisfying the statute of frauds does not have to be an "integration" assented to by both parties (and thus coming within the scope of the parol evidence rule); it can consist of a series of letters or a unilateral statement in a writing signed by "the party to be charged." A single letter addressed to a third person will do, as will a memorandum prepared and signed some time after the date of the oral agreement. Even a memorandum made before the oral contract is formed can satisfy the statute. The memorandum need only be signed by "the party to be charged," and it can be supplied at any time prior to the action brought on the contract (in some states, at any time before the trial). The knowledge or consent of the other party is not required. The "note or memorandum" that satisfies most of the general statutes can thus take almost any form. It does not have to be in English, or written in ink, or on paper—stone will do. Since the essential requirement would seem to be some measure of permanence in the means used, entry into a laptop computer should suffice. We know of no cases involving skywriting in smoke, but we assume this would be insufficient. See Thomas, Legal Responses to Commercial Transactions Employing Novel Communications Media, 90 Mich.L.Rev. 1145 (1991).

The writing must also be "signed" (some statutes say "subscribed") by the party to be charged, but initials or a mark or a rubber stamp will satisfy this requirement (i.e., neither the common law nor the UCC requires a handwritten signature). A typewritten or printed name (a letterhead, for example) is often used and will suffice, though if the typewritten or printed name appears at the top or in the middle of the document, there may be trouble under statutes requiring the name to be "subscribed." E.g., Parma Tile Mosaic & Marble Co. v. Estate of Short, 87 N.Y.2d 524, 663 N.E.2d 633 (1996) (fax machine's automatic imprinting of sender's name at top of each page transmitted is not "an act to authenticate a writing" satisfying requirement that writing be "subscribed"). In any case, under most statutes an intention to adopt or authenticate a writing, manifested at least symbolically, will be given effect. Signature of a principal's name by an authorized agent is also sufficient, except where the agent so authorized is the opposite party to the same contract. (We will return in a moment to agency problems.) It would be difficult to demonstrate that the many judicial dilutions of the statutory requirements, including the leniency shown "signed" or "subscribed," reflect hostility to the statute. The statute itself contains no specific standards or guides, the purpose of preventing "fraud and perjury" is very broad, and the phrase "note or memorandum" itself implies a considerable measure of informality.

As to the contents of the note or memorandum, there is much general language in the older cases to the effect that the writing must contain all the "essential terms and conditions" of the contract, or at least "the substance of the contract." And many courts are reluctant to admit oral evidence for the purpose of showing that an ambiguous document satisfies the statute's writing requirement. A good example is Gagne v. Stevens, 696 A.2d 411 (Me. 1997) (the requirement of a reasonably complete and certain memorandum "relates to the statute's primary, evidentiary purpose[,] [to] prevent enforcement through fraud or perjury of contracts never in fact made"). Such tests as "the substance of the contract" offer little aid in the decision of individual cases. Courts are influenced in doubtful cases by the quality of the corroborative evidence (including oral evidence) from other sources and the degree of forfeiture that may result where the asserted agreement has been partly performed. See, e.g., Central Illinois Light Co. v. Consolidated Coal Co., 349 F.3d 488 (7th Cir.2003). But in general the memorandum should identify:

(1) The parties and their relationship to the transaction (e.g., which is buyer and which is seller). The names do not need to appear in the body of the document; even a name on an envelope can be used to fill in gaps in the document mailed in the envelope. Initials or given names can be used, for it should be remembered that even the longest and fullest name will have to be identified by oral evidence in any event.

(2) The specific asset forming the subject of the contract. This problem arises routinely in contracts for the sale of land. Again, extreme informality has been tolerated if oral evidence shows that the description refers unmistakably to a particular tract and no other. Not all courts would necessarily agree in all cases, but the following have been held sufficient: "the house and lot now occupied by James H. Benham"; "Hodge's place in Stratford, Conn., containing fifteen acres more or less"; "a two-story brick building in Foss, Okla., same being the property heretofore inspected by the first party."

(3) The price, if a price is agreed upon, including the terms of payment if there are terms other than the constructive condition of cash on delivery. The question of price has been confused by the larger and different question of whether the "consideration" must be stated. Some statutes expressly require it to be stated; others expressly declare that it need not be stated; and many, like the original English statute, are entirely silent on the question. The problem has arisen chiefly in contracts of guaranty, where it is possible to have a fairly respectable memorandum without reciting the consideration. But in sales of land and, until the UCC came along, in sales of goods, the money (or other) price to be given in exchange has seemed as essential a part of the subject matter as the land or goods to be sold. How much further it is necessary to go, beyond the crucial terms of parties, subject matter, and price—into express conditions, date or form of conveyance, etc.—we cannot hope to say here. If a client gets you into trouble, you can start with 2 A. Corbin, Contracts §§ 505, 506.

For sales of goods, the UCC has brought a notable relaxation of traditional requirements. The contract of sale need not be in writing (it can be oral); there need only be a document (memorandum) indicating the existence of a contract. The Official Comment on § 2–201(1) states:

> The required writing need not contain all the material terms of the contract and such material terms as are stated need not be precisely stated. All that is required is that the writing afford a basis for believing that the offered oral evidence rests on a real transaction. It may be written in lead pencil on a scratch pad. It need not

indicate which party is the buyer and which the seller. The only term which must appear is the quantity term which need not be accurately stated but recovery is limited to the amount stated. The price, time and place of payment or delivery, the general quality of the goods, or any particular warranties may all be omitted.

Special emphasis must be placed on the permissibility of omitting the price term in view of the insistence of some courts on the express inclusion of this term. . . . In many valid contracts for sale the parties do not mention the price in express terms, the buyer being bound to pay and the seller to accept a reasonable price which the trier of the fact may well be trusted to determine. . . . [F]requently the price is not mentioned since the parties have based their agreement on a price list or catalogue known to both of them and this list serves as an efficient safeguard against perjury. Finally, "market" prices and valuations that are current in the vicinity constitute a similar check. Thus if the price is not stated in the memorandum it can normally be supplied without danger of fraud. Of course if the "price" consists of goods rather than money the quantity of goods must be stated.

Only three definite and invariable requirements as to the memorandum are made by this subsection. First, it must evidence a contract for the sale of goods; second, it must be "signed," a word which includes any authentication which identifies the party to be charged; and third, it must specify a quantity.

There remain two more general issues as to the sufficiency of writings for statute-of-frauds purposes. One is the effect of using an agent. It might be thought that the injection of an agent into the process of preparing or authenticating the memorandum would cause difficulty, but on the whole it does not. The texts of the various statutes usually provide for signature by "the party to be charged or his agent in that behalf" (variations occur in the phrasing). Perhaps a dozen or so states in this country require that the authority of the agent be expressed in a writing, usually as concerns land contracts. In the absence of such express provisions, it is agreed everywhere that oral testimony can be used to prove the agent's authority. Nor will it matter whether the signature by the agent is in the agent's own or the principal's name. Two qualifications are needed: (1) by judicial construction, it is held that the opposite party to the contract cannot be made an agent to sign the memorandum, and (2) if the agent's name is signed, but the memorandum discloses the agency in such a manner as to exclude the agent's personal liability, most courts have said that the memorandum is insufficient unless it also discloses the principal's name. The defect in such a case is not in the *signature* but in the *identification of the parties*. This particular refinement is criticized in 2 A. Corbin, Contracts § 500.

What if only one party has signed? This is not all uncommon (recall the Problem in Chapter 3, p. 351, involving the buyer of sweaters). Standard provisions require signature only by "the party to be charged." This means, of course, that the contract may be enforceable by a party who has not signed against the other party who has. If this is thought to present a problem of mutuality of obligation, the answer commonly given is that this type of case is an exception to any such requirement. In equity actions for specific performance, the sole signer might want to defend on the ground that mutuality of remedy is lacking.

Insofar as the strict requirement of mutuality of remedy survives (it does not in most places), it may raise doubts about equity enforcement against the signer. In most cases today, however, it is clear that courts have the means to provide sufficient assurance that the signing party will not be compelled to perform fully without getting the promised counterperformance.

4. Contemporary Technology—Electronic "Writings"

The making of agreements through electronic data transmission or interchange—commonly known as "EDI"—quite obviously raises questions about compliance with laws requiring evidence of a writing. Common sense will carry one a long way, even in the new age.

What is a "writing" (or "memorandum" of agreement)? Common law views on what it takes to satisfy the statute of frauds were noted above. A formal statement of the accepted wisdom appears in UCC 1–201(46): "written" or "writing" includes "printing, typewriting or any other intentional reduction to tangible form." The residual phrase of the definition ("any other intentional reduction to tangible form") presumably is intended to have a broad reach. One who stores information—including contract terms—in a computer, whether by hard drive or floppy disc, no doubt believes the information is in a "tangible form"; it can be recaptured and read from the machine or, most commonly, printed into a document, an even clearer tangible form. The "writing" thus taken in hand, the printout, differs not all from other "writings" produced by today's electronic technology—e.g., a telegram, telecopy, or telex.

The trouble spot, it may be argued, is EDI which lacks a paper document at either end of the transmission. But presumably a piece of paper indicating that a contract was made can be generated at some point, even after a dispute arises. (As is the case with most data processing activities, records of EDI communications are stored electronically, either internally on a computer or on such magnetic media as tapes or discs.) Then, too, the parties themselves, voluntarily or by agreement, may always exchange paper copies of an electronic communication that involved no piece of paper. And the courts are surely free to conclude that electronic records produced in EDI are sufficiently reliable to satisfy the evidentiary purposes of the statute of frauds. An often-cited study puts it well:

> The important point, from the Statute of Frauds perspective, is that EDI has the capacity to produce the writing on request. Telegrams, telexes, and telecopies differ from EDI documents in that the end result of their electronic transmission is designed to be a paper-based writing. An EDI document transmission is more versatile. It may result in a paper-based writing (a printout) or may be stored in magnetic or other non-paper media at the option of the receiver. Telegrams, telexes, and telecopies have all been accepted as offering circumstantial guaranties of trustworthiness which are equivalent to those which a writing (in the more conventional pencil-and-paper sense) provide. A similar result with respect to EDI (assuming reliable record retention procedures are in place) should not be unexpected. . . The records of EDI transactions reflect a potential for reliability and accuracy that is, at the least, equivalent to the records maintained with regard to the use of the other technologies. The records are retained on a form of media (magnetic tapes or disks) which are identical to the type of media used to record oral conver-

sations, a form which has been accepted as a "writing" in other instances. This message, however stored, constitutes objective, corroborating evidence, apart from the oral testimony of the parties, which demonstrates the possible existence of a contract. Thus, the evidentiary purpose of the writing requirement is met.

Electronic Messaging Services Task Force, The Commercial Use of Electronic Data Interchange—A Report and Model Trading Partner Agreement 45 Bus.Law. 1645, 1686 (1990).

Nor does EDI pose unusual problems for the standard requirement of a writing "signed" by the party against whom enforcement is sought. The UCC, in § 1–201(39), gives a definition which one sees often in statute-of-frauds settings: "signed" means "any symbol executed or adopted by a party with present intention to authenticate a writing." (The widely adopted revision of Article 1, in § 1–201(37), is the same, except "authenticate" is replaced by "adopt or accept.") The Official Comment to this definition underscores that a complete signature is unnecessary, that "authentication" may take any form (a stamp, printing, initials, a thumbprint) and be found on any part of the document (even a letterhead), and that, since no catalog of possible authentications can be given in advance, courts must use "common sense and commercial experience" in passing on such matters. The question, the drafters say, "is always whether the symbol was executed or adopted by the party with present intention to authenticate the writing." The authors of the report quoted above believe that the typical EDI transmission today contains the requisite signature. Why? Because the electronic transmission "will undoubtedly include a name, access code, or other identifier which not only documents the source of the transmission, but also evidences [the sender's] intent to authenticate the transmission." 45 Bus.Law. at 1687–1688.

Recent legislative efforts to keep pace with the technologies of electronic contracting have, in general, approved the substitution of electronic records and authentication for earlier regulation that spoke of writings and signatures. See, e.g., the Uniform Electronic Transactions Act, §§ 2, 7, approved in 1999 by the National Conference of Commissioners on Uniform State Laws and recommended by that body for enactment by the states (many have). Congress has also acted to validate the use of electronic signatures and records in interstate and foreign commerce, in the Electronic Signatures in Global and National Commerce Act, 106 P.L. 229, 114 Stat. 464 (15 U.S.C. § 7001), which is generally comparable to, and defers to state adoptions of, the 1999 Uniform Act.

5. Consequences of Noncompliance

Where there is no sufficient memorandum, and in sales of goods none of the alternative bases for satisfying UCC 2–201 are available, there remain some peculiar problems as to the legal effect of the statute of frauds. Under the standard provisions of the statute, other than the UCC, the usual consequence of noncompliance is that "no action shall be brought." Several states provide that in the absence of a memorandum, the agreement, contract, or promise shall be "void." What do these various provisions mean?

First of all, it is clear everywhere that a noncomplying contract within the statutory classes is not illegal, as would be a contract to commit murder, a contract in unreasonable restraint of trade, etc. Even where the statute describes the agreement, contract, or promise as "void," the making or performance of the oral undertaking is certainly not criminal or offensive to general policy. Indeed, for most purposes, the differences in statutory terminology between "no action shall be brought" and "shall be void" can be ignored. A noncomplying contract within the statute of frauds is, in short, a peculiar hybrid—a not-quite contract, merely lacking a couple of legal chromosomes. This appears from a variety of simple tests:

(1) Suppose that, despite the absence of legal or equitable remedies to compel performance, both parties proceed to perform an oral contract. No one can complain to the prosecuting attorney, and neither party can assert any prejudice through the absence of a memorandum. The oral contract would provide a complete answer, in any court, to a claim for restitution of the performances thus exchanged.

(2) Third parties who interfere with the performance of an oral contract within the statute are liable in tort for damages to whatever extent they would be if the contract were written.

(3) Creditors of one of the parties to an oral contract cannot complain that performance of the contract is a "fraud on creditors."

(4) An oral promise within the statute provides consideration for a counter-promise in almost all the states (there is a small group of states in which the "voidness" stated in the statute produces a contrary result).

(5) As noted, the signing of a memorandum at a later date, at least up to the start of suit on the contract, will make it fully enforceable.

(6) Most courts would say that a plaintiff does not have to plead compliance with the statute, so that failure to allege that there was a writing (or the equivalent, in sales of goods) cannot be taken advantage of by demurrer. There is more disagreement on the question whether a demurrer can be used where the complaint alleges both a contract within the statutory classes and facts showing that it was oral. There is also much disagreement on the question whether proof that the contract is oral can be introduced under a plea of the general issue, but the more common view is that the statute must be specially pleaded to be taken advantage of at all.

(7) If a sufficient memorandum has once been prepared and signed, its later loss or destruction will not prevent enforcement.

All of these elements add up to the conclusion usually expressed, that a noncomplying contract within the statute is still very much a contract; it is merely unenforceable by direct action for enforcement ("no action shall be brought to charge any person upon any agreement"). This suggests a further distinction:

> **Case 24.** On April 1, Thoughtless enters into an oral contract with Sharp for the purchase of lot 32, Blackwood Subdivision, for $30,000. Thoughtless pays Sharp $1,500 and agrees to pay the balance on May 1. On May 1, when Thoughtless tenders the $28,500 balance, Sharp responds that since the contract is oral she does not intend to perform and will keep the $1,500 paid.

Since there is no entry into possession, with improvements or other reliance by Thoughtless, we assume that a plea of the statute will preclude specific performance in equity (recall the "part performance" doctrine applied in Seavey v. Drake, p. 233). It will certainly preclude an action at law for damages for breach of the oral contract. But can Sharp keep the $1,500? No. It is perfectly clear that the statute does not preclude restitution of a part performance rendered by a party not in default, after substantial breach by the other party who has received the performance. To allow restitution in such cases is thought not to undercut the policy behind the statute, since, it is said, the relief given does not amount to "enforcement" of the contract. The ease with which courts slip into this manner of describing the situation is most significant. The oral contract is treated as the measure of rights and duties, and the whole apparatus for determining default and the measure of the benefit conferred is carried over bodily from the oral (unenforceable) contract.

> **Case 25.** The same case as Case 24, except that on May 1 Thoughtless says to Sharp that he has decided to abandon the contract, will pay nothing more, and wants the $1,500 back.

This case shows, better than Case 24, why we called him Thoughtless. There is, of course, much history to support the view that Thoughtless can recover no part of the money paid, since it is his own default that has prevented performance of the oral (unenforceable) contract. Again, the contract provides the measure of rights and duties, and by this measure Thoughtless is clearly in default and deserves very little sympathy. Whether anything could be done for Thoughtless if he had paid much more than $1,500 before his repudiation is a closer question, since modern decisions in many states—e.g., Vines v. Orchard Hills, p. 134—have shown a willingness to aid a defaulter whose part performance significantly exceeds the damage caused the nondefaulter. It is in this type of case, however, that the word "void" in the statute can conceivably make a difference. Most courts confronted with this statutory word have given it the standard interpretation and made it mean merely unenforceable by affirmative action. But in a few states the word "void" is taken at face value in restitution actions, so that the defendant cannot show by way of defense to an action for restitution that the plaintiff has defaulted on the oral and "void" agreement. "Voidness" thus has the strange result of facilitating restitution, and in these few states Thoughtless can likely get the $1,500 back despite his own default.

One final reminder on restitution remedies. Recovery for the value of real estate brokers' services under oral brokerage contracts is a special case. Where a statute requires such contracts to be in writing, it is usually thought that recovery on a theory of restitution comes so close to recovery on the oral agreement that the policy of the statute forbids it.

6. Other Statutes Requiring Writings

Modern statutes have substituted signed writings for the seal in order to validate promises that would otherwise be unenforceable for lack of consideration. Such statutes (applicable, for example, to "firm" offers, releases or modifications of existing contract duties, and waiver or renunciation of a claim or right arising out of a breach) have the effect of enlarging the area of enforceable obligation, though one could say in those situations that a writing is "required" for enforceability if some other needed element, such as consideration, is lacking.

At this point, we are not so much concerned with this type of statute as we are with those which impose a writing requirement on promises that in every other respect meet standard tests of enforceability. This is the effect, obviously, of the statute of frauds in the cases to which it applies. This is also the effect of a considerable number of other statutes. We mention a few by way of reminder:

(1) promises to make testamentary dispositions;

(2) promises to pay for the services of real estate and insurance brokers;

(3) acknowledgments or new promises to extend statutory time limitations for starting actions or to revive debts barred by bankruptcy discharge;

(4) agreements to submit disputes to arbitration;

(5) wage assignments;

(6) agreements to transfer copyright ownership.

The New York legislature has probably been as active as any in interposing requirements of a writing, though statistics are difficult to secure for purposes of comparison since many such requirements are scattered through the statute books, and they are not readily discoverable from the indices. See, e.g., Henry L. Fox Co. v. William Kaufman Organization, Ltd., 74 N.Y.2d 136, 544 N.Y.2d 565, 542 N.E.2d 1082 (1989) ("the [various New York] statutes may require more or less particularity in the writings depending upon the Legislature's perception regarding the risks of false claims inherent in the [particular] contractual setting"). An earlier survey in New York that did not purport to be exhaustive turned up 31 instances in which writings were either used to extend the enforceability of promises or were required for enforceability of promises otherwise valid. Braucher, General Re-examination of the Statute of Frauds, 1953 Report of the New York Law Revision Commission 545. The heterogeneous character of the activities covered is illustrated by a sampling taken from the New York list:

(1) authority of commission merchants to sell on credit;

(2) general assignments for the benefit of creditors;

(3) promises to pay auctioneers commissions of more than a stated percent;

(4) promises of innkeepers to assume liability for more than $500 for property of their guests;

(5) assignments or waivers of mechanics' liens;

(6) chattel mortgages and conditional sales contracts;

(7) consent to the revocation of a trust;

(8) designation of beneficiary of pension, death benefit, or annuity contract; and

(9) security receipts and corporate bonds.

One would expect to find similar provisions in many states, especially as concerns consumer contracts.

Finally, it should be said that § 2–201 of the UCC is supplemented by a separate statute-of-frauds provision for "security agreements" (§ 9–203). Also, as noted earlier, UCC 2A–201(1) has added a statute respecting oral leases of goods. These supplementary clauses need not concern us now.

INDEX

References are to Pages